DogFriendly.com's

CALIFORNIA AND THE WEST DOG TRAVEL GUIDE

4th Edition

by
Tara Kain and Len Kain
DogFriendly.com, Inc.

DogFriendly.com's California and the West Dog Travel Guide, 4th Edition
by Tara Kain and Len Kain

DogFriendly.com, Inc.
6454 Pony Express Trail #33-233
Pollock Pines, CA 95726 USA
1-877-475-2275
email: email@dogfriendly.com
http://www.dogfriendly.com

PLEASE NOTE
Although the authors and publisher have tried to make the information as accurate as possible, they do not assume, and hereby disclaim, any liability for any loss or damage caused by errors, omissions, misleading information or potential travel problems caused by this book, even if such errors or omissions result from negligence, accident or any other cause.

CHECK AHEAD
We remind you, as always, to call ahead and confirm that the applicable establishment is still "dog-friendly" and that it will accommodate your pet.

DOGS OF ALL SIZES
If your dog is over 75-80 pounds, then please call the individual establishment to make sure that they allow your dog. Please be aware that establishments and local governments may also not allow particular breeds.

OTHER PARTIES DESCRIPTIONS
Some of the descriptions have been provided to us by our web site advertisers, paid researchers or other parties.

ISBN 13 - 978-0-9718742-7-5
ISBN 10 - 0-9718742-7-1

Printed in the United States of America

Cover Photographs (top to bottom, left to right):
Toby at Runyon Canyon Off-Leash Area, Los Angeles, CA
Baker Beach, San Francisco, CA
Grand Canyon, AZ
Fun Zone Boat Tours, Newport Beach, CA

Book Contents and Pages

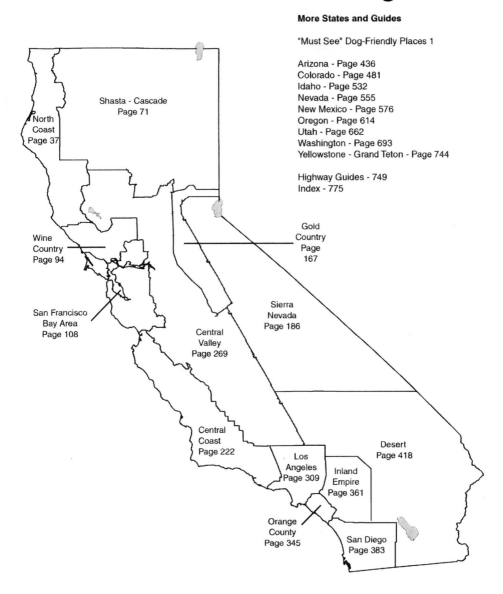

TABLE OF CONTENTS

Introduction

DogFriendly.com's guides have helped over one million dog lovers plan vacations and trips with their dogs. While this guide is full of accommodations, we also strive to have a complete travel guide for pet travelers including dog-friendly attractions, campgrounds, beaches, parks, dog parks, outdoor restaurants, stores and more. This guide focuses on places that allow all well-behaved dogs, regardless of size or breed. And only lodging that allows dogs in your choice of a non-smoking or smoking room is included, therefore not mentioning places that restrict pets to smoking rooms. In this latest edition, there are over 6000 listings in the States of California, Arizona, Colorado, Idaho, Nevada, New Mexico, Oregon, Utah and Washington with dog-friendly attractions, outdoor restaurants, parks, beaches and camping. To inspire you and your four-legged friend, we include photographs of dog-friendly places that have been visited by the authors. As with our previous editions, there are also helpful road trip tips and highway pet-friendly lodging guides to the major highways in the West. Also included is a special section on visiting Yellowstone and Grand Teton in Wyoming and Montana with your dogs. Thank you for selecting our pet travel guide and we hope you spend less time researching and more time actually going places with your dog. Enjoy your dog-friendly travels!

"Must See" Dog-Friendly Places

DogFriendly.com includes in this guide to California and the west 200 "Must See" Dog-Friendly Places. Many of these places include famous landmarks that tourists with or without dogs would want to see on any trips to a region. These include places like the Grand Canyon, Golden Gate Bridge and Hollywood. They also include many exciting attractions that welcome your dog such as Gondola rides, Boat tours, Walking and Ghost tours, Museums, Shopping Centers that are especially dog-friendly and more. These are the places that you should strive to visit with your dog as your visit the various regions in the west with your pup.

About Author Tara Kain

Tara Kain grew up with dogs and has always loved dogs. When she moved away from home, she discovered a whole new world through traveling. But whenever she traveled, the last thing she wanted was to leave her best friend behind. Tara often spent the whole time worrying about her pooch. So she began taking her dog. It was much tougher than she originally thought. Tara would spend several days researching and planning where her dog would be accepted and what else there was to do with her dog, aside from staying in a hotel room. Unfortunately, many places did not allow dogs, especially a large dog like her standard poodle. Many times when she found a supposedly "dog-friendly" hotel or motel, they would allow pets only in smoking rooms. In her opinion, because one travels with a dog should not limit them to a smoking room. So in June of 1998, she began to compile a list of dog-friendly places, notes and photos and began posting them on a web site called DogFriendly.com. This allowed her to easily keep track of the research and also help other dog lovers know about dog-friendly places. Today she still travels with her family, including the family dog. She is devoted to finding the best pet-friendly places and letting others know about them.

Tara has traveled over 150,000 miles across the United States and Canada with her dog. She serves as DogFriendly.com's President and editor-in-chief. She has written a number of magazine articles. Tara has been interviewed by numerous reporters about dog travel, dogs in the workplace and other issues concerning dogs in public places. DogFriendly.com and Tara have been featured in many articles over the years including in most major newspapers. She has appeared on CNN and CBS Television, did a live on-line forum for USA Today and has been a guest on many radio shows. Tara and her family reside in California, in the Sierra Nevada foothills near Sacramento.

About Author Len Kain

Len Kain began traveling with his dog when he was young. His family traveled with a camping trailer and brought along their standard poodle, Ricky. On trips, he found places and attractions that welcomed his best friend. When Len grew up and got his own dog, he continued the tradition of bringing his dog on trips with him. Len and his family have traveled over 150,000 miles across the country on road trips. Today he continues to travel and find fun and exciting dog-friendly places.

Currently, Len serves as DogFriendly.com's Vice President of Sales and Marketing. Len has been quoted numerous times in print, on radio and television about issues relating to traveling with dogs. Prior to joining DogFriendly.com Len served in various executive and management positions in several Silicon Valley and Internet Companies. Len holds a Bachelor of Engineering degree from Stevens Tech in New Jersey, a Master of Science degree from Stanford University and an MBA from the University of Phoenix. Len resides with his family in the Sierra Nevada foothills of California.

Your Comments and Feedback

We value and appreciate your feedback and comments. If you want to recommend a dog-friendly place or establishment, let us know. If you find a place that is no longer dog-friendly, allows small dogs only or allows dogs in smoking rooms only, please let us know. You can contact us using the following information.

Mailing Address and Contact Information:
DogFriendly.com, Inc.
6454 Pony Express Trail #33-233
Pollock Pines, CA 95726 USA
Toll free phone: 1-877-475-2275
email: email@ dogfriendly.com
http://www.dogfriendly.com

How To Use This Guide

General Guidelines

1. Please only travel with a well-behaved dog that is comfortable around other people and especially children. Dogs should also be potty trained and not bark excessively.

2. Always keep your dog leashed unless management specifically tells you otherwise.

3. Establishments listed in this book should allow well-behaved dogs of ALL sizes (at least up to 75 pounds) and in non-smoking rooms. If your dog is over 75-80 pounds, then please call the individual establishment to make sure they will allow your dog. We have listed some establishments which only allow dogs up to 50 pounds, but we try our best to make a note in the comments about the restrictions. All restaurants and attractions we list should allow dogs of all sizes.

4. Accommodations listed do not allow dogs to be left alone in the room unless specified by hotel management. If the establishment does not allow pets to be left alone, try hiring a local pet sitter to watch your dog in the room.

5. All restaurants listed as dog-friendly refer to outdoor seating only. While dogs are not permitted to sit in a chair at a restaurant's outdoor dining table, they should be allowed to sit or lay next to your table. We do not list outdoor restaurants that require your dog to be tied outside of a fenced area (with you at the dining table on one side and your dog on the other side of the fence). In our opinion, those are not truly dog-friendly restaurants. Restaurants listed may have seasonal outdoor seating.

6. Pet policies and management change often, especially within the lodging and restaurant industries. Please always call ahead to make sure an establishment still exists and is still dog-friendly.

7. After purchasing your book, please visit http://www.dogfriendly.com/updates for FREE book updates. We will do our best to let you know which places may no longer be dog-friendly.

Preparation for a Road Trip

A Month Before

If you don't already have one, get a pet identification tag for your dog. It should have your dog's name, your name and phone number. Consider using a cell phone number, a home number and, if possible, the number of where you will be staying.

Get a first aid kit for your dog. It comes in very handy if you need to remove any ticks. The kits are usually available at a pet store, a veterinary office or on the Internet.

If you do not already have a dog harness for riding the car, consider purchasing one for your dog's and your own safety. A loose dog in the car can fly into the windshield, out of the car, or into you and injure you or cause you to lose control of the car. Dog harnesses are usually sold at pet stores or on the Internet.

Make a trip to the vet if necessary for the following:

- A current rabies tag for your dog's collar. Also get paperwork with proof of the rabies vaccine.
- Dogs can possibly get heartworm from mosquitoes in the mountains, rural areas or on hikes. Research or talk to your vet and ask him or her if the area you are traveling to has a high risk of heartworm disease. The vet may suggest placing your dog on a monthly heartworm preventative medicine.
- Consider using some type of flea preventative for your dog, preferably a natural remedy. This is out of courtesy for the dog-friendly hotels plus for the comfort of your pooch.
- Make sure your dog is in good health.

Several Days Before

Make sure you have enough dog food for the duration of the trip.

If your dog is on any medication, remember to bring it along.

Some dog owners will also purchase bottled water for the trip, because some dogs can get sick from drinking water they are not used to. Talk to your vet for more information.

The Day Before

Do not forget to review DogFriendly.com's Etiquette for the Traveling Dog!

Road Trip Day

Remember to pack all of your dog's necessities: food, water, dog dishes, leash, snacks and goodies, several favorite toys, brush, towels for dirty paws, plastic bags for cleaning up after your dog, doggie first aid kit, possibly dog booties if you are venturing to an especially cold or hot region, and bring any medicine your dog might be taking.

Before you head out, put on that doggie seat belt harness.

On The Road

Keep it cool and well ventilated in the car for your dog.

Stop at least every 2-3 hours so your dog can relieve him or herself. Also offer him or her water during the stops.

Never leave your pet alone in a parked car - even in the shade with the window cracked open. According to the Los Angeles SPCA, on a hot day, a car can heat up to 160 degrees in minutes, potentially causing your pet (or child) heat stroke, brain damage, and even death.

If your dog needs medical attention during your trip, check the yellow pages phone book in the area and look under Veterinarians. If you do not see an emergency vet listed, call any local vet even   during the evening hours and they can usually inform you of the closest emergency vet.

Etiquette for the Traveling Dog

So you have found the perfect getaway spot that allows dogs, but maybe you have never traveled with your dog. Or maybe you are a seasoned dog traveler. But do you know all of your doggie etiquette? Basic courtesy rules, like your dog should be leashed unless a place specifically allows your dog to be leash-free. And do you ask for a paper bowl or cup for your thirsty pooch at an outdoor restaurant instead of letting him or her drink from your water glass?

There are many do's and don'ts when traveling with your best friend. We encourage all dog owners to follow a basic code of doggie etiquette, so places will continue to allow and welcome our best friends. Unfortunately all it takes is one bad experience for an establishment to stop allowing dogs. Let's all try to be on our best behavior to keep and, heck, even encourage new places to allow our pooches.

Everywhere...

- Well-Behaved Dogs. Only travel or go around town with a well-behaved dog that is friendly to people and especially children. If your dog is not comfortable around other people, you might consider taking your dog to obedience classes or hiring a professional trainer. Your well-behaved dog should also be potty trained and not bark excessively in a hotel or other lodging room. We believe that dogs should be kept on leash. If a dog is on leash, he or she is easier to bring under control. Also, many establishments require that dogs be on leash and many people around you will feel more comfortable as well. And last, please never leave your dog alone in a hotel or other lodging room unless you have the approval from the establishment's management.

- Leashed Dogs. Please always keep your dog leashed, unless management specifically states otherwise. Most establishments (including lodging, outdoor restaurants, attractions, parks, beaches, stores and festivals) require that your dog be on leash. Plus most cities and counties have an official leash law that requires pets to be leashed at all times when not on your property. Keeping your dog on leash will also prevent any unwanted contact with other people that are afraid of dogs, people that do not appreciate strange dogs coming up to them, and even other dog owners who have a leashed dog. Even when on leash, do not let your pooch visit with other people or dogs unless welcomed. Keeping dogs on leash will also protect them from running into traffic, running away, or getting injured by wildlife or other dogs. Even the most well-behaved and trained dogs can be startled by something, especially in a new environment.

- Be Considerate. Always clean up after your dog. Pet stores sell pooper scooper bags. You can also buy sandwich bags from your local grocery store. They work quite well and are cheap!

At Hotels or Other Types of Lodging...

- Unless it is obvious, ask the hotel clerk if dogs are allowed in the hotel lobby. Also, because of health codes, dogs are usually not allowed into a lobby area while it is being used for serving food like continental breakfast. Dogs may be allowed into the area once there is no food being served, but check with management first.

- Never leave your dog alone in the hotel room. The number one reason hotel management does not allow dogs is because some people leave them in the room alone. Some dogs, no matter how well-trained, can cause damage, bark continuously or scare the housekeepers. Unless the hotel management allows it, please make sure your dog is never left alone in the room. If you need to leave your dog in the room, consider hiring a local pet sitter.

- While you are in the room with your dog, place the Do Not Disturb sign on the door or keep the deadbolt locked. Many housekeepers have been surprised or scared by dogs when entering a room.

- In general, do not let your pet on the bed or chairs, especially if your dog sheds easily and might leave pet hair on the furniture. Some very pet-friendly accommodations will actually give you a sheet to lay over the bed so your pet can join you. If your pet cannot resist coming hopping onto the furniture with you, bring your own sheet.

- When your dog needs to go to the bathroom, take him or her away from the hotel rooms and the bushes located right next to the rooms. Try to find some dirt or bushes near the parking lot. Some hotels have a designated pet walk area.

At Outdoor Restaurants...

- Tie your dog to your chair, not the table (unless the table is secured to the ground). If your dog decides to get up and move away from the table, he or she will not take the entire table.

- If you want to give your dog some water, please ask the waiter/waitress to bring a paper cup or bowl of water for your dog. Do not use your own water glass. Many restaurants and even other guests frown upon this.

- Your pooch should lay or sit next to your table. At restaurants, dogs are not allowed to sit on the chairs or tables, or eat off the tables. This type of activity could make a restaurant owner or manager ban dogs. And do not let your pooch beg from other customers. Unfortunately, not everyone loves dogs!

- About Restaurant Laws regarding dogs at restaurants
State health codes in the United States prohibit all animals except for service animals inside indoor sections of restaurants. In recent years some health departments have begun banning dogs from some outdoor restaurant areas. It is complicated to determine where dogs are and are not allowed outdoors because most State laws are vague. They state something such as "Animals are not allowed on the premises of a food establishment". These laws also define animals to include "birds, vermin and insects" which are always present at outdoor restaurants. Various health departments have various interpretations of where the premises start and stop. Some allow dogs at outdoor areas where food is served, some allow dogs at outdoor areas only where you bring your own food to the table. Some will allow special pet-friendly areas or will allow dogs on the outside of the outer most tables. Any city or county can issue a variance to State law if it wants to allow dogs into outdoor (or indoor) restaurants. This can be done in two ways, directly by the local health department or through a vote of the local government. If a restaurant that you are visiting with your dog cites some curious requirement it is probably due to the health code. Please also understand that in all places the owner of a restaurant has the choice to not allow dogs with the exception of service dogs. The laws are in a state of flux at the moment so please understand that they may change.

According to the California Department of Health Services (CDHS) in Sacramento, since at least 1986 and up until the time of the writing of this book dogs are allowed throughout the State of California to be at any outdoor seating area that does not require that the dog walk through the inside sections. The choice is up to the restaurant owner, not the local health department. In addition, state-wide law prohibits local governments from making this rule harsher. Despite the state-wide laws in California cited above there are still some areas, particularly Santa Barbara, that insist that dogs are not allowed at some areas of outdoor patios. Other states can and do have harsher laws regarding the areas where dogs are allowed. Nationally, Austin, Dallas, Orlando and Alexandria forced law changes to allow dogs at outdoor restaurants when their health departments went too far in banning dogs from outdoor seats. Dogs are now allowed in outdoor areas in these cities through variances (or in Orlando's case) changing Florida state law. For up to date information, and more details, please see http://www.dogfriendly.com/dining .

At Retail Stores...

- Keep a close eye on your dog and make sure he or she does not go to the bathroom in the store. Store owners that allow dogs inside assume that responsible dog owners will be entering their store. Before entering a dog-friendly store, visit your local pet store first. They are by far the most forgiving. If your dog does not go to the bathroom there, then you are off to a great start! If your dog does make a mistake in any store, clean it up. Ask the store clerk for paper towels or something similar so you can clean up any mess.

- In most states dogs are allowed in stores, shops and other private buildings with the exception of grocery stores and restaurants. The decision to allow dogs is the business owner's and you can always ask if you may bring your dog inside. Also in most states packaged foods (bottled sodas, waters, bags of cookies or boxes of snacks) does not cause a store to be classified as a grocery. Even pet stores do sell these items . In many states, drinks such as coffee, tea and water are also allowed. You can order food from a restaurant to a pet-friendly establishment (so long as the establishment is not also the restaurant with the kitchen) in most areas.

At Festivals and Outdoor Events...

Make sure your dog has relieved himself or herself before entering a festival or event area. The number one reason that most festival coordinators do not allow dogs is because some dogs go to the bathroom on a vendor's booth or in areas where people might sit.

Breed Specific Laws and the Effect of These Laws on Travel With Dogs

There has been a trend in cities, counties, states and provinces towards what is known as Breed-Specific Laws (BSL) in which a municipality bans or restricts the freedoms of dog owners with specific breeds of dogs. These laws vary from place to place and are effecting a greater number of dog owners every year. Most people may think that these laws effect only the "Pit Bull" but this is not always the case. Although the majority of dogs effected are pit-bulls other breeds of dogs as well as mixed breeds that include targeted breeds are also named in the various laws in North America. These laws range from registration requirements and leash or muzzle requirements to extreme laws in which the breed is banned from the municipality outright. Some places may even be permitted to confiscate a visitor's dog who unknowingly enters the region with a banned breed.

As of August 29, 2005 the province of Ontario, Canada (including Toronto, Niagara Falls, and Ottawa) passed a very broad breed-specific law banning Pit Bulls and "similar" dogs from the province. The law allows for confiscation of visiting dogs as well as dogs living in Ontario. It is extremely important that people visiting Ontario make sure that they are able to prove that their dog is not a Pit Bull with other documentation. Various cities throughout the U.S. and Canada have muzzle requirements for Pit Bulls and other restrictions on targeted breeds as well. Breed-specific laws do get repealed as well. In October, 2005 the city of Vancouver, BC removed its requirement that Pit Bulls be muzzled in public and now only requires dogs with a known history of aggressiveness to be muzzled.

The breed specific laws usually effect pit bull type dogs but are often vaguely written and may also effect mixed breed dogs that resemble the targeted breeds. These laws are always changing and can be passed by cities, counties and even states and provinces. We recommend that travelers with dogs check into whether they are effected by such laws. You may check www.DogFriendly.com/bsl for links to further information on BSL.

DogFriendly.com does not support breed-specific laws. Most people who take their dogs out in public are responsible and those that choose to train a dog to be viscous will simply choose another breed, causing other breeds to be banned or regulated in the future.

Customs Information for Traveling Between the United States and Canada

If you will be traveling between the United States and Canada, identification for Customs and Immigration is required. U.S. and Canadian citizens traveling across the border need the following:

People

- A passport is now required (or will shortly be required depending on your point of entry) to move between the U.S. and Canada. This is a new policy so be sure to have your passport with you. Children also need a passport of their own now.

Dogs

- Dogs must be free of evidence of diseases communicable to humans when possibly examined at the port of entry.

- Valid rabies vaccination certificate (including an expiration date usually up to 3 years from the actual vaccine date and a veterinarian's signature). If no expiration date is specified on the certificate, then the certificate is acceptable if the date of the vaccination is not more than 12 months before the date of arrival. The certificate must show that the dog had the rabies vaccine at least 30 days prior to entry.

- Young puppies must be confined at a place of the owner's choosing until they are three months old, then they must be vaccinated. They must remain in confinement for 30 days after the vaccination.

Traveling with a Dog By Air

Many airlines allow dogs to be transported with the traveling public. Small dogs, usually no more than 15 pounds and with shorter legs, may travel in a carrier in the cabin with you. They must usually be kept under the seat. Any larger dogs must travel in a kennel in the cargo hold. We do not recommend that dogs travel in the cargo hold of airplanes. Most airlines restrict cargo hold pet transportation during very hot and cold periods. Most require that you notify them when making reservations about the pet as they limit the number of pets allowed on each plane and the size of the carriers may vary depending on what type of plane is being used. There are no airlines that we are aware of today that will allow dogs larger than those that fit in a carrier under a seat to fly in the cabin. Service animals are allowed in the cabin and are harnessed during takeoff and landing. Below is a summary of the pet policies for airlines at the time of publication of this book.

Airline	Cabin – Small Dogs Allowed	Cargo – Dogs Allowed	Phone	Fees (US) (each way)	Web Link for More Information - May Change
Air Canada	No	Yes	888-247-2262	$90.00	aircanada.com/en/travelinfo/airport/baggage/pets. html
Alaska Air / Horizon Air	Yes	Yes	800-252-7522	$75.00	alaskaair.com/www2/help/faqs/Pets.asp
America West/ US Airways	Yes	No	800-235-9292	$80.00	usairways.com/customers/travel_policies/pets/
American	Yes	Yes	800-433-7300	Cabin - $80 Cargo - $100	aa.com/content/travelInformation/ specialAssistance/travelingWithPets.jhtml
Continental	Yes	No	800-525-0280	$80.00	continental.com/travel/policies/animals/default.asp
Delta	Yes	Yes	800-221-1212	Cabin - $50 Cargo - $100	delta.com/planning_reservations/special_travel _needs/ pet_travel_information/pet_travel_options/ index.jsp#cargo
Frontier	No	Yes	800-432-1359	$100.00	flyfrontier.com/faq/index.ASP#PP
Independence	Yes	No	800-FLYFLYI	$35.00	flyi.com/tools/policies.aspx#traveling_pets
Jet Blue	Yes	No	800-538-2583	$50.00	jetblue.com/travelinfo/howToDetail.asp?topicId=%278%27
Northwest	Yes	Yes	800-225-2525	$80.00	nwa.com/services/shipping/cargo/products/ppet 2. shtml
Southwest	No	No			
United	Yes	Yes	800-241-6522	Cabin - $80 Cargo - $100	united.com/page/middlepage/0,6823,1047,00.html

* We do not recommend that dogs travel in the cargo hold of airplanes. Temperatures can range from freezing to sweltering and there can be delays on the runways, at the gates and elsewhere. These varying conditions can cause injury or even death to a pet.

Chapter 1

200 "Must See" Dog-Friendly Places

"Must See" California Dog-Friendly Places

Barstow

Calico Ghost Town PO Box 638 Yermo CA   760-254-2122
Dogs are allowed at this old ghost town but not inside the restaurants. Founded in March 1881, it grew to a population of 1,200 with 22 saloons and more than 500 mines. Calico became one of the richest mining towns in California, producing $86 million in silver, $45 million in borax and gold. After 1907, when silver prices dropped and borax mining moved to Death Valley, Calico became a ghost town. Take a self-guided town tour or go for a hike on one of their trails. You and your pooch can also take a guided walking tour (Mon-Fri) with Calico's historian who will examine the history of the miners, the famous 20-mule team and a U.S. Postal Mail dog named Dorsey. The park also offer many festivals throughout the year. Camping and RV hookups are available here. The park is located 8 miles north of Barstow and 3 miles east of Interstate 15.

Big Bear Lake

Bear Valley Stage Lines Village Drive and Pine Knot Avenue Big Bear Lake CA   909-584-2277
http://www.stagelines.com/
This company offers horse drawn carriage rides of the Village, and for special occasions/events they will travel anywhere in the Los Angeles metropolitan area. Dogs are allowed to come along for the ride for no additional fee if they are trained and well behaved. Dogs must be leashed and cleaned up after.

Boat Rentals on Big Bear Lake

Pine Knot Landing-Boat Rentals 439 Pine Knot Road Big Bear Lake CA   909-866-2628
http://www.pineknotlanding.com/
Rent a boat with your pup in beautiful Big Bear Lake. You'll drive your own gas powered pontoon boat which goes up to 15 miles per hour. These are nice boats which have a covering and a good amount of room for your dog to walk around. Remember to bring along some water. If you've never driven a boat, don't worry. The people working there say if you know how to drive a car, you'll be fine. Rent a boat by the hour or day. The rate for 3 hours is about $100. Prices are subject to change. This boat rental company is at Pine Knot Landing \at the end of Pine Knot Road near Hwy 18 (Big Bear Blvd.) There are also other dog-friendly boat rentals.
Woodland Trail / Nature Walk Hwy 38 Big Bear Lake CA   909-866-3437
This is a nature trail with about 20 informational stops. Pick up one of the maps and follow the self-guided 1.5 mile nature walk. This is rated as an easy loop. To get there, (going away from the village), take the Stanfield Cutoff to the other side of the lake and turn left onto Hwy 38. In about 1/2 mile, parking will be on the right.

Carmel

Carmel City Beach Ocean Avenue Carmel CA 831-624-9423
This dog-friendly beach is within walking distance (about 7 blocks) from the quaint village of Carmel. There are a couple of hotels and several restaurants that are within walking distance of the beach. Your pooch is allowed to run off-leash as long as he or she is under voice control. To get there, take the Ocean Avenue exit from Hwy 1 and follow Ocean Ave to the end.

Carmel Walks-Walking Tours Lincoln and Ocean Streets Carmel CA 831-642-2700
http://www.carmelwalks.com
Discover the special charms and secrets of Carmel on this two hour guided walking tour. Walk through award-winning gardens, by enchanting fairy tale cottages and learn the homes, haunts, and history of famous artists, writers, and movie stars. Your leashed dog is welcome to join you. Tours are offered every Saturday at 10am and 2pm. Tuesday thru Friday, the tours are at 10am. The cost is $20 per person and dogs get the tour for free. Prices are subject to change. Reservations are required.

Cypress Inn Lincoln & 7th Carmel CA 831-624-3871 (800-443-7443)
http://www.cypress-inn.com
This hotel is located within walking distance to many dog-friendly outdoor restaurants in the quaint town of Carmel and walking distance to the Carmel City Beach. This is definitely a pet-friendly hotel. Here is an excerpt from the Cypress Inn's web page "Co-owned by actress and animal rights activist Doris Day, the Cypress Inn welcomes pets with open arms -- a policy which draws a high percentage of repeat guests. It's not unusual to see people strolling in and out of the lobby with dogs of all sizes. Upon arrival, animals are greeted with dog biscuits, and other pet pamperings." Room rates are about $125 - $375 per night. If you have more than 2 people per room (including a child or baby), you will be required to stay in their deluxe room which runs approximately $375 per night. There is a $25 per day pet charge.

PortaBella Ocean Ave Carmel CA 831-624-4395
Dogs... come here to be treated first class. Your waiter will bring your pup water in a champagne bucket. They have several outdoor tables with heaters. It's located in downtown near several hotels and within a 15-20 minute walk to the beach.

Carmel City Beach

Carmel City Beach Ocean Avenue Carmel CA 831-624-9423
This beach is within walking distance (about 7 blocks) from the quaint village of Carmel. There are a couple of hotels and several restaurants that are within walking distance of the beach. Your pooch is allowed to run off-leash as long as he or she is under voice control. To get there, take the Ocean Avenue exit from Hwy 1 and follow Ocean Ave to the end.

Fresno

Basin AH1 Dog Park and Pond 4257 W. Alamos Fresno CA 559-621-2900
This is a seasonal dog park which offers a nice wading pool for dogs to use during the summer. The park is open from May through November from 7 am to 10 pm daily. The dog park is located at 4257 W. Alamos at El Capitan. To get to the dog park from Highway 99, exit at Shaw Avenue and head east. In about a mile turn right on El Capitan.

Hollywood - West LA

Hollywood Star's Homes Self-Guided Walking Tour Beverly Hills CA
Want to check out the Star's homes in Beverly Hills with your dog? How about a self-guided walking tour of the Star's homes? All you need is a map and a good starting point. Maps can be purchased at many of the tourist shops on Hollywood Blvd. A good place to begin is at the Will Rogers Memorial Park in Beverly Hills (between Sunset Blvd, Beverly Dr and Canon Drive). It's a small park but still a good place for both of you to stretch your legs before beginning the walk. You can certainly plot out your own tour, but we have a few samples tours that will help you get started. TOUR 1 (approx 1 mile): From the park and Canon Street, turn left (heading west) onto Sunset Blvd. Turn right on Roxbury. Cross Benedict Canyon Rd and the road becomes Hartford Way. Take Hartford Way back to the park. TOUR 2 (approx 3 miles): From the park, head north on Beverly Drive and cross Sunset Blvd. Turn right on Rexford Drive. Turn right on Lomitas Ave and then left onto Crescent Drive. Make a right at Elevado Ave, walk for about 5 blocks and turn right onto Bedford Dr. Then turn left on Lomitas Ave, right on Whittier Dr and left on Greeway. Then turn right on Sunset Blvd and head back to the park.
The Tower-Beverly Hills Hotel 1224 S Beverwil Drive Beverly Hills CA 310-277-2800 (800-421-3212)
This 12 story, luxury hotel offers an upscale destination for business and leisure travelers with an outstanding location to numerous activities and recreation in the Los Angeles/Hollywood areas. Specializing in making you feel at home, they offer elegant accommodations, a heated pool, 24 hour room service, a complete business center, private balconies, an award winning restaurant with patio dining service, and more. Dogs of all sizes are allowed for no additional pet fee. Dogs must be well mannered, and leashed and cleaned up after at all times. Dogs may also join their owners at the outside dining tables.
Chateau Marmont Hotel 8221 Sunset Blvd Hollywood CA 323-656-1010
http://www.chateaumarmont.com/
Modeled after a royal residence in France, grand eloquence awaits guests to this castle on the hill. Some of the features/amenities include a full service bar, gourmet dining either indoor or in a beautiful garden patio setting, many in room amenities, a heated outdoor pool, and personalized services. Dogs up to 100 pounds are allowed. There is a $100 one time additional pet fee per room and a pet policy to sign at check in. Dogs must be well behaved, leashed, cleaned up after, and the Do Not Disturb sign put on the door if they are in the room alone.

Jackson - Gold Country Central

49er Village RV Resort 18265 H 49 Plymouth CA 800-339-6981
http://www.49ervillage.com
Nestled in the Sierra foothills, this park offers spacious, shady sites on tree-lined streets, 2 swimming pools-one year round-heated, an indoor whirlpool spa, and an on-site Deli-Espresso Cafe and Gift Shop, which is open daily at 7 a.m. Up to 3 dogs of any size are allowed for the RV section, and there is no additional fee or deposit. There are 2 pet friendly cabins; 1 dog is allowed in the studio, and up to 2 dogs are allowed in the one bedroom. There is a $100 per pet refundable deposit. Dogs may not be left unattended in the cottages or outside. Dogs must be leashed and cleaned up after. This is an RV only park. There is a dog walk area at the campground. Dogs are allowed in the camping cabins.
Sobon Winery 14430 Shenandoah Rd Plymouth CA 209-245-6554
http://www.sobonwine.com/
This Shenandoah Valley winery serves and sells red and white wines made entirely from organic fruits. Wine Tasting is offered 7 days a week in the tasting room and there is a little museum on the premises. Well-behaved leashed dogs are allowed at the outdoor picnic tables at the winery.

Julian

Julian Downtown and Walking Tour Main Street Julian CA 760-765-1857
You and your pooch can take a self-guided tour of Julian's historical buildings which highlight history from the Gold Rush era to the 1920s. Follow the tour through Main, Second, Third, B, C, and Washington Streets. A map is available at the Julian Chamber of Commerce located on Main and Washington Streets inside the Town Hall. There are also a number of pet-friendly outdoor restaurants and a horse and carriage ride as well as shopping.

Lake Arrowhead

Arrowhead Queen Boat Tours 28200 H 189 Building C100 Lake Arrowhead CA   909-336-6992
This enclosed paddlewheel boat is a great way to view beautiful Lake Arrowhead Lake and to learn about the area from their knowledgeable guides. Dogs are welcome aboard for no additional fee. They suggest that visitors with pets tour during the off-season, or weekdays during the busy summer season. Dogs must be friendly, and under owner's control/responsibility at all times.

Lake Tahoe

Hope Valley Cross Country Ski Center 14255 Hwy 88 Hope Valley CA   530-694-2203 (800-423-9949)
This resort is located 30 minutes south of South Lake Tahoe. You can rent cross-country skis at the at the ski center which is located at the dog-friendly Sorensen's Resort. After renting the skis, you can either take your dog on some advanced uphill trails next to the rental center or drive about a mile down the road for some easier trails. The trails are located in the Toiyabe National Forest and are not groomed. The Burnside Lake Trail is a flat, 14 mile cross-country loop trail around the lake. A smaller loop, about 4-5 miles, can be found at the Sawmill Trail. The rental center will be able to provide directions and/or maps.
The Village At Squaw Valley Squaw Valley Olympic Valley CA   530-584-6267
http://www.thevillageatsquaw.com
This European style village is very dog-friendly. You can ride the Gondola in the summer with your dog, take in a pet boutique store Tails by the Lake, enjoy numerous outdoor restaurants with your pup and browse the various stores with your leashed dog. There is a miniature golf course sprinkled throughout the walkways where kids and adults can play mini-golf with your dog along for the fun. And throughout the summer there are events such as music festivals and outdoor movies on a large screen where you and your dog are welcome for most events. Check out their website at http://www.thevillageatsquaw.com for more information and event schedules. The village is located at Squaw Valley USA just off Highway 89 between Tahoe City and Truckee in the north Tahoe area.

Squaw Valley USA-Gondola

Borges Sleigh and Carriage Rides P.O. Box 5905 Stateline NV   775-588-2953
http://www.sleighride.com/
Take your pooch on a carriage or sleigh ride in Lake Tahoe. The carriage rides start in the casino area between Harveys and Horizon, and in front of Embassy Suites. The sleigh rides begin in the field next to Caesars Tahoe (on the corner of hwy 50 and Lake Parkway). The carriages and sleighs are pulled by their 2000 pound Blond

Belgium horses or one of their rare American- Russian Baskhir Curlies which have been featured in Pasadena's Tournament of Rose Parade over the past few years. Carriage rides open noon until sunset daily, weather permitting. Prices are $15 per adult $7.50 per child under 11. Sleigh rides are given during the winter. Sleigh rides are open 10:00am to sunset (about 4:45pm). Sleigh rides are $15 per Adult $7.50 per child under 11.

Tahoe Cross Country Ski Area Country Club Drive Tahoe City CA 530-583-5475
http://www.tahoexc.org
This ski resort offers two groomed dog trails for people who want to cross country ski with their pooch. While dogs must be leashed at the trailhead and the parking lot, they can be off-leash under direct voice control on the trails. They welcome dogs on about 5 miles of groomed trails, including beginner and intermediate terrain. The dog-friendly trails are the BlueTrail and the Special Green Trail. They do not allow skijoring on either trail. The dog trails are open on Monday through Friday from 8:30am to 5pm, and on weekends and holidays from 3pm to 5pm. Dog passes are $3.00 per dog per day with a two dog per party maximum. Complimentary poop bags are provided.

North Beach at Zephyr Cove Resort 460 Highway 50 Zephyr Cove NV 775-588-6644
Dogs are not allowed at the main beach at the Zephyr Cove Resort. They are allowed on leash, however, at the north beach at the resort. There is a $5.00 parking fee for day use. When you enter Zephyr Cover Resort head to the right (North) to the last parking area and walk the few hundred feet to the beach. The North Beach is located just into the National Forest. There usually are cleanup bags on the walkway to the beach but bring your own in case they run out. This is a nice beach that is used by a lot of people in the summer. The cabins at Zephyr Cove Resort also allow dogs.

Long Beach Area

Long Beach Dog Beach Zone between Roycroft and Argonne Avenues Long Beach CA 562-570-3100
http://www.hautedogs.org/
This 3 acre off-leash unfenced dog beach is the only off-leash dog beach in Los Angeles County. It is open daily from 6am until 8pm. It opened on August 1, 2003. The "zone" is 235 yards along the water and 60 yards deep. There is a fresh water fountain called the "Fountain of Woof" which is located near the restrooms at the end of Granada Avenue, near the Dog Zone. Only one dog is allowed per adult and dog owners are entirely responsible for their dog's actions. The beach is located between Roycroft and Argonne avenues in Belmont Shore, Long Beach. It is a few blocks east of the Belmont Pier and Olympic pool. From Ocean Blvd, enter at Bennett Avenue for the beachfront metered parking lot. The cost is 25 cents for each 15 minutes from 8am until 6pm daily. Parking is free after 5pm in the beachfront lot at the end of Granada Avenue. You can check with the website http://www.hautedogs.org for updates and additional rules about the Long Beach Dog Beach Zone.

Los Angeles

Kenneth Hahn State Rec Area 4100 S La Cienega Los Angeles CA 323-298-3660
In 1932 this area hosted the 10th Olympiad, and again in 1984 Los Angeles hosted the Olympics with athletes from 140 nations, so as a reminder, 140 trees were planted here to commemorate this event. Other park features/amenities include large landscaped areas, picnic sites, BBQs, playgrounds, a fishing lake, lotus pond/Japanese Garden, gaming fields/courts, and several miles of hiking trails. Dogs are allowed throughout the park and on the trails. Dogs of all sizes are allowed for no additional fee. Dogs must be well behaved, leashed, and cleaned up after.

Laurel Canyon Park 8260 Mulholland Dr. Los Angeles CA
This nice park is located in the hills of Studio City. It is completely fenced with water and even a hot dog stand. To get there, take Laurel Canyon Blvd and go west on Mulholland Blvd. Go about a 1/4 mile and turn left. There is a parking lot below.

Prana Cafe 650 N. La Cienega Blvd Los Angeles CA 310-360-0551
This restaurant is a sleek, casual spot with mostly outdoor seating, and serves food with a bit of an Asian influence. Seeing that there was a desire for pet owner's to be able to dine with their four-legged companions, they set about preparing a doggy menu and purchasing shiny silver bowls for their canine clientele. They are open 8 am to 10 pm daily with a limited menu after 5 pm. Dogs of all sizes are allowed. Dogs must be socially friendly, leashed, and please clean up after your pet.

Runyon Canyon Off-Leash Park

Runyon Canyon Park Mulholland Hwy Los Angeles CA   323-666-5046
From this popular hiking trail and excellent off-leash area you can see views of Hollywood, the Wilshire District, and the skyscrapers of downtown L.A. This park has mostly off-leash and some on-leash hiking trails. It is about a 2 mile round-trip from end to end in the park. The top of the trail is located off Mulholland Hwy (about 2 miles east of Laurel Canyon Blvd) at Desmond Street in the Hollywood Hills. The bottom part of the trail is located at the end of Fuller Ave. Parking is available on the street. The trailhead might be kind of tricky to find from Fuller, but you'll probably see other people going to or coming from the trail.

SkyBark 1026 S Santa Fe Avenue Los Angeles CA   213-891-1722
http://www.skybark.com
This unique club sits atop a building giving a 360 degree view of downtown Los Angeles, and was born from a desire for a place to unwind and have a few drinks with others who wanted a socializing place to go with their canine companions, too. They also wanted to make a difference for animals in distress, so each event benefits animal related needs. Events are usually about one time a month with a different charity each time to benefit. There is a full bar, live music/DJs, dancing, and catered food for owners and pets. For pets, there is a play area with several hundred square feet of grass and toys, an animal potty area, waiter service, a full bar with healthy drinks in their own special martini glasses, and places to lounge around. This venue has quickly become popular, and is spreading nationwide with other bars opening in Las Vegas and Boston. Tickets, in advance, are usually $20 per person and $10 per dog. Dogs must be well mannered.

Mammoth Lakes

Cross Country Skiing Mammoth Visitor Center Mammoth Lakes CA
Want to cross country ski with your pup? Follow this plan: Rent some skis and boots at the Ski Renter (760-934-6560) located next to the Shell Gas Station on Hwy 203 (by Old Mammoth Rd). Walk or drive the skis a block or two over to the Mammoth Visitor Center / Inyo National Forest. There are several trails that start at the Visitor Center. From there I've been told you can join up to Shady Rest Park which offers more miles of cross country skiing trails (beginner trails - not too steep.) And of course, take your dog with you since this is a dog-friendly National Forest. Just listen carefully and watch out for any snowmobilers. Dogs should be leashed.

Mammoth Mountain-Gondola #1 Minaret Road Mammoth Lakes CA   760-934-0745 (800-MAMMOTH)
http://www.mammothmountain.com/
Want some awesome views of Mammoth Mountain and the surrounding areas? During the summer, you and your dog can hop on the Gondola (Cable Car) ride. You'll climb about 2,000 feet to the top of the mountain. Once there, you can enjoy a nice 1 1/2 - 2 hour hike down or take the Gondola back down the mountain. Dogs should be leashed.

Marin - North Bay

Bodega Bay Sportsfishing Center 1500 Bay Flat Road Bodega Bay CA   707-875-3344
This sports fishing center offers a variety of trips, boats, and supplies for your trip. They are located in the Porto Bodega RV Park and Marina, where dogs are also allowed. Dogs of all sizes are welcome aboard mostly on the weekdays when they are not so busy, and they suggest you bring a doggy life jacket. There is no additional pet fee. Dogs must be well behaved, under owner's control, and leashed and cleaned up after at all times.

Mendocino

Mendocino Coast Botanical Gardens 18220 N. Highway 1 Fort Bragg CA   707-964-4352
http://www.gardenbythesea.org/
This botanical garden is the only public garden in the continental United States fronting directly on the ocean. Well-behaved, leashed dogs are welcome. The gardens offer everything from colorful displays to thunderous waves. The mild maritime climate makes it a garden for all seasons, attracting gardeners and nature lovers alike. You are welcome to bring a picnic lunch to enjoy on the grounds.
Casper Beach RV Park and Campground 14441 Point Cabrilla Mendocino CA   707-964-3306
This RV park is located in one of the most picturesque coastal regions anywhere in the US, with such amenities as an arcade, an onsite grocery & novelty store, and host to a variety of land and water recreation. Dogs of all sizes are allowed for an additional fee of $2 per night per per pet. Dogs must be very friendly, quiet, well behaved, leashed, and cleaned up after. The camping and tent areas also allow dogs. There is a nice dog-friendly beach right across from the campground where you can walk your leashed dog. The campground is about five miles north of Mendocino.
Catch a Canoe Rentals 44850 Comptche-Ukiah Rd Mendocino CA   707-937-5615
http://www.stanfordinn.com/canoes.html
This canoe rental shop is located on the grounds of the dog-friendly Stanford Inn by the Sea. Feel free to walk into the shop with your pooch. If you are staying at the inn, it's a five minute walk to the shop. If you are staying at another hotel, there is ample parking. If your pup is over 50 pounds, he or she is more than welcome, but the folks at the shop will warn you that if your dog is a land-lover or decides to make a quick turn in the canoe, the whole party may become very wet. However, this dog-friendly rental shop has even modified a Mad River Winooski to create an incredibly stable canoe especially designed for dogs. Interior carpet, water bowl and a dog biscuit is included. The river you will be canoeing on is close to the ocean and it does contain alot of salt water, so make sure you bring separate water for you and your dog. Check with the shop for water conditions, but in general this is a calm river - no white water rafting here.
Stanford Inn by the Sea and Spa 44850 Comptche Ukiah Rd and Highway One Mendocino CA   707-937-5615 (800-331-8884)
http://www.stanfordinn.com
This resort is specially designed to accommodate travelers with pets. The inn is rustic and elegant. Amenities include feather beds, wood burning fireplaces, antiques, sofas, televisions with VCRs and DVDs. The resort offers complimentary breakfast featuring a choice from organic selections of omelets, waffles, burritos, and more. A large pool, sauna and Jacuzzi are protected from the fog by a solarium. Massage in the Forest provides massage and body work and yoga. The Inn's Catch A Canoe & Bicycles, too! offers kayaking and canoeing on Big River Estuary as well as mountain biking and. Special canoes are set-up to provide secure footing for your dog as well as a bowl of fresh water (Big River is tidal and for eight miles and therefore salty). The Ravens vegetarian/vegan restaurant serves organic cuisine. Well behaved pets may join you at breakfast or dinner in a dining area created especially for them. Feed and water dishes, covers to protect bedding and furniture, sleeping beds and treats are provided in the rooms. There is a $25 pet fee per stay.

Monterey

Monterey Recreation Trail various (see comments) Monterey CA
Take a walk on the Monterey Recreation Trail and experience the beautiful scenery that makes Monterey so famous. This paved trail extends for miles, starting at Fisherman's Wharf and ending in the city of Pacific Grove. Dogs must be leashed. Along the path there are a few small beaches that allow dogs such as the one south of Fisherman's Wharf and another beach behind Ghirardelli Ice Cream on Cannery Row. Along the path you'll find a few more outdoor places to eat near Cannery Row and by the Monterey Bay Aquarium. Look at the Restaurants section for more info.
Randy's Fishing Trips 66 Old Fisherman's Wharf #1 Monterey CA   800-251-7440
http://www.randysfishingtrips.com/
This fishing and whale viewing cruiser offers fully narrated tours of this region that is as rich in marine life as it is in its history. Dogs of all sizes are welcome to come aboard when they are not busy. During the week and the slow part of the season are good times to plan a trip. There is no additional fee for dogs. Dogs must be friendly, boat wise, and they must be leashed at all times and cleaned up after. Please bring your own clean up supplies.

Dogs are not allowed to loiter on the wharf by the shops.

Mount Shasta

Railroad Park Resort 100 Railroad Park Road Dunsmuir CA   530-235-4440
http://www.rrpark.com/
Spend a night or more inside a restored antique railroad car at this unique resort. Dogs are allowed for an additional $10 per day. This resort also offers RV hookup spaces.

Napa Valley

Old Faithful Geyser 1299 Tubbs Lane Calistoga CA   707-942-6463
http://www.oldfaithfulgeyser.com
Your well-behaved dog is welcome to accompany you to this natural phenomena. Just keep him or her away from the hot water. This geyser is one of only three Old Faithful geysers in the world, erupting about every 40 minutes on a yearly average. The water is 350 degrees hot and shoots about 60 feet into the air for about three to four minutes, then recedes. To see the geyser, you and your pup will need to walk through the main entrance and gift shop. Purchase the tickets at the gift shop and then walk to the geyser area to watch Old Faithful erupt. There is also a snack bar and picnic areas onsite. The admission price is $6 per adult, $5 per senior, $2 per children 6-12 and FREE for dogs. Prices are subject to change.
Petrified Forest 4100 Petrified Forest Rd. Calistoga CA   707-942-6667
http://www.petrifiedforest.org
Geologists call this petrified forest, "one of the finest examples of a pliocene fossil forest in the world." The petrified forest was created from a long ago volcanic eruption, followed by torrential rains which brought giant mudflows of volcanic ash from the eruption site to entomb the felled giants/trees. The 1/2 mile round trip meadow tour shows some of the petrified trees. Your leashed dog is welcome. Admission prices are $5 for adults, less for seniors and children, and FREE for dogs. Prices are subject to change.
The Farm Restaurant 4048 Sonoma Highway Napa CA   707-299-4900
http://www.thecarnerosinn.com/
Located at the Carneros Resort among the vineyards and orchards, this newly opened eatery offers cuisine that reflects the unique characteristics of the area. They have a large outdoor dining area with table service, and your pet may join you on their patio. Dogs must be well mannered, under owner's control at all times, leashed, and cleaned up after. Another eatery on the property, the Boon Fly Café also offers bench seating outside for visitors with dogs, and to go lunches.
Mumm Napa Winery 8445 Silverado Trail Rutherford CA   800-686-6272
http://mummnapa.com/
This winery offers outside table service on their terrace (weather permitting), spectacular views, a knowledgeable staff, an art gallery, annual events, and a gift store. Your well behaved dog is welcome to explore the grounds with you or join you on the terrace. They usually have doggy treats available and are happy to get a bowl of water for your pooch. Dogs must be leashed and cleaned up after at all times.
Beringer Vineyards 2000 Main Street St Helena CA   707-963-4812
This busy vineyard specializes in offering a large selection of wines for every occasion and every budget, feature daily historic tours and educational seminars, and hold food and wines events often throughout the year. Dogs are welcome around the grounds, at outdoor seating areas, and at the one outside tasting room area; they are not allowed in buildings. Dogs must be well mannered, under owner's control at all times, leashed, and cleaned up after.

Ojai

Casitas Boat Rentals 11311 Santa Ana Road Oak View CA   805-649-2043
You, your family and your dog can go for a boat adventure on Lake Casitas. Pontoon and row boat rentals are available and your dog is welcome to accompany you. Boating on the lake is only permitted during daylight hours. There are four floating restrooms for people on the lake. Lake Casitas is a drinking water reservoir and does not allow swimming by people or dogs. Dogs must be on-leash throughout the Lake Casitas Rec Area and may not go within 50 feet of the lake.
Ojai Valley Inn and Spa 905 Country Club Road Ojai CA   805-646-2420 (888-697-8780)
http://www.ojairesort.com/
This award-winning historic resort is elegance inside and out with 220 tree-shaded acres that include luxury accommodations, a premier championship golf course, a comprehensive 31,000 square foot spa village, and a first-of-its-kind artist cottage where local artists inspire and help guests to create in a variety of medias. In addition to several amenities, they also offer in room dining, handcrafted picnics, a cocktail lounge, and several dining options featuring California Central Coast cuisine prepared with locally harvested, seasonal foods and herbs. Dogs of all sizes are allowed but they must be acknowledged at the time of reservations. There is a $50 per night additional pet fee per room for the first 3 nights for a total of no more than $150. Dogs must be quiet,

9

leashed, cleaned up after, and crated when left alone in the room.

Orange County Beaches

Huntington Dog Beach Pacific Coast Hwy (Hwy 1) Huntington Beach CA 714-841-8644
http://www.dogbeach.org
This beautiful beach is about a mile long and allows dogs from 5 am to 10 pm. Dogs must be under control but may be off leash and owners must pick up after them. Dogs are only allowed on the beach between Golden West Street and Seapoint Ave. Please adhere to these rules as there are only a couple of dog-friendly beaches left in the entire Los Angeles area. The beach is located off the Pacific Coast Hwy (Hwy 1) at Golden West Street. Please remember to pick up after your dog... the city wanted to prohibit dogs in 1997 because of the dog waste left on the beach. But thanks to The Preservation Society of Huntington Dog Beach (http://www.dogbeach.org), it continues to be dog-friendly. City ordinances require owners to pick up after their dogs.

The Park Bench Cafe 17732 Golden West Dr Huntington Beach CA 714-842-0775
This is the most dog-friendly restaurant we have found yet. Your dog will absolutely feel welcome here. Dogs also have their own special menu. It's actually on the people's menu, but includes items like Hot Diggity Dog (hot dog a la carte), Bow Wow Chow (skinless chicken), Annabelle's Treat (chopped bacon bits) and Doggie Kibble (dog kibble for dogs that don't eat table food). For those especially pampered pups, order the Chili Paws (single scoop of Vanilla ice cream) for dessert. This restaurant can arrange special events like Poochie Parties for your dog and a minimum of six of his or her best friends. The party menu has a mouth-watering array of foods for dogs. They do ask that your dog stay off the tables and chairs. But with all the other canine amenities, pooches don't get upset about that rule. The people food here is quite tasty too. They serve a full breakfast ranging from omelets to pancakes and Belgium waffles. Lunch includes a variety of hamburgers and sandwiches. This cafe is located in Huntington Central Park at 17732 Golden West Drive between Slater Dr and Talbert Ave. Hours are Tuesday through Friday from 8am-2pm, Saturday and Sunday from 8am-3pm, and closed on Mondays. Come and enjoy the food and atmosphere.

Fashion Island Mall 1133 Newport Center Dr Newport Beach CA 800-495-4753
Fashion Island Mall is known as Southern California's premier open-air shopping center. And they allow dogs. Some of the stores allow your well-behaved dog inside. Please always ask the store clerk before bringing your dog inside, just in case policies have changed. You can also shop at the numerous outdoor retail kiosks located throughout the mall. Work up an appetite after walking around? Try dining at the fast food court located upstairs which has many outdoor seats complete with heaters or at a number of outdoor restaurants.

Newport's Fun Zone Boat Tours

Fun Zone Boat Tours 6000 Edgewater Place Newport Beach CA   949-673-0240
http://newportbeach.com/funzoneboats
The people here are very dog-friendly and welcome your pup on several of their boat tours. The narrated trips range in length from 45 to 90 minutes and can include a harbor, sea lion and Lido Island tour. The prices range from $6.00 to $9.00 and less for children. Prices are subject to change. Boat tours depart every half hour seven days a week. They do have a summer and winter schedule, so please call ahead for the hours. Whale watching tours are also available from January through March. The Fun Zone Boat Co. is located at the end of Palm Street next to the Ferris Wheel.
Newport Dunes RV Park 1131 Back Bay Drive Newport Beach CA   949-729-3863 (800-765-7661)
http://www.newportdunes.com
This waterfront resort features lush grounds, many amenities, and a variety of land and water recreation. Dogs of all sizes are allowed for an additional $2 per night per pet for the nightly fee, and an additional $5 per night per pet for the weekly fee. Dogs may not be left unattended, and they must be leashed and cleaned up after. Dogs are not allowed on the beach or anywhere on the sand. There are some breed restrictions. The camping and tent areas also allow dogs. There is a dog walk area at the campground.

Palo Alto - Peninsula

Stanford Shopping Center 680 Stanford Shopping Center Palo Alto CA   650-617-8585 (800-772-9332)
http://www.stanfordshop.com/
Stanford Shopping Center is the Bay Area's premier open-air shopping center. This dog-friendly mall has a beautiful outdoor garden environment. Thirty-five varieties of trees are represented by 1,300 specimens throughout the mall. There are hundreds of hanging baskets and flower-filled planters located in four microclimates. We have found that many of the stores do allow well-behaved dogs inside. However, please ask the store clerk before bringing your dog inside each store just in case their policies have changed. Depending on the season, there will be many outdoor tables adjacent to the food stands and cafes. Here you can order the food inside and then enjoy it with your pup at one of the outside tables.

Perris

Orange Empire Railway Museum 2201 South A Street Perris CA   951-657-2605
http://www.oerm.org/
Home to the West's largest collection of railway locomotives, streetcars, freight/passenger cars, interurban electric cars, buildings, and other objects dating from the 1870's, this museum also educates the public of the rail history and offers a variety of interactive programs. You can ride or drive a locomotive, have a special caboose birthday party, visit the museum store, picnic, or take self-guided or guided tours. Dogs of all sizes are welcome. Dogs are allowed throughout the grounds; they are not allowed in the gift shop. Dogs must be well mannered, leashed, and cleaned up after.

Pioneertown

Pioneertown Pioneertown Road Pioneertown CA   760-964-6549
http://www.pioneertown.com/f-index.htm
Because the town was also built as a movie set to be a complete old west town, numerous Western stars and movie star greats of the past spent a lot of time here. The movie sets that were used in filming also provided homes for the actors and crew and with an emphasis placed on experiencing the old west, this place is like stepping back to the 1800's. The town has its own pioneer posse, and offers seasonal old west reenactments, dozens of shops and exhibits to explore, western cooking, a motel that accepts dogs, and a lot more. Dogs are welcome all around town, and they may even end up with their picture on the website. They are not allowed in buildings. Dogs must be leashed at all times and cleaned up after. Please carry supplies.

Placerville - Highway 50 Corridor

Jack Russell Brewing Company 2380 Larsen Drive Camino CA   530-644-4722
http://www.jackrussellbrewing.com/
You and your best friend are welcome at this English farm-style brewery located near Placerville in the Sierra Foothills between Sacramento and Lake Tahoe. Adjacent to the brewery is a picnic area where you can enjoy a variety of hand-crafted beers. They also have homemade root beer. The founding mascot, a Jack Russell Terrier named Boomer, is on the beer label. The brewery is open on the weekends and during the summer they sometimes have live entertainment outside and English-style meat pies. Dogs are welcome outside including the picnic areas.
High Hill Ranch 2901 High Hill Rd. Placerville CA   530-644-1973
Every fall from September to Christmas the region around Camino known as Apple Hill hosts half a million

visitors to the apple farms and wineries of the region. There are a number of farms and wineries open to visitors with activities, rides, crafts booths and much more. High Hill Ranch is one of the largest of these farms and offers pony rides, fishing, crafts, food and apple pies. Your leashed dog is welcome to the outside areas in High Hill Ranch and most of the other ranches in the area. See the detailed listings around Camino and Placerville for more ranches and activities in Apple Hill.

Sweetie Pie's 577 Main Street Placerville CA 530-642-0128
Try the fresh cinnamon rolls at this restaurant. They also serve a delicious variety of food for breakfast and lunch. They are open 7 days a week from 6:30am to 4pm. They usually do not serve food outside during the winter. It is located on Main Street (between Bedford and Clay Streets), east of historic downtown Placerville.

Porterville

Sequoia National Forest 1839 South Newcomb Street Porterville CA 559-784-1500 (877-444-6777)
Named for the world's largest tree, this forest is home to 38 groves of the giant sequoias, as well as impressive granite monoliths, glacier torn canyons, lush meadows, and rushing rivers. There are also several features/attractions here, some of which include; a 50 mile auto route (Kings Canyon Scenic Byway) that descends into one of North America's deepest canyons; several lookout stations-including the highest lookout (Bald Mountain) in the southern Sierra Nevadans; there are 3 National Recreation Trails, 45 miles of the Pacific Crest National Scenic Trail, and more than 800 miles of maintained roads/over a 1,000 miles of trails. There is a wide variety of year round land and water recreational opportunities. Your dog is welcome here at Sequoia National Forest (not to be confused with the less than dog-friendly Sequoia National Park). Dogs must be friendly, well behaved, on no more than a 6 foot leash, cleaned up after, and inside an enclosed vehicle or tent at night. Dogs may go on all the trails and throughout the park; they are not allowed on developed swimming beaches or in park buildings.

Redding

Turtle Bay Exploration Park 840 Auditorium Drive Redding CA 800-TURTLEBAY (887-8532)
http://www.turtlebay.org/
This amazing exploration park is 300 acres of educational and entertaining activities with a focus on relationships between humans and nature through the telling of the region and its peoples. It is home to the translucent Sundial Bridge, a free-standing, technical marvel spanning the Sacramento River that connects the north and south campuses of the park. There is also a historical railroad exhibit, an arboretum that extends over 200 acres, a series of climate display gardens, a medicinal garden, children's garden, a variety of several other gardens, and much more. Dogs are allowed throughout most of the park, in the gardens, the bridge, and on the hiking trails. They are not allowed at Paul Bunyan's Forest Camp or in the museum. Dogs must be leashed and cleaned up after at all times. There are doggy clean-up supplies on site.

Redwood National and State Parks

Redwood National and State Parks 1111 Second Street Crescent City CA 707-464-6101
http://www.nps.gov/redw/
The National and State Parks do not allow dogs on any trails but some of the beaches and campgrounds welcome dogs. Pets are allowed on Crescent Beach, Gold Bluffs Beach and the Freshwater Spit Lagoon. The campgrounds that allow pets include Jedediah Smith Redwoods State Park campground, Prairie Creek Redwoods State Park campground and Gold Bluffs Beach campground. One way to see a number of redwood groves with dogs is to take the Newton B. Drury Scenic Bypass off of Highway 101. You may see large elk grazing near the parking lots as you drive through the park. Dogs are also allowed to walk along some gravel roads. Two roads that can be walked along with dog include Cal Barrel Road (3 miles long) and Howland Hill Rd (6 miles long). These roads will usually not be too crowded with cars except at the busiest times. Old growth Redwood groves line these gravel roads. Pets must be leashed and attended at all times and please clean up after them.

Trees of Mystery 15500 Highway 101 N. Klamath CA 800-638-3389
http://www.treesofmystery.net
Located in the center of the Redwood National and State Parks, this attraction allows leashed dogs everywhere people are welcome. They have an 8/10ths of a mile groomed interpretive trail through the awe-inspiring Redwoods of California. Also located here is a world-class Native American Museum and a gondola which takes you and your pooch on an aerial ride through the redwood forest canopy. They are located along Highway 101 in Klamath. Klamath is 36 miles south of the Oregon border and 260 miles north of Santa Rosa.

Sacramento

American River Parkway   Sacramento CA 916-875-6672

The American River Parkway is a very popular recreation trail for locals and visitors. There are over 32 miles of paved and dirt paths that stretch from Folsom Lake in the Sierra Foothills to Old Sacramento in downtown Sacramento. It is enjoyed by hikers, wildlife viewers, boaters, equestrians and bicyclists. And of course, by dogs. Dogs must be on leash. There are various starting points, like the Folsom Lake State Recreation Area in Folsom or just north of downtown Sacramento. To start just north of downtown, take Hwy 5 north of downtown and exit Richards Blvd. Turn left onto Richards Blvd. Then turn right on Jibboom Street. Take Jibboom St to the parking lot.

Top Hand Ranch Carriage Rides in Old Sacramento

Old Sacramento Historic Area between I and L Streets Sacramento CA 916-442-7644
http://www.oldsacramento.com/
Old Sacramento is a state historic park located in downtown Sacramento, next to the Sacramento River. This National Registered Landmark covers 28 acres and includes a variety of shops and restaurants (see Restaurants). Take the self-guided audio tour of Old Sacramento and learn about life in the 1860's. There are nine audio stations ($.50 per station) placed throughout Old Sacramento. The California State Railroad Museum is also located here. Dogs aren't allowed inside the museum, but there are several locomotives outside. You and your pup can investigate these large trains outside of the museum. Dogs are allowed on the horse and carriage rides located throughout town. Top Hand Ranch Carriage Rides will be more than happy to take you and your well-behaved pup on their carriages. (see Attractions). Old Sacramento is located in downtown Sacramento, between I and L Streets, and Interstate 5 and the Sacramento River. Parking garages are located at 3rd and J Streets or at Capitol Mall and Front Streets. There is a minimal fee for parking.
Sheraton Grand Sacramento Hotel 1230 J St. (13th & J St) Sacramento CA 916-447-1700 (888-625-5144)
The elegant and dog-friendly Sheraton Grand Sacramento Hotel is located directly across the street from the Capitol Park and within easy walking distance of Downtown Plaza and Old Sacramento. Dogs of all sizes are allowed. Pet rooms are on the sixth floor. Dogs are not allowed to be left alone in the room.

San Diego

Otay Ranch Town Center Eastlake Pkwy At Olympic Pkwy Chula Vista CA 619-656-9100
http://www.otayranchtowncenter.com
This upscale outdoor mall opened in October, 2006. It was the first new mall opened in the San Diego area in 20 years. It is pet-friendly and it even has a dog park on the premises next to the Macy's. Many stores allow dogs inside but you will need to ask first. There are poop bags available at the mall and many stores have water dishes for dogs. There is also a vet located at the mall. To get to the mall and dog park from San Diego go south on the 805 Freeway to the Orange Avenue Exit. Head east on Orange Avenue which will become Olympic

Parkway. Go 4 miles east to the mall.

Loews Coronado Bay Resort

Loews Coronado Bay Resort 4000 Coronado Bay Road Coronado CA   619-424-4000
All well-behaved dogs of any size are welcome. This upscale hotel offers their "Loews Loves Pets" program which includes special pet treats, local dog walking routes, and a list of nearby pet-friendly places to visit. There are no pet fees and loads of pet-friendly activities on the premises including various boat rentals and tours.
Dog Beach Point Loma Blvd. Ocean Beach CA 619-221-8900
Dogs are allowed to run off leash at this beach anytime during the day. This is a very popular dog beach which attracts lots and lots of dogs on warm days. To get there, take Hwy 8 West until it ends and then it becomes Sunset Cliffs Blvd. Then make a right turn onto Point Loma Blvd and follow the signs to Ocean Beach's Dog Beach.
Campland on the Bay 2211 Pacific Beach Drive San Diego CA   800-422-9386
http://www.campland.com/
This RV park is located on Mission Bay, across the water from Sea World. They offer beach front, bay view or primitive sites. Amenities include boat slips, a boat launch, store with a market, game room and a laundry room. Dogs of all sizes are allowed for an additional fee of $3 per night per pet. They must be leashed and please clean up after them. Dogs may not be left unattended outside, and they are not allowed on the beach. The camping and tent areas also allow dogs. There is a dog walk area at the campground.
Family Kayak Adventure Center 4217 Swift Avenue San Diego CA   619-282-3520
http://familykayak.com
This company offers guided kayaking adventure tours to people of all ages and abilities. For beginners they offer paddles on flat water in stable tandem kayaks that hold one to four people. All equipment and instruction is provided for an enjoyable first outing. Well-behaved dogs are also welcome. There is even a "Dog Paddles" tour which is an evening tour on Mission Bay that includes quality time on the water and on Fiesta Island's leash free area.
Hotel Solamar 453 6th Avenue San Diego CA   619-531-8740 (877-230-0300)
http://www.hotelsolamar.com/
This hip luxury boutique hotel features a vibrant décor, a great location to the area's best shopping, dinning, and entertainment, and a full list of amenities for the business or leisure traveler. They feature elegantly appointed rooms, an evening wine hour, 24 hour room service from the adjacent J6Restaurant and J6Bar, a pool and spa, and several in-room amenities. Dogs of all sizes are welcome for no additional pet fee. Dogs must be friendly, quiet, leashed and cleaned up after, and the Dog in Room sign put on the door if they are in the room alone.
Seaforth Boat Rentals 1641 Quivira Road San Diego CA   619-223-1681
http://www.seaforthboatrental.com/

This boat rental/adventure tour company feature over 200 watercraft rentals available at 3 locations. They offer a wide variety of adventure packages, including manned or unmanned rentals, sailing lessons, fishing excursions/tournaments, remote or on-site picnicking, whale watching, and they will even organize beach parties. Dogs of all sizes are welcome on the boat rentals for no additional fee. Dogs must be friendly, well behaved, under owner's control at all times, and leashed and cleaned up after.

San Diego County North

Witch Creek Winery 2906 Carlsbad Blvd/H 101 Carlsbad CA   760-720-7499
This winery focuses on handcrafted wines that are rich, full bodied, and well balanced. They have two tasting rooms; one in Carlsbad and the other one in Julian, California. They consider themselves dog-friendly, and your pet is welcome to go wherever you can go, including the tasting room in Carlsbad. Dogs must be well behaved, and leashed and cleaned up after at all times.
California Surf Museum 223 N Coast H Oceanside CA   760-721-6876
http://www.surfmuseum.org/
This interesting museum is a resource and educational center to gather, preserve, and document the art, culture and heritage of this lifestyle sport for generations to come. Well mannered dogs are welcome at this small museum; they must be leashed and under owner's control at all times.

San Francisco

Baker Beach Lincoln Blvd and Bowley St/Golden Gate Nat'l Rec Area San Francisco CA   415-561-4700
This dog-friendly beach in the Golden Gate National Recreation Area has a great view of the Golden Gate Bridge. Dogs are permitted off leash under voice control on Baker Beach North of Lobos Creek; they must be leashed South of Lobos Creek. The beach is located approx. 1.5 to 2 miles south of the Golden Gate Bridge. From Lincoln Avenue, turn onto Bowley Street and head towards the ocean. There is a parking lot next to the beach. This is a clothing optional beach, so there may be the occasional sunbather.
Fort Funston/Burton Beach Skyline Blvd./Hwy 35 San Francisco CA
http://www.nps.gov/goga/
This is a very popular dog-friendly park and beach. In the past, dogs have been allowed off-leash. However, currently all dogs must be on leash. Fort Funston is part of the Golden Gate National Recreation Area. There are trails that run through the dunes & ice plant from the parking lot above with good access to the beach below. It overlooks the southern end of Ocean Beach, with a large parking area accessible from Skyline Boulevard. There is also a water faucet and trough at the parking lot for thirsty pups. It's located off Skyline Blvd. (also known Hwy 35) by John Muir Drive. It is south of Ocean Beach. Thanks to one of our readers for this info. Expect to see lots and lots of dogs having a great time. But not to worry, there is plenty of room for everyone.
Golden Gate Bridge P.O. Box 9000, Presidio Station San Francisco CA   415-921-5858
http://goldengatebridge.org
The walk across the Golden Gate Bridge is a unique and stirring experience, and the views of the city and bay are worth the 1.7 mile walk. Visitors may access the bridge sidewalks during daylight hours, and hours vary by the season. The southeast parking area offers visitor services, such as a café, gift center, renovated gardens, and scenic vistas. Dogs are permitted on the bridge as long as they are under owner's control at all times, and they must be leashed and cleaned up after. Please carry clean-up supplies for your dog.
Golden Gate Park Off Leash Dog Areas Stanyan & Great Highway San Francisco CA   415-751-8987
Listed among the world's greatest urban parks at over 1,000 acres, there are grassy meadows, wooded trails, secluded lakes, open groves, gardens, museums, and four official, legal off leash dog areas. (1) The Southeast area is located in a wooded strip of land bounded by 3rd Ave., 7th Ave., North of Lincoln Way, and South of Martin Luther King Blvd. It is small, not well marked, with lots of traffic and foxtails in the Spring, so the Big Rec locale is the de facto mixed-use off-leash area. Enter Lincoln Way at 7th or 9th Avenue, and the area used is located above/behind the athletic fields. This area is preferred because it is safer and easier to use. (2) The Northeast section is at Fulton and Willard in a Natural Area of 0 .2 acres. This park is near the intersection of Stanyan & Fulton Streets, and is a small, little used area with no fences and prone to heavy traffic. (3) The Southcentral area is bounded by Martin Luther King Drive, Middle Drive and 34th and 38th Avenues; 4.4 acres. This dog friendly knoll has become the last immediate off leash area for people in the outer district. (4) The Northcentral area near 38th Ave. and Fulton (Fenced, training area; 1.4 acres) is the bay areas largest, fenced, exclusive-use off-leash area. It is located behind the Bison pens and West of Spreckles Lake. You can walk in near 39th Avenue and Fulton, or drive in from 38th Ave. The area is surrounded by a low fence that larger dogs could jump and they suggest that this play area may be more suitable for dogs that are in training or not under voice control. Dogs under 4 months old are not allowed, and females in heat should be leashed, and they are not allowed in the single use areas. Dogs must be under control and cleaned up after at all times.
Hotel Diva 440 Geary Street San Francisco CA   800-553-1900
http://www.hoteldiva.com/
At the hub of Union Square, this ultra modern hotel offers exceptional personalized service for the leisure or business traveler, and a convenient location for a wide variety of shopping, entertainment, and dining

opportunities. One dog up to 70 pounds is allowed for an additional one time pet fee of $75. This is a Personality Hotel property and one of four local hotels that offer the "Every Doggie is a Diva Package" with prices starting at $189 per night. This deluxe package includes the overnight accommodations (so no additional $75 fee), a bottle of water, a designer pet bowl, a personalized dog tag, a plush sheep skin throw, a 1 hour VIP dog walking tour highlighting favored parks and fire hydrants (Monday through Friday-noon to 1pm), and a Petco amenity box with treats, biscuits, 2 flavors of dog food, and a red paw print bandana. Dogs must be leashed, cleaned up after, and crated if left alone in the room.

Vampire Tour of San Francisco Nob Hill, Corner of California and Tayor Streets San Francisco CA   866-4-BITTEN (424-8836)

This self-proclaimed vampire hostess leads guests on about a 2 hour unique journey of history and entertainment of the Vampires of the city. Although the tour is open all year, it is a good idea to check ahead if there is inclement weather. This has become a popular attraction, especially around Halloween, so reservations are also suggested. Well mannered dogs are welcome to join this tour because the only building they enter is the Fairmont Hotel, and they are pet friendly. There is no additional fee; dogs must be under owner's control at all times, be leashed, and please carry supplies to clean up after your pet.

Waterfront Carriage Rides Jefferson Street San Francisco CA   415-771-8687

Want to tour San Francisco in style? Take an elegant horse and carriage ride with your well-behaved dog. They'll take you and your pup on a tour of Fisherman's Wharf. The carriages are located by Pier 41.

San Jose

Rock Bottom Restaurant & Brewery 1875 S Bascom Ave Campbell CA   408-377-0707

This dog-friendly restaurant is located in the Pruneyard Shopping Center. The Campbell-Los Gatos path is within walking distance. Water is provided for your pet. There is a nice outdoor seating area with heaters.

Cypress Hotel 10050 S. DeAnza Blvd. Cupertino CA   408-253-8900

http://www.thecypresshotel.com/

Well-behaved dogs of all sizes are welcome at this pet-friendly hotel. The boutique hotel offers both rooms and suites. Hotel amenities include complimentary evening wine service, an a 24 hour on-site fitness room. There are no pet fees, just sign a pet liability form.

Santana Row 368 Santana Row San Jose CA   408-551-4611

http://www.santanarow.com

This European style community with nearly 100 shops beneath condos is dog-friendly. There are clean up bags located at various spots for your dog throughout Santana Row. There are a number of dog-friendly stores and outdoor restaurants and sidewalk cafes in Santana Row. Please ask each individual store if you may bring your dog in. Santana Row is located in the heart of Silicon Valley on Stevens Creek Blvd just west of I-880.

San Luis Obispo

Cambria Shores Inn 6276 Moonstone Beach Drive Cambria CA   805-927-8644 (800-433-9179)

http://www.cambriashores.com

Dogs are allowed for a $10.00 per night per dog fee. Pets must be leashed and never left alone. The inn offers local pet sitting services and provide treats for dogs.

Pismo Coast Village RV Park 165 S Dolliver Street Pismo Beach CA   805-773-1811 (888-RV-BEACH (782-3224))

http://www.pismocoastvillage.com/

This 26 acre RV park is located right on the dog-friendly Pismo State Beach. There are 400 full hookup sites each with satellite TV. RVs up to 40 feet can be accommodated. Nestled right on the beach and beautifully landscaped, park amenities include a general store, arcade, guest laundry, guest modem access in lobby, heated pool, bicycle rentals and miniature golf course. The maximum stay is 29 consecutive nights. Well-behaved leashed dogs of all sizes are allowed, up to a maximum of three pets. People need to clean up after their pets. There is no pet fee. Dogs may not be left unattended outside. This RV only campground is open all year. There are some breed restrictions. There is a dog walk area at the campground.

Pismo State Beach Grand Ave. Pismo Beach CA 805-489-2684

Leashed dogs are allowed on this state beach. This beach is popular for walking, sunbathing, swimming and the annual winter migration of millions of monarch butterflies (the park has the largest over-wintering colony of monarch butterflies in the U.S.). To get there from Hwy 101, exit 4th Street and head south. In about a mile, turn right onto Grand Ave. You can park along the road.

Novo Restaurant 726 Higuera Street San Luis Obispo CA   805-543-3986

http://www.novorestaurant.com

This restaurant in downtown San Luis Obispo offers creekside dining on its patio. Well-behaved, leashed dogs are allowed on the outside patio. The restaurant serves Brazilian, Mediterranean and Asian foods. It opens for lunch at 11 am and remains open through dinner.

Santa Barbara

Santa Barbara Botanical Garden 1212 Mission Canyon Road Santa Barbara CA   805-682-4726
This beautiful botanical garden is located on 65 acres in historic Mission Canyon and they allow dogs in the garden and on the trails. This garden features over 1,000 species of rare and indigenous California plants. There are five and a half miles of scenic trails that take you through meadows and canyons, across historic Mission Dam, and along ridge-tops that offer sweeping views of the California Islands. The garden is about a 15-20 minute drive from downtown Santa Barbara.
Santa Barbara Electric Car Rental 101 State Street Santa Barbara CA   805-962-2585
http://www.wheelfunrentals.com/
This premier recreational rental outlet offers a wide variety of rental vehicles for various uses. Dogs are allowed in the electric car rentals for no additional pet fee as long as the car is returned clean. Dogs must be well behaved, and leashed and cleaned up after at all times.

Shasta - Trinity National Forest

Estrellita Marina 49160 State Highway 3 Trinity Center CA   530-286-2215
Rent a patio/pontoon boat with your pooch on Lake Trinity. There is a 4 hour minimum for boat rentals and pricing starts at about $75 for 4 hours. This full service marina includes a country store, launch ramp and gas. Well-behaved dogs are allowed on the boats. The marina also rent houseboats and well-behaved dogs are welcome on those too.

Solvang

Solvang Village

Solvang Village 1500-2000 Mission Drive Solvang CA   800-468-6765
http://www.solvang.org/
As the Solvang Visitor's Bureau states, "Visiting Danes have described Solvang as 'more like Denmark than Denmark' - a remarkable tribute to the town's passion for Danish architecture, cuisine and customs." Solvang is a quaint shopping village and a great place to walk with your dog. Several stores along Mission Drive are dog-friendly like The Book Loft and Lemo's Feed & Pet Supply (please always verify that stores are dog-friendly by asking the clerk before entering). There are also many dog-friendly restaurants in town including bakeries that have mouth watering goodies. Sunset Magazine recently voted Solvang as one of the '10 Most Beautiful Small

Towns' in the Western United States.

Sonoma

Sebastiani Vineyards and Winery 389 Fourth Street East Sonoma CA   800-888-5532
http://www.sebastiani.com/home.asp
Dogs of all sizes are welcome to explore the vineyard and enjoy the picnic area with their owners. Small dogs that can be carried are allowed in the tasting room. They provide water bowls outside all the time, and anchored leash extensions. They are open daily from 10 am to 5 pm. Dogs must be well behaved, leashed at all times, and please clean up after your pet.
Mutt Lynch Winery 1960 Dry Creek Road Healdsburg CA   707-942-6180
http://www.muttlynchwinery.com/
This small one woman winery is usually open only by appointment. However, by combining humor, a love of dogs and passion for wine, this winery offers such items as the "Big Dog" wines, or their Merlot Over and Play Dead, and their annual Dog Days of Summer festival is a fun event for pet and owner with a dog art exhibit, good food, and music. They also have other related events. Dogs are welcome throughout the winery, and they must be leashed at all times and cleaned up after.
Russian River Adventures Canoe Rentals 20 Healdsburg Ave Healdsburg CA   707-433-5599 (800-280-7627 (SOAR))
Take a self-guided eco-adventure with your pooch. Rent an inflatable canoe and adventure along the Russian River. The SOAR 16 is the largest model and is great for taking children and dogs. There are many refreshing swimming holes along the way. Dogs and families of all ages are welcome. Be sure to call ahead as reservations are required.
Pacific Coast Air Museum 2330 Airport Blvd Santa Rosa CA   707-575-7900
http://pacificcoastairmuseum.org/
Well-behaved, leashed dogs are allowed in the museum. The museum offers both indoor and outdoor exhibits.

Sonora - Gold Country South

Columbia State Historic Park Parrotts Ferry Rd. Columbia CA   209-532-0150
The popular Columbia State Historic Park represents a gold rush town of the 1850-1870 time period. In 1945 the State Legislature made this site a State Historic Park in order to preserve a typical Gold Rush town, an example of one of the most colorful eras in American history. The town's old Gold Rush-era business district has been preserved with many shops and restaurants. The proprietors of the shops are dressed in mid 1800s period clothing. Activities include viewing over a dozen historic structures, shopping, picnic facilities and a few hiking trails. One of the trails, The Karen Bakerville Smith Memorial Trail is a self-guided 1/2 mile loop trail which was dedicated to a teacher. The trail is located by the historic school building and there is a brochure describing the plants and surroundings. The park operates daily from 9am to 5 pm. They are closed on Thankgiving and Christmas days. Admission is free. Your leashed dog is welcome. It is located on Parrotts Ferry Road, between Hwy 4 and Hwy 49 (near Sonora).

Temecula

Baily Vineyard 33440 La Serena Way Temecula CA   951-676-WINE (9463)
http://www.bailywinery.com/
Grapes are brought to this winery's state-of-the-art production facility from 32 acres of grapes grown in 4 different sites in the Temecula Valley. The restaurant on site (Carol's) offers patio dining service, and a selection of luncheon salads, sandwiches, grilled fish and steak, and pasta dishes. Dogs are allowed around the grounds, and at the outside dining area, but not in the tasting room. Dogs must be well behaved, and leashed and cleaned up after at all times.

Ventura - Oxnard

Eric Ericsson's on the Pier 668 Harbor Blvd Ventura CA   805-643-4783
http://www.ericericssons.com/
Located on the edge of the dog-friendly Ventura Pier (one of the longest piers in California, they offer a variety of California cuisine and "seafood prepared at it's best". They are open 7 days a week; from 11 am to 10 pm Sunday through Thursday, and from 11 am to 11 pm Friday and Saturday. All well behaved, leashed dogs are allowed to join their owners on the patio. Just go into the restaurant (without your dog) and the hostess will seat you and your pet on the patio.

Yorkville

Yorkville Cellars 25701 H 128 Yorkville CA   707-894-9177
http://www.YorkvilleCellars.com
This vineyard has been CCOF certified since 1986, and they are a recipient of prestigious "Masters of Organics" award. Their free tasting room is located in the middle of the estate vineyards, and they are open daily from 11 am to 6 pm. Your well behaved, leashed dog is welcome to explore the vineyard with you; they are allowed in some of the buildings and the picnic area as well. They would also like your dog to be cat friendly, and that you clean up after your pet.

Yosemite

Yosemite Mountain Sugar Pine Railroad

Yosemite Mountain Sugar Pine Railroad 56001 Highway 41 Fish Camp CA 559-683-7273
http://www.ymsprr.com/
Hop aboard a four mile railroad excursion with your pooch and enjoy a narrative ride through the Sierra National Forest. One of their steam engines is the heaviest operating narrow gauge Shay locomotive in use today. Well-behaved leashed dogs are welcome. The railroad is located near Yosemite Park's south gate on Highway 41.
Yosemite National Park PO Box 577 Yosemite National Park CA   209-372-0200
http://www.nps.gov/yose
This 750,000 acre park is one of the most popular national parks in the country. Yosemite's geology is world famous for its granite cliffs, tall waterfalls and giant sequoia groves. As with most national parks, pets have limited access within the park. Pets are not allowed on unpaved or poorly paved trails, in wilderness areas including hiking trails, in park lodging (except for some campgrounds) and on shuttle buses. However, there are still several nice areas to walk with your pooch and you will be able to see the majority of sights and points of interest that most visitors see. Dogs are allowed in developed areas and on fully paved trails, include Yosemite Valley which offers about 2 miles of paved trails. From these trails you can view El Capitan, Half Dome and Yosemite Falls. You can also take the .5 mile paved trail right up to the base of Bridalveil Fall which is a 620 foot year round waterfall. The best time to view this waterfall is in the spring or early summer. The water thunders down and almost creates a nice rain at the base. Water-loving dogs will be sure to like this attraction. In general dogs are not allowed on unpaved trails, but this park does make the following exceptions. Dogs are allowed on the Meadow Loop and Four Mile fire roads in Wawona. They are also allowed on the Carlon Road and on the Old Big Oak Flat Road between Hodgdon Meadow and Hazel Green Creek. Dogs must be on a 6 foot or less leash and attended at all times. People must also clean up after their pets. For a detailed map of Yosemite, visit their web site at http://www.nps.gov/yose/pphtml/maps.html. The green dots show the paved trails. There are four main entrances to the park and all four lead to the Yosemite Valley. The park entrance fees are as follows: $20 per vehicle, $40 annual pass or $10 per individual on foot. The pass is good for 7 days. Prices are subject to

change. Yosemite Valley is open year round and may be reached via Highway 41 from Fresno, Highway 140 from Merced, Highway 120 from Manteca and in late spring through late fall via the Tioga Road (Highway 120 East) from Lee Vining. From November through March, all park roads are subject to snow chain control (including 4x4s) or temporary closure at any time due to hazardous winter driving conditions. For updated 24 hour road and weather conditions call (209) 372-0200.

Yreka

Blue Goose Steam Excursion Train 300 East Miner Street Yreka CA   530-842-4146 (800-973-5277)
http://www.yrekawesternrr.com/
The Blue Goose excursion train rides on railroad tracks that were built in 1888. The train travels over Butcher Hill in Yreka and then down through the scenic Shasta Valley with Mt. Shasta in the view. The train then crosses over the Shasta River and continues on to the old cattle town of Montague. The distance is about 7.5 miles one way and takes approximately 1 hour to arrive. Upon arrival in Montague, passengers disembark the train and will have about 1.5 hours for lunch and to explore the historic town of Montague. During lunchtime, the train is pushed back in preparation for the return trip to Yreka. The train returns to pick up passengers about 15 minutes before departure. The total round trip time for this ride is about 3.5 hours. Trains run from Memorial Day Weekend to the end of October on a limited schedule. Well-behaved leashed dogs that are friendly towards people and children are welcome. They ask that you please keep your pooch out of the aisles once on the train.

"Must See" Arizona Dog-Friendly Places

Camp Verde

Montezuma Castle National Monument 2800 Montezuma Castle H Camp Verde AZ   928-567-3322
http://www.nps.gov/moca/
This park is home to one of the best preserved cliff dwellings in North America. The 20 room, 5 story cliff dwelling sits high above a creek in a limestone recess, and served as a "high-rise apartment building" for Sinagua Indians over 600 years ago. Exhibits along the self-guiding trail describe the cultural and natural history of the site and a diorama/audio program shows the interior view of the cliff dwellings. Dogs must be on no more than a six foot leash at all times and cleaned up after. Dogs may not be left unattended in the park or in automobiles. They are open every day of the year, including Christmas day. Winter hours: 8 AM to 5 PM; Summer hours (May 30th through Labor Day): 8 AM to 6 PM MST.

Grand Canyon

Grand Canyon National Park Hwy 64 Grand Canyon AZ   928-638-7888
http://www.nps.gov/grca/
The Grand Canyon, located in the northwest corner of Arizona, is considered to be one of the most impressive natural splendors in the world. It is 277 miles long, 18 miles wide, and at its deepest point, is 6000 vertical feet (more than 1 mile) from rim to river. The Grand Canyon has several entrance areas, but the most popular is the South Rim. Dogs are not allowed on any trails below the rim, but leashed dogs are allowed on the paved rim trail. This dog-friendly trail is about 2.7 miles each way and offers excellent views of the Grand Canyon. Remember that the elevation at the rim is 7,000 feet, so you or your pup may need to rest more often than usual. Also, the weather can be very hot during the summer and can be snowing during the winter, so plan accordingly. And be sure you or your pup do not get too close to the edge! Feel like taking a tour? Well-behaved dogs are allowed on the Geology Walk. This is a one hour park ranger guided tour and consists of a leisurely walk along a 3/4 mile paved rim trail. They discuss how the Grand Canyon was created and more. The tour departs at 11am daily (weather permitting) from the Yavapai Observation Station. The Grand Canyon park entrance fee is currently $25.00 per private vehicle, payable upon entry to the park. Admission is for 7 days, includes both South and North Rims, and covers the entrance fee only.
Supai and the Havasupai Reservation P. O. Box 10/Indian Road 18 Supai AZ   928-448-2141
http://www.havasupaitribe.com/index.htm
Want to take your dog down to the Colorado River in the Grand Canyon but, of course, this is not allowed by the National Park Service? Instead, just down river from Grand Canyon National Park is the Havasupai Indian Reservation, which shares the Canyon with the National Park. The canyon and the campgrounds are accessible only by foot, pack animals and helicopter. Leashed dogs may accompany you on the trails into the canyon, to the water falls, the campground and the Colorado River. They are not allowed in the lodge. Please clean up after your dog throughout the reservation. It is suggested that you inquire ahead as there is only limited space at the campground and there is an eight mile hike down into the canyon to the campground. Dogs are also allowed on the helicopters. For more information see the detailed listings.
The Planes of Fame Air Museum 755 Mustang Way Valle AZ   928-635-1000
http://www.planesoffame.org/menu.php This air museum is dedicated to collecting, restoring, displaying, and

preserving aircraft and memorabilia for the educational benefit of present and future generations. There are over 150 aircraft at its two locations; the main facility is in Chino, California. The displayed aircraft spans the history of manned flight, from a replica of the Chanute Hang Glider of 1896, to modern space flight. It also includes vehicles from numerous milestone achieving test and research flights. Hours are from 9am to 5pm everyday (Closed Thanksgiving & Christmas Day). Well behaved dogs of all sizes are allowed throughout the property for no additional fee. Dogs must be leashed, under owners' control at all times, and cleaned up after.

Lake Havasu

The London Bridge 314 London Bridge Road (Lake Havasu City Visitor's Center) Lake Havasu City AZ   928-453-8883
The London Bridge was built in 1831, and after many long years in service, it was relocated to Lake Havasu City, Arizona, and dedicated on October 10, 1971. There is a walkway along the bridge so that you and your pet can walk across this piece of history and enjoy the view of the lake. Dogs must be leashed at all times, and please clean up after your pet.

Page - Lake Powell

Lake Powell - Glen Canyon Recreation Area   Page AZ   435-684-7400
http://www.nps.gov/glca/
Beautiful Lake Powell is called America's Natural Playground and is home to the world's largest natural bridge (standing 290 feet high), the Rainbow Bridge National Monument. The Wahweap Lodge, located in Page, rents powerboats for sight-seeing on the lake. Rent and drive your own boat, and your dog is welcome to join you. If you rent a boat, there is a one half mile trail to the Rainbow Bridge from the Rainbow Bridge courtesy dock. Also at Lake Powell near Bullfrog, there is a 3 mile round-trip hiking trail called Pedestal Alley. For boat rentals, the Wahweap Lodge is located 2.5 miles SE of US 89 at Lake Powell. The best time to visit the lake is during the fall season when temperatures are mild.
Navajo Village 1235 Copper Mine Road Page AZ 928-660-0304
http://www.navajovillage.com/home.html
This Navajo Village is an authentic re-creation of a traditional Navajo homesite that tells the living history of the Navajo people through oral story telling, music, dance, their art, and even their food preparation. Share the beauty of their harmony, relationships, industry, and creativity through the various programs they offer. They offer mini or grand tours for individuals or groups. Their season is from April through October, and during the busy times, they are usually open all day. If it is during a slow time, the tours start at 4 pm. Well behaved dogs on lead are welcome for no additional fee. Please clean up after your pet.
Wahweap Lodge and Marina 100 Lakeshore Drive Page AZ 928-645-2433
The lodge offers a fine dining restaurant, gift shop, pool, lounge, and spectacular views of Lake Powell. Pets are allowed for an additional fee of $20 per night per room. Pets must be on a leash at all times when outside the room, and they are not to be left unattended or tied up outside on the patio or balcony. Dogs must be attended to or removed for housekeeping. If your pet is accustomed to being on the bed, they request you ask for a sheet to put over the bedspread. There is also a marina on site where they rent watercraft. Your pet may join you on a boat ride if you rent an 18' or 19' personal craft, as they are not allowed on the tour boats.

Phoenix

Biltmore Fashion Park 2502 E. Camelback Rd. Phoenix AZ   602-955-8400
Well-behaved leashed dogs are welcome at this outdoor shopping mall and most of the stores are pet-friendly. Some of the stores that allow dogs include Macy's, Sak's Fifth Avenue, Restoration Hardware, Pottery Barn, Godiva Chocolatier, The Sharper Image, Williams-Sonoma, Three Dog Bakery, and Baily, Banks & Biddle.

Phoenix Area

Carefree Resort and Villas 37220 Mule Train Road Carefree AZ   480-488-5300 (888-488-9034)
For a luxurious vacation getaway, a wedding, or a special business event, Carefree Resort wants your stay to be carefree. Backed by spectacular desert landscapes and mountain vistas, this full service resort and spa features spacious single and double guest rooms, luxury suites, casitas, and elegant condominiums in a private gated community. They are considered a premier golfing destination, and there is convenient access to 16 of Arizona's finest golf courses. They also offer such amenities as tennis courts/instruction, 3 pools, a clubhouse, fitness center, a grocery service, gourmet dining, room service, and a day spa and salon that offer a variety of massages and body treatments. Dogs of all sizes are allowed. There is a $50 one time fee per pet. Dogs must be quiet, leashed, cleaned up after, and the Do Not Disturb sign put on the door or a contact number left with the front desk if they are in the room alone.
Goldfield Ghost Town 4650 N Mammoth Mine Road Goldfield AZ   480-983-0333

http://www.goldfieldghosttown.com
Step back in time at this authentic 1890's ghost town, where you and your pet can ride on the only narrow gauge railroad in operation in Arizona (36 inches), tour through the mine together, pan for gold, witness an old west gun fight, or attend a chili cook-off. The only place pets are not allowed are in the shops on main street or in the general store. Dogs must be on lead at all times. Pet owners are asked to bring their own clean up bags, and to dispose of waste properly.

Sedona

Adventure Company Jeep Tours 336 H 179 Sedona AZ 928-204-1973
http://www.sedonajeeptours.com/
This company offers 4-wheeling fun in their convertible jeeps with a variety of tours of Sedona's spectacular red rock country. They offer the history of the amazing geological process responsible for the incredible scenery. You will also learn about the Native American and pioneer history, and the diverse plant and animal life of the area. Your well behaved dog is allowed to journey with you as long as none of the other riders object. There is also the option of renting out the jeep for your party only. If your dog is a large breed and needs a seat, there may be the cost of a child's ticket for the pet. Dogs must be leashed at all times and cleaned up after.

Superior

Boyce Thompson Arboretum State Park 223 H 60 Superior AZ 520-689-2811
This 323 acre park is Arizona's oldest and largest botanical garden. They feature the plants of the desert, a streamside forest, panoramic views, various natural habitats and wildlife, a desert lake, specialty gardens, and more. They also offer an interpretive center, a demonstration garden, visitor center, guided tours, picnic grounds with tables, gift shop, and restrooms. Well behaved dogs of all sizes are allowed for no additional fee. They must be kept on a short lead, under owner's control at all times, and cleaned up after. Dogs are not allowed anywhere in the water or in the gift shop. They are allowed throughout the rest of the park, and may even join their owners on the guided tours. The park is open daily from 8:00 a.m. to 5:00 p.m (October 1 - April 30). Summer hours are from 6:00 a.m. to 3:00 p.m. (May 1 - September 30).

Tombstone

1880 Historic Tombstone 70 miles from Tucson Tombstone AZ 800-457-3423 (800-457-3423)
http://www.tombstone1880.com/
This historic Western town is one of the most famous and glamorized mining towns in America. Prospector Ed Schieffelin was told he would only find his tombstone in the San Pedro Valley. He named his first silver claim Tombstone, and it later became the name of the town. The town is situated on a mesa at an elevation of 4,540 feet. While the area became notorious for saloons, gambling houses and the O.K. Corral shootout, in the 1880s Tombstone had become the most cultivated city in the West. Surviving the Great Depression and relocation of the County Seat to Bisbee, in the 1930s Tombstone became known as "The Town Too Tough To Die." You an your leashed dog are welcome to take a step back in time and walk along the wooden sidewalks and dirt streets. Here is a side note about the town: dogs are not allowed inside the O.K. Corral shoot-out area. This historic town is a must visit when you go to Arizona!

Tucson

Trail Dust Town 6541 E Tanque Verde Road Tucson AZ 520-296-4551
http://www.traildusttown.com/
Originally constructed as a movie set, this town has been a Tucson landmark for over 40 years, and is considered a premier "in-town" western town. It features wooden boardwalks and red brick streets, the Fiesta del Presidio carousel, a town square with a centerpiece gazebo, and a lot more. There is a variety of activities and recreation such as the Wild Wild West street shows or panning for gold. Dogs are allowed throughout the town, but they are not allowed inside the shops or museum. Dogs must be kept leashed, under owners' control at all times, and cleaned up after.
Westward Look Resort 245 East Ina Road Tucson AZ 520-297-1151 (800-722-2500)
http://www.westwardlook.com
This resort comes highly recommended from one of our readers. They said it was the most pet-friendly resort around and they can't say enough good things about it. This former 1912 guest ranch, now a desert resort hideaway, is nestled in the foothills of Tucson's picturesque Santa Catalina Mountains. It offers guests a Southwestern experience on 80 desert acres. They have walking trails at the resort, tennis, swimming pools and much more. Special room rates can be as low as $69 during certain times and seasons. There is a $50 one time additional pet fee.

Winslow

Homolovi Ruins State Park State Route 87 Winslow AZ   928-289-4106
This site is Arizona's first archaeological state park. Homolovi, a Hopi word meaning 'place of the little hills,' consists of four major pueblo sites thought to have been occupied between A.D. 1200 and 1425 by ancestors of today's Hopi Indians. Homolovi sites I and II are accessible to visitors. Your leashed dog is welcome to view the sites with you. Just stay on the trail because there are rattlesnakes in the area. The park is located five miles northeast of Winslow on State Route 87. Tale I-40 to Exit 257, then go 1.3 miles north on Highway 87.

"Must See" Colorado Dog-Friendly Places

Boulder

Boulder Creek Winery 6440 Odell Place Boulder CO   303-516-9031
This is a winery that offers modern technology with old world artistry in handcrafting traditional and private reserve wines. They also offer a variety of wine related gift items from their tasting room. Hours vary through the seasons, and they are closed the month of January. Dogs are allowed in and around the tasting room. They are not allowed in the winery or on the tours. Dogs must be friendly and well behaved. If your dog is under firm voice control, they may be off lead, and please clean up after your pet.

Canon City

Buckskin Joe Frontier Town and Railway 1193 Fremont County Road 3A Canon City CO   719-275-5149
http://www.buckskinjoe.com/
This old west town takes you to back to the wild frontier through a series of activities and settings. The "little train" is open-topped and offers a big view of this dramatic gorge country. After the train ride, head back into town for a variety of activities, reenactments, food, and fun. Hours and days open vary throughout the seasons. This place is pet friendly; they even let your four-legged friends ride the train, go into all the shops, or belly up to the bar at the Silver Dollar Saloon for something cool to drink. They are not allowed in the restaurant; however, the same menu is served in the bar. They ask that you take extra care with your dog around the other animals in town and during the gunfights. Dogs must be leashed and cleaned up after at all times.
Royal Gorge Bridge & Park 4218 Fremont County Road 3A Canon City CO   719-275-7507
http://www.royalgorgebridge.com/
Known as the Grand Canyon of Colorado, this park offers a variety of thrill rides, several attractions such as the Mountain Man Encampment, a Visitor's Center, petting zoo, a wildlife park, the world's highest suspension bridge that offers unparalleled views of all over-but especially down, and much more. They also offer live daily entertainment, shopping, and a variety of food choices. Dogs are allowed throughout the park as long as they are kept leashed at all times, and cleaned up after. Dogs are not allowed on any of the rides.

Clark

Steamboat Lake Marina P. O. Box 867/County Road 62 Clark CO   970-879-7019
http://www.steamboatlakemarina.com/
Located In the scenic Steamboat Lake State Park at 8,100 feet, this marina services a 1,100 surface acre, beautiful man made lake. They offer boat rentals (seasonal), fuel, a convenience store, and freshly made foods in the summer. If requested at the time of reservation, some of the pontoon boats have gas grills on board for no extra charge. Dogs are allowed on the rentals, and they are usually most comfortable on the pontoon boats. There is no additional fee for your pet unless there is excessive cleaning needed, then, there is a $25 cleaning fee. Dogs must be under owner's control and cleaned up after at all times.

Colorado Springs

Pikes Peak Toll Road P.O. Box 1575-MC060 Colorado Springs CO   719-385-PEAK (800-318-9505)
The Pikes Peak Toll Road allows you to drive your car up to the top of Pikes Peak at an altitude of over 14,000 feet. You may bring your dog with you. Dogs are not allowed on the Cog Railway. Dogs need to be on leash when outside of your car. There are a number of trails at various altitudes where leashed dogs may accompany you. Please keep in mind that the air is very thin at 14,000 feet. Before venturing up to this altitude, you should check with any appropriate doctors and veterinarians. At the summit, do not let your dog off-leash as it is very unsafe to exercise your dog at this altitude. It will take you up to around three hours to make the round trip up the mountain. To get to the toll road from Interstate 25 take Highway 24 West to the toll road.
Manitou Cliff Dwellings Museum Cliff Dwelling Road Manitou Springs CO   719-685-5242
http://www.cliffdwellingsmuseum.com/

These authentic Anasazi cliff dwellings have been preserved under a protective red sandstone overhang, and are considered a rare historical treasure. In addition to the ruins, there are reproductions of a stone mesa-top building, an Anasazi baking oven, a nature walk with well-labeled native flowers/herbs/trees, and a 3 story Pueblo-style building that houses the museum and gift shop. From June through August a snack bar and picnic patio are available. Well behaved, leased dogs are allowed throughout the preserve, and please clean up after your pet.

Denver

Tennyson Gallery and Sherlock Hound Pet Deli 4329 Stuart St Denver CO 303-433-3274
http://www.tennysongallery.com
This dog-friendly art gallery and attached pet deli makes for an interesting combination. The Tennyson Gallery is very dog-friendly. There are many events held here including Saturday morning dog socials with coffee for the people and snacks for the dogs. Sandwiches are available to be ordered from the deli across the street. On some days there are speakers at the gallery.
Buffalo Bills Gravesite and Museum 987 1/2 Look-Out Mountain Road Golden CO 303-526-0744
http://www.buffalobill.org/
On the top of Lookout Mountain, among the wildlife, breezes, and Ponderosa Pines, per his request, is the gravesite of Buffalo Bill Cody. Today visitors can enjoy the panoramic view from 2 observation decks adjacent to his burial site, tour the comprehensive museum and gift store, join in on one of the planned yearly events, walk along the nature trails, or just rest and enjoy the concessions that offer a variety of foods and drink. Dogs of all sizes are allowed. They must be leashed at all times, and please bring supplies to clean up after them quickly. Dogs are not allowed in the park buildings, but they are allowed on the grounds and the trails.
Aspen Grove Shopping Center 7301 S Santa Fe Drive Littleton CO 303-794-0640
http://www.shopaspengrove.com/
This open air shopping center offers the finest of national specialty shops and restaurants in a convenient, safe, pleasing environment, and with great views of Colorado too. Your well-behaved pet is welcome here, and there are more than 2 dozen stores that display the yellow "Pet Friendly" triangle sign. There are poop-n-scoop stations throughout the mall so that you may clean up after your pet quickly. Dogs must be kept leashed at all times.

Fort Collins

Grave of Annie the Railroad Dog 201 Peterson St Fort Collins CO
Annie, the Railroad Dog, was adopted by the Colorado and Southern Railway people in 1934. She was sick and was nursed back to health at the railway depot. For years she remained at the depot, greeting trains and visitors. Annie died in 1948 and was buried a few yards from the depot. There is a statue of Annie in front of the library at 201 Peterson St. The gravesite is at the nearby intersection of Mason Street and LaPorte Avenue. The site is designated a national landmark. Both you and your dog can view the statue and gravesite of Fort Collin's most famous dog.

Gunnison

Monarch Crest Tram H 50 between Salida and Gunnison CO 719-539-4091
This tram's four passenger gondolas climb from the 11,312 foot Monarch Pass to the Continental Divide at an altitude of over 12,000 feet, and offer some of the most spectacular views anywhere in the world. They are open daily from 8:30 am to 5:30 pm, with few exceptions. Your dog is allowed to join you on the ride for no additional fee. Dogs must be leashed, and please bring your own poop-n-scoop supplies.

Idaho Springs

Argo Gold Mill and Museum 2350 Riverside Drive Idaho Springs CO 303-567-2421
http://www.historicargotours.com/
An experienced guide takes you through the history of the tunnel that took 17 years to go the 4.5 miles to town, the mine and mill showing live demonstrations of crushing/milling/rock drilling, and at the end of the tour--free gold panning instructions with a pan of free gold ore to try your luck. You might also want to buy a sack of guaranteed gold or gemstone ore, as there are a variety of gems to be found. Dogs are allowed to tour the mine, mill, and grounds. Water bowls are provided for thirsty four-legged guests. Dogs must be friendly, well trained, and be able to climb stairs. Dogs must be leashed and cleaned up after at all times.

Leadville

Piney Creek Nordic Center 259 County Road 19 Leadville CO 719-486-1750

http://www.tennesseepass.com/skiing.htm
This rental center is located off Highway 24 between Leadville and Vail. Dogs are allowed on any of the 25km of groomed and maintained trails. Pets are not allowed inside the nordic center and need to be leashed when on the property. Once on the trails, dogs can be off-leash under direct voice control. Please clean up after your pet.

Marble

Ute Meadows Nordic Center 2880 County Road 3 Marble CO   970-963-5513
http://www.utemeadows.com
This nordic center welcomes dogs on their cross country and snowshoe trails. The cross country trails are groomed. There is a $3 daily "tail-fee" for dogs and a maximum of 2 dogs per skier. Dogs can be off-leash on the trails but need to be under direct voice control. You can rent cross-country skis or snowshoes from the nordic center. If you are looking for a place to stay, the Ute Meadows Bed and Breakfast Inn allows pets. They are located next to the nordic center. This center is located 2 hours east of Grand Junction and 4 hours west of Denver. From Interstate 70, take Highway 82 south towards Aspen. Go 12 miles then at Carbondale take Highway 133 south towards Redstone. Go 5 miles past Redstone and turn left on County Road 3. Go 3 more miles and turn right just after you cross the Crystal River bridge.

Mosca

Great Sand Dunes National Park and Preserve 11999 Highway 150 Mosca CO   719-378-6300
http://www.nps.gov/grsa/index.htm
The dunes of Great Sand Dunes National Park rise over 750 feet high. Dogs are allowed throughout the park and must be on leash. You must clean up after your dog and dogs may not be left unattended in the park. Leashed dogs are also welcome in the campgrounds. The park features auto touring, camping fishing, hiking, and more.

Palisade

Colorado Cellars Winery 3553 E Road Palisade CO   970-464-7921
http://www.coloradocellars.com/
This winery is Colorado's oldest and largest winery, and they offer a wide variety of wines, meads, ports, and more. They are open Monday to Friday from 9 am to 5 pm; Saturday from 10 am to 5 pm, and closed on Sunday. Dogs are allowed in and around the tasting room, but they are not allowed in the vineyards. They must be leashed, and please clean up after your pet.

Silverton

Triangle Jeep Rentals 864 Greene Street Silverton CO   877-522-2354
The staff here will share their vast knowledge of this area with you by providing you with a map of the area, going over the routes with you, and offering instructions when needed. There are over 500 miles of jeep roads offering a variety of vistas, waterfalls, wildlife, ghost towns, and snow-laden peaks. Your dog is allowed to join you on the jeep rental for no additional charge. However, they are quite strict regarding dog hair. If the jeep only needs the regular clean up from the trip, there is no charge; however, if they have to clean a lot of dog hair, they charge $25 per hour-firm. There are no size or weight restrictions. Dogs must be under owner's control at all times.

Snowmass Village

Blazing Adventures P. O. Box 5068 Snowmass Village CO   800-282-7238
http://www.BlazingAdventures.com/
This outdoor adventure company offers a wide range of exciting summer and winter guided tours; some of which include jeep tours, rafting, hiking or biking tours, sunset dinners, and fishing excursions. They couple these tours with a unique selection of environmental, educational, and historical lectures. They offer years of experience and will custom tailor your adventure according to your needs. They will allow dogs on most of the tours; however, it would have to be a "private trip". There is no additional fee for the dog, and they must be leashed at all times.

Steamboat Springs

Silver Bullet Gondola Rides Gondola Square Steamboat Springs CO   970-879-0740
Dogs are allowed to join their owners on this incredibly scenic ride of lush mountain sides with blankets of wildflowers, and long distance vistas. The gondola is open daily (weather permitting), and is located at the base of Mt Werner. At the top of the mountain there are several trails to explore. Tickets are available at the Main

Ticket Office or Ride Sports from 9:00am to 5:00pm; lift hours vary by season and day. Dogs are allowed to ride the gondola in the summer only and free of charge. They must be leashed at all times, and please clean up after your pet.

Telluride

Mountain Lodge Telluride 457 Mountain Village Blvd. Telluride CO   866-368-6867
http://www.mountainlodgetelluride.com
This rustic pet-friendly lodge is located in Telluride's Mountain Village Resort community with views of the San Juan Mountains. There are 125 dog-friendly rooms in the lodge. There is a $25 per day pet fee up to a maximum of $100 per stay. The lodge offers pet beds, bowls and treats to their dog visitors and have pet pick-up stations around the property.

"Must See" Idaho Dog-Friendly Places

Bonner's Ferry

Copper Falls Self-Guided Nature Trail Forest Road 2517 Bonner's Ferry ID   208-267-5561
Located in the Bonner's Ferry Ranger District, this great family hike of just under a mile takes you to a spectacular overlook of the Copper Falls then takes you on an easy loop back along the creek. There is an information and registration box at the trailhead that offers pamphlets. Dogs are allowed on this trail. They must be under owner's control, and leashed and cleaned up after at all times. The Copper Creek Campground nearby also allows pets.

Cottonwood

Dog Bark Park Inn 2421 H 95 Cottonwood ID   208-962-3647
http://dogbarkparkinn.com/index.htm
Definitely a unique traveling experience! The inn is built into the shape of a 30 foot tall Beagle and its 12 foot tall "puppy". They offer a 2nd floor private deck with sleeping accommodations for four, a cozy reading nook in the dog's nose, and an extended continental breakfast. The owners' obvious love of dogs shows in the folk-art style wooden canine carvings (over 60 different breeds) that are offered in their gift store. Carvings from real or still life (like pictures), and tours of the studio where they are made are also available. They are open seasonally and at times close when business may take them away, so call ahead. Dogs of all sizes are welcome for an additional $10 per night per pet. Dogs may not be left alone in the room at any time, or on the beds, and they must be well behaved, leashed and cleaned up after.

Donnelly

Tamarack Resort Nordic Center 2099 West Mountain Road Donnelly ID   208-325-1002
This nordic center offers 22km of daily groomed trails and 15km of snowshoe trails. Dogs are welcome on all of the trails. They can be off-leash if under direct voice control. There is a $3 per day dog trail pass. This nordic center is located about 2.5 hours from Boise.

Horseshoe Bend

Cascade Raft Company 7050 H 55 Horseshoe Bend ID   208-793-2221
http://www.cascaderaft.com/
This rafting company offers a variety of trips so that you can enjoy river rafting at its best; whether whitewater thrills or a cool float. They will allow a dog on board, but you must provide your own doggy lifejacket. Their season usually lasts from the end of April to the first couple of weeks in September. There is no additional fee for your pet. Dogs must be very well mannered, under owner's control at all times, leashed, and cleaned up after.

Kellogg

Silver Mountain Gondola 610 Bunker Avenue Kellogg ID   208-783-1111
http://www.silvermt.com/
This gondola is 3.1 miles long; the longest single stage people carrier in the world. Dogs are allowed on the gondola in the summer only, but they are allowed in the gondola village at the base of the mountain year round. There is no additional fee for your pet on the gondola ride, and there are a variety of hiking trails available. They are also allowed at the Morning Star Lodge here. Dogs must be under owner's control at all times, and be leashed and cleaned up after.

Riggins

Heavens Gate Observation Site/Hells Canyon Forest Road 517 Riggins ID   208-628-3916
Located in Hell's Canyon by way of Heaven's Gate, this is one of 3 routes to the edge of the canyon. This short path winds to the Heaven's Gate Lookout and an incredible four state vista with several impressive points of interest. The Forest Road 517 is a steep gravel road that climbs from 2,500 feet to 7,200 feet and is not viable for large trailers or trucks. Dogs are permitted at the look-out point and at stops along the way. Dogs must be leashed and cleaned up after.

Twin Falls

Shoshone Falls Park Road 3300 East Twin Falls ID   208-736-2265
The falls at this park drop 212 feet and are higher than Niagara Falls. They are considered one of the most spectacular natural beauties on the Snake River. There is a variety of land and water recreation, and some of the amenities include large shaded grass areas, picnicking, playgrounds, hiking trails, restrooms, a concession stand, boat ramp, and a scenic overlook. Dogs of all sizes are allowed for no additional fee. Dogs must be under owner's control, and leashed and cleaned up after at all times.

"Must See" Nevada Dog-Friendly Places

Beatty

Rhyolite Ghost Town off Highway 374 Beatty NV   760-786-3200
http://www.nps.gov/deva/rhyolite.htm
In 1904 two prospectors found quartz all over a hill which was "full of free gold". Soon the rush was on and camps were set up in the area including the townsite called Rhyolite. The name was derived from the silica-rich volcanic rock in the area. The most prominent mine in the area was the Montgomery Shoshone mine which prompted everyone to move to Rhyolite. This boomtown once had a 3 story building, a stock exchange, board of trade, red light district, hotels, stores, a school for 250 children, an ice plant, two electric plants, foundries, machine shops and a miner's union hospital. Today you can see several remnants of Rhyolite. The 3 story building still has some walls standing and so does an old jail. A privately owned train depot was restored and so was the Bottle House. The Bottle House was made out of whiskey bottles by a miner. This house was restored in 1925 by Paramount Pictures. Rhyolite is located 35 miles from the Furnace Creek Visitor Center in Death Valley National Park. Drive towards Beatty, Nevada. Before you reach Beatty, take a paved road north (left) from Highway 374. It will take you right into the ghost town. Pets are allowed but must be leashed. Please clean up after your pet. Remember to watch out for rattlesnakes.

Las Vegas

District at Green Valley Ranch 2240 Village Walk Drive Henderson NV   702-564-8595
http://www.thedistrictatgvr.com/
Thanks for a reader for recommending this dog-friendly shopping district in Henderson. She says "This place is all about dogs. Each store has water and dog biscuits out front." Many stores allow dogs inside but please remember to ask first.
Loews Lake Las Vegas Resort 101 Montelago Boulevard Henderson NV   702-567-6000
This upscale resort on the shores of Lake Mead offers all the luxuries. All well-behaved dogs of any size are welcome. This upscale hotel resort offers their "Loews Loves Pets" program which includes special pet treats, local dog walking routes, and a list of nearby pet-friendly places to visit. The hotel is about 30 minutes from the Las Vegas Strip. There is a $25 one time additional pet fee. To get to the hotel take I-215 east until it ends into Lake Mead Blvd and proceed 7 miles on Lake Mead Blvd. The hotel will be on the left and you can follow the signs.
Dog Fancier's Park 5800 E. Flamingo Rd. Las Vegas NV   702-455-8200
Dog Fancier's Park is a 12 acre park that allows canine enthusiasts to train their dogs off leash. Owner's must still have control over their dogs and may be cited if their dogs (while off leash) interfere with other animals training at the park. This dog park has benches, poop bags and water taps.
Red Rock Canyon National Area Charleston Blvd/159 Las Vegas NV   702-363-1921
http://www.nv.blm.gov/redrockcanyon
Located just 20-25 minutes west of downtown Las Vegas is the beautiful Red Rock Canyon National Conservation Area. This preserve has over 60,000 acres and includes unique geological formations. There is a popular 13 mile one-way scenic loop road that winds around the park, providing sightseeing, vistas and overlooks. Many of the hiking trails begin off this road. Leashed dogs are allowed on most of the trails. Some of the trails they are not allowed on are more like rock climbing expeditions than hiking trails. There are a variety of

hiking trails ranging from easy to difficult. The visitor center is open daily and should have trail maps. On the trails, be aware of extreme heat or cold. Also watch out for flash floods, especially near creeks and streams. According to the BLM (Bureau of Land Management), violent downpours can cause flash flooding in areas untouched by rain. Do not cross low places when water is running through a stream. The park entrance fee is $5 per vehicle and $5 per dog. To get there from downtown Las Vegas, take Charleston Blvd./159 and head west.

Reno

Atlantis Casino Resort Spa 3800 S Virigina Street Reno NV   775-825-4700 (800-723-6500)
Dogs of all sizes are allowed in the Motor Lodge section of this casino hotel. There is a $25 one time fee per pet. Dogs must be kept on leash and cleaned up after. Please place the Do Not Disturb sign on the door if there is a pet alone in the room.
Pyramid Lake Hwy 445 Sutcliffe NV   775-574-1000
Pyramid Lake is located in an Indian reservation, but visitors to the lake are welcomed guests of the Pyramid Lake Tribe of the Paiute Indians. Your leashed dog is also welcome. The lake is a beautiful contrast to the desert sandstone mountains which surround it. It is about 15 miles long by 11 miles wide, and among interesting rock formations. Pyramid Lake is Nevada's largest natural lake. It is popular for fishing and photography. The north end of the lake is off-limits to visitors because it is a sacred area to the Paiutes. There is a beach area near the ranger's station in Sutcliffe. Be careful when wading into the water, as there are some ledges which drop off into deeper water. Also, do not wade in the water at the south end of the lake because the dirt acts like quick sand. The lake is about 35-40 minutes north of Reno, off Hwy 445.

Virginia City

Virginia City Hwy 341 Virginia City NV   775-847-0311
http://www.virginiacity-nv.com/
This small town was built in the late 1800s and was a booming mining town. The restored Old Western town now has a variety of shops with wooden walkways. Dogs are allowed to window shop with you. Dogs are also welcome to ride the Virginia & Truckee Steam Train with you. Virginia City is located about 30-40 minutes south of Reno.

"Must See" New Mexico Dog-Friendly Places

Albuquerque

New Mexico Ghost Tours 303 Romero Street NW Albuquerque NM   505-249-7827
http://www.nmghosttours.com/
The Ghost walk of Old Town Albuquerque is an outdoor walking tour that takes visitors to reputed haunted sites and the sites that is under investigation by the Southwest Ghost Hunter's Association. The tours last about an hour and a half are available year round, and knowledgeable guides, historical accuracy, and their stellar reputation has made a name for this tour. Your well-behaved dog is welcome to join you on this outdoor tour, and there is no additional fee. Dogs must be under owner's control at all times, be leashed, and please carry supplies to clean up after your pet.
Sandia Man Cave Cibola National Forest Placitas NM   505-281-3304
Explore a cave with your dog. From the Highway 165 exit, go towards Placitas. The paved road ends and becomes an unimproved mountain road as you enter Cibola National Forest. The road is fairly rough and muddy and becomes frozen as you reach the 7-8000 foot elevation. The parking area is unmarked but it is the only one around. After paying a $3 parking fee walk north out of the parking lot and take a 10 minute hike up a wide and fairly easy, flat trail. Take a flashlight with you because not much of cave will be visible in daylight. Dogs on leash may go with you to the caves.

Aztec

Aztec Museum and Pioneer Village 125 N Main Avenue Aztec NM   505-334-9829
Three replicated buildings and 10 original buildings depict life as it was in the 1880's, and include a log cabin, a general store, post office, sheriff's office, church, bank, school, and a doctor's office. The museum displays authentic pioneer/native American artifacts. Dogs are welcome, but they must be cat and critter friendly as there are other pets in residence. They can walk through the village and surrounding area, but they are not allowed in the museum. Dogs must be well behaved, and leashed and cleaned up after at all times.

Carrizozo

Valley of Fires Recreation Area U.S. 380 Carrizozo NM   505-648-2241
Valley of Fires is adjacent to the spectacular Malpais Lava Flow. It was created about 1500 years ago when Little Black Peak erupted. The lava flowed into the Tularosa Basin, filling the valley with molten rock. The lava flow is now rock that is 4-6 miles wide by 44 miles long and 160 feet deep. This lava flow is the youngest formation of this type in the continental U.S. Dogs on leash are allowed on the self-guided paved 3/4 mile each way Malpais Nature Trail. From the trail you can view the lava rock, and native plants and animals. Valley of Fires is located on U.S. Highway 380, four miles west of Carrizozo, NM. There is a minimal fee for parking.

Chimayo

High Road Market Place HC 64 Box 12/Santuario Drive Chimayo NM   505-351-1078
This marketplace highlights high quality crafts and fine art created by over 100 local artists, and once a year many open their homes and studios to share their creations and the bounty of traditional fall foods. There are maps available for other sites along the High Road between Taos and Santa Fe at the Visitor's Center in Taos, the Marketplace, and at sites along the self-guided tour. Dogs are allowed to walk the grounds of the marketplace, and some of the stores will also let them come inside. Dogs must be very well behaved, and leashed and cleaned up after at all times.

Clayton

Clayton Lake State Park 141 Clayton Road Clayton NM   505-374-8808 (800-NMPARKS (667-2757))
Rolling grasslands, volcanic rocks, and sandstone bluffs all characterize this 471 acre park with a 170 surface acre lake, but the real pull here is the internationally significant dinosaur trackway that contains more than 500 footprints dating back more than 100 million years. Many have been preserved and identified, and a boardwalk trail with extensive signage tells of the ancient visitors here. The park is also home to a variety of plant/bird/animal life, and land and water recreation. Dogs of all sizes are allowed for no additional fee. Dogs must be leashed and cleaned up after at all times.

Lincoln

Lincoln Historic Town Highway 380 Lincoln NM
The town of Lincoln was built in the 1800's and today it is a National Historic Landmark. The Lincoln County war took place here, which was a fight between cowboys/ranchers and banker/politicians. Billy the Kid was one of the cowboys who fled during this battle. He was later found and brought back to Lincoln. While waiting for his trial, he escaped from the Lincoln County Courthouse. Today there are over 40 historic buildings throughout the town. You and your pup can go on a self-guided walking tour of Lincoln. Just pick up a map from the Visitor Center located on Hwy 380. There is a minimal fee for the map.

Madrid

Old Coal Mine Museum 2846 Highway 14 Madrid NM   505-473-0743
The Old Coal Mine Museum is located on 3 acres of what was once the epicenter of the Madrid mining operation. Here you will find a fully restored railroad engine, impressive collection of mining equipment, tools of trade, household goods and a blacksmith's shop, as well as industrial sized machinery. Dogs are welcome at this mostly outdoor museum. There is a minimal entrance fee. The museum is located in the city of Madrid, about an hour south of Santa Fe. If you are driving between Santa Fe and Albuquerque, take Highway 14 and visit this attraction in Madrid.

Ramah

El Morrow National Monument HC 61 Box 43/Monument Drive Ramah NM   505-783-4226
http://www.nps.gov/elmo
Located at an elevation of over 7,000 feet, this monument boasts a massive mesa-point that rises 200 feet above the valley floor with a 1/2 mile loop trail leading to an historic pool, and more than 2000 inscriptions and petroglyphs. If you continue to the top of the mesa for a 2 mile round trip hike, you will be met with breathtaking views and the ancestral Puebloan ruins. Dogs are allowed on the trails, but they must stay on the trails, and be leashed and under owners control at all times. Dogs must be cleaned up after in the campground area, the park, and on the trails. Pets are not permitted in the visitor center, but they ask that you stop there first before going in to get directions/instructions. There is a picnic area at the visitor center where pets are allowed.

Red River

Enchanted Forest Cross Country Ski Area P. O. Box 219 Red River NM 505-754-2374
http://www.enchantedforestxc.com/
This is the state's largest full service cross country ski area with about 20 miles of groomed areas for various skiing, and about 10 miles for snowshoeing, but they have provided an area especially for our canine companions. There are about 3 miles of a smooth, groomed trail for easier skiing/snowshoers, and varies from 6 to 12 feet that guests with or without pets may use. They expect guests to use the doggie waste bags they have provided along the way. Dogs must be leashed in the parking areas, and under strict voice command if off lead on the trails.

Roswell

International UFO Museum & Research Center 114 N. Main Street Roswell NM 505-625-9495
http://www.iufomrc.com/
Ever wondered if there is extraterrestrial life out there? Curious about the famous 'Roswell Incident'? The Tourism Association of New Mexico has awarded this museum the 1996 "Top Tourist Destination of New Mexico." You and your dog are absolutely welcome inside this very popular and large UFO Museum and Research Center. They have many dog visitors every day. At the museum you can view exhibits about The Roswell Incident, Crop Circles, Ragsdale Crash Site, Ancient Cultures, Worldwide Sighting Map and a Childrens Area. You can also sit and view videos (with your pup, of course) in their small theatre room. After viewing the exhibits, your pup is welcome in the gift shop too. Admission is free, but donations are always welcome.

Santa Fe

Galloping Galleries 22B Stacy Rd Santa Fe NM 505-988-7016
http://www.gallopinggalleries.com/
This company provides CD road trips of New Mexico's landscape, history, diverse cultures, and cultural events, and then they combine them with the local myths and legends of the area. The CD's are also interlaced with music from local musicians, and includes information such as where the last chance for gas or food is, and more. This is a fun and casual way to discover New Mexico from your own car.
Ten Thousand Waves Japanese Spa and Resort 3451 Hyde Park Road Santa Fe NM 505-992-5003
http://www.tenthousandwaves.com
Ten Thousand Waves is a Japanese style spa in the mountains above Santa Fe with outdoor and indoor hot tubs, facials, spa services, and many types of massage. There are 13 guest houses, most with fireplaces and either enclosed courtyards or decks. Some have full kitchens and/or separate bedrooms. The resort is about ten minutes from downtown. Pets are $20 per night for one or more.

Socorro

Very Large Array (VLA) Radio Telescope U.S. Hwy 60 Socorro NM 505-835-7000
The VLA is one of the world's premier astronomical radio observatories. It consists of 27 antennas arranged in a huge Y pattern up to 22 miles across. Dogs are not allowed in the visitor's center, but you can take your pup on the self-guided walking tour. This is where part of the movie Contact, starring Jodie Foster, was filmed. The VLA is located 50 miles west of Socorro on U.S. Highway 60. From U.S. 60, turn South on NM 52, then West on the VLA access road, which is well marked. Signs will point you to the Visitor Center. The tour is free, but donations are welcome.

Steins

Steins Railroad Ghost Town Interstate 10, Exit 3 Steins NM 505-542-9791
When traveling along I-10 in New Mexico, near the Arizona border, be sure to stop at this ghost town. Steins Railroad Ghost Town was once a thriving railroad station town named after Captain Stein, a U.S. Army officer, who was the first Anglo witness to sign a treaty with the Apaches. At the town's peak, between 1905 to 1945, Steins supported 1300 residents. Take a step back in time and walk through the preserved Old West frontier town with your pup. You can purchase some souvenirs and cold drinks at the Steins Mercantile or purchase a guided tour for $2.50 per person. The self-guided tour is free. This is a nice place to stop when traveling along I-10. Just be sure to keep your dog leashed because there are several cats on the premises.

"Must See" Oregon Dog-Friendly Places

Bend

Mount Bachelor Ski Resort 13000 SW Century Drive Bend OR 800-829-2442

http://mtbachelor.com/
As one of North Americas' largest ski resorts, skiers, snowboarders, and Nordic skiers will find great conditions with plenty of snow, a large terrain, short lift lines, great value, 4 different terrain parks, and an Olympic size superpipe. Mt. Bachelor is nearly 3700 acres of varied terrain atop the high desert of the Central Cascades in the Deschutes National Forest. They also offer tubing, snowshoeing, dog sledding, and they host the North American Pond Skimming Championships each year. They are open from mid-November to Memorial Day for the ski season, and from July 1st through Labor Day for summer sight-seeing. Dogs of all sizes are allowed throughout the year. In the summer, your pet can even ride the chair lift, and is allowed throughout the park. In the winter, there are some ski trails and trails that dogs can be on. Dogs must be leashed at all times, and cleaned up after. Dogs must be friendly and well behaved.

Cannon Beach

Ecola State Park Highway 101 Cannon Beach OR   503-436-2844
According to the Oregon State Parks Division, this park is one of the most photographed locations in Oregon. To reach the beach, you will need to walk down a trail. Restrooms, hiking and primitive campgrounds are available at this park. There is a $3 day use fee. Leashed dogs are allowed on the beach. Dogs are also allowed on hiking trails and campgrounds. They must be on a six foot or less leash at all times and people are required to clean up after their pets. On beaches located outside of Oregon State Park boundaries, dogs might be allowed off-leash and under direct voice control, please look for signs or postings. This park is located off U.S. Highway 101, 2 miles north of Cannon Beach.

Depoe Bay

Dockside Charters Whale Watching PO Box 1308/ Coast Guard Place Depoe Bay OR   541-765-2445
http://www.docksidedepoebay.com/
Experienced professionals, wanting their visitors to have the best time they can, thought ocean charters should be a more personal experience, and have implemented several ideas to make the trips fun and enjoyable. Although dogs are not allowed on the fishing charters, they are allowed on the whale watching tours. This is the closest port along the path of the migrating Gray Whales and the summer feeding grounds for numerous other whales. Dogs up to about 70 pounds are allowed for no additional fee. Dogs must be friendly and well behaved. They must be on a leash at all times. The cruises are approximately an hour and a half, and run seasonally. Schedules and times vary.

Diamond Lake

Diamond Lake Resort 350 Resort Drive Diamond Lake OR   541-793-3333
http://www.diamondlake.net
This resort has 8 miles of groomed cross-country ski trails and 50 miles of ungroomed trails. They rent skis and snowmobiles. The cross-country ski and snowmobiles trails are separate. Dogs are allowed on almost all of the cross-country ski trails. Pets need to be leashed at the resort and on the trails. If you are looking for a place to stay, the resort allows pets in both their cabins and motel rooms.

Hood River

Pheasant Valley Vineyard 3890 Acree Drive Hood River OR   866-357-WINE (9463)
http://www.pheasantvalleywinery.com/
This winery gets rave reviews for their award-winning wines and picturesque setting. There is a certified organic pear and apple orchard also on site, and a very nice Bed and Breakfast Inn. Wine gift packs, accessories, and souvenirs are available in their gift shop. They are open daily April through October from 11 am to 6 pm, and from November through March from 11 am to 5 pm. Well behaved, friendly dogs of all sizes are allowed. Dogs must be leashed, cleaned up after, and under owners' control at all times. They are not allowed in the buildings, but they can be out on the covered patio or lawns, and walked around with their owners. They are not allowed at the Bed and Breakfast Inn; however, they have a 2 bedroom, full sized cottage where up to 2 dogs (no size restriction) are allowed for no additional fee.

Portland

Hoyt Arboretum 4000 SW Fairview Blvd Portland OR   503-865-8733
http://www.hoytarboretum.org/
Hoyt Arboretum covers 185 ridge top acres, is home to a collection of trees representing more than 1,100 species gathered from around the world, and features 12 miles of trails winding through what they call "a living museum". The Visitor Center is at the heart of the Arboretum and they offer maps, trail guides, and park

information. There are tours, classes, and special events throughout the year also. Free guided tours, part of Portland Parks and Recreation's Green Walk series, are offered the first Saturday of each month from April through October. The grounds are open 6:00 a.m. to 10:00 p.m. daily. The Visitor Center is open from 9 a.m. to 4 p.m. Monday through Friday; 9 a.m. to 3 p.m. on Saturday; and closed Sundays and major holidays. They say that all dogs are welcome in the Arboretum "as long as they are accompanied by a sensible human", and if your pet(s) is thirsty after the drive, they have a water dish out front to greet them. Dogs must be friendly, well behaved, leashed, and cleaned up after. Dogs are allowed throughout the park on all the trails.

Lucky Labrador Brewing Co. 915 SE Hawthorne Blvd. Portland OR   503-236-3555
http://www.luckylab.com
This dog-friendly brew pub has a labrador retriever as their mascot and on their beer labels. At the outside seating area, your pooch can relax at your feet while you unwind with some beer or food. The pub offers a nice variety of food including veggie and meat sandwiches, bentos (chicken or veggies over rice), soup and more. Of course, if you love beer, you will also have to try their ales like the Black Lab Stout, the Dog Day India Pale Ale or the Top Dog Extra Special Pale Ale. And if you visit during the month of October, don't miss their Dogtoberfest usually held on a Saturday. They celebrate the pub's anniversary on this day. The highlight of the day is the dog wash, which helps to raise money for dog-related causes or dog organizations. For treats, humans can try a special Dogtoberfest ale and doggies can get dog cookies and biscuits. The pub might even have a band for musical entertainment as well. Please keep pets leashed.

Oaks Park Amusement Park 7100 SE Oaks Parkway Portland OR   503-233-5777
http://www.oakspark.com/
Surrounded by stately Oak trees, and one of the oldest continuously operating amusement parks in America, this amusement park really has something for everyone. They've got thrill rides, kid's rides, bumper cars, carnival games, a roller skating rink, all the usual carnival treats, and many events and celebrations throughout the year. The park is closed on Monday and the hours and times vary month by month. Your pet is allowed to join you at the park for no additional fee. They are not allowed in buildings. Dogs must be friendly, well behaved, leashed at all times, and cleaned up after. Owners assume full responsibility for their pet.

Portland Walking Tours SW Broadway and Yamhill Portland OR   503-774-4522
Take an award-winning guided outdoor walking tour of Portland. Their most popular tour is called The Best of Portland. This 2 to 2.5 hour morning tour features an overview of Portland including history, architecture, artwork, and more. The tour goes through downtown Portland, the Cultural District, Historic Yamhill and along the riverfront. Tours are held rain or shine on Friday, Saturday and Sunday at 10:30am and 3pm, from April through November. The cost is $15 per person and free for dogs and young children. At the beginning of the tour, the guide will ask if everyone is okay with dogs. If there is anyone in your tour that is uncomfortable around dogs, you might have to keep your pooch away from that person by staying on the other side of the group. The overwhelming majority of people on these tours are okay with dogs. All tours leave from the Pioneer Courthouse Square. Please note that they strongly recommend reservations, even a week or two in advance.

Salem

The Oregon Garden 879 W Main Street Silverton OR   877-674-2733
http://www.oregongarden.org
Popular and educational, this 80 acre botanical garden displays thousands of plants in more than 20 specialty gardens. There is an amphitheater for their annual summer concert series, picnic areas and a café, a seasonal tram that allows you to get on and off anywhere in the gardens, and they are also host to many other planned events and activities throughout the year. Some of the spectacular scenery includes an educational forest with a 400 year old Oak tree, a children's garden, a refreshing water garden, a rose garden with a fountain and a view, a sensory garden, the Lewis and Clark garden, and many more, but unusual for public gardens-there is a Pet-Friendly Garden where "Max" the yellow lab (statue) welcomes all the canine guests. Dogs of all sizes are allowed throughout the park for no additional fee, and they can ride the tram too. Dogs must be on no more than an 8 foot leash, be well behaved, and cleaned up after at all times.

"Must See" Utah Dog-Friendly Places

Bryce Canyon

Red Canyon Park P. O. Box 80/H 12 Panguitch UT   435-676-9300
The beautiful Red Canyon Park can serve as a dog-friendly substitute to see the rock formations that make Bryce Canyon famous. Dogs are not allowed on any trails at Bryce Canyon but are allowed on leash throughout Red Canyon Park. The park sits at a 7,400 foot altitude in a Ponderosa Pine setting surrounded by striking red and pink Limestone formations that rival those of the National Park. There are a variety of extensive trail systems for multi-use, many scenic overlooks (one allows visitors to see 3 different states), and a visitor's center. Dogs of all sizes are allowed for no additional fee. Dogs must be well behaved, leashed, and cleaned up after at all times. Dogs are allowed throughout the park and on the trails by the park. They are not allowed in park buildings, or on

the trails leading into the nearby Bryce Canyon National Park.

Farmington

Lagoon Amusement Park and Pioneer Village 375 N Lagoon Drive Farmington UT   801-451-8000
http://www.lagoonpark.com/
This amusement park offers dozens of rides and attractions, shops, games, a state-of-the-art waterpark, 2 high-tech go-kart tracks, an X-Venture Zone (extreme rides), a lagoon, and lots of delicious eating. They also offer an active live entertainment program, and the Pioneer Village, an 1800's frontier community with all the artifacts to transport you back in time. They are open daily from about May 5th to August 22, and then open mostly weekends until closed for the season. Dates and times are subject to change and closing times may vary. They have an extended opening for FRIGHTMARES, from September 29th to October 28th, opening on Friday's at 6 pm and on the weekend at 11 am. This yearly event offers several spooky fun activities for all ages. Dogs of all sizes are allowed to explore this fun place. They are not allowed in the waterpark, on the rides or in buildings, but they are allowed on the midway, around the grounds, and through the village. Dogs must be leashed and cleaned up after at all times. There is also a full service RV and campground on site where dogs are allowed for no additional fee.

Kanab

Frontier Movie Town 297 W Center Street Kanab UT   800-551-1714
http://www.frontiermovietown.com/
Some 300 movies and TV shows were filmed here, giving it the name of "Utah's Little Hollywood", where several movie sets were left behind with lots of memorabilia. They offer a gift shop, museum, an Old West Costume rental shop, an all you can eat cowboy-style dinner buffet with tin plates and cups (or have coffee and a light snack from their cook shack), and a photo shop. Friendly dogs of all sizes are allowed. They can walk through the gift shop to get to the Frontier Movie Town. Your pet is welcome to join you at the picnic tables, on the grass under the trees, and around the park. They keep a bucket of doggy treats and water available for four-legged travelers. Dogs must be leashed and cleaned up after at all times, and they are not allowed in the cook shack.

Moab

Red River Canoe Company 1371 Main Street/N H 191 Moab UT   800-753-8216
http://www.redrivercanoe.com/
There are several types of tours through this visually striking area on the waterways of the Colorado Plateau, guided and unguided. They open daily at 8:30 am from March through October. Dogs are not allowed on guided tours, but they are allowed on self-guided canoe rentals. There are many places on the river to pull over along the way for you and your pooch to hike, picnic, or just explore. Dogs must be under owners control at all times, and be sure to pack enough water and food for your pet as well.

Monument Valley

Goulding's Tours 1000 Main Street Monument Valley UT   435-727-3231
This tour company has Navajo Indian guides which take you on a full day or half day tour of the area. The tours include Anasazi ruins, petroglyphs, movie locations, 1,000 foot monoliths, and Indian hogans. Tour prices for half a day are $40 per person and full day are $70 per person. Children under 8 years old receive a discount off the adult price. Well-behaved leashed dogs are allowed on the tours. There is no charge for a small dog but if you have a larger dog that takes up more space, they may charge extra. You can make a reservation by calling or by signing up at the pet-friendly Goulding's Lodge or campgrounds.
Monument Valley Navajo Tribal Park P. O. Box 360289 Monument Valley UT   435-727-5870
Rich in natural and cultural history, this great valley is home to sandstone masterpieces towering to 1,000 feet and surrounded by miles of mesas and buttes, shrubs, trees, and windblown sand. There is a scenic drive through this park; the hours for Summer-(May-Sept) 6:00am - 8:30pm, and Winter-(Oct - Apr) 8:00am - 4:30pm. In summer, the visitor center features the Haskenneini Restaurant, which specializes in both native Navajo and American cuisines, and film/snack/souvenir shop. There are year-round restroom facilities. Dogs of all sizes are allowed for no additional fee. Dogs must be leashed at all times, cleaned up after, and under owner's control. Dogs are allowed throughout the park; they are not allowed in buildings.

Promontory

Golden Spike National Historical Site 6200 N 22300 W Promontory UT   435-471-2209
http://www.nps.gov/gosp/home.html
This historic site commemorates the driving of the last spike on May 10, 1869 of the first transcontinental

railroad, and illustrates the social, economic, and political impacts this accomplishment has meant to the growth and westward development of America. The Visitor's Center is open daily from 9 am to 5 pm. The activities range from regularly scheduled ranger programs, engine house tours, living history programs, reenactments, films to view, picnicking, a 1 ½ mile walking trail, and locomotive demonstrations are offered seasonally. Dogs are welcome throughout the park, with the exception of the Visitor's Center. Dogs must be leashed and cleaned up after at all times.

Salt Lake City

Carriage for Hire across from Crossroads Mall Salt Lake City UT   801-363-8687
Take a carriage ride through downtown Salt Lake City. Most of the carriages will allow a well-behaved dog. The horse and carriages cost about $40 for a half hour ride. They give rides on weekdays from about 10am to 4pm and then again from 6pm to 11pm. During the weekends they are usually open for carriage rides all day.
Ensign Peak Trail Ensign Vista Drive Salt Lake City UT   801-972-7800
Located just a short drive from downtown, this 1/2 mile trail offers panoramic views of the valley and the lake. It also offers some historical value. This peak was used by Indians, pioneers and explorers. Brigham Young, along with eight other pioneers, climbed to this summit on July 26, 1847, two days after the Mormon pioneers arrived in the Salt Lake Valley. They used this peak to view their surroundings. The trail leads up to a stone monument located at the peak. The elevation gain is about 400 feet. Dogs must be on a leash. To get there, drive north on East Capitol Blvd. and go past the State Capitol Building. Continue for about 8 blocks and then turn left on Ensign Vista Drive.
Wheeler Historic Farm 6351 S 900 E Salt Lake City UT   801-264-2241
http://www.wheelerfarm.com
This historical, working farm (a restoration of the turn of the century dairy farm of Henry J. Wheeler) represents the rural lifestyle in Salt Lake County from 1890-1920 and showcases the best farming methods of the Progressive Era. It is comprised of 75 acres and is on both the state and National Register of Historic Places. They offer a variety of planned seasonal activities, farmhouse tours, historic demonstrations, exhibits, and environmental educational programs. The grounds are open from dawn to dusk everyday, and office hours are from 9 am to 5 pm, Monday through Saturday. Friendly dogs on leash are welcome, and please clean up after your pet.

"Must See" Washington Dog-Friendly Places

Chehalis

Chehalis-Centralia Railroad 1101 Sylvenus Street Chehalis WA   360-748-9593
http://www.steamtrainride.com/index.html
Operating over a nine mile section of tract through scenic hills, farmland, and many wooden trestles, this restored steam powered train will provide a pleasant, relaxing journey back in time. This company currently runs only one of a few steam powered standard gauge tourist railroads in the state. Your pet is welcome to join you for no additional fee when they are not very busy and/or when the train cars are not full. Dogs must be well behaved, leashed, and please bring supplies to clean up after your pet.

Chelan

Chelan Airways 1328 West Woodin Ave/H Alt 97 Chelan WA   509-682-5555
http://www.chelanairways.com/
This company has been providing air transportation and sightseeing tours for over 60 years to the Lake Chelan area, an area that offers spectacular contrasts in geography and topography. Cradled in the deepest gorge in North America, the lake begins deep inside the North Cascades and reaches 55 miles into the desert of N. Central Washington. Dogs are allowed on the small planes if they will be comfortable and well behaved. There is no additional fee if they do not take a paying seat. Dogs must be leashed and please carry supplies to clean up after your pet.

Clarkston

Snake Dancer Excursions 1550 Port Drive, Suite B (Below Roosters Landing) Clarkston WA   509-758-8927
http://www.snakedancerexcursions.com/
These jet boat tours of the Hells Canyon have been offering a variety of scenic tours since 1970. Some of the features/amenities include whitewater rapids, historic sites, exposed lava flows, petroglyphs, incredible scenery, abundant wildlife, and a tasty home-made buffet style lunch. Dogs are allowed on some of the tours (if ok with other passengers) for no additional fee, or you can schedule a customized tour. You must provide your pooch

with their own doggy life jacket. Dogs must be attended to at all times, well behaved, leashed, and cleaned up after.

Mount Baker - Glacier

Mt. Baker Lodging 7463 Mt. Baker Highway Glacier WA   360-599-2453 (1-800-709-7669)
http://www.mtbakerlodging.com/
Private vacation rental homes located at the gateway to Mt. Baker. There are a wide variety of rental homes to choose, from honeymoon getaways and family cabins, to accommodations for group retreats and family reunions. All properties are privately owned, unique and completely self-contained.

Port Townsend

Sidewalk Tours Old City Hall Port Townsend WA   360-385-1967
You can enjoy these expertly guided living history walking tours of this culturally rich area with your pooch. Dogs usually take the tour of the waterfront where they get a few pit stops at the water along the way. Tours begin at the Old City Hall on Water and Madison Streets and are by appointment. Dogs must be friendly, leashed, and please bring supplies to clean up after your pet when in town.

Ruston

Fort Nisqually 5400 N Pearl Street Ruston WA   253-591-5339
http://www.fortnisqually.org/
Located in Point Defiance Park, this living history museum recreates life in the early 1800's in the first European settlement on Puget Sound. Workers from all over came to this area for the fur trade and brought with them quite a diverse trade and agricultural market. The fort also plays host to other events during the year, and their hours vary with the seasons. Dogs are welcome at the park, and at this mostly outdoor museum. Dogs are not allowed to go inside any of the buildings, and they must be leashed and cleaned up after at all times.

San Juan Island

San Juan Island National Historic Park 125 Spring Street Friday Harbor WA   360-378-2902
http://www.nps.gov/sajh/
Leashed dogs are welcome on the hiking trails. Some of the trails are self-guided tours of the area and buildings. Dogs on leash are also allowed at South Beach, which is located at the American Camp. Dogs are not allowed inside the Visitor's Center.

Seattle

Fun Forest Amusement Park 305 Harrison Street Seattle WA   206-728-1586
http://www.funforest.com
This amusement park sits at the base of the Seattle Space needle and was originally the midway for the 1962 World's Fair. In addition to the midway and a host of thrill rides, there is an entertainment pavilion and the Seattle Center House, a vast food court. Days and hours of operation vary with the seasons. There is no admission fee, and dogs are welcome throughout the park, with the exception of the Center House food court. Dogs must be well behaved, and leashed and cleaned up after at all times.
Sand Point Magnuson Park Dog Off-Leash Beach and Area 7400 Sand Point Way NE Seattle WA   206-684-4075
This leash free dog park covers about 9 acres and is the biggest fully fenced off-leash park in Seattle. It also offers an access point to the lake where your pooch is welcome to take a dip in the fresh lake water. To find the dog park, take Sand Point Way Northeast and enter the park at Northeast 74th Street. Go straight and park near the playground and sports fields. The main gate to the off-leash area is located at the southeast corner of the main parking lot. Dogs must be leashed until you enter the off-leash area.

Snoqualmie

Northwest Railway Museum 38625 SE King Street Snoqualmie WA   425-888-3030
http://www.trainmuseum.org/
This is the largest and most comprehensive railway museum in the state, and they offer interpretive programs/displays on the history, operation, and importance of the railway. Although dogs are not allowed in the buildings or on the train, they are allowed around the grounds. Dogs must be leashed and cleaned up after.

Union Gap

Central Washington Agricultural Museum 4508 Main Street Union Gap WA   509-457-8735
Located on 15 acres in a city park, this museum has collected an extensive history of Central Washington's agriculture, which is still recognized as one of the most productive agricultural areas in the nation. They constructed an outer ring of semi-open buildings to display numerous exhibits, and farm equipment. There is also an operating windmill and a railroad exhibit. Dogs are allowed to walk the grounds, but they are not allowed in enclosed buildings. Dogs must be leashed, and please have supplies to clean up after your pet. Hours vary with the season.

White Pass

White Pass Ski Area 48935 H 12 White Pass WA   509-672-3101
http://www.skiwhitepass.com/
This snow/ski resort offers a wide variety of terrain for all ability levels, ski/snowboard instruction, and they are family oriented and offer fun events throughout the year. Dogs are allowed at this resort and can be on the trails. During their winter season, dogs are only allowed on the cross country ski trails after 3:30 on Thursday, Friday, and Saturday, and all day on Monday through Wednesday. During the summer (off-season months) there is unlimited use. Dogs may be unleashed when on the cross country trails if they will respond to voice control. Dogs must be leashed and cleaned up after at all times when in the resort area.

Yakima

McAllister Museum of Aviation 2008 S 16th Avenue Yakima WA   509-457-4933
http://mcallistermuseum.org/
Operating for 73 years, this flight school was one of the longest running flight schools in the Northwest. Now a museum, they host various events throughout the year, and on Saturdays you will usually find local pilots hanging out there who love to share their aviation history. Dogs are allowed to explore the museum with you. Dogs must be well behaved, leashed, and please have supplies to clean up after your pet.

Chapter 2

California - North Coast
Dog Travel Guide

Albion

Campgrounds and RV Parks

Albion River Campground and Fishing Village 34500 Hwy 1 Albion CA 7 0 7-937-0606
http://www.albionrivercampground.com/
Located along side the Albion River on the beautiful Mendocino coast, this campground offers a variety of recreational pursuits, a small store, restaurant, a boat dock, and a nice sandy beach. Some other amenities include on-site RV rentals, picnic tables, fire rings, showers and restrooms. Dogs of all sizes are allowed for an additional fee of $2 per pet. Dogs must be leashed and cleaned up after at all times, and they may not be left unattended on the camp site or in a vehicle. There is a steep hill down from Highway 1 to the campground. Dogs are allowed throughout the park and on the beach. The camping and tent areas also allow dogs. There is a dog walk area at the campground.

Vacation Home Rentals

The Doors North Hwy 1 Albion CA 707-937-9200 (800-525-0049)
This vacation home rental is dog-friendly. There are no additional pet fees. Please call to make reservations.

Arcata

Accommodations

Best Western Arcata Inn 4827 Valley West Blvd Arcata CA 707-826-0313 (800-780-7234)
Dogs of all sizes are allowed. There is a $10 per night pet fee per pet. Smoking and non-smoking are available for pet rooms.
Comfort Inn 4701 Valley W Blvd Arcata CA 707-826-2827 (877-424-6423)
Dogs of all sizes are allowed. There is a $5 per night per pet additional fee for dogs under 25 pounds, a $10 per night per pet additional fee for dogs 25 pounds or over, and a credit card must be on file. Dogs may only be left alone in the room if they will be quiet and well behaved. Dogs must be leashed and cleaned up after.
Hotel Arcata 708 Ninth Street Arcata CA 707-826-0217 (800-344-1221)
http://www.hotelarcata.com
This hotel comes highly recommended from one of our readers who says "In Arcata, just north of Eureka, we stayed in an old refurbished hotel, the Hotel Arcata. It's in the center of town, right on the town square. Ask for a room that doesn't face the square, as it can get noisy at night. Bringing a dog into the elevator is fun." There is a $5 per day additional pet fee.
Motel 6 - Arcata - Humboldt University 4755 Valley West Boulevard Arcata CA 707-822-7061 (800-466-8356)
One well-behaved family pet per room. Guest must notify front desk upon arrival. Guest is liable for any damages. In consideration of all guests, pets must never be left unattended in the guest rooms.
Quality Inn 3535 Janes Road Arcata CA 707-822-0409 (877-424-6423)
Dogs of all sizes are allowed. There is a $10 per night pet additional fee. Dogs may be left alone in the room only if they will be quiet, well behaved, and it is only for a short period. Dogs must be on leash when out of the room and cleaned up after.
Super 8 Arcata 4887 Valley W Blvd Arcata CA 707-822-8888 (800-800-8000)
Dogs of all sizes are allowed. There is a $5 per night pet fee per pet. Smoking and non-smoking rooms are available for pet rooms.

Beaches

Mad River Beach County Park Mad River Road Arcata CA 707-445-7651
Enjoy walking or jogging for several miles on this beach. Dogs on leash are allowed. The park is located about 4-5 miles north of Arcata. To get there, take Highway 101 and exit Giuntoli Lane. Then go north onto Heindon Rd. Turn left onto Miller Rd. Turn right on Mad River Road and follow it to the park.
Clam Beach County Park Highway 101 McKinleyville CA 707-445-7651
This beach is popular for fishing, swimming, picnicking and beachcombing. Of course, there are also plenty of clams. Dogs on leash are allowed on the beach and at the campgrounds. There are no day use fees. The park is located off Highway 101, about eight miles north of Arcata.

Parks

Arcata Community Forest 11th and 14th Streets Arcata CA   707-822-3619
Leashed dogs are allowed on this 600+ acre park which offers 18 trails. The trails range from 1/10 of a mile to almost 2 miles long. The park is located on the east side of the City of Arcata, accessible from Redwood Park located at the east ends of 11th and 14th Streets; on the southern side from Fickle Hill Road, which begins at the east end of 11th and 7th Streets at Bayside Road; and from the east end of California Street which connects with L.K. Wood Blvd. north of Humboldt State University.

Avenue Of The Giants

Accommodations

Miranda Gardens Resort 6766 Avenue of the Giants Miranda CA   707-943-3011
http://www.mirandagardens.com/
The cottages are surrounded by flowering gardens and surrounded by ancient redwoods. From this resort, you can take day trips to the Avenue of the Giants or the Lost Coast. All cottages are non-smoking. Children are welcome and the resort has a children's play area. Pets are allowed in certain cabins and there is a $50 one time pet charge.

Campgrounds and RV Parks

Benbow Valley RV Resort and Golf Course 7000 Benbow Drive Garberville CA   707-923-2777 (866) BENBOWRV (236-2697))
http://www.benbowrv.com
This beautiful full service resort offers many amenities in addition to a wide variety of recreation. Dogs of all sizes are allowed for an additional $3 per night per pet. Dogs may not be left unattended outside, and left inside only if they will be quiet and well behaved. Dogs must be on no more than a 6 foot leash and be cleaned up after. They are also adjacent to a state park where there are several hiking trails. This is an RV only park. This campground is closed during the off-season. There is a dog walk area at the campground.

Richardson Grove Campground 750 Hwy 101 Garberville CA   70 7-247-3380
http://www.redwoodfamilycamp.com/
This well kept camp area also offers a chapel on site and a variety of family and age-appropriate church camps. Some of the amenities include a general store, high-speed internet, a laundry, showers, and restrooms. Dogs of all sizes are allowed for no additional fee. They must have a current license and proof of vaccinations. Dogs must be under owner's immediate control, and leashed and cleaned up after at all times. Pets may not be left unattended on site, and they must be walked in the designated areas only. Although sites are on a 1st come 1st served basis, reservations are suggested between June 1st and October 1st. The camping and tent areas also allow dogs. There is a dog walk area at the campground.

Humboldt Redwoods State Park P.O. Box 100/17119 Avenue of the Giants Weott CA   707-946-2409 (800-444-PARK (7275))
http://www.humboldtredwoods.org/
Of the 3 developed camp areas, Albee Creek, Burlington, and Hidden Springs, only Burlington is open year round. They can all be accessed from the Avenue of the Giants. Some of the amenities at this scenic park include fire rings, picnic tables, coin-operated showers, flush toilets, and potable water. Dogs are welcome for no additional pet fees. Dogs must have current tags, and be on no more than a 6 foot leash and cleaned up after at all times. They are not allowed in trail, environmental, or group camps. Dogs are allowed in the developed areas/roads, the picnic areas, and the campground. They are not allowed on any of the trails or in the back country, and they must be inside at night. The camping and tent areas also allow dogs. There is a dog walk area at the campground. There are no electric or water hookups at the campgrounds.

Humboldt Redwoods State Park Campgrounds 17119 Avenue of the Giants (Hwy 254) Weott CA   707-946-2409 (800-444-PARK (7275))
There are several campgrounds located in this park including Albee Creek, Burlington and Hidden Springs Campgrounds. Tent and RV sites are available. Camp amenities include picnic tables, fire rings, showers and flush toilets. While dogs are not allowed on the trails, they are allowed in the campgrounds and on miles of fire roads and access roads. These paths are used mainly for mountain biking, but dogs are allowed too. There are both steep and gently sloping fire roads. Some of the fire roads are located next to the Albee Creek Campground. Pets must be on no more than a 6 foot leash, and cleaned up after. There is no additional pet fee, but dogs must have proof of their shots. Dogs must be quiet, well behaved, and inside at night. They are not allowed in park buildings. The park is located about 45 miles south of Eureka and 20 miles north of Garberville The camping and tent areas also allow dogs. There is a dog walk area at the campground. There are no electric or water hookups at the campgrounds.

Attractions

One Log House

One Log House 705 US Hwy 101 Garberville CA 707-247-3717
This espresso and gift shop hosts the One Log House, a house built inside of a single 13 foot diameter redwood tree. You can get an espresso to drink outside with your pet after viewing the home.

Avenue of the Giants Highway 101 Phillipsville CA 707-722-4291
This 33 mile drive offers spectacular views of redwoods and some very unique redwood trees, including some of the biggest trees in the world. You and your pooch might be able to drive your car through a redwood tree or two (depending on the size of your car). There is a fee to drive through some of the trees. The auto tour can be taken from the northbound or southbound direction. Allow about 1-2 hours, depending on stops and any traffic. From the north start at the Pepperwood/Jordan Creek exit off Highway 101 and from the south, start at the Phillipsville exit off Highway 101. The auto tour map can be picked up at either entrance. Dogs are not allowed on the trails in the state park, but they are allowed on fire roads and access roads in the Humboldt Redwoods State Park. One of the access points to the fire roads is at Albee Creek Campground.

Parks

Benbow Lake State Recreation Area 1600 Highway 101 Garberville CA 707-923-3238
Leashed dogs are allowed. The park consists of about 1,200 acres with campsites and a large day-use picnic area. Hiking, picnicking and camping are popular summer time activities, while salmon and steelhead fishing are popular in the winter.

Humboldt Redwoods State Park

Humboldt Redwoods State Park Avenue of the Giants Weott CA 707-946-2409
This park is located along the scenic Avenue of the Giants. While dogs are not allowed on the trails, they are allowed in the campgrounds and on miles of fire roads and access roads. These paths are used mainly for mountain biking, but dogs are allowed too. There are both steep and gently sloping fire roads. Some of the fire roads are located next to the Albee Creek Campground. Pets on leash are allowed and please clean up after them. The park is located along the Avenue of the Giants, about 45 miles south of Eureka and 20 miles north of Garberville.

Boonville

Accommodations
Boonville Hotel Highway 128 Boonville CA 707-895-2210
This historic hotel was built in 1862. Dogs and children are allowed in the Bungalow and the Studio rooms which are separate from the main building. Both of these rooms are in the Creekside building with private entrances and yards. Room rates start at $225 per night and there is a $15 per day pet charge. Please note that their restaurant is closed on Tuesdays and Wednesdays. This hotel is in Anderson Valley, which is located 2 1/2 hours north of San Francisco.

Attractions
Anderson Valley Brewing Company 17700 Hwy 253 Boonville CA 707-895-BEER (895-2337)
http://www.avbc.com
Home to various events and activities throughout the year, this top-award winning brewery features carefully crafted ales of the highest caliber. They also have an 18 hole Disc Golf Course right on the grounds, and a gift shop and visitor center. Dogs are welcome around the grounds and on the course; they are not allowed in the buildings. Dogs must be well mannered, leashed, and cleaned up after.

Boont Berry Farm

Boont Berry Farm 13980 Hwy 128 Boonville CA   707-895-3441
This organic farm and store has even been seen on TV as a "Pet Friendly Place" and welcome their four-legged visitors. Dogs are allowed around the farm and store areas. They must be friendly, leashed and cleaned up after at all times.
Zina Hyde Cunningham Winery 14077 Hwy 128 Boonville CA   707-895-9462
http://www.zinawinery.com/
Some of the specialties of this scenic winery include a Bordeaux Cepage blend, Carignane, Sauvignon Blanc, Zinfandel, and Petite Sirah. Dogs are allowed around the property, but not in the tasting room. Dogs must be well behaved, and leashed and cleaned up after.

Outdoor Restaurants

Redwood Cafe 13980 Hwy 128 Boonville CA   707-895-3441
Offering good American favorites and fresh from the orchard pies, this eatery offers indoor or outdoor dining options. You can order and pick from an outside window. Dogs are welcome at the outer tables; they must be under owner's control, and be leashed and cleaned up after at all times.

Crescent City

Accommodations

Town House Motel 444 US Hwy 101S Crescent City CA   707-464-4176
Well behaved and friendly dogs are allowed. There is a $10 per night per pet fee and there is only 1 pet friendly room available. There are some breed restrictions.

Campgrounds and RV Parks

Crescent City KOA 4241 Hwy 101N Crescent City CA   707-464-5744 (800-562-5754)
http://www.koa.com/where/ca/05102/
This 17 acre campground has 10 acres of camping in the redwood forest. It offers ice cream socials, pancake breakfasts, movie nights, hayrides, snack bar, bike rentals and a maximum pull through length of 60 feet with 50 amp service. Dogs of all sizes are allowed for no additional fee. Dogs must be under owner's control and visual observation at all times. Dogs must be quiet, well behaved, and be on no more than a 6 foot leash at all times, or otherwise contained. Dogs may not be left unattended outside the owner's camping equipment. There are some

breed restrictions. The camping and tent areas also allow dogs. There is a dog walk area at the campground. Dogs are allowed in the camping cabins.

De Norte Coast Redwoods State Park 7 miles S of Crescent City off Hwy 101 Crescent City CA   707-464-6101, ext. 5064

This predominately old growth coastal forest park is known for its steep topography and lush natural setting, and they offer guided tours, exhibits, and a variety of recreational pursuits. Dogs of all sizes are allowed. There are no additional pet fees. Dogs must be leashed and cleaned up after. Dogs are not allowed on the nature trails, but they are allowed on the beach on lead. No swimming, due to high danger, is allowed. This campground is closed during the off-season. The camping and tent areas also allow dogs. There is a dog walk area at the campground. There are no electric or water hookups at the campgrounds.

Jedediah Smith Campground 1440 Hwy 199 Crescent City CA   707-464-6101 (800-444-PARK (7275))
http://www.nps.gov/redw/camping.html

This campground is located in the Jedediah Smith Redwoods State Park and offers 106 RV or tent sites in an old growth redwood forest. RVs must be 36 feet or less. Camp amenities include restrooms, showers, fire pits, dump station and bear-proof lockers. While dogs are not allowed on any park trails, they are allowed in the campground and at the beach. They are also allowed to walk on or along Walker Road which is just west of the campground. Pets must be on no more than a 6 foot leash and attended at all times. Please clean up after your pets. There are no additional pet fees. The camping and tent areas also allow dogs. There is a dog walk area at the campground. There are no electric or water hookups at the campgrounds.

Jedediah Smith Redwoods State Park 9 miles east of Crescent City on Highway 199. Crescent City CA   707-464-6101, ext. 5112

This predominately old growth coastal forest of redwoods is home to the last major free flowing river in California. The park is abundant with animal and plant life and offers a variety of interpretive programs, guided tours, and recreational pursuits. Dogs of all sizes are allowed. There are no additional pet fees. Dogs must be leashed and cleaned up after. Dogs are not allowed on the trails, but they are allowed on the beach on lead. The camping and tent areas also allow dogs. There is a dog walk area at the campground. There are no electric or water hookups at the campgrounds.

Mill Creek Campground 1375 Elk Valley Road Crescent City CA   707-464-9533 (800-444-PARK (7275))
http://www.nps.gov/redw/camping.html

This park is located in a second growth Redwood forest, and offers guided walks, campfire programs, and a variety of recreational pursuits. Dogs of all sizes are allowed. There are no additional pet fees. Dogs must be on no more than a 6 foot leash and cleaned up after. Dogs are not allowed on the beach. They are allowed on the trails unless otherwise marked. This campground is closed during the off-season. The camping and tent areas also allow dogs. There is a dog walk area at the campground. There are no electric or water hookups at the campgrounds.

Panther Flat Campground mile post 16.75 on Highway 199 Gasquet CA   707-457-3131

This park, located next to the Middle Fork of Smith River, is the largest Smith River NRA campground, and offers botanical areas, various trails, and a variety of recreational pursuits. Dogs of all sizes are allowed. There are no additional pet fees. Dogs must be leashed and cleaned up after. Dogs are allowed on the trails unless otherwise marked. They are not allowed to go on the National or State Park trails that connect in areas to this park. The camping and tent areas also allow dogs. There is a dog walk area at the campground. There are no electric or water hookups at the campgrounds.

Panther Flat Campground Mile Post 16.75 Hwy 199 Gasquet CA   707-442-1721 (877-444-6777)

This campground is located in the Smith River National Recreation Area and is part of the Six Rivers National Forest. The campground offers 39 tent and RV sites. RVs up to 40 feet are allowed. Amenities include flush restrooms, pay shower, potable water, picnic tables, grills, fishing, and sites with river and scenic views. Pets on leash are allowed at no additional fee, and please clean up after them. Dogs are allowed on the trails in the National Forest on lead but not on State Park trails. The camping and tent areas also allow dogs. There is a dog walk area at the campground. There are no electric or water hookups at the campgrounds.

Beaches

Beachfront Park Front Street Crescent City CA   707-464-9507

Dogs are allowed at park and the beach, but must be leashed. Please clean up after your pets. To get there, take Highway 101 to Front Street. Follow Front Street to the park.

Crescent Beach Enderts Beach Road Crescent City CA   707-464-6101
http://www.nps.gov/redw/home.html

While dogs are not allowed on any trails in Redwood National Park, they are allowed on a couple of beaches, including Crescent Beach. Enjoy beachcombing or bird watching at this beach. Pets are also allowed at road accessible picnic areas and campgrounds. Dogs must be on a 6 foot or less leash and people need to pick up after their pets. The beach is located off Highway 101, about 3 to 4 miles south of Crescent City. Exit Enderts Beach Road and head south.

Parks

Myrtle Creek Trail Highway 199 Gasquet CA   707-442-1721
This trail is located in the Smith River National Recreation Area and is part of the Six Rivers National Forest. The trail is an easy 1 mile interpretive hiking path. The elevations range from 250 to 500 feet. From this trail you can also access the Smith River. Pets on leash are allowed and please clean up after them. The trail is located 8 miles west of Gasquet at Milepost 7.0. Park on the south (river) side of the highway. Use caution when crossing Highway 199 to reach the trailhead.

Outdoor Restaurants
Beacon Burger 160 Anchor Way Crescent City CA   707-464-6565
Well-behaved leashed dogs are allowed at the outdoor seating area.
Betterbean Espresso 315 M Street Crescent City CA   707-465-1248
Well-behaved leashed dogs are allowed at the outdoor seating area.
Bistro Gardens 110 Anchor Way Crescent City CA   707-464-5627
Let them know that you want to sit outside and they will bring out a table. Well-behaved leashed dogs are welcome at the outdoor seating area.
Glen's Bakery and Restaurant 722 3rd Street Crescent City CA   707-464-2914
This restaurant has one outdoor table and well-behaved leashed dogs are allowed.
Good Harvest Cafe 700 Northcrest Drive Crescent City CA   707-465-6028
Well-behaved leashed dogs are allowed at the outdoor seating area.
Los Compadres Mexican Food 457 Highway 101 Crescent City CA   707-464-7871
Well-behaved leashed dogs are allowed at the outdoor seating area.
Surfside Grill & Brewery 400 Front Street Crescent City CA   707-464-7962
Well-behaved leashed dogs are allowed at the outdoor seating area.

Elk

Accommodations
The Greenwood Pier Inn 5928 S Hwy 1 Elk CA   707-877-9997
Dogs of all sizes are allowed. There is a $15 per night per pet additional fee.
The Griffin House Inn 5910 Hwy 1 Elk CA   707-877-3422
Dogs of all sizes are allowed. There is a $20 one time fee per room, and there is only 1 pet friendly room available.
The Griffin House Inn 5910 S Hwy 1 Elk CA   707-877-1820
http://www.griffinhouseinn.com/
Some of the amenities at this inn include a hearty breakfast delivered to your cottage door, wood burning stoves with firewood, private decks, and an on-site restaurant and pub. There is only one pet friendly cottage so be sure to declare your pet at the time of the reservation; this cottage also has a back yard. Dogs up to 75 pounds are allowed for an additional fee of $20 per pet per stay. Dogs must be leashed and cleaned up after at all times. The reservation number is 707-877-3422.

Eureka

Accommodations
Best Western Bayshore Inn 3500 Broadway Eureka CA   707-268-8005 (800-780-7234)
Dogs of all sizes are allowed. There is a $40 one time pet fee per visit. Smoking and non-smoking are available for pet rooms.
Discovery Inn 2832 Broadway Eureka CA   707-441-8442
There is a $7 per day additional pet fee.
Motel 6 - Eureka 1934 Broadway Street Eureka CA   707-445-9631 (800-466-8356)
One well-behaved family pet per room. Guest must notify front desk upon arrival. Guest is liable for any damages. In consideration of all guests, pets must never be left unattended in the guest rooms.
The Eureka Inn 518 Seventh Street Eureka CA   707-442-6441 (800-862-4906)
http://www.eurekainn.com
This inn has been named a National Historical Place, and is a member of Historic Hotels of America. Dogs are allowed on the first floor and there is no pet fee. They have allowed well-behaved St. Bernards here before.

Campgrounds and RV Parks

Eureka KOA 4050 N Hwy 101 Eureka CA   707-822-4243   (800-562-3136)
http://www.koa.com/where/ca/05122/
Located along Humboldt Bay in the heart of the giant redwood country, this well-kept park offers a maximum length pull-through of 70 feet with 50 amp service. Some amenities include cable TV, two playgrounds, a swimming pool, family hot tub, adults-only hot tub, horseshoe pits, rental bikes, a camp store, and ice cream socials during the summer months. Dogs of all sizes are allowed for an additional fee of $3 per night per pet. Dogs must be under owner's control and visual observation at all times. Dogs must be quiet, well behaved, and be on no more than a 6 foot leash at all times, or otherwise contained. Dogs may not be left unattended outside the owner's camping equipment. There are some breed restrictions. The camping and tent areas also allow dogs. There is a dog walk area at the campground. Dogs are allowed in the camping cabins.

Stores
Petco Pet Store 3300 Broadway St Eureka CA   707-445-1256
Your licensed and well-behaved leashed dog is allowed in the store.
Restoration Hardware 417 Second Street Eureka CA   707-443-3152
Utilizing the finest of products, this store features a large selection of home restoration products. Your leashed, well behaved dog is welcome to join you in the store. They must be housebroken and under owner's control at all times.

Beaches
Samoa Dunes Recreation Area New Navy Base Road Samoa CA   707-825-2300
The Bureau of Land Management oversees this 300 acre sand dune park. It is a popular spot for off-highway vehicles which can use about 140 of the park's acres. Dogs are allowed on leash or off-leash but under voice control. Even if your dog runs off-leash, the park service requests that you still bring a leash just in case. To get there, take Highway 255 and turn south on New Navy Base Road. Go about four miles to the parking area.

Parks

Fort Humboldt State Historic Park

Fort Humboldt State Historic Park 3431 Fort Avenue Eureka CA   707-445-6567
This old military post was established in 1853 to assist in resolving conflicts between Native Americans and settlers who were searching for gold. Dogs are not allowed inside any buildings but they can walk through the outdoor exhibits and view historic logging equipment. There is also a grassy bluff area where you can walk your dog. Pets must be on leash and please clean up after them. The park is located south of Eureka off Highway

101. Go east on Highland Avenue for one block.
Six Rivers National Forest 1330 Bayshore Way Eureka CA   707-442-1721
http://www.fs.fed.us/r5/sixrivers/
This national forest covers almost 1 million acres of land which ranges in elevation from sea level to almost 7,000 feet. Please see our listings in this region for dog-friendly hikes and/or campgrounds.

Outdoor Restaurants
Hana Sushi Restaurant 2120 4th Street Eureka CA   707-444-3318
Well-behaved dogs are welcome this Japanese restaurant's outdoor seating area. Dogs need to be leashed.

Los Bagels

Los Bagels 403 Second Street Eureka CA   707-442-8525
http://www.losbagels.com
This bakery offers a variety of breads, bagels and pastries. It is located in Eureka's historic Old Town. Well-behaved, leashed dogs are allowed at the outside tables.
Starbucks Coffee 1117 Myrtle Avenue Eureka CA   707-445-2672
http://www.starbucks.com/
Fuel up with some coffee and pastries at Starbucks. Well-behaved, leashed dogs are allowed at the outside tables.

Ferndale

Accommodations
Collingwood Inn 831 Main Street Ferndale CA   707-786-9219
Dogs of all sizes are allowed. There is a $25 per pet per stay fee and a pet policy to sign at check in.

Fortuna

Accommodations
Best Western Country Inn 2025 Riverwalk Dr Fortuna CA   707-725-6822 (800-780-7234)

Dogs of all sizes are allowed. There is a $10 one time per pet fee per visit. Smoking and non-smoking are available for pet rooms.

Attractions
Fortuna Depot Museum 3 Park St Fortuna CA 707-725-7645
The museum contains the history of the Eel River Valley. Museum collections include memorabilia from railroad, farm and war eras. There is also a doll collection. Well-behaved, leashed dogs are allowed, just keep them right next to you.

Outdoor Restaurants
Shotz Coffee 1665 Main Street Fortuna CA 707-725-8000
This coffee shop offers a table and bench outside where guests may sit with their pet. Dogs must be under owner's control at all times, leashed, and cleaned up after.

Garberville

Accommodations
Dean Creek Resort Motel 4112 Redwood Drive Redway CA 707-923-2555 (877-923-2555)
Located along the Eel River in Giant Redwood country, and only three miles from the famous "Avenue of the Giants", this resort offers a long list of amenities and recreation. Pets are allowed for an additional fee of $6 per night per pet for the motel. There is an RV park on site where dogs are an additional $1.50 per night per pet. Dogs may not be left unattended at any time, either in the motel or in the RV park. Dogs are allowed on the trails and on the beach. Dogs must be leashed and cleaned up after. Please check with the resort for breed restrictions.

Campgrounds and RV Parks
Dean Creek Resort 4112 Redwood Drive Redway CA 707-923-2555
http://www.deancreekresort.com/
Located on the Eel River, this campground is located just 3 miles from the Avenue of the Giants attraction. River front sites are available for both RVs and tent camping. Many of the RV sites have full hookups with 50 amp service available. All sites have picnic tables and barbecue grills. Other amenities include a pool, spa, sauna, coin laundry, mini-mart, meeting room, game room, playground, and restrooms. Pets are allowed but must be leashed at all times. There is an additional $1.50 per night per pet fee for the tent or RV sites. There is a $6 per night per pet additional fee for the motel rooms. Dogs may not be left unattended at any time. There are some breed restrictions. The camping and tent areas also allow dogs. There is a dog walk area at the campground.

Gualala

Accommodations
Mar Vista Cottages 35101 S Hwy 1 Gualala CA 707-884-3522 (877-855-3522)
http://www.marvistamendocino.com/
This inn offers 12 housekeeping cottages with kitchens and an organic garden to harvest from. They will also stock the cottages with any essential needs if you call ahead. There are breathtaking ocean and coastal views with a short walk to the beach, 9 acres of scenic grounds, and hiking trails. Dogs of all sizes are welcome for an additional one time fee of $35 for one pet, and $50 if there are two pets. Dogs are allowed around the grounds, on the trails, and at the beach. Dogs must be at least 2 years old and completely housebroken; they are not permitted on the beds and furniture, and they may not be left alone in the cottage at any time. Dogs may be off lead only if they are under good voice control as there are other dogs and animals in residence. Dogs must be friendly, well behaved, and cleaned up after at all times.
Surf Motel 39170 S. Highway 1 Gualala CA 707-884-3571
http://www.gualala.com
There is a $10 per day pet charge.

Campgrounds and RV Parks
Gualala Point Regional Park 42401 Coast Highway 1 Gualala CA 707-785-2377
This 195 acre park offers spectacular scenery, wide open meadows along coastal forest, a Visitor Center, an

extensive trail system, sandy beaches, and a variety of land and water recreation. Dogs are allowed for an additional $1 per night per pet. A rabies certificate is required, and dogs must be on a leash no longer than 6 feet and cleaned up after at all times. The campground sits among majestic redwood trees adjacent to the Gualala River, and in addition to the beautiful surroundings, the park provides potable water, a modern restroom, showers, and a dump station. The camping and tent areas also allow dogs. There is a dog walk area at the campground. There are no electric or water hookups at the campgrounds.

Gualala Point Regional Park Campgrounds 42401 Coast Hwy 1 Gualala CA 707-785-2377
This dog-friendly park offers sandy beaches, hiking trails and 20 campsites. RVs are permitted and there is a dump station. Dogs are allowed but must be on a 6 foot or less leash at all times, be cleaned up after, and have proof of rabies vaccination. There is an additional fee of $1 per night per pet. Reservations are taken by telephone at 707-565-CAMP(2267). The camping and tent areas also allow dogs. There is a dog walk area at the campground. There are no electric or water hookups at the campgrounds.

Vacation Home Rentals
Ocean View Properties P.O. Box 1285 Gualala CA 707-884-3538
http://www.oceanviewprop.com/
Ocean View Properties offers vacation home rentals on The Sea Ranch and Mendocino Coast. Some of their vacation homes are pet-friendly. They offer a wide variety of special vacation home rentals, located on the oceanfront, oceanside and hillside at The Sea Ranch. Each of the rental homes has a fully equipped kitchen, a fireplace or wood stove, blankets, pillows, and telephones. Most have hot tubs, televisions, VCR's, radios, CD/cassette players, and washer/dryers. Guests provide kindling, bed linens, and towels. With advance notice, linens can be rented and maid service can be hired. Please call and ask them which rentals are dog-friendly.

Sea Ranch Vacation Homes P.O. Box 246 Gualala CA 707-884-4235
http://www.searanchrentals.com/
Rent a vacation home for the weekend, week or longer along the coast or on a forested hillside. Some of their 50 homes allow well-behaved dogs.

Serenisea Vacation Homes 36100 Highway 1 S. Gualala CA 707-884-3836
http://www.serenisea.com
Serenisea maintains and manages a number of vacation homes and cottages in this community on the Mendocino coast. Some of them allow dogs of all sizes.

Beaches
Gualala Point Regional Park Beach 42401 Coast Highway 1 Gualala CA 707-565-2041
This county park offers sandy beaches, hiking trails, campsites, picnic tables and restrooms. Dogs are allowed on the beach, on the trails, and in the campground, but they must be on a 6 foot or less leash. People also need to clean up after their pets. There is a $3 day use fee.

Hopland

Attractions
Brutocao Cellars and Vineyards 13500 Hwy 101 Hopland CA 707-744-1664
http://brutocaocellars.com/
This scenic vineyard offers outside dining at their restaurant, The Crushed Grape, and a variety of great wines, but they also offer a membership program so that you can produce your own label. From the start to the finish with a custom-designed label bearing your name, you get to learn, and be involved as much as you would like, in the winemaking process. Dogs are welcome. They must be leashed and cleaned up after. Dogs are not allowed in the tasting room, but they can sit with you at the outside dining tables.

Leggett

Attractions
Leggett Drive Thru Tree Hwy 1 and Hwy 101 Leggett CA
Want to drive your car through a tunnel built into a redwood tree. If your car isn't too wide you can do this at the Leggett Drive Thru Tree. From 101 take the turn-off at Hwy 1 towards Ft Bragg and immediately turn left onto Drive-Thru-Tree Road. The entrance is on your right in about 1/4 mile. There is a $5 fee to enter per vehicle. There is also a gift shop and picnic tables at the site.

Leggett Drive Thru Tree

Parks

Standish-Hickey State Recreation Area 69350 Highway 101 Leggett CA 707-925-6482
While dogs are not allowed on the trails, they are allowed on a few fire roads. The fire roads are not passable during the winter because of the river, but are fine during the summer months. The fire roads are located near the campground and near the main swimming hole. Dogs are also allowed in the water. Pets must be on leash and please clean up after them. The park is located 1.5 miles north of Leggett on Highway 101.

Manchester

Campgrounds and RV Parks

Manchester Beach/Mendocino Coast KOA 44300 Kinney Road Manchester CA 707-882-2375 (800-562-4188)
http://www.koa.com/where/ca/05182/
There is a variety of land and water recreation at this park located on a spectacular five-mile stretch of sand beach on the Mendocino Coast. Dogs of all sizes are allowed for no additional fee. Dogs must be under owner's control and visual observation at all times. Dogs must be quiet, well behaved, and be on no more than a 6 foot leash at all times, or otherwise contained. Dogs may not be left unattended outside the owner's camping equipment. There are some breed restrictions. The camping and tent areas also allow dogs. There is a dog walk area at the campground. Dogs are allowed in the camping cabins.

Mendocino

Accommodations

Beachcomber Motel 1111 N. Main Street Fort Bragg CA 707-964-2402 (800-400-SURF)
http://www.thebeachcombermotel.com/
This ocean front motel is next to a walking, jogging, and cycling trail that stretches for miles along the coast.
Many rooms have ocean views. They allow well-behaved dogs up to about 75-80 pounds. There is an additional
$10 per day pet charge.

Cleone Gardens Inn 24600 N. Hwy 1 Fort Bragg CA 707-964-2788 (800-400-2189)
http://www.cleonelodgeinn.com/
This park-like inn is on 5 acres. There are three pet rooms and an additional pet charge of $6 per day.

Delamere Seaside Cottages 16821 Ocean Drive Fort Bragg CA 707-964-3175
http://www.delamerecottages.com
These two small pet-friendly cottages are located on the Mendocino Coast and have nice ocean views. One
cottage has two decks and the other has a gazebo. Your well-behaved dog is welcome.

Pine Beach Inn 16801 N Hwy 1 Fort Bragg CA 888-987-8388
http://www.pinebeachinn.com/index.html
Located on 11 lush, tranquil acres with its own private beach and cove, this scenic inn also features easy access
to several other recreational activities, shopping, and dining. Some of the amenities include a large lawn with a
gazebo, 2 championship tennis courts, and a restaurant (south of the border cuisine) and full bar. Dogs of all
sizes are allowed for an additional $10 per night per pet. Dogs may not be left alone in the rooms, and they must
be leashed and cleaned up after.

Quality Inn and Suites Tradewinds 400 S Main Street Fort Bragg CA 707-964-4761 (877-424-6423)
Dogs of all sizes are allowed. There is a $10 per night per pet additional fee. Dogs must be leashed, cleaned up
after, and the Do Not Disturb sign put on the door if they are alone in the room.

Rendezvous Inn 647 N Main Street Fort Bragg CA 707-964-8142
Dogs of all sizes are allowed. There are no additional pet fees. There are only 2 pet friendly rooms available.

Shoreline Cottages 18725 N Hwy 1 Fort Bragg CA 707-964-2977
Adult dogs only are allowed, no puppies. There is a $10 per pet per stay pet fee.

The Rendezvous Inn and Restaurant 647 North Main Street Fort Bragg CA 707-964-8142 (800-491-8142)
http://www.rendezvousinn.com/
A romantic and elegant destination, this beautifully crafted 1897 home offers charm, relaxation, beautiful
gardens, a large sunny guest parlor, and an inviting ambiance. They can also tailor your stay with a food and
wine pairing. Their award-winning restaurant offers French gourmet dining in a casual but elegant atmosphere,
an extensive wine list, and seasonal outdoor dining where your four-legged companion may join you. Dogs of all
sizes are welcome for no additional fee. Dogs must be leashed and cleaned up after.

Little River Inn 7901 N Hwy 1 Littleriver CA 707-937-5942
Dogs of all sizes are allowed. There is a $25 plus tax fee per pet per stay and a pet policy to sign at check in.

S. S. Seafoam Lodge 6751 N Hwy 1 Littleriver CA 707-937-1827
http://www.seafoamlodge.com/
This lodge comprises a total of 8 separate buildings with 24 guest accommodations and a conference center.
Located on 6 acres of coastal gardens and pines, there are spectacular ocean views and a private cove and
beach access. Some of the amenities include a Continental breakfast delivered to your room, private baths and
decks, a hot tub, and conference facilities. Dogs of all sizes are allowed for an additional fee of $10 per night per
pet. Dogs may not be left alone in the room at any time, and they must be well mannered, leashed, and cleaned
up after.

Blackberry Inn 44951 Larkin Road Mendocino CA 707-937-5281 (800-950-7806)
http://www.blackberryinn.biz/
Located at one of California's most beautiful locations overlooking the Mendocino Bay, this country inn offers
ocean views, finely appointed rooms with fresh cut flowers daily from their garden, and a Continental breakfast.
There are 2 pet-friendly rooms available, and dogs must be friendly as there are other animals (wild and
domestic) on the property. Dogs are allowed for an additional fee of $10 per night per pet. Dogs may not be left
alone in the rooms or in cars on the property at any time, and they must be leashed and cleaned up after.

Inn at Schoolhouse Creek

Inn at Schoolhouse Creek 7051 N. Highway 1 Mendocino CA   707-937-5525 (800-731-5525)
http://www.schoolhousecreek.com
With 8+ acres of ocean view gardens, meadows, forest, hiking trails and a secluded beach cove you and your pets will truly feel like you've gotten away from it all. To help your pets get in the vacation mood they will be welcomed with their own pet basket that includes a bed, towel, blanket and a treat. At the end of your day, relax in the ocean view hot tub.

Little River Inn

Little River Inn 7901 Highway One Mendocino CA   707-937-5942 (888-INN-LOVE)
http://www.littleriverinn.com
This coastal resort has oceanview rooms, some with fireplaces and Jacuzzis. There are gardens to walk through and breakfast and dinner are available in the restaurant. Pets are $25 per night, per pet.

MacCallum House

MacCallum House 45020 Albion Street Mendocino CA   707-937-0289 (800-609-0492)
http://www.maccallumhouse.com
Pets of all varieties are welcomed at the MacCallum House Inn, located in the heart of the Mendocino Village. Pets are allowed in the cottages and Barn and are provided with blankets and sheets. The original Victorian mansion, built in 1882 by William H. Kelley, was a wedding gift to his daughter, Daisy MacCallum, and is a historic landmark. Rooms include a full breakfast and a complimentary wine hour is served in the Grey Whale Bar featuring wines from throughout the California wine country. Children are also welcome.
Mendocino Seaside Cottages 10940 Lansing St Mendocino CA   707-485-0239
http://www.romancebythesea.com/
Accommodations have jacuzzi spas, wet bars,& fireplaces. It is located within easy walking distance of Mendocino.
Pacific Mist Inn and Cabins 6051 Highway One Mendocino CA   707-937-1543 (800-955-6478)
http://www.pacificmistinn.com
These cabins and inn allow dogs. The cabins have kitchenettes and there is a spa.

The Blair House Inn 45110 Little Lake Street Mendocino CA   707-937-1800 (800-699-9296)
http://www.blairhouse.com/
Although built in 1888, this home has been called a "Victorian Treasure", and it still offers luxury surroundings, beautifully appointed rooms, gardens and ocean vistas. Room rates include breakfast and a complimentary bottle of wine. They have one pet-friendly cottage, and dogs of all sizes are allowed for an additional fee of $10 per night per pet. Dogs may not be left alone in the cottage at any time, and they must be well mannered, leashed, and cleaned up after.

Stanford Inn by the Sea and Spa

TOP 200 PLACE **Stanford Inn by the Sea and Spa** 44850 Comptche Ukiah Rd and Highway One Mendocino CA 707-937-5615 (800-331-8884)
http://www.stanfordinn.com
This resort is specially designed to accommodate travelers with pets. The inn is rustic and elegant. Amenities include feather beds, wood burning fireplaces, antiques, sofas, televisions with VCRs and DVDs. The resort offers complimentary breakfast featuring a choice from organic selections of omelets, waffles, burritos, and more. A large pool, sauna and Jacuzzi are protected from the fog by a solarium. Massage in the Forest provides massage and body work and yoga. The Inn's Catch A Canoe & Bicycles, too! offers kayaking and canoeing on Big River Estuary as well as mountain biking and. Special canoes are set-up to provide secure footing for your dog as well as a bowl of fresh water (Big River is tidal and for eight miles and therefore salty). The Ravens vegetarian/vegan restaurant serves organic cuisine. Well behaved pets may join you at breakfast or dinner in a dining area created especially for them. Feed and water dishes, covers to protect bedding and furniture, sleeping beds and treats are provided in the rooms. There is a $25 pet fee per stay.

Campgrounds and RV Parks
Dolphin Isle Marina 32399 Basin Drive Fort Bragg CA 707-964-4113 (866-964-4113)
http://www.dolphinisle.com/
This lush vacation spot features beautiful views of the Noyo River, and they offer a full service marina, a deli with patio dining, a store, free wireless internet service, and RV camping. The camp area offers showers and a laundry room. Dogs of all sizes are allowed for no additional fee. They are allowed throughout the park and at the deli patio dining area. Dogs must be well behaved, leashed and cleaned up after. This RV park is closed during the off-season. There is a dog walk area at the campground.
Pomo RV Park and Campground 17999 Tregoning Lane Fort Bragg CA 707-964-3373
http://www.infortbragg.com/pomorvpark
This small scenic park offers a good variety of recreational opportunities. They have a "major holiday dog policy", wherein dogs must remain on the owners campsite only. No walking of dogs in the park is allowed on major holidays and dogs may not be left alone on campsites for any reason. Dogs of all sizes are allowed for an additional $1 per night per dog. Dogs must be leashed and cleaned up after. There are some breed restrictions. The camping and tent areas also allow dogs. There is a dog walk area at the campground.
Van Damme State Park 8125 N Hwy 1 Littleriver CA 707-937-5804 (800-444-PARK (7275))
Covering almost 2000 acres of beach and uplands on the Mendocino Coast, this park offers a variety of camp sites; some are on a 1st come 1st served basis, but reservations are suggested. The park offers a visitor center, wi-fi, showers, restrooms, picnic areas, and a dump station. Dogs of all sizes are allowed for no additional fee. Dogs may be on paved roads, fire roads, on the beach, and in the campground area; they are not allowed on the trails. Dogs must be under owner's immediate control, and leashed and cleaned up after at all times. The camping and tent areas also allow dogs. There is a dog walk area at the campground. There are no electric or

water hookups at the campgrounds.

Casper Beach RV Park and Campground

TOP 200 PLACE Casper Beach RV Park and Campground 14441 Point Cabrilla Mendocino CA   707-964-3306
This RV park is located in one of the most picturesque coastal regions anywhere in the US, with such amenities as an arcade, an onsite grocery & novelty store, and host to a variety of land and water recreation. Dogs of all sizes are allowed for an additional fee of $2 per night per per pet. Dogs must be very friendly, quiet, well behaved, leashed, and cleaned up after. The camping and tent areas also allow dogs. There is a nice dog-friendly beach right across from the campground where you can walk your leashed dog. The campground is about five miles north of Mendocino.
Navarro River Redwoods State Park Hwy 128 Mendocino CA 707-895-3141
Paralleling the Navarro River and Highway 128 is this 673 acre park that offers outstanding natural beauty, walking paths through redwood groves, and access to the Pacific Ocean. Camping is on a 1st come 1st served basis at the 25 developed sites and the 10 beach sites. There are restrooms but no drinking water available. Dogs of all sizes are allowed for no additional fee, and they are allowed throughout the park, on the trails, and on the beach. Dogs must be leashed at all times and be cleaned up after. This RV park is closed during the off-season. The camping and tent areas also allow dogs. There is a dog walk area at the campground. There are no electric or water hookups at the campgrounds.

Vacation Home Rentals
Harbor View Seasonal Rental Call to arrange. Fort Bragg CA   760-438-2563
Watch the boats go in and out of the harbor and listen to the sea lions and fog horns from this dog-friendly vacation rental. This 3,000 square foot house is entirely furnished. The main floor has a living room, dining room, kitchen, 2 bedrooms, 1 bathroom and a deck with a view of the harbor. The upstairs has a large master suite with a deck and a view of the bridge and ocean. The yard has redwood trees and even deer wandering through. This area is popular for year-round fishing. The rental is available throughout the year. Please call to inquire about rates and available dates.

Abigails Bed & Breakfast

Abigails Bed & Breakfast P.O. Box 150, 499 Howard St. Mendocino CA   707-937-4892 (800-531-7282)
http://www.abigailsmendocino.com
Pets are welcome in both Abigails Bed & Breakfast and the Whitegate Inn cottage. They are not allowed in the main house. The cottage has 4 bedrooms and 3 baths. Stroll with your dog in beautiful Mendocino and nearby state parks.
Coastal Getaways 10501 Ford Street POB1355 Mendocino CA   707-937-9200 (800-525-0049)
http://www.coastgetaways.com
Coastal Getaways has over 5 vacation homes that allow dogs. Most of the homes have ocean front views and one is located in the quaint village of Mendocino. The rates range from $140 to $250 and up per night. They also have weekly rates. For more information, please call 800-525-0049.
Mendocino Coast Reservations Call to Arrange Mendocino CA   707-937-5033 (800-262-7801)
http://www.mendocinovacations.com
Mendocino Coast Reservations manages around nine pet friendly properties in the Mendocino area. There is a $35 additional pet fee.
Sweetwater Spa & Inn 44840 Main Street Mendocino CA   707-937-4076 (800-300-4140)
http://www.sweetwaterspa.com/
Sweetwater Spa & Inn offers a unique variety of accommodations, including cabin and vacation home rentals. They give dog treats at check-in as well as sheets for the guests to cover furniture and towels for wet paws in the rainy season. Some of the rentals are located in the village of Mendocino. The other rentals are located around the Mendocino area. There is a two night minimum on weekends and three night minimum on most holidays. All units are non-smoking. Your well-behaved dog is welcome. Room rates start at the low $100s and up. There is a $15 per day additional pet fee.

Attractions

All Aboard Adventures 32400 N Harbor Drive, Noyo Harbor Fort Bragg CA   707-964-1881
http://www.allaboardadventures.com/
This 45 foot charter boat offers deep sea fishing, whale watching, or cruises of the bay and harbor. Dogs are allowed on all the tours except for the Salmon fishing tours. There is no additional pet fee. They suggest you bring your own dogs life jacket, and any supplies you may need for the care or clean-up of your pet. Dogs must be well behaved and leashed at all times.

All Aboard Adventures

Anchor Charter Boats and the Lady Irma II 780 N Harbor Drive Fort Bragg CA 707-964-4550
A licensed, experienced owner and crew offer a variety of ocean faring activities and fishing trips, and they will usually take about 20 people out at a time. A dog 50 pounds or under is welcome on the boat as long as it is not full or nearly full. Dogs must be very well behaved, crated or leashed at all times, and cleaned up after. There is no additional pet fee.

Mendocino Coast Botanical Gardens

TOP 200 PLACE Mendocino Coast Botanical Gardens 18220 N. Highway 1 Fort Bragg CA 707-964-4352
http://www.gardenbythesea.org/
This botanical garden is the only public garden in the continental United States fronting directly on the ocean. Well-behaved, leashed dogs are welcome. The gardens offer everything from colorful displays to thunderous waves. The mild maritime climate makes it a garden for all seasons, attracting gardeners and nature lovers alike. You are welcome to bring a picnic lunch to enjoy on the grounds.

Catch a Canoe Rentals

TOP 200 PLACE Catch a Canoe Rentals 44850 Comptche-Ukiah Rd Mendocino CA 707-937-5615
http://www.stanfordinn.com/canoes.html
This canoe rental shop is located on the grounds of the dog-friendly Stanford Inn by the Sea. Feel free to walk into the shop with your pooch. If you are staying at the inn, it's a five minute walk to the shop. If you are staying at another hotel, there is ample parking. If your pup is over 50 pounds., he or she is more than welcome, but the folks at the shop will warn you that if your dog is a land-lover or decides to make a quick turn in the canoe, the whole party may become very wet. However, this dog-friendly rental shop has even modified a Mad River Winooski to create an incredibly stable canoe especially designed for dogs. Interior carpet, water bowl and a dog biscuit is included. The river you will be canoeing on is close to the ocean and it does contain alot of salt water, so make sure you bring separate water for you and your dog. Check with the shop for water conditions, but in general this is a calm river - no white water rafting here.

Shopping Centers

Mendocino Village Main Street at Lansing Street Mendocino CA
This quaint village is filled with interesting shops, outdoor cafes and beautiful walks along the Mendocino coast in the Mendocino Highlands. There are also a number of dog-friendly B&Bs in town.

Beaches
Caspar Beach 14441 Point Cabrillo Drive Caspar CA 707-937-5804
Dogs on leash are allowed at this sandy beach across from the Caspar Beach RV Park. The beach is located about 4 miles north of Mendocino. Please clean up after your dog.
MacKerricher State Park Highway 1 Fort Bragg CA 707-964-9112
Dogs are allowed on the beach, but not on any park trails. Pets must be leashed and people need to clean up after their pets. Picnic areas, restrooms and campsites (including an ADA restroom and campsites), are

available at this park. The park is located three miles north of Fort Bragg on Highway 1, near the town of Cleone.

Mendocino Village

Noyo Beach Off-Leash Dog Beach

Noyo Beach Off-Leash Dog Beach North Harbor Drive Fort Bragg CA

http://www.frankhartzell.com/MCDOG
The dog beach is located at the north side of where the Noyo River enters the Pacific Ocean. To get to the dog beach, turn EAST (away from the ocean) on N. Harbor Drive from Highway 1. N. Harbor will go down to the river and circle under Highway 1 to the beach. The beach was organized by MCDOG (Mendocino Coast Dog Owners Group) which is now working on an off-leash dog park for the Mendocino area.

Big River Beach N. Big River Road Mendocino CA 707-937-5804
This small beach is located just south of downtown Mendocino. There are two ways to get there. One way is to head south of town on Hwy 1 and turn left on N. Big River Rd. The beach will be on the right. The second way is to take Hwy 1 and exit Main Street/Jackson heading towards the coastline. In about 1/4-1/2 mile there will be a Chevron Gas Station and a historic church on the left. Park and then walk behind the church to the trailhead. Follow the trail, bearing left when appropriate, and there will be a wooden staircase that goes down to Big River Beach. Dogs must be on leash.

Van Damme State Beach

Van Damme State Beach Highway 1 Mendocino CA
This small beach is located in the town of Little River which is approximately 2 miles south of Mendocino. It is part of Van Damme State Park which is located across Highway 1. Most California State Parks, including this one, do not allow dogs on the hiking trails. Fortunately this one allows dogs on the beach. There is no parking fee at the beach and dogs must be on leash.

Parks

Mendocino Headlands State Park off Hesser Drive Mendocino CA
This trail (1-2 miles each way) is located next to the village of Mendocino and it follows the Mendocino peninsula and coastline on bluffs above the beach. The trail is part of the Mendocino Headlands State Park. To get there, take Hwy 1, exit Main Street/Jackson toward the coastline. When Main Street ends, turn right onto Hesser Drive. Go 4 blocks and turn left to continue on Hesser Drive. There are many trailheads or starting points along Hesser Drive, but in the summer, watch out for foxtails.

Mendocino Headlands State Park

Outdoor Restaurants

Cafe One 753 N Main Street Fort Bragg CA   707-964-3309
This cafe has a few outdoor tables and well-behaved leashed dogs are allowed.
Home Style Cafe 790 S. Main Street Fort Bragg CA   707-964-6106
This cafe has two outdoor picnic tables and well-behaved leashed dogs are allowed.
Laurel Deli 401 N Main Street Fort Bragg CA   707-964-7812
Well-behaved leashed dogs are allowed at the outdoor seating area.
Nemo's Fish Market 2410 N Harbor Dr Fort Bragg CA   707-964-1600
Dogs up to medium sizes are allowed at the outdoor tables.
Piaci Pub and Pizzeria 120 W. Redwood Avenue Fort Bragg CA   707-961-1133
Alcohol drinks are not allowed outside but you are welcome to dine at the outdoor tables with your well-behaved leashed dog.
Rendezvous Inn and Restaurant 647 North Main Street Fort Bragg CA   707-964-8142
http://www.rendezvousinn.com/
Located at the romantic Rendezvous Inn, this award-winning eatery is open to the public for dinner Wednesday through Sunday. Although a real gourmet restaurant, they feature an elegant yet casual atmosphere and delicious French fare with an extensive wine list. They offer indoor and outdoor dining service. Dogs are allowed at the outdoor tables. They must be well behaved, under owner's control at all times, leashed, and cleaned up after. Reservations are suggested, especially for guests with pets. Dogs are also allowed at the Inn.
Lu's Kitchen 45013 Ukiah Street Mendocino CA   707-937-4939
Dogs are allowed at the outdoor tables.

Mendo Burgers

Mendo Burgers 10483 Lansing Street Mendocino CA 707-937-1111
Look carefully or you might miss it. This place is located behind the Mendocino Bakery and Cafe. This very dog-friendly place usually has a water bucket for dogs next to the front door. If they don't, ask them and they'll be happy to get your pooch some water.

Mendocino Cafe

Mendocino Cafe 10451 Lansing Street Mendocino CA 707-937-6141
Lunch and dinner are served at this cafe. The food is great, but if you go for dinner, come early as they may not serve outside when it gets dark and chilly. They do have food to go if you arrive too late.
Ravens Restaurant Coast Highway and Comptche Ukiah Road Mendocino CA 707-937-5615
This award winning restaurant is located at the pet-friendly Stanford Inn in Mendocino. It has outdoor seating for people with dogs. The restaurant serves mostly organic produce and vegan cuisine along with organic wines.
The Moosse Cafe 390 Kasten Mendocino CA 707-937-4323
This restaurant features elegant, innovative North Coast cuisine with Mediterranean influences. Soups and decadent desserts are homemade, and wines and beers are carefully selected to highlight their seasonal and daily lunch and dinner specials. They provide indoor and outdoor seating with ocean and garden views. Dogs are allowed at the outdoor tables. They must be well behaved, under owner's control at all times, leashed, and cleaned up after.

Philo

Accommodations
Anderson Valley Inn 8480 Hwy 128 Philo CA 707-895-3325
Dogs only, and of all sizes are allowed. There is a $25 one time fee for 1 dog and a 2nd dog would be an additional $10 one time fee. No pit bulls are allowed, and dogs must be on a leash at all times. Dogs may not be left alone at any time.
Highland Ranch 18941 Philo Greenwood Rd. Philo CA 707-895-3600
http://www.highlandranch.com/home.html
This 125 year old ranch house sits along the mountainside among majestic trees with 8 individually decorated cabins nestled around it. At this country resort you can take in a wide variety of land and water recreation and activities, a massage, a yoga class, trek a hundred miles of multi-use trails, or take part in a myriad of other events. They also feature good home-cooked meals served family-style in the main house. Dogs of all sizes are welcome for no additional fee. They are greeted with treats, and some towels and blankets that they'll need after a day of enjoying country life. Dogs must be well mannered, leashed, and cleaned up after.

Attractions
Christine Woods Vineyards 3155 Hwy 128 Philo CA 707-895-2115
Specializing in Pinot Noir, this winery is one of the few that grow their own grapes and make all their wines on site from their own grapes. Dogs are allowed on the grounds but not in the tasting room. Dogs must be well behaved, leashed, and cleaned up after at all times.
Handley Cellars 3151 Hwy 128 Philo CA 707-895-3876
http://www.handleycellars.com/index.jsp
Open year round, this company features wines that pair well with Asian, African, and New World cuisine. They have a beautiful garden courtyard area where dogs are welcome. It is ok to walk through the building with your dog to get to the courtyard. Dogs must be well behaved, and leashed and cleaned up after at all times.
Handley Cellars 3151 Hwy 128 Philo CA 707-895-3876
This winery specializes in Pinot Noir, Chardonnay, and Gewurztraminer wines, and feature a beautiful fenced garden courtyard by their tasting room for those who also might like to picnic. Dogs are welcome around the grounds and in the courtyard where they are even met with water and treats. Dogs must be friendly, well mannered, and leashed and cleaned up after at all times.
Husch Vineyards 4400 Hwy 128 Philo CA 1-800-55-HUSCH(555-8724)
http://huschvineyards.com/
This small, family owned and operated winery produces 18 different wines plus some specialty wines. The converted 1800's pony barn works well for the tasting room, and they offer a picnic area on the deck or at a table under one of the many grape arbors. Dogs are welcome on the grounds and picnic areas, just not in the buildings. Dogs must be well behaved, leashed, and cleaned up after.

Potter Valley

Parks
Milk Ranch Loop Potter Valley CA 530-934-3316
This trail is 9.5 miles long and is rated moderate. Located in the Mendocino National Forest at an elevation of 5,200 feet, this trail is one of the most popular loops on Snow Mountain. The route offers dense red fir forests, meadows and a barren peak. The Milk Ranch meadow is private property, but the landowner allows horse and

foot travelers to pass through on the trail. They just request that no camps be set up within the posted portion of the meadow. Pets are allowed on the trail. They must be leashed in the campground, but are allowed off-leash under voice control on the trail. Please clean up after your pets. The loop can be started at the Summit Springs Trailhead. To get there from Ukiah, take Highway 101 North then take Highway 20 East towards Upper Lake/Williams. Go about 5 miles and turn left onto Potter Valley Road towards Potter Valley. Turn right on Forest Service Road M8 towards Lake Pillsbury. The road towards the lake is not paved. The trail starts near the lake at the Summit Springs Trailhead. Dogs are also allowed at the lake but should be leashed.

Redwood National and State Parks

Accommodations

Motel Trees

Motel Trees 15495 Highway 101 South Klamath CA 707-482-3152
This motel is located directly across Highway 101 from the dog-friendly Trees of Mystery attraction. The motel offers pet rooms and allows all well-behaved dogs. There is a $5 per pet per night fee. They have a AAA 2 diamond rating.

Campgrounds and RV Parks

Mystic Forest RV Park 15875 Hwy 101 Klamath CA 707-482-4901
http://www.mysticforestrv.com/
This scenic camp area offers a natural environment with lots of shade trees and grass. Some of the amenities include a gift shop, small store, a club house, recreation room, a laundry, showers and restrooms, lots of hiking trails, and an 18-hole miniature golf course. Dogs of all sizes are allowed for no additional fee. Dogs must be under owner's immediate control, leashed, cleaned up after, and they may not be left unattended in vehicles or outside. Dogs are allowed throughout the park and on the trails. The camping and tent areas also allow dogs. There is a dog walk area at the campground.
Elk Prairie Campground 127011 Newton B. Drury Scenic Parkway Orick CA 707-464-6101 (800-444-PARK (7275))
This campground is located in Prairie Creek Redwoods State Park. While dogs are not allowed on any park trails or the beach, they are allowed at this campground. There are 75 RV or tent sites which are next to a prairie and old growth redwood forest. RVs must be less than 27 feet. Camp amenities include restrooms, showers, fire pits, dump station and bear-proof lockers. Located just north of the campground is Cal Barrel Road. Dogs can walk

on or along this 3 mile gravel road. There are not too many cars that travel along this road. Pets must be on no more than a 6 foot leash and attended to at all times. Please clean up after your pet. The camping and tent areas also allow dogs. There is a dog walk area at the campground. There are no electric or water hookups at the campgrounds.

Gold Bluffs Beach Campground Davidson Road Orick CA 707-464-6101
http://www.nps.gov/redw/camping.html
This campground is located in Prairie Creek Redwoods State Park. While dogs are not allowed on any park trails, they are allowed at this campground and the adjoining beach. There are 29 tent sites and 25 RV sites at the beach. RVs must be less than 24 feet long and 8 feet wide. All sites are on a first-come, first-served basis. Camp amenities include restrooms, solar showers and fire pits. Pets must be leashed and attended at all times. Please clean up after your pets. Dogs are not allowed on any established trails. They are allowed in parking lots, the campground, picnic areas, paved roads, and must stay within 100 feet of the roads. Although the campground is open year round, call ahead, as sometimes the roads are closed for repairs. The camping and tent areas also allow dogs. There is a dog walk area at the campground. There are no electric or water hookups at the campgrounds.

Emerald Forest of Trinidad 753 Patrick's Point Drive Trinidad CA 707-677-3554 (888-677-3800)
http://cabinsintheredwoods.com/
This well kept campground covers 12 acres of redwood forest and is less than a mile from Trinidad Bay. Some of the amenities include a gift shop, playground, an arcade, laundry facilities, an outdoor pavilion with barbecues, gaming areas, and a dump station. Dogs are allowed in 2 of the cabins for an additional fee of $10 per night per pet, and 1 medium dog or 2 small dogs (15 pound limit each) are allowed per cabin. Dogs are not allowed in the tent area. There is no additional pet fee for RV camping or size restrictions. Dogs may not be left unattended, and they must be leashed and cleaned up after at all times. There is a dog walk area at the campground. Dogs are allowed in the camping cabins.

Patrick's Point State Park 4150 Patrick's Point Drive Trinidad CA 707-677-3570
Located in the heart of the coastal redwood country, this park is a mix of dense forests and wildflower filled meadows. They feature a recreated Yurok Village, a Native American Plant Garden, fully developed picnic areas with barbecues and restrooms, and interpretive programs in the summer. Dogs are allowed for no additional fee. They are allowed at the lagoons, and in developed and paved areas only; they are not allowed on the trails or the beaches. Dogs must be inside an enclosed vehicle or tent at night, be on no more than a 6 foot leash, and cleaned up after. There are three family campgrounds with a total of 124 campsites; they each have a table, stove, cupboard, and water and restrooms nearby. Group campsites are also available. The camping and tent areas also allow dogs. There is a dog walk area at the campground. There are no electric or water hookups at the campgrounds.

Attractions

Trees of Mystery

TOP 200 PLACE **Trees of Mystery** 15500 Highway 101 N. Klamath CA 800-638-3389
http://www.treesofmystery.net
Located in the center of the Redwood National and State Parks, this attraction allows leashed dogs everywhere
people are welcome. They have an 8/10ths of a mile groomed interpretive trail through the awe-inspiring
Redwoods of California. Also located here is a world-class Native American Museum and a gondola which takes
you and your pooch on an aerial ride through the redwood forest canopy. They are located along Highway 101 in
Klamath. Klamath is 36 miles south of the Oregon border and 260 miles north of Santa Rosa.

Beaches

Crescent Beach - Del Norte SP Enderts Beach Rd Crescent Beach CA 707-464-6101
http://www.nps.gov/redw/home.html
Dogs are allowed on the ocean beach at Crescent Beach in the Del Norte Coast Redwoods State Park. They are
not allowed on any trails within the Redwood National or State Parks. Pets are also allowed at road accessible
picnic areas and campgrounds. Dogs must be on a 6 foot or less leash and people need to pick up after their
pets. To get to the beach take Enderts Beach Road South from Highway 101 just south of Crescent City.

Freshwater Lagoon Beach - Redwood NP

Freshwater Lagoon Beach - Redwood NP Highway 101 south end of Redwood National Park Orick CA 707-
464-6101
http://www.nps.gov/redw/home.html
Dogs are allowed on the ocean beaches around Freshwater Lagoon, but not on any trails within Redwood
National Park. Picnic tables are available at the beach. Pets are also allowed at road accessible picnic areas and
campgrounds. Dogs must be on a 6 foot or less leash and people need to pick up after their pets. The beach is
located off Highway 101 behind the Redwood Information Center at the south end of the Redwood National Park.
The parking area for the beach is about 2 miles south of Orick. Some portions of this beach are rather rocky but
there are also sandy portions as well.
Gold Bluffs Beach - Redwood NP Davison Road Orick CA 707-464-6101
http://www.nps.gov/redw/home.html
Dogs are allowed on this beach, but not on any trails within this park. Picnic tables and campgrounds are
available at the beach. Pets are also allowed at road accessible picnic areas and campgrounds. Dogs must be
on a 6 foot or less leash and people need to pick up after their pets. The beach is located off Highway 101. Take
Highway 101 heading north. Pass Orick and drive about 3-4 miles, then exit Davison Rd. Head towards the coast
on an unpaved road (trailers are not allowed on the unpaved road).
Trinidad State Beach Highway 101 Trinidad CA 707-677-3570
Dogs are unofficially allowed at College Cove beach, as long as they are leashed and under control. The

residents in this area are trying keep this beach dog-friendly, but the rules can change at any time. Please call ahead to verify.

Parks

Redwood National and State Parks

TOP 200 PLACE **Redwood National and State Parks** 1111 Second Street Crescent City CA   707-464-6101
http://www.nps.gov/redw/
The National and State Parks do not allow dogs on any trails but some of the beaches and campgrounds welcome dogs. Pets are allowed on Crescent Beach, Gold Bluffs Beach and the Freshwater Spit Lagoon. The campgrounds that allow pets include Jedediah Smith Redwoods State Park campground, Prairie Creek Redwoods State Park campground and Gold Bluffs Beach campground. One way to see a number of redwood groves with dogs is to take the Newton B. Drury Scenic Bypass off of Highway 101. You may see large elk grazing near the parking lots as you drive through the park. Dogs are also allowed to walk along some gravel roads. Two roads that can be walked along with dog include Cal Barrel Road (3 miles long) and Howland Hill Rd (6 miles long). These roads will usually not be too crowded with cars except at the busiest times. Old growth Redwood groves line these gravel roads. Pets must be leashed and attended at all times and please clean up after them.
Patrick's Point State Park 4150 Patrick's Point Drive Trinidad CA   707-677-3570
Located in the heart of the coastal redwood country, this park is a mix of dense forests and wildflower filled meadows. They feature a recreated Yurok Village, a Native American Plant Garden, fully developed picnic areas with barbecues and restrooms, and interpretive programs in the summer. Dogs are allowed for no additional fee. They are allowed at the lagoons, and in developed and paved areas only; they are not allowed on the trails or the beaches. Dogs must be inside an enclosed vehicle or tent at night, be on no more than a 6 foot leash, and cleaned up after.

Redwood Valley

Attractions
Elizabeth Vineyards 8591 Colony Drive Redwood Valley CA   707-485-9009
http://www.elizabethvineyards.com/

Redwood Valley is blessed with excellent soil and a favorable climate, giving the grapes the unique flavor and character of the region. The vineyard is open by appointment only, and during harvest they are almost to busy for visitors. They suggest also checking out the other events in which they participate on their website. Dogs are welcome on the grounds when you do visit the vineyard, but they are not allowed in the tasting room. Dogs must be leashed and cleaned up after at all times.
Gabrielli Winery 10950 West Road Redwood Valley CA   707-485-1221
This winery is not usually open during harvest time, but they reopen the first of the year, so they suggest to be sure and call before coming out to make sure they are open. Usually they are open from 10 am to 4 pm Monday through Friday, and all other times by appointment. Well behaved dogs are welcome on the grounds, but not in the tasting room. Dogs must be leashed and cleaned up after at all times.

Sea Ranch

Accommodations
Sea Ranch Lodge 60 Sea Walk Drive Sea Ranch CA   707-785-2371 (800-SEA-RANCH (732-7262))
http://www.searanchlodge.com/
Shinning with a natural rustic elegance along a dramatic ocean side location, this award-winning 20 room lodge is an idyllic retreat for special events, and the business or leisure traveler. Some the features/amenities include miles of scenic hiking trails, a full breakfast, exquisite wining and dining with the freshest ingredients available and ocean views, and Concierge Services. Friendly dogs of all sizes are allowed for an additional one time fee of $50 per pet. Dogs must be leashed and cleaned up after at all times, and pet rooms are located on the 1st floor only. Canine guests receive a welcome package that includes a welcome note with suggestions for activities, a cookie, bottled water, a cushy bed, a furniture cover, food/water bowls, and a place mat.

Ukiah

Accommodations
Days Inn 950 North State St Ukiah CA   707-462-7584 (800-329-7466)
There is a $10 per day per pet fee.
Motel 6 - Ukiah 1208 South State Street Ukiah CA   707-468-5404 (800-466-8356)
One well-behaved family pet per room. Guest must notify front desk upon arrival. Guest is liable for any damages. In consideration of all guests, pets must never be left unattended in the guest rooms.

Campgrounds and RV Parks
Cow Mountain Recreation Area/Ukiah Field Office 2550 North State Street Ukiah CA   707-468-4000
http://www.blm.gov/ca/ukiah/cowmtn.html
Dogs are allowed at the North Cow Mountain portion of this recreation area off Mill Creek Road; the South area is mostly for off-road vehicles. Dogs of all sizes are allowed for no additional fee. Dogs must be under owner's control at all times, and leashed and cleaned up after. Campsites are on a first-come, first-served basis and some of the amenities include tables, barbecues, fire grates, and pit toilets; there is no potable water. The camping and tent areas also allow dogs. There is a dog walk area at the campground. There are no electric or water hookups at the campgrounds.
Lake Mendocino Recreation Area 1160 Lake Mendocino Drive Ukiah CA   707-462-7581 (877-444-6777)
http://www.lakemendocino.com/camping.htm
Created by the construction of the Coyote Dam, this beautiful lake recreation area is set among rolling hills and oak groves near the headwaters of the Russian River offering plenty of hiking trails. The lake has more than 1,800 surface acres, and there is a wide variety of land and water recreational opportunities. Dogs of all sizes are allowed for no additional fee. Dogs must be on no more than a 6 foot leash and be cleaned up after. Dogs are allowed throughout the park and on the trails. There are 3 main campgrounds (offering more than 200 campsites) each with different features; 2 of them have pay showers, 2 shares an amphitheater, 1 has an 18-hole golf course, and all have potable water, picnic tables, and a fire ring. Most sites can be reserved up to 240 days in advance at the 877-444-6777 number. The camping and tent areas also allow dogs. There is a dog walk area at the campground. There are no electric or water hookups at the campgrounds.

Parks
Cache Creek Recreation Area 2550 N State Street/Ukiah Field Office Ukiah CA   707-468-4000
Rich in natural and cultural history, this day-use primitive recreation area has no developed camp areas or facilities and is located along Highways 20 and 16. It is maintained and managed for wildlife habitat, rare plants,

the protection of archaeological resources, and to provide primitive recreational opportunities including offering multi-use trails, wildlife viewing, river running, hunting, and fishing. Dogs of all sizes are allowed for no additional fee. Dogs must be under owner's control at all times. They may be off lead if they are under voice command. Please clean up after your pet, especially on the trails.

Cow Mountain Recreation Area/Ukiah Field Office 2550 North State Street Ukiah CA 707-468-4000
http://www.blm.gov/ca/ukiah/cowmtn.html
Dogs are allowed at the North Cow Mountain portion of this recreation area off Mill Creek Road; the South area is mostly for off-road vehicles. There are a variety of recreational opportunities available, a rifle range, and 17 miles of foot trails. Dogs of all sizes are allowed for no additional fee. Dogs must be under owners control at all times, and leashed and cleaned up after.

Lake Mendocino Recreation Area 1160 Lake Mendocino Drive Ukiah CA 707-462-7581 (877-444-6777)
http://www.lakemendocino.com/camping.htm
Created by the construction of the Coyote Dam, this beautiful lake recreation area is set among rolling hills and oak groves near the headwaters of the Russian River offering plenty of hiking trails. The lake has more than 1,800 surface acres, and there is a wide variety of land and water recreational opportunities. Dogs of all sizes are allowed for no additional fee. Dogs must be on no more than a 6 foot leash and be cleaned up after. Dogs are allowed throughout the park and on the trails.

Outdoor Restaurants

Porter Street BBQ

Porter Street BBQ 225 E Perkins Street Ukiah CA 707-468-9222
This barbecue eatery offers indoor and outdoor service (weather permitting), and welcomes your pet to join you at the outer tables. They will even be glad to serve your pup with a rib bone. Dogs must be friendly, well behaved, and leashed and cleaned up after.

Westport

Accommodations

Howard Creek Ranch Inn B&B 40501 N. Highway 1 Westport CA 707-964-6725
http://www.howardcreekranch.com/
Howard Creek Ranch is a historic, 40 acre ocean front farm located about 5-6 hours north of San Francisco. Accommodations include cabins, suites and rooms. It is bordered by miles of beach and mountains. They offer

award winning gardens, fireplaces or wood stoves, farm animals, a hot tub, and a sauna. Dog-friendly beaches nearby include Westport Union Landing State Beach in Westport, MacKerricher State Park 3-4 miles north of Fort Bragg and the 60 mile Sinkyone Wilderness Area (Lost Coast). Outdoor restaurants nearby are Jenny's Giant Burgers and Sea Pal (in Fort Bragg). Room rates are $80 and up (includes a full hearty ranch breakfast). There is a $10 plus tax per day pet charge. Certain dog rules apply: don't leave your dog alone in the room, dogs must be supervised and attended at all times, bring towels to clean up your pooch if he/she gets dirty from outside, clean up after your dog, and if your dog will be on the bed, please use a sheet to cover the quilt (sheets can be provided). The inn is located 3 miles north of Westport.

Campgrounds and RV Parks
Westport Beach RV and Camping 37700 N Hwy 1 Westport CA 707-964-2964
http://www.westportbeachrv.com/
This 30 acre camping area offers several camp areas that immerse visitors in the natural beauty that is unique to the Mendocino Coast. There is a large sandy beach; beach site campers may build their own fire on the beach, and sites along the creek offer picnic tables and fire rings at each site. There is a coin laundry, phone/internet hookup, showers, restrooms, gaming areas/courts, a playground, and club house. Dogs of all sizes are allowed for an additional $2 per night per pet. We suggest that RVs approach Westport from the south on Highway 1. Dogs must be leashed and cleaned up after at all times. Dogs are allowed on the beach and throughout the park. The camping and tent areas also allow dogs. There is a dog walk area at the campground.

Beaches
Westport-Union Landing State Beach Highway 1 Westport CA 707-937-5804
This park offers about 2 miles of sandy beach. Dogs must be on a 6 foot or less leash at all times and people need to clean up after their pets. Picnic tables, restrooms (including an ADA restroom) and campsites are available at this park. Dogs are also allowed at the campsites, but not on any park trails. The park is located off Highway 1, about 2 miles north of Westport or 19 miles north of Fort Bragg.

Whitehorn

Campgrounds and RV Parks
Nadelos Campground Chemise Mountain Road Whitehorn CA 707-825-2300
http://www.blm.gov/ca/
This campground offers 8 walk-in tent sites ranging from 50 to 300 feet from the parking lot. The sites are shaded by Douglas fir trees and are set along a small mountain stream. Campground amenities include picnic tables, vault toilets, drinking water and fire rings. Day use parking for the dog-friendly Chemise Mountain Trail is located at this campground. Sites are $8 per day with a maximum of 14 days per stay. Pets are allowed but must be leashed in the campground. If off leash on the trails, they must respond to voice command and not chase wildlife. Dogs may not be left unattended. To get there, take Highway 101 to Redway. Go west on Briceland/Shelter Cove Road for 22 miles and then head south on Chemise Mountain Road for 1.5 miles. Travel time from Highway 101 is about 55 minutes. The camping and tent areas also allow dogs. There is a dog walk area at the campground. There are no electric or water hookups at the campgrounds.
Wailaki Campground Chemise Mountain Road Whitehorn CA 707-825-2300
http://www.blm.gov/ca/
This campground offers 13 tent and trailer sites along a small mountain stream amidst large Douglas fir trees. Large RVs are not recommended on the roads to this campground. Day use parking for the dog-friendly Chemise Mountain Trail is located at this campground. Camp amenities include picnic tables, grills, water and restrooms. Sites are $8 per day with a maximum of 14 days per stay. Pets are allowed but must be leashed in the campground. If off leash on the trails, they must respond to voice command and not chase wildlife. Dogs may not be left unattended. To get there, take Highway 101 to Redway, go west on Briceland/Shelter Cove Road for 22 miles, and then head south on Chemise Mountain Road for 2 miles. Travel time from Highway 101 is about 55 minutes. This campground is closed during the off-season. The camping and tent areas also allow dogs. There is a dog walk area at the campground. There are no electric or water hookups at the campgrounds.

Parks
Chemise Mountain Trail Chemise Mountain Road Whitehorn CA 707-825-2300
This trail is about 1.5 miles long and involves an 800 foot climb. At the top of the trail you will see vistas of the coastline and inland mountain ranges. This trail is popular with hikers and mountain bikers. Pets are required to be leashed in the campgrounds. On the trails there is no leash requirement but your dog needs to be under direct voice control. There is a $1 day use fee. To get there, take Highway 101 to Redway. Go west on Briceland/Shelter Cove Road for 22 miles and then head south on Chemise Mountain Road for just over 1.5

miles. Trailhead parking is available at the Wailaki or Nadelos Campgrounds. Travel time from Highway 101 is about 55 minutes.

Yorkville

Accommodations

The Other Place and the Long Valley Ranch P.O. Box 49 Yorkville CA 707-894-5322
Dogs of all sizes are allowed. There is no additional pet fee for 2 pets. If there are more than 2 pets the fee is $25 per night per pet

Attractions

Meyer Family Cellars 19750 Hwy 128 Yorkville CA 707-895-2341
http://www.meyerfamilycellars.com/
Located in the rolling oak-laden hills of Anderson Valley, this scenic winery produces a popular unique solera-style, tawny port wine. There offer picnic areas and gardens, and your pet is welcome to join you on the grounds. Dogs must be friendly, and leashed and cleaned up after at all times.

TOP 200 PLACE **Yorkville Cellars** 25701 Hwy 128 Yorkville CA 707-894-9177
http://www.YorkvilleCellars.com
This vineyard has been CCOF certified since 1986, and they are a recipient of prestigious "Masters of Organics" award. Their free tasting room is located in the middle of the estate vineyards, and they are open daily from 11 am to 6 pm. Your well behaved, leashed dog is welcome to explore the vineyard with you; they are allowed in some of the buildings and the picnic area as well. They would also like your dog to be cat friendly, and that you clean up after your pet.

Chapter 3

California - Shasta Cascades Dog Travel Guide

Alturas - Modoc National Forest

Accommodations

Best Western Trailside Inn 343 N Main St Alturas CA   530-233-4111 (800-780-7234)
Dogs of all sizes are allowed. There is a $5 per night pet fee per pet. Smoking and non-smoking are available for pet rooms.
Sunrise Motel & RV Park 54889 Highway 200 West Cedarville CA   530-279-2161
Located at the base of the dog-friendly Modoc National Forest, this motel offers all non-smoking rooms. There are no pet fees. If you are out during the day and cannot bring your pooch with you, they do have an outdoor kennel available for an extra $5.

Campgrounds and RV Parks

Blue Lake Campground Forest Service Road 64 Likely CA 530-233-5811
This campground is located along Blue Lake at a 6,000 foot elevation in the Modoc National Forest. There are 48 RV and tent sites, several of which are located directly on the lake. RVs up to 32 feet are allowed. There is a $7 per vehicle fee. Amenities include picnic tables, fire pits, vault toilets and piped water. A boat ramp is located near the campground. Rowboats, canoes and low powered boats are allowed on the lake. The 1.5 mile Blue Lake National Recreation Trail begins at this campsite. Dogs on leash are allowed at the campgrounds, on trails and in the water. There are no additional pet fees. Please clean up after your pets. This campground is closed during the off-season. The camping and tent areas also allow dogs. There is a dog walk area at the campground. There are no electric or water hookups at the campgrounds.
Mill Creek Falls Campground Mill Creek Road Likely CA 530-233-5811
This campground is located in the Modoc National Forest at an elevation of 5,700 feet. There are 19 RV and tent sites. There is a $6 per night fee. Amenities include picnic tables, fire pits, vault toilets and drinking water. The Clear Lake Trail begins here and provides access into the South Warner Wilderness. Dogs on leash are allowed at the campgrounds, on trails and in the water. Please clean up after your pets. To get there from the town of Likely, go 9 miles east on Co. Rd. #64. Then go northeast on West Warner Road for 2.5 miles. Go east on Mill Creek access road for 2 more miles. This campground is closed during the off-season. The camping and tent areas also allow dogs. There is a dog walk area at the campground. There are no electric or water hookups at the campgrounds.

Attractions

Surprise Valley Back Country Byway Highway 299 Cedarville CA 530-279-6101
If you are up for some adventure, try this 93 mile driving tour which traverses by many points of interest in the Great Basin Desert. The loop begins and ends in Cedarville and takes a minimum of three hours and longer if you make any stops. The Bureau of Land Management offers a 32 page self-guided Byway Tour Guide which tells about the historic and prehistoric stories of Surprise Valley. It includes details about fossils and wildlife. The byway is paved in California and is a gravel road in Nevada which can be passable by all vehicles when the road is dry. Dogs on leash are allowed. Please clean up after your dog. Contact the following BLM office for a map and more details: BLM, Surprise Field Office, 602 Cressler Street, Cedarville, CA 96104, 530-279-6101. The office is open Monday through Friday.

Parks

Modoc National Forest 800 West 12th Street Alturas CA 530-233-5811
http://www.fs.fed.us/r5/modoc/
This national forest covers over 1.9 million acres of land which ranges in elevation from 4,300 to 9,934 feet. Please see our listings in this region for dog-friendly hikes and/or campgrounds.
Blue Lake National Recreation Trail Forest Service Road 64 Likely CA 530-233-5811
This 1.5 mile one way trail is located at Blue Lake, in the Modoc National Forest, at an elevation of 6,000 feet. At least 90 percent of the trail is shaded by white fir and massive ponderosa pine trees. The trailhead begins at the Blue Lake Campground and ends at the boat ramp. Dogs on leash are allowed at the campgrounds, on the trail and in the water. Please clean up after your pets. The trail is located is 16 miles from the small town of Likely. From Highway 395 go east on Forest Service Road 64. At about 10 miles you will come to a road junction. Stay on Forest Service Road 64 for the remaining 6 miles.
Clear Lake Trail Mill Creek Rd. Likely CA 530-233-5811
This trail is located in the Modoc National Forest at an elevation of 5,700 feet. At .5 miles into the trail, you will reach Mills Creek Falls. Beyond that the trail serves as a major entry way to the trails of the South Warner

Wilderness. Dogs on leash are allowed on the trail and in the water. Please clean up after your pets. To get there from the town of Likely, go 9 miles east on Co. Rd. #64. Then go northeast on West Warner Road for 2.5 miles. Go east on Mill Creek access road for 2 more miles. The trailhead is located in the Mill Creek Falls Campground.

Anderson

Accommodations
AmeriHost Inn 2040 Factory Outlets Dr Anderson CA   530-365-6100

Burney

Campgrounds and RV Parks
McArthur-Burney Falls Memorial State Park 24898 Hwy 89 Burney CA   530-335-2777 (800-444-PARK (7275))
Formed from volcanic activity, this park also has a rich natural and cultural history, and the park's showcase is the beautiful 129 foot Burney Falls flowing from springs at 100 million gallons a day. There is a variety of land and water recreation and activities to pursue, exhibits, and the park now has Wi-Fi service. Dogs of all sizes are allowed for no additional fee. Dogs are not allowed on the trails or on the beach. Dogs must be under owner's control at all times, and be leashed and cleaned up after. There are 128 family campsites and 7 primitive sites. Amenities include picnic tables, restrooms, showers, and a dump station. The camping and tent areas also allow dogs. There is a dog walk area at the campground. There are no electric or water hookups at the campgrounds.

Parks
McArthur-Burney Falls Memorial State Park 24898 Hwy 89 Burney CA   530-335-2777 (800-444-PARK (7275))
Formed from volcanic activity, this park also has a rich natural and cultural history, and the park's showcase is the beautiful 129 foot Burney Falls flowing from springs at 100 million gallons a day. There is a variety of land and water recreation and activities to pursue, exhibits, and the park now has Wi-Fi service. Dogs of all sizes are allowed for no additional fee. Dogs are not allowed on the trails or on the beach. Dogs must be under owners control at all times, and be leashed and cleaned up after.

Chico

Accommodations
Chico Oxford Suites 2035 Buisness Lane Chico CA   530-899-9090 (800-870-7848)
http://www.oxfordsuiteschico.com/
This hotel offers a variety of beautiful rooms, a full country breakfast buffet, an evening reception with two complimentary beverages and light hors d'ouevres. Also featured are a 24 hour gift/snack shop, business center, and an outdoor pool and Jacuzzi. Dogs up to about 75 pounds are allowed for an additional $35 one time pet fee per room. Dogs may only be left alone in the room if they will be quiet and well behaved, and a contact number is left with the front desk. Dogs must be leashed or crated, and cleaned up after.
Esplanade Bed & Breakfast 620 The Esplanade Chico CA   530-345-8084
http://now2000.com/esplanade/
Built in 1915, this Craftsman Bungalow has been completely restored. This B&B is located just steps from downtown Chico and Chico State University. Each room has a private bathroom and cable television. Enjoy their hearty breakfast served in the dining room or on the patio. Well-behaved dogs are allowed with a $20 refundable deposit. Children are also allowed.
Holiday Inn 685 Manzanita Ct Chico CA   530-345-2491 (877-270-6405)
There is a $30 one time pet fee per visit.
Motel 6 - Chico 665 Manzanita Court Chico CA   530-345-5500 (800-466-8356)
One well-behaved family pet per room. Guest must notify front desk upon arrival. Guest is liable for any damages. In consideration of all guests, pets must never be left unattended in the guest rooms.
Music Express Inn Bed and Breakfast 1091El Monte Avenue Chico CA   530-891-9833
http://now2000.com/musicexpress/

This B&B is located near the dog-friendly Bidwell Park, the third largest municipal park in the United States. The B&B offers nine rooms all with private baths, refrigerators and microwaves. All rooms are non-smoking. A well-behaved dog is allowed, but must be leashed when outside your room. Pets must be attended at all times. There are no pet fees. Children are also allowed.
Super 8 Chico 655 Manzanita Ct Chico CA 530-345-2533 (800-800-8000)
Dogs of all sizes are allowed. There is a $4 per night pet fee per pet. Dogs are not allowed to be left alone in the room. Smoking and non-smoking rooms are available for pet rooms.

Stores
Petco Pet Store 2005 Whitman Avenue Chico CA 530-899-1422
Your licensed and well-behaved leashed dog is allowed in the store.

Parks
Bidwell Park Highway 99 Chico CA 530-895-4972
This park exceeds 3,600 acres, making it the third largest municipal park in the United States. The park is comprised of three major sections: Lower Park, Middle Park and Upper Park. Lower Park has children's playgrounds, natural swimming areas, and vehicle-free roads for runners, cyclists, rollerbladers and walkers. Middle Park features ball-playing fields, picnic areas, the "World of Trees" walk, which is accessible to the physically challenged, and the park's environmental and informational headquarters. Upper Park remains relatively untouched with majestic canyons overlooking Big Chico Creek, which contains some of the most spectacular swimming areas in Northern California. Dogs on leash are allowed. Please clean up after them.

Outdoor Restaurants
Baja Fresh Mexican Grill 2072 E. 20th St. Chico CA 530-896-1077
http://www.bajafresh.com
This Mexican restaurant is open for lunch and dinner. They use fresh ingredients and making their salsa and beans daily. Some of the items on their menu include Enchiladas, Burritos, Tacos Salads, Quesadillas, Nachos, Chicken, Steak and more. Well-behaved leashed dogs are allowed at the outdoor tables.
Bellachinos 800 Bruce Road Chico CA 530-892-2244
This restaurant welcomes dogs on their outdoor patio which has music and a fountain. Dogs should be leashed.
Cafe Flo 365 E 6th Street Chico CA 530-892-0356
Well-behaved leashed dogs are allowed at the outdoor seating area.
Cal Java 2485 Notre Dame Blvd. Chico CA 530-893-2662
Leashed dogs are welcome at their outdoor tables.
California Pasta Production 118 W East Ave Chico CA 530-343-6999
Well-behaved leashed dogs are allowed at their perimeter tables.
Celestino's Pasta and Pizza 1354 East Ave Chico CA 530-345-7700
Well-behaved leashed dogs are allowed at the outdoor seating area.
Dog House 1008 W Sacramento Avenue Chico CA 530-894-3641
Well-behaved leashed dogs are allowed at the outdoor seating area.
La Cantera 3524 State Highway 32 Chico CA 530-345-1048
Well-behaved leashed dogs are allowed at the outdoor seating area.
Leftcoast Pizza Co 800 Bruce Road Chico CA 530-892-9000
Well-behaved leashed dogs are allowed at the outdoor seating area.
Moxie's Cafe & Gallery 128 Broadway Street Chico CA 530-345-0601
Well-behaved leashed dogs are allowed at the outdoor seating area.
S & S Organic Produce and Natural Foods 1924 Mangrove Avenue Chico CA 530-343-4930
This natural food store has an onsite deli. Well-behaved leashed dog are allowed at the outdoor tables.
Shubert's Ice Cream 178 E 7th Street Chico CA 530-342-7163
This ice cream shop allows pets at their outdoor tables. Will even give ice cream to your pet for free.
Spiteri's Delicatessen 971 East Avenue Chico CA 530-891-4797
Well-behaved leashed dogs are allowed at the outdoor seating area.

Corning

Accommodations
Best Western Inn-Corning 2165 Solano St Corning CA 530-824-2468 (800-780-7234)
Dogs of all sizes are allowed. There is a $10 per night pet fee per pet. Smoking and non-smoking are available for pet rooms.
Comfort Inn 910 Hwy 99W Corning CA 530-824-5200 (877-424-6423)

Dogs of all sizes are allowed. There is a $10 per night per pet additional fee. Dogs must be leashed and cleaned up after.
Holiday Inn Express Hotel & Suites 3350 Sunrise Way Corning CA   530-824-6400 (877-270-6405)
Dogs of all sizes are allowed. There is a $10 per day pet fee.

Campgrounds and RV Parks
Woodson Bridge State Rec Area 25340 South Avenue Corning CA   530-839-2112 (800-444-PARK (7275))
This beautiful oak woodland park along the Sacramento River is home to a dense native riparian forest that is also a winter home to the Bald Eagle. The park also offers various recreational opportunities. Dogs of all sizes are allowed. There are no additional pet fees. Dogs must be on no more than a 6 foot leash, and cleaned up after. Dogs are not allowed on the beach or on the trails, and they must be inside at night. The camping and tent areas also allow dogs. There is a dog walk area at the campground. There are no electric or water hookups at the campgrounds.
Woodson Bridge State Recreation Area 25340 South Avenue Corning CA   530-839-2112 (800-444-7275)
This beautiful oak wooded park sits along the Sacramento River, and is home to one of the last remaining riparian habitats in California. Fishing and birding are popular here, as are a variety of land and water recreation, and there is easy access to a boat launch ramp across the road. Dogs are allowed for no additional fee. They must be on no more than a 6 foot leash and be cleaned up after at all times. Dogs may be at your campsite and on paved areas only; they are not allowed on the trails. On the east side of the park there are 37 family campsites and a group campsite; the west bank has a boat-in campsite. They are on a first come first served basis when not on reservations. Some the amenities include fire rings, a laundry, restrooms, and showers. The camping and tent areas also allow dogs. There is a dog walk area at the campground. There are no electric or water hookups at the campgrounds.

Klamath National Forest

Campgrounds and RV Parks
East Fork Campground Salmon River Road Forks of Salmon CA   530-468-5351
This Klamath National Forest campground has 9 camp sites with no water but there are vault toilets. There is no charge for a camp site. Hiking from the East Fork Campground provides access to the lakes in the Caribou Basin, Rush Creek, and Little South Fork drainages. The campground is located 27 miles southwest of Callahan next to the East and the South Forks of the Salmon River. It sits at a 2,600 foot elevation. Dogs of all sizes are allowed at no additional fee. Dogs may not be left unattended outside, except for short periods, and only if they will be quiet and well behaved. Dogs must be leashed in camp and cleaned up after. Dogs are allowed on the trails, and they may be off lead on the trails if they will respond to voice command. This campground is closed during the off-season. The camping and tent areas also allow dogs. There is a dog walk area at the campground. There are no electric or water hookups at the campgrounds.
Bridge Flat Campground Scott River Road Fort Jones CA   530-468-5351 (877-444-6777)
This Klamath National Forest campground offers 4 camp sites with no water but there are vault toilets. There are no fees. Popular activities include hiking and fishing. The campground is open from May to October. The Kelsey Trail begins at this camp site. The campground is located on the Scott River approximately 17 miles from Fort Jones towards the town of Scott Bar, at a 2,000 foot elevation. Dogs must be on lead at all times in developed sites. They may be off lead on the trails if they are under voice control. Dogs may not be left unattended outside, except for short periods. This campground is closed during the off-season. The camping and tent areas also allow dogs. There is a dog walk area at the campground. There are no electric or water hookups at the campgrounds.
Norcross Campground Elk Creek Road Happy Camp CA   530-493-1777
This 6 site campground is located in the Klamath National Forest at an elevation of 2,400 feet. Amenities include vault toilets. The campground is open from May to October. This campground serves as a staging area for various trails that provide access into the Marble Mountain Wilderness. The trails are used by hikers and horseback riders. Dogs must be leashed in the campground. On trails, pets must be either leashed or off-leash but under direct voice control. Please clean up after your pets. Dogs may not be left unattended outside your unit, except for short periods. The campsite is located 16 miles south of Happy Camp on Elk Creek Road. This campground is closed during the off-season. The camping and tent areas also allow dogs. There is a dog walk area at the campground. There are no electric or water hookups at the campgrounds.

Parks
Kelsey Trail Scott River Road Fort Jones CA   530-468-5351
The historic Kelsey Trail offers excellent opportunities for scenic day hikes or longer trips into the Marble Mountain Wilderness. The trail is located in the Klamath National Forest and begins at the Bridge Flat

Campground. The campground is located on the Scott River approximately 17 miles from Fort Jones towards the town of Scott Bar, at a 2,000 foot elevation. Dogs should be on leash.

Lake Shasta

Accommodations
Sugarloaf Cottages Resort 19667 Lakeshore Drive Lakehead CA   800-953-4432
http://www.shastacabins.com/
These cottages are located near the shore of Lake Shasta and have air conditioning, heating, bathrooms, linens and complete kitchens, but no phones, televisions or maid service. They charge a $5 per night pet fee and allow only one pet per unit.
Tsasdi Resort Cabins 19990 Lakeshore Dr. Lakehead CA 530-238-2575
All cabins have private baths, linens, cable TV, air conditioning, heating, outdoor barbeque and private decks, most of which overlook Shasta Lake. There is a $10 per day pet fee. In order for them to continuing being pet-friendly, they ask that all pets be kept on a leash and not be left unattended in the cabins or on the decks. Please clean up after your pets.

Campgrounds and RV Parks
Antler's RV Park and Campground 20682 Antlers Road Lakehead CA   530-238-2322 (800-42-6849)
http://www.antlersrvpark.com/
located on beautiful Shasta Lake, this park offers a multitude of amenities and recreational opportunities. Dogs of all sizes are allowed for an additional $3 per night per pet or $15 per week per pet. Dogs may not be left unattended, and they must be leashed and cleaned up after. Pets must have vaccination papers for Parvo, Rabies and Distemper in order to stay at park. These are required at check-in. The camping and tent areas also allow dogs. There is a dog walk area at the campground.
Antlers RV Park and Campground 20682 Antlers Road Lakehead CA   530-238-2322 (800-642-6849)
http://www.antlersrvpark.com/
This camping area is located on beautiful Shasta Lake, and they provide some fun activities such as movies Tuesday thru Sunday, Monday night bingo, and a Sunday all-you-can-eat pancake breakfast. Other amenities include a playground, ball field/courts, a horseshoe pit, a convenience store with a great deck providing scenic views, a pool, laundry facilities, picnic tables, fire pits, a snack bar, hot showers, and lake access. Dogs of all sizes are allowed for no additional fee. Dogs must be leashed and cleaned up after at all times. The camping and tent areas also allow dogs. There is a dog walk area at the campground.
Castle Crags State Park Castle Creek Road Lakehead CA 530-235-2684 (800-444-7275)
Named for 6,000-feet tall glacier-polished crags, this park features a variety of land and water recreation, activities, and interpretive and campfire programs are offered in summer. Dogs are allowed for no additional fee. They must be under owner's control at all times, be on no more than a 6 foot leash, and cleaned up after. Dogs are not permitted on the trails, except for the campground/river trail to the picnic area, or in park buildings, and they must be inside a vehicle or tent at night. The park provides 76 developed campsites and six environmental campsites, each with a table, stove and food storage locker; restrooms and showers are nearby. The camping and tent areas also allow dogs. There is a dog walk area at the campground. There are no electric or water hookups at the campgrounds.
Lakeshore Inn and RV 20483 Lakeshore Drive Lakehead CA   530-238-2003
This campground has tall pine and oak trees and overlooks Shasta Lake. Septic and cable TV are available at some of the sites. Other amenities include a large swimming pool, mini store, gift shop, playground, picnic area, video game room, showers, guest laundry, dump station and handicap bathrooms. Well-behaved dogs are welcome. Pets should be quiet and please clean up after them. There is a $1 per day per pet fee. Dogs may not be left unattended, and they must be leashed at all times. Dogs are allowed on the trails. The camping and tent areas also allow dogs. There is a dog walk area at the campground.
Shasta Lake RV Resort and Campground 20433 Lakeshore Drive Lakehead CA   530-238-2370 (800-3-SHASTA (374-2782))
http://www.shastarv.com/
This RV resort and campground is located on Lake Shasta. The campground is on Shasta-Trinity National Forest land. RVs up to 60 feet are allowed. Amenities include hot showers, swimming pool, private boat dock, playground, grocery store, and more. Well-behaved leashed dogs are allowed for an additional $1 per night per pet. Please clean up after your pets. There are some breed restrictions. The camping and tent areas also allow dogs. There is a dog walk area at the campground.
Hirz Bay Campground Gilman Road Shasta Lake CA 530-275-1587 (877-444-6777)
This campground is located in the Shasta-Trinity National Forest at an elevation of 1,100 feet. The campground offers 37 tent and RV campsites. RVs up to 30 feet are allowed. Amenities include drinking water, accessible restrooms, flush toilets and boat ramp. Fishing, swimming and boating are popular activities at the campground.

The camp is open year round. Dogs are allowed in the lake, but not at the designated swimming beaches. Pets must be leashed and please clean up after them. The camping and tent areas also allow dogs. There is a dog walk area at the campground. There are no electric or water hookups at the campgrounds.

Attractions
Self Guided Audio Cassette Tour 204 West Alma St Lake Shasta CA 530-926-4511
This free audio cassette tour is available when you travel the Upper Sacramento River Canyon on Interstate 5, between Mt. Shasta and Anderson in scenic Northern California. The tape and its original sound track are keyed to I-5 exit signs traveling at 65 mph. The tapes tell a colorful story filled with details of more than a century of traveling and recreating in the canyon. Pick up and drop off the free "Sacramento Canyon Auto Tour" audio cassette tape. If you are traveling south on I-5, you can pick up a tape at the Mt. Shasta Ranger Station located at 204 West Alma St. in Mt. Shasta. You can drop off your southbound tape at either the Shasta Lake Ranger Station on the east side of I-5 at the Mountain Gate exit or the California Welcome Center in Anderson, located at 1699 Highway 273, adjacent to I-5. Going north, you can pick up a tape at the California Welcome Center in Anderson and drop it off at the Mt. Shasta Ranger Station. There is even an after hours drop box in Mt. Shasta.

Parks
Castle Crags State Park Castle Creek Road Lakehead CA 530-235-2684 (800-444-7275)
Named for 6,000-feet tall glacier-polished crags, this park features a variety of land and water recreation, activities, and interpretive and campfire programs are offered in summer. Dogs are allowed for no additional fee. They must be under owners control at all times, be on no more than a 6 foot leash, and cleaned up after. Dogs are not permitted on the trails, except for the campground/river trail to the picnic area, or in park buildings, and they must be inside a vehicle or tent at night.

Shasta Lake

Shasta Lake Redding CA 530-365-7500
Dogs on leash are allowed on the trails and in the lake. There are miles of trails near this beautiful lake. The easiest trail to reach from Interstate 5 is the Bailey Cove Trail. For a map of all trails, stop at the Visitors Center and Ranger's Station located just south of the lake on Interstate 5 at the Wonderland Blvd exit in Mountain Gate. The Visitor's Center is about 8 miles north of Redding.
Hirz Bay Trail Gilman Road Shasta Lake CA 530-275-1587
This 1.6 mile easy rated trail is located in the Shasta-Trinity National Forest. The trail follows the shoreline and crosses several cool, shady creeks. It also provides scenic vistas of the lake. The trailhead is located at Hirz Bay Campground which is 10 miles from Interstate 5 on Gilman Road. Dogs are allowed in the lake, but not at the designated swimming beaches. Pets must be leashed and please clean up after them.

Lassen Volcanic Area

Accommodations

Child's Meadow Resort 41500 Highway 36E Mill Creek CA 530-595-3383
Dogs are allowed in this all season resort. Located between the towns of Susanville and Red Bluff, this quiet resort is on 18 acres of picturesque meadows and streams at the end of the Shasta/Cascade Mountain Range. The resort is just 9 miles from the southwest entrance to Lassen Volcanic National Park. RV hookups are available at the resort. There is no pet charge.
Budget Host Frontier Inn 2685 Main St Susanville CA 530-257-4141

River Inn 1710 Main St Susanville CA 530-257-6051
There is an $11 per day additional pet fee. One large dog per room is allowed.

Campgrounds and RV Parks

Hat Creek Campground Hwy 89 Hat Creek CA 530-336-5521 (877-444-6777)
This campground is located in the Lassen National Forest at an elevation of 4,300 feet. The camp offers 75 campsites. Camp amenities include water, fire rings, picnic tables and restrooms. Most sites are available on a first-come, first-served basis. Some sites can be reserved. Dogs on leash are allowed at the campground and on trails. Please clean up after your dog. Dogs must be quiet, well behaved, and have current shot records. This campground is closed during the off-season. The camping and tent areas also allow dogs. There is a dog walk area at the campground. There are no electric or water hookups at the campgrounds.
Butte Lake, Lassen Volcanic National Park PO Box 100, Mineral CA 530-595-4444 (877-444-6777)
This park, at 6,100 feet, sits amid a variety of landscapes and recreational pursuits. Dogs of all sizes are allowed. There are no additional pet fees. Dogs may not be left unattended outside, and they must be leashed and cleaned up after. Dogs are allowed only on paved roads, and in the developed areas of the campground. Dogs are not allowed on the trails. The campsite is located 17 miles from Old Station on Highway 44 East, then 6 miles south on a dirt road. This campground is closed during the off-season. The camping and tent areas also allow dogs. There is a dog walk area at the campground. There are no electric or water hookups at the campgrounds.
Lassen Volcanic National Park Campgrounds 36050 Hwy 36 Mineral CA 530-595-4444
This park offers many campgrounds, with the largest campground having 179 sites. Trailers up to 35 feet are permitted, and all sites are on a first-come, first-served basis. Pets must be leashed and attended at all times. Please clean up after your pet. Dogs must be well behaved, and have current shot records. Dogs are permitted on established roadways, in campgrounds, picnic areas, and in other developed areas. Dogs are not allowed on any trails or hikes in this park, but see our Lassen National Forest listing for nearby dog-friendly hiking, sightseeing and additional camping. This campground is closed during the off-season. The camping and tent areas also allow dogs. There is a dog walk area at the campground. There are no electric or water hookups at the campgrounds.
Cave Campground Hwy 89 Old Station CA 530-336-5521 (877-444-6777)
This campground is located in the Lassen National Forest near the Subway Cave where you and your pooch can explore an underground lava tube. The camp is at an elevation of 4,300 feet and offers 46 campsites. Camp amenities include water, fire rings, picnic tables and restrooms. Most sites are available on a first-come, first-served basis. Some sites can be reserved. Dogs on leash are allowed at the campground and on trails. Please clean up after your dog. Dogs must be quiet, well behaved, and have current shot records. This campground is closed during the off-season. The camping and tent areas also allow dogs. There is a dog walk area at the campground. There are no electric or water hookups at the campgrounds.
Mt Lassen/Shingletown KOA 7749 KOA Road Shingletown CA 530-474-3133 (800-562-3403)
http://www.koa.com/where/ca/05147/
Located at an elevation of 3,900 feet, this twelve acre campground offers both tent and RV sites in the pines. The maximum length for pull through sites is 60 feet. Sites have 30 amp service available. Other amenities include LP gas, free modem dataport, snack bar, swimming pool during the summer, and a deli. Dogs of all sizes are allowed for no additional fee. Dogs must be under owner's control and visual observation at all times. Dogs must be quiet, well behaved, and be on no more than a 6 foot leash at all times, or otherwise contained. Dogs may not be left unattended outside the owner's camping equipment. There is a large field where dogs may be off lead if they are well trained, and under voice command. There are some breed restrictions. This campground is closed during the off-season. The camping and tent areas also allow dogs. There is a dog walk area at the campground.
Goumas Campground, Eagle Lake 477-050 Eagle Lake Road Susanville CA 530-257-4188 (877-444-6777)
This primitive campground, at 5,600 feet and near Eagle Lake, offers great scenery and a host of recreational pursuits. Dogs of all sizes are allowed. There are no additional pet fees. Dogs must be on no more than a 6 foot leash at all times in the camp areas, but they may be off lead on the trails if they are under voice command and

well behaved. Please clean up after your pet. This campground is closed during the off-season. The camping and tent areas also allow dogs. There is a dog walk area at the campground. There are no electric or water hookups at the campgrounds.

Merrill Campground, Eagle Lake 477050 Eagle Lake Road Susanville CA   530-257-4188 (877-444-6777)
Located at the south end of Eagle Lake at 5,100 feet, this park offers great scenery and a variety of land and water recreation. Dogs of all sizes are allowed. There are no additional pet fees. Dogs may not be left unattended, and they must be leashed and cleaned up after. Dogs are allowed on the trails. This campground is closed during the off-season. The camping and tent areas also allow dogs. There is a dog walk area at the campground. There are no water hookups at the campgrounds.

Parks
Lassen Volcanic National Park PO Box 100 Mineral CA   530-595-4444
http://www.nps.gov/lavo/
This national park does not really have much to see or do if you bring your pooch, except for staying overnight at the campgrounds. However, the dog-friendly Lassen National Forest surrounds the national park. At the national forest you will be able to find dog-friendly hiking, sightseeing and camping. Pets must be leashed and attended at all times. Please clean up after your pet.
Biz-Johnson Trail 2950 Riverside Drive Susanville CA   530-257-0456
This 25 mile trail follows the old Fernley and Lassen Branch Line of the Southern Pacific Railroad. It begins in Susanville at 4,200 feet and climbs 1,300 feet to a high point of 5,500 feet. Following the Susan River, the trail crosses over the river many times and passes through a former railroad tunnel. During the winter the trail's upper segment, located west of Highway 36, is used for cross-country skiing. Dogs on leash are allowed. Please clean up after your dog. To check on current trail conditions, call the Eagle Lake BLM Field Office at 530-257-0456. To get there from Alturas, take Highway 36 to Susanville. Follow Main Street to the stop light at the bottom of the hill by historic Uptown Susanville. Turn left on Weatherlow Street which becomes Richmond Road. Follow Richmond Road .5 miles across Susan River to Susanville Railroad Depot Trailhead and Visitor Center.
Lassen National Forest Highways 44 and 89 Susanville CA   530-257-4188
http://www.fs.fed.us/r5/lassen
Within this forest you can explore a lava tube, watch prong-horn antelope, drive four-wheel trails into high granite country or discover spring wildflowers on foot. Dogs are allowed on leash. If you want to check out a lava tube take a self-guided tour of the Subway Cave. Be sure to bring a flashlight, as there are no other sources of light underground. Subway Cave is located near the town of Old Station, 1/4 mile north of the junction of Highway 44 & 89 across from Cave Campground. The temperature inside the cave remains a cool 46 degrees F. year around. The cave is open late May through October and closed during the winter months. Or try a hike instead. Try the Spattercone Trail which explores the volcanic landscape and how life adapts to it. Three of the four kinds of volcanoes in the world can be seen along the Spattercone Trail. The trailhead and parking area are located at the Sanitary Dump Station across the highway form Hat Creek Campground on Highway 89 in Old Station. The trail has a round-trip distance of 1.5 miles. This trail is not shaded, so during the summer, try an early morning or late afternoon walk. For information about other miles of trails throughout this beautiful forest, stop by any National Forest Offices in Susanville including the Eagle Lake Ranger District Office located at 477-050 Eagle Lake Road in Susanville.

Lava Beds Area

Campgrounds and RV Parks
Eagles Nest RV Park 634 County Road 97A Tionesta CA   530-664-2081
http://www.eaglesnestrvpark.com/
This RV park is located 24 miles south of the town of Tulelake and 2 miles off Highway 139. Amenities include 20 full hookup pull through sites, showers, restrooms, a guest laundry, clubhouse with pool table, satellite TV, and a book exchange. Grassy tent sites are also available. Well-behaved leashed dogs are welcome for no additional fee. Please clean up after your pets. This campground is closed during the off-season. The camping and tent areas also allow dogs. There is a dog walk area at the campground.
Indian Well Campground 1 Indian Well Tulelake CA   530-667-8100
This campground, located in the Lava Beds National Monument, offers 40 campsites for tents and small to medium sized RVs. Amenities include water and flush toilets. Campsites are available on a first-come, first-served basis. Pets must be on no more than a 6 foot leash and attended at all times. Please clean up after your pet. Dogs may not be left unattended. Dogs are not allowed on any trails or hikes in this park, but see our Modoc National Forest listings in this region for nearby dog-friendly hiking, sightseeing and additional camping. The camping and tent areas also allow dogs. There is a dog walk area at the campground. There are no electric or water hookups at the campgrounds.
Medicine Lake Campground County Road 49 Tulelake CA   530-667-2246

Located in the Modoc National Forest at 6,700 feet, this camp area gives everyone a view of the 640 acre tree-lined lake, and the fascinating surrounding landscape created from ancient volcanic activity. There is a variety of land and water recreational activities available and close access to other points of interest. Dogs of all sizes are allowed for no additional fee. Dogs must be on no more than a 6 foot leash at all times, and be leashed and cleaned up after. Dogs are allowed throughout the park and on the trails. Campsites are on a first-come, first-served basis and some of the amenities include tables and grills, vault toilets (wheelchair friendly), and water. This RV park is closed during the off-season. The camping and tent areas also allow dogs. There is a dog walk area at the campground. There are no electric or water hookups at the campgrounds.

Medicine Lake Campground Forest Service Road 44N38 Tulelake CA   530-233-5811
This campground is located on the shores of Medicine Lake at a 6,700 foot elevation in the Modoc National Forest. There are 22 RV and tent sites. RVs up to 22 feet are allowed, and amenities include picnic tables, fire pits, vault toilets and potable water. Dogs on leash are allowed at the campgrounds and in the water. Please clean up after your pets. There is a $7 per vehicle fee. This campground is closed during the off-season. The camping and tent areas also allow dogs. There is a dog walk area at the campground. There are no electric or water hookups at the campgrounds.

Attractions

Medicine Lake Highlands Forest Road 49 Tulelake CA   530-233-5811
Medicine Lake is an area of moderately sloping to steep mountains. It was formed by a volcano and is one of North America's most unique geological areas. One feature is that it has no known outlets but yet its water remains clean and clear. It lies within the volcanic caldera of the largest shield volcano in North America. Obsidian and pumice are common in the highlands. For thousands of years Native Americans have used these substances to make tools and other objects. More recently astronauts prepared in the pumice fields for their first landing on the moon. To get there from the town of Tulelake, take Highway 139 south and follow the signs to the Tulelake National Wildlife Refuge. Then go south through the Lava Beds National Monument. Follow the signs along Forest Road 49 to Medicine Lake. This route is part of the Modoc Volcanic Scenic Byway.

Volcanic Historic Loop State Route 139 Tulelake CA   530-233-5811
This self-guided auto tour takes you through an area of "rocks that float and mountains of glass" and into one of the most unique geological regions in North America. The tour begins in the town of Tulelake and heads south on State Route 139. At CR97 head west and go into the town of Tionesta. Head another 12 miles west and you will come to Glass Mountain. The glass flow is from glassy dacite and rhyolitic obsidian that flowed from the same vent simultaneously without mixing. At nearby Medicine Lake you can camp, sightsee, swim, fish or take photos. Medicine Lake was once the center of a volcano. Native Americans believed that the lake had special healing powers. About 4.5 miles southeast of the lake is the Burnt Lava Flow. It is estimated to be about 200 years old which makes it the youngest lava flow in the area. The tour continues, but goes into the Lava Beds National Monument which only allows dogs in parking lots and along roads. In the national forest, which is the majority of this tour, dogs on leash are allowed on trails and in lake waters. Please clean up after your pets. For more information including maps, contact the Modoc National Forest office at 800 West 12th Street, Alturas, CA 96101, 530-233-5811.

Parks

Lava Beds National Monument 1 Indian Well Tulelake CA   530-667-2282
http://www.nps.gov/labe/
This national park does not really have much to see or do if you bring your pooch, except for staying overnight at the Indian Well Campground. However, the dog-friendly Modoc National Forest surrounds the national park. At the national forest you will be able to find dog-friendly hiking, sightseeing and camping. See our Modoc National Forest listing in this region for more details. Pets must be leashed and attended at all times. Please clean up after your pet.

Medicine Lake Campground County Road 49 Tulelake CA   530-667-2246
Located in the Modoc National Forest at 6,700 feet, this camp area gives everyone a view of the 640 acre tree-lined lake, and the fascinating surrounding landscape created from ancient volcanic activity. There is a variety of land and water recreational activities available and close access to other points of interest. Dogs of all sizes are allowed for no additional fee. Dogs must be on no more than a 6 foot leash at all times, and be leashed and cleaned up after. Dogs are allowed throughout the park and on the trails.

Mount Shasta

Accommodations

Dunsmuir Lodge

Dunsmuir Lodge 6604 Dunsmuir Avenue Dunsmuir CA   530-235-2884 (877-235-2884)
http://www.dunsmuirlodge.net/
Located in a mountain setting on 4 landscaped acres with a beautiful meadow and great mountain views, this lodge offers country log home decor and all rooms open out to a central courtyard. Dogs of all sizes are allowed. There is no fee for 1 or 2 dogs; for a 3rd dog there is a $15 per night additional pet fee. Dogs may not be left alone in the rooms at any time, and there are designated areas to walk your pet.

Railroad Park Resort

TOP 200 PLACE **Railroad Park Resort** 100 Railroad Park Road Dunsmuir CA   530-235-4440
http://www.rrpark.com/
Spend a night or more inside a restored antique railroad car at this unique resort. Dogs are allowed for an
additional $10 per day. This resort also offers RV hookup spaces.
Century House Inn 433 Lawndale Court McCloud CA   530-964-2206
http://www.mccloudcenturyhouse.com/
Gracefully resting along the southern slope of Mount Shasta among green lawns and tall pines in the town's
historic district, this retreat features elegant, individually decorated rooms, and many have porches or decks.
Dogs of all sizes are allowed, but they must be declared at time of reservation prior to arrival. There is no fee for
1 pet; for 2 dogs or more there is an additional fee of $10 per night per pet. Dogs must be leashed and cleaned
up after at all times, and be removed or crated for housekeeping.
Stoney Brook Inn 309 W Colombero Road McCloud CA   800-369-6118
There are only 2 pet friendly suites available; 1 dog is allowed in one, and in the other, 2 pets are allowed. There
is a $17 one time additional fee per pet.
Dream Inn Bed and Breakfast 326 Chestnut Street Mount Shasta CA   530-926-1536
http://home.att.net/~dreaminn
Dogs (and children) are welcome at this bed and breakfast inn. The Victorian home, built in 1904 and completely
restored, is located at 3,500 ft. in downtown Mount Shasta. Lying at the base of 14,162 ft. Mount Shasta, they are
surrounded by National Forest. The inn offers 4 bedrooms with shared bathrooms. The owners also have a dog
on the premises. There are no pet fees.
Econo Lodge 908 S. Mt. Shasta Blvd. Mount Shasta CA   530-926-3145
http://www.econolodge.com
There is an additional $5 per day pet charge. There is a limit of one dog per room.
Mount Shasta Ranch Bed and Breakfast 1008 W. A. Barr Rd. Mount Shasta CA   530-926-3870
http://www.stayinshasta.com
Dogs are allowed at this ranch style house bed and breakfast built in 1923. This B&B offers 12 bedrooms
including a cottage. Five of the rooms have private bathrooms. There is a $10 one time per stay, per pet fee.
Children are also welcome.
Mountain Air Lodge 1121 S Mount Shasta Blvd Mount Shasta CA   530-926-3411
There is an additional $7 per day pet charge.
Swiss Holiday Lodge 2400 S. Mt. Shasta Blvd. Mount Shasta CA   530-926-3446
There is an additional $5 per day pet charge.
Comfort Inn Central 1844 Shastina Drive Weed CA   530-938-1982 (877-424-6423)
Dogs of all sizes are allowed. There is a $10 per night per pet additional fee. Dogs may not be left alone in the
rooms, and they must be leashed and cleaned up after.
Holiday Inn Express 1830 Black Butte Drive Weed CA   530-938-1308 (877-270-6405)
There is a $10 one time pet fee. A well-behaved large dog is okay.
Lake Shastina Golf Resort 5925 Country Club Drive Weed CA   530-938-3201
http://www.lakeshastinagolfresort.net/
Dogs are allowed in some of the condos at this 18 hole golf course resort. There is a $25 one time pet charge.
Motel 6 - Weed - Mount Shasta 466 North Weed Boulevard Weed CA   530-938-4101 (800-466-8356)
One well-behaved family pet per room. Guest must notify front desk upon arrival. Guest is liable for any
damages. In consideration of all guests, pets must never be left unattended in the guest rooms.

Campgrounds and RV Parks
Railroad Park Resort 100 Railroad Park Road Dunsmuir CA   530-235-4440
http://www.rrpark.com/rvpark/
This RV park is located at the foot of the grand Castle Crags, and their features/amenities include a swimming
hole, a game room, flush toilets, hot showers, laundry facilities, and a group barbecue pit. Dogs of all sizes are
allowed for no additional fee. Dogs must be friendly, leashed, and cleaned up after. This RV park is closed
during the off-season. The camping and tent areas also allow dogs. There is a dog walk area at the campground.
Fowlers Campground Hwy 89 McCloud CA   530-964-2184
This campground has 39 sites available on a 1st come 1st served basis. Water and vault toilets are on site.
Dogs of all sizes are allowed for no additional fee; they must be leashed and cleaned up after at all times when in
a developed site, and in areas where posted. Dogs are not allowed in the wilderness area at the base of Mt
Shasta. This RV park is closed during the off-season. The camping and tent areas also allow dogs. There is a
dog walk area at the campground. There are no electric or water hookups at the campgrounds.
Lake Siskiyou Camp Resort 4239 W. A. Barr Rd Mount Shasta CA   530-926-2618 (888-926-2618)
http://www.lakesis.com/
This recreational and camping area sits on 250 forested acres along side a pristine 430 acre sailing lake. There
is a large grocery/deli/gift shop and marina, and the campground has 360 overnight sites, laundry facilities, a
dump station, restrooms with showers, free family outdoor movies, and a rec hall. Dogs of all sizes are allowed

for an additional fee of $2 per day per pet. Dogs must be leashed and cleaned up after at all times, and they may not be left unattended on a camp site. Dogs are allowed throughout the park, except they are not allowed in the lodging (rentals), picnic areas, or the beach. This RV park is closed during the off-season. The camping and tent areas also allow dogs. There is a dog walk area at the campground.

Mount Shasta KOA 900 N Mt Shasta Blvd Shasta City CA   530-926-4029 (800-562-3617)
http://www.koa.com/where/ca/05108/
There is a variety of land, water, and air recreation at this scenic alpine park. The campground also offers 80 foot pull through sites with 50 amp, cable, LP gas, snack bar, and swimming pool. Dogs of all sizes are allowed for no additional fee. Dogs must be under owner's control and visual observation at all times. Dogs must be quiet, well behaved, and be on no more than a 6 foot leash at all times, or otherwise contained. Dogs may not be left unattended outside the owner's camping equipment. There are some breed restrictions. The camping and tent areas also allow dogs. There is a dog walk area at the campground. Dogs are allowed in the camping cabins.

Cross Country Ski Resorts

Mt. Shasta Ski Park Nordic Center

Mt. Shasta Ski Park Nordic Center Highway 89 Mount Shasta CA   530-925-1131
http://www.skipark.com/nordic.html
This resort is located 65 miles north of Redding, 10 miles east of Interstate 5, off Highway 89. The cross country ski center is about one mile before Mt. Shasta's downhill ski area. You can rent skis or snowshoes from the center and then enjoy about 9km of ungroomed snowshoe packed backcountry trails. The trails might be tough for cross country skiing but they are also popular for snowshoeing. It is recommended that dogs be leashed when crossing trails but can be off-leash under direct voice control when on the trails. On the weekends, these trails can have lots of dogs on them. The center is open daily from 9am to 4pm.

Outdoor Restaurants
Cafe Maddalena 5801 Sacramento Avenue Dunsmuir CA   530-235-2725
http://www.cafemaddalena.com/
Well-behaved leashed dogs are allowed at the outdoor seating area.
Cornerstone Bakery & Cafe 5759 Dunsmuir Avenue Dunsmuir CA   530-235-4677
Well-behaved leashed dogs are allowed at the outdoor seating area.
Lalo's Mexican Restaurant 520 N Mount Shasta Blvd Mount Shasta CA   530-926-5123
This Mexican eatery offers seasonal outdoor patio seating. Dogs are allowed at the outdoor tables. They must be well behaved, under owner's control at all times, leashed, and cleaned up after.

Paradise

Accommodations
Comfort Inn Central 5475 Clark Road Paradise CA 530-876-0191 (877-424-6423)
Dogs of all sizes are allowed. There is a $10 per night per pet additional fee. Dogs must be crated when left alone in the room, and leashed and cleaned up after.
Ponderosa Gardens Motel 7010 The Skyway Paradise CA 530-872-9094
True to its name, this motel features a garden like setting, a pool and Jacuzzi, gift shop, picnic grounds, and a continental breakfast. Dogs of all sizes are allowed for an additional fee of $6 per night per pet. Dogs may not be left alone in the room at any time, and they must be leashed and cleaned up after.

Plumas National Forest - Quincy

Accommodations
Lake Oroville Bed and Breakfast 240 Sunday Drive Berry Creek CA 530-589-0700
Dogs are welcome, but should be okay around other dogs. The owner has dogs and cats on the premises. There is a $10 per day pet fee. Children are also welcome.
La Porte Cabin Rentals Main Street and Pike Road/P. O. Box 225 La Porte CA 530-675-0850
http://www.laportecabins.com/index.html
This mountain retreat features clean, fully-equipped cabins and a bunkhouse; all with complete kitchens so just bring your own cuisine. There is satellite TV available, and the cabins have private porches. Dogs of all sizes are allowed for no additional fee. Dogs may only be left alone in the rooms if they will be quiet and well mannered, and they must be leashed and cleaned up after.
Bucks Lake Lodge 23685 Bucks Lake Quincy CA 530-283-2262
There is a $10 per day additional pet fee. Dogs are allowed in the cabins, but not the motel section. The cabins are not designated as smoking or non-smoking. Thanks to one of our readers for this recommendation.

Campgrounds and RV Parks
Upper Jamison Creek Campground 310 Johnsville Road Blairsden CA 530-836-2380
This campground is located in the scenic Sierra Plumas Eureka State Park at the foot of Eureka Mountain. Dogs of all sizes are allowed at no additional fee. Dogs may not be left unattended, and they must be quiet, leashed, and cleaned up after. Dogs are not allowed on the trails; they are allowed on Jamison Trail Road or in the back country on lead. This campground is closed during the off-season. The camping and tent areas also allow dogs. There is a dog walk area at the campground. There are no electric or water hookups at the campgrounds.
Silver Lake Campground Forest Road 24N29X/Silver Lake Bucks Lake CA 530-283-0555
This tent only campground is located in the Plumas National Forest and offers 8 campsites and vault toilets. There is no water available. Campsites are on a first-come, first-served basis. The trailhead for the Gold Lake Trail is located at this campground. In the campground dogs must be on leash. On the trails, dogs on leash or off-leash but under direct voice control are allowed. Dogs may not be left unattended. From the turn-off, travel 6.4 miles on Road 24N29X, a gravel road. This campground is closed during the off-season. The camping and tent areas also allow dogs. There is a dog walk area at the campground. There are no electric or water hookups at the campgrounds.
Little Beaver Campground, Feather River District off Forest Road 120/La Porte Road La Porte CA 530-534-6500 (877-444-6777)
This campground is located at the Little Grass Valley Reservoir Recreation Area in the Plumas National Forest. There are 120 campsites, some of which offer prime lakeside sites. Amenities include water, flush toilets, trailer space, and an RV dump station. Dogs are allowed in the campgrounds, on trails and in the water. In the campground dogs must be on leash. On the trails, dogs on leash or off-leash but under direct voice control are allowed. Dogs may not be left unattended outside. Please clean up after your pet. This campground is closed during the off-season. The camping and tent areas also allow dogs. There is a dog walk area at the campground. There are no electric or water hookups at the campgrounds.
Buck's Lake Recreation Area Bucks Lake Road Quincy CA 530-283-0555 (877-444-6777)
This recreation area of 1,827 acres sits at an elevation of over 5,100 feet and provides a wide variety of year round land and water recreational activities. There are several businesses surrounding the 103,000 acre-feet Buck's Lake, with an assortment of services available. The park also offers 4 boat launch areas and access to the Pacific Crest Trail. Dogs of all sizes are allowed for no additional fee. Dogs must be leashed and cleaned up after. They are not allowed in the public swim areas; they are allowed on the trails. There are about 63 camp sites on a first come first served basis and 3 group sites that can be reserved, each with piped water and

restroom facilities with the exception of Lower Bucks Lake. This RV park is closed during the off-season. The camping and tent areas also allow dogs. There is a dog walk area at the campground. There are no electric or water hookups at the campgrounds.

Pioneer RV Park 1326 Pioneer Road Quincy CA   530-283-0796 (888-216-3266)
This pet-friendly RV park is located in the Sierra Nevada Mountains between Lassen National Park and Lake Tahoe. They have over 60 sites on 6.5 acres. RV sites have long wide pull through sites, picnic tables, 30 or 50 amp service, and satellite TV. Tent campers are also welcome. Other amenities include a laundry room, LP gas, rec room with DSL and WI-FI, big screen TV, books exchange and a ping-pong table. They are located about 1.5 miles from downtown Quincy and right next to a county park which has an Olympic size swimming pool and a playground. Well-behaved leashed dogs of all sizes are allowed. There is a covered dog kennel available for your use and a dog wash area. People need to clean up after their pets. There is no pet fee. There is a large area outside the park for walking your pet. The camping and tent areas also allow dogs.

Parks

Yellow Creek Trail Highway 70 Belden CA   530-283-0555
This trail is located in the Plumas National Forest and is an easy one way 1.4 mile trail. This day hike ends in a box canyon. Dogs on leash or off-leash but under direct voice control are allowed. Please clean up after your pets. The trailhead is location about 25 miles west of Quincy on Highway 70. It is to the right of the Ely Stamp Mill rest area, across from Belden.

Bald Mountain Trail Road #57 Berry Creek CA   530-534-6500
This trail is located in the Plumas National Forest and is a short one way .5 mile hike through the forest to impressive rock formations. The elevation ranges from 3100 feet to 3270 feet. Big Bald Rock provides great views of Oroville Lake and the Sacramento Valley. The trail is usually open for hiking from February to December, weather permitting. Dogs on leash or off-leash but under direct voice control are allowed. Please clean up after your pets. To get there from Oroville, take Highway 162 east. Drive for about 17-18 miles and turn right onto Bald Rock Road. Drive for about 5.8 on the gravel road. Then turn left at the Big Bald Rock turn-off and go .1 miles.

Plumas-Eureka State Park Johnsonville Road Blairsden CA   530-836-2380
Dogs are allowed on one trail which is called the Grass Lake Trail. This 3.8 mile trail climbs steadily to the Pacific Crest Trail passing several lakes. Pets must be on leash and please clean up after them. The trailhead is at the Jamison Mine. To get there take Johnsonville Road (County Road A14) off Highway 89 in Graeagle. Go about 4.5 miles to the unimproved Jamison Mine Road. There should be a sign on the left for the Jamison Mine/Grass Lake Trail. Continue another 1.5 miles to the parking area.

Lakeshore Trail off La Porte Road Brownsville CA
This trail is located in the Plumas National Forest and is an easy but long 13.5 mile hike around the Little Grass Valley Reservoir. The trail is at a 5,100 foot elevation and is heavily used by hikers. In some areas the trail becomes a walk along the beach. Dogs on leash are allowed on the trail and in the water. The trail is usually open for hiking from early June to early September, weather permitting. Please clean up after your pets. To get there from Oroville, take Highway 162 east. Drive for about 7 miles and then turn right onto Forbestown Road (Challenge Cut-Off). Drive 16.6 miles and then turn left on La Porte Road. Go 27.4 miles and then make a right at Road #57 (South Fork Rec Area).

Gold Lake Trail Forest Road 24N29X Bucks Lake CA   530-283-0555
This trail is located in the Plumas National Forest and is an easy one way 1.5 mile trail. This trail provides access to the Bucks Lake Wilderness and the Pacific Crest Trail. At Bucks Lake swimming and fishing are popular activities. Dogs on leash or off-leash but under direct voice control are allowed. Dogs are allowed on the trails and in the water. Please clean up after your pets. To get there from Quincy, go west 9.2 miles on Bucks Lake Road. Turn right on a gravel road, 24N29X (Silver Lake sign). Go 6.4 miles to the lake and the Silver Lake Campground. The trail begins at the campground.

Chambers Creek Trail Highway 70 Pulga CA   530-283-0555
This trail is located in the Plumas National Forest and is a moderate one way 4.2 mile trail. There are some great waterfalls at the bridge. It takes about 2 to 3 hours to reach the bridge and a total of 6 hours to the top of the trail. Dogs on leash or off-leash but under direct voice control are allowed. Please clean up after your pets. The trailhead is location about 40 miles west of Quincy on Highway 70, or about 40 miles from Oroville.

Buck's Lake Recreation Area Bucks Lake Road Quincy CA   530-283-0555 (877-444-6777)
This recreation area of 1,827 acres sits at an elevation of over 5,100 feet and provides a wide variety of year round land and water recreational activities. There are several businesses surrounding the 103,000 acre-feet Buck's Lake, with an assortment of services available. The park also offers 4 boat launch areas and access to the Pacific Crest Trail. Dogs of all sizes are allowed for no additional fee. Dogs must be leashed and cleaned up after. They are not allowed in the public swim areas; they are allowed on the trails.

Plumas National Forest 159 Lawrence Street Quincy CA   530-283-2050
http://www.fs.fed.us/r5/plumas/
This national forest covers over 1.1 million acres of land which ranges in elevation from around 2,000 to over 7,000 feet. Please see our listings in this region for dog-friendly hikes and/or campgrounds.

Outdoor Restaurants

Stoney's Country Burgers 11 Lindan Avenue Quincy CA   530-283-3911
http://www.stoneyscountryburger.com/
This country burger eatery offers indoor and outdoor dining. Dogs are allowed at the outdoor tables. Dogs must be under owner's control at all times, leashed, and cleaned up after.

Portola

Campgrounds and RV Parks

Grasshopper Flat Campground Grizzley Flat Road (Road 112) Portola CA   530-836-2575 (877-444-6777)
This park on Lake Davis in the Sequoia National Forest offers varied habitats, ecosystems, and a wide variety of land and water recreation. Dogs may not be left unattended, and they must be leashed at all times and cleaned up after. Dogs are allowed on the trails unless otherwise marked, and in developed areas. Dogs are not allowed in any park buildings. This campground is closed during the off-season. The camping and tent areas also allow dogs. There is a dog walk area at the campground.

Red Bluff

Accommodations

Comfort Inn 90 Sale Lane Red Bluff CA   530-529-7060 (877-424-6423)
Dogs of all sizes are allowed. There is a $15 per night per pet additional fee. Dogs must be quiet, well behaved, leashed, cleaned up after, and the Do Not Disturb sign put on the door if they are in the room alone.
Motel 6 - Red Bluff 20 Williams Avenue Red Bluff CA   530-527-9200 (800-466-8356)
One well-behaved family pet per room. Guest must notify front desk upon arrival. Guest is liable for any damages. In consideration of all guests, pets must never be left unattended in the guest rooms.
Sportsman's Lodge 768 Antelope Blvd Red Bluff CA   530-527-2888
http://www.rbsportsmanlodge.com/
Some of the amenities at this lodge include refrigerators in all the rooms and a swimming pool. Dogs of all sizes are allowed. There is a $7 additional fee per pet for a small to medium dog; the fee may be higher for larger or heavily-haired dogs. Dogs may not be left unattended in the rooms at any time, and they must be well behaved, leashed, and cleaned up after.
Travelodge 38 Antelope Blvd Red Bluff CA   530-527-6020
There is a $6 per day pet fee.

Parks

Red Bluff Recreation Area 825 North Humboldt Avenue Red Bluff CA   530-934-3316
The popular Red Bluff Recreation Area is part of the Mendocino National Forest. The recreation area includes the Lake Red Bluff Trail (1.5 mi.), which is accessible and paved. The trail travels along the Sacramento River and through a wildlife viewing area. Popular activities at the lake include boating, water skiing, swimming, camping and fishing. The facilities include accessible restrooms with showers, a boat ramp and campground. Dogs are allowed including on the trails and in the water but pets should be leashed. The park is located just east of the city of Red Bluff in the Sacramento Valley. If you are heading North on I-5, take the Highway 36 East exit towards Central Red Bluff/Chico. Continue of Antelope Blvd for less than 1/2 mile and turn right on Sale Lane. The park is open year round unless there is flooding or high winds.
Samuel Ayer/Dog Island Park 1360 Main Street Red Bluff CA   530-527-2605
This day-use park offers multi-use trails, fishing on the Sacramento River, a large group barbecue area, horseshoe pits, picnic areas with fire pits, and restrooms. Dogs of all sizes are allowed; they must be leashed and cleaned up after at all times.

Redding

Accommodations

Best Western Hospitality House Motel 532 N Market St Redding CA   530-241-6464 (800-780-7234)
Dogs of all sizes are allowed. There is a $10 per night pet fee per pet. Reservations are recommended due to limited rooms for pets. Only non-smoking rooms used for pets.

Bridge Bay Resort 10300 Bridge Bay Road Redding CA   530-275-3021 (800-752-9669)
This is a complete resort that offers a full-service marina with tackle and bait, small boats and houseboat rentals, dining, a lounge, gift shop, convenience store, banquet rooms, a pool, and lakeside accommodations. Dogs of all sizes are welcome for an additional fee of $10 per night per pet, plus a $50 deposit if paying by cash. There is no additional pet fee for the dogs on the boats. Dogs may be left alone in the rooms for a short time if they are house-trained and they will be quiet and well behaved. Dogs must be leashed and cleaned up after at all times.
Fawndale Lodge and RV Resort 15215 Fawndale Road Redding CA   800-338-0941
http://members.aol.com/fawnresort/
Nestled in the pines, this lodge offers acres of lawn, a pool and easy access to many recreational activities. All rooms are non-smoking. There is a $1 per day pet charge.
Holiday Inn Express 1080 Twin View Blvd Redding CA   530-241-5500 (877-270-6405)
There is a $25 one time pet fee.
La Quinta Inn Redding 2180 Hilltop Drive Redding CA   530-221-8200 (800-531-5900)
Dogs of all sizes are allowed. There are no additional pet fees. Dogs may not be left unattended at any time, and they must be leashed and cleaned up after.
Motel 6 - Redding Central 1640 Hilltop Drive Redding CA   530-221-1800 (800-466-8356)
One well-behaved family pet per room. Guest must notify front desk upon arrival. Guest is liable for any damages. In consideration of all guests, pets must never be left unattended in the guest rooms.
Motel 6 - Redding North 1250 Twin View Boulevard Redding CA   530-246-4470 (800-466-8356)
One well-behaved family pet per room. Guest must notify front desk upon arrival. Guest is liable for any damages. In consideration of all guests, pets must never be left unattended in the guest rooms.
Motel 6 - Redding South 2385 Bechelli Lane Redding CA   530-221-0562 (800-466-8356)
One well-behaved family pet per room. Guest must notify front desk upon arrival. Guest is liable for any damages. In consideration of all guests, pets must never be left unattended in the guest rooms.
Ponderosa Inn 2220 Pine St Redding CA   530-241-6300 (800-626-1900)
There is a $15 per night pet fee per small pets. There is a $25 per night pet fee per large pets. Smoking and non-smoking are available for pet rooms.
Quality Inn 2059 Hilltop Drive Redding CA   530-221-6530 (877-424-6423)
Dogs of all sizes are allowed. There is a $15 one time additional pet fee per room. Dogs may be left alone in the room only if they will be quiet and well behaved. Dogs must be leashed, cleaned up after, and a contact number left with the front desk if they are in the room alone.
River Inn 1835 Park Marina Drive Redding CA   530-241-9500 (800-995-4341)
This inn is adjacent to the Sacramento River and has a private grass area next to their lake. There is a $6 per day pet charge. Thanks to one of our readers for recommending this inn.
Shasta Lodge 1245 Pine Street Redding CA   530-243-6133
There is a $20 refundable pet deposit. There is also a $5 per day pet fee.

Campgrounds and RV Parks
Mountain Gate RV Park 14161 Holiday Road Redding CA   530-283-0769 (888-216-3266)
http://www.mt-gatervpark.com/
This RV park's amenities include full RV hookups, lighted grounds, large pull through sites, a convenience store, video rentals, cable TV, pool, rec room with pool table, email station, laundry, showers, restrooms, dump station, easy I-5 access, and an off lead, fenced pet area. Well-behaved leashed dogs are allowed. Please clean up after your pets. There is an additional fee of $1 per night per pet. The park is located 7 miles north of Redding. There are some breed restrictions. There is a dog walk area at the campground. There are special amenities given to dogs at this campground.
Redding RV Park 11075 Campers Court Redding CA   530-241-0707 (800-428-2089)
This scenic RV only park offers 110 paved, landscaped sites, barbecues, swimming pools, laundry facilities, a recreation room with pool tables, a convenience store, and a dump station. Dogs of all sizes are welcome for no additional fee. Dogs must be well behaved, and leashed and cleaned up after at all times. There is a dog walk area at the campground.
Sacramento River RV Resort 6596 Riverland Drive Redding CA   530-365-6402
http://www.sacramentoriverrvresort.com
This is an RV only park located along the Sacramento River. No number or size restrictions are set on dogs for a one or two night stay, and there is no additional fee. For stays of one week or longer, there can be no more than 2 dogs and they can not be over 25 pounds, also for no additional fee. Dogs must be leashed and cleaned up after. There are some breed restrictions. There is a dog walk area at the campground.

Stores
Petco Pet Store 1603 East Hilltop Drive Redding CA   530-226-1200
Your licensed and well-behaved leashed dog is allowed in the store.

Parks

Sacramento River Trail North Market Street Redding CA   530-224-6100
This trail attracts people of all ages, from the walkers and joggers to bicyclists and fisherman looking for an ideal angling spot. The complete trail, round-trip, is approximately 6 miles and can easily be walked in a couple of hours. It is located along the Sacramento River from the North Market Street bridge to Keswick Dam. There are also several access points to the paved trail in Caldwell Park.
Shasta-Trinity National Forest 3644 Avtech Pkwy Redding CA   530-226-2500
http://www.fs.fed.us/r5/shastatrinity/
This national forest covers over 2 million acres of land which ranges in elevation from 1,000 to 14,162 feet. Please see our listings in this region for dog-friendly hikes and/or campgrounds.

Turtle Bay Exploration Park

TOP 200 PLACE **Turtle Bay Exploration Park** 840 Auditorium Drive Redding CA   800-TURTLEBAY (887-8532)
http://www.turtlebay.org/
This amazing exploration park is 300 acres of educational and entertaining activities with a focus on relationships between humans and nature through the telling of the region and its peoples. It is home to the translucent Sundial Bridge, a free-standing, technical marvel spanning the Sacramento River that connects the north and south campuses of the park. There is also a historical railroad exhibit, an arboretum that extends over 200 acres, a series of climate display gardens, a medicinal garden, children's garden, a variety of several other gardens, and much more. Dogs are allowed throughout most of the park, in the gardens, the bridge, and on the hiking trails. They are not allowed at Paul Bunyan's Forest Camp or in the museum. Dogs must be leashed and cleaned up after at all times. There are doggy clean-up supplies on site.

Off-Leash Dog Parks

Benton Dog Park 1700 Airpark Drive Redding CA   530-941-8200
http://www.bentondogpark.com/
This fenced off-lead dog park is located on 2.30 acres. Dogs of all sizes are welcome, they must be leashed when out of the off-lead area, and please clean up after your pet.

Benton Dog Park

Outdoor Restaurants

Burrito Bandito 8938 Airport Road Redding CA   530-222-6640
Well-behaved leashed dogs are allowed at the outdoor seating area.
Chevys Fresh Mex 1691 Hilltop Drive Redding CA 530-223-5797
Well-behaved leashed dogs are allowed at the outdoor bar patio tables.
Chico's Tecate Grill 913 Dana Drive Redding CA 530-223-3299
Dogs are welcome at the outdoor tables and they give dogs a bowl of water. Pets should be on leash.
Coffee Creek Juice and Java 2380 Athens Avenue Redding CA   530-229-7500
Well-behaved leashed dogs are allowed at the outdoor seating area.
Espresso Joe's 2143 Hilltop Drive Redding CA 530-223-1198
Well-behaved leashed dogs are allowed at the outdoor seating area.
In-n-Out 1275 Dana Dr Redding CA 800-786-1000
This restaurant serves fast food. Dogs are allowed at the outdoor tables.
La Gondola 632 N Market Street Redding CA 530-244-6321
Well-behaved leashed dogs are allowed at the outdoor seating area.
La Palomar Mexican Dining 2586 Churn Creek Road Redding CA   530-222-1208
Well-behaved leashed dogs are allowed at the outdoor seating area.
Manhattan Bagel 913 Dana Drive Redding CA 530-222-2221
Well-behaved leashed dogs are allowed at the outdoor seating area.
Market St Pizza and Deli 871 N Market Street Redding CA   530-242-0675
Well-behaved leashed dogs are allowed at the outdoor seating area.
Nick's Bella Vista Grill 21442 Highway 299 Redding CA 530-549-3042
Well-behaved leashed dogs are allowed at the outdoor seating area.
Sandwichery 1341 Tehama Street Redding CA 530-246-2020
Well-behaved leashed dogs are allowed at the outdoor seating area.
Togos 1030 East Cypress Avenue Ste B Redding CA 530-222-9212
This restaurant serves deli-type food. Dogs are allowed at the outdoor tables.
Wall Street Pizza 1165 Hartnell Avenue Redding CA 530-221-7100
Well-behaved leashed dogs are allowed at the outdoor seating area.

Shasta

Attractions

Shasta State Historic Park 15312 Hwy 299 W Shasta CA 530-243-8194
This historic park pays tribute to the "Queen City of the Northern Mines"; a main shipping area for supplies and gold from the 1849 rush, and includes the old brick remains of the buildings. There are exhibits, interpretive programs, picnic areas, and an unparalleled collection of historic California artwork on display. Dogs of all sizes are allowed throughout the park, at the picnic areas, and on the trails; they are not allowed in the museum. Dogs must be well mannered, leashed, and cleaned up after at all times.

Shasta - Trinity National Forest

Accommodations

Becker's Bounty Lodge and Cottage HCR #2 Box 4659 Coffee Creek CA 530-266-3277
http://www.beckersbountylodging.com/
The lodge is a secluded mountain hideaway at the edge of the one-half million acre Trinity Alps Wilderness. Dogs are not allowed on the furniture. There is a $50 one time pet charge.
Lewiston Valley RV Park 4789 Trinity Dam Blvd. Lewiston CA 530-778-3942
http://www.lewistonca.com/lewvally.htm
This RV park is on 8 acres and offers 7 pull through sites and 2 back-in sites. The sites have 50 amp service. Amenities include a seasonal heated pool. Within walking distance is a family style restaurant, gas station and mini-mart. Well-behaved leashed dogs are allowed. There is no pet fee.
Best Western Weaverville Victorian Inn 1709 Main St Weaverville CA 530-623-4432 (800-780-7234)
Dogs of all sizes are allowed. There are no additional pet fees. Reservations are recommended due to limited rooms for pets. Smoking and non-smoking are available for pet rooms.

Campgrounds and RV Parks

Lakeview Terrace Resort Trinity Dam Blvd Lewiston CA 530-778-3803
http://www.lakeviewterraceresort.com/
This resort overlooks Lewiston Lake and features an RV park and cabin rentals. RV spaces feature pull through sites, tables and barbecues. Most of the pull through sites offer a lake view. Other amenities include a laundry facility, restrooms and showers. Well-behaved quiet leashed dogs are welcome, up to two pets per cabin or RV. Pets are not allowed in the swimming pool area and cannot not be left alone at any time, either in your RV or at the cabins. Please clean up after your pet. There is no pet fee if you stay in an RV space, but there is a $10 per day fee for pets in the cabins. Dogs may not be left unattended in the cabins, or outside your RV. There are some breed restrictions. There is a dog walk area at the campground.
Clark Springs Campground Off Hwy 3 Trinity Center CA 530-623-2121 (877-444-6777)
This campground is located in the Shasta-Trinity National Forest at an elevation of 2,400 feet. The campground offers 21 tent and RV campsites. RVs up to 25 feet are allowed, and amenities include a swimming beach, boat ramp, drinking water, picnic sites, wheelchair access and flush toilets. Fishing, swimming, boating and hiking are popular activities at the campground. The Trinity Lakeshore trailhead is located here. Dogs are allowed on the trails and in the lake water but only on non-designated swimming areas. Pets must be leashed at all times in camp, and please clean up after them. Dogs may be off lead on the trails only if they are under strict voice control, and they will not chase. This campground is closed during the off-season. The camping and tent areas also allow dogs. There is a dog walk area at the campground. There are no electric or water hookups at the campgrounds.
Hayward Flat Campground Hwy 3 Trinity Center CA 530-623-2121 (877-444-6777)
This campground is located on the west side of the East Fork arm of Trinity Lake in the Shasta-Trinity National Forest. The campground is at an elevation of 2,400 feet and offers 94 tent and RV campsites. RVs up to 40 feet are allowed, and amenities include drinking water and flush toilets. Fishing, swimming and boating are popular activities at the campground. Dogs may not be left unattended outside. Pets must be leashed at all times in the camp areas, and please clean up after them. Dogs may be off lead on the trails if they are under strict voice command and will not chase. This campground is closed during the off-season. The camping and tent areas also allow dogs. There is a dog walk area at the campground. There are no electric or water hookups at the campgrounds.
Wyntoon Resort 60260 Hwy 3 Trinity Center CA 530-266-3337 (800-715-3337)
http://www.wyntoonresort.com/
This 90 acre wooded resort is located at the north end of Lake Trinity and offers both RV and tent sites. The RV sites are tree shaded with 30 or 50 amp service, and will accommodate RVs up to 60 feet. Tent sites are located under pine and cedar trees and have picnic tables and barbecues. Other camp amenities include a swimming pool, clubhouse, snack bar, ping-pong, showers and laundry facilities. Well-behaved leashed pets are always

welcome. Please clean up after your pet. There is a $1 per day pet fee. Dogs may not be left unattended. The camping and tent areas also allow dogs. There is a dog walk area at the campground.

Shasta Trinity National Forest Campgrounds P.O.Box 2303/Hwy 3 Weaverville CA 530-286-2666 (877-444-6777)
http://www.campersonline.com/
There are 19 campgrounds here with sites along rivers, lakes, or nestled among the trees, and a variety of services/amenities are available depending on the site locations. Dogs of all sizes are welcome for no additional pet fees. Dogs must be under owner's immediate control, and be leashed and cleaned up after at all times. Dogs are allowed on the trails but not on the beaches. The camping and tent areas also allow dogs. There is a dog walk area at the campground.

Sidney Gulch RV Park 504 N Main Street/Hwy 299 Weaverville CA 530-623-6621 (800-554-1626)
This 4.9 acre park offers 40 level sites in a mountain setting, and some of the amenities include showers and restrooms, laundry facilities, and a recreation room with a full kitchen. Dogs of all sizes are allowed for no additional pet fee. Dogs must be leashed and cleaned up after, and they may not be left unattended on site at any time. Dogs are allowed throughout the park, but not in buildings. The camping and tent areas also allow dogs. There is a dog walk area at the campground.

Brandy Creek RV Campground P. O. Box 188 Whiskeytown CA 530-246-1225 (800-365-CAMP (2267))
This campground is part of the Whiskeytown National Recreation Area which allows dogs on trails, in the lake and on non-swimming beaches only. The camp offers paved parking spots for RVs along an access road. There are no hookups, and generators are allowed, but not during the quiet time which is usually from 10pm to 6am. All sites are on a first-come, first-served basis. Dogs must be leashed, or crated, and attended at all times. Please clean up after your pet. The campground is open all year. The camping and tent areas also allow dogs. There is a dog walk area at the campground. There are no electric or water hookups at the campgrounds.

Oak Bottom Campgrounds Oak Bottom Road Whiskeytown CA 530-359-2269 (800-365-CAMP (2267))
This campground offers tent sites next to Whiskeytown Lake. The campground is part of the Whiskeytown National Recreation Area which allows dogs on trails, in the lake and on non-swimming beaches only. The camp also offers RV sites. Generators are allowed but not during the quiet time which is usually from 10pm to 6am. During the summer reservations are required and dogs are on a first-come, first-served basis. Dogs must be leashed at all times while in the camp areas. Dogs may be off lead on trails only if they will respond to voice command and will not chase. Please clean up after your pet. Dogs may not be left unattended. The camping and tent areas also allow dogs. There is a dog walk area at the campground. There are no electric or water hookups at the campgrounds.

Vacation Home Rentals

Blackberry Creek Garden Cottage On SR-3 Coffee Creek CA 530-266-3502
There is a $15 per day additional pet fee. According to a reader "We just spent a week at this wonderful cottage, and it is a little piece of heaven for you and your dog. Nestled under the pines, cedars and redwoods the cottage has everything you need for the perfect vacation in the woods. Down the road is the greatest swimming hole in the Trinity River, and great hikes await you in every direction. Our dogs did not want to leave and neither did we.
"

Attractions

Trinity Alps Marina Fairview Marina Rd. Lewiston CA 530-286-2282
http://www.trinityalpsmarina.com
Rent a houseboat on Lake Trinity with your well-behaved dog. There is a $75 one time pet fee.

TOP 200 PLACE Estrellita Marina 49160 State Highway 3 Trinity Center CA 530-286-2215
Rent a patio/pontoon boat with your pooch on Lake Trinity. There is a 4 hour minimum for boat rentals and pricing starts at about $75 for 4 hours. This full service marina includes a country store, launch ramp and gas. Well-behaved dogs are allowed on the boats. The marina also rent houseboats and well-behaved dogs are welcome on those too.

Parks

Trinity Lakeshore Trail Highway 3 Trinity Center CA 530-623-2121
This easy to moderate hike follows the western shore of Trinity Lake. The four mile trail runs from Clark Springs Campground to a private resort. There are a few short, steep stretches along the route. The trail offers shade and goes through an old-growth forest. Please stay on the trail when walking through private facilities. The majority of this trail is in the Shasta-Trinity National Forest. The trailhead at the Clark Springs Campground which is located 18 miles north of Weaverville off Highway 3. Pets should be leashed and please clean up after them.

Whiskeytown National Recreation Area P.O. Box 188 Whiskeytown CA 530-246-1225
http://www.nps.gov/whis/
The main highlight of this park is Whiskeytown Lake. Popular activities include swimming, sailing, water-skiing, scuba diving and fishing. The land surrounding the lake offers ample opportunities for hiking, mountain biking

and horseback riding. Dogs are allowed on the trails, in the campgrounds and in the water at non-swim beaches which are beaches without sand. Pets are not allowed on the sandy swimming beaches or inside any buildings. Dogs must be leashed and attended at all times. Please clean up after your pet. This recreation area is located on Highway 299 near Highway 5.

Six Rivers National Forest

Accommodations
Ziegler's Trails End 1 Main St, P.O. Box 150 Hyampom CA 530-628-4929 (800-566-5266)
http://www.zieglerstrailsend.com/
These cabins are on the South Fork of the Trinity River. This is in the middle of the dog-friendly Six Rivers National Forest.

Parks
Ruth Lake Recreation Area Lower Mad River Rd, south of Hwy 36 Mad River CA 800-500-0285
Dogs on leash are allowed on the trails and in the lake. RV and camp sites are available with reservations.

Yreka

Accommodations
Best Western Miner's Inn 122 E Miner St Yreka CA 530-842-4355 (800-780-7234)
Dogs of all sizes are allowed. There is a $10 per night pet fee per pet. Smoking and non-smoking are available for pet rooms.
Comfort Inn 1804 E Fort Jones Road Yreka CA 530-842-1612 (877-424-6423)
One dog of any size is allowed. There is a $20 refundable deposit plus a $10 per night additional pet fee. Dogs may not be left alone in the rooms, and they must be leashed and cleaned up after.
Days Inn 1804 B Fort Jones Rd Yreka CA 530-842-1612 (800-329-7466)
There is a $20 refundable pet deposit.
Motel 6 - Yreka 1785 South Main Street Yreka CA 530-842-4111 (800-466-8356)
One well-behaved family pet per room. Guest must notify front desk upon arrival. Guest is liable for any damages. In consideration of all guests, pets must never be left unattended in the guest rooms.
Relax Inn 1210 S Main Street Yreka CA 530-842-2791
Dogs of all sizes are allowed. There is a $5 per night per pet additional fee.

Campgrounds and RV Parks
Tree of Heaven Campground, Klamath National Forest 1312 Fairlane Road Yreka CA 530-468-5351 (877-444-6777)
This park features great river access, a Birding Nature Trail and various recreation. Dogs of all sizes are allowed. There are no additional pet fees. Dogs must be leashed and cleaned up after. Dogs are allowed on the trails. The camping and tent areas also allow dogs. There is a dog walk area at the campground. There are no electric or water hookups at the campgrounds.

Attractions
TOP 200 PLACE **Blue Goose Steam Excursion Train** 300 East Miner Street Yreka CA 530-842-4146 (800-973-5277)
http://www.yrekawesternrr.com/
The Blue Goose excursion train rides on railroad tracks that were built in 1888. The train travels over Butcher Hill in Yreka and then down through the scenic Shasta Valley with Mt. Shasta in the view. The train then crosses over the Shasta River and continues on to the old cattle town of Montague. The distance is about 7.5 miles one way and takes approximately 1 hour to arrive. Upon arrival in Montague, passengers disembark the train and will have about 1.5 hours for lunch and to explore the historic town of Montague. During lunchtime, the train is pushed back in preparation for the return trip to Yreka. The train returns to pick up passengers about 15 minutes before departure. The total round trip time for this ride is about 3.5 hours. Trains run from Memorial Day Weekend to the end of October on a limited schedule. Well-behaved leashed dogs that are friendly towards people and children are welcome. They ask that you please keep your pooch out of the aisles once on the train.

Parks

Klamath National Forest 1312 Fairlane Road Yreka CA   530-842-6131
http://www.r5.fs.fed.us/klamath
This forest has over 1,700,000 acres of land throughout Siskiyou County in California and Jackson County in Oregon. Dogs should be on leash. Hiking from East Fork Campground provides access to the lakes in the Caribou Basin, Rush Creek, and Little South Fork drainages. The campground is located 27 miles southwest of Callahan next to the East and the South Forks of the Salmon River, at a 2,600 foot elevation. From the Bridge Flat Campground, the historic Kelsey Trail offers excellent opportunities for scenic day hikes or longer trips into the Marble Mountain Wilderness. The campground is located on the Scott River approximately 17 miles from Fort Jones, at a 2,000 foot elevation. For more details, call or visit the Salmon River Ranger District, 11263 N. Highway 3,Fort Jones, (530) 468-5351. The Klamath National Forest offers miles of other hiking trails. For maps and more information on trails throughout this forest, please contact the forest office in Yreka.

Chapter 4

California - Wine Country
Dog Travel Guide

Napa Valley

Accommodations

Calistoga Ranch 580 Lommel Road Calistoga CA   707-254-2800
http://www.calistogaranch.com/
Nestled away in a private canyon, this 157 acre luxury resort is a great getaway with oak tree covered hills, a stream and private lake, and a private restaurant. Some of the amenities include natural spring-fed mineral pools, a heated outdoor pool, miles of hiking trails, 24 hour room service, a variety of indoor and outdoor spaces so visitors get to fully enjoy the surroundings, and much more. Dogs of all sizes are allowed for a $125 one time additional pet fee per room. Dogs must be well behaved, leashed, and cleaned up after.
Hillcrest Country Inn 3225 Lake County Hwy Calistoga CA   707-942-6334
http://www.bnbweb.com/hillcrest
Hillcrest is a country home secluded on a hilltop with a view of vineyards and the Napa Valley. Rooms have fireplaces,balconys, some jacuzzi tubs for 2 and HBO. There is swimming, hiking and fishing on 36 acres. Breakfast is served on weekends. There is an outdoor hot tub and a large cold water pool. Dogs of all sizes are allowed.
Meadowlark Inn 601 Petrified Forest Road Calistoga CA   707-942-5651 (800-942-5651)
http://www.meadowlarkinn.com/
On 20 scenic acres in the heart of wine country is this elegant Inn with gardens, hiking trails, meadows, forests, and horses grazing in pastures. Other features/amenities include a clothing optional mineral pool, hot tub, sauna, in-house massages, well appointed rooms, and a full, gourmet breakfast. Dogs of all sizes are welcome for no additional fee. Dogs must be very well behaved, leashed, and cleaned up after at all times.
Pink Mansion Bed and Breakfast 1415 Foothill Blvd. Calistoga CA   707-942-0558
http://www.pinkmansion.com
This restored 1875 home offers modern amenities for wine country travellers. The Pink Mansion has been featured in The Wine Spectator, Best Places To Kiss and the New York Post. Dogs are allowed in one of their six rooms. Each room has a private bathroom. There is a $30 per day pet charge.
Beazley House Bed & Breakfast Inn 1910 First Street Napa CA   707-257-1649
http://www.beazleyhouse.com
This Bed and Breakfast is located in a residential area in historic downtown Napa. There is a $25 per day per dog charge, with a maximum of 2 dogs.
Daughters Inn 1938 First Street Napa CA   707-253-1331 (866-253-1331)
http://www.daughtersinn.com
This circa 1900 B&B is located in downtown Napa. There is a $25 per day per dog pet fee. Up to two dogs are allowed per room. Your dog will receive a dog basket upon arrival.
Napa River Inn 500 Main Street Napa CA   707-251-8500
http://www.napariverinn.com/
This beautiful inn sits on 2.5 picturesque acres along the Napa River, is on the National Registry of Historic Places, and offer top amenities to visitors and their pets. They participate in a pet VIP program which gives your pooch their own in-house care package too. It includes a blanket, feeding mat with stainless steel bowls, a Cab-Bone-Nay dog biscuit made with real wine, and a supply of doggy clean up bags. Small to medium sized dogs are welcome for an additional $25 per night per pet. Dogs must be well mannered, leashed, and cleaned up after. Dogs may only be left alone in the room if they will be quiet and they are in a kennel.
The Chablis Inn 3360 Solono Ave Napa CA   707-257-1944 (800-443-3490)
http://www.chablisinn.com
There is a 150 pound limit for dogs. There is a $10 per day additional pet fee. All rooms are non-smoking.
The Napa Inn Bed and Breakfast 1137 Warren Street Napa CA   707-257-1444
http://www.napainn.com
Located on a quiet street in historic, downtown Napa, this inn is within an easy walking distance of shops and restaurants. Dogs are allowed in one room, the garden cottage. This private cottage is decorated in French Provincial prints. It has a queen size bed, sofa, fireplace, French doors overlooking a private flower garden, skylight, wet bar with refrigerator and microwave, and an outdoor spa. It sleeps up to four people. There is a $20 per day pet charge.
El Bonita Motel 195 Main Street St Helena CA   707-963-3216 (800-541-3284)
http://www.elbonita.com/
Amenities at this motel include a continental breakfast, pool, whirlpool, sauna, and over two acres of peaceful gardens. Room amenities include microwaves, refrigerators, and more. Room rates start at about $130 per night and up. There is a $5 per day pet charge.
Harvest Inn One Main Street St Helena CA   707-963-9463 (800-950-8466)

http://www.harvestinn.com/
This inn is nestled among 8-acres of award winning landscape. Most guest rooms feature wet bars, unique brick fireplaces and private terraces. Amenities include two outdoor heated pools and whirlpool spas and jogging and bike trails bordering the grounds. Dogs are allowed in the standard rooms. There is a $75 one time pet charge.
Vintage Inn 6541 Washington St. Yountville CA 707-944-1112 (800-351-1133)
http://www.vintageinn.com
This inn is located in the small town of Yountville and is located within walking distance of several dog-friendly restaurants. Amenities at this pet-friendly inn include a continental champagne breakfast, afternoon tea, coffee & cookies, a heated pool, two tennis courts, and award winning gardens. Room amenities include a wood burning fireplace in every room, refrigerator with a chilled welcome bottle of wine, terry robes, nightly turn down service, hair dryer, in room iron & ironing board and more. If you need to leave your room, but can't take your pooch with you, the concierge can arrange for a dog sitter. They also have a list of nearby dog-friendly outdoor restaurants. Room rates start at about $200 per night and up. There is a $30 one time pet charge.
Yountville Inn 6462 Washington Street Yountville CA 707-944-5600
Dogs of all sizes are allowed. There is a $100 one time fee per room and a pet policy to sign at check in.

Campgrounds and RV Parks
Napa County Fairgrounds Campground 1435 Oak Street Calistoga CA 707-942-5111
Located at the fairgrounds, this campground offers 46 RV/tent sites. RV sites are parallel in the parking lot and tent sites are located on an adjacent lawn. RV sites have full hookups (some have sewer). Other amenities include restrooms, showers, potable water and disabled accessible. Dogs are allowed but must be on a 10 foot or less leash. Dogs must be well behaved, and please clean up after your pet. For reservations call 707-942-5221. The camping and tent areas also allow dogs. There is a dog walk area at the campground.
Putah Creek Resort 7600 Knoxville Road Napa CA 707-966-0794
This park of many mini-peninsulas along Lake Berryessa allows for lots of accessible shoreline along with land and water recreation. Dogs of all sizes are allowed for an additional $2 per night per pet. Dogs may only be left unattended on your site if they have secure water and food, will be quiet, and well behaved. Dogs must be leashed at all times and cleaned up after. There are some breed restrictions. The camping and tent areas also allow dogs. There is a dog walk area at the campground.

Vacation Home Rentals
Combining Luxury and Comfort in Napa Valley Email or Call to Arrange Napa CA 707-227-2276
http://www.napahomeawayfromhome.com
This dog-friendly two bedroom home is located minutes from wineries and historic downtown Napa. There is a large fenced yard and covered patio.
Napa Valley Country Cottage Mt Veeder Rd Napa CA 707-226-6621
http://www.napavalleycasa.com
This one bedroom country cottage is located on 12 acres in the heart of Napa Valley wine country. The house has a full kitchen, Living room with Satellite TV,CD player, and a stereo. The property has walking paths, a seasonal creek, and gardens in a wooded setting. The property is fenced and has electric gates. They accept any well behaved pets. Pets are not to be left unattended.

Attractions
Chateau Montelena 1429 Tubbs Lane Calistoga CA 707-942-5105
http://www.montelena.com/
This award winning vineyard offers a variety of wines. Dogs are allowed on the grounds, by the water fountain, and there is a nice walk down to the lake that pooches really seem to like. Dogs are not allowed in the buildings. Dogs must be well mannered, under owner's control, and be leashed and cleaned up after at all times.
Cuvaison Winery 4550 Silverado Trail Calistoga CA 707-942-6266
Well-behaved leashed dogs are allowed in the tasting room and at the outdoor picnic areas.
Dutch Henry Winery 4300 Silverado Trail Calistoga CA 707-942-5771
http://www.dutchhenry.com/
Although a small family-owned and operated winery, they specialize in artisan Bordeaux varietals in very limited releases, and are known for their Napa Valley Estate Cabernet Sauvignon. Your well behaved canine companion is welcome on the grounds and will most likely be greeted by the winery's four-legged companions. There are picnic areas and places for dogs to play; they are not allowed inside the winery. Dogs must be leashed and cleaned up after.
Graeser Winery 255 Petrified Forest Road Calistoga CA 707-942-4437
http://www.graeserwinery.com
Canine visitors to this winery may be met by the resident great dane, Jack. The winery welcomes visiting dogs as long as they are friendly towards other dogs and people. There are picnic tables on the front patio and a table on top of the hill.

Old Faithful Geyser

TOP 200 PLACE **Old Faithful Geyser** 1299 Tubbs Lane Calistoga CA 707-942-6463
http://www.oldfaithfulgeyser.com
Your well-behaved dog is welcome to accompany you to this natural phenomena. Just keep him or her away from the hot water. This geyser is one of only three Old Faithful geysers in the world, erupting about every 40 minutes on a yearly average. The water is 350 degrees hot and shoots about 60 feet into the air for about three to four minutes, then recedes. To see the geyser, you and your pup will need to walk through the main entrance and gift shop. Purchase the tickets at the gift shop and then walk to the geyser area to watch Old Faithful erupt. There is also a snack bar and picnic areas onsite. The admission price is $6 per adult, $5 per senior, $2 per children 6-12 and FREE for dogs. Prices are subject to change.

TOP 200 PLACE **Petrified Forest** 4100 Petrified Forest Rd. Calistoga CA 707-942-6667
http://www.petrifiedforest.org
Geologists call this petrified forest, "one of the finest examples of a pliocene fossil forest in the world." The petrified forest was created from a long ago volcanic eruption, followed by torrential rains which brought giant mudflows of volcanic ash from the eruption site to entomb the felled giants/trees. The 1/2 mile round trip meadow tour shows some of the petrified trees. Your leashed dog is welcome. Admission prices are $5 for adults, less for seniors and children, and FREE for dogs. Prices are subject to change.

Clos Du Val Winery 5330 Silverado Trail Napa CA 800-993-9463
http://www.closduval.com
Dogs on leash are allowed in the tasting room and on the property. The hours are 10am-5pm Monday-Sunday.

Darioush Winery 4240 Silverado Trail Napa CA 707-257-2345
http://www.darioush.com/winery.html
This breathtaking estate is 22,000 square feet, and the first winery in America to merge together architecture, design, and Persian culture reminiscent of the grand buildings of ancient times. The lush, varied landscape is laced with continuous gardens, water fountains, and the visitor center offers a unique tasting experience with indoor or outdoor seating. The winery is noted for its Bordeaux style estate wines. Dogs are allowed at the outdoor tables and around the grounds; they are not allowed inside the winery. Dogs must be well behaved, under owner's control at all times, leashed, and cleaned up after.

Hess Collection Winery 4411 Redwood Road Napa CA 707-255-1144
http://www.hesscollection.com/
This winery specializes in wines that embody the unique distinctive growing factors of Mount Veeder. Dogs are allowed on the grounds and bench areas; they are not allowed in the tasting room. Dogs must be well mannered, and leashed and cleaned up after at all times.

Pine Ridge Winery 5901 Silverado Trail Napa CA 707-252-9777
http://www.pineridgewinery.com/

This winery specializes in wines that embody the unique distinctiveness of the Napa Valley region. Dogs are allowed on the grounds and bench areas; they are not allowed in the tasting room. Dogs must be well mannered, and leashed and cleaned up after at all times.

Frogs Leap Winery 8815 Conn Creek Road Rutherford CA   707-963-4704
http://www.frogsleap.com
Utilizing organically grown grapes and traditional winemaking techniques, this award winning winery strives to produce wines that reflect the unique characteristics of the Napa Valley. Dogs are allowed on the grounds and gardens, but not in buildings. Dogs must be very well mannered, and leashed and cleaned up after.

TOP 200 PLACE Mumm Napa Winery 8445 Silverado Trail Rutherford CA   800-686-6272
http://mummnapa.com/
This winery offers outside table service on their terrace (weather permitting), spectacular views, a knowledgeable staff, an art gallery, annual events, and a gift store. Your well behaved dog is welcome to explore the grounds with you or join you on the terrace. They usually have doggy treats available and are happy to get a bowl of water for your pooch. Dogs must be leashed and cleaned up after at all times.

Sullivan Vineyards 1090 Galleron Rd Rutherford CA   707-963-9646
Well-behaved leashed dogs are allowed in the tasting room and at the picnic table. They have three dogs on the premises.

TOP 200 PLACE Beringer Vineyards 2000 Main Street St Helena CA   707-963-4812
This busy vineyard specializes in offering a large selection of wines for every occasion and every budget, feature daily historic tours and educational seminars, and hold food and wines events often throughout the year. Dogs are welcome around the grounds, at outdoor seating areas, and at the one outside tasting room area; they are not allowed in buildings. Dogs must be well mannered, under owner's control at all times, leashed, and cleaned up after.

Casa Nuestra Winery 3451 Silverado Trail North St Helena CA   866-844-WINE
Dogs are welcome in the picnic area. The winery has five dogs that "work" here as greeters, but they all work different days.

Rustridge 2910 Lower Chiles Valley Rd St Helena CA   707-965-2871
Well-behaved leashed dogs are allowed in the tasting room and in the picnic area. The owner also has four dogs on the premises.

V. Sattui Winery 1111 White Lane St Helena CA   707-963-7774
http://www.vsattui.com/
Established in 1885, this family owned, award-winning winery sits in the heart of the Napa Valley, and their wines can only be purchased by mail order or by a visit to the estate. Also on site are a cheese shop and deli, and 2 1/2 acres of tree-shaded picnic grounds. Dogs are allowed around the grounds and at the picnic area; they may only be in buildings if they are being carried in a carrier. Dogs must be well behaved, under owner's control at all times, leashed, and cleaned up after.

V. Sattui Winery 1111 White Lane St Helena CA   707-963-7774
Dogs are welcome in the picnic area. This winery also has an onsite deli. This winery has lawn picnic benches and a shaded area.

Domain Chandon One California Drive Yountville CA   707-944-2280
http://www.chandon.com/
This secluded winery offers a variety of sparkling wines, regular events, and beautifully landscaped grounds. Dogs are allowed on the grounds and the terrace, but not in buildings. Dogs must be well mannered, and leashed and cleaned up after.

Stores
Petco Pet Store 3284 Jefferson St Napa CA   707-224-7662
Your licensed and well-behaved dog is allowed in the store.
Fideaux 1312 Main Street St Helena CA   707-967-9935
Well-behaved leashed dogs are welcome to accompany you into Fideaux. The store boasts dog specialty items and gifts. It is located in the center of St. Helena.

Off-Leash Dog Parks
Canine Commons Dog Park Alston Park - Dry Creek Road Napa CA   707-257-9529
This fenced 3 acre dog park has water, benches, and pooper scoopers. The dog park is located in Alston Park which has about 100 acres of dog-friendly on-leash trails. Thanks to one of our readers for recommending this park. To get there from Napa, take Hwy 29 North and exit Redwood Rd. Turn left on Redwood Rd and then right on Dry Creek Rd. The park will be on the left.
Shurtleff Park Dog Park Shetler Avenue Napa CA   707-257-9529
This park offers an off-leash exercise area. Dogs must be under voice control at all times. The park is located on Shetler Avenue, east of Shurtleff Avenue.

Outdoor Restaurants

Buster's BBQ 1207 Foothills Blvd Calistoga CA   707-942-5605
This American-style barbecue eatery specializes in slow cooked links, ribs, steaks, and home baked items. They have an outdoor seating area, just go inside to order. Your pet is welcome to join you at the outdoor tables. Dogs must be well behaved, under owner's control, and leashed at all times.

Home Plate Cafe Hwy 128 & Petrified Forest Rd. Calistoga CA   707-942-5646
You and your pup can enjoy hamburgers or chicken sandwiches at this cafe. The restaurant is located near the Old Faithful Geyser.

Angele 540 Main Street Napa CA   707-252-8115
This restaurant serves French/Gourmet food. Dogs are allowed at the outdoor tables. Water and treats are provided for your pet.

Bistro Don Giovanni 4110 Howard Street Napa CA   707-224-3300
http://www.bistrodongiovanni.com/
A traditional wood burning fireplace, romantic outdoor terraces, an Italian and Country French menu influenced by the local region, gardens, and a showpiece water fountain surrounded by manicured lawns, bring a touch of the Tuscan Valley ambiance to this Napa Valley restaurant. Dogs are welcome to explore the grounds and are allowed on the outdoor patio. Dogs must be well mannered, under owner's control at all times, leashed, and cleaned up after.

Boon Fly Cafe 4048 Sonoma Highway Napa CA   707-299-4872
This café serves freshly prepared, modern cuisine that reflects the unique characteristics of the area. They are open for breakfast and lunch with fresh baked items and will also pack lunches to go. There are some benches outside where you and your pet may sit to enjoy your meal; just order inside. There is also another restaurant on the property called the Farm Restaurant with a large outdoor seating area with table service where dogs are also allowed. Dogs must be well mannered, under owner's control at all times, leashed, and cleaned up after.

Napa General Store Restaurant 540 Main Street Napa CA   707-259-0762
http://www.napageneralstore.com/
This store and restaurant offers a unique shopping experience, and great outdoor dining along the Napa River featuring Asian and American cuisine. Your well behaved dog is welcome to join you at the outdoor tables. Dogs must be leashed and under owner's control at all times.

TOP 200 PLACE **The Farm Restaurant** 4048 Sonoma Highway Napa CA   707-299-4900
http://www.thecarnerosinn.com/
Located on the Carneros Resort among the vineyards and orchards, this newly opened eatery offers cuisine that reflects the unique characteristics of the area. They have a large outdoor dining area with table service, and your pet may join you on their patio. Dogs must be well mannered, under owner's control at all times, leashed, and cleaned up after. Another eatery on the property, the Boon Fly Café also offers bench seating outside for visitors with dogs, and to go lunches.

Rutherford Grill 1180 Rutherford Road Rutherford CA   707-963-1792
This is definitely a dog-friendly restaurant. They usually bring out treats for your dog while you dine at the lovely outdoor patio. The food is great. Rutherford is north of Napa, just beyond Oakville and just south of St. Helena. Thanks to one of our readers for recommending this restaurant.

Cindy's Backstreet Kitchen 1327 Railroad Ave St Helena CA   707-963-1200
This restaurant serves American food. Dogs are allowed at the outdoor tables.

Silverado Brewing Company 3020 St Helena Hwy N/Hwy 29 St Helena CA   707-967-9876
http://silveradobrewingcompany.com/
The historic Freemark Abbey Winery building provides a picturesque setting for this unique dining and entertaining experience. In addition to the beers they brew, you might like the home-brewed Root Beer and Cream Soda. There is seasonal outdoor seating. Your pet is welcome to join you at the outdoor tables. Dogs must be well behaved, under owner's control, and leashed at all times.

Tra Vigne Cantinetta 1050 Charter Oak Avenue St Helena CA   707-963-4444
This Italian wine bar features more than 50 wines by the glass and is known for having wines for retail sale that are considered impossible to find. The Italian fare can be paired with its compliment wine, and they offer outdoor courtyard seating. Just order inside, and they will bring your order to you. Dogs must be well mannered, under owner's control at all times, leashed, and cleaned up after. There is also a pizzeria on site that has outdoor seating for visitors with dogs.

Bouchon 6534 Washington Street Yountville CA   707-944-8037
This eatery offers excellent French bistro cuisine in a Parisian atmosphere. They are open late nights, and offer a full bar and bar dining, an outdoor patio with service, great views, and a wide variety of wines. Your pet is welcome to join you at the outdoor tables. Dogs must be well behaved, under owner's control, and leashed at all times. They prefer only one dog on the patio at a time, so they ask that you call ahead and make reservations.

Compadres Mexican Grill 6539 Washington St. Yountville CA   707-944-2406
This restaurant has an enjoyable outdoor patio with heaters and shade umbrellas.

Hurley's Restaurant 6518 Washington Street Yountville CA   707-944-2345
http://www.hurleysrestaurant.com/
Serving fresh seasonal wine country cuisine with a Mediterranean flair, this eatery is also popular for their "wild

game" dishes and wonderful wine and food pairings. They feature a full bar with a large open patio for outside dining, weather permitting, and they also host several fun events through the year. Your pet is welcome to join you at the outdoor tables. Dogs must be well behaved, under owner's control, and leashed at all times.

Napa Valley Grille 6795 Washington Street Yountville CA 707-944-8686

This popular eatery offers a seasonally changing menu of refined American wine country cuisine, patio dining with vineyard views, an extensive wine collection, and an exhibition kitchen. Your pet is welcome to join you on the patio. Dogs must be well behaved, under owner's control, and leashed at all times.

PJ Steak and Seafood 6725 Washington Street Yountville CA 707-945-1000

http://www.pjsteak.com/

This steak and seafood eatery pairs fine American cuisine and wines with flavors reminiscent of Southern France. They have a beautiful outdoor seating area with service and outdoor heaters. You and your pet are welcome at the outdoor tables. Dogs must be well behaved, under owner's control, and leashed at all times.

Pacific Blues Cafe 6525 Washington Street Yountville CA 707-994-4455

Serving a full flavored menu of American favorites with some regional influences, they are open from 8:30 am until 10 pm daily. They have a beautiful outdoor seating area with service. Your pet is welcome to join you at the outdoor tables. Dogs must be well behaved, under owner's control, and leashed at all times.

Sonoma

Accommodations

Creekside Inn & Resort 16180 Neeley Rd Guerneville CA 707-869-3623

http://www.creeksideinn.com

Dogs are allowed in one of their cottages. During the summer it books up fast, so please make an early reservation. The inn will be able to help you find some pet-friendly hiking trails and beaches nearby.

Ferngrove Cottages 16650 Hwy 116 Guerneville CA 707-869-8105

This charming retreat offers cottages nestled among redwoods and colorful gardens. Some of the amenities include spa tubs, fireplaces and skylights, a delicious extended continental breakfast, pool and sun deck, a barbecue and picnic area, individual decks or patios, and it is only a short walk to the river/beaches and town. Dogs of all sizes are allowed. There is a $15 per night per pet additional fee. Dogs may not be left alone in the room, and they must be well behaved, leashed, and cleaned up after. Pit Bulls are not allowed.

River Village Resort and Spa 14880 River Road Guerneville CA 888-342-2624

http://www.rivervillageresort.com

This inn is located just minutes from the Russian River. At this inn, dogs are allowed in certain cottages and there is a $10 per day pet fee. Please do not walk pets on the lawn. Children are also welcome.

Best Western Dry Creek Inn 198 Dry Creek Rd Healdsburg CA 707-433-0300 (800-780-7234)

Dogs of all sizes are allowed. There is a $20 per night pet fee per pet. Smoking and non-smoking are available for pet rooms.

Duchamp Hotel 421 Foss Street Healdsburg CA 707-431-1300

http://www.duchamphotel.com

This hotel, located in Healdsburg, allows dogs in two of their cottages. Every cottage features a king bed, oversized spa shower, private terrace, fireplace, mini bar, and more. Children over 16 years old are allowed. The entire premises is non-smoking. Dogs are not allowed in the pool area and they request that you take your dog away from the cottages and hotel when they go to the bathroom.

Birmingham Bed and Breakfast 8790 Hwy 12 Kenwood CA 707-833-6996 (800-819-1388)

http://www.birminghambb.com/

This beautiful 1915 inn is now a Historic Landmark and allows guests a visit to an elegant past; whether it's a stroll through the 2 acres of trees, berry patches, and gardens, or just resting on the big wrap around porch enjoying the amazing view. There is one pet friendly cottage that was built onto the original water tower, and is spacious with many features and amenities, including a fenced-in back yard. Dogs of all sizes are welcome for an additional fee of $10 per night per pet and a pet policy to sign at check in. Since there is a dog that lives on site, they ask that guests check in before removing pets from their car. Dogs may not be left alone in the cottage, and they must be friendly, well behaved, and leashed and cleaned up after at all times.

Grandma's House Bed and Breakfast 20280 River Blvd Monte Rio CA 707-865-1865

This dog-friendly bed and breakfast inn is located on the Russian River. The inn offers three rooms, all with private bathrooms. Each room also includes a private phone line, TV and VCR, refrigerator, microwave, and more. One of the rooms is handicapped accessible. Clean, well-behaved dogs may accompany their owners, with advance notice, for $10 per dog per day. There is a $75 damage and cleaning deposit, refundable (if not needed) at departure. Owners are expected to clean up behind their dog on the grounds. Pooper-scooper bags are available for this purpose. Dogs must not be left unattended in the room for long periods. Owners are responsible for not letting their dog disturb other guests and making sure their dog is not destructive to the property.

Inn at Occidental 3657 Church Street Occidental CA 707-874-1047 (800-522-6324)

http://www.innatoccidental.com/
Set among towering redwoods, this completely restored Victorian inn offers world class comfort and elegance in a country setting. Some of the amenities/features include a welcoming veranda, antiques, a complimentary Sonoma-harvest gourmet breakfast, an afternoon hors d'oeuvre and wine reception, private baths, fireplaces, and spa tubs. They offer a spacious cottage for guests with pets. Dogs of all sizes are allowed for an additional $25 per night per pet. Dogs must be kenneled when left unattended in the cottage, and they must be well behaved, leashed, and cleaned up after. Dogs are not allowed on the furnishings.
Occidental Hotel 3610 Bohemian Hwy Occidental CA   707-874-3623
There is an $8.70 per day pet fee for each pet. Dogs must be on leash and may not be left alone in the rooms.
Doubletree One Doubletree Drive Rohnert Park CA   707-584-5466
There is a fee of $15 per night per pet if the dogs are under 50 pounds, and you can have up to three dogs. The fee is $25 per night per pet if the dogs are over 50 pounds, and you can have up to two dogs.
Motel 6 - Rohnert Park 6145 Commerce Boulevard Rohnert Park CA   707-585-8888 (800-466-8356)
One well-behaved family pet per room. Guest must notify front desk upon arrival. Guest is liable for any damages. In consideration of all guests, pets must never be left unattended in the guest rooms.
Best Western Garden Inn - Santa Rosa 1500 Santa Rosa Avenue Santa Rosa CA   707-546-4031 (800-780-7234)
http://www.thegardeninn.com
Dogs up to 50 pounds are allowed at this hotel in the heart of the Sonoma Valley wine region. A maximum of two dogs per room are allowed with a $15 per night pet fee.
Days Inn 3345 Santa Rosa Ave Santa Rosa CA   707-568-1011 (800-329-7466)
There is a $10 per day additional pet fee.
Holiday Inn Express 870 Hopper Ave Santa Rosa CA   707-545-9000 (877-270-6405)
Dogs of any size are allowed. There is a $20 one time pet fee. There are a few pet rooms in the hotel, some of which are non-smoking.
Los Robles Lodge 1985 Cleveland Ave Santa Rosa CA   707-545-6330 (800-255-6330)
http://www.bluejaylodge.com/page7.html
Dogs are allowed, but not in the poolside rooms or executive suites. There is a $10 per day pet charge.
Motel 6 - Santa Rosa North 3145 Cleveland Avenue Santa Rosa CA   707-525-9010 (800-466-8356)
One well-behaved family pet per room. Guest must notify front desk upon arrival. Guest is liable for any damages. In consideration of all guests, pets must never be left unattended in the guest rooms.
Motel 6 - Santa Rosa South 2760 Cleveland Avenue Santa Rosa CA   707-546-1500 (800-466-8356)
One well-behaved family pet per room. Guest must notify front desk upon arrival. Guest is liable for any damages. In consideration of all guests, pets must never be left unattended in the guest rooms.
Santa Rosa Motor Inn 1800 Santa Rosa Ave Santa Rosa CA   707-523-3480
There is a $10 per day pet fee and a refundable pet deposit.
The Days Inn 3345 Santa Rosa Avenue Santa Rosa CA   707-545-6330 (800-329-7466)
This inn offers a complimentary breakfast and swimming pool in addition to other amenities. Dogs of all sizes are allowed for a $25 per night per pet additional fee. Dogs must be quiet and removed or crated for housekeeping. Dogs must be leashed and cleaned up after.
Best Western Sonoma Valley Inn 550 2nd St W Sonoma CA   707-938-9200 (800-780-7234)
Dogs of all sizes are allowed. There is a $30 one time pet fee per visit and $15 extra for a 2nd pet. Only non-smoking rooms used for pets.
Renaissance Lodge at Sonoma 1325 Broadway Sonoma CA   707-935-6600
Dogs of all sizes are allowed. There is a $75 one time fee per room and a pet policy to sign at check in.

Campgrounds and RV Parks
Cloverdale KOA 1166 Asti Ridge Road Cloverdale CA   707-894-3337 (800-562-4042)
http://www.koa.com/where/ca/05275/
This park is nestled among 100-year-old oak, eucalyptus and evergreen trees, and some of the amenities include a hillside pool and spa, nature trail, pond, gymnastics playground, and various land and water recreation. Dogs of all sizes are allowed for no additional fee. Dogs must be under owner's control and visual observation at all times. Dogs must be quiet, well behaved, and be on no more than a 6 foot leash at all times, or otherwise contained. Dogs may not be left unattended outside the owner's camping equipment. There are some breed restrictions. The camping and tent areas also allow dogs. There is a dog walk area at the campground. Dogs are allowed in the camping cabins.
Casini Ranch Family Campground 22855 Moscow Road Duncans Mills CA   707-865-2255 (800-451-8400)
http://www.casiniranch.com
This beautiful family campground lies along the Russian River, offers great scenery, fishing, trails, and a variety of recreation. Dogs of all sizes are allowed for an additional $1 per night per pet. Dogs may not be left unattended, and they must be quiet, leashed at all times, and cleaned up after. Dogs must be inside at night, and they are not allowed in the livestock areas. Dogs are allowed on the trails on lead. The camping and tent areas also allow dogs. There is a dog walk area at the campground.
Dawn Ranch Lodge 16467 Hwy 116 Guerneville CA   707-869-0656

http://www.fifes.com/
Located on 15 acres and among redwood trees, this guest ranch offers individual cabins, cottages and tent camping. Amenities include a pool, volleyball court, gym and onsite massages. Well-behaved dogs of all sizes are allowed in the campsites, cabins, and cottages for an additional fee of $50 per stay. Dogs are allowed on the trails nearby and on the beach. This campground is closed during the off-season. There is a dog walk area at the campground.
Spring Lake Regional Park Campgrounds 5585 Newanga Avenue Santa Rosa CA 707-785-2377
This 320 acre regional park with a 72 acre lake, offers 27 campsites and miles of easy walking trails. RVs are permitted and there is a dump station. Dogs are allowed at an additional $1 per night per pet. They must be on a 6 foot or less leash and proof of a rabies vaccination is required. Dogs are not allowed around the swimming lagoon area. For reservations call 707-565-CAMP(2267). To get to the campground, take Hoen Avenue east, cross Summerfield Road, left at the stop sign (Newanga Avenue) into park. This campground is closed during the off-season. The camping and tent areas also allow dogs. There is a dog walk area at the campground. There are no electric or water hookups at the campgrounds.

Vacation Home Rentals
Russian River Getaways 14075 Mill Street, P.O. Box 1673 Guerneville CA 707-869-4560 (800-433-6673)
http://www.rrgetaways.com/
This company offers about 40 dog-friendly vacation homes in Russian River wine country with leash free beaches nearby. There are no pet fees and no size limits for dogs. There is a $75 refundable pet deposit.
Baywood Gardens Inn 6952 Giovanetti Rd. Healdsburg CA 707-887-1400
A vacation rental located in a quiet valley in Sonoma wine country. Various size dog beds and dog dishes are available.

Attractions
TOP 200 PLACE **Sebastiani Vineyards and Winery** 389 Fourth Street East Sonoma CA 800-888-5532
http://www.sebastiani.com/home.asp
Dogs of all sizes are welcome to explore the vineyard and enjoy the picnic area with their owners. Small dogs that can be carried are allowed in the tasting room. They provide water bowls outside all the time, and anchored leash extensions. They are open daily from 10 am to 5 pm. Dogs must be well behaved, leashed at all times, and please clean up after your pet.
Topolos Vineyards 5700 Gravenstein Hwy N. Forestville CA 707-887-1575
http://www.topolos.com/
Dogs are allowed in the tasting room. The tasting room is open 11 am to 5:30 pm daily.
Arrowood Vineyards and Winery 14347 Sonoma H Glen Ellen CA 707-935-2600
http://www.arrowoodvineyards.com/
This picturesque winery features a good variety of wines using grapes grown exclusively from Sonoma County. They have a nice tasting room that opens into a wrap-around veranda that overlooks the vineyards and vistas beyond. Dogs are welcome on the veranda and around the grounds. Dogs must be well behaved, leashed, and cleaned up after.
Benziger Family Winery 1883 London Ranch Road Glen Ellen CA 707-935-3000
http://www.benziger.com/
This 85 acre winery specializes in organic and Biodynamic winegrowing practices producing wines with an accent on more flavor, intensity, and site-specific vineyard traits. A deck with tables and chairs allows a nice area to rest. Dogs are welcome on the grounds and on the deck. Dogs must be well mannered, leashed, and cleaned up after. They are not allowed in the tasting room.
Jack London State Historic Park 2400 London Ranch Road Glen Ellen CA 707-938-5216
This park is a memorial to adventurer/writer Jack London, and is home to various personal artifacts and the cottage residence where he lived and tended various agriculture projects while producing a variety of famous writings. They offer a variety of trails, exhibits, programs, and tours. There are two first come first served picnic areas and one group picnic area. Dogs are allowed at the picnic areas, and on the trails to the Wolf House ruins and Beauty Ranch as far as the silos. Dogs must be under owner's control at all times, and leashed and cleaned up after.
F. Korbel and Brothers Champagne Cellars 13250 River Road Guerneville CA 707-824-7000
Well-behaved leashed dogs are allowed at the outdoor picnic area.
Dry Creek Vineyard 3770 Lambert Bridge Road Healdsburg CA 707-433-1000
http://www.drycreekvineyard.com/
This award winning vineyard produces an impressive list of wines using the "small batch" method, and they are known for producing some of California's best Fume Blancs and Zinfandels. There are benches outside for visitors to sit and enjoy the lush surroundings of the vineyard. Dogs are welcome on the grounds; they must be well behaved, leashed, and cleaned up after. Dogs are not allowed in the tasting room.
Foppiano Vineyards 12707 Old Redwood Highway Healdsburg CA 707-433-7272
http://www.lfoppiano.com.

Dogs are allowed at the picnic area and on the self-guided vineyard tour.
Lambert Bridge Winery 4085 W. Dry Creek Rd Healdsburg CA 800-975-0555
http://www.lambertbridge.com/
Dogs are allowed in the wine tasting room and the large picnic grounds. The winery is open daily from 10:30 am to 4:30 pm.

TOP 200 PLACE Mutt Lynch Winery 1960 Dry Creek Road Healdsburg CA 707-942-6180
http://www.muttlynchwinery.com/
This small one woman winery is usually open only by appointment. However, by combining humor, a love of dogs and passion for wine, this winery offers such items as the "Big Dog" wines, or their Merlot Over and Play Dead, and their annual Dog Days of Summer festival is a fun event for pet and owner with a dog art exhibit, good food, and music. They also have other related events. Dogs are welcome throughout the winery, and they must be leashed at all times and cleaned up after.

Quivira Vineyards 4900 W Dry Creek Road Healdsburg CA 707-431-8333
http://www.quivirawine.com/
This small, family owned winery believes in crafting wines that capture and accentuate the delicious, lively fruit flavors that is characteristic of their wines, and they were recently certified for using Biodynamic agricultural growing methods. There are benches for those wanting to sit outside and picnic tables. Dogs are allowed on the grounds and the picnic area; they are not allowed in the tasting room. Dogs must be well mannered, leashed, and cleaned up after.

Rodney Strong Vineyards 11455 Old Redwood H Healdsburg CA 707-433-6511
http://www.rodneystrong.com/
This award winning winery is committed to crafting exceptional wines sourced from 12 unique vineyards and four of Sonoma County's distinct growing appellations. There is a lawn and picnic area for visitors to enjoy that is surrounded by acres of beautiful vineyards. Dogs must be well behaved, leashed, and cleaned up after. Dogs are allowed on the lawn and at the picnic area, but they are not allowed in buildings.

TOP 200 PLACE Russian River Adventures Canoe Rentals 20 Healdsburg Ave Healdsburg CA 707-433-5599 (800-280-7627 (SOAR))
Take a self-guided eco-adventure with your pooch. Rent an inflatable canoe and adventure along the Russian River. The SOAR 16 is the largest model and is great for taking children and dogs. There are many refreshing swimming holes along the way. Dogs and families of all ages are welcome. Be sure to call ahead as reservations are required.

Deloach Vineyards 1791 Olivet Road Santa Rosa CA 707-526-9111
http://www.deloachvineyards.com.
Dogs are allowed at the picnic area.

Hanna Winery 5353 Occidental Road Santa Rosa CA 707-575-3371
Well-behaved, leashed dogs are allowed in the tasting room and in the picnic area.

Martini and Prati Wines 2191 Laguna Road Santa Rosa CA 707-823-2404
Well-behaved, leashed dogs area allowed at the picnic area.

Matanzas Creek Winery 6097 Bennet Valley Road Santa Rosa CA 707-528-6464
http://www.matanzascreek.com/
This scenic winery is dedicated to offering exceptionally crafted wines sourced from Sonoma County's finest vineyards. They also offer gardens carefully planned and planted to attractively appear as part of the native landscape, a picnic area, and a deck with benches. Well behaved dogs are allowed. Dogs must be leashed and cleaned up after at all times. Dogs are not allowed in the tasting room.

TOP 200 PLACE Pacific Coast Air Museum 2330 Airport Blvd Santa Rosa CA 707-575-7900
http://pacificcoastairmuseum.org/
Well-behaved, leashed dogs are allowed in the museum. The museum offers both indoor and outdoor exhibits.

Taft Street Winery 2030 Barlow Lane Sebastopol CA 707-823-2404
Dogs are allowed on the picnic deck.

Sebastiani Vineyards and Winery 389 Fourth Street East Sonoma CA 800-888-5532
http://www.sebastiani.com
Well-behaved dogs are allowed on and off leash at the outdoor tables and property. Water bowls and cleanup stations are provided. They ask that dogs stay out of the fountain. This is a very dog friendly winery.

Martinell Vineyards 3360 River Road Windsor CA 707-525-0570
Dogs are allowed at the picnic area.

Stores

PetSmart Pet Store 575 Rohnert Park Expry. Rohnert Park CA 707-586-1891
Your licensed and well-behaved leashed dog is allowed in the store.
Petco Pet Store 2765 Santa Rosa Avenue Santa Rosa CA 707-566-7900
Your licensed and well-behaved leashed dog is allowed in the store.
Three Dog Bakery 526 Broadway Sonoma CA 707-933-9780
http://www.threedog.com

Three Dog Bakery provides cookies and snacks for your dog as well as some boutique items. You well-behaved, leashed dog is welcome.

Beaches

Cloverdale River Park 31820 McCray Road Cloverdale CA 707-565-2041
This park is located along the Russian River and offers seasonal fishing and river access for kayaks and canoes. There are no lifeguards at the beach area. Dogs are allowed, but must be on a 6 foot or less leash. They can wade into the water, but cannot really swim because pets must remain on leash. There is a $3 per car parking fee.

Healdsburg Memorial Beach 13839 Old Redwood Highway Healdsburg CA 707-565-2041
This man-made swimming beach is located on the Russian River. Dogs are allowed at this park, but must be on a 6 foot or less leash. They can wade into the water, but cannot really swim because pets must remain on leash. People are urged to swim only when lifeguards are present, which is usually between Memorial Day and Labor Day. The beach area also offers picnic tables and a restroom. There is a $3 to $4 parking fee per day, depending on the season.

Sea Ranch Coastal Access Trails Highway 1 Sea Ranch CA 707-785-2377
Walk along coastal headlands or the beach in Sea Ranch. There are six trailhead parking areas which are located along Highway 1, south of the Sonoma Mendocino County Line. Access points include Black Point, Bluff Top Trail, Pebble Beach, Stengal Beach, Shell Beach and Walk on Beach. Dogs must be on a 6 foot or less leash. There is a $3 per car parking fee. RVs and vehicles with trailers are not allowed to use the parking areas.

Parks

Jack London State Historic Park 2400 London Ranch Road Glen Ellen CA 707-938-5216
This park is a memorial to the famous writer and adventurer Jack London. He lived here from 1905 until his death in 1916. Dogs on leash are allowed around the ranch and historic buildings, but not inside. Pets are also allowed on the Wolf House Trail which is a 1.2 mile round trip trail. Please clean up after your pet. The park is located about 20 minutes north of Sonoma.

Sonoma Valley Regional Park 13630 Sonoma Highway Glen Ellen CA 707-565-2041
This 162 acre park offers both paved and dirt trails which are used for hiking, bicycling and horseback riding. Dogs are allowed but must be on a 6 foot or less leash. The Elizabeth Anne Perrone Dog Park is also located within this park and allows dogs to run leash-free within the one acre. There is a $3 parking fee.

Crane Creek Regional Park 5000 Pressley Road Rohnert Park CA 707-565-2041
http://www.sonoma-county.org/parks
Located just east of Sonoma State University, this 128 acre foothills park offers hiking and bicycling trails. There are picnic tables and restrooms at the trailhead. Dogs must be kept on a 6 foot or less leash. There is a $3 per car parking fee.

Hood Mountain Regional Park 3000 Los Alamos Road Santa Rosa CA 707-565-2041
This 1,450 acre wilderness park offers bicycling, equestrian and rugged hiking trails for experienced hikers in good physical condition. Dogs are allowed at this park, but must be on a 6 foot or less leash. Access to the park is on Los Alamos Road which is a very narrow and winding road. There is a $3 per car parking fee.

Spring Lake Regional Park 391 Violetti Drive Santa Rosa CA 707-785-2377
This 320 acre park with a 72 acre lake offers miles of easy walking trails and a campground. Dogs are allowed but must be on a 6 foot or less leash and proof of a rabies vaccination is required.

Joe Rodota Trail Petaluma Avenue Sebastopol CA 707-565-2041
This is a 2.8 mile paved trail that runs parallel to an abandoned railway line. There are agricultural ranches and farms along the trail. Dogs are allowed, but must be on a 6 foot or less leash. Parking is available in the town of Sebastopol, at the trailhead located off of Petaluma Avenue.

Ragle Ranch Regional Park 500 Ragle Road Sebastopol CA 707-565-2041
This 157 acre park offers walking trails, sports courts, picnic areas and a children's playground. Dogs are allowed, but must be on a 6 foot or less leash. There is a $3 per car parking fee.

Maxwell Farms Regional Park 100 Verano Avenue Sonoma CA 707-565-2041
This 85 acre park offers meadow nature trails on 40 acres, multi-use fields for soccer and softball, a children's playground and picnic areas. Dogs are allowed but must be on a 6 foot or less leash. There is a $3 parking fee.

Foothill Regional Park 1351 Arata Lane Windsor CA 707-565-2041
Hiking, bicycling, horseback riding and fishing are popular activities at this 211 acre park. Dogs must be kept on a 6 foot or less leash. No swimming, wading or boating is allowed on the lakes. There is a $3 per car parking fee.

Off-Leash Dog Parks

Elizabeth Anne Perrone Dog Park 13630 Sonoma Highway Glen Ellen CA 707-565-2041
This one acre fenced dog run is located in the dog-friendly Sonoma Valley Regional Park. The dog park has a doggie drinking fountain, and a gazebo which provides shade for both people and dogs.

Dog Park-Deturk Park 819 Donahue Street Santa Rosa CA 707-543-3292
http://ci.santa-rosa.ca.us

This dog park is fully fenced.
Dolye Community Park Dog Park 700 Doyle Park Drive Santa Rosa CA 707-543-3292
http://ci.santa-rosa.ca.us
This dog park is fully fenced.
Galvin Community Park Dog Park 3330 Yulupa Avenue Santa Rosa CA 707-543-3292
http://ci.santa-rosa.ca.us
This dog park is fully fenced.
Northwest Community Dog Park 2620 W. Steele Lane Santa Rosa CA 707-543-3292
Thanks to one of our readers who writes "Wonderful dog park. 2 separately fenced areas (one for little dogs too... It's all grassy and some trees and right near the creek. Also a brand new childrens play area (one for big kids and one fenced for toddlers). This dog park is sponsored by the Peanut's comics creator Charles M. Schultz's estate."
Rincon Valley Community Park Dog Park 5108 Badger Road Santa Rosa CA 707-543-3292
http://ci.santa-rosa.ca.us
This dog park is fully fenced.

Outdoor Restaurants
Jalos Taqueria 7600 Commerce Blvd Cotati CA 707-795-7600
This restaurant serves Mexican food. Dogs are allowed at the outdoor tables.
Redwood Cafe 8240 Old Redwood Highway Cotati CA 707-795-7868
This restaurant serves American food. Dogs are allowed at the outdoor tables.
Cape Fear Cafe 25191 Main Street/Hwy 116 Duncans Mills CA 707-865-9246
Fine dining with a Cajun flair is featured here. They offer weekend brunches, and lunch and dinners (closed daily from 2:30 to 5 pm). Service is available at their outdoor seating where your pet is welcome to join you. Dogs must be attended to at all times, friendly, and leashed.
Russian River Pub 11829 River Road Forestville CA 707-887-7932
http://russianriverpub.com/default.aspx
This family style pub has new owners but still serve their famous chicken wings and the Ultimate Pub Burger. They provide service at their outdoor patio where your pet is welcome to join you. Dogs must be friendly, attended to at all times, and leashed.
Garden Court Cafe & Bakery 13875 Sonoma Highway 12 Glen Ellen CA 707-935-1565
http://www.gardencourtcafe.com/
Well-behaved dogs may accompany owners on the enclosed patio. They have a special dog menu as well. The outdoor patio is only open on the weekends. Its hours are 7:30 am to 2 pm.
Charizma Wine Lounge & Deli 16337 Main Street/Hwy 116 Guerneville CA 707-869-0909
http://www.charizmawinelounge.com/
This restaurant has placed a few tables and chairs on the sidewalk out front so that your four legged companion can be with you. They are open Monday, Tuesday, Thursday, and Friday from 10 a.m. to 9 p.m.; Wednesday from 10 a.m. to 3 p.m., and Saturday and Sunday from 8 a.m. to 9 p.m. Dogs must be well behaved, leashed, and cleaned up after quickly.
Korbel Deli & Market 13250 River Road Guerneville CA 707-824-7313
Well-behaved leashed dogs are allowed at the outdoor seating area.
Main Street Station Ristorante, Cabaret & Pizzeria, 16280 Main Street Guerneville CA 707-869-0501
http://www.mainststation.com/
This restaurant offers fun and food with an Italian flair. Your pet is welcome to sit with you at the outdoor tables. They must be attended to at all times, well behaved, and leashed.
Roadhouse Restaurant at Dawn Ranch Lodge 16467 River Road Guerneville CA 707-869-0656
This restaurant offers a variety of wines from the Russian River area, a full bar and contemporary California cuisine. They offer outside dining on their deck, and your pet is welcome to join you. Dogs must be attended to at all times, well behaved, and leashed.
Triple R Bar and Grill, Russian River Resort 16390 4th Street Guerneville CA 707-869-0691
This bar and grill serves dinner and weekend brunch with a reasonably-priced menu of American favorites. Service is offered at outdoor table seating where your pet is welcome to join you. Dogs must be attended to at all times, well behaved, and leashed.
Dry Creek General Store 3495 Dry Creek Rd Healdsburg CA 707-433-4171
http://www.dcgstore.com/
Enjoy a breakfast sandwich or a variety of sandwiches for lunch including turkey, roast beef, ham and veggie. Dogs are welcome at the outdoor tables.
Giorgio's Pizzeria 25 Grant Avenue Healdsburg CA 707-433-1106
Dogs are allowed at the outdoor tables. The outdoor tables are on a covered deck.
Union Hotel Restaurant 3731 Main Street Occidental CA 707-874-3444
This restaurant specializes in fine Italian food and homemade pizzas, and they offer a beautiful garden patio for those who would like outdoor dining. Dogs are allowed to join you on the patio. They must be attended to at all times, well behaved, and leashed.

Baja Fresh Mexican Grill 451 Rohnert Pk. Expressway West Rohnert Park CA 707-585-2252
http://www.bajafresh.com
This Mexican restaurant is open for lunch and dinner. They use fresh ingredients and making their salsa and beans daily. Some of the items on their menu include Enchiladas, Burritos, Tacos Salads, Quesadillas, Nachos, Chicken, Steak and more. Well-behaved leashed dogs are allowed at the outdoor tables.
Golden B Cafe 101 Golf Course Drive Rohnert Park CA 707-585-6185
Dogs are allowed at the outdoor tables.
Chevy's Fresh Mex 24 4th Street Santa Rosa CA 707-571-1082
Dogs are allowed at the outdoor seats. The restaurant is in Railroad Square, next to the train station.
Flying Goat Coffee 10 4th Street Santa Rosa CA 707-575-1202
Dogs are allowed at the outdoor seats. The coffee shop is in Railroad Square in Santa Rosa, next to the train station.
Sonoma Valley Bagel 2194 Santa Rosa Ave Santa Rosa CA 707-579-5484
Dogs are allowed at the outdoor tables, which are covered.
Whole Foods Market 1181 Yulupa Ave. Santa Rosa CA 707-575-7915
http://www.wholefoods.com/
This natural food supermarket offers natural and organic foods. Order some food from their deli without your dog and bring it to an outdoor table where your well-behaved leashed dog is welcome. Dogs are not allowed in the store including the deli at any time.
Animal House Cafe 171 Pleasant Hill Ave Sebastopol CA 707-823-1800
This cafe serves deli-type food and coffee. Dogs are allowed at the outdoor tables. Water and treats are provided for your pet.
Pasta Bella 796 Gravenstein Highway Sebastopol CA 707-824-8191
This Italian restaurant is open daily for lunch and dinner, and serves brunch on Sundays. Well-behaved leashed dogs are allowed at the outdoor tables. Thanks to one of our readers for recommending this dog-friendly restaurant!
Stella's Cafe 4550 Gravenstein Hwy S Sebastopol CA 707-823-6637
http://www.stellascafe.net/
Although located in a rural country setting, your dining experience is a blending of flavors from Asia, the Middle East, New Orleans, and Europe with local and Sonoma County wines. They offer service on the veranda and your pet is welcome to join you. Dogs must be attended to at all times, well behaved, and leashed.
Whole Foods Market 6910 McKinley St. Sebastopol CA 707-829-9801
http://www.wholefoods.com/
This natural food supermarket offers natural and organic foods. Order some food from their deli without your dog and bring it to an outdoor table where your well-behaved leashed dog is welcome. Dogs are not allowed in the store including the deli at any time.
Harmony Club 480 First Street East Sonoma CA 707-996-9779
http://www.ledsonhotel.com/dining.html
This gourmet restaurant and wine bar is located at the elegant Ledson Hotel, and feature a seasonally changing lunch and dinner menu. You can dine at their outside sidewalk tables where they offer service, a heated patio, and live music drifting from the inside. Your friendly dog is welcome to join you on the patio. Dogs must be well mannered, under owner's control at all times, leashed, and cleaned up after.
La Casa 121 E Spain Street Sonoma CA 707-996-3406
http://www.lacasarestaurant.com/
This Mexican restaurant offers a generous made-from-scratch menu with traditional favorites and regional specialties, and a full bar. Well behaved dogs are welcome at the bar patio, and table service is offered. Dogs must be under owner's control at all times and be leashed.

Sonoma Coast

Accommodations

Jenner Inn 10400 Hwy 1 Jenner CA 707-865-2377
http://www.jennerinn.com/index.html
Located where the Russian River meets the Pacific Ocean, this unique resort features rooms, suites, and cottages set in historic houses and cottages with something to fit everyone's budget. A full country breakfast is included, and cafe dining is also available. Dogs of all sizes are allowed for a $35 one time additional fee per pet. They have only four pet friendly rooms, and dogs may not be left alone in the room at any time. Dogs must be well behaved, leashed, and cleaned up after.

Campgrounds and RV Parks

Salt Point State Park 2050 Hwy 1 Jenner CA 707-847-3221
Enjoy panoramic views and the dramatic sounds of the surf at this park that offers a variety of sights and recreational activities. This park is also home to one of the first underwater parks in California. Dogs of all sizes are allowed at the campgrounds and in any of the developed areas. Dogs are not allowed on the trails or on the beaches, and they must be inside at night. There is no additional pet fee. Dogs must be leashed and cleaned up after at all times. Campsites are all equipped with a fire ring, picnic tables, and a food locker except for the overflow camping area. There is drinking water and restrooms, but there are no showers or a dump station. The camping and tent areas also allow dogs. There is a dog walk area at the campground. There are no electric or water hookups at the campgrounds.

Stillwater Cove Regional Park Campgrounds 22455 Hwy 1 Jenner CA 707-847-3245
This 210 acre park offers 17 campsites. RVs are permitted and there is a dump station. The park also features a small beach, great views of the Pacific Ocean, picnic tables and restrooms. Dogs are allowed but must be on a 6 foot or less leash and proof of a rabies vaccination is required. There is an additional fee of $1 per night per pet. Please clean up after your pet. The camping and tent areas also allow dogs. There is a dog walk area at the campground. There are no electric or water hookups at the campgrounds.

Beaches

Stillwater Cove Regional Park 22455 Highway 1 Jenner CA 707-565-2041
This 210 acre park includes a small beach, campground, picnic tables, and restrooms. The park offers a great view of the Pacific Ocean from Stillwater Cove. Dogs are allowed on the beach, and in the campground, but they must be on a 6 foot or less leash. People also need to clean up after their pets. There is a $3 day use fee. The park is located off Highway 1, about 16 miles north of Jenner.

Sonoma Coast State Beach Highway 1 Salmon Creek CA 707-875-3483
Dogs on leash are allowed at some of the beaches in this state park. Dogs are allowed at Shell Beach, Portuguese Beach and Schoolhouse Beach. They are not allowed at Goat Rock or Salmon Creek Beach due to the protected seals and snowy plovers. Please clean up after your pets. While dogs are allowed on some of the beaches and campgrounds, they are not allowed on any hiking trails at this park.

Parks

Salt Point State Park 2050 Hwy 1 Jenner CA 707-847-3221
Enjoy panoramic views and the dramatic sounds of the surf at this park that offers a variety of sights and recreational activities. This park is also home to one of the first underwater parks in California. Dogs of all sizes are allowed at the campgrounds and in any of the developed areas. Dogs are not allowed on the trails or on the beaches, and they must be inside at night. There is no additional pet fee. Dogs must be leashed and cleaned up after at all times.

Chapter 5

California - San Francisco Bay Area Dog Travel Guide

Gilroy

Accommodations
Motel 6 - Gilroy 6110 Monterey Highway Gilroy CA   408-842-6061 (800-466-8356)
One well-behaved family pet per room. Guest must notify front desk upon arrival. Guest is liable for any damages. In consideration of all guests, pets must never be left unattended in the guest rooms.

Attractions
Bonfante Gardens Family Theme Park Kennel 3050 Hecker Pass Hwy Gilroy CA   408-840-7100
http://www.bonfantegardens.com/
The park, designed to educate guests and to foster a greater appreciation of horticulture, features over forty rides, attractions, educational exhibits, majestic gardens, an event plaza, a unique kid's splash garden, a variety of interactive educational and performance experiences for youth, and more. All the rides and attractions are built around a beautifully designed landscape featuring many different varieties of trees, flowers, water elements and rock formations. However, the real attraction here is the one of a kind Circus Trees that were rescued and moved to this park. Using intricate grafting techniques, these amazing trees were coiled, scalloped, woven, and spiral shaped from Sycamore, Box Elder, Ash, and Spanish Cork trees. Dogs are not allowed in the park; however, there is a free kennel at the entrance with a latch gate. The kennel space is limited, only dog owners are allowed in this area, and they must provide the pet's food and water. The kennel is open Monday through Thursday from 10 am to 6 pm, and on Friday from 10 am to 7 pm. Park hours vary depending on the season.

Stores
PetSmart Pet Store 6755 Camini Arroyo Gilroy CA   408-848-1383
Your licensed and well-behaved leashed dog is allowed in the store.
Petco Pet Store 8767 San Ysidro Avenue Gilroy CA   408-846-2844
Your licensed and well-behaved leashed dog is allowed in the store.

Marin - North Bay

Accommodations
Bodega Bay and Beyond 575 Coastal Hwy One Bodega Bay CA   707-875-3942
Dogs of all sizes are allowed. There is a a $50 per room per stay fee and a pet policy to sign at check in.
Inn Marin 250 Entrada Drive Novato CA   415-883-5952 (800-652-6565)
http://innmarin.com/
Inn Marin invites both business and leisure travelers. Nestled in a beautiful resort setting and richly restored, this inn welcomes your best friend. Amenities include a large outdoor heated pool and spa, garden patio area with barbecue, exercise facility, guest laundry facility and a continental breakfast. Rooms include data ports, voice mail and two line speaker phone, iron and ironing board, and handicapped rooms/facilities are available. They are located just off Highway 101, perfect for the business or tourist traveler. There is a $20 one time pet fee. You are required to bring a crate if you plan to leave your dog alone in the room.
Travelodge 7600 Redwood Blvd Novato CA   415-892-7500
There is a $10 per day pet fee. Dogs are allowed on the first floor only.
Bear Valley Inn 88 Bear Valley Road Olema CA   415-663-1777
Offering a step into an elegant past, this nicely appointed historic 1910 inn offers a great location for other local attractions and recreational activities, including hundreds of miles of multi-use trails. Dogs are welcome in the cottage but not the main house. The cottage has a nice deck and offers a full kitchen supplied with homemade granola, fresh fruit and yogurt, and coffee and organic teas. There is an additional pet fee of $20 per room per stay. Dogs must be well mannered, leashed, cleaned up after, and crated when left alone in the cottage.
Olema Inn 10,000 Sir Francis Drake Blvd Olema CA   415-663-9559
http://www.theolemainn.com/index.html
Only moments from beautiful coastline, this restored inn offers elegant rooms, exceptional fine dining from a mostly organic menu, a splendid outdoor patio, lush gardens, and more. Dogs of all sizes are allowed for no additional fee. Dogs must be well mannered, leashed, and cleaned up after.
Motel 6 - Petaluma 1368 North McDowell Boulevard Petaluma CA   707-765-0333 (800-466-8356)
One well-behaved family pet per room. Guest must notify front desk upon arrival. Guest is liable for any damages. In consideration of all guests, pets must never be left unattended in the guest rooms.
Petaluma KOA Campground 20 Rainsville Road Petaluma CA   707-763-1492

Well behaved dogs of all sizes are allowed, however if your dog is over 30 pounds there is a 1 week maximum stay. There is a pet policy to sign at check in and there are no additional pet fees. Pit bulls or heavy barkers are not allowed.

Quality Inn 5100 Montero Way Petaluma CA   707-664-1155 (877-424-6423)
Dogs of all sizes are allowed. There can be up to 2 large or 3 small to medium dogs per room. There is a $15 per night per room additional fee. Dogs must be leashed, cleaned up after, and the Do Not Disturb sign put on the door and a contact number left with the front desk if they are in the room alone.

Sheraton Sonoma County - Petaluma 745 Baywood Dr. Petaluma CA   707-283-2888 (888-625-5144)
Dogs of all sizes are allowed. Pet rooms are available on the first floor only. You must sign a pet policy when checking in with a dog. Dogs are not allowed to be left alone in the room.

Point Reyes Station Inn Bed and Breakfast 11591 Highway One, Box 824 Point Reyes Station CA   415-663-9372
http://www.pointreyesstationinn.com/
They offer private, romantic rooms with thirteen foot vaulted ceilings, whirlpool baths, fireplaces and views of rolling hills. This inn is located at the gateway of the Point Reyes National Seashore. Well-behaved dogs are welcome and there is no extra pet charge. Children are also welcome.

Tree House Bed and Breakfast Inn 73 Drake Summit, P.O. Box 1075 Point Reyes Station CA   415-663-8720

http://www.treehousebnb.com/
This inn offers a secluded and peaceful getaway in West Marin. It is located on the tip of Inverness Ridge with a view of Point Reyes Station. The Point Reyes National Seashore is nearby. All three rooms have a private bathroom. Pets and children are always welcome. Smoking is allowed outdoors. There are no pet fees.

Campgrounds and RV Parks

Bodega Bay RV Park 2001 Hwy 1 Bodega Bay CA   707-875-3701 (800-201-6864)
Steeped in history and a natural beauty, this park is the only full service park in the area, and they offer 72 sites on 51/2 wind-protected acres. Some features include wi-fi, a restaurant, hot showers and restrooms, a laundry, dump station, gaming courts, and they are host to various celebrations and events throughout the year. Dogs of all sizes are allowed for no additional fee. Dogs must be friendly, well behaved, leashed and cleaned up after. Pit Bulls are not allowed. There is a dog walk area at the campground.

Bodega Dunes Campground 3095 Hwy 1 Bodega Bay CA   707-875-3483 (800-444-7275)
This campground is located in one of the largest beach parks in the state, and offers miles of hiking trails, whale-watching sites, various nature habitats, and a variety of land and water recreation. Dogs of all sizes are allowed. There are no additional pet fees. Dogs must be on no more than a 6 foot leash at all times and cleaned up after. Dogs must be inside at night, and they are not allowed on beach adjacent to the campground or on trails. The camping and tent areas also allow dogs. There is a dog walk area at the campground. There are no electric or water hookups at the campgrounds.

Doran Regional Park Campgrounds 201 Doran Beach Road Bodega Bay CA   707-875-3540
Walk to the beach from your campsite! There are over 100 campsites in this park which features 2 miles of sandy beach. There is a dump station for RVs. Dogs are allowed for an additional fee of $1 per night per pet. Dogs must be on no more than a 6 foot leash at all times, and proof of a rabies vaccination is required. They may not be left unattended unless they will be quiet and well behaved. The number for reservations is 707-565-CAMP(2267). The camping and tent areas also allow dogs. There is a dog walk area at the campground. There are no electric or water hookups at the campgrounds.

Porto Bodega Marina and RV Park 1500 Bay Flat Road Bodega Bay CA   707-875-2354
This RV park offers 58 RV sites and is located along 16 acres of the bay near a marina where there are a variety of recreation and hiking opportunities available. There is also a sports fishing center on site that allows dogs to go on their boats. Dogs are allowed for no additional fee. Dogs must be well behaved, under owner's control, and leashed and cleaned up after at all times. There is a dog walk area at the campground.

Westside Regional Park Campground 2400 Westshore Road Bodega Bay CA   707-875-3540
This park offers 38 campsites. Fishing is the popular activity at this park. Dogs are allowed but must be on a 6 foot or less leash at all times, and proof of a rabies vaccination is required. There is an additional $1 per night per pet. Dogs may not be left unattended outside unless they will be quiet and well behaved. The camping and tent areas also allow dogs. There is a dog walk area at the campground. There are no electric or water hookups at the campgrounds.

Lawsons Landing Campground 137 Marine View Dr Dillon Beach CA   707-878-2726
This campground is located along the sand dunes a short distance from the Pacific Ocean and Tomales Bay. There are rest rooms but no shower facilities and there are dump stations. Dogs on leash are allowed in the campground and on the beach. There are no electric or water hookups at the campsite. During wet times the campground may be closed so for information on current conditions call 707-878-2443.

Samuel P. Taylor State Park 8889 Sir Francis Drake Blvd Lagunitas CA   415-488-9897 (800-444-PARK (7275))
This park is home to a unique contrast of coastal redwood groves, open grassland and flowers. Amenities include water, tables, grills, flush toilets and showers. Dogs of all sizes are allowed at no additional fee. While

dogs are not allowed on the hiking trails, they are allowed on the bike trail that runs about six miles through the park. The path is nearly level and follows the Northwest Pacific Railroad right-of-way. The trail is both paved and dirt and it starts near the park entrance. Dogs are also allowed in the developed areas like the campgrounds. Pets must be leashed, and please clean up after your pet. Dogs may not be left unattended. The camping and tent areas also allow dogs. There is a dog walk area at the campground. There are no electric or water hookups at the campgrounds.

Novato RV Park 1530 Armstrong Avenue Novato CA 415-897-1271 (800-733-6787)
http://www.novatorvpark.com/
Nestled in a quiet country setting just minutes from all the attractions of the bay cities, this park offers modern amenities, and various recreation. Dogs of all sizes are allowed. There are no additional pet fees. Dogs may not be left unattended outside, and they must be quiet, well behaved, leashed, and cleaned up after. This is an RV only park. There is a dog walk area at the campground.

Olema Ranch Campground 10155 Hwy 1 Olema CA 415-663-8001 (800-655-CAMP (2267))
http://www.olemaranch.com
This full service park features both natural forest and open meadow camp sites, a laundry, rec hall, store, Post Office, and a wide variety of activities and recreation. Dogs of all sizes are allowed for an additional $1 per night per pet. Dogs must be on no more than an 8 foot leash at all times and cleaned up after. The camping and tent areas also allow dogs. There is a dog walk area at the campground.

San Francisco North/Petaluma KOA 20 Rainsvile Road Petaluma CA 707-763-1492 (800-562-1233)
http://www.koa.com/where/ca/05330/
Just north of the Golden Gate, this scenic country-style campground offers tours of the city, a petting farm, a full recreational program, swimming pool, hot tub, cable TV, and a snack bar. Friendly dogs of all sizes are allowed for no additional fee. Dogs must be under owner's control and visual observation at all times. Dogs must be quiet, well behaved, and be on no more than a 6 foot leash at all times, or otherwise contained. Dogs may not be left unattended outside the owner's camping equipment, and must be brought inside at night. There are some breed restrictions. The camping and tent areas also allow dogs. There is a dog walk area at the campground.

Vacation Home Rentals

Rosemary Cottage 75 Balboa Ave Inverness CA 415-663-9338
http://www.rosemarybb.com/
Dogs are welcome at the Rosemary Cottage and The Ark Cottage. Families are also welcome. The Rosemary Cottage is a two room cottage with a deck and garden. It is adjacent to the Point Reyes National Seashore. The Ark Cottage is a two room cottage tucked in the forest a mile up the ridge from the village of Inverness. There is a $25 one time pet charge for one dog or a $35 one time pet charge for two dogs.

Beach Front Retreat 90 Calle Del Ribera Stinson Beach CA 415-383-7870
http://www.beachtime.org
This vacation home rental offers 3 bedrooms, 2 baths, a fireplace and a beach deck with barbecue. You can view the ocean from the balcony located next to the master bedroom. There is an additional $50 one time per stay pet charge

Attractions

TOP 200 PLACE Bodega Bay Sportsfishing Center 1500 Bay Flat Road Bodega Bay CA 707-875-3344
This sports fishing center offers a variety of trips, boats, and supplies for your trip. They are located in the Porto Bodega RV Park and Marina, where dogs are also allowed. Dogs of all sizes are welcome aboard mostly on the weekdays when they are not so busy, they they suggest you bring a doggy life jacket. There is no additional pet fee. Dogs must be well behaved, under owner's control, and leashed and cleaned up after at all times.

Petaluma Adobe State Historic Park 3325 Adobe Road Petaluma CA 707-762-4871
This old adobe ranch building, the largest private hacienda in California between 1834 and 1846, was the center of activity on one of the most prosperous private estates established during the Mexican period. The park offers shaded picnic areas with views of farmland and oak-studded hills. Leashed dogs are allowed at the park, but not inside the buildings. Once a year, usually in May, is Living History Day at this park. Volunteers dress up in authentic clothing. You will find Mexican vaqueros, musicians, blacksmiths, carpenters and more. Try brick-making, basketry, corn-grinding, candlemaking and more. The park is located a twenty minute drive from Sonoma. It is at the east edge of Petaluma, off Highway 116 and Adobe Road.

Petaluma Self-Guided Film Walking Tour Keller St. and Western Ave. Petaluma CA 707-769-0429
Commercial and feature film producers love to step back in time to Petaluma's town charm. Petaluma's iron front buildings are frequently the backdrop for film sets. The Film Tour will lead you through the streets to locations of films like American Grafitti, Peggy Sue Got Married, Heroes,Howard the Duck,Shadow of A Doubt, and Basic Instinct. To begin the tour, park in the city garage at the corner of Keller Street and Western Avenue. The Riverfront at the foot of Western Avenue was where the police car was hurled into the water in Howard the Duck. This was also a film site for Explorers. Nearby, 120 Petaluma Blvd. North (Bluestone Main Building) was the site of Bodell's Appliances in Peggy Sue Got Married where Charlie worked for his father. The Mystic Theater, 23 Petaluma Blvd. North near B St. starred as the State Movie Theater in American Graffiti. Walk down Petaluma

Blvd. South to H Street. The end of H Street at the Petaluma River was Lovers Lane for Peggy Sue and her boyfriend. Head back to D Street, turning Left on D and head west to 920 D Street. The upstairs bedroom was used in Explorers, and a 20 foot tree was imported from Los Angeles for the boyfriend to climb to the girl's bedroom. Commercials for General Electric, Levi's, and catalog stills for the local Biobottoms company were shot here. At Brown Court off D Street, is an area that has a look that is a favorite with commercial producers, including Orville Redenbacher Popcorn. At 1006 D Street was Charlie's house in Peggy Sue Got Married. Backtrack down D Street to Sixth Street and go north towards town. St. Vincent's Church and neighborhood at Howard/Sixth and Liberty Streets were used for scenes in the TV remake of Shadow of a Doubt with Mark Harmon and Basic Instinct with Michael Douglas and Sharon Stone. The big white house at 226 Liberty Street, on the east side of Liberty near Washington Street was Peggy Sue's house in Peggy Sue Got Married. For more information, please visit the Petaluma Visitor Center at 800 Baywood Drive, Suite #1 in Petaluma or call 707-769-0429. The Visitor Center is located a the northwest corner of Highway 116 (Lakeville Hwy.) and Baywood Drive next to the Petaluma Marina. Take the Lakeville Hwy 116 exit off Hwy 101.

River Walk Near D St. bridge and Washington St. Petaluma CA 707-769-0429
You and your pooch can take an almost 2.5 mile stroll on the River Walk. This walk will take you around the riverfront which was once a bustling river port, and is now a favorite weekend yachting destination. There are numerous species of birds that inhabit this area. For more details of the walk, pick up a brochure at the Petaluma Visitor Center at 800 Baywood Drive, Suite #1 in Petaluma or call 707-769-0429. The Visitor Center is located a the northwest corner of Highway 116 (Lakeville Hwy) and Baywood Drive next to the Petaluma Marina. Take the Lakeville Hwy 116 exit off Hwy 101.

Shopping Centers

Petaluma Village Factory Outlet 2200 Petaluma Blvd N. Petaluma CA 707-778-9300
Dogs are allowed on leash in the shopping center. Whether they are allowed in the stores or not is up to the individual stores. Dogs may sit with you at the outdoor tables while you eat at some of the food places.

Stores

Petco Pet Store 208 Vintage Way Novato CA 415-898-9416
Your licensed and well-behaved leashed dog is allowed in the store.
Petco Pet Store 165 North McDowell Blvd Petaluma CA 707-775-3149
Your licensed and well-behaved leashed dog is allowed in the store.
Petco Pet Store 375 Third St San Rafael CA 415-457-5262
Your licensed and well-behaved leashed dog is allowed in the store.

Beaches

Doran Regional Park 201 Doran Beach Road Bodega Bay CA 707-875-3540
This park offers 2 miles of sandy beach. It is a popular place to picnic, walk, surf, fish and fly kites. Dogs are allowed but must be on a 6 foot or less leash and proof of a rabies vaccination is required. There is a minimal parking fee. The park is located south of Bodega Bay.
Agate Beach Elm Road Bolinas CA 415-499-6387
During low tide, this 6 acre park provides access to almost 2 miles of shoreline. Leashed dogs are allowed.
Muir Beach Hwy 1 Muir Beach CA
Dogs on leash are allowed on Muir Beach with you. Please clean up after your dog on the beach. To get to Muir Beach from Hwy 101 take Hwy 1 North from the north side of the Golden Gate Bridge.
Point Reyes National Seashore Olema CA 415-464-5100
http://www.nps.gov/pore/
Leashed dogs (on a 6 foot or less leash) are allowed on four beaches. The dog-friendly beaches are the Limantour Beach, Kehoe Beach, North Beach and South Beach. Dogs are not allowed on the hiking trails. However, they are allowed on some hiking trails that are adjacent to Point Reyes. For a map of dog-friendly hiking trails, please stop by the Visitor Center. Point Reyes is located about an hour north of San Francisco. From Highway 101, exit at Sir Francis Drake Highway, and continue west on Sir Francis Drake to Olema. To find the Visitor Center, turn right in Olema onto Route 1 and then make a left onto Bear Valley Road. The Visitor Center will be on the left.
Upton Beach Highway 1 Stinson Beach CA 415-499-6387
Dogs not allowed on the National Park section of Stinson Beach but are allowed at Upton Beach which is under Marin County's jurisdiction. This beach is located north of the National Park. Dogs are permitted without leash but under direct and immediate control.

Parks

Westside Regional Park 2400 Westshore Road Bodega Bay CA 707-565-2041
Located on Bodega Bay, this park is a popular spot for fishing. Dogs are allowed but must be on a 6 foot or less leash and proof of a rabies vaccination is required. To get there from Highway 1, take Eastshore Road.

Deer Park Porteous Avenue Fairfax CA   415-499-6387
Leashed dogs are allowed at this park including the nature trails. The 54 acre park is located in a wooded setting.

Mill Valley-Sausalito Path Almonte Blvd. Mill Valley CA
This multi-purpose path is used by walkers, runners, bicyclists and equestrians. Dogs on leash are allowed. The path is located in the Bothin Marsh Open Space Preserve.

Mount Tamalpais State Park 801 Panoramic Highway Mill Valley CA   415-388-2070
While dogs are not allowed on most of the trails, they are allowed on the Old Stage Road. This path is about .5 to .75 miles and leads to the Marin Municipal Water District Land which allows dogs on their trails. Dogs must be leashed on both the state park and the water district lands. Please clean up after your pets. To get there, take Highway 101 north of San Francisco's Golden Gate Bridge. Then take Highway 1 to the Stinson Beach exit and follow the signs up the mountain.

Muir Woods National Monument Highway 1/Muir Woods Exit Mill Valley CA   415-388-2595
http://www.nps.gov/muwo/index.htm
Dogs must be on leash and must be cleaned up after on the Muir Beach coastal trail. Dogs are not allowed in the woods.

Bolinas Ridge Trail Drake Blvd Olema CA
Dogs on leash may accompany you on the Bolinas Ridge Trail. The trailhead is about 1 mile from the Pt Reyes National Seashore Visitor Center in Olema. Dogs are not allowed on trails in Pt Reyes (see Point Reyes National Seashore) so this is the closest trail available. The trailhead is one mile up Drake Blvd from Olema on the right. Parking is at the side of the road.

Civic Center Lagoon Park Civic Center Drive San Rafael CA   415-499-6387
This 20 acre park has an 11 acre lagoon which is used for fishing and non-motorized boating. The park also has picnic areas and a children's playground. Leashed dogs are allowed.

John F. McInnis Park Smith Ranch Road San Rafael CA   415-499-6387
This 440 acre parks offers nature trails, sports fields, and a golf course. Dogs are allowed not allowed on the golf course. Pets are allowed off leash but must be under immediate verbal control at all times. Owners must also carry a leash and pick up after their pets.

Samuel P. Taylor State Park Sir Francis Drake Blvd. San Rafael CA
While dogs are not allowed on the hiking trails, they are allowed on the bike trail that runs about six miles through the park. The path is nearly level and follows the Northwest Pacific Railroad right-of-way. The trail is both paved and dirt and it starts near the park entrance. Dogs are also allowed in the developed areas like the campgrounds. Pets must be leashed and please clean up after your pet. The park is located north of San Francisco, 15 miles west of San Rafael on Sir Francis Drake Blvd.

Off-Leash Dog Parks

Canine Commons Doherty, East of Magnolia Larkspur CA   415-927-5110
http://www.ci.larkspur.ca.us/3053.html
This fenced dog park is located in Piper Park. The park is run by the Larkspur Park and Recreation Department. In 2006, the dog park is temporarily closed for construction, but is expected to open by Spring of 2007.

Mill Valley Dog Run Sycamore Ave At Camino Alto Mill Valley CA
This large, 2 acre fenced dog park in Bayfront Park in Mill Valley even has drains installed. It is located on Sycamore, east of Camino Alto.

Ohair Park Dog Park Novato Blvd at Sutro Novato CA
http://
This no-frills fenced dog park is located in the Neil Ohair Park in Novato. The park has been organized by the D.O.G.B.O.N.E. Dog Park Group which is looking to improve the park.

Rocky Memorial Dog Park W. Casa Grande Road Petaluma CA   707-778-4380
Your dog can run leash-free in this 9 acre fenced dog park. To get there, take Lakeville Hwy. (Hwy 116) east, and turn west on Casa Grande Rd.

Field of Dogs Civic Center Drive behind the Marin County Civic Center San Rafael CA
http://fieldofdogs.org
The Field Of Dogs off-leash dog park is located behind the Marin County Civic Center. To get there from 101, take the N. San Pedro Road exit east. Turn left onto Civic Center Drive and the dog park is on the right. The park is open during daylight hours, is fenced and is 2/3 acres in size.

Sausalito Dog Park Bridgeway and Ebbtide Avenues Sausalito CA
http://www.dogpark-sausalito.com/
This fenced dog park is 1.3 acres complete with lighting, picnic tables, benches, a dog drinking water area, and a scooper cleaning station. On some days, this very popular park has over 300 dogs per day.

Outdoor Restaurants

Coast Cafe 46 Wharf Road Bolinas CA   415-868-2298
http://www.bolinascafe.com/

This eatery offers Northern California cuisine specializing in organic and fresh local products with casual indoor or outdoor dining service. Dogs are allowed at the outdoor tables in the front of the cafe. They must be well behaved, under owner's control at all times, leashed, and cleaned up after.

Coast Cafe 46 Wharf Rd Bolinas CA   415-868-2224

Dogs are allowed at the outside tables. Bolinas usually has a large number of dogs walking around with their owners. It is a bit off the beaten path, about 10 minutes from Highway 1.

Smiley's Schooner Saloon 41 Wharf Road Bolinas CA   415-868-1311

http://www.coastalpost.com/smileys/

This bar has been recognized by the California Historical Society as one of 14 continually operating bars in the state since the 1800's. In addition to libations, they also offer a variety of live entertainment, board games, a pool table, light meals and snacks, pastries, and espressos. They offer outside seating; just go inside to order and pick up food items (alcohol not permitted at outer tables). Dogs are allowed at the outdoor tables. They must be well behaved, under owner's control at all times, leashed, and cleaned up after.

A.G. Ferrari Foods 107 Corte Madera Town Ctr Corte Madera CA   415-927-4347

Dogs are allowed at the outdoor tables. The restaurant is at the Corte Madera Town Center Shopping Center.

Baja Fresh Mexican Grill 100 Corte Madera Town Center Corte Madera CA   415-924-8522

http://www.bajafresh.com

This Mexican restaurant is open for lunch and dinner. They use fresh ingredients and making their salsa and beans daily. Some of the items on their menu include Enchiladas, Burritos, Tacos, Quesadillas, Nachos, Chicken, Steak and more. Well-behaved leashed dogs are allowed at the outdoor tables.

Book Passage Bookstore and Cafe 51 Tamal Vista Corte Madera CA   415-927-1503

Dogs are allowed at the outdoor tables.

World Wrapps 208 Corte Madera Town Center Corte Madera CA   415-927-3663

Dogs are allowed at the outdoor tables. This is a quick service restaurant providing healthy and flavorful alternatives to traditional fast food. They offer gourmet low fat wrapped meals with multi-cultural ingredients. They also serve smoothies.

Fairfax Scoop 63 Broadway Blvd Fairfax CA   415-453-3130

Organic ice cream can't get much better than this. There is a bench out front that you can sit there with your pooch and enjoy a treat. Dogs must be leashed, and please clean up after your pet.

Priscilla's Pizza 12781 Sir Francis Drake Blvd. Inverness CA   415-669-1244

Located in downtown Inverness, this restaurant serves pizza, pasta, sandwiches, salads, desserts and more. The outdoor seating offers a bay view. Dogs are allowed at the outdoor tables.

Vladimir's Czechoslovakian Restaurant 12785 Sir Francis Drake Blvd. Inverness CA   415-669-1021

This restaurant is located in downtown Inverness and dogs are allowed at the outdoor tables. The restaurant has a well covered patio with heaters.

Willie's Cafe 799 College Ave Kentfield CA   415-455-9455

This cafe serves American food. Dogs are allowed at the outdoor tables.

Baja Fresh Mexican Grill 924 Diablo Ave. Novato CA   415-897-4122

http://www.bajafresh.com

This Mexican restaurant is open for lunch and dinner. They use fresh ingredients and making their salsa and beans daily. Some of the items on their menu include Enchiladas, Burritos, Tacos Salads, Quesadillas, Nachos, Chicken, Steak and more. Well-behaved leashed dogs are allowed at the outdoor tables.

Boca Restaurant 340 Ignacio Blvd Novato CA   415-883-0901

http://www.bocasteak.com

Dogs are allowed at the outside tables.

Maya Palenque Restaurant 349 Enfrente Rd Novato CA   415-883-6292

Dogs are allowed at the outdoor tables, which are covered.

Apple Box 224 B Street Petaluma CA   707-762-5222

Dogs are allowed at the outdoor seats on the patio. It overlooks the Petaluma River near the Riverwalk.

Lombardi's Downtown Deli and BBQ 139 Petaluma Blvd N. Petaluma CA   707-763-6959

http://www.lombardisbbq.com

Dogs are allowed at the outdoor tables.

Cowgirl Creamery 80 Fourth Street Point Reyes Station CA   415-663-9335

http://www.cowgirlcreamery.com/

This creamery offers award winning organic cheeses in a wide variety of flavors and styles from the local area, and from other corners of North America and Europe. They also offer the region's finest natural foods and other products, from prepared dishes, fresh, organic fruits and vegetables, wines and cheeses, as well as cheese accessories. There is seating outside where your dog may join you. Just order and pick up inside. Dogs must be well behaved, under owner's control, and leashed and cleaned up after at all times.

Pine Cone Diner 60 4th Street Point Reyes Station CA   415-663-1536

This eatery serves local, fresh American food for breakfast and lunch daily. There is seating outside where your dog may join you, weather permitting. Dogs must be well behaved, under owner's control, and leashed at all times.

Ristorante La Toscana 3751 Redwood Hwy. San Rafael CA   415-492-9100

Dogs are allowed at the outdoor tables. This Italian restaurant features pasta, veal, seafood, rabbit and a full bar.

Whole Foods Market 340 Third Street San Rafael CA   415-451-6333
http://www.wholefoods.com/
This natural food supermarket offers natural and organic foods. Order some food from their deli without your dog and bring it to an outdoor table where your well-behaved leashed dog is welcome. Dogs are not allowed in the store including the deli at any time.
Cafe Trieste 1000 Bridgeway Sausalito CA   415-332-7660
Dogs are allowed at the outdoor tables.
Scoma's 588 Bridgeway Sausalito CA   415-332-9551
Dogs are allowed at the outdoor tables. This restaurant is located on the waterfront and offers a great view of the San Francisco Bay. Seafood is their specialty.
Parkside Cafe 43 Arenal Avenue Stinson Beach CA   415-868-1272
http://www.parksidecafe.com/
This eatery serves American favorites, pizza, barbecue, and gourmet dishes with service for both indoor and outdoor dining (weather permitting). Dogs are permitted at the outdoor tables. Dogs must be well behaved, under owner's control, and leashed and cleaned up after at all times.
Sand Dollar Restaurant 3458 Shoreline Highway Stinson Beach CA   415-868-0434
In operation since 1921, this eatery is open 7 days a week, and features classic American cuisine and seafood. They have a separate porch area with benches for visitors with pets; just order and pick-up inside. Dogs must be well behaved, under owner's control, and leashed and cleaned up after at all times.
Shark's Deli 1600 Tiburon Blvd Tiburon CA   415-435-9130
Dogs are allowed at the outdoor tables.
Tomales Bakery 27000 Highway One Tomales CA   707-878-2429
This bakery offers a variety of breads and pastries plus calzones and more. They have a few outdoor tables and dogs are allowed at the outdoor tables.
Route 1 Diner 14450 Highway 1 Valley Ford CA   707-876-9600
Dogs are allowed at the outdoor seats.

Vets and Kennels
Pet Emergency & Specialty 901 Francisco Blvd E San Rafael CA   415-456-7372
Monday - Friday 5:30 pm to 8 am, 24 hours on weekends.

Morgan Hill

Accommodations
Residence Inn by Marriott 18620 Madrone Parkway Morgan Hill CA   408-782-8311
Dogs up to 100 pounds are allowed. There is a $75 one time fee and a pet policy to sign at check in.

Campgrounds and RV Parks
Parkway Lakes RV Park 100 Ogier Avenue Morgan Hill CA   408-779-0244
This 110 RV space park offers a pool, mini mart, wi-fi, club house, laundry, showers, and more. Dogs of all sizes are allowed for an additional fee of $1 per night per pet. Dogs must be leashed and cleaned up after. There is an area just outside the park for walking your pet. There are some breed restrictions. The camping and tent areas also allow dogs.

Stores
Petco Pet Store 313 Vineyard Town Center Morgan Hill CA   408-778-7838
Your licensed and well-behaved leashed dog is allowed in the store.

Oakland - East Bay

Accommodations
Best Western Heritage Inn 1955 East 2nd St Benecia CA   707-746-0401 (800-780-7234)
Dogs of all sizes are allowed. There is a $25 one time per pet fee per visit. Smoking and non-smoking are available for pet rooms.
Beau Sky Hotel 2520 Durant Ave Berkeley CA   510-540-7688
This small hotel offers personalized service. Some rooms have balconies. If your room doesn't, you can sit at the chairs and tables in the patio at the front of the hotel. Your small, medium or large dog will feel welcome here

because they don't discriminate against dog size. It is located close to the UC Berkeley campus and less than a block from the popular Telegraph Ave (see Attractions). There aren't too many hotels in Berkeley, especially around the campus. So if you are going, be sure to book a room in advance. To get there from Hwy 880 heading north, take the Hwy 980 exit towards Hwy 24/Walnut Creek. Then take the Hwy 24 exit on the left towards Berkeley/Walnut Creek. Exit at Claremont Ave and turn left onto Claremont Ave. Make a slight left onto College Ave. Turn left onto Haste St. Turn right onto Telegraph Ave and then right onto Durant. The hotel will be on the right. There are no additional pet fees. All rooms are non-smoking.

Golden Bear Motel 1620 San Pablo Ave Berkeley CA   510-525-6770
This motel has over 40 rooms. Eight of the rooms have two-bedroom units and there are four two-bedroom cottages with kitchens. Parking is free. To get there from Hwy 80 heading north, exit University Ave. Turn right onto University Ave, and then left on San Pablo Ave. The motel is on the left. There is a $10 per day additional pet fee.

Holiday Inn Express 2532 Castro Valley Blvd Castro Valley CA   510-538-9501 (877-270-6405)
Dogs of all sizes are allowed. There is a $20 one time per pet fee per visit. Smoking and non-smoking rooms are available for pets.

Holiday Inn 1050 Burnett Ave Concord CA   925-687-5500 (877-270-6405)
Dogs of all sizes are allowed. There is a $10 per day additional pet fee.

Woodfin Suite Hotel 5800 Shellmound Emeryville CA   510-601-5880
All rooms are suites and all are non-smoking. Hotel amenities include a pool, exercise facility, complimentary video movies or books and a complimentary breakfast buffet. There is a $5 per day pet fee and a $150 refundable pet deposit. All well-behaved dogs are welcome.

Extended Stay America 1019 Oliver Road Fairfield CA   707-438-0932
Dogs of all sizes are allowed. There is a $25 fee for the first night, and a $75 one time fee starting the 2nd night per room.

Motel 6 - Fairfield North 1473 Holiday Lane Fairfield CA   707-425-4565 (800-466-8356)
One well-behaved family pet per room. Guest must notify front desk upon arrival. Guest is liable for any damages. In consideration of all guests, pets must never be left unattended in the guest rooms.

La Quinta Inn & Suites Fremont 46200 Landing Pkwy. Fremont CA   510-445-0808 (800-531-5900)
Dogs of all sizes are allowed. There are no additional pet fees. Dogs must be quiet, well behaved, leashed and cleaned up after.

Motel 6 - Fremont North 34047 Fremont Boulevard Fremont CA   510-793-4848 (800-466-8356)
One well-behaved family pet per room. Guest must notify front desk upon arrival. Guest is liable for any damages. In consideration of all guests, pets must never be left unattended in the guest rooms.

Motel 6 - Fremont South 46101 Research Avenue Fremont CA   510-490-4528 (800-466-8356)
One well-behaved family pet per room. Guest must notify front desk upon arrival. Guest is liable for any damages. In consideration of all guests, pets must never be left unattended in the guest rooms.

Comfort Inn 24997 Mission Boulevard Hayward CA   510-538-4466 (877-424-6423)
http://www.comfortinnhayward.com
Newly renovated guestrooms. Every room has a microwave & refrigerator, hairdryer, iron & ironing board, two 2-line phones with voice mail, coffeemaker, and 27" TV's with expanded cable & HBO.

Motel 6 - Hayward 30155 Industrial Parkway Southwest Hayward CA   510-489-8333 (800-466-8356)
One well-behaved family pet per room. Guest must notify front desk upon arrival. Guest is liable for any damages. In consideration of all guests, pets must never be left unattended in the guest rooms.

Vagabond Inn 20455 Hesperian Blvd. Hayward CA   510-785-5480
http://www.vagabondinn.com
This two story motel offers a heated pool and spa. To get there from Hwy 880 heading north, exit A Street/San Lorenzo. Turn left onto A Street. Then turn right onto Hesperian Blvd. There is a $10 per day additional pet fee per pet.

Motel 6 - Livermore 4673 Lassen Road Livermore CA   925-443-5300 (800-466-8356)
One well-behaved family pet per room. Guest must notify front desk upon arrival. Guest is liable for any damages. In consideration of all guests, pets must never be left unattended in the guest rooms.

Residence Inn by Marriott 1000 Airway Blvd Livermore CA   925-373-7252
Dogs of all sizes are allowed. There is a $75 plus tax one time fee, and a pet policy to sign at check in. Please remove pet or kennel for housekeeping.

Motel 6 - Newark 5600 Cedar Court Newark CA   510-791-5900 (800-466-8356)
One well-behaved family pet per room. Guest must notify front desk upon arrival. Guest is liable for any damages. In consideration of all guests, pets must never be left unattended in the guest rooms.

Residence Inn by Marriott 35466 Dumbarton Court Newark CA   510-739-6000
Dogs of all sizes are allowed. There is a $75 one time fee, and a pet policy to sign at check in.

Woodfin Suite Hotel 39150 Cedar Blvd. Newark CA   510-795-1200
All well-behaved dogs are welcome. Every room is a suite with a full kitchen. Hotel amenities include free video movies and a complimentary hot breakfast buffet. There is a $50 one time per stay pet fee.

La Quinta Inn Oakland Airport/Coliseum 8465 Enterprise Way Oakland CA   510-632-8900 (800-531-5900)
Dogs of all sizes are allowed. There are no additional pet fees. Dogs must be leashed and cleaned up after.

Motel 6 - Oakland - Embarcadero 1801 Embarcadero Oakland CA   510-436-0103 (800-466-8356)

One well-behaved family pet per room. Guest must notify front desk upon arrival. Guest is liable for any damages. In consideration of all guests, pets must never be left unattended in the guest rooms.
Motel 6 - Oakland Airport 8480 Edes Avenue Oakland CA   510-638-1180 (800-466-8356)
One well-behaved family pet per room. Guest must notify front desk upon arrival. Guest is liable for any damages. In consideration of all guests, pets must never be left unattended in the guest rooms.
Motel 6 - Pinole 1501 Fitzgerald Drive Pinole CA   510-222-8174 (800-466-8356)
One well-behaved family pet per room. Guest must notify front desk upon arrival. Guest is liable for any damages. In consideration of all guests, pets must never be left unattended in the guest rooms.
Motel 6 - Pittsburg 2101 Loveridge Road Pittsburg CA 925-427-1600 (800-466-8356)
One well-behaved family pet per room. Guest must notify front desk upon arrival. Guest is liable for any damages. In consideration of all guests, pets must never be left unattended in the guest rooms.
Residence Inn by Marriott 700 Ellinwood Way Pleasant Hill CA 925-689-1010
Dogs of all sizes are welcome. There is a $100 one time fee, and a pet policy to sign at check in.
Candlewood Suites 5535 Johnson Drive Pleasanton CA 925-463-1212 (877-270-6405)
Dogs up to 75 pounds are allowed. There is a $75 one time pet fee.
Crowne Plaza 11950 Dublin Canyon Rd Pleasanton CA 925-847-6000 (877-270-6405)
Dogs of all sizes are allowed. There is a $25 one time per pet fee per visit. Smoking and non-smoking rooms are available for pets.
Motel 6 - Pleasanton 5102 Hopyard Road Pleasanton CA 925-463-2626 (800-466-8356)
One well-behaved family pet per room. Guest must notify front desk upon arrival. Guest is liable for any damages. In consideration of all guests, pets must never be left unattended in the guest rooms.
Residence Inn by Marriott 11920 Dublin Canyon Road Pleasanton CA 925-227-0500
Pets of all sizes are allowed. There is a $75 one time fee, and a pet policy to sign at check in.
Residence Inn by Marriott 1071 Market Place San Ramon CA 925-277-9292
Dogs of all sizes are allowed. There is a $75 one time fee and a pet policy to sign at check in.
San Ramon Marriott 2600 Bishop Drive San Ramon CA 925-867-9200 (800-228-9290)
Dogs of all sizes are allowed. There can be up to 2 large or 3 small to medium dogs per room. There is a $75 one time additional pet fee per room. Dogs may not be left alone in the room at any time, and they must be leashed and cleaned up after.
Crowne Plaza 32083 Alvarado-Niles Road Union City CA 510-489-2200 (877-270-6405)
Dogs of all sizes are allowed. There are no additional pet fees. Smoking and non-smoking rooms are available for pets.
Embassy Suites Hotel Walnut Creek 1345 Treat Blvd. Walnut Creek CA 925-934-2500
Dogs up to 75 pounds are allowed. There is a $75 one time pet fee per visit and a $15 per night additional pet fee. Dogs are not allowed to be left alone in the room.
Motel 6 - Walnut Creek 2389 North Main Street Walnut Creek CA 925-935-4010 (800-466-8356)
One well-behaved family pet per room. Guest must notify front desk upon arrival. Guest is liable for any damages. In consideration of all guests, pets must never be left unattended in the guest rooms.

Campgrounds and RV Parks
Del Valle Regional Park 7000 Del Valle Road Livermore CA 510-562-2267
http://www.ebparks.org/parks/delval.htm
This park of almost 4,000 acres sits along a lake surrounded by rolling hills. It is a popular area for nature study, a variety of land and water recreation, and for hiking. It also serves as an entrance to the Ohlone Wilderness Trail. Dogs of all sizes are allowed for an additional $2 per night per pet, and they must have current tags, rabies, and shot records. Dogs may not be left unattended at any time, and they must be on no more than a 6 foot leash and cleaned up after. Dogs are not allowed on the beach. The gates at this park close each night at 10 pm. There are some breed restrictions. This campground is closed during the off-season. The camping and tent areas also allow dogs. There is a dog walk area at the campground. There are no electric hookups at the campgrounds.
Anthony Chabot Regional Park 9999 Redwood Road Oakland CA 510-562-2267
With almost 5,000 acres this beautiful park features an amphitheater, naturalist-led campfire programs, a marksmanship range, and a full range of activities and recreation. Dogs of all sizes are allowed for an additional $2 per night per pet. Dogs may not be left unattended, and they must be leashed, and cleaned up after at all times. Dogs are not allowed on the beach. The gates at this park close at 10 pm. The camping and tent areas also allow dogs. There is a dog walk area at the campground.

Attractions
Rosenblum Cellars 2900 Main Street Alameda CA 510-865-7007
http://www.rosenblumcellars.com/
Well-behaved dogs are allowed at the outdoor tables. The tasting room hours are 12pm-5pm daily.
Redwood Valley Railway Tilden Park Berkeley CA 510-548-6100
http://www.redwoodvalleyrailway.com

Dogs on leash are allowed to ride the miniature train for free. They do warn it is a noisy ride.

Telegraph Ave Telegraph Ave Berkeley CA

Telegraph Avenue in Berkeley is a colorful multi-cultural center. There are numerous boutiques, street vendors, artists and street performers set up along the sidewalks of Telegraph Avenue between Bancroft Way and Dwight Way. It can be quite busy here, so make sure your pup is okay in crowds. Thanks to one of our readers for the following information: "There is an ordinance prohibiting more than two 'stationary' dogs within ten feet of each other on a certain part of Telegraph Avenue. This ordinance is aimed at the homeless, and I've never personally seen it enforced in the two or so years of existence... The most likely consequence of violating the ordinance is being asked to move your dog. A more serious concern to me would be bringing a not-yet-fully immunized young puppy to the area, where it might me more likely to get parvo, etc/ from a dog that has not received much if any veterinary care." To get there from Hwy 880 heading north, take the Hwy 980 exit towards Hwy 24/Walnut Creek. Then take the Hwy 24 exit on the left towards Berkeley/Walnut Creek. Exit at Claremont Ave and turn left onto Claremont Ave. Make a slight left onto College Ave. Turn left onto Dwight Way. Then turn right onto Telegraph Ave. Parking can be very difficult except maybe during the summer and University holidays.

Eugene O'Neill National Historic Site PO Box 280 Danville CA 925-838-0249

http://www.nps.gov/euon/index.htm

Dogs must be on leash and must be cleaned up after on the grounds. Dogs are not allowed in any buildings. Home of America's only Nobel Prize winning playwright.

Marina Boat Rentals

Marina Boat Rentals Del Valle Road Livermore CA 925-373-0332

http://www.ebparks.org/parks/delval.htm

Rent a patio boat with your dog and explore Lake Del Valle. Each patio boat holds up to 6 people. There is a 10 mph speed limit on the lake. It costs about $70 for 2 hours or less. All day rentals are available for $100. They do require a $100 refundable deposit (credit card okay). Prices are subject to change. The rentals are available from 6am-5pm, seven days a week, weather permitting. This lake is about 5 miles long and is located in Del Valle Regional Park, about 10 miles south of Livermore. To get there from Hwy 580 heading east, exit S. Vasco Road. Turn right onto Vasco and head south. When Vasco ends, turn right onto Tesla Rd. Then turn left onto Mines Rd. Turn right onto Del Valle Road. Follow Del Valle Rd to the park entrance.

Juan Bautista de Anza National Historic Trail 1111 Jackson Street #700 Oakland CA 510-817-1438

http://www.nps.gov/juba/index.htm

Dogs on leash are allowed on most of the trails. You must respect state park rules and private property rules within California and Arizona. The trail features touring trail by car, bicycle, or foot depending on area. This trail commemorates the route followed by Juan Bautista de Anza, a Spanish commander, in 1775-76 when he led a contingent of 30 soldiers and their families to the San Francisco Bay.

Western Aerospace Museum 8260 Boeing St., Building 621 Oakland Airport Oakland CA 510-638-7100

The museum is located at historic Oakland Airport, North Field, in a 1940 wooden and corrugated metal military-type hanger. This site was the take-off point for many famous flights, including the first several flights across the Pacific. The museum has indoor and outdoor exhibit areas. Well-behaved, leashed dogs are welcome. Please make sure your pooch relieves himself before going into the museum, including the outdoor museum. The museum is open Wednesday through Sunday and on most holidays except for Christmas and New Year's Day). Hours are 10am to 4pm. There is a minimal admission fee.

Shopping Centers

Jack London Square

Jack London Square Broadway & Embarcadero Oakland CA   510-814-6000
http://www.jacklondonsquare.com
Historic Jack London Square was named after the famous author, who spent his early years in Oakland. In the 1800's, this waterfront was one of Oakland's main shipping ports. Today it is a shopping village with shops, restaurants, entertainment and more. While at the village, you and your dog can take a self-guided history walk by following the distinctive bronze wolf tracks in the walkway. The walk begins at Heinold's First and Last Chance Saloon. At the village you will also find musical entertainment Sunday afternoons in the courtyard. Be aware that on Sundays, from 10am-2pm, there is a Farmer's Market in the main walkway (center and north end of the village). Dogs are not allowed in the market and the security attendants will remind you. The market pretty much fills up the main walkway, so it is tough to walk around it. There are some dog-friendly outdoor restaurants located at the village. To get there from Hwy 880 heading north, exit Broadway. Turn left onto Broadway. Follow Broadway into Jack London Square.

Stores

Petco Pet Store 2310 South Shore Center Alameda CA   510-864-1844
Your licensed and well-behaved leashed dog is allowed in the store.
PetSmart Pet Store 1001 Eastshore Hwy Albany CA   510-524-1518
Your licensed and well-behaved leashed dog is allowed in the store.
PetSmart Pet Store 5879 Lone Tree Way Antioch CA   925-755-8504
Your licensed and well-behaved leashed dog is allowed in the store.
Avenue Books 2904 College Avenue Berkeley CA   510-549-3532
Thanks to one of our readers who writes "So dog-friendly, they offer doggie biscuits!" They are located in the Elmwood district and are open 7 days a week.
Restoration Hardware 1733 Fourth Street Berkeley CA   510-526-6424
http://www.restorationhardware.com/

Petco Pet Store 3735 East Castro Valley Blvd Castro Valley CA   510-886-4466
Your licensed and well-behaved leashed dog is allowed in the store.
PetSmart Pet Store 1700 Willow Pass Rd Concord CA   925-687-7199
Your licensed and well-behaved leashed dog is allowed in the store.
Petco Pet Store 1825 Salvio St Concord CA   925-827-3338

Your licensed and well-behaved leashed dog is allowed in the store.
PetSmart Pet Store 6960 Amador Plaza Rd Dublin CA   925-803-8370
Your licensed and well-behaved leashed dog is allowed in the store.
Petco Pet Store 11976 Dublin Blvd Dublin CA   925-803-4045
Your licensed and well-behaved leashed dog is allowed in the store.
Petco Pet Store 420 El Cerrito Plaza El Cerrito CA   510-528-7919
Your licensed and well-behaved leashed dog is allowed in the store.
Petco Pet Store 1370 Holiday Lane Ste A Fairfield CA   707-427-8162
Your licensed and well-behaved leashed dog is allowed in the store.
PetSmart Pet Store 39410 Argonaut Way Fremont CA   510-790-1459
Your licensed and well-behaved leashed dog is allowed in the store.
Petco Pet Store 3780 Mowry Avenue Fremont CA   510-742-0573
Your licensed and well-behaved leashed dog is allowed in the store.
Petco Pet Store 3517 Mount Diablo Blvd Lafayette CA   925-284-1756
Your licensed and well-behaved leashed dog is allowed in the store.
Petco Pet Store 1170 Arnold Drive Ste 115 Martinez CA   925-370-6060
Your licensed and well-behaved leashed dog is allowed in the store.
PetSmart Pet Store 4655 Century Blvd Pittsburg CA   925-706-9975
Your licensed and well-behaved leashed dog is allowed in the store.
PetSmart Pet Store 3700 Klose Way Bldg 4 Richmond CA   510-758-8990
Your licensed and well-behaved leashed dog is allowed in the store.
PetSmart Pet Store 15555 E 14th St San Leandro CA   510-317-1880
Your licensed and well-behaved leashed dog is allowed in the store.
Petco Pet Store 2005 Crow Canyon Place San Ramon CA   925-275-2111
Your licensed and well-behaved leashed dog is allowed in the store.
Petco Pet Store 31090 Dyer St Union City CA   510-477-9235
Your licensed and well-behaved leashed dog is allowed in the store.
Petco Pet Store 1301 South California St Walnut Creek CA   925-988-9370
Your licensed and well-behaved leashed dog is allowed in the store.
Restoration Hardware 1460 Mt Diablo Blvd Walnut Creek CA   925-906-9230
http://www.restorationhardware.com/
Your well-behaved leashed dog is allowed inside this store. They love having dogs in the store!

Parks

Benicia State Recreation Area Interstate 780 Benicia CA   707-648-1911
This park covers 720 acres of marsh, grassy hillsides and rocky beaches along the narrowest portion of the
Carquinez Strait. Dogs on leash are allowed. Cyclists, runners, walkers and roller skaters enjoy the park's 2
miles of road and bike paths. Picnicking, bird watching and fishing are also attractions. The recreation area is 1.5
miles west of the outskirts of Benicia on I-780. Cars can enter the park through a toll gate.
Tilden Regional Park Grizzly Peak Blvd. Berkeley CA   510-562-PARK
http://www.ebparks.org/parks/tilden.htm
This regional park has over 2,000 acres including Lake Anza. Dogs must be on leash in the parking areas, picnic
areas, lawns and developed areas. Your dog can run off-leash in other areas and trails, just make sure they are
under voice control and you must carry a leash. Your dog should be under voice control around bicyclists and
equestrians - this has been the biggest area of conflict for unleashed dogs. At Lake Anza, dogs are not allowed
at swimming pools or swim beaches. But you should be able to find a non-swim beach where your dog can play
and swim in the water. The park can be reached via Canon Drive, Shasta Road, or South Park Drive, all off
Grizzly Peak Boulevard in Berkeley.

Coyote Hills Regional Park

Coyote Hills Regional Park Patterson Ranch Rd. Fremont CA   510-562-PARK
http://www.ebparks.org/parks/coyote.htm
This regional park has Ohlone Indian shellmound sites with fascinating archaeological resources. This Indian site can be viewed from the Chochenyo Trail. For a longer hike, try the 3.5 mile long Bayview bike trail. There are many other numerous trails that wind through the park which offer scenic vistas of the San Francisco Bay. Dogs must be on leash. They are not allowed in the seasonal wetlands, marshes, or the Visitor Center lawn area. But there are plenty of dog-friendly trails around to satisfy you and your pup. Coyote Hills is at the west end of Patterson Ranch Road/ Commerce Drive in Fremont. From I-880, take Highway 84 west, exit at Paseo Padre Parkway and drive north. Turn left on Patterson Ranch Road (parking fee).

Sunol Regional Wilderness Geary Rd. Fremont CA   510-562-PARK
http://www.ebparks.org/parks/sunol.htm
This park is home to the Ohlone Wilderness Trail and Little Yosemite. The Wilderness Trail is at least 7 miles long in each direction. It spans the length of the park and connects up to the Mission Peak Regional Preserve. Hikers who cross into the San Francisco Water Department lands that connect Mission Peak Regional Preserve, Sunol, Ohlone Regional Wilderness and Del Valle Regional Park must carry an Ohlone Wilderness Trail map/permit. Little Yosemite is a scenic gorge on the Alameda Creek. It is open to the public through a lease agreement with the San Francisco Water Department, who owns the property. The Canyon View Trail is about 1.5 miles each way and leads into Little Yosemite. There are approximately 6-7 other popular trails ranging from 1.2 miles to over 7 miles. Dogs must be on leash in the parking areas, picnic areas, lawns and developed areas. Your dog can run off-leash on most of the trails, just make sure they are under voice control and you must carry a leash. Check with the ranger as to which trails require your dog to be leashed. To get there from the Fremont area, drive north on I-680 and exit at Calaveras Road. Turn right on Calaveras and proceed to Geary Road, which leads directly into the park.

Garin and Dry Creek Regional Parks Garin Ave Hayward CA
http://www.ebparks.org/parks/garin.htm
There are over 3,000 acres of land between these two parks. Combined, these parks have over 20 miles of unpaved trails. You'll also find several creeks that run through the parks. To get there from Mission Blvd, take Garin Rd to the park entrance. There is a minimal fee for parking.

Bethany Reservoir State Recreation Area off Grant Line Road Livermore CA   209-874-2056
This park offers activities like fishing and windsurfing. There is also a bike trail that follows the California Aqueduct. Leashed dogs are allowed on the trails. The person we spoke at the park office believes that dogs are also allowed in the lake. Please clean up after your pets. The recreation area is northeast of Livermore, 7 miles off Interstate 580 at the Grant Line Road exit.

Del Valle Dog Run Del Valle Road Livermore CA   510-562-PARK
http://www.ebparks.org/parks/delval.htm
This dog run is located in Del Valle Regional Park. Here your dog can walk leash free along the trail with you. Del Valle Regional Park is over 3,997 acres of land and it includes a five mile long lake. To get there from Hwy 580 heading east, exit S. Vasco Road. Turn right onto Vasco and head south. When Vasco ends, turn right onto

Tesla Rd. Then turn left onto Mines Rd. Turn right onto Del Valle Road. Follow Del Valle Rd to the park entrance. The dog run is to the right of the marina.

Del Valle Regional Park Del Valle Road Livermore CA 510-562-PARK
http://www.ebparks.org/parks/delval.htm
This park is over 3,997 acres of land and it includes a five mile long lake. The park is in a valley surrounded by oak-covered hills. Miles of trails surround the lake. If you would rather view the scenery from the water, you and your dog can rent a patio boat at the Marina Boat Rentals (see Attractions). Dogs must be on leash in the parking areas, picnic areas, lawns and developed areas. Your dog can run off-leash in other areas and on trails, just make sure they are under voice control and you must carry a leash. Your dog should be under voice control around bicyclists and equestrians - this has been the biggest area of conflict for unleashed dogs. Dogs are not allowed at swimming pools or swim beaches. But with a 5 mile long lake, you should be able to find a non-swim beach where your dog can play in the water. To get there from Hwy 580 heading east, exit S. Vasco Road. Turn right onto Vasco and head south. When Vasco ends, turn right onto Tesla Rd. Then turn left onto Mines Rd. Turn right onto Del Valle Road. Follow Del Valle Rd to the park entrance.

Ohlone Regional Wilderness Del Valle Rd Livermore CA 510-562-PARK
http://www.ebparks.org/parks/ohlone.htm
This park's centerpiece is the 3,817-foot Rose Peak, just 32 feet lower than Mount Diablo. Surrounding Rose Peak are 9,156 acres of grassy ridges, flowered in season. Wildlife found at this park includes golden eagles, mountain lions, and tule elk. The wilderness trail through this park is 28 miles of mountain and canyon terrain in southern Alameda County. Your dog is allowed to run off-leash, as long as he or she is under voice control. There are several entrances to this park and the trail, including the Del Valle Regional Park (off Del Valle Rd) and the Sunol Regional Wilderness (off Geary Rd).

Sycamore Grove Park Wetmore Road Livermore CA 510-373-5700
This park has over 360 acres and provides walking paths, jogging paths and picnic areas. There are many kinds of wildlife here such as deer, fox, bobcat, hawks and more. Dogs must be on leash. To get there from Hwy 580 heading east, take the First Street exit. Turn right and follow First Street until it turns into Holmes Ave. Then turn left onto Wetmore Road. The park entrance is on the right. There is a minimal fee for parking.

John Muir National Historic Site 4202 Alhambra Avenue Martinez CA 925-228-8860
http://www.nps.gov/jomu/
While dogs are not allowed in any buildings or on the nature trails, they are allowed on the adjacent Mt. Wanda fire road trail. Hike up to the top and back with your pooch. Pets must be leashed and rangers actively patrol the area and will issue citations to anyone who has their dog off leash. To get to the trail, park at the historic site or at the Park and Ride lot on Franklin Canyon and Alhambra. Please clean up after your pet.

Lake Merritt Lakeside Drive Oakland CA
http://www.lakemerritt.com/
This park and lake is in the center of Oakland. Dogs are not allowed inside the park or lake. However, if you keep your dog leashed, you can walk the perimeter (furthest outside) sidewalk. You'll want to remember this rule, since a $270 ticket could be imposed if you venture into the park. It has a nice approximately 3 mile perimeter path that winds around the lake. It is a popular walking, jogging and biking path. To get there from Hwy 880 heading north, take the Oak Street exit towards Lakeside Drive. Turn right onto Oak Street. Oak Street becomes Lakeside Drive. There is ample parking.

Shadow Cliffs Stanley Blvd. Pleasanton CA 510-562-PARK
http://www.ebparks.org/parks/shadow.htm
Special thanks to one of our readers for the info on this great dog-friendly park. This 296-acre park includes an 80-acre lake. Dogs must be on leash in the parking areas, picnic areas, lawns and developed areas. Your dog can run off-leash in other areas and trails, just make sure they are under voice control and you must carry a leash. Your dog should be under voice control around bicyclists and equestrians - this has been the biggest area of conflict for unleashed dogs. Dogs are not allowed at swimming pools or swim beaches. But you should be able to find a non-swim beach where your dog can play and swim in the water. To get there, from I-580 take the Santa Rita Road south, turn left onto Valley Ave, then left onto Stanley Blvd. Turn right off Stanley into the park. There is a minimal entrance fee.

Wildcat Canyon Regional Park 5755 McBride Richmond CA 510-562-PARK (7275)
http://www.ebparks.org/parks/wildcat.htm
Rich in natural and cultural history, this park of over 2,400 acres supports an assortment of plant and animal life, and offers a variety of land and water recreational pursuits, and interpretive programs. There are picnic areas, restrooms, and lots of trails to walk. Dogs of all sizes are allowed throughout the park except where noted. Dogs must be on no more than a 6 foot leash, and be cleaned up after at all times. Dogs are not allowed in any swim areas, park buildings, or the Tilden's Nature Area.

San Miguel Park Off-leash hours Los Cerros Avenue at San Carlos Drive Walnut Creek CA 925-943-5899x232
San Miguel Park is a 4 acre city park with a playground, sports and walking trails. Dogs are allowed to be off-leash and under voice control in the park until 9 am. After 9 am dogs must be on-leash. From Ygnacio Valley Rd turn south onto San Carlos Drive and turn right onto Los Cerros Ave to the park.

Off-Leash Dog Parks

Cesar Chavez Park Off-Leash Dog Area 11 Spinnaker Way Berkeley CA 510-981-6700
There is an off-leash dog area in the north side of the park. Your dog must be leashed while walking to and from this area, and dogs must be cleaned up after. Bags are available at the park. To get to the park from Berkeley go over I-80 on University Ave. From I-80 exit University Avenue and go west towards the bay. However, you will have to turn around on University Avenue if coming from the south.

Ohlone Dog Park Hearst Avenue Berkeley CA
This is a relatively small dog park. At certain times, there can be lots of dogs here. The hours are 6am-10pm on weekdays and 9am-10pm on weekends. The park is located at Hearst Ave, just west of Martin Luther King Jr. Way. There is limited street parking.

Castro Valley Dog Park 4660 Crow Canyon Castro Valley CA 510-881-6700
http://geocities.com/cvdogpark/
The Castro Valley Dog Run has two fenced areas, one for larger dogs and one for small dogs. There are two parking lots, rest rooms, an open lawn area and picnic tables. The park is open during daylight hours daily. The dog park is located in Earl Warren Park. Exit I 580 at Crow Canyon and head north.

Paw Patch in Newall Community Park Clayton Rd & Newhall Pkwy Concord CA 925-671-3329
This fenced dog park is located in Newhall Community Park in Concord. To get to the park from Clayton Road or Turtle Creek Road head south on Newhall Parkway. Local dog groups frequently meet at the dog park.

Central Park Dog Park 1110 Stevenson Blvd Fremont CA 510-494-4800
Thanks to one of our readers who writes: "Fenced, fresh water on demand, plenty of free parking, easy to find, all grass." Pet waste disposal bags are available at the park. The dog park is open from sunrise to 10 pm. The park is located on one acre, is adjacent to the Central Park Softball Complex with access off of Stevenson Blvd. To get there from I 680 head north on Mission Blvd and turn left on Stevenson Blvd. The park is on the left. From I 880 take Stevenson Blvd east to the park on the right.

Livermore Canine Park Murdell Lane Livermore CA
This dog park is located in Max Baer Park. It has several trees and a lawn. To get there from downtown Livermore, head west on Stanely Blvd. Turn left on Isabel Ave. Then turn left onto Concannon Blvd (if you reach Alden Ln, you've passed Concannon). Turn left on Murdell Lane and the park will be on the right.

Hardy Dog Park 491 Hardy Street Oakland CA 510-238-PARK
This 2 acre dog park in fully fenced. Dogs must be on-leash outside of the park. The park is located on Hardy Street at Claremont Avenue in the Rockridge District. It is just under the 24 Freeway.

Point Isabel Regional Shoreline

Point Isabel Regional Shoreline Isabel Street Richmond CA 510-562-PARK
This 20 plus acre park is a dog park that is not completely fenced, but has paved paths, grass and beach access

to the bay. If your pooch likes chasing birds, beware... dogs sometimes run over to the bird sanctuary which is close to the freeway. Other activities at this park include bay fishing, jogging and running trails, birdwatching, kite flying and picnicking. Thanks to one of our readers for providing us with this great information. From I-80 (the Eastshore Freeway) in Richmond, take Central Avenue west to Point Isabel, adjacent to the U.S. Postal Service Bulk Mail Center.

Muirwood Dog Exercise Area 4701 Muirwood Drive Pleasanton CA 925-931-5340
This 3/4 acre fenced dog park is located in Muirwood Community Park. To get to the park, exit I-680 at Stoneridge Dr and head west. Turn left on Springdale Avenue and left again on Muirwood Drive. The park will be on the left.

Del Mar Dog Park Del Mar and Pine Valley San Ramon CA 925-973-3200
To get to this fenced dog park, take I-680 to Alcosta, exit east, and turn left onto Broadmoor. Turn left onto Pine Valley and left on Del Mar.

Memorial Park Dog Run Bollinger Canyon Road at San Ramon Valley Blvd San Ramon CA 925-973-3200
This fenced dog park is just over one acre in size and is located within San Ramon's Memorial Park. It has shade and benches. From I-680 exit Bollinger Canyon Rd, go west and cross San Ramon Valley Blvd and park on the left.

Drigon Dog Park Mission Blvd at 7th Street Union City CA 510-471-3232x702
The Drigon Dog Park is open from 6 am to 10 pm except for Mondays. It is closed all day Monday for cleaning. The dog park has separate fenced areas for small and large dogs. There are agility tunnels and climbing items available at the park. The park is sometimes closed due to wet weather. To get to the park from I-880 take Decoto Road to Mission Blvd and head south on Mission to the park. From I-680 take Mission Blvd north to the park.

Outdoor Restaurants
Tucker's Super-Creamed Ice Cream 1349 Park Street Alameda CA 510-522-4960
http://www.tuckersicecream.com/#
This ice creamery usually has an outdoor table by the front door where you and your pooch can enjoy an ice cream. Dogs must be attended to at all times, well behaved, and leashed.

Cugini Restaurant 1556 Solano Ave Albany CA 510-558-9000
Your dog is welcome to join you for dinner at this restaurant. They serve a variety of wood-fired pizzas. It is located on Solano Ave, which is a shopping area.

Schmidts Pub 1492 Solano Avenue Albany CA 510-525-1900
Dogs are allowed at the outdoor tables at this bar.

Bel Forno 1400 Shattuck Ave Berkeley CA 510-644-1601
Open for breakfast and lunch, this cafe serves omelets, pastries, salads, soups, sandwiches and more. They have 5-6 outdoor tables. It is located northwest of the UC Berkeley campus.

Cafe Trieste 2500 San Pablo Ave Berkeley CA 510-548-5198
Dogs are allowed at the outdoor tables.

French Hotel Cafe 1538 Shattuck Ave Berkeley CA 510-548-9930
You and your dog are welcome at the outdoor tables. The cafe is located northwest of the UC Berkeley campus.

Homemade Cafe 2454 Sacramento St Berkeley CA 510-845-1940
This restaurant serves American food. Dogs are allowed at the outdoor tables.

Pasta Shop 1786 4th Street Berkeley CA 510-528-1786
This restaurant serves Italian food. Dogs are allowed at the outdoor tables.

Tacubaya 1788 4th Street Berkeley CA 510-525-5160
This restaurant serves Mexican food. Dogs are allowed at the outdoor tables.

Whole Foods Market 3000 Telegraph Ave. Berkeley CA 510-649-1333
http://www.wholefoods.com/
This natural food supermarket offers natural and organic foods. Order some food from their deli without your dog and bring it to an outdoor table where your well-behaved leashed dog is welcome. Dogs are not allowed in the store including the deli at any time.

Skipolini's Pizza 1033 Diablo St Clayton CA 925-672-1111
This restaurant serves Pizza and pasta. Dogs are allowed at the outdoor tables.

Cafe A 1515 Broadway Concord CA 925-825-2800
http://www.cafeasap.com
Dogs are allowed at the outdoor tables.

Baja Fresh Mexican Grill 4550 Tassajara Rd. Dublin CA 925-556-9199
http://www.bajafresh.com
This Mexican restaurant is open for lunch and dinner. They use fresh ingredients and making their salsa and beans daily. Some of the items on their menu include Enchiladas, Burritos, Tacos Salads, Quesadillas, Nachos, Chicken, Steak and more. Well-behaved leashed dogs are allowed at the outdoor tables.

Baja Fresh Mexican Grill 1450 Travis Blvd Fairfield CA 707-432-0460
http://www.bajafresh.com
This Mexican restaurant is open for lunch and dinner. They use fresh ingredients and making their salsa and

beans daily. Some of the items on their menu include Enchiladas, Burritos, Tacos Salads, Quesadillas, Nachos, Chicken, Steak and more. Well-behaved leashed dogs are allowed at the outdoor tables.
Camille's Sidewalk Cafe 24375 Southland Drive Hayward CA 510-783-8801
A vision of healthier, tastier foods inspired the idea for the freshly made salads, gourmet wraps and sandwiches, drinks, desserts, and coffees that are offered at all of Camille's Cafes. Dogs are allowed to sit with you at your outdoor table. Dogs must be attended to at all times, well behaved, and leashed.
Baja Fresh Mexican Grill 3596 Mt. Diablo Blvd. Lafayette CA 925-283-8740
http://www.bajafresh.com
This Mexican restaurant is open for lunch and dinner. They use fresh ingredients and making their salsa and beans daily. Some of the items on their menu include Enchiladas, Burritos, Tacos Salads, Quesadillas, Nachos, Chicken, Steak and more. Well-behaved leashed dogs are allowed at the outdoor tables.
Chow Restaurant 53 Lafayette Circle Lafayette CA 925-962-2469
This restaurant serves American food. Dogs are allowed at the outdoor tables.
Uncle Yu's Szechuan 999 Oak Hill Rd Lafayette CA 925-283-1688
This restaurant serves Szechuan food. Dogs are allowed at the outdoor tables.
Altamonte Pass Cafe 7633 Southfront Road Livermore CA 925-960-0636
http://www.altamontpasscafe.com
Well-behaved leashed dogs are allowed at the outdoor seating area. They offer specialty coffee drinks, snacks, beverages, sandwiches, and pastries for breakfast, lunch and corporate catering.
Baja Fresh Mexican Grill 2298 Las Positas Livermore CA 925-245-9888
http://www.bajafresh.com
This Mexican restaurant is open for lunch and dinner. They use fresh ingredients and making their salsa and beans daily. Some of the items on their menu include Enchiladas, Burritos, Tacos Salads, Quesadillas, Nachos, Chicken, Steak and more. Well-behaved leashed dogs are allowed at the outdoor tables.
Bruno's Italian Cuisine 2133 First Street Livermore CA 925-371-3999
Well-behaved leashed dogs are allowed at the outdoor seating area.
Cafe Paradiso 53 Wright Brothers Avenue Livermore CA 925-371-2233
Well-behaved leashed dogs are allowed at the outdoor seating area.
Chevys Fresh Mex 4685 First Street Livermore CA 925-960-0071
Well-behaved leashed dogs are allowed at the outdoor seating area.
Manpuku 4363 First Street Livermore CA 925-371-9038
Well-behaved leashed dogs are allowed at the outdoor seating area. This restaurant serves Oriental cuisine.
New York Pizza 853 E Stanley Blvd Livermore CA 925-447-4992
Well-behaved leashed dogs are allowed at the outdoor seating area.
Panama Bay Coffee Co. 2115 First Street Livermore CA 925-245-1700
Well-behaved leashed dogs are allowed at the outdoor seating area.
Una Mas Taqueria 1476 First Street Livermore CA 925-606-5120
http://www.unamas.com/
Well-behaved leashed dogs are allowed at the outdoor seating area.
La Beau's Louisiana kitchen 436 Fairy Street Martinez CA 925-229-9232
Dogs are allowed at the outdoor tables.

Heinolds First & Last Chance 56 Jack London Sq Oakland CA 510-839-6761
Dogs are welcome at the outdoor tables of this bar. The saloon serves beer, wine and cocktails. Heinold's First and Last Chance Saloon is where the famous author, Jack London, borrowed his entrance fee for college from the proprietor. This bar is the starting point for the self-guided history walk of Jack London Square (see Attractions).
Italian Colors Ristorante 2220 Mountain Boulevard Oakland CA 510-482-8094
Dogs are allowed at the outdoor tables.
Tony Roma's 55 Washington St Oakland CA 510-271-1818
http://www.tonyromas.com/ .
This restaurant is famous for its barbecue ribs. They also serve chicken, steak, seafood and delicious desserts. It is located in the dog-friendly Jack London Square (see Attractions).
Zazoo's Restaurant 30 Jack London Sq Oakland CA 510-986-5454
Located on the waterfront, this restaurant serves seafood, pasta, burgers, kabobs, omelets, salads and more. Try the tasty kabobs. It is located in the dog-friendly Jack London Square (see Attractions).
Shelby's 2 Theater Square Orinda CA 925-254-9687
This restaurant serves American food. Dogs are allowed at the outdoor tables.
360 (Degrees) Gourmet Burritos 4220 Rosewood Drive Pleasanton CA 925-225-9306
Well-behaved leashed dogs are allowed at the outdoor seating area.
Baci Restaurant 500 Main Street Pleasanton CA 925-600-0600
Well-behaved leashed dogs are allowed at the outdoor seating area.
Baja Fresh Mexican Grill 2457 Stoneridge Mall Ste. Pleasanton CA 925-251-1500
http://www.bajafresh.com
This Mexican restaurant is open for lunch and dinner. They use fresh ingredients and making their salsa and

beans daily. Some of the items on their menu include Enchiladas, Burritos, Tacos Salads, Quesadillas, Nachos, Chicken, Steak and more. Well-behaved leashed dogs are allowed at the outdoor tables.
Erik's Deli 4247 Rosewood Drive Pleasanton CA 925-847-9755
Well-behaved leashed dogs are allowed at the outdoor seating area.

Heinolds First & Last Chance

High Tech Burrito 349 Main Street Pleasanton CA 925-462-2323
Well-behaved leashed dogs are allowed at the outdoor seating area.
New York Pizza 690 Main Street Pleasanton CA 925-484-4757
Well-behaved leashed dogs are allowed at the outdoor seating area.
New York Pizza and Deli 5321 Hopyard Road Pleasanton CA 925-847-1700
Well-behaved leashed dogs are allowed at the outdoor seating area.
Rising Loafer Cafe & Bakery 428 Main Street Pleasanton CA 925-426-0822
Well-behaved leashed dogs are allowed at the outdoor seating area.
TGI Fridays 3999 Santa Rita Road Pleasanton CA 925-225-1995
Well-behaved leashed dogs are allowed at the outdoor seating area.
Tomo Sushi Bar & Grill 724 Main Street Pleasanton CA 925-600-9136
Well-behaved leashed dogs are allowed at the seats on the front patio, but not on the back patio.
Baja Fresh Mexican Grill 132 Sunset Drive San Ramon CA 925-866-6667
http://www.bajafresh.com
Your dog is welcome here! This Mexican restaurant is open for lunch and dinner. They use fresh ingredients and making their salsa and beans daily. Some of the items on their menu include Enchiladas, Burritos, Tacos Salads, Quesadillas, Nachos, Chicken, Steak and more. Well-behaved leashed dogs are allowed at the outdoor tables.
Whole Foods Market 100 Sunset Drive San Ramon CA 925-355-9000
http://www.wholefoods.com/
This natural food supermarket offers natural and organic foods. Order some food from their deli without your dog and bring it to an outdoor table where your well-behaved leashed dog is welcome. Dogs are not allowed in the store including the deli at any time.
Baja Fresh Mexican Grill 1271-1273 S. California Blvd. Walnut Creek CA 925-947-0588
http://www.bajafresh.com
This Mexican restaurant is open for lunch and dinner. They use fresh ingredients and making their salsa and beans daily. Some of the items on their menu include Enchiladas, Burritos, Tacos Salads, Quesadillas, Nachos, Chicken, Steak and more. Well-behaved leashed dogs are allowed at the outdoor tables.
Pacific Bay Coffee Co and Micro-Roastry 1495 Newell Ave Walnut Creek CA 925-935-1709

This cafe serves coffee,smoothies and pastries. Dogs are allowed at the outdoor tables.
Whole Foods Market 1333 E. Newell Walnut Creek CA   925-274-9700
http://www.wholefoods.com/
This natural food supermarket offers natural and organic foods. Order some food from their deli without your dog and bring it to an outdoor table where your well-behaved leashed dog is welcome. Dogs are not allowed in the store including the deli at any time.

Events
Oakland A's Dog Day at the Park 7000 Coliseum Way Oakland CA   510-638-4900
The annual Dog Days of Summer Event is an A's baseball game at which dogs may attend with their owners. Dogs and their owners can watch the game together from the Plaza Reserve and pooches receive an Oakland A's bandana and a goodie bag. Dogs must be well behaved, leashed, and cleaned up after at all times.

Day Kennels
PetsHotel by PetsMart Day Kennel 39410 Argonaut Way Fremont CA
http://www.petsmart.com/PETsHOTEL/
This PetSmart pet store offers day care, day camp and overnight care. You may drop off and pick up your dog 7 am - 9 pm M-S, Sunday 8 am - 7 pm. Dogs are required to have proof of current rabies, DPP and bordatella vaccines.

Vets and Kennels
Pet Emergency Treatment Service 1048 University Ave Berkeley CA   510-548-6684
Monday - Friday 6pm to 8am, Noon Saturday to 8 am Monday.
Veterinary Emergency Clinic 1410 Monument Blvd Concord CA   925-798-2900
Monday - Friday 6pm to 8am, 24 hours weekends and holidays.
Ohlone Veterinary Emergency 1618 Washington Blvd Fremont CA   510-657-6620
Monday - Friday 6pm to 8am, 24 hours weekends and holidays.
Alameda County Emergency Pet Hospital 14790 Washington Ave San Leandro CA   510-352-6080
Monday - Friday 6pm to 8am, 24 hours weekends and holidays.

Palo Alto - Peninsula

Accommodations
Motel 6 - San Francisco - Belmont 1101 Shoreway Road Belmont CA   650-591-1471 (800-466-8356)
A well-behaved large dog is okay. There are no additional pet fees for a regular room. For a suite, there is a $10 per day pet fee up to a maximum of $50 per visit.
Crowne Plaza, San Francisco International Airport 1177 Airport Blvd Burlingame CA   877-252-1558 (877-270-6405)
http://www.sfocp.com
Dogs of all sizes are allowed. There is a $100 refundable pet deposit.
Doubletree 835 Airport Blvd Burlingame CA   650-344-5500
Dogs up to 50 pounds are allowed. There is a $20 one time fee per pet and a pet policy to sign at check in.
Embassy Suites Hotel San Francisco Airport/Burlingame 150 Anza Blvd. Burlingame CA   650-342-4600
Dogs of all sizes are allowed. There is a $50 one time pet fee per visit. Dogs are not allowed to be left alone in the room.
Red Roof Inn - San Francisco Airport 777 Airport Boulevard Burlingame CA   650-342-7772 (800-RED-ROOF)
One well-behaved dog is up to about 80 pounds is allowed. There are no additional pet fees.
San Francisco Airport Marriott 1800 Old Bayshore H Burlingame CA   650-692-9100 (800-228-9290)
Dogs of all sizes are allowed. There is a $75 one time additional pet fee per room. Dogs must be leashed, cleaned up after, removed or accompanied for housekeeping, and the Pet in Room sign put on the door if they are in the room alone.
Vagabond Inn 1640 Bayshore Highway Burlingame CA   650-692-4040 (800-522-1555)
http://www.vagabondinn.com
This motel overlooks the San Francisco Bay. It is located just south of the airport and about 16 miles from downtown San Francisco. All rooms include coffee makers, cable television and air conditioning. Pets are an additional $10 per day.
Four Seasons Hotel Silicon Valley 2050 University Ave. East Palo Alto CA   650-566-1200
Dogs of all sizes are allowed. There are no additional pet fees. Dogs are not allowed to be left alone in the room.
Comfort Inn 2930 N Cabrillo H Half Moon Bay CA   650-712-1999 (877-424-6423)

Dogs of all sizes are allowed. There is a $20 one time fee per room. Dogs must be leashed, cleaned up after, and the Do Not Disturb sign put on the door if they are in the room alone.
Holiday Inn Express 230 S Cabrillo Hwy Half Moon Bay CA 650-726-3400 (877-270-6405)
http://www.holiday-inn.com
Amenities at this motel include a deluxe complimentary continental breakfast. There is an additional $10 per day per pet charge. All rooms in the hotel are non-smoking.
Clarion Hotel San Francisco Airport 401 E Millbrae Avenue Millbrae CA 650-692-6363 (877-424-6423)
One dog of any size is allowed. There are no additional pet fees. Dogs must be quiet, well behaved, leashed, cleaned up after, and the Do Not Disturb sign put on the door if they are in the room alone. A contact number also needs to left with the front desk.
Residence Inn by Marriott 1854 El Camino West Mountain View CA 650-940-1300
Dogs of all sizes are allowed. There is a $75 one time fee per pet, and a pet policy to sign at check in. They also request a credit card to be on file.
Tropicana Lodge 1720 El Camino Real Mountain View CA 650-961-0220
Pets may not be left alone in the rooms.
Motel 6 - Palo Alto 4301 El Camino Real Palo Alto CA 650-949-0833 (800-466-8356)
One well-behaved family pet per room. Guest must notify front desk upon arrival. Guest is liable for any damages. In consideration of all guests, pets must never be left unattended in the guest rooms.
Sheraton Palo Alto Hotel 625 El Camino Real Palo Alto CA 650-328-2800 (888-625-5144)
Dogs of all sizes are allowed. You must sign a pet policy. Dogs are not allowed to be left alone in the room.
The Westin Palo Alto 675 El Camino Real Palo Alto CA 650-321-4422 (888-625-5144)
Dogs up to 80 pounds are allowed. There are no additional pet fees. Dogs are not allowed to be left alone in the room.

Hotel Sofitel

Hotel Sofitel 223 Twin Dolphin Dr Redwood City CA 650-598-9000
http://www.sofitel.com
This nice 8 story dog-friendly hotel is located off Hwy 101 and Marine World Parkway. There is a $25 one time pet fee.
Staybridge Suites 1350 Huntington Avenue San Bruno CA 650-588-0770 (877-270-6405)
Dogs of any size are allowed. There is a $100 one time pet fee. In addition, there is a $10 per day pet additional pet fee for each of the first 7 days.
Residence Inn by Marriott 2000 Winward Way San Mateo CA 650-574-4700
Pets of all sizes are allowed. There is a $75 plus tax one time fee per pet and a pet policy to sign at check in.
Embassy Suites Hotel San Francisco Airport South 250 Gateway boulevard South San Francisco CA 650-589-3400
Dogs of all sizes are allowed. There is a $50 one time pet fee per visit. Dogs are not allowed to be left alone in the room.
Howard Johnson Express Inn 222 South Airport Blvd. South San Francisco CA 650-589-9055 (800-446-

4656)
Dogs of all sizes are welcome. There is a $10 per day pet fee.
La Quinta Inn San Francisco Airport 20 Airport Blvd. South San Francisco CA   650-583-2223 (800-531-5900)
Dogs of all sizes are allowed. There are no additional pet fees. Dogs must be leashed and cleaned up after. Be sure to inform the front desk you have a pet, and put the Do Not Disturb sign on the door if the dog is alone in the room.
Motel 6 - San Francisco Airport 111 Mitchell Avenue South San Francisco CA   650-877-0770 (800-466-8356)
One well-behaved family pet per room. Guest must notify front desk upon arrival. Guest is liable for any damages. In consideration of all guests, pets must never be left unattended in the guest rooms.
Vagabond Inn 222 S. Airport Blvd South San Francisco CA   650-589-9055
Amenities include microwaves and refrigerators in some rooms. There is a $10 per day pet charge. This inn was formerly a Howard Johnson Inn.

Campgrounds and RV Parks
Butano State Park Campground Off Hwy 1 4.5 miles SE of Pescadero Pescadero CA   650-879-2040 (800-444-7275)
The campground can accept RVs up to 27 feet, and camp amenities include picnic tables, water and vault toilets. While dogs are not allowed on the park trails, they are allowed in the campground, picnic area, all paved roads, and on miles of fire roads. Mountain biking is also allowed on the fire roads. Pets must be on a 6 foot or less leash at all times. Please clean up after them. The camping and tent areas also allow dogs. There is a dog walk area at the campground. There are no electric or water hookups at the campgrounds.

Vacation Home Rentals
Estancia del Mar Cottages San Mateo County Coastside Pescadero CA   650-879-1500
http://www.a1vacations.com/edm/1/
Enjoy a romantic getaway or a family vacation at one of the six cottages that overlook the ocean. Dogs are allowed as well as children. Estancia del Mar is also a working horse ranch where the owners breed, raise and train purebred Peruvian Paso horses.

Attractions
Santa's Tree Farm 78 Pilarcitos Creek Road Half Moon Bay CA 650-726-2246
http://members.aol.com/DSare/index.htm
Well-behaved leashed dogs are allowed at this farm, but please note that the owners and/or employees reserve the right to request that your dog wait in the car if your pup misbehaves. Be watchful of others, especially children who may be frightened of dogs. They are open year-round. Santa's Tree Farm offers complimentary candy canes, hot apple cider, and of course, a great selection of Christmas trees. To get there from Hwy 280, take Hwy 92 West towards Half Moon Bay. Hwy 92 becomes Half Moon Bay Road. Go approximately 4 miles and then make a right turn onto Pilarcitos Creek Road.
Hewlett-Packard Garage 367 Addison Ave Palo Alto CA
The HP Garage is known as the birthplace of Silicon Valley. You and your pup can see where William Hewlett and David Packard started HP. Please note that the house is now a private residence, so you'll need to view it from the sidewalk only.

Shopping Centers
Downtown Palo Alto University Ave Palo Alto CA
Downtown Palo Alto is a nice area to walk with your leashed dog. There are many shops and outdoor restaurants that line University Ave. Some of the stores allow dogs inside, like Restoration Hardware. However, please ask the store clerk before bringing your dog inside each store just in case their policies have changed. Enjoy lunch or dinner at one of the many nearby outdoor cafes (see Restaurants).

TOP 200 PLACE Stanford Shopping Center 680 Stanford Shopping Center Palo Alto CA   650-617-8585 (800-772-9332)
http://www.stanfordshop.com/
Stanford Shopping Center is the Bay Area's premier open-air shopping center. This dog-friendly mall has a beautiful outdoor garden environment. Thirty-five varieties of trees are represented by 1,300 specimens throughout the mall. There are hundreds of hanging baskets and flower-filled planters located in four micro climates. We have found that many of the stores do allow well-behaved dogs inside. For a list of dog-friendly stores, please look at our stores category. However, please ask the store clerk before bringing your dog inside each store just in case their policies have changed. Depending on the season, there will be many outdoor tables adjacent to the food stands and cafes. Here you can order the food inside and then enjoy it with your pup at one of the outside tables.

Stores

Petco Pet Store 1919 El Camino Real Mountain View CA   650-966-1233
Your licensed and well-behaved leashed dog is allowed in the store.
Bang & Olufsen Stanford Shopping Center Palo Alto CA   650-322-2264
http://www.bang-olufsen.com/
Your well-behaved leashed dog is allowed inside this store.
Bloomingdale's Stanford Shopping Center Palo Alto CA   650-463-2000
http://www.bloomindales.com/
Your well-behaved leashed dog is allowed inside this store.
Books Inc. Stanford Shopping Center Palo Alto CA   650-321-0600
Your well-behaved leashed dog is allowed inside this store.
Giants Dugout Stanford Shopping Center Palo Alto CA   650-323-9790
Your well-behaved leashed dog is allowed inside this store.
Going in Style Travel Accessories Stanford Shopping Center Palo Alto CA   650-326-2066
http://www.goinginstyle.com/
Your well-behaved leashed dog is allowed inside this store.
Hear Music Stanford Shopping Center Palo Alto CA   650-473-9142
http://www.hearmusic.com/
Your well-behaved leashed dog is allowed inside this store.
Kenneth Cole Mens & Womens Shoes & More Stanford Shopping Center Palo Alto CA   650-853-8365
http://www.kennethcole.com/
Your well-behaved leashed dog is allowed inside this store.
Lady Foot Locker Stanford Shopping Center Palo Alto CA   650-325-2301
http://www.ladyfootlocker.com/
Your well-behaved leashed dog is allowed inside this store.
Macy's and Macy's Mens Store Stanford Shopping Center Palo Alto CA   650-326-3333
http://www.macys.com/
Your well-behaved leashed dog is allowed inside this store.
Neiman Marcus 400 Stanford Shopping Center Palo Alto CA   650-329-3300
http://www.neimanmarcus.com
This famous department store, which sells everything from clothing to home furnishings, allows your well-behaved leashed dog to shop with you. It is located in Stanford Shopping Center, which is very dog-friendly.
Nordstrom Stanford Shopping Center Palo Alto CA   650-323-5111
http://www.nordstrom.com/
Your well-behaved leashed dog is allowed inside this store.
Postal Annex Stanford Shopping Center Palo Alto CA   650-324-8082
http://www.postalannex.com/
Your well-behaved leashed dog is allowed inside this store.
Pottery Barn Stanford Shopping Center Palo Alto CA   650-473-0449
http://www.potterybarn.com/
Your well-behaved leashed dog is allowed inside this store.
Restoration Hardware 281 University Avenue Palo Alto CA   650-328-4004
http://www.restorationhardware.com/
They love having dogs in the store!
The Discovery Channel Store Stanford Shopping Center Palo Alto CA   650-321-9833
http://shopping.discovery.com/
Your well-behaved leashed dog is allowed inside this store.
The Sharper Image Stanford Shopping Center Palo Alto CA   650-322-5488
http://www.sharperimage.com/
Your well-behaved leashed dog is allowed inside this store.
Petco Pet Store 520 Woodside Rd Redwood City CA   650-364-6077
Your licensed and well-behaved leashed dog is allowed in the store.
Petco Pet Store 1150 El Camino Real #167 San Bruno CA   650-589-3757
Your licensed and well-behaved leashed dog is allowed in the store.
PetSmart Pet Store 3520 S El Camino Real San Mateo CA   650-577-9010
Your licensed and well-behaved leashed dog is allowed in the store.
Petco Pet Store 3012 Bridgepointe Parkway San Mateo CA   650-357-9480
Your licensed and well-behaved leashed dog is allowed in the store.

Beaches

Blufftop Coastal Park Poplar Street Half Moon Bay CA   650-726-8297
Leashed dogs are allowed at this beach. The beach is located on the west end of Poplar Street, off Highway 1.

Montara State Beach Highway 1 Half Moon Bay CA   650-726-8819
Dogs on leash are allowed at this beach. Please clean up after your pets. The beach is located 8 miles north of Half Moon Bay on Highway 1. There are two beach access points. The first access point is across from Second Street, immediately south of the Outrigger Restaurant. The second access point is about a 1/2 mile north on the ocean side of Highway 1. Both access points have steep paths down to the beach.
Surfer's Beach Highway 1 Half Moon Bay CA   650-726-8297
Dogs on leash are allowed on the beach. It is located at Highway 1 and Coronado Street.
Esplanade Beach Esplanade Pacifica CA   650-738-7381
This beach offers an off-leash area for dogs. To get to the beach, take the stairs at the end of Esplanade. Esplanade is just north of Manor Drive, off Highway 1.
Bean Hollow State Beach Highway 1 Pescadero CA   650-879-2170
This is a very rocky beach with not much sand. Dogs are allowed but must be on a 6 foot or less leash. Please clean up after your pets. The beach is located 3 miles south of Pescadero on Highway 1.

Parks
Pacifica State Beach Highway 1 Pacifica CA   650-738-7381
This wide crescent shaped beach is located off Highway 1 in downtown Pacifica. Dogs on leash are allowed and please clean up after them.
Greer Dog Park 1098 Amarillo Avenue Palo Alto CA   650-329-2261
This is a fenced off leash dog exercise park. Dogs on leash are allowed in the rest of the park.
Palo Alto Baylands Preserve San Antonio Road Palo Alto CA   650-329-2506
The Palo Alto Baylands Preserve is a flat mostly unpaved 5 mile loop trail. Leashed dogs are allowed, unless posted in special bird nesting areas. There are several entrance points. One of the main starting points is from Hwy 101 heading north, exit San Antonio Road and turn right. San Antonio Road will bring you directly into the start of the Preserve. Please note that there is an adjacent park on the right which is a City of Mountain View park that does not allow dogs. However, no need to worry, the dog-friendly Palo Alto side has plenty of trails for you and your pooch to walk or run.

Stanford University

Stanford University Palm Drive Palo Alto CA   408-225-0225
Stanford University has miles of tree covered sidewalks and paths that wind through the campus. There is also a park at the end of Palm Drive which is a small but popular hang out for locals and their leashed dogs on warm days . To get there from downtown Palo Alto, take University Ave west toward the hills. University Ave turns into Palm Drive. There are tree lined walking paths along this street. The park is at the end of Palm. Ample parking is available.

Butano State Park Highway 1 Pescadero CA 650-879-2040
This 2,200 acre park is located in a secluded redwood-filled canyon. While dogs are not allowed on the trails, they are allowed in the campground and on miles of fire roads. Mountain biking is also allowed on the fire roads. Pets must be on a 6 foot or less leash. Please clean up after them. The park is located on the San Mateo Coast off Highway 1. To get there go 4.5 miles southeast of Pescadero via Pescadero and Cloverdale Roads.
Windy Hill Preserve Hwys 84 and 35 Portola Valley CA 650-691-1200
http://www.openspace.org/WINDY.html
At this park there are views of the Santa Clara Valley, San Francisco and the ocean. This preserve features grassy meadows and redwood, fir, and oak trees. Leashed dogs are allowed on designated trails. Directions: From Hwy 280, take Hwy 84 west (La Honda Rd). Go about 2.3 miles to Hwy 35 (Skyline Blvd). The main parking is at the intersection of Hwys 84 and 35. Another starting option is to park at the Portola Valley Town Hall and begin there.

Pulgas Ridge Open Space Preserve

Pulgas Ridge Open Space Preserve Edmonds Road Redwood City CA 650-691-1200
http://www.openspace.org/PULGAS.html
This park has about 293 acres and some great trails. There are are about 3 miles of trails that will provide moderate to strenuous exercise. Leashed dogs are allowed on the trails. The park offers some nice shade on warm days. To get there from Interstate 280, take the Edgewood Road exit. Travel 0.75 miles northeast on Edgewood Road toward San Carlos and Redwood City. Turn left (north) on Crestview Drive, and then immediately turn left on Edmonds Road. Limited roadside parking is available along Crestview Drive and Edmonds Road.

Off-Leash Dog Parks
City of Belmont Dog Park 2525 Buena Vista Avenue Belmont CA 650-365-3524
This dog park is located at the Cipriani Elementary School.
Bayside Park Dog Park 1125 South Airport Blvd Burlingame CA 650-558-7300
This dog park is over 570 feet long. It is in the back of the parking area and then you have to walk about 1/8 mile down a path to the off-leash dog park.
Foster City Dog Run Foster City Blvd at Bounty Foster City CA
There is a separate dog area for small dogs and large dogs at this off leash dog park. The parks are about 1/2 an acre in size. There are tables and benches. The dog park is located in Boat Park at the corner of Bounty Drive and Foster City Blvd.
Coastside Dog Park Wavecrest Road Half Moon Bay CA 650-726-8297
http://www.coastdogs.org
This fenced, public off-leash dog park is supported by citizen volunteers. The dog park is located at Smith Field, at the western end of Wavecrest Road. The organization that runs the park would appreciate a $20 annual membership from locals that use the park regularly but it is not mandatory.

Mountain View Dog Park Shoreline Blvd at North Rd Mountain View CA
http://mvdp.org
This fenced, off leash dog park is located across from Shoreline Ampitheatre at the entrance to Shoreline Park. Dogs are not allowed in Shoreline Park itself.
Hoover Park 2901 Cowper St Palo Alto CA 650-329-2261
This is a small off leash dog exercise area. Dogs on leash are allowed in the rest of the park.
Mitchell Park/Dog Run 3800 Middlefield Rd Palo Alto CA 650-329-2261
Located in Mitchell Park at 3800 Middlefield Rd (between E. Charleston and E. Meadow) Note: It can be tough to find at first. The dog run is closer to E. Charleston by the baseball fields and over a small hill.
Shores Dog Park Radio Road Redwood City CA
http://www.shoredogs.org
This dog park (opened Nov/Dec 98) was funded by Redwood City residents. To get there from Hwy 101, take Holly/Redwood Shores Parkway Exit. Go east (Redwood Shore Parkway). Turn right on Radio Road (this is almost at the end of the street). The park will be on the right. Thanks to one of our readers for this information.
San Bruno Dog Park Commodore Lane and Cherry Ave San Bruno CA 650-877-8868
San Bruno moved its dog park to this new location. The dog park has two fenced areas for large and small dogs, water for dogs and people, benches, bags to clean up and shade. If your dog doesn't like loud noises, beware of the large jets taking off from San Francisco Airport less than 2 miles away. The dog park is located in Commodore Park the intersection of I-280 and I-380. Take the 280 San Bruno Avenue exit east and turn left on Cherry Avenue to the park.
Heather Dog Exercise Area 2757 Melendy Drive San Carlos CA 650-802-4382
This 1.5 acre park offers a small area where dogs can run off-leash as well as an on-leash hiking trail. Access the park through the Heather School parking lot.
Pulgas Ridge Off-Leash Dog Area Edmonds Road and Crestview Drive San Carlos CA 650-691-1200
Most of Pulgas Ridge Open Space Preserve allows dogs on leash. There is a large, seventeen acre area in the center of the preserve that allows dogs off-leash under voice control. Please check the signs for the appropriate boundries of the off-leash area. To get to the preserve, take I-280 to Edgewood Rd. Head east on Edgewood and turn left on Crestview. Immediately after that turn, turn left onto Edmonds to the entrance to the preserve.

Outdoor Restaurants
Coyote Cafe 1003 Alameda de las Pulgas Belmont CA 650-595-1422
This restaurant serves Mexican food. Dogs are allowed at the outdoor tables. Water is provided for your pet.
Copenhagen Bakery and Cafe 1216 Burlingame Ave Burlingame CA 650-342-1357
Dogs are allowed at the outdoor tables.
La Scala 1219 Burlingame Ave Burlingame CA 650-347-3035
Dogs are allowed at the outdoor tables.
Baja Fresh Mexican Grill 1031 East Hillsdale Blvd. Foster City CA 650-358-8632
http://www.bajafresh.com
This Mexican restaurant is open for lunch and dinner. They use fresh ingredients and making their salsa and beans daily. Some of the items on their menu include Enchiladas, Burritos, Tacos Salads, Quesadillas, Nachos, Chicken, Steak and more. Well-behaved leashed dogs are allowed at the outdoor tables.
El Torito Mexican Restaurant and Cantina 388 Vintage Park Drive Foster City CA 650-574-6844
This eatery serves up authentic Mexican food. Your pet is welcome to join you at the outside tables. Dogs must be well behaved, attended to at all times, and leashed.
Portofino Grill 929-A Edgewater Blvd Foster City CA 650-570-6099
This restaurant serves gourmet-style food. Dogs are allowed at the outdoor tables.
3 Zero Café 46 Cabrillo Hwy N Half Moon Bay CA 650-728-1411
This cafe is located in the airport terminal building adjacent to the parking lot. This dog-friendly place is popular with the locals. You can watch the small aircraft taking off from the outdoor seats. Thanks to one of our readers who recommended this cafe. The cafe is open for breakfast and lunch everyday except Mondays. The hours are 6:30 am to 2:00 pm, weekends to 4:00 pm.
Casey's Cafe 328 Main Street Half Moon Bay CA 650-560-4880
Dogs are allowed at the outdoor tables.
Half Moon Bay Brewery 390 Capistrano Road Half Moon Bay CA 650-728-2739
This restaurant serves American food. Dogs are allowed at the outdoor tables.
Half Moon Bay Coffee Company 20 Stone Pine Rd #A Half Moon Bay CA 650-726-3664
Dogs are allowed at the outdoor tables.
It's Italia Pizzeria 40 Stone Pine Rd Half Moon Bay CA 650-726-4444
Dogs are allowed at the outdoor tables.
Three-Zero Cafe 9850 Hwy 1 Half Moon Bay CA 650-728-1411
http://www.3-zero.com/toppage11.htm
Eight years in a row this restaurant won "Best Breakfast on the Coast". They offer indoor and outdoor dining- weather permitting. Dogs are allowed at the outdoor tables. Dogs must be under owner's control at all times, leashed, and cleaned up after.

Cafe Borrone 1010 El Camino Real Menlo Park CA 650-327-0830
There is a large outdoor seating area where dogs are welcome. There are umbrellas for shade. The coffee house is open for breakfast lunch and dinner except on Sunday when it is open until 5 pm.
Amici's East Coast Pizza 790 Castro Street Mountain View CA 650-961-6666
Dogs are allowed at the outdoor tables.
Clarkes Charcoal Broiler 615 W El Camino Real Mountain View CA 650-967-0851
Enjoy their hamburgers, steak or chicken sandwiches.
La Salsa Restaurant 660 San Antonio Rd Mountain View CA 650-917-8290
This restaurant has several kinds of tacos and burritos to choose from.
Le Boulanger 650 Castro St #160 Mountain View CA 650-961-1787
Dogs are allowed at the outdoor tables.
Posh Bagel 444 Castro Street #120 Mountain View CA 650-968-5308
Dogs are allowed at the outdoor tables.
Baja Fresh Mexican Grill 3990 El Camino Real Palo Alto CA 650-424-8599
http://www.bajafresh.com
This Mexican restaurant is open for lunch and dinner. They use fresh ingredients and making their salsa and beans daily. Some of the items on their menu include Enchiladas, Burritos, Tacos Salads, Quesadillas, Nachos, Chicken, Steak and more. Well-behaved leashed dogs are allowed at the outdoor tables.
Golden Wok 451 S California Ave Palo Alto CA 650-327-2222
Choose from a variety of Chinese appetizers and dishes like pot stickers, egg rolls, meat and vegetarians dishes, noodles and more. Then are open for lunch and dinner, but come early since they only have a few outdoor tables.
Izzy's Brooklyn Bagels 477 S California Ave Palo Alto CA 650-329-0700
This bagel shop has a wide variety of bagels and pastries.
Joanie's Cafe 447 S California Ave Palo Alto CA 650-326-6505
If you come here for breakfast, you can order a variety of dishes like Belgium waffles, pancakes and more. They also serve sandwiches for lunch.

Spalti Ristorante

Spalti Ristorante 417 S California Ave Palo Alto CA 650-327-9390
This nice Italian restaurant has outdoor heaters to keep you and your pup warm. Sidewalk and patio seating are available. They are open for lunch and dinner.
St. Michael's Alley 806 Emerson St. Palo Alto CA 650-326-2530
http://www.stmikes.com
This restaurant has dog-friendly outdoor seating and they love dogs. The owners also have two dogs. They serve brunch, lunch and dinner. For brunch they offer omelets, French toast, pancakes and more. The lunch menu has

a wide variety of appetizers, entrees, sandwiches and pizza. The dinner menu includes entrees like NY Steak, chicken, pasta and much more.

Taxi's Hamburgers 403 University Ave Palo Alto CA 650-322-8294
If you like burgers, then you'll definitely need to have lunch or dinner here. They serve big juicy hamburgers, great fries, and shakes (lowfat and nonfat shakes too.)

Whole Foods Market 774 Emerson Street Palo Alto CA 650-326-8676
http://www.wholefoods.com/
This natural food supermarket offers natural and organic foods. Order some food from their deli without your dog and bring it to an outdoor table where your well-behaved leashed dog is welcome. Dogs are not allowed in the store including the deli at any time. They have one square picnic table located under an awning.

Half Moon Bay Brewing Company 390 Capistrano Rd Princeton CA 650-728-BREW
Thanks to one of our readers who writes: "A great setting south of San Francisco to spend the day walking your dog on the beautiful San Mateo Coastal Beaches. You can enjoy an open air meal with your furry friend sitting beside you in a fun and relaxed patio with music and friendly service."

City Pub 2620 Broadway Redwood City CA 650-363-2620
http://www.city-pub.com/html/home.html
Dogs are allowed at the outside tables. They will bring your dog a bowl of water as well. They serve burgers, other food and many beers.

Diving Pelican Cafe 650 Bair Island Rd #102 Redwood City CA 650-368-3668
http://www.divingpelican.com/
According to a reader "Great outdoor deck-like seating. Awesome place for brunch." Dogs need to be leashed at the outdoor deck.

Whole Foods Market 1250 Jefferson Avenue Redwood City CA 650-367-1400
http://www.wholefoods.com/
This natural food supermarket offers natural and organic foods. Order some food from their deli without your dog and bring it to an outdoor table where your well-behaved leashed dog is welcome. There are two outdoor eating areas. Dogs are not allowed in the store including the deli at any time.

Ristorante Piacere 727 Laurel Street San Carlos CA 650-592-3536
http://www.americandreams.com/piacere/
This fine Italian restaurant serves you outside either at the tables next to the sidewalk or if you prefer, up on the patio. The seating area is covered and has outdoor heaters. If you are looking for an elegant place to take your pooch, this is it. Afterwards, you can stroll down to the pet store that is about 1/2 block away.

Whole Foods Market 1010 Park Place San Mateo CA 650-358-6900
http://www.wholefoods.com/
This natural food supermarket offers natural and organic foods. Order some food from their deli without your dog and bring it to an outdoor table where your well-behaved leashed dog is welcome. Dogs are not allowed in the store including the deli at any time.

Day Kennels

PetsHotel by PetsMart Day Kennel 2440 E. Charleston Rd. Mountain View CA
http://www.petsmart.com/PETsHOTEL/
This PetSmart pet store offers day care, day camp, and overnight care. Dogs may be dropped off and picked up during the hours of 7 am - 7 pm M-S, Sunday 9 am - 6 pm. Dogs must have proof of current rabies, DPP and bordatella vaccinations.

Vets and Kennels

Emergency Veterinary Clinic 3045 Middlefield Rd Palo Alto CA 650-494-1461
Monday - Thursday 6 pm to 8 am, Friday 6 pm - Monday 8 am.

San Francisco

Accommodations

Campton Place Hotel 340 Stockton Street San Francisco CA 415-781-5555
http://www.camptonplace.com
This dog-friendly hotel holds many awards including "Top 100 Hotels in the World" by Conde Nast Traveler. Room rates are approximately $230 to $345 a night. There is a $35 per day additional pet fee.

Crowne Plaza - Union Square 480 Sutter Street San Francisco CA 415-398-8900 (877-270-6405)
Dogs up to 100 pounds are allowed. There is a $100 refundable pet deposit. Pets are not allowed on the executive floors.

Days Inn - Lombard St 2358 Lombard Street San Francisco CA 415-922-2010 (800-329-7466)

There is a $10 per day pet fee. A well-behaved large dog is okay. Dogs may not be left alone in the rooms and you are responsible for any damage to the room by your pet.

Four Seasons Hotel San Francisco 757 Market St. San Francisco CA   415-633-3000
Dogs of all sizes are allowed. There are no additional pet fees. Dogs are not allowed to be left alone in the room.

Halcyon Hotel 649 Jones Street San Francisco CA   415-929-8033
Dogs of all sizes are allowed. There is a $50 refundable pet deposit.

Harbor Court Hotel 165 Steuart Street San Francisco CA   415-882-1300
http://www.harborcourthotel.com/
Well-behaved dogs of all sizes are welcome at this pet-friendly hotel. Amenities include a complimentary evening wine reception, and an adjacent fitness room. There are no pet fees, just sign a pet liability form.

Holiday Inn Select 750 Kearny Street San Francisco CA   415-433-6600 (877-270-6405)
Dogs of all sizes are allowed. There is a $50 one time pet fee per visit. Smoking and non-smoking rooms are available for pets.

Hotel Beresford Arms 701 Post Street San Francisco CA   415-673-2600 (800-533-6533)
Although listed on the National Register of Historic Places, this hotel offers guests many modern conveniences and luxuries, including a great location to several nearby attractions. Amenities/features include well appointed rooms and suites, Jacuzzi bathtubs, complimentary morning coffee/tea and pastries, and a complimentary afternoon tea and wine social. One dog is allowed per room; there is no additional pet fee. Dogs may not be left alone in the room, and they must be leashed and cleaned up after at all times.

Hotel Cosmo 761 Post Street San Francisco CA   415-673-6040
http://www.hotel-cosmo.com/
Well-behaved dogs of all sizes are welcome at this pet-friendly hotel. The boutique hotel offers both rooms and suites. Hotel amenities include a complimentary evening wine service. There are no pet fees, just sign a pet liability form.

TOP 200 PLACE **Hotel Diva** 440 Geary Street San Francisco CA   800-553-1900
http://www.hoteldiva.com/
At the hub of Union Square, this ultra modern hotel offers exceptional personalized service for the leisure or business traveler, and a convenient location for a wide variety of shopping, entertainment, and dining opportunities. One dog up to 70 pounds is allowed for an additional one time pet fee of $75. This is a Personality Hotel property and one of four local hotels that offer the "Every Doggie is a Diva Package" with prices starting at $189 per night. This deluxe package includes the overnight accommodations (so no additional $75 fee), a bottle of water, a designer pet bowl, a personalized dog tag, a plush sheep skin throw, a 1 hour VIP dog walking tour highlighting favored parks and fire hydrants (Monday through Friday-noon to 1pm), and an amenity box with treats, biscuits, 2 flavors of dog food, and a red paw print bandana. Dogs must be leashed, cleaned up after, and crated if left alone in the room.

Hotel Metropolis 25 Mason Street San Francisco CA   800-553-9100
http://www.hotelmetropolis.com/
This 1930, 105 room hotel will indulge your senses with a bit of paradise featuring rich fabrics, bright colors, custom furnishings, and each floor of this 10 story hotel gives reflection to the elements of earth, wind, fire, or water. They feature many in room amenities, exceptional personalized service for the leisure or business traveler, and a convenient location for a wide variety of shopping, entertainment, and dining opportunities. One dog up to 70 pounds is allowed for an additional one time pet fee of $75. This is a Personality Hotel property and one of four local hotels that offer the "Every Doggie is a Diva Package" with prices starting at $189 per night. This deluxe package includes the overnight accommodations (so no additional $75 fee), a bottle of water, a designer pet bowl, a personalized dog tag, a plush sheep skin throw, a 1 hour VIP dog walking tour highlighting favored parks and fire hydrants (Monday through Friday-noon to 1pm), and a Petco amenity box with treats, biscuits, 2 flavors of dog food, and a red paw print bandana. Dogs must be leashed, cleaned up after, and crated if left alone in the room.

Hotel Monaco 501 Geary Street San Francisco CA   415-292-0100
Dogs of all sizes are allowed. There is a pet policy to sign at check in and there are no additional pet fees.

Hotel Palomar 12 Fourth Street San Francisco CA   415-348-1111
http://www.hotelpalomar.com/
Well-behaved dogs of all sizes are welcome at this pet-friendly hotel. The boutique hotel offers both rooms and suites. Hotel amenities include room service, an on-site 24 hour fitness room and complimentary high speed Internet access. There are no pet fees, just sign a pet liability form. Pets cannot be left alone in the room.

Hotel Triton 342 Grant Avenue San Francisco CA   415-394-0500
http://www.hoteltriton.com
Well-behaved dogs of all sizes are welcome at this pet-friendly hotel. The boutique hotel offers both rooms and suites. Hotel amenities include a complimentary evening wine reception, room service, and a 24 hour on-site fitness room. There are no pet fees, just sign a pet liability form.

Hotel Union Square 114 Powell Street San Francisco CA   800-553-1900
http://www.hotelunionsquare.com/
Known as the city's original boutique-style hotel, and graced with a great location in Union Square right on the cable car line, this striking 1913 hotel offers 131 stylish guest rooms with full private baths, a 1930's Art Deco

lobby, beautiful jewel toned décor, and many in-room amenities. One dog up to 70 pounds is allowed for an additional one time pet fee of $75. This is a Personality Hotel property and one of four local hotels that offer the "Every Doggie is a Diva Package" with prices starting at $189 per night. This deluxe package includes the overnight accommodations (so no additional $75 fee), a bottle of water, a designer pet bowl, a personalized dog tag, a plush sheep skin throw, a 1 hour VIP dog walking tour highlighting favored parks and fire hydrants (Monday through Friday-noon to 1pm), and an amenity box with treats, biscuits, 2 flavors of dog food, and a red paw print bandana. Dogs must be leashed, cleaned up after, and crated if left alone in the room.

Kensington Park Hotel 450 Post Street San Francisco CA   800-553-9100
http://www.kensingtonparkhotel.com/
This stylish hotel offers luxury, modern day conveniences, 92 richly detailed-finely appointed rooms, exceptional personalized service for the leisure or business traveler, and a convenient location for a wide variety of shopping, entertainment, and dining opportunities. They are also home to the Farallon Restaurant; an attraction in and of itself. One dog up to 70 pounds is allowed for an additional one time pet fee of $75. This is a Personality Hotel property and one of four local hotels that offer the "Every Doggie is a Diva Package" with prices starting at $189 per night. This deluxe package includes the overnight accommodations (so no additional $75 fee), a bottle of water, a designer pet bowl, a personalized dog tag, a plush sheep skin throw, a 1 hour VIP dog walking tour highlighting favored parks and fire hydrants (Monday through Friday-noon to 1pm), and an amenity box with treats, biscuits, 2 flavors of dog food, and a red paw print bandana. Dogs must be leashed, cleaned up after, and crated if left alone in the room.

Marina Motel - on Lombard Street 2576 Lombard St. San Francisco CA   415-921-9406 (800-346-6118)
http://www.marinamotel.com/
All friendly dogs are welcome regardless of size. Walk to the Golden Gate Bridge along Crissy Field beach five blocks away. Miles of hiking trails in the historical Presidio Park are nearby. All rooms have refrigerators, coffee makers, irons and hair dryers. There is no pet fee for stays of one week or longer otherwise there is a $10/night pet fee. Dogs may not be left unattended in the room at any time. There is free garage parking for overnight guests of the hotel.

Monticello Inn 127 Ellis Street San Francisco CA   415-392-8800
http://www.monticelloinn.com
Well-behaved dogs of all sizes are welcome at this pet-friendly hotel. The boutique hotel offers both rooms and suites. Hotel amenities include complimentary evening wine service, evening room service, hotel library with magazines, newspapers and books, and a Borders Books and Music room service. There are no pet fees, just sign a pet liability form.

Palace Hotel 2 New Montgomery Street San Francisco CA   415-512-1111
There is a $75 one time pet fee. This is a Sheraton Hotel.

Prescott Hotel 545 Post Street San Francisco CA   415-563-0303
http://www.prescotthotel.com/
Well-behaved dogs of all sizes are allowed at this pet-friendly hotel. The luxury boutique hotel is located in Union Square and offers both rooms and suites. Hotel amenities include room service and an on-site 24 hour fitness room. There are no pet fees, just sign a pet liability form.

San Francisco Lofts 1501 Mariposa, Suite 328 San Francisco CA   415-810-3322
Dogs of all sizes are allowed. There is a pet policy to sign at check in and there are no additional pet fees.

San Francisco Marriott Fisherman's Wharf 1250 Columbus Avenue San Francisco CA   415-775-7555 (800-228-9290)
Dogs of all sizes are allowed. There is a $100 one time additional pet fee per room. Dogs may be left for short periods alone in the room only if they will be quiet and a contact number is left with the front desk. Dogs must be leashed and cleaned up after.

Serrano Hotel 405 Taylor Street San Francisco CA   415-885-2500
http://www.serranohotel.com
This luxury boutique hotel near Union Square allows dogs of all sizes. There is an evening hospitality hour and a fitness room. There are no additional pet fees.

Sheraton Fisherman's Wharf Hotel 2500 Mason St. San Francisco CA   415-362-5500 (888-625-5144)
Dogs up to 80 pounds are allowed. Only 5 rooms are available in the hotel for dogs. You must sign a pet policy. Dogs are not allowed to be left alone in the room.

The Inn San Francisco 943 S Van Ness Avenue San Francisco CA   415-641-0188
Well behaved, friendly, dogs of all sizes are allowed. There are no additional pet fees. Dogs may not be left alone at any time and they are not allowed in the gardens.

The Laurel Inn 444 Presidio Ave. San Francisco CA   415-567-8467
http://www.thelaurelinn.com/
This pet-friendly hotel is a boutique hotel in San Francisco's atmospheric Pacific Heights neighborhood. Amenities include a complimentary continental breakfast served daily in the lobby, free indoor parking, laundry and valet service, room service from Dine-One-One and more.

The Palace Hotel 2 New Montgomery St. San Francisco CA   415-512-1111
Dogs up to 80 pounds are allowed. There is a $100 nonrefundable pet fee per visit. Dogs are restricted to 1st and 2nd floor rooms only. Dogs are not allowed to be left alone in the room.

The W San Francisco 181 3rd St. San Francisco CA   415-777-5300

Dogs of all sizes are allowed. There is a $100 nonrefundable one time pet fee per visit. Dogs are allowed in the living room of the hotel cafe and there is a special menu available at the cafe. Dogs are not allowed to be left alone in the room.

Campgrounds and RV Parks

Candlestick RV Park 650 Gilman Avenue San Francisco CA   415-822-2299 (800-888-CAMP (2267))
This modern park is next to it's namesake stadium and near local Bay-Area attractions. It has shuttles to downtown San Francisco, a game room, and laundry. Dogs of all sizes are allowed. There are no additional pet fees. Dogs may not be left unattended outside, and may only be left inside if they will be quiet and comfortable. Dogs must be leashed and cleaned up after. Dogs are not allowed in buildings. The RV park sits along side a state park with miles of trails, and dogs are allowed on the trails except where indicated. The camping and tent areas also allow dogs. There is a dog walk area at the campground.

Transportation Systems

BART (Bay Area Rapid Transit) Regional San Francisco CA   888-968-7282
http://www.bart.gov
A small dog in an enclosed carrier is allowed on BART trains.
SF Municipal Railway (MUNI) Throughout City San Francisco CA   415-673-6864
http://www.sfmuni.com
Both small and large dogs are allowed on cable cars, historic streetcars and trolley buses. People must pay the same fare for their dog that they do for themselves. Dogs are allowed to ride on Muni vehicles from 9 a.m. to 3 p.m. and from 7 p.m. to 5 a.m. on weekdays, and all day on Saturdays, Sundays, and holidays. Only one of dog may ride per vehicle. Dogs must be muzzled and on a short leash or in a small closed container.

Attractions

Barbary Coast Trail   San Francisco CA   415-775-1111
http://www.barbarycoasttrail.com/
The Barbary Coast Trail is a 3.8-mile walk through historic San Francisco. Bronze medallions and arrows in the sidewalk mark the trail and guide you to 20 of the City's most important historic sites. It was created by the San Francisco Historical Society. Begin the self-guided walking tour at the Old U.S. Mint building on the corner of Mission and 5th Street. Along the trail you will find historic Union Square, the oldest Chinatown in North America, Plymouth Square, the Pony Express site and more.

Fisherman's Wharf Shopping

Coit Tower 1 Telegraph Hill Blvd San Francisco CA   415-362-0808
Sitting atop Telegraph Hill is this beautiful monument believed to be in remembrance for the fire fighters who fought the 1906 earthquake fire. The beautiful grounds overlook the Bay Bridge, Golden Gate Bridge, Pier 39, Fisherman's Wharf, and it also gives an impressive view of the city at night. Inside the tower are a history museum, murals, and a greater view of the city. Dogs are allowed on the grounds and around the walking areas; they are not allowed inside the tower. Dogs must be under owner's control at all times, and be leashed and cleaned up after.

Fisherman's Wharf Shopping Jefferson Street San Francisco CA
Fisherman's Wharf is a classic tourist attraction. The walkways follow the bayshore and are complete with all types of street vendors and performers. It's a great dog-friendly place to walk your dog as long as your pup doesn't mind crowds. You can start at Ghirardelli Square and walk along the bayshore to Jefferson Street. Some of the piers don't allow dogs, but there are plenty of things to see and do on Jefferson Street.

Fort Point National Historic Site Fort Mason, Building 201 San Francisco CA   415-556-1693
http://www.fopo/index.htm
Dogs on leash are allowed on the property of Fort Point. They are not allowed in any buildings. The park area is open sunrise to sunset.

Golden Gate Bridge

TOP 200 PLACE Golden Gate Bridge P.O. Box 9000, Presidio Station San Francisco CA   415-921-5858
http://goldengatebridge.org
San Francisco's landmark for most visitors can also be the landmark for four legged tourists as well. The walk across the Golden Gate Bridge is a unique and stirring experience, and the views of the city and bay are worth the 1.7 mile walk. Visitors may access the bridge sidewalks during daylight hours, and hours vary by the season. The southeast parking area offers visitor services, such as a café, gift center, renovated gardens, and scenic vistas. Dogs are permitted on the bridge as long as they are under owner's control at all times, and they must be leashed and cleaned up after. Please carry clean-up supplies for your dog.

Pac Bell Park 24 Willie Mays Plaza San Francisco CA   415-972-2000
There is a viewing deck along the water where you can view a few minutes of the game from way out in right field without entering the ballpark. You may take a leashed and well-behaved dog here. Also, one game a year the bleachers are open to you and your well-behaved pup. It is usually in August and is known as Dog Days of Summer. Get tickets early.

TOP 200 PLACE Vampire Tour of San Francisco Nob Hill, Corner of California and Tayor Streets San Francisco CA   866-4-BITTEN (424-8836)
This self-proclaimed vampire hostess leads guests on about a 2 hour unique journey of history and entertainment of the Vampires of the city. Although the tour is open all year, it is a good idea to check ahead if there is inclement weather. This has become a popular attraction, especially around Halloween, so reservations are also suggested. Well mannered dogs are welcome to join this tour. There is no additional fee; dogs must be under owner's control at all times, be leashed, and please carry supplies to clean up after your pet.

TOP 200 PLACE **Waterfront Carriage Rides** Jefferson Street San Francisco CA   415-771-8687
Want to tour San Francisco in style? Take an elegant horse and carriage ride with your well-behaved dog. They'll take you and your pup on a tour of Fisherman's Wharf. The carriages are located by Pier 41.

Shopping Centers

Ghirardelli Square Shopping Center

Ghirardelli Square Shopping Center 900 North Point Street San Francisco CA   415-775-5500
http://www.ghirardellisq.com/
Back in 1893, the famous Ghirardelli chocolate factory occupied these buildings. Today, it is a popular shopping center with numerous shops including the dog-friendly Beastro By the Bay (your dog is welcome inside this unique animal motif gift store). At Ghirardelli Square, you and your pup can take the self-guided outside walking tour and learn about the area's history. Just pick up a free map at the information booth at the west end of Fountain Plaza.

Stores

PetSmart Pet Store 315 Gellert Blvd Daly City CA   650-997-0395
Your licensed and well-behaved leashed dog is allowed in the store.
Le Video 1231 and 1239 9th Avenue San Francisco CA   415-566-3606
http://www.levideo.com/
Your well-behaved leashed dog is allowed inside this store.
Macy's 170 O'Farrell Street San Francisco CA   415-397-3333
http://www.macys.com
This Macy's store offers clothing, housewares, electronics and much more. Well-behaved leashed dogs are allowed in the store. It is located on O'Farrell between Powell and Stockton Streets at Union Square.
Neiman Marcus 150 Stockton Street San Francisco CA 877-634-6264
http://www.neimanmarcus.com
This famous department store, which sells everything from clothing to home furnishings, allows your well-behaved leashed dog to shop with you.
Pawtrero Hill Bathhouse and Feed Store and Dog Bath 199 Mississippi Street San Francisco CA   415-863-7297
http://www.pawtrero.com/
This store offers natural and specialized foods, toys, gifts, grooming supplies, natural and homeopathic supplements, collars and leashes, and they have 2 state of the art bathing stations. They are open from 11 am to 7 pm Monday through Friday; from 11 am to 6 pm on Saturday, and from Noon to 5 pm on Sunday. Your well behaved pet is welcome to explore the store with you, and if they respond to voice command, they can be off lead.

Petco Pet Store 1591 Sloat Blvd San Francisco CA   415-665-3700
Your licensed and well-behaved leashed dog is allowed in the store.
Petco Pet Store 1685 Bryant St San Francisco CA   415-863-1840
Your licensed and well-behaved leashed dog is allowed in the store.
Petco Pet Store 2598 Taylor St San Francisco CA   415-440-0423
Your licensed and well-behaved leashed dog is allowed in the store.
Saks Fifth Avenue 384 Post Street San Francisco CA   415-986-4300
http://www.saksfifthavenue.com
This upscale department store at Union Square allows well-behaved dogs, but they need to be kept on a short
leash.
South Paw Bathhouse and Feed Store and Dog Bath 199 Brannan Street San Francisco CA   415-882-7297

http://www.pawtrero.com/
This store offers natural and specialized foods, toys, gifts, grooming supplies, natural and homeopathic
supplements, collars and leashes, and they have 2 state of the art bathing stations. They are open from 11 am to
7 pm Monday through Friday; from 11 am to 6 pm on Saturday, and from Noon to 5 pm on Sunday. Your well
behaved pet is welcome to explore the store with you, and if they respond to voice command, they can be off
lead.
Williams-Sonoma 340 Post Street San Francisco CA   415-362-9450
http://www.williamssonoma.com
Located at Union Square, this store offers cookware, cutlrey, electronics, food and more. Well-behaved leashed
dogs are allowed in the store.

Beaches

Baker Beach

TOP 200 PLACE **Baker Beach** Lincoln Blvd and Bowley St/Golden Gate Nat'l Rec Area San Francisco CA
415-561-4700
This dog-friendly beach in the Golden Gate National Recreation Area has a great view of the Golden Gate
Bridge. Dogs are permitted off leash under voice control on Baker Beach North of Lobos Creek; they must be
leashed South of Lobos Creek. The beach is located approx. 1.5 to 2 miles south of the Golden Gate Bridge.
From Lincoln Avenue, turn onto Bowley Street and head towards the ocean. There is a parking lot next to the
beach. This is a clothing optional beach, so there may be the occasional sunbather.

TOP 200 PLACE **Fort Funston/Burton Beach** Skyline Blvd./Hwy 35 San Francisco CA
http://www.nps.gov/goga/

This is a very popular dog-friendly park and beach. In the past, dogs have been allowed off-leash. However, currently all dogs must be on leash. Fort Funston is part of the Golden Gate National Recreation Area. There are trails that run through the dunes & ice plant from the parking lot above with good access to the beach below. It overlooks the southern end of Ocean Beach, with a large parking area accessible from Skyline Boulevard. There is also a water faucet and trough at the parking lot for thirsty pups. It's located off Skyline Blvd. (also known Hwy 35) by John Muir Drive. It is south of Ocean Beach. Thanks to one of our readers for this info. Expect to see lots and lots of dogs having a great time. But not to worry, there is plenty of room for everyone.

Lands End Off Leash Dog Area El Camino Del Mar San Francisco CA   415-561-4700
Owned and operated by the Golden Gate National Recreation Area, Lands End is everything west of and including the Coast Trail, and is an extraordinary combination of parkland, natural areas, and dramatic coastal cliffs. It offers great hiking, ocean and city views, a museum, the ruins of the Sutro Baths, and includes the Sutro Heights Park (dogs must be on lead in this area). This area can be accessed at Merrie Way for the cliffside paths, and at this entrance or the large lot at the end of El Camino Del Mar off Point Lobos for the Coast Trail and beaches. Dogs must be on leash on the Coast Trail, under firm voice control when in off leash areas, and they must be cleaned up after.

Ocean Beach Great Hwy San Francisco CA   415-556-8642
You'll get a chance to stretch your legs at this beach which has about 4 miles of sand. The beach runs parallel to the Great Highway (north of Fort Funston). There are several access points including Sloat Blvd., Fulton Street or Lincoln Way. This beach has a mix of off-leash and leash required areas. Thanks to the San Francisco Dog Owners Group (SFDOG) for providing the following information: Dogs must be on leash on Ocean Beach between Sloat Blvd and Stairwell #21 (roughly at Fulton). North of Fulton to the Cliff House and South of Sloat for several miles are still okay for off-leash dogs, however parts of these areas may be impassible at high tide. The Golden Gate National Rec Area (GGNRA) strictly enforces the on-leash area between Sloat and Fulton. They usually give no warning tickets ($50 fine). As with all other leash required areas, we encourage dog owners to comply with the rules.

Parks

Alta Plaza Park Clay Street San Francisco CA
This park is bordered by Jackson, Clay, Steiner and Scott streets. It is across from the tennis courts. The first Sunday of every month is Pug Day at this park. It's a casual meeting of pug owners which takes place at the north end of park, usually between 3:30 - 5:00, weather permitting. At the gathering, there can be 20-50 pugs. Dogs need to be on leash but residents are trying to make it a legal off-leash area.

Candlestick Point State Recreation Area Next to Monster Park San Francisco CA 415-671-0145
This park offers views of the San Francisco Bay. Amenities include hiking trails, picnic areas, fishing, a fitness course for seniors, and special cultural and educational programs planned throughout the year. Dogs are allowed at the park and on the trails. Pets must be on a 6 foot or less leash, with the exception of the leash free areas. The off-leash areas are the big dirt lots near Monster Park where sports fans park on game days. The off-leash areas are not available on game days. Please clean up after your pet. The park is located next to Monster Park. Take the Monster Park exit from Highway 101.

Crissy Field Park Mason Street San Francisco CA   415-561-4700
http://www.crissyfield.org/
This 100 acre shoreline park is part of the Golden Gate National Recreation Area. Enjoy scenic views of the Golden Gate Bridge while you walk or jog along the paved paths. Off leash areas include the beaches along the waterline and the large, grassy landing field, with the exception of the West beach nearest to Fort Point where they must be leashed. They must be under firm voice control when not on lead. Dogs must be leashed when not in the off lead areas, and they must be cleaned up after at all times. Dogs are not allowed in the fenced restoration zones or the lagoon area. The park is located north of Mason Street and southeast of the Golden Gate Bridge.

Golden Gate National Recreation Area   San Francisco CA   415-556-0560
http://www.nps.gov/goga/
This dog-friendly Recreation Area spans 76,500 acres of land and water. It starts at the coastline south of San Francisco, goes into San Francisco and then north of the Golden Gate Bridge. Many of the San Francisco beaches and parks are part of this Rec Area including Baker Beach, Fort Funston and Ocean Beach. One of the trails is located south of Baker Beach. From Lincoln Avenue, turn onto Bowley Street and head towards the ocean. There is a parking lot next to the beach. Dogs must be on leash.

Presidio of San Francisco Hwy 1/Park Presidio Blvd. San Francisco CA   415-561-4323
http://www.nps.gov/prsf/
This land was an Army base and is now a dog-friendly national park (borders up to the Golden Gate Recreation Area.) The park has over 500 historic buildings and miles of nice hiking trails. Leashes may or may not be required as this issue is going back and forth in the courts currently. It's located south of the Golden Gate Bridge. From the Bridge and Hwy101, take Hwy 1 south. It will turn into Park Presidio Blvd. You can also enter the park from Arguello Blvd.

Off-Leash Dog Parks

Alamo Square Off Leash Dog Park Scott Street, between Hayes and Fulton Streets San Francisco CA 415-831-2084
Dogs may be off leash under voice control in the Western half of this 5 1/2 acre multi-use park; it is not fenced in. The Eastern half of the park is on-leash. This park offers beautiful panoramic views and rolling hills, and is the second largest legal off-leash area in San Francisco.

Alta Plaza Off Leash Dog Park Steiner and Clay Street San Francisco CA 415-831-2084
http://sfdog.org/do/city_ne.htm#ap
This many tiered, Pacific Heights park takes up one square block, and from the top of the park you can enjoy panoramic views of the city. It is bordered by Jackson, Clay, Steiner and Scott streets, and is across from the tennis courts. The first Sunday of every month is Pug Day at this park. It's a casual meeting of pug owners which takes place at the north end of park, usually between 3:30 - 5:00, weather permitting. At the gathering, there can be 20-50 pugs. The legal off-leash area is well marked with paint on the pathways. Dogs should be leashed when not in this area, and they must be cleaned up after at all times.

Bernal Heights Off Leash Dog Park Bernal Heights and Esmerelda San Francisco CA 415-831-2084
This popular park is the largest official DPA/off-leash area in San Francisco. It is on a rocky steep hill, and is accessible via narrow, single track trails. They are situated such that you can walk for up to an hour without retracing any steps. There are also paved trails, an abundance of nature to enjoy, and great views of the city. You can enter either at the parking lot located at Folsom Street at Bernal Heights Ave or at the end of Bernal Heights Ave where the street dead-ends (on the South side of the hill). Dogs must be cleaned up after at all times.

Brotherhood Mini Off Leash Dog Park Brotherhood Way San Francisco CA 415-831-2084
This small park is located on Public Works property along Brotherhood Way at Head Street, and covers about an 1/8 of an acre. Dogs can run off leash in the designated dog park. Please clean up after your pet.

Buena Vista Off Lead Dog Park Buena Vista West at Central Avenue San Francisco CA 415-831-2084
http://sfdog.org/do/city_nw.htm#bv
This is the city's oldest park and is basically a giant one acre hill offering expansive views at the top. It is a popular destination location because of its size and safety/isolation from traffic, for the most part. The legal off-leash area is hardly used by dog walkers because it is not safe being so close to the road and most would prefer the enjoyment of the fantastic trail experience Buena Vista offers. You can enter the park at the intersection of Buena Vista Ave. and Central St. or at any of the other park entrances along Buena Vista Ave. The off-leash area is located in a lower area, along the Western side of the park near Central Ave. Dogs must be leashed in the off leash areas, and please clean up after your pet.

Corona Heights 16th and Roosevelt San Francisco CA 415-831-2084
This park is for those who enjoy the climb as much as the view. To get there, go almost to the top of 17th Street and take a right on Roosevelt and follow it around to another right on Levant. It is located adjacent to the Field Museum. There is a green area used by local dog-walkers and pet owners in addition to the fenced-in area to allow the dogs to socialize and run off-leash. Extended walking is required and be prepared for dirt/off road and steep walks at this park. Dogs must be on leash when not in the off lead area, and always please clean up after your pet.

Crocker Amazon Off Leash Dog Park At Geneva Avenue and Moscow Street San Francisco CA 415-831-2084
This 1.8 acre park is located in the northern part of the park, adjacent to the community garden. This is an unfenced area so dogs must be under firm voice control, and please clean up after your pet.

Delores Off Lead Dog Park 19th Street and Delores Street San Francisco CA 415-831-2084
This area is a large, grassy, gently sloping and sometimes hilly, mixed use park, with gorgeous views of the city from the top half. There are 6 tennis courts, a basketball court, 2 soccer fields, a playground, and a club house with public restrooms. As a popular relaxation/recreation area, it does tend to be quite crowed on weekends. Also, since there is no fenced in off-lead area, it is a good idea to stay away from the streets, and please clean up after your pet.

Douglass Park, Upper Field Off Leash Dog Area 27th and Douglass Streets San Francisco CA 415-831
http://www.sfdog.org/do/city_se.htm
This great multi-use neighborhood park offers a wonderful, grassy place for dogs to play off-leash. Dogs must be under firm voice control as there are no fenced in areas, and please clean up after your pet.

Eureka Valley Off Leash Dog Park 100 Collingwood Street San Francisco CA 415-695-5012
This small neighborhood recreation park of 2 acres is known for its gymnasium, playground structure, athletic field, and excellent recreational programs. The fenced in off lead area is East of the baseball diamond and adjacent to the tennis courts. Dogs must be cleaned up after, and leashed when out of the fenced area.

Fort Miley Off Lead Dog Area Point Lobos and 48th Avenues San Francisco CA 415-561-4700
Owned and operated by the Golden Gate National Recreation Area, this area is actually a combination of 3 parks entities, which are Land's End, Lincoln Park, and Fort Miley. There is a large parking and viewing area at the end of El Camino Del Mar off Point Lobos Avenue, and this is where you can take one of the paths to the above. An easier access from the Veteran's Administration Hospital parking lot is also available. Fort Miley is home to the historical ruins of a fully recessed military armament. A large open lawn encloses a recessed bunker that is

sunny and has great views over the Ocean Beach and Richmond area. It is a nice place to picnic and is one of the only multi-use open field areas here. There are plenty of areas to explore, and your pet may be off lead, except where marked. Please be sure to clean up after your pet.

Glen Park Off Leash Dog Area 400 O'Shaughnessy Blvd San Francisco CA 415-337-4705

This large, natural canyon area is a well used neighborhood park with wonderful trails throughout where there are edible berries to find and a variety of naturescapes to enjoy. Although not an official DPA yet is a great place to walk your dog. They request that you keep the dogs out of the newly planted areas and the seasonal "creek". Enter the park at Bosworth and O'Shaughnessy Blvd. Please clean up after your pet.

Golden Gate Park Fenced Dog Run Fulton Street San Francisco CA

This dog run is completely fenced in and has water bowls for thirsty dogs.Located at 38th Ave & Fulton Street.

TOP 200 PLACE Golden Gate Park Off Leash Dog Areas Stanyan & Great Highway San Francisco CA 415-751-8987

Listed among the world's greatest urban parks at over 1,000 acres, there are grassy meadows, wooded trails, secluded lakes, open groves, gardens, museums, and four official, legal off leash dog areas. (1) The Southeast area is located in a wooded strip of land bounded by 3rd Ave., 7th Ave., North of Lincoln Way, and South of Martin Luther King Blvd. It is small, not well marked, with lots of traffic and foxtails in the Spring, so the Big Rec locale is the de facto mixed-use off-leash area. Enter Lincoln Way at 7th or 9th Avenue, and the area used is located above/behind the athletic fields. This area is preferred because it is safer and easier to use. (2) The Northeast section is at Fulton and Willard in a Natural Area of 0 .2 acres. This park is near the intersection of Stanyan & Fulton Streets, and is a small, little used area with no fences and prone to heavy traffic. (3) The Southcentral area is bounded by Martin Luther King Drive, Middle Drive and 34th and 38th Avenues; 4.4 acres. This dog friendly knoll has become the last immediate off leash area for people in the outer district. (4) The Northcentral area near 38th Ave. and Fulton (Fenced, training area; 1.4 acres) is the bay areas largest, fenced, exclusive-use off-leash area. It is located behind the Bison pens and West of Spreckles Lake. You can walk in near 39th Avenue and Fulton, or drive in from 38th Ave. The area is surrounded by a low fence that larger dogs could jump and they suggest that this play area may be more suitable for dogs that are in training or not under voice control. Dogs under 4 months old are not allowed, and females in heat should be leashed, and they are not allowed in the single use areas. Dogs must be under control and cleaned up after at all times.

Jefferson Square Off Lead Dog Park Eddy and Laguna Streets San Francisco CA 415-831-2084

The legal off-leash area is a gently sloping grassy park located on the Northwest side of Jefferson Square Park at the corner of Eddy and Laguna. Dogs must be cleaned up after at all times.

Lafayette Park Washington/Clay/Laguna San Francisco CA 415-831-2084

The legal off-leash area at this park is quite small and located on a slope adjacent to a busy street, so dogs must be under firm voice control. It is near Sacramento Street between Octavia and Gough Streets, and offers beautiful views of downtown. It is suggested to use caution by the steep slope that leads down to heavy traffic on Sacramento Street. This large city park has lots of trees, hills, and is a great place for walking. Dogs must be leashed when not in the off-leash area, and they must be cleaned up after at all times.

McKinley Off Leash Dog Park 20th Street and Vermont San Francisco CA 415-666-7005

This park is a small neighborhood park with a playground, grassy areas- often frequented by dogs and their owners, walking paths, and great views of the city to the west and south. Dogs must be cleaned up after at all times.

McLaren Park Off Leash Dog Areas 1600 Geneva Avenue San Francisco CA 415-831-2084

This park of about 60 acres has two locations for off lead. The top section at the North end of the park is bounded by Shelly Drive with a fence at the roadway, trails, an open area, a natural area, and a reservoir. Dogs are not allowed at the group picnic or children's play area, and leash restrictions apply during performances at the Amphitheater. The South entrance is accessible via the 1600 block of Geneva or Sunnydale. Dogs are not allowed in sensitive habitat areas, they must be leashed when not in the off leash areas, and cleaned up after at all times.

Mountain Lake Off Leash Dog Park 12th Avenue and Lake Street San Francisco CA 415-666-7005

Although small, this popular park has a strong local dog community. The off-leash area is at the Eastern corner of the park on the opposite end of the lake area. You can enter at 8th Avenue and Lake Street, but for wheelchair access and the doggy water fountain, enter one block west at 9th Avenue. Dogs must be leashed when not in the off-leash area, and they must be cleaned up after at all times.

Pine Lake Off Leash Dog Park Sloat Boulevard & Vale Street San Francisco CA 415-831-2700

This park's lake is one of only 3 natural lakes left in San Francisco. The off leash area is on the second terrace of the park, west, and shares a boundary with Stern Grove Park, which also has an off leash area. There is a 1/5 mile trail from the Pine Lake DPA to the Stern Grove DPA. Dogs must be on leash when not in off lead areas, and they must be cleaned up after at all times.

Pine Lake/Stern Grove Trail Between Hwy 1(Stern Grove) and Wawona (Pine Lake) San Francisco CA 415-252-6252

This off leash trail runs west from the Pine Lake Meadow DPA to the Stern Grove DPA. Dogs must be cleaned up after.

Portrero Hill Mini Off Leash Dog Park 22nd Street and Arkansas San Francisco CA 415-695-5009

This .04 acre park is located on 22nd Street between Arkansas and Connecticut Streets and offers a great view of the bay. The area is unfenced so dogs must be under firm voice control. Dogs must be leashed when not in the off leash area, and be cleaned up after at all times.

St Mary's Off Leash Dog Park 95 Justin Drive San Francisco CA   415-695-5006

This 3 tiered multi-use park offers a fenced-in dog park with grassy and paved areas on the lower level (below the playground), benches, and canine and human water fountains. It is frequently closed (locked shut) during rain or wet seasons. Dogs must be on leash when not in off lead areas, and they must be cleaned up after at all times.

Stern Grove Off Leash Dog Park 19th Avenue and Wawona Avenue San Francisco CA   415-252-6252

Stern Grove is said to be one of the most peaceful getaways in the city. It's foggy sunsets and woodsy retreat belies being in a big city. There are picnic tables, horseshoe courts, walking trails, and it is surrounded by fir, redwood, and eucalyptus trees. There is also a 1/5 mile off leash trail that connects this park to the Pine Lake Park, and the 2 parks comprise an area of about 64 acres. Dogs must be leashed when not in off leash areas, and they must be cleaned up after at all times.

Upper Noe Off Lead Dog Park 30th and Church Street San Francisco CA   415-831-2084

This park is located at the eastern end of the Upper Noe Recreation Center behind and along the baseball field, and can be accessed at 30th Street between Church and Sanchez Streets. This is a rather small fenced in dog park with a dirt floor, and may not give the amenities or exercise room wanted, however it still gets a lot of use, and upgrades are planned for this area.

Walter Haas Playground and Dog Park Diamond Heights and Addison Street San Francisco CA   415-831-2084

This 4 acre park offers great views of downtown and the East Bay, an open lawn, basketball court, playgrounds, and a fenced, off leash dog area located in the Northeast section on the upper terrace of the park. This area is accessed from Diamond Heights Blvd. Dogs must be leashed when not in the off-leash area, and they must be cleaned up after at all times.

West Pacific Avenue Park Pacific Avenue and Lyon Street San Francisco CA   415-831-2084

Dogs can be off lead under voice control along the corridor from West Pacific Avenue at the Broadway Street entrance to the 14th Avenue gate. They must be leashed in the forest and fields east of Lover's Lane and North of the Ecology Trail. This is one of the only off leash trail experiences remaining in the Presidio, however, it is adjacent to roads.

Outdoor Restaurants

24th Street Cafe and Grill 3853 24th Street San Francisco CA   415-282-1213

Dogs are allowed at the outdoor tables.

B44 Bistro 44 Belden Place San Francisco CA   415-986-6287

http://www.b44.citysearch.com/

This restaurant specializes in Spanish dishes and serves seafood, chicken and steak entrees as well as a vegetarian sandwich. They are open for lunch Monday through Friday from 11:30am until 2 :30pm. They serve dinner Monday through Saturday from 5:30pm until midnight. Well-behaved leashed dogs are allowed at the outdoor tables. The restaurant is located near Union Square on Belden Place which is a pedestrian only alley (no cars allowed).

Baja Fresh Mexican Grill 30 Fremont St San Francisco CA   415-369-9760

http://www.bajafresh.com

This Mexican restaurant is open for lunch and dinner. They use fresh ingredients and making their salsa and beans daily. Some of the items on their menu include Enchiladas, Burritos, Tacos Salads, Quesadillas, Nachos, Chicken, Steak and more. Well-behaved leashed dogs are allowed at the outdoor tables.

Bechelli's 2346 Chestnut St San Francisco CA   415-346-1801

Dogs are allowed at the outdoor tables.

Blissful Bites 397 Arguello Blvd San Francisco CA   415-750-9460

Dogs are allowed at the outdoor tables.

Blue Danube Coffee House 306 Clement St San Francisco CA   415-221-9041

There is an outside counter where you can sit with your dog.

Cafe De La Presse 352 Grant Ave San Francisco CA   415-398-2680

It is located next to the Hotel Triton and Chinatown. This cafe also serves beer. Dogs are allowed at the outdoor tables.

Cafe Divine 1600 Stockton Street San Francisco CA   415-986-3414

Dogs are allowed at the outdoor tables.

Cafe Niebaum-Coppola 916 Kearny Street San Francisco CA   415-291-1700

Dogs are allowed at the outdoor tables.

Cafe Triste 601 Vallejo Street San Francisco CA   415-392-6739

Dogs are allowed at the outdoor tables.

Calzone's 430 Columbus Ave San Francisco CA   415-397-3600

http://www.calzonesf.com

Located in North Beach, this Euro bistro features pasta, pizza and much more. Well-behaved, leashed dogs are allowed at the outdoor tables. The restaurant is open everyday from 9am-1am.

Camille's Sidewalk Cafe One Market Plaza, 30 Mission Street San Francisco CA   415-348-1514
A vision of healthier, tastier foods inspired the idea for the freshly made salads, gourmet wraps and sandwiches, drinks, desserts, and coffees that are offered at all of Camille's Cafes. Dogs are allowed to sit with you at your outdoor table. Dogs must be attended to at all times, well behaved, and leashed.
Chez Spencer Restaurant 82 14th St San Francisco CA   415-864-2191
This restaurant serves French food. Dogs are allowed at the outdoor tables.
Cioppino's 400 Jefferson Street San Francisco CA   415-775-9311
http://sfoportco.com/cio/location.html
Cioppino's offers soups, salads, pastas, pizzas, entrees with fish, meat and chicken, and of course Cioppino. Well-behaved leashed dogs are allowed at the outdoor tables. The restaurant is located in the Fisherman's Wharf area, on the corner of Jefferson and Leavenworth Streets across from the historic Cannery Building. They serve food 365 days of the year, from 11am to 10pm.
Coffee Bean and Tea Leaf 2201 Fillmore St San Francisco CA   415-447-9733
This coffee shop is very popular with the dogs. Dogs are allowed at the outdoor tables.
Coffee Roastery 2191 Union Street San Francisco CA   415-922-9559
Dogs are allowed at the outdoor tables.
Crepes a Go Go 2165 Union St San Francisco CA   415-928-1919
Dogs are allowed at the outdoor tables.
Dolores Park Cafe 18th and Dolores San Francisco CA   415-621-2936
Dogs are allowed at the outdoor tables.
Dylan's Pub 2301 Folsom St San Francisco CA   415-641-1416
This pub allows dogs inside. Water is provided.
Farley's 1315-18th Street San Francisco CA   415-648-1545
This cafe serves coffee and pastries. Dogs are allowed at the outdoor tables.
Flippers 482 Hayes Street San Francisco CA   415-552-8880
Dogs are allowed at the outdoor tables.
Ghirardelli Ice Cream Fountain Ghirardelli Square San Francisco CA   415-771-4903
Come here to taste some of the best ice cream around. It's in Ghirardelli Square by the Clock Tower on the first floor (by Larkin Street). This place is almost always crowded, but there are several outdoor tables. You'll need to order inside and then grab one of the outdoor tables.
Judy's Cafe 2268 Chestnut St #248 San Francisco CA   415-922-4588
Dogs are allowed at the outdoor tables.
La Mediterranee 288 Noe Street San Francisco CA   415-431-7210
http://www.cafelamed.com
Dogs are allowed at the outdoor tables.

Lou's Pier 47 Restaurant

Lou's Pier 47 Restaurant 300 Jefferson St San Francisco CA   415-771-5687
http://www.louspier47.com/

This cajun seafood restaurant opens daily at 11am. Lou's is located in the Fisherman's Wharf area on Jefferson by Jones Street. They have live bands seven days a week and you might be able to hear the music from outside. Well-behaved leashed dogs are allowed at the outdoor tables.

LuLu's Restaurant 816 Folsom Street San Francisco CA 415-495-5775
This restaurant serves American and seafood. Dogs are allowed at the outdoor tables. Water is provided for your pet.

Martha & Brothers Coffee Company 1551 Church Street San Francisco CA 415-648-1166
Dogs are allowed at the outdoor tables.

Meze's 2373 Chestnut Street San Francisco CA 415-409-7111
Dogs are allowed at the sidewalk table, not on the patio.

Mona Lisa 353 Columbus Ave San Francisco CA 415-989-4917
Dogs are allowed at the outdoor tables.

Noe's Bar 1199 Church Street San Francisco CA 415-282-4007
Dogs are allowed at the outside tables and may be allowed inside as well.

Panta Rei 431 Columbus San Francisco CA 415-591-0900
This restaurant serves Italian food. Dogs are allowed at the outdoor tables.

Park Chow 12 49th Avenue San Francisco CA 415-665-9912
Dogs are allowed at the outdoor tables.

Peet's Coffee 2156 Chestnut St San Francisco CA 415-931-8302
Dogs are allowed at the outdoor tables.

Peet's Coffee and Tea 2197 Fillmore St San Francisco CA 415-563-9930
This coffee shop is very popular with pups and their people.

Plouf 40 Belden Place San Francisco CA 415-986-6491
http://www.plouf.citysearch.com/
This French seafood bistro specializes in mussels, unique appetizers, salads, seafood entrees and grilled meats. They are open Monday through Wednesday for lunch from 11:30am to 3pm and for dinner from 5:30pm to 10pm. On Thursday through Saturday, they are open for lunch from 11am to 3pm and for dinner from 3pm to midnight. Well-behaved leashed dogs are allowed at the outdoor tables. The restaurant is located near Union Square on Belden Place which is a pedestrian only alley (no cars allowed).

Pluto's Fresh Food 3258 Scott St San Francisco CA 415-775-8867
Dogs are allowed at the outdoor tables.

Polly Ann Ice Cream 3142 Noriega St San Francisco CA 415-664-2472
This ice cream shop allows dogs at the outdoor tables.

Pompei's Grotto 340 Jefferson St San Francisco CA 415-776-9265
http://www.mcn.org/a/pompei/
This restaurant specializes in seafood but also serves meat and chicken entrees. Pompei's Grotto is located in the Fisherman's Wharf area on Jefferson Street by Jones Street. Well-behaved leashed dogs are allowed at the outdoor tables.

Rogue Ales Public House 673 Union San Francisco CA 415-362-7880
This restaurant and bar serves American food. Dogs are allowed at the outdoor tables.

Royal Ground Coffee 2060 Fillmore St San Francisco CA 415-567-8822
Dogs are allowed at the outdoor tables.

The Curbside Cafe 2417 California St San Francisco CA 415-929-9030
http://www.sfcurbside.com
This restaurant serves French and California cuisine. Dogs are allowed at the outdoor tables.

The Curbside Cafe II 2769 Lombard St San Francisco CA 415-921-4442
http://www.sfcurbside.com
This restaurant serves French and California cuisine. Dogs are allowed at the outdoor tables.

Ti Couz 3108 16th St San Francisco CA 415-252-7373
Dogs are allowed at the outdoor tables.

Events

SF Giants Dog Days of Summer at AT&T Park 24 Willie Mays Plaza San Francisco CA 415-972-2361
http://www.sfgiants.com
This annual event has been held for over 8 years now. During an August San Francisco Giants game the Giants along with the San Francisco SPCA allow people to bring their dogs to a baseball game in the bleacher seats. There is also a dog parade on the field before the game. See the San Francisco Giants website or call the Giants for specifics.

The Bark and Wine Ball 888 Brannan Street San Francisco CA 415-522-3535
This unique, annual Spring ball benefits the neediest of animals arriving at the shelter, and is presented by CLAW (Critter Lovers At Work). This is one of the few times that you can take your dog to an indoor event with a buffet. Take your pup and go dancing, enjoy the cocktails, a silent auction, inspiring orchestrated music, and more. Dogs must be leashed, and under the owner's control and care at all times.

Vets and Kennels
All Animals Emergency Hospital 1333 9th Ave San Francisco CA   415-566-0531
Monday - Friday 6 pm to 8 am, Saturday noon - Monday 8 am.

San Jose

Accommodations
Motel 6 - San Jose- Campbell 1240 Camden Avenue Campbell CA   408-371-8870 (800-466-8356)
One well-behaved family pet per room. Guest must notify front desk upon arrival. Guest is liable for any damages. In consideration of all guests, pets must never be left unattended in the guest rooms.
Residence Inn by Marriott 2761 S Bascom Avenue Campbell CA   408-559-1551
Dogs of all sizes are allowed. There is a $75 one time fee and a pet policy to sign at check in.
TownePlace Suites 700 E Campbell Avenue Campbell CA   408-370-4510 (800-257-3000)
This extended stay inn offers 95 well appointed suites, each with a full kitchen and living room area, is only minuets from numerous companies and popular attractions, and staff is available 24/7 to make the business or leisure traveler feel right at home. They also have a spa, barbecue area, and a large park and trails close by. Dogs of all sizes are allowed for an additional one time pet fee of $75 per room, and there is a pet policy to sign at check in. Dogs may not be left alone in the rooms, and they must be leashed and cleaned up after at all times.
TOP 200 PLACE **Cypress Hotel** 10050 S. DeAnza Blvd. Cupertino CA   408-253-8900
http://www.thecypresshotel.com/
Well-behaved dogs of all sizes are welcome at this pet-friendly hotel. The boutique hotel offers both rooms and suites. Hotel amenities include complimentary evening wine service, an a 24 hour on-site fitness room. There are no pet fees, just sign a pet liability form.
Residence Inn by Marriott 4460 El Camino Real Los Altos CA   650-559-7890
Dogs of all sizes are allowed. There is a $75 one time fee per pet, and a pet policy to sign at check in.
Best Western Brookside Inn 400 Valley Way Milpitas CA   800-995-8834 (800-780-7234)
Dogs of all sizes are allowed. There is a $10 per night pet fee per pet. Smoking and non-smoking are available for pet rooms.
Candlewood Suites 40 Ranch Drive Milpitas CA   408-719-1212 (877-270-6405)
Dogs of all sizes are allowed. There is a $75 one time pet fee. In addition, there is a $10 per day pet fee.

Fairmont Hotel in San Jose

Embassy Suites Hotel Milpitas - Silicon Valley 901 E. Calaveras Boulevard Milpitas CA   408-942-0400
Dogs of all sizes are allowed. There is a $50 one time pet fee per visit. Dogs are not allowed to be left alone in the room.
Residence Inn by Marriott 1501 California Circle Milpitas CA   408-941-9222
Dogs of all sizes are allowed. There is a $75 one time fee, and a pet policy to sign at check in.
Sheraton San Jose Hotel 1801 Barber Lane Milpitas CA   408-943-0600 (888-625-5144)
Dogs of all sizes are allowed. You must sign a pet policy. Dogs are not to be left alone in the rooms.
TownePlace Suites Milpitas Silicon Valley 1428 Falcon Drive Milpitas CA   408-719-1959
Dogs of all sizes are allowed. There is a $75 one time pet fee per visit.
Clarion Hotel San Jose Airport 1355 N 4th Street San Jose CA   408-453-5340 (877-424-6423)
One dog of any size is allowed. There is a $10 per night additional pet fee. Dogs must be quiet, well behaved, leashed, cleaned up after, and crated when left in the room alone.
Fairmont Hotel 170 S Market Street San Jose CA   408-998-1900 (800-257-7544)
http://www.fairmont.com/sanjose/
This luxury hotel offers 731 beautifully appointed guest rooms and 74 suites, and being set in the high-tech Silicon Valley, they are fully equipped for the business traveler. Vacationers can enjoy the historic grandeur of the inn and its close proximity to several recreational activities. Some of the features include several dining options, a lounge, pool and spa, and many in room amenities. Dogs of all sizes are allowed for an additional one time fee of $75 per pet. Dogs may not be left alone in the room at any time, and they must be leashed and cleaned up after.

Hilton Downtown San Jose

Hilton Downtown San Jose 300 Almaden Blvd San Jose CA   408-287-2100
Dogs of all sizes are allowed. There is a $100 refundable deposit and a pet policy to sign at check in.
Homewood Suites 10 W Trimble Rd San Jose CA   408-428-9900
http://www.homewoodsuites.com
This inn is located in north San Jose, near Milpitas. The inn offers kitchens in each room. There are about half a dozen restaurants next door in a strip mall, many of which have outdoor seating. They require a $275 deposit, and $200 is refundable. The $75 fee is a one time pet charge.
Howard Johnson Express Inn 1215 South 1st St. San Jose CA   408-280-5300 (800-446-4656)
Well-behaved dogs of all sizes are allowed. There is a $5 per day additional pet fee.
Motel 6 - San Jose Airport 2081 North 1st Street San Jose CA   408-436-8180 (800-466-8356)
One well-behaved family pet per room. Guest must notify front desk upon arrival. Guest is liable for any damages. In consideration of all guests, pets must never be left unattended in the guest rooms.
Motel 6 - San Jose South 2560 Fontaine Road San Jose CA   408-270-3131 (800-466-8356)

One well-behaved family pet per room. Guest must notify front desk upon arrival. Guest is liable for any damages. In consideration of all guests, pets must never be left unattended in the guest rooms.
Residence Inn by Marriott 6111 San Ignacio Avenue San Jose CA 408-226-7676
Dogs of all sizes are allowed. There is a $75 one time fee and a pet policy to sign at check in.
Candlewood Suites 481 El Camino Road Santa Clara CA 403-241-9305 (877-270-6405)
Dogs up to 80 pounds are allowed. There is a $75 one time pet fee per visit. Smoking and non-smoking rooms are available for pets.
Guesthouse Inn & Suites 2930 El Camino Real Santa Clara CA 408-241-3010
All rooms have microwaves and refrigerators. There is a $10 per day additional pet fee.
Madison Street Inn 1390 Madison Street Santa Clara CA 408-249-5541
http://www.madisonstreetinn.com/
This attractive inn sits on one third acre of lush greens and gardens and features a pool and spa, fine dining, a house with a parlor and six guest rooms. Dogs of all sizes are allowed for a $75 refundable pet deposit. Dogs must be quiet, well mannered, and leashed and cleaned up after.
Motel 6 - Santa Clara 3208 El Camino Real Santa Clara CA 408-241-0200 (800-466-8356)
One well-behaved family pet per room. Guest must notify front desk upon arrival. Guest is liable for any damages. In consideration of all guests, pets must never be left unattended in the guest rooms.
Santa Clara Marriott 2700 Mission College Blvd Santa Clara CA 408-988-1500 (800-228-9290)
Dogs of all sizes are allowed. There is a $100 refundable pet deposit per room. Dogs must be leashed, cleaned up after, and either crated or the Do Not Disturb sign put on the door, and the front desk informed if they are in the room alone.
Vagabond Inns 3580 El Camino Real Santa Clara CA 408-241-0771
Dogs of all sizes are allowed. There is a $10 per night per pet additional fee.
Comfort Inn 1071 E El Camino Real Sunnyvale CA 408-244-9000 (877-424-6423)
One dog up to 60 pounds is allowed. There is a $10 per night additional pet fee. Dogs may not be left alone in the room, and they must be leashed and cleaned up after.
Motel 6 - Sunnyvale North 775 North Mathilda Avenue Sunnyvale CA 408-736-4595 (800-466-8356)
One well-behaved family pet per room. Guest must notify front desk upon arrival. Guest is liable for any damages. In consideration of all guests, pets must never be left unattended in the guest rooms.
Motel 6 - Sunnyvale South 806 Ahwanee Avenue Sunnyvale CA 408-720-1222 (800-466-8356)
One well-behaved family pet per room. Guest must notify front desk upon arrival. Guest is liable for any damages. In consideration of all guests, pets must never be left unattended in the guest rooms.
Residence Inn by Marriott 750 Lakeway Sunnyvale CA 408-720-1000
Dogs of all sizes are allowed. There is a $75 one time fee and a pet policy to sign at check in.
Residence Inn by Marriott 1080 Stewart Drive Sunnyvale CA 408-720-8893
Dogs of all sizes are allowed. There is a $75 one time fee and a pet policy to sign at check in.
Sheraton Sunnyvale Hotel 1100 North Mathilda Ave. Sunnyvale CA 408-745-6000 (888-625-5144)
Dogs up to 80 pounds are allowed. You must sign pet policy. Dogs are not allowed to be left alone in the room.
Staybridge Suites 900 Hamlin Court Sunnyvale CA 408-745-1515 (877-270-6405)
Dogs of all sizes are allowed. There is a $150 one time pet fee.
The Maple Tree Inn 711 El Camino Real Sunnyvale CA 408-720-9700 (800-423-0243)
http://www.mapletreeinn.com
Located in the heart of Silicon Valley, this pet friendly hotel features a fitness room and complimentary high-speed Internet access. The hotel allows dogs of all sizes. There is a $10 per night pet fee per pet.
TownePlace Suites Sunnyvale Mountain View 606 S Bernardo Avenue Sunnyvale CA 408-733-4200
Dogs of all sizes are allowed. There is a $75 one time pet fee per visit.
Woodfin Suite Hotel 635 E. El Camino Real Sunnyvale CA 408-738-1700
All well-behaved dogs are welcome. All rooms are suites with full kitchens. Hotel amenities include a heated pool. There is a $5 per day pet fee.

Attractions

Ron's Tours / Pedicab Service Call to Arrange. San Jose CA 408-859-8961
Providing pedicab taxi and tour services for the downtown area of San Jose. The pedicab can also be hired for weddings and other special events. Dogs ride free.

Shopping Centers

Santana Row

TOP 200 PLACE **Santana Row** 368 Santana Row San Jose CA   408-551-4611
http://www.santanarow.com
This European style community with nearly 100 shops beneath condos is dog-friendly. There are clean up bags located at various spots for your dog throughout Santana Row. There are a number of dog-friendly stores and outdoor restaurants and sidewalk cafes in Santana Row. Please ask each individual store if you may bring your dog in. Santana Row is located in the heart of Silicon Valley on Stevens Creek Blvd just west of I-880.

Stores

Metropooch 241 E Campbell Avenue Campbell CA   408-379-2275
http://metropooch.com/
This pet gift store has a great variety of items to explore with your pooch. They offer tasty treats, fun toys, birthday cakes, clothing, collars, leashes, pillows, and more. They are open Mondays 11 am to 7 pm; Tuesdays through Fridays 10 am to 7 pm; and Saturdays 10 am to 6 pm. Dogs must be leashed.
PetSmart Pet Store 850 W Hamilton Ave Campbell CA   408-374-9321
Your licensed and well-behaved leashed dog is allowed in the store.
PetSmart Pet Store 20558 Stevens Creek Blvd Cupertino CA   408-725-9530
Your licensed and well-behaved leashed dog is allowed in the store.
Petco Pet Store 444 N Santa Cruz Avenue Los Gatos CA   408-395-7074
Your licensed and well-behaved leashed dog is allowed in the store.
PetSmart Pet Store 175 Ranch Dr Milpitas CA   408-956-1044
Your licensed and well-behaved leashed dog is allowed in the store.
Gussied Up Dog Boutique 1310 Lincoln Avenue San Jose CA   408-279-2544
This is a rather large store a wide variety of gifts, treats, and supplies. Your leashed (or carried), well behaved pet is allowed to explore the store with you. They are open 7 days a week from 10 am to 7 pm.
Hahn's Lighting Store 260 E Virginia St San Jose CA   408-295-1755
Your well-behaved leashed dog is allowed inside this store.
Happy Go Lucky Dog Boutique 925 Blossom Hill Road San Jose CA   408-360-0508
http://www.happygoluckydogs.com/
Located in the Oakridge Mall, there is an outer door so your pet can join you to explore this pet friendly store. They offer designer dog collars, dog carriers, dog beds, fun toys, hip doggie clothes, healthy snacks and more at competitive prices. Dogs must be leashed, but if they are well behaved and will respond to voice control, they

151

may be off lead in the store. They are open from 10 am to 9:30 pm Monday to Friday; 10 am to 9 pm on Saturday, and from 11 am to 7 pm on Sunday.

PetSmart Pet Store 607 Coleman Ave San Jose CA 408-920-0316
Your licensed and well-behaved leashed dog is allowed in the store.
Petco Pet Store 4698 Meridian Avenue San Jose CA 408-269-2481
Your licensed and well-behaved leashed dog is allowed in the store.
Petco Pet Store 500 El Paseo De Saratoga San Jose CA 408-866-7387
Your licensed and well-behaved leashed dog is allowed in the store.
Wilson Motor Sports 1980 Kingman Avenue San Jose CA 408-371-9199
Your well-behaved leashed dog is allowed inside this store. We are a dog-friendly environment and welcome all animal owners.
Petco Pet Store 2775 El Camino Real Santa Clara CA 408-423-9110
Your licensed and well-behaved leashed dog is allowed in the store.
PetSmart Pet Store 770 E El Camino Real Sunnyvale CA 408-773-0215
Your licensed and well-behaved leashed dog is allowed in the store.
Petco Pet Store 160 East El Camino Real Sunnyvale CA 408-774-0171
Your licensed and well-behaved leashed dog is allowed in the store.

Parks

Los Gatos Creek Park Dell Avenue Campbell CA 408-356-2729
This 80 acre park has a small lake, a couple of ponds, picnic benches, barbecues and restroom facilities. The Campbell-Los Gatos Creek Trail runs through the park which goes to the Los Gatos Vasona Park and downtown Los Gatos. Leashed dogs are welcome at this park and on the Creek Trail.

Los Gatos Creek Trail

Los Gatos Creek Trail various-see comments Campbell CA 408-356-2729
The Los Gatos Creek Trail is about 7 miles long each way. Most of it is paved until you enter the path at downtown Los Gatos heading towards the Lexington Reservoir County Park. You can gain access to the trail at numerous points. Some of the popular starting sites are at the Campbell Park in Campbell (Campbell Ave & Gilman Ave), Los Gatos Park in Campbell (Dell Ave & Hacienda Ave), Vasona Lake Park in Los Gatos (Blossom Hill Rd between Highway 17 & University Ave), and downtown Los Gatos (Main Street & Maple Ln-near Hwy 17).
Fremont Older Preserve Prospect Road Cupertino CA 650-691-1200
http://www.openspace.org/OLDER.html
This preserve offers excellent views of the Santa Clara Valley. There are about 9 miles of trails. Dogs must be leashed. One of the popular hikes starts at Prospect Road, goes to Hunter's Point and then continues to Seven

Springs Loop. On a hot day, you may want to bring some water with you. Here are directions to the park: From Hwy 280, take DeAnza Blvd south towards Saratoga. After crossing Hwy 85, you will soon come to Prospect Road. Turn right onto Prospect. Go about 1.5 miles on Prospect. Before Prospect Road ends, turn left onto a one lane road (should be signs to Fremont Older). There is parking for approximately 15 cars.

Los Gatos Creek Reservoir Trail

Los Gatos Creek Reservoir Trail University Avenue Los Gatos CA   408-356-2729
This is a popular hike with about 5-7 miles of trails. There is a nice combination of fire roads and single track trails with streams. A loop trail begins at University Ave (by Hwy 17). The fire road trail parallels Hwy 17 for a while until you reach the Lexington Reservoir. Across the street from the parking lot (the one w/the portable restrooms) by the Reservoir, the trail continues. You'll hike uphill to the top and then back towards the bottom where you started. There are several forks in the trail. Always stay to the left and you'll be back where you started.

Vasona Lake Park Blossom Hill Rd Los Gatos CA   408-356-2729
Your dog is welcome at this 151 acre park. This is a very popular park during the summer because of the nice lake, green landscape, walking trails and picnic tables. There are six miles of paved trails that wind through the park. The paved trails join the Los Gatos Creek Park to the south and the Los Gatos Creek Trail to the north. In the summer, there is usually a hot dog stand by the childen's playground. Your pup can also get his or her paws wet in the lake. The easiest spot is near the playground. The park is located on Blossom Hill Road between University Ave and Hwy 17 (no Hwy exit here). From southbound Hwy 17, take the Saratoga-Los Gatos (Hwy 9) exit and head east/right. At University Avenue, turn right. Turn right again at Blossom Hill and the park will be on the left. There is a fee for parking.

Dixon Landing Park Milmont Drive Milpitas CA
Dixon Landing Park is a relatively small park, but has much to offer. There are numerous picnic tables, a children's playground, tennis courts and a basketball court. You can grab food to go at one of the restaurants near Dixon Landing Rd and Milmont Drive, then bring it back to enjoy at the picnic tables. This park is a few blocks away (heading west) from the Levee Path. To get there from Hwy 880 heading north, exit Dixon Landing Rd. At the light, turn left then make a right onto Dixon Landing Rd. Turn right onto Milmont Dr/California Circle. The park will be on the right.

Ed Levin County Park 3100 Calveras Blvd. Milpitas CA   408-262-6980
http://www.parkhere.org
Dogs are allowed on the Bay Area Ridge Trail from Sandy Wool Lake to Mission Peak. They are not allowed on any other trails in the park. Dogs must be leashed, except when in the off-leash dog park.

Anderson Lake/Park Cochrane Rd. Morgan Hill CA   408-779-3634
The 2,365 acre Anderson Lake/Park also features the Coyote Creek Parkway's multiple use trails. Dogs on a 6 foot leash are allowed. Anderson Lake and the picnic areas along the Coyote Creek are located off of Cochrane

Road in Morgan Hill, east of Highway 101.

Almaden Quicksilver McAbee Ave. San Jose CA 408-268-8220
http://www.parkhere.org/prkpages/aq.htm
This park encompasses over 3900 acres. Dogs are allowed on a 6 foot leash. During early spring the park offers a wildflower display. Remnants of the mining era also offer a look at the mining operations of the 1800's. The park may be accessed from three areas. The McAbee entrance at the north end of the park can be accessed off McAbee Road. This entrance is accessible to pedestrians and equestrians only. Turn south off Camden Avenue and follow McAbee Road until it ends (.6 miles). Only street parking is available. The Mockingbird Hill entrance is accessed off Mockingbird Hill Lane. This entrance is accessible to pedestrians and equestrians only. From Highway 85, take the Almaden Expressway exit south 4.5 miles to Almaden Road. Proceed .5 miles on Almaden Road to Mockingbird Hill Lane, turn right and continue .4 miles to the parking entrance is accessible to all users, including bicyclists. From Almaden Expressway, proceed 3 miles along Almaden Road through the town of New Almaden to the unpaved staging area on the right.

Coyote Creek Parkway various-see comments San Jose CA 408-225-0225
The Coyote Creek Trail is approximately 13 miles each way. The north end is paved and popular with bicyclists, rollerbladers and hikers. The sound end (south of Metcalf Rd) has an equestrian dirt trail that parallels the paved trail. Leashed dogs are allowed on both the paved and dirt trails. You can gain access to the trail at numerous points. The south trail access has parking off Burnett Ave. From Hwy 101 South, exit Cochrane Rd. Turn right on Cochrane. Then turn right on Monterey Hwy (Hwy 82). Right on Burnett Ave and the parking will be at the end of Burnett. The north trail access has parking at Hellyer Park. From Hwy 101, exit Hellyer Ave and head west. Continue straight, pay at the booth and then park. There is also parking at Silver Creek Valley Blvd for north trail access. Take Hwy 101 and exit Silver Creek Valley Blvd. Head east (toward the hills). Parking will be on the right.

Guadalupe River Park & Gardens 715 Spring Street San Jose CA 408-298-7657
http://www.grpg.org/
The river park is a 3-mile section of land that runs along the banks of the Guadalupe River in the heart of downtown, and adjacent to the park are the gardens, together providing 150 acres open to the public. The Heritage Rose Garden has over 3,700 varieties of roses, and has been further developed to include 2.6 miles of trails, over 15,000 trees, 9,000 shrubs, and 60,000 ground cover plants, and is also beneficial in providing the town with 100 year flood protection. Dogs of all sizes are welcome. Dogs must be on lead at all times, cleaned up after, and all must stay on the paths.

Santa Teresa County Park San Vicente Avenue San Jose CA 408-268-3883
Dogs are allowed on a 6 foot leash. This diverse 1,688 acre park, located ten miles south of downtown San Jose, is rich in history and offers spectacular views from its trails located above the Almaden and Santa Clara Valleys. The secluded upland valleys of the park provide a quiet place for exploring the natural environment minutes away from the surrounding developed areas. From San Jose, follow Almaden Expressway until it ends. Turn right onto Harry Road, then turn left onto McKean Road. Travel approximately 1.3 miles to Fortini Road. Turn left onto Fortini Road toward the Santa Teresa Hills. At the end of Fortini Road, turn left onto San Vicente Avenue. A ten car parking area is located on the right about 500 feet from Fortini Road.

Off-Leash Dog Parks

Los Gatos Creek County Dog Park 1250 Dell Avenue Campbell CA 408-866-2105
The dog park offers separate fenced off-leash areas for large and small dogs. Water for dogs, benches for people, and pooper scoopers are at the park. The dog park is located in Los Gatos Creek Park. If you park at the Dell Avenue parking area to access the park there is a $5 parking fee. Alternatively, you can walk in from Dell Avenue or by a pedestrian bridge over the 17 freeway. The location of the dog park is between the ponds and San Tomas Expressway, just east of 17.

City of Milpitas Dog Park 3100 Calveras Blvd. Milpitas CA 408-262-6980
http://www.parkhere.org
This dog park has separate sections for small and large dogs. The dog park is run by the City of Milpitas, but it is located at Ed Levin County Park. The dog park is located off Calaveras Blvd. Turn onto Downing Road and head toward Sandy Wool Lake. Go uphill by the lake until you come to the dog park.

Delmas Dog Park Park Avenue and Delmas Avenue San Jose CA 408-535-3570
http://www.sjparks.org/dogparks.asp
Delmas Dog Park opened in February, 2006. It is completely fenced and nearly 1/2 an acre in size. The dog park is a joint venture between the City of San Jose and the Santa Clara Valley Transportation Authority. The dog park is located just under Highway 87 one block south of San Carlos Street on Dalmas Avenue just south of downtown.

Fontana Dog Park Golden Oak Way at Castello Drive San Jose CA 408-535-3570
http://www.sjparks.org/dogparks.asp
Fontana Dog Park is a fenced dog park with two sections. It is closed on Tuesdays and some Fridays for maintainence. There are benches and bags provided to clean up after your dog.

Hellyer Park/Dog Run Hellyer Ave San Jose CA 408-225-0225
This two acre dog park has a nice lawn and is completely fenced. It is closed Wednesdays for maintenance. The

dog park is located at the northeast end of Hellyer Park, near the Shadowbluff group area. There is a minimal fee for parking. To get there, take Hwy 101 to Hellyer Ave. Exit and head west on Hellyer. Continue straight, pay at the booth and drive to the parking lot where the dog park is located.

Los Gatos Creek County Dog Park

Santa Clara Dog Park

Miyuki Dog Park Santa Teresa Boulevard San Jose CA   408-277-4573
This dog park is almost one half acre. There is a rack where dog owners can leave spare toys for other pups to use. All dogs that use this off-leash park must wear a current dog license and proof of the rabies vaccine. The park is open from sunrise to one hour after sunset.
Ryland Dog Park First Street at Bassett Street San Jose CA   408-535-3570
http://www.sjparks.org/dogparks.asp
This dog park is located in Ryland Park which is a few blocks north of Julian Street on North First Street. The dog park is on the west side of Ryland Park and is under the Coleman Avenue overpass. This gives it shade and protection from rain. It has a gravel surface.
Santa Clara Dog Park 3450 Brookdale Drive Santa Clara CA   408-615-2260
The Santa Clara Dog Park was originally located on Lochnivar Ave. but has moved to a new location at 3450 Brookdale Drive right across the park from the original location. This park is completely fenced. Weekday hours are from 7am to a 1/2 hour after sunset and weekend hours are from 9am to a 1/2 hour after sunset.
Las Palmas Park/Dog Park 850 Russett Drive Sunnyvale CA   408-730-7506
After your pup finishes playing with other dogs at this dog park, you can both relax by the pond at one of the many picnic tables. It's located at 850 Russett Drive (by Remington Avenue and Saratoga-Sunnyvale Rd).

Outdoor Restaurants

Baja Fresh Mexican Grill 1976 S. Bascom Ave Campbell CA   408-377-2600
http://www.bajafresh.com
This Mexican restaurant is open for lunch and dinner. They use fresh ingredients and making their salsa and beans daily. Some of the items on their menu include Enchiladas, Burritos, Tacos Salads, Quesadillas, Nachos, Chicken, Steak and more. Well-behaved leashed dogs are allowed at the outdoor tables.
Camille's Sidewalk Cafe 1700 S Bascom Avenue Campbell CA   408-559-0310
http://www.camillescafe.com/
The vision of healthier, tastier foods enjoyed in a garden setting inspired the freshly made salads, gourmet wraps and sandwiches, drinks, desserts, and coffees that are offered at all of Camille's Cafes. Dogs are allowed to sit with you at your table. Dogs must be attended to at all times, well behaved, and leashed.
Le Boulanger Bakery 1875 S Bascom Ave Campbell CA   408-369-1820
This bakery is located in the Pruneyard Shopping Center. The Campbell-Los Gatos path is within walking distance.

Rock Bottom Restaurant & Brewery

TOP 200 PLACE **Rock Bottom Restaurant & Brewery** 1875 S Bascom Ave Campbell CA   408-377-0707
This dog-friendly restaurant is located in the Pruneyard Shopping Center. The Campbell-Los Gatos path is within

walking distance. Water is provided for your pet. There is a nice outdoor seating area with heaters.
Stacks 139 E Campbell Ave Campbell CA   408-376-3516
This restaurant serves breakfast food. Dogs are allowed at the outdoor tables.
The Kings Head Pub & Restaurant 201 Orchard City Drive Campbell CA   408-871-2499
http://www.thekingshead.com/
Thanks to one of our readers for recommending this dog-friendly restaurant. The restaurant has lots of outdoor
seating with a shady deck.
Yiassoo 2180 S Bascom Ave Campbell CA   408-559-0312
Delicious Greek food.
Baja Fresh Mexican Grill 20735 Stevens Creek Blvd Cupertino CA   408-257-6141
http://www.bajafresh.com
This Mexican restaurant is open for lunch and dinner. They use fresh ingredients and making their salsa and
beans daily. Some of the items on their menu include Enchiladas, Burritos, Tacos Salads, Quesadillas, Nachos,
Chicken, Steak and more. Well-behaved leashed dogs are allowed at the outdoor tables.
Cafe Society 21265 Stevens Creek Blvd #202 Cupertino CA   408-725-8091
This coffee shop serves coffee and pastries. Dogs are allowed at the outdoor tables.
Whole Foods Market 20830 Stevens Creek Blvd. Cupertino CA   408-257-7000
http://www.wholefoods.com/
This natural food supermarket offers natural and organic foods. Order some food from their deli without your dog
and bring it to an outdoor table where your well-behaved leashed dog is welcome. Dogs are not allowed in the
store including the deli at any time.
Three Degrees Restaurant and Bar 140 S Santa Cruz Avenue Los Gatos CA   408-884-1054
This restaurant offers contemporary California cuisine and wines in a comfortable, kicked back setting. They are
located inside the Toll House Hotel and also offer service on their spacious patio. Your well behaved dog is
welcome to join you for outside dining. Dogs must be attended to and leashed at all times.
Whole Foods Market 15980 Los Gatos Blvd. Los Gatos CA   408-358-4434
http://www.wholefoods.com/
This natural food supermarket offers natural and organic foods. Order some food from their deli without your dog
and bring it to an outdoor table where your well-behaved leashed dog is welcome. Dogs are not allowed in the
store including the deli at any time.
Willow Street Pizza 20 S. Santa Cruz Ave Los Gatos CA   408-354-5566
There is a large outdoor seating area with heat lamps. The hours are 11:30 am to 10 pm, 11 pm on Friday and
Saturday.
Bento Xpress 23 N. Milpitas Blvd Milpitas CA   408-262-7544
http://www.bentoxpress.com
This restaurant offers quick Japanese cuisine. Dogs are allowed at the outdoor tables.
Erik's Deli Cafe 148 N. Milpitas Blvd Milpitas CA   408-262-7878
This cafe offers sandwiches, soup, stew, chili and more. Dogs are allowed at the outdoor tables.
Giorgio's Italian Food and Pizza 643 S Calaveras Blvd Milpitas CA   408-942-1292
This restaurant serves Italian food. Dogs are allowed at the outdoor tables.
Amato Pizzeria 6081 Meridian Avenue #A San Jose CA   408-997-7727
http://www.amatopizzeria.com/index.html
This pizzeria has some nice tables and chairs out front where you can sit with your pet and enjoy the fair. Dogs
must be well behaved, leashed, and please clean up after your pet.
Baja Fresh Mexican Grill 1708 Oakland Road San Jose CA   408-436-5000
http://www.bajafresh.com
This Mexican restaurant is open for lunch and dinner. They use fresh ingredients and making their salsa and
beans daily. Some of the items on their menu include Enchiladas, Burritos, Tacos Salads, Quesadillas, Nachos,
Chicken, Steak and more. Well-behaved leashed dogs are allowed at the outdoor tables.
Ben and Jerry's 377 Santana Row #1120 San Jose CA   408-423-8115
This ice cream parlour allows pets at the outdoor tables.
Bill's Cafe 1115 Willow Street San Jose CA   408-294-1125
Bill's cafe has outdoor seating for you and your dog. Dogs sometimes get biscuits and water.
Blowfish Sushi to Die For 355 Santana Row #1010 San Jose CA   408-345-3848
This restaurant serves Asian food. Dogs are allowed at the outdoor tables.
Britannia Arms 173 W Santa Clara Street San Jose CA   408-278-1400
Dogs are allowed at the outdoor tables.
Camille's Sidewalk Cafe 864 Blossom Hill Road San Jose CA   408-363-1515
A vision of healthier, tastier foods inspired the idea for the freshly made salads, gourmet wraps and sandwiches,
drinks, desserts, and coffees that are offered at all of Camille's Cafes. Dogs are allowed to sit with you at your
outdoor table. Dogs must be attended to at all times, well behaved, and leashed.
Camille's Sidewalk Cafe 90 Skyport Drive San Jose CA   408-436-5333
A vision of healthier, tastier foods inspired the idea for the freshly made salads, gourmet wraps and sandwiches,
drinks, desserts, and coffees that are offered at all of Camille's Cafes. Dogs are allowed to sit with you at your
outdoor table. Dogs must be attended to at all times, well behaved, and leashed.

Casa Vicky's Catering and Cafe 792 E Julian St San Jose CA   408-995-5488
This restaurant serves Mexican food. Dogs are allowed at the outdoor tables.
Coffee on the Patio 1305-I North Bascom Ave San Jose CA   408-296-1112
This coffee shop serves deli-type food and pastries. Dogs are allowed at the outdoor tables.
Consuelo Mexican Bistro 377 Santana Row #1125 San Jose CA   408-260-7082
This restaurant serves Mexican food. Dogs are allowed at the outdoor tables.
Left Bank Restaurant 377 Santana Row San Jose CA   408-984-3500
http://www.leftbank.com/
This sidewalk cafe offers a seasonally-changing French menu, a happy hour, and a Sunday brunch. Your pet is welcome to join you on the sidewalk patio. Dogs must be attended to at all times, well behaved, and leashed.
Noah's Bagels 1578 S Bascom Ave San Jose CA   408-371-8321
Dogs are allowed at the outdoor seats.
Pamela's East Side Cafe 2122 McKee Road San Jose CA   408-254-4000
This restaurant serves American food. Dogs are allowed at the outdoor tables.
Pasta Pomodoro 378 Santana Row #1130 San Jose CA   408-241-2200
This restaurant serves Italian and sandwich type food. Dogs are allowed at the outdoor tables.
Pizza Antica 334 Santana Row #1065 San Jose CA   408-557-8373
This restaurant serves Italian food. Dogs are allowed at the outdoor tables.
Riga European Bakery and Cafe 1338-3 The Alameda San Jose CA   408-947-7442
This cafe serves European food. Dogs are allowed at the outdoor tables.
Sonoma Chicken Coop 31 North Market Street San Jose CA   408-287-4098
http://www.sonomachickencoop.com/
Located in San Pedro Square, this restaurant allows dogs at their outdoor tables. Thanks to one of our readers for recommending this restaurant.
Straits 333 Santana Row San Jose CA   408-246-6320
This restaurant serves American food. Dogs are allowed at the outdoor tables.
The Loft Bar and Bistro 90 S Second Street San Jose CA   408-291-0677
This American restaurant with a Mediterranean twist offers a variety of dining areas and 2 bar areas. They offer service at the street level patio where dogs are allowed. Dogs must be attended to at all times, well behaved, and leashed.
Willow Street Wood Fired Pizza 1072 Willow St San Jose CA   408-971-7080
This restaurant serves Italian food. Dogs are allowed at the outdoor tables.
Yankee Pier 378 Santana Row #1100 San Jose CA   408-244-1244
This restaurant serves seafood. Dogs are allowed at the outdoor tables.
Baja Fresh Mexican Grill 3950 Rivermark Plaza Santa Clara CA   408-588-4060
http://www.bajafresh.com
This Mexican restaurant is open for lunch and dinner. They use fresh ingredients and making their salsa and beans daily. Some of the items on their menu include Enchiladas, Burritos, Tacos Salads, Quesadillas, Nachos, Chicken, Steak and more. Well-behaved leashed dogs are allowed at the outdoor tables.
Pizz'a Chicago 1576 Halford Ave Santa Clara CA   408-244-2246
They have delicious deep dish style pizza. They only have 3 outdoor tables, so try to arrive before the lunch or dinner rush. Once there, you and your pup can enjoy being served pizza at the covered tables. This is a good place to go even if it's raining, because the tables are well covered.
Tony & Alba's Pizza & Pasta 3137 Stevens Creek Blvd Santa Clara CA   408-246-4605
Great food and nice outdoor seating. They have warm outdoor heat lamps. If for some reason they don't have them turned on, just ask one of the folks working there and they'll be happy to turn them on.
Fibbar Magees Irish Pub 1565 Murphy Avenue Sunnyvale CA   408-749-8373
You and your dog are welcome at the outdoor tables at this Irish Pub. It is located in the Murphy's Station area, across from the Sunnyvale Town Center Mall.
Scruffy Murphys Irish Pub 187 S Murphy Ave Sunnyvale CA   408-735-7394
Enjoy the great Irish food at this pub. They have just one outdoor table, so arrive early to ensure a seat with your pup. This restaurant is located in the Murphy's Station area, across from the Sunnyvale Town Center Mall. You can eat at the outdoor table, but the pub cannot server drinks outside.

Events
Bark in the Park William and South 16th Streets San Jose CA   408-793-5125
http://www.barksanjose.org/
This huge annual September fundraising event at William Street Park is sponsored by the Naglee Park neighborhood's Campus Community Association in central San Jose. Thousands of people and dogs attend this event, which may be the largest pet event in the west each year. A $5 donation per registered dog is requested. Festivities include doggy demonstrations, contests, performances, live music, specialty and food vendors, and much more. Dogs must be leashed and cleaned up after at all times.

Pet Sitters

Guardian Petsitting Service Please Call or Email at robinrmh@aol.com . San Jose CA   408-394-3320
http://guardianpetsitting.com
Visits start at $24. Dog walking available. Mid-day dog walking and overnight petsitting available upon special request. Member Better Business Bureau, Licensed, Bonded, and Insured.

Day Kennels

PetsHotel by PetsMart Day Kennel 607 Coleman Ave. San Jose CA
http://www.petsmart.com/PETsHOTEL/
This PetSmart pet store offers day camp only. You can drop off and pick up your dog between the hours of 7 am - 7 pm, M-S, Sunday 9 am - 5 pm. Dogs are required to have proof of current rabies, DPP and bordatella vaccinations.

Vets and Kennels

United Emergency Animal Clinic 1657 S Bascom Ave Campbell CA   408-371-6252
Monday - Friday 6 pm to 8 am, 24 hours on weekends.
Emergency Animal Clinic 5440 Thornwood Dr. San Jose CA   408-578-5622
Monday - Friday 6 pm to 8 am, 24 hours on weekends.

Santa Cruz

Accommodations

Apple Lane Inn B&B 6265 Soquel Drive Aptos CA   831-475-6868 (800-649-8988)
http://applelaneinn.com/
You and your well-behaved dog are allowed at this Victorian farmhouse built in the 1870s. It is situated on over 2 acres with fields, gardens, and apple orchards. There are also many farm animals such as horses, chickens, goats, ducks and geese. They have three double rooms and two suites with antique furniture. Each of the five rooms have private baths. Room stay includes a full breakfast, and afternoon and evening refreshments. Rates are $120 per night and up. There is a $25 charge for a dog, extra person or crib. No smoking is allowed indoors. This bed and breakfast is located on Soquel Drive, near Cabrillo Jr. College. From Hwy 17 south, exit Hwy 1 south towards Watsonville. Take the Park Avenue/New Brighton Beach exit. Turn left onto Park Ave. Turn right onto Soquel. It will be near Atherton Drive and before Cabrillo College.
Redwood Croft B&B 275 Northwest Drive Bonny Doon CA   831-458-1939
http://www2.cruzio.com/~cummings/ .
This bed and breakfast, located in the Santa Cruz Mountains, is set on a sunny hill amidst the redwood forest. It is the perfect country getaway, especially since they allow dogs. They are very dog-friendly. This B&B has two rooms each with a private bath and full amenities. The Garden Room has its own entrance, private deck with a secluded 7 foot Jacuzzi spa, full-size bed, wood-burning stone fireplace and a sky-lighted loft with a queen futon. The West Room is sunny and spacious, has a California king bed and large bathroom with a double shower and roman tub. Room stay includes a lavish country breakfast. Room rates are $145 per night. The dog-friendly Davenport Beach (see Parks) is only about 10-15 minutes away. Call the inn for directions or for a brochure.
Best Western Capitola By-the-Sea Inn & Suites 1435 41st Avenue Capitola CA   831-477-0607 (800-780-7234)
http://www.bestwesterncapitola.com/
This award winning hotel is well-located to many other attractions and recreational opportunities, and offer 574 beautifully appointed rooms with many in-room amenities. Dogs of all sizes are welcome for no additional fee as the fee is included in the pet specific rooms. Dogs may not be left alone in the room at any time, and they must be leashed and cleaned up after.
Capitola Inn 822 Bay Ave Capitola CA   831-462-3004
This inn is located a few blocks from Capitola Village. They offer 56 rooms with either a private patio or balcony. There is a $20 per day pet charge.
Buck's Beach Bungalow 341 35th Avenue Santa Cruz CA   831-476-0170
Dogs of all sizes are allowed. There is a pet policy to sign at check in and there are no additional pet fees.
Casa Del Barco 108 7th Avenue Santa Cruz CA   650-491-0036
Dogs only are allowed here and in all sizes. There is a $500 refundable deposit per stay and a pet policy to sign at check in.
Continental Inn 414 Ocean Street Santa Cruz CA   831-429-1221 (800-343-6941)
http://www.continentalinnsantacruz.com/
Elegant, yet affordable, this inn is only minutes from several other local attractions. Some of the amenities include a complimentary continental breakfast and morning paper, an outdoor heated pool and spa, and several

in-room extras. Dogs of all sizes are allowed for an additional $10 per night per pet. Dogs may not be left alone in the room, and they must be leashed and cleaned up after.

Edgewater Beach Motel 525 Second Street Santa Cruz CA   831-423-0440   (888-809-6767)
http://www.edgewaterbeachmotel.com/
This motel has ocean views, beach views, and 17 uniquely designed suites (for one to eight people). Some of the rooms have ocean views, microwaves, refrigerators. A couple of the rooms have fireplaces, private lawns and full kitchens. Non-smoking rooms are available. While dogs are not allowed on the Boardwalk or on the nearby beach, they are allowed on the West Cliff Drive Walkway. Walk to the waterfront, then go north (away from the Boardwalk) along the sidewalk on the street closest to the ocean. It will become a walkway that is used by walkers, joggers and bicyclists. If you walk about 1 1/2 - 2 miles, you'll reach several dog beaches (see Parks). To get to the motel, take Hwy 17 south. Take the Hwy 1 North exit. Then take the Ocean St exit on the left towards the beaches. Head towards the beach on Ocean St and then turn right on San Lorenzo Blvd. Turn left on Riverside Ave and then right on 2nd St. The motel will be on the left. Ample parking is available in their parking lot. There is a $20 one time additional pet fee.

Guesthouse International 330 Ocean Street Santa Cruz CA   831-425-3722
There is a $10 per day pet fee.

Best Western 6020 Scott's Valley Drive Scotts Valley CA   831-438-6666 (800-780-7234)
Dogs of all sizes are allowed. There can be one large dog or 2 small dogs per room. There is a $100 refundable pet deposit per room. Dogs must be leashed, cleaned up after, and the front desk informed if they are in the room alone.

Hilton 6001 La Madrona Drive Scotts Valley CA   831-440-1000
Dogs of all sizes are allowed, however, if it is a very large dog, you may need manager's approval. There is a $25 per night per room fee and a pet policy to sign at check in.

Blue Spruce Inn Bed and Breakfast 2815 Main Street Soquel CA   831-464-1137
http://bluespruce.com
A well-behaved dog is allowed in the Secret Garden Room. This room offers a private enclosed garden that includes an outdoor hot tub for two, a small sitting area with gas fireplace and comfortable reading chairs, private bathroom and more. There is a $25 one time pet charge. Please abide by the following pet rules. If your dog will be allowed on the furniture, please cover it first with a sheet. If you take your pooch to the dog beach, please rinse him or her off in the outside hot and cold shower before entering the room. This bed and breakfast does offer a VIP (Very Important Pets) program for your pooch. This includes a dog bone, water bowl and poop bags upon arrival.

Campgrounds and RV Parks

New Brighton State Beach 1500 Park Avenue Capitola CA   831-464-6330 (800-444-7275)
Rich in natural and cultural history, this park also has various marine and land habitats to explore and a variety of recreational opportunities. Dogs of all sizes are allowed. There are no additional pet fees. Dogs may not be left unattended outside, and they must be on no more than a 6 foot leash at all times, and cleaned up after. Dogs are allowed to walk on the beach. The camping and tent areas also allow dogs. There is a dog walk area at the campground.

Big Basin Redwoods State Park 21600 Big Basin Way Old Creek CA   831-338-8860 (800-444-PARK (7275))
http://www.bigbasin.org
This park is California's oldest park and is home to the largest continuous stand of ancient coast redwoods south of the bay area. It offers a wide variety of recreation and other activities. Dogs of all sizes are allowed. There are no additional pet fees. Dogs may not be left unattended at any time, and they must be leashed and cleaned up after. Dogs are allowed in the picnic area, the campground area, on paved roads, and the North escape road only. Dogs are not allowed anywhere at Rancho del Oso or on any other trails or interior roads. They must be kept in the RV or tent at night. Check at Park Headquarters for scheduled guided "dog walks", which are informative group hikes that give dog owners a chance to take their dogs along while learning about redwood ecology and park history. The camping and tent areas also allow dogs. There is a dog walk area at the campground. There are no electric or water hookups at the campgrounds.

Vacation Home Rentals

Redtail Ranch by the Sea Call to Arrange. Santa Cruz CA   831-429-1322
http://www.redtailranch.com/
This 3 bedroom, 1 1/2 bath ranch house is located on a 72 acre horse ranch, the Redtail Ranch. The house features a 180 degree ocean view of the Monterey Bay and views of the coastal hills. The house sleeps 1 to 8 people and comes with a complete full kitchen. The home is located about a 5 minute drive to local beaches, a 1 hour drive to Monterey, Carmel and Big Sur, and a 1 1/2 hour scenic coastal drive to San Francisco. The rental is available year-round for nightly, weekly, and extended vacation rentals.

Beachnest Vacation Rentals Call to Arrange Sunset Beach State Park CA   831-722-0202
http://www.beachnest.com

These vacation rentals are located in the middle of Sunset State Beach with views of the Monterey Bay Marine Sanctuary. Dogs are not allowed on Sunset State Beach but there are a number of dog-friendly beaches within a few miles. There are no additional pet fees.

Attractions

Bonny Doon Vineyard 10 Pine Flat Road Bonny Doon CA   831-425-4518
Dogs are allowed only at the outside seating areas. They must be controlled and on leash. There is no wine tasting fee. The wine tasting room is open daily from 11 am to 5 pm except on most holidays.
Roaring Camp & Big Trees RR P.O.Box G-1 Felton CA   831-335-4484
http://www.roaringcamprr.com/
As of the summer of 1999, dogs are required to wear muzzles on this train ride but not on the grounds. They provide free muzzles you can borrow. At Roaring Camp you will find daily musical entertainment (Old Western style) and a couple of outdoor cafes that serve burgers, chicken sandwiches and more. They also hold many seasonal events here like a Harvest Fair and Steam Festival. The train ride takes you into the beautiful Santa Cruz Mountains. This is America's last steam-powered passenger railroad with year-round passenger service. They operate daily from 11am to 5pm. To get there, take Hwy 17 to the Scotts Valley Mount Hermon Road exit. Stay on Mount Hermon Road until it ends. Turn left onto Graham Hill Road. Roaring Camp is 1/4 mile ahead on the right.

De Laveaga Park Disc Golf

De Laveaga Park Disc Golf Branciforte Santa Cruz CA
Santa Cruz is quickly gaining recognition for being home to one of disc golf's premier courses. Disc golf is similar to golf with clubs and balls, but the main difference is the equipment. Discs are shot into elevated baskets/holes. Your leashed dog is allowed to go with you on this course (pick up after your pooch). Rangers patrol the park frequently and will fine any dog owner that doesn't have their dog on a leash or doesn't clean up after their pup. This course has 27 baskets and is part of an over 1200 acre park which allows dogs. If you do not have any discs, you can purchase them at various locations in the Santa Cruz area. You can purchase discs at Play it Again Sports in Soquel, on Soquel Ave right past Capitola Ave. Another place that sells discs is Johnny's Sports in downtown Santa Cruz. New discs cost about $8.00 to $12.00 depending on the make and model. To get to the park, take Hwy 17 south to Santa Cruz and exit Hwy 1 south (towards Watsonville). Take the first exit, Morrissey Blvd (the exit has a sharp 90 degree turn). Turn right at the stop sign, and then go to the end of the street where it dead ends at Branciforte. Turn right. Go over Hwy 1, stop at the stop sign, and continue straight up the hill. Follow the signs to the De Laveaga Golf Course. Go approx. 1/4 mile past the club house and the disc golf parking will be on the right. The first hole is across the road in the Oak Grove. Maps should be available.
Harbor Water Taxis Lake Avenue Santa Cruz CA   831-475-6161

The water taxis run inside the Santa Cruz Harbor only. The taxis are small barges (flat-bottomed boats). They have several very short hops across and around the harbor. It's something fun to do while walking around the harbor. If you are on the east side of the harbor by Lake Ave., you and your dog can take the taxi across the harbor to dine at Aldo's Restaurant (see Restaurants). There is more parking by Lake Ave than by Aldos. The taxi's are seasonal, usually running from May through October. There are several spots around the harbor where you can catch the water taxis and there is a minimal fee for the taxi. To get there from Hwy 17 heading south, take the Ocean Street exit on the left towards the beaches. Turn left onto East Cliff Drive. Go straight to go onto Murray Street. Turn right on Lake Avenue (East Santa Cruz Harbor). Take Lake Ave until it ends near Shamrock Charters. There is a minimal fee for parking.

Lighthouse Point Surfer's Museum W. Cliff Dr Santa Cruz CA 831-420-6289
This lighthouse is home to California's first surfing museum. Well-behaved, leashed dogs are allowed inside. It is open from noon to 6pm daily, except it is closed on Tuesdays. The museum is located on West Cliff Drive, about a 5-10 minute drive north of the Santa Cruz Boardwalk.

Santa Cruz Harley Davidson Motorcyles 1148 Soquel Ave Santa Cruz CA 831-421-9600
http://www.santacruzharley.com/
Well-behaved, leashed dogs are allowed in the store and the museum. They have dogs come into the store all the time. The museum, located inside the store, features vintage motorcycles, memorabilia, photos and more. Located at the corner of Soquel and Seabright.

Stores

PetSmart Pet Store 490 River St Santa Cruz CA 831-429-2780
Your licensed and well-behaved leashed dog is allowed in the store.

Beaches

Rio Del Mar Beach Rio Del Mar Aptos CA 831-685-6500
Dogs on leash are allowed at this beach which offers a wide strip of sand. From Highway 1, take the Rio Del Mar exit.

Davenport Beach Hwy 1 Davenport CA 831-462-8333
This beautiful beach is surrounded by high bluffs and cliff trails. Leashes are required. To get to the beach from Santa Cruz, head north on Hwy 1 for about 10 miles.

Manresa State Beach San Andreas Road Manresa CA 831-761-1795
Surfing and surf fishing are both popular activities at this beach. Dogs are allowed on the beach, but must be leashed. To get there from Aptos, head south on Highway 1. Take San Andreas Road southwest for several miles until you reach Manresa. Upon reaching the coast, you will find the first beach access point.

East Cliff Coast Access Points East Cliff Drive Santa Cruz CA 831-454-7900
There are many small dog-friendly beaches and coastal access points that stretch along East Cliff Drive between 12th Avenue to 41st Avenue. This is not one long beach because the water comes up to cliffs in certain areas and breaks it up into many smaller beaches. Dogs are allowed on leash. Parking is on city streets along East Cliff or the numbered avenues. To get there from Hwy 17 south, take the Hwy 1 exit south towards Watsonville. Take the exit towards Soquel Drive. Turn left onto Soquel Avenue. Turn right onto 17th Avenue. Continue straight until you reach East Cliff Drive. From here, you can head north or south on East Cliff Drive and park anywhere between 12th and 41st street to access the beaches.

Its Beach West Cliff Drive Santa Cruz CA 831-429-3777
Your dog can go leash free from sunrise to 10am and 4pm until sunset. It is not a large beach, but enough for your water loving dog to take a dip in the water and get lots of sand between his or her paws. According to the sign, dogs are not allowed between 10am and 4pm. It is located on West Cliff Drive, just north of the Lighthouse, and south of Columbia Street. It is also across from the Lighthouse Field off-leash area. To get there, head south on Hwy 17. Take the Hwy 1 North exit, heading towards Half Moon Bay and Hwy 9. Merge onto Mission Street (Hwy 1). Turn left onto Swift Street. Then turn left on West Cliff Drive. The beach and limited parking will be on the right.

Mitchell's Cove Beach West Cliff Drive at Almar Santa Cruz CA 831-420-5270
Dogs are allowed off-leash on Mitchell's Cove Beach between sunrise and 10 am and from 4 pm to sunset. They must be on-leash during other hours. The beach is along West Cliff Drive between Woodward and Almar. While off-leash dogs must be under voice control.

Seabright Beach Seabright Ave Santa Cruz CA 831-429-2850
This beach is located south of the Santa Cruz Beach Boardwalk and north of the Santa Cruz Harbor. Dogs are allowed on leash. Fire rings are available for beach bonfires. It is open from sunrise to sunset. To get there from Hwy 17 south, exit Ocean Street on the left towards the beaches. Merge onto Ocean Street. Turn left onto East Cliff Drive and stay straight to go onto Murray Street. Then turn right onto Seabright Ave. Seabright Ave will take you to the beach (near the corner of East Cliff Drive and Seabright).

Twin Lakes State Beach East Cliff Drive Santa Cruz CA 831-429-2850
This beach is one of the area's warmest beaches, due to its location at the entrance of Schwann Lagoon. Dogs are allowed on leash. The beach is located just south of the Santa Cruz Harbor where Aldo's Restaurant is

located. Fire rings for beach bonfires, outdoor showers and restrooms are available. It is open from sunrise to sunset. To get there from Hwy 17 south, exit Ocean Street on the left towards the beaches. Merge onto Ocean Street. Turn left onto East Cliff Drive and stay straight to go onto Murray Street. Murray Street becomes Eaton Street. Turn right onto 7th Avenue.

Parks

Forest of Nisene Marks Aptos Creek Road Aptos CA   831-763-7062
Dogs on leash are allowed in part of this park. They are allowed on a beautiful wooded trail that parallels the gravel Aptos Creek Road (on the left or west side of the road only). A good starting point is at the park entrance booth. Park after paying the minimal day use fee and then join the trail next to the parking lot. On this trail, head into the park (north). Dogs are allowed on the dirt trail up to the Steel Bridge (about 1 mile each way). You can continue on Aptos Creek Rd to the Porter Family Picnic Area, but dogs need to stay on the road (cars also allowed). The dirt trail up to the bridge is usually the best hiking trail that allows dogs and it includes several trails that divert towards the creek. Here your pup can enjoy playing in the water. To get there from Hwy 17, exit Hwy 1 south towards Watsonville. Drive through Santa Cruz and Capitola on Hwy 1 and then exit at the Seacliff Beach/Aptos exit. Turn left onto State Park Drive. Then turn right on Soquel Avenue. After going under the train bridge, you'll soon turn left onto Aptos Creek Rd. It's a small street, so be careful not to miss it. Drive up this road until you reach the park entrance booth.

Henry Cowell State Park Highway 9 Felton CA   831-335-4598
Dogs are allowed in the picnic area, the campground, and on Pipeline Road, Graham Hill Trail, and Meadow Trail. They are not allowed on any other trails or interior roads. Dogs must be leashed. The park is near Felton on Highway 9 in the Santa Cruz Mountains. Traveling from San Jose to the main entrance: Take Highway 17 towards Santa Cruz. After you go over the mountains, turn right on Mt. Hermon Road. Follow Mt. Hermon road until it ends at Graham Hill Road. Turn right, and go to the next stop light (Highway 9). Turn left on Highway 9 and go through downtown Felton. The park entrance will be a half mile down on your left. You can park outside and walk a half mile into the park, or you can drive in and pay a fee.

Lighthouse Field West Cliff Drive Santa Cruz CA   831-429-3777
Your dog can go leashless from sunrise to 10am and 4pm until sunset. Leashes are required between 10am and 4pm. This open field is across from the West Lighthouse Beach where dogs can run leash-free during certain hours. This field is not fenced and there are several busy streets nearby, so if your dog runs off-leash, make sure he or she is very well trained. It is located on West Cliff Drive, just north of the Lighthouse, and south of Columbia Street. It is also across from the West Lighthouse Beach. To get there, head south on Hwy 17. Take the Hwy 1 North exit, heading towards Half Moon Bay and Hwy 9. Merge onto Mission Street (Hwy 1). Turn left onto Swift Street. Then turn left on West Cliff Drive. Limited parking will be on the right or on other sides of the field.

West Cliff Drive Walkway

West Cliff Drive Walkway West Cliff Drive Santa Cruz CA 831-429-3777
This is a popular paved walking path that follows the beautiful Santa Cruz coastline. It is about 2 miles long each way and is frequented by walkers, runners, bicyclists and of course, dogs. It is located on West Cliff Drive, north of the Santa Cruz Beach Boardwalk and south of Natural Bridges State Beach. While dogs are not allowed on either the Boardwalk or the State Beach, there is a dog beach along this path called West Lighthouse Beach. There are several areas where you can park near the path. The easiest is by the north end of the path: Heading south on Hwy 17, take the Hwy 1 North exit towards Half Moon Bay and Hwy 9. Merge onto Mission Street (Hwy 1). Turn left onto Swift Street. Then turn right on West Cliff Drive. Turn right onto Swanton Blvd. Parking is available on Swanton Blvd. If you prefer to park closer to the Boardwalk, follow these directions: From Hwy 17 heading south, take the Hwy 1 North exit towards Half Moon Bay and Hwy 9. Merge onto Chestnut Street. Turn left onto Laurel Street, then right onto Center Street. Make a slight left onto Washington Street and Washington will become Pacific Avenue. Then turn right onto Beach Street. There is limited metered parked available near the Municipal Wharf.

Off-Leash Dog Parks
Polo Grounds Dog Park 2255 Huntington Avenue Aptos CA 831-454-7900
http://www.scparks.com
This one acre off leash dog park is fenced and includes water and benches. The park is open during daylight hours. To get there, take Highway 1 and exit at Rio Del Mar. Go left over the freeway and turn right onto Monroe Avenue (second stop light). After Monroe turns into Wallace Avenue, look for Huntington Drive on the left. Turn left on Huntington and the park entrance will be on the left.
University Terrace Dog Run Meder Street and Nobel Drive Santa Cruz CA 831-420-5270
Dogs are allowed off leash in University Terrace from sunrise to 10 am and from 4 pm to sunset. They are allowed on-leash from 10 am to 4 pm. The park is on the corner of Meder Street and Noble Drive. Please check the signs for the off-leash area in the park.
Scotts Valley Dog Park Bluebonnet Road Scotts Valley CA 831-438-3251
http://www.svdogpark.org/
This off leash dog park is located in the Skypark complex next to the soccer fields. The dog park offers 1.2 fully enclosed acres which is divided into two sections. One section is for small dogs under 25 pounds, puppies or shy dogs. The other section is for all dogs but primarily for larger and more active dogs. Other amenities include water bowls, wading pools, tennis balls, other dog toys, drinking fountains, shaded seating, plastic bags and pooper scoopers. To get there from Highway 17, take the Mt. Hermon exit and follow Mt. Hermon Road straight. Pass two stoplights and take the second right into the shopping center at the movie theatre sign. Go about .1 miles and turn left on Bluebonnet Road. The dog park is on the left.

Outdoor Restaurants

Britannia Arms Restaurant 8017 Soquel Drive Aptos CA 831-688-1233
Britannia Arms Restaurant and Pub serves some great British food and beer. They have one table in front, but the majority of tables are in the back. The seats on the back patio have shade umbrellas. This restaurant is located close to the Forest of Nisene Marks State Park (see Parks). To get there from Hwy 17, exit Hwy 1 south towards Watsonville. Drive through Santa Cruz and Capitola on Hwy 1 and then exit at the Seacliff Beach/Aptos exit. Turn left onto State Park Drive. Then turn right on Soquel Avenue. The restaurant will be on the left.

Cole's Bar-B-Q 8059 Aptos Street Aptos CA 831-662-1721
This award winning barbecue establishment has one table outside for customers who bring their canine companions with them. Dogs must be attended to at all times, well behaved, and leashed.

Spanky's 9520 Hwy 9 Ben Lomond CA 831-336-8949
This breakfast and lunch restaurant is decorated with Spanky and The Gang, and also has outdoor dining. Your dog is allowed to sit with you outside. Dogs must be attended to at all times, well behaved, and leashed.

Whale City Bakery 490 Hwy 1 Davenport CA 831-423-9803
This bakery, bar and grill is located in the small town of Davenport which is about 10-15 minutes north of Santa Cruz. They are open early for breakfast. The Davenport Beach (see Parks) is across the highway from the restaurant. To get there from Hwy 17 south, exit Hwy 1 north. Drive about 10-15 minutes until you reach the town of Davenport. The restaurant will be on the right near Ocean Street.

La Bruschetta 5447 Hwy 9 Felton CA 831-335-3337
Dogs are welcome on the outside patio of this restaurant that specializes in Italian cuisine. Dogs must be well behaved, leashed, and cleaned up after.

New Leaf Felton 6240 Hwy 9 Felton CA 831-335-7322
The New Leaf stores specialize in natural health and beauty products, and believe in foods for optimum health; their deli reflects this. Dogs are not allowed in the store, but you may go in and order from the deli and sit at the tables outside with your dog. Dogs must be attended to, well behaved, and leashed.

Rocky's Cafe 6560 Hwy 9 Felton CA 831-335-4637
Located in a beautiful old house set among the trees, this breakfast and lunch restaurant also has outdoor service on the veranda. Your pet is welcome, and dogs must be attended to at all times, well behaved, and leashed.

Aldo's Harbor Restaurant

Aldo's Harbor Restaurant 616 Atlantic Avenue Santa Cruz CA 831-426-3736
Aldo's outdoor dining area overlooks the Santa Cruz Harbor. They are open for breakfast and lunch. After dining here, you can go for a walk around the harbor. To get there from Hwy 17 south, exit Ocean Street on the left

towards the beaches. Merge onto Ocean Street. Turn left onto East Cliff Drive and stay straight to go onto Murray Street. Then turn right onto Seabright Ave. Turn left on Atlantic Ave. The road ends by the restaurant. Limited street parking or harbor parking lots are available.

Black China Cafe and Bakery 1121 Soquel Avenue Santa Cruz CA 831-460-1600
This outdoor café/bakery is combined with a furnishings, accessories, and gift store that sits in front of the café. They specialize in vegetarian food and bakery items. Visitors with dogs can use the back entry to the café by the alley. Dogs must be well behaved, leashed, and cleaned up after at all times.

Cole's Bar-B-Q 2590 Portola Drive Santa Cruz CA 831-476-4424
This award winning barbecue establishment allows your dog to join you at their outdoor tables. They must be attended to at all times, well behaved, and leashed.

Engfer Pizza Works 537 Seabright Ave Santa Cruz CA 831-429-1856
This restaurant serves pizza. Dogs are allowed at the outdoor tables.

Las Palmas Taco Bar 55 Front Street Santa Cruz CA 831-429-1220
This taco bar allows dogs to sit at their outside tables. Dogs must be well behaved, leashed, and cleaned up after.

New Leaf Westside 2351 Mission Street/Hwy 1 Santa Cruz CA 831-426-1306
The New Leaf stores specialize in natural health and beauty products, and believe in foods for optimum health; their deli reflects this. Dogs are not allowed in the store, but you may go in and order from the deli and sit at the tables outside with your dog. Dogs must be attended to, well behaved, and leashed.

Pleasure Pizza 4000 Portola Drive Santa Cruz CA 831-475-4999
This pizza place serves slices and whole pizzas. It is located near the East Cliff Coastal Access Points/Beaches (see Parks). To get there from Hwy 17 south, exit Hwy 1 south towards Watsonville. Take the 41st Avenue exit. Turn right onto 41st Avenue and the restaurant will be at Portola Drive.

Michael's on Main 2591 Main Street Soquel CA 831-479-9777
Known for their back to basics "cutting edge comfort cuisine" in a friendly, casual setting, this restaurant allows dogs on their patio. Dogs must be well behaved, leashed, and cleaned up after.

Vets and Kennels
Santa Cruz Veterinary 2585 Soquel Dr Santa Cruz CA 831-475-5400
24 hours for emergencys. 8 - 5 pm for routine visits.

Vallejo

Accommodations
Motel 6 - Vallejo - Maritime North 597 Sandy Beach Road Vallejo CA 707-552-2912 (800-466-8356)
One well-behaved family pet per room. Guest must notify front desk upon arrival. Guest is liable for any damages. In consideration of all guests, pets must never be left unattended in the guest rooms.
Motel 6 - Vallejo - Six Flags East 458 Fairgrounds Drive Vallejo CA 707-642-7781 (800-466-8356)
One well-behaved family pet per room. Guest must notify front desk upon arrival. Guest is liable for any damages. In consideration of all guests, pets must never be left unattended in the guest rooms.
Motel 6 - Vallejo - Six Flags West 1455 Marine World Parkway Vallejo CA 707-643-7611 (800-466-8356)
One well-behaved family pet per room. Guest must notify front desk upon arrival. Guest is liable for any damages. In consideration of all guests, pets must never be left unattended in the guest rooms.

Stores
Petco Pet Store 161 Plaza Drive Vallejo CA 707-649-8081
Your licensed and well-behaved leashed dog is allowed in the store.

Off-Leash Dog Parks
Wardlaw Dog Park Redwood Pkwy at Ascot Pkwy Vallejo CA
http://www.wardlawdogpark.com/
Located in Blue Rock Springs Corridor Park, the dog park is 2.2 acres in size and fully fenced. There is a separate area for small, shy or older dogs. There is a 2 mile walking path in Blue Rock Springs Park where you can take your leashed dog. From I-80 take the Redwood Pkwy East exit. Turn right on Ascot Parkway to the park.

Chapter 6

California - Gold Country
Dog Travel Guide

Auburn - Gold Country North

Accommodations

Foothills Motel 13431 Bowman Road Auburn CA   530-885-8444 (800-292-5694)
This motel offers microwaves, refrigerators, HBO/cable TV, and a barbecue, gazebo and picnic area next to the pool. Dogs of all sizes are allowed for an additional $10 per night per pet, and there is a pet policy to sign. Dogs may not be left alone in the room, and they must be leashed and cleaned up after.
Motel 6 - Auburn 1819 Auburn Ravine Road Auburn CA   530-888-7829 (800-466-8356)
One well-behaved family pet per room. Guest must notify front desk upon arrival. Guest is liable for any damages. In consideration of all guests, pets must never be left unattended in the guest rooms.
Travelodge 13490 Lincoln Way Auburn CA   530-885-7025
There is a $10 per day pet fee.
Downieville Carriage House Inn 110 Commercial Street Downieville CA   530-289-3573
This 9 room inn is located in historic downtown Downieville and is open year round. Well-behaved dogs are allowed. Dogs should be able to get along well with other guests, as this is a house. There is a $15 per day pet fee.
Downieville Loft 208 Main Street Downieville CA   510-501-2516
This amazing retreat along the Yuba River offers many features and amenities, some of which include 2,700 feet of retreat space on 2 levels, 8 full-size skylights, all custom made furniture, a large well equipped kitchen with river views, 2 fireplaces and bathrooms, and excellent summer swimming and fishing just steps from the loft. Dogs of all sizes are welcome for an additional fee of $10 per night per pet. Dogs are not allowed on the furnishings, and they must be leashed and cleaned up after. Dogs may not be left alone in the loft.
Durgan Flat Inn 121 River Street Downieville CA   530-289-3308
Dogs of all sizes are allowed. There are no additional pet fees with a credit card on file. There is a pet policy to sign at check in and they request you kennel your dog when out of the room.
Grass Valley Courtyard Suites 210 N Auburn Street Grass Valley CA   530-272-7696
http://www.gvcourtyardsuites.com/
This luxurious getaway offers a great location to several local points of interest, individually decorated guest rooms with fully equipped kitchens, fireplaces, a heated pool and spa, many in-room amenities, and an intimate lounge where guests may enjoy a continental breakfast or an evening of wine and hors d'oeuvres. Dogs of all sizes are welcome and receive their own canine cuddler to use during their stay. There is an additional $25 per pet per stay for dogs under 40 pounds, and an additional $50 per pet per stay for dogs over 40 pounds. Dogs may not be left alone in the room at any time, and they must be leashed and cleaned up after; they have provided a doggy station with a scooper and receptacles.
Swan Levine House Bed and Breakfast 328 South Church Street Grass Valley CA   916-272-1873
This renovated historic house was built in 1880. It was originally owned by a local merchant who made his fortune by selling mining equipment. He sold it to a doctor who converted the house into a hospital and it served as a community medical center until 1968. There are four rooms, each with a private bath. They have one room available for guests who bring a large dog. Dogs are not to be left alone in the room. There is a $15 per day pet charge. They are also kid-friendly. They do have a cat that resides in the house.
The Outside Inn 575 E. Broad Street Nevada City CA   530-265-2233
http://www.outsideinn.com/
This inn is located in a quiet residential neighborhood two blocks from downtown Nevada City. This completely renovated 1940's era motor court features never smoked in rooms under tall pines. Children and pets are welcome. There is a $10 per night pet charge.

Campgrounds and RV Parks

Auburn Gold Country RV (formally KOA) 3550 KOA Way Auburn CA   530-885-0990 (866-820-8362)
http://www.auburngoldcountryrvpark.com
Dogs of all sizes are allowed for no additional fee at this recreational park. Dogs may not be left unattended, and they must be leashed and cleaned up after. They are not allowed in the pool or playground areas, or in park buildings. There are some breed restrictions. The camping and tent areas also allow dogs. There is a dog walk area at the campground.
Rocky Rest Campground Hwy 49 Downieville CA   530-288-3231
This 10 site campground is located at the Yuba River District in the Tahoe National Forest at a 2,200 foot elevation. Amenities include piped water and vault toilets. The North Yuba trailhead is located at this campground. Pets must be leashed in the campsite and please clean up after your pets. Dogs are not allowed to be left unattended outside. This campground is closed during the off-season. The camping and tent areas also

allow dogs. There is a dog walk area at the campground. There are no electric or water hookups at the campgrounds.

French Meadows Reservoir Campground Mosquito Ridge Road Foresthill CA   530-367-2224
Located in the Tahoe National Forest, this 75 site campground is at an elevation of 5,300 feet. The campground is next to the French Meadows Reservoir. Camp amenities include piped water and flush/vault toilets. Pets are allowed but must be leashed in the campground. The campsite is located 36 miles east of Foresthill on Mosquito Ridge Road. Call to make a reservation. Dogs are allowed on the trails. This campground is closed during the off-season. The camping and tent areas also allow dogs. There is a dog walk area at the campground. There are no electric or water hookups at the campgrounds.

Robinson Flat Campground Foresthill Divide Road Foresthill CA   530-367-2224
This campground is located at an elevation of 6,800 feet in the Tahoe National Forest, near the Little Bald Mountain Trail. The campground offer 14 sites (7 family sites and 7 equestrian sites) on a first-come, first-served basis. Amenities include well water and vault toilets. There is no fee. Pet must be on leash in the campground. Please clean up after your pets. To get there, go 28 miles from Foresthill on Foresthill Divide Road to Robinson Flat. This campground is closed during the off-season. The camping and tent areas also allow dogs. There is a dog walk area at the campground. There are no electric or water hookups at the campgrounds.

Lodgepole Campground Lake Valley Reservoir Nevada City CA   916-386-5164
This 35 site campground is located in the Tahoe National Forest and is managed by PG&E. The campsite is located at an elevation of 5,800 feet. Pets must be leashed in the campground must be cleaned up after. There is a $1 per night per pet additional fee. To get there from I-80, take the Yuba Gap exit for .4 miles. Go around Lake Valley Reservoir for 1.2 miles. Then take right fork 2.5 miles. This campground is closed during the off-season. The camping and tent areas also allow dogs. There is a dog walk area at the campground. There are no electric or water hookups at the campgrounds.

South Yuba Campground North Bloomfield Road Nevada City CA   916-985-4474
This campground has 16 sites for tents or RVs. Camp amenities include picnic tables, fire grills, piped water, pit toilets and garbage collection. The cost per site is $5 per night with a 14 day maximum stay. Sites are available on a first-come, first-served basis. Dogs may not be left unattended outside, and they must be leashed and cleaned up after. Dogs are allowed on the trails. After traveling about 10 miles on N Bloomfield Road, and you come to the one lane bridge at Edwards Crossing, go about 1.5 miles on a dirt/gravel road to the campground and trailhead. Trailers and motorhomes should take Highway 49 and then turn right at the junction of Tyler Foote Road. At the intersection of Grizzly Hill Road turn right and proceed to North Bloomfield Road. This campground is closed during the off-season. The camping and tent areas also allow dogs. There is a dog walk area at the campground. There are no electric or water hookups at the campgrounds.

South Yuba Campground North Bloomfield Road Nevada City CA   919-985-4474
This campground has 16 sites for tents or RVs. Camp amenities include picnic tables, fire grills, piped water, pit toilets and garbage collection. The cost per site is $5 per night with a 14 day maximum stay, and are on a first-come, first-served basis. The South Yuba River Recreation Area is located about 10 miles northeast of Nevada City. Once turned on North Bloomfield Road, drive 10 miles to the South Yuba Recreation Area. From the one lane bridge at Edwards Crossing, go about 1.5 miles on a dirt/gravel road to the campground and trailhead. Trailers and motorhomes should take Highway 49 and then turn right at the junction of Tyler Foote Road. At the intersection of Grizzly Hill Road turn right and proceed to North Bloomfield Road. Dogs of all sizes are allowed at no additional fee. Dogs may not be left unattended outside, and they must be leashed and cleaned up after. Dogs are allowed on the trails. This campground is closed during the off-season. The camping and tent areas also allow dogs. There is a dog walk area at the campground. There are no electric or water hookups at the campgrounds.

Attractions

Empire Mine State Historic Park 10791 East Empire Street Grass Valley CA   530-273-8522
This park is home to one of the oldest, largest, deepest, longest, and richest gold mines in California. The park consists of over 800 acres and has eight miles of trails. Dogs on leash are allowed in the park and on the trails.

Nevada City Horse & Carriage downtown Nevada City Nevada City CA   530-265-9646
Well-behaved dogs are allowed to ride in this horse and carriage with their family.

Parks

Auburn State Recreation Area Highway 49 or Auburn-Foresthill Rd. Auburn CA   530-885-4527
Dogs on leash are allowed everywhere except at Lake Clementine. Located in the heart of the gold country, this recreation area covers over 35,000 acres along 40 miles of the North and Middle Forks of the American River. Major recreational uses include hiking, swimming, boating, fishing, camping, mountain biking, gold panning and off-highway motorcycle riding. One of the more popular trails is the Western States National Recreation Trail. It hosts the Tevis Cup Endurance Ride and Western States100 Endurance Run each summer. The park is located south of Interstate 80, stretching from Auburn to Colfax. The main access is from Auburn, either on Highway 49 or the Auburn-Foresthill Road.

Stevens Trail North Canyon Way Colfax CA   916-985-4474

This 4.5 mile trail is a popular year-round hiking, mountain biking and horseback riding trail which follows the northwestern slope of the North Fork of the American River. The trail offers a gentle slope that is suitable for novice hikers. Along the trail you can enjoy great views of the river, pass by several mine shafts, and see the China Wall built by Chinese laborers during the Gold Rush era in the 1850s. Please stay away from the mines because they are extremely dangerous and unstable. In April and May there should be a nice wildflower display. Leashed dogs are welcome. Please clean up after your dog. To get there from Sacramento, head east on Highway 80 towards Colfax. Take the North Canyon Way exit. Take this road past the Colfax cemetery to the trailhead. On weekends and in high use season, parking may be very limited.

North Yuba Trail Highway 49 Downieville CA 530-288-3231
This 7.5 mile moderate rated trail is located in the Tahoe National Forest. Pets must be either leashed or off-leash but under direct voice control. Please clean up after your pets. The trail is located on Highway 49, 7.5 miles west of Downieville at the Rocky Rest Campground.

Big Trees Loop Mosquito Ridge Road Foresthill CA 530-367-2224
This .5 mile easy trail is located in the Tahoe National Forest and is a popular interpretive trail. The trail is accessible when the road is open, generally from late May to early November. Pets on leash are allowed and please clean up after them. To get there from Foresthill, take Mosquito Ridge Road 24 miles to Road 16.

French Meadows Reservoir Mosquito Ridge Road Foresthill CA 530-367-2224
Activities at this reservoir include fishing, boating, swimming, picnicking, hiking, and viewing scenery. Dogs are allowed in the water. Pets must be either leashed or off-leash but under direct voice control. Please clean up after your pets. The reservoir is located in the Tahoe National Forest, 36 miles east of Foresthill on Mosquito Ridge Road.

Little Bald Mountain Trail Foresthill Divide Road Foresthill CA 530-367-2224
This trail is located in the Tahoe National Forest and is a 3.39 mile moderate rated trail. The trail is open from May to November, weather permitting. Pets must be either leashed or off-leash but under direct voice control. Please clean up after your pets. To get there, go 28 miles from Foresthill on Foresthill Divide Road to Robinson Flat and park in the day use area.

Sugar Pine Trail Foresthill Divide Road Foresthill CA 530-367-2224
This popular 3.5 mile easy trail goes around Sugar Pine Reservoir. Dogs are allowed on the trail and in the water on non-designated swim beaches. Pets must be either leashed or off-leash but under direct voice control. Please clean up after your pets. The primary season for this trail is usually from May to October. This trail is located in the Tahoe National Forest. To get there from Foresthill, go 18 miles northeast on Foresthill Divide Road.

Salmon Lakes Trail Road 38 Nevada City CA 530-265-4531
This 2 mile easy rated trail is located in the Tahoe National Park. It used by hikers, mountain bikers and equestrians. Pets must be leashed in the campground and please clean up after them. To get there from I-80 at Yuba Gap, go south for .3 miles and turn right toward Lodgepole Campground. After 1.1 miles, turn right on Road 19 (unpaved). After 2 miles turn left on Road 38. The trailhead is 2 miles ahead and .5 miles past Huysink Lake.

South Yuba Trail North Bloomfield Road Nevada City CA 916-985-4474
This 12 mile trail is popular with hikers, runners, mountain bikers and horseback riders. The trail offers pine tree covered canyons, gentle slopes and open meadows. Along the trail you will see historic flumes and waterworks. Leashed dogs are welcome. Please clean up after your dog. The South Yuba River Recreation Area is located about 10 miles northeast of Nevada City. From Nevada City, take Highway 49 north to North Bloomfield Road. Drive 10 miles to the South Yuba Recreation Area. From the one lane bridge at Edwards Crossing, go about 1.5 miles on a dirt/gravel road to the campground and trailhead. Trailers and motorhomes should take Highway 49 and then turn right at the junction of Tyler Foote Road. At the intersection of Grizzly Hill Road turn right and proceed to North Bloomfield Road.

Tahoe National Forest 631 Coyote Street Nevada City CA 530-265-4531
http://www.fs.fed.us/r5/tahoe/
This national forest includes the Lake Tahoe Basin Management Area. Elevations range from 1,500 feet up to 9,400 feet. Please see our listings in the Gold Country and Sierra Nevada region for dog-friendly hikes and/or campgrounds.

Outdoor Restaurants

Awful Annies 160 Sacramento Street Auburn CA 530-888-9857
http://awfulannies.com/
This restaurant specializes in American, homemade, freshly prepared foods. Open 7 days a week from 8 am to 3 pm for breakfast and lunch, and from 5 to 8:30 pm Thursday, Friday, and Saturday for dinner. Dogs are welcome to join you on their veranda. Dogs must be attended to at all times, well behaved, and leashed.

Bootleggers Tavern and Grill 210 Washington St Auburn CA 530-889-2229
http://www.worldint.com/bootleggers/
This restaurant is located in historic Auburn in the original City Hall which was built in 1870. Leashed dogs are welcome at the outdoor tables during the summer.

Ikeda's 13500 Lincoln Way Auburn CA 530-885-4243
http://www.ikedas.com/auburn.htm

Award winning hamburgers, homemade soups and fair, a country market with local grown fruits and vegetables, and a bakery for fresh goods are all to be found at this restaurant. There is outdoor seating, just order and pick up your food inside. Dogs are allowed on the patio. They must be attended to at all times, well behaved, and leashed.

La Bou 2150 Grass Valley Hwy Auburn CA 530-823-2303
Dogs are allowed at the outdoor tables.
Lou La Bonte's 13460 Lincoln Way Auburn CA 530-885-9193
They offer Continental and American cuisine. Dogs are allowed at the outdoor tables.
Maidu Market and South Side Caffe 631 Auburn-Folsom Rd Auburn CA 530-823-1717
This cafe allows dogs at the outdoor tables. They serve doughnuts, bagels and expresso for breakfast. For lunch they offer barbecue sandwiches, salads and soups.
Open Door Cafe 891 Lincoln Way Auburn CA 530-887-9970
Dogs are allowed at the outdoor tables.
Tio Pepe's 216 Washington Street Auburn CA 530-888-6445
Dogs are allowed at the outdoor tables.
Drooling Dog BBQ and Catering 212 N Canyon Way Colfax CA 530-346-8883
212 N. Canyon Way
This barbecue and catering restaurant offers patio seating when the weather is good so that you can dine with your own "drooling dog". Dogs must be attended to at all times, well behaved, and leashed.
Bubba's Bagels 11943 Nevada City Hwy Grass Valley CA 530-272-8590
Dogs are allowed at the outdoor table.
Cousin Jack Pastries 100 S Auburn St Grass Valley CA 530-272-9230
Dogs are allowed at the covered outdoor tables. The restaurant is in downtown Grass Valley.
California Organics 135 Argall Way Nevada City CA 530-265-9392
This market and café features healthy, organic, foods for breakfast, lunch, and dinner dining. They offer patio dining where your pet may join you. Dogs must be attended to at all times, well behaved, and leashed.
Ike's Quarter Cafe 401 Commercial Street Nevada City CA 530-265-6138
This café specializes in offering free range meats, organic coffees (locally roasted), eggs, grains, and vegetables. They feature an extensive beer and wine list and patio dining service. Your pet is welcome to join you at the outdoor tables. Dogs must be attended to at all times, well behaved, and leashed.
New Moon Cafe 203 York Street Nevada City CA 530-265-6399
http://www.thenewmooncafe.com/#
This café offers sophisticated dining with a small town atmosphere, variety in their season-changing menu, and natural/organic foods that are prepared fresh daily, including the breads and deserts. Your pet is welcome to join you at the outside tables. Dogs must be attended to at all times, well behaved, and leashed.
Posh Nosh 318 Broad St Nevada City CA 530-265-6064
This restaurant serves gourmet-style/health food. Dogs are allowed at the outdoor tables.
Wisdom Cafe and Gallery 426 Broad St Nevada City CA 530-265-4204
Dogs are not allowed on the patio, but there is one table near the back door. There is a water bowl for your dog next to this table.

Jackson - Gold Country Central

Accommodations
Old Well Motel 15947 State Highway 49 Drytown CA 209-245-6467
This motel is located near the Shenandoah Valley. There is a $5 per day additional pet fee.
Amador Motel 12408 Kennedy Flat Rd Jackson CA 209-223-0970
This motel has a large backyard, not completely enclosed, where you can walk your dog. They allow all well-behaved dogs. There are no additional pet fees.
Jackson Gold Lodge 850 N. State Hwy 49 Jackson CA 209-223-0486
http://www.jacksongoldlodge.com/
This lodge has been dog-friendly for years. They allow dogs in the motel rooms and in the cottages. They have eight duplex cottages, each with a separate living room, kitchen, dining room, bedroom and patio. Amenities include a free continental breakfast. Dogs are an additional $10 per day. There are no designated smoking or non-smoking cottages.
The St. George Hotel 16104 Main Street Volcano CA 209-296-4458
http://www.stgeorgehotel.com/
A well-behaved large dog is allowed in one of the bungalow rooms. The non-smoking pet-friendly room has hardwood floors, a queen bed, a private bath and garden views. Upon arrival, your pooch will receive treats and an extra blanket. There is a $20 per day pet charge.

Jackson Gold Lodge

Campgrounds and RV Parks

49er Village RV Resort

TOP 200 PLACE **49er Village RV Resort** 18265 Hwy 49 Plymouth CA   800-339-6981
http://www.49ervillage.com
Nestled in the Sierra foothills, this park offers spacious, shady sites on tree-lined streets, 2 swimming pools-one year round-heated, an indoor whirlpool spa, and an on-site Deli-Espresso Cafe and Gift Shop, which is open daily at 7 a.m. Up to 3 dogs of any size are allowed for the RV section, and there is no additional fee or deposit. There are 2 pet friendly cabins; 1 dog is allowed in the studio, and up to 2 dogs are allowed in the one bedroom. There is a $100 per pet refundable deposit. Dogs may not be left unattended in the cottages or outside. Dogs must be leashed and cleaned up after. This is an RV only park. There is a dog walk area at the campground. Dogs are allowed in the camping cabins.

Acorn Campground 2713 Hogan Dam Road Valley Springs CA   209-772-1343 (877-444-6777)
This campground, along New Hogan Lake on the Calaveras River, features an amphitheater, an interpretive trail, hiking trails, and various recreation opportunities. Dogs of all sizes are allowed. There are no additional pet fees. Dogs must be on no more than a 6 foot leash and cleaned up after. Dogs are allowed on the trails, but they are not allowed at Wrinkle Cove. The camping and tent areas also allow dogs. There is a dog walk area at the campground. There are no electric or water hookups at the campgrounds.

Attractions

Drytown Cellars 16030 Highway 49 Drytown CA   209-245-3500
http://www.drytowncellars.com/
This winery is dedicated to producing high quality, well balanced, intensely flavored California wines that are affordable, and good for every day consumption. Dogs are welcome here, and there are a couple of vineyard dogs to welcome your canine companion. Dogs are allowed on the grounds and even in the tasting room. Dogs must be leashed and cleaned up after at all times.

French Hill Winery 8032 S Main Street Mokelumne Hill CA   209-728-0638
http://www.frenchhill.com/
French Hill specializes in Cal-Italia varietals and ultra-premium wines, which has resulted in numerous awards. Friendly dogs are welcome to explore the winery and the tasting room. Dogs must be leashed and cleaned up after at all times.

Indian Grinding Rock State Historic Park 14881 Pine Grove - Volcano Road Pine Grove CA   209-296-7488
This park preserves a great outcropping of marbleized limestone with 1185 mortar holes, the largest collection of bedrock mortars anywhere in North America. Visitors can find many petroglyphs here. Dogs on leash are allowed at the historic site, but not on any trails. The park is located off Highway 88.

Convergence Vineyards

Convergence Vineyards 14650 Hwy 124 Plymouth CA   209-245-3600

Located where 3 creeks converge together into one running river, this winery features hand-crafted wines made in small batches that are sold directly from their vineyard. Dogs are welcome at the winery, around the grounds, and on the covered patio; they are not allowed in the tasting room. Dogs must be friendly and well behaved as there are other pets in residence. Please keep your dog leashed and clean up after your pet.

Deaver Vineyards 12455 Steiner Road Plymouth CA 209-245-4099
http://www.deavervineyard.com/index.html
Family owned/operated, and in production for more than 100 years, they offer award winning wines (some from vines more than 120 years old), a gift shop and a picnic area. Dogs are allowed around the grounds and at the picnic area, but not in the tasting room. Dogs must be well behaved, and leashed and cleaned up after at all times. They did state there may be a few friendly neighborhood dogs that also like to check out the picnic area when they think food is available.

Montevina Wines 20680 Shenandoah School Road Plymouth CA 209-245-6942
Dogs are allowed at the outdoor tables in their patio. The hours are 11 - 4 daily.

Nine Gables Vineyard & Winery 10778 Shenandoah Road Plymouth CA 209-245-3949
http://www.9gables.com/
Small batch fermentation with a hands-on approach is this winery's formula for maximum extraction of flavors, colors, and aromas. Dogs must be very friendly as there are other dogs on site that are anxious to meet new visitors. Dogs are allowed around the grounds and in the tasting room. Dogs must be leashed and cleaned up after at all times.

Renwood Winery 12225 Steiner Road Plymouth CA 209-245-6979
http://www.renwood.com/
Using old-world and hand crafted winemaking techniques, this vineyard showcases wines that come from some of the world's oldest and most renowned vineyards in the Shenandoah Valley. Complimentary and reserve tasting is available daily from 10:30 am to 4:30 pm. Dogs are allowed on the grounds and will probably like a roll on the grassy lawn, but they are not allowed in the tasting room. Dogs must be leashed, and please bring supplies to clean up after your pet.

TOP 200 PLACE **Sobon Winery** 14430 Shenandoah Rd Plymouth CA 209-245-6554
http://www.sobonwine.com/
This Shenandoah Valley winery serves and sells red and white wines made entirely from organic fruits. Wine Tasting is offered 7 days a week in the tasting room and there is a little museum on the premises. Well-behaved leashed dogs are allowed at the outdoor picnic tables at the winery.

Sutter Creek

Sutter Creek Highway 49 Sutter Creek CA 209-267-5647
http://www.suttercreek.org/
Sutter Creek, named for John Sutter of Gold Rush fame, is a well preserved 1850's western town in California's

174

Gold Country. There is a half mile long downtown along Highway 49 with staired sidewalks and a variety of shops including wine tasting, ice cream, and for your dog, a Three Dog Bakery. There are also other stores that may allow your dog inside if you ask and some cafes with outdoor seats.
Sutter Creek Wine Tasting 85 Main Street Sutter Creek CA 209-267-5838
Dogs may sit with you at the outdoor picnic bench or the two small tables in the front while you sample the wines from a local group of growers.

Stores
Paws and Claws 30 Main Street Jackson CA 209-223-3970
http://www.dressapet.net
In addition to a selection of gifts you will also find decorator pet collars & leashes at this store. Your pet is welcome on leash or you can carry them in. They are open 10 am to 5 pm 7 days a week.
Three Dog Bakery 16 Eureka St. Sutter Creek CA 209-267-1500
http://www.threedog.com/
This dog cookie bakery is located in the historic town of Sutter Creek. Bring your dog in for a variety of goodies prepared and baked just for your best friend.

Parks
W.F. Detert Park Hwy 49 Jackson CA
This is a small but nice city park that allows leashed dogs. It has some picnic tables and a children's playground. It is located on Hwy 49, between the Jackson Gold Lodge and historic downtown Jackson.

Outdoor Restaurants
Mel & Faye's Drive In 205 N. State Hwy 49 Jackson CA 209-223-0853
This diner is open for breakfast, lunch and dinner. They have several outdoor covered picnic tables and benches where you and your pup can enjoy the American-style food. If it gets too chilly, they have an outdoor heater. The diner is located on Hwy 49, near historic downtown Jackson.
88 Burgers 19845 State Highway 88 Pine Grove CA 209-296-7277
Dogs are allowed at the outdoor tables.
Cafe at the Park 18265 Hwy 49 Plymouth CA 209-245-6981
This cafe serves sandwiches, pastries, and ice cream. They are located at the entrance of the 49er RV Park in Plymouth. The dog-friendly outdoor seating is located behind the cafe. They are open weekdays from 7am to 8pm and weekends from 7am to 10pm. It is off Hwy 49, across the street from the Pokerville Market.
Gold Country Cafe 17830 State Highway 49 Plymouth CA 209-245-6218
Dogs are allowed at the outdoor tables.
Marlene and Glen's Diner 18726 Highway 49 Plymouth CA 209-245-5778
Dogs are allowed at the outdoor seats.
Sutter Creek Coffee 20 Eureka Street Sutter Creek CA 209-267-5550
Dogs are allowed on the patio seats in front. Dogs are not allowed at the tables on the porch.

Placerville - Highway 50 Corridor

Accommodations
Golden Lotus Bed and Breakfast Inn 1006 Lotus Road Coloma CA 530-621-4562
This pre-Victorian B&B, located in the historic town of Coloma, is surrounded by herb gardens. Dogs are allowed in one of their rooms. Dogs must be well-behaved and owners must agree to pay for any damages. There is a $20 per day additional pet fee.
American River Bed and Breakfast Inn Main and Orleans Streets Georgetown CA 530-333-4499
http://www.americanriverinn.com
They have certain pet rooms and you need to call in advance to make a reservation. All rooms are non-smoking. There is a refundable pet deposit.
Kyburz Resort Motel 13666 Highway 50 Kyburz CA 530-293-3382
http://www.kyburzresort.com
Nestled among the pines along 300 feet of the South Fork of the American River, this motel is located in the heart of the El Dorado National Forest. It is located about 30 minutes east of Placerville and about 15-20 minutes

from Apple Hill. Well-behaved dogs are allowed and they must be leashed when outside your room. There is a $10 per day pet fee.

Best Western Placerville Inn 6850 Greenleaf Dr Placerville CA 530-622-9100 (800-780-7234)
There is a $20 per night pet fee per pet. Smoking and non-smoking are available for pet rooms.

Fleming Jones Homestead B&B 3170 Newtown Road Placerville CA 530-344-0943
http://www.robinsnestranch.com
This historic homestead is a B&B at a working miniature horse ranch. It is located 5 minutes from Placerville and near the Apple Hill farms that are open to the public each fall. Well-behaved dogs are welcome in the Woodshed and Bunkhouse rooms of the B&B. There is a $10 per day per dog. Dogs may not be left unattended and guests are responsible for any damages caused by their pets.

Campgrounds and RV Parks

Ice House Campground Forest Road 32 Pollock Pines CA 530-644-2349 (877-444-6777)
This 83 site campground is located in the El Dorado National Forest at an elevation of 5,500 feet. It is located near the Ice House Bike Trail. Camp amenities include restrooms, water, picnic tables, swimming, bicycling, hiking and more. Pets on leash are allowed in the campground, on the trails and in the water. Please clean up after your pets. Dogs are not allowed on trails into Desolation Valley. This campground is closed during the off-season. The camping and tent areas also allow dogs. There is a dog walk area at the campground. There are no electric or water hookups at the campgrounds.

Sly Park Campground 4771 Sly Park Road Pollock Pines CA 530-644-2792 (866-SLY-PARK (759-7275))
The wooded Sly Park Recreation Area offers 159 campsites at an elevation of 3,500 feet. Site amenities include a table, barbecue and fire ring. Camp amenities include water, vault toilets, and a dump station at the park entrance. Pets on leash are allowed in the campground and on trails including the 8 to 9 mile trail which surround the lake. Dogs are not allowed in the lake. There is an additional fee of $2 per night per pet. Although open year round, call first in winter as snow causes road closures. The camping and tent areas also allow dogs. There is a dog walk area at the campground. There are no electric or water hookups at the campgrounds.

Wench Creek Campground Ice House Road/Forest Road 3 Pollock Pines CA 530-644-2349
This campground is located in the El Dorado National Forest next to Union Valley Reservoir and offers 100 tent and RV campsites. Camp amenities include restrooms, water, swimming, bicycling, and hiking. Dogs are allowed in the campground, on the trails, and in the water. Pets should be leashed and please clean up after them. Dogs are not allowed to go into Desolation Valley. This campground is closed during the off-season. The camping and tent areas also allow dogs. There is a dog walk area at the campground. There are no electric or water hookups at the campgrounds.

Placerville KOA 4655 Rock Barn Road Shingle Springs CA 530-676-2267 (800-562-4197)
http://www.koa.com/where/ca/05429/
Located close to other attractions, this park offers 110 foot pull-through sites with 50 amp service, a store, petting zoo, playground, pond, swimming pool, sauna/spa, cable, wi-fi, and more. Dogs of all sizes are allowed for no additional fee. Dogs must be under owner's control and visual observation at all times. Dogs must be quiet, well behaved, and be on no more than a 6 foot leash at all times, or otherwise contained. Dogs may not be left unattended outside the owner's camping equipment, and must be brought inside at night. There is a fenced in dog run area where your pet may be off lead. There are some breed restrictions. The camping and tent areas also allow dogs. There is a dog walk area at the campground. There are special amenities given to dogs at this campground.

Attractions

Argyres Orchard 4220 N. Canyon Rd. Camino CA 530-644-3862
Located in Apple Hill, this ranch is open mid-September through October. Leashed dogs are allowed outside. You can pick your own apples and grapes at this ranch.

Bodhaine Ranch 2315 Cable Road Camino CA 530-644-1686
http://www.bodhaineranch.com/
This apple hill farm is a California Certified Organic Grower, and their bake shop offers a variety of tasty baked treats, hearty meals, and gourmet coffees. There are picnic tables on the grounds and on the terrace for outside dining. They also host an organic farmer's market every weekend from June to Christmas, and feature arts and crafts from local artisans. Dogs of all sizes are welcome. They must be leashed and cleaned up after at all times.

Bolster's Hilltop Ranch

Bolster's Hilltop Ranch 2000 Larsen Drive Camino CA   530-644-2230
http://www.bolsters.net
Located in Apple Hill, this ranch is open daily June through the beginning of December. Leashed dogs are allowed outside. This ranch offers u-pick blueberries from June through August including a Blueberry Festival in June (blueberry plants available), u-pick apples on the weekends from September to November, outdoor arts & crafts booths, barbecue, picnic area, pumpkins, Christmas trees and more.

Celtic Gardens Organic Farm 4221 North Canyon Road Camino CA   530-647-0689
This organic farm sells mostly wholesale (produce only-no pie shop) and are open only a short time to the public before they usually sell out of product. Table grapes become available sometime in August when they partially open; then by September they are open for about a month before they close until the next season. Your well behaved, leashed dog is allowed to explore the farm with you. Dogs must be cleaned up after at all times.

Denver Dan's 4344 Bumblebee Ln. Camino CA   530-644-6881
Located in Apple Hill, this ranch is open during the fall season, September through mid-December. They are closed on Tuesdays and only open Friday, Saturday and Sunday from late November through December. Leashed dogs are allowed outside. This ranch offers a bake shop, candy & caramel apples, gift shop, picnic area and u-pick apples.

Grandpa's Cellar 2360 Cable Rd. Camino CA   530-644-2153
Located in Apple Hill, this ranch is open daily during the fall season, September through mid-December. Leashed dogs are allowed outside. The owners have an old black lab on the premises. This ranch offers a bake shop, country store, nature trail, and on the weekends only, an outdoor craft fair and barbecue.

Honey Bear Ranch 2826 Barkley Road Camino CA   530-644-3934
http://www.honeybearranch.com/
This apple tree farm features an eatery with outside seating, craft booths during the harvest season, and they also produces an ancient rare fruit known as medlar. Your dog is welcome to check out the grounds, but they are not allowed in the buildings. Dogs must be leashed and cleaned up after at all times.

Honey Bear Ranch 2826 Barkley Rd. Camino CA   530-644-3934
Located in Apple Hill, this ranch is open during the fall season, September through December. Open daily September through October, and weekends only November through mid-December). Leashed dogs are allowed outside and you need to clean up after them. This ranch offers a restaurant with outdoor dining, bake shop, fudge kitchen, general store with antiques & crafts, and a picnic area with outdoor arts & crafts booths and live music.

Jack Russell Brewing Company

TOP 200 PLACE **Jack Russell Brewing Company** 2380 Larsen Drive Camino CA 530-644-4722
http://www.jackrussellbrewing.com/
You and your best friend are welcome at this English farm-style brewery located near Placerville in the Sierra
Foothills between Sacramento and Lake Tahoe. Adjacent to the brewery is a picnic area where you can enjoy a
variety of hand-crafted beers. They also have homemade root beer. The founding mascot, a Jack Russell Terrier
named Boomer, is on the beer label. The brewery is open on the weekends and during the summer they
sometimes have live entertainment outside and English-style meat pies. Dogs are welcome outside including the
picnic areas.
Kids, Inc. 3245 N. Canyon Rd. Camino CA 530-622-0084
http://www.kidsincapples.com
Located in Apple Hill, this ranch is open during the fall season. Open all week during September and October
and open weekends only in November through mid-December. Leashed dogs are allowed outside. This ranch
offers a bake shop, gift shop, antiques, grassy picnic area, farm animals, nature trail, family activities, apples,
pumpkins and Christmas trees.
Mother Lode Orchards 4341 N. Canyon Rd. Camino CA 530-644-5101
http://www.motherlodeorchards.com/
Located in Apple Hill, this ranch is open during the fall season, September through December. Open weekends
only in November through mid- December. Leashed dogs are allowed outside including at the picnic tables. This
ranch offers over 30 varieties of fruit and vegetables, pumpkins and Christmas trees. The owner also has a dog
on the premises.
O'Hallorans Apple Trail Ranch 2261 Cable Rd. Camino CA 530-644-3389
Located in Apple Hill, this ranch is open during the fall season (September through mid-December). Leashed
dogs are allowed outside. This ranch offers a fruit store, handmade crafts, nature trail, picnic area, u-pick
pumpkin patch, and cut & choose Christmas trees.
Plubell's Family Orchard 1800 Larsen Dr. Camino CA 530-647-0613
Located in Apple Hill, this ranch is open during the fall season, September through mid-November. Leashed
dogs are allowed outside. This ranch offers fresh produce, a grassy picnic area, nature walk, pumpkin patch and
on weekends a barbecue, miniature horse & wagon rides and more.
Stone's Throw Vineyard & Winery 3541 North Canyon Rd. Camino CA 530-622-5100
Leashed dogs are allowed at the picnic area. The owners also have their own dogs on the premises. Their wine
tasting is open Thursday through Sunday year-round (except major holidays).
Summerfield Berry Farm 4455 Pony Express Trail Camino CA 530-647-2833
Located in Apple Hill, this ranch is open mid-June through mid-November on Fridays, Saturdays and Sundays.
Leashed dogs are allowed in the u-pick fruit area and picnic area. You can pick fresh raspberries and
blackberries.

Gold Country Carriages Hwy 49 Coloma CA 530-622-6111
Dogs and families are welcome on this horse and carriage ride located at Marshall Gold Discovery State Park in Coloma on Hwy 49 (see Attractions for more information about the park). They offer tours of historic Coloma. Dogs need to stay on the floor of the carriage, not on the seat.

Marshall Gold Discovery State Park Hwy 49 Coloma CA 530-622-3470
http://www.windjammer.net/coloma/
This is the place where James W. Marshall found some shining flecks of gold in the tailrace of a sawmill he was building for himself and John Sutter in 1848. This began the famous Gold Rush era. The park has a replica of the sawmill and a number of historic buildings. Gold Country Carriage operates frequently on Hwy 49 at this park and dogs are welcome to join their family on this horse and carriage ride (see Attractions). Dogs on leash are welcome at several trails near the river. They are allowed in the picnic areas, but not allowed in the hiking trails across the street from the river side. Throughout the year the park has many special events, and dogs are welcome at most of the outdoor events. The park is located in Coloma on Highway 49 between Placerville and Auburn. It is open year round from 8am to sunset. There is a minimal fee for parking and for dogs.

Venezio Winery & Vineyard 5821 Highway 49 Coloma CA 530-885-WINE
http://www.venezio.com/
Leashed and well-behaved dogs are allowed in the picnic area. This vineyard is nestled in the lovely Coloma Valley, 3.5 miles from the dog-friendly Marshall Gold Discovery State Park. From Placerville, take Hwy 49 north. Go past the town of Coloma, and the winery will be on the right.

Charles B. Mitchell Vineyards 8221 Stoney Creek Road Fair Play CA 800-704-WINE
http://www.charlesbmitchell.com/
Leashed dogs are allowed in the picnic area. The owners have an older dog that resides on the premises. From E-16, take Fair Play Rd. east. Turn right on Stoney Creek Rd. The winery will be on the left.

Oakstone Winery 6440 Slug Gulch Rd. Fair Play CA 530-620-5303
http://www.oakstone-winery.com/
Well-behaved, leashed dogs are allowed in both of their picnic areas. From E-16, turn onto Fair Play Rd. Turn right on Slug Gulch Rd.

Perry Creek Vineyards 7400 Perry Creek Rd. Fair Play CA 530-620-5175
http://www.perrycreek.com/
Well-behaved, leashed dogs are allowed at the picnic area. Their tasting room opens to the spacious outdoor verandah picnic area. From E-16, turn onto Fair Play Rd. Turn left onto Perry Creek Rd. Winery will be on the left.

Latcham Vineyards 2860 Omo Ranch Road Mount Aukum CA 530-620-6642
http://www.latcham.com
Leashed dogs are allowed at the picnic tables. The winery is located on the north slope of a valley in Mt. Aukum. From E-16, take Omo Ranch Rd east. The winery will be on the right.

Abel's Apple Acres 2345 Carson Rd. Placerville CA 530-626-0138
Located in Apple Hill, this ranch is open daily, September through Christmas Eve. Leashed dogs are allowed outside. This ranch offers a bake shop, fudge, homemade caramel, barbecue, fresh apples, gift store, outdoor arts & crafts booths, pony & horse rides, duck pond, picnic area, hay maze & hay rides, and pumpkin patch.

Apple Creek Ranch 2979 Carson Rd. Placerville CA 530-644-5073
Located in Apple Hill, this ranch is open during apple season, usually mid-September through October. Leashed dogs are allowed outside. This ranch offer fresh apples.

Boa Vista Orchards 2952 Carson Rd. Placerville CA 530-622-5522
http://www.boavista.com/
This ranch is open year round (closed on Christmas Day). Dogs are not allowed in the store, but are allowed at the picnic tables. Dogs must be leashed. At the tables, you and your pooch can enjoy goodies from their bakery, like a fresh apple pie with ice cream or try their barbecue sandwiches on the weekends. They also have outdoor arts and crafts booths during the fall, on the weekends.

Boeger Winery 1709 Carson Road Placerville CA 530-622-8094
http://www.boegerwinery.com/
Well-behaved leashed dogs are allowed at the picnic tables at this winery. People can bring some of the wine to the picnic tables to taste. The winery is one of the oldest family owned and operated wineries in the Sierra Foothills of Northern California. They are open 10a.m.-5p.m. daily.

Gold Hill Vineyard 5660 Vineyard Lane Placerville CA 530-626-6522
http://www.goldhillvineyard.com/
Dogs are allowed at the picnic tables near the tasting room. They allow well-behaved and leashed dogs outside. From Hwy 50, take Cold Springs Rd. north (towards Coloma). Turn right on Vineyard Lane.

High Hill Ranch

TOP 200 PLACE **High Hill Ranch** 2901 High Hill Rd. Placerville CA   530-644-1973
Located in Apple Hill, this ranch is open daily during the fall season (September through December). Leashed dogs are allowed outside. They offer a bake shop (with lunch on the weekends), a cider mill, wine tasting, outdoor arts & crafts booths, a picnic area overlooking the Sierra Nevada mountains, trout fishing, pony rides (weekends only), a fudge shop and a farm shop including fresh apples and produce, apple butter, dried fruits, gift packs and more.

Hooverville Orchards 1100 Wallace Rd. Placerville CA 530-622-2155
Open daily year-round, this orchard offers peaches, nectarines, plums, apricots, cherries, apples, avocados, pumpkins, vegetables and more. They also have a bake shop and a picnic area. Leashed dogs are allowed at the picnic area.

Lava Cap Winery 2221 Fruitridge Road Placerville CA   530-621-0175
http://www.lavacap.com/
Well-behaved, leashed dogs are allowed at the tables on their deck. Relax on the deck with a picnic and savor the scenic view of their vineyard. They are located just 5 minutes from Hwy 50. From Placerville, exit Schnell School Rd. (at the exit, head north by turning left at stop sign), turn right onto Carson Rd, turn left on Union Ridge, then veer right on Hassler Rd, then left on Fruitridge Rd.

Placerville Downtown Area Main Street & Hwy 49 Placerville CA
Placerville is a historic gold rush town that was established in the late 1840's. The town got its name from the placer gold deposits found in its hills and river beds. Today, Placerville serves as a hub for activities in the gold country including the Marshall Gold Discovery State Historic Park, Apple Hill farms, white water rafting on the American River, and the nearby wine country. You can still see this town's historic charm when you visit downtown Placerville. There you will find many shops, some of which may allow well-behaved dogs inside. You can also stroll down the sidewalks and see a number of buildings that were build over a hundred years ago. There are outdoor events held in historic downtown Placerville throughout the year and many of these events allow well-behaved leashed dogs.

Sierra Vista Winery & Vineyard 4560 Cabernet Way Placerville CA   530-622-7841
http://www.sierravistawinery.com
Leashed and well-behaved dogs are allowed in the picnic area. The picnic grounds offer a beautiful view of The Sierra Nevada mountains. From Pleasant Valley Road, turn right onto Leisure Lane. The winery is at the end of Leisure Lane.

Harris Tree Farm 2640 Blair Road Pollock Pines CA 530-644-2194
http://www.applehill.com/harris.htm
Harris Tree Farm features 30 acres of Christmas trees plus a variety of fruits and home-made goodies. They are open every year from August through December 24.

Stores

Act 1 Video & Music 1345 Broadway Placerville CA   530-621-1919
Your leashed, well-behaved dog is allowed inside the store. Here you can rent your favorite video or browse through their selection of music CDs. The store is located across the street from the Mountain Democrat Newspaper building.
Doggles Pet Boutique 416 Main Street Placerville CA   530-622-9663
http://www.doggles.com/index.html
Doggles Pet Boutique features "Doggles", or goggles for dogs. They also feature gifts for dogs and dog lovers alike, as well as dog cookies. Your well-behaved, leashed dog is welcome.

Parks

Dave Moore Nature Area Highway 49 Coloma CA   916-985-4474
http://www.ca.blm.gov/folsom/dmna.html
This nature area features a one mile loop and about half of the trail is wheelchair, walker and stroller accessible. It starts at the parking lot and goes down to the South Fork of the American River and back, passing through several types of habitat. Located in the heart of the historic Gold Rush area, the trail is lined with remnants from about 150 years ago when Chinese laborers channeled the creek water by hand with a pick and shovel to find gold. Leashed dogs are welcome. Please clean up after your dog. To get there from Sacramento, take Highway 50 east towards Placerville. In Shingle Springs, take the Ponderosa Road exit and go over the freeway bridge to the stop sign (located just north of Highway 50). Turn right onto North Shingles Road and go 3 miles. Turn left at the Y in the road onto Lotus Road. Continue for 5 miles heading north. At Highway 49 turn left and cross the bridge at the river. Continue for about 1 mile along Highway 49. Turn left at the cobblestone wall. There are no park fees, but donations are accepted.
El Dorado Trail Mosquito Rd. Placerville CA
This part of the El Dorado Trail is a nice paved path that is popular with runners and walkers. Leashed dogs are allowed. The trail was originally 2 miles each way for a total of 4 miles, but the trail has been expanded a few extra miles. Most of the path is wide enough that there is a dirt trail paralleling the paved trail. It is located near historic downtown Placerville. To get there from Hwy 50 heading east, exit Broadway and turn right. When Broadway ends, turn right onto Mosquito Rd and go back under the freeway. At the second street, turn left. If you go too far, you'll end up going back onto Hwy 50. The trail will be on the right. Park along the street.
Eldorado National Forest 100 Forni Road Placerville CA   530-622-5061
http://www.fs.fed.us/r5/eldorado/
This national forest covers over 590,000 acres of land which ranges in elevation from 1,000 feet in the foothills to more than 10,000 feet along the Sierras. Please see the listings in our Sierra Nevada region for dog-friendly hikes and/or campgrounds.
Gold Bug Park 2635 Gold Bug Lane Placerville CA   530-642-5207
http://www.goldbugpark.org
Gold Bug Park is a 60 acre park that was once the home of many gold mines. Your leashed dog is allowed at the picnic areas and on the trails, but is not allowed into the mine.
Cedar Park Trail Sly Park Road Pollock Pines CA 530-644-2349
This easy paved trail, set amongst pine and conifer trees, has two small paved loops which total 1.2 miles in length. The elevation ranges from about 3,640 to 3,700 feet. Pets must be leashed and please clean up after them. The trail is located in the Eldorado National Forest. From Highway 50 in Pollock Pines, take Sly Park Road south (away from the Safeway). Drive about 6 miles to the parking area and trailhead on the left side of the road. There is ample parking.
Sly Park/Jenkinson Lake 4771 Sly Park Road Pollock Pines CA   530-644-2545
This beautiful wooded recreation area is at an elevation of 3500 feet. There is an 8 mile loop trail that circles Jenkinson Lake. It is a popular park for hiking, horseback riding, fishing and camping. Leashed dogs are allowed on the trails and in the campgrounds. The west side of the park (next to the campgrounds) offers wide fire road trails, while the east side has single track trails. Be sure to check your pup for ticks after walking here. The park is open from sunrise to sunset. It is located about 30 minutes from Placerville. To get there from Hwy 50, take the Sly Park Rd exit and turn right. Drive about 5-10 minutes and the park will be on the left.

Outdoor Restaurants

Forrester Restaurant 4110 Carson Road Camino CA   530-644-1818
Dogs are allowed at the outdoor tables. The restaurant has outdoor tables only in the summer. They request you come in the back way to the outside deck and that you choose one of the back tables.
Mountain Mike's Pizza 3600 Carson Rd #C Camino CA   530-644-6000
Dogs are allowed at the outdoor tables.
Argonaut Cafe Hwy 49 Coloma CA
Thanks to one of our readers who writes: "Located in the Marshall Gold Discovery State Historic Park, The Argonaut serves up sandwiches, sodas, candy, pie, ice cream, coffee and more. Dogs are allowed in the outdoor dining area of the porch which spans two sides of the building."

Sutter Center Market 378 Highway 49 Coloma CA   530-626-0849
In addition to selling gifts and food items, this market also has a deli where you can order pastries, sandwiches, burritos, ice cream and more. It is located near the dog-friendly Marshall Gold Discovery State Park (see Parks). Dogs are allowed at the outdoor picnic tables.

Bella Bru Coffee Company 3941 Park Drive #50 El Dorado Hills CA   916-933-5454
Dogs are allowed at the outdoor tables.

Juice It Up 4355 Town Center Blvd, #113 El Dorado Hills CA   916-941-7140
Dogs are allowed at the outdoor tables.

Mama Ann's Deli & Bakery 4359 Town Center Blvd #111 El Dorado Hills CA   916-939-1700
Dogs are allowed at the outdoor tables.

Masque Ristorante 3909 Park Drive El Dorado Hills CA   916-933-8555
http://www.masqueristorante.com/
In addition to featuring award winning food and ambiance, this Italian restaurant also has a retail shop offering specialty food products and a variety of wines. Your pet is welcome to join you at the outside tables on the cafe side of the restaurant. Place your order inside, and they will bring your order to your table. Dogs must be attended to at all times, well behaved, and leashed.

Quiznos Sub 4361 Town Center Blvd, Suite #113 El Dorado Hills CA   916-939-7833
Dogs are allowed at the outdoor tables.

Steve's Place Pizza & Pasta 3941 Park Drive, #100 El Dorado Hills CA   916-939-2100
Dogs are allowed at the outdoor tables.

Z's Wine Bar and Bistro 879 Embarcadero Dr., Suite 7 El Dorado Hills CA   916-933-3227
This wine bar and eatery offers tasty seafood, meats, and specialty foods in a casual yet elegant setting. They offer outside dining service, where your pet may join you as long as there is no objection from any other guest. Dogs must be quiet and well behaved, under owner's control at all times, and leashed.

Creekside Cantina 451 Main Street #10 Placerville CA   530-626-7966
Dogs are allowed at the outdoor tables.

Dairy Depot 4601 Missouri Flat Rd Placerville CA   530-622-8548
Dogs are allowed at the outdoor tables.

Noah's Ark 535 Placerville Drive Placerville CA   530-621-3663
This natural food market has outdoor tables where your well-behaved leashed dog is welcome. During the week they usually have pre-made vegan sandwiches and hot slices of organic veggie pizza. You will need to pick up your food inside and bring it to your outside table.

Pizza Factory 4570 Pleasant Valley Road Placerville CA   530-644-6043
http://www.pizzafactory.com/
This restaurant serves a variety of pizzas, pasta and salad. Well-behaved leashed dogs are allowed at the outdoor tables.

Quiznos Sub 545 Main Street Placerville CA   530-626-0274
Dogs are allowed at the outdoor tables.

Quiznos Sub 3967 Missouri Flat Road Placerville CA   530-622-7878
Dogs are allowed at the outdoor tables.

Starbucks 541 Main Street Placerville CA   530-642-8229
Dogs are allowed at the outdoor tables, and they have water bowls set out for pets.

Straw Hat Pizza 3970 Missouri Flat Rd Placerville CA   530-626-8511
Dogs are allowed at the outdoor tables.

TOP 200 PLACE Sweetie Pie's 577 Main Street Placerville CA   530-642-0128
Try the fresh cinnamon rolls at this restaurant. They also serve a delicious variety of food for breakfast and lunch. They are open 7 days a week from 6:30am to 4pm. They usually do not serve food outside during the winter. It is located on Main Street (between Bedford and Clay Streets), east of historic downtown Placerville.

Teriyaki Junction 1216 Broadway Placerville CA   530-295-1413
This Japanese restaurant serves bento dishes, teriyaki, and sushi. There are 5-6 tables outside where you can enjoy lunch or dinner. The tables are also shared by Baskin Robbins. To get there from Hwy 50 heading east, take the Broadway exit and turn left. Then turn right into the shopping complex, near the McDonalds.

The Steak Out 1234 Broadway Placerville CA   530-642-8217
This restaurant serves Greek cuisine, including broiled steak, chicken and lamb kabobs. Or try the homemade gourmet custom wraps. The hours are from 11am until 9pm. To get there from Hwy 50 heading east, take the Broadway exit and turn left. Then turn right into the shopping complex.

Caffeine Cuisine 4056 Mother Lode Dr Shingle Springs CA   530-676-2623
Dogs are allowed at the outdoor tables.

Vets and Kennels

Mother Lode Pet Emergency Clinic 4050 Durock Rd Cameron Park CA   530-676-9044
Monday - Thursday 6 pm to 8 am, Friday 6 pm to 8 am Monday.

Sonora - Gold Country South

Accommodations

Best Western Cedar Inn and Suites 444 S Main St Angels Camp CA 209-736-4000 (800-780-7234)
Dogs of all sizes are allowed. There is a $10 per night pet fee per pet. Dogs have to be over one year old. Reservations are recommended due to limited rooms for pets. Only non-smoking rooms used for pets.
Ebbetts Pass Lodge 1173 Highway 4, Box 2591 Arnold CA 209-795-1563
There is a $5 per day pet charge.
49er RV Ranch 23223 Italian Bar Road Columbia CA 209-532-4978
Dogs of all sizes are allowed. There are no additional pet fees.
Columbia Gem Motel 22131 Parrotts Ferry Rd Columbia CA 209-532-4508
http://www.columbiagem.com/business/gem/
This dog-friendly motel offers gracious, country hospitality, comfort and privacy. The motel is set on a sunny park-like acre beneath towering, majestic pines, cedars and sequoias, which provide a shady umbrella over their 6 cozy log cabins and 4 motel rooms. For a little extra, they can provide the perfect getaway with champagne on ice, flowers, wine, cheese, crackers, chocolates, or bubble bath waiting for you in your room. They can also arrange breakfast in bed or can help with any other ideas. The motel is located within walking distance (about 1 mile) from the popular dog-friendly Columbia State Historic Park. The Gold Mine Winery/Micro-Brewery is located about 1 block away from the motel. The winery has a nice outdoor covered patio and lawn area. They have free wine and beer tasting and they also make pizza from scratch, any way you like it. The management are of the belief that people who travel with their "best friends" are responsible pet owners and a pleasure to have as guests at The Gem. Dog owners are not penalized with an extra fee here. Instead, management has a simple, common sense pet regulation form they have each owner read and sign. Dogs are not to be left unattended in the rooms.
National Hotel 18183 Main Street Jamestown CA 209-984-3446
Dogs up to 75 pounds are allowed. There is a $15 per night per pet additional fee.
Royal Hotel Bed and Breakfast 18239 Main Street Jamestown CA 209-984-5271
Dogs are not allowed in the hotel, but are allowed in one of the private cottages. This hotel is located in historic Jamestown, near Yosemite National Park. There is a $10 per day pet charge.
The National Hotel 18183 Main Street Jamestown CA 209-984-3446
http://www.national-hotel.com
Established in 1859, this is one of the oldest continuously operating hotels in California. Taking a day trip or going for a hike? Just ask for a picnic basket the day before and their chef will provide you with a meal to take with you and enjoy next to a cool Sierra Nevada stream or at one of the many picnic areas throughout the dog-friendly Stanislaus National Forest. There is a $10 per day pet charge. All rooms are non-smoking.
Best Western Sonora Oaks 19551 Hess Avenue Sonora CA 800-532-1944 (800-780-7234)
Dogs of all sizes are allowed. There is a $20 one time per pet fee per visit. Reservations are recommended due to limited rooms for pets. Only non-smoking rooms used for pets.
Sonora Aladdin Motor Inn 14260 Mono Way (Hwy 108) Sonora CA 209-533-4971
http://www.aladdininn.com
This motel's rooms offer Southwest decor with king or queen sized beds, table & chairs, refrigerators, coffee makers, climate control, cable TV & HBO, and direct dial phones with free local & credit card calls. They also feature a guest laundry. Dogs are welcome with a $5 one time charge. The motel is about an hour and a half from Yosemite.

Campgrounds and RV Parks

49er RV Ranch 23223 Italian Bar Road Columbia CA 209-532-4978 (800-446-1333)
http://www.49rv.com/
This RV only park is located within a short distance to the dog-friendly Columbia State Historic Park. Park amenities offers full hookups, cable TV, a store, laundry, propane and a modem hookup in the store. Dogs of all sizes are allowed for no additional fee. They ask you take your pet to the pet walk area to do their business, and that you clean up after your pet at all times. Dogs may not be left unattended, and they must be well behaved, and leashed. There is a dog walk area at the campground.
Vallecito Regional Park 37349 County Route S-2 Vallecito CA 760-765-1188 (877-565-3600)
Rich in natural and cultural history, this park has been called a beautiful oasis in the desert. It offers a wide variety of recreational pursuits. Dogs of all sizes are allowed for an additional $1 per night per pet, and they must have current tags, rabies, and shot records. Dogs may not be left unattended at any time, and they must be on no more than a 6 foot leash and cleaned up after. Dogs are not allowed on the trails, but they may be walked on the payment and along side the roads on leash. This campground is closed during the off-season. The camping and tent areas also allow dogs. There is a dog walk area at the campground. There are no electric or water hookups at the campgrounds.

Attractions

Columbia State Historic Park

TOP 200 PLACE **Columbia State Historic Park** Parrotts Ferry Rd. Columbia CA 209-532-0150
The popular Columbia State Historic Park represents a gold rush town of the 1850-1870 time period. In 1945 the State Legislature made this site a State Historic Park in order to preserve a typical Gold Rush town, an example of one of the most colorful eras in American history. The town's old Gold Rush-era business district has been preserved with many shops and restaurants. The proprietors of the shops are dressed in mid 1800s period clothing. Activities include viewing over a dozen historic structures, shopping, picnic facilities and a few hiking trails. One of the trails, The Karen Bakerville Smith Memorial Trail is a self-guided 1/2 mile loop trail which was dedicated to a teacher. The trail is located by the historic school building and there is a brochure describing the plants and surroundings. The park operates daily from 9am to 5 pm. They are closed on Thankgiving and Christmas days. Admission is free. Your leashed dog is welcome. It is located on Parrotts Ferry Road, between Hwy 4 and Hwy 49 (near Sonora).

Railtown 1897 State Historic Park Highway 49 Jamestown CA 209-984-3953
This park is home to one of America's last authentic, operating railroad roundhouses. Still a popular Hollywood location site, Railtown 1897 has been called "the most photographed railroad in the world." "Petticoat Junction," "The Wild, Wild West," "High Noon," "The Virginian," and "Unforgiven" were all filmed here. Movie crews also produced the railroad sequences in "Back to the Future Part III" at Railtown. Dogs on leash are allowed in the park, but not on the trains.

Black Sheep Winery West end of Main Street Murphys CA 209-728-2157
http://www.blacksheepwinery.com/
This winery specializes in zinfandel, with production also of sauvignon, sauvignon blanc and a second label called True Frogs Lily Pad Red. Well behaved dogs are welcome. Dogs must be leashed and cleaned up after at all times.

Rocco's Com'e Bella Winery 457-C Algiers Murphys CA 209-728-9030
This scenic winery believes in developing wines in the old Italian way, and they specialize in Mission, Zinfandel, Cabernet Sauvignon, and Chardonnay. Their Mission wine, though, is produced from descendants of the first vines ever planted in California. Dogs are welcome here and many enjoy the park like setting and walking by the nearby stream. There is also a table out back for a picnic or just a rest. Dogs must be well behaved, and leashed and cleaned up after at all times.

Stevenot Winery 2690 San Domingo Road Murphys CA 209-728-0638
http://www.stevenotwinery.com/
This premier winery is located in an area that has been an esteemed wine grape growing region since the mid

1800s, and they offer complimentary tasting of their world class wines. Dogs are welcome to join you on the grounds, the lawns, or at the picnic area under the grape arbor. Dogs must be well behaved, leashed, and cleaned up after.

Mark Twain Cabin Jackass Hill Rd. Tuttletown CA

This replica of Mark Twain's cabin has the original chimney and fireplace. During 1864-1865, young Mark Twain was a guest of the Gillis Brothers. While he stayed at this cabin, he gathered material for The Jumping Frog of Calaveras County (this book brought him fame) and for Roughing It. The cabin is located near Sonora, approximately 1 mile northwest of Tuttletown off Hwy 49. There are several parking spots next to the cabin.

Stores

Sierra Nevada Adventure Company (SNAC) 2293 Highway 4 Arnold CA   209-795-9310
http://www.snacattack.com/
This store carries outdoor gear and clothing for kayaking, rock-climbing, hiking, cross-country skiing and more. They always encouraged dog owners to bring their pets into the store to try on dog packs, dog lifevests, and more! It comes highly recommended from one of our readers and her Australian Shepherd.

Parks

Utica Park Hwy 49 Angels Camp CA   209-736-2187
Utica Park was built in 1954 on the site of the Utica Mine after the ground had been leveled and shafts filled to the 60 foot level. Today it is a great park for having a picnic or watching the kids have fun in the large playground area. The historic Lightner Mine at this park operated from 1896-1915. It produced over $6 million dollars in ore. The mine was filled, but you will still see some of the equipment that was used above ground. The park is located off Hwy 49, just north of downtown Angels Camp.

Calaveras Big Trees State Park Highway 4 Arnold CA   209-795-2334
Just three species of redwood trees remain; the dawn redwood in central China; the coast redwood along the coast of northern California and southern Oregon; and the Sierra redwoods which grow at Calaveras Big Trees State Park and other widely scattered groves along the western slope of the Sierra Nevada. These redwood trees have evolved from the Mesozoic Era, the time when dinosaurs roamed the Earth. Dogs are not allowed on the trails, but are allowed on the dirt fire roads. There are miles of fire roads at this park. They are used by hikers, bicyclists and equestrians. Dogs must be on leash. The state park is about a 35 minute drive from Angel's Camp on Highway 4.

Red Hills Area Hiking Red Hills Road Chinese Camp CA   916-985-4474
This 7,000 acres of public land has just over 17 miles of trails with various loops. Elevations vary between 750 and 1,750 feet. This is a popular area for hunting, hiking, horseback riding and wildflower viewing. Leashed dogs are welcome. Please clean up after your dog. There are no park fees. The land is located near Highways 49 and 120. From Sonora, take Highway 49 south 15 miles to Chinese Camp. Then drive south on Red Hills Road for .5 miles.

Stanislaus National Forest 19777 Greenley Road Sonora CA   209-532-3671
http://www.fs.fed.us/r5/stanislaus/
This national forest covers almost 900,000 acres of land which ranges in elevation from 1,200 to over 10,000 feet. Please see our listings in the Sierra Nevada region for dog-friendly hikes and campgrounds.

Outdoor Restaurants

La Hacienda Restaurant 51 N. Main Street Angels Camp CA   209-736-6711
Dogs are allowed at the outdoor seats on the covered deck.

Giant Burger 846 Highway 4 Arnold CA   209-795-1594
Dogs are allowed at the outdoor tables.

Pablito's of the Mother Lode 925 Highway 4 # J Arnold CA   209-795-3303
Dogs are allowed at the outdoor seats.

Columbia Frosty 22652 Parrotts Ferry Rd Columbia CA   209-532-6773
Dogs are allowed at the tables outside.

The Lickskillet 11256 State Street Columbia CA   209-536-9599
This nice restaurant is located in the Columbia State Historic Park and allows your dog to dine with you at the outdoor tables. The tables are on the lawn and some are in the shade. Thanks to one of our readers for recommending this restaurant. She writes "..wanted to let you know about (this) extremely dog-friendly restaurant... We sat at a table on the lawn, in the shade, with a bowl of water for the dogs. And the food was wonderful - both of us were delighted with our dinners."

Historic National Hotel 18187 Main St Jamestown CA   209-984-3446
This restaurant serves Mediteranean food. Dogs are allowed at the outdoor tables.

Pizza Plus 18251 Main St Jamestown CA   209-984-3700
Dogs on leash are allowed at the outdoor seats.

Pine Tree Restaurant 19601 Hess Ave Sonora CA   209-536-6065
Dogs are allowed at the outdoor tables.

Chapter 7

California - Sierra Nevada Mountains Dog Travel Guide

Bear Valley - Arnold

Vacation Home Rentals
The Topanga Treehouse Call to Arrange Dorrington CA 415-488-0278
This two bedroom, two bath vacation rental is located on Highway 4 between Arnold and Bear Valley. It sleeps 4 people. Well behaved dogs are welcome with a $100 refundable security deposit. Dogs should be groomed and have flea control. Dog beds, dog bowls and treats are provided.

Big Pine

Accommodations
Big Pine Motel 370 S Main St Big Pine CA 760-938-2282
There is a $4 per day additional pet fee.
Bristlecone Motel 101 N. Main St. Big Pine CA 760-938-2067
According to one of our website readers "Neat,inexpensive rooms with kitchens or fridge and microwave. Barbecue and fish cleaning area. Easy day trip to the ancient Bristlecone Pine Forest, which is extremely dog friendly."

Campgrounds and RV Parks
Big Pine Creek Campground Glacier Lodge Road Big Pine CA 760-873-2500 (877-444-6777)
This 36 site campground is located in the Inyo National Forest at an elevation of 7,700 feet. Amenities include water and space for RVs. For hiking, the trailheads for the Big Pine Canyon Trails are located here. The fee for a campsite is $13. Pets must be leashed while in the campground and please clean up after your pets. They may be off lead in the back country if they are under voice command. Dogs may not be left unattended outside, and only left inside if they will be comfortable, quiet, and well behaved. This campground is closed during the off-season. The camping and tent areas also allow dogs. There is a dog walk area at the campground. There are no electric or water hookups at the campgrounds.
Glacier Lodge RV Park Glacier Lodge Road Big Pine CA 760-938-2837
This campground offers tent camping and some RV spaces with full hookups. Amenities include a general store and nearby hiking and fishing. Dogs are also allowed in the cabins for an extra $15 per pet per stay. The Big Pine Canyon trailheads are located here which offer miles of dog-friendly on or off-leash hiking trails. Pets must be leashed in the campground and please clean up after them. This rv park is closed during the off-season. The camping and tent areas also allow dogs. There is a dog walk area at the campground. Dogs are allowed in the camping cabins.
Grandview Campground White Mountain Road Big Pine CA 760-873-2500
This campground is in Bristlecone Pine Forest, at 8,600 feet, in the White Mountain area of Inyo National Forest. There are no services or water available here. Dogs of all sizes are allowed at no additional fee. Dogs may not be left unattended, and they must be leashed and cleaned up after. When out of camp, on the trails, dogs may be off lead if no one is around, and they are under voice control. This campground is closed during the off-season. The camping and tent areas also allow dogs. There is a dog walk area at the campground. There are no electric or water hookups at the campgrounds.

Parks
Big Pine Canyon Trails Glacier Lodge Road Big Pine CA 760-873-2500
http://www.fs.fed.us/r5/inyo
These trails start and an elevation of 7,800 feet and go up to 12,400 feet. There are about 15 miles of trails. The trails lead into the dog-friendly John Muir Wilderness. One of the closest lakes, Willow Lake, is a 4 mile hike from the trailhead. At the campgrounds pets must be on a 6 foot or less leash. While hiking on the trails, pets must be on leash or under voice command at all times. Dogs are also allowed in the lake. Please clean up after your pets. This trail is located in the Inyo National Forest. To get there from Highway 395, exit in Big Pine and go 11 miles west on Glacier Lodge Road.
John Muir Wilderness Trails Glacier Lodge Road Big Pine CA 760-873-2500
http://www.fs.fed.us/r5/inyo
The wilderness trails are located in the Inyo National Forest and can be accessed from many points, including the Big Pine Canyon Trails near Big Pine. See our listing for Big Pine Creek Canyon Trail. From these trailheads,

there are about 9 miles of hiking trails and several campgrounds. To get there from Highway 395, exit in Big Pine and go 11 miles west on Glacier Lodge Road.

Bishop

Accommodations

Bishop Village Motel 286 W Elm Street Bishop CA 888-668-5546
Dogs of all sizes are allowed. There is a $10 per night per pet additional pet fee.
Comfort Inn 805 N Main Street Bishop CA 760-873-4284 (877-424-6423)
Dogs of all sizes are allowed. There is a $5 per night per pet additional fee. Dogs may only be left alone in the room if they will be quiet, well behaved, and the Do Not Disturb sign is placed on the door. Dogs must be leashed and cleaned up after.
Motel 6 - Bishop 1005 North Main Street Bishop CA 760-873-8426 (800-466-8356)
One well-behaved family pet per room. Guest must notify front desk upon arrival. Guest is liable for any damages. In consideration of all guests, pets must never be left unattended in the guest rooms.
Rodeway Inn 150 E Elm Street Bishop CA 760-873-3564
There is a $5 per day pet fee. Dogs are allowed in certain rooms only.
Vagabond Inn 1030 N Main Street Bishop CA 760-873-6351
There is a $5 per day pet fee.

Campgrounds and RV Parks

Four Jeffrey Campground South Lake Road Bishop CA 760-873-2500 (877-444-6777)
This 106 site campground is located in the Inyo National Forest at an elevation of 8,100 feet. Amenities include water, space for RVs and a dump station. For hiking, the Bristlecone Pine Forest is located nearby and offers many dog-friendly trails. The fee for a campsite is $14. Pets must be leashed while in the campground and please clean up after your pets. Dogs must be quiet and friendly. This campground is closed during the off-season. The camping and tent areas also allow dogs. There is a dog walk area at the campground. There are no electric or water hookups at the campgrounds.

Attractions

Bristlecone Pine Forest White Mountain Rd Bishop CA 760-873-2500
This forest, located in the Inyo National Forest, is home to the world's oldest known trees. They are the ancient bristlecone pines. Some of these trees were growing when the Egyptians built the pyramids over four thousand years ago. At the Schulman Grove Visitor's Center, there are picnic areas, restrooms, outdoor exhibits and two self-guided nature trails. You can also get information on hiking trails in the area from the visitor's center. Open daily from Memorial Day through October, weather permitting. July through September are usually the best months for hiking in the White Mountains. Dogs are allowed on leash. Driving time from Big Pine to Schulman Grove is approximately 45 minutes on paved roads. Take Highway 168 east 12 miles from Big Pine to White Mtn Road. Turn left and drive ten miles to the Schulman Grove Visitor Center. The Bristlecone Pines can be viewed from the parking area of the visitor center and along three nature trails.

Parks

Hilton Lakes Trail Rock Creek Canyon Rd. Bishop CA 760-873-2500
http://www.fs.fed.us/r5/inyo
This trail is located in the Inyo National Forest. It starts at an elevation of 9,600 feet and goes up to 10,720 feet over 5.25 miles. From the trailhead you can hike to several lakes. At the campgrounds pets must be on a 6 foot or less leash. While hiking on the trails, pets must be on leash or under voice command at all times. Please clean up after your pets. To get there from Highway 395, exit at Tom's Place. Go up Rock Creek Canyon Road. The trail starts before the Rock Creek Pack Station on the road to Mosquito Flat.
Inyo National Forest 351 Pacu Lane, Suite 200 Bishop CA 760-873-2400
http://www.fs.fed.us/r5/inyo/
This national forest covers thousands of acres of land ranging in elevations up to 14,246 feet in the White Mountain Range which is located near Mt. Whitney. Please see our listings in the Sierra Nevada region for dog-friendly hikes and/or campgrounds.
Little Lakes Trail Rock Creek Canyon Rd. Bishop CA 760-873-2500
http://www.fs.fed.us/r5/inyo
This trail is located in the Inyo National Forest. It starts at an elevation of 10,300 feet and the first 1.5 miles of the trail goes up to 10,440 to Heart Lake. From there you can go several more miles up to elevations around 11,000 feet. At the campgrounds pets must be on a 6 foot or less leash. While hiking on the trails, pets must be on leash or under voice command at all times. Please clean up after your pets. To get there from Highway 395, exit at

Sierra Nevada Mountains - Please always call ahead to make sure that an establishment is still dog-friendly

Tom's Place. Go up Rock Creek Canyon Road to the end, about 10 miles to the Mosquito Flat parking.

Vets and Kennels
Bishop Veterinary Hospital 1650 N. Sierra Highway Bishop CA 760-873-5801
Weekdays 9 - noon, 2 - 5 pm. Saturday 9 - noon by appt. Emergency doctor on call 24 hours.

Bridgeport

Accommodations
Walker River Lodge 100 Main Street Bridgeport CA 760-932-7021
Well behaved dogs of all sizes are allowed. There is a pet policy to sign at check in and there are no additional pet fees.

Campgrounds and RV Parks
Honeymoon Flat P. O. Box 631/Twin Lakes Road Bridgeport CA 760-932-7070
This campground is in the Twin Lakes Recreation Area of the Sierra Nevada Mountain Range, and there are a variety of recreational pursuits. Dog of all sizes are allowed at no additional fee. Dogs must be leashed in the camp areas, and cleaned up after at all times. Dogs may be off lead when hiking if they are under voice control, however, they may not be off lead at any time on the Robinson Head Creek Trail. This campground is closed during the off-season. The camping and tent areas also allow dogs. There is a dog walk area at the campground. There are no electric or water hookups at the campgrounds.

Attractions
Bodie State Historic Park State Route 270 Bridgeport CA 760-647-6445
This park is a ghost town. It looks much the same today as it did 50 years ago. Bodie is now listed as one of the worlds 100 most endangered sites by the World Monuments Watch. A self guided brochure describing a brief history of each building is available at the park. Dogs are welcome but must be on a leash at all times. From Highway 395 seven miles south of Bridgeport, take State Route 270. Go east 10 miles to the end of the pavement and continue 3 miles on an un-surfaced road to Bodie. The last 3 miles can at times be rough. Reduced speeds are necessary.

Camptonville

Parks
Rebel Ridge Trail Marysville Road Camptonville CA 530-288-3231
This 1.6 mile moderate rated trail is open all year. Pets must be either leashed or off-leash but under direct voice control. Please clean up after your pets. It is located in the Tahoe National Forest, on Marysville Road, .6 miles west of Highway 49.

Coleville

Accommodations
Andruss Motel 106964 Highway 395 Coleville CA 530-495-2216

Campgrounds and RV Parks
Sonora Bridge Campground Sonora Bridge Road Coleville CA 760-932-7070
Dogs of all sizes are allowed. There are no additional pet fees. Dogs may not be left unattended, and they must be leashed and cleaned up after. Dogs may be off lead on the trails only if they will respond to voice command and will not chase wildlife. Dogs are not allowed on the trails that go into Yosemite. This campground is closed during the off-season. The camping and tent areas also allow dogs. There is a dog walk area at the campground. There are no electric or water hookups at the campgrounds.

Crowley Lake

Campgrounds and RV Parks
Crowley Lake Campground Crowley Lake Drive Crowley Lake CA 760 873-2503
This campground is located in open high desert country at 7,000 feet and has 47 tent and RV sites available. Please note that there are no trees and the winds can be strong. The area overlooks Crowley Lake which is a popular site for fishing. The campground is usually open from late April until the end of October. Camp amenities include 4 pit toilets and pull through trailer spaces. All sites are first-come, first-served. This campsite is managed by the BLM (Bureau of Land Management), and there is a $5 per night camping fee. Dogs are allowed at no additional fee, but please keep them under control, and leashed in camp. The closest convenience stores are located in Mammoth Lakes, about 10 miles north of the campground or at a very small store in the Crowley Lake area. After exiting Hwy 395, go west through the Crowley Lake community for about 2 miles. At Crowley Lake Drive turn north and go about 2 miles. This campground is closed during the off-season. The camping and tent areas also allow dogs. There is a dog walk area at the campground. There are no electric or water hookups at the campgrounds.

Dinkey Creek

Campgrounds and RV Parks
Dinkey Creek Campground Dinkey Creek Road Dinkey Creek CA 559-297-0706 (877-444-6777)
This campground is next to Dinkey Creek in the Sierra National Forest. The campground is on a large sandy flat above the river and shaded by cedar and pine trees at an elevation of 5,400 feet. There are 128 tent and RV sites. RVs up to 35 feet are allowed. Amenities include piped water, flush toilets, picnic tables and grills. There are several trails that start at this campground. Dogs are allowed at the campgrounds, on trails, and in the water, but only at non-designated swimming beaches. Pets must be leashed and please clean up after them. Dogs must be quiet and well behaved. This campground is closed during the off-season. The camping and tent areas also allow dogs. There is a dog walk area at the campground. There are no electric or water hookups at the campgrounds.

Graeagle

Accommodations
Gray Eagle Lodge 5000 Gold Lake Rd. Graeagle CA 800-635-8778 (800-635-8778)
http://www.grayeaglelodge.com/
Stay in a rustic cabin at this mountain getaway located in the Sierra Mountains, about 1.5 hours north of Truckee. There are many hiking trails within a short walk from the cabins. There are over 40 alpine lakes nearby. There is a $20 per pet, per day, fee with a maximum of 2 pets per cabin. Guests are expected to follow guidelines provided by the lodge and will sign a pet policy form upon arrival. Dogs up to 50 pounds are allowed.

Campgrounds and RV Parks
Lakes Basin Campground County Road 519 Graeagle CA 530-836-2575 (877-444-6777)
Glaciers formed the special geological features of this park that is located in the Plumas National Forest, and it is known for it's spectacular scenery and numerous clear lakes. Amenities include water, vault toilets and trailer space. Located at this campground is the trailhead for the Grassy Lake Trail. In the campground dogs must be on leash. On the trails, dogs on leash or off-leash, but under direct voice control, are allowed. Owners must clean up after their pets. This campground is closed during the off-season. The camping and tent areas also allow dogs. There is a dog walk area at the campground. There are no electric or water hookups at the campgrounds.

Parks
Grassy Lake Trail County Road 519 Graeagle CA 530-836-2575
This trail is located in the Plumas National Forest and is an easy one way .8 mile trail. This trail starts at an elevation of 6,320 feet and goes past Grassy Lake. It then crosses Gray Eagle Creek to join with the Long Lake Trail. If you continue on this trail, you can hike another 3 miles one way on a moderate rated trail. Long Lake

Trail gradually climbs to Long Lake. Dogs on leash or off-leash but under direct voice control are allowed. Dogs are allowed on the trails and in the water. Please clean up after your pets. The trailhead is located in the Lakes Basin Campground. The campground is located 9 miles southwest of Graeagle on County Road 519.

Independence

Accommodations
Independence Courthouse Motel 157 N Edwards Street Independence CA 760-878-2732
There is a $6 per day additional pet fee. All rooms are non-smoking.
Ray's Den Motel 405 N Edwards St Independence CA 760-878-2122
There is a $6 per day additional pet fee.
Wilder House Bed & Breakfast 325 Dusty Lane Independence CA 760-878-2119
http://www.wilderhouse.com

Campgrounds and RV Parks
Goodale Creek Campground Aberdeen Cutoff Road Independence CA 760-872-5000
This campground is located at a 4,000 foot elevation on a volcanic flow, next to Goodale Creek. It offers great views of the Sierra Nevada Mountains. There are 62 tent and RV sites available, 5 pit toilets, picnic tables and campfire rings/stands. The campground is usually open from late April to the end of October. There are no fees, no hookups and no drinking water. All sites are on a first-come, first-served basis. Be aware of rattlesnakes in the area, especially during the summer months. The closest convenience stores are located in the towns of Independence and Big Pine. Dogs are allowed at the campground, but please keep them under control, and they must be leashed and cleaned up after. Dogs are allowed on the trails on lead. The camping and tent areas also allow dogs. There is a dog walk area at the campground. There are no electric or water hookups at the campgrounds.

Parks
Manzanar National Historic Site P.O. Box 426 Independence CA 760-878-2932
http://www.nps.gov/manz/
This site was one of ten camps where Japanese and Japanese American citizens were interned during World War II. It is located at the base of the Sierra Nevada mountains and has been identified as the best preserved camp. Dogs are allowed at the site, on the self-guided walking tour which takes about 1-2 hours, and on the 3.2 mile self-guided auto tour. A tour description and map is available at the camp entrance. Pets must be on leash and please clean up after them. The park is open all year and there is no parking fee. It is located off Highway 395, 12 miles north of Lone Pine and 5 miles south of Independence.

Johnsondale

Campgrounds and RV Parks
Redwood Meadow Campground Off Mountain Road 50 on Western Divide H/M 107 Johnsondale CA 559-539-2607 (877-444-6777)
This campground is located in the Sequoia National Forest at an elevation of 6,100 feet. It is across the road from the Trail of a Hundred Giants. The campground offers 15 tent and small RV sites. RVs up to 16 feet are allowed. Vault toilets are located at the camp. Ideal camping is from May to October. Pets must be on no more than a 6 foot leash and attended to at all times. Please clean up after your pet. The campsite is located about 45 miles northwest of Kernville. This campground is closed during the off-season. The camping and tent areas also allow dogs. There is a dog walk area at the campground. There are no electric or water hookups at the campgrounds.

Parks
Trail of a Hundred Giants off Mountain Road 50 Johnsondale CA 559-539-2607
This trail is located in the Giant National Sequoia Monument which is part of the Sequoia National Forest. The universally accessible trail meanders through over 125 giant sequoias in the Long Meadow Grove. The estimated age of the trees here are estimated between 500 and 1,500 years old. Pets must be leashed and attended at all times. Please clean up after your pet. The trail is located about 45 miles northwest of Kernville. From Kernville, take State Mountain Road 99 north to Johnsondale. Go west on 50 to the Western Divide

Highway turnoff. Go 2 miles to the Redwood Meadow Campground. The trail is located across the road from the campground.

June Lake

Accommodations

Big Rock Resort Big Rock Road at Boulder Drive June Lake CA 760-648-7717
http://www.bigrockresort.net
Dogs of all sizes are allowed in some of these one to three bedroom cabins right on June Lake. A maximum of one dog is allowed per cabin. There is a $15 per day additional pet fee. All cabins are non-smoking.
Double Eagle Resort and Spa 5587 Highway 158 June Lake CA 760-648-7004
http://www.doubleeagle.com
The combination of running streams, towering pines, and spectacular mountain scenery add to the beauty of this resort. They offer cabins and luxury rooms, wood-burning fireplaces or stoves, fully equipped kitchens, and the cabins have their own outside deck with furnishings and a barbecue. Other features include a picnic area and fly-fishing pond, an indoor Olympic-sized swimming pool, a full-service creekside spa and fitness center, an in-house restaurant that also offers healthy spa selections, and a full-service bar. Dogs of all sizes are allowed for an additional $15 per night per pet up to a total amount of $50 for the stay. Dogs must be quiet, well behaved, leashed, and cleaned up after.
June Lake Villager Inn 2640 Hwy 158 June Lake CA 760-648-7712 (800-655-6545)
http://www.junelakevillager.com/
Just minutes from several other activities and recreational pursuits, this mountain resort offers wonderful views, a variety of rooms/cabins (some with wood burning stoves or fireplaces), a seasonal indoor Jacuzzi, and in summer; a patio, barbecue, fish cleaning station, and they will freeze your catch as well. One or two dogs are allowed per room depending on the size of the room. There is no additional pet fee with a credit card on file; however, dogs are accepted by advance reservation only. Dogs must be leashed, cleaned up after, and removed or crated for housekeeping.

Campgrounds and RV Parks

June Lake RV Park 155 Crawford Avenue June Lake CA 760-648-7967
This full service campground is located between June Lake and Gulf Lake in the June Lake area. The campground is within walking distance of both lakes. There are full hook ups, cable TV, and a laundry room. This is an RV campground only; tent camping is not allowed. There are no public bathrooms or showers. Dogs are allowed, they must be on a leash at all times. Dogs must be picked up after. The campground is open from April through October annually.
Pine Cliffs Resort P.O. Box 38 June Lake CA 760-648-7558
Pine Cliff Resort RV park is located right on June Lake. It is a full-service campground with a general store, propane, a laundry, and showers. Dogs are allowed in the campground in RVs and in tents. They must be leashed and cleaned up after.
Silver Lake Resort 6957 Hwy 158 June Lake CA 760-648-7572
This resort, located on the shore of Silver Lake, offers great views and amenities that include a general store, cafe, showers, restrooms, laundry room and picnic area. Well-behaved dogs of all sizes are allowed at no additional fee. Dogs must be leashed, and walked outside of the park, and please clean up after your pet in the Sierra National Forest. The resort is open from the end of April to mid-October. This is an RV only park. This campground is closed during the off-season. The camping and tent areas also allow dogs. There is a dog walk area at the campground.

Parks

June Lake Area of Inyo National Forest Highway 158 (June Lake Loop) June Lake CA   760-647-3044
This popular resort area is known for skiing in winter (both downhill and cross-country) and hiking and enjoying the four lakes along the June Lake Loop in the summer. These lakes are June Lake, Gulf Lake, Sliver Lake, and Grant Lake. There are a number of marinas at the lakes which may allow your dog on some of their boat rentals. This entire area is within the Inyo National Forest, which allows dogs throughout the forest on leash. Dogs are not supposed to swim in any of the lakes but they are allowed on leash up to them and on boats in the lakes. There are many hiking trails in the area, however, if you are planning a long hike make sure that you keep your dog out of land in Yosemite National Park, where dogs are not allowed. They need to stay in the National Forest.

Kernville

Accommodations

Falling Waters River Resort 15729 Sierra Way Kernville CA 760-376-2242
Two dogs of any size are welcome, but 3 dogs are allowed if they are all small. There is a $10 per night per pet fee and dogs may only be left unattended for short periods.
River View Lodge 2 Sirreta Street Kernville CA 760-376-6019
Dogs of all sizes are allowed. There is a $20 per night per room fee and a pet policy to sign at check in.

Campgrounds and RV Parks

Rivernook Campground 14001 Sierra Way Kernville CA 760-376-2705
This park is nestled in 60 wooded acres along the scenic Kern River and offers a variety of land and water recreation. Dogs of all sizes are allowed. There are no additional pet fees. Dogs may not be left unattended outside, and left inside only if they will be quiet, well behaved, and physically comforable. Dogs must be leashed and cleaned up after. The camping and tent areas also allow dogs. There is a dog walk area at the campground.
Lake Isabella RV Resort 11936 Hwy 178 Mountain Mesa CA 800-787-9920
http://www.lakeisabellarv.com/home.htm
This picturesque, RV only park, is located along Lake Isabella, and amenities include more than 40 miles of open shoreline, a full service marina, and a pool. Dogs of all sizes are allowed for an additional $1 per night per pet. Dogs may not be left unattended outside, and they must be brought in at night, leashed, and cleaned up after. There are some breed restrictions. There is a dog walk area at the campground.
Isabella Lake KOA 15627 Hwy 178 Weldon CA 760-378-2001 (800-562-2085)
Located near the dog-friendly Isabella Lake, this campground offers both tent sites and RV spaces. Well-behaved leashed dogs of all sizes are allowed. People need to clean up after their pets. There is no pet fee. Site amenities include a maximum length pull through of 40 feet and 30 amp service available. Other amenities include LP gas, an entrance gate, free modem dataport, snack bar and a seasonal swimming pool, playground, and adult pub. There are some breed restrictions. The camping and tent areas also allow dogs. There is a dog walk area at the campground.

Parks

Lake Isabella Highways 155 and 178 Lake Isabella CA 661-868-7000
This lake is set at an elevation of over 2,500 feet and with a surface area of 11,200 acres it is Kern County's largest body of year round water. The lake is a popular spot for fishing and boating. Dogs are allowed at the lake and in the lake but must be on leash. Please clean up after your pets. There are nearby dog-friendly Sequoia National Forest trails within driving distance, including the Trail of a Hundred Giants. See our listing for this trail or call the Greenhorn Rangers District at 760-379-5646 for details.

Kirkwood

Cross Country Ski Resorts

Kirkwood Cross Country Ski Center Highway 88 Kirkwood CA 209-258-7248
http://www.kirkwood.com/
This ski resort allow dogs on two cross-country ski trails. They are the High Trail, located behind the Kirkwood Inn Restaurant, and the Inner Loop on the meadow. Dogs need to be leashed or can be off-leash but under direct voice control. Please clean up after your pet. Adult passes are about $20 per day, children $6 per day and doggie passes are $20 per day. Kirkwood is located about 45 minutes from South Lake Tahoe, on Highway 88. The closest pet-friendly lodging to Kirkwood, that we know of, is in South Lake Tahoe. Thanks to one of our readers for recommending this attraction.

Parks

Meiss Lake Trail Highway 88 Kirkwood CA 530-622-5061
This 4 mile moderate rated trail is used by both hikers and equestrians. Bicycling is prohibited. Take the Pacific Crest Trail one mile to the ridge, which offers great views and a wildflower display around mid-summer. Hike another three miles to Meiss Lake. The trailhead is located on the north side of Highway 88, immediately west of the Carson Pass Information Center. There is a parking fee. Pets must be leashed and please clean up after them.

Lake Tahoe

Accommodations

Shinneyboo Creek Cabin Resort 11820 Eagle Lakes Road Cisco CA 530-587-5160
http://www.shinneyboocreek.com
These secluded cabins are located in the High Sierra, surrounded by the Tahoe National Forest. There is a $10 per pet per day additional pet fee.

Tahoe Biltmore Lodge #5 Hwy 28 (Hwy 28 and Stateline) Crystal Bay NV 775-831-0660 (800-BILTMORE (245-6673))
This inn offers 92 affordable, well appointed rooms and suites, and there are also some cottages available overlooking the lake. Amenities include room service, an outdoor spa and seasonal pool, a long list of entertainment and special events throughout the year, a nightclub, and 2 restaurants. Dogs of all sizes are allowed for a refundable deposit of $100 and an additional fee of $20 per night per pet. Dogs must be crated or removed for housekeeping, and crated when left alone in the room. Dogs must be leashed and cleaned up after at all times.

Sorensen's Resort 14255 Highway 88 Hope Valley CA 530-694-2203 (800-423-9949)
http://www.sorensensresort.com/
This secluded mountain resort is located in beautiful Hope Valley which is about 30 minutes south of South Lake Tahoe. Dogs are allowed in several of the cabins. The dog-friendly cabins sleep from two up to four people. Each cabin has a wood-burning stove (for heat) and kitchen. The Hope Valley Cross Country Ski Rentals are located on the premises (see Attractions). Hiking is available during the summer on the trails of the Toiyable National Forest. There are also several nearby lakes. Cabin rates start at $85 per night and go up to about $450 for a large bedroom cabin. There are no additional pet fees.

3 Peaks Resort and Beach Club 931 Park Avenue South Lake Tahoe CA 800-957-5088
The 3 Peaks Resort and Beach Club is a family resort near the center of South Lake Tahoe. All pets are welcome for a $15 per night fee. Pets cannot be left unattended and must be kept on a leash when out of the room.

7 Seas Inn 4145 Manzanita Ave South Lake Tahoe CA 530-544-7031 (800-800-SEAS)
http://www.sevenseastahoe.com
This motel is located one block from the casinos and near Heavenly Ski Resort. There is a 2000 Square foot dog run and pet sitting is available.

Alder Inn 1072 Ski Run Blvd South Lake Tahoe CA 530-544-4485 (800-544-0056)
http://www.alderinntahoe.com
Minutes from Heavenly Valley Ski Resort and the casinos. All rooms have a small refrigerator and microwave. There is a $10.00 per night pet fee.

Colony Inn at South Lake Tahoe 3794 Montreal Road South Lake Tahoe CA 530-544-6481
http://gototahoe.com/rooms/colony.html
The Colony Inn at South Lake Tahoe is located just 1.5 blocks from Harrah's and the other casinos and just down the street from Heavenly Ski Resort. Want to experience the beautiful outdoors? The Colony Inn's backyard is National Forest Land, featuring dog-friendly hiking, mountain biking, and peace and quiet. There is a $25 refundable pet deposit, and pets cannot be left unattended in the rooms.

Fireside Lodge 515 Emerald Bay Rd. South Lake Tahoe CA 530-544-5515 (800-My-Cabin)
http://www.tahoefiresidelodge.com/
This inn offers log cabin style suites. The rooms have a unique "Country Mountain" theme decor with crafted fireplaces, and custom woodwork. Each room offers a microwave, refrigerator and coffee-maker, private bath w/shower, cable TV and VCR with numerous free videos available in their Gathering Room. Full kitchen units are available as well as private 1 to 4 bedroom cabins, off the property. There is a $20 per day pet charge.

Hollys Place 1201 Rufus Allen Blvd. South Lake Tahoe CA 530-544-7040 (800-745-7041)
http://www.hollysplace.com
This resort and retreat has 5 cabins on 2.5 fenced acres near South Lake Tahoe. There is a pet fee of $15 per night per dog.

Inn at Heavenly B&B 1261 Ski Run Boulevard South Lake Tahoe CA 530-544-4244 (800-692-2246)
http://www.innatheavenly.com/
You and your dog are welcome at this log-cabin style bed and breakfast lodge. The property is all dog-friendly and dogs are allowed everywhere but their Gathering Room. They offer 14 individual rooms each with a private bath and shower. Room conveniences include refrigerators, microwaves and VCRs. Some rooms have a fireplace. Three to four bedroom cabins are also available. The lodge is located on a 2-acre wooded park complete with picnic areas, barbecues and log swings. Continental breakfast is served and snacks are available throughout the day. One large dog is allowed per room and pet charges apply. Room rates range from the low to mid $100s per night. Call for cabin prices. The owners have friendly dogs on the premises. The lodge is located in South Lake Tahoe. There is a $20 per day pet fee per pet.

Motel 6 - South Lake Tahoe 2375 Lake Tahoe Boulevard South Lake Tahoe CA 530-542-1400 (800-466-8356)
One well-behaved family pet per room. Guest must notify front desk upon arrival. Guest is liable for any

damages. In consideration of all guests, pets must never be left unattended in the guest rooms.

Spruce Grove Cabins & Suites P.O. Box 16390 South Lake Tahoe CA 530-544-0549 (800-777-0914)
http://www.sprucegrovetahoe.com
Spruce Grove Cabins puts you amidst a mountain resort off of Ski Run Blvd. at the foot of Heavenly Ski Area and within walking distance to the center of Lake Tahoe. Children and well-behaved dogs are welcome. This dog friendly retreat offers a fully fenced acre of land that is next to an open field of pine trees.

Spruce Grove Cabins and Suites 3599 Spruce Ave South Lake Tahoe CA 530-544-6481
Well behaved dogs of all sizes are allowed. There is a $10 per night fee for one dog any size; each pet thereafter is an additional $5 per night per pet fee. There is a pet policy to sign at check in. There is also a large fenced area for a safe place to off-leash your pet.

Tahoe Tropicana 4132 Cedar Avenue South Lake Tahoe CA 530-541-3911
Dogs of all sizes are allowed. There is a $5 per night per pet additional fee Sunday through Thursday, and $10 per night per pet additional fee Friday and Saturday nights.

The Nash Cabin 3595 Betty Ray South Lake Tahoe CA 415-759-6583
Dogs of all sizes are allowed. There are no additional pet fees.

Holiday House 7276 North Lake Blvd Tahoe Vista CA 530-546-2369 (800-294-6378)
http://www.tahoeholidayhouse.com
This lodge in North Tahoe welcomes you and your dog. The hotel is located 1 mile west of the Hwy 267/Hwy 28 intersection near restaurants and activities.

Rustic Cottages 7449 N Lake Blvd Tahoe Vista CA 530-546-3523
Dogs of all sizes are allowed. There is a $15 per night per pet fee and dogs may not be left unattended. They request to clean up after your pet, keep it leashed, and they are not allowed on the furniture.

Norfolk Woods Inn 6941 West Lake Blvd. Tahoma CA 530-525-5000
http://www.norfolkwoods.com/
This inn only allows dogs in the cabins...but your pup won't mind. They have wonderful cozy cottages with kitchens. They only have 4 cabins, so call ahead. Also note that the entire premises is smoke free. Located directly in front of this inn is the Tahoe bike trail where you and your pup can walk or run for several miles. The trail is mostly paved except for a small dirt path section. The inn is located approx. 8-9 miles south of Tahoe City on Hwy 89. There is a $10 per day additional pet fee per pet.

Tahoma Lodge 7018 West Lake Blvd Tahoma CA 530-525-7721
Dogs only are allowed and up to 75 pounds. There is a $10 per night per pet fee, and they ask you kennel your dog when out. There are some breed restrictions.

Zephyr Cove Resort

Tahoma Meadows Bed and Breakfast 6821 W. Lake Blvd. Tahoma CA 530-525-1553

http://www.tahomameadows.com/
A well-behaved dog is allowed only if you let them know in advance that you are bringing your dog. Pets are allowed in one of their cabins, the Mountain Hideaway (previously known as Dogwood). There is an extra $25 one time pet charge per stay, plus a security deposit.
The Inn at Truckee 11506 Deerfield Drive Truckee CA   530-587-8888 (888-773-6888)
http://www.innattruckee.com
The Inn at Truckee specializes in relaxed accommodations and fun filled days for Truckee Tahoe Visitors. North Lake Tahoe resorts are located within a few minutes of this inn's doorstep. There is a $11 per day pet charge.
Zephyr Cove Resort 460 Highway 50 Zephyr Cove NV   775-588-6644
http://www.tahoedixie2.com/Resort.html
Thanks to one of our readers for recommending this resort. Dogs are allowed in the cabins but not in the lodge or cabin number one. That still leaves a nice selection of cabins to choose from. There is a $10 per day pet fee. This resort is located near South Lake Tahoe on the Nevada side. Dogs are allowed on the beaches at the northern side of the resort about a two block walk from the cabins.

Campgrounds and RV Parks
D. L. Bliss State Park Hwy 89 South Lake Tahoe CA   530-525-9529 (800-444-7275)
This park, at 6,200 feet, offers an impressive panoramic view of Lake Tahoe and the Tahoe Valley and a variety of recreational opportunities. Dogs are allowed in the parks at no additional fee. However, they must be kept on a leash during the day and in an enclosed vehicle or tent at night. Due to the possible danger to wildlife and other park visitors, dogs are not permitted on the trails, beaches or in the Vikingsholm area. The camping and tent areas also allow dogs. There is a dog walk area at the campground. There are no electric or water hookups at the campgrounds.
Encore Tahoe Valley RV Resort 1175 Melba Drive South Lake Tahoe CA 877-717-8737
Located in South Lake Tahoe, this campground sits among towering pines and mountain vistas, and some of their amenities include volleyball and tennis courts, seasonal heated outdoor pool, pool table, playground, video game center, general store, laundry facilities, modem hookups and even a dog run. Well-behaved leashed (at all times) dogs are welcome. Please clean up after your pet. There is no pet fee. Dogs may not be left unattended. The camping and tent areas also allow dogs. There is a dog walk area at the campground.
Fallen Leaf Campground Fallen Leaf Lake Road South Lake Tahoe CA   530-543-2600 (877-444-6777)
This campground is at a 6,377 foot elevation and is located in the Lake Tahoe Management Basin Unit of the National Forest. The camp offers 250 sites and 17 are available on a first-come, first-served basis. The maximum RV length allowed is 40 feet. Amenities include water, flush toilets, fire rings, picnic tables and barbecues. There are miles of trails which begin at or near this campground. Pets on leash are allowed at no additional fee, but not at the beach; they are allowed to swim in the lake. Please clean up after your pets. Dogs are allowed on the trails. Access to the campgrounds is on a rough paved road. A regular passenger car will make it, but go slow. This campground is closed during the off-season. The camping and tent areas also allow dogs. There is a dog walk area at the campground. There are no electric or water hookups at the campgrounds.
Lake Tahoe-South Shore KOA 760 North Highway 50 South Lake Tahoe CA   530-577-3693 (800-562-3477)
http://www.koa.com/where/ca/05148/
Surrounded by tall pines with a creek running through, this campground offers a variety of land and water recreation with amenities that include cable TV, 60 foot pull through sites with 30 amp, LP gas, wi-fi, swimming pool, and tours. Dogs of all sizes are allowed for an additional fee of $4 per night per pet. Dogs must be under owner's control and visual observation at all times. Dogs must be quiet, well behaved, and be on no more than a 6 foot leash at all times, or otherwise contained. Dogs may not be left unattended outside the owner's camping equipment. There are some breed restrictions. This campground is closed during the off-season. The camping and tent areas also allow dogs. There is a dog walk area at the campground.
Meeks Bay Campground Hwy 89 Tahoe City CA   530-543-2600 (877-444-6777)
This campground is at 6,225 feet elevation and is located in the Lake Tahoe Management Basin Unit of the National Forest. The camp offers 40 tent and RV sites. The maximum RV length allowed is 20 feet. Amenities include water, flush toilets, fire rings, picnic tables and barbecues. Pets on leash are allowed but not at the beach. Please clean up after your pets. Dogs are allowed on the trails. The camp is about 10 miles south of Tahoe City, located near D.L. Bliss State Park. This campground is closed during the off-season. The camping and tent areas also allow dogs. There is a dog walk area at the campground. There are no electric or water hookups at the campgrounds.
D. L. Bliss State Park Hwy 89/South Lake Tahoe Tahoma CA   530-525-7277 (800-444-7275)
Donated by the D. L. Bliss family in 1929, this park of 744 acres displays the grandeur of the mountain building processes of Mother Earth and offers visitors spectacular views of the surrounding area and deep into the lake. Dogs of all sizes are only allowed in developed areas, picnic grounds, and on paved roads. They are not allowed on the trails, beaches, or in the Vikingsholm area, and they must be inside a tent or vehicle from the hours of 10 pm to 6 am. Dogs must be under owner's control at all times, be on no more than a 6 foot leash, and be cleaned up after. There are 268 family campsites and a group camp between the D.L. Bliss State Park and Emerald Bay, reserved-or on a 1st come/1st serve basis and the sites each have a table, cupboard, and stove. There are restrooms and hot showers nearby. This RV park is closed during the offseason. The camping and tent areas

also allow dogs. There is a dog walk area at the campground. There are no electric or water hookups at the campgrounds.

Emerald Bay State Park Hwy 89/South Lake Tahoe Tahoma CA 530-541-3030 (800-444-7275)
A National Natural Landmark, this beautiful state park is rich in its natural beauty, history, and geology, and features Vikingsholm, one of the best examples of Scandinavian architecture in the western hemisphere. The park is also home to Lake Tahoe's only island, Fannette Island, and there are a variety of recreational opportunities to pursue. Dogs of all sizes are allowed in developed areas, picnic grounds, and on paved roads. They are not allowed on the trails, beaches, or in the Vikingsholm area, and they must be inside a tent or vehicle from the hours of 10 pm to 6 am. Dogs must be under owner's control at all times, be on no more than a 6 foot leash, and be cleaned up after. There are 268 family campsites and a group camp between the D.L. Bliss State Park and Emerald Bay, reserved-or on a 1st come/1st serve basis and the sites each have a table, cupboard, and stove. There are restrooms and hot showers nearby. This RV park is closed during the offseason. The camping and tent areas also allow dogs. There is a dog walk area at the campground. There are no electric or water hookups at the campgrounds.

General Creek Campground West Shore Lake Tahoe Tahoma CA 530-525-7982 (800-444-7275)
This park is located in the Sugar Pine Point State Park, offering various habitats to explore, miles of trails, and a variety of land and water recreation. Dogs of all sizes are allowed at no additional fee. Dogs must be kept on a leash no longer than six feet and under control at all times. They are not permitted in buildings or beaches. Dogs are allowed on all paved trails. Dogs must be confined to a vehicle or tent from 10:00 p.m. to 6:00 a.m. This campground is closed during the off-season. The camping and tent areas also allow dogs. There is a dog walk area at the campground.

Lakeside Campground Off Hwy 89 Truckee CA 530-587-3558 (877-444-6777)
This 30 site campground is located in the Tahoe National Forest at an elevation of 5,741 feet. Camp amenities include vault toilets. There is no water. Sites are $13 per night. The campground is located next to the reservoir and activities include fishing and swimming. Pets are allowed at no additional fee, and they must be leashed in the campground. Dogs must be cleaned up after. They may be off lead on the trails only if they are under voice control. This campground is closed during the off-season. The camping and tent areas also allow dogs. There is a dog walk area at the campground. There are no electric or water hookups at the campgrounds.

Logger Campground, Truckee District 9646 Donner Pass Road Truckee CA 530-587-3558
http://www.fs.fed.us/r5/tahoe
Located high in the northern Sierra Nevada mountain range, this park offers great scenery, interpretive exhibits, miles of trails, and a variety of recreation. Dogs of all sizes are allowed. There are no additional pet fees. Dogs must be leashed in the camp areas, and cleaned up after. Dogs may be off lead on the trails if they are under voice control. This campground is closed during the off-season. The camping and tent areas also allow dogs. There is a dog walk area at the campground. There are no electric or water hookups at the campgrounds.

Camp at the Cove 760 Hwy 50 Zephyr Cove NV 775-589-4907 (800-23-TAHOE (238-2463))
http://www.zephyrcove.com
Located in spectacular scenery, this award winning resort campground offers a wide variety of amenities and recreational opportunities. Dogs of all sizes are allowed at no additional fee for tent or RV sites. There is a $15 per night per pet additional fee for the cabins. Dogs may not be left unattended outside, or in a tent. They may be left in an RV if they will be quiet and well behaved. Dogs are not allowed on the beach or in the buildings. The camping and tent areas also allow dogs. There is a dog walk area at the campground. Dogs are allowed in the camping cabins.

Zephyr Cove RV Park and Campground 760 Hwy 50 Zephyr Cove NV 775-589-4922 (800-23-TAHOE (238-2463))
This campground is located within minutes of South Lake Tahoe and Stateline. RV site amenities include telephone lines, cable TV, picnic tables, fire rings, bear proof lockers, barbecues, and spectacular scenery. There is also a restaurant, coffee bar, general store and gift shop, and a full service marina. RVs up to 40 feet can be accommodated. Tent sites are either drive-in or walk-in sites, some of which offer lake views. Well-behaved dogs on leash are allowed for no additional fee for the tent or RV sites. There is an additional fee of $15 per night per pet for the cabins. Dogs may not be left unattended in the cabins. Dogs must be leashed and cleaned up after, and they are not allowed on the beach. The camping and tent areas also allow dogs. There is a dog walk area at the campground. Dogs are allowed in the camping cabins.

Vacation Home Rentals

Agate Bay Realty Lake Tahoe Call to Arrange North Lake Tahoe CA 530-546-4256 (800-550-6740)
http://www.agatebay.com
These vacation rentals are located in North Tahoe. Many of the homes are dog-friendly, and some offer lake views or easy access to beaches.

Enchanted Vacation Properties Call to Arrange North Lake Tahoe CA 530-546-2066
These vacation rentals are located on the north side of Lake Tahoe. Dogs of all sizes are welcome. Pet amenities include dog beds, dog bowls and treats, dog toys and a doggie guest book. There are no pet fees.

Buckingham Properties Lake Tahoe Call to Arrange South Lake Tahoe CA 530-542-1114 (800-503-0051)
http://www.BuckinghamTahoeRentals.com

This company offers elegant and unique vacation rentals which allow dogs. Their properties range from deluxe cabins to luxurious lakefront homes. The homes are located on the south shore from Glenbrook in Nevada to Camp Richardson in California.

Hal & Pat's Lake Tahoe Mountain Home 3745 Forest Ave. South Lake Tahoe CA 520-405-0242
http://www.halnpat.com
Located at the base of Heavenly Ski Resort and half a mile from the casinos this pet-friendly vacation rental offers rom for ten, high speed Internet and 4 bedrooms and three baths. There is a fully fenced yard. Dogs are welcome to join you for your Tahoe vacation.

Stonehenge Vacation Properties Call to Arrange. South Lake Tahoe CA 800-822-1460 (800-822-1460)
http://www.tahoestonehenge.com/
This vacation rental company offers several elegant and unique dog-friendly vacation homes located around South Lake Tahoe.

Tahoe Keys Resort 599 Tahoe Keys Blvd South Lake Tahoe CA 530-544-5397 (800-698-2463)
http://www.petslovetahoe.com
They feature approximately 50 pet friendly cabins, condos and homes in South Lake Tahoe. All dogs receive treats upon check-in. A $25.00 pet fee is taken per reservation. There is also a $100.00 refundable security deposit upon check in.

TahoeWoods Lodging See Website or Call South Lake Tahoe CA 415-444-0777
These three vacation homes in South Lake Tahoe feature at least 5 bedrooms and access to the Tahoe National Forest.

Percy's Place Email or call to arrange Tahoe City CA 510-898-2962
http://www.percysplace.com
Percy's Place is a 3-bedroom, 2-bath home just outside Tahoe City. The rental is a short walk to a US Forest Service trail. Dogs of all sizes are allowed. Please email percy@percysplace.com to make reservations.

Tahoe Lake And Mountain Properties P.O. Box 8258 Tahoe City CA 530-386-1622
http://www.tahoelamp.com
This vacation rental company on the west side of the lake provides pet-friendly vacation rentals. There are no additional pet fees and dogs of all sizes are welcome. Dogs may not be left alone in the rentals.

Tahoe Moon Properties P.O. Box 7521 Tahoe City CA 530-581-2771 (866-581-2771)
http://www.tahoemoonproperties.com
They have over 15 beautiful homes that allow well-behaved dogs. All of the houses are close to Tahoe City or ski areas. Bath and bed linens are provided. There are a few dog rules; no dogs on the furniture, dogs are not to be left alone in the house, you must clean up after your dog and pet owners are responsible for any damages. Rates start at $150 per night with a 2 night minimum. There is a $30 per dog charge.

Waters of Tahoe Vacation Properties PO Box 312 Tahoe Vista CA 530-546-8904 (800-215-8904)
http://www.watersoftahoe.com
These vacation homes are near the Tahoe National Forest and the lake. They provide pet amenities such as a dog basket with treats, toys, an extra leash, dog bowls and other miscellaneous goodies.

Andrea's Unsurpassed Truckee Vacation Rentals Call to Arrange Truckee CA 530-582-8703
http://www.truckeevacations.net
These vacation rental cottages at Donner Lake or a full size home that sleeps from 2 - 12 are available in the Truckee area. Dogs are welcome.

Attractions

Mountain High Weddings PO Box 294 Homewood CA 530-525-9320
http://mountainhighweddings.com/
Want to get married AND have your pooch with you to enjoy that special moment? Mountain High Weddings performs ceremonies on the North and West Shores of Lake Tahoe and they invite you to bring your dog. They have performed many ceremonies where rings were taken off the collars of special canine ring bearers. Couples have been married on skis on top of a mountain, under the full moon on the lake, or at a small intimate dinner party in the middle of a meadow. The weddings can be as traditional or unique as you desire. So if you are getting ready to tie the knot, now you can include your pooch in the wedding party.

Ann Poole Weddings, Nature's Chapel P.O. Box 3768 Olympic Valley CA 530-412-5436
http://www.tahoeminister.com
This business offers Lake Tahoe and Bay Area Weddings. Make it a special day by bringing your dog along with you. Here is an excerpt from the Wedding Minister: "You are planning to marry the Love of Your Life... so naturally, you will bring your 'best friend' to your wedding, won't you? Dogs do great at weddings... they are excellent ring bearers or proudly stand up with you, with flowers around their collars. They seem to simply KNOW that this is a Special Day for you and that they have an important part in it." They have many Wedding locations to choose from. You can choose your own unique location or have your wedding in a wedding chapel, nestled in the woods, or at one of their favorite locations like on a cliff overlooking beautiful Lake Tahoe, surrounded by tall pine trees.

Squaw Valley Chapel 440 Squaw Peak Road Olympic Valley CA 530-525-4714
This chapel, supported by a local congregation of the United Church of Christ, welcomes persons of all faiths,

and is very open to having your dog be part of the wedding ceremony. The chapel can seat up to 120 people and offers a piano and a CD and tape player sound system. They can also refer you to local florists, photographers and musicians if needed.

Squaw Valley USA-Gondola 1910 Squaw Valley Rd Olympic Valley CA   530-583-5585 (888 SNOW 3-2-1)
http://www.squaw.com
This is a summer only attraction. Dogs are allowed in the Gondola/Cable Car, but make sure your best friend is not claustrophobic. You can take the cable car from the parking lot (6,200 ft elevation) to High Camp (8,200 ft elevation). Once at the top, your well-behaved leashed pooch is welcome inside the lobby and the gift shop. Want some exercise? From High Camp, hike down the mountain along the ski path. Want a more strenuous hike? Try hiking up to High Camp. Squaw Valley is located off Hwy 89 on the northwest shore of Lake Tahoe. Dogs are not allowed on the cable car on the 4th of July weekend because of the crowds and fireworks. Squaw Valley does have special events during the summer, like Full Moon Hikes and Stargazing at High Camp. Dogs are welcome at both events.

The Village At Squaw Valley

TOP 200 PLACE The Village At Squaw Valley Squaw Valley Olympic Valley CA   530-584-6267
http://www.thevillageatsquaw.com
This European style village is very dog-friendly. You can ride the Gondola in the summer with your dog, take in a pet boutique store Tails by the Lake, enjoy numerous outdoor restaurants with your pup and browse the various stores with your leashed dog. There is a miniature golf course sprinkled throughout the walkways where kids and adults can play mini-golf with your dog along for the fun. And throughout the summer there are events such as music festivals and outdoor movies on a large screen where you and your dog are welcome for most events. Check out their website at http://www.thevillageatsquaw.com for more information and event schedules. The village is located at Squaw Valley USA just off Highway 89 between Tahoe City and Truckee in the north Tahoe area.

Tahoe Keys Boat Rentals 2435 Venice Drive E. South Lake Tahoe CA 530-544-8888
Rent a boat and cruise around on beautiful Lake Tahoe with your pup. Dogs are allowed as long as you clean up any 'accidents' your pup may do on the boat. Boat rentals can be seasonal, so please call ahead. It's located in Tahoe Keys. To get there from Hwy 89 north, take Hwy 50 east. Turn left onto Tahoe Keys Blvd and then right at Venice Drive East. Park at the end of Venice Drive and follow the signs to the rental office.

Tahoe Sport Fishing 900 Ski Run Boulevard South Lake Tahoe CA 530-541-5448
http://www.tahoesportfishing.com
This company offers sport fishing charters in the morning or afternoon and your pooch can go with you. Travel from the south shore up to the north shore of Lake Tahoe and back. They have six fishing boats ranging from 30 to 45 foot boats. They will clean and bag the fish (trout) you catch. They can even suggest local restaurants that

will cook your fresh catch for you. Call ahead to make a reservation. Rates for the morning charter are $80 per person and for the afternoon charter are $70 per person.

Tahoe Keys Boat Rentals

TOP 200 PLACE **Borges Sleigh and Carriage Rides** P.O. Box 5905 Stateline NV 775-588-2953
http://www.sleighride.com/
Take your pooch on a carriage or sleigh ride in Lake Tahoe. The carriage rides start in the casino area between Harveys and Horizon, and in front of Embassy Suites. The sleigh rides begin in the field next to Caesars Tahoe (on the corner of hwy 50 and Lake Parkway). The carriages and sleighs are pulled by their 2000 pound Blond Belgium horses or one of their rare American- Russian Baskhir Curlies which have been featured in Pasadena's Tournament of Rose Parade over the past few years. Carriage rides open noon until sunset daily, weather permitting. Prices are $15 per adult $7.50 per child under 11. Sleigh rides are given during the winter. Sleigh rides are open 10:00am to sunset (about 4:45pm). Sleigh rides are $15 per Adult $7.50 per child under 11.
Reel Deal Sport Fishing & Lake Tours P.O. Box 7724 Tahoe City CA 530-581-0924
This dog-friendly fishing charter runs year-round. After your fishing trip, they will clean the fish for you. They also offer lake tours during the summer months. Rates are $75 per person during the winter and $80 per person during the summer. Dogs are allowed on both the fishing tour and the lake tours.
Truckee River Raft Rentals 185 River Road Tahoe City CA 530-581-0123
http://www.truckeeriverraft.com
Your pooch is welcome to join you on a self-guided river rafting adventure. They just ask that your dog doesn't keep going in and out of the raft constantly because their nails can damage the raft. Enjoy a 2-3 hour leisurely, self guided, 5-mile float on the Truckee River from Tahoe City to the River Ranch Bar, Restaurant & Hotel. From there you can catch a free shuttle bus back to your car any time until 6 p.m. daily.

Cross Country Ski Resorts

TOP 200 PLACE **Hope Valley Cross Country Ski Center** 14255 Hwy 88 Hope Valley CA 530-694-2203 (800-423-9949)
This resort is located 30 minutes south of South Lake Tahoe. You can rent cross-country skis at the at the ski center which is located at the dog-friendly Sorensen's Resort. After renting the skis, you can either take your dog on some advanced uphill trails next to the rental center or drive about a mile down the road for some easier trails. The trails are located in the Toiyabe National Forest and are not groomed. The Burnside Lake Trail is a flat, 14 mile cross-country loop trail around the lake. A smaller loop, about 4-5 miles, can be found at the Sawmill Trail. The rental center will be able to provide directions and/or maps.
Taylor Creek/Fallen Leaf-XCountry Ski off Highway 89 South Lake Tahoe CA
The Taylor Creek/Fallen Leaf area provides the newcomer to cross-country skiing an opportunity to enjoy winter

adventure. Developed for the beginner, this well marked series of trails allows skiers to explore an area of forest with the knowledge that other people are near and there is no avalanche danger. The terrain is mostly flat and provides an excellent day tour for the whole family. The developed trails cover a large area and although heavily used, are not congested. The loop trail traverses through open meadows and aspen groves. To get there, take Highway 89 north from South Lake Tahoe approximately 3-1/2 miles to the Taylor Creek Sno-Park. Snowmobiles are not allowed. You'll need to bring your own cross-country skis.

Blackwood Canyon Rd-XCountry Ski off Highway 89 Tahoe City CA
Picturesque scenery can be seen along this unmarked road winding through Blackwood Canyon. Follow the road to an obvious junction and stay to the right. This path will lead you to a beautiful meadow where snowmobiles are not allowed. For a longer, more strenuous outing, continue upward to Barker Pass. Snowmobiles are allowed on this part of the trail. Take Highway 89 three miles south of Tahoe City to Blackwood Canyon Road, across from Kaspian Picnic Area. Continue to the Blackwood Canyon Sno-Park. You'll need to bring your own cross-country skis.

Page Meadow-XCountry Ski & Snowshoeing off Highway 89 Tahoe City CA
Try this pleasant ski or snowshoeing trip through a meadow surrounded by a scenic forest. Here are directions from the Lake Tahoe Basin Management Unit: From Highway 89, two miles south of Tahoe City, turn on Fountain Ave. just north of William Kent Campground. Turn right on Pine Ave., left on Tahoe Park Heights Dr., right on Big Pine Dr. and left on Silvertip. Park along the street where the snowplowing ends. Parking is extremely limited. Ski down the road to the meadow. There are no designated trails. Snowmobiles are not allowed. You'll need to bring your own skis or snowshoes.

TOP 200 PLACE **Tahoe Cross Country Ski Area** Country Club Drive Tahoe City CA 530-583-5475
http://www.tahoexc.org
This ski resort offers two groomed dog trails for people who want to cross country ski with their pooch. While dogs must be leashed at the trailhead and the parking lot, they can be off-leash under direct voice control on the trails. They welcome dogs on about 5 miles of groomed trails, including beginner and intermediate terrain. The dog-friendly trails are the BlueTrail and the Special Green Trail. They do not allow skijoring on either trail. The dog trails are open on Monday through Friday from 8:30am to 5pm, and on weekends and holidays from 3pm to 5pm. Dog passes are $3.00 per dog per day with a two dog per party maximum. Complimentary poop bags are provided.

Stores

Bone Jour-Gift Store 521 North Lake Blvd. Tahoe City CA 530-581-2304
http://www.bone-jour.com
Dogs are welcome inside this specialty gift store for dogs, cats and people. They also have a selection of dog treats and toys. It is on the second story near Fiamma Restaurant. Bone Jour is located in Tahoe City on Hwy 28 which is on the northwest shore of Lake Tahoe.

Beaches

Coon Street Beach Coon Street Kings Beach CA
Located at the end of Coon Street, on the east side of Kings Beach is a small but popular dog beach. There are also picnic tables, barbecues and restrooms at this beach.

Kiva Beach Hwy 89 South Lake Tahoe CA 530-573-2600
This small but lovely beach is a perfect place for your pup to take a dip in Lake Tahoe. Dogs must be on leash. To get there from the intersection of Hwys 89 and 50, take Hwy 89 north approx 2-3 miles to the entrance on your right. Follow the road and towards the end, bear left to the parking lot. Then follow the path to the beach.

Pebble Beach/Dog Beach Hwy 89 Tahoe City CA
This beach is not officially called "pebble beach" but it is an accurate description. No sand at this beach, but your water-loving dog won't mind. The water is crisp and clear and perfect for a little swimming. It's not a large area, but it is very popular with many dogs. There is also a paved bike trail that is parallel to the beach. There was no official name posted for this beach, but it's located about 1-2 miles south of Tahoe City on Hwy 89. From Tahoe City, the beach and parking will be on your left. Dogs should be on leash on the beach.

TOP 200 PLACE **North Beach at Zephyr Cove Resort** 460 Highway 50 Zephyr Cove NV 775-588-6644
Dogs are not allowed at the main beach at the Zephyr Cove Resort. They are allowed on leash, however, at the north beach at the resort. There is a $5.00 parking fee for day use. When you enter Zephyr Cover Resort head to the right (North) to the last parking area and walk the few hundred feet to the beach. The North Beach is located just into the National Forest. There usually are cleanup bags on the walkway to the beach but bring your own in case they run out. This is a nice beach that is used by a lot of people in the summer. The cabins at Zephyr Cove Resort also allow dogs.

North Beach at Zephyr Cove Resort

.

Parks

Lake Tahoe State Park/Spooner Lake Hwy 28 Glenbrook NV   775-831-0494
http://www.state.nv.us/stparks/lt.htm
This hiking trail is known as the world famous "Flume Trail". This is one of the most beautiful places in the world to mountain bike. But as a hiker, you'll hardly notice the bicyclists because this trail is so long and a good portion of the path consists of nice wide fire trails. It starts at Spooner Lake and the entire loop of the Flume Trail is about 25 miles which can satisfy even the most avid hiker. For a shorter hike, try the trail that loops around Spooner Lake. For a longer 10-12 mile out and back hike, start at Spooner Lake and hike up to Marlette Lake. Although there is a rise in elevation, it's not a rock climbing path as most of this is a fire road trail. Even if you are used to hiking 10 miles, don't forget about the altitude which will make you tired quicker. Also, do not forget to bring enough water and food. To get to the start of the trail, from South Lake Tahoe, take Hwy 50 towards Nevada (north). Then turn left onto Hwy 28. Follow the signs to the Lake Tahoe State Park and Spooner Lake. Parking for Spooner Lake is on the right. There is a parking fee of approx. $5-7. This includes an extra fee for the pup - but well worth it. From South Lake Tahoe, it's about a 25-30 minute drive to Spooner Lake. Dogs must be leashed in the park.

North Tahoe Regional Park National Avenue Kings Beach CA
In the summer this park is used for hiking and during the winter, it's used by cross-country skiers. There are about 3-4 miles of wooded trails at this park. Want to go for a longer hike? There is a National Forest that borders up to this regional park and dogs are allowed on those trails as well. To get there, take Hwy 28 by Kings Beach to Gun Club Road (north). Turn left on Donner Road and then right on National Avenue. There is a large parking lot at the end. Dogs must be on a leash in the park.

Squaw Valley USA 1960 Squaw Valley Rd Olympic Valley CA   530-583-6985 (888 SNOW 3-2-1)
http://www.squaw.com
In the summer (non-snow season) you and your pup can hike on the trails at this ski resort. Both of you will feel very welcome at Squaw. You can take your dog into the lobby to purchase the tickets for the dog-friendly Cable Car ride and/or snacks. As for the trails, there are many miles of hiking trails. One of the main hikes is from High Camp to the main parking lot or visa versa. It's the trail designed for night skiing (follow the light posts). During the summer, Squaw Valley has several dog-friendly events like the Star Gazing and Full Moon Hikes where dogs are welcome. Dogs must be leashed at all times.

Cove East Venice Drive East South Lake Tahoe CA
This short but nice path is located near the boat rentals and Tahoe Keys Resort. It's approximately 1-2 miles and will give your pup a chance to take care of business before hopping on board your rental boat. To get there from Hwy 89 north, take Hwy 50 east. Turn left onto Tahoe Keys Blvd and then right at Venice Drive East. Dogs must

be leashed.

Desolation Wilderness Fall Leaf Lake Road South Lake Tahoe CA 530-644-2349
http://www.fs.fed.us/r5/eldorado/
This wilderness area is located in the Eldorado National Forest and has many access points. One of the trailheads is located at Fallen Leaf Lake. See our Fallen Leaf Lake listing in South Lake Tahoe for more details. Dogs need to be leashed and please clean up after them.

Eagle Falls Hwy 89 South Lake Tahoe CA
This beautiful moderate to strenuous hiking trail in the Desolation Wilderness starts at Hwy 89 and goes up to Eagle Lake. This trail is pretty popular because it's about a 1 mile hike from the road to the lake. If you want a longer hike, you can go another 4-5 miles where there are 3 other lakes. Dogs must be leashed. To get there from the intersection of Hwys 50 and 89, take Hwy 89 north and go approximately 8 miles. The Eagle Falls Picnic Area and parking are on the left. Day and Camping Wilderness Permits are required. Go here early because it is extremely popular and parking spots fill up fast. There is a minimal fee for parking. Dogs must be on leash on the trail.

Echo Lakes Trail off Johnson Pass Road South Lake Tahoe CA
See a variety of alpine lakes on this moderate rated trail. Take Highway 50 to Echo Summit and turn onto Johnson Pass Road. Stay left and the road will lead you to the parking area by Lower Echo Lake. For a short hike, go to the far end of Upper Echo Lake. A longer hike leads you to one of the many lakes further down the trail. Day hikers, pick up your permit at the self serve area just to the left of the Echo Lake Chalet. Dogs should always be on leash.

Fallen Leaf Lake Fallen Leaf Lake Rd off Hwy 89 South Lake Tahoe CA
There are some nice walking trails on the north shore of Fallen Leaf Lake and the surrounding areas. To get there from the intersection of Hwys 89 and 50, take Hwy 89 north approximately 2.5 to 3 miles to Fallen Leaf Lake Rd. Turn left and in about 1/2 mile there will be parking on the right. The Fallen Leaf Lake Trail begins here. For a longer hike, there are two other options. For the first option, instead of taking the trailhead on the right, take the trail on the left side of Fallen Leaf Lake Rd. This trail is also known as the Tahoe Mountain Bike Trail. Option number two is to take Fallen Leaf Lake Rd further to the south side of Fallen Leaf Lake. Park at the Glen Alpine trailhead which offers about 3-4 miles of trails (parking is across from Lily Lake). There is also a trail here that heads off to the Desolation Wilderness which has miles and miles of trails. Dogs should be leashed.

Truckee River Bike Path Hwy 89 Tahoe City CA
This paved path starts at Tahoe City and heads towards Squaw Valley, paralleling Highway 89. It's about 5 miles each way with spots for your water dog to take a dip in the Truckee River (just be careful of any quick moving currents.) To get there, the path starts near the intersection of Hwys 89 and 28 in Tahoe City. You can also join the path 1/2 - 1 mile out of town by heading north on Hwy 89 and then there are 1 or 2 parking areas on the left side which are adjacent to the path. Dogs must be on leash.

D. L. Bliss State Park Hwy 89/South Lake Tahoe Tahoma CA 530-525-7277 (800-444-7275)
Donated by the D. L. Bliss family in 1929, this park of 744 acres displays the grandeur of the mountain building processes of Mother Earth and offers visitors spectacular views of the surrounding area and deep into the lake. Dogs of all sizes are only allowed in developed areas, picnic grounds, and on paved roads. They are not allowed on the trails, beaches, or in the Vikingsholm area, and they must be inside a tent or vehicle from the hours of 10 pm to 6 am. Dogs must be under owners control at all times, be on no more than a 6 foot leash, and be cleaned up after.

Emerald Bay State Park Hwy 89/South Lake Tahoe Tahoma CA 530-541-3030 (800-444-7275)
A National Natural Landmark, this beautiful state park is rich in its natural beauty, history, and geology, and features Vikingsholm, one of the best examples of Scandinavian architecture in the western hemisphere. The park is also home to Lake Tahoe's only island, Fannette Island, and there are a variety of recreational opportunities to pursue. Dogs of all sizes are allowed in developed areas, picnic grounds, and on paved roads. They are not allowed on the trails, beaches, or in the Vikingsholm area, and they must be inside a tent or vehicle from the hours of 10 pm to 6 am. Dogs must be under owners control at all times, be on no more than a 6 foot leash, and be cleaned up after.

Commemorative Overland Emigrant Trail Alder Creek Road Truckee CA 530-587-3558
This 15 mile moderate rated trail is located in the Tahoe National Forest. While the trail is open from May to November, it is most heavily used in the spring. The trail is popular with both hikers and mountain bikers. Pets must be either leashed or off-leash but under direct voice control. To get there from Interstate 80, take the Highway 89 North exit and go 2.3 miles to Alder Creek Road. Turn left and go 3 miles. The trail starts on the south side of the road.

Donner Memorial State Park Highway 80 Truckee CA 530-582-7892
While dogs are not allowed at the China Cove Beach Area and the nature trail behind the museum, they are allowed on the rest of the trails at this park. Dogs are also allowed in the lake. Pets must be on leash at all times and please clean up after them. The park has campgrounds but they are undergoing renovation from 2003 to 2004. It is located off Highway 80 in Truckee.

Glacier Meadow Loop Trail Castle Peak Truckee CA 530-587-3558
This .5 mile easy loop trail is located in the Tahoe National Forest and is used for hiking only. It is a very popular trail from June to October. Pets must be either leashed or off-leash but under direct voice control. To get there from I-80, exit Castle Peak, on the south side of I-80, turn left. The trailhead is on the east side of the parking lot.

Sand Ridge Lake Trail Castle Peak Truckee CA 530-587-3558
This 6 miles one way moderate rated trail is located in the Tahoe National Forest. From June to October, it is heavily used for hiking and horseback riding. Pets must be either leashed or off-leash but under direct voice control. To get there from I-80, exit Castle Peak, on the south side of I-80, turn left. The trailhead is on the east side of the parking lot.
Summit Lake Trail Castle Peak Truckee CA 530-587-3558
This 2 mile easy rate trail is located in the Tahoe National Forest and is popular for hiking, mountain biking and horseback riding. The trail is most frequently used from June to October. Pets must be either leashed or off-leash but under direct voice control. To get there from Interstate 80, exit Castle Peak, on the south side of I-80, turn left. The trailhead is on the east side of the parking lot.

Outdoor Restaurants
Old Post Office Coffee Shop 5245 North Lake Blvd Carnelian Bay CA 530-546-3205
This restaurant is open for breakfast and lunch. They welcome well-behaved dogs at their outdoor seats. Dogs need to be leashed while sitting at the table with you.
Pisanos Pizza 5335 West Lake Blvd Homewood CA 530-525-6464
Enjoy pizza at one of the several outdoor tables. The restaurant (formerly West Side Pizza) is located off Hwy 89 in Homewood (between Tahoe City and Tahoma on the west shore of Lake Tahoe.)
Grog & Grist Market & Deli 800 Tahoe Blvd Incline Village NV 775-831-1123
They have a few tables and some benches outside where your dog is welcome.
T's Rotisserie 901 Tahoe Blvd Incline Village NV 775-831-2832
This restaurant serves rotisserie sandwiches and more. Your dog can sit with you at the outdoor tables.
Brockway Bakery 8710 North Lake Blvd Kings Beach CA 530-546-2431
Grab one of the several outdoor tables at this bakery and enjoy. It's located on Hwy 28 in Kings Beach.
Char-Pit 8732 N Lake Blvd Kings Beach CA 530-546-3171
http://www.char-pit.com
This restaurant serves barbecue. Dogs are allowed at the outdoor tables. The restaurant has outdoor tables only in the summer.
Straddles 9980 N Lake Blvd Kings Beach CA 530-546-3774
This restaurant offers outdoor seating in the summer. Your pet is welcome to join you at the outdoor tables where they will give your canine companion his own water bowl and a doggy biscuit. Dogs must be well behaved, under owner's control, and leashed at all times.
Auld Dubliner The Village at Squaw Valley Olympic Valley CA 530-584-6041
http://www.aulddubliner.com
Auld Dubliner is an authentic Irish Pub was actually built in Ireland, dismantled, shipped to Olympic Valley and reassembled. Enjoy Irish cuisine at the outdoor patio with your dog.
Balboa Cafe The Village at Squaw Valley Olympic Valley CA 530-583-5850
http://www.balboacafe.com
This eleguent American Bistro has a nice outside patio where you and your dog may dine.
Mamasake Sushi The Village at Squaw Valley Olympic Valley CA 530-584-0110
http://www.mamasake.com
This Japanese restaurant in the Village at Squaw Valley has a dog-friendly patio.
Starbucks Coffee The Village at Squaw Valley Olympic Valley CA 530-584-6120
This Starbucks is located near the Gondola in the Village at Squaw Valley and has outdoor seats for you and your dog. You will need to go inside to get the food without your dog.
Big Daddy's Burgers 3490 Lake Tahoe Blvd/Hwy 50 South Lake Tahoe CA 530-541-3465
This eatery specializes in hamburgers and other American type fare. During the summer season they offer outside dining. Your pet is welcome to join you at the outdoor tables. Dogs must be well behaved, under owner's control, and leashed at all times.
Colombo's Burgers A-Go-Go 841 US Hwy 89 Emerald Bay Rd South Lake Tahoe CA 530-541-4646
Dogs are welcome at the outdoor tables.
Izzy's Burger Spa 2591 Highway 50 South Lake Tahoe CA 530-544-5030
Dogs are welcome at the outdoor tables.
Meyer's Downtown Cafe 3200 Highway 50 South Lake Tahoe CA 530-573-0228
This dog-friendly cafe is off Highway 50 in Meyers, before entering South Lake Tahoe.
Nikkis Restaurant 3469 Lake Tahoe Blvd South Lake Tahoe CA 530-541-3354
Dogs are allowed at the outdoor tables. This cafe is located near the shoreline of Lake Tahoe.
Quiznos Sub 1001 Heavenly Village South Lake Tahoe CA 530-544-9600
This specialty sub shop offers outdoor seasonal dining. Your pet is welcome to join you at the outdoor tables. Dogs must be well behaved, under owner's control, and leashed at all times.
Rude Brothers Bakery and Coffee House 3117 Harrison Ave #B South Lake Tahoe CA 530-541-8195
Dogs are allowed at the outdoor tables.
Shoreline Cafe 3310 Lake Tahoe Blvd/Hwy 50 South Lake Tahoe CA 530-541-7858
This eatery serves all American foods, and during the summer they offer outdoor seating. Your pet is welcome to

join you at the outdoor tables. Dogs must be well behaved, under owner's control, and leashed at all times.

Sno-Flake Drive In 3059 Harrison South Lake Tahoe CA   530-544-6377

This is a great place for a burger or chicken sandwich. You can walk up to the outside order window and then sit on the small patio and enjoy your lunch or dinner. To get there from the intersection of Hwys 50 and 89, take Hwy 50 south. It will be on your right at Modesto Ave.

Sprouts Health Foods 3125 Harrison Avenue South Lake Tahoe CA   530-541-6969

Dogs are allowed at the outdoor tables when weather permits.

The Burger Lounge 717 Emerald Bay Rd South Lake Tahoe CA   530-542-4060

Leashed dogs are welcome to sit at the outdoor tables.

Black Bear Tavern 2255 West Lake Blvd. Tahoe City CA   530-583-8626

http://www.blackbearlaketahoe.com

Dogs are allowed at the outdoor tables at this upscale restaurant. The restaurant is located on Hwy 89, south of downtown Tahoe City.

Bridgetender Tavern and Grill 65 West Lake Blvd Tahoe City CA   530-583-3342

This local favorite serves a lunch and dinner menu of burgers, sandwiches, ribs, homemade soups and salads, and offers a full bar in a cozy log cabin setting. There is seasonal outdoor dining with service, and your pet is welcome to join you at the front outdoor tables, but not on the back patio. Dogs must be well behaved, under owner's control, and leashed at all times.

Fiamma 521 North Lake Blvd Tahoe City CA   530-581-1416

This Italian restaurant has a few seats outside where dogs are welcome. Arrive early to get one of the tables.

Front Street Station Pizza 205 River Road Tahoe City CA   530-583-3770

Dogs are allowed at the outdoor seats.

Rosie's Cafe 571 North Lake Blvd Tahoe City CA   530-583-8504

Enjoy a delicious breakfast, lunch or dinner on the porch at this cafe. It's located in Tahoe City off Hwy 28 which is located on the northwest shore of Lake Tahoe.

Syd's Bagelery & Expresso 550 N Lake Blvd Tahoe City CA   530-583-2666

Your dog is welcome at the outdoor picnic tables.

Tahoe House Bakery and Gourmet Store 625 W Lake Blvd Tahoe City CA   530-583-1377

http://www.tahoe-house.com/

They offer fresh baked breads, pastries, coffee drinks, cookies, European style tortes, deli lunches fully prepared meals to go with gourmet chesses, meats and more. Dogs are allowed at the outdoor tables.

The Blue Agave 425 N Lake Blvd Tahoe City CA   530-583-8113

This Mexican eatery has seasonal outdoor seating and service. Dogs are allowed at the outer tables. They must be well behaved, under owner's control, and leashed at all times.

West End Bistro 15628 Donner Pass Road Truckee CA   530-550-7770

http://www.westendcatering.com

This seasonal restaurant draws their culinary inspiration from many cultures. Dogs are allowed at the patio dining area, but not on the outer deck. Dogs must be attended to at all times, well behaved, and leashed.

Events

The Bark Festival The Village at Squaw Valley Olympic Valley CA   530-583-WAGS (9247)

http://tailsbythebay.stores.yahoo.net/

This unique arts and wine festival for pets is an annual September event. Activities consist of live music, fine wines and foods, animal themed art, pet contests, fashion shows, massages and more. The event is held in the Village at Squaw Valley and is brought to you by Tails by the Lake. Friendly dogs of all sizes are welcome. They must be leashed, cleaned up after, and have currant vaccinations and tags.

Pet Sitters

All Tuckered Out Pet Sitting Call To Arrange South Lake Tahoe CA   530-318-8749

http://www.alltuckeredoutpetsitting.com

This South Lake Tahoe pet sitter will come to your hotel, campground or other rental and watch your dog when you are not able to take your pup with you. Call to make reservations.

K.Y.P.S.A.H. Pet Services 10718 Manchester Drive Truckee CA   530-582-1671

http://www.kypsah.com

K.Y.P.S.A.H. is available for doggie day care services and overnight boarding in Truckee.

Zephyr Feed & Boarding 396 Dorla Court Zephyr Cove NV   775-588-3907

mailto:zephyrfeed@aol.com

Zephyr Feed and Boarding offers daycare & overnight boarding while you are in the Lake Tahoe region. Doggie daycare is available by the hour or day, so you can tour around the sites and know your pet is having a day of fun. The kennel is climate controlled inside, full walls for stress free boarding, veterinarian on call, an outside area for potty time, inside exercise runs, and a large playroom.

Vets and Kennels

Carson Tahoe Veterinary Hospital 3389 S. Carson Street Carson City NV   775-883-8238
Weekdays 7:30 am - 6 pm. Emergencys will be seen 24 hours with an additional $60 emergency fee.
Avalanche Natural Health Office for Pets and Kennel 964 Rubicon Trail South Lake Tahoe CA   530-541-3551
This veterinary hospital specializes in alternative medicine. If you need some doggy day care, they also offer a kennel that is open all year, including Sundays. They are very flexible with all aspects of the boarding kennel including hours and accommodating special needs pets usually with no extra charge.

Lone Pine

Accommodations
Alabama Hills Inn 1920 South Main Lone Pine CA   760-876-8700 (800-800-6468)
http://www.ca-biz.com/alabamahillsinn/
There is a $5 per day pet fee. There is a large grass area near the hotel to walk your dog. The area around the hotel is where many Western films have been made.
Best Western Frontier Motel 1008 S Main St Lone Pine CA   760-876-5571 (800-780-7234)
Dogs of all sizes are allowed. There are no additional pet fees. Smoking and non-smoking are available for pet rooms.

Campgrounds and RV Parks
Lone Pine Campground Whitney Portal Road Lone Pine CA   760-876-6200 (877-444-6777)
This 43 site campground is located in the Inyo National Forest at an elevation of 6,000 feet. Water is available at the site. There is a $12 fee per campsite. Pets must be leashed while in the campground. Please clean up after your pets. Dogs may not be left unattended. Dogs may be off lead on the trails if they are under good voice control. The camping and tent areas also allow dogs. There is a dog walk area at the campground. There are no electric or water hookups at the campgrounds.
Tuttle Creek Campground Horseshoe Meadows Road Lone Pine CA   760-876-6200
This campground is located at 5,120 feet and is shadowed by some of the most impressive peaks in the Sierra Nevada Mountain Range. The camp is located in an open desert setting with a view of Alabama Hills and Mt. Whitney. There are 85 tent and RV sites, but no potable water. Amenities include 9 pit toilets, stream water, barbecues, fire rings and picnic tables. All sites are based on a first-come, first-served basis. This campground is managed by the BLM (Bureau of Land Management). Pets on leash are allowed and please clean up after them. Dogs may not be left unattended. They may be off lead on the trials if they are under good voice control. To get there go 3.5 miles west of Lone Pine on Whitney Portal Road. Then go 1.5 miles south on Horseshoe Meadows Road and follow the sign to the campsite. This campground is closed during the off-season. The camping and tent areas also allow dogs. There is a dog walk area at the campground. There are no electric or water hookups at the campgrounds.
Whitney Portal Campground, Inyo National Forest Whitney Portal Road Lone Pine CA   760-876-6200 (877-444-6777)
This camp area at 8,000 feet, is located in a national forest, and offers a wide variety of both land and water recreational opportunities. Dogs of all sizes are allowed at no additional fee. Dogs may not be left unattended, and they must be on no more than a 6 foot leash, and cleaned up after. Dogs are allowed on the trails up to the trail camp. This campground is closed during the off-season. The camping and tent areas also allow dogs. There is a dog walk area at the campground. There are no electric or water hookups at the campgrounds.
Wildrose Campground On Corner of Hwy 395 and Hwy 136 Lone Pine CA   760-786-3200
Wildrose is a free campground at 4,100 feet in the Panamint Mountains and is not accessible to vehicles over 25 feet in length. Dogs of all sizes are allowed. There are no additional pet fees. Dogs may not be left unattended outside, and they must be leashed and cleaned up after. Dogs are not allowed off the main road or along side the main road if being walked. Dogs must remain by the vehicle otherwise, and they are not allowed on the trails. The camping and tent areas also allow dogs. There is a dog walk area at the campground. There are no electric or water hookups at the campgrounds.

Attractions
Alabama Hills Movie Road Lone Pine CA   760-876-6222
http://www.lonepinechamber.org
Located west of the town of Long Pine, there is an area called Alabama Hills which features unusual rock formations. Since 1920 this area has been a favorite location for television and movie filmmakers. Over 250 movies, TV episodes and commercials have been filmed in this area. Movies like Gunga Din and Maverick were filmed here. A partial list of stars who have been filmed at Alabama Hills includes Hopalong Cassidy, Roy Rogers, Humphrey Bogard, Susan Hayward, Spencer Tracy, Natalie Wood, Clint Eastwood, Kirk Douglas, John

Wayne, Steve McQueen, Shelly Winters, Luci and Desi Arnaz, Willie Nelson and Mel Gibson. You can take yourself and your pooch on a self-guided auto tour of this area. Go 2.5 miles west of Lone Pine and turn north at Movie Road. At the corner of Movie and Whitney Portal Roads, you will find the Movie Plaque which commemorates the many movies filmed in the nearby hills. Go north .25 miles to the Roy Rogers Movie Flats, an area were hundreds of westerns and other movies were filmed. Go north .25 miles and turn east to Lone Ranger Canyon. This spot is another popular filming area and was where some scenes of the Lone Ranger was filmed. Go 2.25 miles to the southern loop to find Moonscape Views. Turn south on Horseshoe Meadow Road and go 1 mile to Gunga Din Canyon. The classic 1939 movie used locations in the first canyon to the east for filming. Go south for 3 miles to the Tuttle Creek Campground. It used for camping and as a fishing spot. Go 2 miles southeast to view The Needles Formation. It is a sharp spine of rocks north of the housing area. Then take Tuttle Creek Canyon Road down the canyon and back to Lone Pine. Pets on leash are allowed to walk around the view points. Please clean up after your pets. For more information, stop by the InterAgency Visitor Center at the intersection of Highways 395 and 136 in Lone Pine. The center is open daily from 8am to 4:30pm.

Parks
Mt. Whitney Trail Whitney Portal Road Lone Pine CA 760-876-6200
http://www.fs.fed.us/r5/inyo
Dogs are allowed on the first eight miles of the main Mt. Whitney Trail in the Inyo National Forest, but not on the last three miles of the trail leading to the summit which is located in Sequoia/Kings Canyon National Park. Dogs must be leashed on this trail and please clean up after them. The national forest advises that people should be aware of the high elevation affect on dogs. There is no shade or cover available and the heat of the sun at higher elevations can be intense for pets. The trail is located 13 miles west of Lone Pine on Whitney Portal Road.

Long Barn

Campgrounds and RV Parks
Fraser Flat Campground Fraser Flat Road Long Barn CA 209-586-3234
At an elevation of 4,800 feet this campground offers forested sites on the South Fork of the Stanislaus River. There are 34 tent and RV sites with a maximum RV length of 22 feet. There are no hookups. Amenities include piped water, vault toilets, picnic tables and grills. All sites are on a first-come, first-served basis. Pets on leash are allowed and please clean up after them. This campground is located in the Stanislaus National Forest. To get there, drive 3 miles north of Highway 108 at Spring Gap turnoff (Fraser Flat Road). This rv park is closed during the off-season. The camping and tent areas also allow dogs. There is a dog walk area at the campground. There are no electric or water hookups at the campgrounds.

Parks
Sugar Pine Railroad Grade Trail Fraser Flat Road Long Barn CA 209-586-3234
This 3 mile easy rated trail parallels the South Fork of the Stanislaus River and overlays the historic Sugar Pine Railroad System. Pets on leash are allowed and please clean up after them. This trail is located in the Stanislaus National Forest. One access point to this trail is the Fraser Flat Campground. To get there, drive 3 miles north of Highway 108 at Spring Gap turnoff (Fraser Flat Road).

Mammoth Lakes

Accommodations
Convict Lake Resort HCR - 79, Box 204 Mammoth Lakes CA 760-934-3800 (800-992-2260)
http://www.convictlakeresort.com/
Since 1929, this scenic resort area has been a popular get-a-way offering a wide range of services, amenities, land and water recreational opportunities, and a full line-up of planned activities throughout the year. Their on site restaurant features a French country cuisine with an extensive wine list, and indoor and outdoor dining service (weather permitting) where your pet may join you at the outside tables. Some of the resort amenities include a spacious full-service cocktail lounge, barbecue's, fully equipped kitchens, TV with HBO, a multi-functional general store, boat rentals, and a campground (no pet fee). Well mannered dogs of all sizes are allowed for an additional $20 per pet per stay. Dogs must be on no more than a 6 foot leash, and cleaned up after at all times.
Crystal Crag Lodge P.O. Box 88 Mammoth Lakes CA 760-934-2436
This lodge offers cabins at 9,000 feet elevation on beautiful Lake Mary in the dog-friendly Inyo National Forest. Lake Mary is known as one of the best fishing spots in the Eastern Sierra, regularly producing trophy size trout.

You will find a number of other lakes, most of the best hiking trailheads, Lake Mary Store, and some of the best scenery that the Eastern Sierra has to offer within walking distance of your cabin. The cabins, all non-smoking, have full kitchens and baths. Most cabins have living rooms with fireplaces. The lodge also offers 14-foot aluminum boats with or without a motor. Dogs are allowed on the boats as well. Please note that the lodge is only open during the summer season, from about late May to early October. Dogs are allowed for an additional $8 per day charge. Pets must never be left unattended in the cabins.

Mammoth Creek Inn 663 Old Mammoth Road Mammoth Lakes CA 760-934-6162
There is a $25 per day per pet fee. Well-behaved pets are welcome. Just make sure you mention you will be bringing a pet as they have specific "pet-friendly" rooms. Pets may not be left alone in the rooms unless they are trained to stay in a crate. This inn is located within walking distance to grocery and boutique shopping, restaurants, cross country skiing, snowshoe area and Mammoth's biking and running path. Amenities include in room high speed Internet access, limited in room dining, indoor dry sauna, hot tub, and a game, movie and book library.

Motel 6 - Mammoth Lakes 3372 Main Street Mammoth Lakes CA 760-934-6660 (800-466-8356)
One well-behaved family pet per room. Guest must notify front desk upon arrival. Guest is liable for any damages. In consideration of all guests, pets must never be left unattended in the guest rooms.

Shilo Inn 2963 Main Street Mammoth Lakes CA 760-934-4500 (800-222-2244)
Your dog is welcome here. Each room in this motel is a mini-suite complete with microwaves, refrigerators and more. This motel is located across the street from the Visitors Center which has trails that border up to the Shady Rest Park where there are many hiking trails. If you are there in the winter, try some cross-country skiing with your pup. The cross country ski rental store is very close to this motel (see Attractions.) There is a $10 per day additional pet fee per pet.

Sierra Lodge 3540 Main Street Mammoth Lakes CA 760-934-8881
There is a $10 per night pet fee. Amenities include continental breakfast and kitchenettes in the rooms. All rooms are non-smoking.

Swiss Chalet 3776 Viewpoint Road Mammoth Lakes CA 760-934-2403
This inn offers a few pet rooms. All rooms are non-smoking. Dogs must be one year or older and only one pet per room. Pets cannot be left unattended in the room. There is a $5 per day pet fee.

Tamarack Lodge P.O. Box 69/Lake Mary Road Mammoth Lakes CA 760-934-2442 (800-MAMMOTH (626-6684))
http://www.tamaracklodge.com/
This historic lodge has been in operation since 1924 with their cabins and lodge rooms ranging from simple and rustic to deluxe accommodations. On site is the Lakefront Restaurant specializing in blending classic French cuisine with regional influences of the eastern Sierra. There is outdoor dining service when weather permits, and your pooch is allowed to join you on the outer deck. Watercraft rentals, fishing, easy to strenuous hiking trails, and other recreational pursuits are available throughout the summer. Their cabins have private bathrooms, porches, and telephones. Dogs are allowed in the summer and in the cabins only. There is an additional fee of $30 per night per pet. Dogs must be well behaved, under owner's control at all times, and be leashed and cleaned up after.

Campgrounds and RV Parks

Convict Lake Campground HCR - 79, Box 204 Mammoth Lakes CA 760-924-5771 (877-444-6777)
http://www.convictlakeresort.com/
Located at the Convict Lake Resort, this camp area offers 88 sites; 25 of which can be reserved. Some of the amenities include fire rings, water, flush toilets, a dump, and showers. Dogs of all sizes are allowed for no additional fee. Dogs must be on no more than a 6 foot leash, and be cleaned up after. They are allowed on the trails. This RV park is closed during the off-season. The camping and tent areas also allow dogs. There is a dog walk area at the campground. There are no electric or water hookups at the campgrounds.

Lake George Campground Lake George Road Mammoth Lakes CA 760-924-5500
This 16 site campground is located in the Inyo National Forest at an elevation of 9,000 feet. It is located near several trails. The fee for a campsite is $14. The sites are available on a first-come, first-served basis. Pets must be leashed while in the campground and please clean up after them. Dogs may be off lead on the trails only if they are under voice control. To get there from the intersection of Main Street and Hwy 203, take Lake Mary Road to the left. Go past Twin Lakes. You'll see a road that goes off to the left (Lake Mary Loop Rd). Go past this road, you'll want the other end of the loop. When you come to another road that also says Lake Mary Loop Rd, turn left. Then turn right onto Lake George Road and follow it to the campground. This campground is closed during the off-season. The camping and tent areas also allow dogs. There is a dog walk area at the campground. There are no electric or water hookups at the campgrounds.

Lake Mary Campground Lake Mary Loop Road Mammoth Lakes CA 760-924-5500
This 48 site campground is located in the Inyo National Forest at an elevation of 8,900 feet. It is located near several trails. The fee for a campsite is $14. The sites are available on a first-come, first-served basis. Pets must be leashed while in the campground and please clean up after them. Dogs may be off lead on the trails if they will respond to voice command. From Hwy 203, take Lake Mary Road to the left. Pass Twin Lakes and then you'll come to Lake Mary. Turn left onto Lake Mary Loop Road. This campground is closed during the off-season.

The camping and tent areas also allow dogs. There is a dog walk area at the campground. There are no electric or water hookups at the campgrounds.

Mammoth Mountain RV Park P.O. Box 288/Hwy 203 Mammoth Lakes CA 760-934-3822 (800-582-4603)
This RV park offers over 160 tent sites and RV sites with full hookups. Amenities include dump stations, restrooms with hot showers, laundry rooms, picnic tables, indoor heated swimming pool and spa, children's play area and RV supplies. Site rates range from $21 to $34 per night. Rates are subject to change. Pets are welcome but need to be leashed at all times and cannot be left unattended outside, and left inside only if they will be physically comfortable and quiet. There is a $3 per night per pet fee. They are located within walking distance of shops and restaurants. The RV park is open year round. There are some breed restrictions. The camping and tent areas also allow dogs. There is a dog walk area at the campground.

New Shady Rest Campground Sawmill Cutoff Road Mammoth Lakes CA 760-924-5500 (877-444-6777)
This 94 site campground is located in the Inyo National Forest at an elevation of 7,800 feet. It is located near several trails. Amenities include water, flush toilets, fire ring, showers, interpretive programs, and a visitors' center. The fee for a campsite is $13. The sites are available on a first-come, first-served basis. Pets must be leashed while in the campground and please clean up after them. This campground is closed during the off-season. The camping and tent areas also allow dogs. There is a dog walk area at the campground. There are no electric or water hookups at the campgrounds.

Red Meadows Campground Off Hwy 203 Mammoth Lakes CA 760-924-5500
This 56 site campground is located in the Inyo National Forest at an elevation of 7,600 feet. It is near the dog-friendly Devil's Postpile National Monument and hiking trails including the John Muir Trail. Amenities include water. The fee for a campsite is $15, and sites are available on a first-come, first-served basis. Pets must be leashed while in the campground and please clean up after them. From Highway 395, drive 10 miles west on Highway 203 to Minaret Summit. Then drive about 7 miles on a paved, narrow mountain road. This campground is closed during the off-season. The camping and tent areas also allow dogs. There is a dog walk area at the campground. There are no electric or water hookups at the campgrounds.

Twin Lakes Campground, Inyo National Forest Lake Mary Road Mammoth Lakes CA 760-924-5500
This forest campground located at 8,600 feet offers great scenery amid a variety of recreational activities and pursuits. Dogs of all sizes are allowed. There are no additional pet fees. Dogs may not be left unattended, and they must be leashed and cleaned up after. Dogs are allowed on the trails unless otherwise marked. This campground is closed during the off-season. The camping and tent areas also allow dogs. There is a dog walk area at the campground. There are no electric or water hookups at the campgrounds.

Vacation Home Rentals

Villa De Los Pinos #3 3252 Chateau Rd Mammoth Lakes CA 760-722-5369
http://www.mammoth-lakes-condo.com
This is a year-round vacation rental townhouse-style condominium in Mammoth Lakes. The amenities include two downstairs bedrooms, two bathrooms, a large living room, dining room, and kitchen. The condo is fronted by a large deck overlooking the development courtyard (where dogs are allowed off-leash), swimming pool, and Jacuzzi building. All dogs are welcome. The $25 per visit pet fee helps with the cleaning.

Attractions

Hot Creek Geologic Site Hot Creek Hatchery Road Mammoth Lakes CA 760-924-5500
Considered a geologic wonder complete with hot springs, fumaroles, craters, and the ever-changing earth of the area, it is also a natural sanctuary for many kinds of birds and wildlife. Because of the high concentrations of chemicals in the water and the potential danger of scalding water, swimming is not recommended, and visitors must remain on walkways and boardwalks. There is a hatchery here, and long rearing ponds (called raceways) where visitors may view the fish. Dogs are allowed at the site, but are to be kept away from the water. Dogs must be on no more than a 6 foot leash, under owner's control at all times, and be cleaned up after.

TOP 200 PLACE **Mammoth Mountain-Gondola** #1 Minaret Road Mammoth Lakes CA
760-934-0745 (800-MAMMOTH)
http://www.mammothmountain.com/
Want some awesome views of Mammoth Mountain and the surrounding areas? During the summer, you and your dog can hop on the Gondola (Cable Car) ride. You'll climb about 2,000 feet to the top of the mountain. Once there, you can enjoy a nice 1 1/2 - 2 hour hike down or take the Gondola back down the mountain. Dogs should be leashed at all times.

Sierra Nevada Mountains - Please always call ahead to make sure that an establishment is still dog-friendly

Mammoth Mountain

Cross Country Ski Resorts

TOP 200 PLACE **Cross Country Skiing** Mammoth Visitor Center Mammoth Lakes CA
Want to cross country ski with your pup? Follow this plan: Rent some skis and boots at the Ski Renter (760-934-6560) located next to the Shell Gas Station on Hwy 203 (by Old Mammoth Rd). Walk or drive the skis a block or two over to the Mammoth Visitor Center / Inyo National Forest. There are several trails that start at the Visitor Center. From there I've been told you can join up to Shady Rest Park which offers more miles of cross country skiing trails (beginner trails - not too steep.) And of course, take your dog with you since this is a dog-friendly National Forest. Just listen carefully and watch out for any snowmobilers. Dogs should be leashed.

Stores

Mammoth Sporting Goods 425 Old Mammoth Road Mammoth Lakes CA 760-934-3239
http://www.mammothsportinggoods.com/
This sports shop specializes in skiing, biking, hiking, snowboarding, and fishing supplies and your well behaved dogs is welcome to join you in the store. Dogs must be friendly, under owner's control at all times and leashed.
Tailwaggers Dog Bakery & Boutique 452 Old Mammoth Rd Mammoth Lakes CA 760-924-3400
This dog bakery and boutique is the perfect place to find a gift for your pup and anyone who loves dogs.

Parks

Ansel Adams Wilderness off Highway 203 Mammoth Lakes CA 760-934-2289
http://www.fs.fed.us/r5/inyo
The wilderness can be accessed at many points, including the John Muir Trail. See our listing for this trail under the city of Mammoth Lakes. There are miles of on or off-leash hiking opportunities.
Devil's Postpile National Monument Minaret Rd. Mammoth Lakes CA 760-934-2289
http://www.nps.gov/depo
During the summer only, take a bus ride/shuttle to the Devil's Postpile National Monument with your pup. The shuttle is the only way to drive to this National Monument unless you have a camping permit or have a vehicle with 11 people or more. The shuttle begins at the Mammoth Mountain Inn off Hwy 203 and takes you and your dog on a scenic ride along the San Joaquin River to the National Monument. The travel time is about 45 minutes to Reds Meadow (past the Monument), but there are 10 stops along the way to get out and stretch or hike. Once at the Monument, there is a short 1/2 mile walk. The Monument is a series of basalt columns, 40 to 60 feet high, that resembles a giant pipe organ. It was made by hot lava that cooled and cracked 900,000 years ago. The John Muir Trail crosses the monument, so for a longer hike, join up with nearby trails that are in the dog-friendly Inyo National Forest. Dogs should be on a leash.
John Muir Trail off Highway 203 Mammoth Lakes CA 760-934-2289

http://www.fs.fed.us/r5/inyo
This trail crosses the dog-friendly Devil's Postpile National Monument. The John Muir Trail offers miles of hiking trails. Dogs must be on leash at the monument but can be off leash under direct voice control in the Inyo National Forest and Ansel Adams Wilderness. The trailhead is located near the ranger's station at the monument. To get there, you can drive directly to the monument and trailhead ONLY if you have a camping permit or a vehicle with 11 people or more. All day visitors must ride a shuttle bus from the Mammoth Mountain Ski Area at the end of Highway 203. Well-behaved leashed dogs are allowed on the bus. From Highway 395, drive 10 miles west on Highway 203 to Minaret Summit. Then drive 7 miles on a paved, narrow mountain road. Or take the shuttle bus at the end of Highway 203. The bus ride takes about 45 minutes to the monument with several stops along the way.

Lake George Lake George Rd. Mammoth Lakes CA
At Lake George, you can find the trailheads for the Crystal Lake and Mammoth Crest trails. You'll be hiking among the beautiful pine trees and snow covered peaks. The trails start at the north side of Lake George. The hike to Crystal Lake is about a 3 mile round trip. If you want a longer hike, you'll have the option on your way to Crystal Lake. The Mammoth Crest trail is the trail that branches to the right. The Mammoth trail is about a 6 mile round trip and it's a more strenuous trail. To get there from the intersection of Main Street and Hwy 203, take Lake Mary Road to the left. Go past Twin Lakes. You'll see a road that goes off to the left (Lake Mary Loop Rd.). Go past this road, you'll want the other end of the loop. When you come to another road that also says Lake Mary Loop Rd, turn left. Then turn right onto Lake George Rd. Follow this road almost to the end and you should see signs for the Crystal Lake Trail. Dogs should be leashed.

Lake Mary Lake Mary Loop Rd. Mammoth Lakes CA
Here's another lake and hiking trail to enjoy up in the high country. Lake Mary is known as one of the best fishing spots in the Eastern Sierra, regularly producing trophy size trout. After your water dog is done playing in the lake, head to the southeast side of the lake to go for a hike on the Emerald Lake Trail. The trail starts at the Cold Water trailhead next to the Cold Water campgrounds. Take the trail to the right towards Emerald Lake and Sky Meadows. The trail to Emerald Lake is about 1 1/2 miles round trip (out and back). If you continue on to Sky Meadows, then your hike is about 4 miles round trip. To get there from the intersection of Main Street and Hwy 203, take Lake Mary Road to the left. Pass Twin Lakes and then you'll come to Lake Mary. Turn left onto Lake Mary Loop Road and the trailhead is located on the southeast side of the lake. Dogs should be on a leash.

Mammoth Mountain Minaret Rd. Mammoth Lakes CA 760-934-2571 (800-MAMMOTH)
http://www.mammothmountain.com/
You can hike with your dog on "The" Mammoth Mountain in three ways. One way is to take the Gondola ride with your pup (summer only) up to the top of the mountain and then hike down. The second is to hike up the mountain from the parking lot by the Mammoth Mountain Inn and the Gondola. The third option is to start on the backside of the mountain and hike up and then of course down. For the third option, you can start at Twin Lakes (off Lake Mary Rd). The Dragon's Back Trail is on the west side of the lakes (by the campgrounds). Dogs must be leashed.

Shady Rest Park and Trail Sawmill Cutoff Rd. Mammoth Lakes CA 760-934-8983
This park serves as a multi-use recreation park. During the winter it's popular with cross country skiers - yes dogs are allowed. In the summer, you can go for a hike on the 5-6 miles of single track and fire road trails. It's also used by 4x4 off road vehicles too, so just be aware. To get there from the Mammoth Visitor's Center, take Hwy 203 towards town. The first street on your right will be Sawmill Cutoff Road. Turn right and Shady Rest Park is at the end of the road. There are restrooms at this park which can come in handy for the humans before starting out on the trails. Dogs must be leashed.

Tamarack Cross Country Ski Center Lake Mary Road Mammoth Lakes CA 760- 934-2442
http://www.tamaracklodge.com/xcountry/
During the summer and fall (until first snowfall), dogs are allowed at Tamarack. They offer watercraft rentals, fishing, easy to strenuous hiking trails, an eatery, a lodge that allows dogs, and great scenery. Dogs are welcome on the deck of the restaurant. Dogs must be under owner's control at all times, and be leashed and cleaned up after.

Outdoor Restaurants

Base Camp Cafe 3325 Main Street Mammoth Lakes CA 760-934-3900
Dogs are welcome at this cafe! They have a water bowl outside for your pooch.
Giovanni's Pizza 437 Old Mammoth Rd Mammoth Lakes CA 760-934-7563
Dogs are allowed at the outdoor tables.

Vets and Kennels

Alpen Veterinary Hospital 217 Sierra Manor Rd Mammoth Lakes CA 760-934-2291
Monday - Friday 9:30 am - 5:30 pm. Closed Weekends. Vet available in Emergency other hours.
High Country Veterinary Hospital 148 Mountain Blvd Mammoth Lakes CA 760-934-3775
Monday - Friday 9 am - 12 noon, 2 pm - 5 pm. Closed weekends.

Markleeville

Campgrounds and RV Parks

Grover Hot Springs State Park 3415 Hot Springs Road Markleeville CA 530-694-2248
You will find a variety of weather and recreation at this park that is known for its mineral hot springs. Dogs of all sizes are allowed. There are no additional pet fees. Dogs may not be left unattended, and they must be leashed at all times, and cleaned up after. Dogs are not allowed in the pool area, and guests or their dogs are not allowed in the meadows. The camping and tent areas also allow dogs. There is a dog walk area at the campground. There are no electric or water hookups at the campgrounds.

Indian Creek Campground Indian Creek Road Markleeville CA 775-885-6000
Surrounded by pine trees at 5,600 feet, this park covers 160 acres used for recreational pursuits. Dogs of all sizes are allowed. There are no additional pet fees. Dogs may not be left unattended, and they must be leashed at all times, and cleaned up after. Dogs are allowed on the trails. This campground is closed during the off-season. The camping and tent areas also allow dogs. There is a dog walk area at the campground. There are no electric or water hookups at the campgrounds.

McGee Creek

Campgrounds and RV Parks

McGee Creek Campground McGee Creek Road McGee Creek CA 760-873-2500 (877-444-6777)
This 28 site campground is located in the Inyo National Forest at an elevation of 7,600 feet. The campsite is in an open area and adjacent to McGee Creek. Amenities include water, flush toilets and space for RVs. For hiking, the McGee Creek Trail is located within a few miles of the campground. The fee for a campsite is $15. Pets must be leashed while in the campground and please clean up after your pets. This campground is closed during the off-season. The camping and tent areas also allow dogs. There is a dog walk area at the campground. There are no electric or water hookups at the campgrounds.

Parks

McGee Creek Trailhead McGee Creek Road McGee Creek CA 760-873-2500
http://www.fs.fed.us/r5/inyo
This trail is rated moderate to strenuous. It is located in the Inyo National Forest. From the trailhead you can hike to several lakes including Steelhead Lake. Pets must either be leashed or off-leash but under direct voice control. Please clean up after your pets. To get there from Highway 395, take the first exit after Crowley Lake. Go 4 miles heading south on McGee Creek Road to the trailhead.

Mono Lake

Accommodations

Inn at Lee Vining 45 2nd St Lee Vining CA 760-647-6300

Murphey's Hotel 51493 Hwy 395 Lee Vining CA 760-647-6316
There is a $5 per day additional pet fee. Dogs are not to be left alone in rooms.

Campgrounds and RV Parks

Glass Creek Campground Hwy 395 Lee Vining CA 760-873-2408
This 50 site campground is located in the Inyo National Forest at an elevation of 7,600 feet. It is located near several trails. The fee for a campsite is $14. The sites are available on a first-come, first-served basis. Pets must be leashed while in the campground and please clean up after them. The campground is located between Lee Vining and Mammoth Lakes on Highway 395. It is at the intersection of the highway and the Crestview CalTrains Maintenance Station, about one mile north of the Crestview Rest Area. This campground is closed during the off-season. The camping and tent areas also allow dogs. There is a dog walk area at the campground. There are no electric or water hookups at the campgrounds.

Lundy Canyon County Park Campground Lundy Lake Road, Mono Lake Lee Vining CA 760-932-5440
This park, in the Mono Lake area, offers hikers a variety of trails and recreational pursuits. There are also trails to

enter the Ansel Adams and Hoover Wildernesses. Dogs of all sizes are allowed. There are no additional pet fees. Dogs must be leashed at all times and cleaned up after. Dogs are allowed on the trails on lead. This campground is closed during the off-season. The camping and tent areas also allow dogs. There is a dog walk area at the campground. There are no electric or water hookups at the campgrounds.

Attractions
Mono Basin National Forest Scenic Area Hwy 395, 1/2 mile North of Lee Vining Lee Vining CA 760-647-3044
Mono is the westernmost basin of the Basin and Range province, which stretches across western North America between the Rocky Mountains and Sierra Nevada. In the heart of the Basin lies the majestic Mono Lake, a quiet inland sea nestled amidst the Sierra Mountains. Estimated between one million and three million years of age, Mono Lake is one of the oldest continuous lakes in North America. It is a "terminal" lake, which means that it has no outlet water flow. Thus fresh water flows in and can only leave through evaporation. For this reason the lake has a high content of salt. It is nearly three times saltier than the Pacific Ocean and 1,000 more alkaline than fresh water. A chemical twin of Mono Lake exists nowhere in the world; the closest kin would be found no closer than equatorial Africa. There are many trails here. The Lee Vining Creek Nature Trail is about 1 mile long and is located next to the Mono Basin National Forest Scenic Area Visitor Center. You can also get information about other hikes and trails at the visitor's center.

Onyx

Campgrounds and RV Parks
Walker Pass Campground Hwy 178 Onyx CA 661-391-6000
This BLM (Bureau of Land Management) campground has 11 walk-in sites for Pacific Crest Trail hikers and two sites are available for vehicles. Drinking water is available from spring through fall. Hitching racks and corrals are available for horses. There are no reservations or fees but donations are accepted. Dogs are allowed but need to be on leash while in the campground. They are allowed on the trails. The camping and tent areas also allow dogs. There is a dog walk area at the campground. There are no electric or water hookups at the campgrounds.

Parks
Pacific Crest Trail-Owens Peak Segment Highway 178 Onyx CA 661-391-6000
The Owens Peak Segment of the Pacific Crest Trail is managed by the Bureau of Land Management. This section begins at Walker Pass in Kern County and goes 41 miles north to the Sequoia National Forest at Rockhouse Basin. Elevations on this portion range from 5,245 feet at Walker Pass to 7,900 feet on Bear Mountain. The trail offers great views of the surrounding mountains and valleys. Dogs are allowed on the Owen's Peak Segment of the Pacific Crest Trail. Trail conditions can change due to fires, storms and landslides. To confirm current conditions, contact the Bakersfield BLM Office at 661-391-6000. There are many trailheads, but one of the more popular staging areas is at Walker Pass. From Ridgecrest go 27 miles west on Highway 178 to Walker Pass.

Pinecrest

Campgrounds and RV Parks
Boulder Flat, 21 miles east of Pinecrest on Highway 108 Pinecrest CA 209-965-3434
This camp area is located in the Brightman Recreation Area in a forested area along the Stanislaus River. Dogs of all sizes are allowed. There are no additional pet fees. Dogs must be well behaved, leashed in camp, and cleaned up after. Dogs may be off lead on the trails if they are under voice command and will not chase wildlife. Please refrain from taking pets to beach areas to prevent contamination. This campground is closed during the off-season. The camping and tent areas also allow dogs. There is a dog walk area at the campground. There are no electric or water hookups at the campgrounds.
Pinecrest Lake Pinecrest Lake Road Pinecrest CA 209-965-3434
Located in a timbered setting at an elevation of 5,600 feet, this scenic park offers interpretive programs and a variety of land and water recreation. Dogs of all sizes are allowed. There are no additional pet fees. Dogs must be quiet, well behaved, leashed, and cleaned up after. No dogs allowed in Day Use Area (between Pinecrest Lake Road/Pinecrest Avenue and the boat launch and the fishing pier) from May 15 to September 15. This campground is closed during the off-season. The camping and tent areas also allow dogs. There is a dog walk area at the campground. There are no electric or water hookups at the campgrounds.

Riverton

Parks

Ice House Bike Trail Ice House Road Riverton CA 530-644-2349
This 3.1 mile dirt trail winds along the ridge tops and shaded slopes, through old and new forest growths. The trail, located in the Eldorado National Forest at about 5,400 feet, is rated easy and offers great views of the Ice House Reservoir. Both hikers and mountain bikers use this trail. Dogs should be on leash and are allowed on the trail and in the water. To get there from Placerville, take Highway 50 east for 21 miles to Ice House Road turnoff. Turn left and go 11 miles north to the campground turnoff. Then go one mile to the campgrounds. The trail can be accessed from any of the Ice House Reservoir campgrounds or at the intersection of Road 12N06 and Ice House Road which is located about 200 yards north of the turnoff to Big Hill Lookout.

Union Valley Bike Trail Ice House Road Riverton CA 530-644-2349
This 4.8 mile two-lane paved trail is located in the Eldorado National Forest. Elevations range from 4,860 to 5,160 feet. The trail connects all the campgrounds on the east side of Union Valley Reservoir, from Jones Fork to Wench Creek Campgrounds. Parking is available at the campgrounds except for Lone Rock and Azalea Cove. Views and interpretive signs complement this high country trail. Dogs should be on leash and are allowed on the trail and in the water. To get there from Placerville, take Highway 50 east and go 21 miles to Riverton. Turn left on Ice House Road. Go about 19 miles north to the reservoir.

Sequoia National Park

Accommodations

Buckeye Tree Lodge 46,000 Sierra Drive/Hwy 198 Three Rivers CA 559-561-5900
http://www.buckeyetree.com/
This lodge sits in the Kaweah River Canyon along the banks of the Kaweah River. The beautiful grounds offer a grassy lawn, a picnic area on the river surrounded by Sycamore trees, an outdoor pool, and miles of multi-use trails to explore. Dogs of all sizes are allowed for an additional fee of $8 per night per pet. Dogs may not be left alone in the rooms at any time, and they must be well behaved, leashed, and cleaned up after.

Sequoia Village Inn 45971 Sierra Drive/Hwy 198 Three Rivers CA 559-561-3652
http://www.sequoiavillageinn.com/
Neighboring the Sequoia National Park, this inn features spectacular mountain and river scenery, 1.3 acres of native oak trees, grasses, an abundance of wildflowers, and 8 private chalet and/or cottages. Some of the amenities include a seasonal swimming pool and spa, satellite TV, kitchens with basic needs/utilities, and beautiful hand-crafted accommodations. Dogs of all sizes are allowed for an additional fee of $8 per night per pet. Dogs may not be left alone in the rooms at any time, and they must be well behaved, leashed, and cleaned up after.

Wickyup Bed and Breakfast Cottage 22702 Avenue 344 Woodlake CA 559-564-8898
http://www.wickyup.com/
Dogs are allowed in the Calico Room Cottage. It offers bunk beds, a half-bath, and a discrete, enclosed outdoor shower. The cottage is located in the garden and has a private entrance.

Campgrounds and RV Parks

Azalea Campground, Kings Canyon National Park Grant Tree Road Three Rivers CA 559-565-3708
This scenic park, located at 6,500 feet in the Kings Canyon National Park, offers a variety of recreational pursuits. Dogs of all sizes are allowed. There are no additional pet fees. Dogs must be leashed at all times and cleaned up after. Dogs are not allowed on the hiking trails, and must stay in the camp area or on the roads. The camping and tent areas also allow dogs. There is a dog walk area at the campground. There are no electric or water hookups at the campgrounds.

Potwisha Campground, Sequoia and Kings Canyon Nat'l Park 47050 Generals Hwy (Hwy 198) Three Rivers CA 559-565-3341
http://www.nps.gov/seki
Located in a National Forest, this park offers spectacular scenery, varied habitats and elevations, and a wide variety of land and water recreation. Dogs of all sizes are allowed at no additional fee. Dogs may not be left unattended at any time. Keep in mind that dogs are not permitted on park trails and it may be too hot to leave them in the car. It is highly suggested that dogs are not brought to the park in summer as temperatures reach over 110 degrees, and there is poison oak, snakes, and ticks. Dogs are not allowed in the water or on any of the trails. Dogs may be walked in the campground, on walkways or roadways only. Dogs must be leashed at all times and cleaned up after. The camping and tent areas also allow dogs. There is a dog walk area at the

campground. There are no electric or water hookups at the campgrounds.

Sequoia and Kings Canyon National Park Campgrounds 47050 General H Three Rivers CA 559-565-3341

This park offers many campgrounds which range in elevation from 2,100 feet to 7,500 feet. The Lodgepole, Dorst, Grant Grove and Atwell Mill campgrounds are located near giant sequoia groves. The Lodgepole campground, located at 6,700 foot elevation, is one of the largest camps and offers 250 sites. Tent and RV camping is available, with a maximum RV length of 35 feet. Amenities at this campground include a guest laundry, deli, market, gift shop, pay showers, flush toilets and more. Some of the campgrounds are open all year. Pets must be leashed and attended at all times. Please clean up after your pet. Keep in mind that dogs are not permitted on park trails and it may be too hot to leave them in the car. Please see our listings in the towns of Johnsondale and Hume for details about nearby dog-friendly hiking, sightseeing and additional camping. A couple of the camp areas are not accessible to RV's, so research ahead. The camping and tent areas also allow dogs. There is a dog walk area at the campground. There are no electric or water hookups at the campgrounds.

Parks

Sequoia and Kings Canyon National Park 47050 General Highway Three Rivers CA 559-565-3341
http://www.nps.gov/seki/

This national park does not really have much to see or do if you bring your pooch, except for driving through a giant redwood forest in your car and staying overnight at the campgrounds. However, located to the west and south of this national park is the dog-friendly Giant National Sequoia Monument. There you will be able to find dog-friendly hiking, sightseeing and camping. Pets must be leashed and attended at all times. Please clean up after your pet.

Shaver Lake

Campgrounds and RV Parks

Camp Edison at Shaver Lake 42696 Tollhouse Road Shaver Lake CA 559-841-3134

This campground is located at Shaver Lake in the Sierra National Forest and is managed by Southern California Edison. There are 252 campsites with electricity and free cable TV. Amenities include picnic tables, restroom with heated showers, a guest laundry, marina and a general store. Dogs are allowed at the campgrounds, on trails and in the water but only at non-designated swimming beaches. Pets must be leashed and please clean up after them. There is a $5 per night per pet fee. Dogs may not be left unattended, and they must be brought inside at night. The camping and tent areas also allow dogs. There is a dog walk area at the campground.

Dorabelle Campground Dorabella Street Shaver Lake CA 559-297-0706 (877-444-6777)

This campground is next to Shaver Lake in the Sierra National Forest. Some of the sites have lake views and all of the sites have shade from dense pines trees. The camp is at an elevation of 5,500 feet. There are 68 tent and RV sites, and RVs up to 40 feet are allowed. Amenities include water, vault toilets, picnic tables and grills. Be sure to bring some mosquito repellant. There are several trails here that provide access around the lake. Dogs are allowed at the campgrounds, on trails and in the water but only at non-designated swimming beaches. Pets must be leashed and please clean up after them. Dogs may not be left unattended. This campground is closed during the off-season. The camping and tent areas also allow dogs. There is a dog walk area at the campground. There are no electric or water hookups at the campgrounds.

Tom's Place

Campgrounds and RV Parks

East Fork Campground Rock Creek Canyon Road Tom's Place CA 760-873-2500 (877-444-6777)

This 133 site campground is located in the Inyo National Forest at an elevation of 9,000 feet. Amenities include water, flush toilet, picnic tables and space for RVs. For hiking, there are several trailheads nearby including the Hilton Lakes and Little Lakes Valley trails. The fee for a campsite is $15. Pets must be leashed while in the campground and please clean up after them. Dogs may not be left unattended outside. This campground is closed during the off-season. The camping and tent areas also allow dogs. There is a dog walk area at the campground. There are no electric or water hookups at the campgrounds.

Twin Bridges

Parks

Bryan Meadows Trail Bryan Road Twin Bridges CA 530-644-2545
This 4 mile moderate rated trail passes through stands of lodgepole pine and mountain hemlock. From the parking area, hike one mile up Sayles Canyon Trail along the creek to the junction of Bryan Meadows Trail. The trail continues east for about three miles. The elevation ranges from about 7,200 to 8,400 feet. Pets must be leashed and please clean up after them. This trail is located in the Eldorado National Forest. From Highway 50 go about 48 miles east of Placerville. Turn onto the Sierra-At-Tahoe Road and go 2 miles. Turn right onto Bryan Road (17E13). Go another 2.5 miles to the parking area where the trailhead is located.

Pyramid Creek Loop Trail Highway 50 Twin Bridges CA 530-644-2545
This 1.7 mile Eldorado National Forest trail is rated moderate to strenuous. The elevation ranges from 6,120 to 6,400 feet. At the trailhead, begin your hike by heading east and then north up to Pyramid Creek. Turn right (east) at the sign and follow the trail along the creek. The trail offers great views of the American River Canyon, Lover's Leap, Horsetail Falls and other geological interests. Follow the trail north, then loop back south on the old trail bed down to the granite slabs and return to Highway 50. Pets must be leashed and please clean up after them. The trailhead is located on the north side of Highway 50 at Twin Bridges, about .5 miles east of Strawberry.

Yosemite

Accommodations

Yosemite Gold Country Motel 10407 Highway 49 Coulterville CA 209-878-3400
http://www.yosemitegold.com/ygcm/
All rooms are completely furnished with a heater and air conditioner, color TV, telephones, bathroom with tub-shower and free coffee. Your dog is more than welcome here, but he or she must stay on a leash when outside and should use their Doggie Park when going to the bathroom. Also, they require that you do not leave your dog outside unattended. This motel is located about hour from Yosemite Valley (40 min. to the main gate and 20 min. to the valley). There are no additional pet fees.

Yosemite View Lodge Hwy 140 El Portal CA 209-379-2681 (888-742-4371)
Just steps away from the entrance to the National Park, this lodge offers luxury accommodations and many extras. Some of the amenities include private balconies or patios, 1 indoor and 3 outdoor pools, 1 indoor and 5 outdoor spas, a cocktail lounge, gift shop, convenience store, restaurant, and a visitor and guide center. Dogs of all sizes are allowed for an additional fee of $10 per night per pet. Dogs must be leashed and cleaned up after at all times, and they may only be left alone in the room if they will be quiet, well behaved, and the Do Not Disturb sign is put on the door.

Apple Tree Inn at Yosemite 1110 Highway 41 Fish Camp CA 559-683-5111 (888-683-5111)
http://www.appletreeinn-yosemite.com/
This 54 unit inn is nestled among acres of trees. There is dog-friendly hiking right from the property on fire roads in the Sierra National Forest (on Jackson/Big Sandy Road which is also the road to the Yosemite Trails Pack Station). Pets must be leashed on the inn's property and in the forest. The next property over from the inn is the Tenaya Lodge which has several cafes with food to go. The inn is located two miles from the southern entrance to Yosemite National Park (about 45 minutes to Yosemite Valley). There is a $50 one time pet charge.

Narrow Gauge Inn 48571 Highway 41 Fish Camp CA 559-683-7720
http://www.narrowgaugeinn.com/
This inn is located amidst pine trees in the Sierra Mountains. They are located about four miles from the southern entrance to Yosemite National Park (about 45 minutes to Yosemite Valley). There are some trails nearby in the dog-friendly Sierra National Forest near Bass Lake. All rooms are non-smoking. Dogs are allowed in the main level rooms and there is a $25 one time per stay pet fee. Children are also welcome.

Tenaya Lodge 1122 Highway 41 Fish Camp CA 888-514-2167
http://www.tenayalodge.com/
This classic resort with 244 guest rooms and suites has created an elegant retreat with all the modern services. The resort sits on 35 scenic acres only two miles from the south entrance of Yosemite National Park and offers many in-room amenities and a variety of dining choices. One dog up to 75 pounds is allowed per room. There is a $75 one time additional pet fee. Dogs may not be left unattended in the room, and they are not allowed in the shops and restaurants. Dogs must be leashed and cleaned up after at all times. They also offer a canine amenity package that includes treats, disposable mitts, a plush dog bed, water bowl, and a canine concierge fact sheet of fun areas to roam. With advanced booking they can also provide a dog walking/sitting service.

Historic Groveland Hotel 18767 Main Street Groveland CA 209-962-4000 (800-273-3314.)
http://www.groveland.com/
Your dog or cat is welcome at this 1849 historic inn. Country Inns Magazine rated the Groveland Hotel as one of the Top 10 Inns in the United States. The inn is located 23 miles from Yosemite's main gate. Their restaurant can pack a gourmet picnic basket for your day trip to Yosemite. Make your reservations early as they book up

quickly. This inn is located about an hour from Yosemite Valley. There is a $10 per day additional pet fee. All rooms are non-smoking.

Hotel Charlotte 18736 Main Street Groveland CA 209-962-6455
Dogs of all sizes are allowed. There is a $20 per night per pet fee and there is only 1 pet friendly room.

Sunset Inn 33569 Hardin Flat Rd. Groveland CA 209-962-4360
This inn offers three cabins near Yosemite National Park. The cabins are located on two acres and are surrounded by a dog-friendly National Forest at a 4500 foot elevation. All cabins are non-smoking and include kitchens and private bathrooms. Children are also welcome. The Sunset Inn is located just 2 miles from the west entrance to Yosemite, one mile from Highway 120. There is a $20 per day pet charge.

Yosemite Westgate Motel 7633 Hwy 120 Groveland CA 209-962-5281 (800-253-9673)
This motel has one pet room available and it is a non-smoking room. There is a $10 per night pet fee. The motel is located about 40 minutes from Yosemite Valley.

Comfort Inn 4994 Bullion Street Mariposa CA 209-966-4344 (877-424-6423)
Dogs of all sizes are allowed. There is a $15 per night per pet additional fee. Dogs must be leashed, cleaned up after, and the Do Not Disturb sign put on the door if they are in the room alone. Dogs must be removed for housekeeping.

The Mariposa Lodge 5052 Hwy 140 Mariposa CA 209-966-3607 (800-341-8000)
http://www.mariposalodge.com
Thanks to one of our readers for recommending this hotel. Here is what they said about it: "We stayed here after a clogged 4 hour drive from San Jose, CA. Mia at the front desk was courteous and friendly -- not what you always get when you are traveling with a 90 lb dog (black lab). The room was large, new and very nice. Lovely pool and jacuzzi. A little sitting area under a patch of trees with benches. It was very warm and Mia recommended a restaurant where we could sit outside and take our dog. Castillos on 5th Street. Our extra nice waitress brought him water and us an excellent Mexican dinner. Couldn't have been nicer. All in all Mariposa and the hotel was an A+ experience." If you take Highway 140, this motel is located about 50 minutes from Yosemite Valley (45 min. to the main gate and about 10 min. to the valley). Pets are an additional $10 per pet per night.

A Bed of Roses 43547 Whispering Pines Drive Oakhurst CA 559-642-6975 (877-624-7673)
http://www.abedofrosesbandb.com/
Individually, beautifully decorated rooms with private baths, a freshly prepared hearty breakfast, 24 hour cookie jar and snacks, an outdoor swimming pool and hot tub with lighted waterfalls, a petting zoo, and spectacular views are just a few of the features of this inn. Rooms with Jacuzzi tubs, skylights, private outdoor decks, and wood burning stoves, are also available. Although pet rooms are limited, dogs of all sizes are welcome for an additional fee of $20 per night per pet, and advanced reservations are required with a valid credit card. Reservations may be made toll free at 877-624-7673. A throw blanket, extra towels, a comfortable sleeping pad, water bowl, and treats are provided for canine guests. Dogs must be leashed or crated when in common areas, and be cleaned up after at all times. Dogs are not allowed on the furniture in the room or the common use areas, and they are not allowed in the dining room.

Comfort Inn 40480 Hwy 41 Oakhurst CA 559-683-8282 (877-424-6423)
Dogs of all sizes are allowed. There is a $10 per night per pet additional fee. Dogs may not be left alone in the rooms, and they must be leashed and cleaned up after.

High Sierra RV & Mobile Park 40389 Hwy 41 Oakhurst CA 559-683-7662
Dogs of all sizes are allowed. There are no additional pet fees. Dogs may not be left unattended at any time.

Pine Rose Inn Bed and Breakfast 41703 Road 222 Oakhurst CA 559-642-2800 (866-642-2800)
http://www.pineroseinn.com/
The inn is located 13 miles from the south gate of Yosemite National Park, 2 miles from Bass Lake and surrounded by the Sierra National Forest. The entire inn is non-smoking, except for outside. There is a $10 per day pet charge. Dogs and other pets are welcome.

Campgrounds and RV Parks

Lupine/Cedar Bluff Campground County Road 222 on South side of Bass Lake Bass Lake CA 559-877-2218 (877-444-6777)
This campground is next to Bass Lake in the Sierra National Forest. It is at an elevation of 3,400 feet and offers shade from dense pine, oak and cedar trees. There are 113 campsites for tent and RV camping. RVs up to 40 feet are allowed, and amenities include piped water, flush toilets, picnic tables and grills. The campground is open all year. A .5 mile trail called The Way of the Mono Trail, is located near this campground. Dogs are allowed at the campgrounds, on trails and in the water but only at non-designated swimming beaches. Pets must be leashed and please clean up after them. Dogs may not be left unattended outside, and they are not allowed on the beach. Check in at the Bass Lake Campground office before heading to your campsite. The office is located at the west end of the lake near Recreation Point. The camping and tent areas also allow dogs. There is a dog walk area at the campground. There are no electric or water hookups at the campgrounds.

Yosemite/Mariposa KOA 6323 Hwy 140 Midpines CA 209-966-2201 (800-562-9391)
http://www.koa.com/where/ca/05195/
Nestled in the pines, close to Yosemite, this campground offers such amenities as 43 foot pull through sites with 50 amp service, cable TV, swimming pool, mini golf, planned activities, and guided tours. Dogs of all sizes are

allowed for an additional pet fee of $2 per night per pet. Dogs must be under owner's control and visual observation at all times. Dogs must be quiet, well behaved, and be on no more than a 6 foot leash at all times, or otherwise contained. Dogs may not be left unattended outside the owner's camping equipment, and must be brought inside at night. There are some breed restrictions. The camping and tent areas also allow dogs. There is a dog walk area at the campground.

Bridalveil Creek Campground Glacier Point Road Yosemite CA   209/372-0200
This 110 site camp area is about 45 minutes south of the Yosemite Valley at an altitude of 7,200 feet, and all sites are on a first-come, first-served basis; each site has a fire ring, picnic table, and a food storage locker. There is potable water and flush toilets in camp, and a Laundromat and showers nearby. Dogs are allowed here and at 7 more of the 13 campgrounds in Yosemite for no additional pet fee. Dogs may not be left unattended while tied in a campsite, and they must be leashed and cleaned up after at all times. They are not allowed in any group camp areas, on any hiking trails, beaches, in the backcountry, or in public buildings. This RV park is closed during the off-season. The camping and tent areas also allow dogs. There is a dog walk area at the campground. There are no electric or water hookups at the campgrounds.

Crane Flat Campground Big Oak Flat and Tioga Roads Yosemite National Park CA   209-372-0200 (877-444-6777)
Next to the Big Tree Groves and only 17 miles from the Yosemite Valley, it is suggested that you get an early reservation as this popular camp site usually fills up well in advance. It sits at an altitude of 6,200 feet and offers 166 campsites; each site has a fire ring, picnic table, and a food storage locker. There is potable water and flush toilets in camp, and a Laundromat and showers nearby. Dogs are allowed here and at 7 more of the 13 campgrounds in Yosemite for no additional pet fee. Dogs may not be left unattended while tied in a campsite, and they must be leashed and cleaned up after at all times. They are not allowed in any group camp areas, on any hiking trails, beaches, in the backcountry, or in public buildings. For reservations call 877-444-6777. This RV park is closed during the off-season. The camping and tent areas also allow dogs. There is a dog walk area at the campground. There are no electric or water hookups at the campgrounds.

Hodgdon Meadow Campground Big Oak Flat Road Yosemite National Park CA   800-388-2733 (877-444-6777)
Only 25 miles from the Yosemite Valley at an elevation of 4,872 feet, this camp area offers 105 camp sites; each site has a fire ring, picnic table, and a food storage locker. There is potable water and flush toilets in camp, and a Laundromat and showers in the valley. Dogs are allowed here and at 7 more of the 13 campgrounds in Yosemite for no additional pet fee. Dogs may not be left unattended while tied in a campsite, and they must be leashed and cleaned up after at all times. They are not allowed in any group camp areas, on any hiking trails, beaches, in the backcountry, or in public buildings. For reservations call 877-444-6777. The camping and tent areas also allow dogs. There is a dog walk area at the campground. There are no electric or water hookups at the campgrounds.

Tuolumne Meadows Campground Tioga Road Yosemite National Park CA   800-388-2733 (877-444-6777)
This beautiful open meadow area offers 314 campsites at 8,600 feet altitude, and half of the sites can be reserved; the other half is on a 1st come 1st served basis. Each site has a fire ring, picnic table, and a food storage locker with potable water, flush toilets, and a dump station in camp, and groceries, laundry and showers nearby. Dogs are allowed here and at 7 more of the 13 campgrounds in Yosemite for no additional pet fee. Dogs may not be left unattended while tied in a campsite, and they must be leashed and cleaned up after at all times. They are not allowed in any group camp areas, on any hiking trails, beaches, in the backcountry, or in public buildings. For reservations call 877-444-6777. This RV park is closed during the off-season. The camping and tent areas also allow dogs. There is a dog walk area at the campground. There are no electric or water hookups at the campgrounds.

Upper Pines Campground East Yosemite Valley Yosemite National Park CA   800-388-2733 (877-444-6777)
This 238 site campground is located inside the Yosemite Valley. Reservations are required during the busy seasons. Potable water, fire pits, a dump station, showers, and restrooms are available. Dogs are allowed here and at 7 more of the 13 campgrounds in Yosemite for no additional pet fee. Dogs may not be left unattended while tied in a campsite, and they must be leashed and cleaned up after at all times. They are not allowed on any hiking trails, beaches, in the backcountry, or in public buildings. For reservations call 877-444-6777. The camping and tent areas also allow dogs. There is a dog walk area at the campground. There are no electric or water hookups at the campgrounds.

Wawona Campground Highway 41 Yosemite National Park CA   209-375-9531 (877-444-6777)
Located along the south fork of the Merced River, this camp area sits at 4,000 feet and offers 100 campsites; each site has a picnic table and fire pit. There is drinking water, flush toilets, a dump station, and groceries available in the camp area. Dogs are allowed here and at 7 more of the 13 campgrounds in Yosemite for no additional pet fee. Dogs may not be left unattended while tied in a campsite, and they must be leashed and cleaned up after at all times. They are not allowed in any group camp areas, on any hiking trails, beaches, in the backcountry, or in public buildings. For reservations call 877-444-6777. The camping and tent areas also allow dogs. There is a dog walk area at the campground. There are no electric or water hookups at the campgrounds.

White Wolf Campground Tioga Road Yosemite National Park CA   209-379-1899
Sitting at an elevation of 8,000 feet, this campground lies between the Tuolumne River and Tioga Road and offers 87 camp sites on a 1st come 1st served basis; each site has a picnic table, food storage locker, and a fire pit; drinking water and flush toilets are available within the camp area. Dogs are allowed here and at 7 more of

the 13 campgrounds in Yosemite for no additional pet fee. Dogs may not be left unattended while tied in a campsite, and they must be leashed and cleaned up after at all times. They are not allowed in any group camp areas, on any hiking trails, beaches, in the backcountry, or in public buildings. This RV park is closed during the off-season. The camping and tent areas also allow dogs. There is a dog walk area at the campground. There are no electric or water hookups at the campgrounds.

Yosemite Creek Campground Tioga Road/Hwy 120 Yosemite National Park CA 209-379-1899
This tent-camping only park sits at 7,700 feet, offers 75 camp sites available on a 1st come 1st served basis, and provides easy access for fishing in its namesake creek. The 5 mile access road from Tioga Road is not suitable for RVs or large trailers, and all water obtained on site must be treated or boiled before use. Each site has a picnic table, food storage locker, and a fire pit; pit toilets are located in camp. Dogs are allowed here and at 7 more of the 13 campgrounds in Yosemite for no additional pet fee. Dogs may not be left unattended while tied in a campsite, and they must be leashed and cleaned up after at all times. They are not allowed in any group camp areas, on any hiking trails, beaches, in the backcountry, or in public buildings. This RV park is closed during the off-season. There is a dog walk area at the campground. There are no electric or water hookups at the campgrounds.

Vacation Home Rentals

Indian Peak Ranch MountainTop Hideaway Call to arrange Mariposa CA 209-966-5259
http://www.indianpeakranch.com
This mountaintop vacation rental is located on 122 acres. To make reservations or for more information see www.indianpeakranch.com or call.

The Redwoods In Yosemite PO Box 2085; Wawona Station Yosemite National Park CA 209-375-6666
 (888-225-6666)
http://www.redwoodsinyosemite.com
Dog-friendly vacation rentals inside Yosemite National Park offer year-round vacation rentals that range in size from one to six bedrooms. Some of the rentals allow pets, but not all, so please specify your need for a pet unit when you make your reservation. There is a $10/night pet fee (per pet). Please abide by Yosemite's pet regulations, which require that pets be leashed at all times and are not permitted on many Park trails (a couple of exceptions are paved paths in the Valley Floor and a couple of short trails in the south Yosemite area). The rentals are located approximately 10 minutes inside the southern entrance of Yosemite National Park and offer 120 privately owned vacation rentals.

Attractions

Yosemite Mountain Sugar Pine Railroad

TOP 200 PLACE Yosemite Mountain Sugar Pine Railroad 56001 Highway 41 Fish Camp CA 559-683-7273
http://www.ymsprr.com/
Hop aboard a four mile railroad excursion with your pooch and enjoy a narrative ride through the Sierra National Forest. One of their steam engines is the heaviest operating narrow gauge Shay locomotive in use today. Well-behaved leashed dogs are welcome. The railroad is located near Yosemite Park's south gate on Highway 41.

Mount Bullion Vineyard 6947 Hwy 49N Mariposa CA 209-377-8450
The tasting room and tours are by appointment only, and they look forward to showing visitors around the winery. Some of the other amenities include a picnic deck shaded by oak trees, horseshoe pit, and a barbecue area. Your dog is welcome but must be very social and friendly with people and other animals as there are cats, dogs, and chickens roaming about. Dogs must be leashed and cleaned up after at all times.

Millers Landing Resort - Bass Lake 37926 Road 222 Wishon CA 559-642-3633
http://www.millerslanding.com
Dogs on are allowed on the boats. They ask that all dogs be leashed while in the public areas (office, parking lot, etc) but can be off leash on the boats.

Parks

The Way of the Mono Trail off Road 222 Bass Lake CA 559-877-2218
http://www.fs.fed.us/r5/sierra/
On this .5 mile trail you can see authentic Mono Indian grinding holes, plus you will get some great views of Bass Lake. The trail is located next to Bass Lake in the Sierra National Forest. Stop at the Yosemite/Sierra Visitors Bureau at 41969 Highway 41 in Oakhurst for the trail location. The office is open 7 days a week from 8:30am to 5pm.

Shadow of the Giants Trail off Sky Ranch Road Oakhurst CA 559-297-0706
http://www.fs.fed.us/r5/sierra/
This one mile each way self-guided trail is located in the Nelder Grove Giant Sequoia Preservation Area. Along the trail you will see some of the best giant sequoia trees in the state. Pets on leash are allowed and please clean up after them. The trail is located in the Nelder Grove Giant Sequoia Preservation Area. To get there from Oakhurst, go about 5 miles north on Highway 41. Turn right (east) onto Sky Ranch Road. Along Sky Ranch Road you will find Nelder Grove.

Badger Pass Ski Area P.O. Box 578/Badger Pass Road Yosemite National Park CA 209-372-1220
This popular family-friendly ski area offers great scenery, and a variety of activities, festivals, and friendly competitions throughout the season. Although dogs are not allowed on the ski slopes in winter, they are allowed to go anywhere a car can go-being paved roads and developed areas. Dogs must be leashed.

Yosemite National Park

220

TOP 200 PLACE Yosemite National Park PO Box 577 Yosemite National Park CA   209-372-0200
http://www.nps.gov/yose
This 750,000 acre park is one of the most popular national parks in the country. Yosemite's geology is world famous for its granite cliffs, tall waterfalls and giant sequoia groves. As with most national parks, pets have limited access within the park. Pets are not allowed on unpaved trails, in wilderness areas including hiking trails, in park lodging (except for some campgrounds) and on shuttle buses. However, there are still several nice areas to walk with your pooch and you will be able to see the majority of sights and points of interest that most visitors see. Dogs are allowed in developed areas and on fully paved trails, include Yosemite Valley which offers about 2 miles of paved trails. From these trails you can view El Capitan, Half Dome and Yosemite Falls. You can also take the .5 mile paved trail right up to the base of Bridalveil Fall which is a 620 foot year round waterfall. The best time to view this waterfall is in the spring or early summer. The water thunders down and almost creates a nice rain at the base. Water-loving dogs will be sure to like this attraction. In general dogs are not allowed on unpaved trails, but this park does make the following exceptions. Dogs are allowed on the Meadow Loop and Four Mile fire roads in Wawona. They are also allowed on the Carlon Road and on the Old Big Oak Flat Road between Hodgdon Meadow and Hazel Green Creek. Dogs must be on a 6 foot or less leash and attended at all times. People must also clean up after their pets. For a detailed map of Yosemite, visit their web site at http://www.nps.gov/yose/pphtml/maps.html. The green dots show the paved trails. There are four main entrances to the park and all four lead to the Yosemite Valley. The park entrance fees are as follows: $20 per vehicle, $40 annual pass or $10 per individual on foot. The pass is good for 7 days. Prices are subject to change. Yosemite Valley is open year round and may be reached via Highway 41 from Fresno, Highway 140 from Merced, Highway 120 from Manteca and in late spring through late fall via the Tioga Road (Highway 120 East) from Lee Vining. From November through March, all park roads are subject to snow chain controls or closures. For updated 24 hour road and weather conditions call (209) 372-0200.

Outdoor Restaurants
Round-Up BBQ 18745 Back Street Groveland CA   209-962-0806
Dogs are allowed at the outdoor tables.
Pizza Factory 40120 Highway 41 #B Oakhurst CA   559-683-2700
Well-behaved dogs may sit at the outside tables.

Vets and Kennels
Hoof and Paw Veterinary Hospital 41149 Highway 41 Oakhurst CA   559-683-3313
http://www.sierratel.com/hoofnpaw
Oakhurst Veterinary Hospital 40799 Highway 41 Oakhurst CA   559-683-2135

Chapter 8

California - Central Coast Dog Travel Guide

Avila Beach

Beaches
Avila Beach off Avila Beach Drive Avila Beach CA   805-595-5400
This beach is about a 1/2 mile long. Dogs are not allowed between 10am and 5pm and must be leashed.
Olde Port Beach off Avila Beach Drive Avila Beach CA   805-595-5400
This beach is about a 1/4 mile long. Dogs are not allowed between 10am and 5pm and must be leashed.

Big Sur

Campgrounds and RV Parks
Big Sur Campground and Cabins 47000 Hwy 1 Big Sur CA   831-677-2322
This tent and RV campground is set amongst redwood trees along the Big Sur River. Camp amenities include
some pull through sites, a general store, playground, basketball court and more. Well-behaved leashed dogs of
all sizes are allowed in the tent, RV sites, and the tent cabins, but not in the hardwood cabins or around them.
There is an additional fee of $4 per night per pet for the tent or RV sites. There is an additional fee of $12 per
night per pet for the tent cabins. Pets must be attended at all times. People need to clean up after their pets.
They are located about 5 miles from the dog-friendly Pfieffer Beach and 2.5 miles from Big Sur Station. The
camping and tent areas also allow dogs. There is a dog walk area at the campground. Dogs are allowed in the
camping cabins.
Fernwood at Big Sur 47200 Hwy 1 Big Sur CA   831-667-2422
http://www.fernwoodbigsur.com/
Home to a famous and rare Albino Redwood tree, this park provides historic sites, river campsites, a store,
tavern and planned events. One of the many trails here ends at Pfeiffer Falls, a 60-foot high waterfall. Dogs of all
sizes are allowed for an additional fee of $3 per night per pet for the tent or RV sites, and an additional fee of $10
per night per pet for the tent cabins. Dogs may not be left unattended, and they must be leashed and cleaned up
after. Dogs are allowed on the trails unless otherwise marked. The camping and tent areas also allow dogs.
There is a dog walk area at the campground. Dogs are allowed in the camping cabins.
Ventana Big Sur Campground 28106 Hwy 1 Big Sur CA   831-667-2712
http://www.ventanacampground.com/
This 40 acre campground, located in a redwood tree lined canyon, offers 80 camp sites nestled among the trees
and along the edge of the stream. RV's are limited to 22 feet. Well-behaved, quiet, leashed dogs of all sizes are
allowed, maximum of two dogs per site. People need to clean up after their pets. There is a $5 per night pet fee
per dog. This campground is closed during the off-season. The camping and tent areas also allow dogs. There is
a dog walk area at the campground. There are no electric or water hookups at the campgrounds.

Vacation Home Rentals
Big Sur Vacation Retreat off Highway One Big Sur CA   831-624-5339 Ext 13
http://www.thawley.com/bigsur/
Rent this vacation rental by the week or longer. The home is situated on ten acres and at an elevation of 1,700
feet which is usually above the coastal fog and winds. Well-behaved dogs are welcome. No children under 10
years old allowed without the prior consent of the owner. This rental is usually available between June and mid-
October. Rates are about $2300 per week. The home is located about 45 minutes south of Carmel.

Beaches
Pfieffer Beach Sycamore Road Big Sur CA   805-968-6640
Dogs on leash are allowed at this day use beach which is located in the Los Padres National Forest. The beach
is located in Big Sur, south of the Big Sur Ranger Station. From Big Sur, start heading south on Highway 1 and
look carefully for Sycamore Road. Take Sycamore Road just over 2 miles to the beach. There is a $5 entrance
fee per car.

Parks
Los Padres National Forest Big Sur Station #1 Big Sur CA   831-385-5434
http://www.r5.fs.fed.us/lospadres/

While dogs are not allowed in the state park in Big Sur, they are welcome in the adjacent Los Padres National Forest. Dogs should be on leash. One of the most popular trails is the Pine Ridge Trail. This trail is miles long and goes through the Los Padres National Forest to the dog-friendly Ventana Wilderness. To get there, take Highway 1 south, about 25-30 miles south of Carmel. Park at the Big Sur Station for a minimal fee. From the Big Sur Station in Big Sur, you can head out onto the Pine Ridge Trail. The Los Padres National Forest actually stretches over 200 miles from the Carmel Valley all the way down to Los Angeles County. For maps and more information about the trails, contact the Monterey Ranger District at 831-385-5434 or at the Forest Headquarters in Goleta at 805-968-6640.

Carmel

Accommodations
Best Western Carmel Mission Inn 3665 Rio Rd Carmel CA 831-624-1841 (800-780-7234)
Dogs up to 60 pounds are allowed. There is a $35 one time per pet fee per visit. Only non-smoking rooms used for pets.
Carmel Country Inn P.O. Box 3756 Carmel CA 831-625-3263 (800-215-6343)
http://www.carmelcountryinn.com/
This dog-friendly bed and breakfast has 12 rooms and allows dogs in several of these rooms. It's close to many downtown dog-friendly restaurants (see Restaurants). A 20-25 minute walk will take you to the dog-friendly Carmel City Beach. There is a $20 per night per pet charge.
Casa De Carmel Monte Verde & Ocean Ave Carmel CA 831-624-2429
There is an additional fee of $20 per day for 1 pet, and $30 a day for 2 pets.
Coachman's Inn San Carlos St. & 7th Carmel CA 831-624-6421 (800-336-6421)
http://www.coachmansinn.com
Located in downtown, this motel allows dogs. It's close to many downtown outdoor dog-friendly restaurants (see Restaurants). A 20-25 minute walk will take you to the Carmel City beach which allows dogs. There is a $15 per day additional pet fee.

Cypress Inn

TOP 200 PLACE **Cypress Inn** Lincoln & 7th Carmel CA 831-624-3871 (800-443-7443)
http://www.cypress-inn.com
This hotel is located within walking distance to many dog-friendly outdoor restaurants in the quaint town of Carmel and walking distance to the Carmel City Beach. This is definitely a pet-friendly hotel. Here is an excerpt from the Cypress Inn's web page "Co-owned by actress and animal rights activist Doris Day, the Cypress Inn welcomes pets with open arms -- a policy which draws a high percentage of repeat guests. It's not unusual to see people strolling in and out of the lobby with dogs of all sizes. Upon arrival, animals are greeted with dog

biscuits, and other pet pamperings." Room rates are about $125 - $375 per night. If you have more than 2 people per room (including a child or baby), you will be required to stay in their deluxe room which runs approximately $375 per night. There is a $25 per day pet charge.

Happy Landing Inn Monte Verde at 6th Carmel CA 831-624-7917 (800-297-6250)
http://www.carmelhappylanding.com
This dog-friendly B&B is located six blocks from the Carmel leash free beach and in the middle of Carmel-By-The-Sea. Pets of all sizes are allowed. There is a $20 per day pet fee for one pet and $30 per day for two pets.

Hofsas House Hotel San Carlos Street Carmel CA 831-624-2745
There is a $15 per day additional pet fee. The hotel is located between 3rd Ave and 4th Ave in Carmel. Thanks to one of our readers for recommending this hotel.

Lincoln Green Inn PO Box 2747 Carmel CA 831-624-7738
http://www.vagabondshouseinn.com
These cottages are owned and booked through the dog-friendly Vagabond's House Inn in Carmel. One big difference between the two accommodations is that the Vagabond's House does not allow children, whereas the Lincoln Green does allow children. The Lincoln Green is located very close to a beach. All cottages are non-smoking and there is a $20 per day pet fee.

Sunset House Camino Real and Ocean Ave Carmel CA 831-624-4884
http://www.sunset-carmel.com
There is a $20 one time pet fee. Thanks to one of our readers who writes "Great B&B, breakfast brought to your room every morning."

The Forest Lodge Cottages Ocean Ave. and Torres St. (P.O. Box 1316) Carmel CA 831-624-7055
These cottages are surrounded by oak and pine trees among a large garden area. They are conveniently located within walking distance to many dog-friendly restaurants and the dog-friendly Carmel City Beach. There is a $10 one time additional pet fee.

The Tradewinds at Carmel Mission Street at 3rd Avenue Carmel CA 831-624-2776 (800-624-6665)
http://www.tradewindscarmel.com
This motel allows dogs in several of their rooms. They are a non-smoking inn. It's located about 3-4 blocks north of Ocean Ave and close to many outdoor dog-friendly restaurants in downtown Carmel. A 20-25 minute walk will take you to the dog-friendly Carmel City beach. There is a $25 per day pet charge.

Vagabond's House Inn B&B P.O. Box 2747 Carmel CA 831-624-7738 (800-262-1262)
http://www.vagabondshouseinn.com/
This dog-friendly bed and breakfast is located in downtown and has 11 rooms. It's close to many downtown outdoor dog-friendly restaurants. A 20-25 minute walk will take you to the dog-friendly Carmel City beach. Children 12 years and older are allowed at this B&B inn.

Wayside Inn Mission St & 7th Ave. Carmel CA 831-624-5336 (800-433-4732)
http://www.ibts-waysideinn.com/
This motel allows dogs in several of their rooms and is close to many downtown outdoor dog-friendly restaurants. A 20-25 minute walk will take you to the dog-friendly Carmel City beach. Pets are welcome at no extra charge. Dogs up to about 75 pounds are allowed.

Carmel Valley Lodge Carmel Valley Rd Carmel Valley CA 831-659-2261 (800-641-4646)
http://www.valleylodge.com
Your dog will feel welcome at this country retreat. Pet amenities include heart-shaped, organic homemade dog biscuits and a pawtographed picture of Lucky the Lodge Dog. Dogs must be on leash, but for your convenience, there are doggy-hitches at the front door of every unit that has a patio or deck and at the pool. There are 31 units which range from standard rooms to two bedroom cottages. A great community park is located across the street and several restaurants with outdoor seating are within a 5 minute walk. Drive about 15 minutes from the lodge and you'll be in downtown Carmel or at one of the dog-friendly beaches. Dogs are an extra $10 per day and up to two dogs per room. There is no charge for childen under 16. The lodge is located in Carmel Valley. From Carmel, head south on Hwy 1. Turn left on Carmel Valley Rd., drive about 11-12 miles and the lodge will be located at Ford Rd.

Country Garden Inns/Acacia Lodge 102 W Carmel Valley Road Carmel Valley CA 831-659-5361 (800-367-3336)
http://www.countrygardeninns.com/
Individually decorated rooms, a lush garden setting, walking distance to the village, and an outdoor pool/picnic area and spa are just a few of the amenities to be found at this retreat. A generous continental breakfast and a hosted evening wine and cheese hour are also included. Dogs of all sizes are allowed for an additional one time pet fee of $25 per room. Dogs may only be left alone in the room if they will be quiet and well behaved, and they must be leashed and cleaned up after at all times. Dogs are not allowed at the Hidden Valley Inn which is nearby.

Forest Lodge Cottages Corner of Ocean and Torres; P.O. Box 1316 Carmel by the Sea CA 831-624-7023
Dogs of all sizes are allowed. There is a $20 per night fee for one dog, a $30 per night fee for 2 dogs, and a pet policy to sign at check in. They request you exercise and relieve your pet off the grounds.

The Lodge at Pebble Beach 1700 17 Mile Drive Pebble Beach CA 831-624-3811 (800-654-9300)
With a long list of accolades to its name, this elegant inn offers attentive hospitality, world-class luxury suites with a fireplace, and a patio or balcony-each offering stunning views, 4 championship golf courses, and great hiking

trails. Dogs up to 25 pounds are allowed. There are no additional pet fees. Dogs may not be left unattended in the rooms, and they must be leashed and cleaned up after at all times. Dogs are allowed on the trails; they are not allowed on the golf courses.

Campgrounds and RV Parks

Carmel by the River RV Park 27680 Schulte Road Carmel CA 831-624-9329
http://www.carmelrv.com/CarmelRVpark.htm
This RV park is located right next to the river. Amenities include hookups, a basketball court, recreation room and dog walk area. Per Monterey County's Ordinance, the maximum length per stay from April through September is 14 days and from October through March is 8 weeks. Well-behaved quiet dogs of all sizes are allowed, up to a maximum of three pets. Pets must be kept on a short leash and never left unattended in the campsite or in your RV. People need to clean up after their pets. There is a $2 per night per dog pet fee. The owners have dogs that usually stay at the office. There is a dog walk area at the campground.

Attractions

TOP 200 PLACE Carmel Walks-Walking Tours Lincoln and Ocean Streets Carmel CA 831-642-2700
http://www.carmelwalks.com
Discover the special charms and secrets of Carmel on this two hour guided walking tour. Walk through award-winning gardens, by enchanting fairy tale cottages and learn the homes, haunts, and history of famous artists, writers, and movie stars. Your leashed dog is welcome to join you. Tours are offered every Saturday at 10am and 2pm. Tuesday thru Friday, the tours are at 10am. The cost is $20 per person and dogs get the tour for free. Prices are subject to change. Reservations are required.
Seventeen Mile Drive Seventeen Mile Drive Carmel CA
This toll road costs $8 and allows you to access a very scenic section of coastline, walking trails and beaches. Dogs are allowed all along 17 mile drive on leash.

Shopping Centers

Carmel Village Shopping Area Ocean Ave Carmel CA
This shopping expedition is more of a window shopping adventure, however there are some dog-friendly stores throughout this popular and quaint village. Just ask a store clerk before entering into a store with your pooch. We do know that the Galerie Blue Dog (Blue Dog Gallery) located at 6th Ave. and Lincoln St. is dog-friendly. There are also many dog-friendly restaurants throughout the village (see Restaurants).
Crossroads Shopping Center Cabrillo Hwy (Hwy 1) Carmel Valley CA
This is an outdoor shopping mall with many dog-friendly outdoor restaurants and a pet store. While your dog cannot go into the shops, he or she is more than welcome inside the pet store.

Stores

Blue Dog Gallery 6th Ave. and Lincoln St. Carmel CA 831-626-4444
First created in 1984, Blue Dog is based on the mythical "loup garou," a French-Cajun ghost dog, and Tiffany, Rodrique's own pooch who had passed away a few years prior to the notoriety. Blue Dog represents a dog who is between heaven and earth. Ask about the story behind Blue Dog when you visit this gallery. The painter, Rodrique, is an internationally acclaimed painter. Blue Dog will probably look familiar to you because Absolut Vodka and other companies have used it for their marketing campaigns. This gallery usually has some cookies and treats for visiting pooches. Thanks to one of our readers who writes: "A most wonderful place, I called asking for information after Rodrigue did a picture for Neiman Marcus . . . the lady with whom I spoke sent us information plus dog biscuits for our corgi.."
Yellow Dog Gallery Dolores & 5th Ave Carmel CA 831-624-3238
This contemporary art gallery has a large number of dog works and allows your dog to visit with you.

Beaches

TOP 200 PLACE Carmel City Beach Ocean Avenue Carmel CA 831-624-9423
This beach is within walking distance (about 7 blocks) from the quaint village of Carmel. There are a couple of hotels and several restaurants that are within walking distance of the beach. Your pooch is allowed to run off-leash as long as he or she is under voice control. To get there, take the Ocean Avenue exit from Hwy 1 and follow Ocean Ave to the end. You can see a picture of the beach in the "Must See" chapter at the front.

Carmel River State Beach

Carmel River State Beach Carmelo Street Carmel CA 831-624-9423
This beach is just south of Carmel. It has approximately a mile of beach and leashes are required. It's located on Carmelo Street.

Garrapata State Park Highway 1 Carmel CA 831-649-2836
There are two miles of beach front at this park. Dogs are allowed but must be on a 6 foot or less leash and people need to clean up after their pets. The beach is on Highway 1, about 6 1/2 miles south of Rio Road in Carmel. It is about 18 miles north of Big Sur.

Parks

Garland Ranch Regional Park Carmel Valley Rd. Carmel Valley CA 831-659-4488
http://www.mprpd.org/parks/garland.html
This 4,500 acre regional park offers about 5 to 6 miles of dirt single-track and fire road trails. The trail offers a variety of landscapes, with elevations ranging from 200 to 2000 feet. If you are looking for some exercise in addition to the beaches, this is the spot. Dogs must be on a 7 foot or less leash. They can also be under direct voice control which is defined by park management as you having close visual contact of your dog, not letting them run far ahead or behind you, and having a dog that listens to your commands. Dogs are not allowed to bother any wildlife, other people or other dogs. People who violate this regulation may be cited and lose access privileges. Please also clean up after your pet. The park is located 8.6 miles east of Highway 1 on Carmel Valley Road.

Outdoor Restaurants

Anton and Michel Mission Street and 7th Avenue Carmel CA 831-624-2406
This fine dining eatery is considered one of the areas most beautiful and romantic restaurants and they offer an innovative continental cuisine combined with traditional fare giving an emphasis on light and flavorful sauces. There is indoor dining, and, when weather permits, there is outdoor dining on a fountain patio. Dogs are allowed at the outdoor tables in the front of the cafe. They must be well behaved, under owner's control at all times, leashed, and cleaned up after.

Carmel Bistro San Carlos St between 5th and 6th Carmel CA 831-626-6003
This bistro serves CA American food. Dogs are allowed at the outdoor tables. Water is provided and treats at a cost.

Casanova Restaurant Mission & 5th Carmel CA 831-625-0501
http://www.casanovarestaurant.com/ .
This dog-friendly restaurant has several outdoor tables in the front with heaters. It's located in downtown near

several hotels and within a 20-25 minute walk to the dog-friendly beach.

Anton and Michels Restaurant

Flaherty's Seafood Grill Dolores and San Carlos Carmel CA 831-625-1500
This restaurant serves American and seafood. Dogs are allowed at the outdoor tables.
Forge in the Forest 5th and Junipero, SW Corner Carmel CA 831-624-2233
Dogs are allowed to dine in this elegantly designed outdoor patio. Dogs are only allowed at certain tables on the upper patio.
Hog's Breath Inn San Carlos St and 5th Ave Carmel CA 831-625-1044
This restaurant serves American food. Dogs are allowed at the outdoor tables.
Le Coq D'Or Mission between 4th & 5th Carmel CA 831-626-9319
http://www.lecoqdor.com/
Your well-behaved dog is welcome on their heated outdoor patio. This is a European country restaurant that serves an innovative menu of German and French specialties. Your pooch will feel welcome here.
Nico's San Carlos St and Ocean Ave Carmel CA 831-624-6545
This restaurant serves Mediterranean food. Dogs are allowed at the outdoor tables.
Bistro 211 Restaurant 211 The Crossroads Carmel Valley CA 831-625-3030
Dogs are allowed on the outdoor patio. The restaurant is located in the Crossroads Shopping Center in Carmel Valley. A pet store is nearby.
Brunello 3 Del Fino Pl Carmel Valley CA 831-659-9119
Dogs are allowed at the outdoor tables.
Cafe Stravaganza 241 The Crossroads Carmel Valley CA 831-625-3733
Located in the Crossroads Shopping Center in Carmel Valley, this restaurant offers dog-friendly outdoor dining. A pet store is nearby.
Oak Deli 24 W Carmel Valley Rd Carmel Valley CA 831-659-3416
Dogs are allowed at the outdoor tables.
Plaza Linda 9 Del Fino Pl Carmel Valley CA 831-659-4229
This "dog-friendly" restaurant has a sign out front that says so. Sit on the front patio.
The Corkscrew Cafe 55 W Carmel Valley Rd Carmel Valley CA 831-659-8888
http://www.corkscrewcafe.com/home.html
Their daily menu reflects the use of fresh herbs and seasonal produce from their large gardens, paired with local fish and meats. Dogs are allowed at the outdoor tables.

TOP 200 PLACE **PortaBella** Ocean Ave Carmel CA   831-624-4395
Dogs... come here to be treated first class. Your waiter will bring your pup water in a champagne bucket. They have several outdoor tables with heaters. It's located in downtown near several hotels and within a 15-20 minute walk to the beach.

The PortaBella Restaurant

Vets and Kennels
Monterey Peninsula - Salinas Emergency Vet 2 Harris Court Suite A1 Monterey CA   831-373-7374
Monday - Thursday 5:30 pm to 8 am. Friday 5:30 pm to Monday 8 am.

Creston

Accommodations
J & J Guest House 5515 Calumet Lane Creston CA   805-226-9558
Well behaved dogs of all sizes are allowed, but keep in mind it is a fairly small cabin of about 600 square fee. There are no additional pet fees.

Gorda

Campgrounds and RV Parks
Kirk Creek Campground Hwy 1 Gorda CA   831-385-5434
Located in the Los Padres National Forest, this campground is situated on an open bluff 100 feet above sea level and offers great views of the ocean and coastline. The beach is reached by hiking down from the campgrounds. The Kirk Creek trailhead is also located at the campground and leads to the Vicente Flat Trail which offers miles of hiking trails. Dogs are allowed in the campgrounds, on the hiking trails, and on the beach, but they must be leashed. Dogs must be cleaned up after. Be aware that there are large amounts of poison oak on the trails. RVs up to 30 feet are permitted. The campground is located about 25 miles south of Big Sur. There

is no additional fee for pets, but dogs must have proof of rabies vaccinations and current shot records. Dogs may not be left unattended outside, and left inside an RV only if they will be quiet and comfortable. The camping and tent areas also allow dogs. There is a dog walk area at the campground. There are no electric or water hookups at the campgrounds.

Plaskett Creek Campground Hwy 1 Gorda CA 831-385-5434 (877-444-6677)
Located in the Los Padres National Forest, this tent and RV campground is nestled among large Monterey Pine trees. The campsites are within walking distance of the dog-friendly Sand Dollar Beach. Dogs of all sizes are allowed at no additional fee. Dogs may not be left unattended outside, and left inside only if they will be quiet and comfortable. Dogs must be leashed in the campgrounds, on trails, on the beach, and have proof of current shots. The campground is about 5 miles south of the Kirk Creek and about 30 miles south of Big Sur. The camping and tent areas also allow dogs. There is a dog walk area at the campground. There are no electric or water hookups at the campgrounds.

Beaches

Kirk Creek Beach and Trailhead Highway 1 Gorda CA 831-385-5434
Both the Kirk Creek Beach and hiking trails allow dogs. Pets must be leashed. You can park next to the Kirk Creek Campground and either hike down to the beach or start hiking at the Kirk Creek Trailhead which leads to the Vicente Flat Trail where you can hike for miles with your dog. The beach and trailhead is part of the Los Padres National Forest and is located about 25 miles south of Big Sur.

Sand Dollar Beach Highway 1 Gorda CA 805-434-1996
Walk down a path to one of the longest sandy beaches on the Big Sur Coast. This national forest managed beach is popular for surfing, fishing and walking. Dogs must be on leash and people need to clean up after their pets. There is a minimal day use fee. The dog-friendly Plaskett Creek Campground is within walking distance. This beach is part of the Los Padres National Forest and is located about 5 miles south of the Kirk Creek and about 30 miles south of Big Sur.

Willow Creek Beach Highway 1 Gorda CA 831-385-5434
Dogs on leash are allowed at this day use beach and picnic area. The beach is part of the Los Padres National Forest and is located about 35 miles south of Big Sur.

Hollister

Campgrounds and RV Parks

Casa de Fruta, RV Orchard Resort 10031 Pacheco Pass H Hollister CA 408-842-9316 (800-548-3813 (Information))
This RV park is located at a popular roadside orchard resort which features a fruit stand, store, 24 hour restaurant, zoo, rock shop, gold panning, children's train ride, children's playground and picnic areas. Amenities at the RV park include full hookups, pull through sites, shady areas, TV hookups and seasonal tent sites. Well-behaved leashed dogs are allowed. Dogs may not be left unattended. There is a $3 per night pet fee per pet. Please clean up after your pets. The resort is located on Highway 152/Pacheco Pass, two miles east of the Highway 156 junction. The camping and tent areas also allow dogs. There is a dog walk area at the campground.

King City

Accommodations

Motel 6 - King City 3 Broadway Circle King City CA 831-385-5000 (800-466-8356)
One well-behaved family pet per room. Guest must notify front desk upon arrival. Guest is liable for any damages. In consideration of all guests, pets must never be left unattended in the guest rooms.

Campgrounds and RV Parks

San Lorenzo Campground and RV Park 1160 Broadway King City CA 831-385-5964
This campground is located in the dog-friendly San Lorenzo Park where leashed dogs are allowed on the hiking trails. Camp amenities include grassy tent sites, shaded RV spaces, an information center and museum, a walking trail along the river, laundry facilities, a putting green, playground, internet access kiosk, restrooms, and showers. Well-behaved leashed dogs of all sizes are allowed in the campground. Pets must be attended at all times. People need to clean up after their pets. There is a $2 per night per pet fee. Dogs are allowed on the trails, on roads, and at a place on the other side of the levy. The camping and tent areas also allow dogs. There is a dog walk area at the campground.

Parks

San Lorenzo Regional Park 1160 Broadway King City CA   831-385-5964
This park is located in the foothills of the Santa Lucia Mountains and along the Salinas River. Amenities include a walking trail along the river, picnic areas, playgrounds, volleyball courts, softball areas and camping. Dogs are allowed but must be leashed. Please clean up after your pets.

Lompac

Accommodations

Super 8 Lompoc 1020 E Ocean Ave Lompac CA   805-735-6444 (800-800-8000)
Dogs of all sizes are allowed. There is a $10 one time per pet fee per visit. Smoking and non-smoking rooms are available for pet rooms.

Lompoc

Accommodations

Days Inn - Vandenberg Village 3955 Apollo Way Lompoc CA   805-733-5000 (800-329-7466)
There is a $250 refundable deposit and a $20 one time pet fee. Dogs may not be left alone in the rooms.
Motel 6 - Lompoc 1521 North H Street Lompoc CA   805-735-7631 (800-466-8356)
One well-behaved family pet per room. Guest must notify front desk upon arrival. Guest is liable for any damages. In consideration of all guests, pets must never be left unattended in the guest rooms.
Quality Inn and Suites 1621 N H Street Lompoc CA   805-735-8555 (877-424-6423)
Dogs of all sizes are allowed. There can be 1 large or 2 small to medium dogs per room. There is a $25 one time fee per pet, and a pet policy to sign at check in. Dogs must be leashed, cleaned up after, and removed for housekeeping. Dogs must be crated when left alone in the room, and a contact number left with the front desk.

Stores

Petco Pet Store 717 North H St Lompoc CA   805-735-6436
Your licensed and well-behaved leashed dog is allowed in the store.

Parks

La Purisima Mission State Historic Park 2295 Purisima Road Lompoc CA   805-733-3713
This mission was founded in 1787 and is one of the most completely resorted Spanish missions in California. While dogs are not allowed in the buildings, they are allowed on the grounds and on miles of trails. Pets must be on a 6 foot or less leash and please clean up after them. The park is located about 2 miles northeast of Lompoc.

Monterey

Accommodations

Motel 6 - Monterey - Marina 100 Reservation Road Marina CA   831-384-1000 (800-466-8356)
One well-behaved family pet per room. Guest must notify front desk upon arrival. Guest is liable for any damages. In consideration of all guests, pets must never be left unattended in the guest rooms.
Bay Park Hotel 1425 Munras Avenue Monterey CA   831-649-1020
Dogs of all sizes are allowed. There is a $20 per room per stay additional pet fee. Dogs are not allowed to be left alone in the room.
Best Western The Beach Resort 2600 Sand Dunes Dr Monterey CA   831-394-3321 (800-780-7234)
Dogs of all sizes are allowed. There is a $25 one time pet fee per visit. Smoking and non-smoking are available for pet rooms.
El Adobe Inn 936 Munras Ave. Monterey CA   831-372-5409
This inn is located on Munras Ave. about 1/2 mile east of Hwy 1. There is a $10 per day additional pet fee.
Hyatt Regency Monterey 1 Old Golf Course Road Monterey CA   831-372-1234
The warm colors and fireplaces throughout this resort offer a relaxed atmosphere for the business or leisure traveler. Amenities include spacious guestrooms, room service, pools, a golf course, tennis courts, massage

therapy, dining and entertainment, an award winning sports bar, and a 24 hour fully automated business center. Dogs of all sizes are allowed. There is a $50 one time additional pet fee per room. Dogs must be crated when left alone in the room, and they must be leashed and cleaned up after.

Monterey Fireside Lodge 1131 10th Street Monterey CA 831-373-4172 (800-722-2624)
http://www.montereyfireside.com/
All 24 rooms have gas fireplaces. There is an additional $20/day pet charge.

Motel 6 - Monterey 2124 North Fremont Street Monterey CA 831-646-8585 (800-466-8356)
One well-behaved family pet per room. Guest must notify front desk upon arrival. Guest is liable for any damages. In consideration of all guests, pets must never be left unattended in the guest rooms.

Andril Fireplace Cottages 569 Asilomar Blvd Pacific Grove CA 831-375-0994
There is an additional fee of $14 per day for a pet. Well-behaved dogs are allowed.

Lighthouse Lodge and Suites 1249 Lighthouse Ave Pacific Grove CA 831-655-2111

Attractions

La Mirada House and Gardens 720 Via Mirada Monterey CA 831-372-3689
Radiating an ambiance of early California, these magnificent gardens are surrounded by the warmly inviting adobe walls of an elegant home that has been exquisitely furnished to be reminiscent of its early years. Visitors will also enjoy spectacular views of the Monterey Bay. Although dogs are not allowed in the home, they are allowed to stroll through the gardens. Dogs must be well mannered, leashed, and cleaned up after at all times. They are closed on Monday and Tuesday.

Monterey Bay Whale Watch Boat Tours Fisherman's Wharf Monterey CA 831-375-4658
http://www.montereybaywhalewatch.com/
Monterey Bay Whale Watch offers year-round whale watching trips to observe whales and dolphins in Monterey Bay. Tours are 3 - 6 hours. Well-behaved dogs on leash are allowed. The tours are located at Sam's Fishing Fleet on Fisherman's Wharf in Monterey.

Princess Monterey Whale Watch 96 Fishermans Wharf Monterey CA 800-200-2203
This whale watching cruiser offers 2 ½ to 3 hour fully narrated tours by a marine biologist. With one of the largest and most comfortable boats in the bay, they offer plenty of seating in a warm cabin for cold days, a snack bar, and spacious restrooms. Dogs of all sizes are welcome to come aboard when they are not real busy. During the week and the slow part of the season are good times to plan a trip. There is no additional fee for dogs. Dogs must be friendly, boat wise, and they must be leashed at all times and cleaned up after. Please bring your own clean up supplies. Dogs are not allowed to loiter on the wharf by the shops.

TOP 200 PLACE **Randy's Fishing Trips** 66 Old Fisherman's Wharf #1 Monterey CA 800-251-7440
http://www.randysfishingtrips.com/
This fishing and whale viewing cruiser offers fully narrated tours of this region that is as rich in marine life as it is in its history. Dogs of all sizes are welcome to come aboard when they are not busy. During the week and the slow part of the season are good times to plan a trip. There is no additional fee for dogs. Dogs must be friendly, boat wise, and they must be leashed at all times and cleaned up after. Please bring your own clean up supplies. Dogs are not allowed to loiter on the wharf by the shops.

Sea Life Tours 90 Fishermans Wharf Monterey CA 831-372-7150
http://www.sealifetours.com/
This boat allows leashed dogs on its 45 minute tours of the Monterey bay where you can view sea lions and sometimes whales and other sea life.

Ventana Vineyards 2999 Monterey-Salinas Highway, #10 Monterey CA 831-372-7415
http://www.ventanawines.com/
This award-winning winery has certain wines that are unique to Ventana and Meador Estates, such as Beaugravier, Magnus, "Due Amici", and Dry Rosado, in addition to an impressive list of other classics. The old stone house tasting room was built in 1919 and is surrounded now by lush greenery and splashes of color and fragrance from all the potted flowers. There are tables and bench seating on the patio that also has an open-top fireplace, and is a great place for a picnic. Dogs are not allowed in the building, but they are allowed on the patio and around the grounds. Dogs must be friendly, leashed, and cleaned up after.

Stores

Petco Pet Store 960 Del Monte Center Monterey CA 831-373-1310
Your licensed and well-behaved leashed dog is allowed in the store.

Best Friends Pet Wash 167 Central Ave # A Pacific Grove CA 831-375-2477
After a day at the beach with your pup you may want to wash the sand away here at a self serve pet wash.

PetSmart Pet Store 2020 California Ave Sand City CA 831-392-0150
Your licensed and well-behaved leashed dog is allowed in the store.

Beaches

Monterey Recreation Trail

Monterey State Beach

TOP 200 PLACE **Monterey Recreation Trail** various (see comments) Monterey CA
Take a walk on the Monterey Recreation Trail and experience the beautiful scenery that makes Monterey so famous. This paved trail extends for miles, starting at Fisherman's Wharf and ending in the city of Pacific Grove. Dogs must be leashed. Along the path there are a few small beaches that allow dogs such as the one south of Fisherman's Wharf and another beach behind Ghirardelli Ice Cream on Cannery Row. Along the path you'll find a few more outdoor places to eat near Cannery Row and by the Monterey Bay Aquarium. Look at the Restaurants section for more info.
Monterey State Beach various (see comments) Monterey CA 831-649-2836
Take your water loving and beach loving dog to this awesome beach in Monterey. There are various starting points, but it basically stretches from Hwy 1 and the Del Rey Oaks Exit down to Fisherman's Wharf. Various beaches make up this 2 mile (each way) stretch of beach, but leashed dogs are allowed on all of them . If you want to extend your walk, you can continue on the paved Monterey Recreation Trail which goes all the way to Pacific Grove. There are a few smaller dog-friendly beaches along the paved trail.
Asilomar State Beach Along Sunset Drive Pacific Grove CA 831-372-4076
Dogs are permitted on leash on the beach and the scenic walking trails. If you walk south along the beach and go across the stream that leads into the ocean, you can take your dog off-leash, but he or she must be under strict voice control and within your sight at all times.

Parks

El Estero Park Camino El Estero & Fremont St Monterey CA 831-646-3860
This is a city park with a lake, trails around the lake, a children's play area and many places to walk your dog. It's located on the east side of town.
Jacks Peak County Park 25020 Jacks Peak Park Road Monterey CA 831-755-4895
This wooded park offers great views of the Monterey Bay area. You and your dog can enjoy almost 8.5 miles of hiking trails which wind through forests to ridge top vistas. Park amenities include picnic areas and restrooms. There is a $2 vehicle entrance fee during the week and a $3 fee on weekends and holidays. Dogs need to be leashed and please clean up after them.

Outdoor Restaurants

Archie's Hamburgers & Breakfast 125 Ocean View Blvd. Monterey CA 831-375-6939
Enjoy a hamburger or chicken sandwich for lunch and dinner or come early and have some breakfast at this restaurant that overlooks the ocean. The Monterey Recreation Trail is directly across the street.
Captain's Gig Restaurant 6 Fishermans Wharf #1 Monterey CA 831-373-5559
This restaurant has outdoor seating on Fisherman's Wharf in Monterey.
El Palomar Mexican Restaurant 724 Abrego St Monterey CA 831-372-1032
Dogs are allowed at the outdoor tables.
Ghiradelli Ice Cream 660 Cannery Row Monterey CA 831-373-0997
Come here for some of the best tasting ice cream. While there, you have a choice of outdoor seating. They have nice patio seating shaded by a large tree or ocean view seating that is covered. Afterwards you and your pup can enjoy the small beach below (dogs on leash only).
Grill and Ryan Ranch 1 Harris Court Monterey CA 831-647-0390
http://www.grillatryanranch.com
This casual fine dining restaurant allows dogs at the outdoor tables.
Indian Summer 220 Olivier Street Monterey CA 831-372-4744
This restaurant serves Indian food. Dogs are allowed at the outdoor tables.
Jose's Restaurant 638 Wave St Monterey CA 831-655-4419
This restaurant has a few outdoor tables and heaters. Dogs are welcome at these tables.
London Bridge Pub & Restaurant Municipal Wharf Monterey CA 831-655-2879
Enjoy tasty English food at this British Pub located on the Municipal Wharf between Fisherman's Wharf and the Monterey Beaches. They serve lunch outside and possibly dinner depending how cold it gets at night.
Peter B's Brewery & Restaurant 2 Portola Plaza Monterey CA 831-649-4511
This restaurant is located in the Doubletree Hotel just east of Fisherman's Wharf and near the Monterey State Historic Park. They do not always offer the outdoor dining so call ahead. If they are serving outside you can order a good lunch and great beer.
Pino's Italian Cafe & Ice Cream 211 Alvarado St Monterey CA 831-649-1930
This Italian cafe & ice cream/gelato shop has a few outdoor seats and is located between Fisherman's Wharf and the Doubletree Hotel near the Monterey State Historic Park.
Tarpy's Road House 2999 Monterey Salinas Hwy #1 Monterey CA 831-647-1444
This 1800's looking complex is an interesting atmosphere for dining with your dog. There is a courtyard with a large number of outdoor tables. The restaurant is about 5 miles out of town on the Salinas highway.
Trailside Cafe 550 Wave Street Monterey CA 831-649-8600
http://www.trailsidecafe.com
Thanks to one of our readers for recommending this dog-friendly restaurant: "A terrific restaurant we found for

breakfast during our morning walks is the Trailside Cafe. I know you request an address, but i don't have a specific one, except to say it is on the Monterey Rail Trail (Monterey Recreation Trail). ...my pooch loved the ocean view of the trail, but most importantly the special biscuit treats he recieved from the waitstaff when we ordered our wonderful breakfasts. the food is marvelous and staff very good... the patio has a breathtaking view of the pacific.

London Bridge Pub & Restaurant

Morgan's Coffee Shop 498 Washington St Monterey CA 831-373-5601
Turtle Bay Taqueria 431 Tyler St Monterey CA 831-333-1500
Turtle Bay Taqueria is in Old Monterey. It has a few outdoor tables for dining with your pup.
Whole Foods Market 800 Del Monte Center Monterey CA 831-333-1600
http://www.wholefoods.com/
This natural food supermarket offers natural and organic foods. Order some food from their deli without your dog and bring it to an outdoor table where your well-behaved leashed dog is welcome. Dogs are not allowed in the store including the deli at any time.
Bagel Bakery 1132 Forest Ave Pacific Grove CA 831-649-6272
Dogs are allowed at the outdoor tables.
First Awakenings 125 Ocean View Blvd #105 Pacific Grove CA 831-372-1125
Dogs are allowed at the outdoor tables.
Seventeenth Street Grill 617 Lighthouse Ave Pacific Grove CA 831-373-5474
Dogs are allowed at the outdoor tables.
Toasties Cafe 702 Lighthouse Ave Pacific Grove CA 831-373-7543
Toasties Cafe has a large number of outdoor tables for you and your dog.
Bagel Bakery 2160 California Ave Seaside CA 831-392-1581
Dogs are allowed at the outdoor tables.
Jamba Juice 2160 California Ave Seaside CA 831-583-9696
Dogs are allowed at the outdoor tables.

Vets and Kennels
Monterey Peninsula - Salinas Emergency Vet 2 l larris Court Suite A1 Monterey CA 831-373-7374
Monday - Thursday 5:30 pm to 8 am. Friday 5:30 pm to Monday 8 am.

Newbury Park

Accommodations

Motel 6 - Thousand Oaks South 1516 Newbury Rd Newbury Park CA   805-499-0711 (800-466-8356)
One well-behaved family pet per room. Guest must notify front desk upon arrival. Guest is liable for any damages. In consideration of all guests, pets must never be left unattended in the guest rooms.

Outdoor Restaurants

Baja Fresh Mexican Grill 1015 Broadbeck Dr. Newbury Park CA   805-376-0808
http://www.bajafresh.com
This Mexican restaurant is open for lunch and dinner. They use fresh ingredients and making their salsa and beans daily. Some of the items on their menu include Enchiladas, Burritos, Tacos Salads, Quesadillas, Nachos, Chicken, Steak and more. Well-behaved leashed dogs are allowed at the outdoor tables.

Ojai

Accommodations

Oakridge Inn 780 Ventura Avenue Oak View CA   805-649-4018
http://www.oakridgeinn.com/
This great getaway offers 33 spacious, clean, nicely appointed rooms. Some of the features/amenities include a heated pool and spa, complimentary continental breakfast, and a convenient location to several other attractions and activities. Dogs up to 50 pounds are allowed for an additional pet fee of $15 per night per pet. They may require an additional pet deposit for very hairy dogs. Dogs must be quiet, leashed, cleaned up after, and they may not be left alone in the room at any time.

Lavender Inn

Lavender Inn 210 E Matilija Street Ojai CA   805-646-6635
http://www.lavenderinn.com/
This tranquil retreat offers 7 rooms and an attached cottage, each with its own unique décor of bold colors and detail, and it is conveniently located to several other attractions and activities. The private gardens and fountains are breathtaking complete with tall oaks, mountain views, and a wonderful variety of lavenders. A separate building on the property houses an intimate day spa that offer a variety of massages. One dog up to 50 pounds is

allowed for an additional one time fee of $25. They may accept a slightly larger dog in the cottage only. Dogs must be quiet, well behaved, leashed and cleaned up after.

Ojai Valley Inn and Spa

TOP 200 PLACE Ojai Valley Inn and Spa 905 Country Club Road Ojai CA   805-646-2420 (888-697-8780)
http://www.ojairesort.com/
This award-winning historic resort is elegance inside and out with 220 tree-shaded acres that include luxury accommodations, a premier championship golf course, a comprehensive 31,000 square foot spa village, and a first-of-its-kind artist cottage where local artists inspire and help guests to create in a variety of medias. In addition to several amenities, they also offer in room dining, handcrafted picnics, a cocktail lounge, and several dining options featuring California Central Coast cuisine prepared with locally harvested, seasonal foods and herbs. Dogs of all sizes are allowed but they must be acknowledged at the time of reservations. There is a $50 per night additional pet fee per room for the first 3 nights for a total of no more than $150. Dogs must be quiet, leashed, cleaned up after, and crated when left alone in the room.

Campgrounds and RV Parks
Wheeler Gorge Campground 17017 Maricopa Highway Ojai CA   805-640-1977 (877-444-6777)
This campground is located on a year round stream and is shaded by trees running the length of the camp area. There are vault toilets and potable water, and each site has a table, barbecue, and fire ring. A variety of land and water recreation activities are available, and there are interpretive and campfire nature presentations offered in the summer. Dogs of all sizes are allowed for no additional pet fee. Dogs must be under owner's control at all times, and be leashed and cleaned up after. The camping and tent areas also allow dogs. There is a dog walk area at the campground.

Attractions
TOP 200 PLACE Casitas Boat Rentals 11311 Santa Ana Road Oak View CA   805-649-2043
You, your family and your dog can go for a boat adventure on Lake Casitas. Pontoon and row boat rentals are available and your dog is welcome to accompany you. Boating on the lake is only permitted during daylight hours. There are four floating restrooms for people on the lake. Lake Casitas is a drinking water reservoir and does not allow swimming by people or dogs. Dogs must be on-leash throughout the Lake Casitas Rec Area and may not go within 50 feet of the lake.

Casitas Boat Rentals

Shopping Centers

Downtown Ojai

Downtown Ojai E Ojai Ave at S Montgomery St Ojai CA 805-646-8126

http://www.ci.ojai.ca.us

Ojai is a quaint artist town with a number of art studios, boutique shopping and restaurants, many of which have outdoor dining where your dog is welcome. Ask at the stores if your dog may join you. The downtown district is about ten blocks long and stretches along Ojai Avenue in both directions from Libbey Park, which is home to a number of annual outdoor music festivals during the summer months.

Parks

Lake Casitas Rec Area 11311 Santa Ana Road Oak View CA 805-649-2233

Lake Casitas was created as a drinking water reservoir by the creation of the Casitas Dam. It is well known as one of the top bass fishing lakes in America. Hiking, camping and boating are available in the Recreation Area. Dogs must be on a six foot leash at all times. They must be under control and are not allowed within 50 feet of the lake or streams or inside the Water Adventure area. Dogs are allowed in boats on the lake including the rental boats. There is an $8.00 automobile fee to enter the Rec Area and a $1.50 pet fee per pet per day to use the Rec Area. There is camping in the Rec Area for RVs with lots priced from $19 to $50 per night. Full hookups are available.

Cozy Dell Trail Highway 33 Ojai CA

This trail offers great panoramic views of the Ojai Valley. It is about a 4 mile round trip trail and can take a couple of hours to walk. It is rated an easy to moderate trail. The trail might be a little overgrown during certain times of the year. To get there, take Highway 33 north and go about 3.3 miles north of Ojai. The trail begins near the Friends Ranch Packing House. Park on the left side of the highway. Dogs need to be leashed.

Libbey Park

Libbey Park Ojai Ave at Signal Street Ojai CA 805-646-5581

This city park that is home to many events is located in the heart of picturesque Ojai. Dogs must be on leash at all times. The park boasts a music amphitheater, playground and a well-cut grass area. There are clean up bags for dogs located in the park.

Ojai Valley Trail Hwy 33 at Casitas Vista Rd Ojai CA 805-654-3951

This 9.5 mile trail has a paved pedestrian path and a wood-chip bridle path. Dogs are allowed but must always be on leash. The trail parallels Highway 33 from Foster Park, just outside Ventura to Fox Street, in Ojai.

Outdoor Restaurants

Oak Pit Restaurant 820 Ventura Ave Oak View CA 805-649-9903

Dogs are allowed at the outdoor tables.

Antonio's Breakfast Coffee 106 S Montgomery St Ojai CA 805-646-6353

Dogs are allowed at the outdoor tables.

Deer Lodge Tavern

Deer Lodge Tavern 2261 Maricopa Hwy Ojai CA 805-646-4256
http://www.ojaideerlodge.net
Dogs are allowed at the outdoor tables.
Feast Bistro 254 East Ojai Ave. Ojai CA 805-640-9260
http://www.feastofojai.com
Feast Bistro serves healthy American cuisine. Some of their menu is organic. They have outdoor tables with heaters in the back. Dogs are allowed at the outdoor seats.
Jim & Rob's Fresh Grill 535 E Ojai Ave Ojai CA 805-640-1301
Dogs are allowed at the outdoor tables.
Rainbow Bridge Natural Foods Market 211 East Matilija Street Ojai CA 805-646-4017
http://www.rainbowbridgeojai.com
This natural food market has outdoor tables where you may sit with your dog. You will need to get the food yourself as your dog may not enter the store.
Rainbow Bridge Natural Store and Deli 211 E Matilija St Ojai CA 805-646-6623
http://www.rainbowbridgeojai.com
Dogs are allowed at the outdoor tables.
Tottenham Court 242 E. Ojai Avenue Ojai CA 805-646-2339
http://www.tottenhamcourt.com/
Dogs are allowed at the outdoor tables in the garden patio. Lunches and teas are served at this tea room.

Salinas

Accommodations
Motel 6 - Salinas North - Monterey Area 140 Kern Street Salinas CA 831-753-1711 (800-466-8356)
One well-behaved family pet per room. Guest must notify front desk upon arrival. Guest is liable for any damages. In consideration of all guests, pets must never be left unattended in the guest rooms.
Motel 6 - Salinas South - Monterey Area 1257 De La Torre Boulevard Salinas CA 831-757-3077 (800-466-8356)
One well-behaved family pet per room. Guest must notify front desk upon arrival. Guest is liable for any damages. In consideration of all guests, pets must never be left unattended in the guest rooms.
Residence Inn by Marriott 17215 El Rancho Way Salinas CA 831-775-0410
Pets of all sizes are allowed. There is a $75 one time fee, and a pet policy to sign at check in.

Campgrounds and RV Parks

Laguna Seca Campground 1025 Monterey Hwy 68 Salinas CA   831-755-4895 (888-588-2267)
The popular Laguna Seca raceway is the highlight of this park. The park also offers a rifle range and an OHV and Off-Highway Motocross Track. Dogs are not permitted on any of the tracks including the OHV area. Dogs on leash are allowed at the RV and tent campgrounds, and on hiking trails. There is an additional fee of $2 per night per pet. RV sites are paved and offer up to 30 amp service. Tent sites are dirt pads with showers, telephones and a playground within walking distance. Camping fees are subject to change depending on events that are being held at the raceway. Call ahead for rates and reservations. The camping and tent areas also allow dogs. There is a dog walk area at the campground.

Stores

PetSmart Pet Store 1265 N Davis Rd Salinas CA   831-775-0318
Your licensed and well-behaved leashed dog is allowed in the store.

Parks

Toro County Park 501 Monterey-Salinas Highway 68 Salinas CA   831-755-4895
This 4,756 acre park offers over 20 miles of hiking, biking and horseback riding trails. Other park amenities include playgrounds, picnic sites, volleyball courts and an equestrian staging area. There is a $3 vehicle entrance fee during the week and a $5 fee on weekends and holidays. This park is located 6 miles from downtown Salinas and 13 miles from the Monterey Peninsula. Dogs need to be leashed and please clean up after them.

San Luis Obispo

Accommodations

Motel 6 - Atascadero 9400 El Camino Real Atascadero CA   805-466-6701 (800-466-8356)
One well-behaved family pet per room. Guest must notify front desk upon arrival. Guest is liable for any damages. In consideration of all guests, pets must never be left unattended in the guest rooms.
Cambria Pines Lodge 2905 Burton Drive Cambria CA   805-927-4200
This lodge is a 125 room retreat with accommodations ranging from rustic cabins to fireplace suites. It is nestled among 25 acres of Monterey Pines with forested paths and flower gardens. There is a $25 one time pet charge.
TOP 200 PLACE **Cambria Shores Inn** 6276 Moonstone Beach Drive Cambria CA   805-927-8644 (800-433-9179)
http://www.cambriashores.com
Dogs are allowed for a $10.00 per night per dog fee. Pets must be leashed and never left alone. The inn offers local pet sitting services and provide treats for dogs.
Coastal Escapes Inc. 778 Main Street Cambria CA   805-927-3182 (800-578-2100)
http://www.calcoastvacationrentals.com/
There are a couple of hundred listings with this company and not all houses allow dogs. The properties are located in the picturesque communities of Cayucos and Cambria, and offer an impressive diversity of accommodations from secluded forest settings to oceanfront headlands, and a variety of recreational opportunities nearby. Dogs of all sizes are allowed for one time cleaning fees of $75 to $125, depending on the property; the number of dogs allowed per house also depends on the property. Dogs must be house-trained, well behaved, leashed, and cleaned up after both inside and out.
Pine Lodge 2905 Burton Drive Cambria CA   805-927-4200
Dogs of all sizes are allowed. There is a $25 per night per pet fee and a pet policy to sign at check in.
Cayucos Beach Inn 333 South Ocean Avenue Cayucos CA   805-995-2828
There is a $10 one time pet fee. All rooms in the inn are non-smoking. Family pets are welcome. The inn even has a dog walk and dog wash area. Thanks to one of our readers for this recommendation.
Cypress Tree Motel 125 S. Ocean Avenue Cayucos CA   805-995-3917
This pet-friendly 12-unit motel is located within walking distance to everything in town. Amenities include a garden area with lawn furniture and a barbecue. There is a $10 one time pet charge.
Dolphin Inn 399 S Ocean Ave Cayucos CA   805-995-3810
There is a $10 per day pet charge.
Shoreline Inn 1 North Ocean Avenue Cayucos CA   805-995-3681 (800-549-2244)
http://www.centralcoast.com/shorelineinn
This dog-friendly motel is located on the beach (dogs are not allowed on this State Beach). Dogs are allowed in the first floor rooms which have direct access to a patio area. There is a $10 per day charge for dogs.

Bayfront Inn 1150 Embarcadero Morro Bay CA   805-772-5607
http://www.bayfront-inn.com
There is a $10 per day pet charge.
Days Inn 1095 Main Street Morro Bay CA   805-772-2711 (800-329-7466)
There is an $11 per day pet fee.
Motel 6 - Morro Bay 298 Atascadero Road Morro Bay CA   805-772-5641 (800-466-8356)
All well behaved dogs are welcome. There are no additional pet fees.
Pleasant Inn Motel 235 Harbor Street Morro Bay CA   805-772-8521
http://www.pleasantinnmotel.com/
This motel, family owned and operated, is just one block east of the beautiful Morro Bay waterfront and one block
west of old downtown. All rooms are non-smoking. Dogs and cats are welcome for an extra $5 per day.
Motel 6 - Paso Robles 1134 Black Oak Drive Paso Robles CA   805-239-9090 (800-466-8356)
One well-behaved family pet per room. Guest must notify front desk upon arrival. Guest is liable for any
damages. In consideration of all guests, pets must never be left unattended in the guest rooms.
Cottage Inn by the Sea 2351 Price Street Pismo Beach CA   805-773-4617
Dogs of all sizes are allowed. There is a $10 per night per pet fee and a pet policy to sign at check in.
Motel 6 - Pismo Beach 860 4th Street Pismo Beach CA   805-773-2665 (800-466-8356)
One well-behaved family pet per room. Guest must notify front desk upon arrival. Guest is liable for any
damages. In consideration of all guests, pets must never be left unattended in the guest rooms.
Oxford Suites 651 Five Cities Drive Pismo Beach CA   805-773-3773 (800-982-SUITE)
http://www.oxfordsuites.com
This motel is located within a short drive of the dog-friendly Pismo State Beach. Amenities include a year-round
pool & spa, complimentary full breakfast buffet, an evening reception with beverages & light hor d'oeuvres.
Room amenities for the guest suites include a work table, sofa, microwave oven, refrigerator, TV/VCR, and
wheelchair accessibility. There is a $10 per day pet charge. Dogs must never be left unattended in the room,
even if they are in a crate.
Sea Gypsy Motel 1020 Cypress Street Pismo Beach CA   805-773-1801
http://www.seagypsymotel.com/
This motel is located on the beach and they allow dogs of any size. There is a $15 per day pet charge.

Holiday Inn Express

Holiday Inn Express 1800 Monterey Street San Luis Obispo CA   805-544-8600 (877-270-6405)
Amenities include a free breakfast, outdoor pool and free local calls. They are located about one mile from
downtown San Luis Obispo. Well-behaved, leashed dogs of all sizes are welcome. There is a $25 one time per
stay pet fee. Pet rooms are located on the first floor. The entire inn is non-smoking.
Motel 6 - San Luis Obispo North 1433 Calle Joaquin San Luis Obispo CA   805-549-9595 (800-466-8356)

One well-behaved family pet per room. Guest must notify front desk upon arrival. Guest is liable for any damages. In consideration of all guests, pets must never be left unattended in the guest rooms.

Motel 6 - San Luis Obispo South 1625 Calle Joaquin San Luis Obispo CA 805-541-6992 (800-466-8356)
One well-behaved family pet per room. Guest must notify front desk upon arrival. Guest is liable for any damages. In consideration of all guests, pets must never be left unattended in the guest rooms.

Sands Suites & Motel 1930 Monterey Street San Luis Obispo CA 805-544-0500 (800-441-4657)
http://www.sandssuites.com/
This motel is close to Cal Poly. Amenities include a heated pool and spa, free continental breakfast, self serve laundry facilities and wheelchair accessibility. There is a $10 one time pet fee.

Vagabond Inn 210 Madonna Rd. San Luis Obispo CA 805-544-4710 (800-522-1555)
http://www.vagabondinn.com
This motel is located near Cal Poly. Amenities include a heated pool and whirlpool, complimentary continental breakfast, dry cleaning/laundry service and more. There is a $5 per day pet charge.

Best Western Cavalier Oceanfront Resort 9415 Hearst Dr San Simeon CA 805-927-4688 (800-780-7234)
Dogs of all sizes are allowed. There are no additional pet fees. Only non-smoking rooms used for pets.

Motel 6 - San Simeon - Hearst Castle Area 9070 Castillo Drive San Simeon CA 805-927-8691 (800-466-8356)
One well-behaved family pet per room. Guest must notify front desk upon arrival. Guest is liable for any damages. In consideration of all guests, pets must never be left unattended in the guest rooms.

Silver Surf Motel 9390 Castillo Drive San Simeon CA 805-927-4661 (800-621-3999)
http://www.silversurfmotel.com/
This coastal motel is situated around a courtyard in a park like setting. There are beautiful flower gardens, majestic pine trees, and scenic ocean views. Some rooms offer private balconies, fireplaces or ocean views. Amenities include an indoor pool & spa, and guest laundry facility. There is a $10 per day pet charge.

The Cliffs Resort 2757 Shell Beach Road Shell Beach CA 805-773-5000 (800-826-7827)
http://www.cliffsresort.com/hotel/
With a multi-million dollar renovation and a visually stunning location, this award winning resort features a private oceanfront cliff setting with access to the beach, indoor or outdoor dining and many in room amenities. Dogs are welcome on the 1st floor only, and there is a $50 one time additional pet fee per room. Normally one dog is allowed per room, but they may allow 2 dogs if they are 10 pounds or under. Canine guests are greeted with an amenity kit that includes a comfy bed, a clip ID tag, a treat, water, and food and water bowls. Dogs may be left alone in the room only if they will be quiet and well behaved, and they must be removed or crated for housekeeping. Dogs must be leashed and cleaned up after at all times.

Campgrounds and RV Parks

Lake Lopez Recreation Area Campground 6820 Lopez Drive Arroyo Grande CA 805-788-2381
This campground has 354 campsites which overlook the lake or are nestled among oak trees. This lake is popular for fishing, camping, boating, sailing, water skiing, canoeing, bird-watching and miles of hiking trails ranging from easy to strenuous. The marina allows dogs on their boat rentals for an extra $20 fee. Other amenities at the marina include a guest laundry, grocery store and tackle shop. Dogs must be leashed at all times and people need to clean up after their pets. There is an additional fee of $2 per night per pet. Dogs are not allowed in the water, but they are allowed on the trails. Reservations for the campsites are accepted. The camping and tent areas also allow dogs. There is a dog walk area at the campground.

Lake San Antonio Campground 2610 San Antonio Road Bradley CA 805-472-2311 (888-588-2267)
http://www.lakesanantonio.net/
Lake San Antonio is a premier freshwater recreation area, located just 20 miles inland from California's beautiful Central Coast. Lake San Antonio offers year-round activities including picnicking, camping, fishing, hiking, swimming, boating and water-skiing. Dogs of all sizes are allowed at no additional fee. Dogs must be on no more than a 7 foot leash and be cleaned up after. Dogs are allowed on the trails. The camping and tent areas also allow dogs. There is a dog walk area at the campground.

North Beach Campground, Pismo State Beach Park 555 Pier Avenue Oceano CA 805-489-1869 (800-444-7275)
Close to the ocean, sitting inland behind the dunes, is a beautiful campground offering a variety of land and water recreation. Dogs of all sizes are allowed. There are no additional pet fees. Dogs may not be left unattended, and they must be leashed and cleaned up after. Dogs are allowed on the trails on lead. The camping and tent areas also allow dogs. There is a dog walk area at the campground. There are no electric or water hookups at the campgrounds.

Pacific Dunes RV Resort 1025 Silver Spur Place Oceano CA 760-328-4813 (888-908-7787)
Walk to the dog-friendly sand dunes and beach from this campground. Well-behaved leashed dogs are welcome in the tent sites and RV spaces. Please clean up after your pet. There is no pet fee, and dogs are allowed on the trails. The RV sites are pull through or back-in with 50 amp service, water, electric, sewer hookups, cable TV and a picnic table. Other campground amenities include a volleyball court, pool table, basketball courts, horseback riding, barbecue facilities, bicycle and walking paths, general store, laundry facilities, lighted streets, restrooms/showers, modem hookup and a clubhouse. The camping and tent areas also allow dogs. There is a

dog walk area at the campground.

Lake Nacimiento Resort RV and Campgrounds 10625 Nacimiento Lake Drive Paso Robles CA 805-238-3256 (800-323-3839)

http://www.nacimientoresort.com/

This campground offers a variety of amenities and land and water recreation. Dogs are allowed around and in the lake at this campground, but be careful about letting your dog get too far into the water, as there are many boats on the lake. They are also allowed on trails. Pets must be on no more than a 6 foot leash, cleaned up after, and attended at all times. There is a $10 per day charge for dogs. Proof of your dogs' rabies vaccination is required. The camping and tent areas also allow dogs. There is a dog walk area at the campground.

Pismo Coast Village RV Park

TOP 200 PLACE **Pismo Coast Village RV Park** 165 S Dolliver Street Pismo Beach CA 805-773-1811 (888-RV-BEACH (782-3224))

http://www.pismocoastvillage.com/

This 26 acre RV park is located right on the dog-friendly Pismo State Beach. There are 400 full hookup sites each with satellite TV. RVs up to 40 feet can be accommodated. Nestled right on the beach and beautifully landscaped, park amenities include a general store, arcade, guest laundry, guest modem access in lobby, heated pool, bicycle rentals and miniature golf course. The maximum stay is 29 consecutive nights. Well-behaved leashed dogs of all sizes are allowed, up to a maximum of three pets. People need to clean up after their pets. There is no pet fee. Dogs may not be left unattended outside. This RV only campground is open all year. There are some breed restrictions. There is a dog walk area at the campground.

El Chorro Regional Park Campground Hwy 1 San Luis Obispo CA 805-781-5930

This campground offers 62 campsites for tent or RV camping. Some of the RV spaces are pull through sites and can accommodate RVs up to 40 feet. All sites are available on a first-come, first-served basis. Use the self-registration envelopes upon arrival. There are several hiking trails to choose from at this park, from hiking on meadows to walking along a creek. There is an additional fee of $2 per night per pet. Dogs must be leashed at all times on the trails and in the campground. Please clean up after your pets. This park is home to the Dairy Creek Golf Course and features a day use area, barbecue facilities, volleyball courts, an off leash dog park (with two separate areas - one for smaller pets and one for larger pets), horseshoe pits, a botanical garden, softball fields and various hiking trails. The camping and tent areas also allow dogs. There is a dog walk area at the campground.

Santa Margarita KOA 4765 Santa Margarita Lake Road Santa Margarita CA 805-438-5618 (800-562-5619)

http://www.koa.com/where/ca/05224/

Set in a rural setting with panoramic vistas, other amenities offered are 40 foot pull through sites with 30 amp, LP gas, swimming pool, and planned activities. Dogs of all sizes are allowed for no additional fee. Dogs must be under owner's control and visual observation at all times. Dogs must be quiet, well behaved, and be on no more than a 6 foot leash at all times, or otherwise contained. Dogs may not be left unattended outside the owner's camping equipment, and must be brought inside at night. In the cabins, dogs must remain in their carriers at all times. There are some breed restrictions. The camping and tent areas also allow dogs. There is a dog walk area at the campground. Dogs are allowed in the camping cabins.

Santa Margarita Lake Regional Park Camping 4695 Santa Margarita Lake Road Santa Margarita CA 805-781-5930
Primitive boat-in sites are available at this park. This lake is popular for fishing, boating and hiking. Swimming is not allowed at the lake because it is a reservoir which is used for city drinking water. There is a seasonal swimming pool at the park. Hiking can be enjoyed at this park which offers miles of trails, ranging from easy to strenuous. Dogs must be leashed at all times and people need to clean up after their pets. There is an additional fee of $2 per night per pet. Dogs are allowed on the trails. The camping and tent areas also allow dogs. There is a dog walk area at the campground. There are no electric or water hookups at the campgrounds.

Vacation Home Rentals

The Big Red House 370- B Chelsea Lane Cambria CA 805-927-1390
http://www.thebigredhouse.com
The Big Red House is located 2 blocks from the beach. These vacation rentals have an ocean view from each room. There is a $200 refundable pet deposit.

Attractions

Lake Lopez Boat Rentals 6820 Lopez Drive Arroyo Grande CA 805-489-1006
Rent a motor boat or pontoon boat on Lake Lopez and take your dog along with you. Boat rentals start at about $35 for 2 hours and there is a $10 one time per rental pet fee. The rentals are available year-round.
Lake Lopez Recreation Marina 6820 Lopez Drive Arroyo Grande CA 805-489-1006
A dog may accompany their owner on one of their aluminum boats for an additional fee of $20, the cost of a person. Dogs must be leashed, and they are not allowed in the pontoon boats. The marina is open year round.
Le Cuvier Winery 9750 Adelaida Road Paso Robles CA 805-238-5706
Dogs on leash are allowed at this winery in Paso Robles wine country. Its hours are 11 am to 5 pm daily.
Tablas Creek Vineyard 9339 Adelaida Rd Paso Robles CA 805-237-1231
http://tablascreek.com
Dogs are allowed on and off leash at the outdoor tables and property. There are several other dogs there so they have to be able to get along. The hours are 10am-5pm Monday-Sunday.
San Luis Obispo Botanical Garden Post Office Box 4957 San Luis Obispo CA 805-546-3501
http://www.slobg.org/
This dog-friendly botanical garden is devoted to the display and study of the plants and ecosystems of the five Mediterranean-climate zones of the world: parts of California, Chile, Australia, South Africa and the countries surrounding the Mediterranean Sea. Dogs on leash are allowed. Please pick up after them. The garden is located on Highway 1 in El Chorro Regional Park, between San Luis Obispo and Morro Bay. The garden is open during daylight hours and admission is free. On the weekends, there is a dog fee for entering the regional park. There is also an off leash area for your dog to run, just up the street from the garden.

Shopping Centers

Cambria Historic Downtown 1880-2580 Main Street Cambria CA
Cambria was settled in the early 1860s. In the 1880s it was the second largest town in the county, with an active center of shipping, mining, dairy farming, logging, and ranching. The isolation of Cambria occurred in 1894, when railroad lines were extended into San Luis Obispo from the south, resulting in the decline of coastal shipping. The town's main industry today is tourism. Cambria's Historic Downtown includes 22 historic sites which can be viewed on a self-guided walking tour with your dog. A list of the historic sites can be found at their website (http://new.cambria-online.com/historic/index.asp). There are a few outdoor cafes in downtown Cambria where you and your pup can grab some lunch or dinner.

Stores

Reigning Cats and Dogs 816 Main Street, Suite B Cambria CA 805-927-0857
http://www.thelittledoglaughed.com/
Located on the Central Coast of California, near San Luis Obispo, this store specializes in gifts, collectibles, and unique pet gifts and merchandise for both common and uncommon dog breeds. They are usually open seven days a week.
Teresa Belle Gallery 766 Main Street (Hwy 1) Cambria CA 805-927-4556
http://www.teresabelle.com/
This store, only a few blocks from Moonstone Beach on California's Central Coast, features a unique collection of handmade jewelry and contemporary crafts. Dogs of all sizes are welcome to explore the shop with their owners, and their shop dog looks forward to visitors. Dogs must be well behaved and leashed. The store is open

daily from 10 am to 6pm.
Petco Pet Store 2051 Theater Drive Paso Robles CA 805-238-5857
Your licensed and well-behaved leashed dog is allowed in the store.
Petco Pet Store 271 Madonna Rd San Luis Obispo CA 805-596-0836
Your licensed and well-behaved leashed dog is allowed in the store.

Beaches

Cayucos State Beach Cayucos Drive Cayucos CA 805-781-5200
This state beach allows leashed dogs. The beach is located in the small town of Cayucos. To get to the beach from Hwy 1, exit Cayucos Drive and head west. There is a parking lot and parking along the street.
Oceano Dunes State Vehicular Recreation Area Highway 1 Oceano CA 805-473-7220
This 3,600 acre off road area offers 5 1/2 miles of beach which is open for vehicle use. Pets on leash are allowed too. Swimming, surfing, horseback riding and bird watching are all popular activities at the beach. The park is located three miles south of Pismo Beach off Highway 1.
Lake Nacimento Resort Day Use Area 10625 Nacimiento Lake Drive Paso Robles CA 805-238-3256
http://www.nacimientoresort.com/
In addition to the campgrounds and RV area, this resort also offers day use of the lake. Dogs can swim in the water, but be very careful of boats, as this is a popular lake for water-skiing. Day use fees vary by season and location, but in general rates are about $5 to $8 per person. Senior discounts are available. Dogs are an extra $5 per day. Proof of your dog's rabies vaccination is required.

Pismo State Beach

TOP 200 PLACE Pismo State Beach Grand Ave. Pismo Beach CA 805-489-2684
Leashed dogs are allowed on this state beach. This beach is popular for walking, sunbathing, swimming and the annual winter migration of millions of monarch butterflies (the park has the largest over-wintering colony of monarch butterflies in the U.S.). To get there from Hwy 101, exit 4th Street and head south. In about a mile, turn right onto Grand Ave. You can park along the road.
Coastal Access off Hearst Drive San Simeon CA
There is parking just north of the Best Western Hotel, next to the "Coastal Access" sign. Dogs must be on leash.

Parks

Lake Lopez Recreation Area 6820 Lopez Drive Arroyo Grande CA 805-781-5930
This lake has 22 miles of shoreline and is a popular place for fishing, camping, boating, sailing, water skiing, canoeing, birdwatching and hiking. There are miles of hiking trails, ranging from easy to strenuous. The marina

allows dogs on their boat rentals for an extra $10 fee. Dogs must be leashed at all times and people need to clean up after their pets.

Heilmann Regional Park Cortez Avenue Atascadero CA   805-781-5930
This park offers hiking trails, tennis courts and a disc golf course. The Blue Oak trail is 1.3 miles and is an easy multi-use trail. The Jim Green trail is 1.7 miles multi-use trail that is rated moderate. Dogs must be leashed at all times and people need to clean up after their pets.

Lake San Antonio 2610 San Antonio Road Bradley CA   805-472-2311
http://www.lakesanantonio.net/
This park offers a variety of activities including boating, swimming, fishing and miles of hiking trails. Dogs are allowed on the trails and in the water. This park also offers dog-friendly campgrounds. Pets need to be leashed and please clean up after them. There is a $6 day use fee per vehicle.

Lake Nacimiento Lake Nacimiento Drive Paso Robles CA   805-238-3256
There are approximately 170 miles of tree lined shoreline at this lake. This is a popular lake for boating and fishing. It is the only lake in California that is stocked with White Bass fish. There is also a good population of largemouth and smallmouth bass. The lake offers over 400 campsites and RV sites have both full or partial hook ups. Dogs are allowed around and in the lake. They must be on leash and attended at all times. There is a $5 per day charge for dogs. The lake is located west of Hwy 101, seventeen miles north of Paso Robles. Take the 24th Street (G-14 West) exit in Paso Robles and proceed west on G-14 to the lake.

Santa Margarita Lake Regional Park off Pozo Road Santa Margarita CA   805-781-5930
This lake is popular for fishing, boating and hiking. Swimming is not allowed at the lake because it is a reservoir which is used for city drinking water. There is a seasonal swimming pool at the park. Hiking can be enjoyed at this park which offers miles of trails, ranging from easy to strenuous. Dogs must be leashed at all times and people need to clean up after their pets.

Off-Leash Dog Parks

Heilmann Dog Park

Heilmann Dog Park Atascadero CA
http://www.tcsn.net/parks4pups/
The Heilmann Dog Park is almost one acre in size, fenced, and has restrooms for people. From Highway 101 take the Santa Rosa Avenue exit east, turn right (south) on El Camino Real, and left (east) on El Bordo Avenue.

Cambria Dog Park Main Street and Santa Rosa Creek Rd Cambria CA
The fenced Cambria Dog Park is located south of the town center on Main Street. From Highway 1 North or South take Main Street to the dog park.

El Chorro Regional Park and Dog Park Hwy 1 San Luis Obispo CA   805-781-5930

This regional park offers hiking trails, a botanical garden, volleyball courts, softball fields, campground and a designated off-leash dog park. The hiking trails offer scenic views on Eagle Rock and a cool creek walk along Dairy Creek. The Eagle Rock trail is about .7 miles and is rated strenuous. There are two other trails including Dairy Creek that are about 1 to 2 miles long and rated easy. Dogs must be on leash at all times, except in the dog park. To get to the park from Highway 101, head south and then take the Santa Rosa St. exit. Turn left on Santa Rosa which will turn into Highway 1 after Highland Drive. Continue about 5 miles and the park will be on your left, across from Cuesta College.

Nipomo Park Off-Leash Area W. Tefft St and Pomery Rd San Luis Obispo CA   805-781-5930
http://1nora.tripod.com/
This off-leash area in Nipoma Park is not fenced. It is marked by signs and off-leash dogs must remain in the designated area. The park is open during daylight hours. The park is located 3/4 miles west of 101 on W. Tefft St.

Outdoor Restaurants

Baja Fresh Mexican Grill 929 Rancho Pkwy Arroyo Grande CA   805-474-8900
http://www.bajafresh.com
This Mexican restaurant is open for lunch and dinner. They use fresh ingredients and making their salsa and beans daily. Some of the items on their menu include Enchiladas, Burritos, Tacos Salads, Quesadillas, Nachos, Chicken, Steak and more. Well-behaved leashed dogs are allowed at the outdoor tables.

Branch Street Deli 203 E. Branch St Arroyo Grande CA   805-489-9099
This deli allows well-behaved dogs at the outdoor tables.

Old Village Grill 101 E. Branch St Arroyo Grande CA   805-489-4915
This restaurant has several outdoor dog-friendly tables.

Cambria Courtyard Deli 604 Main Street Cambria CA   805-927-3833
http://www.courtyarddeli.com/
Dogs are welcome in the outdoor garden patio. Located in the village of Cambria, this deli offers a variety of cold and hot sandwiches, salads, soups, smoothies and fresh squeezed juices. Try one of the sandwiches like the Mother Nature Veggie, Italian Sub, Big Sur Tuna Avocado, Chicken, Roast Beef or Black Bean Veggie Burger. They are open 7 days a week. Monday through Thursday and on Sunday, they are open from 10:30 to 4pm. On Friday and Saturday they are open from 10:30am to 6pm. Well-behaved leashed dogs are welcome at the outdoor tables.

Madeline's 788 Main St Cambria CA   805-927-4175
This restaurant serves gourmet style food. Dogs are allowed at the outdoor tables. Reservations are required for the two patio tables outside.

Mustache Pete's 4090 Burton Drive Cambria CA   805-927-8589
http://www.mustachepetes.com
Dogs are allowed at the outdoor eating area, which has heaters and a roof. They have been known to bring a bowl of water for the pup as well.

Dorn's Original Breakers Cafe 801 Market Ave Morro Bay CA   805-772-4415
This restaurant serves American and seafood. Dogs are allowed at the outdoor tables.

Big Bubba's BBQ 1125 24th Street Paso Robles CA   805-238-6272
This restaurant serves Mexican food. Dogs are allowed at the outdoor tables.

Chubby Chandler's Pizza 1304 Railroad St. Paso Robles CA   805-239-2141
You and your pup can order some pizza from the outdoor window and then enjoy it at one of their outdoor picnic tables.

Good Ol' Burgers 1145 24th Street Paso Robles CA   805-238-0655
Dogs are allowed at the outdoor tables on the grass and at the side of the building. Your pup will help you enjoy the burgers or the delicious steak sandwich. There is also a little tree house next to the tables for kids to enjoy.

Longboards 1090 Price Street Pismo Beach CA   805-556-0887
This restaurant serves American food. Dogs are allowed at the outdoor tables.

Mo's Smokehouse BBQ 221 Pomeroy Ave Pismo Beach CA   805-773-6193
This restaurant serves Mexican food. Dogs are allowed at the outdoor tables.

Baja Fresh Mexican Grill 1085 Higuera Street San Luis Obispo CA   805-544-5450
http://www.bajafresh.com
This Mexican restaurant is open for lunch and dinner. They use fresh ingredients and making their salsa and beans daily. Some of the items on their menu include Enchiladas, Burritos, Tacos Salads, Quesadillas, Nachos, Chicken, Steak and more. Well-behaved leashed dogs are allowed at the outdoor tables.

Mo's Smokehouse 970 Higuera Street San Luis Obispo CA   805-544-6193
http://www.mosbbq.com/
This authentic hickory-smoked barbeque restaurant serves pork, chicken, turkey and beef. They also have a variety of side orders including onion rings, fires, coleslaw and potato salad. Well-behaved leashed dogs are allowed at the sidewalk tables.

Novo Restaurant

TOP 200 PLACE **Novo Restaurant** 726 Higuera Street San Luis Obispo CA   805-543-3986
http://www.novorestaurant.com
This restaurant in downtown San Luis Obispo offers creekside dining on its patio. Well-behaved, leashed dogs
are allowed on the outside patio. The restaurant serves Brazilian, Mediterranean and Asian foods. It opens for
lunch at 11 am and remains open through dinner.
Pizza Solo 891 Higuera Street San Luis Obispo CA   805-544-8786
http://www.virtualslo.com/pizzasolo/
This restaurant serves gourmet pizzas plus a variety of salads and sandwiches including several chicken and
vegetarian sandwiches. Well-behaved leashed dogs are allowed at the courtyard tables.
Splash Cafe 1491 Monterey Street San Luis Obispo CA   805-544-7567
http://splashbakery.com/
Featuring daily hand-crafted specials, fresh baked goods, designer chocolates, and a bright, cheerful
environment, this eatery offers indoor or outdoor dining options. Your well behaved dog is welcome to join you at
the outer tables. Dogs must be well mannered, and leashed and cleaned up after.
San Simeon Restaurant 9520 Castillo Dr. San Simeon CA   805-927-4604
Dogs are allowed at the outdoor tables at this restaurant.

Vets and Kennels
Central Coast Pet Emergency Clinic 1558 W Branch St Arroyo Grande CA   805-489-6573
Monday - Friday 6 pm to 8 am, 24 hours on weekends.

Splash Cafe – San Luis Obispo

Santa Barbara

Accommodations
Holiday Inn Express Hotel and Suites 5606 Carpinteria Ave Carpinteria CA   805-566-9499 (877-270-6405)
Dogs of all sizes are allowed. There is a $10 per night pet fee per pet. Reservations are recommended due to limited rooms for pets. Only non-smoking rooms used for pets.
Motel 6 - Santa Barbara-Carpinteria North 4200 Via Real Carpinteria CA 805-684-6921 (800-466-8356)
One well-behaved family pet per room. Guest must notify front desk upon arrival. Guest is liable for any damages. In consideration of all guests, pets must never be left unattended in the guest rooms.
Motel 6 - Santa Barbara-Carpinteria South 5550 Carpinteria Avenue Carpinteria CA 805-684-8602 (800-466-8356)
One well-behaved family pet per room. Guest must notify front desk upon arrival. Guest is liable for any damages. In consideration of all guests, pets must never be left unattended in the guest rooms.
Motel 6 - Santa Barbara - Goleta 5897 Calle Real Goleta CA   805-964-3596 (800-466-8356)
One well-behaved family pet per room. Guest must notify front desk upon arrival. Guest is liable for any damages. In consideration of all guests, pets must never be left unattended in the guest rooms.
San Ysidro Ranch 900 San Ysidro Lane Montecito CA 805-969-5046
Dogs of all sizes are allowed. There is a $100 one time fee per pet.
Best Western Beachside Inn 336 W Cabrillo Blvd Santa Barbara CA 805-965-6556 (800-780-7234)
Dogs of all sizes are allowed. There is a $20 per night pet fee per pet. Smoking and non-smoking are available for pet rooms.
Casa Del Mar Hotel 18 Bath Street Santa Barbara CA 805-963-4418 (800-433-3097)
http://www.casadelmar.com
This popular Mediterranean-style inn is within walking distance of several restaurants, shops and parks. Amenities include a relaxing courtyard Jacuzzi and sun deck surrounded by lush gardens year round. All rooms are non-smoking and equipped with a writing desk and chair or table, telephone, color TV with remote control, and private bathroom. There is a 2 or 3 night minimum stay on the weekends. Pets are welcome. They allow up to two pets per room and there is a $10 per pet charge. Pets must never be left alone or unattended, especially in the rooms. Children under 12 are free and there is no charge for a crib. State Street, a popular shopping area, is within walking distance.

Fess Parkers Doubletree Resort 633 E Cabrillo Blvd Santa Barbara CA   805-564-4333
Dogs of all sizes are allowed. There are no additional pet fees.
Four Seasons Resort 1260 Channel Dr. Santa Barbara CA   805-969-2261
Dogs up to 50 pounds are allowed. There are no additional pet fees. Dogs are not allowed to be left alone in the room.
Montecito Del Mar 316 W Montecito St Santa Barbara CA   805-962-2006
There is a $10 per day pet fee. Dogs up to 50 pounds are permitted.
Motel 6 - Santa Barbara - Beach 443 Corona Del Mar Santa Barbara CA   805-564-1392 (800-466-8356)
One well-behaved family pet per room. Guest must notify front desk upon arrival. Guest is liable for any damages. In consideration of all guests, pets must never be left unattended in the guest rooms.
Motel 6 - Santa Barbara - State Street 3505 State Street Santa Barbara CA   805-687-5400 (800-466-8356)
One well-behaved family pet per room. Guest must notify front desk upon arrival. Guest is liable for any damages. In consideration of all guests, pets must never be left unattended in the guest rooms.
San Ysidro Ranch 900 San Ysidro Lane Santa Barbara CA   805-969-5046
http://sanysidroranch.com
This is an especially dog-friendly upscale resort located in Santa Barbara. They offer many dog amenities including a Privileged Pet Program doggie turn down and several miles of trails and exercise areas. Pet Massage Service is available. Choose from the Slow & Gentle Massage or the Authentic Reiki massage for your dog. Dogs are allowed in the freestanding cottages and prices start around $600 and up per night. There is a $100 per pet non-refundable cleaning fee.
Secret Garden Inn & Cottages 1908 Bath Street Santa Barbara CA   805-687-2300
Dogs are allowed in the cabins only. There is a $50 refundable pet deposit.

Campgrounds and RV Parks
El Capitan State Beach 10 Refugio Beach Road Goleta CA   805-968-1033 (800-444-PARK (7275))
Set among sycamores and oaks along El Capitán Creek, this park offers rocky tide pools, a sandy beach, and a variety of land and water recreation. Dogs of all sizes are allowed at no additional fee. Dogs may not be left unattended at any time, and they must be leashed and cleaned up after. Dogs are not allowed on the beach. The camping and tent areas also allow dogs. There is a dog walk area at the campground. There are no electric or water hookups at the campgrounds.
Cachuma Lake Rec Area Hwy 154 Santa Barbara CA   805-686-5054
http://www.cachuma.com
This modern Santa Barbara park is well known for its natural beauty and a variety of recreational opportunities. Dogs of all sizes are allowed for an additional fee of $3 per night per dog. Dogs may not be left unattended, and they must have current rabies and shot records. Dogs must be quiet, well behaved, leashed at all times, and cleaned up after. Dogs may not be closer than 50 feet to the shore. The camping and tent areas also allow dogs. There is a dog walk area at the campground.

Attractions
Chumash Painted Cave State Historic Park Painted Caves Road Goleta CA   805-733-3713
The drawings in this cave are from Chumash Native Americans and coastal fishermen that date back to the 1600s. Dogs are allowed but need to be leashed. Please clean up after your pets. The cave is located in a steep canyon above Santa Barbara. The site is located three miles south of the San Marcos Pass. To get there, take Highway 154 out of Santa Barbara and turn right on Painted Caves Road. The cave is on the left, about two miles up a steep narrow road. There is parking for only one or two vehicles. Trailers and RVs are not advised.
TOP 200 PLACE **Santa Barbara Botanical Garden** 1212 Mission Canyon Road Santa Barbara CA   805-682-4726
This beautiful botanical garden is located on 65 acres in historic Mission Canyon and they allow dogs in the garden and on the trails. This garden features over 1,000 species of rare and indigenous California plants. There are five and a half miles of scenic trails that take you through meadows and canyons, across historic Mission Dam, and along ridge-tops that offer sweeping views of the California Islands. The garden is about a 15-20 minute drive from downtown Santa Barbara.
TOP 200 PLACE **Santa Barbara Electric Car Rental** 101 State Street Santa Barbara CA   805-962-2585
http://www.wheelfunrentals.com/
This premier recreational rental outlet offers a wide variety of rental vehicles for various uses. Dogs are allowed in the electric car rentals for no additional pet fee as long as the car is returned clean. Dogs must be well behaved, and leashed and cleaned up after at all times.
Stearns Wharf Vinters 217-G Stearns Wharf Santa Barbara CA   805-966-6624
Located on California's oldest working wharf, visitors can enjoy the fresh ocean breeze and watch the comings and goings on the waterfront while savoring fine wines from the Santa Ynez Winery. They also offer a variety of cheese plates, fondues, gourmet sandwiches, picnic items, fondues, and coffee and espresso drinks. Dogs are allowed at the outdoor tables. They must be well behaved, under owner's control at all times, leashed, and cleaned up after.

TJ Paws Pet Wash 2601 De La Vina Street Santa Barbara CA 805-687-8772
http://www.tjpaws.com/
This self-serve pet wash can come in very handy after your pup has played around on some dirt trails or in the ocean and sand. Dogs can ruff it during the day and come back to the hotel nice and clean. At TJ Paws, you'll wash and groom your pet yourself, using their supplies and equipment. The staff at TJs will be there if any assistance is required.

Shopping Centers
State Street Shopping Area 100-700 State Street Santa Barbara CA 805-963-2202
In downtown Santa Barbara there are several popular shopping areas. One shopping area is on State Street. Two dog-friendly stores, Big Dog Sportswear and The Territory Ahead, allows dogs inside the store. Another area, an outdoor mall adjacent to State Street, is called the Paseo Nuevo Shopping Center. Here there are several outdoor retail kiosks. State Street shopping is between the 100 and 700 block of State Street between Cabrillo Boulevard and Carrillo Street. Paseo Nuevo is around the 700 block of State Street, between Ortega Street and Canon Perdido Street.

Stores
Big Dog Sportswear Store 6 E. Yanonali Street Santa Barbara CA 805-963-8728
http://www.bigdogs.com/
This factory outlet store allows dogs inside. Big Dogs Sportswear is a Santa Barbara-based company and produces high quality, reasonably priced activewear and accessories for men, women, and children of all ages. No clothes for the pup, but the human clothes have the cool "Big Dog" logo. The store is located at the corner of State Street and Yanonali Street, across from the Amtrak station.
Petco Pet Store 3985 State St Santa Barbara CA 805-964-2868
Your licensed and well-behaved leashed dog is allowed in the store.
Petco Pet Store 19 South Milpas St Santa Barbara CA 805-966-7292
Your licensed and well-behaved leashed dog is allowed in the store.
The Territory Ahead Store 515 State Street Santa Barbara CA 805-962-5558 x181
http://www.territoryahead.com/
The Territory Ahead was founded in 1988 and set out to create a new kind of clothing catalog that offered personality through special fabrics, distinguishing details, and easy, wearable designs. All the men's and women's clothing, as well as many of the accessory and gift items are designed in-house, to offer a collection of merchandise that can't be found anywhere else. The Territory Ahead allows well-behaved dogs inside their flagship store on State Street.

Beaches
Goleta Beach County Park 5990 Sandspit Road Goleta CA 805-568-2460
Leashed dogs are allowed at this county beach. The beach and park are about 1/2 mile long. There are picnic tables and a children's playground at the park. It's located near the Santa Barbara Municipal Airport in Goleta, just north of Santa Barbara. To get there, take Hwy 101 to Hwy 217 and head west. Before you reach UC Santa Barbara, there will be an exit for Goleta Beach.
Arroyo Burro Beach County Park 2981 Cliff Drive Santa Barbara CA 805-967-1300
Leashed dogs are allowed at this county beach and park. The beach is about 1/2 mile long and it is adjacent to a palm-lined grassy area with picnic tables. To get to the beach from Hwy 101, exit Las Positas Rd/Hwy 225. Head south (towards the ocean). When the street ends, turn right onto Cliff Drive. The beach will be on the left.
Arroyo Burro Off-Leash Beach Cliff Drive Santa Barbara CA
While dogs are not allowed off-leash at the Arroyo Burro Beach County Park (both the beach and grass area), they are allowed to run leash free on the adjacent beach. The dog beach starts east of the slough at Arroyo Burro and stretches almost to the stairs at Mesa Lane. To get to the off-leash area, walk your leashed dog from the parking lot to the beach, turn left and cross the slough. At this point you can remove your dog's leash.
Rincon Park and Beach Bates Road Santa Barbara CA
This beach is at Rincon Point which has some of the best surfing waves in the world. In the winter, it is very popular with surfers. In the summer, it is a popular swimming beach. Year-round, leashed dogs are welcome. The beach is about 1/2-1 mile long. Next to the parking lot there are picnic tables, phones and restrooms. The beach is in Santa Barbara County, about 15-20 minutes south of Santa Barbara. To get there from Santa Barbara, take Hwy 101 south and go past Carpinteria. Take the Bates Rd exit towards the ocean. When the road ends, turn right into the Rincon Park and Beach parking lot.

Parks
Beach Walkway Cabrillo Blvd. Santa Barbara CA
We couldn't find the official name of this paved path (it might be part of Chase Palm Park), so we are labeling it the "Beach Walkway". This path parallels the beach. While dogs are not allowed on this beach, they can walk

along the paved path which has grass and lots of palm trees. There are also many public restrooms along the path. The path is about 1.5 miles long each way.

Chase Palm Park 323 E. Cabrillo Boulevard Santa Barbara CA 805-564-5433

This beautiful waterfront city park opened in May 1998. It is about a mile long and has many sections including a carousel, plaza, pavilion, shipwreck playground, the wilds, fountain gateway and casa las palmas. It is on Cabrillo Blvd. between Garden Street and Calle Cesar Chavez Street.

Plaza Del Mar 129 Castillo Street Santa Barbara CA

This city park is about 4 blocks long and is close to several hotels and restaurants. The park is home to the Old Spanish Days Carriage Museum. While dogs are not allowed inside the museum, you can see many of the carriages from the outside.

Shoreline Park 1200 Shoreline Drive Santa Barbara CA

This 1/2 mile paved path winds along the headlands and provides scenic overlooks of Santa Barbara and the ocean. It is located northwest of Leadbetter Beach and Santa Barbara City College.

Off-Leash Dog Parks

Douglas Family Preserve Linda Street Santa Barbara CA 805-564-5418

Once planned to support a major housing development, this beautiful, undeveloped stretch of property was rescued to be enjoyed by all. Features include spectacular ocean and beach views and a great walking path along the bluffs. Dogs are allowed throughout the park and on the trails. Dogs must be under owner's immediate control at all times, and cleaned up after.

Santa Barbara Off-Leash Areas Various Santa Barbara CA 805-564-5418

http://www.sbparks.org/DOCS/dogpark.html

Unlike almost all larger California cities, Santa Barbara does not have any fenced off-leash dog parks nor any off-leash unfenced dog runs that are available throughout the day. However, they do have five unfenced park areas with very limited off-leash hours. Please check the signs to find the off-leash areas and the hours as they may change. The five parks are Toro Canyon Park Meadow, daily (8 am to 10 am, 4 pm - sunset), Patterson Open Space, M - F (8 am to 10 am), Tucker's Grove, M - F (8 am - 10 am, 4 pm - sunset), Tabano Hollow, daily (4 pm to sunset) and Isla Vista Park, M - F (8 am - 10 am, 4 pm - sunset). Please keep in mind that in winter there is not much time between 4 pm and sunset.

Outdoor Restaurants

Beach Grill at Padaro 3765 Santa Claus Lane Carpinteria CA 805-566-3900

This restaurant serves American food. Dogs are allowed at the outdoor tables.

Tony's Italian Dinners and BBQ Ribs 699 Linden Ave Carpinteria CA 805-684-3413

Dogs must be on leash while on the premises. Dogs are allowed at the outdoor tables.

Baja Fresh Mexican Grill 7127 Hollister Ave. Goleta CA 805-685-9988

http://www.bajafresh.com

This Mexican restaurant is open for lunch and dinner. They use fresh ingredients and making their salsa and beans daily. Some of the items on their menu include Enchiladas, Burritos, Tacos Salads, Quesadillas, Nachos, Chicken, Steak and more. Well-behaved leashed dogs are allowed at the outdoor tables.

Jerusalem Garden Cafe 910 Embarcadero Del Norte Goleta CA 805-685-7010

This restaurant serves American and Maylasian food. Dogs are allowed at the outdoor tables.

Baja Fresh Mexican Grill 3851 State Street Santa Barbara CA 805-687-9966

http://www.bajafresh.com

This Mexican restaurant is open for lunch and dinner. They use fresh ingredients and making their salsa and beans daily. Some of the items on their menu include Enchiladas, Burritos, Tacos Salads, Quesadillas, Nachos, Chicken, Steak and more. Well-behaved leashed dogs are allowed at the outdoor tables.

City Kitchen 901 North Milpas Santa Barbara CA 805-892-4483

This restaurant serves American food. Dogs are allowed at the outdoor tables.

Dargan's Irish Pub 18 E. Ortega Street Santa Barbara CA 805-568-0702

http://www.dargans.com/main.html

Dogs are allowed on the outdoor patio. The pub serves food and drinks. It's hours are 4 pm to 2 am Monday to Friday and 11:30 am to 2 am on Saturday and Sunday.

Emilio's Restaurant 324 W Cabrillo Blvd Santa Barbara CA 805-966-4426

http://www.emilios-restaurant.com/

This quaint Italian eatery is located along the waterfront and offers indoor and outdoor dining. Dogs are allowed at the outdoor tables. They must be well behaved, under owner's control at all times, leashed, and cleaned up after.

Italian and Greek Deli 636 State Street Santa Barbara CA 805-962-6815

Dogs are allowed at the outdoor tables.

Jeannine's Bakery and Cafe 3607 State St Santa Barbara CA 805-687-8701

Dogs are allowed at the outdoor tables.

The Summerland Beach Cafe 2294 Lillie Ave Summerland CA 805-969-1019

This restaurant comes highly recommended from one of our readers who says "It is just south of Montecito and Santa Barbara proper. The cafe was recommended by some locals and it is great. The restaurant is situated in an old house and seating extends to a wide porch around the front and side. We sat on the porch with at least 3 other pet families. They brough Willow a water bowl and 2 bones. Lucky dog."

Events

Big Dog Parade and Canine Festival 121 Gray Ave Santa Barbara CA 805-963-8727, Ext:1398
http://www.bigdogs.com/
This is the largest dog parade in the country (with proceeds benefiting our canine companions), and thousands from all over the west come to watch, participate, or compete in this fun event sponsored by the Big Dog Foundation. It is held annually (usually in early June) with the parade beginning at State and De La Guerra Streets with a regalia of costumed canines strutting for the judges and spectators. It ends at the Canine Festival in Old Chase Palm Park where there awaits vendors, activities, celebrities, food, music, and more. Dogs must be well mannered, leashed, and cleaned up after.
The French Festival Poodle Parade Junipero and Alamar Streets at Oak Park Santa Barbara CA 805-564-PARIS (7274)
http://www.frenchfestival.com/
This event is held every Bastille Day, July 14. It is sponsored by the Santa Barbara French Festival, and is the largest French celebration in the Western U.S. with all the sights, sounds, art, foods, wines, and exuberance of France. There is even a model Eiffel Tower. There is a menagerie of free entertainment, but the "Poodle Parade" where every dog can strut their stuff (and their most impressive costumes) is one of the biggest and most fun draws. Dogs must be well mannered, leashed, and cleaned up after. Your dog doesn't have to be a poodle to attend.

Vets and Kennels

CARE Hospital 301 E. Haley St. Santa Barbara CA 805-899-2273
This 24 hour veterinary has a state-of-the-art veterinary center which offers advanced medical and surgical procedures for pets. They have a veterinarian on the premises at all times and a surgeon on call for emergency surgeries.

Santa Maria

Accommodations

Best Western Big America 1725 North Broadway Santa Maria CA 805-922-5200 (800-780-7234)
Dogs of all sizes are allowed. There are no additional pet fees. Smoking and non-smoking are available for pet rooms.
Holiday Inn Hotel & Suites 2100 North Broadway Santa Maria CA 805-928-6000 (877-270-6405)
Dogs up to 50 pounds are allowed. There is a $10 per day additional pet fee.
Motel 6 - Santa Maria 2040 North Preisker Lane Santa Maria CA 805-928-8111 (800-466-8356)
One well-behaved family pet per room. Guest must notify front desk upon arrival. Guest is liable for any damages. In consideration of all guests, pets must never be left unattended in the guest rooms.

Stores

PetSmart Pet Store 2306 S Bradley Rd Santa Maria CA 805-348-1075
Your licensed and well-behaved leashed dog is allowed in the store.

Off-Leash Dog Parks

Woof-Pac Park 300 Goodwin Rd Santa Maria CA 805-896-2344
This three acre fenced dog park opened in 2006 in Waller Park. It is located next to the Hagerman Softball Complex. Its hours are dawn to dusk. From 101 take Betteravia Rd west and turn left onto Orcutt Expy. Turn right into Waller Park.

Santa Nella

Accommodations
Holiday Inn Express 28976 W. Plaza Drive Santa Nella CA 209-826-8282 (877-270-6405)

Dogs of all sizes are allowed. There is an $8.00 per day pet fee. Pets are not allowed in the King Mini Suite Rooms and may not be left alone at the hotel.

Solvang

Accommodations
Motel 6 - Buellton - Solvang Area 333 McMurray Road Buellton CA 805-688-7797 (800-466-8356)
One well-behaved family pet per room. Guest must notify front desk upon arrival. Guest is liable for any damages. In consideration of all guests, pets must never be left unattended in the guest rooms.
Quality Inn 630 Avenue of the Flags Buellton CA 805-688-0022 (877-424-6423)
Dogs of all sizes are allowed. There is a $25 one time additional pet fee per room for a stay of 1 to 7 days. Dogs may not be left alone in the rooms, and they must be leashed and cleaned up after.
Rodeway Inn 630 Ave of Flags Buellton CA 805-688-0022
http://www.rodewayinn.com/
This motel (formerly Econo Lodge) is located about 4 miles from the village of Solvang. Amenities include cable TV and movies. Handicap accessible rooms are available. There is a $25 one time pet charge.
Santa Ynez Valley Marriott 555 McMurray Road Buellton CA 805-688-1000 (800-638-8882)
Dogs of all sizes are allowed. There is a $50 one time fee per pet. Dogs must be leashed, cleaned up after, and the Pet in Room sign put on the door and the front desk informed if they are in the room alone. The provide food and water bowls and a designated pet walking area. Dogs are not allowed on the bed.

Royal Copenhagen Inn

Royal Copenhagen Inn 1579 Mission Drive Solvang CA 800-624-6604
This inn is located in the heart of the Solvang village. Walk to dog-friendly restaurants, stores and parks. Well-behaved dogs are allowed. There is no pet fee.
Wine Valley Inn 1554 Copenhagen Drive Solvang CA 805-688-2111 (800-824-6444)
http://www.winevalleyinn.com/
A luxurious blend of old world ambiance and modern day comforts, this chateau-style retreat offers accommodations for all tastes and budgets. Set among beautifully landscaped courtyards complete with koi ponds, a stone fireplace, and private gardens are individually decorated guest rooms, cottages, and a grand suite, all with many in-room amenities. Dogs of all sizes are allowed for a $100 refundable deposit plus an additional pet fee of $25 per night per pet. Dogs may not be left alone in the room at any time, and they must be leashed and cleaned up after at all times.

Wine Valley Inn

Campgrounds and RV Parks

Flying Flags RV Park and Campground

Flying Flags RV Park and Campground 180 Avenue of the Flags Buellton CA   805-688-3716 (877-RV-FLAGS (783-5247))
http://www.flyingflags.com/
This award winning campground offers beautiful landscaped grounds, grassy pull through sites with up to 50 amp service, wi-fi, a guest laundry, convenience store, snack bar, pool, spa, and playground. Up to 2 dogs are allowed at no additional fee. If there are more than 2 dogs, then there is a $2 per night per pet fee. Dogs must be leashed at all times and cleaned up after. Dogs may not be left unattended outside, and they are not allowed in the pool area, playground, or in buildings. There are some breed restrictions. The camping and tent areas also allow dogs. There is a dog walk area at the campground.

Attractions
LinCourt Vineyards 343 North Refugio Rd Santa Ynez CA   805-688-8381
Dogs are allowed at the outdoor picnic tables.
Buttonwood Farm Winery 1500 Alamo Pintado Rd Solvang CA   805-688-3032

Solvang Horsedrawn Streetcars P.O. Box 531 Solvang CA   805-686-0022
http://www.solvangstreetcar.com
When this streetcar is not too crowed, your well-behaved dog is welcome. They offer a twenty minute guided tour of the beautiful Danish village of Solvang. The tour costs less than $5 per person. Prices are subject to change. The tour starts on Copenhagen Drive, opposite the Blue Windmill.

Solvang Village

TOP 200 PLACE Solvang Village 1500-2000 Mission Drive Solvang CA   800-468-6765
http://www.solvang.org/
As the Solvang Visitor's Bureau states, "Visiting Danes have described Solvang as 'more like Denmark than Denmark' - a remarkable tribute to the town's passion for Danish architecture, cuisine and customs." Solvang is a quaint shopping village and a great place to walk with your dog. Several stores along Mission Drive are dog-friendly like The Book Loft and Lemo's Feed & Pet Supply (please always verify that stores are dog-friendly by asking the clerk before entering). There are also many dog-friendly restaurants in town including bakeries that have mouth watering goodies. Sunset Magazine recently voted Solvang as one of the '10 Most Beautiful Small Towns' in the Western United States.

Stores
Big Dog 485 Alisal Rd #D1-2 Solvang CA   805-693-0899

Your well-behaved, leashed dog may shop with you at this Big Dog shop.
Book Loft 1680 Mission Drive Solvang CA 805-688-6010
Your leashed, well-behaved dog can browse this bookstore with you and sit with you at the outdoor seats of the attached Kaffe Hus.
Lemo's Feed and Pet Supply 1511 Mission Dr Solvang CA 805-693-8180
This feed and pet store in Solvang has some nice treats for your dog, as well as regular dog supplies.

Parks

Santa Ynez Recreation Area Paradise Road Santa Ynez CA 805-967-3481
Dogs on leash are allowed on the nature trails and hikes. There are miles of trails at this park. Other activities include swimming and fishing. This recreation area is actually part of the Los Padres National Forest. From Highway l0l at west end of Santa Barbara, turn north on Highway l54 (San Marcos Pass Road) for about10- l2 miles, then go east on Paradise Road to the Santa Ynez Recreation Area.

Hans Christian Andersen Park

Hans Christian Andersen Park Atterdag Road Solvang CA
You and your leashed pup can enjoy a 1.3 mile round trip hike along meadows lined with majestic oak trees. This park's 50 acres also has picnic facilities, a playground for kids and tennis courts. It is open daily from 8 a.m. to dusk. The park is located within walking distance of the village. It on Atterdag Road, just 3 blocks north of Mission Drive and the village of Solvang.
Nojoqui Falls Park Alisal Road Solvang CA
Nojoqui Falls is a 160+ foot waterfall which towers over the park grounds. It is best viewed after a rainy period. You and your leashed pup can view the waterfall by embarking on an easy 10 minute hike through a wooded canyon. This park also has a sports playing field, playgrounds for kids, and a picnic area. The park is open every day from dawn to dusk. It is located on Alisal Road, just 7 miles south of Solvang on a country road.
Solvang Park Mission Drive Solvang CA
This small city park is located in the middle of the Solvang village. It is a nice spot to rest after walking around town. It is located on Mission Drive at the corner of First Street.

Outdoor Restaurants

Los Olivos Cafe 2879 Grand Ave Los Olivos CA 805-688-7265
Dogs are allowed at the outdoor tables.
Patrick's Side Street Cafe 2375 Alamo Pintado Ave Los Olivos CA 805-686-4004
This restaurant serves American food. Dogs are allowed at the outdoor tables.
Bit O'Denmark 473 Alisal Rd. Solvang CA 805-688-5426

This restaurant allows 1 dog per table (maybe 2, depending on how many other dogs are there). They are open from 9:30am until 9pm.

Giovanni's Italian Restaurant 1988 Old Mission Drive Solvang CA 805-688-1888

This pizza place is located about one mile outside of the village. To get there, head east on Mission Drive/Hwy 246 and it will be on the left. They are open from 11am until 9:30pm. On Friday and Saturday, they are open until 10:30pm.

Greenhouse Cafe 487 Atterdag Road Solvang CA 805-688-8408

Dogs are allowed on the side patios only, not the front patio.

McConnell's Ice Cream 1588 Mission Drive Solvang CA 805-688-9880

They are open daily from 11am until 9pm.

Olsen's Danish Village Bakery 1529 Mission Drive Solvang CA 805-688-6314

The bakery is open from 7:30am until 6pm.

Panino 475 First Street Solvang CA 805-688-0608

One well-behaved dog is okay at the outdoor tables.

River Grill at The Alisal 150 Alisal Rd Solvang CA 805-688-7784

The River Grille has a nice outdoor patio for you and your well-behaved pup to watch the golf course. But beware of stray golf balls.

Subway 1641 Mission Dr Solvang CA 805-688-7650

Dogs are allowed at the outdoor tables.

The Belgian Cafe 1671 Copenhagen Drive Solvang CA 805-688-6630

They only have 1 table outside, so come early. Many people with dogs sit at this outdoor table. The table seats up to 4-5 people. The hours are from 7am until 3pm.

The Big Bopper 1510 Mission Drive Solvang CA 805-688-6018

You and your pup can order food from the outside window. They are open from 11am until 8:30pm.

The Bulldog Cafe

The Bulldog Cafe 1680 Mission Drive Solvang CA 805-686-9770

Dogs are also welcome in the attached bookstore, the Book Loft. Dogs are allowed at the outdoor tables.

The Little Mermaid 1546 Mission Drive Solvang CA 805-688-6141

They serve breakfast, lunch and dinner. The hours are from 7:30am until 9pm. The name was derived from the The Little Mermaid, which is a life-size statue of a mermaid sitting on a rock in the harbor in Denmark. It considered to be a symbol of Denmark, and several smaller copies exist around the globe, including Solvang.

The Touch 475 First Street Solvang CA 805-686-0222

This dog-friendly restaurant serves American style breakfast and lunch. They serve Chinese food for dinner. The owner of this restaurant is a dog lover and has several dogs.

Tower Pizza 436 Alisal Rd, Units C + D Solvang CA 805-688-3036

Dogs are allowed at the outdoor tables.
Viking Garden Restaurant 446C Alisal Rd Solvang CA 805-688-1250
Dogs are allowed at the outdoor tables.

Vets and Kennels
Valley Pet Emergency Clinic 914 W Highway 246 Buellton CA 805-688-2334
Monday - Friday 8 am - 5:30 pm, Saturday 8 am - 5 pm, Closed Sunday.

Ventura - Oxnard

Accommodations
Motel 6 - Camarillo 1641 East Daily Drive Camarillo CA 805-388-3467 (800-466-8356)
One well-behaved family pet per room. Guest must notify front desk upon arrival. Guest is liable for any damages. In consideration of all guests, pets must never be left unattended in the guest rooms.

Casa Sirena Hotel and Resort

Casa Sirena Hotel and Resort 3605 Peninsula Rd Oxnard CA 805-985-6311
There is a $50 one time pet fee. There is an on-site tennis court and an exercise room. Some rooms have views of the Channel Islands Harbor.
Residence Inn by Marriott 2101 W Vineyard Avenue Oxnard CA 805-278-2200
Dogs of all sizes are allowed. There is a 475 one time fee, and a pet policy to sign at check in.
Vagabond Inn 1245 N. Oxnard Blvd. Oxnard CA 805-983-0251
http://www.vagabondinn.com
Amenities at this motel include a free continental breakfast and weekday newspaper. They also have an on-site coffee shop, which might be helpful in getting food to go for the room. Pets are an additional $5 per day.

Crowne Plaza Hotel - Ventura Beach

Crowne Plaza Hotel - Ventura Beach 450 E Harbor Blvd Ventura CA 805-648-2100 (877-270-6405)
Dogs of all sizes are allowed. There is a $30 one time additional pet fee. There are six pet-friendly rooms - all are non-smoking. All are located on the sixth floor of the hotel. The hotel is located very close to the dog-friendly Ventura beaches.

La Quinta Inn Ventura

La Quinta Inn Ventura 5818 Valentine Rd. Ventura CA 805-658-6200 (800-531-5900)
Dogs of all sizes are allowed. There are no additional pet fees. Dogs must be leashed and cleaned up after. Dogs must be crated or attended to for housekeeping.
Motel 6 - Ventura Beach 2145 East Harbor Boulevard Ventura CA 805-643-5100 (800-466-8356)
One well-behaved family pet per room. Guest must notify front desk upon arrival. Guest is liable for any damages. In consideration of all guests, pets must never be left unattended in the guest rooms.
Motel 6 - Ventura South 3075 Johnson Drive Ventura CA 805-650-0080 (800-466-8356)
One well-behaved family pet per room. Guest must notify front desk upon arrival. Guest is liable for any damages. In consideration of all guests, pets must never be left unattended in the guest rooms.
Vagabond Inn 756 E. Thompson Blvd. Ventura CA 805-648-5371
http://www.vagabondinn.com
Amenities at this motel include a free continental breakfast, weekday newspaper, and heated jacuzzi. They also have an on-site coffee shop, which might be helpful in getting food to go for the room. There is a $10 per day pet fee. Dogs are allowed in a few of the non-smoking rooms.

Campgrounds and RV Parks
Evergreen RV Park 2135 N Oxnard Blvd Oxnard CA 805-485-1936
Dogs are welcome at this 90 space RV park for an additional pet fee of $1 per night per pet. The fee is $15 per pet if paying monthly. Dogs may not be left outside unattended, and they must be leashed and cleaned up after at all times. There is a dog walk area at the campground.
Lake Casitas Recreation Area 11311 Santa Ana Road Ventura CA 805-649-2233
http://www.lakecasitas.info/
Along side the lake or up on the hillside nestled among the trees, there are over 400 camp sites to choose from here. Visitors will find a variety of concessions throughout the park, including a seasonal waterpark. All camp sites offer picnic tables and fire rings with children's playgrounds close by; restrooms and showers are located by the front gate and towards the back of the park. Reservations can be made for camp sites at 805-649-1122. Dogs of all sizes are allowed. There is a $1.50 per pet fee for day use, and a $3 additional fee per pet per night for camping. Dogs must be under owner's immediate control, leashed, and cleaned up after at all times. Dogs are allowed throughout the park, but they must be kept at least 50 feet away from the water. The camping and tent areas also allow dogs. There is a dog walk area at the campground.

Ventura Beach RV Resort

Ventura Beach RV Resort 800 W Main Street Ventura CA 805-643-9137
http://venturabeach-rvresort.com/
This camping resort offers 144 paved sites, all with a grassy area, picnic tables, shade trees, and fire rings.

Some of the amenities include a children's playground, laundry facilities, a pool and spa, family activities, gaming tables/courts, an arcade, bike rentals, restrooms and showers, and wi-fi. Dogs of all sizes are allowed for an additional $2 per night per pet, and they must have a current rabies certificate. Dogs may not be left unattended outside at any time, and they must be leashed and cleaned up after. Pit Bulls are not allowed. The camping and tent areas also allow dogs. There is a dog walk area at the campground.

Attractions

Hopper Boat Rentals 3600 Harbor Blvd # 368 Oxnard CA 805-382-1100
This boat rental company, located at Fisherman's Wharf in Oxnard, allows well-behaved dogs on their motor skiff boats. You and your pup can cruise the Channel Islands Harbor between the hours of 10am until dusk. The boat rentals are $45 per hour. Prices are subject to change.

Albinger Archaeological Museum 113 East Main Street Ventura CA 805-648-5823
Well-behaved dogs are allowed. This museum was once the home to five different cultures spanning 3,500 years of history. Learn about the Chumash Indians, Chinese immigrants and others who resided on the site, as well as the archaeological digs uncovered in 1974. The museum is on the National Register of Historic Places. It is open Wednesday through Sunday.

Ventura Pier

Ventura Pier 668 Harbor Blvd Ventura CA
Ventura Pier was originally built in 1872. The wooden pier is about 2000 feet long. On the pier, the restaurant Eric Ericsson's on the Pier has dog-friendly outdoor seating and there is also a snack bar where you can get a quick bite on the pier. Dogs on leash are allowed on the pier.

Shopping Centers

Ventura Harbor Village

Ventura Harbor Village 1559 Spinnaker Drive Ventura CA 805-644-0169
http://www.venturaharborvillage.com
This nice seaside shopping village allows your leashed dog. While dogs are not allowed inside the stores, there are several outdoor dog-friendly restaurants (see Restaurants). During the summer weekends, the village usually has outdoor art exhibits and concerts where your pup is welcome.

Stores

Petco Pet Store 177 West Ventura Blvd Camarillo CA 805-384-5435
Your licensed and well-behaved leashed dog is allowed in the store.
PetSmart Pet Store 2021 N Oxnard Blvd Oxnard CA 805-981-4012
Your licensed and well-behaved leashed dog is allowed in the store.
Petco Pet Store 545 West Channel Islands Blvd Port Hueneme CA 805-984-3470
Your licensed and well-behaved leashed dog is allowed in the store.
PetSmart Pet Store 4840 Telephone Rd Ventura CA 805-650-9191
Your licensed and well-behaved leashed dog is allowed in the store.
Petco Pet Store 4300-A East Main St Ventura CA 805-639-3016
Your licensed and well-behaved leashed dog is allowed in the store.

Beaches

Hollywood Beach various addresses Oxnard CA
This beach is located on the west side of the Channel Islands Harbor. The beach is 4 miles southwest of Oxnard. Dogs must be on leash and owners must clean up after their pets. Dogs are allowed on Hollywood Beach before 9 am and after 5 pm.
Oxnard Shores Beach Harbor Blvd. Oxnard CA
This beach stretches for miles. If you enter at 5th Street and go north, there are no houses and very few people. Dogs must be on leash and owners must clean up after their pets. Thanks to one of our readers for recommending this beach.
Silverstrand Beach various addresses Oxnard CA
This beach is located between the Channel Islands Harbor and the U.S. Naval Construction Battalion Center. The beach is 4 miles southwest of Oxnard. Dogs must be on leash and owners must clean up after their pets. Thanks to one of our readers for recommending this beach.

Harbor Cove Beach West end of Spinnaker Drive Ventura CA   805-652-4550
This beach is considered the safest swimming area in Ventura because of the protection of the cove. Dogs of all sizes are allowed at this beach as well as on the 6 miles of Ventura City Beaches and on the long wooden pier, but they are not allowed on any of the beaches south of the Ventura Pier or on any of the State beaches. Dogs must be leashed and cleaned up after at all times.

Promenade Park Figueroa Street at the Promenade Ventura CA   805-652-4550
This park is a one acre oceanfront park on the site of an old Indian village near Seaside Park. Dogs of all sizes are are allowed at this beach as well as on the 6 miles of Ventura City Beaches and on the long wooden pier, but they are not allowed on any of the beaches south of the Ventura Pier or on any of the State beaches. Dogs must be leashed and cleaned up after at all times.

Seaward Avenue Beach Seaward Avenue Ventura CA   805-652-4550
Dogs are allowed at this beach as well as on the 6 miles of Ventura City Beaches and on the long wooden pier, but they are not allowed on any of the beaches south of the Ventura Pier or on any of the State beaches. Dogs must be leashed and cleaned up after at all times.

Surfer's Point at Seaside Park Figueroa Street at the Promenade Ventura CA   800-483-6215
This park is one of the area's most popular surfing and windsurfing beaches, and it offers showers, picnic facilities and restrooms, and is connected with the Ventura Pier by a scenic landscaped Promenade walkway and the Omer Rains Bike Trail. Dogs are allowed on the 6 miles of Ventura City Beaches and on the long wooden pier, but they are not allowed on any of the beaches south of the Ventura Pier or on any of the State beaches. Dogs must be leashed and cleaned up after at all times.

Parks

Orchard Park Geranium Place Oxnard CA
This small city park has tennis courts and a nice playground for kids. It is located on the corner of Geranium Place and Camelot Way. Dogs must be on leash.

Channel Islands National Park 1901 Spinnaker Drive Ventura CA   805-658-5730
http://www.nps.gov/chis/index.htm
Pets are not allowed on the islands.

Grant Park Brakey Road Ventura CA
The park has a few hiking trails and the Padre Serra Cross. There are some great views of the Ventura Harbor from this park. It is located about 1/2 mile north of Hwy 101, near California Street. Dogs must be on leash.

Ojai Valley Trail Hwy 33 at Casitas Vista Rd Ventura CA   805-654-3951
This 9.5 mile trail has a paved pedestrian path and a wood-chip bridle path. Dogs are allowed but must always be on leash. The trail parallels Highway 33 from Foster Park, just outside Ventura to Fox Street, in Ojai.

Ventura River Trail Old Town Ventura to Foster Park Ventura CA   805-658-4740
This 6.5 mile paved trail heads from Old Town Ventura near Main Street and Hwy 33 along the Ventura River to Foster Park where it hooks up with the Ojai Valley Trail which continues to Ojai nearly 10 miles away. Dogs on leash may share the trail with joggers, bicycles and others.

Off-Leash Dog Parks

Camarillo Grove Dog Park off Camarillo Springs Road East Camarillo CA   805-482-1996
http://www.pvrpd.org
This fenced dog park is about one acre and double gated. Amenities include a water fountain for dogs and people, benches, and a fire hydrant. The dog park is located off Camarillo Springs Road, at the base of the Conejo Grade. Dogs are not allowed in other parts of the park except for the off-leash area.

Arroyo Verde Park, Parks and Recreation Foothill and Day Road Ventura CA   805-658-4740
This park has a designated off-leash area for use at specific times. There are benches and drinking fountains for the dogs and their people. Only well-socialized, dogs are permitted in the off-leash areas. All dogs must be vaccinated for rabies and have a current license, and owners are expected to be responsible for their dogs including keeping them under voice control and cleaning up after them. Their hours are Tuesday through Sunday from 6 to 9 AM, excluding holidays and days reserved for special events.

Camino Real Park At Dean Drive and Varsity Street Ventura CA   805-658-4740
This park has a fenced in area in the southwest corner of the park for dogs and their owners to socialize and exercise. Hours of the dog park are from dawn to dusk, and amenities include drinking fountains for the dogs and their people, benches, and doggie-doo bags. Double gates allow both small and large dogs to come in and out of the area safely. All dogs must be vaccinated for rabies and have a current license, and owners are expected to be responsible for their dogs including keeping them under voice control and cleaning up after them.

Arroyo Verde Park Off-Leash Area

Outdoor Restaurants

Baja Fresh Mexican Grill 1855 Daily Drive Camarillo CA   805-383-6884
http://www.bajafresh.com
This Mexican restaurant is open for lunch and dinner. They use fresh ingredients and making their salsa and beans daily. Some of the items on their menu include Enchiladas, Burritos, Tacos Salads, Quesadillas, Nachos, Chicken, Steak and more. Well-behaved leashed dogs are allowed at the outdoor tables.

Cousins Wine Tasting 2390 Las Posas Rd Camarillo CA   805-445-4424
This restaurant and bar serves American. Dogs are allowed at the outdoor tables.

Baja Fresh Mexican Grill 2350 Vineyard Ave Oxnard CA   805-988-7878
http://www.bajafresh.com
This Mexican restaurant is open for lunch and dinner. They use fresh ingredients and making their salsa and beans daily. Some of the items on their menu include Enchiladas, Burritos, Tacos Salads, Quesadillas, Nachos, Chicken, Steak and more. Well-behaved leashed dogs are allowed at the outdoor tables.

Buon Appetito 2721 Victoria Ave Oxnard CA   805-984-8437
This restaurant allow dogs at their perimeter tables. It is located on Fisherman's Wharf.

Chinese Dumpling House 575 W. Channel Islands Blvd. Port Hueneme CA   805-985-4849
This restaurant is open from 11am until 9pm.

Manhattan Bagel 585 W Channel Islands Blvd. Port Hueneme CA   805-984-3550
This bagel store is open for breakfast and lunch. They have several outdoor seats where you and your pup can enjoy some bagels and cream cheese.

Anacapa Brewing Company 472 E Main Street Ventura CA   805-643-BEER (2337)
http://www.anacapabrewing.com/index.asp
This is Ventura's only restaurant and brewery, or Brewpub. They are open daily at 11:30 a.m. except for Mondays when they open at 5:00 p.m. Well behaved, leashed dogs of all sizes are allowed to join you on the patio while you enjoy handcrafted food and ale.

Baja Fresh Mexican Grill 4726-2 Telephone Road Ventura CA   805-650-3535
http://www.bajafresh.com
This Mexican restaurant is open for lunch and dinner. They use fresh ingredients and making their salsa and beans daily. Some of the items on their menu include Enchiladas, Burritos, Tacos Salads, Quesadillas, Nachos, Chicken, Steak and more. Well-behaved leashed dogs are allowed at the outdoor tables.

Cafe Nouveau 1497 E Thompson Blvd Ventura CA   805-648-1422
This restaurant serves Italian food. Dogs are allowed at the outdoor tables.

TOP 200 PLACE Eric Ericsson's on the Pier 668 Harbor Blvd Ventura CA   805-643-4783

http://www.ericericssons.com/
Located on the edge of the dog-friendly Ventura Pier (one of the longest piers in California, they offer a variety of California cuisine and "seafood prepared at it's best". They are open 7 days a week; from 11 am to 10 pm Sunday through Thursday, and from 11 am to 11 pm Friday and Saturday. All well behaved, leashed dogs are allowed to join their owners on the patio. Just go into the restaurant (without your dog) and the hostess will seat you and your pet on the patio.

Lassen Ventura Market and Deli 4071 E Main Street Ventura CA 805-644-6990
Although dogs are not allowed inside this "healthy choices" store and deli, outside seating is available where you may sit with your pet while you dine or wait for someone shopping. Dogs must be well mannered, leashed, and cleaned up after quickly.

Nature's Grill 566 E Main Street Ventura CA 805-643-2337
Nature's Grill welcomes all well behaved, leashed dogs to join you on their patio. They offer health-minded diners vegetarian and California cuisine. They are open from 11 am to 9 pm 7 days a week.

Pelican Bay Cafe 1575 Spinnaker Dr. Ventura CA 805-658-2228
This cafe is located in the dog-friendly Ventura Harbor Village. The cafe used to be called Lorenzoni's.

Spinnaker Seafood 1583 Spinnaker Dr. Ventura CA 805-658-6220
This seafood restaurant is located in the dog-friendly Ventura Harbor Village.

Tony's Pizzeria 186 E Thompson Blvd Ventura CA 805-643-8425
They welcome all dogs on a leash in the outdoor patio. People just tie their dogs right to the tables and enjoy the pizza. No dogs allowed inside but you can order from the side window. They are located one block from the beach.

Top Hat Burger Palace 299 E Main Street Ventura CA 805-643-9696
This unique hamburger and hot dog stand serves up a bit of nostalgia with good food. They welcome all friendly, leashed dogs to join you on their patio. They are open from 10 am to 7 pm Monday through Saturday, and closed on Sunday.

Events

Pooch Parade Dog Walk and Pet Expo 10 West Harbor Blvd Ventura CA 805-488-7533
http://www.poochparade.org/
Sponsored by the Canine Adoption and Rescue League, the Pooch Parade benefits the Project Second Chance Adoption Programs. It is an annual summer, day long event of fun-filled contests, doggy demonstrations, a pet expo, silent auction, and a beautiful 3 mile round trip Pooch Parade along the Ventura Beach Promenade. All well behaved, leashed dogs are welcome, and please clean up after your pet.

Vets and Kennels

Pet Emergency Clinic 2301 S Victoria Ave Ventura CA 805-642-8562
Monday - Friday 6 pm to 8 am, 24 hours on weekends.

Watsonville

Accommodations

Best Western Rose Garden Inn 740 Freedom Blvd Watsonville CA 831-724-3367 (800-780-7234)
Dogs of all sizes are allowed. There is a $10 one time per pet fee per visit. Only non-smoking rooms used for pets.

Motel 6 - Watsonville - Monterey Area 125 Silver Leaf Drive Watsonville CA 831-728-4144 (800-466-8356)
One well-behaved family pet per room. Guest must notify front desk upon arrival. Guest is liable for any damages. In consideration of all guests, pets must never be left unattended in the guest rooms.

Red Roof Inn - Watsonville 1620 West Beach Street Watsonville CA 831-740-4520 (800-RED-ROOF)
One well-behaved family pet per room. Guest must notify front desk upon arrival. Guest is liable for any damages. In consideration of all guests, pets must never be left unattended in the guest rooms.

Campgrounds and RV Parks

Mount Madonna County Park 7850 Pole Line Road Watsonville CA 408-355-2201
From the towering redwoods to the Monterey Bay, this 3,688 acre park offers great scenery, interpretive exhibits and programs, an amphitheater, access to an extensive 14 mile trail system, a self-guided nature trail, and a variety of recreation. Dogs of all sizes are allowed at no additional fee. Dogs must be on no more than a 6 foot leash, and cleaned up after. Dogs must be in confined areas at night. The camping and tent areas also allow dogs. There is a dog walk area at the campground.

Santa Cruz/Monterey Bay KOA 1186 San Andreas Road Watsonville CA 831-722-0551 (800-562-7701)
http://www.koa.com/where/ca/05113/

This scenic family resort along the coast of Monterey Bay offers a long list of amenities, planned activities, and land and water recreation. Dogs of all sizes are allowed for no additional fee. Dogs must be under owner's control and visual observation at all times. Dogs must be quiet, well behaved, and be on no more than a 6 foot leash at all times, or otherwise contained. Dogs may not be left unattended outside the owner's camping equipment, and must be brought inside at night. Dogs are not allowed in the lodge or the play areas. There are some breed restrictions. The camping and tent areas also allow dogs. There is a dog walk area at the campground. Dogs are allowed in the camping cabins.

Sunset State Beach 201 Sunset Beach Road Watsonville CA   831-763-7062 (800-444-PARK (7275))
http://www.parks.ca.gov/park_list.asp
Dogs of all sizes are allowed. There are no additional pet fees. Dogs may not be left unattended at any time, and they must be leashed and cleaned up after. Dogs are not allowed on the beach. This campground is closed during the off-season. The camping and tent areas also allow dogs. There is a dog walk area at the campground. There are no electric or water hookups at the campgrounds.

Parks
Mount Madonna   Watsonville CA   408-842-2341
This 3,219 acre park is dominated by a redwood forest. The park offers redwood and oak forests as well as meadows. Visitors may choose from 118 drive-in and walk-in first-come, first-served campsites spread throughout four campgrounds. Each site comes equipped with a barbecue pit, food locker and picnic table. Showers (for a small fee) are also available, as well as 17 partial hook-up RV sites. Hikers have access to an extensive 20 mile trail system. Park visitors may learn about areas where Ohlone Indians hunted and harvested. A one mile self-guided nature trail winds around the ruins of cattle baron Henry Miller's summer home. White fallow deer, descendants of a pair donated by William Randolph Hearst in 1932, can be viewed in an enclosed pen. The park is located on Highway 152 (Hecker Pass Road), ten miles west of Gilroy.

Royal Oaks Park 537 Maher Road Watsonville CA   831-755-4895
This 122 acre park offers miles of hiking trails, a playground, picnic areas, basketball, volleyball and tennis courts. There is a $3 vehicle entrance fee during the week and a $5 fee on weekends and holidays. Dogs need to be leashed and please clean up after them.

Off-Leash Dog Parks
Watsonville Dog Park 757 Green Valley Road Watsonville CA   831-454-7900
Watsonville Dog Park is located in the Pinto Lake County Park off of Green Valley Rd at Dalton Lane. Head west on Dalton Lane until you reach the park. The fenced dog park is about 1/3 of an acre.

Outdoor Restaurants
El Alteno 323 Main Street Watsonville CA   831-768-9876
This Mexican food restaurant allows your pet to join you on the outside deck. They just request that you bring your dog when they are not real busy. Dogs must be well behaved, leashed, and cleaned up after.

Chapter 9

California - Central Valley Dog Travel Guide

Bakersfield

Accommodations

Best Western Heritage Inn (Buttonwillow) 253 Trask St Bakersfield CA   661-764-6268 (800-780-7234)
Dogs of all sizes are allowed. There is a $10 per night pet fee per pet. Smoking and non-smoking are available for pet rooms.

Best Western Hill House 700 Truxton Ave Bakersfield CA   661-327-4064 (800-780-7234)
Dogs of all sizes are allowed. There is a $10 per night pet fee per pet. Smoking and non-smoking are available for pet rooms.

Days Hotel and Golf 4500 Buck Owens Blvd Bakersfield CA   661-324-5555
There is a $20 one time pet fee.

Doubletree 3100 Camino Del Rio Court Bakersfield CA   661-323-7111
Dogs of all sizes are allowed. There is a $15 one time pet fee per room.

Holiday Inn Select 801 Truxton Avenue Bakersfield CA   661-323-1900 (877-270-6405)
Dogs of all sizes are allowed. There is a $150 returnable deposit required per room. There is a $50 one time pet fee per visit. Smoking and non-smoking rooms are available for pets.

La Quinta Inn Bakersfield 3232 Riverside Dr. Bakersfield CA   661-325-7400 (800-531-5900)
Dogs of all sizes are allowed. There are no additional pet fees. Dogs must be housebroken, well behaved, leashed, and cleaned up after.

Motel 6 - Bakersfield Convention Center 1350 Easton Drive Bakersfield CA   661-327-1686 (800-466-8356)
One well-behaved family pet per room. Guest must notify front desk upon arrival. Guest is liable for any damages. In consideration of all guests, pets must never be left unattended in the guest rooms.

Motel 6 - Bakersfield East 8223 East Brundage Lane Bakersfield CA   661-366-7231 (800-466-8356)
One well-behaved family pet per room. Guest must notify front desk upon arrival. Guest is liable for any damages. In consideration of all guests, pets must never be left unattended in the guest rooms.

Motel 6 - Bakersfield South 2727 White Lane Bakersfield CA   661-834-2828 (800-466-8356)
One well-behaved family pet per room. Guest must notify front desk upon arrival. Guest is liable for any damages. In consideration of all guests, pets must never be left unattended in the guest rooms.

Quality Inn 1011 Oak Street Bakersfield CA   661-325-0772 (877-424-6423)
Dogs of all sizes are allowed. There is a $10 per night per pet additional fee. Dogs may not be left unattended in the rooms, and they must be leashed and cleaned up after.

Red Lion Bakersfield

Red Lion 2400 Camino Del Rio Court Bakersfield CA 661-327-0681
Dogs of all sizes are allowed. There is a $25 per pet fee for each three day stay and a pet policy to sign at check in.
Residence Inn by Marriott 4241 Chester Lane Bakersfield CA 661-321-9800
Pets of all sizes are welcome. There is a $75 one time fee, and a pet policy to sign at check in.
Rio Bravo Resort 11200 Lake Ming Rd Bakersfield CA 661-872-5000
There is a $50 refundable pet deposit.

Campgrounds and RV Parks

Bakersfield Palms RV Resort 250 Fairfax Road Bakersfield CA 661-366-6700 (888-725-6778 (888-PALMSRV))
http://www.palmsrv.com
This RV only park offers various recreational pursuits, and ready access to other nearby attractions. Dogs of all sizes are allowed. There are no additional pet fees. Dogs may not be left unattended outside, and they must be leashed and cleaned up after. There is a dog walk area at the campground.
Orange Grove RV Park 1452 S Edison Road Bakersfield CA 661-366-4662
http://www.orangegrovervpark.com/
This RV park is on a 40 acre orange grove about eight miles east of Highway 99. Site amenities include pull through sites with up to 50 amp service. Other amenities include a rig and car wash, a children's playground, oranges available from December through March, a swimming pool, laundry facilities, propane, TV/group meeting room and a country store. Well-behaved, leashed dogs are welcome. There are no pet fees. Please clean up after your pet. The camping and tent areas also allow dogs. There is a dog walk area at the campground.
Bakersfield KOA 5101 E Lerdo H Shafter CA 661-399-3107 (800-562-1633)
Large pull through RV spaces and grassy tent sites are available at this campground. RV site amenities include a maximum length pull through of 70 feet and 50 amp service. Other campground amenities include a seasonal swimming pool, modem dataport, and LP gas. Gas stations and 24 hour restaurants are within walking distance. Dogs of all sizes are allowed for no additional fee. Dogs must be under owner's control and visual observation at all times. Dogs must be quiet, well behaved, and leashed at all times or otherwise contained. Dogs may not be left unattended outside the owner's camping equipment. There are some breed restrictions. The camping and tent areas also allow dogs. There is a dog walk area at the campground.
Bakersfield KOA 5101 E Lerdo H Shafter CA 661-399-3107 (800-562-1633)
http://www.koa.com/where/ca/05381/
Some of this park's amenities are free morning coffee, a swimming pool, and large pull thru grass sites with shade trees. Dogs of all sizes are allowed at no additional fee. Dogs may not be left unattended for long periods, and they must be well behaved, leashed and cleaned up after. There are some breed restrictions. The camping and tent areas also allow dogs. There is a dog walk area at the campground.

Stores

PetSmart Pet Store 2661 Oswell St Bakersfield CA 661-873-1092
Your licensed and well-behaved leashed dog is allowed in the store.
PetSmart Pet Store 4100 Ming Ave Bakersfield CA 661-834-1044
Your licensed and well-behaved leashed dog is allowed in the store.
Petco Pet Store 5151 Gosford Rd Bakersfield CA 661-664-6874
Your licensed and well-behaved leashed dog is allowed in the store.
Petco Pet Store 8220 Rosedale Highway Bakersfield CA 661-587-1097
Your licensed and well-behaved leashed dog is allowed in the store.

Parks

Beach Park Oak Street and Rosedale Hwy Bakersfield CA
This city park is a good park to take your dog while in Bakersfield. The Kern River Parkway paved exercise trail passes through here and there are picnic tables and open areas. Dogs must be on leash in the park and on the Kern River Parkway trail.
Hart Park Harrell Highway Bakersfield CA 661-868-7000
http://www.co.kern.ca.us/parks/hart.htm
Hart Park is 8 miles northeast of Bakersfield on Alfred Harrell Highway. It is on 370 acres along the Kern River. There are hiking trails and fishing. Pets are allowed but must always be on leash.
Kern River County Park Lake Ming Road Bakersfield CA 661-868-7000
This park consists of over 1,000 acres and includes a river, a lake, campgrounds and picnic areas. Hills surround the lake, and the Greenhorn Mountains stretch along the eastern horizon. Please note that Kern River currents are very strong at times and can be extremely dangerous. Do not leave children or dogs unattended at the river. The park is located about10 miles northeast of Bakersfield, off the Alfred Harrell Highway on the Lake Ming Road exit. Dogs must be on leash.

Kern River Parkway Oak Street and Rosedale Hwy Bakersfield CA
The Kern River Parkway trail is a paved biking, walking and running trail along the Kern River. It can be entered at many points, including Beach Park at the address listed here. The trail is about 12 miles long. Dogs on leash are permitted.
The Bluffs - Panorama Park Panorama Drive Bakersfield CA
This walking and jogging trail overlooks the oil wells in the valley below. It stretches a number of miles from Bakersfield along Panorama Drive towards Lake Ming and Hart Park. There is also an exercise trail. Dogs on leash are permitted.

Off-Leash Dog Parks

Centennial Park Off-Leash Dog Park

Centennial Park Off-Leash Dog Park On Montclair north of Stockdale Hwy Bakersfield CA 661-326-3866
Centennial Park off-leash dog park, close to Highway 99, is a fenced in dog park that is easily accessible to locals and travelers alike. From Highway 99, take the Stockdale Hwy exit west and turn right onto Montclair. The park is on the right.
Kroll Park Off-Leash Dog Park Kroll Way and Montalvo Dr Bakersfield CA 661-326-3866
This large, fenced off-leash dog park is located near Stockdale Hwy and Gosford on the west side of Bakersfield. To get there from Highway 99, take Stockdale Hwy west to Gosford, turn left and then turn left onto Kroll Way.
University Park Off-Leash Dog Park University Ave east of Columbus Bakersfield CA 661-326-3866
This fenced, off-leash dog park is located in University Park. The park is located on University Ave east of Columbus Street and between Camden and Mission Hills.
Wilson Park Off-Leash Dog Park Wilson Road and Hughes Lane Bakersfield CA 661-326-3866
This fenced off-leash dog park is located in Wilson Park south of central Bakersfield. The park is located on Wilson Road at Hughes Lane. Wilson Road is one major block south of Ming Ave. You can exit and Ming Avenue from Highway 99 and take the access roads to Wilson.

Outdoor Restaurants
Baja Fresh Mexican Grill 9660 Hageman Rd. Bakersfield CA 661-587-8700
http://www.bajafresh.com
This Mexican restaurant is open for lunch and dinner. They use fresh ingredients and making their salsa and beans daily. Some of the items on their menu include Enchiladas, Burritos, Tacos Salads, Quesadillas, Nachos, Chicken, Steak and more. Well-behaved leashed dogs are allowed at the outdoor tables.
Baja Fresh Mexican Grill 9000 Ming Ave. Bakersfield CA 661-665-2252
http://www.bajafresh.com

This Mexican restaurant is open for lunch and dinner. They use fresh ingredients and making their salsa and beans daily. Some of the items on their menu include Enchiladas, Burritos, Tacos Salads, Quesadillas, Nachos, Chicken, Steak and more. Well-behaved leashed dogs are allowed at the outdoor tables.

Black Angus 3601 Rosedale Highway Bakersfield CA 661-324-0814
Dogs are allowed at the outdoor tables.

Cafe Med 4809 Stockdale Hwy Bakersfield CA 661-834-4433
Dogs are allowed at the outdoor tables.

Cottage Sandwich Shoppe 1032 Truxtun Ave Bakersfield CA 661-322-4149
Well-behaved dogs are allowed at the outdoor tables.

Filling Station 1830 24th Street Bakersfield CA 661-323-5120
This is a drive-thru and walk-thru coffee and tea outlet. During spring and summer they have outdoor seats as well.

Jamba Juice 5180 Stockdale Hwy #AB Bakersfield CA 661-322-6722
Dogs are allowed at the outdoor tables.

Los Hermanos 3501 Union Ave Bakersfield CA 661-328-1678
Dogs are allowed at the outdoor tables.

Los Hermanos 8200 Stockdale Hwy #N Bakersfield CA 661-835-7294
Dogs are allowed at the outdoor tables.

Mimi's Cafe 4025 California Ave Bakersfield CA 661-326-1722
Dogs are allowed at the outdoor tables.

Patio Mexican Grill 13001 Stockdale Hwy Bakersfield CA 661-587-6280
Dogs are allowed at the outdoor tables.

Pizza Palace 5482 California Ave Bakersfield CA 661-861-1500
http://www.pizzapalace.net
Dogs are allowed at the outdoor tables.

Plumberry's 13001 Stockdale Hwy Bakersfield CA 661-589-8889
Dogs are allowed at the outdoor tables. They have outdoor tables only in the spring and summer months.

Rosemary's Family Creamery 2733 F Street Bakersfield CA 661-395-0555
Dogs are allowed at the outdoor tables. They have outdoor tables in the spring and summer months only.

Sequoia Sandwich Company 1231 18th Street Bakersfield CA 661-323-2500
Dogs are allowed at the outdoor tables.

Sonic Drive In 1402 23rd Street Bakersfield CA 661-324-9100
Dogs are allowed at the outdoor tables.

Sonic Drive-In 13015 Stockdale Hwy Bakersfield CA 661-587-9400
Dogs are allowed at the outdoor tables.

Sub Station 5464 California Ave Bakersfield CA 661-323-2400
Dogs are allowed at the outdoor tables.

Subway 8346 East Brundage Lane Bakersfield CA 661-366-3300
Dogs are allowed at the outdoor tables.

The Gourmet Shoppe 4801 Stockdale Hwy Bakersfield CA 661-834-5522
Dogs are allowed at the outdoor tables.

Village Grill 2809 F Street Bakersfield CA 661-325-1219
Dogs are allowed at the outdoor tables in the courtyard.

Vets and Kennels

Kern Animal Emergency Clinic 4300 Easton Dr #1 Bakersfield CA 661-322-6019
Monday - Friday 5:30 pm to 8 am, Noon Saturday to 8 am Monday.

Buttonwillow

Accommodations

Motel 6 - Bakersfield - Buttonwillow 20638 Tracy Avenue Buttonwillow CA 661-764-5153 (800-466-8356)
One well-behaved family pet per room. Guest must notify front desk upon arrival. Guest is liable for any damages. In consideration of all guests, pets must never be left unattended in the guest rooms.

Chowchilla

Accommodations

Days Inn Hwy 99 & Robertson Blvd Chowchilla CA   559-665-4821 (800-329-7466)
There is a $5 per day additional pet fee.

Campgrounds and RV Parks
The Lakes RV and Golf Resort 1024 Robetson Blvd Chowchilla CA   866-665-6980
http://www.thelakesrv.com/about.htm
This luxury resort offers many amenities in addition to a wide variety of recreational opportunities. Dogs of all sizes are allowed at no additional fee. Dogs may not be left unattended outside, and they must be quiet, well behaved, on no more than a 6 foot leash, and cleaned up after. Dogs are not allowed in the green belt or pool/spa areas. This campground is closed during the off-season. There is a dog walk area at the campground.

Clear Lake

Accommodations
Edgewater Resort and RV Park 6420 Soda Bay Road Kelseyville CA   707-279-0208 (800-396-6224)
http://www.edgewaterresort.net/
This resort and RV park offers 61 campsites, 6 cabins, and a couple of houses. Some of the amenities include 600 feet of lakefront, a seasonal swimming pool, a 230 foot fishing pier, boat launch, clubhouse, picnic areas, and fire pits. Dogs of all sizes are allowed in the cabins and houses for an additional $10 per night per pet; the fee for RV and tent sites is $2.50 per night per pet. Dogs may not be left unattended outside at any time, may only be left alone in cabins if they are kenneled, and they must have proof of current shots. Dogs must be quiet, well behaved, be inside at night, and leashed and cleaned up after (there is a pet station with bags at the beach). They are not allowed in park buildings or the gated swimming pool area, but they are allowed at the beach. They have provided an "OK-9 Corral outside the general store with fresh water for your pet, and they offer a "pet tag" that says "Guest at Edgewater Resort" with an address and phone number of the resort for a $5 refundable deposit.

Campgrounds and RV Parks
Funtime RV Park, Cabins and Campground 6035 Old Hwy 53 Clear Lake CA   707-994-6267
http://www.funtimervparks.com/
This family campground offers more than 60 sites and tent camping areas for large groups with plenty of shade trees, and many sites are on the waterfront. Some of the amenities include a private beach, swimming pool, barbecues, gaming courts/areas, a boat launch, laundry facilities, hot showers, and picnic tables. They will allow 2 dogs per site provided they are current on all shots and attended to at all times. Dogs must always be leashed and cleaned up after. They are allowed throughout the park, but they are not allowed in cabins, on the beach, docks, or fishing pier. There are some breed restrictions. The camping and tent areas also allow dogs. There is a dog walk area at the campground.
Island RV Park 12840 Island Drive Clearlake Oaks CA   707-998-3940
http://www.islandrvpark.com/
Located on a small island in Clear Lake (you will cross a bridge to get to the island), this RV park offers 30 full hookup sites and 4 tent sites. Amenities include laundry facilities, boat ramps and docks and hot showers. Well-behaved leashed dogs are allowed. Please clean up after them. They do not accept credit cards. The camping and tent areas also allow dogs. There is a dog walk area at the campground.
Clear Lake State Park 5300 Soda Bay Road Kelseyville CA   707-279-4293 (800-444-7275)
This park offers 149 campsites for RV or tent camping, and is located along the shores of California's largest freshwater lake. Amenities include picnic tables, restrooms, showers and grills. While dogs are not allowed on the trails or the swimming beaches at this park, they are allowed in the campgrounds and in the water at non-designated swim areas. One of the non-designated swim beaches is located between campgrounds 57 and 58. Pets must be on leash at all times, and please clean up after them. The park is located 3.5 miles northeast of Kelseyville. The camping and tent areas also allow dogs. There is a dog walk area at the campground. There are no electric or water hookups at the campgrounds.
Edgewater Resort and RV Park 6420 Soda Bay Road Kelseyville CA   707-279-0208 (800-396-6224)
http://www.edgewaterresort.net/
This resort is located in a natural park-like setting with plenty of shade trees in a protected cove on the shores of California's largest natural lake. Some of the amenities include a lakefront clubhouse, cable TV, a general store, a fish cleaning station, gaming areas, spotless restrooms, showers and laundry facilities, picnic tables, barbecues, and fire pits. Well behaved dogs of all sizes are allowed for an additional fee of $2.50 per night per pet for RV and tent camping, and an additional $10 per night per pet for the cabins. Dogs will receive a 'guest at Edgewater Resort' locater tag, and they must be current on all their shots, be friendly, under owner's immediate control, and leashed and quickly cleaned up after at all times. Dogs may not be left outside alone or unattended

anywhere in the park, and they may only be left alone in the cabin if they are kenneled. Dogs are allowed throughout the park and at the beach; they may even go for a supervised off-leash swim if they are under good voice command. They are not allowed in the general store, clubhouse, or the gated pool area, but there is fresh water for thirsty canine visitors outside the store. Dogs must always be brought inside at night. The camping and tent areas also allow dogs. There is a dog walk area at the campground. Dogs are allowed in the camping cabins.

Konocti Vistat Casino Resort and Marina 2755 Mission Rancheria Road Lakeport CA 707-262-1900 (800-FUN-1950 (386-1950))
http://www.kvcasino.com
Located on beautiful, historic Clear Lake, this RV park sits along a casino that has its own 90 slip marina, and there are several recreational activities to explore. Dogs of all sizes are allowed at no additional fee. Dogs may not be left unattended, and they must be leashed and cleaned up after. Dogs are not allowed in the hotel or casino. This is an RV only park. There is a dog walk area at the campground.

Pine Acres Resort

Pine Acres Resort 5328 Blue Lakes Road Upper Lake CA 707-275-2811
http://www.bluelakepineacres.com/
This well kept mountain resort sits along a regularly stocked spring-fed lake, and each of the RV sites has a scenic lake view. Some of the features/amenities include a country store, tackle shop, boat launch, hot showers, and restrooms. Dogs are allowed for an additional $5 per night per pet. Dogs are allowed throughout the park, except they are not allowed in the tent area or in rooms or cottages. Dogs must be leashed and cleaned up after at all times. There is a dog walk area at the campground.

Sunset Campground County Road 301/Forest Road M1 Upper Lake CA 916-386-5164
This campground is located in the Mendocino National Forest and is managed by Pacific Gas and Electric. Camp amenities include 54 tables, 54 stoves, 12 toilets, water, trailer spaces and 27 grills. The Sunset Nature Trail Loop begins at this campground. There is a $12 fee per campsite and an extra $1 per night per pet fee. Dogs on leash are allowed and please clean up after them. This campground is closed during the off-season. The camping and tent areas also allow dogs. There is a dog walk area at the campground. There are no electric or water hookups at the campgrounds.

Parks

Clear Lake State Park Soda Bay Road Kelseyville CA 707-279-4293
While dogs are not allowed on the trails or the swimming beaches at this park, they are allowed in the campgrounds and in the water at non-designated swim areas. One of the non-designated swim beaches is located between campgrounds 57 and 58. Pets must be on leash and please clean up after them. The park is

located is 3.5 miles northeast of Kelseyville.
Mendocino National Forest 10025 Elk Mountain Road Upper Lake CA 707-275-2361
This forest consists of one million acres of mountains and canyons and offers a variety of recreational opportunities like camping, hiking, backpacking, boating, fishing, hunting, nature study, photography, and off highway vehicle travel. Elevations in the forest range from 750 feet to 8092 feet with an average elevation of about 4000 feet. For a map of hiking trails, please visit the Visitor Center at 10025 Elk Mountain Road in the town of Upper Lake.
Sunset Nature Trail Loop County Road 301/Forest Road M1 Upper Lake CA 530-934-3316
This self-guided interpretive trail is an easy .5 mile one way hike. Elevation begins at 1,800 feet and has a 100 foot climb. The trail is located in the Mendocino National Forest, adjacent to a campground. Pets on leash are allowed. Please clean up after your pets. To get there from Upper Lake, take County Road 301 north for 31 miles. The trail begins at the Sunset Campground.

Coalinga

Accommodations
Best Western Big Country Inn 25020 West Dorris Ave Coalinga CA 559-935-0866 (800-780-7234)
Dogs of all sizes are allowed. There is a $10 one time per pet fee per visit. Smoking and non-smoking are available for pet rooms.

Harris Ranch Inn and Restaurant

Harris Ranch Inn and Restaurant 24505 W Dorris Avenue Coalinga CA 800-443-3322
Fine living and dining are combined for a great getaway here. Dogs of all sizes are allowed. There is a $20 one time additional pet fee per pet. Dogs may not be left alone in the room and they must be leashed and cleaned up after. Dogs are not allowed in the pool/spa or restaurant areas.
Motel 6 - Coalinga East 25008 West Dorris Avenue Coalinga CA 559-935-1536 (800-466-8356)
One well-behaved family pet per room. Guest must notify front desk upon arrival. Guest is liable for any damages. In consideration of all guests, pets must never be left unattended in the guest rooms.
Pleasant Valley Inn 25278 W Doris St Coalinga CA 559-935-2063
There is a $5 per day additional pet fee.

Colusa

Parks
Colusa National Wildlife Refuge Hwy 20 at Ohair Road Colusa CA 530-934-2801
This 4,507 acre refuge consists mostly of seasonal wetlands, uplands, restored/maintained habitats for migratory birds and endangered species, and the preservation/maintenance of as much of the indigenous flora and fauna as possible. The area is popular for wildlife viewing, nature photography, hiking, and hunting. There is a 3 mile graveled auto tour that wanders through freshwater wetlands, a 1 mile Discovery Trail walk along dense riparian marshes, and it is home to more than 200,000 ducks and 50,000 geese every winter. Dogs are allowed and they may go just about anywhere their human companions can go. Dogs must be kept under control, leashed, and cleaned up after at all times.

Davis

Accommodations
Best Western University Lodge 123 B Street Davis CA 530-756-7890 (800-780-7234)
Dogs of all sizes are allowed. There are no additional pet fees. Only non-smoking rooms used for pets.
Econo Lodge 221 D Street Davis CA 530-756-1040

Howard Johnson Hotel 4100 Chiles Road Davis CA 530-792-0800 (800-446-4656)
Dogs of all sizes are welcome. There is a $10 per day pet fee. They have one non-smoking pet room, but cannot guarantee it will be available.
Motel 6 - Davis - Sacramento Area 4835 Chiles Road Davis CA 530-753-3777 (800-466-8356)
One well-behaved family pet per room. Guest must notify front desk upon arrival. Guest is liable for any damages. In consideration of all guests, pets must never be left unattended in the guest rooms.
University Inn Bed and Breakfast 340 A Street Davis CA 530-756-8648
All rooms are non-smoking. There are no pet fees. Children are also allowed.
University Park Inn & Suites 1111 Richards Blvd. Davis CA 530-756-0910
Located within walking distance of downtown Davis. They have one pet room available and there is a $10 per night pet charge.

Stores
Petco Pet Store 1341-B W Covell Blvd Davis CA 530-750-0111
Your licensed and well-behaved leashed dog is allowed in the store.
The Cultured Canine 231 G Street #3 Davis CA 530-753-3470
Well-behaved dogs are allowed inside this gift store.

Parks
Community Park 1405 F Street Davis CA
Dogs on leash are permitted in this and most parks in Davis. The park is 28 acres in size.

Off-Leash Dog Parks
Toad Hollow Dog Park 1919 Second Street Davis CA 530-757-5656
Toad Hollow Dog Park is located in Davis on Second Street between L Street and the Pole Line Road bridge. The fenced park is large (about 2 1/2 acres). The dog park will be closed during periods of heavy rains. The dog park is run by the Davis Parks & Community Services Department.

Outdoor Restaurants
Ali Baba Middle Eastern Restaurant 220 3rd Street Davis CA 530-758-2251
This restaurant serves Middle Eastern food. Dogs are allowed at the outdoor tables.
Ben & Jerry's 500 1st St #9 Davis CA 530-756-5964
http://www.benandjerrys.com
This Ben & Jerry's Ice Cream is at the Davis Common in Downtown. Dogs are allowed at the outdoor tables.
Jamba Juice 500 1st Street #3 Davis CA 530-757-8499
http://www.jambajuice.com
This Juice Bar is located at the Davis Common in downtown. Dogs are allowed at the outdoor tables.
Mishka's 514 2nd Street Davis CA 530-759-0811
Dogs are allowed at the outdoor tables.

Psh Bagels 206 F Street Davis CA   530-753-6770
This bagel shop is in downtown Davis. Dogs are allowed at the outdoor tables.

Redrum

Redrum 978 Olive Drive Davis CA   530-756-2142
http://www.murderburger.com/
This burger place is a local favorite in this college town (the original name was Murder Burger and the new name is Redrum Burger). They serve regular hamburgers and ostrich burgers, chicken sandwiches, shakes and more. You can order with your pup from the outside window. Then enjoy the food at the covered seating next to the building or under a large shade tree in the back. To get there from Sacramento, take Hwy 80 south and exit Richards Blvd. Turn right onto Richards Blvd. Then turn left onto Olive Drive.
Steve's Place Pizza, Pasta & Grill 314 F Street Davis CA   530-758-2800
http://www.stevespizza.com
Steve's Place has a nice outdoor seating area for you and your leashed dog.
Subway 4748 Chiles Rd Davis CA   530-753-2141
Dogs are allowed at the outdoor tables.

Delano

Accommodations
Shilo Inn 2231 Girard Street Delano CA   661-725-7551
Your pet is welcome. Amenities include complimentary continental breakfast, in-room iron, ironing board & hair dryer, guest laundry, seasonal outdoor pool & spa. Conveniently located between Fresno & Bakersfield off Highway 99.

Dixon

Accommodations
Best Western Inn Dixon 1345 Commercial Way Dixon CA   707-678-1400 (800-780-7234)
Dogs of all sizes are allowed. There is a $10 one time per pet fee per visit. Smoking and non-smoking are

available for pet rooms.

Firebaugh

Accommodations

Best Western Apricot Inn 46290 W Panoche Rd Firebaugh CA   559-659-1444 (800-780-7234)
Dogs of all sizes are allowed. There is a $5 per night pet fee per pet. Smoking and non-smoking are available for pet rooms.

Fresno

Accommodations

Best Western Garden Court Inn of Fresno 2141 N Parkway Dr Fresno CA   559-237-1881 (800-780-7234)
Dogs of all sizes are allowed. There is a $10 per night pet fee per pet. Smoking and non-smoking are available for pet rooms.
Comfort Inn 5455 W Shaw Avenue Fresno CA   559-275-2374 (877-424-6423)
Dogs of all sizes are allowed. There is a $25 one time additional pet fee per pet. Dogs must be leashed, cleaned up after, and the Do Not Disturb sign put on the door if they are in the room alone.
Days Inn-Parkway 1101 N Parkway Dr Fresno CA   559-268-6211 (800-329-7466)
http://www.daysinn.com
This motel has a playground for the kids. They also have 2 two bedroom suites available. Room rates include a free breakfast. To get there from Hwy 99 south, take the Olive Ave exit. Turn right onto Olive Ave and then left onto North Parkway Drive. The motel will be on the right. There is a $5 per day additional pet fee.
Econo Lodge 445 N Parkway Dr Fresno CA 559-485-5019
A large well-behaved dog is okay. There is a $10 refundable pet deposit.
Holiday Inn Express and Suites 5046 N. Barcus Rd Fresno CA 559-277-5700 (877-270-6405)
There is a $20 one time pet fee per visit.
La Quinta Inn Fresno Yosemite 2926 Tulare Fresno CA   559-442-1110 (800-531-5900)
Dogs of all sizes are allowed. There are no additional pet fees, and there is a pet waiver to sign at check in. Dogs must be leashed and cleaned up after.
Motel 6 - Fresno - Blackstone North 4245 North Blackstone Avenue Fresno CA   559-221-0800 (800-466-8356)
One well-behaved family pet per room. Guest must notify front desk upon arrival. Guest is liable for any damages. In consideration of all guests, pets must never be left unattended in the guest rooms.
Motel 6 - Fresno - Blackstone South 4080 North Blackstone Avenue Fresno CA   559-222-2431 (800-466-8356)
One well-behaved family pet per room. Guest must notify front desk upon arrival. Guest is liable for any damages. In consideration of all guests, pets must never be left unattended in the guest rooms.
Motel 6 - Fresno - SR 99 1240 North Crystal Avenue Fresno CA   559-237-0855 (800-466-8356)
One well-behaved family pet per room. Guest must notify front desk upon arrival. Guest is liable for any damages. In consideration of all guests, pets must never be left unattended in the guest rooms.
Quality Inn 4278 W Ashlan Avenue Fresno CA 559-275-2727 (877-424-6423)
Dogs of all sizes are allowed. There is a $30 per room per stay additional pet fee. Dogs must be leashed and cleaned up after.
Red Roof Inn - Fresno - SR 99 5021 North Barcus Avenue Fresno CA 559-276-1910 (800-RED-ROOF)
One well-behaved family pet per room. Guest must notify front desk upon arrival. Guest is liable for any damages. In consideration of all guests, pets must never be left unattended in the guest rooms.
Red Roof Inn - Fresno North 6730 North Blackstone Avenue Fresno CA 559-431-3557 (800-RED-ROOF)
One well-behaved family pet per room. Guest must notify front desk upon arrival. Guest is liable for any damages. In consideration of all guests, pets must never be left unattended in the guest rooms.
Residence Inn by Marriott 5322 N Diana Avenue Fresno CA 559-222-8900
Dogs of all sizes are allowed. There is a $75 plus tax one time fee, and a pet policy to sign at check in.
Super 8 Fresno/Highway 99 1087 N Parkway Dr Fresno CA 559-268-0741 (800-800-8000)
Dogs up to 60 pounds are allowed. There is a $10 per night pet fee per pet. Smoking and non-smoking rooms are available for pet rooms.
TownePlace Suites Fresno 7127 N Fresno St Fresno CA 559-435-4600
Dogs of all sizes are allowed. There is a $75 one time pet fee per visit.
Travelodge 3093 N Parkway Dr Fresno CA 559-276-7745 (800-276-7745)
This motel shares a lobby with the Knights Inn. There is a $10 per day pet charge. To get there from Hwy 99

south, take the Shields Ave exit. Then turn right onto N Parkway Drive.

University Inn 2655 E Shaw Avenue Fresno CA 559-294-0224

A convenient location to numerous activities and recreation, this inn also offers a free continental breakfast, an outdoor pool and Jacuzzi, and an on-site restaurant. Dogs of all sizes are allowed for an additional pet deposit of $25 per room. Dogs may not be left alone in the rooms, and they must be leashed and cleaned up after.

Campgrounds and RV Parks

Millerton Lake State Recreation Area 47597 Road 145 (campground) 5290 Millerton Road (day use) Friant CA 559-822-2332

This popular park offers lush rolling hills and over 40 miles of shoreline allowing for ample recreational opportunities. Dogs of all sizes are allowed. There are no additional pet fees. Dogs must be on no more than a 6 foot leash and cleaned up after. Dogs are not allowed in park buildings, on trails, or on most beaches. Dogs may be walked in the campgrounds, along the shoreline, or on the side of the roads on lead. The camping and tent areas also allow dogs. There is a dog walk area at the campground.

Stores

PetSmart Pet Store 470 Shaw Ave Clovis CA 559-297-9514

Your licensed and well-behaved leashed dog is allowed in the store.

PetSmart Pet Store 3220 W Shaw Ave Fresno CA 559-277-2220

Your licensed and well-behaved leashed dog is allowed in the store.

Petco Pet Store 4144 North Blackstone Avenue Fresno CA 559-226-4941

Your licensed and well-behaved leashed dog is allowed in the store.

Parks

Sierra National Forest 1600 Tollhouse Road Clovis CA 559-297-0706

http://www.r5.fs.fed.us/sierra/

The dog-friendly Sierra National Forest, just south of Yosemite, consists of 1.3 million acres. Your leashed dog is allowed in this forest and on over 1,000 miles of trails. Just make sure you stay within the Sierra National Forest and do not accidentally cross over to the bordering National Parks which don't allow dogs on hiking trails. The Sierra National Forest trails offer gentle meadows, pristine lakes and streams, and rugged passes in the forest's five wilderness areas. A Wilderness Visitor Permit is required if you plan on hiking into one of the five wilderness areas. In the Sierra National Forest, one of the more popular trails is the Lewis Creek National Recreation Trail. This 3.7 mile hike makes a great day hike as it offers scenic views of waterfalls like the Corlieu and Red Rock Falls. The trail gains 880 feet in elevation from south to north. There are three trailheads along the Lewis Creek Trail. From Oakhurst, take Highway 41 north towards Yosemite National Park. The southernmost trailhead, located 7 miles from Oakhurst, is about 0.5 mile off the highway along the Cedar Valley Road. The middle trailhead is about 3 miles further along Highway 41, at a large turnout just beyond the snow chain station. The northernmost trailhead is just off Highway 41 along the Sugar Pine Road, 500 feet past the bridge on the south side of the road.

Kearny Park 7160 W. Kearney Blvd Fresno CA 559-441-0862

This park consists of over 220 green acres with a variety of plants. The park features several playgrounds, picnic tables, soccer fields, and the Kearny Mansion Museum. The Kearney Mansion was the home of M. Theo Kearney. It was constructed in the early 1900s. Kearny was a key Fresno land developer and agricultural leader. He was known as the "Raisin King of California" and formed the California Raisin Growers' Association. When he passed away in 1906, he donated his entire 5000 acre estate to the University of California. Thus 220 acres were developed into Kearny Park. Dogs on leash are allowed at the park, but not in the museum. The park is located about 7 miles west of Fresno off Kearny Road.

Roeding Park W. Olive Avenue Fresno CA 559-498-1551

This large city park has public tennis courts, an exercise course, barbecue and picnic areas, and playgrounds. Leashed dogs are allowed. There is a minimal fee for parking. The park entrance is on W. Olive Avenue by Hwy 99.

Woodward Park E. Audubon Drive Fresno CA

Leashed dogs are allowed at this regional park. There are over 280 acres for you and your pup to explore. This park has some small hills, lakes and streams. There is also a fenced off-leash area in the park. It is located on the north side of Fresno, near Hwy 41. Take Hwy 41, exit N. Friant Rd to the right. Turn left onto Audubon and the park will be on the right.

Off-Leash Dog Parks

TOP 200 PLACE Basin AH1 Dog Park and Pond 4257 W. Alamos Fresno CA 559-621-2900

This is a seasonal dog park which offers a wading pool for dogs to use during the summer. The park is open from May through November from 7 am to 10 pm daily. The dog park is located at 4257 W. Alamos at El Capitan. To get to the dog park from Highway 99, exit at Shaw Avenue and head east. In about a mile turn right on El Capitan.

Woodward Park Dog Park E. Audubon Drive Fresno CA 559-621-2900
Thanks to one of our readers who writes "Woodward Park now has a wonderful, enclosed area built specifically for dogs to play off-leash. It is located inside the park area and contains toys, water bowls and plastic bags."

Outdoor Restaurants

Baja Fresh Mexican Grill 7675 N. Blackstone Fresno CA 559-431-8811
http://www.bajafresh.com
This Mexican restaurant is open for lunch and dinner. They use fresh ingredients and making their salsa and beans daily. Some of the items on their menu include Enchiladas, Burritos, Tacos Salads, Quesadillas, Nachos, Chicken, Steak and more. Well-behaved leashed dogs are allowed at the outdoor tables.
Dai Bai Dang Restaurant 7736 N Blackstone Ave Fresno CA 559-448-8894
This restaurant serves Chinese food. Dogs are allowed at the outdoor tables.
Revue News 620 E. Olive Avenue Fresno CA 559-499-1844
This news stand also serves coffee and pastries. They are open from 8am-10pm and allow dogs at the outdoor tables. It is located on Olive Avenue between N. Blackstone Avenue and N. Palm Avenue.
Subway 3071 W. Shaw Ave #107 Fresno CA 559-225-6900
Dogs are allowed at the outdoor tables.
TGI Fridays 1077 E. Herndon Avenue Fresno CA 559-435-8443
This casual dining restaurant chain allows well-behaved leashed dogs at the outdoor tables. Thanks to one of our readers for recommending this restaurant.
Whole Foods Market 650 West Shaw Avenue Fresno CA 559-241-0300
http://www.wholefoods.com/
This natural food supermarket offers natural and organic foods. Order some food from their deli without your dog and bring it to an outdoor table where your well-behaved leashed dog is welcome. Dogs are not allowed in the store including the deli at any time.

Day Kennels

PetsHotel by PetsMart Day Kennel 615 W. Hearndon Ave. Clovis CA
http://www.petsmart.com/PETsHOTEL/
This PetSmart pet store offers day care and day camp only. You may drop off and pick up your dog at any time they are open. Their hours are 7 am - 9 pm M-F, Sunday 8 am - 7 pm. Dogs are required to have proof of current rabies, DPP and bordatella vaccinations.

Vets and Kennels

Veterinary Emergency Services 1639 N Fresno St Fresno CA 559-486-0520
Open 24 hours.

Gorman

Accommodations

Econo Lodge 49713 Gorman Post Rd Gorman CA 661-248-6411
There is a $10 per day pet fee.

Gustine

Accommodations

Motel 6 - Santa Nella - Los Banos 12733 South Highway 33 Gustine CA 209-826-6644 (800-466-8356)
One well-behaved family pet per room. Guest must notify front desk upon arrival. Guest is liable for any damages. In consideration of all guests, pets must never be left unattended in the guest rooms.

Hanford

Stores

PetSmart Pet Store 288 N 12th Ave Hanford CA 559-587-0286
Your licensed and well-behaved leashed dog is allowed in the store.

Herald

Attractions
Blue Gum Winery 13637 Borden Road Herald CA 209-748-5669
This winery welcomes owners with canine companions. Dogs must be friendly though, as they also have a dog who likes to greet visitors. Dogs can check out the grounds, but they are not allowed in the buildings. Dogs must be well behaved, leashed, and cleaned up after.

Kettleman City

Accommodations
Best Western Kettleman City Inn and Suites 33410 Powers Dr Kettleman City CA 559-386-0804 (800-780-7234)
Dogs of all sizes are allowed. There is a $5 per night pet fee per pet. Smoking and non-smoking are available for pet rooms.
Super 8 Kettleman City 33415 Powers Drive Kettleman City CA 559-386-9530 (800-800-8000)
Dogs of all sizes are allowed. There is a $10 one time per pet fee per visit. Smoking and non-smoking rooms are available for pet rooms.

Lebec

Parks

Fort Tejon State Historical Park

Fort Tejon State Historical Park Interstate 5 Lebec CA 661-248-6692
Fort Tejon State Historical Park is a nice stop on the Grapevine about 77 miles north of LA. Dogs on leash can roam the grounds, the historical cabins and the small museum.

Lathrop

Accommodations
Days Inn 14750 South Harlan Rd Lathrop CA 209-982-1959 (800-329-7466)
There is a $10 per day pet fee.

Lemoore

Accommodations
Best Western Vineyard Inn 877 East D St Lemoore CA 559-924-1261 (800-780-7234)
Dogs of all sizes are allowed. There is a $50 returnable deposit required per room. Pet must be kept in kennel when left alone. Smoking and non-smoking are available for pet rooms.
Motel 6 - Lemoore 1290 Sierra Circle Lemoore CA 559-925-6100 (800-466-8356)
One well-behaved family pet per room. Guest must notify front desk upon arrival. Guest is liable for any damages. In consideration of all guests, pets must never be left unattended in the guest rooms.

Lincoln

Off-Leash Dog Parks
Lincoln Dog Park Third Street Lincoln CA 916-624-6808
http://www.lincolndogpark.org/
The amenities at this dog park include 2.5 fenced acres for dogs to run off-leash, potable water, handicap accessible, parking, and limited seating. The park is open from dawn to dusk and is closed Wednesdays until 12pm. To get there, take Highway 65 (City of Lincoln) to Third Street. Go west on Third Street 1.8 miles to Santa Clara (just past the big oak tree).

Outdoor Restaurants
Awful Annie's 490 G Street Lincoln CA 916-645-9766
Dogs are allowed at the outdoor tables, which are available during the summer.

Los Banos

Accommodations
Best Western Executive Inn 301 West Pacheco Blvd Los Banos CA 209-827-0954 (800-780-7234)
Dogs of all sizes are allowed. There is a $20 per night pet fee per pet. Smoking and non-smoking are available for pet rooms.
Days Inn 2169 East Pacheco Blvd Los Banos CA 209-826-9690 (800-329-7466)
There is a $5 per day pet fee.
Sunstar Inn 839 W. Pacheco Blvd Los Banos CA 209-826-3805
There is a $10 per day additional pet fee.

Lost Hills

Accommodations
Days Inn 14684 Aloma St Lost Hills CA 661-797-2371 (800-329-7466)

Motel 6 - Lost Hills 14685 Warren Street Lost Hills CA 661-797-2346 (800-466-8356)

One well-behaved family pet per room. Guest must notify front desk upon arrival. Guest is liable for any damages. In consideration of all guests, pets must never be left unattended in the guest rooms.

Campgrounds and RV Parks
Lost Hills RV Park (formally KOA) 14831 Warren Street Lost Hills CA 661-797-2719 (800-562-2793)
Dogs of all sizes are allowed for no additional fee at this RV only park. Dogs must be leashed and cleaned up after. There are some breed restrictions. There is a dog walk area at the campground.

Madera

Accommodations
Days Inn 25327 Ave 16 Madera CA 559-674-8817 (800-329-7466)
There is a $5 per day pet fee.
Madera Valley Inn 317 North G St Madera CA 559-664-0100
Dogs of all sizes are allowed. There is a $15 per night pet fee per pet. Smoking and non-smoking are available for pet rooms.
Motel 6 - Madera 22683 Avenue 18 1/2 Madera CA 559-675-8697 (800-466-8356)
One well-behaved family pet per room. Guest must notify front desk upon arrival. Guest is liable for any damages. In consideration of all guests, pets must never be left unattended in the guest rooms.

Attractions
Mariposa Wine Company 20146 Road 21 Madera CA 559-673-6372
http://www.mariposawine.com/index.html
The combining of four distinctive wineries under one company has made for a wide variety of wines for tasting and purchase. Dogs are allowed on the grounds and on the deck where seating is also available. Dogs must be well behaved, leashed, and cleaned up after.

Outdoor Restaurants
Cole's Books & Bagels 1516 Howard Road Madera CA 559-674-1400
Dogs are allowed at the outdoor tables.

Merced

Accommodations
Motel 6 - Merced North 1410 V Street Merced CA 209-384-2181 (800-466-8356)
One well-behaved family pet per room. Guest must notify front desk upon arrival. Guest is liable for any damages. In consideration of all guests, pets must never be left unattended in the guest rooms.
Travelodge 1260 Yosemite Park Way Merced CA 209-722-6225
There is a $10 per day additional pet fee.
Vagabond Inn 1215 R Street Merced CA 209-722-2737

Modesto

Accommodations
Motel 6 - Modesto 1920 West Orangeburg Avenue Modesto CA 209-522-7271 (800-466-8356)
One well-behaved family pet per room. Guest must notify front desk upon arrival. Guest is liable for any damages. In consideration of all guests, pets must never be left unattended in the guest rooms.
Red Lion 1612 Sisk Road Modesto CA 209-521-1612
Dogs of all sizes are allowed. There is a $50 per pet per stay fee and a pet policy to sign at check in.
Vagabond Inn 2025 W Orangeburg Ave Modesto CA 209-577-8008
A well-behaved large dog is okay.

Stores
PetSmart Pet Store 2100 Mc Henry Ave Modesto CA 209-574-0441
Your licensed and well-behaved leashed dog is allowed in the store.
Petco Pet Store 2021 Evergreen Avenue Modesto CA 209-571-0488
Your licensed and well-behaved leashed dog is allowed in the store.

Outdoor Restaurants
Baja Fresh Mexican Grill 3801 Pelandale Ave Modesto CA 209-545-4111
http://www.bajafresh.com
This Mexican restaurant is open for lunch and dinner. They use fresh ingredients and making their salsa and beans daily. Some of the items on their menu include Enchiladas, Burritos, Tacos Salads, Quesadillas, Nachos, Chicken, Steak and more. Well-behaved leashed dogs are allowed at the outdoor tables.
Baja Fresh Mexican Grill 801 Oakdale Road Ste Modesto CA 209-238-0222
http://www.bajafresh.com
This Mexican restaurant is open for lunch and dinner. They use fresh ingredients and making their salsa and beans daily. Some of the items on their menu include Enchiladas, Burritos, Tacos Salads, Quesadillas, Nachos, Chicken, Steak and more. Well-behaved leashed dogs are allowed at the outdoor tables.

Vets and Kennels
Veterinary Medical Clinic 1800 Prescott Rd Modesto CA 209-527-8844
Monday - Thursday 6 pm - 8 am. Friday 6 pm - Monday 8 am. 24 hours holidays.

New Cuyama

Campgrounds and RV Parks
Selby Campgrounds Soda Lake Road New Cuyama CA 661-391-6000
Primitive camping is available at this campground which is located at the base of the Caliente Mountains and near the dog-friendly Caliente Mountain Access Trail. There are 5 picnic tables and 4 fire pits, but no shade trees. There is no garbage pickup service, electricity or drinking water. Leave vehicles along the edge of the road, do not drive to your chosen campsite. Be aware of rattlesnakes in the area. Dogs on leash are allowed. Dogs may not be left unattended, and please clean up after your dog. The campground is about 14 miles west of New Cuyama off Hwy 166, on Soda Lake Road. There will be signs. Dogs are not allowed at Painted Rock at any time. This campground is closed during the off-season. The camping and tent areas also allow dogs. There is a dog walk area at the campground. There are no electric or water hookups at the campgrounds.

Parks
Caliente Mountain Access Trail Highway 166 New Cuyama CA 661-391-6000
This trail is popular with hikers and mountain bikers. It is also used by hunters who take the trail to get access to adjacent public lands. This open space has a nice display of wildflowers in the Spring. The trailhead is located about 14 miles west of New Cuyama. The trail starts on the north side of the highway after crossing a bridge over the Cuyama River. Dogs are allowed on the trail.

Oregon House

Campgrounds and RV Parks
Collins Lake 7530 Collins Lake Road Oregon House CA 530-692-1600 (800-286-0576)
http://www.collinslake.com/
This is a popular 1600 acre lake and recreation area with a wide range of land and water recreation and activities. Some of the features/amenities include a big sandy swimming beach with beach volleyball, picnic areas, a playground, general store, boat launch, a marina with rentals, and lakeside camping. The camp areas have tables, fire pits, and showers. Dogs of all sizes are allowed for an additional fee of $2 per night per pet. Dogs must be under owner's control, well mannered, leashed, and cleaned up after at all times. Dogs may not be left unattended, and they are not allowed on the swim beach or on the playground. The camping and tent areas also allow dogs. There is a dog walk area at the campground.

Orland

Campgrounds and RV Parks
Black Butte Lake Recreation Area 19225 Newville Road Orland CA   530-865-4781 (877-444-6777)
Located on Stony Creek, this popular recreation area features a 4,460 surface acre lake with 40 miles of shoreline, and during the spring nature puts on a wonderful display of wildflowers. Some of the features/amenities include 3 self-guided nature trails, interpretive programs, well maintained picnic facilities, a playground, and a variety of land and water recreational activities. Dogs of all sizes are allowed for no additional fee. Dogs must be under owner's control at all times, and be leashed and cleaned up after. Dogs are not allowed at the beach. There are two campgrounds available at the lake. Some of the amenities include drinking water, picnic tables, fire pits, phones, and restrooms with showers. The camping and tent areas also allow dogs. There is a dog walk area at the campground. There are no electric hookups at the campgrounds.
Buckhorn Recreation Area 19225 Newville Road Orland CA   530-865-4781 (877-444-6777)
This picturesque park, snuggled in the foothills of north-central California along Black Butte Lake, offers a variety of recreational pursuits and an interpretive trail. Next door is a 75-acre all-terrain park. Dogs of all sizes are allowed at no additional fee. Dogs must be on no more than a 6 foot leash at all times in the camp and trail areas. Dogs may be off lead at the backside of the lake only if they are under voice command. The camping and tent areas also allow dogs. There is a dog walk area at the campground. There are no electric or water hookups at the campgrounds.

Parks
Black Butte Lake Recreation Area 19225 Newville Road Orland CA   530-865-4781 (877-444-6777)
Located on Stony Creek, this popular recreation area features a 4,460 surface acre lake with 40 miles of shoreline, and during the spring nature puts on a wonderful display of wildflowers. Some of the features/amenities include 3 self-guided nature trails, interpretive programs, well maintained picnic facilities, a playground, and a variety of land and water recreational activities. Dogs of all sizes are allowed for no additional fee. Dogs must be under owners control at all times, and be leashed and cleaned up after. Dogs are not allowed at the beach.

Orleans

Attractions
Coates Family Vineyards 3255 Red Cap Road Orleans CA   530-627-3369
The CCOF (California Certified Organic Farmers) have only certified a few wineries as organic and this winery is one of them. The grapes are aged in oak barrels the traditional way in small lots, sulfite free, unfiltered, unrefined, and with perfect growing conditions. Tours are available by reservation by phone or at norman@coatesvineyards.com. Dogs are welcome; they just need to be social and friendly as there are also 5 other happy dogs on site. Dogs must be well behaved, leashed, and cleaned up after.

Oroville

Accommodations
Days Inn 1745 Feather River Blvd Oroville CA   530-533-3297 (800-329-7466)
One large dog per room is okay. There is a $7 per day pet fee.
Motel 6 - Oroville 505 Montgomery Street Oroville CA   530-532-9400 (800-466-8356)
One well-behaved family pet per room. Guest must notify front desk upon arrival. Guest is liable for any damages. In consideration of all guests, pets must never be left unattended in the guest rooms.
Travelodge 580 Oroville Dam Blvd Oroville CA   530-533-7070
There is a $40 refundable pet deposit.

Campgrounds and RV Parks
Oroville State Wildlife Area 945 Oroville Dam Blvd West Oroville CA   530-538-2236
Just outside the city limits sits this wildlife area of almost 12,000 acres of riparian forest bordered by 12 miles of river channels. The area is popular for fishing, birding, and hiking. Dogs of all sizes are allowed for no additional

fee. Dogs must be under owner's control, and leashed and cleaned up after at all times. Primitive camping is allowed; there are restrooms and drinking water available. The camping and tent areas also allow dogs. There is a dog walk area at the campground. There are no electric or water hookups at the campgrounds.
Spenceville Wildlife and Recreation Area Larkin Road Oroville CA 530-538-2236
Fishing and birding are popular at this 11,448 acre park of mostly foothill oak trees and grasslands with creeks and springs found throughout. Dogs of all sizes are allowed for no additional fee. They must be under owner's control at all times, and be leashed and cleaned up after. The camp area is very primitive and provides a vault toilet. The camping and tent areas also allow dogs. There is a dog walk area at the campground. There are no electric or water hookups at the campgrounds.

Parks

Oroville State Wildlife Area 945 Oroville Dam Blvd West Oroville CA 530-538-2236
Just outside the city limits sits this wildlife area of almost 12,000 acres of riparian forest bordered by 12 miles of river channels. The area is popular for fishing, birding, and hiking. Dogs of all sizes are allowed for no additional fee. Dogs must be under owners control, and leashed and cleaned up after at all times.
Spenceville Wildlife and Recreation Area Larkin Road Oroville CA 530-538-2236
Fishing and birding are popular at this 11,448 acre park of mostly foothill oak trees and grasslands with creeks and springs found throughout. Dogs of all sizes are allowed for no additional fee. They must be under owners control at all times, and be leashed and cleaned up after.

Piedra

Campgrounds and RV Parks

Pine Flat Lake Rec Area 28100 Pine Flat Road Piedra CA 559-488-3004
This park of 120 acres is located on the Kings River below Pine Flat Dam, has 5 day use areas in addition to the camp area, and offers a variety of recreational pursuits. Dogs of all sizes are allowed at no additional fee. Dogs may not be left unattended, and they must be on no more than a 6 foot leash at all times, and cleaned up after. Dogs are allowed on the trails. The camping and tent areas also allow dogs. There is a dog walk area at the campground. There are no electric or water hookups at the campgrounds.

Porterville

Accommodations

Motel 6 - Porterville 935 West Morton Avenue Porterville CA 559-781-7600 (800-466-8356)
One well-behaved family pet per room. Guest must notify front desk upon arrival. Guest is liable for any damages. In consideration of all guests, pets must never be left unattended in the guest rooms.

Campgrounds and RV Parks

Sequoia National Forest 1839 South Newcomb Street Porterville CA 559-784-1500 (877-444-6777)
Named for the world's largest tree, this forest is home to 38 groves of the giant sequoias, as well as impressive granite monoliths, glacier torn canyons, lush meadows, and rushing rivers. There are also several features/attractions here, some of which include; a 50 mile auto route (Kings Canyon Scenic Byway) that descends into one of North America's deepest canyons; several lookout stations-including the highest lookout (Bald Mountain) in the southern Sierra Nevadans; there are 3 National Recreation Trails, 45 miles of the Pacific Crest National Scenic Trail, and more than 800 miles of maintained roads/over a 1,000 miles of trails. There is a wide variety of year round land and water recreational opportunities. Your dog is welcome here at Sequoia National Forest (not to be confused with the less than dog-friendly Sequoia National Park). Dogs must be friendly, well behaved, on no more than a 6 foot leash, cleaned up after, and inside an enclosed vehicle or tent at night. Dogs may go on all the trails and throughout the park; they are not allowed on developed swimming beaches or in park buildings. There are more than 50 developed campgrounds, reserved-and first come first served sites that offer a wide variety of different altitudes/features/amenities; all have vault or flush toilets. If you plan to make your own camp, be sure to obtain a campfire permit. The camping and tent areas also allow dogs. There is a dog walk area at the campground. There are no electric or water hookups at the campgrounds.

Parks

TOP 200 PLACE **Sequoia National Forest** 1839 South Newcomb Street Porterville CA 559-784-

1500 (877-444-6777)
Named for the world's largest tree, this forest is home to 38 groves of the giant sequoias, as well as impressive granite monoliths, glacier torn canyons, lush meadows, and rushing rivers. There are also several features/attractions here, some of which include; a 50 mile auto route (Kings Canyon Scenic Byway) that descends into one of North America's deepest canyons; several lookout stations-including the highest lookout (Bald Mountain) in the southern Sierra Nevadans; there are 3 National Recreation Trails, 45 miles of the Pacific Crest National Scenic Trail, and more than 800 miles of maintained roads/over a 1,000 miles of trails. There is a wide variety of year round land and water recreational opportunities. Your dog is welcome here at Sequoia National Forest (not to be confused with the less than dog-friendly Sequoia National Park). Dogs must be friendly, well behaved, on no more than a 6 foot leash, cleaned up after, and inside an enclosed vehicle or tent at night. Dogs may go on all the trails and throughout the park; they are not allowed on developed swimming beaches or in park buildings.

Ripon

Accommodations
La Quinta Inn Ripon 1524 Colony Road Ripon CA   209-599-8999 (800-531-5900)
Dogs of all sizes are allowed. There are no additional pet fees. Dogs must be leashed and cleaned up after.

Sacramento

Accommodations

Lake Natoma Inn

Lake Natoma Inn 702 Gold Lake Drive Folsom CA   916-351-1500
http://www.lakenatomainn.com/
This inn offers 120 guest rooms and 12 Lakeview Suites nestled in a wooded natural environment overlooking Lake Natoma. Enjoy over 20 miles of beautiful bike and dog-friendly walking trails along the American river. This inn is also located next to Historic Folsom. There is a $45 one time per stay pet fee and a $15 per day pet charge per pet.

Motel 6 - Sacramento - North Highlands 4600 Watt Avenue North Highlands CA 916-973-8637 (800-466-8356)
One well-behaved family pet per room. Guest must notify front desk upon arrival. Guest is liable for any damages. In consideration of all guests, pets must never be left unattended in the guest rooms.

AmeriSuites 10744 Gold Center Dr. Rancho Cordova CA 916-635-4799 (800-833-1516)
This is an all-suite hotel. It is six stories with interior corridors. Each suite has either 2 double beds or 1 king bed in the bedroom area. The hotel boosts dog bones for your four legged family members.

Best Western Heritage Inn 11269 Point East Dr Rancho Cordova CA 916-635-4040 (800-780-7234)
Dogs of all sizes are allowed. There is a $20 one time per pet fee per visit. Smoking and non-smoking are available for pet rooms.

Inns of America 12249 Folsom Blvd Rancho Cordova CA 916-351-1213 (800-826-0778)
http://innsofamerica.com/sac12.htm
This motel offers a complimentary continental breakfast. To get there from Sacramento, take Hwy 50 and exit Hazel Ave. Turn right onto Hazel. Then turn right onto Folsom Blvd. The hotel will be on the right. There is a $5 per day additional pet fee.

Motel 6 - Sacramento - Rancho Cordova East 10694 Olson Drive Rancho Cordova CA 916-635-8784 (800-466-8356)
One well-behaved family pet per room. Guest must notify front desk upon arrival. Guest is liable for any damages. In consideration of all guests, pets must never be left unattended in the guest rooms.

Residence Inn by Marriott 2779 Prospect Park Drive Rancho Cordova CA 916-851-1550
Pets of all sizes are allowed. There is a $75 one time fee, and a pet policy to sign at check in.

Best Western Rocklin Park Hotel 5450 China Garden Rd Rocklin CA 916-630-9400 (800-780-7234)
Dogs of all sizes are allowed. There is a $75 one time pet fee per visit. Smoking and non-smoking are available for pet rooms.

Best Western Roseville Inn 220 Harding Blvd Roseville CA 916-782-4434 (800-780-7234)
Dogs of all sizes are allowed. There is a $10 per night pet fee per pet. Dogs are not allowed to be left alone in the room. Smoking and non-smoking are available for pet rooms.

Oxford Suites 130 N Sunrise Ave Roseville CA 916-784-2222 (800-882-SUITE)
This inn features a health club, self-service laundry, heated pool and spa, and video rentals. Each room has a separate living area, 2 phones, 2 TVs, a microwave, refrigerator and more. To get there from Hwy 80, exit Douglas Blvd. and head east. Then turn left on N Sunrise Ave. There is a $15 one time pet fee.

Residence Inn by Marriott 1930 Taylor Road Roseville CA 916-772-5500
Dogs of all sizes are allowed. There is a $75 one time fee, and a pet policy to sign at check in.

Candlewood Suites 555 Howe Ave Sacramento CA 916-646-1212 (877-270-6405)
Dogs of any size are allowed. Only one pet per room is allowed. There is a $75 one time pet fee.

Canterbury Inn Hotel 1900 Canterbury Rd Sacramento CA 916-927-0927
This inn is located about a 5-10 minute drive from Old Sacramento. Guest laundry services are available. To get there from Hwy 160, take the Leisure Lane ramp towards Canterbury Rd. Turn right onto Canterbury Rd. There is a $5 per day additional pet fee.

Clarion Hotel Mansion Inn 700 16th Street Sacramento CA 916-444-8000 (877-424-6423)
One dog of any size is allowed. There is a $35 per night additional pet fee. Dogs must be leashed, cleaned up after, and the Do Not Disturb sign put on the door if they are in the room alone. Arrangements need to be made for housekeeping.

Doubletree 2001 Point West Way Sacramento CA 916-929-8855
Well behaved dogs up to 50 pounds are allowed. There is a $50 one time fee per room and a pet policy to sign at check in.

Holiday Inn 5321 Date Ave Sacramento CA 916-338-5800 (877-270-6405)
Dogs of all sizes are allowed. There is a $25 one time per pet fee per visit. Smoking and non-smoking rooms are available for pets.

Holiday Inn Express 728 16 Street Sacramento CA 916-444-4436 (877-270-6405)
Dogs of any size are allowed. There is a $35 refundable pet deposit. The entire hotel is non-smoking.

Inn At Parkside 2116 6th Street Sacramento CA 916-658-1818 (800-995-7275)
http://innatparkside.com
This pet-friendly Sacramento B&B is located in downtown Sacramento within walking distance of the State Capitol and Old Town.

La Quinta Inn Sacramento Downtown 200 Jibboom St. Sacramento CA 916-448-8100 (800-531-5900)
Dogs of all sizes are allowed. There are no additional pet fees. Dogs must be leashed and cleaned up after.

Motel 6 - Sacamento South 7407 Elsie Avenue Sacramento CA 916-689-6555 (800-466-8356)
One well-behaved family pet per room. Guest must notify front desk upon arrival. Guest is liable for any damages. In consideration of all guests, pets must never be left unattended in the guest rooms.

Motel 6 - Sacramento Central 7850 College Town Drive Sacramento CA 916-383-8110 (800-466-8356)
One well-behaved family pet per room. Guest must notify front desk upon arrival. Guest is liable for any damages. In consideration of all guests, pets must never be left unattended in the guest rooms.

Motel 6 - Sacramento Downtown 1415 30th Street Sacramento CA 916-457-0777 (800-466-8356)
One well-behaved family pet per room. Guest must notify front desk upon arrival. Guest is liable for any

damages. In consideration of all guests, pets must never be left unattended in the guest rooms.

Motel 6 - Sacramento North 5110 Interstate Avenue Sacramento CA   916-331-8100 (800-466-8356)
One well-behaved family pet per room. Guest must notify front desk upon arrival. Guest is liable for any damages. In consideration of all guests, pets must never be left unattended in the guest rooms.

Motel 6 - Sacramento Southwest 7780 Stockton Boulevard Sacramento CA   916-689-9141 (800-466-8356)
One well-behaved family pet per room. Guest must notify front desk upon arrival. Guest is liable for any damages. In consideration of all guests, pets must never be left unattended in the guest rooms.

Motel 6 - Sacramento-Old Sacramento North 227 Jibboom Street Sacramento CA   916-441-0733 (800-466-8356)
One well-behaved family pet per room. Guest must notify front desk upon arrival. Guest is liable for any damages. In consideration of all guests, pets must never be left unattended in the guest rooms.

Red Lion

Red Lion 1401 Arden Way Sacramento CA   916-922-8041
Dogs of all sizes are allowed. There is a $25 per room per stay fee and a pet policy to sign at check in.

Red Roof Inn - Sacramento 3796 Northgate Boulevard Sacramento CA   916-927-7117 (800-RED-ROOF)
One well-behaved family pet per room. Guest must notify front desk upon arrival. Guest is liable for any damages. In consideration of all guests, pets must never be left unattended in the guest rooms.

Residence Inn by Marriott 2410 W El Camino Avenue Sacramento CA   916-649-1300
Dogs of all sizes are allowed. There is a $75 one time fee, and a pet policy to sign at check in.

Residence Inn by Marriott 1530 Howe Avenue Sacramento CA   916-920-9111
Pets of all sizes are allowed. There is a $75 one time fee, and a pet policy to sign at check in. Please do not leave the pet unattended or kennel for housekeeping.

TOP 200 PLACE **Sheraton Grand Sacramento Hotel** 1230 J St. (13th & J St) Sacramento CA   916-447-1700 (888-625-5144)
The dog-friendly Sheraton Grand Sacramento Hotel is located directly across the street from the Capitol Park and within easy walking distance of Downtown Plaza and Old Sacramento. Dogs of all sizes are allowed. Pet rooms are on the sixth floor. Dogs are not allowed to be left alone in the room.

Motel 6 - Sacramento West 1254 Halyard Drive West Sacramento CA   916-372-3624 (800-466-8356)
One well-behaved family pet per room. Guest must notify front desk upon arrival. Guest is liable for any damages. In consideration of all guests, pets must never be left unattended in the guest rooms.

Sheraton Grand Sacramento Hotel

Campgrounds and RV Parks

Beals Point Campground 7806 Folsom-Auburn Road Folsom CA 916-988-0205 (800-444-PARK (7275))
This park, located on shores of Folsom Lake, offers miles of hiking trails, and a wide variety of recreational opportunities. Dogs of all sizes are allowed. There are no additional pet fees. Dogs must be on no more than a 6 foot leash and cleaned up after. Dogs are not allowed at the main swimming beaches. Dogs are allowed on the trails. The camping and tent areas also allow dogs. There is a dog walk area at the campground. There are no electric or water hookups at the campgrounds.

Cal Expo RV Park 1600 Exposition Blvd Sacramento CA 916-263-3000 (877-CAL-EXPO (225-3976))
http://www.calexpo.com/html/rvpark.asp
Centrally located amid an abundance of attractions and recreational opportunities, this park also provides a laundry room, private restroom and showers, and 24 hour security. Dogs of all sizes are allowed. There are no additional pet fees. Dogs may not be left unattended outside, and only inside if they will be physically comfortable, quiet, and well behaved. Dogs must be leashed at all times, and cleaned up after. This is an RV only park. There is a dog walk area at the campground.

Sacramento Metropolitan KOA 3951 Lake Road West Sacramento CA 916-371-6771 (800-562-2747)
http://www.koa.com/where/ca/05151/
This camping area, located close to many other attractions and the state capitol, offer such amenities as 65 foot pull-through sites with 50 amp service, cable, phone, swimming pool, bike rentals, and planned activities. Up to 3 dogs of all sizes are allowed for no additional fee at the tent or RV sites. There is an additional fee of $10 per night per pet for the cabins, and only 2 dogs are allowed. Guests who own any of the known aggressive breeds must sign a waiver. Dogs must be under owner's control and visual observation at all times. Dogs must be quiet, well behaved, and be on no more than a 6 foot leash at all times, or otherwise contained. Dogs may not be left unattended outside the owner's camping equipment, and must be brought inside at night. The camping and tent areas also allow dogs. There is a dog walk area at the campground. Dogs are allowed in the camping cabins.

Transportation Systems

RT (Rapid Transit) Regional Sacramento CA 916-321-2877
http://www.sacrt.com
Small dogs in carriers are allowed on the buses and light rail. The carrier must fit on the person's lap.

Central Valley - Please always call ahead to make sure that an establishment is still dog-friendly

Sacramento Metropolitan KOA

Attractions

Old Towne Folsom

Old Towne Folsom Sutter St & Riley St Folsom CA
This few block area of Folsom represents the historic mid 1800's gold rush days. There are shops, restaurants,

and places to explore. Some of the restaurants will allow your well-behaved, leashed dog at their outdoor tables.
Nimbus Fish Hatchery 2001 Nimbus Rd Rancho Cordova CA 916-358-2884
There is a free self-guided tour of the fish hatchery, where salmon eggs are hatched every year. Your well-behaved dog may accompany you leashed. The hours are daily 9 am - 3 pm.

Capitol Park-Self-Guided Walk

Capitol Park-Self-Guided Walk 10th and L Streets Sacramento CA 916-324-0333
At this park, you can enjoy the historic nostalgia of California's State Capitol. The Capitol Building has been the home of the California Legislature since 1869. While dogs are not allowed inside the Capitol Building, you can walk up to it and around it on the 40 acres known as Capitol Park. This park is home to a variety of different trees from around the world. There is a self-guided tour that explains the origin of the trees and plants. Squirrels are also in abundance here, so be sure to hold on to the leash if your pup likes those little creatures. Capitol Park is located in downtown Sacramento at 10th and L Streets.

TOP 200 PLACE Old Sacramento Historic Area between I and L Streets Sacramento CA 916-442-7644
http://www.oldsacramento.com/
Old Sacramento is a state historic park located in downtown Sacramento, next to the Sacramento River. This National Registered Landmark covers 28 acres and includes a variety of shops and restaurants (see Restaurants). Take the self-guided audio tour of Old Sacramento and learn about life in the 1860's. There are nine audio stations ($.50 per station) placed throughout Old Sacramento. The California State Railroad Museum is also located here. Dogs aren't allowed inside the museum, but there are several locomotives outside. You and your pup can investigate these large trains outside of the museum. Dogs are allowed on the horse and carriage rides located throughout town. Top Hand Ranch Carriage Rides will be more than happy to take you and your well-behaved pup on their carriages. (see Attractions). Old Sacramento is located in downtown Sacramento, between I and L Streets, and Hwy 5 and the Sacramento River. Parking garages are located at 3rd and J Streets or at Capitol Mall and Front Streets. There is a minimal fee for parking.
Scribner Bend Vineyards 9051 River Road Sacramento CA 916-744-1803
http://www.scribnerbend.com/
Located along the Delta, this award winning vineyard offers complimentary wine tasting Friday through Sunday, beautiful landscaped gardens, a courtyard and water fountain, and picnic tables/benches around the grounds. Dogs are allowed on the grounds, but not in the tasting room. Dogs must be leashed and cleaned up after.

Old Sacramento Historic Area

Top Hand Ranch Carriage Rides

Top Hand Ranch Carriage Rides Old Sacramento Sacramento CA 916-655-3444
Top Hand Ranch offers horse and carriage rides in Old Sacramento and around the State Capitol. Your pooch is welcome in the carriage. Prices are subject to change, but when we checked it cost $10 for a 15 minute ride or $30 for a 35 minute ride around Old Sacramento. If you want to tour Sacramento in style, take the horse and carriage from Old Sacramento to the State Capitol Building and back. This ride lasts about 50 minutes and costs $50. The carriage rides are available daily in Old Sacramento. The carriages are located in several spots, but the

main location is at the Old Supreme Court building near J and 2nd Streets. Old Sacramento is located in downtown Sacramento, between I and L Streets, and Hwy 5 and the Sacramento River. Parking garages are located at 3rd and J Streets or at Capitol Mall and Front Streets. There is a minimal fee for parking.

Shopping Centers

Downtown Plaza 547 L Street Sacramento CA 915-442-4000
http://westfield.com/downtownplaza/
This open air mall has great outdoor views and 120 stores in various categories. They also offer a concierge center, a 7 theater cinema complex, a kid's playground, a great imported carousel, several well-known eateries, and is home to Sacramento's only outdoor skating rink. Dogs are allowed to walk through the area, and it is up to the individual stores whether or not they are allowed inside. Dogs must be well mannered at all times, and be leashed and cleaned up after.

Stores

PetSmart Pet Store 6434 Sunrise Blvd Citrus Heights CA 916-729-2866
Your licensed and well-behaved leashed dog is allowed in the store.
Petco Pet Store 6067 Greenback Lane Citrus Heights CA 916-725-2556
Your licensed and well-behaved leashed dog is allowed in the store.
PetSmart Pet Store 8215 Laguna Blvd Elk Grove CA 916-691-3700
Your licensed and well-behaved leashed dog is allowed in the store.
Petco Pet Store 7715 Laguna Blvd Elk Grove CA 916-683-5155
Your licensed and well-behaved leashed dog is allowed in the store.
Petco Pet Store 8840 Madison Avenue Fair Oaks CA 916-863-7387
Your licensed and well-behaved leashed dog is allowed in the store.
PetSmart Pet Store 2705 E Bidwell St Folsom CA 916-984-4748
Your licensed and well-behaved leashed dog is allowed in the store.
Petco Pet Store 855 East Bidwell St Folsom CA 916-984-6141
Your licensed and well-behaved leashed dog is allowed in the store.
PetSmart Pet Store 10830 Olson Dr Rancho Cordova CA 916-851-1813
Your licensed and well-behaved leashed dog is allowed in the store.
PetSmart Pet Store 318 N Sunrise Blvd Roseville CA 916-786-5512
Your licensed and well-behaved leashed dog is allowed in the store.
PetSmart Pet Store 10363 Fairway Dr Roseville CA 916-774-8205
Your licensed and well-behaved leashed dog is allowed in the store.
Petco Pet Store 1917 Douglas Blvd Roseville CA 916-786-8655
Your licensed and well-behaved leashed dog is allowed in the store.
Chez Pooche 900 2nd Street Sacramento CA 916-446-1213
http://www.chezpoocheinc.com/
A variety of fun activities year around, a great selection of designer clothes, all natural gourmet treats, pet strollers, grooming and health supplies, jewelry, pet sitting, and lots more have made this a popular stop for pet lovers and pets. It is located in the popular Old Sacramento area. They will validate your parking ticket with any purchase, and pooches will get a free gourmet treat. Dogs must be under owner's control at all times.
PetSmart Pet Store 1738 Watt Ave Sacramento CA 916-973-8391
Your licensed and well-behaved leashed dog is allowed in the store.
PetSmart Pet Store 7923 E Stockton Blvd Sacramento CA 916-689-3000
Your licensed and well-behaved leashed dog is allowed in the store.
PetSmart Pet Store 3641 Truxel Rd Sacramento CA 916-928-0314
Your licensed and well-behaved leashed dog is allowed in the store.
Petco Pet Store 1878 Arden Way Sacramento CA 916-923-1082
Your licensed and well-behaved leashed dog is allowed in the store.

Parks

Rusch Community Park and Gardens Antelope Road & Auburn Blvd Citrus Heights CA
This is a nice city park with walkways, bridges and views plus a botanical garden to explore. The botanical garden is accessed from Antelope Rd and Rosswood. Dogs must be on leash at all times.

Folsom Lake State Recreation Area

Folsom Lake State Recreation Area various (see comments) Folsom CA   916-988-0205
This popular lake and recreation area is located in the Sierra Foothills. The Folsom Lake State Rec Area is approximately 18,000 acres, of which, 45% is land. Leashed dogs are allowed almost everywhere in this park except on the main beaches (there will be signs posted). But there are many other non-main beaches all around Folsom Lake where your dog is welcome. There are about 80 miles of dog-friendly trails in this park. This park is also adjacent to the American River Parkway, a 32 mile paved and dirt path, which stretches from Folsom Lake to downtown Sacramento. Folsom Lake has various entry points and can be reached via Hwy 80 or Hwy 50. It is located about 25 miles east of Sacramento. From Hwy 80, exit Douglas Blvd in Roseville and head east. From Hwy 50, exit Folsom Blvd. and head north. There is a minimal day use fee.
Gibson Ranch Park Elverta Rd West of Watt Ave North Highlands CA   916-875-6961
http://www.gibson-ranch.com/Gib_Five.htm
This park allows dogs on leash. There are a lot of dirt walking or jogging trails which must be shared with horses as this is predominantly an equestrian park. There is a lake in the center with picnic areas and fishing available.
Orangevale Community Park Oak Ave & Filbert Ave Orangevale CA   916-988-4373
Dogs must be on leash at this city park.
Maidu Park Rocky Ridge Rd & Maidu Dr Roseville CA   916-774-5969
Dogs must be on leash in this new 152 acre park in Roseville.

TOP 200 PLACE **American River Parkway** various (see comments) Sacramento CA   916-875-6672
The American River Parkway is a very popular recreation trail for locals and visitors. There are over 32 miles of paved and dirt paths that stretch from Folsom Lake in the Sierra Foothills to Old Sacramento in downtown Sacramento. It is enjoyed by hikers, wildlife viewers, boaters, equestrians and bicyclists. And of course, by dogs. Dogs must be on leash. There are various starting points, like the Folsom Lake State Recreation Area in Folsom or just north of downtown Sacramento. To start just north of downtown, take Hwy 5 north of downtown and exit Richards Blvd. Turn left onto Richards Blvd. Then turn right on Jibboom Street. Take Jibboom St to the parking lot.

American River Parkway

William Land Park

William Land Park 4000 S Land Park Drive Sacramento CA 916-808-5200
With just over 166 developed acres, this park offers a variety of recreational opportunities and amenities, some of which include family and group picnic areas, gaming courts, playing fields, an adventure play area, an

amphitheater, rock garden, and a jogging path. They are also home to the Sacramento Zoo, Fairytale town, Funderland, and a golf course. Dogs are allowed throughout the park unless otherwise noted. They must be leashed and cleaned up after at all times.

Off-Leash Dog Parks

Carmichael Park and Dog Park Fair Oaks Blvd & Grant Ave Carmichael CA   916-485-5322
This is a one acre off leash dog park. It is located in Carmichael Park which can be accessed from Fair Oaks Blvd in Carmichael. The rest of the park is nice for picnics and other activities. Dogs must be leashed when not inside the dog park.
P.O.O.C.H. Park of Citrus Heights Oak Avenue east of Fair Oaks Citrus Heights CA   916-725-1585
http://www.poochdogpark.com/
The dog park is located in C-Bar-C Park on Oak Ave. east of Fair Oaks and West of Wachtel. The dog park is over 2 acres in size and fenced. Benches are available and there is shade in the park. There is drinking water for dogs and people. For your water loving pups there are hoses and small wading pools in the park. The park is host to a number of dog events annually.
Elk Grove Dog Park 9950 Elk Grove Florin Rd Elk Grove CA 916-405-5600
The fenced dog park is best accessed from the East Stockton Blvd side of Elk Grove Park.From 99 take Grant Line Rd east and go left on East Stockton. The Elk Grove dog parks are monitored and maintained by the Park department and W.O.O.F. (We Offer Off-leash Fun), a dog owners organization in Elk Grove.
Laguna Dog Park 9014 Bruceville Rd Elk Grove CA 916-405-5600
The fenced Laguna Community Dog Park is located on the west side of Laguna Community Park. The small Laguna Community Park is located south of Big Horn Blvd and west of Brucevill Rd. The Elk Grove dog parks are monitored and maintained by the Park department and W.O.O.F. (We Offer Off-leash Fun), a dog owners organization in Elk Grove.
Phoenix Dog Park 9050 Sunset Ave Fair Oaks CA 916-966-1036
http://www.fordog.org
The Phoenix Dog Park is located in Phoenix Park in Fair Oaks. It is just under 2 acres in size and has three separate fenced areas. There is one area for large dogs, one area for small dogs and an area for shy dogs. There are shade structures, benches and a wash-off pad just outside of the dog park. The park is sponsored by FORDOG which stands for Fair Oaks Responsible Dog Owners Group. The park is located on Sunset Avenue east of Hazel. To get to the dog park from Highway 50, take Hazel north to Sunset and turn right. The dog park will be on your right.
West Side Dog Park 810 Oak Lane Rio Linda CA 916) 991-5929
This one acre fenced dog park is located in Westside Park at 810 Oak Lane in Rio Linda.

Marco Dog Park

Marco Dog Park 1800 Sierra Gardens Drive Roseville CA 916-774-5950
RDOG (Roseville Dog Owners Group) helped to establish this 2 acre dog park which is Roseville's first off-leash dog park. This park was named Marco Dog Park in memory of a Roseville Police Department canine named Marco who was killed in the line of duty. The park has a large grassy area with a few trees and doggie fire hydrants. It is closed on Wednesdays from dawn until 3:30pm for weekly maintenance. Like other dog parks, it may also be closed some days during the winter due to mud. To get there from Hwy 80, exit Douglas Blvd. heading east. Go about 1/2 mile and turn left on Sierra Gardens Drive. Marco Dog Park will be on the right.
Bannon Creek Dog Park Bannon Creek Drive near West El Camino Sacramento CA 916-264-5200
http://www.sacto.org/parks/dogpark1.htm
This off leash dog park is in Bannon Creek Park. Its hours are 5am to 10 pm daily. The park is 0.6 acres in size.
Granite Park Dog Park Ramona Avenue near Power Inn Rd Sacramento CA 916-264-5200
http://www.sacto.org/parks/dogpark1.htm
This dog park is in Granite Regional Park. Its hours are 5 am to 10 pm daily. It is 2 acres in size.
Howe Dog Park 2201 Cottage Way Sacramento CA 916-927-3802
Howe Dog Park is completely fenced and located in Howe Park. It has grass and several trees. To get there, take Business Route 80 and exit El Camino Ave. Head east on El Camino Ave. Turn right on Howe Ave. Howe Park will be on the left. Turn left onto Cottage Way and park in the lot. From the parking lot, the dog park is located to the right of the tennis courts.
Partner Park Dog Park 5699 South Land Park Drive Sacramento CA 916-264-5200
http://www.sacto.org/parks/dogpark1.htm
This dog park is located behind the Bell Cooledge Community Center. The park is 2.5 acres and its hours are 5 am to 10 pm daily. There are lights at the park.
Tanzanite Community Park Dog Park Tanzanite Dr at Innovator Dr Sacramento CA 916-808-5200
Tanzanite Community Park Dog Park is located in the Tanzanite Community Park in North Natomas. This new two acre fenced dog park is scheduled to open by the Fall of 2006. The park is located east of Airport Road in the Tanzanite Community Park.
Sam Combs Dog Park 205 Stone Blvd West Sacramento CA 916-617-4620
This fenced off-leash dog park opened in early 2006. There is a separate area for large dogs and small dogs. Take Jefferson Blvd south from the I-80 Freeway, left on Stone Blvd to the park on the left.

Outdoor Restaurants
Bella Bru Coffee Co 5038 Fair Oaks Blvd Carmichael CA 916-485-2883
They allow dogs at their outdoor tables and may even have dog cookies for your pup.
Java Central 7429 Fair Oaks Blvd Carmichael CA 916-972-7800
This coffee shop serves Deli-type food. Dogs are allowed at the outdoor tables. Water and treats are provided for your pet.
Camille's Sidewalk Cafe 5437 Sunrise Blvd Citrus Heights CA 916-961-8882
A vision of healthier, tastier foods inspired the idea for the freshly made salads, gourmet wraps and sandwiches, drinks, desserts, and coffees that are offered at all of Camille's Cafes. Dogs are allowed to sit with you at your outdoor table. Dogs must be attended to at all times, well behaved, and leashed.
Krispy Kreme Doughnuts 7901 Greenback Lane Citrus Heights CA 916-721-3667
http://www.krispykreme.com
Dogs are allowed at the outdoor tables.
Baja Fresh Mexican Grill 7419 Laguna Blvd. Ste 220 Elk Grove CA 916-691-2252
http://www.bajafresh.com
This Mexican restaurant is open for lunch and dinner. They use fresh ingredients and making their salsa and beans daily. Some of the items on their menu include Enchiladas, Burritos, Tacos Salads, Quesadillas, Nachos, Chicken, Steak and more. Well-behaved leashed dogs are allowed at the outdoor tables.
Steve's Place Pizza 11711 Fair Oaks Blvd Fair Oaks CA 916-961-1800
Dogs are allowed at the outdoor tables.
Baja Fresh Mexican Grill 1870 Prairie City Rd. Folsom CA 916-985-2112
http://www.bajafresh.com
This Mexican restaurant is open for lunch and dinner. They use fresh ingredients and making their salsa and beans daily. Some of the items on their menu include Enchiladas, Burritos, Tacos Salads, Quesadillas, Nachos, Chicken, Steak and more. Well-behaved leashed dogs are allowed at the outdoor tables.
Bella Bru Coffee 1115 E Bidwell St #126 Folsom CA 916-983-4003
Dogs are allowed at the outdoor tables.
Coffee Republic 6610 Folsom Auburn Rd Folsom CA 916-987-8001
Dogs are allowed at the outdoor tables.
My Brother Vinney's 718 Sutter St #200 Folsom CA 916-353-0273
Dogs are allowed in the outdoor seats in the back only, not on the front deck.
Pizzeria Classico 702 Sutter St Folsom CA 916-351-1430
Outdoor seating is available during the summer months only.
Rubio's Baja Grill 2776 E Bidwell Street Folsom CA 916-983-0645

Dogs are allowed at the outdoor tables.

Snook's Candies and Ice Cream 731 Sutter Street Folsom CA 916-985-0620

There are benches outside but no tables. Dogs are welcome to join you at these benches.

Yager's Tap House and Grille 727 Traders Lane Folsom CA 916-985-4677

Dogs are allowed at the outdoor tables.

La Bou 4110 Douglas Blvd Granite Bay CA 916-791-2142

Dogs are allowed at the outdoor tables.

The Cellar Cafe 12401 Folsom Blvd Rancho Cordova CA 916-985-0202

Enjoy lunch or dinner at this cafe. It is located in the Nimbus Winery Center. To get there from Sacramento, take Hwy 5 east and exit Hazel Ave. Turn right on Hazel and then left on Folsom Blvd. The cafe is on the left.

Baja Fresh Mexican Grill 2210 Sunset Blvd. Rocklin CA 916-772-1600

http://www.bajafresh.com

This Mexican restaurant is open for lunch and dinner. They use fresh ingredients and making their salsa and beans daily. Some of the items on their menu include Enchiladas, Burritos, Tacos Salads, Quesadillas, Nachos, Chicken, Steak and more. Well-behaved leashed dogs are allowed at the outdoor tables.

Cafe Buonarroti 4800 Granite Dr Ste 1B Rocklin CA 916-632-0100

This restaurant offers fine Italian cuisine, a superb wine menu, and outside dining service. Your pet is welcome to join you on the patio. Dogs must be attended to at all times, well behaved, and leashed.

Jasper's Giant Hamburgers 4820 Granite Dr Rocklin CA 916-624-9055

Dogs are allowed at the outdoor tables.

Baja Fresh Mexican Grill 1850 Douglas Blvd Roseville CA 916-773-2252

http://www.bajafresh.com

This Mexican restaurant is open for lunch and dinner. They use fresh ingredients and making their salsa and beans daily. Some of the items on their menu include Enchiladas, Burritos, Tacos Salads, Quesadillas, Nachos, Chicken, Steak and more. Well-behaved leashed dogs are allowed at the outdoor tables.

Cafe Elletti 2240 Douglas Blvd Roseville CA 916-774-6704

This café and deli offers outside seating service. They are open Monday through Friday from 7:30 am to 3:30 pm. Your pet is welcome to join you on the patio. Dogs must be attended to at all times, well behaved, and leashed.

Dos Coyotes Border Cafe 2030 Douglas Blvd #4 Roseville CA 916-772-0775

Dogs are allowed at the outdoor tables.

Mas Mexican Food 1563 Eureka Roa Roseville CA 916-773-3778

This Mexican style restaurant offers inside and outside dining service. Your pet is welcome to join you on the patio. Dogs must be attended to at all times, well behaved, and leashed.

Pasghetti 1060 Pleasant Grove Blvd. #100 Roseville CA 916-746-8707

http://www.pasghetti.com/

This family oriented Italian restaurant offers quick service, healthy portions, and during warm weather, they offer outdoor seating service. Place your order inside, and they will bring your meal out to your table. Your pet is welcome to join you at the outside tables. Dogs must be attended to at all times, well behaved, and leashed.

Quizno's Classic Subs 1228 Galleria Blvd #130 Roseville CA 916-787-1940

Dogs are allowed at the outdoor tables.

Texas West Bar b Que 1950 Douglas Blvd (at Rocky Ridge) Roseville CA 916-773-7427

http://www.texaswestbbq.com/location.htm

This barbecue restaurant offers dining service on the patio where your pet may join you. Well behaved dogs of all sizes are welcome. Dogs must be attended to at all times, well behaved, and leashed.

Togo's Eatery 1825 Douglas Blvd Roseville CA 916-782-4546

This is a fast food sandwich place. It is within walking distance of Marco Dog Park (see Sacramento Parks). To get there, take Hwy 80 and exit Douglas Blvd. east (towards Folsom). Turn left at the third street which is Sierra Gardens Drive. Then make a left turn into the parking lot. Dogs are allowed at the outdoor tables.

55 Degrees Restaurant 555 Capital Mall, Suite #55 Sacramento CA 916-553-4100

http://www.restaurant55.com

Dogs are allowed at the outdoor tables. This restaurant serves fresh California Cuisine.

Annabelle's Pizza-Pasta 200 J Street Sacramento CA 916-448-6239

Located in Old Sacramento, this restaurant allows dogs at the outdoor seating area in the back of the restaurant. There you will find several picnic tables.

Baja Fresh Mexican Grill 2100 Arden Way Sacramento CA 916-564-2252

http://www.bajafresh.com

This Mexican restaurant is open for lunch and dinner. They use fresh ingredients and making their salsa and beans daily. Some of the items on their menu include Enchiladas, Burritos, Tacos Salads, Quesadillas, Nachos, Chicken, Steak and more. Well-behaved leashed dogs are allowed at the outdoor tables.

Baja Fresh Mexican Grill 2600 Gateway Oaks Dr. Sacramento CA 916-920-5201

http://www.bajafresh.com

This Mexican restaurant is open for lunch and dinner. They use fresh ingredients and making their salsa and beans daily. Some of the items on their menu include Enchiladas, Burritos, Tacos Salads, Quesadillas, Nachos, Chicken, Steak and more. Well-behaved leashed dogs are allowed at the outdoor tables.

Bella Bru Cafe and Catering 4680 Natomas Blvd Sacramento CA 916-928-1770
This café offers American food, a full service bar, and full-service indoor and outdoor dining. Dogs are allowed to join you on the patio. Dogs must be attended to at all times, well behaved, and leashed.
Broiler Steakhouse 1201 K Street, Suite #100 Sacramento CA 916-444-3444
Dogs are allowed at the outdoor tables of this steakhouse.
Cafe Bernardo 2726 Capitol Avenue Sacramento CA 916-443-1180
Dogs are allowed at the outdoor tables. This restaurant serves California Cuisine. This popular restaurant's outdoor seating areas can be packed during nice weather for lunch and on weekends.
Danielle's Creperie 3535 B Fair Oaks Blvd Sacramento CA 916-972-1911
The outdoor tables here are seasonal. Well-behaved dogs on leash are permitted at the outdoor tables.
Gonuls J Street Cafe 3839 J Street Sacramento CA 916-457-1155
http://www.jstreetcafe.com
Dogs are allowed at the outdoor tables. This restaurant serves Mediterranean and California Cuisine.
Hangar 17 Bar and Grill 1630 S Street Sacramento CA 916-447-1717
Dogs are allowed at the outdoor tables.
Hot Rods Burgers 2007 K Street Sacramento CA 916-443-7637
Dogs are allowed at the outdoor tables.
La Bou 5420 Madison Ave Sacramento CA 916-349-1002
They gave our pup a dog cookie at the drive-thru. Dogs are allowed at the outdoor tables.
La Bou 10395 Rockingham Dr Sacramento CA 916-369-7824
Dogs are allowed at the outdoor tables.
Lomo Argentine Grill 1107 Front Street Sacramento CA 916-442-5666
Dogs are allowed at the outdoor tables.
Olive Garden 1780 Challenge Way Sacramento CA 916-649-8305
This restaurant serves Italian food. Dogs are allowed at the outdoor tables.
Original Pete's Pizza, Pasta and Grill 2001 J Street Sacramento CA 916-442-6770
Dogs are allowed at the outdoor tables.
River City Brewing Company 545 Downtown Plaza Ste 1115 Sacramento CA 916-447-2739
This restaurant and bar serves American food. Dogs are allowed at the outdoor tables.
Rubicon Brewing Company 2004 Capitol Avenue Sacramento CA 916-448-7032
Dogs are allowed at the outdoor tables.
Sacramento Natural Foods Cooperative 1900 Alhambra Blvd. Sacramento CA 916-455-2667
http://www.sacfoodcoop.com
Dogs are allowed at the outdoor tables. You will need to go inside without your dog to get your food.
Streets of London Pub 1804 J Street Sacramento CA 916-498-1388
http://www.streetsoflondon.net
Dogs are allowed at the outdoor tables.
Texas West Bar B Que 1600 Fulton Avenue Sacramento CA 916-483-7427
http://www.texaswestbbq.com/
This barbecue restaurant offers dining service on the patio where your pet may join you. Well behaved dogs of all sizes are welcome. Dogs must be attended to at all times, well behaved, and leashed.
The Bread Store 1716 J Street Sacramento CA 916-557-1600
This sandwich shoppe allows dogs at the outdoor patio. The patio is covered.
Whole Foods Market 4315 Arden Way Sacramento CA 916-488-2800
http://www.wholefoods.com/
This natural food supermarket offers natural and organic foods. Order some food from their deli without your dog and bring it to an outdoor table where your well-behaved leashed dog is welcome. Dogs are not allowed in the store including the deli at any time.
Cafe Vienna 1229 Merkley West Sacramento CA 916-371-9560
http://www.viennatonight.com/
This is Sacramento's only Austrian/German Restaurant, and they specialize in homemade, freshly prepared foods. They offer a lunch buffet Monday through Friday from 11 am to 2 pm, and a regular dinner menu Tuesday through Saturday from 5 to 9 pm. On some Saturday nights, they forgo the dinner menu and offer a dinner buffet and dance special. Dogs are welcome to join you on their patio. Someone needs to stay with your pet while you visit the buffet (if during lunch). Dogs must be attended to at all times, well behaved, and leashed.

Events
Doggy Dash 915 I St Sacramento CA 916-383-7387
http://www.sspca.org/Events.html
This annual summer event at William Land Park, sponsored by the Sacramento SPCA, offers a full day of activities for canines and their human companions. It includes a scenic run/walk, specialty vendors, contests, demonstrations, agility shows, and more. Dogs must be leashed and cleaned up after at all times.

Vets and Kennels

Kenar Pet Resort 3633 Garfield Ave Carmichael CA 916-487-5221
Monday - Saturday 7 am - 6 pm, Sunday 3 pm - 6 pm pickup with extra day fee.
Greenback Pet Resort 8311 Greenback Lane Fair Oaks CA 916-726-3400
This kennel is attached to a veterinary clinic. The kennel hours are Monday - Friday 8am to 6 pm, Saturday 8am - 5pm, Sunday 10am - 5pm.
Greenback Veterinary Hospital 8311 Greenback Lane Fair Oaks CA 916-725-1541
There is also an on site kennel - Greenback Pet Resort. This is a 24 hour emergency veterinarian.
Pet Emergency Center 1100 Atlantic St Roseville CA 916-783-4655
The vet is open 24 hours for emergencies.
Emergency Animal Clinic 9700 Business Park Dr #404 Sacramento CA 916-362-3146
Monday - Saturday 9 am - 6 pm, Emergencies handled 24 hours.
Sacramento Emergency Vet Clinic 2201 El Camino Ave Sacramento CA 916-922-3425
Monday - Friday 6 pm to 8 am, 24 hours on the weekend.

Wag Pet Hotel

Wag Pet Hotel 1759 Enterprise Blvd West Sacramento CA 916-373-0300
This new pet kennel is notable for its 24 hour pick up and drop off - making it ideal for Sacramento Visitors who need to drop there dog off for a while if they are unable to take their dog with them. It also features play areas and webcams to check on your pet.

San Juan Bautista

Accommodations

San Juan Inn 410 The Alameda #156 San Juan Bautista CA 831-623-4380
Located near the center of Monterey Peninsula, you'll enjoy excellent nearby hiking trails at this inn. One dog of any size is allowed. There is a $10 per night additional pet fee. Dogs may not be left alone in the room, and they must be leashed and cleaned up after.

Campgrounds and RV Parks

Betabel RV Park 9664 Betabel Road San Juan Bautista CA 831-623-2202 (800-278-7275)
http://www.betabel.com/

Located about 5 miles south of Gilroy, this RV park is set in the quiet countryside. Amenities include 30 or 50 amp service, a mini mart, seasonally heated pool, propane, club/meeting rooms, satellite TV, restrooms, showers and handicapped access. Well-behaved leashed dogs of all sizes are allowed at no additional fee. People need to clean up after their pets. There is no pet fee. Dogs may not be left unattended outside, and they may only be left inside your unit for a short time if they will be quiet and comfortable. There is a large park across from the office where dogs can run off lead if they are well behaved and under voice control. The camping and tent areas also allow dogs. There is a dog walk area at the campground.

Mission Farms RV Park & Campground 400 San Juan Hollister Road San Juan Bautista CA   831-623-4456
Thanks to one of our readers for recommending this campground. Close to the highway, but quiet with lots of shade trees, this RV only park offers pull thru sites, big rig access, cable TV, and laundry. The camp sites are $28 per night. There is a $2 per night per pet fee for each small dog, and there is a $4 per night per pet fee for medium to large dogs. Dogs may not be left unattended, and they must be leashed and cleaned up after. There is a dog walk area at the campground.

Outdoor Restaurants

Flor's Coffee House 304 3rd Street San Juan Bautista CA   831-623-9300
This coffee house offers 2 tables outside where you may sit with your pet. They are open 10 am to 5 pm on Monday; 8 am to 6 pm on Tuesday, 8 am to 7 pm Wednesday and Thursday, and 9 am to 8 pm Friday through Sunday. Dogs must be well behaved, leashed, and cleaned up after.

JJ's Homemade Burgers 100 The Alameda San Juan Bautista CA   831-623-2518
This restaurant offers a variety of hamburgers and all the fixings. They offer outside dining service, and your pet is welcome to join you. Dogs must be attended to at all times, well behaved, and leashed.

Joan and Peter's German Restaurant 322 Third Street San Juan Bautista CA   831-623-4521
http://www.joanandpeter.com/
Open 4 days a week, they specialize in German foods and also offer outside dining service. Your pet is welcome to join you on the outdoor patio. Dogs must be attended to at all times, well behaved, and leashed.

La Casa Rosa 107 Third Street San Juan Bautista CA   831-623-4563
This establishment offers light soufflés and casseroles plus a variety of fresh accompaniments. They are open daily from 11:30 to 3 pm, except Tuesdays, and once in a while they close on a Monday. Your well behaved pet is welcome to join you on their outside patio where they also offer service. Dogs must be attended to and leashed at all times.

Stockton

Accommodations

Holiday Inn 111 East March Lane Stockton CA   209-474-3301 (877-270-6405)
Dogs of all sizes are allowed. There is a $20 per night pet fee per pet. Smoking and non-smoking rooms are available for pets.

La Quinta Inn Stockton 2710 W. March Ln. Stockton CA   209-952-7800 (800-531-5900)
Dogs of all sizes are allowed. There are no additional pet fees. Dogs must be leashed and cleaned up after. The Do Not Disturb sign must be placed on the door if there is a pet alone in the room.

Motel 6 - Stockton - Charter Way West 817 Navy Drive Stockton CA   209-946-0923 (800-466-8356)
One well-behaved family pet per room. Guest must notify front desk upon arrival. Guest is liable for any damages. In consideration of all guests, pets must never be left unattended in the guest rooms.

Motel 6 - Stockton - I-5 Southeast 1625 French Camp Turnpike Road Stockton CA   209-467-3600 (800-466-8356)
One well-behaved family pet per room. Guest must notify front desk upon arrival. Guest is liable for any damages. In consideration of all guests, pets must never be left unattended in the guest rooms.

Motel 6 - Stockton North 6717 Plymouth Road Stockton CA   209-951-8120 (800-466-8356)
One well-behaved family pet per room. Guest must notify front desk upon arrival. Guest is liable for any damages. In consideration of all guests, pets must never be left unattended in the guest rooms.

Residence Inn by Marriott March Lane and Brookside Stockton CA   209-472-9800
Pets of all sizes are allowed. There is a $70 per pet per stay fee and a pet policy to sign at check in.

Travelodge 1707 Fremont St Stockton CA   209-466-7777
There is a $25 refundable pet deposit.

Motel 6 - Tracy 3810 North Tracy Boulevard Tracy CA   209-836-4900 (800-466-8356)
One well-behaved family pet per room. Guest must notify front desk upon arrival. Guest is liable for any damages. In consideration of all guests, pets must never be left unattended in the guest rooms.

Campgrounds and RV Parks

Stockton/Lodi (formally KOA) 2851 East Eight Mile Road Lodi CA 209-334-0309 (800-562-1229)
http://www.stknlodirv.com/
This campground offers a store, a host of amenities, planned activities, and various land and water recreation. Dogs of all sizes are allowed at no additional fee. Dogs may not be left unattended, and they must be on no more than a 6 foot leash. Dogs must be taken to the dog walk area to do their "business", and be cleaned up after at all times. There are some breed restrictions. The camping and tent areas also allow dogs. There is a dog walk area at the campground.

Attractions

Jessie's Grove Winery 1973 W Turner Road Lodi CA 209-368-0880
http://www.jgwinery.com/#
This winery, located along the delta in the foothills of the Sierra Nevada Mountains, specializes in wines that embody the unique distinctive growing factors of the area. They offer events and concerts throughout the year; dogs are not allowed during concerts. Dogs are allowed around the grounds of the winery; they must be friendly, well behaved, and leashed and cleaned up after.
Phillips Farm/ Michael-David Vineyards 4580 Hwy 12 Lodi CA 209-368-7384
http://www.lodivineyards.com/
Six generations of winegrowers have made this an award winning winery, producing some of the finest varietals in California, and they are also know for producing the very popular 7 Deadly Zins and the 6th Sense Syrah. Dogs are allowed to explore the grounds and the large farm area; dogs must be friendly towards farm and domestic animals. Dogs must be well behaved, leashed, and cleaned up after at all times. They are not allowed in the tasting room.

Stores

PetSmart Pet Store 10520 Trinity Pkwy Stockton CA 209-474-9748
Your licensed and well-behaved leashed dog is allowed in the store.
Petco Pet Store 5406 Pacific Avenue Stockton CA 209-478-7726
Your licensed and well-behaved leashed dog is allowed in the store.
PetSmart Pet Store 2477 Naglee Rd Tracy CA 209-836-6080
Your licensed and well-behaved leashed dog is allowed in the store.
Petco Pet Store 2888 West Grant Line Rd Tracy CA 209-830-4476
Your licensed and well-behaved leashed dog is allowed in the store.

Outdoor Restaurants

Baja Fresh Mexican Grill 5350 Pacific Ave Stockton CA 209-477-5024
http://www.bajafresh.com
This Mexican restaurant is open for lunch and dinner. They use fresh ingredients and making their salsa and beans daily. Some of the items on their menu include Enchiladas, Burritos, Tacos Salads, Quesadillas, Nachos, Chicken, Steak and more. Well-behaved leashed dogs are allowed at the outdoor tables.
Baja Fresh Mexican Grill 1855 W. 11th Street Tracy CA 209-834-2252
http://www.bajafresh.com
This Mexican restaurant is open for lunch and dinner. They use fresh ingredients and making their salsa and beans daily. Some of the items on their menu include Enchiladas, Burritos, Tacos Salads, Quesadillas, Nachos, Chicken, Steak and more. Well-behaved leashed dogs are allowed at the outdoor tables.

Vets and Kennels

Associated Veterinary Emergency Hospital 3008 E Hammer Lane #115 Stockton CA 209-952-8387
Monday - Friday 6 pm to 8 am, 24 hours on weekends.

Stonyford

Campgrounds and RV Parks

Letts Lake Campground Forest Road M10 Stonyford CA 530-934-3316
This campground is located in the Mendocino National Forest and is next to a 35 acre lake. Water-based activities include non-motorized boating, trout fishing and swimming. There are 44 campsites and camp amenities include toilets, fire rings, water and trailer space. The access road and camps are suitable for 16 to 20 foot camping trailers. The campground is at an elevation of 4,500 feet. There is a $10 per day campsite fee.

Prices are subject to change. Dogs on leash are allowed at the campground, on trails and in the water at non-designated swimming areas only. The camp is located 19 miles west of Stonyford. This campground is closed during the off-season. The camping and tent areas also allow dogs. There is a dog walk area at the campground. There are no electric or water hookups at the campgrounds.

Tulare

Accommodations
Days Inn 1183 N Blackstone St Tulare CA   559-686-0985 (800-329-7466)
There is a $5 per day pet fee.
Howard Johnson Express Inn 1050 E Rankin Ave Tulare CA   559-688-6671 (800-446-4656)
There is a $6 per day pet fee.
Motel 6 - Tulare 1111 North Blackstone Drive Tulare CA   559-686-1611 (800-466-8356)
One well-behaved family pet per room. Guest must notify front desk upon arrival. Guest is liable for any damages. In consideration of all guests, pets must never be left unattended in the guest rooms.

Turlock

Accommodations
Motel 6 - Turlock 250 South Walnut Avenue Turlock CA   209-667-4100 (800-466-8356)
One well-behaved family pet per room. Guest must notify front desk upon arrival. Guest is liable for any damages. In consideration of all guests, pets must never be left unattended in the guest rooms.

Vacaville

Accommodations
Best Western Heritage Inn 1420 E Monte Vista Ave Vacaville CA   707-448-8453 (800-780-7234)
Dogs of all sizes are allowed. There are no additional pet fees. Smoking and non-smoking are available for pet rooms.
Motel 6 - Vacaville 107 Lawrence Drive Vacaville CA   707-447-5550 (800-466-8356)
One well-behaved family pet per room. Guest must notify front desk upon arrival. Guest is liable for any damages. In consideration of all guests, pets must never be left unattended in the guest rooms.
Residence Inn by Marriott 360 Orange Drive Vacaville CA   707-469-0300
Pets of all sizes are allowed. There is a $75 one time fee per pet and a pet policy to sign at check in.

Campgrounds and RV Parks
Midway RV Park 4933 Midway Road Vacaville CA   707-446-7679 (866-446-7679)
http://www.midwayrvpark.com/
Located in a beautiful rural setting, this park offers a pool, wi-fi, laundry, pull through sites, sewer hook-ups, and is centrally located to several attractions. Dogs of all sizes are allowed for an additional $1 per night per pet. Dogs may not be left unattended outside, and they must be leashed and cleaned up after. This is an RV only park. There are some breed restrictions. There is a dog walk area at the campground.
Vineyard RV Park 4985 Midway Road Vacaville CA   707-693-8797 (866-447-8797)
This nicely landscaped park offers a large enclosed dog walk area, a rec room, wi-fi, laundry room, pool, and a variety of activities and recreation. Dogs of all sizes are allowed for an additional $1 per night per pet by the day, or for an additional $5 per night per pet by the week. Dogs may not be left unattended outside, and they must be leashed and cleaned up after. This is an RV only park. There are some breed restrictions. There is a dog walk area at the campground. There are special amenities given to dogs at this campground.

Stores
PetSmart Pet Store 1621 E Monte Vista Ave Ste B Vacaville CA   707-469-9066
Your licensed and well-behaved leashed dog is allowed in the store.
Petco Pet Store 210 Nut Tree Parkway Vacaville CA   707-448-2020
Your licensed and well-behaved leashed dog is allowed in the store.

Outdoor Restaurants

Baja Fresh Mexican Grill 150 Nut Tree Parkway Vacaville CA 707-446-6736
http://www.bajafresh.com
This Mexican restaurant is open for lunch and dinner. They use fresh ingredients and making their salsa and beans daily. Some of the items on their menu include Enchiladas, Burritos, Tacos Salads, Quesadillas, Nachos, Chicken, Steak and more. Well-behaved leashed dogs are allowed at the outdoor tables.

Visalia

Accommodations

Holiday Inn 9000 W. Airport Drive Visalia CA 559-651-5000 (877-270-6405)
There is a $25 one time pet fee.

Campgrounds and RV Parks

Horse Creek Campgrounds Horse Creek(Lake Kaweah), Hwy 198 Visalia CA 559-597-2301 (800-444-CAMP (2267))
Located on the Kaweah River in the foothills of the central Sierra Nevada Mountains, this park offers interpretive and hiking trails and a variety of land and water recreation. Dogs of all sizes are allowed. There are no additional pet fees. Dogs must be leashed and cleaned up after. Dogs are allowed on the trails. The camping and tent areas also allow dogs. There is a dog walk area at the campground. There are no electric or water hookups at the campgrounds.

Visalia/Fresno South KOA 7480 Avenue 308 Visalia CA 559-651-0544 (800-562-0540)
http://www.koa.com/where/ca/05180/
Amenities include old time charm, a good location, 65 foot pull-through sites with 50 amp service, cable, LP gas, snack bar, and swimming pool. Dogs of all sizes are allowed for no additional fee. Dogs must be under owner's control and visual observation at all times. Dogs must be quiet, well behaved, and be on no more than a 6 foot leash at all times, or otherwise contained. Dogs may not be left unattended outside the owner's camping equipment, and must be brought inside at night. There is a fenced-in dog area where your pets may be off lead. There are some breed restrictions. The camping and tent areas also allow dogs. There is a dog walk area at the campground. There are special amenities given to dogs at this campground.

Stores

PetSmart Pet Store 4240 S Mooney Blvd Visalia CA 559-625-0299
Your licensed and well-behaved leashed dog is allowed in the store.
Petco Pet Store 3444 South Mooney Blvd Visalia CA 559-733-5646
Your licensed and well-behaved leashed dog is allowed in the store.

Parks

Sunset Park Monte Verde and Liserdra Visalia CA 559-713-4300
Thanks to one of our readers who writes "It is a well kept park with plenty of friendly people and dogs."

Westley

Accommodations

Days Inn 7144 McCracken Rd Westley CA 209-894-5500 (800-329-7466)
There is a $10 per day additional pet fee.
Econo Lodge 7100 McCracken Rd Westley CA 209-894-3900
There is a $10 per day pet fee.
Super 8 Westley/Modesto Area 7115 McCracken Road Westley CA 209-894-3888 (800-800-8000)
Dogs of all sizes are allowed. There is a $10 per night pet fee per pet. Smoking and non-smoking rooms are available for pet rooms.

Williams

Accommodations
Comfort Inn 400 C Street Williams CA 530-473-2381 (877-424-6423)
Dogs of all sizes are allowed. There is a $10 per night per pet additional fee. Dogs must be leashed, cleaned up after, and the Do Not Disturb sign put on the door if they are in the room alone.

Holiday Inn Express Hotel and Suites

Holiday Inn Express Hotel and Suites 374 Ruggieri Way Williams CA 530-473-5120 (877-270-6405)
Dogs of all sizes are allowed. There is a $25 one time pet fee per 3 night visit. Smoking and non-smoking rooms are available for pets.
Motel 6 - Williams 455 4th Street Williams CA 530-473-5337 (800-466-8356)
One well-behaved family pet per room. Guest must notify front desk upon arrival. Guest is liable for any damages. In consideration of all guests, pets must never be left unattended in the guest rooms.

Willows

Accommodations
Best Western Golden Pheasant Inn 249 N Humboldt Ave Willows CA 530-934-4603 (800-780-7234)
Dogs of all sizes are allowed. There is a $10 per night pet fee per pet. Smoking and non-smoking are available for pet rooms.
Days Inn 475 N Humboldt Ave Willows CA 530-934-4444 (800-329-7466)
There is a $5 per day additional pet fee.
Motel 6 - Willows 452 Humboldt Avenue Willows CA 530-934-7026 (800-466-8356)
One well-behaved family pet per room. Guest must notify front desk upon arrival. Guest is liable for any damages. In consideration of all guests, pets must never be left unattended in the guest rooms.

Parks
Sacramento National Wildlife Refuge 752 County Road 99W Willows CA 530-934-2801
This day use park is one of the state's premier waterfowl refuges with hundreds of thousands of geese and ducks making their winter home here, and numerous other birds and mammals making it their home year round. The habitat consists of almost 11,000 acres of seasonal marsh lands, permanent ponds, and uplands. There are interpretive kiosks, a six mile auto tour, a two mile walking trail, and benches and restrooms outside the visitor center. Dogs of all sizes are allowed throughout the park and on the trails. Dogs must be under owner's control

at all times, and be leashed and cleaned up after.

Woodland

Accommodations
Holiday Inn Express 2070 Freeway Drive Woodland CA 530-662-7750 (877-270-6405)
Dogs of any size are allowed. There is a $20 per day additional pet fee.
Motel 6 - Woodland - Sacramento Area 1564 East Main Street Woodland CA 530-666-6777 (800-466-8356)
One well-behaved family pet per room. Guest must notify front desk upon arrival. Guest is liable for any damages. In consideration of all guests, pets must never be left unattended in the guest rooms.
Sacramento - Days Inn 1524 East Main Street Woodland CA 530-666-3800 (800-329-7466)
There is a $10 per day pet fee.

Outdoor Restaurants
Morrison's Upstairs Restaurant 428 1/2 1st Street Woodland CA 530-666-6176
This steak and seafood restaurant offers classic American and continental cuisine in a restored former apartment complex, allowing them to offer spacious and comfortable dining. They also offer outside dining service. Your pet is allowed to join you at the outer tables. Dogs must be attended to at all times, well behaved, and leashed.
Steve's Place Pizza Pasta 714 Main Street Woodland CA 530-666-2100
http://www.stevespizza.com/
This pizza pasta restaurant offers outside dining for guests with canine companions. Dogs of all sizes are welcome. They must be attended to at all times, well behaved, and leashed.

Yuba City

Accommodations
Days Inn 700 N Palora Ave Yuba City CA 530-674-1711 (800-329-7466)
There is a $7 per day pet fee.
Motel 6 - Yuba City 965 Gray Avenue Yuba City CA 530-790-7066 (800-466-8356)
One well-behaved family pet per room. Guest must notify front desk upon arrival. Guest is liable for any damages. In consideration of all guests, pets must never be left unattended in the guest rooms.

Stores
PetSmart Pet Store 865 Colusa Ave Yuba City CA 530-822-0623
Your licensed and well-behaved leashed dog is allowed in the store.
Petco Pet Store 1110 Harter Rd Yuba City CA 530-674-1816
Your licensed and well-behaved leashed dog is allowed in the store.

Outdoor Restaurants
Sonic Drive-in 981 Grey Avenue Yuba City CA 530-671-3736
This drive-in hamburger restaurant also offers indoor and outdoor seating. Your pet is welcome to join you at the outdoor tables. You will need to go inside to order. Dogs must be attended to at all times, well behaved, and leashed.
The City Cafe 667 Plumas Street Yuba City CA 530-671-1501
Serving American and international cuisine, this café also offers outside dining on the patio. Dogs of all sizes are allowed. Dogs must be well behaved, attended to at all times, and leashed.

Chapter 10

California - Los Angeles Area Dog Travel Guide

Agua Dulce

Parks

Vasquez Rocks Natural Area Park 10700 W Escandido Canyon Road Agua Dulce CA 661-268-0840
This high desert, 745 acre park offers unique towering rock formations, "Birds of Prey" presentations that begin each October, Star Group parties, and various recreational opportunities. The park features a history trail tour of the Tatavian Indians and Spanish settlers, a seasonal stream, and hiking trails. Dogs are allowed throughout the park and on the trails. Dogs must be on leash and please clean up after them.

Canyon Country

Outdoor Restaurants

Telly's Drive In and Diner 27125 Sierra Hwy Canyon Country CA 661-250-0444
This restaurant serves American and Greek food. Dogs are allowed at the outdoor tables.

Castaic

Campgrounds and RV Parks

Valencia Travel Resort 27946 Henry Mayo Drive (Hwy 126) Castaic CA 661-257-3333
This full service park offers a pool, store, laundry room, meeting room, planned activities, and a variety of recreation. Dogs of all sizes are allowed. There are no additional pet fees. Dogs may not be left unattended outside unless they will be quiet and well behaved. They must be leashed, and cleaned up after. There is also an off-lead dog run area at this RV only park. There are some breed restrictions. There is a dog walk area at the campground.

Catalina Island

Accommodations

Edgewater Beach Front Hotel 415 Crescent Avenue Avalon CA 310-510-0347 (1-866-INCATALINA)
This historic and scenic resort offers cable TV, VCR's, mini refrigerators, microwaves, electrical fire places, and close proximity to shopping, dining, and nightlife. Up to 2 dogs are allowed, however, 3 dogs are allowed if they are very small. There is an additional $50 one time pet fee per room. Dogs must be house trained, quiet, and well behaved. The resort can be seen from the ferry docking area, and is about a 10 minute walk.

Hollywood - West LA

Accommodations

Le Meridien at Beverly Hills 465 S. La Cienaga Blvd. Beverly Hills CA 310-247-0400
Dogs up to 50 pounds are allowed. There is a $150 one time nonrefundable pet fee per visit. Dogs are not allowed to be left alone in the room.

The Tower-Beverly Hills Hotel

TOP 200 PLACE **The Tower-Beverly Hills Hotel** 1224 S Beverwil Drive Beverly Hills CA 310-277-2800 (800-421-3212)
This 12 story, luxury hotel offers an upscale destination for business and leisure travelers with an outstanding location to numerous activities and recreation in the Los Angeles/Hollywood areas. Specializing in making you feel at home, they offer elegant accommodations, a heated pool, 24 hour room service, a complete business center, private balconies, an award winning restaurant with patio dining service, and more. Dogs of all sizes are allowed for no additional pet fee. Dogs must be well mannered, and leashed and cleaned up after at all times. Dogs may also join their owners at the outside dining tables.

Hilton Burbank 2500 Hollywood Way Burbank CA 818-843-6000
Dogs up to 50 pounds are allowed. There is a $25 per night per pet fee and a pet policy to sign at check in. This hotel is 100% non-smoking.

Safari Inn 1911 Olive Avenue Burbank CA 818-845-8586
Dogs of all sizes are allowed. There is a $25 one time fee per room per stay and a pet policy to sign at check in. If you are not paying with a credit card, then there would be a $200 cash refundable pet deposit.

Four Points by Sheraton 5990 Green Valley Circle Culver City CA 310-641-7740 (888-625-5144)
There is a $25 one time pet fee. Dogs are allowed only on the first floor.

Four Points by Sheraton Culver City 5990 Green Valley Circle Culver City CA 310-641-7740 (888-625-5144)
Dogs up to 50 pounds are allowed. There are no additional pet fees. Dogs are not allowed to be left alone in the room.

Radisson Hotel Los Angeles Westside 6161 Centinela Avenue Culver City CA 310-649-1776
Dogs of all sizes are allowed. Dogs are allowed in first floor rooms only. These are all non-smoking rooms. There is a $50 one time pet fee, with a $100 refundable pet deposit.

TOP 200 PLACE Chateau Marmont Hotel 8221 Sunset Blvd Hollywood CA 323-656-1010
http://www.chateaumarmont.com/
Modeled after a royal residence in France, grand eloquence awaits guests to this castle on the hill. Some of the features/amenities include a full service bar, gourmet dining either indoor or in a beautiful garden patio setting, many in room amenities, a heated outdoor pool, and personalized services. Dogs up to 100 pounds are allowed. There is a $100 one time additional pet fee per room and a pet policy to sign at check in. Dogs must be well behaved, leashed, cleaned up after, and the Do Not Disturb sign put on the door if they are in the room alone.

Motel 6 - Los Angeles - Hollywood 1738 North Whitley Avenue Hollywood CA 323-464-6006 (800-466-8356)
One well-behaved family pet per room. Guest must notify front desk upon arrival. Guest is liable for any damages. In consideration of all guests, pets must never be left unattended in the guest rooms.

Sheraton Universal Hotel 333 Universal Hollywood Drive Universal City CA 818-980-1212 (888-625-5144)

Dogs up to 70 pounds are allowed at this luxury hotel near Universal Studios. There are no additional pet fees. Pet Sitting can be arranged by the hotel.

Le Montrose Suites 900 Hammond Street West Hollywood CA   310-855-1115 (800- 776-0666)
http://www.lemontrose.com/
A multi-million dollar renovation transformed this hotel into an elegant, stylish urban retreat with many conveniences for the business or leisure traveler. Some of the features include personalized services, several in-room amenities, a business center, and a beautiful outdoor pool and sunning area. Dogs up to 50 pounds are allowed for an additional $100 one time pet fee per room. Dogs may only be left alone in the room if they will be quiet, well behaved, and a contact number is left with the front desk. They also request that the sliding glass door is closed if a pet is in the room alone. Dogs must be leashed and cleaned up after at all times. Dogs are not allowed in food service areas or on the roof.

Vacation Home Rentals

PET Friendly Hollywood/West Hollywood Call to Arrange Los Angeles - Hollywood Area CA   323-851-6556 (800-422-3272)
Dogs are allowed at this 1 bedroom condo vacation rental 1.5 miles from Laural Canyon Dog Park.

Attractions

TOP 200 PLACE **Hollywood Star's Homes** Self-Guided Walking Tour Beverly Hills CA
Want to check out the Star's homes in Beverly Hills with your dog? How about a self-guided walking tour of the Star's homes? All you need is a map and a good starting point. Maps can be purchased at many of the tourist shops on Hollywood Blvd. A good place to begin is at the Will Rogers Memorial Park in Beverly Hills (between Sunset Blvd, Beverly Dr and Canon Drive). It's a small park but still a good place for both of you to stretch your legs before beginning the walk. You can certainly plot out your own tour, but we have a few samples tours that will help you get started. TOUR 1 (approx 1 mile): From the park and Canon Street, turn left (heading west) onto Sunset Blvd. Turn right on Roxbury. Cross Benedict Canyon Rd and the road becomes Hartford Way. Take Hartford Way back to the park. TOUR 2 (approx 3 miles): From the park, head north on Beverly Drive and cross Sunset Blvd. Turn right on Rexford Drive. Turn right on Lomitas Ave and then left onto Crescent Drive. Make a right at Elevado Ave, walk for about 5 blocks and turn right onto Bedford Dr. Then turn left on Lomitas Ave, right on Whittier Dr and left on Greeway. Then turn right on Sunset Blvd and head back to the park.

Los Angeles Equestrian Center 480 Riverside Drive Burbank CA   818-840-9066
http://www.la-equestriancenter.com/
This is a nice diversion for those pups that enjoy being around horses. Southern California's largest Equestrian Center has a covered arena where many top-rated horse shows are held throughout the year. Your dog is welcome to watch the horse shows if he or she doesn't bark and distract the horses. To see their upcoming events list, check out their website or call 818-840-9066. When there are no shows, you can still walk around on the grounds. There is a horse trail to the right of the main entrance where you can walk your dog. Or if you want to do some shopping, your dog is welcome in 1 of the 2 equestrian stores (which also has some dog treats and toys). The dog-friendly store is called Dominion Saddlery and is located behind the store that is next to the parking lot. They even have water bowls in the store for your pup.

Will Rogers State Hist. Park 1501 Will Rogers State Park Rd. Pacific Palisades CA   310-454-8212
This park was Will Roger's personal home and ranch. Mr. Rogers was famous for his horse and rope tricks. He performed on Broadway and then moved on to Hollywood to star in many movies. The ranch was made into a state historic park in 1944 after the death of Mrs. Rogers and it reflects Will Rogers avid horsemanship. On the ranch there is a large polo field, which is the only outdoor polo field in Los Angeles county and the only field that is regulation size. The polo field has been featured in many movies and TV shows. The ranch buildings and grounds have been maintained to show how the Rogers' family lived back in the late 1920s and 1930s. Today, the grounds are also a working ranch with a variety of western equestrian activities. Leashed dogs are allowed on the property, in the horse barn, and on the Inspiration Point Trail. They are not allowed inside the ranch house. Dogs, along with people and children, should not touch the horses. The ranch staff enforces the leash law and will fine violators $82. The entrance fee to the park is $6 per car and $1 per dog.

Universal Studios Kennel Hollywood Frwy (Hwy 101) Universal City CA   818-508-9600
This isn't really an attraction for your pup, but will allow humans to spend several hours in the world's largest film and TV studio. Universal Studios has a day kennel located at the main entrance. There is no full time attendant, but the kennels are locked. Simply stop at one of the information booths and ask for assistance. There is no fee for this service. At Universal Studios, you can learn how movies are made, visit set and sound stages, and enjoy a variety of special effect rides.

Shopping Centers

Beverly Hills Rodeo Drive Shopping District

Beverly Hills Rodeo Drive Shopping District Rodeo Drive Beverly Hills CA
Rodeo Drive, located in Beverly Hills, is one of the most prestigious and expensive shopping streets in the world. This is the street where the movie "Pretty Woman" starring Julia Roberts was filmed. Many actors and actresses shop along this street. Dogs are welcome to window shop with you. Tiffany & Company is one store we know of which allows dogs inside, at least pooches up to about 50 pounds. Just off of Rodeo Drive is Beverly Drive which is host to many dog-friendly stores such as Anthropologie, Banana Republic, Crate and Barrel, The Gap, Pottery Barn, and Williams-Sonoma. All of these stores allow well-behaved leashed dogs. Find more details about these stores, including addresses, under our Stores section. When you visit this shopping district, please note that it is often very crowded and it can be tough to find a parking spot.

Sunset Plaza 8600 - 8700 Sunset Boulevard (at Sunset Plaza Drive), West Hollywood CA 310-652-2622
This sidewalk mall sits on both sides of the Sunset Strip, between La Cienega and San Vicente Boulevards and feature a number of fashionable boutiques, outdoor cafés, and trendy bistros. Also, don't be surprised to see a celebrity or two. Well mannered dogs are welcome to walk the sidewalk mall area, and some establishments may also allow them. Dogs must be under owner's control, and leashed and cleaned up after at all times.

Stores

Anthropologie 320 North Beverly Dr. Beverly Hills CA 310-385-7390
http://www.anthropologie.com/
Thanks to one of our readers who writes "They have always been especially lovely when Hector and I go in!"
Banana Republic 357 N Beverly Drive Beverly Hills CA 310-858-7900
http://www.bananarepublic.com
This apparel store offers both mens and womens clothing as well as home collection, shoes, accessories and more. Well-behaved leashed dogs are allowed in the store.
Crate and Barrel 438 N. Beverly Drive Beverly Hills CA 310-247-1700
http://www.crateandbarrel.com/
Home furnishings are the focus of this store. Well-behaved leashed dogs are allowed in the store.
Pottery Barn 300 N Beverly Drive Beverly Hills CA 310-860-9506
http://www.potterybarn.com
This store offers stylish and quality home furnishings. Well-behaved leashed dogs are allowed in the store.
The Gap 420 N Beverly Drive Beverly Hills CA 310-274-0461
http://www.gap.com
This store offers clothing for men, women and children. Well-behaved leashed dogs are allowed in the store.
Tiffany & Co. 210 N Rodeo Drive Beverly Hills CA 310-273-8880
http://www.tiffany.com/

This store offers a selection of jewelry, gifts and accessories. Well-behaved leashed dogs up to about 50 pounds are allowed in this store.

Williams Sonoma 339 N. Beverly Drive Beverly Hills CA 310-274-9127
http://www.williamssonoma.com
This store offers cookware, cutlrey, electronics, food and more. Well-behaved leashed dogs are allowed in the store.

Petco Pet Store 5481 Lone Tree Way Brentwood CA 925-308-7307
Your licensed and well-behaved leashed dog is allowed in the store.

Petco Pet Store 3525 W Victory Blvd Burbank CA 818-566-8528
Your licensed and well-behaved leashed dog is allowed in the store.

PetSmart Pet Store 10900 W Jefferson Blvd Culver City CA 310-390-5120
Your licensed and well-behaved leashed dog is allowed in the store.

Petco Pet Store 5347 S Sepulveda Blvd Culver City CA 310-390-7255
Your licensed and well-behaved leashed dog is allowed in the store.

Amoeba Music Store 6400 Sunset Blvd Hollywood CA 323-245-6400
http://www.amoebamusic.com/
This music store has the pet friendly sign right at their door, so you know that you and your canine companion are welcome. Dogs must be well behaved, leashed, and under the owner's control at all times.

Petco Pet Store 508 North Doheny Drive West Hollywood CA 310-275-6012
Your licensed and well-behaved leashed dog is allowed in the store.

Video West 805 Larrabee Street West Hollywood CA 310-659-5762
Very dog friendly video store. Dogs always welcome and usually they have dog biscuits. The owner is a dog lover and is active in dog rescue. The store is open 10am-midnight, 7 days a week.

Parks

Roxbury Park 471 S. Roxbury Dr. Beverly Hills CA 310-285-2537
This city park offers gently rolling green hills and shady areas. The park has large children's playgrounds, tennis courts and other sports courts. Dogs are allowed but must be on a 6 foot or less leash and people are required to clean up after their pets.

Temescal Canyon Park 15601 Sunset Blvd. Pacific Palisades CA 805-370-2301
http://smmc.ca.gov/temtrail.html
There are several trails at this park. Dogs are allowed but must be on a 6 foot or less leash and people need to clean up after their pets. The Sunset Trail is almost a half mile trail that begins at the lower parking lot by Sunset Blvd. It parallels Temescal Creek. The Temescal Loop Trail is about a four and a half mile hike up a canyon. Some areas area steep. If you go about 1.2 miles from the trailhead, you will reach the Temescal waterfall which is seasonal. The park is located at the intersection of Temescal Canyon Road and Sunset Blvd. This park is part of the Santa Monica Recreation Area.

Off-Leash Dog Parks

Culver City Off-Leash Dog Park Duquesne Ave near Jefferson Blvd Culver City CA 310-390-9114
http://www.culvercitydogpark.org
This new dog park opened in April, 2006. Known as the "Boneyard" to the locals, this one acre park has a large dog and a small dog area. There are benches, trees, shade and water fountains. The park is located near Jefferson Blvd on Duquesne Ave in Culver City Park. It is about 3/4 miles east of Overland.

Whitnall Off-Leash Dog Park 5801 1/2 Whitnall Highway North Hollywood CA 818-756-8190
Whitnall Off-Leash Dog Park is located one block west of Cahuenga Blvd on Whitnall. The park has a 50,000 square foot fenced area for large dogs and a 22,000 square foot fenced area for small dogs. The park is open during daylight hours.

Culver City Off-Leash Dog Park

Outdoor Restaurants

Baja Fresh Mexican Grill 475 N. Beverly Drive Beverly Hills CA   310-858-6690
http://www.bajafresh.com
This Mexican restaurant is open for lunch and dinner. They use fresh ingredients and making their salsa and beans daily. Some of the items on their menu include Enchiladas, Burritos, Tacos Salads, Quesadillas, Nachos, Chicken, Steak and more. Well-behaved leashed dogs are allowed at the outdoor tables.
Joan's on 3rd 8350 W Third Street Beverly Hills CA 323-655-2285
This take-out cafe serves deli-type food. Dogs are allowed at the outdoor tables.
Kings Road Expresso Cafe 8361 Beverly Blvd Beverly Hills CA 323-655-9044
This cafe serves coffee and sandwiches. Dogs are allowed at the outdoor tables. Water is provided for your pet.
The Lazy Daisy 9010 Wilshire Blvd Beverly Hills CA 310-859-1111
Dogs are allowed at the outdoor tables.
Urth Cafe 267 S Beverly Dr Beverly Hills CA 310-205-9311
This cafe serves coffee and sandwiches. Dogs are allowed at the outdoor tables.
Baja Fresh Mexican Grill 877 N. San Fernando Blvd. Burbank CA 818-841-4649
http://www.bajafresh.com
This Mexican restaurant is open for lunch and dinner. They use fresh ingredients and making their salsa and beans daily. Some of the items on their menu include Enchiladas, Burritos, Tacos Salads, Quesadillas, Nachos, Chicken, Steak and more. Well-behaved leashed dogs are allowed at the outdoor tables.
La Bamba 2600 North Glenoaks Blvd. Burbank CA 818-846-3358
This Caribbean restaurant allows dogs at the outdoor tables.
Priscilla's Coffee and Tea 4150 W Riverside Street, Suite A Burbank CA 818-843-5707
Dogs are allowed at the outdoor tables.
The Riverside Cafe 1221 Riverside Dr Burbank CA 818-563-3567
This British style bistro allows dogs at its outdoor seats. It is closed Mondays. The restaurant is open for lunch and dinner on Tuesday through Friday, and for brunch, lunch and dinner on weekends. According to a reader dogs get their own bowl of water and maybe a dog bone.
Baja Fresh Mexican Grill 10768 Venice Blvd Culver City CA 310-280-0644
http://www.bajafresh.com
This Mexican restaurant is open for lunch and dinner. They use fresh ingredients and making their salsa and beans daily. Some of the items on their menu include Enchiladas, Burritos, Tacos Salads, Quesadillas, Nachos, Chicken, Steak and more. Well-behaved leashed dogs are allowed at the outdoor tables.
In-N-Out Burgers 7009 Sunset Blvd. Hollywood CA 800-786-1000

We decided to mention this specific In-N-Out Burgers because it's very close to the Hollywood Blvd. Walk of Fame. It's a few blocks south of Hollywood Blvd (Walk of Fame). Head south on Orange Drive which is near the Mann's Chinese Theater. The In-N-Out is near the corner of Sunset Blvd. and Orange. Dogs are allowed at the outdoor tables.

The Cat and Fiddle 6530 Sunset Blvd Hollywood CA 323-468-3800
This restaurant and bar serves British food. Dogs are allowed at the outdoor tables.

Chez Nous 10550 Riverside Drive North Hollywood CA 818-760-0288
Enjoy lunch dining and table service at this restaurant located in North Hollywood. Dogs are allowed at the outdoor tables.

Basix Cafe 8333 Santa Monica Blvd. West Hollywood CA 323-848-2460
http://www.basixcafe.com/
This cafe offers flavor-infused, health-conscious cuisine using the freshest ingredients. Here you can enjoy specialties like fresh-baked breads, pastas, sandwiches, wood-fired pizzas. They also serve breakfast including items like eggs and omelettes, pancakes and more. Well-behaved leashed dogs are allowed at the outdoor tables. Thanks to one of our readers for recommending this dog-friendly cafe.

Champagne Cafe 8917 Santa Monica Blvd West Hollywood CA 310-657-4051
This French cafe serves champagne and french deli food. Dogs are allowed at the outdoor tables.

Joey's Cafe 8301 Santa Monica Blvd/Hwy 2 West Hollywood CA 323-822-0671
This organic eatery offers tasty breakfast, brunch, and lunch items with service both inside and out. Your pet is welcome to join you at the outside tables. Dogs must be well behaved, attended to at all times, and leashed.

Le Pain Quotidien 8607 Melrose Avenue West Hollywood CA 310-854-3700
This cafe serves French and Belgian food. Dogs are allowed at the outdoor tables.

Marix West Hollywood 1108 N. Flores Street West Hollywood CA 323-656-8800
This Tex-Mex restaurant allows well-behaved leashed dogs at their outdoor tables. They are open 11am to 11pm seven days a week.

Miyagi's Sushi Restaurant 8225 Sunset Blvd West Hollywood CA 323-650-3524
http://www.miyagisonsunset.com/
This restaurant serves up Japanese/Asian foods in a rather lively environment. There is outside dining service available. Your pet is welcome to join you at the outside tables. Dogs must be well behaved, attended to at all times, and leashed.

The Courtyard 8543 Santa Monica Blvd West Hollywood CA 310-358-0301
http://www.dinecourtyard.com
This dog-friendly restaurant has an assortment of Spanish dishes. The courtyard is enclosed on three sides and there are heaters for cooler weather. Dogs are allowed at the outdoor seats.

Urth Cafe 8565 Melrose Ave West Hollywood CA 310-659-0628
This cafe serves coffee and deli-type food. Dogs are allowed at the outdoor tables.

Zeke's Smokehouse 7100 Santa Monica Blvd West Hollywood CA 323-850-9353
http://www.zekessmokehouse.com/
This is the place to go for contemporary American comfort food and great tasting barbecue. They offer service for their outdoor dining customers, and will even bring out a bowl of water for your canine companion. Your pet is allowed to join you at the outer tables. Dogs must be attended to at all times, well behaved, and leashed.

Native Foods 1110 1/2 Gayley Avenue Westwood CA 310-209-1055
http://www.nativefoods.com
This restaurants serves organic vegetarian food. Dogs are allowed at the outdoor tables.

Vets and Kennels
Affordable Emergency Clinic 5558 Sepulveda Blvd Culver City CA 310-397-4883
9:30 am - 12 midnight 7 days a week

LA Beach Area

Accommodations
Residence Inn by Marriott 2135 El Segundo Blvd El Segundo CA 310-333-0888
Dogs of all sizes are allowed. There is a $75 one time fee, and a pet policy to sign at check in.

TownePlace Suites LAX/Mahattan Beach 14400 Aviation Blvd Hawthorne CA 310-725-9696
Dogs of all sizes are allowed. There is a $75 one time pet fee per visit.

LeMerigot Hotel-A JWMarriott Beach Hotel and Spa 1740 Ocean Avenue Santa Monica CA 310-395-9700
This hotel has a "Pet Friendly Accommodations Program", and dogs of all sizes are welcome. They offer a unique assortment of boutique amenities, a sitting service, and special food fare for your pet. There is a $150 refundable deposit plus a $35 one time additional fee per pet. Dogs must be leashed, cleaned up after, and the Do Not Disturb sign put on the door if they are in the room alone.

Loews Santa Monica Beach Hotel 1700 Ocean Avenue Santa Monica CA   310-458-6700
All well-behaved dogs of any size are welcome. This upscale hotel offers their "Loews Loves Pets" program which includes special pet treats, local dog walking routes, and a list of nearby pet-friendly places to visit. There are no pet fees.

Sheraton Delfina Santa Monica Hotel 530 West Pico Blvd. Santa Monica CA   310-399-9344 (888-625-5144)
Dogs of all sizes are allowed. Pet rooms are limited to ground floor cabanas. You must sign a pet policy when checking in with a dog. Dogs are not allowed to be left alone in the room.

The Fairmont Miramar Hotel Santa Monica 101 Wilshire Blvd Santa Monica CA   310-576-7777 (800-257-7544)
http://www.fairmont.com/santamonica/
Nestled atop the scenic bluffs of Santa Monica beach, this hotel features historic elegance with all the modern-day conveniences and services. Some of the features/amenities include 302 stylish guest rooms, 32 secluded garden bungalows, casual elegant indoor and outdoor dining, and 24 hour room service. There can be up to 3 dogs in one room if they are all small, otherwise there are only 2 dogs allowed per room. There is a $25 per night per dog additional fee, and a pet policy to sign at check in. Dogs may not be left alone in the room at any time, and they must be leashed and cleaned up after.

Viceroy Hotel 1819 Ocean Avenue Santa Monica CA   310-260-7500
Well behaved dogs of all sizes are allowed. There is a $175 refundable deposit and a pet policy to sign at check in.

Holiday Inn 19800 S Vermont Ave Torrance CA 310-781-9100 (877-270-6405)
Dogs of all sizes are allowed. There are no additional pet fees. Smoking and non-smoking rooms are available for pets.

Residence Inn by Marriott 3701 Torrance Blvd Torrance CA   310-543-4566
Well behaved dogs of all sizes are allowed. There is a $75 one time fee, and a pet policy to sign at check in.

Staybridge Suites 19901 Prairie Avenue Torrance CA   310-371-8525 (877-270-6405)
Dogs of all sizes are allowed. There are no additional pet fees. Smoking and non-smoking rooms are available for pets.

Attractions

Catalina Ferries 13763 Fiji Way , C2 Terminal Building Marina del Rey CA   310-305-7250
http://www.catalinaferries.com/
This ferry provides transportation from Marina Del Rey to Avalon or Two Harbors on Catalina Island and back. You are welcome to take your dog for no additional fee, but he must be muzzled and checked in at the office.

Stores

Petco Pet Store 3901 Inglewood Avenue, Ste G Redondo Beach CA   310-355-1370
Your licensed and well-behaved leashed dog is allowed in the store.

Petco Pet Store 537 North Pacific Coast Highway Redondo Beach CA   310-374-7969
Your licensed and well-behaved leashed dog is allowed in the store.

Petco Pet Store 51-A Peninsula Center Rolling Hills Estates CA   310-377-5560
Your licensed and well-behaved leashed dog is allowed in the store.

Barnes and Noble Bookstore 1201 3rd Street Santa Monica CA   310-260-9110
http://www.barnesandnoble.com/
Your well-behaved leashed dog is allowed inside this store. One of our readers writes "They (dogs) are totally welcome there!"

Petco Pet Store 2910 Wilshire Blvd Santa Monica CA   310-586-1963
Your licensed and well-behaved leashed dog is allowed in the store.

Wagging Tail 1123 Montana Avenue Santa Monica CA   310-656-9663
http://www.wagwagwag.com/
This upscale boutique has dedicated itself to offering unique and one of a kind items for your pooch. They carry paw wear, fresh bakery items, fine art and doggie furniture, jewelry, and even French perfume. They are open from 10 am to 6 pm Monday through Saturday, and Noon to 5 pm on Sunday. Your dog is welcome to explore this store with their owner, and if they are well behaved they may be off lead.

PetSmart Pet Store 3855-59 Sepulveda Blvd Torrance CA   310-316-9047
Your licensed and well-behaved leashed dog is allowed in the store.

Petco Pet Store 24413 Crenshaw Blvd, Ste 8 Torrance CA   310-530-5945
Your licensed and well-behaved leashed dog is allowed in the store.

Parks

El Segundo Recreation Park Grande Ave at Eucalyptus Dr El Segundo CA
This park allows dogs during all hours that the park is open, but they must be on leash at all times. Please clean up after your dogs, so the city continues to allow their presence. This park is bounded by the following streets:

North by E. Pine St, South by Grande Ave, West by Eucalyptus Dr. and East by Penn St. Thanks to one of our readers for recommending this park.

Off-Leash Dog Parks

Redondo Beach Dog Park Flagler Lane and 190th Redondo Beach CA 310-376-9263
http://www.rbdogpark.com
This dog park is located next to Dominguez Park. Local dogs and vacationing dogs are welcome at the dog park. There is a separate section for small dogs and big dogs. It is completely fenced and has pooper scooper bags available. From the PCH take Herondo Street east which will become 190th Street.
Joslyn Park Dog Park 633 Kensington Road Santa Monica CA 310-458-8974
The fenced Joslyn Park dog park includes two areas. One is for small dogs and the other for large dogs.
Memorial Park 1401 Olympic Blvd Santa Monica CA 310-450-1121
There is an off-leash dog run located in this park.
Westminster Dog Park 1234 Pacific Ave Venice CA 310-392-5566
The Westminster Dog Park is 0.8 acres in size and it is open daily from 6 am to 10 pm. There is a smaller fenced area for small dogs. The park is located one block south of Venice Blvd near Centinela Avenue.

Outdoor Restaurants

Martha's Corner 25 22nd St Hermosa Beach CA 310-379-0070
This restaurant serves American food. Dogs are allowed at the outdoor tables.
Johnny Rockets 1550 Rosecrans Ave. Manhattan Beach CA 310-536-9464
Dogs are allowed at the outdoor tables at this Johnny Rockets.
Baja Fresh Mexican Grill 13424 Maxella Avenue Marina Del Rey CA 310-578-2252
http://www.bajafresh.com
This Mexican restaurant is open for lunch and dinner. They use fresh ingredients and making their salsa and beans daily. Some of the items on their menu include Enchiladas, Burritos, Tacos Salads, Quesadillas, Nachos, Chicken, Steak and more. Well-behaved leashed dogs are allowed at the outdoor tables.
Kool Dog Diner 1666 South Pacific Coast Highway Redondo Beach CA 310-944-3232
This dog bakery serves gourmet treats for your pet. Dogs are allowed inside and out.
Whole Foods Market 405 N. Pacific Coast Hwy. Redondo Beach CA 310-376-6931
http://www.wholefoods.com/
This natural food supermarket offers natural and organic foods. Order some food from their deli without your dog and bring it to an outdoor table where your well-behaved leashed dog is welcome. Dogs are not allowed in the store including the deli at any time.
Baja Fresh Mexican Grill 720 Wilshire Blvd. Santa Monica CA 310-393-9313
http://www.bajafresh.com
This Mexican restaurant is open for lunch and dinner. They use fresh ingredients and making their salsa and beans daily. Some of the items on their menu include Enchiladas, Burritos, Tacos Salads, Quesadillas, Nachos, Chicken, Steak and more. Well-behaved leashed dogs are allowed at the outdoor tables.
News Room Cafe 530 Wilshire Street Santa Monica CA 310-319-9100
This casual coffee shop features indoor and outdoor dining service. Dogs are allowed at the outdoor tables. They must be well behaved, under owner's control at all times, leashed, and cleaned up after.
The Lazy Daisy 2300 Pico Blvd Santa Monica CA 310-450-9011
This restaurant serves American food. Dogs are allowed at the outdoor tables. Only open for Breakfast and lunch.
Whole Foods Market 2655 Pacific Coast Highway Torrance CA 310-257-8700
http://www.wholefoods.com/
This natural food supermarket offers natural and organic foods. Order some food from their deli without your dog and bring it to an outdoor table where your well-behaved leashed dog is welcome. Dogs are not allowed in the store including the deli at any time.
Baja Fresh Mexican Grill 245 Main Street Venice CA 310-392-3452
http://www.bajafresh.com
This Mexican restaurant is open for lunch and dinner. They use fresh ingredients and making their salsa and beans daily. Some of the items on their menu include Enchiladas, Burritos, Tacos Salads, Quesadillas, Nachos, Chicken, Steak and more. Well-behaved leashed dogs are allowed at the outdoor tables.
Brick House Cafe 826 Hampton Dr Venice CA 310-581-1639
This restaurant serves American and Mexican food. Dogs are allowed at the outdoor tables.
French Market Cafe 2321 Abbot Kinney Venice CA 310-577-9775
This restaurant serves French deli-type food. Dogs are allowed at the outdoor tables.
The Terrace 7 Washington Blvd Venice CA 310-578-1530
This restaurant serves CA American variety food. Dogs are allowed at the outdoor tables. Water and treats are provided for your pet.

Long Beach Area

Accommodations

Motel 6 - Los Angeles - Bellflower 17220 Downey Avenue Bellflower CA   562-531-3933 (800-466-8356)
One well-behaved family pet per room. Guest must notify front desk upon arrival. Guest is liable for any damages. In consideration of all guests, pets must never be left unattended in the guest rooms.
Motel 6 - Los Angeles - Harbor City 820 West Sepulveda Boulevard Harbor City CA   310-549-9560 (800-466-8356)
One well-behaved family pet per room. Guest must notify front desk upon arrival. Guest is liable for any damages. In consideration of all guests, pets must never be left unattended in the guest rooms.
La Quinta Inn & Suites Buena Park 3 Centerpointe Drive La Palma CA   714-670-1400 (800-531-5900)
Dogs of all sizes are allowed. There are no additional pet fees. Dogs must be quiet, well behaved, leashed and cleaned up after.
Guesthouse International Hotel 5325 E Pacific Coast Highway Long Beach CA   562-597-1341
http://www.guesthouselb.com/
Located by several other attractions and recreational activities, this hotel offers a courtesy shuttle service to the attractions within a 5 mile radius. Some of the features/amenities include 142 spacious, stylish rooms with conveniences for leisure and business travelers, gardens, a complimentary continental breakfast, and a heated, tropically landscaped pool complete with cascading waterfall. Dogs of all sizes are allowed for an additional $10 per night per pet. Dogs may only be left for short periods, and they must be crated and a contact number left with the front desk. Dogs must be leashed and cleaned up after at all times.
Holiday Inn 2640 Lakewood Blvd Long Beach CA   562-597-4401 (877-270-6405)
Dogs are not allowed in the main tower. There is a $25 one time additional pet fee and a $100 refundable deposit.
Long Beach Marriott 4700 Airport Plaza Drive Long Beach CA   562-425-5210 (800-228-9290)
Dogs of all sizes are allowed. There is a $75 refundable deposit per room. Dogs must be quiet, well behaved, leashed, cleaned up after, and a contact number left with the front desk if they are in the room alone.
Motel 6 - Long Beach - International City 1121 East Pacific Coast Highway Long Beach CA   562-591-3321 (800-466-8356)
One well-behaved family pet per room. Guest must notify front desk upon arrival. Guest is liable for any damages. In consideration of all guests, pets must never be left unattended in the guest rooms.
Motel 6 - Los Angeles - Long Beach 5665 East 7th Street Long Beach CA   562-597-1311 (800-466-8356)
One well-behaved family pet per room. Guest must notify front desk upon arrival. Guest is liable for any damages. In consideration of all guests, pets must never be left unattended in the guest rooms.
Renaissance Long Beach Hotel 111 East Ocean Blvd Long Beach CA   562-437-5900
Located in the middle of the entertainment district, this luxury hotel also offers an ideal location to exciting nightlife, shopping, and recreation. Some of their amenities/features include a $5.6 million renovation of all the rooms and suites with an emphasis on casual elegance, 2 restaurants, 24 hour room service, a pool, sauna whirlpool, and highly personalized service. Dogs of all sizes are allowed. There is a $75 one time additional pet fee per pet. Dogs must be kenneled when left alone in the room, and they must be leashed and cleaned up after.
Residence Inn by Marriott 4111 E Willow Street Long Beach CA   562-595-0909
Dogs of all sizes are allowed. There is a $75 one time fee, and a pet policy to sign at check in.
Holiday Inn 111 S. Gaffey St. San Pedro CA   310-514-1414 (877-270-6405)
Dogs of all sizes are allowed. There is a $25 per day pet fee.

Attractions

Catalina Explorer Ferry 100 Aquarium Way, Pine Avenue Pier Long Beach CA   877-432-6276
http://www.catalinaferry.com
Dogs are allowed to go on this ferry that provides service from the greater Los Angeles area to Catalina Island. There is no additional pet fee. Dogs must be leashed and muzzled, or crated. One pet per person is allowed, depending on space. Reservations are suggested. Hours of operation and tour schedules alter with the seasons.
Catalina Express 320 Golden Shore Long Beach CA 800-360-1212
http://www.catalinaexpress.com/
Dogs are allowed on the boats to the Catalina Island at no additional fee. Dogs must be leashed and muzzled or crated while aboard. There is a limit of one pet per person. Reservations are recommended.

Catalina Classic Cruises

Catalina Classic Cruises Berth 95 San Pedro CA 800-641-1004
Dogs are allowed on the boats to the Catalina Island at no additional fee. This boat only run seasonally, and reservations are recommended. Dogs must be leashed and muzzled or crated while aboard. There is a limit of one pet per person.

Stores

Petco Pet Store 5215 Lakewood Blvd Lakewood CA 562-630-2888
Your licensed and well-behaved leashed dog is allowed in the store.
Petco Pet Store 5615 Woodruff Avenue Lakewood CA 562-804-1444
Your licensed and well-behaved leashed dog is allowed in the store.
Ace Billings Paint and Hardware 5004 E 2nd Street Long Beach CA 562-439-2113
This hardware store knows how to treat their four-legged customers too; they can expect doggy treats. Dogs must be friendly, well behaved, under owner's control at all times, leashed, and cleaned up after.
Holly's Hallmark Shop 5012 E 2nd Street Long Beach CA 562-434-5291
http://www.rubios.com/
Friendly, well-behaved dogs are welcome at this card, stationary, and gift shop. Dogs must be under owner's control and leashed at all times.
PetSmart Pet Store 7631 Carson Long Beach CA 562-938-8056
Your licensed and well-behaved leashed dog is allowed in the store.
Petco Pet Store 2304 Bellflower Blvd Long Beach CA 562-594-8865
Your licensed and well-behaved leashed dog is allowed in the store.
Petco Pet Store 6500 Pacific Coast Highway Long Beach CA 562-493-6083
Your licensed and well-behaved leashed dog is allowed in the store.
Runner's High 5375 E Second Street Long Beach CA 562-430-7833
This store is an outfitter for running, walking, and triathlon needs. Well behaved dogs are welcome to come into the store with you. Dogs must be trained, under owners control at all times, and leashed.
Wiskers Pet Beastro and Bowteek 4818 East 2nd Street Long Beach CA 562-433-0707
http://www.wiskers.com/Belmont.html
This specialty retailer hosts special events throughout the year in addition to offering a variety of collars,leads, toys, gifts/games for their owners, treats, pet necessities, and they also offer a pet hand painted portrait service. Pets are welcome and treats are always accessible for pets on their best behavior. Dogs must be housetrained, leashed, and picked up after.
Petco Pet Store 852 North Western Avenue San Pedro CA 310-521-8131
Your licensed and well-behaved leashed dog is allowed in the store.

PetSmart Pet Store 2550 Cherry Ave Signal Hill CA   562-988-0832
Your licensed and well-behaved leashed dog is allowed in the store.

Beaches

Long Beach Dog Beach Zone

TOP 200 PLACE **Long Beach Dog Beach Zone** between Roycroft and Argonne Avenues Long Beach CA 562-570-3100
http://www.hautedogs.org/
This 3 acre off-leash unfenced dog beach is the only off-leash dog beach in Los Angeles County. It is open daily from 6am until 8pm. It opened on August 1, 2003. The "zone" is 235 yards along the water and 60 yards deep. There is a fresh water fountain called the "Fountain of Woof" which is located near the restrooms at the end of Granada Avenue, near the Dog Zone. Only one dog is allowed per adult and dog owners are entirely responsible for their dog's actions. The beach is located between Roycroft and Argonne avenues in Belmont Shore, Long Beach. It is a few blocks east of the Belmont Pier and Olympic pool. From Ocean Blvd, enter at Bennett Avenue for the beachfront metered parking lot. The cost is 25 cents for each 15 minutes from 8am until 6pm daily. Parking is free after 5pm in the beachfront lot at the end of Granada Avenue. You can check with the website http://www.hautedogs.org for updates and additional rules about the Long Beach Dog Beach Zone.

Off-Leash Dog Parks
Recreation Park Dog Park 7th St & Federation Dr Long Beach CA   562-570-3100
http://www.geocities.com/lbdogpark/
Licensed dogs over four months are allowed to run leash-free in this area by the casting pond. As usual with all dog parks, owners are responsible for their dogs and must supervise them at all times. The Recreation Park Dog Park is located off 7th Street and Federation Drive behind the Casting Pond. It is open daily until 10 p.m. Thanks to one of our readers for recommending this park.
Knoll Hill Off-Leash Dog Park 200 Knoll Drive San Pedro CA   310-514-0338
http://www.dogparks.org
This 2.5 acre off-leash dog park is open during daylight hours. This park is located at the south end of the 110 Freeway. Exit 110 at Highway 47 east and exit quickly at N. Front St/Harbor Blvd. Go north on N. Front St to Knoll Drive on the left. The dog park is managed by Peninsula Dog Parks, Inc.

Outdoor Restaurants
George's Greek Deli 318 Pine Ave Long Beach CA   562-437-1184

This restaurant serves Greek food. Dogs are allowed at the outdoor tables.

Rubio's Fresh Mexican Grill 7547 Carson Blvd Long Beach CA   562-496-1892
http://www.rubios.com/
This eatery offers indoor and outdoor dining; just order and pick-up inside. Dogs are allowed at the outdoor tables. Dogs must be well behaved, under owner's control at all times, leashed, and cleaned up after.

Wild Oats Natural Marketplace 6550 E. Pacific Coast Highway Long Beach CA   562-598-8687
http://www.wildoats.com
This full service natural food market offers both natural and organic food. You can get food from the deli and bring it to an outdoor table where your well-behaved leashed dog is welcome.

Events

Haute Dog Easter Parade and Pet Adobtion Fair 4900 E Livingston Drive Long Beach CA   562-439-3316
http://www.hautedogs.org/
For a $10 pre-entry fee per dog ($15 on the day of the event) you can take part in this popular annual Easter Parade sponsored by Haute Dogs, where hundreds of costumed canines present their very best for the judges and thousands of spectators in this 12-block sidewalk pooch parade. The parade begins and ends at Livingston Park, and is just the beginning of a wide variety of contests and events with various prize categories, vendors, an adoption fair, doggie demonstrations, and more. Dogs (no puppies) must have their rabies and vaccinations current, wear ID tags, and be leashed and cleaned up after at all times. No aggressive dogs or dogs in heat are allowed.

Haute Dog Howl'oween Parade 4900 E Livingston Drive Long Beach CA   562-439-3316
http://www.hautedogs.org/
For a $10 entry fee per dog you can take part in this popular annual Howl'oween event sponsored by the Community Action Team and Haute Dogs. Hundreds of dogs present their very best costumes for the judges and thousands of spectators in this 12-block sidewalk pooch parade. The parade begins and ends at Livingston Park, and is just the beginning of a wide variety of contests and events with various prize categories, vendors, an adoption fair, a kids' costume contest, doggie demonstrations, and more. Dogs (no puppies) must have their rabies and vaccinations current, wear ID tags, and be leashed and cleaned up after at all times. No aggressive dogs or dogs in heat are allowed.

Vets and Kennels

Evening Pet Clinic 6803 Cherry Ave Long Beach CA   562-422-1223
Mon - Fri 8 am - 9 pm with certain lunch and dinner breaks, Sat - Sun 12 - 6 pm.

Los Angeles

Accommodations

Pacific Palms Resort and Conference Center One Industry Hills Parkway City of Industry CA   626-810-4455 (800-524-4557)
Sitting on 650 acres of meticulously landscaped grounds with 2 championship golf courses, 17 tennis courts, an Olympic-sized pool, miles of riding and hiking trails, and home to one of the most prestigious conference centers with cutting-edge technology in the US, this resort is a consummate retreat for the business or leisure traveler. Some of the amenities include 292 spacious well-appointed guestrooms and suites each with a balcony and many in-room amenities, and 2 outstanding restaurants and a lounge. Dogs of all sizes are allowed for an additional one time fee of $25 per pet. Dogs must be friendly and well behaved and removed or crated for housekeeping. Dogs must be kept on leash out of the room and cleaned up after at all times.

Embassy Suites Hotel Los Angeles - Downey 8425 Firestone Blvd. Downey CA   562-861-1900
Dogs of all sizes are allowed. There is a $25 per night pet fee per pet. Dogs are not allowed to be left alone in the room.

Beverly Hills Plaza Hotel 10300 Wilshire Blvd Los Angeles CA   310-275-5575 (800-800-1234)
This unique all-suite hotel offers luxury accommodations with a modern European decor and an elegant atmosphere to please the business or leisure traveler. Offering a convenient location to several attractions, they also feature the Le Petit Cafe/Bar, many in-room amenities, a heated outdoor pool with cabanas and a Jacuzzi, private balconies, room service, a 24 hour gift shop and front desk, and a concierge staff. Dogs up to 60 pounds are allowed. There is a $500 refundable deposit plus a $200 one time additional pet fee per pet and a pet policy to sign at check in. Dogs may only be left alone in the room if they will be quiet and well behaved. Dogs must be leashed and cleaned up after at all times.

Beverly Laurel Hotel 8018 Beverly Blvd Los Angeles CA   323-651-2441
There is a $25 per day pet fee. Up to two pets per room are allowed. Thanks to one of our readers who wrote "Our large German Shepherd was welcome."

Four Points by Sheraton Los Angeles International Airport 9750 Airport Blvd. Los Angeles CA   310-645-4600 (888-625-5144)
Dogs up to 50 pounds are allowed. There are no additional pet fees. Dogs are not allowed to be left alone in the room.
Hilton 5711 West Century Blvd Los Angeles CA   310-410-4000
Dogs of all sizes are allowed. There is a $15 per night per pet additional fee.
Holiday Inn 170 N Church Lane Los Angeles CA   310-476-6411 (877-270-6405)
Dogs of all sizes are allowed. There is a $50 one time pet fee per visit. Smoking and non-smoking rooms are available for pets.

Hotel Sofitel

Hotel Sofitel 8555 Beverly Blvd Los Angeles CA   310-278-5444
http://www.sofitel.com
This upscale hotel is located next to West Hollywood and Beverly Hills. You and your dog will feel most welcome at this hotel. Since parking is limited in this area, your car will be valet parked. They open the car doors not only for you, but for your dog too. You can feel comfortable registering at the front desk with your pup at your side and then taking the elevator to the room that awaits you. There is a restaurant at this hotel that has outdoor dining where your dog is also welcome. Room rates run about $150-250 per night, but your dog will be treated first class.
La Quinta Inn & Suites LAX 5249 West Century Blvd Los Angeles CA   310-645-2200 (800-531-5900)
Dogs of all sizes are allowed. There are no additional pet fees, but they request to meet your pet, and to know that you have a pet so as to inform housekeeping. Dogs must be leashed and cleaned up after.
Le Meridien Hotel 465 South La Cienega Blvd. Los Angeles CA   310-247-0400
Dogs up to 50 pounds are allowed. This luxury class hotel is located in one of the most prestigious areas in Los Angeles. They welcome both business and leisure travelers, as well as your dog of any size. Room rates at this first class hotel start at the low $300s per night. They sometimes offer special weekend rates. There is an additional $100 pet fee for the first night and an additional $25 for each additional day.
Los Angeles Airport Marriott 5855 W Century Blvd Los Angeles CA   310-641-5700 (800-228-9290)
Dogs of all sizes are allowed. There are no additional pet fees. Dogs must be quiet, leashed, cleaned up after, and a contact number left with the front desk if they are in the room alone.
Residence Inn by Marriott 1177 S Beverly Drive Los Angeles CA   310-277-4427
Pets of all sizes are welcome. There is an $80 N/R cleaning fee plus $10 per night for one pet; $15 per night for two pets, and an additional $5 per night for each pet thereafter. There is also a pet policy to sign at check in.
Travelodge Hotel at LAX 5547 W. Century Blvd. Los Angeles CA   310-649-4000
http://www.travelodge.com
This inn offers free parking, a feature not found with many of the L.A./West Hollywood hotels. They welcome pets here at this 2 story inn which has interior/exterior corridors, a gift shop and heated pool. It is located about one mile east of the Los Angeles Airport. There is a $10 per day additional pet fee per pet.
Vagabond Inn 3101 S. Figueroa St. Los Angeles CA   213-746-1531 (800-522-1555)

http://www.vagabondinn.com
This motel is located just 2 blocks from the University of Southern California (USC) and 2 miles from the LA Convention Center. It features an outdoor swimming pool, cable television, air conditioning and many more amenities. There is a $10 per day pet fee.

W Los Angeles Westwood 930 Hilgard Avenue Los Angeles CA 310-208-8765
Dogs up to 80 pounds are allowed. There is a $100 one time per stay pet fee and a $25 per night additional pet fee.

Campgrounds and RV Parks

Kenneth Hahn State Rec Area 4100 S La Cienega Los Angeles CA 323-298-3660
In 1932 this area hosted the 10th Olympiad, and again in 1984 Los Angeles hosted the Olympics with athletes from 140 nations, so as a reminder, 140 trees were planted here to commemorate this event. Other park features/amenities include large landscaped areas, picnic sites, barbecues, playgrounds, a fishing lake, lotus pond/Japanese Garden, gaming fields/courts, and several miles of hiking trails. Dogs are allowed throughout the park and on the trails. Dogs of all sizes are allowed for no additional fee. Dogs must be well behaved, leashed, and cleaned up after. There is primitive camping allowed. The camping and tent areas also allow dogs. There is a dog walk area at the campground. There are no electric or water hookups at the campgrounds.

Transportation Systems

Metro Transit Authority 1 Gateway Plaza Los Angeles CA 213-580-7500
http://www.metro.net
Small dogs in an enclosed carrier are allowed on the light rail and buses for no additional fee.

Attractions

Griffith Observatory 2800 East Observatory Road Los Angeles CA 323-664-1181
http://www.griffithobs.org/
This observatory has been a major Los Angeles landmark since 1935. Star-gazing dogs are not allowed inside the Observatory, but you are allowed to walk to the roof (on the outside stairs) and get some great views of the Los Angeles basin and the Hollywood sign. Located across the parking lot from the Observatory is the Griffith Park snack shop and the Mt. Hollywood Trail (about 6 miles of dog-friendly trails). To get to there, take Hwy 5 to the Los Feliz Blvd exit and head west. Turn right on Hillhurst or Vermont Ave (they merge later). Go past the Bird Sanctuary and Greek Theater. Stay on Vermont Ave and you'll come to the Griffith Observatory.

Griffith Park Southern Railroad 4400 Crystal Springs Drive Los Angeles CA 323-664-6788
http://www.gprec.com/
Does your pup want to try a train ride? This small train ride (serving the public since 1948) is popular with kids, but your dog will love it too. The seating area is kind of small and larger dogs will need to sit or stand on the floor by your feet. But don't worry, it's a pretty short ride which goes about 1 mile in distance. It'll give your pup a chance to decide if he/she is made for the rails. It's located in Griffith Park which also has several nice hikes that of course allow dogs. Hungry? There is a small snack stand located nearby with many picnic tables. While you eat lunch, you can watch the kids ride the rental ponies. Griffith Park is pretty large, so to find the train ride, take Los Feliz Blvd (near Hwy 5) to Crystal Springs Drive/Griffith Park Drive. Head north on Crystal Springs and the train ride will be on your right.

Hollywood Walk of Fame 6100-6900 Hollywood Blvd. Los Angeles CA 323-469-8311
Want to see the star that was dedicated to your favorite actor or actress? Then come to the famous Hollywood Walk of Fame on Hollywood Blvd. You'll find about 10-15 blocks of Hollywood stars placed in the sidewalks of Hollywood Blvd. Don't forget to look at the famous Footprints located at the Mann's Chinese Theatre on Hollywood Blvd between Orange Drive and Orchid Ave. Want to see an actor or actress receive their honorary Star? This takes place throughout the year in front of the Hollywood Galaxy General Cinemas on Hollywood Blvd. It may be too crowded for your pup to stand directly in front of the Cinemas, but you can see plenty from across the street. Just make sure your dog is comfortable with crowds yelling and cheering as this will happen when the actor/actress arrives. Our pup was able to see Nicolas Cage receive his Hollywood Star. To find out the schedule of when the next actor/actress will receive their star, look at the Hollywood Chamber of Commerce website at http://www.hollywoodcoc.org or call 323-469-8311. To get to the Hollywood Walk of Fame, take Hwy 101 North past Sunset Blvd. Take the next exit which is Hollywood Blvd and turn left (west). The Hollywood Stars are located on 6100-6900 Hollywood Blvd. between Gower Street and Sycamore Avenue.

TOP 200 PLACE SkyBark 1026 S Santa Fe Avenue Los Angeles CA 213-891-1722
http://www.skybark.com
This unique club sits atop a building giving a 360 degree view of downtown Los Angeles, and was born from a desire for a place to unwind and have a few drinks with others who wanted a socializing place to go with their canine companions, too. They also wanted to make a difference for animals in distress, so each event benefits animal related needs. Events are usually about one time a month with a different charity each time to benefit. There is a full bar, live music/DJs, dancing, and catered food for owners and pets. For pets, there is a play area

with several hundred square feet of grass and toys, an animal potty area, waiter service, a full bar with healthy drinks in their own special martini glasses, and places to lounge around. This venue has quickly become popular, and is spreading nationwide with other bars opening in Las Vegas and Boston. Tickets, in advance, are usually $20 per person and $10 per dog. Dogs must be well mannered.

Hollywood Walk of Fame

You never know who you might see in Hollywood

Travel Town Museum

Travel Town Museum 5200 Zoo Drive Los Angeles CA   323-662-5874
Dogs are allowed on leash throughout the Travel Town Museum in Griffith Park in LA. Here you can see many trains, cars and lots more. Your well-behaved dog is also allowed on the miniature train ride.

Shopping Centers

Century City Shopping Center

Century City Shopping Center 10250 Santa Monica Blvd Los Angeles CA   310-277-3898
This dog-friendly outdoor shopping center, located just one mile from Rodeo Drive in Beverly Hills, is popular with many Hollywood actors and actresses. Your well-behaved dog is allowed inside many of the stores. For a list of dog-friendly stores, please look at our stores category. Your dog is also welcome to join you at the outdoor cafe tables in the food court area.

Stores

Petco Pet Store 17585 Colima Rd City of Industry CA   626-964-1666
Your licensed and well-behaved leashed dog is allowed in the store.
PetSmart Pet Store 12126 Lakewood Blvd Downey CA   562-803-1607
Your licensed and well-behaved leashed dog is allowed in the store.
Petco Pet Store 8580 Firestone Blvd Downey CA   562-861-2093
Your licensed and well-behaved leashed dog is allowed in the store.
Brentano's Books Century City Shopping Center Los Angeles CA   310-785-0204
Your well-behaved leashed dog is allowed inside this store.
Dutton's Brentwood Bookstore 11975 San Vicente Blvd Los Angeles CA   310-476-6263
http://www.duttonsbrentwood.com/
More than a bookstore, they also card cards and CD's, are host to a monthly reading series, special events, and more, and they have also been known to greet their canine visitors with a doggy biscuit. Friendly, well behaved dogs are welcome in the bookstore. They must be house trained, leashed, and under owner's control/responsibility at all times.
Foot Locker Century City Shopping Center Los Angeles CA   310-556-1498
http://www.footlocker.com/
Your well-behaved leashed dog is allowed inside this store.
Gap Century City Shopping Center Los Angeles CA   310-556-1080
http://www.gap.com/
Your well-behaved leashed dog is allowed inside this store.
Illiterature 452 S La Brea Ave Los Angeles CA   323-937-3505
Dogs are allowed but they must be leashed.
Laura Ashley Century City Shopping Center Los Angeles CA   310-553-0807
http://www.laura-ashley.com/
Your well-behaved leashed dog is allowed inside this store.
Le Pet Boutique 189 The Grove Drive Los Angeles CA   323-935-9195
This pet gift store is located in an outdoor mall, so your pooch can join you in checking out all the toys, treats, collars, leads, and a lot more. They are open from 10 am to 9 pm Monday through Friday; from 10 am to 10 pm Friday and Saturday, and from 11 am to 8 pm on Sunday. Dogs must be well behaved and on leash.
Origins Century City Shopping Center Los Angeles CA   310-772-0272
http://www.origins.com/
Your well-behaved leashed dog is allowed inside this store.
Petco Pet Store 1873 Westwood Blvd Los Angeles CA   310-441-2073
Your licensed and well-behaved leashed dog is allowed in the store.
Petco Pet Store 200 S La Brea Ave #C Los Angeles CA   323-934-8444
Your licensed and well-behaved leashed dog is allowed in the store.
Petco Pet Store 8801 S Sepulveda Blvd Los Angeles CA   310-645-7198
Your licensed and well-behaved leashed dog is allowed in the store.
Pottery Barn Century City Shopping Center Los Angeles CA   310-552-0170
http://www.potterybarn.com/
Your well-behaved leashed dog is allowed inside this store.
Restoration Hardware Century City Shopping Center Los Angeles CA   310-551-4995
http://www.restorationhardware.com/
Your well-behaved leashed dog is allowed inside this store.
Rocket Video 726 N La Brea Ave Los Angeles CA   323-965-1100
http://www.rocketvideo.com/
Well-behaved leashed dogs are welcome in this store which is Los Angeles' premier independent video store.
Three Dog Bakery The Grove, 6333 West 3rd Street, #710 Los Angeles CA   323-935-7512
http://www.threedog.com
Three Dog Bakery provides cookies and snacks for your dog as well as some boutique items. You well-behaved, leashed dog is welcome.
Petco Pet Store 1425 North Montebello Blvd Montebello CA   323-724-3194
Your licensed and well-behaved leashed dog is allowed in the store.

Parks

Elysian Park 929 Academy Road Los Angeles CA   805-584-4400

At 600 acres, this is the 2nd largest city park in Los Angeles, and much of the landscape of natural chaparral is crisscrossed with hiking trails. There are barbecue pits, a small man-made lake, restrooms, and a children's play area at the central picnic area.

Griffith Park

Griffith Park Los Feliz Blvd. Los Angeles CA
This is the park that allows dogs on their small trains (see Attractions), has the Griffith Observatory, the famous Hollywood sign and plenty of hiking trails. The Mt. Hollywood Trail is about a 6 mile round trip and can get very hot in the summer season, so head out early or later in the evening during those hot days. There is also a more shaded trail that begins by the Bird Sanctuary. Be careful not to go into the Sanctuary because dogs are not allowed there. Instead go to the trail to the left of the Sanctuary entrance. That trail should go around the perimeter of the Bird Sanctuary. For more trail info, pick up a map at one of the Ranger stations (main Ranger's station is at Crystal Springs/Griffith Park Drive near Los Feliz Blvd). To get to there, take Hwy 5 to the Los Feliz Blvd exit and head west. Turn right on Hillhurst or Vermont Ave (they merge later). The trail by the Bird Sanctuary will be on the right, past the Greek Theater. To get to the Mt. Hollywood Trail, continue until you come to the Griffith Observatory. Park here and the trail is across the parking lot from the Observatory (near the outdoor cafe). Please note that no one is allowed to actually hike to the famous Hollywood sign - it is very well guarded. But from some of the trails in this park, you can get a long distance view of the sign. Dogs must be leashed in the park.

TOP 200 PLACE Kenneth Hahn State Rec Area 4100 S La Cienega Los Angeles CA   323-298-3660
In 1932 this area hosted the 10th Olympiad, and again in 1984 Los Angeles hosted the Olympics with athletes from 140 nations, so as a reminder, 140 trees were planted here to commemorate this event. Other park features/amenities include large landscaped areas, picnic sites, barbecues, playgrounds, a fishing lake, lotus pond/Japanese Garden, gaming fields/courts, and several miles of hiking trails. Dogs are allowed throughout the park and on the trails. Dogs of all sizes are allowed for no additional fee. Dogs must be well behaved, leashed, and cleaned up after.

Kenneth Hahn State Rec Area

Off-Leash Dog Parks

Barrington Dog Park 333 South Barrington Avenue Los Angeles CA 310-476-4866
Barrington Dog Park is located just west of the 405 Freeway at Sunset Blvd. Exit the 405 at Sunset, head west, and then south onto Barrington. This fenced 1 1/2 acre dog park is open during daylight hours.

Griffith Park Dog Park North Zoo Drive Los Angeles CA 323-913-4688
This dog park is located 1/2 mile west of the 134 Fwy at the John Ferraro Soccer Field, next to the Autry Museum and across from the main zoo parking. There are two separate fenced areas, one for larger dogs and the other for small or timid dogs. There is a portable restroom for people.

Herman Park Dog Park 5566 Via Marisol Los Angeles CA 323-255-0370
Herman Park in the Arroyo Seco Dog Park is a 1 1/3 acre fenced dog park with separate areas for large and small dogs. The park is open during daylight hours. The park is located off of the 110 Freeway east on Via Marisol.

TOP 200 PLACE Laurel Canyon Park 8260 Mulholland Dr. Los Angeles CA
This nice dog park is located in the hills of Studio City. It is completely fenced with water and even a hot dog stand. To get there, take Laurel Canyon Blvd and go west on Mulholland Blvd. Go about a 1/4 mile and turn left. There is a parking lot below.

TOP 200 PLACE Runyon Canyon Park Mulholland Hwy Los Angeles CA 323-666-5046
From this popular hiking trail and excellent off-leash area you can see views of Hollywood, the Wilshire District, and the skyscrapers of downtown L.A. This park has mostly off-leash and some on-leash hiking trails. It is about a 2 mile round-trip from end to end in the park. The top of the trail is located off Mulholland Hwy (about 2 miles east of Laurel Canyon Blvd) at Desmond Street in the Hollywood Hills. The bottom part of the trail is located at the end of Fuller Ave. Parking is available on the street. The trailhead might be kind of tricky to find from Fuller, but you'll probably see other people going to or coming from the trail.

Silverlake Dog Park 2000 West Silverlake Blvd. Los Angeles CA
This is one of the best dog parks in the Los Angeles area and it usually averages 30-40 dogs. It is located at approximately 2000 West Silverlake Blvd. It's on the south side of the reservoir in Silverlake, which is between Hollywood and downtown L.A. between Sunset Blvd. and the 5 Freeway. The easiest way to get there is to take the 101 Freeway to Silverlake Blvd. and go east. Be careful about street parking because they ticket in some areas. Thanks to one of our readers for recommending this dog park.

Laurel Canyon Park

Runyon Canyon Park

Los Angeles Area - Please always call ahead to make sure that an establishment is still dog-friendly

Silverlake Dog Park

Outdoor Restaurants

Baja Fresh Mexican Grill 7919 Sunset Blvd. Los Angeles CA 323-436-3844
http://www.bajafresh.com
This Mexican restaurant is open for lunch and dinner. They use fresh ingredients and making their salsa and beans daily. Some of the items on their menu include Enchiladas, Burritos, Tacos Salads, Quesadillas, Nachos, Chicken, Steak and more. Well-behaved leashed dogs are allowed at the outdoor tables.
Baja Fresh Mexican Grill 5757 Wilshire Blvd. Los Angeles CA 323-549-9080
http://www.bajafresh.com
This Mexican restaurant is open for lunch and dinner. They use fresh ingredients and making their salsa and beans daily. Some of the items on their menu include Enchiladas, Burritos, Tacos Salads, Quesadillas, Nachos, Chicken, Steak and more. Well-behaved leashed dogs are allowed at the outdoor tables.
Camille's Sidewalk Cafe 655 S Hope Street Los Angeles CA 213-629-2255
A vision of healthier, tastier foods inspired the idea for the freshly made salads, gourmet wraps and sandwiches, drinks, desserts, and coffees that are offered at all of Camille's Cafes. Dogs are allowed to sit with you at your outdoor table. Dogs must be attended to at all times, well behaved, and leashed.
Cava 8384 West 3rd Street Los Angeles CA 323-658-8898
This restaurant and bar serves American. Dogs are allowed at the outdoor tables.
Crest on Sunset 3725 Sunset Blvd Los Angeles CA 323-660-3645
This restaurant serves American food. Dogs are allowed at the outdoor tables.
Cyberjava Cybercafe 7080 Hollywood Los Angeles CA 323-466-5600
This cafe serves coffee and deli-type food. Dogs are allowed at the outdoor tables. Water and treats are provided for your pet.
Doughboys 8136 W 3rd Street Los Angeles CA 323-651-4202
This restaurant serves American food. Dogs are allowed at the outdoor tables. Water is provided for your pet.
Fred's 62 1850 N Vermont Ave Los Angeles CA 323-667-0062
Dogs are allowed at the outdoor tables.
Good Microbrew and Grill 922 Lucille Avenue Los Angeles CA 323-660-3645
Dogs are allowed at the outdoor tables. They will also provide a bowl of water for your dog.
Griffith Park snack stand Vermont Ave Los Angeles CA
This is a basic snack stand but what makes it nice is the fact that it's in Griffith Park between the Griffith Observatory and the Mt. Hollywood Trail. Your pup can't go in the Observatory, but can walk up the outside stairs to the roof and check out the view of Los Angeles. At the Mt. Hollywood Trail, there is a 6 mile round trip dog-friendly trail. Load up on snacks and water at this stand. To get to there, take Hwy 5 to the Los Feliz Blvd exit

and head west. Turn right on Hillhurst or Vermont Ave (they merge later). Go past the Bird Sanctuary and Greek Theater. Stay on Vermont Ave and you'll come to the Griffith Observatory and snack shop parking.

Hollywood Blvd restaurants Hollywood Blvd. Los Angeles CA
While you are looking at the Stars on the Hollywood Walk of Fame at Hollywood Blvd., you can take a lunch or snack break at one of the many outdoor cafes that line this popular street. Many of them only have a few tables, but you should be able to find one.

Home 1760 Hillhurst Avenue Los Angeles CA 323-669-0211
This American restaurant is open for breakfast, lunch and dinner. They welcome dogs at their outdoor tables. Dogs should be on leash. Thanks to one of our readers for recommending this restaurant.

Il Capriccio on Vermont 1757 N Vermont Avenue Los Angeles CA 323-662-5900
This fine Italian restaurant offers indoor and outdoor dining service. Dogs are allowed at the outdoor tables. They must be well behaved, under owner's control at all times, leashed, and cleaned up after.

Johnnie's New York Pizza 10251 Santa Monica Blvd Los Angeles CA 310-553-1188
This restaurant serves Italian/American food. Dogs are allowed at the outdoor tables on the sidewalk part.

Mel's Drive-In 8585 Sunset Blvd. Los Angeles CA 310-854-7200
This 24 hour West Hollywood restaurant serves you and your pup breakfast, lunch or dinner outside.

TOP 200 PLACE **Prana Cafe** 650 N. La Cienega Blvd Los Angeles CA 310-360-0551
This restaurant is a sleek, casual spot with mostly outdoor seating, and serves food with a bit of an Asian influence. Seeing that there was a desire for pet owner's to be able to dine with their four-legged companions, they set about preparing a doggy menu and purchasing shiny silver bowls for their canine clientele. They are open 8 am to 10 pm daily with a limited menu after 5 pm. Dogs of all sizes are allowed. Dogs must be socially friendly, leashed, and please clean up after your pet.

Sante La Brea 345 N La Brea Los Angeles CA 323-857-0412
http://www.santecuisine.com/
Featuring an eclectic menu of original, alternative foods with plenty of well-balanced, high protein choices, they also have pioneered the concept of "Sante Cuisine", which offers full, rich foods where the absence of fat and dairy doesn't compromise the flavor of the recipe. There are tables out front for customers with pets. Dogs must be well behaved, under owner's control at all times, leashed, and cleaned up after.

Sonora Cafe 180 S La Brea Los Angeles CA 323-857-1800
http://www.sonoracafe.com/
This eatery has established itself as one of Los Angeles' premier Southwestern restaurants offering generous dishes and bold flavors. They have a unique bar menu, an extensive wine list, and offer indoor and outdoor patio service. Dogs are allowed at the outdoor tables. They must be well behaved, under owner's control at all times, leashed, and cleaned up after.

The Back Door Bakery 1710 Silver Lake Blvd Los Angeles CA 323-662-7927
This restaurant is two blocks from the Silver Lake Dog Park, so it gets a regular group of 4 legged customers at the outdoor tables. They have dog biscuits for the dogs. The hours are 7:30 am to 7 pm Tuesday through Sunday.

The Lazy Daisy 11913 Wilshire Blvd Los Angeles CA 310-447-8580
Dogs are allowed at the outdoor tables.

The Pig, Memphis-Style barbecue 612 N. La Brea Ave Los Angeles CA 323-935-1116
This restaurant is very dog friendly. There are a lot of doggy regulars at the "Pig". Closed Mondays. Open from 11 am to at least 10 pm other days. Dogs are welcome to dine with you at the outdoor tables.

Toast Bakery Cafe Inc 8221 W 3rd St Los Angeles CA 323-655-5018
This cage serves deli-type food. Dogs are allowed at the outdoor tables.

Whole Foods Market 11737 San Vicente Blvd. Los Angeles CA 310-826-4433
http://www.wholefoods.com/
This natural food supermarket offers natural and organic foods. Order some food from their deli without your dog and bring it to an outdoor table where your well-behaved leashed dog is welcome. Dogs are not allowed in the store including the deli at any time.

Whole Foods Market 6350 West 3rd Street Los Angeles CA 323-964-6800
http://www.wholefoods.com/
This natural food supermarket offers natural and organic foods. Order some food from their deli without your dog and bring it to an outdoor table where your well-behaved leashed dog is welcome. Dogs are not allowed in the store including the deli at any time.

Whole Foods Market 7871 West Santa Monica Blvd. Los Angeles CA 323-848-4200
http://www.wholefoods.com/
This natural food supermarket offers natural and organic foods. Order some food from their deli without your dog and bring it to an outdoor table where your well-behaved leashed dog is welcome. Dogs are not allowed in the store including the deli at any time.

Whole Foods Market 11666 National Boulevard Los Angeles CA 310-996-8840
http://www.wholefoods.com/
This natural food supermarket offers natural and organic foods. Order some food from their deli without your dog and bring it to an outdoor table where your well-behaved leashed dog is welcome. Dogs are not allowed in the

store including the deli at any time. The market is located at the corner of National and Barrington.
Whole Foods Market 1050 S. Gayley Los Angeles CA   310-824-0858
http://www.wholefoods.com/
This natural food supermarket offers natural and organic foods. Order some food from their deli without your dog and bring it to an outdoor table where your well-behaved leashed dog is welcome. Dogs are not allowed in the store including the deli at any time.

Vets and Kennels
Animal Emergency Clinic 1736 S Sepulveda Blvd #A Los Angeles CA   310-473-1561
Monday - Friday 6 pm - 8 am. 24 hours weekends and holidays.
Eagle Rock Emergency Pet Clinic 4252 Eagle Rock Blvd Los Angeles CA   323-254-7382
Monday - Friday 6 pm - 8 am. Saturday 12 noon - Monday 8 am.

Malibu

Campgrounds and RV Parks
Leo Carrillo State Park Campground 35000 Pacific Coast Hwy (Hwy 1) Malibu CA   818-880-0350 (800-444-PARK (7275))
This campground offers tent and RV camping near the dog-friendly (leashes only and certain sections only) beach, tide pools, marine viewing, interpretive programs, and a variety of recreational activities. The campsites are located on the inland side of Highway 1. You can walk to the beach along a road that goes underneath the highway. Dogs on leash are allowed in the campgrounds and on a certain section of the beach. Please clean up after you pets. Dogs are not allowed in the rocky tide pool area, or on the back country trails. The camping and tent areas also allow dogs. There is a dog walk area at the campground. There are no electric or water hookups at the campgrounds.
Malibu Beach RV Park 25801 Pacific Coast Hwy Malibu CA   310-456-6052 (800-622-6052)
http://www.maliburv.com/
This ocean park provide many amenities, some of which are a rec room, video game room, an outdoor game room, marine life viewing, hiking trails, and various other land and water recreational activities. Dogs of all sizes are allowed for an additional fee of $3 per night per pet. Dogs may not be left unattended, and they must be leashed at all times, and cleaned up after. This is an RV only park. There are some breed restrictions. There is a dog walk area at the campground.

Beaches
Leo Carrillo State Beach Hwy 1 Malibu CA   818-880-0350
This beach is one of the very few dog-friendly beaches in the Los Angeles area. In a press release dated November 27, 2002, the California State Parks clarified the rules for dogs at Leo Carrillo State Beach. We thank the State Parks for this clear announcement of the regulations. Dogs are allowed on a maximum 6 foot leash when accompanied by a person capable of controlling the dog on all beach WEST (up coast) of lifeguard tower 3 at Leo Carrillo State Park, Staircase Beach, County Line Beach, and all Beaches within Point Mugu State Park. Dogs are NOT allowed EAST of lifeguard tower 3 at Leo Carrillo State Beach at any time. And please note that dogs are not allowed in the tide pools at Leo Carrillo. There should be signs posted. A small general store is located on the mountain side of the freeway. Here you can grab some snacks and other items. The park is located on Hwy 1, approximately 30 miles northwest of Santa Monica. We ask that all dog people closely obey these regulations so that the beach continues to be dog-friendly.

Parks
Circle X Ranch Yerba Buena Road Malibu CA   805-370-2301
There are both easy and strenuous trails at this park. The Backbone Trail is a strenuous 3 mile round trip hike which starts at an elevatio of 2,050 feet. This trail offers views on the Conejo and San Fernando Valleys and the Pacific Coast. This trail continues to Point Mugu State Park but dogs are not allowed on those trails. The Grotto Trail is a 3.5 mile round trip trail rated moderate to strenuous. The trail is all downhill from the starting point which means you will be hiking uphill when you return. The Canyon View Trail is almost 2 miles and is rated easy to moderate. There are many access points to this trail, but one is located .3 miles east of the Ranger Station on Yerba Buena Road. Dogs are allowed but must be leashed and people need to clean up after their pets. To get there go about 5.4 miles north on Yerba Buena Road from Highway 1. This park is part of the Santa Monica Recreation Area.
Escondido Canyon Park Winding Way Malibu CA   805-370-2301
http://smmc.ca.gov/escontral.html
The Escondido Falls trail is a little over 4 miles long. The trailhead is reached by a one mile walk up the road

from the parking lot. The trail will cross the creek several times before opening up to grassland. You will see the waterfall about one mile from the trailhead. Hiking, horseback riding, and mountain bicycling are popular activities at the park. Dogs on a 6 foot or less leash are allowed and people need to clean up after their pets. The park is located in Malibu, about one mile from the Pacific Coast Highway on Winding Way. This park is part of the Santa Monica Recreation Area.

Santa Clarita Woodlands Park 5750 Ramiraz Canyon Road Malibu CA   310-589-3200
A very important park with concern to the wildlife habitat corridor that it provides, it also supplies 4000 acres of recreational land. Some of the features/amenities include globally unique combinations of tree species, lush greenery and spring wildflowers, abundant bird and wildlife, year round streams, a nature center, hiking and multi-use trails, and picnic areas. Dogs are allowed throughout the park and on the trails. Dogs must be under owner's immediate control, leashed, and cleaned up after at all times.

Solstice Canyon Park Corral Canyon Road Malibu CA   805-370-2301
This park is a wooded, narrow coastal canyon which offers five trails, ranging from easy to moderate hikes. One of the trails is called the Solstice Canyon Trail. This is an easy 2.1 mile round trip walk which passes by the Keller House which is believed to be the oldest existing stone building in Malibu. Dogs are allowed on the trails but must be leashed and people need to clean up after their pets. To get there from the Pacific Coast Highway 1, go through Malibu and turn inland onto Corral Canyon Road. In about .25 miles the entrance will be on your left at a hairpin curve in the road. This park is part of the Santa Monica Recreation Area.

Newhall

Parks

Placerita Canyon Nature Center 19152 Placerita Canyon Road Newhall CA   661-259-7721
This 350 acre nature park is one of the first places where gold was discovered in California. An early frontier cabin called Walker's Cabin is located at this park. Hiking trails are accessible for wheelchairs and strollers. The paved trail is about .3 miles. Dogs must be on leash and please clean up after them.

William S. Hart Regional Park 24151 N. San Fernando Road Newhall CA   661-259-0855
This 265 acre ranch was donated to the public by William S. Hart, also known as "Two Gun Bill". He was a popular cowboy actor during the silent film era. The park includes a western art museum and barnyard animals including wild buffalo. Dogs are allowed at the park and on trails, but not inside any buildings. Pets must be leashed and please clean up after them.

Pasadena - East LA

Accommodations

Motel 6 - Los Angeles - Arcadia/Pasadena 225 Colorado Place Arcadia CA   626-446-2660 (800-466-8356)
One well-behaved family pet per room. Guest must notify front desk upon arrival. Guest is liable for any damages. In consideration of all guests, pets must never be left unattended in the guest rooms.

Residence Inn by Marriott 321 E Huntington Drive/Gateway Arcadia CA   626-446-6500
Pets of all sizes are allowed. There is a $75 one time fee, and a pet policy to sign at check in.

Motel 6 - Los Angeles - Baldwin Park 14510 Garvey Avenue Baldwin Park CA   626-960-5011 (800-466-8356)
One well-behaved family pet per room. Guest must notify front desk upon arrival. Guest is liable for any damages. In consideration of all guests, pets must never be left unattended in the guest rooms.

Motel 6 - Los Angeles - El Monte 3429 Peck Road El Monte CA   626-448-6660 (800-466-8356)
One well-behaved family pet per room. Guest must notify front desk upon arrival. Guest is liable for any damages. In consideration of all guests, pets must never be left unattended in the guest rooms.

Vagabond Inn 120 W. Colorado Street Glendale CA   818-240-1700
http://www.vagabondinn.com
This motel is located near Universal Studios. Amenities include a complimentary breakfast and during the week, a free USA Today newspaper. There is a $10 per day pet fee.

Motel 6 - Los Angeles - Norwalk 10646 Rosecrans Avenue Norwalk CA   562-864-2567 (800-466-8356)
One well-behaved family pet per room. Guest must notify front desk upon arrival. Guest is liable for any damages. In consideration of all guests, pets must never be left unattended in the guest rooms.

Days Inn - Pico Rivera 6540 S. Rosemead Blvd Pico Rivera CA   562-942-1003 (800-329-7466)
There is a $15 per day pet fee.

Motel 6 - Los Angeles - Rosemead 1001 South San Gabriel Boulevard Rosemead CA   626-572-6076 (800-466-8356)
One well-behaved family pet per room. Guest must notify front desk upon arrival. Guest is liable for any

damages. In consideration of all guests, pets must never be left unattended in the guest rooms.
Motel 6 - Los Angeles - Santa Fe Springs 13412 Excelsior Drive Santa Fe Springs CA   562-921-0596 (800-466-8356)
One well-behaved family pet per room. Guest must notify front desk upon arrival. Guest is liable for any damages. In consideration of all guests, pets must never be left unattended in the guest rooms.
Motel 6 - Los Angeles - Whittier 8221 South Pioneer Boulevard Whittier CA   562-692-9101 (800-466-8356)
One well-behaved family pet per room. Guest must notify front desk upon arrival. Guest is liable for any damages. In consideration of all guests, pets must never be left unattended in the guest rooms.

Attractions

Frisbee Golf Course Oak Grove Drive Pasadena CA
http://members.aol.com/throwgolf
This disc golf course in Pasadena is the world's first disc golf course. It is an extremely popular course, with over 100 golfers playing daily during the week and twice that on the weekends. If you are a beginner, this might not be the right course for you, but you can watch some of the pros at work. Disc golf is similar to golf with clubs and balls, but the main difference is the equipment. Discs are shot into elevated baskets/holes. Your dog is allowed to go with you on this course, just watch out for flying discs. Dogs must be leashed and poop bags/scoopers are necessary. During the summer months, there can be rattlesnakes, so make sure your dog stays leashed. You'll also want to keep your pup away from the ground squirrels (they can potentially be rabid). This course is located in Hahamongna Watershed Park (formerly Oak Grove Park). If you don't have any discs, you can purchase them online at http://www.gottagogottathrow.com. The prices range from $8-12. Directions to the course are on their website. The park is off Hwy 210 near Altadena.

Shopping Centers

Old Town Pasadena 100W-100E Colorado Blvd. Pasadena CA
http://www.oldpasadena.com/oldpas/
Old Town Pasadena is Pasadena's premier shopping and dining district. This area is a nice place to walk around with your pup. While dogs are not allowed inside the stores, they can sit at one of the many dog-friendly outdoor cafes and dine with you (see our restaurant listings). A major portion of the popular annual Rose Parade takes place on this part of Colorado Boulevard. The shopping area is the 100 West to 100 East blocks of Colorado Blvd., and between Marengo & Pasadena Avenues.

Stores

PetSmart Pet Store 2568 W Commonwealth Ave Alhambra CA   626-284-3390
Your licensed and well-behaved leashed dog is allowed in the store.
Petco Pet Store 12601 Towne Center Drive Cerritos CA   562-924-3018
Your licensed and well-behaved leashed dog is allowed in the store.
Petco Pet Store 231 North Glendale Avenue Glendale CA   818-548-0411
Your licensed and well-behaved leashed dog is allowed in the store.
Petco Pet Store 475 Foothill Blvd La Canada CA   818-790-3165
Your licensed and well-behaved leashed dog is allowed in the store.
PetSmart Pet Store 3347 E Foothill Blvd Pasadena CA   626-351-8434
Your licensed and well-behaved leashed dog is allowed in the store.
Petco Pet Store 845 South Arroyo Parkway Pasadena CA   626-577-2600
Your licensed and well-behaved leashed dog is allowed in the store.
Saks Fifth Avenue 35 N De Lacey Ave Pasadena CA   626-396-7100
Leashed, well - behaved dogs are allowed in the store.
Three Dog Bakery 24 Smith Alley Pasadena CA   626-440-0443
http://www.threedog.com/
Your pup is invited inside this dog bakery store which is located in Old Town Pasadena. Here he or she can choose from a variety of special dog cookies and pastries. The goodies look yummy enough for people to eat, but remember they are for dogs, not for humans. After your pup has indulged in the treats, both of you can dine at one of the many dog-friendly outdoor restaurants located within walking distance (see Restaurants).
Petco Pet Store 7262 N Rosemead Blvd San Gabriel CA   626-287-9847
Your licensed and well-behaved leashed dog is allowed in the store.
Petco Pet Store 1050 West Covina Parkway West Covina CA   626-813-9040
Your licensed and well-behaved leashed dog is allowed in the store.
Petco Pet Store 13420 Whittier Blvd Whittier CA   562-907-2300
Your licensed and well-behaved leashed dog is allowed in the store.

Parks

Angeles National Forest 701 N Santa Anita Ave Arcadia CA   626-574-1613
http://www.fs.fed.us/r5/angeles/
This national forest covers over 650,000 acres and is known as the backyard playground to the metropolitan area of Los Angeles. Elevations range from 1,200 to 10,064 feet. Please see our listings in this region for dog-friendly hikes and/or campgrounds.

Deukemjian Wilderness Park 5142 Dunsmore Avenue Glendale CA   818-548-2000
Sitting on 700 acres of chaparral-covered slopes at the northernmost part of the city, this park has a variety of multi-use trails available for first time and experienced hikers, a year round stream, and great views. Dogs are allowed throughout the park and on the trails. Dogs must be under owner's immediate control, leashed, and cleaned up after at all times.

Santa Fe Dam Recreation Area 15501 E. Arrow Highway Irwindale CA   626-334-1065
This 836 acre park has a 70 acre lake which popular for sailing and fishing. The lake is stocked with bass, trout and catfish. Other park amenities include picnic areas and hiking and biking trails. Dogs are allowed on the hiking trails, but not in the lake. Pets must be leashed and people need to clean up after their pet.

Brookside Park 360 N Arroyo Blvd Pasadena CA   626-744-4386
A 61.1 acre park, and the city's largest fully maintained park, is located just south of the Rose Bowl Stadium, and offers a variety of recreational opportunities. Some of the park's features/amenities include lighted gaming fields, picnic areas-most with barbecue pits, drinking fountains, playground areas, and restrooms. Dogs of all sizes are allowed. They must be well mannered, and leashed and cleaned up after at all times.

Eaton Canyon Nature Center 1750 N Altadena Drive Pasadena CA   626-398-5420
http://www.ecnca.org/
This 190 acre day-use park is considered to be a zoological, botanical, and geological wonderland, and there are also a variety of recreational opportunities available. Some of the features/amenities include a nature center/gift shop, hiking trails, and restrooms. Dogs of all sizes are allowed for no additional fee. Dogs must be under owner's control at all times, and be leashed and cleaned up after.

Hahamongna Watershed Oak Grove Drive Pasadena CA
The Hahamongna Watershed Park (formerly Oak Grove Park) allows leashed dogs on the trails and on the world's first disc golf course. During the summer months, there can be rattlesnakes here, so make sure your dog stays leashed. You'll also want to keep your pup away from the ground squirrels. Some squirrels in this mountain range have been known to carry rabies. Aside from being a very popular disc golf course, this park is also very popular with bird watchers. To get there from Hwy 210, take the Berkshire Ave. exit and head east. Turn left onto Oak Grove Drive and the park will be on the right. To get to one of the trails, follow the signs to the disc golf course. After going downhill, turn right and the trail begins.

Whittier Narrows Nature Center 1000 N. Durfee Ave. South El Monte CA   626-575-5523
This park has over 200 acres of natural woodland and includes four lakes which offer a winter sanctuary for migrating waterfowl. Dogs are allowed on the trails, but not in the water. Pets must be leashed and please clean up after them.

Whittier Narrows Recreation Area 823 Lexinton-Gallatin Road South El Monte CA   310-589-3200
This 1,400 acre day use park offers a wide variety of land and water recreational opportunities, in addition to hosting carnivals, festivals, and dog shows. Some of the features/amenities include fishing lakes, comfort stations, gaming courts/fields, playgrounds, picnicking areas, and hiking and multi-use trails. Dogs are allowed throughout the park and on the trails. Dogs must be under owner's immediate control, leashed, and cleaned up after at all times.

Off-Leash Dog Parks

Arcadia Dog Park Second Avenue and Colorado Blvd Arcadia CA   626-574-5400
The fenced dog park is located in Eisenhower Park in Arcadia. The park is open from 7 am to 10 pm daily. On even numbered days the park is reserved for small dogs. On odd numbered days it is open to large dogs. The park is near I-210 at the Santa Anita Ave exit. Go north on Santa Anita, turn right on E Foothill and go right on 2nd Ave to the park.

Alice Frost Kennedy Off-Leash Dog Area 3026 East Orange Grove Blvd Pasadena CA   626-744-4321
The dog park is located in Vina Vieja Park. It is open during daylight hours and is 2.5 acres and fenced. There is a large dog area and a small dog area. The dog park has a grass surface with no herbicides used. The park is maintained by the City of Pasadena and capital improvements are done by POOCH, a dog group in Pasadena. To get to the dog park from I-210 exit at Sierra Madre Blvd and head east. Turn right onto Orange Grove Blvd to the dog park.

Outdoor Restaurants

Matt Denny's Ale House 145 E Huntington Dr Arcadia CA   626-462-0250
This restaurant and bar serves American food. Dogs are allowed at the outdoor tables.

Picasso's Cafe 6070 N. Irwindale Ave. Irwindale CA   626-969-6100
http://www.picassoscafe.com .

The owners of this restaurant are very dog-friendly. This restaurant was one of the sponsors in the spcaLA's 1999 Petelethon. Your pup is welcome to dine with you at the outdoor tables. They serve a full breakfast and lunch. Also enjoy some great dessert from their bakery. The hours are Monday through Friday from 7am-2:30pm. To get there from the 210 Freeway, exit Irwindale and head south. Turn right at Gateway Business and Picasso's is on the corner.

Baja Fresh Mexican Grill 2637 Foothill Blvd La Crescenta CA 818-541-0568
http://www.bajafresh.com
This Mexican restaurant is open for lunch and dinner. They use fresh ingredients and making their salsa and beans daily. Some of the items on their menu include Enchiladas, Burritos, Tacos Salads, Quesadillas, Nachos, Chicken, Steak and more. Well-behaved leashed dogs are allowed at the outdoor tables.

Frank and Joe's Southern Smokehouse 110 E Colorado Blvd Monrovia CA 626-357-1616
This restaurant serves Cajun barbecue food. Dogs are allowed at the outdoor tables.

All India Cafe 39 S Fair Oaks Ave Pasadena CA 626-440-0309
Dogs are allowed at the outdoor tables.

Baja Fresh Mexican Grill 899 E. Del Mar Pasadena CA 626-792-0446
http://www.bajafresh.com
This Mexican restaurant is open for lunch and dinner. They use fresh ingredients and making their salsa and beans daily. Some of the items on their menu include Enchiladas, Burritos, Tacos Salads, Quesadillas, Nachos, Chicken, Steak and more. Well-behaved leashed dogs are allowed at the outdoor tables.

Barney's Ltd 93 W. Colorado Blvd. Pasadena CA 626-577-2739
This restaurant has good chili, salads, sandwiches and a large selection of beers. Your pup is welcome to join you at the outdoor tables.

Camille's Sidewalk Cafe 285 E Green Street Pasadena CA 626-440-1212
A vision of healthier, tastier foods inspired the idea for the freshly made salads, gourmet wraps and sandwiches, drinks, desserts, and coffees that are offered at all of Camille's Cafes. Dogs are allowed to sit with you at your outdoor table. Dogs must be attended to at all times, well behaved, and leashed.

Gaucho Grill 121 W. Colorado Blvd. Pasadena CA 626-683-3580
This restaurant allows dogs to dine with you at their outdoor tables.

Il Fornaio 24 W Union Pasadena CA 626-683-9797
This Italian restaurant features fine dining, wines to compliment your meal from local wineries, and a bakery counter showcasing award-winning baked goods and branded products. There are several seating options; there is a seating area just outside the bakery for guests with pets. Dogs must be well behaved, under owner's control at all times, leashed, and cleaned up after.

Jake's Diner & Billiards 38 W. Colorado Blvd. Pasadena CA 626-568-1602
Come here for some English-style meat pies, burgers or just a beer. Dogs are welcome to join their people and the restaurant staff will even bring out some water for your pup.

Jones Coffee Roasters 537 S Raymond Ave Pasadena CA 626-564-9291
This cafe serves coffee and pastries. Dogs are allowed at the outdoor tables.

Kabuki Japanese Restaurant 88 W. Colorado Blvd. Pasadena CA 626-568-9310
http://www.kabukirestaurants.com
You are welcome to dine with your dog at the outdoor tables.

Malagueta 43 E. Colorado Blvd. Pasadena CA 626-564-8696
http://www.malaguets.net
The outdoor tables are pretty close together, but your dog is welcome to join you for lunch or dinner.

Mi Piace 25 E Colorado Blvd Pasadena CA 626-795-3131
This restaurant serves Italian food. Dogs are allowed at the outdoor tables.

Sorriso Ristorante 168 W Colorado Blvd Pasadena CA 626-793-2233
http://www.sorrisopasadena.com/
This modern Italian supper club offers fine Italian dining, seafood, steaks, and a stylish martini bar that serves over 20 specialty martinis. They feature indoor and outdoor courtyard dining service, and there is also outdoor seating by the front door. Dogs are allowed at the outside tables in the front of the restaurant. They must be well behaved, under owner's control at all times, leashed, and cleaned up after.

South Lake Italian Kitchen 524 S Lake Avenue Pasadena CA 626-792-5984
This restaurant offers a wide range of pastas, pizzas, salads, sandwiches, and is decorated throughout with a dog motif. They welcome your well behaved pet to join you at one of their tables outside. Dogs must be leashed and cleaned up after. There are open Monday through Saturday from 11:30 am to 9 pm.

Wok n Roll 46 E. Colorado Blvd. Pasadena CA 626-304-1000
Not only does this restaurant allow your dog, they will also bring him or her water. Dogs are allowed at the outdoor tables.

Fair Oaks Pharmacy and Soda Fountain 1526 Mission St South Pasadena CA 626-799-1414
This cafe inside a pharmacy serves deli-type food. Dogs are allowed at the outdoor tables.

Baja Fresh Mexican Grill 13582 Whittier Blvd Whittier CA 562-464-5900
http://www.bajafresh.com
This Mexican restaurant is open for lunch and dinner. They use fresh ingredients and making their salsa and beans daily. Some of the items on their menu include Enchiladas, Burritos, Tacos Salads, Quesadillas, Nachos,

Chicken, Steak and more. Well-behaved leashed dogs are allowed at the outdoor tables.

Day Care Centers
Doggy Time 815 N Fair Oaks Ave Pasadena CA   626-449-3644
http://www.doggytime.com
This full service dog care facility offers cage-free daycare, short-term boarding, grooming and a dog supply store.

Day Kennels
PetsHotel by PetsMart Day Kennel 15618 Whittwood Lane Whittier CA   562-902-1394
http://www.petsmart.com/PETsHOTEL/
This PetSmart pet store offers day camp, day care and overnight care. You can drop off and pick up your dog during the hours of 7 am - 7 pm M-S, Sunday 7 am - 6 pm. Dogs are required to have current proof of rabies, DPP and bordatella vaccinations.

Vets and Kennels
Emergency Pet Clinic 3254 Santa Anita Ave El Monte CA   626-579-4550
Monday - Friday 6 pm to 8 am, Noon Saturday to 8 am Monday.
Animal Emergency Clinic 831 Milford St Glendale CA   818-247-3973
Mon - Tues 8 am - 7 pm. Wed - Fri 8 am - 6 pm, Sat 8 am - 12 noon, Closed Sunday.
Crossroads Animal Emergency Hospital 11057 Rosecrans Ave Norwalk CA   562-863-2522
Monday - Thursday 6 pm to 8 am, Friday 6 pm to 8 am Monday.
Animal Emergency Clinic 2121 E Foothill Blvd Pasadena CA   626-564-0704
Monday - Friday 6 pm - 8 am. Saturday 12 noon - Monday 8 am.

Piru

Campgrounds and RV Parks
Olive Grove Campground 4780 Piru Canyon Road Piru CA   805-521-1500
http://www.lake-piru.org/
Located at Lake Piru, this campground allows well-behaved leashed dogs in the developed campgrounds, but not in the water. However, dogs are allowed on a boat on the water. The Marina rents pontoon boats and dogs are allowed on the rentals. Campsite amenities including laundry facilities, showers, water, picnic areas and dumping stations. Five of the RV sites have hookups. There is a $2 per day pet fee, and dogs must have current shot records. Please clean up after your pets. Dogs may not be left unattended outside. The camping and tent areas also allow dogs. There is a dog walk area at the campground.

Attractions
Lake Piru Marina 4780 Piru Canyon Road Piru CA   805-521-1231
http://www.lake-piru.org/
While dogs are not allowed in the water at Lake Piru, they are allowed on a boat on the water. This marina rents pontoon boats starting at $65 for 4 hours. Well-behaved dogs are allowed on the boats.

San Fernando Valley

Accommodations
Motel 6 - Canoga Park 7132 De Soto Avenue Canoga Park CA   818-883-6666 (800-466-8356)
One well-behaved family pet per room. Guest must notify front desk upon arrival. Guest is liable for any damages. In consideration of all guests, pets must never be left unattended in the guest rooms.
Staybridge Suites 21902 Lassen St Chatsworth CA   818-773-0707 (877-270-6405)
Dogs of all sizes are allowed. There is a $50 one time pet fee per visit for one bed suites. There is a $200 one time pet fee per visit for two bed suites. Smoking and non-smoking rooms are available for pets.
Motel 6 - Los Angeles - Van Nuys/Sepulveda 15711 Roscoe Boulevard North Hills CA   818-894-9341 (800-466-8356)
One well-behaved family pet per room. Guest must notify front desk upon arrival. Guest is liable for any damages. In consideration of all guests, pets must never be left unattended in the guest rooms.
Motel 6 - Simi Valley 2566 North Erringer Road Simi Valley CA 805-526-3533 (800-466-8356)

One well-behaved family pet per room. Guest must notify front desk upon arrival. Guest is liable for any damages. In consideration of all guests, pets must never be left unattended in the guest rooms.
Motel 6 - Los Angeles - Sylmar 12775 Encinitas Avenue Sylmar CA 818-362-9491 (800-466-8356)
One well-behaved family pet per room. Guest must notify front desk upon arrival. Guest is liable for any damages. In consideration of all guests, pets must never be left unattended in the guest rooms.
Hilton 6360 Canoga Avenue Woodland Hills CA 818-595-1000
Dogs up to 50 pounds are allowed. There is a $50 per night per pet fee and a pet policy to sign at check in.
Warner Center Marriott 21850 Oxnard Street Woodland Hills CA 818-227-6126
http://www.warnercentermarriott.com
You and your dog are welcome at this Marriott hotel in the heart of the west San Fernando Valley. The hotel is located just off Highway 101 near Topanga Plaza and the Promenade Mall. There is a one time non-refundable $50 pet fee.
Warner Center Marriott Woodland Hills 21850 Oxnard Street Woodland Hills CA 818-887-4800 (800-228-9290)
Dogs of all sizes are allowed. There is a $50 one time additional pet fee per room. Dogs must be leashed, cleaned up after, and the Do Not Disturb sign put on the door and a contact number left with the front desk if they are in the room alone.

Attractions
Paramount Ranch Cornell Road Agoura Hills CA 805-370-2301
Part of the Santa Monica National Recreation Area, Paramount Ranch is a Western Town movie set that has been used in hundreds of televisions shows and movies. Most recently the set was used to film the television show, Dr. Quinn, Medicine Woman from 1991 to 1998. You and your leashed pooch can walk around the set and explore the Western Town. Just remember the town is a movie set only so walk carefully on the boardwalks and do not lean or climb on the buildings. There are also a few trails located in this 700 acre park. The Coyote Canyon Trail is an easy .5 mile round trip which follows a small chaparral-covered canyon and climbs to a small knoll overlooking the valley. It is located on the west side of the Western Town. The Medea Creek Trail is an easy .75 mile round trip which loops through the streamside and oak woodlands. From this trail you an reach the Overlook Trail which is another .5 mile one way moderate climb. The Medea Creek Trail starts at the southern end of the parking area. To get to the park take the Ventura Freeway/101 to the Kanan exit and head south for . 75 miles. Turn left onto Cornell Way and continue south for 2.5 miles to the main entrances on the right side.
Los Encinos State Historic Park 16756 Moorpark Street Encino CA 818-784-4849
http://www.lahacal.org/losencinos.html
This park covers 5 acres and includes several historic buildings. The park contains exhibits on early California ranch life. The springs at this site attracted Native Americans for centuries. The spot later became a stagecoach stopover and a Basque sheepherder's home before construction of the rancho buildings. While dogs are not allowed inside the buildings, they are allowed to walk (leashed) on the grounds. The park is closed on Monday and Tuesday. The rest of the week, the park is open from 10am-5pm.
The Dogs Gallery 31139 Via Colinas, Suite 204 Westlake Village CA 818-707-8070
http://www.thedogsgallery.com/
This fine art gallery offers 2,000 square feet of contemporary paintings, sculptures and photographs of dogs and other animals. North American artists are featured. Well-behaved leashed dogs are welcome at the art gallery. There are a couple of dogs on the premises but they are usually put in the office when there are dog visitors.

Stores
Petco Pet Store 6615 Fallbrook Avenue Canoga Park CA 818-883-0210
Your licensed and well-behaved leashed dog is allowed in the store.
Petco Pet Store 17919 Ventura Blvd Encino CA 818-343-1124
Your licensed and well-behaved leashed dog is allowed in the store.
Petco Pet Store 8800 Tampa Avenue Northridge CA 818-993-1871
Your licensed and well-behaved leashed dog is allowed in the store.
Petco Pet Store 19869 Rinaldi St Porter Ranch CA 818-368-3062
Your licensed and well-behaved leashed dog is allowed in the store.
Three Dog Bakery 14545 Ventura Blvd Sherman Oaks CA 818-304-0440
http://www.threedog.com
Three Dog Bakery provides cookies and snacks for your dog as well as some boutique items. You well-behaved, leashed dog is welcome.
PetSmart Pet Store 455 E Cochran St Simi Valley CA 805-306-1912
Your licensed and well-behaved leashed dog is allowed in the store.
Petco Pet Store 12800 Ventura Blvd Studio City CA 818-506-6416
Your licensed and well-behaved leashed dog is allowed in the store.
Petco Pet Store 5850 Sepulveda Blvd Van Nuys CA 818-997-4009
Your licensed and well-behaved leashed dog is allowed in the store.

PetSmart Pet Store 5766 Lindero Canyon Rd Westlake Village CA 818-865-8626
Your licensed and well-behaved leashed dog is allowed in the store.
PetSmart Pet Store 22914 Victory Blvd Woodland Hills CA 818-340-2816
Your licensed and well-behaved leashed dog is allowed in the store.
Petco Pet Store 21943-21947 Ventura Blvd Woodland Hills CA 818-346-9397
Your licensed and well-behaved leashed dog is allowed in the store.

Parks

Peter Strauss Ranch Mulholland Highway Agoura Hills CA 805-370-2301
http://www.nps.gov/samo/maps/peter.htm
The Peter Strauss Trail is an easy .6 mile round trip trail which traverses through chaparral and oak trees. Dogs are allowed on the trail but must be leashed and people need to clean up after their pets. From the Ventura Freeway/101, take the Kanan exit and head south for 2.8 miles to Troutdale Rd. Turn left onto Troutdale Rd and then left on Mulholland Highway. This park is part of the Santa Monica Recreation Area.
Rocky Oaks Park Mulholland Highway Agoura Hills CA 805-370-2301
This park offers an open grassland area with oak groves and small rock outcroppings. There are four trails ranging from 100 yards to just over one mile and are rated easy to moderate. Dogs are allowed on the trails but must be leashed and people need to clean up after their pets. To get there take the Ventura Freeway/101 to Kanan Road. Head south on Kanan and then turn right on Mulholland Highway. Then make a right into the parking lot. This park is part of the Santa Monica Recreation Area.
Beilenson Park Lake Balboa 6300 Balboa Blvd Encino CA 818-756-9743
This park consists of large grass fields, sports fields and a nice lake. There is an approximate 1 mile walk around the lake perimeter. You and your leashed pup are welcome to explore this 70+ acre park. To get there, take the Balboa Blvd exit from Hwy 101. Head north on Balboa.
San Vicente Mountain Park 17500 Mulholland Drive Encino CA 310-589-3200
This 10.2 acre park is a historical military site, complete with a radar tower that features 360 degree spectacular views, making it a great place for sunsets. There are self-guided interpretive displays, restrooms, drinking water, picnic tables, and a large network of multi-use trails. The park is located about a 10 minute walk along a dirt road from the parking area. Dogs are allowed at this park; they must be leashed, under owner's immediate control, and cleaned up after at all times.
O'Melveny Park Orozco Street Granada Hills CA
This 600+ acre park has a nice variety of single track and fire road hiking trails. The park is popular with bird watchers, mountain bikers, hikers and leashed dogs. The best way to get there is from Hwy 118. Take the Balboa Blvd. exit and head north. Go about 1.5 to 2 miles and turn left onto Orozco. Take this road to the park.
Hansen Dam 11770 Foothill Blvd. Lakeview Terrace CA 818-756-8190
This 1,437-acre basin has lots of hills and grassy meadows. There are several large picnic areas and firepits, and a children's play area. There wasn't much water in the lake but your leashed pup will have lots of land to roam. To get there, take Hwy 210 and exit Foothill Blvd south. The park will be on your left.
Angeles National Forest Little Tujunga Canyon Rd. San Fernando CA 626-574-1613
This forest is over 690,000 acres and covers one-fourth of the land in Los Angeles County. We have selected a couple of trails near San Fernando Valley ranging from 2.5 to 3 miles. Dogs are allowed on leash or leash free but under voice control. Both of the trails are single-track, foot trails. The first trail is called Gold Creek Trail. It is about 2.5 miles long. The second trail is called Oaks Springs Trail and it is about 3 miles long. To get there from Hwy 215, take the Foothill Blvd. exit and head north towards the mountains. Turn left onto Little Tujunga Canyon Rd. You will see the Little Tujunga Forest Station on the left. After you pass the station, continue on Little Tujunga Canyon Rd. Go about 1-1.5 miles and then turn right onto Gold Creek Rd. Go about 1 mile and on the right you will see the trailhead for Oak Springs Trail. If you continue to the end of Gold Creek Rd, you will see the trailhead for Gold Creek Trail. There should be parking along the road.
Van Nuys/Sherman Oaks Park 14201 Huston St Sherman Oaks CA 818-783-5121
This park has an approximate 1.5 mile walking and jogging path that winds through and around the sports fields. There are also many picnic tables near the Recreation Center. To get there from Hwy 101, take the Van Nuys exit and head north.
Corriganville Park 7001 Smith Road Simi Valley CA 805-584-4400
Once owned by a cowboy actor and used as a western setting for hundreds of movies and TV shows in the 1940's and 50's, this 190 acre day use park now offers visitors several recreational activities, hiking trails, picnic areas, park benches, restrooms, and drinking fountains. Dogs are allowed throughout the park and on the trails. Dogs must be under owner's immediate control, leashed, and cleaned up after at all times.

Off-Leash Dog Parks

Sepulveda Basin Dog Park 17550 Victory Blvd. Encino CA 818-756-7667
Sepulveda Basin Dog Park is located near the Sepulveda Dam Rec Area. It consists of 5 acres of legal off-leash roaming that is fully fenced. There is a smaller area for small dogs that is about half an acre. The dog park is near the junction of I 405 with Highway 101. It is at the corner of White Oak Ave and Victory Blvd. There is

parking for about 100 cars at the location.

Outdoor Restaurants

Adobe Cantina 29100 Agoura Rd Agoura Hills CA   818-991-3474
http://www.venturabiz.com/adobecantina/
Dogs are allowed at a couple of the outdoor perimeter tables at this Mexican restaurant.
Telly's Diner 27125 Sierra Hwy Canyon Country CA   661-250-0444
Thanks to one of our readers who writes: "Traditional diner fare and Greek dishes. Breakfast, lunch, dinner."
Baja Fresh Mexican Grill 16542 Ventura Blvd Encino CA   818-907-9998
http://www.bajafresh.com
This Mexican restaurant is open for lunch and dinner. They use fresh ingredients and making their salsa and beans daily. Some of the items on their menu include Enchiladas, Burritos, Tacos Salads, Quesadillas, Nachos, Chicken, Steak and more. Well-behaved leashed dogs are allowed at the outdoor tables.
Cha Cha Cha 17499 Ventura Boulevard Encino CA   818-789-3600
They have one outdoor table and your pooch is welcome. This restaurant serves contemporary Caribbean and California cuisine.
More Than Waffles 17200 Ventura Blvd. Encino CA   818-789-5937
Dogs are allowed at the outdoor tables. This restaurant is open for breakfast, lunch and dinner. In addition to their huge selection of breakfast favorites like Belgian Waffles, omelettes and pancakes, this restaurant also offers a great selection of foods for lunch and dinner.
Rubio's Restaurant 17200 Ventura Blvd Encino CA   818-784-1497
This popular chain serves a variety of Mexican food like tacos, burritos and more.
Zeke's Smokehouse Restaurant 2209 Honolulu Avenue Montrose CA   818-957-7045
http://www.zekessmokehouse.com/
This is the place to go for contemporary American comfort food and great tasting barbecue. They offer service for their outdoor dining customers, and will even bring out a bowl of water for your canine companion. Your pet is allowed to join you at the outer tables. Dogs must be attended to at all times, well behaved, and leashed.
Whole Foods Market 19340 Rinaldi Northridge CA   818-363-3933
http://www.wholefoods.com/
This natural food supermarket offers natural and organic foods. Order some food from their deli without your dog and bring it to an outdoor table where your well-behaved leashed dog is welcome. Dogs are not allowed in the store including the deli at any time.
Baja Fresh Mexican Grill 19701 Rinaldi St. Porter Ranch CA   818-831-3100
http://www.bajafresh.com
This Mexican restaurant is open for lunch and dinner. They use fresh ingredients and making their salsa and beans daily. Some of the items on their menu include Enchiladas, Burritos, Tacos Salads, Quesadillas, Nachos, Chicken, Steak and more. Well-behaved leashed dogs are allowed at the outdoor tables.
Prism Bistro 9695 Sunland Blvd Shadow Hills CA   818-352-0041
This restaurant serves American food. Dogs are allowed at the outdoor tables.
Baja Fresh Mexican Grill 14622 Ventura Blvd. Sherman Oaks CA   818-789-0602
http://www.bajafresh.com
This Mexican restaurant is open for lunch and dinner. They use fresh ingredients and making their salsa and beans daily. Some of the items on their menu include Enchiladas, Burritos, Tacos Salads, Quesadillas, Nachos, Chicken, Steak and more. Well-behaved leashed dogs are allowed at the outdoor tables.
Solleys Deli 4578 Van Nuys Blvd Sherman Oaks CA   818-905-5774
This deli is located several blocks from the Van Nuys/Sherman Oaks Park.
Whole Foods Market 12905 Riverside Drive Sherman Oaks CA   818-762-5548
http://www.wholefoods.com/
This natural food supermarket offers natural and organic foods. Order some food from their deli without your dog and bring it to an outdoor table where your well-behaved leashed dog is welcome. Dogs are not allowed in the store including the deli at any time.
Whole Foods Market 4520 Sepulveda Boulevard Sherman Oaks CA   818-382-3700
http://www.wholefoods.com/
This natural food supermarket offers natural and organic foods. Order some food from their deli without your dog and bring it to an outdoor table where your well-behaved leashed dog is welcome. Dogs are not allowed in the store including the deli at any time.
Baja Fresh Mexican Grill 2679 Tapo Cyn Rd Simi Valley CA   805-581-6001
http://www.bajafresh.com
This Mexican restaurant is open for lunch and dinner. They use fresh ingredients and making their salsa and beans daily. Some of the items on their menu include Enchiladas, Burritos, Tacos Salads, Quesadillas, Nachos, Chicken, Steak and more. Well-behaved leashed dogs are allowed at the outdoor tables.
Camille's Sidewalk Cafe 12265 Ventura Blvd, # 101 Studio City CA   818-623-9009
A vision of healthier, tastier foods inspired the idea for the freshly made salads, gourmet wraps and sandwiches, drinks, desserts, and coffees that are offered at all of Camille's Cafes. Dogs are allowed to sit with you at your

outdoor table. Dogs must be attended to at all times, well behaved, and leashed.

Gaucho Grill 12050 Ventura Blvd. Studio City CA 818-508-1030

This Argentinian restaurant is located on the second floor of a strip mall in Studio City. The outdoor seats are pretty popular during the lunch and dinner rush hours, so try to come a little early to ensure a seat.

Killer Shrimp 4000 Colfax Avenue Studio City CA 818-508-1570

Although they offer a rather short menu, this eatery's claim to fame is its rich, spicy broth with fresh Louisiana shrimp, along with a good selection of beer and wine. Your well behaved dog is welcome to join you at the outside tables. Dogs must be attended to all times and leashed.

Louise's Trattoria 12050 Ventura Blvd. Studio City CA 818-762-2662

This Italian restaurant is located on the second floor of a strip mall in Studio City. The outdoor seats are pretty popular during the lunch and dinner rush hours, so try to come a little early to ensure a seat.

Studio Yogurt 12050 Ventura Blvd Studio City CA 818-508-7811

This yogurt shops allows dogs at the outdoor tables.

Teru Sushi 1194 Ventura Blvd Studio City CA 818-763-6201

http://www.terusushi.com/

This popular sushi bar also features a good variety of fine Japanese cuisine. They offer 3 dining areas, including an outdoor Japanese garden setting with a koi pond and a waterfall. Dogs are allowed at the outdoor tables. They must be well behaved, under owner's control at all times, leashed, and cleaned up after.

Big Jim's 8950 Laurel Canyon Blvd Sun Valley CA 818-843-0213

Thanks to one of our readers who writes: "Outdoor patio is shady with plants and a fountain. Steaks, Mexican, Sunday Champagne Brunch."

Baja Fresh Mexican Grill 10760 Riverside Drive Toluca Lake CA 818-762-7326

http://www.bajafresh.com

This Mexican restaurant is open for lunch and dinner. They use fresh ingredients and making their salsa and beans daily. Some of the items on their menu include Enchiladas, Burritos, Tacos Salads, Quesadillas, Nachos, Chicken, Steak and more. Well-behaved leashed dogs are allowed at the outdoor tables.

Priscilla's Gourmet Cafe 4150 Riverside Dr Toluca Lake CA 818-843-5707

This cafe serves deli-type food and coffee. Dogs are allowed at the outdoor tables. Walk up window available so that pets don't have to be left alone.

Springboc Bar and Grill 16153 Victory Blvd Van Nuys CA 818-988-9786

http://www.springbokbar.com

This restaurant serves American food. Dogs are allowed at the outdoor tables.

Baja Fresh Mexican Grill 30861 Thousand Oaks Blvd. Westlake Village CA 818-889-1347

http://www.bajafresh.com

This Mexican restaurant is open for lunch and dinner. They use fresh ingredients and making their salsa and beans daily. Some of the items on their menu include Enchiladas, Burritos, Tacos Salads, Quesadillas, Nachos, Chicken, Steak and more. Well-behaved leashed dogs are allowed at the outdoor tables.

Jack's Restaurant and Deli 966 South Westlake Blvd Westlake Village CA 805-495-8181

This restaurant serves American food. Dogs are allowed at the outdoor tables. Water is provided and dog biscuits are on the menu.

Baja Fresh Mexican Grill 19960 Ventura Blvd. Woodland Hills CA 818-888-3976

http://www.bajafresh.com

This Mexican restaurant is open for lunch and dinner. They use fresh ingredients and making their salsa and beans daily. Some of the items on their menu include Enchiladas, Burritos, Tacos Salads, Quesadillas, Nachos, Chicken, Steak and more. Well-behaved leashed dogs are allowed at the outdoor tables.

Baja Fresh Mexican Grill 5780 Canoga Avenue Woodland Hills CA 818-347-9033

http://www.bajafresh.com

This Mexican restaurant is open for lunch and dinner. They use fresh ingredients and making their salsa and beans daily. Some of the items on their menu include Enchiladas, Burritos, Tacos Salads, Quesadillas, Nachos, Chicken, Steak and more. Well-behaved leashed dogs are allowed at the outdoor tables.

La Fontana di Trevi 21733 Ventura Blvd Woodland Hills CA 818-888-0206

There is a covered outdoor seating area for you and your pup.

My Brother's BBQ 21150 Ventura Blvd Woodland Hills CA 818-348-2020

The barbecue smoke coming from this restaurant will attract any barbecue lover. They have several outdoor tables where your pup can join you for lunch or dinner.

Pickwick's Pub 21010 Ventura Blvd Woodland Hills CA 818-340-9673

Dogs are allowed at the outdoor tables.

Whole Foods Market 21347 Ventura Blvd. Woodland Hills CA 818-610-0000

http://www.wholefoods.com/

This natural food supermarket offers natural and organic foods. Order some food from their deli without your dog and bring it to an outdoor table where your well-behaved leashed dog is welcome. Dogs are not allowed in the store including the deli at any time.

Golden State Wok 21028 Victory Blvd Woodlawn Hills CA 818-884-1369

This restaurant serves Chinese food. Dogs are allowed at the outdoor tables.

Vets and Kennels

Affordable Animal Emergency Clinic 16907 San Fernando Mission Granada Hills CA   818-363-8143
Monday - Friday 6 pm - Midnight for appointments, Midnight to 8 am for emergencies. Saturday 1:30 pm - Monday 8 am. You must call ahead during emergency hours after midnight.
Emergency Animal Clinic 14302 Ventura Blvd Sherman Oaks CA   818-788-7860
24 hours everyday.
Animal Emergency Center 11740 Ventura Blvd Studio City CA   818-760-3882
Monday - Friday 6 pm to 8 am, Saturday 2 pm - Monday 8 am.

Santa Clarita

Accommodations

Residence Inn by Marriott 25320 The Old Road Santa Clarita CA 661-290-2800
Dogs of all sizes are allowed. There is a $75 one time fee per pet plus $10 per night per pet and a pet policy to sign at check in.

Stores

PetSmart Pet Store 24965 Pico Canyon Rd Stevenson Ranch CA   661-260-3990
Your licensed and well-behaved leashed dog is allowed in the store.
Starpups Depot 25818 Hemingway Avenue Stevenson Ranch CA   661-255-2208
http://www.starpupsdepot.com/
This is an upscale dog boutique that caters to discerning dogs and their people, and they offer a large selection of gifts, toys, treats, and even birthday cakes. They are open from 10 am to 7 pm Tuesday through Friday; 10 am to 6 pm on Saturday; 11 am to 5 pm on Sunday, and closed Mondays. Well behaved, leashed dogs are allowed to explore the store with their owners.

Thousand Oaks

Accommodations

Holiday Inn 1320 Newbury Road Thousand Oaks CA   805-499-5910 (877-270-6405)
Dogs of all sizes are allowed. There is a $30 one time per pet fee per visit. Smoking and non-smoking rooms are available for pets.
Thousand Oaks Inn 75 W. Thousand Oaks Blvd. Thousand Oaks CA   805-497-3701
This motel allows both dogs and cats. They have a $75 non-refundable pet deposit.

Stores

Petco Pet Store 140 West Hillcrest Drive, Ste 101 Thousand Oaks CA   805-777-7554
Your licensed and well-behaved leashed dog is allowed in the store.

Parks

Ahmanson Ranch Park 26135 Mureau Road Calabasas CA   818-878-4225
http://smmc.ca.gov/
This park is part of the Santa Monica Mountains Conservancy and allows leashed dogs on the trails. Please clean up after your pets. No hunting is allowed in the park. In the past, some movies have been filmed at this ranch, including Gone With The Wind. The easiest access to the trails is at the north end of Las Virgenes Road. In early 2004 there are plans to having a parking area at the end of Victory Blvd. in Woodland Hills.
Santa Monica Mountains National Recreation Area 401 West Hillcrest Drive Thousand Oaks CA   805-370-2301
http://www.nps.gov/samo/index.htm
Dogs on leash are allowed in the park. They must stay on trails, roads and campgrounds. They are not allowed in any buildings or undeveloped areas. This park features fishing, hiking, camping, swimming, and more.
Wildwood Regional Park Ave. De Los Arboles Thousand Oaks CA
This park has hiking trails that run along a beautiful hill and streams (the streams have water at certain times of the year). It makes for a great morning hike in the summer. Leashed dogs are allowed on the trails. There are also picnic tables at the park. During the winter (rainy season), the trails are subject to flash flooding. To get there from the 101 freeway, take the Lynn Road exit and head north. Turn left onto Avenida de los Arboles. Go

until you reach Wildwood School. Park there and take the trail to the left of the parking lot. It will take you to a large wooden "Fort". Go past or through the fort to the trails. Thanks to one of our readers for recommending this park.

Off-Leash Dog Parks
Calabasas Bark Park Las Virgines Road Calabasas CA
Thanks to one of our readers for recommending this dog park. It is located on Las Virgines Road, south of the Agoura Road and Las Virgines Road intersection. This fenced dog park is open from 5 am to 9 pm daily. There is a separate fenced children's play area next to the dog park.
Thousand Oaks Dog Park Avenida de las Flores Thousand Oaks CA 805-495-6471
http://www.pvrpd.org
This 3.75 acre enclosed dog park has a separate section for large dogs and small dogs. Amenities include picnic tables and three drinking fountains. The dog park is located at Avenida de las Flores, at the northwest quadrant of Conejo Creek.

Outdoor Restaurants
Red Robin Gourmet Burgers 24005 Calabasas Rd Calabasas CA 818-223-8112
This restaurant serves American food. Dogs are allowed at the outdoor tables.
Baja Fresh Mexican Grill 595 N Moorpark Rd Thousand Oaks CA 805-778-0877
http://www.bajafresh.com
This Mexican restaurant is open for lunch and dinner. They use fresh ingredients and making their salsa and beans daily. Some of the items on their menu include Enchiladas, Burritos, Tacos Salads, Quesadillas, Nachos, Chicken, Steak and more. Well-behaved leashed dogs are allowed at the outdoor tables.
Thousand Oaks Meat Locker 2684 E Thousand Oaks Blvd Thousand Oaks CA 805-495-3211
The Meat Locker tempts barbecue lovers with their large outdoor barbecue. Dogs are allowed at the outdoor tables.
Baja Fresh Mexican Grill 22815 Victory Blvd. Ste C West Hills CA 818-704-4267
http://www.bajafresh.com
This Mexican restaurant is open for lunch and dinner. They use fresh ingredients and making their salsa and beans daily. Some of the items on their menu include Enchiladas, Burritos, Tacos Salads, Quesadillas, Nachos, Chicken, Steak and more. Well-behaved leashed dogs are allowed at the outdoor tables.

Vets and Kennels
Pet Emergency Clinic 2967 N Moorpark Rd Thousand Oaks CA 805-492-2436
Monday - Friday 6 pm to 8 am, 24 hours on weekends.

Topanga

Outdoor Restaurants
Abuelitas Restaurant 137 South Topanga Canyon Blvd Topanga CA 310-455-8788
This restaurant serves Mexican food. Dogs are allowed at the outdoor tables.

Valencia

Stores
Petco Pet Store 26501 Bouquet Canyon Rd Saugus CA 661-297-6936
Your licensed and well-behaved leashed dog is allowed in the store.

Outdoor Restaurants
Baja Fresh Mexican Grill 23630 W. Valencia Blvd. Valencia CA 661-254-6060
http://www.bajafresh.com
This Mexican restaurant is open for lunch and dinner. They use fresh ingredients and making their salsa and beans daily. Some of the items on their menu include Enchiladas, Burritos, Tacos Salads, Quesadillas, Nachos, Chicken, Steak and more. Well-behaved leashed dogs are allowed at the outdoor tables.
Cabo Cabana 25710 The Old Road Valencia CA 661-222-7022
Thanks to one of our readers who recommended this restaurant. The restaurant serves Mexican food.
Wahoo's Fish Taco 24230 Valencia Blvd Valencia CA 661-255-5138
This restaurant serves Mexican food. Dogs are allowed at the outdoor tables.

Chapter 11

California - Orange County
Dog Travel Guide

Anaheim Resort Area

Accommodations

Anaheim Marriott

Anaheim Marriott 700 W Convention Way Anaheim CA 714-750-8000 (800-228-9290)
Dogs of all sizes are allowed. There is a $50 one time additional pet fee per room. Dogs must be leashed, cleaned up after, and placed in a crate or the bathroom if they are left in the room alone.
Best Western Anaheim Hils 5710 East La Palma Anaheim CA 714-779-0252 (800-780-7234)
Dogs of all sizes are allowed. There is a $15 per night pet fee per pet. Smoking and non-smoking are available for pet rooms.
Embassy Suites Hotel Anaheim - North near Disneyland 3100 E. Frontera Anaheim CA 714-632-1221
Dogs of all sizes are allowed. There is a $50 one time pet fee per visit. Dogs are not allowed to be left alone in the room.
Hilton 777 Convention Way Anaheim CA 714-750-4321
Dogs up to 40 pounds are allowed. There is a pet policy to sign at check in, there are no additional fees, and dogs are not allowed to be left alone in the room.
Motel 6 - Anaheim - Fullerton East 1440 North State College Boulevard Anaheim CA 714-956-9690 (800-466-8356)
One well-behaved family pet per room. Guest must notify front desk upon arrival. Guest is liable for any damages. In consideration of all guests, pets must never be left unattended in the guest rooms.
Red Roof Inn - Anaheim Maingate 100 Disney Way Anaheim CA 714-520-9696 (800-RED-ROOF)
One well-behaved dog up to about 80 pounds is allowed. There are no additional pet fees.
Residence Inn by Marriott 1700 S Clementine Street Anaheim CA 714-533-3555
Dogs of all sizes are welcome. There is a $75 plus tax one time fee, and they request a credit card on file.
Staybridge Suites 1855 South Manchester Avenue Anaheim CA 714-748-7700 (877-270-6405)
Dogs of all sizes are allowed. There is a $150 one time additional pet fee.
Motel 6 - Buena Park-Knotts/Disneyland 7051 Valley View Street Buena Park CA 714-522-1200 (800-466-8356)
One well-behaved family pet per room. Guest must notify front desk upon arrival. Guest is liable for any

damages. In consideration of all guests, pets must never be left unattended in the guest rooms.

Red Roof Inn - Buena Park 7121 Beach Boulevard Buena Park CA 714-670-9000 (800-RED-ROOF)
One well-behaved family pet per room. Guest must notify front desk upon arrival. Guest is liable for any damages. In consideration of all guests, pets must never be left unattended in the guest rooms.

Woodfin Suite Hotel 5905 Corporate Ave Cypress CA 714-828-4000
All rooms are non-smoking. All well-behaved dogs are welcome. Every room is a suite with wetbars or full kitchens. Hotel amenities include a pool, exercise facility, complimentary video movies, and a complimentary hot breakfast buffet. There is a $5 per day pet fee and you will need to sign a pet waiver.

Fullerton Marriott at California State University 2701 E Nutwood Avenue Fullerton CA 714-738-7800 (800-228-9290)
Dogs up to 50 pounds are allowed. There is a $100 refundable deposit plus a $20 per night per pet additional fee. Dogs must be well behaved, leashed, cleaned up after, removed or accompanied for housekeeping, and the Do Not Disturb sign put on the door if they are in the room alone.

Anaheim Marriott Suites 12015 Harbor Blvd Garden Grove CA 714-750-1000 (800-228-9290)
Dogs of all sizes are allowed. There is a $15 per night per pet additional fee, and a pet policy to sign at check in. Dogs may not be left alone in the room, and they must be leashed and cleaned up after.

Candlewood Suites 12901 Garden Grove Blvd Garden Grove CA 714-539-4200 (877-270-6405)
Dogs of any size are allowed. There is a $75 one time pet fee for stays up to 15 days. For longer stays, the pet fee is $150.

Residence Inn by Marriott 11931 Harbor Blvd Garden Grove CA 714-591-4000
Dogs of all sizes are welcome. There is a $60 per pet per stay fee, and a pet policy to sign at check in.

Residence Inn by Marriott 4931 Katella Avenue Los Alamitos CA 714-484-5700
Dogs up to 75 pounds are allowed. There is a $75 one time fee, and a pet policy to sign at check in.

Motel 6 - Anaheim Stadium - Orange 2920 West Chapman Avenue Orange CA 714-634-2441 (800-466-8356)
One well-behaved dog up to about 80 pounds is allowed. There are no additional pet fees.

Candlewood Suites 2600 S. Red Hill Avenue Santa Ana CA 949-250-0404 (877-270-6405)
Dogs up to 80 pounds are allowed. There is a $75 one time pet fee per visit.

La Quinta Inn Santa Ana 2721 Hotel Terrace Santa Ana CA 714-540-1111 (800-531-5900)
Dogs up to 75 pounds are allowed. There are no additional pet fees. Dogs must be leashed, cleaned up after, and removed for housekeeping.

Motel 6 - Santa Ana 1623 East 1st Street Santa Ana CA 714-558-0500 (800-466-8356)
One well-behaved family pet per room. Guest must notify front desk upon arrival. Guest is liable for any damages. In consideration of all guests, pets must never be left unattended in the guest rooms.

Quality Suites, John Wayne Airport 2701 Hotel Terrace Drive Santa Ana CA 714-641-8936
Dogs of all sizes are allowed. There is a $25 per day per room additional pet fee. Dogs must be leashed when out of the room, and cleaned up after. Please put the Do Not Disturb sign on the door if there is a pet in the room alone, and make arrangements for housekeeping.

Red Roof Inn - Irvine - Orange County Airport 1717 East Dyer Road Santa Ana CA 949-261-1515 (800-RED-ROOF)
One well-behaved family pet per room. Guest must notify front desk upon arrival. Guest is liable for any damages. In consideration of all guests, pets must never be left unattended in the guest rooms.

Red Roof Inn - Santa Ana 2600 North Main Street Santa Ana CA 714-542-0311 (800-RED-ROOF)
One well-behaved family pet per room. Guest must notify front desk upon arrival. Guest is liable for any damages. In consideration of all guests, pets must never be left unattended in the guest rooms.

Motel 6 - Stanton 7450 Katella Avenue Stanton CA 714-891-0717 (800-466-8356)
One well-behaved family pet per room. Guest must notify front desk upon arrival. Guest is liable for any damages. In consideration of all guests, pets must never be left unattended in the guest rooms.

Motel 6 - Westminster North 13100 Goldenwest Street Westminster CA 714-895-0042 (800-466-8356)
One well-behaved family pet per room. Guest must notify front desk upon arrival. Guest is liable for any damages. In consideration of all guests, pets must never be left unattended in the guest rooms.

Motel 6 - Westminster South - Long Beach 6266 Westminster Avenue Westminster CA 714-891-5366 (800-466-8356)
One well-behaved family pet per room. Guest must notify front desk upon arrival. Guest is liable for any damages. In consideration of all guests, pets must never be left unattended in the guest rooms.

Campgrounds and RV Parks

Canyon RV Park at Featherly 24001 Santa Ana Canyon Road Anaheim CA 714-637-0210
http://www.canyonrvpark.com/about.htm
This RV only park is situated on the Santa Ana River surrounded by mature cottonwood and sycamore trees. They have 140 RV hookup sites. Other amenities include a pool, playground, laundry, acres of wilderness and trees, bike trails, and an amphitheater. This park is about 14 miles from Disneyland. Well-behaved leashed dogs are welcome for an additional $1 per day. Please clean up after your pets. There are some breed restrictions. There is a dog walk area at the campground.

Attractions

Disneyland Kennel 1313 Harbor Blvd Anaheim CA   714-781-4565
http://disney.go.com/Disneyland/
Disneyland is really more of an attraction for people, but we thought we would mention it because of their kennel. The great folks at Disneyland offer a day kennel for your pup while the rest of the family enjoys the theme park. There is a full time attendant at the kennels and the kennel hours are the same as the park hours. The cost is $15 for the whole day and you can come and walk your dog or just say hi as many times as you want. Just be sure to get your hand stamped for in/out park privileges. The cast members (Disneyland employees) suggest that you might want to bring a favorite blanket for your pup to lay on if he or she is used to that. The kennel is located to the right of the main Disneyland entrance/ticket booths. Please note the following special information: When driving to Disneyland, follow the signs to the main parking lot. At the parking garage toll booth, tell the attendant that you have a dog and would like to use the RV/Oversize parking lot so you can be within closer walking distance to the kennels. From this parking lot, you can either walk to the main entrance of Disneyland (about 10-15 minutes) or take the parking lot tram from the parking lot to the entrance. Dogs are allowed on the parking lot tram, just make sure they are in the middle of the seat so they won't fall out during the ride. Once you arrive at Disneyland, make sure you walk your dog straight to the kennels. Dogs are not allowed in Downtown Disney and the security guards will remind you of this. If you are approached by a guard, just ask where the kennels are and they will point you in the right direction. Since August 28, 2006 dogs boarded at the Disneyland Kennel are required to show proof of rabies and distemper vaccines from the dogs vet. This is due to an Orange County requirement placed on kennels in the county.

Stores

Petco Pet Store 430 North Euclid St Anaheim CA   714-635-1714
Your licensed and well-behaved leashed dog is allowed in the store.
Petco Pet Store 8092 East Santa Ana Canyon Rd Anaheim CA   714-998-6833
Your licensed and well-behaved leashed dog is allowed in the store.
PetSmart Pet Store 8321 La Palma Ave Buena Park CA   714-739-2100
Your licensed and well-behaved leashed dog is allowed in the store.
Petco Pet Store 6020 Ball Rd Buena Park CA   714-828-4600
Your licensed and well-behaved leashed dog is allowed in the store.
PetSmart Pet Store 1411 S Harbor Blvd Fullerton CA   714-992-5116
Your licensed and well-behaved leashed dog is allowed in the store.
Barnes and Noble Bookstore 791 S Main Street Orange CA   714-558-0028
Well-behaved, leashed dogs may accompany shoppers in the bookstore or at the outdoor tables at the coffee shop.
Petco Pet Store 1824 E Katella Avenue Orange CA   714-289-1400
Your licensed and well-behaved leashed dog is allowed in the store.
PetSmart Pet Store 2140 E 17th St Santa Ana CA   714-480-0620
Your licensed and well-behaved leashed dog is allowed in the store.
Petco Pet Store 3327 S Bristol St Santa Ana CA   714-979-3802
Your licensed and well-behaved leashed dog is allowed in the store.
Petco Pet Store 13942 Newport Avenue Tustin CA   714-669-9030
Your licensed and well-behaved leashed dog is allowed in the store.
Petco Pet Store 6761 Westminster Blvd Westminster CA   714-799-4558
Your licensed and well-behaved leashed dog is allowed in the store.

Parks

Santa Ana River Path E. La Palma Ave. Anaheim CA
This path stretches for about 20 miles each way. The trail parallels the Santa Ana River. In most spots, there are two sets of trails, one for bikes and one for horses. Dogs are allowed on either trail (paved and dirt). Parking is available at the Yorba Regional Park which is located on E. La Palma Avenue between the Imperial Hwy (Hwy 90) and S. Weir Canyon Rd. There is a minimal fee for parking.
Yorba Regional Park E. La Palma Ave. Anaheim CA   714-970-1460
This regional park has 175 acres with several streams and four lakes. There are also over 400 picnic tables and over 200 barbecue stoves. If you want an longer walk or jog, the park is adjacent to the twenty mile long Santa Ana River Bike Path and Trail. The park is located on E. La Palma Avenue between the Imperial Hwy (Hwy 90) and S. Weir Canyon Rd. There is a minimal fee for parking.
Irvine Regional Park 1 Irvine Park Rd Orange CA   714-633-8074
Located in the foothills, this is California's oldest regional park. With over 470 acres, this park has a variety of Oak and Sycamore groves, streams, a pond, a paved trail, picnic tables and barbecues. There are also several historical sites and plaques located throughout the park. Maps are available from the park ranger at the main entrance. Because this park is also a wilderness area with mountain lions, park rules state that minors must be

under adult supervision at all times. Dogs must be leashed. There is a minimal parking fee.

Peters Canyon Regional Park Canyon View Ave Orange CA 714-973-6611
This park has over 350 acres of coastal sage scrub, woodlands, a freshwater marsh, and a 55 acre reservoir. They have a variety of dirt paths and trails (approx. 2-3 miles) which are frequented by hikers, mountain bikers, equestrians and of course, leashed dogs. All trails are closed for three days following rainfall. To get there from Hwy 5 or Hwy 405, take the Jamboree Road exit north. Then turn left at Canyon View Ave. Proceed 1/4 mile to the park entrance and parking lot. Maps should be available at a stand near the parking lot.

Centennial Regional Park 3000 W Edinger Avenue Santa Ana CA 714-571-4200
This large, day-use park features a 10 acre lake stocked with fish and an historic trail that follows the original path of the Santa Ana River. There are picnic areas, restrooms, and several multi-use trails. Dogs are allowed throughout the park and on the trails. Dogs must be well behaved, leashed, and cleaned up after at all times.

Off-Leash Dog Parks

Yorba Dog Park 190 S Yorba Street Orange CA 714-633-2980
http://www.orangedogpark.com/
There is a separate small dog section at this park, and until there are benches installed, lawn chairs may be brought into the park and set along the fence that separates the big dog/small dog areas. Chairs must be taken out each night. The park is closed for maintenance on Wednesdays.

Outdoor Restaurants

Rubios Baja Grill 520 N Euclid St Anaheim CA 714-999-1525
This restaurant serves Mexican food. Dogs are allowed at the outdoor tables

Subway Sandwiches 514 N Euclid Street Anaheim CA 714-535-3444
Dogs are allowed at the outdoor tables.

Baja Fresh Mexican Grill 7855 La Palma Blvd. Buena Park CA 714-521-9500
http://www.bajafresh.com
This Mexican restaurant is open for lunch and dinner. They use fresh ingredients and making their salsa and beans daily. Some of the items on their menu include Enchiladas, Burritos, Tacos Salads, Quesadillas, Nachos, Chicken, Steak and more. Well-behaved leashed dogs are allowed at the outdoor tables.

Byblos Mediterranean Cafe 129 W Chapman Ave Orange CA 714-538-7180
Dogs are allowed at the outdoor tables.

Krispy Kreme Doughnuts 330 The City Dr S Orange CA 714-769-4330
Dogs are allowed at the outdoor tables.

The Filling Station 201 N Glassell St Orange CA 714-289-9714
This restaurant serves American food. Dogs are allowed at the outdoor tables.

Two's Company 22 Plaza Square Orange CA 714-771-7633
Dogs are allowed at the outdoor tables.

Whole Foods Market 14945 Holt Ave. Tustin CA 714-731-3400
http://www.wholefoods.com/
This natural food supermarket offers natural and organic foods. Order some food from their deli without your dog and bring it to an outdoor table where your well-behaved leashed dog is welcome. Dogs are not allowed in the store including the deli at any time.

Lazy Dog Cafe 16310 Beach Blvd Westminster CA 714-848-4300
This restaurant serves American, Italian, and Asian food. Dogs are allowed at the outdoor tables. Water is provided for your pet.

Vets and Kennels

Orange County Emergency Pet Hospital 12750 Garden Grove Blvd Garden Grove CA 714-537-3032
Monday - Friday 6pm to 8am, Noon Saturday to 8 am Monday.

Orange County Beaches

Accommodations

Holiday Inn 3131 S, Bristol Street Costa Mesa CA 714-557-3000 (877-270-6405)
Dogs up to 50 pounds are allowed. There is a $50 one time additional pet fee. Dogs are allowed on the first floor,which is non-smoking.

Motel 6 - Costa Mesa 1441 Gisler Avenue Costa Mesa CA 714-957-3063 (800-466-8356)
One well-behaved family pet per room. Guest must notify front desk upon arrival. Guest is liable for any damages. In consideration of all guests, pets must never be left unattended in the guest rooms.

Residence Inn by Marriott 881 W Baker Street Costa Mesa CA 714-241-8800

Dogs of all sizes are welcome. There is a $75 plus tax one time fee, and a pet policy to sign at check in.
The Westin South Coast Plaza 686 Anton Blvd. Costa Mesa CA 714-540-2500 (888-625-5144)
Dogs up to 80 pounds are allowed. There are no additional pet fees.
Vagabond Inn 3205 Harbor Blvd Costa Mesa CA 714-557-8360
http://www.vagabondinn.com/
This motel offers a complimentary continental breakfast. The Bark Park dog park is located nearby. There is a
$5 per day pet fee.
Residence Inn by Marriott 9930 Slater Avenue Fountain Valley CA 714-965-8000
Pets of all sizes are allowed. There is a $75 one time fee, and a pet policy to sign at check in.

Campgrounds and RV Parks

Bolsa Chica State Beach Campground Pacific Coast H Huntington Beach CA 714-377-5691 (800-444-7275)
Most RVs can be accommodated at this campground, just let them know when making a reservation if your RV
is over 25 feet. Tent camping is not allowed. Pets on leash are allowed and please clean up after them. While
dogs are not allowed on this state beach, they are allowed on several miles of paved trails that follow the coast.
Dogs are also allowed at the adjacent Huntington Dog Beach. The campground is located on the Pacific Coast
Highway between Golden West to Warner Avenue. There is a dog walk area at the campground.
Huntington By the Sea 21871 Newland Huntington Beach CA 714-536-8316 (800-439-3486)
http://www.huntingtonbythesea.com
If you love the beach and everything about it, then you will love this RV park, which also provides a host of
amenities. Dogs of all sizes are allowed. There are no additional pet fees. Dogs may not be left unattended
outside, and they must be leashed and cleaned up after. This is an RV only park. There are some breed
restrictions. There is a dog walk area at the campground.

Newport Dunes RV Park

TOP 200 PLACE **Newport Dunes RV Park** 1131 Back Bay Drive Newport Beach CA 949-729-3863 (800-765-7661)
http://www.newportdunes.com
This waterfront resort features lush grounds, many amenities, and a variety of land and water recreation. Dogs of
all sizes are allowed for an additional $2 per night per pet for the nightly fee, and an additional $5 per night per
pet for the weekly fee. Dogs may not be left unattended, and they must be leashed and cleaned up after. Dogs
are not allowed on the beach or anywhere on the sand. There are some breed restrictions. The camping and tent
areas also allow dogs. There is a dog walk area at the campground.

Attractions

Boat Rentals of America 510 E Edgewater Newport Beach CA   949-673-7200
http://www.boats4rent.com/
There are a total of 3 boat rental locations in the Southern California area where they offer a variety of safe, reliable watercraft and many recreational boating options. Dogs are welcome aboard the harbor power boat rentals for no additional pet fee as long as the boat is left clean. Dogs must be under owner's control, and leashed and cleaned up after at all times.

Fun Zone Boat Tours

TOP 200 PLACE **Fun Zone Boat Tours** 6000 Edgewater Place Newport Beach CA   949-673-0240
http://newportbeach.com/funzoneboats
The people here are very dog-friendly and welcome your pup on several of their boat tours. The narrated trips range in length from 45 to 90 minutes and can include a harbor, sea lion and Lido Island tour. The prices range from $6.00 to $9.00 and less for children. Prices are subject to change. Boat tours depart every half hour seven days a week. They do have a summer and winter schedule, so please call ahead for the hours. Whale watching tours are also available from January through March. (see Attractions). The Fun Zone Boat Co. is located at the end of Palm Street next to the Ferris Wheel.
Fun Zone Boat-Whale Watching Tours 600 Edgewater Place Newport Beach CA   949-673-0240
http://newportbeach.com/funzoneboats
These nice folks allow dogs on their whale watching boat tours. The tour guide has a golden retriever that rides with him. He asks that your dog be friendly around other dogs and remain leashed while on the boat. He might also limit the number of dogs on the tour depending on how all the pups get along with each other. The whale watching tours are seasonal and last from January through the end of March. Tours are $12 per person for 2 hours. The boat departs for the tour twice per day, so please call ahead for hours. Fun Zone Boat Co. is located off Balboa Blvd. in Balboa (near Newport Beach). It's next to the Balboa Fun Zone and Ferris Wheel.
Marina Water Sports-Boat Rentals 600 E Bay Ave Newport Beach CA   949-673-3372
Want to drive your own rental boat on Newport Bay? This company allows dogs on their pontoon boats. These are flat bottom boats usually with canopies on top which are great for dogs. Rental rates start at $45-50 per hour. They are located on Bay Ave next to the Balboa Fun Zone/Ferris Wheel near Washington Ave and Palm St.

Shopping Centers

Fashion Island Mall

TOP 200 PLACE **Fashion Island Mall** 1133 Newport Center Dr Newport Beach CA 800-495-4753
Fashion Island Mall is known as Southern California's premier open-air shopping center. And they allow dogs.
Some of the stores allow your well-behaved dog inside. Please always ask the store clerk before bringing your
dog inside, just in case policies have changed. For a list of dog-friendly stores, please look at our stores
category. You can also shop at the numerous outdoor retail kiosks located throughout the mall. Work up an
appetite after walking around? Try dining at the fast food court located upstairs which has many outdoor seats
complete with heaters.

Stores

PetSmart Pet Store 620 West 17th St Costa Mesa CA 949-764-9277
Your licensed and well-behaved leashed dog is allowed in the store.
Petco Pet Store 1815 Newport Blvd Costa Mesa CA 949-722-6316
Your licensed and well-behaved leashed dog is allowed in the store.
PetSmart Pet Store 17940 Newhope St Fountain Valley CA 714-241-0317
Your licensed and well-behaved leashed dog is allowed in the store.
Petco Pet Store 16055 Brookhurst St Fountain Valley CA 714-839-2544
Your licensed and well-behaved leashed dog is allowed in the store.
PetSmart Pet Store 7600 Edinger Ave Huntington Beach CA 714-842-5253
Your licensed and well-behaved leashed dog is allowed in the store.
Petco Pet Store 8909 Adams Avenue Huntington Beach CA 714-964-4717
Your licensed and well-behaved leashed dog is allowed in the store.
Petco Pet Store 5961 Warner Avenue Huntington Beach CA 714-846-7331
Your licensed and well-behaved leashed dog is allowed in the store.
Anthropologie Fashion Island Mall Newport Beach CA 949-720-9946
http://www.anthropologie.com/
Your well-behaved leashed dog is allowed inside this store.
Barnes and Noble Fashion Island Mall Newport Beach CA 949-759-0982
http://www.barnesandnoble.com/
Your well-behaved leashed dog is allowed inside this store.
Bebe Fashion Island Mall Newport Beach CA 949-640-2429
http://www.bebe.com/
Your well-behaved leashed dog is allowed inside this store.
Bloomingdale's Fashion Island Mall Newport Beach CA 949-729-6600
http://www.bloomingdales.com/

Your well-behaved leashed dog is allowed inside this store.
Georgiou Fashion Island Mall Newport Beach CA 949-760-2558
Your well-behaved leashed dog is allowed inside this store. They told us on the phone that "We always welcome dogs!".
Neiman Marcus 601 Newport Center Drive Newport Beach CA 949-759-1900
http://www.neimanmarcus.com
This famous department store, which sells everything from clothing to home furnishings, allows your well-behaved leashed dog to shop with you. It is located in Fashion Island Shopping Center, which is very dog-friendly.
Petco Pet Store 1280 Bison Avenue Newport Beach CA 949-759-9520
Your licensed and well-behaved leashed dog is allowed in the store.
Pottery Barn Fashion Island Mall Newport Beach CA 949-644-2406
http://www.potterybarn.com/
Your well-behaved leashed dog is allowed inside this store.
Restoration Hardware Fashion Island Mall Newport Beach CA 949-760-9232
http://www.restorationhardware.com/
Your well-behaved leashed dog is allowed inside this store.
Robinsons-May Fashion Island Mall Newport Beach CA 949-644-2800
http://www.mayco.com/
Your well-behaved leashed dog is allowed inside this store.
Sharper Image Fashion Island Mall Newport Beach CA 949-640-8800
http://www.sharperimage.com/
Your well-behaved leashed dog is allowed inside this store.
St. Croix Fashion Island Mall Newport Beach CA 949-760-8191
http://www.stcroixshop.com/
Your well-behaved leashed dog is allowed inside this store.
The Limited Fashion Island Mall Newport Beach CA 949-720-9891
Your well-behaved leashed dog is allowed inside this store.
Three Dog Bakery 924 Avacado Newport Beach CA 949-760-3647
http://www.threedog.com
Bring your pup here for a real treat. This is a bakery specifically for canines. They have a variety of baked goodies ranging from cookies to cakes for your dog. Come into the store and let your dog drool over the selections.
Victoria's Secret Fashion Island Mall Newport Beach CA 949-721-9606
http://www.victoriassecret.com/
Your well-behaved leashed dog is allowed inside this store.

Beaches

Corona Del Mar State Beach Iris Street and Ocean Blvd. Corona Del Mar CA 949-644-3151
This is a popular beach for swimming, surfing and diving. The sandy beach is about a half mile long. Dogs are allowed on this beach during certain hours. They are allowed before 9am and after 5pm, year round. Pets must be on a 6 foot or less leash. Tickets will be issued if your dog is off leash.
Corona Del Mar State Beach Iris Street and Ocean Blvd. Corona Del Mar CA 949-644-3151
This is a popular beach for swimming, surfing and diving. The sandy beach is about a half mile long. Dogs are allowed on this beach during certain hours. They are allowed before 9am and after 5pm, year round. Pets must be on a 6 foot or less leash. Tickets will be issued if your dog is off leash.
TOP 200 PLACE **Huntington Dog Beach** Pacific Coast Hwy (Hwy 1) Huntington Beach CA 714-841-8644
http://www.dogbeach.org
This beautiful beach is about a mile long and allows dogs from 5 am to 10 pm. Dogs must be under control but may be off leash and owners must pick up after them. Dogs are only allowed on the beach between Golden West Street and Seapoint Ave. Please adhere to these rules as there are only a couple of dog-friendly beaches left in the entire Los Angeles area. The beach is located off the Pacific Coast Hwy (Hwy 1) at Golden West Street. Please remember to pick up after your dog... the city wanted to prohibit dogs in 1997 because of the dog waste left on the beach. But thanks to The Preservation Society of Huntington Dog Beach (http://www.dogbeach.org), it continues to be dog-friendly. City ordinances require owners to pick up after their dogs.
Newport and Balboa Beaches Balboa Blvd. Newport Beach CA 949-644-3211
There are several smaller beaches which run along Balboa Blvd. Dogs are only allowed before 9am and after 5pm, year round. Pets must be on a 6 foot or less leash and people are required to clean up after their pets. Tickets will be issued if your dog is off leash. The beaches are located along Balboa Blvd and ample parking is located near the Balboa and Newport Piers.

Huntington Dog Beach

Parks

Talbert Nature Preserve Victoria Street Costa Mesa CA 949-923-2250
http://www.ocparks.com/Talbert/
This 180 acre park offers hiking trails. Dogs on a 6 foot or less leash are allowed and please clean up after them.
Huntington Central Park Golden West Street Huntington Beach CA 949-960-8847
This city park is over 350 acres with six miles of trails. There are expansive lawns, lots of trees and two lakes.
Huntington Lake is by Inlet Drive between Golden West and Edwards Streets and next to Alice's Breakfast in the
Park Restaurant. Talbert Lake is off Golden West near Slater Ave and Gothard St. The Huntington Dog Park is
located within this park.
Upper Newport Bay Regional Park University Dr & Irvine Ave Newport Beach CA 949-640-1751
This regional park borders the Newport Back Bay and consists of approximately 140 acres of open space. This
coastal wetland is renowned as one of the finest bird watching sites in North America. During winter migration,
there can be tens of thousands of birds at one time. It is also home to six rare or endangered bird species. The
park has a 2-3 mile one-way paved path that is used by walkers, joggers and bicyclists. Additional dirt trails run
along the hills. You can park at a variety of points along the road, but many people park at Irvine Ave and
University Dr. Dogs must be leashed in the park.

Off-Leash Dog Parks

Bark Park Dog Park Arlington Dr Costa Mesa CA 949-73-4101
http://www.cmbarkpark.org
Located in Tewinkle Park, this two acre dog park is fully fenced. It is open from 7am until dusk every day except
for Tuesday, which is clean-up day. The park is located near the Orange County Fairgrounds on Arlington Drive,
between Junipero Drive and Newport Blvd.
Huntington Beach Dog Park Edwards Street Huntington Beach CA 949-536-5672
http://www.hbdogpark.org/
This dog park has a small dog run for pups under 25 pounds and a separate dog run for the larger pooches. It's
been open since 1995 and donations are always welcome. They have a coin meter at the entrance. The money
is used to keep the park maintained and for doggie waste bags. If you want to go for a walk with your leashed
pup afterwards, there many walking trails at the adjacent Huntington Central Park.
Arbor Dog Park Lampson Avenue at Heather St. Seal Beach CA 562-799-9660
This entirely fenced dog park is 2 1/2 acres in size. It has a number of large shade trees. There is water for
people and dogs. The dog park is open during all daylight hours weather permitting except that it is closed on

Thursdays from 8 am until noon for maintenance. To get to the dog park, take Valley View Street from the 22 or 405 Freeways north. Turn left on Lampson Avenue. You will have to turn right to the dog park which is directly behind the building at 4665 Lampson Avenue.

Outdoor Restaurants

Baja Fresh Mexican Grill 3050 E. Coast Hwy Corona Del Mar CA   949-760-8000
http://www.bajafresh.com
This Mexican restaurant is open for lunch and dinner. They use fresh ingredients and making their salsa and beans daily. Some of the items on their menu include Enchiladas, Burritos, Tacos Salads, Quesadillas, Nachos, Chicken, Steak and more. Well-behaved leashed dogs are allowed at the outdoor tables.

Caffe Panini 2333 E Pacific Coast Hwy Corona Del Mar CA   949-675-8101
Come here for breakfast, lunch and on some nights, dinner. They have several outdoor tables where you can dine with your pup. They are open Sunday through Wednesday from 6am until 3pm and on Thursday through Saturday from 6am until 10pm.

Baja Fresh Mexican Grill 3030 Harbor Blvd Costa Mesa CA   949-675-2252
http://www.bajafresh.com
This Mexican restaurant is open for lunch and dinner. They use fresh ingredients and making their salsa and beans daily. Some of the items on their menu include Enchiladas, Burritos, Tacos Salads, Quesadillas, Nachos, Chicken, Steak and more. Well-behaved leashed dogs are allowed at the outdoor tables.

Golden Truffle 1767 Newport Blvd Costa Mesa CA   949-645-9858
Dogs are allowed at the outdoor tables.

Rainbow Bridge Store and Deli 225 East 17th Street Costa Mesa CA   949-631-4741
This natural food market offers natural and organic food plus a kitchen where you can order a smoothie, sandwiches and more. Well-behaved leashed dogs are allowed at their outdoor tables.

Side Street Cafe 1799 Newport Blvd Ste A105 Costa Mesa CA   949-650-1986
This restaurant serves American food. Dogs are allowed at the outdoor tables. WAter is provided for your pet.

Alice's Breakfast in the Park Huntington Central Park Huntington Beach CA   714-848-0690
Dine at one of the several picnic tables at this restaurant which is located next to the Huntington Lake in Huntington Central Park. There are lots of ducks and other birds around, so your pup will be entertained. Try one of the delicious breakfast items like the fresh baked cinnamon rolls, pancakes, or omelets. For lunch, they have hamburgers and sandwiches. Breakfast and lunch are served all day. They are open daily from 7am until 1:30pm. It's located in Huntington Central Park, where Inlet Drive and Central Park Dr (Varsity Dr) meet.

Java City Bakery Cafe 18685 Main St #G Huntington Beach CA   714-842-5020
This cafe serves bakery type food. Dogs are allowed at the outdoor tables.

Spark Woodfire Grill 300 Pacific Coast H Huntington Beach CA   714-960-0996
For ocean front, casual dining, this award-wining steak and seafood, dinner-only house, is the place. They feature a large terrace with an open fire pit, contemporary American cuisine specializing in wood-fire grilling and slow roasting, and an extensive wine selection with a full bar offering more than 50 specialty Martinis. They offer indoor and outdoor dining service, and dogs are allowed at the outer tables. They must be social, well behaved, under owner's control at all times, leashed, and cleaned up after. They suggest for guests with pets to call ahead as there are many times that the outside deck is booked for private event or large parties.

Taste of France 7304 Center Ave Huntington Beach CA   714-895-5305
Dogs are allowed at the outdoor tables.

TOP 200 PLACE **The Park Bench Cafe** 17732 Golden West Dr Huntington Beach CA   714-842-0775
This is THE most dog-friendly restaurant we have found yet. Your dog will absolutely feel welcome here. They even have a separate Doggie Dining Area. And if these tables are full (which they normally are), the nice folks will try to accommodate you and your pooch at the perimeter tables of the other seating area which is next to the dog dining area. Dogs also have their own special menu. It's actually on the people's menu, but includes items like Hot Diggity Dog (hot dog a la carte), Bow Wow Chow (skinless chicken), Annabelle's Treat (chopped bacon bits) and Doggie Kibble (dog kibble for dogs that don't eat table food). For those especially pampered pups, order the Chili Paws (single scoop of Vanilla ice cream) for dessert. This restaurant can arrange special events like Poochie Parties for your dog and a minimum of six of his or her best friends. The party menu has a mouth-watering array of foods for dogs. They do ask that your dog stay off the tables and chairs. But with all the other canine amenities, pooches don't get upset about that rule. The people food here is quite tasty too. They serve a full breakfast ranging from omelets to pancakes and Belgium waffles. Lunch includes a variety of hamburgers and sandwiches. This cafe is located in Huntington Central Park at 17732 Golden West Drive between Slater Dr and Talbert Ave. Hours are Tuesday through Friday from 8am-2pm, Saturday and Sunday from 8am-3pm, and closed on Mondays. Come and enjoy the food and atmosphere.

Baja Fresh Mexican Grill 1324 Bison Avenue Newport Beach CA   949-759-0010
http://www.bajafresh.com
This Mexican restaurant is open for lunch and dinner. They use fresh ingredients and making their salsa and beans daily. Some of the items on their menu include Enchiladas, Burritos, Tacos Salads, Quesadillas, Nachos, Chicken, Steak and more. Well-behaved leashed dogs are allowed at the outdoor tables.

The Park Bench Cafe

Charlie's Chili 102 McFadden Place Newport Beach CA 949-675-7991
This restaurant serves American food. Dogs are allowed at the outdoor tables.
Francoli 1133 Newport Center Dr Newport Beach CA 949-721-1289
This restaurant is located in the dog-friendly Fashion Island Mall. It is located next to Macy's. They serve salads, sandwiches, pasta and more.
Park Avenue Cafe 501 Park Avenue Newport Beach CA 949-673-3830
Dogs are allowed at the outdoor tables. Thanks to one of our readers for recommending this cafe.
Sabatino Restaurant 251 Shipyard Way Newport Beach CA 949-723-0621
Reminiscent of a relaxing European café complete with outdoor dining, this Italian bistro cafe offer foods rich and hearty in flavor, a good variety of seafood, and plenty of ambiance. The outdoor patio area has heat lamps, and dogs are allowed at the outdoor tables. They must be well behaved, under owner's control at all times, leashed, and cleaned up after.
Wilma's Patio 203 Marine Avenue Newport Beach CA 949-675-5542
http://www.wilmaspatio.com/index.htm
A casual, family dining eatery, they offer fresh, homemade favorites of American and Mexican cuisine with a wide selection of dishes for breakfast, lunch, and diner. Dogs are allowed at the outdoor tables. They must be well behaved, under owner's control at all times, leashed, and cleaned up after.

Orange County North

Accommodations
Residence Inn by Marriott 125 S Festival Drive Anaheim Hills CA 714-974-8880
Dogs of all sizes are welcome. There is a $75 plus tax one time fee, and a pet policy to sign at check in. They also ask that you make arrangements for housekeeping.
Woodfin Suites 3100 E Imperial H Brea CA 714-579-3200
Dogs of all sizes are allowed. There is a $5 per night per pet fee and a pet policy to sign at check in.
Residence Inn by Marriott 700 W Kimberly Ave Placentia CA 714-996-0555
Dogs of all sizes are welcome. There is a $75 one time fee, and a pet policy to sign at check in.

Stores
PetSmart Pet Store 2465 E Imperial Hwy Brea CA 714-256-0205

Your licensed and well-behaved leashed dog is allowed in the store.
Petco Pet Store 2500 Imperial Highway, Ste 114 Brea CA 714-255-8162
Your licensed and well-behaved leashed dog is allowed in the store.
Petco Pet Store 1201 W Whittier Blvd La Habra CA 562-690-0410
Your licensed and well-behaved leashed dog is allowed in the store.
PetSmart Pet Store 5521 Mirage St Yorba Linda CA 714-637-8088
Your licensed and well-behaved leashed dog is allowed in the store.

Outdoor Restaurants

Baja Fresh Mexican Grill 5781 E. Santa Ana Canyon Rd. Anaheim Hills CA 714-685-9386
http://www.bajafresh.com
This Mexican restaurant is open for lunch and dinner. They use fresh ingredients and making their salsa and beans daily. Some of the items on their menu include Enchiladas, Burritos, Tacos Salads, Quesadillas, Nachos, Chicken, Steak and more. Well-behaved leashed dogs are allowed at the outdoor tables.
Baja Fresh Mexican Grill 2445 Imperial Hwy. Suite H Brea CA 714-671-9992
http://www.bajafresh.com
This Mexican restaurant is open for lunch and dinner. They use fresh ingredients and making their salsa and beans daily. Some of the items on their menu include Enchiladas, Burritos, Tacos Salads, Quesadillas, Nachos, Chicken, Steak and more. Well-behaved leashed dogs are allowed at the outdoor tables.
Schlotzsky's Deli 2500 E. Imperial Hwy #196 Brea CA 714-256-1100
Dogs are allowed at the outdoor tables.

Day Kennels

PetsHotel by PetsMart Day Kennel 2465 E. Imperial Highway Brea CA 714-256-0396
http://www.petsmart.com/PETsHOTEL/
This PetSmart pet store offers day care, day camp and overnight care. You can drop your dog off and pick up your dog between the hours of 7 am - 9 pm M-F, Sunday 8 am - 6 pm. Dogs are required to have proof of current rabies, DPP and Bordatella vaccinations.

Orange County South

Accommodations

Seaside Inn 34862 Pacific Coast Hwy. Capistrano Beach CA 949-496-1399 (800-25-BEACH)
http://www.seaside-inn.com
There is a $25 one time pet fee.
Doubletree 34402 Pacific Coast Highway Dana Point CA 949-661-1100
Dogs of all sizes are allowed. There is a $30 per night per room fee and a pet policy to sign at check in.
Candlewood Suites 16150 Sand Canyon Ave Irvine CA 949-788-0500 (877-270-6405)
Dogs up to 80 pounds are allowed. There is a $75 one time pet fee for stays of up to 15 days. For longer stays there is a $150 pet fee.
Hilton 18800 MacArthur Blvd Irvine CA 949-833-9999
Dogs up to 50 pounds are allowed. There is a $50 per pet per stay additional fee.
Residence Inn by Marriott 2855 Main Street Irvine CA 949-261-2020
Dogs of all sizes are allowed. There is a $75 one time fee, and a pet policy to sign at check in.
Residence Inn by Marriott 10 Morgan Irvine CA 949-380-3000
Dogs of all sizes are allowed. There is a $75 plus tax one time fee, and a pet policy to sign at check in.
Carriage House Bed and Breakfast 1322 Catalina Street Laguna Beach CA 949-494-8945 (888-335-8945)
http://www.carriagehouse.com
The Carriage House, a country style bed & breakfast, was built in the early 1920's and is a designated landmark. They are located one mile south of downtown Laguna Beach in a quiet neighborhood. Well-mannered, flea protected, friendly dogs over 18 months old are allowed at an extra charge of $10 per pet per night. Please cover the beds with your own blanket, or ask for a sheet, if your dog sleeps on the bed. Towels are provided upon request for your pet. Never leave your pet unattended, unless they are "crated" and you'll need to leave a cell phone or number where you can be reached. Owners are responsible for any damages caused by pets. There is also a resident dog & cat on the property. Dogs must always be leashed in Laguna, even on the beach. There is a dog park for off-leash exercise in Laguna Canyon (closed on Wednesday's year round). During the summer, dogs are allowed on the beach from June 1-September 16 before 8 a.m. and after 6 p.m. only.
Casa Laguna Inn 2510 S. Coast Hwy Laguna Beach CA 949-494-2996 (800-233-0449)
http://www.casalaguna.com/
This Spanish-style bed and breakfast sits on a hillside with views of the ocean. It was voted Orange County's

Best B&B four years in a row. The rooms are decorated with a blend of antique and contemporary furnishings. There are 15 guest rooms plus several guest suites and cottages. While in Laguna Beach, browse the variety of specialty shops or dine at one of the dog-friendly restaurants. Interested in a stroll on the beach? Main Beach (certain dog hours) is a short drive from the inn. There is a $25 per day additional pet fee.

Vacation Village 647 S Costal H Laguna Beach CA 949-494-8566
One dog up to 75 pounds is allowed. There is a $10 per night per pet additional fee.

Candlewood Suites 3 South Pointe Drive Lake Forest CA 949-598-9105 (877-270-6405)
Dogs up to 80 pounds are allowed. There is a $75 pet fee for stays up to 15 days. for longer stays, the pet fee is $150.

Holiday Inn 111 S. Ave. De Estrella San Clemente CA 949-361-3000 (877-270-6405)
There is a $10 per day pet fee.

Campgrounds and RV Parks

Doheny State Beach Park 25300 Dana Point Harbor Drive Dana Point CA 949-496-6172 (800-444-PARK (7275))
This park, nestled among the trees on the ocean, offers exhibits, various other programs, and a variety of land and water recreation. Dogs of all sizes are allowed. There are no additional pet fees. Dogs must be leashed and cleaned up after. Dogs are not allowed on the beach. The camping and tent areas also allow dogs. There is a dog walk area at the campground. There are no electric or water hookups at the campgrounds.

San Clemente State Beach 3030 El Avenida Del Presidente San Clemente CA 949-492-3156 (800-444-PARK (7275))
Set among the sandstone cliffs on the ocean, this park is home to many species of land and marine life. The park offers interpretive exhibits and programs and a variety of recreational activities. Dogs of all sizes are allowed. There are no additional pet fees. Dogs may not be left unattended, and they must be well behaved, on no more than a 6 foot leash, and cleaned up after. Dogs must be brought inside at night. Dogs are not allowed on the trails or on the beach. The camping and tent areas also allow dogs. There is a dog walk area at the campground.

Attractions

Catalina Express 34675 Golden Lantern Dana Point CA 800-360-1212
http://www.catalinaexpress.com/
Dogs are allowed on the boats to the Catalina Island at no additional fee. Dogs must be leashed and muzzled or crated while aboard. There is a limit of one pet per person.

Shopping Centers

Irvine Spectrum Center 71 Fortune Drive Irvine CA 877-ISC-4FUN
http://www.shopirvinespectrumcenter.com
Dogs on leash are allowed to walk through the shopping areas. They are allowed at many outdoor restaurants if they are well-behaved. Some stores may allow dogs inside if you ask.

Stores

PetSmart Pet Store 26761 Aliso Creek Rd Aliso Viejo CA 949-643-2285
Your licensed and well-behaved leashed dog is allowed in the store.

PetSmart Pet Store 3775 Alton Pkwy Irvine CA 949-252-9027
Your licensed and well-behaved leashed dog is allowed in the store.

Petco Pet Store 15333 Culver Plaza Irvine CA 949-262-1400
Your licensed and well-behaved leashed dog is allowed in the store.

PetSmart Pet Store 23602 El Toro Rd Lake Forest CA 949-768-6373
Your licensed and well-behaved leashed dog is allowed in the store.

Petco Pet Store 24332 Rockfield Blvd Lake Forest CA 949-859-6590
Your licensed and well-behaved leashed dog is allowed in the store.

Petco Pet Store 25592 El Paseo Mission Viejo CA 949-348-2310
Your licensed and well-behaved leashed dog is allowed in the store.

PetSmart Pet Store 30515 Avenida De Las Flores Rancho Santa Margarita CA 949-766-7746
Your licensed and well-behaved leashed dog is allowed in the store.

Petco Pet Store 30682 Santa Margarita Parkway Rancho Santa Margarita CA 949-888-0478
Your licensed and well-behaved leashed dog is allowed in the store.

Three Dog Bakery 118 S. El Camino Real San Clemente CA 949-218-3364
http://www.threedog.com
Three Dog Bakery provides cookies and snacks for your dog as well as some boutique items. You well-behaved, leashed dog is welcome.

PetSmart Pet Store 33963 Doheny Park Rd San Juan Capistrano CA 949-443-5336

Your licensed and well-behaved leashed dog is allowed in the store.
Petco Pet Store 32391 Camino Capistrano #A San Juan Capistrano CA 949-240-9388
Your licensed and well-behaved leashed dog is allowed in the store.

Beaches

Main Beach

Main Beach Pacific Hwy (Hwy 1) Laguna Beach CA 949-497-3311
Dogs are allowed on this beach between 6pm and 8am, June 1 to September 16. The rest of the year, they are allowed on the beach from dawn until dusk. Dogs must be on a leash at all times.

Parks

Holy Jim Historic Trail Trabuco Canyon Road Mission Viejo CA 909-736-1811
This trail is part of the Cleveland National Forest. It is about a 4.5 mile hike on a combination of fire roads and single track trails. You can see a small waterfall on this trail which is best viewed in early spring. This trail is used by both hikers and mountain bikers. Pets on leash are allowed and please clean up after them. To get there from Highway 5, exit El Toro Road and head north (away from the coast). Take Live Oak Canyon Road to the right, then turn left onto Trabuco Canyon Road.
O'Neill Regional Park 30892 Trabuco Canyon Road Trabuco Canyon CA 949-923-2260
http://www.ocparks.com/oneillpark/
This heavily wooded park offers hiking trails. Dogs on a 6 foot or less leash are allowed and please clean up after them.

Off-Leash Dog Parks

Central Bark 6405 Oak Canyon Irvine CA 949-724-7740
Thanks to one of our readers who writes: "Irvine's dog park is open daily from 6:30 am to 9 pm, closed Wednesdays." The dog park is located next to the Irvine Animal Care Center and is a 2.8 acre fenced dog park. There is a separate area for small dogs and water for your dog.
Laguna Beach Dog Park Laguna Canyon Rd at El Toro Rd Laguna Beach CA
This dog park, known by the locals as Bark Park, is open six days a week and closed on Wednesdays for clean-up. The park is open from dawn to dusk. The park will be closed during and after heavy rains.
Laguna Niguel Pooch Park Golden Latern Laguna Niguel CA
This fully enclosed dog park is located in the city of Laguna Niguel, which is between Laguna Beach and Dana Point. The park is operated by the City of Laguna Niguel's Parks and Recreation Department. It is located on

Golden Latern, next to fire station 49. From the Pacific Coast Highway in Dana Point, go up Goldern Latern about 2 miles. Thanks to one of our readers for this information.

San Clemente Dog Park 310 Avenida La Pata San Clemente CA

San Clemente Dog Park has two fenced areas, one for large dogs and one for small dogs. The park has benches and water for dogs.

Outdoor Restaurants

JACKShrimp 26705 Aliso Creek Rd. Aliso Viejo CA   949-448-0085

Cajun food and shrimp are the focus here at JACKShrimp. Enjoy the Spiced Shrimp Caesar Salad, Mardi Gras Pasta, Jammin Jambalaya or Butterfly Shrimp Sandwich. Dogs are allowed at the outdoor tables.

Baja Fresh Mexican Grill 13248 Jamboree Rd. Irvine CA   714-508-7777

http://www.bajafresh.com

This Mexican restaurant is open for lunch and dinner. They use fresh ingredients and making their salsa and beans daily. Some of the items on their menu include Enchiladas, Burritos, Tacos Salads, Quesadillas, Nachos, Chicken, Steak and more. Well-behaved leashed dogs are allowed at the outdoor tables.

Britta's Cafe 4237 Campus Drive Irvine CA   949-509-1211

This restaurant serves California cuisine. Dogs are allowed at the outdoor tables.

Corner Bakery Cafe 13786 Jamboree Rd Irvine CA   714-734-8270

Dogs are allowed at the outdoor seats.

Mother's Market & Kitchen 2963 Michelson Drive Irvine CA

http://www.mothersmarket.com/

This natural food market offers natural and organic food plus a kitchen where you can order a smoothie, sandwiches and more. Well-behaved leashed dogs are allowed at their outdoor tables.

Food Village 211-217 Broadway St Laguna Beach CA

The Food Village consists of several different restaurants like Gina's Pizza, El Pollo Loco and more. All of these restaurants share the same 8-10 tables. Just order food inside and grab one of the tables outside. It's located on Broadway St at Pacific Coast Hwy.

Madison Squar and Garden Cafe 320 North Coast Hwy Laguna Beach CA   949-494-0137

This restaurant serves breakfast and deli-type food. Dogs are allowed at the outdoor tables.

Zinc Cafe and Market 350 Ocean Avenue Laguna Beach CA   949-494-6302

http://www.zinccafe.com/

A sophisticated eatery with an extensive breakfast, lunch, and dinner menu, they also offer a market with a large variety of to-go salads, entrees, breads, desserts, grocery items, as well as carefully selected items to compliment the home kitchen and pantry. They offer indoor and outdoor patio dining; just order and pick-up inside. Dogs are allowed at the outdoor tables. They must be well behaved, under owner's control at all times, leashed, and cleaned up after.

Baja Fresh Mexican Grill 26548 Moulton Park Way Laguna Hills CA   949-360-4222

http://www.bajafresh.com

This Mexican restaurant is open for lunch and dinner. They use fresh ingredients and making their salsa and beans daily. Some of the items on their menu include Enchiladas, Burritos, Tacos Salads, Quesadillas, Nachos, Chicken, Steak and more. Well-behaved leashed dogs are allowed at the outdoor tables.

Fresca's Mexican Grill 22681 Lake Forest Dr Lake Forest CA   949-837-8397

This restaurant serves Mexican food. Dogs are allowed at the outdoor tables.

Baja Fresh Mexican Grill 27620 Marguerite Pkwy Ste C Mission Viejo CA   949-347-9033

http://www.bajafresh.com

This Mexican restaurant is open for lunch and dinner. They use fresh ingredients and making their salsa and beans daily. Some of the items on their menu include Enchiladas, Burritos, Tacos Salads, Quesadillas, Nachos, Chicken, Steak and more. Well-behaved leashed dogs are allowed at the outdoor tables.

Skimmer's Panini Grill 25290 Marguerite Pkwy Mission Viejo CA   949-855-8500

This small neighborhood cafe loves to have dogs site outside on the front patio.

Taco Mesa 27702 Crown Valley Parkway Mission Viejo CA   949-364-1957

This restaurant serves Mexican food. Dogs are allowed at the outdoor tables.

Baja Fresh Mexican Grill 979 Avenida Pico San Clemente CA   949-361-4667

http://www.bajafresh.com

This Mexican restaurant is open for lunch and dinner. They use fresh ingredients and making their salsa and beans daily. Some of the items on their menu include Enchiladas, Burritos, Tacos Salads, Quesadillas, Nachos, Chicken, Steak and more. Well-behaved leashed dogs are allowed at the outdoor tables.

Vets and Kennels

Animal Urgent Care Clinic 28085 Hillcrest Mission Viejo CA   949-364-6228

Monday - Friday 6pm to 8am, Noon Saturday to 8 am Monday.

Chapter 12

California - Inland Empire Dog Travel Guide

Arrowbear

Campgrounds and RV Parks
Green Valley Campground Green Valley Lake Road Arrowbear CA   909-337-2444 (877-444-6777)
This 36 site campground is located in the San Bernardino National Forest. RVs up to 22 feet are allowed. The lake offers fishing, swimming and boating. Trails are located nearby. Dogs of all sizes are allowed for no additional fee. Dogs may not be left unattended outside, and they must be on no more than a 6 foot leash at all times, and cleaned up after. Dogs are allowed on the trails. This campground is closed during the off-season. The camping and tent areas also allow dogs. There is a dog walk area at the campground. There are no water hookups at the campgrounds.

Parks
Crab Creek Trail off Green Valley Road Arrowbear CA   909-337-2444
This 2.5 mile moderate rated trail is located in the San Bernardino National Forest. On the trail, you may have to cross Deep Creek. Do not attempt to cross the creek when the water is high as it is too dangerous. Pets are allowed but must be on a 6 foot or less leash. Please clean up after them. The trailhead is located at Forest Road 3N34, west of the Crab Flats Campground. To get there take 330 north and go through Running Springs and Arrowbear to Green Valley Road. Turn left and go about 4 miles to the Crab Flats Campground sign at Forestry (dirt road). Turn left and go about 4.5 miles.
Crabflats Trail off Green Valley Road Arrowbear CA   909-337-2444
This 1.3 mile long moderate rated trail is located in the San Bernardino National Forest. The trail descends and joins up with the Pacific Crest Trail west of the Holocomb Crossing Trail Camp. Pets are allowed but must be on a 6 foot or less leash. Please clean up after them. The trailhead is located at Forest Road 3N34, west of the Crab Flats Campground. To get there take 330 north and go through Running Springs and Arrowbear to Green Valley Road. Turn left and go about 4 miles to the Crab Flats Campground sign at Forestry (dirt road). Turn left and go about 4.5 miles.
Pacific Coast National Scenic Trail off Green Valley Road Arrowbear CA   909-337-2444
The 40 mile one way moderate rated trail is located in the San Bernardino National Forest. Pets are allowed but must be on a 6 foot or less leash. Please clean up after them. One entry point to this trail is at Forest Road 3N16, which is near the Crab Flats Campground. To get there take 330 north and go through Running Springs and Arrowbear to Green Valley Road. Turn left and go about 4 miles to the Crab Flats Campground sign at Forestry (dirt road). Turn left and go about 4.5 miles.

Arrowbear Lake

Campgrounds and RV Parks
Crab Flats Campground Forest Road 3N16 Arrowbear Lake CA   909-337-2444
This San Bernardino National Forest campground is located at an elevation of 6,200 feet in tall pine, oak and cedar trees. It is a popular campsite and off-highway vehicle staging area. Off-road and hiking trails are located near this campground. Tent and small RV sites are available, with a maximum RV length of 15 feet. Sites are available on a first-come, first-served basis. Pets on leash are allowed and please clean up after them. Dogs are allowed on the trails. From Green Valley Road exit turn left and go about 4 miles to the Crab Flats Campground sign at Forestry (dirt road). Turn left and go about 4.5 miles. The camping and tent areas also allow dogs. There is a dog walk area at the campground. There are no electric or water hookups at the campgrounds.

Banning

Accommodations
Travelodge 1700 W. Ramsey Street Banning CA   909-849-1000
A well-behaved large dog is allowed. There is a $5 per day pet charge.

Beaumont

Campgrounds and RV Parks

Country Hills RV Park 14711 Manzanita Park Road Beaumont CA 951-845-5919 (800-203-5662)
http://www.countryhillsrv.com/
This country like park is close to many local attractions and offers a variety of services and recreational
opportunities. Dogs of all sizes are allowed for an additional $1 per night per pet. Dogs may not be left
unattended outside, and left inside only if they will be well behaved and physically comfortable. Dogs must be
leashed and cleaned up after. No Pit Bulls are allowed. This is an RV only park. There are some breed
restrictions. There is a dog walk area at the campground.

Big Bear Lake

Accommodations

Best Western Big Bear Chateau 42200 Moonridge Rd Big Bear Lake CA 909-866-6666 (800-780-7234)
Dogs of all sizes are allowed. There is a $30 per night pet fee per first pet. There is a $15 per night pet fee per 2
or more pets. Smoking and non-smoking are available for pet rooms.
Big Bear Cabins California 43630 Rainbow Lane Big Bear Lake CA 888-336-2891
http://www.bigbearcabinscalifornia.com
There is a $10 per day pet fee. Pets may not be left unattended in the cottages. According to a reader "4 cozy,
clean and comfortable cottages on 40 acres adjoining BLM land. Very relaxed, run by nice people. Plenty of
leash-free hiking right from your door."
Big Bear Frontier Resort and Hotel 40472 Big Bear Blvd Big Bear Lake CA 800-420-4693
http://www.big-bear-cabins.com
The Big Bear Frontier is a group of cabins and motel rooms nestled in a beautiful mountain setting. The Big Bear
Frontier is located on Big Bear Lake. It is located within easy walking distance of Big Bear Village. Amenities
include pool, jacuzzi, gym and more. There is a $15 per night pet fee. Pets may not be left unattended and must
be kept on a leash when out of the room.
Eagle's Nest Lodge 41675 Big Bear Blvd. Big Bear Lake CA 909-866-6465 (888-866-6465)
http://www.bigbear.com/enbb/
There are 5 cabins and only 1 allows dogs, but it is a pretty nice cabin. It's called the Sierra Madre and includes a
kitchen, fireplace and separate bedroom. You can order breakfast delivered to the room for an additional $10 per
person.
Grey Squirrel Resort 39372 Big Bear Blvd Big Bear Lake CA 909-866-4335 (800-381-5569)
http://www.greysquirrel.com
This dog-friendly resort has cabins that accommodate from 1-2 people up to 20 people. They have a heated
pool, indoor spa, basketball and horseshoes. Some of the cabins have fireplaces and kitchens. All units have
VCRs and microwaves. There is a $10 per day additional pet fee.
Holiday Inn 42200 Moonridge Rd Big Bear Lake CA 909-866-6666 (877-270-6405)
There is a $15 per day pet fee. Dogs may not be left alone in the room.
Majestic Moose Lodge 39328 Big Bear Blvd/Hwy 18 Big Bear Lake CA 909-866-9586 (877-585-5855)
http://www.majesticmooselodge.com/
This getaway offers 20 unique cabins/rooms, and is nestled on 2 acres of lush park-like grounds among tall pine
trees with plenty of indoor and outdoor recreational opportunities available. Some of the amenities include
fireplaces and kitchens/kitchenettes, cable TV, VCRs, and large covered porches. Housebroken dogs of all sizes
are allowed for an additional cash pet deposit of $100. Treats, a pet coverlet (to keep dog hair off the furniture),
and waste bags are available at the front desk for their four-legged guests. Dogs must be kenneled when left alone in the room, and they must be leashed and
cleaned up after at all times.
Motel 6 - Big Bear 42899 Big Bear Boulevard Big Bear Lake CA 909-585-6666 (800-466-8356)
One well-behaved family pet per room. Guest must notify front desk upon arrival. Guest is liable for any
damages. In consideration of all guests, pets must never be left unattended in the guest rooms.
Mtn. Resort Adventure Hostel PO Box 1951 Big Bear Lake CA 909-866-8900
According to the people at the Hostel "Rent beds or private rooms in our cozy hostel overlooking Big Bear Lake.
Fenced grass yard for dogs to play in. All dogs welcome as long as they are friendly with our dogs."
Robin Hood Resort 40797 Lakeview Drive Big Bear Lake CA 909-866-4643 (800-990-9956)
http://www.robinhoodresort.info/
This full service resort is located in a great little village across from Big Bear Lake that also offers a variety of
entertainment, shops, dining, a small park, and a marina. Some of the amenities/features include an on-site

restaurant with 3 dining rooms and outdoor dining, complimentary continental breakfast on the weekends, a banquet center, 2 taverns, in-room spas/fireplaces/kitchenettes, and wood-burning fireplaces. There are 2 pet-friendly rooms, and dogs of all sizes are allowed for no additional fee. Dogs must be quiet, well behaved, leashed, cleaned up after, and they may not be left alone in the room at any time.

Shore Acres Lodge

Shore Acres Lodge 40090 Lakeview Drive Big Bear Lake CA   909-866-8200 (800-524-6600)
This resort has 11 cabins and is next to Big Bear Lake and has its own private boat dock. Other amenities include barbecues, volleyball, a children's playground, pool and spa.

Timberline Lodge

Timber Haven Lodge 877 Tulip Lane Big Bear Lake CA 909-866-7207
Dogs are welcome in designated cabins. There is a $15 per dog per night pet fee. Ask about the pet policy when making reservations.
Timberline Lodge 39921 Big Bear Blvd. Big Bear Lake CA 909-866-4141 (800-803-4111)
http://www.thetimberlinelodge.com/
The "Pets Welcome" sign at the main entrance will let you know your pup is more than welcome here. Some of the 13 cabins have fireplaces and full kitchens. There is also a playground for kids. There is a $10 per day additional pet fee per pet.
Wildwood Resort 40210 Big Bear Blvd. Big Bear Lake CA 909-878-2178 (888-294-5396)
http://www.wildwoodresort.com/
This cabin resort has about 15 cabins of various sizes. Most rooms have fireplaces and all cabins have private picnic benches and barbecues. There is also a pool & spa and if your pup is well-behaved, he or she can be tied to the rails on the inside of the pool area. It's a close drive to town and to some of the parks and attractions. Not too many restaurants within walking distance, but there is a local service that delivers food - check with the front desk. This is a nice place to relax and unwind. There is a $10 per day additional pet fee. There are no designed smoking or non-smoking cabins.
Quail Cove P.O. Box 117 Fawnskin CA 800-595-2683
http://www.quailcove.com/
This lodge offers rustic and cozy cabins in a quiet wooded surrounding on Big Bear Lake. They are located within walking distance to several restaurants, markets, marinas and some of the hiking trails and fishing spots. Pets are always welcome. There is a $10 per day pet charge. Never leave your pet unattended in the cabin.
Quail Cove Lakeside Lodge 39117 Northshore Drive Fawnskin CA 909-866-8874 (800-595-2683)
Dogs of all sizes are allowed. There is a $20 per pet per stay fee and a credit card needs to be on file.

Campgrounds and RV Parks
Holloway's RV Park 398 Edgemoor Road Big Bear Lake CA 909-8666-5706 (800-448-5335)
http://www.bigbearboating.com/
This RV park offers large level sites with a nice view of Big Bear Lake. RV sites offer tables, barbecues, and TV cable. Park amenities include a small convenience store, restrooms, showers, laundry room, playground with horseshoes, basketball and boat rentals. Dogs are allowed at the campgrounds and on the boat rentals. Pets must be leashed and please clean up after them. There is a dog walk area at the campground.
Pineknot Campground Bristlecone Big Bear Lake CA 909-866-3437 (800-280-CAMP (2267))
http://www.fs.fed.us/r5/sanbernardino/
This 52 site campground is part of the San Bernardino National Forest. It is located at an elevation of 7,000 feet. RV spaces have a maximum length of 45 feet. Amenities include water, flush toilets and picnic areas. Pets must be on leash and cannot be left unattended. Please clean up after your pets. The campground is on Bristlecone near Summit Blvd. Call to make a reservation. The camping and tent areas also allow dogs. There is a dog walk area at the campground. There are no electric or water hookups at the campgrounds.
Serrano Campground 4533 N Shore Drive Big Bear Lake CA 909-866-3437 (877-444-6777)
This camp area is situated among tall pines on the North Shore of Bear Lake, and some of their new facilities include showers, toilets, and telephones. Dogs of all sizes are allowed. There are no additional pet fees. Dogs may not be left unattended, and they must be leashed and cleaned up after. The camping and tent areas also allow dogs. There is a dog walk area at the campground.
Big Bear Shores RV Resort and Yacht Club 40751 North Shore Lane Fawnskin CA 909-866-4151
http://www.bigbearshores.com
This gated resort offers a fully equipped private health club in addition to other recreational pursuits. Dogs of all sizes are allowed at an additional $10 per night per pet. Dogs may not be left unattended outside, and not left inside unless they will be quiet and well behaved. Dogs must be leashed and cleaned up after. Dogs are allowed on the trails. There is a dog walk area at the campground.
Hanna Flat Campground Rim of the World Drive Fawnskin CA 909-382-2790 (877-444-6777)
This 88 site campground, of tall pines, wildflowers and wild roses, is located in the San Bernardino National Forest at an elevation of 7,000 feet. RVs up to 40 feet are allowed. Amenities include picnic tables, fire rings, paved parking, flush toilets and trash dumpster. The Hanna Flat Trailhead is located at this camp. Pets on leash are allowed and please clean up after them. Dogs may not be left unattended. To get there take Highway 18 to Big Bear Lake Dam. Go straight, do not cross over the dam. Highway 18 becomes Highway 38. Go the Fawnskin Fire Station and turn left onto the Rim of the World Drive. Go about 2.5 miles on a dirt road to the campsite. This campground is closed during the off-season. The camping and tent areas also allow dogs. There is a dog walk area at the campground. There are no electric or water hookups at the campgrounds.
Holcomb Valley Campground 40971 North Shore Drive Fawnskin CA 909-866-3437
This tent and RV campground is located in the historic Holcomb Valley about a mile from the Belleville Ghost Town. See our listing under Big Bear Lake for more information about the ghost town. There is no water at the campsite. Camp amenities include toilets. The sites are on a first-come, first-served basis. Pets are allowed but must be leashed at all times, picked up after, and they cannot be left unattended. Watch out for rattlesnakes,

especially during the warm summer months. The campground is located in the San Bernardino National Forest. Dogs are allowed on the trails on lead. The camping and tent areas also allow dogs. There is a dog walk area at the campground. There are no electric or water hookups at the campgrounds.

Vacation Home Rentals

Big Bear Cool Cabins Book Online Big Bear Lake CA   909-866-7374 (800-550-8779)
http://www.bigbearcoolcabins.com
Big Bear Lake vacation rentals on or near the lake and ski slopes - all with fireplace, bbq, kitchen, and many with hot tubs, pool tables, docks, and more. Professional cleaning, fresh towels, and linens provided. No extra pet fee for responsible pet owners.
Big Bear Luxury Properties Call to Arrange Big Bear Lake CA   909-866-4691 (888-866-4618)
http://www.bigbearlp.com
These vacation rentals in Big Bear vary from rustic cabins to lakefront homes. Contact them for a pet-friendly rental.
Mountain Lodging Unlimited 41135 Big Bear Blvd Big Bear Lake CA   909-866-5500 (800-487-3168)
http://www.bigbearmtnlodging.com
Dogs are allowed in some of the vacation rentals, cabins, and motels. They will tell you which rentals allow dogs.

Attractions

TOP 200 PLACE **Bear Valley Stage Lines** Village Drive and Pine Knot Avenue Big Bear Lake CA   909-584-2277
http://www.stagelines.com/
This company offers horse drawn carriage rides of the Village, and for special occasions/events they will travel anywhere in the Los Angeles metropolitan area. Dogs are allowed to come along for the ride for no additional fee if they are trained and well behaved. Dogs must be leashed and cleaned up after.
Belleville Ghost Town Holcomb Valley Road Big Bear Lake CA
Belleville Ghost Town, located in Holcomb Valley, is one of the old Southern California ghost towns. To get there, you'll take a dirt road, but it is rated a 2 wheel drive road meaning you don't necessarily need a 4WD. At the ghost town, you'll find the old saloon, mining equipment, hanging tree, mines, graves and foundations. This ghost town is located within a National Forest which means you and your pup are welcome to walk or hike on almost any of the trails (the Pacific Crest Trail is the exception). To get there from the northeast corner of Big Bear Lake, take Hwy 38 east and turn left onto Van Dusen Canyon Road. Once on this road, you'll travel about 4-5 miles on a dirt road. When the road ends (there is a campground to the left), turn right on Holcomb Valley Road. The ghost town of Belleville will be approx. less than 1 mile on the right. Go during the late spring through fall when there is no snow.
Big Bear Marina 500 Paine Road Big Bear Lake CA   909-866-3218
http://www.bigbearmarina.com/
At Big Bear Marina you can rent fishing boats for a fishing trip on the lake. Dogs are only allowed on the fishing boats, not the other types of boats rented here.
Holloway's Marina 398 Edgemoor Road Big Bear Lake CA   909-866-5706 (800-448-5335)
http://www.bigbearboating.com/
Here you and your pup can rent a covered pontoon boat or a fishing boat for a morning, afternoon, or day on the lake.
Holloway's Marina 398 Edgemoor Road Big Bear Lake CA   909-866-5706 (800-448-5335)
TOP 200 PLACE **Pine Knot Landing-Boat Rentals** 439 Pine Knot Road Big Bear Lake CA   909-866-2628
http://www.pineknotlanding.com/
Rent a boat with your pup in beautiful Big Bear Lake. You'll drive your own gas powered pontoon boat which goes up to 15 miles per hour. These are nice boats which have a covering and a good amount of room for your dog to walk around. Remember to bring along some water. If you've never driven a boat, don't worry. The people working there say if you know how to drive a car, you'll be fine. Rent a boat by the hour or day. The rate for 3 hours is about $100. Prices are subject to change. This boat rental company is at Pine Knot Landing which is located at the end of Pine Knot Road near Hwy 18 (Big Bear Blvd.)
Pleasure Point Landing 603 Landlock Landing Rd Big Bear Lake CA   909-866-2455
You can rent boats here for boating on Big Bear Lake.

Cross Country Ski Resorts

Big Bear Bikes/Snowshoes 41810 Big Bear Blvd. Big Bear Lake CA   909-866-2224
Rent some snowshoes and go for a snowy mountain hike with your best friend. Big Bear Bikes rents snowshoes and cross-country skis. After picking up the snow gear ($10-15) and the National Forest Adventure Pass for parking ($5), head over to the forest trail off Mill Creek Rd (by the Alpine Slides). Prices are subject to change. The rental shop will be able to provide directions and/or maps. Once at the trail, you'll be able to go snowshoeing for miles.

Pine Knot Landing-Boat Rentals

Beaches

Big Bear Lake Beaches

Big Bear Lake Beaches Hwy 38 Big Bear Lake CA
There are various beaches along the lake on Hwy 38. You can get to any of the beaches via the Alpine Pedal
Path. To get there, (going away from the village), take the Stanfield Cutoff to the other side of the lake and turn

left onto Hwy 38. In about 1/4 - 1/2 mile, parking will be on the left.

Parks

Alpine Pedal Path

Alpine Pedal Path Hwy 38 Big Bear Lake CA
This path is mostly paved and is about a 4-5 mile round trip. Throughout most of the path, there are various access points to the lake and various beaches. The beginning of the path is located off of the Stanfield Cutoff (bridge over Big Bear Lake, close to the village). For easier access, (going away from the village), take the Stanfield Cutoff to the other side of the lake and turn left onto Hwy 38. In about 1/4 - 1/2 mile, parking will be on the left.

Cougar Crest Trail Highway 38 Big Bear Lake CA   909-866-3437
Within the San Bernardino National Forest this trail is well known to visitors and residents alike. Leashed dogs are allowed throughout the San Bernardino Forest Trails in Big Bear. The trailhead is located on Highway 38 west of Big Bear. There is parking at the trailhead. The trail heads two miles up and connects to the Pacific Crest Trail on which you can extend your hike significantly should you desire. The trail offers spectacular views of the lake valley. The Cougar Crest Trail is strenuous and please bring enough water for dogs and people.

Grout Bay Trail Hwy 38 Big Bear Lake CA   909-866-3437
This hiking trail is about 3-5 miles each way and is rated easy to moderate. To get there from the village, head west on Hwy 18. Take Hwy 38 to the right, towards the northwest corner of the lake. The trail begins by the Grout Bay Picnic Area.

Pine Knot Trail Tulip Lane Big Bear Lake CA   909-866-3437
This hiking trail is about 3 miles each way and is rated moderate to difficult. To get there from the village, head west on Hwy 18 and turn left onto Tulip Lane. The trail begins by the Alpine Glen Picnic Area. Remember, to park here, you'll need a Forest Day Pass. Check with your hotel or some of the stores in the village for info on where to purchase this pass.

TOP 200 PLACE **Woodland Trail / Nature Walk** Hwy 38 Big Bear Lake CA   909-866-3437
This is a nature trail with about 20 informational stops. Pick up one of the maps and follow the self-guided 1.5 mile nature walk. This is rated as an easy loop. To get there, (going away from the village), take the Stanfield Cutoff to the other side of the lake and turn left onto Hwy 38. In about 1/2 mile, parking will be on the right.

Hanna Flat Trail Rim of the World Drive Fawnskin CA   909-337-2444
This 9 mile round trip moderate rated trail is located in the San Bernardino National Forest. Pets on leash are allowed and please clean up after them. This trail is closed every year from November 1 to April 1 due to the bald eagle wintering habitat. To get there take Highway 18 to Big Bear Lake Dam. Go straight, do not cross over the dam. Highway 18 becomes Highway 38. Go the Fawnskin Fire Station and turn left onto the Rim of the World

Drive. Go about 2.5 miles on a dirt road to the campsite and trailhead.

Woodland Trail / Nature Walk

Outdoor Restaurants
Alpine High Country Cafe 41546 Big Bear Blvd Big Bear Lake CA   909-866-1959
They have one outdoor table.
Big Bear Mountain Brewery 40260 Big Bear Blvd Big Bear Lake CA   909-866-2337
Dogs are allowed at the outdoor tables.
Boo Bear's Den Restaurant 572 Pine Knot Big Bear Lake CA   909-866-3667
This restaurant serves California cuisine and features a nice outdoor dining area during the warmer months.
Dogs are allowed at the outdoor tables. They must be well behaved, under owner's control at all times, leashed, and cleaned up after.
Kujos Restaurant 41799 Big Bear Blvd Big Bear Lake CA   909-866-6659
http://www.kujosblt.com
Dogs up to medium sizes are allowed at the outdoor tables.
Log Cabin Restaurant and Bar 39976 Big Bear Blvd/Hwy 18 Big Bear Lake CA   909-866-3667
This German restaurant is also known for their great breakfasts, and they offer a nice outdoor dining area that is open when weather permits. Dogs are allowed at the outdoor tables. They must be well behaved, under owner's control at all times, leashed, and cleaned up after.
Nottingham's Restaurant and Tavern 40797 Lakeview Drive Big Bear Lake CA   909-866-4644
http://www.nottinghams.info/
In addition to dining on great California cuisine, guests will be surrounded by unique antiques and entertained by the rich history of these historic surroundings. They offer 5 distinct dining areas, including a courtyard that seats 20 and has a water fountain with free wireless Internet (weather permitting). Dogs are allowed at the outdoor tables. They must be well behaved, under owner's control at all times, leashed, and cleaned up after.
The Mandoline Bistro 40701 Village Drive Big Bear Lake CA   909-866-4200
Dogs are welcome at the outdoor tables. Thanks to one of our readers for recommending this restaurant. They have a variety of entrees including Tequila Chicken Fettuccine, Grilled Alaskan Salmon and Filet Minon. They are open daily for dinner and lunch is served on the weekends.
Village Pizza 40568 Village Dr Big Bear Lake CA   909-866-8505
This pizza place is within walking distance to Big Bear Village.

Vets and Kennels
Bear City Animal Hospital 214 Big Bear Blvd W Big Bear City CA   909-585-7808
Monday - Friday 7:30 am - 6 pm. Closed Weekends.
VCA Lakeside Animal Hospital 42160 N Shore Dr Big Bear City CA   909-866-2021
Monday - Saturday 8 am - 6 pm. Sunday 9 am - 5 pm.

Idyllwild

Accommodations
Silver Pines Lodge 25955 Cedar St Idyllwild CA   909-659-4335
http://www.silverpinesidyllwild.com/
This lodge sits on 1 1/2 acres of wooded pine forest overlooking Strawberry Creek. The lodge is approximately 2 blocks from the main village of Idyllwild where there are many eateries and shops. Each cabin is individually decorated and has its own unique features. Most rooms have fireplaces and about half have kitchens. Every room has its own refrigerator, bathroom, color cable TV and complimentary coffee. Dogs are welcome in all of the cabins, except the Foley Cabin. There is a $10 one time pet charge. They also ask that you please abide by the following pet rules. Never leave pets alone in the room. Pets should not go on the beds or furniture. Keep your dog leashed when on the property. Clean up after your pooch. Please wipe off your pets paws if it's snowy, rainy or muddy outside (they provide dog towels).
Tahquitz Inn 25840 Highway 243 Idyllwild CA   909-659-4554 (877-659-4554)
http://www.tahquitzinn.com
This inn is located in the heart of Idyllwild and allows all well-behaved dogs. They offer one and two bedroom suites with a separate bedroom, kitchen and porches. The inn has also been a location for several Hollywood film shoots. All of their rooms accommodate dogs and there is a $10 per day pet charge.
The Fireside Inn 54540 N Circle Drive Idyllwild CA   877-797-FIRE (3473)
http://www.thefireside-inn.com/
Surrounded by the natural landscape of the San Jacinto Mountains, this comfortable inn offers 7 duplex cottages and a private cottage. Some of the amenities include wood-burning fireplaces in all cottages, outdoor seating, barbecue and picnic areas, and daily feeding of the birds and small animals of the area. Dogs of all sizes are allowed for an additional $20 one time pet fee per room. Dogs may not be left alone in the room at any time, and they must be leashed and cleaned up after.

Vacation Home Rentals
Stellar Summit Cabin Call to arrange Idyllwild CA   626-482-6006
http://www.stellarsummitcabin.com
This secluded cabin is perched high on a hill in Idyllwild. There is a fenced deck, loft, jacuzzi and views. There is a $15 pet fee per visit.

Attractions
Annual Plein Air Festival North Circle Drive Idyllwild CA   866-439-5278
http://www.artinidyllwild.com/
Idyllwild is rated as one of the 100 Best Small Art Towns in America. Once a year there is a festival, usually held on a Saturday in the beginning of September, where artists create original works of art in the streets of the Idyllwild. Leashed dogs are welcome to accompany you at this outdoor event. For more details, please contact the Art Alliance of Idyllwild at 866-439-5278.

Parks
Humber Park Fern Valley Road Idyllwild CA   909-659-2117
The Devil's Slide Trail begins at this park. It is rated as a moderately difficult trail. The trail goes for about 6 miles and there is about a 3,000 foot elevation gain. Day passes are required. To get there, take Highway 243 to North Circle Drive. Turn right onto South Circle Drive, and then left to Fern Valley Road. Follow the signs to Humber Park.
Idyllwild Park Nature Center Highway 243 Idyllwild CA   909-659-3850
http://www.idyllwildnaturecenter.net/
This park offers 5 1/2 miles of hiking trails. Most of the trails are rated as easy, with the exception of one steep trail. Dogs are allowed, but need to be leashed. Your dog will also need to have a current rabies identification tag. The day use fees are $2 per person, $2 per dog and $1 per child. The park is located on Highway 243, about one mile northwest of Idyllwild.

Outdoor Restaurants
Joanne's Restaurant and Bar 25875 N Village Drive Idyllwild CA 951-659-0295
Well-behaved, leashed dogs are allowed at the outdoor tables.
Oma's European Restaurant 54241 Ridgeview Drive Idyllwild CA 951-659-2979
http://www.omabakery.com/
This restaurant offers European cuisine in a scenic setting. They are open for breakfast and lunch. Well-behaved,leashed dogs are allowed at the outdoor tables.

Lake Arrowhead

Accommodations
Arrowhead Saddleback Inn PO Box 1890 Lake Arrowhead CA 800-858-3334 (800-358-8733)
http://www.lakeArrowhead.com/saddleback/
This historic inn was originally constructed in 1917 as the Raven Hotel. It is now totally restored and a historical landmark. The inn is located at the entrance of the Lake Arrowhead Village. Dogs are allowed in some of the cottages. The cottages feature stone fireplaces, double whirlpool baths, heated towel racks and refrigerators. There is an $8 per day pet fee. Dog owners also need to sign a pet agreement.
Arrowhead Tree Top Lodge 27992 Rainbow Drive Lake Arrowhead CA 909-337-2311 (800-358-TREE)
http://www.lakeArrowhead.com/treetop/
This inn is nestled among the tall pines on four acres of heavily forested grounds. You and your pup can enjoy a stroll on their private nature trail or find a spot at Deep Creek to sit, relax and watch the squirrels and birds. Amenties include microwaves in each of the rustic alpine rooms. It is located within walking distance of the Lake Arrowhead Village. There is an $8 per day pet fee.
Gray Squirrel Inn 326 State Hwy 173 Lake Arrowhead CA 909-336-3602 (888-719-3563)
http://www.graysquirrelinn.com/
This inn is near Lake Arrowhead and has ten guest rooms. Room amenities include mini-refrigerators and coffee makers. Dogs are welcome in some of the rooms. There are no additional pet fees.
Prophet's Paradise B&B 26845 Modoc Lane Lake Arrowhead CA 909-336-1969
This bed and breakfast has five stories which cascade down its alpine hillside. This provides guests with privacy and intimate decks. All rooms have private baths. Amenities include a gym, a pool room, ping-pong, and darts, a horseshoe pit and a nearby hiking trail. Room rates start at $100 per night and include a gourmet breakfast. Your well-behaved dog is welcome. The owners also have pets. There are no additional pet fees.

Campgrounds and RV Parks
North Shore Campground Torrey Road Lake Arrowhead CA 909-337-2444 (877-444-6777)
This 27 site campground is located in the San Bernardino National Forest at 5,300 feet. RVs up to 22 feet are allowed and there are no hookups. The trailhead for the North Shore National Recreation Trail is located at this campground. Pets on leash are allowed at no additional fee, and please clean up after them. Dogs are allowed on the trails. The camp is located near the north shore of Lake Arrowhead, about two miles northeast of the village. To get there from the Lake Arrowhead Marina, go east on Torrey Road. At the first left, take the dirt road to Forest Road 2N25 to the trailhead. This campground is closed during the off-season. The camping and tent areas also allow dogs. There is a dog walk area at the campground. There are no electric or water hookups at the campgrounds.
Dogwood Campground Hwy 18 Rimforest CA 909-337-2444 (877-444-6777)
This 93 site campground is located in the San Bernardino National Forest at 5,600 feet. RVs up to 22 feet are allowed. Amenities include water, showers, and a dump station. The camp is located less than a mile from Rimforest and 3 miles from Lake Arrowhead. Pets on leash are allowed at no additional fee, and please clean up after them. Dogs are allowed on the trails. This campground is closed during the off-season. The camping and tent areas also allow dogs. There is a dog walk area at the campground. There are no electric or water hookups at the campgrounds.

Attractions
TOP 200 PLACE **Arrowhead Queen Boat Tours** 28200 Hwy 189 Building C100 Lake Arrowhead CA 909-336-6992
This enclosed paddlewheel boat is a great way to view beautiful Lake Arrowhead Lake and to learn about the area from their knowledgeable guides. Dogs are welcome aboard for no additional fee. They suggest that visitors with pets tour during the off-season, or weekdays during the busy summer season. Dogs must be friendly, and under owner's control/responsibility at all times.
Lake Arrowhead Village 28200 Highway 189 Lake Arrowhead CA 909-337-2533

http://www.lakearrowheadvillage.com/
This outdoor shopping resort features unique specialty and factory outlet stores. While dogs are not allowed in the stores (with the exception of the Big Dogs store), it is a nice place to walk with your pup. During the summer there are usually outdoor events next to the lake. Dogs must be leashed and you must clean up after your dog.
Children's Forest Keller Peak Road Sky Forest CA   909-338-5156
In 1993, San Bernardino National Forest set aside a 3,400-acre site within the forest to create the first Children's Forest in the United States. Forty children and teenagers from around the country were selected and brought to work with key Forest Service staff and other experts to design a trail and interpretive exhibits that teach young people about the Forest. Dogs are not allowed on the guided tour, but you and your pooch can take a self-guided tour on the 1/2 mile paved interpretive trail. Children's Forest is located off Highway 18 at Keller Peak Road, east of Running Springs in the San Bernardino Mountains.

Stores
Big Dogs Sportswear 28200 Hwy 189 Lake Arrowhead CA   909-336-1998
http://www.bigdogs.com
This retail store sells sportswear for people and allows well-behaved dogs inside. It is located in the Lake Arrowhead Village.
Coach Factory Store 28200 Highway 189 Lake Arrowhead CA   909-337-2678
Well-behaved leashed dogs are allowed inside this store.
Jockey International 28200 Highway 189 Lake Arrowhead CA   909-337-8813
Well-behaved leashed dogs are allowed inside this store.
Mountain Haus Interiors 28200 Highway 189 Lake Arrowhead CA   909-336-3581
Well-behaved leashed dogs are allowed inside this store.
Photo Express 28200 Highway 189 Lake Arrowhead CA   909-337-3224
Well-behaved leashed dogs up to about 75 pounds are allowed inside this store. They can take a photo of you, any other people with you and your dog between 10am and 3pm daily. Photos are ready the same day at 4pm.
Wildflowers 28200 Highway 189 Lake Arrowhead CA   909-337-8248
Well-behaved leashed dogs are allowed inside this store.

Parks
Indian Rock Trail Highway 173 Lake Arrowhead CA   909-337-2444
This .5 mile easy walk is located in the San Bernardino National Forest. The trail takes you to large stone slabs that were used by the Serrano Indians to grind acorns into flour. Pets on leash are allowed and please clean up after them. To get there take Highway 173 north to the Rock Camp Station.
North Shore National Recreation Trail Torrey Road Lake Arrowhead CA   909-337-2444
This 1.7 mile moderate rated trail is located in the San Bernardino National Forest. The trail descends to Little Bear Creek and then goes to Forest Road 2N26Y. Pets on leash are allowed and please clean up after them. To get there from the Lake Arrowhead Marina, go east on Torrey Road. At the first left, take the dirt road to Forest Road 2N25 to the trailhead.

Lake Elsinore

Stores
PetSmart Pet Store 29227 Central Ave Lake Elsinore CA   951-245-0267
Your licensed and well-behaved leashed dog is allowed in the store.
Petco Pet Store 18290 Collier Avenue Lake Elsinore CA   951-471-8166
Your licensed and well-behaved leashed dog is allowed in the store.

Murrieta

Stores
PetSmart Pet Store 25290 Madison Ave Murrieta CA   951-696-9847
Your licensed and well-behaved leashed dog is allowed in the store.

Perris

Accommodations

Motel 6 - Hemet 3885 West Florida Avenue Hemet CA   951-929-8900 (800-466-8356)
One well-behaved family pet per room. Guest must notify front desk upon arrival. Guest is liable for any damages. In consideration of all guests, pets must never be left unattended in the guest rooms.

Campgrounds and RV Parks

Lake Perris Campgrounds 17801 Lake Perris Drive Perris CA   951-657-0676 (800-444-7275)
This campground offers 434 campsites including two RV areas with full hookups. While dogs are not allowed in the lake or within 100 feet of the water, they are allowed on miles of trails including the bike trail that loops around the lake. Pets must be on no more than a 6 foot leash, and please clean up after them. Dogs may not be left unattended. The camping and tent areas also allow dogs. There is a dog walk area at the campground.
Luiseno Campground, Lake Perris State Rec Area 17801 Lake Perris Drive Perris CA   951-940-5603 (800-444-PARK (7275))
This campground sits among the white sands and blue waters of Lake Perris and offers a wide variety of land and water recreation. Animals must be leashed (6 foot or less leash), caged, or in a tent, motor home, or vehicle at all times, and can not be left unattended. Visitors are responsible for clean-up after their pets. No body contact with the water is allowed, and dogs may not be on the trails or the beach. The camping and tent areas also allow dogs. There is a dog walk area at the campground.

Attractions

TOP 200 PLACE Orange Empire Railway Museum 2201 South A Street Perris CA   951-657-2605
http://www.oerm.org/
Home to the West's largest collection of railway locomotives, streetcars, freight/passenger cars, interurban electric cars, buildings, and other objects dating from the 1870's, this museum also educates the public of the rail history and offers a variety of interactive programs. You can ride or drive a locomotive, have a special caboose birthday party, visit the museum store, picnic, or take self-guided or guided tours. Dogs of all sizes are welcome. Dogs are allowed throughout the grounds; they are not allowed in the gift shop. Dogs must be well mannered, leashed, and cleaned up after.

Stores

PetSmart Pet Store 2771 Florida Ave W Hemet CA   951-925-8400
Your licensed and well-behaved leashed dog is allowed in the store.
Petco Pet Store 2545 West Florida Avenue Hemet CA   951-652-3437
Your licensed and well-behaved leashed dog is allowed in the store.

Parks

Lake Perris State Recreation Area off Cajalco Expressway Lakeview CA   909-657-0676
While dogs are not allowed in the lake or within 100 feet of the water, they are allowed on miles of trails including the bike trail that loops around the lake. Pets must be leashed and please clean up after them. Pets are also allowed in the campgrounds. The park is located 11 miles south of Riverside via Highway 60 or Interstate 215.
Harford Springs Reserve Gavilan Road Perris CA   909-684-7032
This 325 acre park offer hiking and equestrian trails. The park is located about 7 miles west of Perris, 2 miles south of Cajalco Road on Gavilan Road. Dogs must be leashed and please clean up after them.

Phelan

Accommodations

Best Western Cajon Pass 8317 US Hwy 138 Phelan CA   760-249-6777 (800-780-7234)
Dogs of all sizes are allowed. There is a $25 one time per pet fee per visit. Reservations are recommended due to limited rooms for pets. Only non-smoking rooms used for pets.

Pomona - Ontario

Accommodations

Motel 6 - Chino - Los Angeles Area 12266 Central Avenue Chino CA   909-591-3877 (800-466-8356)
One well-behaved family pet per room. Guest must notify front desk upon arrival. Guest is liable for any damages. In consideration of all guests, pets must never be left unattended in the guest rooms.

Motel 6 - Los Angeles - Hacienda Heights 1154 South 7th Avenue Hacienda Heights CA   626-968-9462 (800-466-8356)
One well-behaved family pet per room. Guest must notify front desk upon arrival. Guest is liable for any damages. In consideration of all guests, pets must never be left unattended in the guest rooms.

Country Inns & Suites by Carlson 231 North Vineyard Avenue Ontario CA   909-937-6000
Dogs of all sizes are allowed. There is a $50 one time additional pet fee. Some rooms have full kitchens and wireless high-speed Internet access. There is an outdoor pool and a fitness center.

Holiday Inn 3400 Shelby Street Ontario CA   909-466-9600 (877-270-6405)
http://www.holiday-inn.com
Amenities include a heated pool, spa, exercise room, sauna, billiards, ping-pong tables, video games and basketball courts. Rooms include refrigerators with free juices and bottled water, microwave ovens with free popcorn, hair dryers, and iron/ironing boards. There is a $25 one time pet fee.

La Quinta Inn & Suites Ontario Airport 3555 Inland Empire Blvd Ontario CA   909-476-1112 (800-531-5900)
Dogs of all sizes are allowed. There are no additional pet fees, but a credit card must be on file. Dogs must be crated if left alone in the room, and be leashed and cleaned up after.

Motel 6 - Ontario Airport 1560 East 4th Street Ontario CA   909-984-2424 (800-466-8356)
One well-behaved family pet per room. Guest must notify front desk upon arrival. Guest is liable for any damages. In consideration of all guests, pets must never be left unattended in the guest rooms.

Red Roof Inn - Ontario Airport 1818 East Holt Boulevard Ontario CA   909-988-8466 (800-RED-ROOF)
One well-behaved family pet per room. Guest must notify front desk upon arrival. Guest is liable for any damages. In consideration of all guests, pets must never be left unattended in the guest rooms.

Residence Inn by Marriott 2025 Convention Center Way Ontario CA   909-937-6788
Dogs of all sizes are allowed. There is a $75 one time fee, and a pet policy to sign at check in.

Motel 6 - Los Angeles - Pomona 2470 South Garey Avenue Pomona CA   909-591-1871 (800-466-8356)
One well-behaved family pet per room. Guest must notify front desk upon arrival. Guest is liable for any damages. In consideration of all guests, pets must never be left unattended in the guest rooms.

Sheraton Suites Fairplex 601 West McKinley Ave. Pomona CA   909-622-2220 (888-625-5144)
Dogs of all sizes are allowed. Pet rooms are available on the second floor only. You must sign a pet policy when checking in with a dog. Dogs are not allowed to be left alone in the room.

Shilo Inn 3200 Temple Ave Pomona CA 909-598-0073 (800-222-2244)
http://www.shiloinns.com
Amenities include a complimentary breakfast buffet, outdoor pool & spa, guest laundry, fitness center and fresh fruit, popcorn & coffee. Rooms include microwaves, refrigerators, hair dryers, iron/ironing boards and more. There is a $10 per day additional pet fee.

Motel 6 - Los Angeles - Rowland Heights 18970 East Labin Court Rowland Heights CA   626-964-5333 (800-466-8356)
One well-behaved family pet per room. Guest must notify front desk upon arrival. Guest is liable for any damages. In consideration of all guests, pets must never be left unattended in the guest rooms.

Motel 6 - Los Angeles - San Dimas 502 West Arrow Highway San Dimas CA   909-592-5631 (800-466-8356)
One well-behaved family pet per room. Guest must notify front desk upon arrival. Guest is liable for any damages. In consideration of all guests, pets must never be left unattended in the guest rooms.

Red Roof Inn - San Dimas 204 North Village Court San Dimas CA   909-599-2362 (800-RED-ROOF)
One well-behaved family pet per room. Guest must notify front desk upon arrival. Guest is liable for any damages. In consideration of all guests, pets must never be left unattended in the guest rooms.

Campgrounds and RV Parks

East Shore RV Park 1440 Camper View Road San Dimas CA   909-599-8355 (800-809-3778)
http://www.eastshorervpark.com/
This family RV park offers over 500 full hookup paved sites including some pull through sites. Site amenities include a grassy area, view sites, and full hookups with 20, 30 or 50 amp service. Park amenities include picnic areas, children's playground, laundry room, swimming pool, general store and market, video rentals, basketballs and volleyballs, email station, restrooms and 24 hour check-in. Well-behaved dogs are allowed in the RV park, but not in the tenting area. Pets must be leashed and please clean up after them. There is a $2 per day pet fee. Dogs may not be left unattended. This RV park is open year-round. There is a dog walk area at the campground.

Stores

Petco Pet Store 7221 Haven Avenue Alta Loma CA   909-945-5881
Your licensed and well-behaved leashed dog is allowed in the store.

PetSmart Pet Store 11945 Central Ave Chino CA 909-628-6665
Your licensed and well-behaved leashed dog is allowed in the store.
Petco Pet Store 3820 Grand Avenue Chino CA 909-364-9807
Your licensed and well-behaved leashed dog is allowed in the store.
PetSmart Pet Store 13001 Peyton Dr Chino Hills CA 909-627-4849
Your licensed and well-behaved leashed dog is allowed in the store.
PetSmart Pet Store 1314 N Azusa Ave Covina CA 626-967-6099
Your licensed and well-behaved leashed dog is allowed in the store.
PetSmart Pet Store 21050 Golden Springs Diamond Bar CA 909-595-0097
Your licensed and well-behaved leashed dog is allowed in the store.
PetSmart Pet Store 12483 Limonite Ave Mira Loma CA 951-685-1927
Your licensed and well-behaved leashed dog is allowed in the store.
Barnes and Noble Bookstore 9041 Central Avenue Montclair CA 909-621-5553
Well-behaved and leashed or carried dogs are allowed in this Barnes and Noble bookstore located off Highway 10 at Central Ave.
Petco Pet Store 9197-G Central Avenue Montclair CA 909-624-9868
Your licensed and well-behaved leashed dog is allowed in the store.
Petco Pet Store 101 E Foothill Blvd Ste 5 Pomona CA 909-596-7670
Your licensed and well-behaved leashed dog is allowed in the store.
Petco Pet Store 822 West Arrow Highway San Dimas CA 909-394-2037
Your licensed and well-behaved leashed dog is allowed in the store.
PetSmart Pet Store 1935 N Campus Ave Upland CA 909-981-4139
Your licensed and well-behaved leashed dog is allowed in the store.

Parks

Cucamonga-Guasti Park 800 N. Archibald Ave. Ontario CA 909-945-4321
This regional park allows leashed dogs. There is a nice path that winds along the lake which is a popular fishing spot. There is a minimal day use fee.
Ganesha Park McKinley Ave Pomona CA
It is not a large park, but is a nice place to walk with your dog. The park also has several playground and picnic areas. Dogs must be leashed.
Schabarum Regional Park 17250 E. Colima Road Rowland Heights CA 626-854-5560
This 640 acre wilderness park offers open space, picturesque canyons and rolling hills. Popular activities at the park including hiking, biking and horseback riding. Park amenities include an 18 station fitness trail, picnic areas, equestrian center, playgrounds and sports fields. There is a parking fee on weekends, holidays and during special events. Dogs are allowed at the park and on the hiking trails. Pets must be leashed and people need to clean up after their pet.
Frank Bonelli Park 120 Via Verde Road San Dimas CA 909-599-8411
This 1,980 acre park has a 250 acre lake for swimming, water skiing, wind surfing, sailing and fishing. The lake is stocked with trout, bluegill, catfish, and largemouth bass. Park amenities include hiking trails, playgrounds and food stands. There is a parking fee on weekends, holidays and during special events. Dogs are allowed at the park and on the hiking trails, but not in the water or at the beach area. Pets must be leashed and people need to clean up after their pet.
San Dimas Canyon Nature Center 1628 N. Sycamore Canyon Road San Dimas CA 909-599-7512
This 1,000 plus acre park offers a variety of nature trails. There is a minimal parking fee. Dogs are allowed on the trails, but must be leashed. Please clean up after your dog.

Off-Leash Dog Parks

Pooch Park 100 S. College Avenue Claremont CA
http://www.claremontpoochpark.org
This park has lots of grass and trees and a ravine for the dogs to climb up and down. There is a 3 foot fence around the park. The Pooch Park is located in College Park, just south of the Metrolink tracks on S. College Avenue.
San Dimas Dog Park 301 Horsethief Canyon Rd San Dimas CA 909-394-6230
http://www.sandimasdogpark.org/
The fenced dog park is open during daylight hours. The park is closed on Wednesday afternoons for cleaning. The dog park is located in the Horsethief Canyon Park which is one mile north of the 210 Freeway.
Baldy View Dog Park 11th Street at Mountain Ave. Upland CA 909-931-4280
http://www.uplanddogpark.com/
The 1.3 acre Baldy View Dog Park has two fenced areas for large and small dogs. To get to the dog park, which is in Baldy View Park, take the I-10 to Mountain Ave. Head north on Mountain Ave and turn right on 11th Street. The park will be on your left.

Outdoor Restaurants
Aruffo's Italian Cuisine 126 Yale Ave Claremont CA 909-624-9624
Dogs are allowed at the outdoor tables.
Danson's Restaurant 109 Yale Ave Claremont CA 909-621-1818
This restaurant serves American and Mexican food. Dogs are allowed at the outdoor tables.
Some Crust Bakery 119 Yale Avenue Claremont CA 909-621-9772
Dogs are allowed at the outdoor tables.
Village Grill 148 Yale Ave Claremont CA 909-626-8813
Dogs are allowed at the outdoor tables.
Aoki Japanese Restaurant 2307 D Street La Verne CA 909-593-2239
Dogs are allowed at the outdoor tables.
Cafe Allegro 2124 3rd Street La Verne CA 909-593-0788
Dogs are allowed at the outdoor tables.
Casa Garcia's Grill 2124 Bonita Ave La Verne CA 909-593-9092
Dogs are allowed at the outdoor tables.
Phoenix Garden 2232 D Street #101 La Verne CA 909-392-2244
Dogs are allowed at the outdoor tables.
Baja Fresh Mexican Grill 929 N. Milliken Ave Ste C Ontario CA 909-484-6200
http://www.bajafresh.com
This Mexican restaurant is open for lunch and dinner. They use fresh ingredients and making their salsa and beans daily. Some of the items on their menu include Enchiladas, Burritos, Tacos Salads, Quesadillas, Nachos, Chicken, Steak and more. Well-behaved leashed dogs are allowed at the outdoor tables.
In-N-Out Burger 1891 E. G Street Ontario CA 800-786-1000
http://www.in-n-out.com/
This In-N-Out Burger has an outside window where you can place an order with your pup.
Joey's Pizza 790 N. Archibald Ave. Ontario CA 909-944-6701
Pizza, salads, lasagna and more are served at this restaurant which has dog-friendly outdoor seating. It is located next to Cucamonga Regional Park (see Parks).
Roady's Restaurant 160 W. Bonita Ave San Dimas CA 909-592-0980
Dogs are allowed at the outdoor tables.

Events
Inland Valley Humane Society Dog Walk 120 Via Verde, Bonelli Park San Dimas CA 909-623977
This pledge walk is an annual event where you and your pet (or even those without pets) walk a scenic 1, 2, or 3 mile route through Bonelli Park to benefit the animals of the IVHS and S.P.C.A. Thousands attend this event, usually held in May, because in addition to the cause, there are prizes, games and activities for dogs and their owners, a pancake breakfast, live music, a variety of vendors, and a lot more. Dogs must be well mannered, leashed, and cleaned up after at all times.

Vets and Kennels
East Valley Emergency Pet Clinic 938 N Diamond Bar Blvd Diamond Bar CA 909-861-5737
Monday - Friday 6 pm to 8 am, Saturday 12 noon to 8 am Monday.
Emergency Pet Clinic of Pomona 8980 Benson Ave Montclair CA 909-981-1051
Monday - Friday 6 pm to 8 am, Noon Saturday to 8 am Monday.

Riverside

Accommodations
Motel 6 - Corona 200 North Lincoln Avenue Corona CA 951-735-6408 (800-466-8356)
One well-behaved family pet per room. Guest must notify front desk upon arrival. Guest is liable for any damages. In consideration of all guests, pets must never be left unattended in the guest rooms.
Comfort Inn 23330 Sunnymead Blvd Moreno Valley CA 951-242-0699 (877-424-6423)
Dogs of all sizes are allowed. There can be up to 2 large or 3 small to medium dogs per room. There is a $10 per night per pet additional fee. Dogs must be quiet, leashed, cleaned up after, and the front desk informed if there is a pet alone in the room.
Econo Lodge 24412 Sunnymead Blvd Moreno Valley CA 909-247-6699
There is a $50 refundable pet deposit and a $5 per day pet fee.
Best Western of Riverside 10518 Magnolia Ave Riverside CA 951-359-0770 (800-780-7234)
Dogs of all sizes are allowed. There is a $100 returnable deposit required per room. There is a $10 per night pet fee per pet. Smoking and non-smoking are available for pet rooms.

Motel 6 - Riverside East 1260 University Avenue Riverside CA 951-784-2131 (800-466-8356)
One well-behaved family pet per room. Guest must notify front desk upon arrival. Guest is liable for any damages. In consideration of all guests, pets must never be left unattended in the guest rooms.
Motel 6 - Riverside South 3663 La Sierra Avenue Riverside CA 951-351-0764 (800-466-8356)
One well-behaved family pet per room. Guest must notify front desk upon arrival. Guest is liable for any damages. In consideration of all guests, pets must never be left unattended in the guest rooms.
Motel 6 - Riverside West 6830 Valley Way Rubidoux CA 951-681-6666 (800-466-8356)
One well-behaved family pet per room. Guest must notify front desk upon arrival. Guest is liable for any damages. In consideration of all guests, pets must never be left unattended in the guest rooms.

Attractions
Citrus State Historic Park Van Buren Blvd. Riverside CA 909-780-6222
This 400-acre historic park recognizes the importance of the citrus industry in southern California. In the early 1900s, "Citrus was King" and there was a "second Gold Rush" which brought potential citrus barons to California. The park, which is reminiscent of a 1900s city park, has demonstration groves, an interpretive structure and picnic areas. Today it is also a working citrus grove and continues to produce high-quality fruits. Dogs are not allowed in the buildings, but are welcome to walk leashed on the grounds, including several trails around the groves. The park is located in Riverside, one mile east of Highway 91. It at the corner of Van Buren Blvd. and Dufferin Ave.

Stores
PetSmart Pet Store 573 Mckinley St Corona CA 951-340-0501
Your licensed and well-behaved leashed dog is allowed in the store.
Petco Pet Store 3485 Grand Oaks Corona CA 951-808-4765
Your licensed and well-behaved leashed dog is allowed in the store.
PetSmart Pet Store 2828 Campus Pkwy Riverside CA 951-653-8482
Your licensed and well-behaved leashed dog is allowed in the store.
Petco Pet Store 3384 Tyler St Riverside CA 951-688-8886
Your licensed and well-behaved leashed dog is allowed in the store.
Petco Pet Store 8974 Trautwein Rd Riverside CA 951-697-4024
Your licensed and well-behaved leashed dog is allowed in the store.

Parks
Box Springs Mountain Reserve Pigeon Pass Road Riverside CA 909-684-7032
This 1,155 acre park offers hiking and equestrian trails. The park is located 5 miles east of Riverside off Highway 60 and Pigeon Pass Road. Dogs must be leashed and please clean up after them.
Hidden Valley Wildlife Arlington Avenue Riverside CA 909-785-6362
Dogs on leash are allowed at this wildlife reserve. It is a popular spot for birdwatching and walking. There is a minimal fee for day use. This reserve is part of the Santa Ana River Regional Park. To get there from the 91 Fwy, go east to the city of Riverside. Exit on La Sierra Ave. and turn left (north). La Sierra dead-ends into Arlington. Bear left at the signal. Drive past the hills until you come to the sign that says "Hidden Valley." Take the first dirt road to the right.
Mount Rubidoux Park Mt. Rubidoux Drive Riverside CA
This park is the highest point in downtown Riverside. It is a popular hiking trail which offers a spectacular 360 degree view of Riverside. Dogs on leash are allowed on the trails. To get there from downtown Riverside, take Mission Inn Avenue northeast (towards the Santa Ana River). Turn left (west) onto Redwood Street. Continue straight to stay on Redwood (otherwise you will go onto University Ave). Turn right on 9th Street and follow it to the park.
Rancho Jurupa Park Crestmore Road Riverside CA 909-684-7032
This 350 acre park is part of the Santa Ana River Regional Park and has more than 10 miles of hiking and equestrian trails. There are also horseshoe pits and picnic areas. To get there from downtown Riverside, take Mission Inn Ave northwest (towards the Santa Ana River). Go over the river and turn left at Crestmore Road. Follow this road to the park entrance. There is a minimal fee for parking and for dogs. Dogs must be leashed.

Off-Leash Dog Parks
Butterfield Park Dog Park 1886 Butterfield Drive Corona CA 909-736-2241
This .8 acre fenced off-leash dog area is located in Butterfield Park. The dog park is well-shaded with benches, a picnic table and a doggie drinking fountain. From the 91 Freeway, take the Maple Street exit and go north. Maple will dead end at Smith Street. Go left on Smith Street about .5 miles to Butterfield Drive. Then turn left to Butterfield Park just across the street from the airport. Thanks to one of our readers for recommending this dog park.
Carlson Dog Park Mission Inn Ave Riverside CA 909-715-3440

This dog park is located near the river. It is also near Mt. Rubidoux Park, which is a good place for hiking before or after your visit to the dog park. To get to the dog park, take the 91 freeway to Mission Inn St. and go west through downtown Riverside past Market St. The park is on the south side just after you cross a large bridge but before you get to the riverbed. Thanks to one of our readers for recommending this dog park.
Pat Merritt Dog Park Limonite Frontage Rd at Avenue Juan Bautista Riverside CA 951-358- 7387
http://www.rcdas.org/parks.htm
This two section fenced dog park is located at the Limonite Frontade Rd in the Jurupa Hills area. There is a section for large dogs and a separate section for small dogs.
Riverwalk Dog Park Pierce Street and Collett Avenue Riverside CA 951-358- 7387
http://www.rcdas.org/parks.htm
Riverwalk Dog Park is divided into two areas for large and small dogs. The park has water, cleanup bags and benches. There is not much shade in the park yet as the trees that have been planted there are still small. To get to the dog park from the 91 Freeway exit at Magnolia and head north on Pierce. Pierce will turn into Esplanade but Pierce will head off to the left. Follow Pierce by turning left to the dog park.

Outdoor Restaurants
Camille's Sidewalk Cafe 163 W Ontario, Suite 101 Corona CA 951-736-6816
A vision of healthier, tastier foods inspired the idea for the freshly made salads, gourmet wraps and sandwiches, drinks, desserts, and coffees that are offered at all of Camille's Cafes. Dogs are allowed to sit with you at your outdoor table. Dogs must be attended to at all times, well behaved, and leashed.
Rubio's Baja Grill 110 Hidden Valley Pkwy Norco CA 909-898-3591
Dogs are allowed at the outdoor tables.
Antonious Pizza 3737 Main Street Riverside CA 909-682-9100
This pizza place, which has dog-friendly outdoor seating, is located in downtown Riverside.

Vets and Kennels
Animal Emergency Clinic 12022 La Crosse Ave Grand Terrace CA 909-783-1300
Monday - Friday 6 pm to 8 am, 24 hours on weekends and holidays.

Running Springs

Cross Country Ski Resorts
Green Valley Nordic Ski Area PO Box 2990 Running Springs CA 909-867-2600
http://www.rimnordic.com
This ski area is located off Highway 18 in the San Bernardino Mountains, about 90 miles from Los Angeles and 125 miles from San Diego. While dogs are not allowed at Rim Nordic, they are welcome on the Green Valley trails. When renting your skis, ask them about their "doggie rules" that you and your pooch will need to follow. The trails are usually groomed. Call ahead to make sure they have received enough snow to be open.

San Bernardino

Accommodations
Days Inn 2830 Iowa Ave Colton CA 909-788-9900 (800-329-7466)
A well-behaved large dog is okay. There is a $5 per day additional fee.
Motel 6 - Fontana 10195 Sierra Avenue Fontana CA 909-823-8686 (800-466-8356)
One well-behaved family pet per room. Guest must notify front desk upon arrival. Guest is liable for any damages. In consideration of all guests, pets must never be left unattended in the guest rooms.
TownePlace Suites Ontario Airport 9645 Milliken Avenue Rancho Cucamonga CA 714-256-2070
Dogs of all sizes are allowed. There is a $75 one time pet fee per visit.
Best Western Sandman Motel 1120 W Colton Ave Redlands CA 909-793-2001 (800-780-7234)
Dogs of all sizes are allowed. There is a $50 returnable deposit required per room. Reservations are recommended due to limited rooms for pets. Smoking and non-smoking are available for pet rooms.
Best Western Empire Inn 475 W Valley Blvd Rialto CA 909-877-0690 (800-780-7234)
There is a $10 per night pet fee per small pet. There is a $10 per night pet fee per large pet. Smoking and non-smoking are available for pet rooms.
Hilton 285 E Hospitality Lane San Bernardino CA 909-889-0133
Dogs up to 50 pounds are allowed. There is a $250 deposit, $200 of which is refundable and a pet policy to sign

at check in.

Motel 6 - San Bernardino North 1960 Ostrems Way San Bernardino CA 909-887-8191 (800-466-8356)
One well-behaved family pet per room. Guest must notify front desk upon arrival. Guest is liable for any damages. In consideration of all guests, pets must never be left unattended in the guest rooms.

Motel 6 - San Bernardino South 111 West Redlands Boulevard San Bernardino CA 909-825-6666 (800-466-8356)
One well-behaved family pet per room. Guest must notify front desk upon arrival. Guest is liable for any damages. In consideration of all guests, pets must never be left unattended in the guest rooms.

Stores

PetSmart Pet Store 15042 Summit Ave Fontana CA 909-463-2900
Your licensed and well-behaved leashed dog is allowed in the store.

PetSmart Pet Store 10940 Foothill Blvd Rancho Cucamonga CA 909-481-8700
Your licensed and well-behaved leashed dog is allowed in the store.

Petco Pet Store 27580 West Lugonia Avenue Redlands CA 909-335-0249
Your licensed and well-behaved leashed dog is allowed in the store.

PetSmart Pet Store 595 E Hospitality Lane San Bernardino CA 909-383-1055
Your licensed and well-behaved leashed dog is allowed in the store.

Parks

Prospect Park Cajon Street Redlands CA 909-798-7572
Prospect Park is a 11.4 acre natural park with trails and picnic facilities. Dogs on leash are allowed.

San Bernardino National Forest 1824 S. Commercenter Circle San Bernardino CA 909-382-2600
http://www.fs.fed.us/r5/sanbernardino/
This national forest covers over 600,000 acres of land which ranges in elevation from 2,000 to 11,502 feet. Please see our listings in this region for dog-friendly hikes and/or campgrounds.

Off-Leash Dog Parks

Loma Linda Dog Park Beaumont Ave and Mountain View Ave. Loma Linda CA
There are two fenced areas at this dog park. One is for large dogs and one is for small dogs. The dog park is open during daylight hours. The dog park is on the side of a hill so it can get slick after rain. From I-10 take Mountain View south to Beaumont. Turn left on Beaumont and the park is on the right.

Wildwood Dog Park 536 E. 40th St San Bernardino CA
Thanks to one of our readers who writes: "We have 3.5 acres divided into 2 large areas & 1 smaller area just for little and older dogs. The larger areas are rotated to help reduce wear & tear on the turf. Amenities include: Fencing, Benches, Handicapped Access, Lighting, Parking, Poop Bags, Restrooms, Shelter, Trash Cans, Water Available. Current Shots & License Required. We are also double-gated for Safety."

Outdoor Restaurants

Baja Fresh Mexican Grill 745 E. Hospitality Lane Ste C San Bernardino CA 909-890-1854
http://www.bajafresh.com
This Mexican restaurant is open for lunch and dinner. They use fresh ingredients and making their salsa and beans daily. Some of the items on their menu include Enchiladas, Burritos, Tacos Salads, Quesadillas, Nachos, Chicken, Steak and more. Well-behaved leashed dogs are allowed at the outdoor tables.

Temecula

Accommodations

Comfort Inn-Wine Country 27338 Jefferson Avenue Temecula CA 951-296-3788 (877-424-6423)
Dogs of all sizes are allowed. There is a $20 per night per pet additional fee. Dogs must be quiet, well behaved, leashed, cleaned up after, and the Do Not Disturb sign put on the door if they are in the room alone. Dogs must be removed for housekeeping.

Motel 6 - Temecula - Rancho California 41900 Moreno Drive Temecula CA 951-676-7199 (800-466-8356)
One well-behaved family pet per room. Guest must notify front desk upon arrival. Guest is liable for any damages. In consideration of all guests, pets must never be left unattended in the guest rooms.

Campgrounds and RV Parks

Pechanga RV Resort 45000 Pechanga Parkway Temecula CA 951-587-0484 (877-997-8386)

http://www.pechangarv.com/index.asp
This RV only resort is located at the Pechanga Casino. They offer 168 sites with 20, 30 and 50 amp service, cable TV, 25 pull through sites, 3 internet access stations, a heated pool, two spas, and an attractive patio area with a full barbecue adjoining the recreation room. Well behaved, friendly dogs are allowed for no additional fee. Dogs may not be left unattended, and they must be leashed and cleaned up after. If dogs are not cleaned up after, they will ask visitors to leave. There are some breed restrictions. There is a dog walk area at the campground.
Vail Lake Wine Country RV Resort 38000 Hwy 79 S Temecula CA 951-303-0173 (866-VAIL LAKE (824-5525))
This RV resort is located in the country, about 15 minutes from Interstate 15. There are several hiking trails throughout the RV park where you can walk with your dog. There is no additional pet fee. Dogs may not be left unattended, and they must be leashed and cleaned up after. There is a dog walk area at the campground.

Attractions

TOP 200 PLACE **Baily Vineyard** 33440 La Serena Way Temecula CA 951-676-WINE (9463)
http://www.bailywinery.com/
Grapes are brought to this winery's state-of-the-art production facility from 32 acres of grapes grown in 4 different sites in the Temecula Valley. The restaurant on site (Carol's) offers patio dining service, and a selection of luncheon salads, sandwiches, grilled fish and steak, and pasta dishes. Dogs are allowed around the grounds, and at the outside dining area, but not in the tasting room. Dogs must be well behaved, and leashed and cleaned up after at all times.
Falkner Winery 40620 Calle Contento Temecula CA 951-676-8231
http://www.falknerwinery.com/
The wines here display a similar taste of full fruit flavors with a soft, clean finish, and they offer both inside and outside wine tasting areas, a grassy tree-lined picnic area with tables, and a gift shop that offers unique gifts and foods for hungry/thirsty visitors. Dogs are allowed around the grounds, but not in the tasting room or the outside dining area of the Pinnacle Restaurant. Dogs must be well behaved, and leashed and cleaned up after at all times.
Filsinger Vineyards and Winery 39050 De Portola Rd Temecula CA 909-302-6363
Dogs are allowed at the outdoor picnic tables.
Keyways Vineyard and Winery 37338 De Portola Rd Temecula CA 909-302-7888
Dogs are allowed at the outdoor picnic tables.
Maurice Car'rie Winery 34225 Rancho California Rd Temecula CA 909-676-1711
Dogs are allowed at the outdoor picnic area. There are usually several outdoor arts and crafts vendors at the winery.
Maurice Carrie Vineyard 34225 Rancho California Road Temecula CA 951-676-1711
http://www.mauricecarriewinery.com/
This winery features award wining wines, picnic grounds where you can dine on their specialty of baked brie in Sourdough, a unique gift shop, and a new Pineapple flavored Champagne. Dogs are allowed around the grounds, but not in the tasting room. Dogs must be well behaved, and leashed and cleaned up after at all times.
Miramonte Winery 33410 Rancho California Road Temecula CA 951-506-5500
http://www.miramontewinery.com/
This award winning winery's wine program is maturing with a clear focus on southern Rhone varietals. They regularly host special events, and offer one of the most stunning views in the valley. Dogs must be friendly though, as they also have a dog who likes to greet visitors. Dogs can check out the grounds and the tasting room. Dogs must be well behaved, leashed, and cleaned up after.
Mount Palomar Winery 33820 Rancho California Road Temecula CA 951-676-5047
This winery operates on 40 acres producing all the wines that are created on the property, and they can all be sampled at the Guest Center, which also has a gift shop and deli. Their emphasis is on classic, Bordeaux style blends and Italian varieties, and they have been the recipient of numerous awards. Dogs are allowed around the grounds, picnic area, and patio, but not in the winery. Dogs must be well behaved, and leashed and cleaned up after at all times.
Oak Mountain Winery 36522 Via Verde Temecula CA 951-699-9102
http://www.oakmountainwinery.com/
This winery combines century old wine making techniques with modern day technology to produce a variety of award wining wines. Dogs are welcome on the grounds, but not in the tasting room. Dogs must be well behaved, leashed, and cleaned up after.
Old Town Temecula Front Street Temecula CA
Old Town Temecula is a quaint historic area with wooden sidewalks where you and your leashed dog can walk. There are shops and some restaurants with outdoor seating.
Stuart Cellars 33515 Rancho California Road Temecula CA 888-260-0870
http://www.stuartcellars.com/main.html
This enterprise has been the recipient of many award winning wines, and continues to incorporate the rich wine making traditions of the Old World with a bit of California flair. They also offer a nice picnic area on spacious

grounds overlooking the Temecula Valley. Dogs are allowed around the grounds and the picnic area, but not in the tasting room. Dogs must be well behaved, and leashed and cleaned up after at all times.
Temecula Hills Winery 47200 De Portola Road Temecula CA 951-767-3450
http://www.temeculahillswinery.com/
Specializing in Zinfandel, Syrah, Viognier, Mourvedre and Cabernet Sauvignon varietals, this winery, sitting atop the hills in Temecula, also offers some very spectacular views. Dogs are welcome around the ground and in the picnic area, but not in the buildings. Dogs must be well behaved, leashed, and cleaned up after.
Van Roekel Winery 34567 Rancho California Rd Temecula CA 909-699-6961
Dogs are allowed at the picnic area.

Stores
PetSmart Pet Store 32413 Hwy 79 Temecula CA 951-302-1209
Your licensed and well-behaved leashed dog is allowed in the store.
Petco Pet Store 40474 Winchester Rd Temecula CA 951-296-0388
Your licensed and well-behaved leashed dog is allowed in the store.

Parks
Duck Pond Rancho California and Ynez Rd Temecula CA 909-836-3285
Dogs on leash are allowed in the park. Owners must pick up after their dog.
Lake Skinner Recreation Area Rancho California Road Temecula CA 909-926-1541
This 6,040 acre park features a lake, hiking trails, equestrian trails and camping. Dogs are allowed on the trails and in the campgrounds, but not in the lake or within 50 feet of the lake. Dogs must be on a 6 foot or less leash and please clean up after them. To get there, take Highway 15 to Rancho California Road and go north 10 miles. There is a minimal fee for day use of the park.
Sam Hicks Park Old Town Temecula Temecula CA 909-836-3285
Dogs are allowed on leash. Owners must pick up after their pets.

Off-Leash Dog Parks
Temecula Dog Exercise Area 44747 Redhawk Parkway Temecula CA 951-694-6444
Tomecula's first dog park was opened in 2006 in the Redhawk Community Park. The fenced park is divided into two areas, one for large dogs and one for small dogs. To get to the dog park from Interstate 15 take Highway 79 east and turn right onto Redhawk Parkway.

Outdoor Restaurants
Aloha J's 27497 Ynez Rd Temecula CA 951-506-9889
Dogs are allowed at the outdoor tables.
Baja Fresh Mexican Grill 40688 Winchester Rd Temecula CA 909-719-1570
http://www.bajafresh.com
This Mexican restaurant is open for lunch and dinner. They use fresh ingredients and making their salsa and beans daily. Some of the items on their menu include Enchiladas, Burritos, Tacos Salads, Quesadillas, Nachos, Chicken, Steak and more. Well-behaved leashed dogs are allowed at the outdoor tables.
Carol's Restaurant 33440 La Serena Way Temecula CA 951-676-9243
http://www.bailywinery.com/carols.html
This restaurant is on the site of the Baily Vineyard. They offer patio dining service, and a selection of luncheon salads, sandwiches, grilled fish and steak, and pasta dishes. Dogs are allowed around the grounds, and at the outside dining area, but not in the tasting room. Dogs must be well behaved, and leashed and cleaned up after at all times.
Front Street Bar and Grill 28699 Old Town Front Street Temecula CA 951-676-9567
This restaurant serves American food. Dogs are allowed at the outdoor tables.
Mad Madeline's Grill 28495 Front Street Temecula CA 951-699-3776
Dogs are allowed at the outdoor tables.
Marie Callender's 29363 Rancho California Rd Temecula CA 951-699-9339
Dogs are allowed at the outdoor tables.
Scarcella's Italian Grille 27525 Ynez Rd Temecula CA 951-676-5450
Dogs are allowed at the outdoor tables.
Temecula Pizza Company 44535 Bedford Ct # D Temecula CA 951-694-9463
Dogs are allowed at the outdoor tables.

Vets and Kennels
Emergency Pet Clinic 27443 Jefferson Ave Temecula CA 909-695-5044
Monday - Friday 6 pm to 8 am, 24 hours on weekends.

Victorville

Accommodations
Days Suites 14865 Bear Valley Rd Hesperia CA 760-948-0600
There is a $7 per day pet fee.
Howard Johnson Express Inn 16868 Stoddard Wells Rd. Victorville CA 760-243-7700 (800-446-4656)
Dogs of all sizes are welcome. There is a $10 per day pet fee per pet.
Motel 6 - Victorville 16901 Stoddard Wells Road Victorville CA 760-243-0666 (800-466-8356)
One well-behaved family pet per room. Guest must notify front desk upon arrival. Guest is liable for any
damages. In consideration of all guests, pets must never be left unattended in the guest rooms.
Red Roof Inn - Victorville 13409 Mariposa Road Victorville CA 760-241-1577 (800-RED-ROOF)
One well-behaved family pet per room. Guest must notify front desk upon arrival. Guest is liable for any
damages. In consideration of all guests, pets must never be left unattended in the guest rooms.

Campgrounds and RV Parks
Victorville/Inland Empire KOA 16530 Stoddard Wells Road Victorville CA 760-245-6867 (800-562-3319)
http://www.koa.com/where/ca/05114/
A shady get-away in the high desert, this park offers a maximum pull through of 75 feet with 30 amp, LP gas,
seasonal swimming pool, several planned activities, and bike rentals. Dogs of all sizes are allowed for no
additional fee. Dogs must be under owner's control and visual observation at all times. Dogs must be quiet, well
behaved, and be on no more than a 6 foot leash at all times, or otherwise contained. Dogs may not be left
unattended outside the owner's camping equipment, and must be brought inside at night. Only dogs that are
house trained are allowed in the cabins, and they must not be left inside unattended. There are some breed
restrictions. The camping and tent areas also allow dogs. There is a dog walk area at the campground. Dogs are
allowed in the camping cabins.

Stores
PetSmart Pet Store 12624 Amargosa Rd Victorville CA 760-955-1030
Your licensed and well-behaved leashed dog is allowed in the store.
Petco Pet Store 17150 Bear Valley Rd Victorville CA 760-241-8137
Your licensed and well-behaved leashed dog is allowed in the store.

Winchester

Campgrounds and RV Parks
Lake Skinner Campground 37101 Warren Road Winchester CA 951-926-1541 (800-234-PARK (7275))
The campground is located in a 6,040 acre park which features a lake, hiking/interpretive trails, equestrian trails,
seasonal swimming pool, launch ramps, boat rentals, and a camp store. Dogs are allowed on the trails and in
the campgrounds, but not in the lake or within 50 feet of the lake. Dogs must be on a 6 foot or less leash and
please clean up after them. There is an additional fee of $2 per night per pet.

Yucaipa

Campgrounds and RV Parks
Yacaipa Regional Park 33900 Oak Glen Road Yucaipa CA 909-790-3127
Sitting on 885 acres in the foothills of the San Bernardino Mountains, this park offers a wide variety of land and
water recreation. Dogs of all sizes are allowed for an additional $1 per night per pet. Dogs must be leashed and
cleaned up after. The camping and tent areas also allow dogs. There is a dog walk area at the campground.

Chapter 13

California - San Diego Area Dog Travel Guide

Campo

Campgrounds and RV Parks

Lake Morena County Park 2550 Lake Morena Drive Campo CA 619-579-4101 (877-565-3600)
This park is a combination of desert, coastal, and mountain habitats. It supports a wide variety of plant and animal life. Dogs of all sizes are allowed for an additional $1 per night per pet, and they must have current tags, rabies, and shot records. Dogs may not be left unattended at any time, and they must be on no more than a 6 foot leash and cleaned up after. Dogs are not allowed on the trails, but they may be walked on the payment and along side the roads on leash. The camping and tent areas also allow dogs. There is a dog walk area at the campground.
Lake Moreno County Park 2550 Lake Moreno Drive Campo CA 858-565-3600
This park of just over 3,200 acres has the distinction because of it's location to have the characteristics of desert, coastal and mountain habitats. It is home to a vast variety of plants, birds, and wildlife. There is a good variety of land and water recreation, many hiking trails including a piece of the Pacific Crest Trail, and they also provide boat rentals; dogs are allowed on the boats. Dogs of all sizes are allowed for camping for an additional fee of $1 per night per pet. Dogs must be leashed and cleaned up after at all times. They are allowed throughout the park and on the trails; they are not allowed at the cabins. The camp area offers 86 individual sites (58 with hook-ups) cozily situated in a majestic grove of oak trees. Some of the amenities include a playground, picnic table, barbecues, and restrooms. The camping and tent areas also allow dogs. There is a dog walk area at the campground.

Parks

Lake Moreno County Park 2550 Lake Moreno Drive Campo CA 858-565-3600
This park of just over 3,200 acres has the distinction because of it's location to have the characteristics of desert, coastal and mountain habitats. It is home to a vast variety of plants, birds, and wildlife. There is a good variety of land and water recreation, many hiking trails including a piece of the Pacific Crest Trail, and they also provide boat rentals; dogs are allowed on the boats. Dogs of all sizes are allowed for camping for an additional fee of $1 per night per pet. Dogs must be leashed and cleaned up after at all times. They are allowed throughout the park and on the trails; they are not allowed at the cabins.

Guatay

Campgrounds and RV Parks

Laguna Campground Sunrise H Pine Valley CA 619-445-6235 (877-444-6777)
This 104 site campground is located in the Cleveland National Forest. It is located at an elevation of 5,600 feet and offers both tent and RV sites. RVs up to 40 feet are allowed. Flush toilets are available at this campground. Pets must be on no more than a 6 foot leash at all times, cleaned up after, and contained at night. There are no additional pet fees. The camping and tent areas also allow dogs. There is a dog walk area at the campground. There are no electric or water hookups at the campgrounds.

Stores

Tryyn Wooden Spoon Gallery 27540 Old Hwy 80 Guatay CA 619-473-9030
http://www.Tryyn.SanDiego411.net
Located on the road from I-8 to Julian, this shop has crafted spoons, wine, jewelry, and other items. Your well-behaved, potty trained dog is allowed inside on leash.

Parks

Big Laguna Trail Sunrise Highway Pine Valley CA 619-445-6235
http://www.fs.fed.us/r5/cleveland
This 6.7 mile easy rated trail is located in the Cleveland National Forest. The trail elevation changes from 5,400 to 5,960 feet. It is a popular trail for hiking, horseback riding and mountain biking. The trail is open year round except during winter storms. Pets on leash are allowed and please clean up after them. To reach the upper end, take Sunrise Highway from I-8 (near Pine Valley) and drive north 13.5 miles to just past the second cattle guard on the highway. Vehicles should park on either side of the highway on the paved turnouts. The access to the Big

Laguna trail is via the Nobel Canyon trail that departs the western turnout and is marked by a small sign. Follow the Nobel Canyon trail about 100 yards to reach the Big Laguna trail junction. The other end of the Big Laguna trail makes a junction with the Pacific Crest Trail about .25 miles northeast of the Laguna Station (the Forest Service fire station).

Julian

Accommodations

Apple Tree Inn

Apple Tree Inn 4360 Highway 78 Julian CA 800-410-8683
http://www.julianappletreeinn.com
This is a small country motel located near the historic gold mining town of Julian. Families are always welcome. There is a $10 per day pet charge and a $50 refundable pet deposit.

Campgrounds and RV Parks
Cuyamaca Ranch State Park Campgrounds 12551 Hwy 79 Descanso CA 760-765 -0755 (800-444-PARK (7275))
This scenic park has two family campgrounds, and some of the amenities include a picnic table, fire ring, barbecue, restrooms with pay showers, and water located near each site. Campsites are $20 per night May 15 through September 15, and $15 the rest of the season. There is an eight person maximum per site. You may bring your own padlock if you wish to lock the cabin during your stay. Dogs are allowed at no additional fee, but restricted to the campgrounds, picnic areas, paved roads, and the Cuyamaca Peak Fire Road. Dogs must be leashed and cleaned up after. They may not be left unattended at any time. This park is located about 15 miles south of the town of Julian. The camping and tent areas also allow dogs. Dogs are allowed in the camping cabins. There are no electric or water hookups at the campgrounds.
Lake Cuamaca 15027 Hwy 79 Julian CA 760-765-0515 (877-581-9904)
http://www.lakecuyamaca.org/
This campground has 40 RV sites, 14 tent sites, and 2 cabins located next a popular fishing lake. There is a 3.5 mile trail surrounding the lake. Dogs on leash are welcome both in the campground and on the trail, but they are not allowed in the water and must stay at least 50 feet from the shore. Dogs are, however, allowed to go on the rental boats. People must clean up after their pets. The camping and tent areas also allow dogs. There is a dog walk area at the campground. Dogs are allowed in the camping cabins.

Pinezanita Trailer Ranch and Campground

Pinezanita Trailer Ranch and Campground 4446 Hwy 79 Julian CA   760-765-0429
http://www.pinezanita.com/
They have a fishing pond which is stocked with blue gill and catfish. You can find fishing tackle and bait in the Campground Registration Office. Dogs are not allowed in the cabins, but they are welcome to stay with you at your RV, trailer, or campsite. There is a $2 per day per pet charge. Pets must be on a 6 foot or shorter leash at all times. Noisy pets are cause for eviction. Carry plastic bags or a pooper scooper and pick up after your pet. The camping and tent areas also allow dogs. There is a dog walk area at the campground.
Stagecoach Trails RV Equestrian and Wildlife Resort 7878 Great Southern Overland Stage Route of 1849 Julian CA   760-765-2197 (877-TWO CAMP (896-2267))
http://www.stagecoachtrails.com
This scenic desert resort park has an historical, natural, cultural history to share in addition to many amenities and recreational pursuits. Dogs of all sizes are allowed at no additional fee. Dogs may not be left unattended, and they must be quiet, well behaved, leashed, and cleaned up after. Dogs are allowed on the trails unless otherwise indicated. This is an RV only park. There is a dog walk area at the campground.
William Heise County Park 4945 Heise Park Road Julian CA   760-765-0650 (877-565-3600)
Dogs of all sizes are allowed for an additional $1 per night per pet, and they must have current tags, rabies, and shot records. Dogs may not be left unattended at any time, and they must be on no more than a 6 foot leash and cleaned up after. Dogs are not allowed on the trails, but they may be walked on the payment and along side the roads on leash. The camping and tent areas also allow dogs. There is a dog walk area at the campground. There are no water hookups at the campgrounds.

Vacation Home Rentals
San Diego Backcountry Retreat Call to Arrange Descanso CA   888-894-4626
http://haylapa.1888twlgman.com
The Haylapa House is located on a small ranch east of San Diego. The Haylapa is one large open room. It has a full kitchen and bathroom. Outside, it has a fenced area for your dog and nearby hiking.
Flat Top Mountain Retreat Call to Arrange. Julian CA   800-810-1170
http://www.julianflattop.com
Secluded mountain vacation home on eight acres. Located 1 1/2 miles north of the old gold mining town of Julian. This home has panoramic views of the mountain countryside to the ocean. There are three bedrooms, sleeping 8 people, and 3 decks for viewing the peaceful surroundings and wildlife including deer, and wild turkey birds. The minimum stay is two nights.
Pine Haven Cabin Rental Call to Arrange. Julian CA   760-726-9888
http://www.pinehavencabin.com/

Enjoy this dog-friendly mountain getaway on 1.25 acres. The entire lot is securely fenced, offering your pet the freedom to run off-leash. The cabin has one bedroom plus a small loft upstairs, a bathroom with a tiled walk-in shower (no tub), and a fully equipped kitchen. The cabin sleeps 2 people and is off a small private lane, so you will have lots of privacy. No smoking allowed. For reservations call Teresa at 760-726-9888 or email to pinehavencabin@sbcglobal.net.

Attractions

Country Carriages

Country Carriages Washington and Main St Julian CA   760-765-1471
Reservations are recommended on the weekends. Your dog is welcome. The carriage rides go a mile out of town and back. The driver points out historic sites on the way.
J. Jenkins Winery 12555 Julian Orchards Drive Julian CA   760-765-3267
http://www.jenkinswinery.com/
This winery set out with a goal to produce beautiful unique wines, and now they offer them in their tasting room that is open Saturdays and Sundays from 11am to 5 pm or by appointment. There is outside seating available, and dogs are allowed on the grounds, but not usually in the buildings. Dogs must be friendly, and leashed and cleaned up after at all times.

TOP 200 PLACE **Julian Downtown and Walking Tour** Main Street Julian CA   760-765-1857
You and your pooch can take a self-guided tour of Julian's historical buildings which highlight history from the Gold Rush era to the 1920s. Follow the tour through Main, Second, Third, B, C, and Washington Streets. A map is available at the Julian Chamber of Commerce located on Main and Washington Streets inside the Town Hall. There are also a number of pet-friendly outdoor restaurants and a horse and carriage ride as well as shopping.
Menghini Winery 1150 Julian Orchards Drive Julian CA   760-765-2072
This winery produces a variety of premium wines. The tasting room is open daily from 10 am to 4 pm, and they also have a nice picnic area. Dogs are allowed around the grounds, but not in the tasting room. Dogs must be well behaved, and leashed and cleaned up after at all times.

Parks

Cuyamaca Ranch State Park 12551 Highway 79 Descanso CA   760-765-0755
http://www.cuyamaca.statepark.org
Leashed dogs are allowed on the paved Cuyamaca Peak Fire Road and the Los Caballos/Stonewall Mine Road trails. Bicycles and horseback riders are also allowed on these trails. Dogs are not allowed on any other trails in the park. The Cuyamaca Peak Fire Road is approximately 3.5 miles and goes all the way to the top of the park.

The Cuyamaca Peak Fire Road begins at Hwy 79 about 1/4 mi south of the Paso Picacho Campground (the road is also accessible from the campground).

Outdoor Restaurants

Apple Alley Bakery 2122 Main Street Julian CA   760-765-2532
Dogs are allowed at the outdoor tables in the year-round patio. The bakery is open for breakfast and lunch, seven days a week. They offer apple pies made from fresh apples, pastries, cookies and more.
Buffalo Bills 2603 B Street Julian CA   760-765-1560
This restaurant specializes in buffalo burgers and apple pie. Dogs of all sizes are allowed on the patio. Dogs must be leashed and cleaned up after. They are open weekdays: 7:30 a.m. to 2 p.m. and weekends: 7:30 a.m. 5 p.m.
Julian Pie Company 2225 Main Street Julian CA   760-765-2449
http://www.julianpie.com/
This pie company welcomes visitors with a door handles that says, "Begin Smelling", and their pies are popular for their variety and freshness. Pets are welcome to come into the store with their owners. Dogs must be friendly, leashed, and under owner's control at all times.
Margarita's 2018 Main Street Julian CA   760-765-3980
This restaurant serves Mexican and American food and is open for breakfast, lunch and dinner. Dogs are allowed at the outdoor tables. The tables are usually out in late spring through summer.
The Bailey Wood Pit Barbecue Main and A Streets Julian CA   760-765-3757
Dogs are allowed at the outdoor tables. Tables are seasonal.

The Julian Grille

The Julian Grille 2224 Main Street Julian CA   760-765-0173
This eatery sets in a restored cottage, and features steaks, seafood, prime rib, and outdoor dining. They are open daily for lunch and from Tuesday through Sunday for diner. Your pet is welcome to join you at the outside tables. Dogs must be well behaved, attended to at all times, and leashed.
Wynola Pizza Express 4355 Hwy 78/79 Julian CA   760-765-1004
This eatery offers wood-fired gourmet pizza and live music on Saturday nights. They offer outside dining where your pet is welcome to join you. Dogs must be well behaved, attended to at all times, and leashed.

Potrero

Campgrounds and RV Parks

Potrero County Park 24800 Potrero Park Drive Potrero CA   619-478-5212 (877-565-3600)
Dotted with hundred-year-old coastal oak trees and rich in natural and cultural history, this park at 2,600 feet, offers a wide variety of habitats and recreational activities. Dogs of all sizes are allowed for an additional $1 per night per pet, and they must have current tags, rabies, and shot records. Dogs may not be left unattended at any time, and they must be on no more than a 6 foot leash and cleaned up after. Dogs are not allowed on the trails, but they may be walked on the payment and along side the roads on leash. The camping and tent areas also allow dogs. There is a dog walk area at the campground.

Ramona

Campgrounds and RV Parks

Dos Picos County Park 17953 Dos Picos Park Road Ramona CA   760-789-2220 (877-565-3600)
This park, located in a small valley sheltered by nearby mountains, is full of plant and animal life, and offers various trails and recreational pursuits. Dogs of all sizes are allowed for an additional $1 per night per pet, and they must have current tags, rabies, and shot records. Dogs may not be left unattended at any time, and they must be on no more than a 6 foot leash and cleaned up after. Dogs are not allowed on the trails, but they may be walked on the payment and along side the roads on leash. The camping and tent areas also allow dogs. There is a dog walk area at the campground.

San Diego

Accommodations

Motel 6 - San Diego - Chula Vista 745 E Street Chula Vista CA   619-422-4200 (800-466-8356)
One well-behaved family pet per room. Guest must notify front desk upon arrival. Guest is liable for any damages. In consideration of all guests, pets must never be left unattended in the guest rooms.
Coronado Bay Resort 4000 Coronado Bay Road Coronado CA   619-424-4000
Dogs of all sizes are allowed. There is a $25 one time fee per room and a pet policy to sign at check in.
Coronado Island Marriott Resort 2000 Second Street Coronado CA   619-435-3000 (800-228-9290)
Dogs of all sizes are allowed. There is a $75 one time additional fee per pet. Dogs must be leashed, cleaned up after, and a contact number left with the front desk if they are alone in the room.
Crown City Inn 520 Orange Ave Coronado CA   619-435-3116
http://www.crowncityinn.com/
This inn is located in beautiful Coronado which is across the harbor from downtown San Diego. Walk to several outdoor restaurants or to the Coronado Centennial Park. Room service is available. Pet charges are $8 per day for a designated pet room and $25 per day for a non-designat
TOP 200 PLACE Loews Coronado Bay Resort 4000 Coronado Bay Road Coronado CA   619-424-4000
All well-behaved dogs of any size are welcome. This upscale hotel offers their "Loews Loves Pets" program which includes special pet treats, local dog walking routes, and a list of nearby pet-friendly places to visit. There are no pet fees.
Motel 6 - San Diego - El Cajon 550 Montrose Court El Cajon CA   619-588-6100 (800-466-8356)
One well-behaved family pet per room. Guest must notify front desk upon arrival. Guest is liable for any damages. In consideration of all guests, pets must never be left unattended in the guest rooms.
Quality Inn Suites 1250 El Cajon Blvd El Cajon CA   619-588-8808 (877-424-6423)
Dogs of all sizes are allowed. There is a $10 per night per pet additional fee. Dogs may not be left alone in the rooms, and they must be leashed and cleaned up after.
Thriftlodge 1220 W Main Street El Cajon CA   619-442-2576
Dogs of all sizes are allowed. There is a $10 per night per pet additional fee.
Andrea Villa Inn 2402 Torrey Pines Rd La Jolla CA   858-459-3311
http://www.andreavilla.com/
Nestled in the heart of beautiful La Jolla, this inn is conveniently located near cosmopolitan shopping and dining experiences. The beaches of La Jolla Shores are within easy walking distance. There is a $25 one time pet charge.
La Jolla Village Lodge 1141 Silverado Street La Jolla CA   858-551-2001
There is a $20 one time pet fee. Thanks to a reader for recommending this hotel.

Loews Coronado Bay Resort

La Valencia Hotel 1132 Prospect Street La Jolla CA 858-454-0771 (800-451-0772)
http://www.lavalencia.com/
This resort hotel blends European flair and old Southern California charm and hospitality with all the modern day amenities. Dogs up to 40 pounds are allowed for an additional one time pet fee of $75. Dogs must be quiet, well mannered, leashed, cleaned up after, and the Do Not Disturb sign put on the door if they are in the room alone.
Residence Inn by Marriott 8901 Gilman Drive La Jolla CA 858-587-1770
Dogs of all sizes are welcome, but only 2 large pets or 3 small pets are allowed per room. There is a $75 one time fee, and a pet policy to sign at check in.
San Diego Marriott La Jolla 4240 La Jolla Village Drive La Jolla CA 858-587-1414 (800-228-9290)
Dogs of all sizes are allowed. There are no additional pet fees. Dogs must be leashed, cleaned up after, and a contact number left with the front desk if they are in the room alone.
Motel 6 - San Diego - La Mesa 7621 Alvarado Road La Mesa CA 619-464-7151 (800-466-8356)
One well-behaved family pet per room. Guest must notify front desk upon arrival. Guest is liable for any damages. In consideration of all guests, pets must never be left unattended in the guest rooms.
Best Western Lamplighter Inn and Suites 6474 El Cajon Blvd San Diego CA 619-582-3088 (800-780-7234)
Dogs of all sizes are allowed. There is a $10 per night pet fee per pet. Smoking and non-smoking are available for pet rooms.
Double Tree Club San Diego 1515 Hotel Circle South San Diego CA 619-881-6900 (800-489-9671)
http://www.doubletreeclubsd.com
The Double Tree Club San Diego welcomes your well behaved dog.
Doubletree 7450 Hazard Center Drive San Diego CA 619-297-5466
Dogs of all sizes are allowed. There is a $50 one time pet fee per room.
Harborview Inn and Suites 550 W Grape Street San Diego CA 619-233-7799
This 3 story hotel is only minutes from a variety of attractions and recreational opportunities. Some of the amenities include a free continental breakfast, room service, and accommodations for both the business and leisure traveler. Dogs of all sizes are welcome for a $10 per night per pet additional fee. Dogs may not be left unattended in the room at any time, and they must be quiet, leashed, and cleaned up after.
Holiday Inn on the Bay 1355 N Harbor Dr San Diego CA 619-232-3861 (877-270-6405)
http://www.basshotels.com/holiday-inn
This Holiday Inn has a 5 and 14 story building which overlooks the harbor. Across the street from the hotel is a harborside walkway. Well-behaved dogs of all sizes are welcome. There is a $25 one time per stay pet fee ($100 pet deposit of which $75 is refundable and $25 is the pet fee.) Pets are allowed in non-smoking and smoking rooms.
Homestead Suites 7444 Mission Valley Rd San Diego CA 619-299-2292

There is a $75 one time pet fee per visit.

TOP 200 PLACE Hotel Solamar 453 6th Avenue San Diego CA 619-531-8740 (877-230-0300)
http://www.hotelsolamar.com/
This hip luxury boutique hotel features a vibrant décor, a great location to the area's best shopping, dinning, and entertainment, and a full list of amenities for the business or leisure traveler. They feature elegantly appointed rooms, an evening wine hour, 24 hour room service from the adjacent J6Restaurant and J6Bar, a pool and spa, and several in-room amenities. Dogs of all sizes are welcome for no additional pet fee. Dogs must be friendly, quiet, leashed and cleaned up after, and the Dog in Room sign put on the door if they are in the room alone.

La Quinta Inn San Diego Rancho Penasquitos 10185 Paseo Montril San Diego CA 858-484-8800 (800-531-5900)
Dogs up to 60 pounds are allowed. There are no additional pet fees, but a credit card must be on file. Dogs must be crated when left alone in the room or place the Do Not Disturb sign on the door. Dogs must be leashed and cleaned up after.

Motel 6 - San Diego - Hotel Circle 2424 Hotel Circle North San Diego CA 619-296-1612 (800-466-8356)
One well-behaved family pet per room. Guest must notify front desk upon arrival. Guest is liable for any damages. In consideration of all guests, pets must never be left unattended in the guest rooms.

Motel 6 - San Diego Airport/Harbor 2353 Pacific Highway San Diego CA 619-232-8931 (800-466-8356)
One well-behaved family pet per room. Guest must notify front desk upon arrival. Guest is liable for any damages. In consideration of all guests, pets must never be left unattended in the guest rooms.

Motel 6 - San Diego Downtown 1546 2nd Avenue San Diego CA 619-236-9292 (800-466-8356)
One well-behaved family pet per room. Guest must notify front desk upon arrival. Guest is liable for any damages. In consideration of all guests, pets must never be left unattended in the guest rooms.

Motel 6 - San Diego North 5592 Clairemont Mesa Boulevard San Diego CA 858-268-9758 (800-466-8356)
One well-behaved family pet per room. Guest must notify front desk upon arrival. Guest is liable for any damages. In consideration of all guests, pets must never be left unattended in the guest rooms.

Ocean Villa Inn 5142 West Point Loma Blvd San Diego CA 619-224-3481 (800-759-0012)
http://www.oceanvillainn.com
Ocean Villa Inn is in the Ocean Beach district near the Dog Beach. They allow pets in all of their downstairs rooms with a $100.00 refundable deposit and a one time per stay fee of $25.00.

Old Town Inn 4444 Pacific H San Diego CA 619-260-8024 (800-643-3025)
http://www.oldtown-inn.com/oldtown.htm
This scenic inn offers deluxe and economy units, a complimentary continental breakfast, heated swimming pool, close proximity to several attractions and recreational opportunities, and beautiful well-kept grounds. Dogs up to 50 pounds are allowed for an additional fee of $10 per night per pet. Dogs may not be left alone in the room, and they must be leashed and cleaned up after.

Pacific Inn Hotel & Suites 1655 Pacific Hwy San Diego CA 619-232-6391
There is a $10 per day additional pet fee.

Premier Inn 2484 Hotel Circle Place San Diego CA 619-291-8252
http://www.premierinns.com
There is no pet fee.

Premier Inn 3333 Channel Way San Diego CA 619-223-9500
http://www.premierinns.com
There is no pet fee.

Red Lion 2270 Hotel Circle N San Diego CA 619-297-1101
Dogs up to 75 pounds are allowed. There is a $75 refundable pet deposit.

Residence Inn by Marriott 5400 Kearny Mesa Road San Diego CA 858-278-2100
Pets of all sizes are welcome. There is a $75 one time fee, and a pet policy to sign at check in.

Residence Inn by Marriott 1865 Hotel Circle S San Diego CA 619-881-3600
Dogs of all sizes are allowed. There is a $75 one time fee, and a pet policy to sign at check in.

Residence Inn by Marriott 11002 Rancho Carmel Drive San Diego CA 858-673-1900
Dogs of all sizes are allowed. There is a $75 one time fee, and a pet policy to sign at check in.

Residence Inn by Marriott 12011 Scripps Highland Drive San Diego CA 858-635-5724
Dogs of all sizes are allowed. There is a $75 one time fee and a pet policy to sign at check in.

Residence Inn by Marriott 5995 Pacific Mesa Court San Diego CA 858-552-9100
Dogs of all sizes are allowed. There is a $75 one time fee and a pet policy to sign at check in.

Sheraton San Diego Hotel and Marina 1380 Harbor Island Drive San Diego CA 619-291-2900 (888-625-5144)
Dogs up to 80 pounds are allowed. There are no additional pet fees.

Sheraton Suites San Diego 701 A. Street San Diego CA 619-696-9800 (888-625-5144)
Dogs up to 80 pounds are allowed. There are no additional pet fees.

Staybridge Suites 6639 Mira Mesa Blvd San Diego CA 858-453-5343 (877-270-6405)
There is a $75 one time pet fee.

Staybridge Suites 1110 A Street San Diego CA 619-795-4000 (877-270-6405)
There is a $75 one time pet fee.

Staybridge Suites 11855 Ave of Industry San Diego CA   858-487-0900 (877-270-6405)
There is a $150 one time pet fee.
Staybridge Suites 1110 A Street San Diego CA 619-795-4000 (877-270-6405)
Dogs of all sizes are allowed. There is a $150 one time pet fee.

Sheraton San Diego Hotel and Marina

Staybridge Suites 6639 Mira Mesa Blvd San Diego CA   858-453-5354 (877-270-6405)
Dogs of all sizes are allowed. There is a $75 one time fee per room and a pet policy to sign at check in.
Staybridge Suites 1110 A Street San Diego CA 619-795-4000 (877-270-6405)
One dog of any size is allowed. There is a $75 one time fee and a pet policy to sign at check in.
Vagabond Inn-Point Loma 1325 Scott St. San Diego CA 619-224-3371 (800-522-1555)
http://www.vagabondinn.com
This motel is located less than five miles from downtown San Diego and Sea World. It is close to the popular
Dog Beach in Ocean Beach. The motel features an outdoor swimming pool, family unit rooms, cable television
and more hotel amenities. Dogs up to about 70-75 pounds are allowed and there is an additional $10 per day pet
fee.
W San Diego 421 West B. Street San Diego CA   619-231-8220
Dogs up to 80 pounds are allowed. There is a $100 one time per stay pet fee and a $25 per night pet charge.
Motel 6 - San Ysidro - San Diego 160 East Calle Primera San Ysidro CA   619-690-6663 (800-466-8356)
One well-behaved family pet per room. Guest must notify front desk upon arrival. Guest is liable for any
damages. In consideration of all guests, pets must never be left unattended in the guest rooms.

Campgrounds and RV Parks
Sweetwater Summit Regional Park 3218 Summit Meadow Road Bonita CA 619-472-7572 (877-565-3600)
This park offers spectacular views from the summit, various habitats to explore, and offers a wide variety of
recreational pursuits. Dogs of all sizes are allowed for an additional $1 per night per pet, and they must have
current tags, rabies, and shot records. Dogs may not be left unattended at any time, and they must be on no
more than a 6 foot leash and cleaned up after. Dogs are not allowed on the trails, but they may be walked on the
payment and along side the roads on leash. The camping and tent areas also allow dogs. There is a dog walk
area at the campground.
San Diego Metro 111 N 2nd Avenue Chula Vista CA 619-427-3601 (800-562-9877)
http://www.koa.com/where/ca/05112/
Only minutes from world class attractions, this resort campground also offers landscaped grounds, 65 feet pull
through sites with 50 amp, cable TV, swimming pool, hot tub, sauna, and a variety of planned activities and

recreation. Dogs of all sizes are allowed for no additional fee. There is a $50 refundable pet deposit for the cabins. Dogs must be under owner's control and visual observation at all times. Dogs must be quiet, well behaved, and be on no more than a 6 foot leash at all times, or otherwise contained. Dogs may not be left unattended outside the owner's camping equipment, and must be brought inside at night. There are some breed restrictions. The camping and tent areas also allow dogs. There is a dog walk area at the campground.

Sunland RV Resort - San Diego 7407 Alvarado Road La Mesa CA   619-469-4697 (877-787-6386)
http://www.sdrvresort.com/default.asp
In addition to an abundance of land and water recreation, this beautiful RV park offers all the amenities of a luxury resort. Dogs of all sizes are allowed for an additional fee of $3 per night per pet. Dogs may not be left unattended outside, and they must be leashed and cleaned up after. Dogs are not allowed in the buildings. This is an RV only park. There are some breed restrictions. There is a dog walk area at the campground.

Lake Jennings County Park 10108 Bass Road Lakeside CA   619-443-2004 (877-565-3600)
This popular park offers great scenery, an amphitheater, various programs and exhibits, and a wide variety of recreational pursuits. Dogs of all sizes are allowed for an additional $1 per night per pet, and they must have current tags, rabies, and shot records. Dogs may not be left unattended at any time, and they must be on no more than a 6 foot leash and cleaned up after. Dogs are not allowed on the trails, but they may be walked on the payment and along side the roads on leash. The camping and tent areas also allow dogs. There is a dog walk area at the campground.

Campland on the Bay

TOP 200 PLACE **Campland on the Bay** 2211 Pacific Beach Drive San Diego CA   800-422-9386
http://www.campland.com/
This RV park is located on Mission Bay, across the water from Sea World. They offer beach front, bay view or primitive sites. Amenities include boat slips, a boat launch, store with a market, game room and a laundry room. Dogs of all sizes are allowed for an additional fee of $3 per night per pet. They must be leashed and please clean up after them. Dogs may not be left unattended outside, and they are not allowed on the beach. The camping and tent areas also allow dogs. There is a dog walk area at the campground.

Santee Lakes Recreation Preserve 9310 Fanita Parkway San Diego CA   619-596-3141
http://www.santeelakes.com
This large park, also a prime bird habitat, offers 2 swimming pools, a spa, 7 scenic lakes-stocked, a laundry with shower facilities, a clubhouse, watercraft rentals, 5 playgrounds including the Kiwanis Playground for children with disabilities, and miles of paved trails. Dogs of all sizes are allowed for an additional fee of $1 per night per pet. Dogs may not be left unattended outside, and they must be leashed and cleaned up after. Dogs are allowed ONLY on the pet walks around lakes 6 and 7 and in the campground. Dogs are not allowed in any of the day use areas. The camping and tent areas also allow dogs. There is a dog walk area at the campground.

Vacation Home Rentals

The Hohe's Beach House 4905 Dixie Drive San Diego CA   858-273-0324
The Hohe House is a non-smoking 2 bedroom/2 bath, Ocean View, vacation rental in the Pacific Beach neighborhood. The Hohe House sleeps 6 and is fully furnished with all linens provided. There is a 4 night minimum during the low season, $200 nightly, (Mid-Sept to Mid-June), and rates vary for low to high season, from $1275 to $1875 weekly. A $350 refundable, security deposit is required to reserve a week's stay. There is a $10 per night pet fee. Well-behaved dogs over 18 months and under 80 pounds are welcome.

Transportation Systems

Metropolitan Transit System Regional San Diego CA   619-233-3004
Small dogs in enclosed carriers are allowed on the buses and light rail. You must be able to transport your dog and the carrier by yourself, and you need to hold the carrier on your lap. Noise or odor may give cause for refusal to transport the animal.

Attractions

Action Sport Rentals 1775 Mission Bay San Diego CA   619-275-8945
http://www.actionsportrentals.com/
This sports rental company offers a wide variety of watercraft for rent, fishing charters and equipment, and also bicycles and skate rentals. The marina has a bait and tackle shop, and a deli and market. Dogs of all sizes are welcome on the boat rentals for no additional fee; they must have their own doggie life jackets. Dogs must be friendly, well behaved, under owner's control at all times, and leashed and cleaned up after.
Cinderella Carriage Rides   San Diego CA   619-239-8080
You and your dog can enjoy a carriage ride throughout downtown San Diego. The horse and carriages are located in the Gaslamp Quarter at 5th and F Streets, or call ahead and get a carriage to pick you up from your downtown hotel. The rides are from 6pm-11pm. Rates start at $15 for about a 10 minute ride and go up to $95 for 60 minutes. Prices are subject to change. The carriages hold 3-4 people plus a dog. They accept cash or credit card.

Old Town State Historic Park

TOP 200 PLACE **Family Kayak Adventure Center** 4217 Swift Avenue San Diego CA   619-282-3520
http://familykayak.com
This company offers guided kayaking adventure tours to people of all ages and abilities. For beginners they offer paddles on flat water in stable tandem kayaks that hold one to four people. All equipment and instruction is

provided for an enjoyable first outing. Well-behaved dogs are also welcome. There is even a "Dog Paddles" tour which is an evening tour on Mission Bay that includes quality time on the water and on Fiesta Island's leash free area.

Gaslamp Quarter Guided Walking Tour 410 Island Avenue San Diego CA   619-233-4692
http://www.gaslampquarter.org/
The historical focal point of this 16 1/2 block district is the William Heath Davis Historic House Museum, where visitors can get information on the walking tours, the museum, and self-guided maps. The foundation began as a way promote and preserve the history and culture of the Gaslamp Quarter. Dogs are welcome on the guided walking tours for no additional fee as long as other guests don't mind, and so far that has never been a problem. They just ask that dogs be friendly and that you call ahead if you have a pet. Dogs are welcome for no additional fee. Dogs must be under owner's control, and leashed and cleaned up after at all times.

Old Town State Historic Park San Diego Ave & Twiggs St San Diego CA 619-220-5422
Old Town demonstrates life in the Mexican and early American periods of 1821 to 1872 (including 5 original adobe buildings). There are shops, several outdoor cafes and live music. Since pups are not allowed inside the buildings, you can shop at the many outdoor retail kiosks throughout the town. There are several food concessions where you can order the food and then take it to an outdoor table. After walking around, relax with your best friend by listening to a variety of live music. If your dog wants to see more trees and green grass, take a quick drive over to Presidio Park which is close to Old Town (see Parks).

San Pasqual Winery 515 Santa Fe Street San Diego CA 858-270-7550
http://www.sanpasqualwinery.com/
This micro-winery produces handcrafted wines in small lots from grapes grown in the Guadalupe Valley in Baja, California. They are open Saturday and Sunday for walk in complimentary wine tasting during the summer; from September 3rd to December 2nd, they are open by appointment, and then they open for regular hours again. Your pet is welcome to join you here and in the tasting room as well. They do not have any picnic facilities. Dogs must be leashed and cleaned up after at all times.

SeaWorld of California-Kennels 1720 South Shore Rd. San Diego CA 619-226-3901
This may not be your dog's idea of an attraction, but it is nice to know that SeaWorld has day kennels at the main entrance of their Adventure Park. The kennels are attended at all times and you can visit your dog throughout the day when you need a break from the attractions. The day boarding is open the same hours as the park and cost only $5 for the whole day. Kennels range in size from small to large. Thanks to one of our San Diego readers for telling us about this.

Seaforth Boat Rentals

TOP 200 PLACE **Seaforth Boat Rentals** 1641 Quivira Road San Diego CA   619-223-1681
http://www.seaforthboatrental.com/
This boat rental/adventure tour company feature over 200 watercraft rentals available at 3 locations. They offer a

wide variety of adventure packages, including manned or unmanned rentals, sailing lessons, fishing excursions/tournaments, remote or on-site picnicking, whale watching, and they will even organize beach parties. Dogs of all sizes are welcome on the boat rentals for no additional fee. Dogs must be friendly, well behaved, under owner's control at all times, and leashed and cleaned up after.

Shopping Centers

Otay Ranch Town Center

Horton Plaza Shopping Center

TOP 200 PLACE **Otay Ranch Town Center** Eastlake Pkwy At Olympic Pkwy Chula Vista CA 619-656-9100
http://www.otayranchtowncenter.com
This upscale outdoor mall opened in October, 2006. It was the first new mall opened in the San Diego area in 20 years. It is pet-friendly and it even has a dog park on the premises next to the Macy's. Many stores allow dogs inside but you will need to ask first. There are poop bags available at the mall and many stores have water dishes for dogs. There is also a vet located at the mall. To get to the mall and dog park from San Diego go south on the 805 Freeway to the Orange Avenue Exit. Head east on Orange Avenue which will become Olympic Parkway. Go 4 miles east to the mall.
Horton Plaza Shopping Center 324 Horton Plaza San Diego CA 619-239-8180
http://westfield.com/hortonplaza/
This outdoor shopping center features 196 stores, a variety of dining options and entertainment, annual activities, concierge services, and more. Dogs are allowed to walk the mall. Dogs must be well behaved, under owner's control at all times, and leashed and cleaned up after.

Stores

PetSmart Pet Store 820 Paseo Del Rey Chula Vista CA 619-656-0071
Your licensed and well-behaved leashed dog is allowed in the store.
PetSmart Pet Store 1840 Main Ct Chula Vista CA 619-397-0605
Your licensed and well-behaved leashed dog is allowed in the store.
Petco Pet Store 1142 Broadway Chula Vista CA 619-476-8064
Your licensed and well-behaved leashed dog is allowed in the store.
Petco Pet Store 925 Orange Avenue Coronado CA 619-437-6557
Your licensed and well-behaved leashed dog is allowed in the store.
PetSmart Pet Store 865 Jackman St El Cajon CA 619-442-0600
Your licensed and well-behaved leashed dog is allowed in the store.
Petco Pet Store 2510 Jamacha Rd El Cajon CA 619-670-9688
Your licensed and well-behaved leashed dog is allowed in the store.
Petco Pet Store 540 N 2nd St El Cajon CA 619-441-5200
Your licensed and well-behaved leashed dog is allowed in the store.
PetSmart Pet Store 8657 Villa La Jolla Dr La Jolla CA 858-535-9175
Your licensed and well-behaved leashed dog is allowed in the store.
Restoration Hardware 4405 La Jolla Village Drive La Jolla CA 858-784-0575
http://www.restorationhardware.com/
Your well-behaved leashed dog is allowed inside this store.
Petco Pet Store 8501 Fletcher Parkway La Mesa CA 619-337-0701
Your licensed and well-behaved leashed dog is allowed in the store.
Le Travel Store 745 4th Avenue San Diego CA 619-544-0005
This store has been outfitting world, and local, travelers with gear and gifts for over 30 years, and they offer an impressive variety of any travel related needs. Your well behaved, leashed dog is welcome to enter the store with you. Dogs must be under owner's control at all times.
Lucky Dog 415 Market St San Diego CA 619-696-0364
Your well-behaved leashed dog is welcome to accompany you into this dog boutique store.
Neiman Marcus 7027 Friars Road San Diego CA 619-692-9100
http://www.neimanmarcus.com
This famous department store, which sells everything from clothing to home furnishings, allows your well-behaved leashed dog to shop with you. It is located in Fashion Valley Center.
PetSmart Pet Store 3396 Murphy Canyon Rd San Diego CA 858-571-0300
Your licensed and well-behaved leashed dog is allowed in the store.
PetSmart Pet Store 3610 Rosecrans St San Diego CA 619-523-4177
Your licensed and well-behaved leashed dog is allowed in the store.
Petco Pet Store 10410 Friars Rd San Diego CA 619-563-0071
Your licensed and well-behaved leashed dog is allowed in the store.
Petco Pet Store 11160 Rancho Carmel Drive San Diego CA 858-451-8347
Your licensed and well-behaved leashed dog is allowed in the store.
Petco Pet Store 3994-A Clairemont Mesa Blvd San Diego CA 858-483-4100
Your licensed and well-behaved leashed dog is allowed in the store.
Petco Pet Store 1210 West Morena Blvd San Diego CA 619-275-5100
Your licensed and well-behaved leashed dog is allowed in the store.
Petco Pet Store 8290 Mira Mesa Blvd San Diego CA 858-693-1131
Your licensed and well-behaved leashed dog is allowed in the store.
Spanish Village Art Center 1770 Village Place San Diego CA 619-233-9050
http://www.spanishvillageart.com/

This art center showcases 37 working artist studios in a series of stores that open to a garden courtyard setting, and at times many of the artist work outside of their studios. Dogs are allowed in the garden courtyard area, and it is up to individual studios as to whether a dog may enter. Dogs must be well mannered, and may not relieve themselves anywhere within the courtyard. Dogs must be leashed and under owner's control at all times.
The Original Paw Pleasers Bakery 1220 Cleveland Ave San Diego CA   619-293-PAWS
http://www.pawpleasers.com
Has your dog every dreamed of going to a bakery where the fresh baked cookies and cakes are made just for canines? Your pup will be sure to drool over the specialty goodies like Tail Waggin' Treats, Bark-La-Va, Carob Brownies, Birthday Cakes and more. The cakes look perfect enough for human consumption, but they are actually for dogs. You'll be able to tell from the sign, "Pets Welcome, Owners Optional", that your pooch is more than welcome to peruse and drool over the treats. And if your pup is thirsty, these nice folks will provide a bowl of water. Also, make sure your pet tries the dog and cat yogurt bar with soft-serve frozen yogurt and a toppings bar that includes freeze-dried liver. The yogurt bar is available weekends in May & June and open daily in July & August. When in San Diego, be sure to stop by. If you don't have time, you can order via phone at 888-670-PAWS.

Beaches

Coronado Dog Beach

Coronado Dog Beach 100 Ocean Blvd Coronado CA   619-522-7342
Coronado's Dog Beach is at the north end of Ocean Blvd. Just north of the famous Hotel del Coronado (unfortunately dogs are not allowed at the hotel)the area that is designated off leash is marked by signs. The off-leash beach is open 24 hours. Dogs must be supervised and cleaned up after. Dogs must be leashed outside of the off-leash area and fines are very steep for any violations. There are also fines for not cleaning up after your dog at the dog beach. Food and Pet Treats are not allowed at the beach.
Imperial Beach Seacoast Drive at Imperial Beach Blvd Imperial Beach CA   619-424-3151
Dogs on leash are allowed on the portions of the beach that are north of Palm Avenue and south of Imperial Beach Blvd. They are not allowed on the beach between Palm Avenue and Imperial Beach Blvd.
La Jolla Shores Beach Camino Del Oro La Jolla CA   619-221-8900
Leashed dogs are allowed on this beach and the adjacent Kellogg Park from 6pm to 9am. The beach is about 1/2 mile long. To get there, take Hwy 5 to the La Jolla Village Drive exit heading west. Turn left onto Torrey Pines Rd. Then turn right onto La Jolla Shores Drive. Go 4-5 blocks and turn left onto Vallecitos. Go straight until you reach the beach and Kellogg Park.
Point La Jolla Beaches Coast Blvd. La Jolla CA   619-221-8900
Leashed dogs are allowed on this beach and the walkway (paved and dirt trails) from 6pm to 9am. The beaches

and walkway are at least a 1/2 mile long and might continue further. To get there, exit La Jolla Village Drive West from Hwy 5. Turn left onto Torrey Pines Rd. Turn right on Prospect and then park or turn right onto Coast Blvd. Parking is limited around the village area.

Ocean Beach Dog Beach

Fiesta Island

TOP 200 PLACE Dog Beach Point Loma Blvd. Ocean Beach CA   619-221-8900
Dogs are allowed to run off leash at this beach anytime during the day. This is a very popular dog beach which attracts lots and lots of dogs on warm days. To get there, take Hwy 8 West until it ends and then it becomes Sunset Cliffs Blvd. Then make a right turn onto Point Loma Blvd and follow the signs to Ocean Beach's Dog Beach.
Ocean Beach Point Loma Blvd. Ocean Beach CA   619-221-8900
Leashed dogs are allowed on this beach from 6pm to 9am. The beach is about 1/2 mile long. To get there, take Hwy 8 West until it ends and then it becomes Sunset Cliffs Blvd. Then make a right turn onto Point Loma Blvd and follow the signs to Ocean Beach Park. A separate beach called Dog Beach is at the north end of this beach which allows dogs to run off-leash.
Fiesta Island Fiesta Island Road San Diego CA   619-221-8900
On this island, dogs are allowed to run off-leash anywhere outside the fenced areas, anytime during the day. It is mostly sand which is perfect for those beach loving hounds. You might, however, want to stay on the north end of the island. The south end was used as the city's sludge area (mud and sediment, and possibly smelly) processing facility. The island is often used to launch jet-skis and motorboats. There is a one-way road that goes around the island and there are no fences, so please make sure your dog stays away from the road. About half way around the island, there is a completely fenced area on the beach. Please note that the fully enclosed area is not a dog park. The city of San Diego informed us that is supposed to be locked and is not intended to be used as a dog park even though there may occasionally be dogs running in this off-limits area.

Parks

Bayshore Bikeway

Bayshore Bikeway Silver Strand Blvd. Coronado CA
If you are in Coronado and really want to stretch your legs, you can go for a run or walk on the Bayshore Bikeway. The path is about 6 miles long each way. It starts by the Glorietta Bay Park and continues south along Silver Strand Blvd. There's not too much shade along this path, so your pup might not want to go on a hot day. Dogs need to be leashed.
Centennial & Tidelands Parks Orange Ave and First St. Coronado CA
We have combined these two parks because there is a scenic 1/2 - 1 mile path between them. Both of these parks provide nice photo opportunities of downtown San Diego and the San Diego Bay. Dogs must be leashed.

Tijuana River National Estuarine Research Reserve

Tijuana River National Estuarine Research Reserve 301 Caspian Way Imperial Beach CA   619-575-3613
This research center works to monitor, improve, and educate about the estuaries and watersheds. The visitor center provides maps for trails and picnic areas where dogs are allowed. Dogs are allowed for no additional fee, they must be under owner's control at all times, and be leashed and cleaned up after. Dogs are not allowed on the beach.
Balboa Park El Prado St San Diego CA   619-235-1121
http://www.balboapark.org
Balboa Park is a 1200 acre urban cultural park located just east of downtown. Dogs must be leashed and under control of the owner at all times, including on the trails and in the canyons. The park is known for its brilliant displays of seasonal flowers, an award-winning rose garden, shady groves of trees, and meandering paths. Many of Balboa Park's museums are magnificent Spanish Colonial Revival buildings, originally constructed for the 1915-1916 Panama-California Exposition. If you are interested in the architecture, you and your pup can take an outdoor walking tour around the various buildings. Work up an appetite after walking around? There is a concession stand called In the Park. It has many outdoor seats and is located at the corner of Village Place and Old Globe Way. For a map of the park, stop by the Visitors Center on El Prado St near Hwy 163. There is also an unfenced dog run on the west side of the park by El Prado and Balboa Drive.
Cabrillo National Monument 1800 Cabrillo Memorial Drive San Diego CA   619-557-5450
http://www.nps.gov/cabr
This day-use park is rich in cultural and natural resources, and because of its location, it features a rather biologically diverse ecosystem creating habitats for a vast variety of plant, bird, marine life, and wildlife. The park rests on 160 acres at the southern-most tip of a peninsula, and is open every day of the year. Dogs are allowed here on leash, and they must be cleaned up after. Dogs are allowed in the dirt lot parking area at the lower end of the park, and on the trails to the tide pools only. The best time for viewing the tide pools is in the winter. Dogs are not allowed on any other trails, at the main parking lot where the visitor center is, or the lighthouse.
Cleveland National Forest 10845 Rancho Bernardo Rd., Suite 200 San Diego CA   858-673-6180
http://www.fs.fed.us/r5/cleveland/
This national forest covers 460,000 acres and offers 356 miles of trails. Please see our listings in this region for dog-friendly hikes and/or campgrounds.
Embarcadero Marina Park North and South Foot of Kettner (N) or Marina Park Way (S), Port of San Diego San Diego CA   619-686-6225
This small but popular public park is split in half by the entrance from San Diego Bay into Embarcadero Marina, and is bordered by Seaport Village and the San Diego Convention Center. Set between two peninsulas, there is great scenery, ample parking, a fishing pier, multi-use paths, exercise stations, gaming courts, gazebos, and a concessionaire. Dogs are welcome; they must be well behaved, leashed and cleaned up after at all times.
Harbor Island 2036 Harbor Island Drive San Diego CA   619-686-6200

This day use park is located near the west end of the island and offers visitors spectacular panoramic views of the bay and its activities. There is a shoreline path for hikers as well as a route for bikers. Dogs are allowed at the picnic area and on the trails. Dogs must be under owner's control, and leashed and cleaned up after at all times.

Mission Bay Park Mission Bay Drive San Diego CA   619-221-8900
Leashed dogs are allowed in this park from 6pm to 9am. There are over 20 miles of beaches that make up this park (including Fiesta Island). If you come during the above mentioned hours, there is also a nice path that meanders through the grass and trees.

Mission Beach & Promenade Mission Blvd. San Diego CA   619-221-8900
Leashed dogs are allowed on this beach and promenade walkway from 6pm to 9am. It is about 3 miles long and located west of Mission Bay Park.

Mission Trails Regional Park

Mission Trails Regional Park 1 Father Junipero Serra Trail San Diego CA   619-668-3275
http://www.mtrp.org/
This 6,000 acre regional park has a nice variety of trails ranging from an easy 1 mile loop to a strenuous 5 mile hike with elevation gains of up to 1150 feet. Dogs are allowed, but must be leashed at all times. Don't forget to bring enough water since it can get pretty warm here year-round. The park is located off Mission Gorge Rd at the corners of Father Junipero Serra Trail and Echo Dell Rd. It is located about 8-9 northeast of downtown San Diego. Maps are available at the Visitor and Interpretive Center on Father Junipero Serra Trail.

Park at the Park Ninth Avenue at J Street San Diego CA
This 2.7 acre grassy park offers a panoramic view of Petco Park, the San Diego Padres baseball stadium. It is located beyond the outfield fences. The park is dog-friendly most of the time, except during baseball games when an admission fee of $5 is charged and dogs are not permitted. They are allowed to attend one Padres game each year at Petco Park's "Dog Days of Summer" event. Please clean up after your dog.

Presidio Park Jackson St San Diego CA   619-235-1100
This is a nice park for your pup to stretch his or her legs before or after you visit Old Town State Historic Park which is located about 2-3 blocks away. Dogs must be leashed in the park.

Sunset Cliffs Park Sunset Cliffs Boulevard San Diego CA   619-235-1100
This park was named for its spectacular sunset vistas and it covers 68 acres of bluffs and walking paths that tower above the Pacific Ocean. Sunset Cliffs Boulevard is also popular for the coastal scenic drive that begins at Adair Street and runs south to Ladera Street. In winter, from high on the bluffs you can see migrating whales. The day use is an overview area and there are only portable restrooms available. Dogs are allowed here and on the bluff trails; they must be under owner's control at all times, leashed, and cleaned up after.

Tecolote Canyon Natural Park

Tecolote Canyon Natural Park Tecolote Road San Diego CA   619-581-9952
This is a very nice natural park with over 6 miles (12 round trip) of walking, running or mountain biking trails. There are nine entry points into the park, but we recommend you start at the Visitors and Nature Center where you can pick up a trail map from the ranger. If you start at the Nature Center, most of the trail (first five miles) is relatively flat. It gets steeper in the last mile and there could be some creek crossings. From the Nature Center, follow the path which will take you past a golf course. At the end of the golf course, you'll need to take Snead Ave which will join up with the rest of the path. There might be a few more street crossings, but the majority of the walk is on the dirt trail. With the all the natural surroundings it seems like it is far from the city, but it's located only 6-7 miles from downtown. To get there, take Tecolote Road until it ends. Dogs must be on leash in the park.
Manning Park Manning Park San Ysidro CA   805-969-0201
The park is open 8 am to Sunset. Dogs on leash are allowed throughout the city park.

Off-Leash Dog Parks
Dog Park at Otay Ranch Town Center Eastlake Pkwy At Olympic Pkwy Chula Vista CA   619-656-9100
This dog park opened in Oct, 2006 in the new Otay Ranch Town Center which is also pet-friendly. The fenced, 10,000 square foot dog park is located next to the Macy's at the outdoor mall. To get to the mall and dog park from San Diego go south on the 805 Freeway to the Orange Avenue Exit. Head east on Orange Avenue which will become Olympic Parkway. Go 4 miles east to the mall.
Montevalle Park Dog Park 840 Duncan Ranch Road Chula Vista CA   619-691-5269
This dog park is fully fenced and is located in the 29 acre Montevalle Park. The park is grassy and there are separate areas for small dogs and large dogs. There are drinking fountains for dogs and cleanup bags are also available. From I-805 take H Street east for about 6 miles. It will become Proctor Valley Rd go an additional 1 mile and turn right onto Duncan Ranch Rd to the park.
Wells Park & Off-Leash Dog Park 1153 E. Madison Ave El Cajon CA   619-441-1680
This fenced dog park has two separate off-leash areas for large dogs and small dogs. Exit I-8 at Mollison Avenue and head south one block and then left on Madison Ave. The park will be on your right in a few blocks.
Harry Griffen Park 9550 Milden Street La Mesa CA   619-667-1307
Thanks to one of our readers who writes: "A leash-free dog area - very nice area of the park and no restrictions on dog size."
Dusty Rhodes Dog Park Sunset Cliffs Blvd. Ocean Beach CA   619-236-5555
This dog park is located in Dusty Rhodes Neighborhood Park. The park is on Sunset Cliffs Blvd. between Nimitz and West Point Loma.

Dog Park at Otay Ranch Town Center

Balboa Park Dog Run

Balboa Park Dog Run Balboa Dr San Diego CA   619-235-1100
http://www.balboapark.org/rules.html
The dog-friendly Balboa Park has set aside a portion of land for an off leash dog run. It's not fenced, so make

sure your pup listens to voice commands. It is located between Balboa Drive and Hwy 163.

Capehart Dog Park Felspar at Soledad Mountain Rd San Diego CA   619-525-8212

This one acre fenced dog park has a separate area for large and small dogs. There is water for dogs and people and benches. The dog park is open 24 hours. It is located in Capehart Park at the corner of Felspar and Soledad Mountain Rd. This is just off the I-5 at Mission Bay Dr west toward Garnet Ave. Then turn right on Soledad Mountain Rd.

Doyle Community Park 8175 Regents Road San Diego CA 619-525-8212

This dog park offers two fenced areas for large and small dogs. It is open 24 hours but there are no lights. The park is located behind the Doyle Community Center. From I-5 take La Jolla Village Dr east to Regents Rd. Turn right on Regents to the park.

Grape Street Park Off-Leash Area Grape Street at Granada Ave San Diego CA   619-525-8212

This is a non-fenced five acre legal off-leash area for certain hours. Currently, the hours are Monday thru Friday 7:30 am to 9 pm, and on weekends and holidays from 9 am to 9 pm. The Grape Street off-leash area is on the eastern boundry of Balboa Park. From Fern Street/30th Street go east on Grape Street to the street ends.

Kearny Mesa Dog Park 3170 Armstrong Street San Diego CA   619-525-8212

http://kmdogpark.com/

This dog park is fenced and is one acre in size. It is open 24 hours and there is some lighting from the nearby ball fields. Parking can be difficult during the day due to the nearby Mesa College. The dog park can be accessed from the 163 freeway (south of 805) at Mesa College Dr. Go west on Mesa College Drive to Armstrong. Turn left on Armstrong to the park.

Maddox Dog Park 7815 Flanders Dr San Diego CA   619-525-8212

This 2/3 acre fenced dog park is located in Maddox Neighborhood Park. The park is located just south of Mira Mesa Blvd. Go south on Parkdale Ave and turn right onto Flanders.

Rancho Bernardo Off-Leash Park 18448 West Bernardo Drive San Diego CA   858-538-8129

http://ranchobernardodogpark.com/

The dog park is 2.66 acres divided into three separate fenced areas. There are benches, clean-up bags and shade in each area. To get to the park from I-15 take the West Bernardo/Pomerado Road exit. Go to the west and the park is on your right in about 1/4 mile. The dog park is in the southern end of the park.

Torrey Highlands Park Landsdale Drive at Del Mar Heights Road San Diego CA   619-525-8212

http://www.ourdogpark.com/

This one acre dog park is located in Torrey Highlands Park. To get to the dog park from I-5 take Del Mar Heights Rd East 1.2 miles. Turn left on Lansdale and left immediately into the park.

Outdoor Restaurants

Cucina Italiana 4705-A Clairemont Drive Clairemont CA   858-274-9732

This eatery features authentic Italian cuisine from many regions, house-made breads, freshly prepared foods, and a heated patio. They are located at the Clairemont Square Shopping Center near the movie multiplex, and weekends can be quite busy. Your pet is welcome to join you at the outside tables. Dogs must be attended to at all times, well behaved, and leashed.

Cafe 1134 1134 Orange Ave Coronado CA   619-437-1134

Cafe 1134 offers coffee and a full bistro menu. Dogs are allowed at the outdoor tables.

McP's Irish Pub and Grill 1107 Orange Avenue Coronado CA   619-435-5280

http://www.mcpspub.com/

This authentic Irish pub serves up popular Irish dishes and beer and offers live entertainment nightly. They offer service on the patio, and when it is cold they turn on the patio heaters. Your friendly pet is welcome to join you at the outside tables. Dogs must be attended to at all times, well behaved, and leashed

Rhinoceros Cafe and Grill

Rhinoceros Cafe and Grill 1166 Orange Ave Coronado CA 619-435-2121
The folks we spoke with here said they are very dog-friendly. For lunch and dinner, they serve steaks, ribs, chicken and pasta dishes seven days a week. Breakfast is served on the weekends. Dogs are welcome at the outdoor tables.

Spiro's Gyros 1201 First Street Coronado CA 619-435-1225
This restaurant offers casual dining with a view and classic Greek food. There is patio seating, but go inside to order and pick up your meal. Dogs must be quiet, well behaved, under owners control at all times, and leashed.

Tartine 1106 1st Street Coronado CA 619-435-4323
This restaurant serves deli-type food and coffee. Dogs are allowed at the outdoor tables.

Villa Nueva 956 Orange Ave Coronado CA 619-435-4191
Come to this bakery and deli for breakfast, lunch or dinner. Dogs are allowed at the outdoor tables.

Elijah's 8861 Villa La Jolla Drive La Jolla CA 858-455-1461
Dogs are allowed at the outdoor tables.

French Pastry Shop 5550 La Jolla Blvd La Jolla CA 858-454-9094
In addition to featuring delicious French bakery treats, they also serve breakfast, lunch, and dinners offering fresh, homemade food, and patio dining. Your pet is welcome to join you at the outside tables. Dogs must be attended to at all times, well behaved, and leashed.

Girard Gourmet 7837 Girard Avenue La Jolla CA 858-454-3321
http://www.girardgourmet.com/
This award winning gourmet eatery offers a wide variety of freshly prepared baked goods (their specialty being custom made cookies for all occasions), a seasonally influenced menu, homemade soups/quiches/deserts, and great comfort food for breakfast, lunch, and dinner. They have an outdoor dining area where guests may sit with their pet; just go inside to order and pickup. Dogs must be well mannered, under owner's control at all times, and leashed.

Harry's Coffee Shop 7545 Girard Avenue La Jolla CA 858-454-7381
http://www.harryscoffeeshop.com/
This breakfast and lunch restaurant serves up old-fashioned American food as well as espresso and fountain drinks. They are open daily from 6 am to 3 pm, and they also offer patio seating. Your pet is welcome to join you at the outside tables. Dogs must be attended to at all times, well behaved, and leashed.

La Jolla Beachhouse Brewery 7536 Fay Ave La Jolla CA 858-456-6279
This restaurant and bar serves American. Dogs are allowed at the outdoor tables.

Sante Ristorante 7811 Herschel Avenue La Jolla CA 858-454-1315
http://www.santeristorante.com/
This fine dining establishment features the finest in Italian cuisine, and during the autumn season, they offer fresh truffle selections. They have several outside dining options; dogs are welcome on the back patio during

lunch service. Dogs must be attended to at all times, well behaved, and leashed.

The 910 Restaurant and Bar 910 Prospect St La Jolla CA 858-454-2181

Located in the Grand Colonial Inn, Putnam's serves breakfast, lunch, dinner and Sunday brunch. They offer contemporary world cuisine by an award-winning chef. Dogs are allowed at the outdoor tables.

Whole Foods Market 8825 Villa La Jolla Drive La Jolla CA 858-642-6700

http://www.wholefoods.com/

This natural food supermarket offers natural and organic foods. Order some food from their deli without your dog and bring it to an outdoor table where your well-behaved leashed dog is welcome. Dogs are not allowed in the store including the deli at any time. The market is located at the corner of Villa La Jolla and Nobel Drive.

Yummy Maki Yummy Box 3211 Holiday Ct # 101A La Jolla CA 858-587-9848

This eatery specializes in oriental cuisine and offer indoor and outdoor dining service. Dogs are allowed at the outer tables. They must be under owner's control at all times, be well behaved, and leashed.

Zenbu Sushi Bar & Restaurant 7660 Fay Avenue La Jolla CA 858-454-4540

This eatery has been called the hot spot for all things fresh and Asian. They offer indoor and outdoor dining, weather permitting. Dogs are welcome at the outer tables. Dogs must be well behaved, attended to at all times, and leashed.

Seau's 1640 Camino del Rio North Mission Valley CA 619-291-7328

This place is one of the city's premier sports-themed eateries offering several large TV viewing screens. They serve contemporary American grill cuisine as well as pizza, pasta, and sushi. Your pet is welcome to join you at the outside tables. Dogs must be well behaved, attended to at all times, and leashed.

Tazablanca 3946 Illinois Street North Park CA 619-294-8292

http://www.tazablancarestaurant.com/

This restaurant serves up authentic Cuban cuisine and live Latin music Thursday through Saturday. They offer outside dining service; just let them know inside that you are there. Your pet is welcome to join you at the outside tables. Dogs must be attended to at all times, well behaved, and leashed.

Bar-B-Que House 5025 Newport Avenue Ocean Beach CA 619-222-4311

http://www.barbquehouse.com/

Located in the heart of Ocean Beach just up the street from the water, this award- winning barbecue restaurant offers slow cooked recipes made from scratch. Your pet is welcome to join you at the outside tables. Place and pick up your order inside. Dogs must be attended to at all times, well behaved, and leashed.

Baja Fresh Mexican Grill 3369 Rosecrans San Diego CA 619-222-3399

http://www.bajafresh.com

This Mexican restaurant is open for lunch and dinner. They use fresh ingredients and making their salsa and beans daily. Some of the items on their menu include Enchiladas, Burritos, Tacos Salads, Quesadillas, Nachos, Chicken, Steak and more. Well-behaved leashed dogs are allowed at the outdoor tables.

Baja Fresh Mexican Grill 120 W. Washington St. San Diego CA 619-497-1000

http://www.bajafresh.com

This Mexican restaurant, located in the Hillcrest area, is open for lunch and dinner. They use fresh ingredients and making their salsa and beans daily. Some of the items on their menu include Enchiladas, Burritos, Tacos Salads, Quesadillas, Nachos, Chicken, Steak and more. Well-behaved leashed dogs are allowed at the outdoor tables.

Baja Fresh Mexican Grill 9015 Mira Mesa Blvd San Diego CA 858-577-0590

http://www.bajafresh.com

This Mexican restaurant is open for lunch and dinner. They use fresh ingredients and making their salsa and beans daily. Some of the items on their menu include Enchiladas, Burritos, Tacos Salads, Quesadillas, Nachos, Chicken, Steak and more. Well-behaved leashed dogs are allowed at the outdoor tables.

Baja Fresh Mexican Grill 3737 Murphy Cyn Rd San Diego CA 858-277-5700

http://www.bajafresh.com

This Mexican restaurant is open for lunch and dinner. They use fresh ingredients and making their salsa and beans daily. Some of the items on their menu include Enchiladas, Burritos, Tacos Salads, Quesadillas, Nachos, Chicken, Steak and more. Well-behaved leashed dogs are allowed at the outdoor tables.

Baja Fresh Mexican Grill 845 Camino De La Reina San Diego CA 619-295-1122

http://www.bajafresh.com

This Mexican restaurant is open for lunch and dinner. They use fresh ingredients and making their salsa and beans daily. Some of the items on their menu include Enchiladas, Burritos, Tacos Salads, Quesadillas, Nachos, Chicken, Steak and more. Well-behaved leashed dogs are allowed at the outdoor tables.

Bareback Grill 4640 Mission Blvd San Diego CA 858-274-7117

Organic hamburgers imported from New Zealand are among the fare at this bar in the Mission Beach area. They have a couple of outdoor seats where you can eat and drink with dog in tow.

Boardwalk Bistro 3704 Mission Blvd San Diego CA 858-488-9484

This cafe is located near Mission Bay. Well-behaved, leashed dogs are allowed at the outdoor tables.

Cafe 222 222 Island Street San Diego CA 619-236-9902

This restaurant serves American food. Dogs are allowed at the outdoor tables.

Cafe Pacifica 2414 San Diego Avenue San Diego CA 619-291-6666

http://www.cafepacifica.com/

This eatery is the recipient of the DiRoNa Award (a distinguished dining accolade), and they feature contemporary seafood cuisine, steaks, and pasta dishes complimented with the distinct flavor of local produce and herbs. When weather permits there is a table with an awning in front of the restaurant where customers with pets may enjoy their meal. Dogs must be well behaved, under owner's control at all times, leashed, and cleaned up after.

Champagne French Bakery Cafe 12955 El Camino Real San Diego CA   858-792-2222
http://www.champagnebakery.com
Located in the Del Mar Highlands Town Center, this restaurant allows well-behaved leashed dogs at the outdoor tables. Thanks to one of our readers for recommending this cafe.

City Delicatessen 535 University Ave San Diego CA 619-295-2747
This restaurant is located in the Hillcrest area and serves a variety of sandwiches. Well-behaved, leashed dogs are allowed at the outdoor tables.

Costa Brava 1653 Garnet Avenue San Diego CA   858-273-1218
http://www.costabravasd.com/
This restaurant and tapes bar brings the traditional cuisine of Spain to San Diego. They offer service on the patio, and your pet is welcome to join you there. Dogs must be attended to at all times, well behaved, and leashed.

El Indio 3695 India Street San Diego CA   619-299-0333
http://www.el-indio.com/
This Mexican eatery has been family owned and operating since 1940, and they offer a wide variety of dishes, including vegetarian choices. They feature indoor and outdoor patio dining. Dogs are allowed at the outer tables. Dogs must be well behaved, under owner's control at all times, leashed, and cleaned up after.

Gulf Coast Grill 4130 Park Blvd San Diego CA   619-295-2244
http://www.gulfcoastgrill.com/
Gulf Coast Grill serves lunch and dinner daily. The specialty is southern and southwestern cuisine. Dogs may dine with you on the outside patio.

Hudson Bay Seafood 1403 Scott Street San Diego CA   619-222-8787
This restaurant serves seafood. Dogs are allowed at the outdoor tables. Water and treats are provided for your pet.

Kemo Sabe 3958 Fifth Ave. San Diego CA   619-220-6802
Located in the Hillcrest area, this restaurant serves food that is influenced by Asian and New Mexican cuisines. They have about 6 outdoor tables and you will need to sign up on a waiting list if all tables are taken. Well-behaved, leashed dogs are allowed at the outside tables.

King's Fish House 825 Camino de la Reina San Diego CA   619-574-1230
http://kingsfishhouse.com/
Specializing in seafood at is best, steaks, freshly prepared salads, desserts, and a daily and seasonally changing menu, this restaurant also offers a full bar and outdoor patio service. Your pet is welcome to join you at the outside tables. Dogs must be attended to at all times, well behaved, and leashed.

Korky's Ice Cream and Coffee 2371 San Diego Avenue San Diego CA   619-297-3080
http://www.korkys.biz/
Home to world famous Niederfranks handmade ice cream, this old-fashioned ice cream parlor comes with the modern comforts of a neighborhood coffee house, and for a quick bite they also offer sandwiches, salads, and pastries. Your pet is welcome to join you at the outside tables. Dogs must be attended to at all times, well behaved, and leashed.

Lamont Street Grill 4445 Lamont Street San Diego CA   858-270-3060
This steak and seafood grill offers up California comfort food with a Mexi/Asian/Cajun flavor. In addition to a full bar, they feature an extensive California wine list. They offer service at the outside tables, and your pet is welcome to join you there. Dogs must be attended to at all times, well behaved, and leashed.

Oggi's Pizza 2245 Fenton Parkway San Diego CA   619-640-1072
This restaurant serves Italian food. Dogs are allowed at the outdoor tables.

Saffron Thai Grilled Chicken 3137 India Street San Diego CA 619-574-0177
http://www.sumeiyu.com/rest.htm
This eatery specializes in traditional Thai grilled chicken in the style of the northeastern region of Thailand in addition to many other tasty items. They offer indoor and outdoor dining service. Dogs are allowed at the outer tables. Dogs must be well behaved, under owner's control at all times, leashed, and cleaned up after.

Terra Bar and Restaurant 3900 Vermont Street San Diego CA   619-293-7088
http://www.terrasd.com/
This restaurant specializes in fine American cuisine featuring signature dishes with local and regional products. They are also host to wine/special events and cooking classes during the month, and offer patio dining service. Your pet is welcome to join you at the outside tables. Dogs must be attended to at all times, well behaved, and leashed.

The Alamo 2502 San Diego Ave San Diego CA 619-296-1112
This Mexican restaurant serves some tasty dishes and is located next to Old Town State Historic Park. Dogs are allowed at the outdoor tables.

The Bean Bar Coffee House and Drive-Thru 3111 Hancock St San Diego CA 619-299-3241

This coffee shop allows dogs at the outdoor tables. Water and treats are provided for your pet.

The Prado Restaurant 1549 El Prado San Diego CA 619-557-9441

Located in the heart of Balboa Park and in one of the city's most beautiful buildings, they offer indoor and outdoor patio dining service, superb wines, exquisite foods, elegant ambiance, and great service. Dogs are allowed at the patio tables. Dogs must be well behaved, under owner's control at all times, leashed, and cleaned up after.

Trattoria Fantastica 1735 India Street San Diego CA 619-234-1735

Dogs are allowed at the tables on the front patio.

Trattoria la Strada 702 Fifth Street San Diego CA 619-239-3400

http://trattorialastrada.com/

This fine Italian restaurant offers an authentic Tuscan menu. They offer a full service patio, and your pet is welcome to join you at the outside tables. Dogs must be well behaved, attended to at all times, and leashed.

Uncle Joe's Pizzeria 4591 El Cajon Blvd San Diego CA 619-584-2535

This pizzeria offers outside dining service. Your pet is welcome to join you at the outside tables. Dogs must be attended to at all times, well behaved, and leashed.

Whole Foods Market 711 University Avenue San Diego CA 619-294-2800

http://www.wholefoods.com/

This natural food supermarket offers natural and organic foods. Order some food from their deli without your dog and bring it to an outdoor table where your well-behaved leashed dog is welcome. Dogs are not allowed in the store including the deli at any time.

Zia's Bistro 1845 India Street San Diego CA 619-234-1344

This restaurant serves Italian food. Dogs are allowed at the outdoor tables.

The Pennant! 2893 Mission Blvd South Mission Beach CA 858-488-1671

Known as the quintessential beach bar, they also serve a variety of snacks and sandwiches, and are only open on the weekends. Dogs are allowed on the outer deck. They must be well behaved, under owner's control at all times, leashed, and cleaned up after.

Events

SD Padres Dog Days of Summer at Petco Park 100 Park Blvd San Diego CA 619-795-5000

http://sandiego.padres.mlb.com

The San Diego Padres open Petco Park to dog owners one day a year for their annual "Dog Days of Summer" game. There is a dog parade before the game and then you can sit in a section of the ballpark with your dog. The 2007 event is scheduled for August 14. The date will vary each year. Please contact the Padres for details and schedules. Throughout the year, there is a 2.5 acre park beyond the center field fence with a panoramic view of Petco Park. Dogs on leash are allowed in this park with you although it is off-limits to dogs during baseball games and a $5 admission charge is made for people.

San Diego Kayaking Tours 2246 Avenida de la Playa San Diego CA 866 HB KAYAK (425-2925)

Tours usually begin from the La Jolla Shores shop on the 3rd Saturday of each month for this unguided outdoor kayaking excursion with your pooch around the La Jolla Bay. Your pup's life jacket is included, and there is no additional pet fee. Dogs (and owners) must be able to swim, and they suggest it is better if dogs have swam in an ocean or a lake before. Dogs must be under owner's control and care at all times. Reservation are definitely recommended as prices, times, and locations may change and weather may be a factor.

Day Kennels

PetsHotel by PetsMart Day Kennel 8657 Villa la Jolla Dr. La Jolla CA

http://www.petsmart.com/PETsHOTEL/

This PetSmart pet store offers day care, day camp and overnight care. You may drop off and pick up your dog during during the hours of 7 am - 7 pm M-S, Sunday 7 am - 6:30 pm. Dogs are required to have proof of current rabies, DPP and bordatella vaccinations.

Vets and Kennels

Animal ER of San Diego 5610 Kearny Mesa Rd San Diego CA 858-569-0600

Monday - Friday 6 pm to 8 am, 24 hours on weekends.

Animal Emergency Clinic 13240 Evening Creek Dr S San Diego CA 858-748-7387

24 hours everyday.

Emergency Animal Clinic 2317 Hotel Cir S # A San Diego CA 619-299-2400

Monday - Friday 6 pm to 8 am, 24 hours on weekends.

San Diego County North

Accommodations

Inns of America 751 Raintree Carlsbad CA 760-931-1185
There is a $10 one time pet fee.
Motel 6 - Carlsbad Downtown 1006 Carlsbad Village Drive Carlsbad CA 760-434-7135 (800-466-8356)
One well-behaved family pet per room. Guest must notify front desk upon arrival. Guest is liable for any
damages. In consideration of all guests, pets must never be left unattended in the guest rooms.
Motel 6 - Carlsbad South 750 Raintree Drive Carlsbad CA 760-431-0745 (800-466-8356)
One well-behaved pet is welcome. There are no additional pet fees, just let them know that you have a pet.
Quality Inn and Suites 751 Raintree Drive Carlsbad CA 760-931-1185 (877-424-6423)
Dogs of all sizes are allowed. There is a $10 per night per pet additional fee. Dogs may not be left alone in the
room, and they must be leashed and cleaned up after. Dogs are not allowed in the pool or breakfast areas.
Red Roof Inn - Carlsbad 6117 Paseo del Norte Carlsbad CA 760-438-1242 (800-RED-ROOF)
One well-behaved family pet per room. Guest must notify front desk upon arrival. Guest is liable for any
damages. In consideration of all guests, pets must never be left unattended in the guest rooms.
Residence Inn by Marriott 2000 Faraday Avenue Carlsbad CA 760-431-9999
Pets of all sizes are allowed. There is a $75 one time fee, and a pet policy to sign at check in.
West Inn and Suites 4970 Avenida Encinas Carlsbad CA 760-208-4929 (866-375-4705)
This boutique style, 4 star hotel offers the ultimate in luxury surroundings and recreational activities for both the
business and leisure traveler. Some of the amenities include 2 fine dining restaurants, pool and Jacuzzi, a
business center, library, and an on-site pantry. They are also close to the beach and several attractions. Dogs of
all sizes are allowed. There is a $75 per night per pet additional fee. Dogs may not be left alone in the room, and
they must be leashed and cleaned up after.
Hilton 15575 Jimmy Durante Blvd Del Mar CA 858-792-5200
Dogs up to 100 pounds are allowed. There is a $200 deposit, $150 of which is refundable, and a pet policy to
sign at check in.
Best Western Encinitas Inn and Suites at Moonlight Beach 85 Encinitas Blvd Encinitas CA 760-942-
7455 (800-780-7234)
Dogs of all sizes are allowed. There is a $50 one time pet fee per visit. Smoking and non-smoking are available
for pet rooms.
Holiday Inn Express 607 Leucadia Blvd Encinitas CA 760-944-3800 (877-270-6405)
Dogs of any size are allowed. There is a $20 per day additional pet fee.
Quails Inn Hotel 1025 La Bonita Drive Lake San Marcos CA 760-744-0120
There is a $10 per day pet fee. This resort has a number of golf packages available.
La Quinta Inn San Diego - Oceanside 937 N. Coast Highway Oceanside CA 760-450-0730 (800-531-5900)
Dogs of all sizes are allowed. There are no additional pet fees. Dogs may not be left unattended, and they must
be leashed and cleaned up after.
Motel 6 - Oceanside 3708 Plaza Drive Oceanside CA 760-941-1011 (800-466-8356)
One well-behaved family pet per room. Guest must notify front desk upon arrival. Guest is liable for any
damages. In consideration of all guests, pets must never be left unattended in the guest rooms.
Motel 6 - Oceanside Downtown 909 North Coast Highway Oceanside CA 760-721-1543 (800-466-8356)
One well-behaved family pet per room. Guest must notify front desk upon arrival. Guest is liable for any
damages. In consideration of all guests, pets must never be left unattended in the guest rooms.
Best Western Country Inn (San Diego) 13845 Poway Rd Poway CA 858-748-6320 (800-780-7234)
Dogs of all sizes are allowed. There is a $15 one time pet fee per week. Smoking and non-smoking are available
for pet rooms.
La Quinta Inn San Diego Vista 630 Sycamore Ave. Vista CA 760-727-8180 (800-531-5900)
Dogs of all sizes are allowed. There are no additional pet fees. Dogs may not be left unattended, and they must
be leashed and cleaned up after.

Campgrounds and RV Parks

San Elijo State Beach Campground 2050 Coast H Cardiff CA 760-753-5091 (800-444-7275)
This campground offers RV sites with limited hookups. RVs up to 26 feet can use the hookup sites and RVs up
to 35 feet are allowed. They offer both inland and ocean view spaces. While dogs are not allowed at this beach,
you can walk to the dog-friendly Cardiff State Beach. The beach is about 1 mile south of Cardiff. Dogs may not
be left unattended, and they must be leashed and cleaned up after. There are some breed restrictions. The
camping and tent areas also allow dogs. There is a dog walk area at the campground.
Guajome County Park 3000 Guajome Lake Road Oceanside CA 858-565-3600
Rich in natural and cultural history, this historic 557 acre park features a wide diversity of plant, bird, and wildlife,
spring-fed lakes, scenic picnic areas, trails, a gazebo and an enclosed pavilion that overlooks the lake. There is
a variety of land and water recreational opportunities to explore. Dogs of all sizes are allowed for an additional
fee of $1 per pet. Dogs must have current tags or shot records, be on no more than a 6 foot leash, and be
cleaned up after. Dogs must remain in developed and paved areas; they are not allowed on the trails. The camp
area has 35 developed sites, restrooms, hot showers, fire rings, and a dump station. There are 4 sites that will

accommodate larger trailers. The camping and tent areas also allow dogs. There is a dog walk area at the campground.

Guajome County Park 3000 Guajome Lake Road Oceanside CA   760-724-4489 (877-565-3600)
Rich in natural and cultural history, this park is home to a variety of diverse habitats for plant and animal life. Dogs of all sizes are allowed for an additional $1 per night per pet, and they must have current tags, rabies, and shot records. Dogs may not be left unattended at any time, and they must be on no more than a 6 foot leash and cleaned up after. Dogs are not allowed on the trails, but they may be walked on the payment and along side the roads on leash. There are some breed restrictions. The camping and tent areas also allow dogs. There is a dog walk area at the campground.

Paradise by the Sea RV Resort 1537 S Coast H Oceanside CA   760-439-1376
http://www.paradisebythesearvresort.com/
Set between the beautiful Pacific Ocean and historic Highway 101, this park features beach and pool swimming, a rec room, hot showers, restroom and laundry facilities, and a convenience store. Dogs of all sizes are allowed for an additional fee of $1 per night per pet. Dogs may not be left unattended, and they must be leashed and cleaned up after. Dogs are not allowed on the beach. This is an RV only park. There are some breed restrictions. There is a dog walk area at the campground.

Vacation Home Rentals

Casa Leucadia Call to Arrange Encinitas CA   760-633-4497
This large vacation rental in Encinitas can sleep up to 13 people. It consists of a main house and two separate suites. There is a nice yard and dogs are welcome.

Attractions

Carlsbad Village Carlsbad Village Drive Carlsbad CA
Carlsbad Village has a number of shops and restaurants that are dog-friendly. Its about 4 blocks long and 2 blocks wide.

Legoland Kennel One Legoland Drive Carlsbad CA   760-918-5346
http://www.legoland.com/California.htm
This amusement park offers a trilling variety of rides, shows and attractions. Although dogs are not allowed in the park they are allowed in the kennels that are provided out front. Individual kennels are provided, and there is a $15 refundable deposit for the key. Water and dishes are provided; they request that you bring food, blankets, and whatever comfort toys along for your pet.

TOP 200 PLACE **Witch Creek Winery** 2906 Carlsbad Blvd/Hwy 101 Carlsbad CA   760-720-7499
This winery focuses on handcrafted wines that are rich, full bodied, and well balanced. They have two tasting rooms; one in Carlsbad and the other one in Julian, California. They consider themselves dog-friendly, and your pet is welcome to go wherever you can go, including the tasting room in Carlsbad. Dogs must be well behaved, and leashed and cleaned up after at all times.

California Surf Museum

TOP 200 PLACE **California Surf Museum** 223 N Coast H Oceanside CA   760-721-6876
http://www.surfmuseum.org/
This interesting museum is a resource and educational center to gather, preserve, and document the art, culture and heritage of this lifestyle sport for generations to come. Well mannered dogs are welcome at this small museum; they must be leashed and under owner's control at all times.

Stores
Petco Pet Store 3239 Camino De Los Coches Carlsbad CA   760-753-0814
Your licensed and well-behaved leashed dog is allowed in the store.
Dexter's Deli 1229 Camino Del Mar Del Mar CA   858-792-3707
http://dextersdeli.com/
Specializing in natural food diets, fresh baked treats and cakes and a selection of dog and cat toys and gifts.
Petco Pet Store 2749 Via De La Valle Del Mar CA   858-259-0110
Your licensed and well-behaved leashed dog is allowed in the store.
PetSmart Pet Store 1034 N El Camino Real Encinitas CA   760-436-1220
Your licensed and well-behaved leashed dog is allowed in the store.
Petco Pet Store 154 Encinitas Blvd Encinitas CA   760-632-6600
Your licensed and well-behaved leashed dog is allowed in the store.
PetSmart Pet Store 3420 Marron Oceanside CA   760-729-4546
Your licensed and well-behaved leashed dog is allowed in the store.
Petco Pet Store 2445 West Vista Way Oceanside CA   760-967-7387
Your licensed and well-behaved leashed dog is allowed in the store.
Petco Pet Store 3875 Mission Avenue Oceanside CA   760-754-1400
Your licensed and well-behaved leashed dog is allowed in the store.
Petco Pet Store 13375 Poway Rd Poway CA   858-679-2020
Your licensed and well-behaved leashed dog is allowed in the store.
PetSmart Pet Store 1740 University Dr Vista CA   760-630-3544
Your licensed and well-behaved leashed dog is allowed in the store.
Petco Pet Store 520 Hacienda Drive Vista CA   760-631-5770
Your licensed and well-behaved leashed dog is allowed in the store.

Beaches
Cardiff State Beach Old Highway 101 Cardiff CA   760-753-5091
This is a gently sloping sandy beach with warm water. Popular activities include swimming, surfing and beachcombing. Dogs on leash are allowed and please clean up after your pets. The beach is located on Old Highway 101, one mile south of Cardiff.
Del Mar Beach Seventeenth Street Del Mar CA   858-755-1556
Dogs are allowed on the beach as follows. South of 17th Street, dogs are allowed on a 6 foot leash year-round. Between 17th Street and 29th Street, dogs are allowed on a 6 foot leash from October through May (from June through September, dogs are not allowed at all). Between 29th Street and northern city limits, dogs are allowed without a leash, but must be under voice control from October through May (from June through September, dogs must be on a 6 foot leash). Owners must clean up after their dogs.
Rivermouth Beach Highway 101 Del Mar CA
This beach allows voice controlled dogs to run leash free from September 15 through June 15 (no specified hours). Leashes are required during mid-summer tourist season from mid June to mid Sept. Fans of this beach are trying to convince the Del Mar City council to extend the leash-free period to year round. The beach is located on Highway 101 just south of Border Avenue at the north end of the City of Del Mar. Thanks to one of our readers for recommending this beach.

Parks
Guajome County Park 3000 Guajome Lake Road Oceanside CA   858-565-3600
Rich in natural and cultural history, this historic 557 acre park features a wide diversity of plant, bird, and wildlife, spring-fed lakes, scenic picnic areas, trails, a gazebo and an enclosed pavilion that overlooks the lake. There is a variety of land and water recreational opportunities to explore. Dogs of all sizes are allowed for an additional fee of $1 per pet. Dogs must have current tags or shot records, be on no more than a 6 foot leash, and be cleaned up after. Dogs must remain in developed and paved areas; they are not allowed on the trails.

Off-Leash Dog Parks
Encinitas Park D Street Encinitas CA
Thanks to one of our readers who recommends the following two dog parks in Encinitas Park. Encinitas Viewpoint Park, on "D" Street at Cornish Drive, off-leash dogs permitted 6:00-7:30 AM and 4:00-6:00 PM on

MWF only. Other days of the week, dogs must be on leash. Orpheus Park, on Orpheus Avenue at Union Street, off-leash dogs permitted 6:00-7:30 AM and 4:00-6:00 PM on MWF only. Other days of the week, dogs must be on leash.

Rancho Coastal Humane Society Dog Park 389 Requeza Street Encinitas CA   760-753-6413

The dog park at the humane society has limited hours. It is open on Tuesday and Thursdays from 2 pm to 5 pm and 11 am - 5 pm on Saturday and Sunday. The dog park is fenced, with separate areas for large and small dogs. There are benches and water for dogs and people. To get to the dog park from I-5 heading north take the Santa Fe Drive exit to Regal Rd and then left on Requeza Street. From I-5 south, exit Encinitas Blvd. Turn left onto Encinitas Blvd, right on Westlake and right onto Requeza Street.

Oceanside Dog Park 2905 San Luis Rey Rd Oceanside CA   760-757-4357

http://www.nchumane.org/news/dogpark.php

The first off-leash dog park in Oceanside is located next to the North County Humane Society buiding. The fenced park is open from 7 am to 7 pm except for Wednesday when it is closed for maintenance.

Poway Dog Park 13094 Civic Center Drive Poway CA

This 1 3/4 acre dog park is open from sunrise to 9:30 pm. The park is lighted at night. There are three separate fenced areas. From the I-15 freeway take Poway Rd east 3.9 miles. Turn right on Bowron and park at the lot at the end of the road.

Outdoor Restaurants

Boar Cross'n Bar and Grill 390 Grand Ave Carlsbad CA   760-729-2989

This is a bar that requires human visitors to be 21. However, dogs don't have to be this old and they are welcome on the patio in the back. Dogs are allowed at the outdoor tables during the daytime, but not at night. Dogs are not allowed when bands are playing as the patio is closed.

Cafe Elysa 3076 Carlsbad Blvd Carlsbad CA   760-434-4100

Dogs are allowed at the outdoor tables.

Grand Deli 595 Grand Ave Carlsbad CA   760-729-4015

Dogs are allowed at the outdoor tables.

Gregorio's Restaurant 300 Carlsbad Village Dr #208 Carlsbad CA   760-720-1132

http://www.gregoriosrestaurant.com

This Italian and Pizza restaurant allows dogs at the outdoor seats.

Pizza Port 571 Carlsbad Village Dr Carlsbad CA   760-720-7007

This pizza house and brewery has heaters outside for their visitors with dogs.

Tom Giblin's Irish Pub 640 Grand Ave Carlsbad CA   760-729-7234

This restaurant and bar serves American food. Dogs are allowed at the outdoor tables.

Village Grille 2833 State Street Carlsbad CA   760-729-3601

Here you can order food from an outside window with your pup. Dogs are allowed at the outdoor tables.

Vinaka Cafe 300 Carlsbad Village Dr #211 Carlsbad CA   760-720-7890

Dogs are allowed at the outdoor tables.

Tom Giblin's Irish Pub 640 Grand Avenue Carlsbad Village CA   760-729-7234

http://www.tomgiblins.com/

This authentic Irish pub offers a variety of American and Irish foods, indoor/outdoor service, premium draft beers with many specialty drinks, and live traditional and contemporary Irish music. Your pet is welcome to join you at the outside tables. Dogs must be attended to at all times, well behaved, and leashed.

Americana 1454 Camino Del Mar Del Mar CA   858-794-6838

This restaurant serves American food. Dogs are allowed at the outdoor tables.

Del Mar French Pastry Cafe 1140 Camino Del Mar Del Mar CA   858-481-8622

Dogs are allowed at the outdoor tables.

En Fuego Cantina & Grill 1342 Camino del Mar Del Mar CA   858-792-6551

Enjoy dining with your dog at the tables in the nicely designed patio. Thanks to one of our readers for recommending this restaurant.

Pacifica Breeze Cafe 1555 Camino Del Mar #209 Del Mar CA   858-509-9147

Dogs are allowed at the outdoor tables.

Stratford Court Cafe 1307 Stratford Court Del Mar CA   858-792-7433

Thanks to one of our readers who writes: "This is THE dog-friendly restaurant in Del Mar. All seating outdoor and you and your dog can order at a walk-up counter. They even offer home-made dog biscuits and have a stack of water bowls. Only a few minutes drive from the off-leash Rivermouth beach, so there are always lots of dogs. Breakfast and lunch only - California cuisine."

Baja Fresh Mexican Grill 194 El Camino Real Blvd Encinitas CA   760-633-2262

http://www.bajafresh.com

This Mexican restaurant is open for lunch and dinner. They use fresh ingredients and making their salsa and beans daily. Some of the items on their menu include Enchiladas, Burritos, Tacos Salads, Quesadillas, Nachos, Chicken, Steak and more. Well-behaved leashed dogs are allowed at the outdoor tables.

Encinitas Cafe 531 S Coast Hwy 101 Encinitas CA   760-632-0919

This restaurant serves Mexican food. Dogs are allowed at the outdoor tables.

Firenze Trattoria 162 S Rancho Santa Fe Road Encinitas CA   760-944-9000
http://www.firenzetrattoria.com/
This upscale restaurant features the finest in Italian cuisine, an extensive wine list, and a flower adorned patio.
Service is provided on the patio where your pet is welcome to join you. Dogs must be well behaved, attended to
at all times, and leashed.
Sazio Italian Restorante 1560 Leucadia Blvd Encinitas CA   760-635-7774
Dogs are allowed at the outdoor tables.
St Germain's Cafe 1010 S Coast Hwy 101 Encinitas CA   858-509-9293
This café offers traditional fair for breakfast (served all day) and lunch. There is ample outside seating with
service, but it can be pretty busy on the weekends. Your pet is welcome to join you at the outside tables. Dogs
must be attended to at all times, well behaved, and leashed.
BB's Cafe 1938 Coast Highway Oceanside CA   760-722-7337
This restaurant serves American food. Dogs are allowed at the outdoor tables.
Daphne's Greek Cafe 409 Mission Avenue Oceanside CA   760-967-6679
Dogs are allowed at the outdoor tables.
Hill Street Coffee House 524 S Coast Hwy Oceanside CA   760-966-0985
This restaurant serves American, vegetarian and more types of food. Dogs are allowed at the outdoor tables.
Ol Smoky 608 Mission Ave Oceanside CA   760-439-4763
Dogs are allowed at the outdoor tables.
Rice Garden 401 Mission Ave #B110 Oceanside CA   760-721-4330
Dogs are allowed at the outdoor tables.
Robins Nest Cafe 280 S Harbor Oceanside CA   760-722-7837
http://www.robinsnestcafe.com/
This café offers fresh, home style cooking and dining along the water's edge where you can watch the goings on
of the harbor. There is a waterfront boardwalk dining area that extends around the café, and they offer service
indoor or outdoor, and your well behaved dog is welcome to join you at the outer tables. Dogs must be under
owner's control at all times, and be leashed and cleaned up after.
The Motorcycle Cafe 624 S Coast Highway Oceanside CA   760-433-1829
This restaurant serves American food. Dogs are allowed at the outdoor tables.
Pacific Coast Grill 437 S Highway 101 #112 Solana Beach CA   858-794-4632
This restaurant serves American and seafood. Dogs are allowed at the outdoor tables.
Zinc Cafe and Market 132 S Cedros Solana Beach CA   858-793-5436
http://www.zinccafe.com/
This breakfast and lunch eatery offers California cuisine from 7 am to 4 pm daily. They have outside tables
where your pet is welcome to join you. You will need to place your order inside. Dogs must be attended to at all
times, well behaved, and leashed.
Baja Fresh Mexican Grill 620 Hacienda Dr. Vista CA   760-643-0110
http://www.bajafresh.com
This Mexican restaurant is open for lunch and dinner. They use fresh ingredients and making their salsa and
beans daily. Some of the items on their menu include Enchiladas, Burritos, Tacos Salads, Quesadillas, Nachos,
Chicken, Steak and more. Well-behaved leashed dogs are allowed at the outdoor tables.

San Diego I-15 Corridor

Accommodations
Castle Creek Inn Resort 29850 Circle R Way Escondido CA   760-751-8800 (800-253-5341)

Comfort Inn 1290 W Valley Parkway Escondido CA   760-489-1010 (877-424-6423)
Dogs of all sizes are allowed. There is a $15 per night per pet additional fee for dogs under 50 pounds, and a
$25 per night per pet additional fee for dogs over 50 pounds. Dogs must be well behaved, leashed, cleaned up
after, and the Do Not Disturb sign put on the door if they are in the room alone. Dogs must be removed for
housekeeping.
Motel 6 - Escondido 900 North Quince Street Escondido CA   760-745-9252 (800-466-8356)
One well-behaved family pet per room. Guest must notify front desk upon arrival. Guest is liable for any
damages. In consideration of all guests, pets must never be left unattended in the guest rooms.
Palm Tree Lodge Motel 425 W Mission Avenue Escondido CA   760-745-7613
This hotel offers 38 guest rooms (some with kitchens or fireplaces), an outdoor pool and a restaurant on site.
Dogs of all sizes are allowed. There is a $20 per night additional pet fee for one dog, and $30 per night for 2
dogs. Dogs may not be left alone in the rooms, and they must be well behaved, leashed, and cleaned up after.

Campgrounds and RV Parks

Sunland RV Resorts 1740 Seven Oaks Road Escondido CA   760-740-5000 (800-331-3556)
http://www.sunlandrvresorts.com
This lushly landscaped resort park is a favorite family and pet-friendly retreat, and they have a pet walking and play area, many amenities, and a variety of recreational opportunities. Dogs of all sizes are allowed for an additional $3 per night per pet. Dogs must be leashed at all times, and cleaned up after. Dogs are not allowed in buildings or the pool area. There are some breed restrictions. There is a dog walk area at the campground. There are special amenities given to dogs at this campground.

Attractions
Orfila Vineyards 13455 San Pasqual Road Escondido CA   760-738-6500
http://www.orfila.com/
With about 900 Medals since 1994, this award winning winery also offers caterers, event staff, manicured lawns, flowering gardens, picnic areas, a gift shop and tasting room, all with a view of the mountains and cascading vineyards. Dogs are allowed around the grounds, but not in the tasting room or grape growing areas. Dogs must be well behaved, and leashed and cleaned up after at all times.
Orfila Vineyards 13455 San Pasqual Rd Escondido CA   760-738-6500
Open Daily from 10 am - 6 pm most of the year. They close at 5 pm in the winter. Dogs are allowed in the outdoor areas.
Palomar Observatory County Road S-6 Palomar Mountain CA   760-742-2100
The observatory is located within the Cleveland National Forest on Palomar Mountain at an elevation of 5000 feet. Dogs on leash may accompany you on the self-guided tour and on the grounds including the gallery to view the 200 inch telescope. To reach Palomar exit Interstate 15 at Highway 76 east. Take S-6 to the left in 25 miles up the mountain to Palomar. The hours are 9 am - 4 pm daily except Christmas and Christmas eve. The gift shop is only open on weekends except in July and August.
Bernardo Winery 13330 Easeo Del Verano Rancho Bernardo CA   858-487-1866
http://www.bernardowinery.com/
In addition to a selection of red, white, and dessert wines, this fully functional 116 year old winery offers an award winning café, an espresso/coffee cottage, more than 12 village shops scattered about, live jazz on Sundays, and a courtyard with beautiful Mediterranean gardens. Dogs are allowed to join you around the grounds and on the patio; they are usually not allowed in buildings. Dogs must be well behaved, and leashed and cleaned up after at all times.

Stores
Petco Pet Store 1000 West Valley Parkway Escondido CA   760-781-1600
Your licensed and well-behaved leashed dog is allowed in the store.

Parks
San Pasqual Battlefield State Historical Park 15808 San Pasqual Valley Road Escondido CA   760-737-2201
This historic park honors the soldiers who fought here and stands as a reminder of the passions that can drive countries to bloodshed, and not as a monument to the Mexican-American war. There are interpretive exhibits/programs, nature and hiking trails, picnic areas, restrooms, and a visitor center. The park is only open on Saturday and Sunday, but during the week you can park on the street and walk into the park. Dogs of all sizes are allowed. Dogs must be on no more than a 6 foot leash, and leashed and cleaned up after at all times. Dogs are allowed throughout the park and on the trails.
Observatory National Recreational Trail Observatory Campground Palomar Mountain CA   760-788-0250
This trail is located in the dog-friendly Cleveland National Forest. The 2. 2 mile trail offers a pleasant hike to the Palomar Observatory site. It meanders through pine and oak woodlands and offers some great views of the Mendenhall and French Valleys. There is a 200 foot elevation gain, with a starting elevation of 4800 feet. Dogs are allowed on leash. From San Diego, drive north on I-15 to Highway 76 (Oceanside-Pala exit) Head east on Hwy 76 to S6 and drive north toward Palomar Mountain. Follow S6 to Observatory Campground. Trailhead parking is near the amphitheater inside the campground (follow the signs). The trailhead is adjacent to the amphitheater. Vehicles must display a Forest Adventure Pass. The pass can be purchased from local vendors and from the Forest Service Offices. Call (760) 788-0250 for a list of forest offices.

Off-Leash Dog Parks
Mayflower Dog Park 3420 Valley Center Road Escondido CA
Mayflower Dog Park is a 1.5 acre fenced area for off-leash dog play.

Outdoor Restaurants
Baja Fresh Mexican Grill 890 W Valley Parkway Escondido CA   760-480-9997

http://www.bajafresh.com
This Mexican restaurant is open for lunch and dinner. They use fresh ingredients and making their salsa and beans daily. Some of the items on their menu include Enchiladas, Burritos, Tacos Salads, Quesadillas, Nachos, Chicken, Steak and more. Well-behaved leashed dogs are allowed at the outdoor tables.
Firehouse Broiler 1019 S. Main Ave Fallbrook CA 760-728-8008
Dogs are allowed at the outdoor tables.
Greek Style Chicken 904 S. Main Ave Fallbrook CA 760-723-8050
Dogs are allowed at the outdoor tables.
Me and Charlies Bakery and Coffee 945 S. Main Ave Fallbrook CA 760-728-1491
Dogs are allowed at the outdoor tables.
Baja Fresh Mexican Grill 11980-11976 Bernardo Plaza Dr. Rancho Bernardo CA 858-592-7788
http://www.bajafresh.com
This Mexican restaurant is open for lunch and dinner. They use fresh ingredients and making their salsa and beans daily. Some of the items on their menu include Enchiladas, Burritos, Tacos Salads, Quesadillas, Nachos, Chicken, Steak and more. Well-behaved leashed dogs are allowed at the outdoor tables.
Old California Coffee House 1080 W. San Marcos Blvd #176 San Marcos CA 760-744-2112
Dogs are allowed at the outdoor tables.
Tony Roma's 1020 W San Marcos Blvd #124 San Marcos CA 760-736-4343
Dogs are allowed at the outdoor tables.

Vets and Kennels
Veterinary Urgent Care 2525 S Centre City Pkwy Escondido CA 760-738-9600
Monday - Friday 6 pm to 8 am, Friday 6pm - Monday 8 am.

Santa Ysabel

Campgrounds and RV Parks
Lake Henshaw Resort 26439 Hwy 76 Santa Ysabel CA 760-782-3487
http://www.lakehenshawresort.com/
Lake Henshaw Resort, located at a lake which rests at the foot of the Palomar Mountains, is a great place for fishermen of all levels. Some of the amenities include a sparkling pool and spa, children's playground, grocery store with all your fishing needs, clubhouse, laundry facilities, and restaurant. Dogs of all sizes are allowed at an additional $2 per night per pet. Dogs are not allowed on the furniture in the cabins and they may not be left unattended. Dogs are allowed to walk along the lakeshore and to go in the water. The camping and tent areas also allow dogs. There is a dog walk area at the campground. Dogs are allowed in the camping cabins.

Outdoor Restaurants
Dudley's Bakery 30218 Hwy 78 Santa Ysabel CA 760-765-0488
http://www.dudleysbakery.com/
Offering tasty treats warm from the oven and a nice picnic table in a grassy area, makes this a favorite for visitors with canine companions. Well behaved, leashed dogs are welcome to enter the store with their owner. Dogs must be under owner's control and be cleaned up after at all times.

Santee

Stores
PetSmart Pet Store 9896 Mission Gorge Rd Santee CA 619-448-1921
Your licensed and well-behaved leashed dog is allowed in the store.
Petco Pet Store 9745 Mission Gorge Rd Santee CA 619-449-1668
Your licensed and well-behaved leashed dog is allowed in the store.

Warner Springs

Parks
Barker Spur Trail Forest Road 9S07 Warner Springs CA 760-788-0250

This 3.4 mile moderate rated trail is located in the Cleveland National Forest. The trail elevation changes from 4,000 to 5,100 feet. It is open from early spring through late fall. Pets on leash are allowed and please clean up after them. To get there, take Highway 79 south toward Warner Springs. At about 2 miles southeast of Sunshine Summit take Forest Road 9S07 west. In about 7 miles the trailhead sign will be found on the left side of the road. Parking is in the wide area along the road. (Vehicles must display a Forest Adventure Pass.)

Chapter 14

California Desert
Dog Travel Guide

Baker

Campgrounds and RV Parks

Hole in the Wall Campground Black Canyon Road Baker CA   760-928-2562
http://www.nps.gov/moja
This desert park, located in the scenic Mojave National Preserve, offers various recreational pursuits to its visitors. Dogs of all sizes are allowed. There are no additional pet fees. Dogs must be on no more than a 6 foot leash and cleaned up after. Dogs must be brought in at night, and they are allowed on the trails on lead. The camping and tent areas also allow dogs. There is a dog walk area at the campground. There are no electric or water hookups at the campgrounds.
Mohave National Preserve Campgrounds Black Canyon Road Baker CA   760-252-6101
http://www.nps.gov/moja/mojareca.htm
This park offers two family campgrounds with elevations ranging from 4,400 feet to 5,600 feet. The campgrounds offer tent camping and one camp offers spaces for RVs. The campsites are usually booked during deer hunting season. Spaces are available on a first-come, first-served basis. Dogs of all sizes are allowed at no additional fee. Dogs must be leashed in camp and cleaned up after. Dogs may be off lead only if they are under voice control and will not chase. Dogs are allowed on the trails, and can even go in the visitor's center. Contact the park for campground locations and more details. The camping and tent areas also allow dogs. There is a dog walk area at the campground. There are no electric or water hookups at the campgrounds.

Parks

Mohave National Preserve 72157 Baker Road Baker CA   760-255-8800
http://www.nps.gov/moja/
Located in the heart of the Mohave Desert, this 1.6 million acre park offers rose-colored sand dunes, volcanic cinder cones and Joshua tree forests. The park offers hundreds of miles of dirt roads to explore the land in your own 4 wheel drive vehicle. There are many hiking opportunities including the Teutonia Peak Hike. This trail lets you explore a dense Joshua tree forest on the way to a peak on Cima Dome. The 4 mile roundtrip trail is located 10.5 miles south of I-15 on Cima Road. Dogs are allowed on trails and in the campgrounds. They must be leashed except dogs that are being used for hunting. Please clean up after your pet. For more park details and information, including maps, visit the Baker Desert Information Center in Baker. They are open all year from 9am to 5pm.

Barstow

Accommodations

Days Inn 1590 Coolwater Lane Barstow CA   760-256-1737 (800-329-7466)
There is a $10 per day pet fee.
Econo Lodge 1230 E. Main Street Barstow CA   760-256-2133
One large well-behaved dog is permitted per room. There is a $5 per day pet fee.
Holiday Inn Express 1861 W. Main St. Barstow CA   760-256-1300 (877-270-6405)
http://www.holiday-inn.com
This 3 story motel, located along Historic Route 66, offers rooms with microwaves, refrigerators, iron/ironing boards, hair dryers and data ports. There is $20 refundable pet deposit.
Holiday Inn Express Hotel and Suites 2700 Lenwood Road Barstow CA   760-253-9200 (877-270-6405)
Dogs of all sizes are allowed. There is a $25 returnable deposit required per room. Smoking and non-smoking rooms are available for pets.
Motel 6 - Barstow 150 Yucca Avenue Barstow CA   760-256-1752 (800-466-8356)
One well-behaved family pet per room. Guest must notify front desk upon arrival. Guest is liable for any damages. In consideration of all guests, pets must never be left unattended in the guest rooms.
Quality Inn 1520 E Main Street Barstow CA   760-256-6891 (877-424-6423)
Dogs of all sizes are allowed. There is a $10 per night per pet additional fee. Dogs may only be left alone in the room if they will be quiet, well behaved, and the Do Not Disturb sign is put on the door. Dogs must be leashed and cleaned up after.
Red Roof Inn - Barstow 2551 Commerce Parkway Barstow CA   760-253-2121 (800-RED-ROOF)
One well-behaved family pet per room. Guest must notify front desk upon arrival. Guest is liable for any damages. In consideration of all guests, pets must never be left unattended in the guest rooms.

Super 8 Barstow 170 Coolwater Lane Barstow CA 760-256-8443 (800-800-8000)
Dogs of all sizes are allowed. There is a $5 per night pet fee per pet. Smoking and non-smoking rooms are available for pet rooms.

Campgrounds and RV Parks

Rainbow Basin Natural Area Fossil Bed Road Barstow CA 760-252-6060
http://www.blm.gov/ca/barstow/basin.html
This park offers a diverse landscape of hills, canyons, washes, multi-colored rock walls, and mesas that are ever changing in color and light. The park has geological and paleontological importance, an auto tour of an Area of Critical Environmental Concern, and a variety of recreational activities to pursue. Dogs are allowed throughout the park and on the trails. Dogs must be under owner's immediate control, leashed, and cleaned up after at all times. Camping is permitted only at Owl Canyon on a first come first served basis, and each site has a table, shelter, and campfire grates. Pit toilets are located in the campground. There is no potable water. The camping and tent areas also allow dogs. There is a dog walk area at the campground. There are no electric or water hookups at the campgrounds.

Barstow/Calico KOA 35250 Outer Hwy 15 Yermo CA 760-254-2311 (800-562-0059)
http://www.koa.com/where/ca/05233/
This campground is located in a desert setting about 3.5 miles from the dog-friendly Calico Ghost Town. RV site amenities include a maximum pull through length of 70 feet and 50 amp service. Other camp amenities include a seasonal swimming pool, free modem dataport, LP gas, snack bar, pavilion/meeting room, and dog walking area. Dogs of all sizes are allowed for no additional fee. Dogs must be under owner's control and visual observation at all times. Dogs must be quiet, well behaved, and be on no more than a 6 foot leash at all times or otherwise contained. Dogs may not be left unattended outside the owner's camping equipment. Dogs are not allowed in the pool or playground areas, and may not be tied to trees. There are some breed restrictions. The camping and tent areas also allow dogs. There is a dog walk area at the campground.

Barstow/Calico KOA 35250 Outer Hwy 15 Yermo CA 760-254-2311 (800-562-0059)
http://www.koa.com/where/ca/05233/
In a convenient location midway between Los Angeles and Las Vegas, this KOA provides easy access to dozens of desert attractions and activities. Amenities include 70 foot pull through sites with 50 amp, LP Gas, modem dataport, snack bar, and a swimming pool. Dogs of all sizes are allowed for no additional fee. Dogs must be under owner's control and visual observation at all times. Dogs must be quiet, well behaved, and be on no more than a 6 foot leash at all times, or otherwise contained. Dogs may not be left unattended outside the owner's camping equipment, and must be brought inside at night. Dogs are not allowed in the pool area, buildings, or playgrounds, and they may not be tied to trees. There are some breed restrictions. The camping and tent areas also allow dogs. There is a dog walk area at the campground.

Attractions

Calico Early Man Site Minneola Road Barstow CA 760-252-6000
In 1942 amateur archaeologists discovered what they believed to be primitive stone tools at this site. Archaeologists have classified the site as a possible stone tool workshop, quarry and camp site for early nomadic hunters and gatherers. It is estimated that the soil at this site may date back to over 200,000 years. The site is open on Wednesday from 12:30pm to 4:30pm and Thursday through Sunday from 9am to 4:30pm. Guided tours are available on Wednesday at 1:30pm and 3:30pm, and on Thursday through Sunday at 9:30am, 11:30am, 1:30pm and 3:30pm. There is a $5 fee per person and less for children and seniors. Well-behaved leashed dogs are allowed. Please clean up after your dog.

Route 66 Mother Road Museum 681 North First Ave Barstow CA 760-255-1890
http://barstow66museum.itgo.com/
The museum offers a collection of historic photographs and artifacts related to Route 66 and the Mojave Desert Communities. Displays include the development of the U.S. Route 66 from early pioneer trails and railroads to automotive history, businesses and sites. Well-behaved, leashed dogs are welcome. The museum is open Friday through Sunday from 11am-4pm. Admission is free. The museum is located in the historic Casa del Desierto Harvey House.

TOP 200 PLACE Calico Ghost Town PO Box 638 Yermo CA 760-254-2122
Dogs are allowed at this old ghost town but not inside the restaurants. Founded in March 1881, it grew to a population of 1,200 with 22 saloons and more than 500 mines. Calico became one of the richest mining towns in California, producing $86 million in silver, $45 million in borax and gold. After 1907, when silver prices dropped and borax mining moved to Death Valley, Calico became a ghost town. Today, Calico is one of the few remaining original mining towns of the western United States. It was preserved by Walter Knott (founder of Knott's Berry Farm and a relative of the owner of Calico's Silver King mine). Mr. Knott donated Calico Ghost Town to the County of San Bernardino in 1966, and it remains alive and well as a 480-acre County Regional Park. Live events like gunfights and living history reenactments are common at the park. Take a self-guided town tour or go for a hike on one of their trails. You and your pooch can also take a guided walking tour (Mon-Fri) with Calico's historian who will examine the history of the miners, the famous 20-mule team and a U.S. Postal

Mail dog named Dorsey. The park also offer many festivals throughout the year. Camping and RV hookups are available here. The park is located 8 miles north of Barstow and 3 miles east of Interstate 15.

Parks
Mojave National Preserve 2701 Barstow Road Barstow CA   760-252-6100
http://www.nps.gov/moja/index.htm
Dogs on leash are allowed in the park. This park features nearby camping, auto touring, hiking, climbing, and more.
Rainbow Basin Natural Area Fossil Bed Road Barstow CA   760-252-6060
http://www.blm.gov/ca/barstow/basin.html
This park offers a diverse landscape of hills, canyons, washes, multi-colored rock walls, and mesas that are ever changing in color and light. The park has geological and paleontological importance, an auto tour of an Area of Critical Environmental Concern, and a variety of recreational activities to pursue. Dogs are allowed throughout the park and on the trails. Dogs must be under owner's immediate control, leashed, and cleaned up after at all times.

Outdoor Restaurants
Baja Fresh Mexican Grill 2854 Lenwood Rd Barstow CA   760-253-2505
http://www.bajafresh.com
This Mexican restaurant is open for lunch and dinner. They use fresh ingredients and making their salsa and beans daily. Some of the items on their menu include Enchiladas, Burritos, Tacos Salads, Quesadillas, Nachos, Chicken, Steak and more. Well-behaved leashed dogs are allowed at the outdoor tables.

Blythe

Accommodations
Best Western Sahara Motel 825 W Hobson Way Blythe CA   760-922-7105 (800-780-7234)
Dogs of all sizes are allowed. There are no additional pet fees. Only non-smoking rooms used for pets.
Comfort Suites Colorado River 545 E Hobson Way Blythe CA   760-922-9209 (877-424-6423)
Dogs of all sizes are allowed. There is a $10 per night per pet additional fee. There can be up to 2 large dogs or up to 3 small to medium dogs per room. Please put the Do Not Disturb sign on the door if there is a pet alone in the room.
Holiday Inn Express 600 W Donlon St Blythe CA   760-921-2300 (877-270-6405)
Dogs of all sizes are allowed. There is a $10 per night pet fee per pet under 20lbs. There is a $20 per night pet fee per pet over 20lbs. Smoking and non-smoking rooms are available for pets.
Motel 6 - Blythe 500 West Donlon Street Blythe CA   760-922-6666 (800-466-8356)
One well-behaved family pet per room. Guest must notify front desk upon arrival. Guest is liable for any damages. In consideration of all guests, pets must never be left unattended in the guest rooms.

Campgrounds and RV Parks
Collis Mayflower Park 4980 Colorado River Road Blythe CA   760-922-4665 (800-234-PARK (7275))
This scenic recreational park features 152 camp sites, a day use picnic area, gaming areas, a boat launch, restrooms, showers, and a dump station. Spaces are available on a 1st come 1st served basis, although reservations can be made. Dogs of all sizes are welcome for an additional $1 per pet per day; there is no pet fee if the stay is a week or longer. Dogs must be under owner's control, and be leashed and cleaned up after at all times. The camping and tent areas also allow dogs. There is a dog walk area at the campground.
Reynolds Riviera Resort 14100 Riviera Drive Blythe CA   760-922-5350
Located along the Colorado River, this park offers more than 300 full service sites and park models, a heated pool, spa, laundry facilities, an arcade, and a community center. Dogs of all sizes are welcome for no additional fee. They are allowed throughout the park. Dogs must be under owner's immediate control, and leashed and cleaned up after at all times. The camping and tent areas also allow dogs. There is a dog walk area at the campground.

Borrego Springs

Campgrounds and RV Parks
Culp Valley Primitive Camp, Anza Borrego State Park Off Montezuma Valley Road/HS 22 Borrego

Springs CA   760-767-5311
Located in the Anza Borrego park, this park allows dogs of all sizes at no additional fee. Dogs may not be left unattended at any time, and they must be on no more than a 6 foot leash, and cleaned up after. Dogs are not allowed on the hiking trails; they may be walked on paved or dirt roads, or in the camp area. The camping and tent areas also allow dogs. There is a dog walk area at the campground. There are no electric or water hookups at the campgrounds.

Parks
Anza-Borrego Desert State Park Highway 78 Borrego Springs CA   760-767-5311
Dogs are not allowed on any trails. They are allowed in day use areas and on over 500 miles of dirt roads. The roads can be used by cars but there is usually not too much traffic. Pets must be leashed and please clean up after them. The park is located about a 2 hour drive from San Diego, Riverside and Palm Springs off Highways S22 and 78.

California City

Campgrounds and RV Parks
Sierra Trails RV Park 21282 Hwy 14N California City CA   877-994-7999
http://www.sierratrailsrv.com/
This RV only park offers shade trees, cement patios, lawns, barbecue grills and picnic tables at each site, a heated pool in summer, a rec room, restrooms with showers and a laundry. Dogs of all sizes are allowed at no additional fee. Dogs may not be left unattended outside, and they must be leashed at all times, and cleaned up after. They ask that you walk your pet along the outside of the park, and in another area close by. There are some breed restrictions.

Death Valley

Accommodations
Stovepipe Wells Village Motel Hwy 190 Death Valley CA   760-786-2387
The Village Motel is a short distance from some of the most photographed sand dunes in the world. They offer such amenities as comfortable ground floor guest rooms, a Restaurant and Saloon, general store and gift shop, service station, private landing strip, and an on-site RV park. Dogs of all sizes are allowed for an additional $20 refundable deposit for the motel rooms; there is no fee or deposit for dogs in the RV park. Dogs may not be left unattended in motel rooms. Dogs must be leashed and cleaned up after. Dogs are allowed in public places only; they are not allowed on trails or in canyon areas.
Panamint Springs Resort Highway 190 Panamint Springs CA   775-482-7680
http://www.deathvalley.com/
There is a $5 per day additional pet fee. The resort is located on Highway 190, 48 miles east of Lone Pine and 31 miles west of Stovepipe Wells.

Campgrounds and RV Parks
Death Valley National Park Campgrounds Hwy 190 Death Valley CA   760-786-3200 (800-365-CAMP (2267))
There are 10 campgrounds to choose from at this park, ranging from 196 feet below sea level to 8,200 feet above sea level. The Emigrant campground, located at 2,100 feet, offers tent camping only. This free campground offers 10 sites with water, tables and flush toilets. The Furnace Creek campground, located at 196 feet below sea level has 136 sites with water, tables, fireplaces, flush toilets and a dump station. Winter rates are $18 per night and less for the summertime. There are no hookups and some campgrounds do not allow generators. The Stovepipe Wells RV Campground is managed by the Stovepipe Wells Resort and offers 14 sites with full hookups but no tables or fireplaces. See our listing in Death Valley for more information about this RV park. About half of the campgrounds are open all year. Pets must be leashed and attended at all times. Please clean up after your pets. Dogs are not allowed on any trails in Death Valley National Park, but they can walk along roads. Pets are allowed up to a few hundred yards from the paved and dirt roads. The camping and tent areas also allow dogs. There is a dog walk area at the campground.
Stovepipe Wells Village Campgrounds and RV Park Hwy 190 Death Valley CA   760-786-2387
http://www.stovepipewells.com/
In addition to the motel, this establishment also offers a campground and RV park with full hookups. The main building has a restaurant, saloon, gift shops and swimming pool. They are located in the Death Valley National Park. Well-behaved leashed dogs are allowed for no additional fee in the camp area and there is no set number

of dogs. There is a $20 refundable deposit for the motel, and only 2 dogs are allowed. Dogs are allowed in public areas only, and they are not allowed on the trails or in the canyon areas. The camping and tent areas also allow dogs. There is a dog walk area at the campground.

Parks
Death Valley National Park Highway 190 Death Valley CA 760-786-2331
http://www.nps.gov/deva
Death Valley is one of the hottest places on Earth, with summer temperatures averaging well over 100 degrees Fahrenheit. It is also the lowest point on the Western Hemisphere at 282 feet below sea level. Average rainfall here sets yet another record. With an average of only 1.96 inches per year, this valley is the driest place in North America. Because of the high summer heat, the best time to visit the park is during the winter. Even though dogs are not allowed on any trails, you will still be able to see the majority of the sights and attractions from your car. There are several scenic drives that are popular with all visitors, with or without dogs. Dante's View is a 52 mile round trip drive that takes about 2 hours or longer. Some parts of the road are graded dirt roads and no trailers or RVs are allowed. On this drive you will view scenic mudstone hills which are made of 7 to 9 million year old lakebed sediments. You will also get a great view from the top of Dantes View. Another scenic drive is called Badwater. It is located about 18 miles from the Visitor Center and can take about 1.5 to 2 hours or longer. On this drive you will view the Devil's Golf Course where there are almost pure table salt crystals from an ancient lake. You will also drive to Badwater which is the lowest point in the Western Hemisphere at 282 feet below sea level. Dogs are allowed at view points which are about 200 yards or less from roads or parking lots. Pets must be leashed and attended at all times. Please clean up after your pets. While dogs are not allowed on any trails in the park, they can walk along roads. Pets are allowed up to a few hundred yards from the paved and dirt roads. Stop at the Furnance Creek Visitor Center to pick up a brochure and more information. The visitor center is located on Highway 190, north of the lowest point.

Outdoor Restaurants
Panamint Springs Resort Hwy 190 Death Valley CA 775-482-7680
This restaurant serves a variety of food. Dogs are allowed at the outdoor tables.

El Centro

Accommodations
Motel 6 - El Centro 395 Smoketree Drive El Centro CA 760-353-6766 (800-466-8356)
One well-behaved family pet per room. Guest must notify front desk upon arrival. Guest is liable for any damages. In consideration of all guests, pets must never be left unattended in the guest rooms.

Campgrounds and RV Parks
Desert Trails RV Park and Golf Course 225 Wake Avenue El Centro CA 760-352-PARK (7275)
http://www.deserttrailsrv.com/
Each season brings a variety of recreational activities at this park. It is a bird watchers haven in the winter months. Some of the features/amenities here include a pool and spa, laundry and restroom facilities, cable TV, a recreation room, and a 9-hole executive golf course. Dogs of all sizes are allowed for no additional fee, and there is a special dog run for canine visitors. Dogs must be well mannered, and leashed and cleaned up after at all times. Dogs are not allowed on the golf course. There are some breed restrictions. There is a dog walk area at the campground.

Attractions
Tumco Historic Townsite Ogilby Road El Centro CA 760-337-4400
Located in the mountains east of El Centro, is an abandoned gold mine town called Tumco. Today a few buildings and mine shafts remain. The mine shafts have very steep drop offs and are dangerous, so make sure you and your pooch stay clear of them. Also be aware of rattlesnakes in the area. It is best to visit during the fall, winter or spring months when it is not too hot. The remote site is managed by the Bureau of Land Management. Dogs must be on leash and please clean up after your dogs. To get there from Highway 8, east of El Centro, take Highway S34 North.

Joshua Tree National Park

Accommodations

Joshua Tree 6426 Valley View Street Joshua Tree CA 760-366-2212
Well behaved dogs of all sizes are allowed. There are no additional pet fees.
Joshua Tree Highlands Houses P. O. Box 1107/ Fleur Road Joshua Tree CA 760-366-3636
http://www.joshuatreehighlandshouse.com/
Four distinct fully furnished and equipped vacation houses are offered; they each sit on their own 5 acres and are all adjacent to the west entrance of the breathtaking Joshua Tree National Park. (Dogs are allowed at the park with restrictions.) Dogs of all sizes are allowed for an additional one time fee of $35 per pet plus a $75 refundable deposit. Dogs must be very well mannered, and leashed and cleaned up after at all times
29 Palms Inn 73950 Inn Avenue Twentynine Palms CA 760-367-3505
http://www.29palmsinn.com/
A natural high mountain desert oasis, this wonderful retreat is located on 30 acres of natural preserve and offers a variety of well- appointed accommodations and amenities. They also have a great garden to supply their seasonally influenced restaurant with fresh new tastes of the seasons, and there is dining inside or at the poolside tables. Dogs of all sizes are allowed for an additional one time fee of $35 per pet. Dogs may only be left alone if they will be well behaved, and they must be leashed and cleaned up after.
Circle C Lodge 6340 El Rey Avenue Twentynine Palms CA 760-367-7615 (800-545-9696)
http://www.circleclodge.com/
The lush private oasis setting of this 12 room lodge offers a wonderful contrast to the spectacular views it provides of the Mojave Desert. Some of the amenities include a continental breakfast, fully equipped kitchenettes with private baths, a garden courtyard with barbecue, heated pool, and spa, and it is a great starting point for several other local attractions. There is only 1 pet room available here, so reservations well in advance are suggested. Dogs of all sizes are allowed for an additional fee of $15 per night per pet. Dogs may not be left alone in the room at any time, and they must be leashed and cleaned up after at all times.
Harmony Hotel 71161 29 Palms H/Hwy 62 Twentynine Palms CA 760-367-3351
http://www.harmonymotel.com/
Known as the perfect location for both artistic inspiration and dramatic visual beauty, this motel offers close proximity to several other attractions and recreational pursuits, an outdoor pool and spa, art from those inspired here, and several amenities for a comfortable stay. Dogs of all sizes are allowed for an additional fee of $15 per night per pet with a credit card on file. Dogs must be tick and flea free, house-trained, and friendly. Dogs may not be left alone in the room, and they must be leashed and cleaned up after at all times.
Motel 6 - Twentynine Palms 72562 Twentynine Palms Highway Twentynine Palms CA 760-367-2833 (800-466-8356)
One well-behaved family pet per room. Guest must notify front desk upon arrival. Guest is liable for any damages. In consideration of all guests, pets must never be left unattended in the guest rooms.
Super 8 Yucca Val/Joshua Tree Nat Pk Area 57096 29 Palm Hwy Yucca Valley CA 760-228-1773 (800-800-8000)
Dogs of all sizes are allowed. There is a $20 returnable deposit required per room. Smoking and non-smoking rooms are available for pet rooms.

Campgrounds and RV Parks

29 Palms RV Resort 4949 Desert Knoll Twentynine Palms CA 760-367-3320
http://www.29palmsgolf.com/
This RV resort is located less than 10 minutes from the Joshua Tree National Park visitor center. RV sites include shade trees, and they can accommodate large motorhomes and trailers. Park amenities include a recreation hall, fitness room, tennis courts, shuffle board, heated indoor pool, laundry, showers, and restrooms. You can stay for a day, a week, or all winter. Pets on leash are welcome. There is no pet fee, just clean up after your dog. They also provide a fenced-in dog run area. Dogs may not be left unattended outside. The camping and tent areas also allow dogs. There is a dog walk area at the campground. There are special amenities given to dogs at this campground.
Joshua Tree National Park Campgrounds 74485 National Park Drive Twentynine Palms CA 760-367-5500 (800-365-CAMP (2267))
There are nine campgrounds at this park which range from 3,000 foot to 4,500 foot elevations. Many have no fees and offer pit toilets. Only a few of the campgrounds offer water and flush toilets. Generators are not allowed between the hours of 10pm and 6am, and they are only allowed for 3 two hour periods each day. Dogs of all sizes are allowed at no additional fee. Dogs may not be left unattended, and they must be leashed and cleaned up after. Dogs are not allowed on the trails, but they are allowed on all paved roads, and the paved trail by the Visitor's Center. The camping and tent areas also allow dogs. There is a dog walk area at the campground. There are no electric or water hookups at the campgrounds.

Parks

Joshua Tree National Park 74485 National Park Drive Twentynine Palms CA 760-367-5500
http://www.nps.gov/jotr

Dogs are not allowed on the trails, cannot be left unattended, and must be on leash. However, they are allowed on dirt and paved roads including the Geology Tour Road. This is actually a driving tour, but you'll be able to see the park's most fascinating landscapes from this road. It is an 18 mile tour with 16 stops. The park recommends taking about 2 hours for the round trip. At stop #9, about 5 miles out, there is room to turnaround if you do not want to complete the whole tour.

Lancaster

Accommodations
Best Western Antelope Valley Inn 44055 N Sierra Hwy Lancaster CA   661-948-4651 (800-780-7234)
Dogs of all sizes are allowed. There is a $35 one time per pet fee per visit. Smoking and non-smoking are available for pet rooms.
Motel 6 - Lancaster 43540 17th Street West Lancaster CA   661-948-0435 (800-466-8356)
One well-behaved family pet per room. Guest must notify front desk upon arrival. Guest is liable for any damages. In consideration of all guests, pets must never be left unattended in the guest rooms.

Stores
PetSmart Pet Store 44551 Valley Central Way Lancaster CA   661-942-7330
Your licensed and well-behaved leashed dog is allowed in the store.

Outdoor Restaurants
Camille's Sidewalk Cafe 43901 15th Street W Lancaster CA   661-940-5878
A vision of healthier, tastier foods inspired the idea for the freshly made salads, gourmet wraps and sandwiches, drinks, desserts, and coffees that are offered at all of Camille's Cafes. Dogs are allowed to sit with you at your outdoor table. Dogs must be attended to at all times, well behaved, and leashed.

Mojave

Accommodations
Best Western Desert Winds 16200 Sierra Hwy Mojave CA   661-824-3601 (800-780-7234)
Dogs of all sizes are allowed. There is a $10 one time per pet fee per visit. Smoking and non-smoking are available for pet rooms.
Econo Lodge 2145 SR 58 Mojave CA   661-824-2463
There is a $5 per day pet fee.
Motel 6 - Mojave 16958 State Route 58 Mojave CA   661-824-4571 (800-466-8356)
One well-behaved family pet per room. Guest must notify front desk upon arrival. Guest is liable for any damages. In consideration of all guests, pets must never be left unattended in the guest rooms.

Needles

Accommodations
Days Inn and Suites 1215 Hospitality Lane Needles CA   760-326-5836 (800-329-7466)

Econo Lodge 1910 N. Needles Hwy Needles CA   760-326-3881
There is a $5 per day pet fee.
Motel 6 - Needles 1420 J Street Needles CA   760-326-3399 (800-466-8356)
One well-behaved family pet per room. Guest must notify front desk upon arrival. Guest is liable for any damages. In consideration of all guests, pets must never be left unattended in the guest rooms.
Travelers Inn 1195 3rd Street Hill Needles CA   760-326-4900

Campgrounds and RV Parks
Moabi Regional Park Campgrounds Park Moabi Road Needles CA   760-326-3831
This park has a campground with 35 RV sites with full hookups, 120 sites with partial hookups, and unlimited

tent sites. The sites are situated in the main section of the park and along 2.5 miles of shoreline. The park is located on the banks of the Colorado River and is popular for camping, fishing, boating, swimming and water skiing. Dogs can go into the water but they strongly advise against it because there are so many fast boats in the water. Dogs must be leashed and please clean up after them. There is an additional fee of $1 per night per pet. The camping and tent areas also allow dogs. There is a dog walk area at the campground.

Needles KOA 5400 National Old Trails H Needles CA 760-326-4207 (800-562-3407)
http://www.koa.com/where/ca/05366/
This desert oasis park offers 90 foot pull through sites with 50 amp service, LP gas, snack bar, swimming pool, and guided tours. Dogs of all sizes are allowed for no additional fee. Dogs must be under owner's control and visual observation at all times. Dogs must be quiet, well behaved, and be on no more than a 6 foot leash at all times, or otherwise contained. Dogs may not be left unattended outside the owner's camping equipment, and must be brought inside at night. Dogs are not allowed in the pool area or buildings. There are some breed restrictions. The camping and tent areas also allow dogs. There is a dog walk area at the campground. Dogs are allowed in the camping cabins.

Parks

Havasu National Wildlife Refuge Box 3009 (Mojave County Road 227) Needles CA 760-326-3853
This refuge is one of more than 500 managed by the Fish and Wildlife Service, and is dedicated to conserving our wildlife heritage. Various habitats provide for a wide variety of plant, bird, and animal species. The refuge office hours are 8am-4pm Monday through Friday, and they suggest you come in there first for brochures and any updates on the area. Dogs of all sizes are allowed. Dogs must be kept on lead at all times and cleaned up after. Dogs are allowed throughout the park, but may not chase or disturb the wildlife in any way.

Olancha

Accommodations

Ranch Motel 2051 S Highway 395 Olancha CA 760-764-2387

Palm Springs

Accommodations

Comfort Suites 69151 E Palm Canyon Drive/Hwy 111 Cathedral City CA 760324-5939 (877-424-6423)
Dogs of all sizes are allowed. There is a $10 per night per pet additional fee. Dogs must be leashed, cleaned up after, and the Do Not Disturb sign put on the door if they are in the room alone. Dogs must be removed for housekeeping.

Doral Desert Princess Resort 67967 Vista Chino Cathedral City CA 760-322-7000 (888-FUN-IN-PS (386-4677))
http://www.doralpalmsprings.com/
This 4-star golf resort offers elegance and comprehensive services for the business or leisure traveler. Some of the features include 27 holes of championship golf, 285 luxury guestrooms and suites, conference and banquet facilities, room service, pool/Jacuzzi/sauna, a gift shop, and golf and tennis shops. Dogs of all sizes are allowed for an additional $75 one time fee per pet. Dogs are placed in first floor rooms, and they may only be left alone in the room if they will be quiet and well behaved. Dogs must be leashed and cleaned up after at all times.

Best Western Date Tree Hotel 81-909 Indio Bvd Indio CA 760-347-3421 (800-780-7234)
Dogs of all sizes are allowed. There is a $10 per night pet fee per pet. Smoking and non-smoking are available for pet rooms.

Holiday Inn Express 84-096 Indio Springs Pkwy Indio CA 760-342-6344 (877-270-6405)
There is a $25 one time pet fee. There are 2 pet rooms in the hotel, both are non-smoking.

Motel 6 - Indio - Palm Springs Area 82195 Indio Boulevard Indio CA 760-342-6311 (800-466-8356)
One well-behaved family pet per room. Guest must notify front desk upon arrival. Guest is liable for any damages. In consideration of all guests, pets must never be left unattended in the guest rooms.

Palm Shadow Inn 80-761 Highway 111 Indio CA 760-347-3476
http://www.palmshadowinn.com/
A well-behaved large dog is okay. Nestled among date palm groves, there are eighteen guest rooms which overlook nearly three acres of lawns, flowers and citrus trees. There is a $5 per day pet charge.

Royal Plaza Inn 82347 Hwy 111 Indio CA 760-347-0911 (800-228-9559)
http://www.royalplazainn.com/

This motel offers a laundry room, whirlpool and room refrigerators. There is a $10 per day additional pet fee.

Motel 6 - Palm Springs North 63950 20th Avenue North Palm Springs CA 760-251-1425 (800-466-8356)
One well-behaved family pet per room. Guest must notify front desk upon arrival. Guest is liable for any damages. In consideration of all guests, pets must never be left unattended in the guest rooms.

Comfort Suites 39-585 Washington Street Palm Desert CA 760-360-3337 (877-424-6423)
Dogs up to 40 pounds are allowed. There is a $20 one time fee per room. Dogs may not be left alone in the room, and they must be leashed and cleaned up after.

Motel 6 - Palm Desert - Palm Springs Area 78100 Varner Road Palm Desert CA 760-345-0550 (800-466-8356)
One well-behaved family pet per room. Guest must notify front desk upon arrival. Guest is liable for any damages. In consideration of all guests, pets must never be left unattended in the guest rooms.

Residence Inn by Marriott 38305 Cook Street Palm Desert CA 760-776-0050
Dogs of all sizes are allowed. There is a $75 one time fee, and a pet policy to sign at check in.

The Inn at Deep Canyon 74470 Abronia Trail Palm Desert CA 760-346-8061 (800-253-0004)
http://www.inn-adc.com/
This hotel features a palm garden, pool and fully-equipped kitchenettes. They have pet-friendly rooms available. There is a $10 per day additional pet fee.

7 Springs Resort and Hotel Palm Springs 950 N. Indian Canyon Dr. Palm Springs CA 800-585-3578
http://www.palm-springs-hotels.cc
7 Springs Inn and Suites offers a variety of accommodations in the heart of Palm Springs. Enjoy fully furnished suites with Kitchens, free daily Continental Breakfast, Heated Pool, Jacuzzi, barbecue area, Remote control T.V., direct dial telephones, free parking. Close to area shopping, restaurants, casinos, golf, tennis, and indian canyons. Pets are welcome for a $15 per night fee. Pets cannot be left unattended and must be kept on a leash when out of the room.

Casa Cody Country Inn

Casa Cody Country Inn 175 S. Cahuilla Rd. Palm Springs CA 760-320-9346
http://www.casacody.com
This is a quaint romantic historic inn that was founded in the 1920s. The founder, Harriet Cody, was a cousin of Buffalo Bill. The inn is nestled against the mountains and has adobe buildings. The rooms have fireplaces, kitchens and private patios. There is a $10 per day pet charge.

Hilton

Hilton 400 E Tahquitz Canyon Way Palm Springs CA   760-320-6868
Dogs up to 50 pounds are allowed. There is a $25 per night per pet fee up to a maximum charge of $75 per pet per stay and a pet policy to sign at check in.
La Serena Villas 339 South Belardo Road Palm Springs CA   760-325-3216
These dog-friendly villas cater to those who prefer a relaxing, secluded hideaway in Palm Springs. Built in the 1930's, the villas are nestled in the foothills of the San Jacinto Mountains. Palm Springs Village is within walking distance. Your pet is welcome. There is a $10 per day pet charge. Pets must be on leash and please pick up after your dog.
Le Parker Meridien Palm Springs 4200 East Palm Canyon Drive Palm Springs CA   760-770-5000
Dogs off all sizes are allowed. There is a $150 per night fee. Leashed dogs are allowed at the outdoor restaurant. Dogs are not allowed to be left alone in the room.
Motel 6 - Palm Springs Downtown 660 South Palm Canyon Drive Palm Springs CA   760-327-4200 (800-466-8356)
One well-behaved family pet per room. Guest must notify front desk upon arrival. Guest is liable for any damages. In consideration of all guests, pets must never be left unattended in the guest rooms.
Motel 6 - Palm Springs East-E Palm Canyon 595 East Palm Canyon Drive Palm Springs CA   760-325-6129 (800-466-8356)
One well-behaved family pet per room. Guest must notify front desk upon arrival. Guest is liable for any damages. In consideration of all guests, pets must never be left unattended in the guest rooms.
Orchid Tree Inn 261 South Belardo Road Palm Springs CA   760-325-2791
This inn has two pet rooms. Dogs must be attended at all times and leashed when outside the room. There is a $250 refundable pet deposit.
Palm Springs Hotels Caliente Tropics Resort 411 E. Palm Canyon Drive Palm Springs CA   800-658-5975
http://www.calientetropics.com
Well-behaved dogs up to 60 pounds are allowed. Leashed pets are allowed in the lawn and pool areas. Pets may not be left alone in the rooms. There is no smoking indoors at the Caliente Tropics Resort.
Palm Springs Riviera Resort 1600 North Indian Canyon Drive Palm Springs CA   760-327-8311
This 24 acre full service resort with 476 guest rooms allows well-behaved dogs of all sizes. Each room features oversized beds, individually controlled central air conditioning and heating units, small refrigerators, irons and ironing boards and multi-line phones with dataports. Amenities at the resort include an 18-hole putting course, nine tennis courts, a volleyball and basketball court and a workout room. They are located one mile from Palm Canyon Drive. There is a $20 per day pet fee and a $200 refundable pet deposit.
San Marino Hotel 225 West Baristo Road Palm Springs CA   800-676-1214
http://www.sanmarinohotel.com/
The hotel, a favorite of writers and artists, is the closest lodging to the Palm Springs historic shopping area. Dogs

are allowed, but not in the poolside rooms. There is a $10 per day pet charge.

Super 8 Lodge - Palm Springs 1900 N. Palm Canyon Drive Palm Springs CA   760-322-3757 (800-800-8000)
http://www.innworks.com/palmsprings
$10/stay for up to 3 dogs in one room. FREE 8-minute long distance call each night. FREE continental breakfast. Coffee maker, refrigerator, night light, clock/radio, safe in each room. Outdoor pool. On-site guest laundry. Kids 12 & under stay free. Off I-10, from West take Hwy 111 (N. Palm Canyon Drive); from East take Indian Avenue. Next to Billy Reed's restaurant.

Vacation Palm Springs 1401 N Palm Canyon Drive, Suite 201 Palm Springs CA   760-778-7832
Dogs of all sizes are allowed. There is a $60 per room per stay fee and a pet policy to sign at check in.

Red Roof Inn - Palm Springs - Thousand Palms 72215 Varner Road Thousand Palms CA   760-343-1381 (800-RED-ROOF)
One well-behaved family pet per room. Guest must notify front desk upon arrival. Guest is liable for any damages. In consideration of all guests, pets must never be left unattended in the guest rooms.

Campgrounds and RV Parks

Palm Springs Oasis RV Resort 36-100 Date Palm Drive Cathedral City CA   800-680-0144
Amidst spectacular views, this parks' amenities include a clubhouse, 2 swimming pools, a spa, an 18 hole executive golf course, and tennis courts to name just a few. Dogs of all sizes are allowed. There are no additional pet fees. Dogs may not be left unattended, and they must be leashed and cleaned up after. The camping and tent areas also allow dogs. There is a dog walk area at the campground.

Indian Wells RV Resort 47-340 Jefferson Street Indio CA   800-789-0895
This RV only resort offers many amenities such as three swimming pools, two spas, shuffleboard courts, basketball courts, pavilion with gas grills, billiards, horseshoes, fitness area, library, modem hookup, putting green, laundry facility, computer center and even a dog run. Site amenities include full hook-ups with 50 amp service, electric, water, sewer, paved pad and patio, and phone service for stays of 30 days or longer. Well-behaved leashed dogs are welcome. Please clean up after your pet. There is no pet fee. Dogs may not be left unattended outside. There is a dog walk area at the campground.

Attractions

Palm Canyon Drive/Star Walk

Palm Canyon Drive/Star Walk Palm Canyon Drive Palm Springs CA
http://www.palmsprings.com/stars/
Take a stroll down historic Palm Canyon Drive (between Tahquitz and Ramon) with your dog. The street is lined with beautiful palm trees and all kinds of restaurants and specialty shops including the Cold Nose, Warm Heart store (see Attractions). If you want to see some stars, Hollywood-style stars, this is the place to be. The Palm Springs Walk of Stars is dedicated to honoring many Hollywood celebrities that have come to Palm Springs.

Come see if your favorite actor or actress has a dedicated star in the sidewalk of Palm Canyon Drive. If you want to watch a celebrity receive his/her star, look at the Star Walk website (http://www.palmsprings.com/stars/) or call 760-322-1563 for a current list of upcoming star dedications (date, time and address included.)

Oasis Date Gardens 59111 Hwy 111 Indio CA 800-827-8017
You and your dog are welcome to walk through the date gardens at Oasis. They also have picnic tables outside where you can enjoy the dates and a variety of date products. Dogs must be leashed.

Moorten Botanical Garden 1701 S Palm Drive Palm Springs CA 760-327-6555
www.moortengarden.com
Although a small private garden, there are over 3000 desert plants from around the world; some not found anywhere else. There is also a petrified tree, dinosaur fossils, a green house, and a dog that lives on site that looks forward to friendly four-legged visitors. Dogs must be well mannered, and leashed and cleaned up after at all times.

Shopping Centers

El Paseo Shopping District El Paseo Drive Palm Desert CA
World famous as the Rodeo Drive of the Desert, the El Paseo Shopping District is a beautifully maintained picture-postcard floral and statue-filled mile with over 300 world class shops, award-winning restaurants, boutiques, galleries, jewelers, and more. It is up to individual stores whether pets are allowed to enter their store. Your well mannered pooch is welcome to join you exploring this wonderful area. Dogs must be leashed, and please clean up after your pet at all times.

Palm Canyon Shopping District Palm Canyon Drive/Hwy 111 Palm Springs CA
The historic Palm Canyon Drive runs between the 300 block and the 1,400 block of S Canyon Drive and it is considered a cultural artery of the city. The area features an abundance of shops, restaurants, pubs, art galleries, and boutiques. It is up to individual stores whether pets are allowed to enter. Also, on both sides of the Palm Canyon Drive and on adjacent streets visitors can view the 250 sidewalk stars of some of the world?s greatest entertainment personalities. Your well mannered pooch is welcome to join you exploring this great area. Dogs must be leashed, and please clean up after your pet at all times.

Stores

PetSmart Pet Store 79375 Hwy 111 La Quinta CA 760-771-4058
Your licensed and well-behaved leashed dog is allowed in the store.

PetSmart Pet Store 72-630 Dinah Shore Dr Palm Desert CA 760-328-4630
Your licensed and well-behaved leashed dog is allowed in the store.

Petco Pet Store 72453 Highway 111 Palm Desert CA 760-341-3541
Your licensed and well-behaved leashed dog is allowed in the store.

Three Dog Bakery 73-613 Hwy 111 Palm Desert CA 760-776-9899
http://www.threedog.com
Three Dog Bakery provides cookies and snacks for your dog as well as some boutique items. You well-behaved, leashed dog is welcome.

Cold Nose, Warm Heart-Gift Store 187 S. Palm Canyon Drive Palm Springs CA 760-327-7747 (877-327-7747)
http://www.doggoneit.net
Enjoy browsing inside this specialty gift store with your pup. (The previous name of the store was "Dog Gone It.") They have all kinds of gifts for dog lovers. And your dog is welcome on leash in the store. This store is located at the main shopping area (Palm Canyon Drive) in downtown Palm Springs. They are open daily from 10am until 6pm.

PetSmart Pet Store 5601 Ramon Rd E Palm Springs CA 760-325-9711
Your licensed and well-behaved leashed dog is allowed in the store.

Parks

Lake Cahuilla Recreation Area Avenue 58 Indio CA 760-564-4712
Come here to sit by the lake, walk around it or on one of the many trails at this 710 acre park. There are also 50 campsites at the park. The park is located in Indio, 4 miles southeast of La Quinta. To get there, take Interstate 10 to Washington St., south on Washington 3 miles to Highway 111, east on 111, 2 miles to Jefferson Street, south on Jefferson, 3 miles to Avenue 54, east on Avenue 54 one mile to Madison Street, south on Madison 2 miles to Avenue 58, west on Avenue 58 one mile to the park. There is a day use fee. Dogs must be leashed.

Magnesia Park Palm Desert Comm. Park Palm Desert CA 760-347-3484
Enjoy walking through this shaded park or having lunch at one of the many picnic tables. It's located in the city of Palm Desert at Magnesia Falls Drive and Portola Avenue. Dogs must be leashed.

California Desert - Please always call ahead to make sure that an establishment is still dog-friendly

Lake Cahuilla Recreation Area

Lykken Trail

Lykken Trail Ramon Road Palm Springs CA
When you begin this hike, there is a choice of two trails (one is pretty steep) which eventually join together up the mountain. The hike is a total of 6 miles round trip and includes a 1,000 foot elevation gain. This trail provides excellent views. It is located at the west end of Ramon Road. Dogs must be leashed. There are many rattlesnakes in the area.

Off-Leash Dog Parks

Civic Center Dog Park 73-510 Fred Waring Dr Palm Desert CA   760-346-0611
The Civic Center Dog Park is open from Dawn to 11 pm and is lighted at night. It is about 3/4 acres in size and has two separate fenced areas for large and small dogs. The dog park is located in Civic Center Park on Fred Waring Drive between Monterey Avenue and Portola Ave.
Joe Mann Dog Park 77820 California Dr Palm Desert CA   760-346-0611
The dog park is a fenced 1/3 acre area. It has no separate area for small dogs. The park is located about 1 mile south of I-10 at Washington Street. Heading south on Washington Street turn right on Avenue of the States and left on California Drive to the dog park.
Palm Springs Dog Park 222 Civic Dr North Palm Springs CA   760-322-8362
This fenced dog park is complete with green grass, trees, and fire hydrants. The dog park is on 1.6 acres. It's located at 222 Civic Drive North behind City Hall.

Outdoor Restaurants

Native Foods 73-890 El Paseo Palm Desert CA   760-836-9396
http://www.nativefoods.com
This restaurants serves organic vegetarian food. Dogs are allowed at the outdoor tables.
Cafe Totonaca 555 South Sunrise Way Palm Springs CA   760-323-9487
This restaurant serves healthy cuisine. Dogs are allowed at the outdoor tables.
Hair of the Dog English Pub 238 N Palm Canyon Dr Palm Springs CA   760-323-9890
This English Pub has a couple of outdoor tables which are pretty close together, but your dog is welcome.
Jamba Juice 111 S. Palm Canyon Drive Palm Springs CA   760-327-3151
http://www.jambajuice.com/
This fruit bar offers a variety of smoothies and fruit juices. Well-behaved leashed dogs are allowed at the outdoor tables.
Native Foods 1775 E. Palm Canyon Drive Palm Springs CA   760-416-0070
http://www.nativefoods.com/home.html
This restaurant serves organic vegetarian dishes. Dogs are welcome at the outdoor seats. The hours are 11:30 am to 9:30 pm except Sunday when the restaurant is closed.
New York Pizza Delivery 260 N. Palm Canyon Drive Palm Springs CA   760-778-6973
This pizza restaurant allows well-behaved leashed dogs at their outdoor tables.
Peabody's Coffee Bar 134 S Palm Canyon Dr Palm Springs CA   760-322-1877
Bring yourself and your dog for breakfast, lunch or dinner at this restaurant and coffee bar.
Pomme Frite 256 S. Palm Canyon Drive Palm Springs CA   760-778-3727
http://www.pomme-frite.com/
This bistro features Belgian and French food. They are open six days a week for dinner and both lunch and dinner is served on the weekends. The restaurant is closed on Tuesdays. Well-behaved leashed dogs are allowed at the outdoor tables.
Shermans Deli and Bakery 401 Tahquitz Canyon Way Palm Springs CA   760-325-1199
Enjoy bagels and bakery treats or choose from their selection of hot or cold sandwiches.
Spencer's Restaurant 701 West Baristo Road Palm Springs CA   760-327-3446
http://www.spencersrestaurant.com/
This restaurant features California Continental Cuisine. Well-behaved leashed dogs are allowed at the outdoor tables. The restaurant is located four blocks west of Palm Canyon Drive on Baristo. Thanks to one of our readers for recommending this restaurant.
Starbucks 682 S. Palm Canyon Drive Palm Springs CA   760-323-8023
http://www.starbucks.com
This coffee shop allows well-behaved leashed dogs at their outdoor tables.

Pet Sitters

In the Doghouse Pet Day Care 4711-B E. Palm Canyon Drive Palm Springs CA   760-324-5013
http://www.IntheDoghousellc.com
This pet day care center offers 2,500 square feet of indoor activities. There is a separate room for large dogs and small dogs. Dogs must have proof of vaccines, male dogs must be neutered and females cannot be in heat.

Vets and Kennels

Animal Emergency Clinic 72374 Ramon Rd Thousand Palms CA   760-343-3438
Monday - Friday 5 pm to 8 am, Saturday noon - Monday 8 am.

Palmdale

Accommodations

Motel 6 - Palmdale 407 West Palmdale Boulevard Palmdale CA 661-272-0660 (800-466-8356)
One well-behaved family pet per room. Guest must notify front desk upon arrival. Guest is liable for any damages. In consideration of all guests, pets must never be left unattended in the guest rooms.
Super 8 Palmdale 200 W Palmdale Blvd Palmdale CA 661-273-8000 (800-800-8000)
Dogs of all sizes are allowed. There is a $10 per night pet fee per pet. Smoking and non-smoking rooms are available for pet rooms.

Stores

PetSmart Pet Store 39523 S 10th St West Palmdale CA 661-947-8900
Your licensed and well-behaved leashed dog is allowed in the store.
Petco Pet Store 39522 10th St West, Ste A Palmdale CA 661-267-2447
Your licensed and well-behaved leashed dog is allowed in the store.

Outdoor Restaurants

Baja Fresh Mexican Grill 39332 10th St. W. Palmdale CA 661-947-1682
http://www.bajafresh.com
This Mexican restaurant is open for lunch and dinner. They use fresh ingredients and making their salsa and beans daily. Some of the items on their menu include Enchiladas, Burritos, Tacos Salads, Quesadillas, Nachos, Chicken, Steak and more. Well-behaved leashed dogs are allowed at the outdoor tables.

Events

Rattlesnake Avoidance Clinic P. O. Box 3174 Quartz Hill CA
This annual Spring Rattlesnake Avoidance clinic in the Palmdale area is sponsored by Jin-Sohl Jindo Dog Rescue. It offers a pro-active training method for keeping dogs safe from rattlesnakes, which are common on hiking trails throughout Southern California and most of the U.S. The fee is $70 per dog and proceeds go to the rescue and placement of Jindo dogs. Pre-registration is required. Email snakeclinic@hotmail.com for more information. Dogs must be leashed and under owner's control and care at all times.

Vets and Kennels

Animal Emergency Clinic 1055 W Avenue M #101 Lancaster CA 661-723-3959
Monday - Friday 6 pm to 8 am, Saturday noon - Monday 8 am.

Pearblossom

Campgrounds and RV Parks

South Fork Campground Big Rock Creek Road/Forest Road 4N11A Pearblossom CA 661-296-9710
This 21 site campground is located in the Angeles National Forest at an elevation of 4,500 feet. There are both tent and small RV sites up to 16 feet. Amenities include vault toilets. There are many hiking trails nearby including one which leads to the dog-friendly Devil's Punchbowl County Park. Well behaved dogs on leash are allowed and please clean up after them. Dogs may not be left unattended outside, and only left inside if they will be quiet and comfortable. The camping and tent areas also allow dogs. There is a dog walk area at the campground. There are no electric or water hookups at the campgrounds.

Parks

Devil's Punchbowl Nature Center 28000 Devil's Punchbowl Road Pearblossom CA 661-944-2743
This 1,310 acre nature park offers unusual rock formations and is just one mile away from the famous San Andreas fault. The park elevation starts at 4,200 feet and climbs up to 6,500 feet. There are miles of trails rated easy to strenuous. The visitor center is open daily from 9am to 4pm. There is no charge for parking. Dogs must be on leash and please clean up after them.

Pioneertown

Accommodations

Pioneer Town Motel 5040 Curtis Road Pioneertown CA   760-365-4879
All of this rustic motel's 20 rooms are decorated with the authentic charm of an era past, but updated with Satellite TV, HBO, a kitchen area, microwave, a refrigerator, and shaded seating areas where you can enjoy the views. Because the town was built also as a movie set to be a complete old west town, many Western stars and movie star greats of the past have slept in these rooms while shooting films here. Dogs of all sizes are allowed. There is a $10 per night per pet additional fee. Dogs may not be left alone in the rooms, and they must be leashed and cleaned up after.

Attractions

TOP 200 PLACE **Pioneertown** Pioneertown Road Pioneertown CA   760-964-6549
http://www.pioneertown.com/f-index.htm
Because the town was also built as a movie set to be a complete old west town, numerous Western stars and movie star greats of the past spent a lot of time here. The movie sets that were used in filming also provided homes for the actors and crew and with an emphasis placed on experiencing the old west, this place is like stepping back to the 1800's. The town has its own pioneer posse, and offers seasonal old west reenactments, dozens of shops and exhibits to explore, western cooking, a motel that accepts dogs, and a lot more. Dogs are welcome all around town, and they may even end up with their picture on the website. They are not allowed in buildings. Dogs must be leashed at all times and cleaned up after. Please carry supplies.

Rancho Mirage

Accommodations

Motel 6 - Palm Springs - Rancho Mirage 69570 SR 111 Rancho Mirage CA   760-324-8475 (800-466-8356)
One well-behaved family pet per room. Guest must notify front desk upon arrival. Guest is liable for any damages. In consideration of all guests, pets must never be left unattended in the guest rooms.
Rancho Las Palmas Marriott Resort and Spa 41000 Bob Hope Drive Rancho Mirage CA   760-568-2727 (800-458-8786)
Dogs of all sizes are allowed. There is a $75 one time additional pet fee per room. Dogs must be leashed, cleaned up after, removed or accompanied for housekeeping, and the Do Not Disturb sign put on the door if they are in the room alone.

Outdoor Restaurants

Baja Fresh Mexican Grill 71-800 Highway 111, Ste A-116 Rancho Mirage CA   760-674-9380
http://www.bajafresh.com
This Mexican restaurant is open for lunch and dinner. They use fresh ingredients and making their salsa and beans daily. Some of the items on their menu include Enchiladas, Burritos, Tacos Salads, Quesadillas, Nachos, Chicken, Steak and more. Well-behaved leashed dogs are allowed at the outdoor tables.

Ridgecrest

Accommodations

Motel 6 - Ridgecrest 535 South China Lake Boulevard Ridgecrest CA   760-375-6866 (800-466-8356)
One well-behaved family pet per room. Guest must notify front desk upon arrival. Guest is liable for any damages. In consideration of all guests, pets must never be left unattended in the guest rooms.

Campgrounds and RV Parks

Fossil Falls Campground Cinder Road Ridgecrest CA   760-384-5400
This park, rich in prehistoric and modern history, features a rugged and primitive landscape as a result of ancient volcanic activity. Dogs of all sizes are allowed. There are no additional pet fees. Dogs must be leashed at all times and cleaned up after. Dogs are allowed on the trails; take caution around the cliff areas. The camping and tent areas also allow dogs. There is a dog walk area at the campground. There are no electric or water hookups at the campgrounds.

Tehachapi

Accommodations
Best Western Mountain Inn 418 W Tehachapi Blvd Tehachapi CA 661-822-5591 (800-780-7234)
Dogs of all sizes are allowed. There are no additional pet fees. Reservations are recommended due to limited rooms for pets. Smoking and non-smoking are available for pet rooms.
Travelodge 500 Steuber Rd Tehachapi CA 661-823-8000
There is a $7 per day pet fee.

Parks
Tehachapi Mountain Park Highway 58 Tehachapi CA 661-868-7000
This 5,000 acre park offers views of the Tehachapi Mountains, the dividing line between the San Joaquin Valley and the Los Angeles Basin. The Nuooah Nature Trail is an interesting interpretative 1/4 mile trail. The park is located between Bakersfield and Mojave. It is 8 miles southwest of the town of Tehachapi and is on the southern side of Hwy. 58. Dogs must be on leash.

Chapter 15

Arizona
Dog Travel Guide

Ajo

Parks
Cabeza Prieta Wildlife Refuge 1611 N 2nd Avenue Ajo AZ   520-387-6483
http://www.fws.gov/refuges/profiles/index.cfm?id=22571
Most of this 1,000-square-mile refuge is designated wilderness where temperatures may top 100 degrees for more than 100 days at a time. Although a water challenged area, there are as many as 420 plant species and more than 300 kinds of wildlife. This park offers a free lecture series from November to March, interpretive trails, hunting, opportunities for wildlife observation, and primitive camping. Before entering the refuge, you must obtain a free, valid Refuge Entry Permit and sign a Military Hold Harmless Agreement There are no facilities for gasoline, sanitation, or potable water. They suggest you bring two gallons of water per day, per person, plus water for your pet. A large part of the refuge falls within the air space of a Military training base, and there may closures of the park during training exercises. Normally, the park is open from Monday through Friday, and closed weekends. Well behaved, friendly dogs of all sizes are allowed. Dogs are allowed throughout the park. They may not be left unattended, and they must be leashed at all times and cleaned up after.
Organ Pipe Cactus National Monument 10 Organ Pipe Drive Ajo AZ   520-387-6849
http://www.nps.gov/orpi/index.htm
Dogs on leash are allowed in the campground, paved roadways, and the Palo Verde Trail. Dogs are not allowed on any other trails.

Alpine

Cross Country Ski Resorts
Hannagan Meadow Lodge HC 61, PO Box 335 Alpine AZ   928-339-4370
http://www.hannaganmeadow.com
This resort is located 22 miles south of Alpine on US 191/Coronado Trail. While dogs are not allowed at the lodge during the winter months they are allowed in the cabins during the summer. Dogs are also allowed on the cross-country ski trails. Rent skis from the lodge and then take your pooch on a cross-country ski adventure. Dogs need to be leashed while on the lodge property, but can be taken off-leash under direct voice control on the Apache-Sitgreaves National Forest trails. The trails are sometimes groomed by the national forest service.

Amando

Campgrounds and RV Parks
Mountain View RV Ranch 2843 E Frontage Road Amando AZ   520-398-9401
http://www.mtviewrvranch.com
Dogs of all sizes are allowed. There are no additional pet fees. Dogs must be quiet, well behaved, leashed, and cleaned up after. The camping and tent areas also allow dogs. There is a dog walk area at the campground. Dogs are allowed in the camping cabins.

Apache Junction

Campgrounds and RV Parks
La Hacienda RV Resort 1797 W 28th Avenue Apache Junction AZ   480-982-2808
http://www.lahaciendarv.com
One dog up to 60 pounds, or 2 dogs up to 10 pounds each are allowed. There are no additional pet fees. Dogs may not be left unattended outside, and they must be quiet, well behaved, leashed, and cleaned up after. There are some breed restrictions. There is a dog walk area at the campground.
Lost Dutchman State Park 6109 N. Apache Trail Apache Junction AZ   480-982-4485
This park is located at the base of the Superstition Mountains, and there are many year round recreational activities and trails to explore. Dogs are allowed at no additional fee. Dogs may not be left unattended, and they must be leashed and cleaned up after. The camping and tent areas also allow dogs. There is a dog walk area at the campground. There are no electric or water hookups at the campground.
Mesa/Apache Junction KOA 1540 S Tomahawk Road Apache Junction AZ   480-982-4015 (800-562-3404)

http://www.koa.com
Dogs of all sizes are allowed, and there are no additional pet fees for tent or RV sites. There is a $25 refundable deposit for the cabins and only 2 dogs are allowed. Dogs may not be left unattended, and they must be leashed and cleaned up after. There are some breed restrictions. The camping and tent areas also allow dogs. There is a dog walk area at the campground. Dogs are allowed in the camping cabins.
Superstition Sunrise 702 S Meridian Apache Junction AZ   480-986-4524
http://www.azrvresort.com
This park is mostly close to 55 or older, no children. Dogs of all sizes are allowed. There are no additional pet fees. Dogs must be leashed and cleaned up after. There is a fenced in area for off lead. Dogs must be walked in the designated pet areas only, and not to the office or other non-pet areas. There is a dog walk area at the campground.
Weaver's Needle Travel Trailor Resort 250 S Tomahawk Road Apache Junction AZ   480-982-3683
http://www.weaversneedle.com
Dogs of all sizes are allowed. There are no additional pet fees. Dogs must be leashed and cleaned up after, and there is a fenced in dog park on site. Dogs must be walked in designated areas for pets only and not in the rest of the park where campers do not have dogs. There is a dog walk area at the campground.

Parks
Lost Dutchman State Park 6109 N Apache Trail Apache Junction AZ   480-982-4485
Named after the fabled lost gold mine, this desert park, at 2000 feet, is located at the base of the Superstition Mountains, a place of mystery and legend since early times. The park offers a variety of hiking trails of varying difficulty, nature trails, visitors' center, picnic facilities with restrooms, and special programs throughout the year. Well behaved dogs of all sizes are allowed. Dogs must be leashed at all times and cleaned up after. Dogs may not be left unattended in the park or in automobiles. Dogs are allowed throughout the park and on the trails, but not in public buildings. There is also a 70 unit campground (no hook-ups) with a dump station and showers that allow pets for no additional fee.

Avondale

Stores
PetSmart Pet Store 1561 N Dysart Rd Avondale AZ   623-547-0889
Your licensed and well-behaved leashed dog is allowed in the store.
Petco Pet Store 10190 West McDowell Rd Avondale AZ   623-936-4034
Your licensed and well-behaved leashed dog is allowed in the store.

Benson

Accommodations
Motel 6 - Benson 637 South Whetstone Commerce Drive Benson AZ   520-586-0066 (800-466-8356)
One well-behaved family pet per room. Guest must notify front desk upon arrival. Guest is liable for any damages. In consideration of all guests, pets must never be left unattended in the guest rooms.
Super 8 Benson 855 N Ocotillo Rd Benson AZ   520-586-1530 (800-800-8000)
Dogs of all sizes are allowed. There is a $10 returnable deposit required per room. Smoking and non-smoking rooms are available for pet rooms.

Campgrounds and RV Parks
Benson KOA 180 W Four Feathers Benson AZ   520-586-3977 (800-562-6823)
http://www.koa.com
Dogs of all sizes are allowed, and there are no additional pet fees for tent or RV sites. There is a $5 one time fee per pet for the cabins. Dogs may not be left unattended outside, and they must be leashed and cleaned up after. The camping and tent areas also allow dogs. There is a dog walk area at the campground. Dogs are allowed in the camping cabins.
Butterfield RV Resort and Observatory 251 S Ocotillo Benson AZ   520-586-4400
http://www.rv-resort.com
Dogs of all sizes are allowed. There are no additional pet fees. Dogs must be leashed and cleaned up after. There is a fenced in area for dogs where they can be off lead. There is a dog walk area at the campground.
Kartchner Caverns State Park 2980 S Hwy 90 Benson AZ   520-586-2283
The guided cave tours are a main attraction at this park and reservations for the caves are suggested. Other

attractions at this park include the Discovery Center, interactive displays, an amphitheater, and a variety of hiking trails. Dogs are allowed at no additional fee. Dogs must be leashed and cleaned up after. Dogs are not allowed in the Discovery Center or other park buildings. The camping and tent areas also allow dogs. There is a dog walk area at the campground. There are no water hookups at the campground.

Bisbee

Vacation Home Rentals
Sleepy Dog Guest House 212A Opera Drive Bisbee AZ   520-432-3057
http://www.sleepydogguesthouse.com
There is a one bedroom and two bedroom guest house overlooking Bisbee. No credit cards, smoking outside only. There are no additional pet fees.

Black Canyon City

Campgrounds and RV Parks
Black Canyon City KOA 19600 E St Joseph Road Black Canyon City AZ   623-374-5318
http://www.koa.com
Dogs of all sizes are allowed. There are no additional pet fees. Dogs may not be left unattended, and they must be quiet, leashed, and cleaned up after. There are some breed restrictions. The camping and tent areas also allow dogs. There is a dog walk area at the campground.

Bowie

Attractions
Fort Bowie National Historic Site 3203 South Old Fort Bowie Road Bowie AZ   520-847-2500
http://www.nps.gov/fobo/index.htm
Dogs on leash are allowed at the historic site. The site features hiking, picnicking, and more. The park advises you to stay on the trail due to sticker bushes that can get twisted in your dog's fur.

Buckeye

Accommodations
Days Inn Buckeye 25205 West Yuma Rd Buckeye AZ   623-386-5400 (800-329-7466)
Dogs of all sizes are allowed. There is a $10 one time per pet fee per visit.

Camp Verde

Accommodations
Comfort Inn 340 N Goswick Way Camp Verde AZ   928-567-9000 (877-424-6423)
Dogs of all sizes are allowed. There is a $15 one time additional pet fee per room, and a pet waiver to sign. Dogs may not be left unattended, and they must be leashed and cleaned up after.
Days Inn Camp Verde 1640 W Finnie Flat Rd Camp Verde AZ   928-567-3700 (800-329-7466)
Dogs of all sizes are allowed. There is a $10 one time per pet fee per visit. Reservations are recommended due to limited rooms for pets.

Campgrounds and RV Parks
Trails End RV Park 983 Finney Flat Road Camp Verde AZ   928-567-0100
http://www.trailsend-rvpark.com
Dogs of all sizes are allowed. There are no additional pet fees. Dogs must be leashed and cleaned up after.

There is a dog walk area at the campground.

Zane Grey RV Park 4500 E Hwy 260 Camp Verde AZ   928-567-4320 (800-235-0608)
http://www.zanegreyrvpark.com/
This beautifully landscaped RV park is close to several attractions in the area, and they offer large clean restrooms, showers, spa, laundry facilities, and propane. Dogs of all sizes are allowed for no additional fee. Dogs may not be left alone at any time, and they must be leashed and cleaned up after. There is a dog walk area at the campground.

Zane Grey RV Park 4500 E Hwy 260 Camp Verde AZ   928-567-4320 (800-235-0608)
http://www.zanegreyrvpark.com/
This beautifully landscaped RV park is close to several attractions in the area, and they offer large clean restrooms, showers, spa, laundry facilities, and propane. Dogs of all sizes are allowed for no additional fee. Dogs may not be left alone at any time, and they must be leashed and cleaned up after. There is a dog walk area at the campground.

Attractions

Montezuma Castle National Monument PO Box 219 Camp Verde AZ   928-567-3322
http://www.nps.gov/moca/index.htm
Dogs on leash are allowed on trails of the trails here. Please pick up after your dog.

Parks

Fort Verde State Historical Park 125 Holloman Street Camp Verde AZ   928-567-3275
This historic Park was a primary army base, and is the best preserved example of an Indian Wars era fort in Arizona. Rich in cultural and American history, they offer living history presentations, special craft and building projects, historic house museums furnished in 1880s period, picnic tables, restrooms, and RV parking. They are ADA accessible, and open 8:00 a.m. - 5:00 p.m. every day. The park is closed on Christmas Day. Dogs of all sizes are allowed. Dogs may not be left unattended anywhere in the park or in automobiles. Dogs must be leashed and cleaned up after. They are allowed throughout the park except in buildings.

TOP 200 PLACE **Montezuma Castle National Monument** 2800 Montezuma Castle H Camp Verde AZ
928-567-3322
http://www.nps.gov/moca/
This park is home to one of the best preserved cliff dwellings in North America. The 20 room, 5 story cliff dwelling sits high above a creek in a limestone recess, and served as a "high-rise apartment building" for Sinagua Indians over 600 years ago. Exhibits along the self-guiding trail describe the cultural and natural history of the site and a diorama/audio program shows the interior view of the cliff dwellings. Dogs must be on no more than a six foot leash at all times and cleaned up after. Dogs may not be left unattended in the park or in automobiles. They are open every day of the year, including Christmas day. Winter hours: 8 AM to 5 PM; Summer hours (May 30th through Labor Day): 8 AM to 6 PM MST.

Tuzigoot National Monument PO Box 219 Camp Verde AZ   928-634-5564
http://www.nps.gov/tuzi/index.htm
Dogs must be on leash and must be cleaned up after in the park and on trails.

Casa Grande

Accommodations

Days Inn Casa Grande 5300 N Sunland Gin Rd Casa Grande AZ   520-426-9240 (800-329-7466)
Dogs of all sizes are allowed. There is a $8 one time pet fee per visit.

Holiday Inn 777 N Pinal Ave Casa Grande AZ   520-426-3500 (877-270-6405)
There are no additional pet fees.

Motel 6 - Casa Grande 4965 North Sunland Gin Road Casa Grande AZ   520-836-3323 (800-466-8356)
One well-behaved family pet per room. Guest must notify front desk upon arrival. Guest is liable for any damages. In consideration of all guests, pets must never be left unattended in the guest rooms.

Super 8 Casa Grande 2066 E Florence Blvd Casa Grande AZ   520-836-8800 (800-800-8000)
Dogs of all sizes are allowed. There is a $10 per night pet fee per pet. Smoking and non-smoking rooms are available for pet rooms.

Campgrounds and RV Parks

Buena Tierra RV Park and Campground 1995 S Cox Road Casa Grande AZ   520-836-3500
http://www.campgroundbuenatierra.com
Dogs of all sizes are allowed. There are no additional pet fees. Dogs may not be left unattended outside or left

out at night. Dogs must be quiet, well behaved, leashed, and cleaned up after. The camping and tent areas also allow dogs. There is a dog walk area at the campground.
Palm Creek Golf and RV Resort 1110 N Hennes Road Casa Grande AZ   800-421-7004
http://www.palmcreekgolf.com
Dogs up to 55 pounds are allowed. There are no additional pet fees. This is a 55 or over park, and one person can be 41 or over. There is a pet section where dogs are allowed, and they are allowed in the park model rentals. Dogs must be on no more than a 6 foot leash, except in the dog runs, and they must be cleaned up after. There is a dog walk area at the campground.

Catalina

Accommodations
Super 8 Catalina/Tucson Area 15691 N Oracle Rd Catalina AZ   520-818-9500 (800-800-8000)
Dogs of all sizes are allowed. There is a $5 per night pet fee per pet. Smoking and non-smoking rooms are available for pet rooms.

Chinle

Accommodations
Best Western Canyon de Chelly Inn 100 Main St Chinle AZ   928-674-5874 (800-780-7234)
Dogs of all sizes are allowed. There is a $5.70 per night pet fee per pet. Smoking and non-smoking rooms available.

Parks
Canyon de Chelly National Monument PO Box 588 Chinle AZ   928-674-5500
http://www.nps.gov/cach/index.htm
Dogs on leash are allowed in campsites, roads that lead up to overlooks and parking lot. Dogs are not allowed in canyons or trails.

Coolidge

Attractions
Casa Grande Ruins National Monument 1100 Ruins Drive Coolidge AZ   520-723-3172
http://www.nps.gov/cagr/index.htm
Dogs must be on leash and must be cleaned up after at the monument. Dogs are not allowed in any buildings.

Cornville

Campgrounds and RV Parks
Lo Lo Mai Springs 11505 Lo Lo Mai Road Cornville AZ   928-634-4700
http://www.lolomai.com
Dogs of all sizes are allowed. There is a $3 per night per pet additonal fee for tent and RV sites, and there is a $5 per night per pet additional fee for cabins. Dogs may not be left unattended at any time, and they must be leashed and cleaned up after. The camping and tent areas also allow dogs. There is a dog walk area at the campground. Dogs are allowed in the camping cabins.
Lo Lo Mai Springs Outdoor Resort 11505 Lo Lo Mai Road Cornville AZ   928-634-4700
http://www.lolomai.com/
Abundant springs in this area provides lush foliage creating a rich oasis for recreation in the high desert. Amenities offered at this campground include hot showers, a spring fed pond, clean restrooms, a heated swimming pool, jacuzzi, convenience store, club house, children's playground, ball and game courts, and a variety of recreational pursuits. Dogs of all sizes are allowed. There is a $3 per night per pet additional fee for the campground or the cabins. Dogs are not allowed in the cottages. Dogs must be leashed and cleaned up after.

Dogs are allowed throughout the park, but not at the pool or in buildings. The camping and tent areas also allow dogs. There is a dog walk area at the campground. Dogs are allowed in the camping cabins.
Lo Lo Mai Springs Outdoor Resort 11505 Lo Lo Mai Road Cornville AZ   928-634-4700
http://www.lolomai.com/
Abundant springs in this area provides lush foliage creating a rich oasis for recreation in the high desert. Amenities offered at this campground include hot showers, a spring fed pond, clean restrooms, a heated swimming pool, jacuzzi, convenience store, club house, children's playground, ball and game courts, and a variety of recreational pursuits. Dogs of all sizes are allowed. There is a $3 per night per pet additional fee for the campground or the cabins. Dogs are not allowed in the cottages. Dogs must be leashed and cleaned up after. Dogs are allowed throughout the park, but not at the pool or in buildings. The camping and tent areas also allow dogs. There is a dog walk area at the campground. Dogs are allowed in the camping cabins.

Attractions
Oak Creek Vineyards and Winery 1555 N Page Springs Road Cornville AZ   928-649-0290
This winery was established in 2002 and features six wine grape varieties. They are open Wednesday to Sunday from 11:00 a.m. to 5:00 p.m for wine tasting and tours. Friendly, well behaved dogs on leash are allowed, and please clean up after your pet. Dogs can go where people can go outside; they are not allowed in the buildings.

Cottonwood

Campgrounds and RV Parks
Dead Horse Ranch State Park 675 Dead Horse Ranch Road Cottonwood AZ   928-634-5283
This park along the Verde River Greenway, shares a unique ecosystem, in that their Cottonwood/Willowriparian gallery forest is one of less than 20 riparian type zones in the world. There are also many trails to explore. Dogs are allowed at no additional fee. Dogs may not be left unattended, and they must be leashed and cleaned up after. Dogs are not allowed in park buildings or ramadas. The camping and tent areas also allow dogs. There is a dog walk area at the campground.

Douglas

Accommodations
Motel 6 - Douglas 111 16th Street Douglas AZ   520-364-2457 (800-466-8356)
One well-behaved family pet per room. Guest must notify front desk upon arrival. Guest is liable for any damages. In consideration of all guests, pets must never be left unattended in the guest rooms.

Attractions
Slaughter House Ranch National Historic Landmark 6151 Geronimo Trail Douglas AZ   520-558-2474
The life of a turn-of-the-century cattle baron is preserved in this original Arizona ranch home that provides authentic displays of turn-of-the-century life. There is also a wash house, icehouse, granary, a pond, artesian wells, and commissary on the grounds. There is no food service available here. The museum is open to the public Wednesday through Sunday from 10 am-3 pm. Dogs of all sizes are allowed to tour the farm and the outer buildings. They must be on lead at all times and cleaned up after. Dogs are not allowed in the main museum.

Eager

Accommodations
Best Western Sunrise Inn 128 N Main St Eager AZ   928-333-2540 (800-780-7234)
Dogs of all sizes are allowed. There is a $10 per night pet fee per pet. Smoking and non-smoking rooms available.

Ehrenberg

Accommodations

Best Western Flying J Motel I-10 Exit 1, S Frontage Rd Ehrenberg AZ   928-923-9711 (800-780-7234)
Dogs up to 60 pounds are allowed. There is a $20 per night pet fee per pet. Smoking and non-smoking rooms available. Reservations are recommended due to limited rooms for pets.

Eloy

Accommodations

Red Roof Inn - Eloy 4015 West Outer Drive Eloy AZ   520-466-2522 (800-RED-ROOF)
One well-behaved family pet per room. Guest must notify front desk upon arrival. Guest is liable for any damages. In consideration of all guests, pets must never be left unattended in the guest rooms.

Flagstaff

Accommodations

Best Western Kings House Motel 1560 East Route 66 Flagstaff AZ   928-774-7186 (800-780-7234)
Dogs of all sizes are allowed. There is a $15 per night pet fee per pet. Smoking and non-smoking rooms available.
Comfort Inn 2355 S Beulah Blvd Flagstaff AZ   928-774-2225 (877-424-6423)
Dogs of all sizes are allowed. There is a $5 per night per pet additional fee. Dogs may not be left unattended, and they must be quiet, well behaved, leashed, and cleaned up after.
Days Inn Flagstaff East 3601 E Lockett Rd Flagstaff AZ   928-527-1477 (800-329-7466)
Dogs of all sizes are allowed. There is a $10 one time per pet fee per visit. Reservations are recommended due to limited rooms for pets.
Days Inn Flagstaff Hwy 66 1000 West Rte 66 Flagstaff AZ   928-774-5221 (800-329-7466)
Dogs of all sizes are allowed. There is a $10 per night pet fee per pet. Reservations are recommended due to limited rooms for pets.
Holiday Inn 2320 E Lucky Lane Flagstaff AZ   928-714-1000 (877-270-6405)
There is a $25 one time pet fee per visit. Dogs are permitted up to 100 pounds.
Howard Johnson Inn 3300 E. Rt. 66 Flagstaff AZ   800-437-7137 (800-446-4656)
Dogs of all sizes are welcome. There is a $7 one time pet fee.
La Quinta Inn & Suites Flagstaff 2015 South Beulah Blvd. Flagstaff AZ   928-556-8666 (800-531-5900)
Dogs of all sizes are allowed. Dogs must be well behaved, leashed, and cleaned up after.
Motel 6 - Flagstaff - Butler Ave 2010 East Butler Avenue Flagstaff AZ   928-774-1801 (800-466-8356)
One well-behaved family pet per room. Guest must notify front desk upon arrival. Guest is liable for any damages. In consideration of all guests, pets must never be left unattended in the guest rooms.
Motel 6 - Flagstaff East - Lucky lane 2440 East Lucky Lane Flagstaff AZ   928-774-8756 (800-466-8356)
One well-behaved family pet per room. Guest must notify front desk upon arrival. Guest is liable for any damages. In consideration of all guests, pets must never be left unattended in the guest rooms.
Motel 6 - Flagstaff West-Woodlands Village 2745 South Woodlands Village Flagstaff AZ   928-779-3757 (800-466-8356)
One well-behaved family pet per room. Guest must notify front desk upon arrival. Guest is liable for any damages. In consideration of all guests, pets must never be left unattended in the guest rooms.
Quality Inn 2500 E Lucky Lane Flagstaff AZ   928-226-7111 (877-424-6423)
Dogs of all sizes are allowed. There is a $15 per night per room additional pet fee. Dogs must be leashed and cleaned up after. The Do Not Disturb sign needs to be put on the door if there is a pet in the room alone.
Quality Inn 2000 S Milton Road Flagstaff AZ   928-774-8771 (877-424-6423)
Dogs of all sizes are allowed. There is a $10 per night per pet additional fee. Dogs must be leashed and cleaned up after.
Residence Inn by Marriott 3440 N. Country Club Drive Flagstaff AZ   928-526-5555
Dogs of all sizes are allowed. There is a $7.50 per night fee to a maximum of $75, and a pet policy to sign at check in.
Sleep Inn 2765 S Woodlands Village Blvd Flagstaff AZ   928-556-3000 (877-424-6423)
Dogs of all sizes are allowed. There is a $20 per night per room additional pet fee. Dogs must be crated when left alone in the room and then for no more than an hour. Dogs must be leashed and cleaned up after.

Campgrounds and RV Parks

Coconino National Forest 1824 S Thompson Street Flagstaff AZ   928-527-3600
http://www.fs.fed.us/r3/coconino/
This diverse forest, of 1,821,495 acres, offers alpine tundra, pine forest, high mountain desert and a variety of land and water recreation. Dogs of all sizes are allowed at no additional fee. Dogs may not be left unattended, and they must be leashed at all times, and cleaned up after in camp areas. The camping and tent areas also allow dogs. There is a dog walk area at the campground. There are no electric or water hookups at the campground.

Flagstaff KOA 5803 N Hwy 89 Flagstaff AZ   928-526-9926 (800-562-3524)
http://www.flagstaffkoa.com
Dogs of all sizes are allowed. There are no additional pet fees. Dogs may not be left unattended outside, and they must be leashed and cleaned up after. The camping and tent areas also allow dogs. There is a dog walk area at the campground. Dogs are allowed in the camping cabins.

Woody Mountain Campground and RV Park 2727 W Hwy 66 Flagstaff AZ   928-774-7727
http://www.woodymountaincampground.com
Dogs of all sizes are allowed. There are no additional pet fees. Dogs may not be left unattended, and they must be quiet, leashed, and cleaned up after. This RV park is closed during the off-season. The camping and tent areas also allow dogs. There is a dog walk area at the campground.

Cross Country Ski Resorts

Flagstaff Nordic Center PO Box 1718 Flagstaff AZ   928-220-0550
http://flagstaffnordiccenter.com
Situated in the Coconino National Forest, 15 miles northwest of Flagstaff, this center is the premier cross-country ski location in Arizona. They are located at an elevation of 8,200 feet. Dogs are allowed on the Skijoring Trail which is a 5.7km beginner and intermediate cross-country ski trail. Rent skis at the center and then head out on the trail. Dogs need to be leashed or on a harness. The trail is generally groomed. If you are looking for a place to stay, the center also has a green (off the grid) yurt rental in the national forest. Pets are allowed in the yurt only with prior permission and cannot be left unattended. Access to the yurt may require a four wheel drive vehicle. Call for more details. To get to the Nordic center from Flagstaff, follow the Highway 180 signs towards the Grand Canyon. They are located along Highway 180 at Mile Marker 232.

Stores

PetSmart Pet Store 1121 S Plaza Way Flagstaff AZ   928-213-1737
Your licensed and well-behaved leashed dog is allowed in the store.

Parks

Sunset Crater Volcano National Monument 6400 N Hwy 89 Flagstaff AZ   928-526-1157
http://www.nps.gov/sucr/index.htm
Dogs on leash are allowed in the park areas. Dogs are not allowed on the trails. You may not leave pets in vehicles in the park.

Walnut Canyon National Monument 6400 N Hwy 89 Flagstaff AZ   928-526-1157
http://www.nps.gov/waca/index.htm
Dogs on leash are allowed on paved roads and picnic areas only. Dogs are not allowed in buildings or on park trails.

Wupatki National Monument 6400 N Hwy 89 Flagstaff AZ   928-526-1157
http://www.nps.gov/wupa/index.htm
Dogs on leash are allowed in the parking areas and picnic areas. Dogs are not allowed in the buildings or on the park trails.

Off-Leash Dog Parks

Bushmaster Dog Park 3150 N. Alta Vista Flagstaff AZ
This fenced dog park has separate areas for small and large dogs. It is about 1 1/2 acres in size. From I-40 exit at Country Club Drive, head north to Route 66 west. Immediately turn right onto Lockett to Bushmaster Park on your left.

Thorpe Park Bark Park 191 N. Thorpe Road Flagstaff AZ   928-779-7690
http://www.flagstaff.az.gov
This 1.5 acre dog park is double-gated and has benches, picnic tables, and a water fountain.

Fort McDowell

Campgrounds and RV Parks
Eagle View RV Resort 9605 N Fort McDowell Road Fort McDowell AZ   480-836-5310
http://www.eagleviewresort.com
Dogs of all sizes are allowed. There are no additional pet fees. Dogs must be leashed and cleaned up after.
There is a dog walk area at the campground.

Fredonia

Parks
Pipe Spring National Monument 406 North Pipe Spring Road Fredonia AZ   928-643-7105
http://www.nps.gov/pisp/index.htm
Dogs on leash are allowed on the picnic grounds and paved areas. Dogs are not allowed in the fort, unpaved
trails, or garden.

Ganado

Attractions
Hubbell Trading Post National Historic Site PO Box 150 Ganado AZ   928-755-3475
http://www.nps.gov/hutr/index.htm
Dogs must be on leash and must be cleaned up after at the site. Dogs are not allowed in any buildings.

Gila Bend

Accommodations
Best Western Space Age Lodge 401 E Pima Gila Bend AZ   928-683-2273 (800-780-7234)
Dogs of all sizes are allowed. There are no additional pet fees. Smoking and non-smoking rooms available.

Globe

Accommodations
Comfort Inn at Round Mountain Park 1515 South Street Globe AZ   928-425-7575 (877-424-6423)
Dogs of all sizes are allowed. There can be up to 3 small to medium or 2 large dogs per room. There is a $10
per night per pet additional fee. Dogs may not be left unattended, and they must be leashed and cleaned up
after.
Motel 6 - Globe 1699 East Ash Street Globe AZ   928-425-5741 (800-466-8356)
One well-behaved family pet per room. Guest must notify front desk upon arrival. Guest is liable for any
damages. In consideration of all guests, pets must never be left unattended in the guest rooms.

Grand Canyon

Accommodations
Red Feather Lodge Highway 64 Grand Canyon AZ   800-538-2345
http://www.redfeatherlodge.com
This motel is located just one mile south of the south entrance to the Grand Canyon National Park. Pets are
welcome, but they must not be left unattended in the room. There is a $50 refundable pet deposit and a $10 pet
fee per night per pet.
Days Inn Williams 2488 W Rt 66 Williams AZ   928-635-4051 (800-329-7466)
Dogs of all sizes are allowed. There is a $10 returnable deposit required per room.
Highlander Motel 533 W. Bill Williams Avenue Williams AZ   928-635-2541 (800-800-8288)
There is a $5/day pet charge. Room prices are in the $50 range. This motel is about 1 hour from the Grand

Canyon.

Holiday Inn 950 N. Grand Canyon Blvd Williams AZ 928-635-4114 (877-270-6405)
There are no additional pet fees.

Motel 6 - Williams East - Grand Canyon 710 West Bill Williams Avenue Williams AZ 928-635-4464 (800-466-8356)
One well-behaved family pet per room. Guest must notify front desk upon arrival. Guest is liable for any damages. In consideration of all guests, pets must never be left unattended in the guest rooms.

Motel 6 - Williams West - Grand Canyon 831 West Route 66 Williams AZ 928-635-9000 (800-466-8356)
One well-behaved family pet per room. Guest must notify front desk upon arrival. Guest is liable for any damages. In consideration of all guests, pets must never be left unattended in the guest rooms.

Quality Inn Mountain Ranch & Resort 6701 E Mountain Ranch Road Williams AZ 928-635-2693 (877-424-6423)
Dogs of all sizes are allowed. There is a $25 one time additional pet fee per room. Dogs must be crated when left alone in the room, and leashed and cleaned up after.

Campgrounds and RV Parks

Ash Fork RV Park 783 W Old Route 66 Ash Fork AZ 928-637-2521
Dogs of all sizes are allowed. There are no additional pet fees. Dogs must be leashed and cleaned up after. The camping and tent areas also allow dogs. There is a dog walk area at the campground.

TOP 200 PLACE Supai and the Havasupai Reservation P. O. Box 10/Indian Road 18 Supai AZ 928-448-2141
http://www.havasupaitribe.com/index.htm
Want to take your dog down to the Colorado River in the Grand Canyon but, of course, this is not allowed by the National Park Service? Instead, just downriver from Grand Canyon National Park is the Havasupai Indian Reservation, which shares the Canyon with the National Park. And here, your dog may enter the canyon with you. The strikingly beautiful, secluded canyon sits at the west end of the Grand Canyon and is accessible only by foot, horseback, or helicopter. The entrance fee is $35 per person, and everything is carry in/carry out, or pack animals can be hired. Only a limited number of persons may visit the Havasu Canyon at a time, so advance inquiry is suggested. There is a large parking lot about 64 miles from the turn-off onto Indian Road 18 where visitors may park at Hualapai Hilltop. This is a trailhead with no services. Here you may start the 8 mile hike to the Supai Village in the canyon where there is a small café, lodge, general store, museum, and a post office that is the only office to still receive mail via Pony Express. The trail is moderately difficult and starts off steep with switchbacks for about the first 1 1/2 miles with narrow canyon passages before it levels out. The name Havasupai means 'People-Of-The Blue-Green-Waters' and the Havasu Creek is a year around spring-fed stream that will astonish visitors with the 4 powerful main waterfalls and deeply colored turquoise pools that it supplies. You first pass Supai Falls as you are nearing the village; then Navajo Falls is about 1 1/2 miles past the village. Just before you reach the campground about 2 miles past the village is the very popular, spectacular double waterfall of the Havasu Falls with a great swimming hole. Then, about 2 miles past the campground is Mooney Falls with the highest drop of 200 feet, but also the most difficult to access. The hiking trails of the Reservation include the hike in from Hualapai Hilltop to the village, to the camp area, and from the campgrounds to the Colorado River which is about 8 miles from the camp area. There is no hiking allowed in Cataract Canyon or off the main trails. Dogs of all sizes are allowed for no additional fees. Dogs must be under owner's control, and leashed and cleaned up after at all times. Dogs may not be left unattended at any time, and dog owners accept full responsibility for their pet. Dogs are allowed to take the helicopter ride in for about $25 for a small to medium dog; it may be more for a large dog. Their website is www.airwesthelicopters.com. Dogs are not allowed at the lodge or in the village buildings. Campers must pack all supplies and refuge in and out of the canyon. The camp area is primitive but rich with lush vegetation and shade trees. Amenities include spring water (treat or purify 1st), composting toilets, picnic tables, and night security during tourist season. The fee for tent camping is $10 per person, and no additional pet fee is required. There are no electric or water hookups at the campgrounds.

Flintstones Bedrock City Junction 64 and 180 Williams AZ 928-635-2600
http://www.bedrockcityaz.com
Dogs of all sizes are allowed. There are no additional pet fees. Dogs may be off leash at the site if the dog is well behaved and will stay on the site regardless of what passes by. They must be on leashed when walked and dogs must be cleaned up after. The camping and tent areas also allow dogs. There is a dog walk area at the campground. There is a little amusement park on the premises where your dog can go with you on leash.

Grand Canyon/Williams KOA 5333 Hwy 64 Williams AZ 928-635-2307 (800-562-5771)
http://www.koa.com
Dogs of all sizes are allowed. There are no additional pet fees. Dogs may not be left unattended, and they must be quiet, leashed, and cleaned up after. There are some breed restrictions. This RV park is closed during the off-season. The camping and tent areas also allow dogs. There is a dog walk area at the campground. Dogs are allowed in the camping cabins.

Kaibab National Forest Railroad Blvd Williams AZ 928-635-8200
http://www.fs.fed.us/r3/kai/
This picturesque forest of 1.6 million acres borders both the north and south rims of the Grand Canyon. It is the

largest contiguous ponderosa pine forest in US and its diverse ecosystems support a large variety of plants, fish, mammals, bird species, and recreation. Dogs of all sizes are allowed at no additional fee. Dogs may not be left unattended except for shore periods, and they must be leashed and cleaned up after in camp areas. Dogs may be off lead on the trails if no one is around, they will not chase wildlife, and are under strict voice command. The camping and tent areas also allow dogs. There is a dog walk area at the campground. Dogs are allowed in the camping cabins. There are no electric or water hookups at the campground.

Williams/Circle Pines KOA 1000 Circle Pines Road Williams AZ   928-635-2626 (800-562-9379)
http://www.circlepineskoa.com
Dogs of all sizes are allowed. There are no additional pet fees. Dogs may not be left unattended outside, and they must be leashed and cleaned up after. Dogs must be crated when left in a cabin. There are some breed restrictions. The camping and tent areas also allow dogs. There is a dog walk area at the campground. Dogs are allowed in the camping cabins.

Attractions

TOP 200 PLACE **The Planes of Fame Air Museum** 755 Mustang Way Valle AZ   928-635-1000
http://www.planesoffame.org/menu.php
This air museum is dedicated to collecting, restoring, displaying, and preserving aircraft and memorabilia for the educational benefit of present and future generations. There are over 150 aircraft at its two locations; the main facility is in Chino, California. The displayed aircraft spans the history of manned flight, from a replica of the Chanute Hang Glider of 1896, to modern space flight. It also includes vehicles from numerous milestone achieving test and research flights. Hours are from 9am to 5pm everyday (Closed Thanksgiving & Christmas Day). Well behaved dogs of all sizes are allowed throughout the property for no additional fee. Dogs must be leashed, under owners' control at all times, and cleaned up after.

Historic Route 66 Driving Tour Bill Williams Avenue Williams AZ
Route 66 was the main route between Los Angeles and Chicago during the 1920's through the 1960's. It was completely paved in 1938. This historic route symbolizes the American adventure and romance of the open road. Begin your self-guided driving tour on Bill Williams Avenue in Williams. This portion of Route 66 is considered "America's Main Street," where you will find gas stations, restaurants, shops and motels that have served travelers since the 1920's. Then head east on Old 66 to the I-40 interchange. Continue east on I-40 for 6 miles. Take the Pittman Valley exit and left left, pass over I-40, and turn right onto historic Route 66. This portion of the road was originally paved in 1939. Stop and park at the Oak Hill Snowplay Area. You and your pooch can take a 2 mile round trip hike to the Keyhole Sink petroglyphs. After your walk, continue driving and you will come to a community called Parks. Located here is a country store that has been in operation since about 1910. At this point you can turn around and head back to Williams via I-40. Directions and descriptions are from the USDA Forest Service in Williams, Arizona.

Parks

TOP 200 PLACE **Grand Canyon National Park** Hwy 64 Grand Canyon AZ   928-638-7888
http://www.nps.gov/grca/
The Grand Canyon, located in the northwest corner of Arizona, is considered to be one of the most impressive natural splendors in the world. It is 277 miles long, 18 miles wide, and at its deepest point, is 6000 vertical feet (more than 1 mile) from rim to river. The Grand Canyon has several entrance areas, but the most popular is the South Rim. Dogs are not allowed on any trails below the rim, but leashed dogs are allowed on the paved rim trail. This dog-friendly trail is about 2.7 miles each way and offers excellent views of the Grand Canyon. Remember that the elevation at the rim is 7,000 feet, so you or your pup may need to rest more often than usual. Also, the weather can be very hot during the summer and can be snowing during the winter, so plan accordingly. And be sure you or your pup do not get too close to the edge! Feel like taking a tour? Well-behaved dogs are allowed on the Geology Walk. This is a one hour park ranger guided tour and consists of a leisurely walk along a 3/4 mile paved rim trail. They discuss how the Grand Canyon was created and more. The tour departs at 11am daily (weather permitting) from the Yavapai Observation Station. The Grand Canyon park entrance fee is currently $25.00 per private vehicle, payable upon entry to the park. Admission is for 7 days, includes both South and North Rims, and covers the entrance fee only.

Supai and the Havasupai Reservation P. O. Box 10/Indian Road 18 Supai AZ   928-448-2141
http://www.havasupaitribe.com/index.htm
Want to take your dog down to the Colorado River in the Grand Canyon but, of course, this is not allowed by the National Park Service? Instead, just downriver from Grand Canyon National Park is the Havasupai Indian Reservation, which shares the Canyon with the National Park. And here, your dog may enter the canyon with you. The strikingly beautiful, secluded canyon sits at the west end of the Grand Canyon and is accessible only by foot, horseback, or helicopter. The entrance fee is $35 per person, and everything is carry in/carry out, or pack animals can be hired. Only a limited number of persons may visit the Havasu Canyon at a time, so advance inquiry is suggested. There is a large parking lot about 64 miles from the turn-off onto Indian Road 18 where visitors may park at Hualapai Hilltop. This is a trailhead with no services. Here you may start the 8 mile hike to the Supai Village in the canyon where there is a small café, lodge, general store, museum, and a post office that

is the only office to still receive mail via Pony Express. The trail is moderately difficult and starts off steep with switchbacks for about the first 1 1/2 miles with narrow canyon passages before it levels out. The name Havasupai means 'People-Of-The Blue-Green-Waters' and the Havasu Creek is a year around spring-fed stream that will astonish visitors with the 4 powerful main waterfalls and deeply colored turquoise pools that it supplies. You first pass Supai Falls as you are nearing the village; then Navajo Falls is about 1 1/2 miles past the village. Just before you reach the campground about 2 miles past the village is the very popular, spectacular double waterfall of the Havasu Falls with a great swimming hole. Then, about 2 miles past the campground is Mooney Falls with the highest drop of 200 feet, but also the most difficult to access. The hiking trails of the Reservation include the hike in from Hualapai Hilltop to the village, to the camp area, and from the campgrounds to the Colorado River which is about 8 miles from the camp area. There is no hiking allowed in Cataract Canyon or off the main trails. Dogs of all sizes are allowed for no additional fees. Dogs must be under owner's control, and leashed and cleaned up after at all times. Dogs may not be left unattended at any time, and dog owners accept full responsibility for their pet. Dogs are allowed to take the helicopter ride in for about $25 for a small to medium dog; it may be more for a large dog. Their website is www.airwesthelicopters.com. Dogs are not allowed at the lodge or in the village buildings.

Kaibab National Forest 800 South 6th Street Williams AZ 928-635-8200
http://www.fs.fed.us/r3/kai/
Dogs on leash are allowed on many trails throughout this national forest. Hiking trails range greatly in difficulty, from easy to very difficult. A couple of the more popular trails are the Keyhole Sink Trail and the Bill Williams Mountain Trail. The Keyhole Sink Trails is an easy trail that is 2 miles round trip. Walk through a ponderosa pine forest until you reach a box canyon. At the canyon, you will find petroglyphs (prehistoric sketches on the rock), that are about 1,000 years old. The message suggests that the area was an important hunting ground. To get there from Williams, take I-40 east to the Pitman Valley Exit (#171). Turn left and cross over the Interstate. Proceed east on Historic Route 66 for about 2 miles to the Oak Hill Snowplay Area. The trail begins on the north side of the road. Park in the lot provided. The Bill Williams Mountain Trail is rated moderate and is about 4 miles long. The trailhead starts at 7,000 feet. To get there, go west from downtown Williams on Bill Williams Avenue about one mile; turn left at Clover Hill and proceed along the frontage road to the turnoff to Williams Ranger District office. Follow the signs to the trailhead.

Outdoor Restaurants

Grand Canyon Snack Bars Grand Canyon National Park Grand Canyon AZ
Dogs are permitted at the outdoor benches at park operated snack bars located at the South Rim area. Please note that these snack bars typically have benches only and not tables. There were no other restaurants we found at the Grand Canyon that had outdoor tables. The closest outdoor dining we found was in Williams, Arizona.

Cruiser's Cafe 233 West Route 66 Williams AZ 928-635-2445
http://www.thegrandcanyon.com/cruisers/
This cafe is located on Old Route 66 in historic downtown Williams. The cafe is located in a renovated gas station and displays hundreds of Route 66 memorabilia items. Dogs are allowed at the outdoor tables.

Subway Sandwiches 1050 North Grand Canyon Blvd. Williams AZ 928-635-0955
Dogs are allowed at the outdoor table.

The Route 66 Place 417 East Route 66 Williams AZ 928-635-0266
http://www.route66place.com
Dogs are allowed at the outdoor tables. This cafe is named after the Old Route 66, which was the main route between Los Angeles and Chicago during the 1920's through the 1960's.

Greer

Accommodations

Big Ten Resort Cabins 45 Main Street Greer AZ 928-735-7578
http://www.bigtencabins.com
These are rustic Cabins located in the cozy town of Greer in the center of the White Mountains in AZ. They are located 13 Miles from Sunrise Ski Resort & many other outdoor activities. Some ammenities include Satellite TV/VCR/DVD, fireplaces and bar-b-cues. Well behaved dogs are welcome for $15 each per night.

Cross Country Ski Resorts

Sunrise Park Resort PO Box 117 Greer AZ 928-735-7669
http://www.sunriseskipark.com
This resort is located off 260 near Show Low, in the White Mountains, about 218 miles from Phoenix and 230 miles from Tucson. While dogs are not allowed at the lodge, they are allowed on the cross-country ski trails. Rent some skis from the lodge and then take your dog on any of the trails that range from .5 to 2.9 miles. The

trails are groomed and dogs need to be leashed.

Heber

Accommodations
Best Western Sawmill Inn 1877 Hwy 260 Heber AZ   928-535-5053 (800-780-7234)
Dogs of all sizes are allowed. There is a $10 per night pet fee per pet. Smoking and non-smoking rooms available.

Hereford

Parks
Coronado National Memorial 4101 E Montezuma Canyon Road Hereford AZ   520-366-5515
http://www.nps.gov/coro/
A memorial park dedicated to its explorer, Coronado. There is auto touring, picnicking, hiking, bird watching, and a museum. Dogs are not allowed in buildings, in caves, or on most all the trails. They are allowed on all paved roads, and on the Crest Trail the 5.3 miles one way to Miller Peak (elevations: 6575 feet to 9456 feet at Miller Peak) and into the National Forest. The trailhead is across the road at the northeast end of the Montezuma Pass parking area. The trail climbs for 2 miles to the northwestern boundary of the Memorial, where it enters the Coronado National Forest. There it continues along the crest of the Huachuca Mountains to the turnoff for Miller Peak, the highest peak in the Huachucas. Dogs must be kept leashed at all times, and cleaned up after. Dogs may not be left unattended anywhere in the park or in automobiles.

Huachuca

Campgrounds and RV Parks
Mountain View RV Park 99 W Vista Lane Huachuca AZ   800-772-4103
http://www.mountainviewrvpark.com
Dogs of all sizes are allowed. There are no additional pet fees. Dogs may not be left unattended outside, and they must be leashed and cleaned up after. There are some breed restrictions. The camping and tent areas also allow dogs. There is a dog walk area at the campground.

Jacob Lake

Campgrounds and RV Parks
Kaibab Campervillage Forest Road #461 Jacob Lake AZ   928-643-7804
http://www.kaibabcampervillage.com
Dogs of all sizes are allowed. There are no additional pet fees. Dogs may not be left unattended, and they must be leashed and cleaned up after. This RV park is closed during the off-season. The camping and tent areas also allow dogs. There is a dog walk area at the campground.

Kingman

Accommodations
Best Western Kings Inn and Suites 2930 E Route 66 Kingman AZ   928-753-6101 (800-780-7234)
Dogs of all sizes are allowed. There is a $8 one time pet fee per visit per pet. Smoking and non-smoking rooms available.
Days Inn 3381 E Andy Devine Kingman AZ   928-757-7337 (800-329-7466)
Dogs of all sizes are allowed. There is a $10 per night pet fee per pet.
Days Inn Kingman/West 3023 Andy Devine Kingman AZ   928-753-7500 (800-329-7466)

Dogs of all sizes are allowed. There is a $10 one time per pet fee per visit.
Mohave Inn 3016 E Andy Devine Kingman AZ 928-753-9555
Dogs of all sizes are allowed. There is a $5 per night per pet additional fee.
Motel 6 - Kingman East 3351 East Andy Devine Avenue Kingman AZ 928-757-7151 (800-466-8356)
One well-behaved family pet per room. Guest must notify front desk upon arrival. Guest is liable for any damages. In consideration of all guests, pets must never be left unattended in the guest rooms.
Motel 6 - Kingman West 424 West Beale Street Kingman AZ 928-753-9222 (800-466-8356)
One well-behaved family pet per room. Guest must notify front desk upon arrival. Guest is liable for any damages. In consideration of all guests, pets must never be left unattended in the guest rooms.
Quality Inn 1400 E Andy Devine Avenue Kingman AZ 928-753-4747 (877-424-6423)
Dogs of all sizes are allowed. There is a $10 per night per pet additional fee. Dogs must be leashed, cleaned up after, and crated or removed for housekeeping.
Super 8 Kingman 3401 E Andy Devine Ave Kingman AZ 928-757-4808 (800-800-8000)
Dogs of all sizes are allowed. There is a $10 one time per pet fee per visit. Smoking and non-smoking rooms are available for pet rooms.

Campgrounds and RV Parks
Kingman KOA 3820 N Roosevelt Kingman AZ 928-757-4397 (800-562-3991)
http://www.koa.com
Dogs of all sizes are allowed. There are no additional pet fees. There is, however, a $20 refundable deposit for the cabins. Dogs must be leashed and cleaned up after. There are some breed restrictions. The camping and tent areas also allow dogs. There is a dog walk area at the campground. Dogs are allowed in the camping cabins.

Stores
Petco Pet Store 3320 Stockton Hill Rd Kingman AZ 928-681-4101
Your licensed and well-behaved leashed dog is allowed in the store.

Lake Havasu

Accommodations
Best Western Lake Place Inn 31 Wings Loop Lake Havasu AZ 928-855-2146 (800-780-7234)
Dogs of all sizes are allowed. There is a $5 per night pet fee per pet. Smoking and non-smoking rooms available.
Motel 6 - Lake Havasu City 2176 Birch Square Lake Havasu AZ 928-855-5566 (800-466-8356)
One well-behaved family pet per room. Guest must notify front desk upon arrival. Guest is liable for any damages. In consideration of all guests, pets must never be left unattended in the guest rooms.
Hampton Inn 245 London Bridge Rd Lake Havasu City AZ 928-855-4071
Dogs of all sizes are allowed. There is a $10 per night per room fee, the rooms are on the 1st and 4th floors, and dogs are not to be left alone in the room.
Island Inn Hotel 1300 W McCulloch Blvd Lake Havasu City AZ 928-680-0606 (800-243-9955)
http://rentor.com/hotels/islanlin.htm
There is a $10 per day pet charge.
Motel 6 - Lake Havasu City Airport 111 London Bridge Road Lake Havasu City AZ 928-855-3200 (800-466-8356)
One well-behaved family pet per room. Guest must notify front desk upon arrival. Guest is liable for any damages. In consideration of all guests, pets must never be left unattended in the guest rooms.
Motel 6 - Parker 604 California Avenue Parker AZ 928-669-2133 (800-466-8356)
One well-behaved family pet per room. Guest must notify front desk upon arrival. Guest is liable for any damages. In consideration of all guests, pets must never be left unattended in the guest rooms.

Campgrounds and RV Parks
Cattail Cove State Park P. O. Box 1990 Lake Havasu City AZ 928-855-1223
This 2,000 acre park offers a beach, boat ramp, an amphitheater, 61 campsites, and a variety of year around land and water recreation. If you have your own watercraft, there are an additional 28 campsites along the water's edge. Dogs of all sizes are allowed at no additional fee. Dogs must be leashed at all times, and cleaned up after. Dogs may not be left unattended at any time. The camping and tent areas also allow dogs. There is a dog walk area at the campground.
Cattail Cove State Park P. O. Box 1990 Lake Havasu City AZ 928-855-1223
This 2,000 acre park offers a beach, boat ramp, an amphitheater, 61 campsites, and a variety of year around

land and water recreation. If you have your own watercraft, there are an additional 28 campsites along the water's edge. Dogs of all sizes are allowed at no additional fee. Dogs must be leashed at all times, and cleaned up after. Dogs may not be left unattended at any time. The camping and tent areas also allow dogs. There is a dog walk area at the campground.

Islander RV Resort 751 Beachcomer Blvd Lake Havasu City AZ   928-680-2000
http://www.islanderrvresort.com
Dogs of all sizes are allowed. There is a $1 per night per pet additional fee. Dogs are not allowed to be left unattended outside, and they must be leashed and cleaned up after. This is an adult only park. There are some breed restrictions. There is a dog walk area at the campground.

Lake Havasu State Park 699 London Bridge Road Lake Havasu City AZ   928-855-2784
This park is home to the Mohave Sunset Walking Trail and the Arroyo-Camino Interpretive Garden that showcases the variety of life in and around the park. Dogs are allowed at no additional fee. Dogs must be leashed, cleaned up after, and water and shade must be provided. The camping and tent areas also allow dogs. There is a dog walk area at the campground.

Buckskin Mountain State Park 5476 Hwy 95 Parker AZ 928-667-3231
This scenic campground sits along an 18-mile stretch of the Colorado River between Parker Dam and Headgate Dam. The park has different activities planned throughout the year. There are ranger led hikes, weekly speakers, ice cream socials, boating safety classes, and campfire programs. They also offer basketball and volleyball courts, a playground, clothing boutique, restaurant, camp store, arcade, restrooms, and a gas dock. Dogs of all sizes are allowed for no additional fee. They may not be left unattended at any time, and they must be leashed at all times, and cleaned up after. Dogs are not allowed in the cabaña area or on the beach from the day use area to the cabañas. At the River Island area, dogs are allowed in the water, but must be kept on right side of boat ramp. Well behaved dogs on lead are allowed on the variety of trails and throughout the rest of the park. The camping and tent areas also allow dogs. There is a dog walk area at the campground.

Buckskin Mountain State Park 5476 Hwy 95 Parker AZ 928-667-3231
This scenic campground sits along an 18-mile stretch of the Colorado River between Parker Dam and Headgate Dam. The park has different activities planned throughout the year. There are ranger led hikes, weekly speakers, ice cream socials, boating safety classes, and campfire programs. They also offer basketball and volleyball courts, a playground, clothing boutique, restaurant, camp store, arcade, restrooms, and a gas dock. Dogs of all sizes are allowed for no additional fee. They may not be left unattended at any time, and they must be leashed at all times, and cleaned up after. Dogs are not allowed in the cabaña area or on the beach from the day use area to the cabañas. At the River Island area, dogs are allowed in the water, but must be kept on right side of boat ramp. Well behaved dogs on lead are allowed on the variety of trails and throughout the rest of the park. The camping and tent areas also allow dogs. There is a dog walk area at the campground.

Attractions

A-1 Watercraft Rentals 1435 Countryshire Ave #103 Lake Havasu City AZ   928-855-8088
http://www.championrentals.com/
Dogs are allowed on their 24 foot pontoon boats for no additional fee. There is a 10 person limit to each boat, and a dog counts as one rider. They open at 9 am and are open year round.

TOP 200 PLACE **The London Bridge** 314 London Bridge Road (Lake Havasu City Visitor's Center) Lake Havasu City AZ   928-453-8883
The London Bridge was built in 1831, and after many long years in service, it was relocated to Lake Havasu City, Arizona, and dedicated on October 10, 1971. There is a walkway along the bridge so that you and your pet can walk across this piece of history and enjoy the view of the lake. Dogs must be leashed at all times, and please clean up after your pet.

Parks

Cattail Cove State Park P. O. Box 1990 Lake Havasu City AZ   928-855-1223
This 2,000 acre park offer a beach, boat ramp, an amphitheater, and a variety of year round land and water recreation. Day use is from sunrise to 10 pm. Dogs must be leashed at all times, and cleaned up after. Dogs may not be left unattended at any time. There is also a campground here where pets are allowed for no additional fee.

Bill Williams River National Wildlife Refuge 60911 H 95 Parker AZ 928-667-4144
This 6,105-acre refuge has a rich natural and cultural history. Dogs of all sizes are allowed for no additional fee. Dogs must be kept leashed at all times, and cleaned up after. Dogs are allowed throughout the park on the trails or just along side the trails. Dogs may not be left unattended at any time.

Buckskin Mountain State Park 5476 H 95 Parker AZ 928-667-3231
This scenic park sits along an 18-mile stretch of the Colorado River between Parker Dam and Headgate Dam. They have different activities throughout the year. There are ranger led hikes, weekly speakers, ice cream socials, boating safety classes, and campfire programs. They also offer basketball and volleyball courts, a playground, clothing boutique, restaurant, camp store, arcade, and a gas dock. Dogs of all sizes are allowed for no additional fee. They may not be left unattended at any time, and they must be leashed at all times, and cleaned up after. Dogs are not allowed in the cabaña area or on the beach from the day use area to the

cabañas. At the River Island area, dogs are allowed in the water, but must be kept on right side of boat ramp. Well behaved dogs on lead are allowed on the variety of trails and throughout the rest of the park. There is also tent and RV camping at this park, and pets are allowed for no additional fee.

Off-Leash Dog Parks
Lions Dog Park 1340 McCulloch Blvd. Lake Havasu City AZ 928-453-8686
This dog park is located with the London Bridge Beach park. The grassy off-leash area is completely fenced and offers a water feature, hydrants, benches, and shade. Dogs are not allowed along the Bridgewater Channel, parking lots or other areas of London Bridge Beach. Dogs must be on leash when outside the off-leash area.

Outdoor Restaurants
Javelina Cantina 1420 McCulloch Drive Lake Havasu City AZ 928-855-8226
http://www.javelinacantina.com
Well behaved dogs are allowed to join you on the patio by the outer tables. They serve South of the Boarder food. Dogs are not allowed to go through the building. Dogs must be leashed and cleaned up after.
Oasis Grill 401 English Village Lake Havasu City AZ 928-854-3223
Your pet may join you on the outdoor patio at this restaurant, and they even provide a water bowl for your thirsty dog. Dogs are not allowed to go through the building, and they must be leashed at all times, and cleaned up after.

McNeal

Campgrounds and RV Parks
Double Adobe 5057 W Double Adobe Road McNeal AZ 520-364-4000
http://www.doubleadobe.com
Dogs of all sizes are allowed. There are no additional pet fees. Dogs must be well behaved, leashed, and cleaned up after. The camping and tent areas also allow dogs. There is a dog walk area at the campground.

Munds Park

Campgrounds and RV Parks
Munds Park RV Resort 17550 Munds Ranch Road Munds Park AZ 928-286-1309
http://www.mundsparkrv.com
Dogs of all sizes are allowed. There are no additional pet fees. Dog may be off lead on the trails with voice command, and be leashed and cleaned up after when in the park. This RV park is closed during the off-season. The camping and tent areas also allow dogs. There is a dog walk area at the campground.

Nogales

Accommodations
Best Western Siesta Motel 673 N Grand Ave Nogales AZ 520-287-4671 (800-780-7234)
Dogs of all sizes are allowed. There is a $5 per night pet fee per pet. Smoking and non-smoking rooms available.
Motel 6 - Nogales 141 W Mariposa Road Nogales AZ 520-281-2951 (800-466-8356)
One well-behaved family pet per room. Guest must notify front desk upon arrival. Guest is liable for any damages. In consideration of all guests, pets must never be left unattended in the guest rooms.

Page - Lake Powell

Accommodations
Best Western Arizonainn 716 Rimview Dr Page AZ 928-645-2466 (800-780-7234)
Dogs of all sizes are allowed. There is a $10 per night pet fee per pet. Smoking and non-smoking rooms

available.
Days Inn Lake Powell 961 N Hwy 89 Page AZ   928-645-2800 (800-329-7466)
Dogs of all sizes are allowed. There is a $10 per night pet fee per pet.
Motel 6 - Page P.O. Box 4450 Page AZ   928-645-5888 (800-466-8356)
One well-behaved family pet per room. Guest must notify front desk upon arrival. Guest is liable for any damages. In consideration of all guests, pets must never be left unattended in the guest rooms.
Quality Inn at Lake Powell 287 N Lake Powell Blvd Page AZ   928-645-8851 (877-424-6423)
Dogs of all sizes are allowed. There are no additional pet fees. Dogs must be quiet, well behaved, leashed, and cleaned up after. The Do Not Disturb sign needs to be placed on the door if there is a pet in the room alone.
TOP 200 PLACE **Wahweap Lodge and Marina** 100 Lakeshore Drive Page AZ   928-645-2433
The lodge offers a fine dining restaurant, gift shop, pool, lounge, and spectacular views of Lake Powell. Pets are allowed for an additional fee of $20 per night per room. Pets must be on a leash at all times when outside the room, and they are not to be left unattended or tied up outside on the patio or balcony. Dogs must be attended to or removed for housekeeping. If your pet is accustomed to being on the bed, they request you ask for a sheet to put over the bedspread. There is also a marina on site where they rent watercraft. Your pet may join you on a boat ride if you rent an 18' or 19' personal craft, as they are not allowed on the tour boats.

Campgrounds and RV Parks
Page-Lake Powell Campground 849 S Copper Mine Road Page AZ   928-645-3374
http://www.pagecampground.com
Dogs of all sizes are allowed. There are no additional pet fees. Dogs may not be left unattended outside, and they must stay off the grass, be leashed and cleaned up after. The camping and tent areas also allow dogs. There is a dog walk area at the campground.
Wahweap RV Park and Campground 100 S Lake Shore Drive Page AZ   888-486-4679
http://www.lakepowell.com
Dogs of all sizes are allowed. There are no additional pet fees. Dogs may not be left unattended, and they must be leashed and cleaned up after. There is also a lodge on site where pets are allowed in the standard rooms. There is a dog walk area at the campground.

Attractions
Antelope Canyon Adventures 104 Lake Powell Blvd Page AZ   928-645-5501
http://www.jeeptour.com/
Located on Navajo land, the tours offered here into the petrified sand dunes are smooth and spectacular enough to attract all ages. Soft ethereal curves, waves, and arches create amazing, unusual textures and patterns along the canyon walls, and when sunlight hits the literally billions of crystals infused through the sandstone, there is quite a light show. Tours depart at 8:00 am, 10:00 am, 12 noon, 2:00 pm and 4:00 pm, and weather is not a factor. Tours are about 1 1/2 hours long, and a good deal of the time is exploring the canyon. One dog up to about 35 pounds is allowed on the jeep tours, as long as other passengers do not object and there is room. They say no one has objected yet, and just ask that dogs be friendly and well behaved. Dogs must be leashed and cleaned up after at all times.
TOP 200 PLACE **Lake Powell - Glen Canyon Recreation Area** Page AZ   435-684-7400
http://www.nps.gov/glca/
Beautiful Lake Powell is called America's Natural Playground and is home to the world's largest natural bridge (standing 290 feet high), the Rainbow Bridge National Monument. The Wahweap Lodge, located in Page, rents powerboats for sight-seeing on the lake. Rent and drive your own boat, and your dog is welcome to join you. If you rent a boat, there is a one half mile trail to the Rainbow Bridge from the Rainbow Bridge courtesy dock. Also at Lake Powell near Bullfrog, there is a 3 mile round-trip hiking trail called Pedestal Alley. For boat rentals, the Wahweap Lodge is located 2.5 miles SE of US 89 at Lake Powell. The best time to visit the lake is during the fall season when temperatures are mild.
TOP 200 PLACE **Navajo Village** 1235 Copper Mine Road Page AZ   928-660-0304
http://www.navajovillage.com/home.html
This Navajo Village is an authentic re-creation of a traditional Navajo homesite that tells the living history of the Navajo people through oral story telling, music, dance, their art, and even their food preparation. Share the beauty of their harmony, relationships, industry, and creativity through the various programs they offer. They offer mini or grand tours for individuals or groups. Their season is from April through October, and during the busy times, they are usually open all day. If it is during a slow time, the tours start at 4 pm. Well behaved dogs on lead are welcome for no additional fee. Please clean up after your pet.
Wahweap Lodge and Marina Boat Rentals 100 Lakeshore Drive Page AZ   928-645-2433
You can relax on a half day smooth water raft trip, tour the rapids, or rent a houseboat that can sleep up to 12 people. The houseboats come with an assortment of amenities. There are also eight day and 14 day expeditions where you will cover almost 300 river miles, and negotiate nearly 200 exciting rapids safely, and in first class comfort. Their season runs from April through September. Dogs are not allowed on the tour boats, but they are

allowed to be on an individual boat rental. Dogs may not be left unattended at any time, and they must be leashed and cleaned up after. There is also a lodge on site that offers a fine dining restaurant, gift shop, lounge, and spectacular views of Lake Powell. Pets are allowed for an additional fee of $20 per night per room. Pets must be on a leash at all times when outside the room, and they are not to be left unattended in the room or tied up outside on the patio or balcony. Dogs must be attended to or removed for housekeeping. If your pet is accustomed to being on the bed, they request you ask for a sheet to put over the bedspread.

Parks
Rainbow Bridge National Monument PO Box 1507 Page AZ   928-608-6404
http://www.nps.gov/rabr/index.htm
Pets are not allowed on the short hike and boat to the monument. Permission must be granted by the tribe to hike the 17 mile trail to the site.

Patagonia

Campgrounds and RV Parks
Patagonia Lake State Park 400 Patagonia Lake Road Patagonia AZ   520-287-6965
This park has a variety of water and land recreation, trails, and the Sonoita Creek State Natural Area is now open to the public. Dogs are allowed at no additional fee. Dogs may not be left unattended, they must be on no more than a 6 foot leash, and be cleaned up after. Dogs are not allowed in the public swim areas. The camping and tent areas also allow dogs. There is a dog walk area at the campground.

Payson

Accommodations
Motel 6 - Payson 101 West Phoenix Street Payson AZ   928-474-4526 (800-466-8356)
One well-behaved family pet per room. Guest must notify front desk upon arrival. Guest is liable for any damages. In consideration of all guests, pets must never be left unattended in the guest rooms.

Petrified Forest

Accommodations
Best Western Adobe Inn 615 W Hopi Dr Holbrook AZ   928-524-3948 (800-780-7234)
Dogs of all sizes are allowed. There is a $10 per night pet fee per pet. Smoking and non-smoking rooms available.
Best Western Arizonian Inn 2508 Navajo Blvd Holbrook AZ   928-524-2611 (800-780-7234)
Dogs of all sizes are allowed. There is a $30 returnable deposit required per room. Smoking and non-smoking rooms available.
Holiday Inn Express 1308 E Navajo Blvd Holbrook AZ   928-524-1466 (877-270-6405)
There is a $10 per visit additional pet fee.
Motel 6 - Holbrook 2514 Navajo Boulevard Holbrook AZ   928-524-6101 (800-466-8356)
One well-behaved family pet per room. Guest must notify front desk upon arrival. Guest is liable for any damages. In consideration of all guests, pets must never be left unattended in the guest rooms.

Campgrounds and RV Parks
Holbrook/Petrified Forest KOA 102 Hermosa Drive Holbrook AZ   928-524-6689 (800-562-3389)
http://www.koa.com
Dogs of all sizes are allowed. There are no additional pet fees. Dogs must be leashed and cleaned up after. The camping and tent areas also allow dogs. There is a dog walk area at the campground.

Parks
Petrified Forest National Park Entrances on Hwy 40 and Hwy 180 Petrified Forest National Park AZ   928-524-6228
http://www.nps.gov/pefo/

The Petrified Forest is located in northeastern Arizona and features one of the world's largest and most colorful concentrations of petrified wood. Also included in the park's 93,533 acres are the multi-hued badlands of the Painted Desert, archeological sites and displays of 225 million year old fossils. Your leashed dog is welcome on all of the paved trails and scenic overlooks. Take a walk on the self-guided Giant Logs trail or view ancient petroglyphs from an overlook. The entrance fee is $10 per private vehicle.

Phoenix

Accommodations

Best Western Bell Hotel 17211 N Black Canyon Hwy Phoenix AZ   602-993-8300 (800-780-7234)
Dogs of all sizes are allowed. There is a $10 per night pet fee per pet. Smoking and non-smoking rooms available.
Best Western InnSuites Hotel and Suites 1615 E Northern Ave Phoenix AZ   602-997-6285 (800-780-7234)
Dogs of all sizes are allowed. There is a $25 one time pet fee per visit. Smoking and non-smoking rooms available.
Candlewood Suites 11411 North Black Canyon Highway Phoenix AZ   602-861-4900 (877-270-6405)
Dogs up to 100 pounds are allowed. There is a $75 one time pet fee for stays up to 2 weeks. For longer stays, there is a $150 one time pet fee.
Clarion Hotel Phoenix Tech Center 5121 E La Puenta Avenue Phoenix AZ   480-893-3900 (877-424-6423)
Dogs of all sizes are allowed. There is a $25 one time additional pet fee per room. Dogs may not be left unattended, and they must be leashed and cleaned up after.
Crowne Plaza 2532 W. Peoria Ave Phoenix AZ   602-943-2341 (877-270-6405)
Exit I-17 at Peoria Ave. There are no additional pet fees.
Days Inn Phoenix Airport 3333 E Van Buren Phoenix AZ   602-244-8244 (800-329-7466)
Dogs of all sizes are allowed. There is a $20 one time per pet fee per visit.
Embassy Suites Hotel Phoenix - Biltmore 2630 E. Camelback Phoenix AZ   602-955-3992
Dogs up to 50 pounds are allowed. There is a $25 one time pet fee per visit. Dogs are not allowed to be left alone in the room.
Embassy Suites Hotel Phoenix Airport at 24th Street 2333 East Thomas Road Phoenix AZ   602-957-1910
Dogs of all sizes are allowed. There is a $15 per night pet fee per pet. Dogs are not allowed to be left alone in the room.
Hilton 10 East Thomas Road Phoenix AZ   602-222-1111
Dogs of all sizes are allowed. There is a $200 refundable deposit and a pet policy to sign at check in.
Hilton 7677 North 16th Street Phoenix AZ   602-997-2626
Dogs of all sizes are allowed. There is a $75 refundable deposit and a pet policy to sign at check in.
Hilton 11111 North 7th Street Phoenix AZ   602-866-7500
Dogs of all sizes are allowed. There is a $75 refundable deposit and a pet policy to sign at check in.
Holiday Inn - West 1500 N 51st Ave Phoenix AZ   602-484-9009 (877-270-6405)
There is a $25 one time pet fee.
Holiday Inn Express Hotel & Suites 15221 S. 50th St Phoenix AZ   480-785-8500 (877-270-6405)
There is no additional pet fee.
Holiday Inn Select - Airport 4300 E. Washington St Phoenix AZ   602-273-7778 (877-270-6405)
There is a $100 refundable pet deposit.
La Quinta Inn Phoenix Sky Harbor Airport North 4727 E Thomas Rd Phoenix AZ   602-956-6500 (800-531-5900)
Dogs of all sizes are allowed. There are no additional pet fees. Dogs must be leashed and cleaned up after. Please put the "Do Not Disturb" sign on the door if there is a dog alone in the room uncrated.
La Quinta Inn Phoenix Thomas Road 2725 N. Black Canyon Hwy. Phoenix AZ   602-258-6271 (800-531-5900)
Dogs of all sizes are allowed. Dogs must be well behaved, leashed, and cleaned up after.
Lexington Hotel at City Square 100 W Clarendon Ave Phoenix AZ   602-279-9811
There is a $100 refundable deposit required for dogs.
Motel 6 - Phoenix - Black Canyon 4130 North Black Canyon Highway Phoenix AZ   602-277-5501 (800-466-8356)
One well-behaved family pet per room. Guest must notify front desk upon arrival. Guest is liable for any damages. In consideration of all guests, pets must never be left unattended in the guest rooms.
Motel 6 - Phoenix - Sweetwater 2735 West Sweetwater Avenue Phoenix AZ   602-942-5030 (800-466-8356)
One well-behaved family pet per room. Guest must notify front desk upon arrival. Guest is liable for any damages. In consideration of all guests, pets must never be left unattended in the guest rooms.
Motel 6 - Phoenix Airport 214 South 24th Street Phoenix AZ   602-244-1155 (800-466-8356)
One well-behaved family pet per room. Guest must notify front desk upon arrival. Guest is liable for any damages. In consideration of all guests, pets must never be left unattended in the guest rooms.

Motel 6 - Phoenix East 5315 East Van Buren Street Phoenix AZ   602-267-8555 (800-466-8356)
One well-behaved family pet per room. Guest must notify front desk upon arrival. Guest is liable for any damages. In consideration of all guests, pets must never be left unattended in the guest rooms.
Motel 6 - Phoenix North - Bell Rd 2330 West Bell Road Phoenix AZ   602-993-2353 (800-466-8356)
One well-behaved family pet per room. Guest must notify front desk upon arrival. Guest is liable for any damages. In consideration of all guests, pets must never be left unattended in the guest rooms.
Motel 6 - Phoenix Northern Avenue 8152 North Black Canyon Highway Phoenix AZ   602-995-7592 (800-466-8356)
One well-behaved family pet per room. Guest must notify front desk upon arrival. Guest is liable for any damages. In consideration of all guests, pets must never be left unattended in the guest rooms.
Motel 6 - Phoenix West 1530 North 52nd Drive Phoenix AZ   602-272-0220 (800-466-8356)
One well-behaved family pet per room. Guest must notify front desk upon arrival. Guest is liable for any damages. In consideration of all guests, pets must never be left unattended in the guest rooms.
Pointe Hilton Squaw Peak Resort 7677 N 16th Street Phoenix AZ   602-997-2626 (800-947-9784)
http://www.pointehilton.com/
Offering the best in luxury accommodations, this award-winning resort features a variety of fun activities and amenities for the business and leisure travelers. The amenities include 563 well appointed suites, 48,000 square feet of meeting space, 3 restaurants, a putting course, gaming courts, and a 9-acre waterpark. Dogs of all sizes are welcome. There is a refundable room deposit of $50 for small dogs, $75 for medium dogs, and $100 for large dogs. Dogs must be leashed and cleaned up after at all times, and they must be removed or crated for housekeeping.
Pointe Hilton Tapatio Cliffs 11111 N 7th Street Phoenix AZ   602-866-7500 (800-947-9784)
http://www.pointehilton.com/
Nestled atop a desert mountain preserve with miles of scenic trails, this award winning resort features variety of fun activities and amenities for the business and leisure travelers, and is also home to the Lookout Mountain Golf Club. Some of the amenities include 547 elegantly appointed suites, 65,000 square feet of meeting space, 5 restaurants, a golf instruction academy, and a 3 1/2 acre water wonderland village. Dogs of all sizes are allowed for a $75 refundable deposit. Dogs must be leashed and cleaned up after at all times, and they must be removed or crated for housekeeping.
Red Roof Inn - Phoenix - Camelback 502 Camelback Road Phoenix AZ   602-264-9290 (800-RED-ROOF)
One well-behaved family pet per room. Guest must notify front desk upon arrival. Guest is liable for any damages. In consideration of all guests, pets must never be left unattended in the guest rooms.
Red Roof Inn - Phoenix Bell Road 17222 North Black Canyon Freeway Phoenix AZ   602-866-1049 (800-RED-ROOF)
One well-behaved family pet per room. Guest must notify front desk upon arrival. Guest is liable for any damages. In consideration of all guests, pets must never be left unattended in the guest rooms.
Red Roof Inn - Phoenix West 5215 West Willetta Street Phoenix AZ   602-233-8004 (800-RED-ROOF)
One Dog up to 80 pounds is allowed. There are no additional pet fees.
Residence Inn by Marriott 8242 N. Black Canyon Freeway Phoenix AZ   602-864-1900
Dogs of all sizes are welcome. There is a $75 one time fee, and a pet policy to sign at check in.
Residence Inn by Marriott 801 N. 44th Street Phoenix AZ   602-273-7221
Dogs up to medium size are welcome. There is a $75 per stay fee, and a pet policy to sign at check in.
Sheraton Crescent Hotel 2620 West Dunlop Avenue Phoenix AZ   602-943-8200 (888-625-5144)
Dogs up tp 60 pounds are allowed. There are no additional pet fees. Dogs are not allowed to be left alone in the room.
Sleep Inn Airport 2621 S 47th Place Phoenix AZ   480-967-7100 (877-424-6423)
Dogs of all sizes are allowed. There is a $25 one time fee per pet. Dogs must be leashed and cleaned up after. The Do Not Disturb sign needs to be on the door if there is a pet alone in the room.
Sleep Inn North 18235 N 27th Avenue Phoenix AZ   602-504-1200 (877-424-6423)
Dogs of all sizes are allowed. There is a $15 per night per pet additional fee. Dogs may not be left unattended, and they must be leashed and cleaned up after.
Studio 6 - PHOENIX - DEER VALLEY 18405 North 27th Avenue Phoenix AZ   602-843-1151 (800-466-8356)
One well-behaved family pet per room. Guest must notify front desk upon arrival. Guest is liable for any damages. In consideration of all guests, pets must never be left unattended in the guest rooms.
Super 8 Phoenix/West I-10 1242 N 53rd Ave Phoenix AZ   602-415-0888 (800-800-8000)
Dogs of all sizes are allowed. There is a $15 per night pet fee per pet. Smoking and non-smoking rooms are available for pet rooms.
TownePlace Suites Phoenix Metrocenter Mall/I-17 9425 N Black Canyon Freeway Phoenix AZ   602-943-9510
Dogs of all sizes are allowed. There is a $75 one time pet fee per visit.

Campgrounds and RV Parks

Covered Wagon RV Park 6540 N Black Canyon H Phoenix AZ   602-242-2500
Dogs of all sizes are allowed. There is a $1 per night per pet additional fee. Dogs may not be left unattended,

and they must be leashed and cleaned up after. There are some breed restrictions. The camping and tent areas also allow dogs. There is a dog walk area at the campground.

Desert Sands RV Park 22036 N 27th Avenue Phoenix AZ   623-869-8186
http://www.desertsandsrvpark.com
Dogs of all sizes are allowed. There are no additional pet fees. Dogs may not be left unattended, and they must be leashed and cleaned up after. There are some breed restrictions. There is a dog walk area at the campground.

Desert Shadows RV Resort 19203 N 29th Avenue Phoenix AZ   623-869-8178 (800-595-7290)
http://www.arizonarvresorts.com
Dogs of all sizes are allowed. There are no additional pet fees. Dogs are to be walked along the path just outside the front gate, and they must be leashed and cleaned up after. This is an adult resort and at least one person must be 55 or older. Dogs are not allowed in the park models. There are some breed restrictions. There is a dog walk area at the campground.

Destiny RV Resort 416 N Citrus Road Phoenix AZ   623-853-0537
http://www.destinyrv.com
Dogs of all sizes are allowed, but there can only be 2 average sized dogs or 3 if all small. There are no additional pet fees. Dogs are not allowed to be tied to the trees or tables, and may not be left unattended outside. Dogs must be on no more than a 6 foot leash and cleaned up after. There is a fenced in area for off lead, and there is a Bark Park about 4 miles from the resort. There are some breed restrictions. There is a dog walk area at the campground.

Pioneer RV Resort 36408 N Black Canyon H Phoenix AZ   800-658-5895
http://www.arizonarvresort.com
Dogs of all sizes are allowed. There are no additional pet fees. Dogs must be leashed and cleaned up after. There are some breed restrictions. There is a dog walk area at the campground. This is a 55 plus park so one person must be 55 or older.

Tonto National Forest 2324 E. McDowell Road Phoenix AZ   602-225-5200
The fifth largest forest in the US with almost 3 million acres offers a wide range of ecosystems, habitats and spectacular scenery. It also supports a large variety of plants, animals, and recreation. Dogs of all sizes are allowed at no additional fee. Dogs may not be left unattended, and they must have current rabies, shot records, and license. Dogs must be leashed at all times and cleaned up after in camp areas. Dogs are allowed on the trails. The camping and tent areas also allow dogs. There is a dog walk area at the campground. There are no electric or water hookups at the campground.

Attractions

Deer Valley Rock Art Center 3711 West Deer Valley Rd. Phoenix AZ   623-582-8007
Run by Arizona State University, this 47 acre attraction offers a self-guided walking tour to an archeological site where you can view petroglyphs with your pooch. The Hedgpeth Hills site has over 1,500 petroglyphs on almost 600 boulders. Researchers believe the petroglyphs are 200 to 2,000 years old. Dogs are not allowed inside the building, but can accompany you on the self-guided trail. A map of the trail is included with admission. Pets must be leashed and please clean up after your pet.

Pioneer Living History Village 3901 West Pioneer Road Phoenix AZ   623-465-1052
http://www.pioneer-arizona.com
This living history museum offers over 90 acres of an old 1800's village with original buildings and historically accurate reproductions. You will find costumed interpreters, cowboys, lawmen, Victorian ladies plus a working blacksmith shop and more. There are also "shootouts" that start daily at 11:30am. Well-behaved leashed dogs are welcome. The village is located 30 minutes north of Phoenix. This attraction is open year-round, but the best time is during the winter when it's not too hot for your dog to walk around. Winter hours are from mid-September through the end of May.

Shopping Centers

TOP 200 PLACE **Biltmore Fashion Park** 2502 E. Camelback Rd. Phoenix AZ   602-955-8400
Well-behaved leashed dogs are welcome at this outdoor shopping mall and most of the stores are pet-friendly. Some of the stores that allow dogs include Macy's, Sak's Fifth Avenue, Restoration Hardware, Pottery Barn, Godiva Chocolatier, The Sharper Image, Williams-Sonoma, Three Dog Bakery, and Baily, Banks & Biddle.

Stores

Petco Pet Store 16835 East Shea Blvd Ste 105 Fountain Hills AZ   480-836-8919
Your licensed and well-behaved leashed dog is allowed in the store.
PetSmart Pet Store 10825 N Tatum Blvd Phoenix AZ   480-367-9680
Your licensed and well-behaved leashed dog is allowed in the store.
PetSmart Pet Store 17035 N 7th Ave Phoenix AZ   602-375-7939
Your licensed and well-behaved leashed dog is allowed in the store.

PetSmart Pet Store 2020 N 75th Ave Phoenix AZ   623-873-1130
Your licensed and well-behaved leashed dog is allowed in the store.
PetSmart Pet Store 3865 E Thomas Rd Phoenix AZ   602-797-0478
Your licensed and well-behaved leashed dog is allowed in the store.
PetSmart Pet Store 1949 E Camelback Rd Phoenix AZ   602-248-8809
Your licensed and well-behaved leashed dog is allowed in the store.
PetSmart Pet Store 21001 N Tatum Blvd Phoenix AZ   480-513-4262
Your licensed and well-behaved leashed dog is allowed in the store.
PetSmart Pet Store 10450 N 31st Ave Ste 101 Phoenix AZ   602-331-0131
Your licensed and well-behaved leashed dog is allowed in the store.
PetSmart Pet Store 1745 W Bethany Home Rd Phoenix AZ   602-841-2507
Your licensed and well-behaved leashed dog is allowed in the store.
Petco Pet Store 4535 East Thomas Rd Phoenix AZ   602-840-9113
Your licensed and well-behaved leashed dog is allowed in the store.
Petco Pet Store 2784 West Peoria Avenue Phoenix AZ   602-504-1202
Your licensed and well-behaved leashed dog is allowed in the store.
Petco Pet Store 4727 East Bell Rd #37 Phoenix AZ   602-923-9814
Your licensed and well-behaved leashed dog is allowed in the store.
Petco Pet Store 2501 West Happy Valley Rd, Ste 6 Phoenix AZ   623-580-5018
Your licensed and well-behaved leashed dog is allowed in the store.
Petco Pet Store 6135 N 35th Avenue Phoenix AZ   602-995-7040
Your licensed and well-behaved leashed dog is allowed in the store.
Three Dog Bakery 2442 E Camelback Road #8 Phoenix AZ   602-522-2333
http://www.threedog.com
Three Dog Bakery provides cookies and snacks for your dog as well as some boutique items. You well-behaved, leashed dog is welcome.

Parks

North Mountain Area 7th Street Phoenix AZ   602-262-6862
http://phoenix.gov/PARKS/hikenort.html
North Mountain is over 2,100 feet and offers panoramic views of Phoenix. There are a variety of trails rated easy to difficult. The trailheads for two of the easy to moderate trails are located at the north end of Mountain View Park at 7th Avenue and Cheryl Drive. The North Mountain National Trail is rated moderate to difficult hiking and the trailhead is located at the Maricopa picnic area off 7th Street (not 7th Avenue). Parking is available. Pets must be leashed and please clean up after them.
Papago Park Van Buren Street and Galvin Parkway Phoenix AZ   602-256-3220
This park of 1,200 acres has easy trails and a natural landscape in addition to a variety of recreational pursuits. There is an archery range, an exercise course of 1.7 miles, over 7 acres of fishing lagoons, a ranger station that is near the Hole In The Rock, a softball complex, an orienteering course, picnic facilities, and unusual rock formations that took millions of years to form. The park is open from 6 am to 10 pm daily. Dogs are allowed for no additional fee. Dogs must be leashed at all times and it is important that you clean up after your pet. They are allowed throughout the park on all the trails.
Piestewa Peak/Dreamy Draw Area Squaw Peak Drive Phoenix AZ   602-262-6862
http://phoenix.gov/PARKS/hikesqua.html
Piestewa Peak (formally Squaw Peak) is 2,608 feet high and is one of the best known peaks in Phoenix. The summit trail does not allow dogs or horses, all other trails in the park allow leashed dogs. To take your dog up most of the summit for the views you can use the 3 3/4 mile Freedom Trail which is a more gradual slope than the Summit Trail. There are several other easy trails as well as difficult ones on which you may take your dog. Some of the trails begin off Squaw Peak Drive. Parking is available. Pets must be leashed and please clean up after them.
Reach 11 Recreation Area Cave Creek Road Phoenix AZ   602-262-6862
http://phoenix.gov/PRL/r11.html
This 1,500 acre park is about 7 miles long and less than 1/2 mile wide. The park runs along the north side of the Central Arizona Project canal. There are about 18 miles of multi-use trails to enjoy. In general the trails are flat and easy. The trails run the length of the recreation area from Cave Creek Road east to Scottsdale Road. Access points include Cave Creek Road, Tatum Blvd., Scottsdale Road and 56th Street. Pets must be leashed and please clean up after them.
South Mountain Park/Preserve 10919 South Central Avenue Phoenix AZ   602-495-0222
http://phoenix.gov/PARKS/hikesoth.html
This park of mostly undeveloped desert has many hiking trails that wind through a variety of habitats and picturesque geographic formations. The diverse ecosystems support a large variety of plants, animals, bird species, and recreation. There is also an educational center and museum at the visitor's center. The park is open daily from 5:30 am to 11pm. Dogs of all sizes are allowed for no additional fee. Dogs may not be left unattended at any time. It is also very important that dogs are on lead and under owners' control at all times, and

cleaned up after.

Off-Leash Dog Parks

Desert Vista Off-Leash Dog Park 11800 North Desert Vista Fountain Hills AZ   480-816-5152
http://www.adog.org
This 12 acre park offers a dog park for off-leash romping. The area is fully fenced with multi-station watering
fountains and shade structures. Paws in the Park, an annual dog festival, is held at this park. The park is located
on Saguaro Blvd., between Tower Drive and Desert Vista. To get there, head east on Shea Blvd. Turn left onto
Saguaro Blvd. Go 1.5 miles and turn right onto Desert Vista. Turn left immediately onto Saguaro Blvd. Go about .
2 miles and then turn right onto Tower Drive. The park is on the right. Thanks to ADOG (Association of Dog
Owners Group) for the directions. The hours are from sunrise to sunset.

Grovers Basin Dog Park 20th Street at Grovers Ave Phoenix AZ   602-262-6696
This dog park is 2.3 acres in total divided between a large and small dog area. Both areas are fenced. There are
no dog water fountains at the park.

Mofford Sports Complex Dog Park 9833 N. 25th Avenue Phoenix AZ   602-261-8011
This fenced dog park is divided into separate areas for small dogs and large dogs. It is open from 6:30 am to 10
pm daily. The dog park may be closed in periods of heavy rain. There is water for dogs, shade trees and
benches. The dog park is located on N. 25th Avenue just north of Dunlap.

Pecos Park Dog Park 48th Street Phoenix AZ   602-262-6862
http://phoenix.gov/PARKS/dogparks.html
This two acre dog park is fully fenced with double-gates and a separate area for small and large dogs. Pecos
Park is located at 48th Street and Pecos Parkway. Enter from 48th Street via Chandler Blvd. The dog park is
located at the southeast corner of the park.

PetsMart Dog Park 21st Avenue Phoenix AZ   602-262-6971
http://phoenix.gov/PARKS/dogparks.html
This fully fenced dog park has over 2.5 grassy acres. Amenities include a water fountain and two watering
stations for dogs, benches, bag dispensers and garbage cans. This off-leash park is located in Washington Park
on 21st Avenue north of Maryland (between Bethany Home and Glendale roads).

Steele Indian School Dog Park 7th Street at Indian School Road Phoenix AZ   602-495-0739
This off-leash dog park opened in June of 2006. The 2 acre park is divided between fenced areas for large and
small dogs. Park in the parking lot on the west side of 7th Street just north of Indian School Rd.

Outdoor Restaurants

Aunt Chilada's 7330 N. Dreamy Draw Drive Phoenix AZ   602-944-1286
http://www.auntchiladas.com/
This Southwestern restaurant offers a variety of food including quesadillas, soup, salads, tacos, enchiladas,
fajitas, and burritos. Well-behaved leashed dogs are allowed at the outdoor tables.

Baja Fresh Mexican Grill 1615 E Camelback Rd Ste F Phoenix AZ   602-263-0110
http://www.bajafresh.com/
This Mexican restaurant chain offers a variety of items on their menu including burritos, tacos, salads,
quesadillas, fajitas, and enchiladas. Well-behaved leashed dogs are allowed at the outdoor tables.

Baja Fresh Mexican Grill 430 East Bell Rd. Phoenix AZ   602-843-6770
http://www.bajafresh.com/
This Mexican restaurant chain offers a variety of items on their menu including burritos, tacos, salads,
quesadillas, fajitas, and enchiladas. Well-behaved leashed dogs are allowed at the outdoor tables.

Baja Fresh Mexican Grill 50 N. Central Ave Phoenix AZ   602-256-9200
http://www.bajafresh.com/
This Mexican restaurant chain offers a variety of items on their menu including burritos, tacos, salads,
quesadillas, fajitas, and enchiladas. Well-behaved leashed dogs are allowed at the outdoor tables.

Bamboo Club 2596 E. Camelback Rd. Phoenix AZ   602-955-1288
This restaurant offers Pacific Rim food, including Thailand, Korean, Vietnam, and Chinese. Well-behaved
leashed dogs are allowed at the outdoor tables. This restaurant is located in the dog-friendly Biltmore Fashion
Park.

Christopher's Fermier Brasserie 2584 E. Camelback Rd. Phoenix AZ   602-522-2344
http://www.fermier.com
This restaurant offers a combination French and American cuisine. Some of their specialty items include house-
smoked salmon, and lightly smoked truffle-cured sirloin. Well-behaved leashed dogs are allowed at the outdoor
tables. This restaurant is located in the dog-friendly Biltmore Fashion Park.

Coffee Plantation 2468 E. Camelback Rd. Phoenix AZ   602-553-0203
This is a tropical coffeehouse and bean store. They offer cofee, espresso, iced drinks, fresh Artisan Breads,
Baguettes, specialty bread loaves and more. Well-behaved leashed dogs are allowed at the outdoor tables. This
restaurant is located in the dog-friendly Biltmore Fashion Park.

Duck and Decanter 1651 East Camelback Road Phoenix AZ   602-274-5429

http://www.duckanddecanter.com
This restaurant offers a variety of sandwiches, salads, and soups. Some of their Signature Sandwiches include The Duckling with smoked duck, The Pocket with your choice of meat, and Where's the Beef which is their veggie sandwich. Well-behaved leashed dogs are allowed at the outdoor tables. The restaurant is located to the east of Albertson's, behind Copenhagen Furniture.

Haagen-Dazs 2454 E. Camelback Rd. Phoenix AZ   602-508-8053
http://www.haagendazs.com
This popular ice cream shop offers a variety of ice creams, sorbet, frozen yogurt, sundaes, banana split, specialty shakes, espresso, and ice cream cakes. Well-behaved leashed dogs are allowed at the outdoor tables. This restaurant is located in the dog-friendly Biltmore Fashion Park.

Honey Baked Ham and Co and Cafe 4635 E Cactus Road Phoenix AZ   602-996-0600
This restaurant serves American food. Dogs are allowed at the outdoor tables.

NYPD Pizza 1949 E Camelback Rd Phoenix AZ   602-294-6969
This restaurant serves Italian food. Dogs are allowed at the outdoor tables. Patios have misters to keep your pets cool.

Rock Bottom Brewery and Restaurant 14205 S 50th St Phoenix AZ   480-598-1300
This restaurant and bar serves American food and microbrews. Dogs are allowed at the outdoor tables.

Rubio's Fresh Mexican Grill 4340 E. Indian School Rd., Ste. 1 Phoenix AZ   602-508-1732
http://www.rubios.com/
This Mexican restaurant chain serves items like chargrilled steak and chicken burritos, tacos, quesadillas, seafood including lobster, shrimp, Mahi-Mahi, and their famous fish taco. Well-behaved leashed dogs are allowed at the outdoor tables.

Rubio's Fresh Mexican Grill 4747 East Bell Road #17 Phoenix AZ   602-867-1454
http://www.rubios.com/
This Mexican restaurant chain serves items like chargrilled steak and chicken burritos, tacos, quesadillas, seafood including lobster, shrimp, Mahi-Mahi, and their famous fish taco. Well-behaved leashed dogs are allowed at the outdoor tables.

Sam's Cafe 2566 E. Camelback Rd. Phoenix AZ   602-954-7100
http://www.sams-cafe.com
This restaurant specializes in Southwestern cuisine and welcomes dogs to their outdoor patio. Their entrees include the Fire Grilled Tuna, Desert Fire Pasta, Blackened Salmon Caesar, Grilled Vegetable Paella and the classic Southwest steak. Well-behaved leashed dogs are welcome at the outdoor tables. This restaurant is located in the dog-friendly Biltmore Fashion Park.

The Capital Grille 2502 E. Camelback Rd. Phoenix AZ   602-952-8900
http://www.thecapitalgrille.com
This steak house offers dry aged steaks, North Atlantic lobsters and fresh seafood. Well-behaved leashed dogs are allowed at the outdoor tables. This restaurant is located in the dog-friendly Biltmore Fashion Park.

The Farm at South Mountain 6106 South 32nd Street Phoenix AZ   602-276-6360
http://www.thefarmatsouthmountain.com/
This restaurant specializes in organic and natural foods. All seating is outdoors, either in their patio under pecan trees or at picnic tables. An organic garden is on the premises and they often use ingredients from it. They serve sandwiches, salads, and baked goods. Well-behaved leashed dogs are allowed at the outdoor tables. The restaurant is open daily weather permitting from 8am to 3pm, except they are closed on Mondays.

Vintage Market 2442 B East Camelback Rd. Phoenix AZ   602-955-4444
This cafe also has a wine bar and gourmet gift shop. They are open for dinner. Well-behaved leashed dogs are allowed at the outdoor tables. This restaurant is located in the dog-friendly Biltmore Fashion Park.

Wild Oats Natural Marketplace 3933 E. Camelback Rd. Phoenix AZ   602-954-0584
http://www.wildoats.com
This natural food market has a deli with outdoor seats. Well-behaved leashed dogs are allowed at the outdoor tables.

Willow House 149 W Mcdowell Rd Phoenix AZ   602-252-0272
This coffee shop serves pastries and coffee. Dogs are allowed at the outdoor tables.

Phoenix Area

Accommodations

Boulders Resort 34631 N Tom Darlington Rd Carefree AZ   480-488-9009
http://www.wyndham.com/Boulders/
There is a one-time $100 dog fee.

TOP 200 PLACE Carefree Resort and Villas 37220 Mule Train Road Carefree AZ   480-488-5300 (888-488-9034)

For a luxurious vacation getaway, a wedding, or a special business event, Carefree Resort wants your stay to be carefree. Backed by spectacular desert landscapes and mountain vistas, this full service resort and spa features spacious single and double guest rooms, luxury suites, casitas, and elegant condominiums in a private gated community. They are considered a premier golfing destination, and there is convenient access to 16 of Arizona's finest golf courses. They also offer such amenities as tennis courts/instruction, 3 pools, a clubhouse, fitness center, a grocery service, gourmet dining, room service, and a day spa and salon that offer a variety of massages and body treatments. Dogs of all sizes are allowed. There is a $50 one time fee per pet. Dogs must be quiet, leashed, cleaned up after, and the Do Not Disturb sign put on the door or a contact number left with the front desk if they are in the room alone.

Comfort Inn 255 N Kyrene Road Chandler AZ 480-705-8882 (877-424-6423)
Dogs of all sizes are allowed. There is a $10 per night per pet additional fee. Dogs must be leashed and cleaned up after. Dogs may only be left alone in the room if they will be quiet, well behaved, and the Do Not Disturb sign is put on the door.

Comfort Inn Chandler 255 N. Kyrene Road Chandler AZ 480-705-8882 (877-424-6423)
http://www.tristarhotels.com/ci-chandler
This hotel offers a free full hot breakfast daily, wireless high speed internet access,a heated outdoor pool, cable TV with expanded HBO and laundry facilities. There are no additional pet fees.

Red Roof Inn - Phoenix Chandler 7400 West Boston Avenue Chandler AZ 480-857-4969 (800-RED-ROOF)
One well-behaved family pet per room. Guest must notify front desk upon arrival. Guest is liable for any damages. In consideration of all guests, pets must never be left unattended in the guest rooms.

Sheraton Wild Horse Pass Resort & Spa 5594 W. Wild Horse Pass Blvd. Chandler AZ 602-225-0100 (888-625-5144)
Dogs up to 80 pounds are allowed. Dogs are restricted to rooms on the first floor only. There are no additional pet fees. Dogs are not allowed to be left alone in the room.

Windmill Inn of Chandler 3535 W Chandler Blvd Chandler AZ 480-812-9600
There is no additional pet fee. There is a special pet section of the hotel.

Best Western Inn Phoenix-Glendale 7116 N 59th Ave Glendale AZ 623-939-9431 (800-780-7234)
Dogs of all sizes are allowed. There is a $10 per night pet fee per pet. Smoking and non-smoking rooms available.

Best Western Phoenix Goodyear Inn 55 N Litchfield Rd Goodyear AZ 623-932-3210 (800-780-7234)
Dogs of all sizes are allowed. There is a $10 per night pet fee per pet. Smoking and non-smoking rooms available.

Hampton Inn 2000 N Litchfield Road Goodyear AZ 623-536-1313
Dogs of all sizes are allowed. There are no additional pet fees, however there must be a credit card on file. Dogs are not allowed to be left alone in the room.

Holiday Inn Express 1313 N. Litchfield Rd Goodyear AZ 623-535-1313 (877-270-6405)
Dogs of any size are permitted. There is a $25 refundable pet deposit.

Super 8 Goodyear/Phoenix Area 1710 N Dysart Rd Goodyear AZ 623-932-9622 (800-800-8000)
Dogs of all sizes are allowed. There is a $50 returnable deposit required per room. Reservations are recommended due to limited rooms for pets. Smoking and non-smoking rooms are available for pet rooms.

Arizona Golf Resort 425 S Power Road Mesa AZ 480-832-3202
http://www.azgolfresort.com/
There are no additional pet charges.

Days Inn Mesa Country Club 333 West Juanita Ave Mesa AZ 480-844-8900 (800-329-7466)
Dogs of all sizes are allowed. There is a $10 one time per pet fee per visit.

Holiday Inn Hotel and Suites 1600 S Country Club Mesa AZ 480-964-7000 (877-270-6405)
There is a $20 one time pet fee.

Homestead Village 1920 W Isabella Mesa AZ 480-752-2266
There is a $75 one time pet fee.

Motel 6 - Phoenix Mesa - Country Club Dr 336 West Hampton Avenue Mesa AZ 480-844-8899 (800-466-8356)
One well-behaved family pet per room. Guest must notify front desk upon arrival. Guest is liable for any damages. In consideration of all guests, pets must never be left unattended in the guest rooms.

Motel 6 - Phoenix Mesa - Main St 630 West Main Street Mesa AZ 480-969-8111 (800-466-8356)
One well-behaved family pet per room. Guest must notify front desk upon arrival. Guest is liable for any damages. In consideration of all guests, pets must never be left unattended in the guest rooms.

Motel 6 - Phoenix Mesa - US 60 1511 South Country Club Drive Mesa AZ 480-834-0066 (800-466-8356)
One well-behaved family pet per room. Guest must notify front desk upon arrival. Guest is liable for any damages. In consideration of all guests, pets must never be left unattended in the guest rooms.

Residence Inn by Marriott 941 W. Grove Ave. Mesa AZ 480-610-0100
Dogs up to 100 pounds are welcome. There is a $75 one time fee, and a pet policy to sign at check in.

Hermosa Inn 5532 N Palo Cristi Rd Paradise Valley AZ 602-955-8614
http://www.hermosainn.com/home.asp
There is a $50 refundable pet deposit.

Holiday Inn Express Hotel & Suites 16771 N. 84th Avenue Peoria AZ 623-853-1313 (877-270-6405)

Dogs of all sizes are allowed. There is a $50 refundable pet deposit. Pet owners must sign a pet waiver.
La Quinta Inn & Suites Phoenix West Peoria 16321 North 83rd Ave. Peoria AZ 623-487-1900 (800-531-5900)
Dogs of all sizes are allowed. There are no additional pet fees. Dogs must be leashed and cleaned up after.
3 Palms Resort Oasis Scottsdale 7707 E. McDowell Rd Scottsdale AZ 800-450-6013
http://www.scottsdale-resort-hotels.com
The hotel is located directly on El Dorado Park with miles of lakes and lawns. The hotel is near Old Town Scottsdale. Hotel provides rooms and suites, some with full kitchens.
Caleo Resort and Spa 4925 North Scottsdale Rd Scottsdale AZ
This Kimpton boutique hotel allows dogs of all sizes. It is located in the heart of Old Towne. There are no additional pet fees.
Caleo Resort and Spa 4925 N Scottsdale Road Scottsdale AZ 480-945-7666 (800-528-7867)
http://www.caleoresort.com/
This boutique style luxury resort and spa creates a tropical ambiance with its lush garden courtyard, open-air architecture, and the Mediterranean-inspired lagoon and sandy beach pool surrounded by cabanas. Other features/amenities include a contemporary American bistro with indoor and outdoor dining, room service, and a hosted evening wine hour. Dogs of all sizes are allowed for no additional fee. Dogs must be well mannered, and leashed and cleaned up after at all times.
Camelback Inn-JW Marriott Resort & Spa 5402 E Lincoln Drive Scottsdale AZ 480-948-1700 (800-24-CAMEL (242-2635))
Dogs of all sizes are allowed. There are no additional pet fees. Dogs must be leashed, cleaned up after, and removed or crated for housekeeping.
Comfort Suites Old Town Scottsdale 3275 N Drinkwater Blvd Scottsdale AZ 480-946-1111 (877-424-6423)
Dogs of all sizes are allowed. There are no additional pet fees. Dogs must be well behaved, leashed, and cleaned up after. The Do Not Disturb sign needs to be on the door if there is a pet alone in the room.
Country Inns & Suites by Carlson 10801 N 89th Place Scottsdale AZ 480-314-1200
Dogs of all sizes are allowed. There is a $50 one time additional pet fee.
Four Seasons Scottsdale 10600 East Crescent Moon Dr. Scottsdale AZ 480-515-5700
Dogs up to 15 pounds are allowed. There are no additional pet fees. Dogs are not allowed to be left alone in the room.
Hampton Inn 4415 N Civic Center Plaza Scottsdale AZ 480-942-9400
Dogs of all sizes are allowed. There is a $50 one time fee per stay.
Homestead Village 3560 N Marshall Way Scottsdale AZ 480-994-0297
There is a $75 one time pet fee.
Inn at the Citadel 8700 E Pinnacle Peak Rd Scottsdale AZ 480-585-6133
This B&B is located in an adobe-like complex of stores and next to the foothills of Pinnacle Peak. There are no additional pet fees.
La Quinta Inn & Suites Phoenix Scottsdale 8888 E. Shea Blvd. Scottsdale AZ 480-614-5300 (800-531-5900)
Dogs of all sizes are allowed. There are no additional pet fees. Dogs may not be left unattended, and they must be leashed and cleaned up after.
Motel 6 - Scottsdale 6848 E Camelback Road Scottsdale AZ 480-946-2280 (800-466-8356)
One well-behaved family pet per room. Guest must notify front desk upon arrival. Guest is liable for any damages. In consideration of all guests, pets must never be left unattended in the guest rooms.
Pima Inn and Suites 7330 N Pima Rd Scottsdale AZ 480-948-3800
There is a $10 one time pet fee. Dogs are not allowed in the lobby.
Residence Inn by Marriott 6040 N. Scottsdale Road Scottsdale AZ 480-948-8666
Dogs of any size are welcome. There is a $75 one time fee, and a pet policy to sign at check in.
Scottsdale Marriott at McDowell Mountains 16770 N Perimeter Drive Scottsdale AZ 480-502-3836 (800-288-6127)
Dogs up to 50 pounds are allowed. There is a $50 per night per room additional pet fee. Dogs may not be left alone in the room, and they must be leashed and cleaned up after.
Sleep Inn 16630 N. Scottsdale Rd Scottsdale AZ 480-998-9211 (877-424-6423)
http://www.sleepinn.com/hotel/A7812
This hotel has 107 rooms which have either 2 double beds or one King bed. They offer a deluxe continental breakfast, outdoor heated pool, spa, and fitness room. They accept all types of pets and charge a $10 per day fee for the first 5 days of your stay. No deposits are required.
Sleep Inn 16330 N Scottsdale Road Scottsdale AZ 480-998-9211 (877-424-6423)
Dogs of all sizes are allowed. There is a $10 per night per pet additional fee. Dogs may not be left alone in the room at any time, and they must be well behaved, leashed, and cleaned up after.
TownePlace Suites Scottsdale 10740 N 90th Street Scottsdale AZ 480-551-1100
Dogs of all sizes are allowed. There is a $75 one time pet fee per visit.
Hampton Inn 14783 W Grand Avenue Surprise AZ 623-537-9122
Dogs of all sizes are allowed. There is a $50 one time fee and a pet policy to sign at check in. They also request you kennel your pet when out.

Candlewood Suites 1335 W Baseline Road Tempe AZ   480-777-0440 (877-270-6405)
Dogs of all sizes are allowed. There is a $75 one time pet fee for stays up to 2 weeks. There is a $150 one time pet fee for stays over 2 weeks.
Comfort Inn and Suites 1031 E Apache Blvd Tempe AZ   480-966-7202 (877-424-6423)
Dogs of all sizes are allowed. There is a $50 refundable deposit per room. Dogs may not be left unattended, and they must be leashed and cleaned up after.
Country Inns & Suites by Carlson 1660 W Elliot Rd Tempe AZ   480-345-8585
Dogs of all sizes are allowed. There is a $55 additional pet fee every two nights. There is a $250 pet fee for stays over two weeks.
Hampton Inn 1429 N Scottsdale Road Tempe AZ   480-675-9799
Dogs of all sizes are allowed. There is a $50 per pet per stay fee and dogs are not to be left alone in the room.
Holiday Inn - Tempe 915 E. Apache Blvd Tempe AZ   480-968-3451 (877-270-6405)
One well-behaved large dog is okay. There are no additional pet fees.
Motel 6 - Phoenix Tempe - Arizona State U 1612 North Scottsdale Road Tempe AZ   480-945-9506 (800-466-8356)
One well-behaved family pet per room. Guest must notify front desk upon arrival. Guest is liable for any damages. In consideration of all guests, pets must never be left unattended in the guest rooms.
Motel 6 - Phoenix Tempe - Broadway - ASU 513 West Broadway Road Tempe AZ   480-967-8696 (800-466-8356)
One well-behaved family pet per room. Guest must notify front desk upon arrival. Guest is liable for any damages. In consideration of all guests, pets must never be left unattended in the guest rooms.
Motel 6 - Phoenix Tempe - Priest Dr - ASU 1720 South Priest Drive Tempe AZ   480-968-4401 (800-466-8356)
All well-behaved dogs are welcome. There are no additional pet fees.
Red Roof Inn - Phoenix Airport 2135 West 15th Street Tempe AZ   480-449-3205 (800-RED-ROOF)
One well-behaved family pet per room. Guest must notify front desk upon arrival. Guest is liable for any damages. In consideration of all guests, pets must never be left unattended in the guest rooms.
Residence Inn by Marriott 5075 S. Priest Drive Tempe AZ   480-756-2122
Dogs of any size are welcome. There is a $75 one time fee, and a pet policy to sign at check in.
Sheraton Phoenix Airport Hotel Tempe 1600 South 52nd St. Tempe AZ   480-967-6600 (888-625-5144)
Dogs up to 75 pounds are allowed. There is a $75 one time refundable pet fee per visit. Dogs are not allowed to be left alone in the room.
Studio 6 - TEMPE 4909 South Wendler Drive Tempe AZ   602-414-4470 (800-466-8356)
All well-behaved dogs are welcome. There is a $10 per day pet fee up to a maximum of $50 per visit.
TownePlace Suites Tempe 5223 S Priest Drive Tempe AZ   480-345-7889
Dogs of all sizes are allowed. There is a $75 one time pet fee per visit.
Motel 6 - Phoenix Sun City - Youngtown 11133 Grand Avenue Youngtown AZ   623-977-1318 (800-466-8356)
One well-behaved family pet per room. Guest must notify front desk upon arrival. Guest is liable for any damages. In consideration of all guests, pets must never be left unattended in the guest rooms.

Campgrounds and RV Parks

Mesa Spirit 3020 E Main Street Mesa AZ   480-832-1770
http://www.mesaspirit.com
Dogs of all sizes are allowed. There are no additional pet fees. Dogs must be quiet, well behaved, leashed and cleaned up after. Dogs must remain in the pet section of the campground. At least one person must be 55 years or older to stay at this resort. There is a dog walk area at the campground.
Silveridge RV Resort 8265 E Southern Mesa AZ   480-373-7000 (800-354-0054)
http://www.silveridge.com
Dogs of all sizes are allowed. There are no additional pet fees. Dogs must be leashed and cleaned up after, and they must stay in the pet section of the campground. At least one person must be 55 or older to stay at this resort. There is a dog walk area at the campground.

Attractions

TOP 200 PLACE **Goldfield Ghost Town** 4650 N Mammoth Mine Road Goldfield AZ   480-983-0333
http://www.goldfieldghosttown.com
Step back in time at this authentic 1890's ghost town, where you and your pet can ride on the only narrow gauge railroad in operation in Arizona (36 inches), tour through the mine together, pan for gold, witness an old west gun fight, or attend a chili cook-off. The only place pets are not allowed are in the shops on main street or in the general store. Dogs must be on lead at all times. Pet owners are asked to bring their own clean up bags, and to dispose of waste properly.

Stores

PetSmart Pet Store 808 W Warner Rd Chandler AZ   480-786-4464
Your licensed and well-behaved leashed dog is allowed in the store.
PetSmart Pet Store 2840 W Chandler Blvd Chandler AZ   480-782-7727
Your licensed and well-behaved leashed dog is allowed in the store.
PetSmart Pet Store 2860 E Germann Rd Chandler AZ   480-722-1358
Your licensed and well-behaved leashed dog is allowed in the store.
PetSmart Pet Store 855 N 54th St Chandler AZ   480-785-7526
Your licensed and well-behaved leashed dog is allowed in the store.
Petco Pet Store 1860 West Chandler Blvd Chandler AZ   480-792-6330
Your licensed and well-behaved leashed dog is allowed in the store.
Petco Pet Store 1415 East Warner Rd Gilbert AZ   480-558-4588
Your licensed and well-behaved leashed dog is allowed in the store.
Petco Pet Store 1015 Baseline Rd Gilbert AZ   480-813-4297
Your licensed and well-behaved leashed dog is allowed in the store.
PetSmart Pet Store 7290 W Bell Rd Glendale AZ   623-334-3600
Your licensed and well-behaved leashed dog is allowed in the store.
PetSmart Pet Store 5707 W Northern Ave Glendale AZ   623-931-6743
Your licensed and well-behaved leashed dog is allowed in the store.
Petco Pet Store 6090 West Behrend Drive Glendale AZ   623-376-0621
Your licensed and well-behaved leashed dog is allowed in the store.
Petco Pet Store 9480 West Northern Avenue Glendale AZ   623-877-2730
Your licensed and well-behaved leashed dog is allowed in the store.
PetSmart Pet Store 1733 S Stapley Rd Mesa AZ   480-539-8552
Your licensed and well-behaved leashed dog is allowed in the store.
PetSmart Pet Store 6932 E Hampton Mesa AZ   480-830-7282
Your licensed and well-behaved leashed dog is allowed in the store.
PetSmart Pet Store 6632 E McKellips Rd Mesa AZ   480-325-4578
Your licensed and well-behaved leashed dog is allowed in the store.
PetSmart Pet Store 4920 S Power Rd Mesa AZ   480-279-3860
Your licensed and well-behaved leashed dog is allowed in the store.
Petco Pet Store 2027 E University Mesa AZ   480-827-1187
Your licensed and well-behaved leashed dog is allowed in the store.
Petco Pet Store 1540 West Southern Mesa AZ   480-834-9088
Your licensed and well-behaved leashed dog is allowed in the store.
Petco Pet Store 2090 S Power Rd Mesa AZ   480-854-1550
Your licensed and well-behaved leashed dog is allowed in the store.
PetSmart Pet Store 9960 N 91st Ave Peoria AZ   623-486-8700
Your licensed and well-behaved leashed dog is allowed in the store.
PetSmart Pet Store 10030 N 90th St Scottsdale AZ   480-391-1647
Your licensed and well-behaved leashed dog is allowed in the store.
Petco Pet Store 8910 East Indian Bend Rd Scottsdale AZ   480-368-8015
Your licensed and well-behaved leashed dog is allowed in the store.
PetSmart Pet Store 13764 W Bell Rd Surprise AZ   623-546-8500
Your licensed and well-behaved leashed dog is allowed in the store.
PetSmart Pet Store 1315 W Elliot Rd Tempe AZ   480-961-9710
Your licensed and well-behaved leashed dog is allowed in the store.
Petco Pet Store 1835 E Guadalupe #112 Tempe AZ   480-820-0603
Your licensed and well-behaved leashed dog is allowed in the store.

Off-Leash Dog Parks

Shawnee Bark Park 1400 W. Mesquite Chandler AZ   480-782-2727
The Shawnee Bark Park is a fenced dog park. The park is open from 6:30 am to 10:30 pm daily. Children under 12 are not allowed in the dog park.
Snedigar Bark Park 4500 S. Basha Rd Chandler AZ   480-782-2727
The Snedigar Bark Park is a fenced dog park. Located at the Snedigar Sportsplex, the dog park is open from 6:30 am to 10:30 pm daily. Children under 12 are not allowed in the dog park.
West Chandler Bark Park 250 S. Kyrene Rd Chandler AZ   480-782-2727
The West Chandler Bark Park is a fenced dog park. Located in West Chandler Park, the dog park is open from 6:30 am to 10:30 pm daily. Children under 12 are not allowed in the dog park.
Cosmo Dog Park 2502 E. Ray Road Gilbert AZ   480-503-6200
Thanks to a reader who writes "This is a brand new park that just opened in July '06. It has one amazing feature - a fenced man made doggie beach with small rocks instead of sand and a small pier for the dogs to jump off of

and into the water." For the dogs who prefer dry land there is also a four acre dog park. There are lights for night use and hoses to clean your dog. The dog park is open from 6 am to 10 pm. The dog park is located on the north-east corner of Ray Road and Greenfield.

Dog Park at Crossroads 2155 E. Knox Rd Gilbert AZ   480-503-6200
The Dog Park at Crossroads is open from 6 am to 10 pm daily. It is 2 acres and fenced. It is partially lit for night use. There are tables and benches. There are separate areas for large and small dogs. Crossroads Park is located on the west side of Greenfield Road, north of Ray. To get to the park go west on Knox Rd from Greenfield.

Foothills Park Dog Park 57th Avenue and Union Hills Drive Glendale AZ   623-930-2820
This fenced dog park is located in Foothills Park in Glendale. The dog park is located next to the Foothills Library parking lot.

Northern Horizon Dog Park 63rd and Northern Avenue Glendale AZ   623-930-2820
This dog park is located in Northern Horizon Park. It has a large fenced in area for larger dogs and a smaller play area for small dogs.

Saguaro Ranch Dog Park 63rd Avenue Glendale AZ
This fully fenced dog park has a large grassy area with trees, fire hydrants, benches and even a doggie drinking fountain. The park is located at 63rd Avenue and Mountain View Road. The off-leash area is just north of the west parking lot and just south of the softball complex. Thanks to one of our readers for recommending this dog park!

Quail Run Park Dog Park 4155 E. Virginia Mesa AZ   480-644-2352
This park offers a completely fenced 3 acre dog park. Amenities include separate areas for timid and active dogs, park benches, water fountains for people and dogs, and doggie poop bags. The dog park is closed every Thursday for maintenance. Dogs must be on leash when outside the off-leash area.

Chaparral Park Dog Park 5401 N. Hayden Road Scottsdale AZ   480-312-2353
This park offers a two acre fenced designated off-leash area for dogs. The temporary off-leash area is on Hayden Road, north of Jackrabbit. The permanent dog park will be located on the southeast corner of Hayden and McDonald Drives after the water treatment facility is completed. Dogs must be on leash when outside the dog park.

Horizon Park Dog Park 15444 N. 100th Street Scottsdale AZ   480-312-2650
This park offers a designated off-leash area for dogs. The park is located at 100th Street and Thompson Peak. Dogs must be on leash when outside the off-leash area.

Vista del Camino Park Dog Park 7700 E. Roosevelt Street Scottsdale AZ   480-312-2330
This park offers a designated off-leash area for dogs. The park is located at Hayden and Roosevelt. Dogs must be on leash when outside the off-leash area.

Creamery Park 8th Street and Una Avenue Tempe AZ   480-350-5200
This park offers a designated off-leash area for dogs. Dogs must be on leash when outside the off-leash area.

Jaycee Park 5th Street and Hardy Drive Tempe AZ   480-350-5200
This park offers a small designated off-leash area for dogs. Dogs must be on leash when outside the off-leash area.

Mitchell Park Mitchell Drive and 9th Street Tempe AZ   480-350-5200
This park offers a designated off-leash area for dogs. Dogs must be on leash when outside the off-leash area.

Papago Park Curry Road and College Avenue Tempe AZ   480-350-5200
This park offers a designated off-leash area for dogs. Dogs must be on leash when outside the off-leash area.

Tempe Sports Complex Dog Park Warner Rd & Hardy Dr Tempe AZ   480-350-5200
This fenced dog park is open from 6 am to 10 pm. It is located at the Tempe Sports Complex.

Outdoor Restaurants

Dooby's Grill 2909 Dobson Rd Chandler AZ   480-756-0469
This restaurant serves Middle Eastern food. Dogs are allowed at the outdoor tables.

Iguana Mack's 1371 N Alma School Rd Chandler AZ   480-899-6735
This restaurant serves American food. Dogs are allowed at the outdoor tables. They have misters in the summer and heat lamps in the winter for you and your pet.

Starbucks 20249 North 67th Ave #B Glendale AZ   623-362-9288
This coffee shop serves hot and cold drinks and pastries. Dogs are allowed at the outdoor tables. Water bowls are provided for your pet.

Starbucks 7410 W Bell Rd #310 Glendale AZ   623-878-1717
This coffee shop serves drinks and pastries. Dogs are allowed at the outdoor tables. Water bowls are provided for your pets.

Honey Baked Ham and Co and Cafe 6736 E Baseline Rd Mesa AZ   480-854-3300
This restaurant serves American food. Dogs are allowed at the outdoor tables.

The Mesa Monastery 4810 East McKillips Mesa AZ   480-474-4477
This restaurant and bar provides American food that you cook on a grill. Dogs are allowed at the outdoor tables. Dogs must be on a leash at all time and must cleaned up after.

Baja Fresh Mexican Grill 4032 N. Scottsdale Rd, Ste 1 Scottsdale AZ   480-429-8270

http://www.bajafresh.com/
This Mexican restaurant chain offers a variety of items on their menu including burritos, tacos, salads, quesadillas, fajitas, and enchiladas. Well-behaved leashed dogs are allowed at the outdoor tables.
Muze Bistro 15680 N Pima Rd Scottsdale AZ 480-222-3366
This restaurant serves Seafood and American food. Dogs are allowed at the outdoor tables. A dish of water and a cookie are provided for your pet.
Rubio's Fresh Mexican Grill 15704 N. Pima Rd., #C8 & 9 Scottsdale AZ 480-348-0195
http://www.rubios.com/
This Mexican restaurant chain serves items like chargrilled steak and chicken burritos, tacos, quesadillas, seafood including lobster, shrimp, Mahi-Mahi, and their famous fish taco. Well-behaved leashed dogs are allowed at the outdoor tables.
Rubio's Fresh Mexican Grill 32415 N. Scottsdale Road, Ste. C Scottsdale AZ 480-575-7280
http://www.rubios.com/
This Mexican restaurant chain serves items like chargrilled steak and chicken burritos, tacos, quesadillas, seafood including lobster, shrimp, Mahi-Mahi, and their famous fish taco. Well-behaved leashed dogs are allowed at the outdoor tables.
Sugar Daddy's 3102 N. Scottsdale Rd. Scottsdale AZ 480-970-6556
http://www.sugardaddysaz.com
This dog-friendly restaurant offers eclectic food where canjun meets southwestern flavors. Menu items include starters like Coconut Shrimp and Black Bean Quesadillas, and salads like the Southwest Chicken Salad and the Mediterranean Calamari Salad. Entrees and meals include sandwiches, pizza and pasta. The restaurant has a 5,000 square foot temperature controlled patio with six air conditioning units, misters and heaters. Well-behaved leashed dogs are welcome at the outdoor tables. They serve water to pooches. Sugar Daddy's also offers a Sunday brunch from 10am until 4pm where your leashed pooch is also welcome. They have lots of food and a "Build Your Own Bloody Mary Bar." From 1pm until 6pm there is live music on the patio. There is also a complimentary coffee station and all of the tips go to the Association of Dog Owners Group (ADOG). This non-profit organization is dedicated to promoting the Fountain Hills off-leash dog park and responsible pet ownership. This restaurant is open for lunch and dinner.
Veneto Trattoria 6137 N Scottsdale Road #B115 Scottsdale AZ 480-948-9928
This restaurant serves Italian food. Dogs are allowed at the outdoor tables.
Baja Fresh Mexican Grill 414 W. University Drive Tempe AZ 480-446-3116
http://www.bajafresh.com/
This Mexican restaurant chain offers a variety of items on their menu including burritos, tacos, salads, quesadillas, fajitas, and enchiladas. Well-behaved leashed dogs are allowed at the outdoor tables.
Rubio's Fresh Mexican Grill 1712 East Guadalupe Rd., Ste. 109 Tempe AZ 480-897-3884
http://www.rubios.com/
This Mexican restaurant chain serves items like chargrilled steak and chicken burritos, tacos, quesadillas, seafood including lobster, shrimp, Mahi-Mahi, and their famous fish taco. Well-behaved leashed dogs are allowed at the outdoor tables.
The Boathouse 5394 S Lakeshore Drive Tempe AZ 480-820-0660
Dogs are allowed at the outdoor tables.

Events
People and Pooch Pajama Party 37220 Mule Train Road Carefree AZ 480-497-8296
This annual event sponsored by Friends for Life Animal Sanctuary to benefit our four-legged companions kicks off the May "Be Kind to Animals Week" with this unique pajama party full of food, fun, raffles, shelter tours, movies, and more. Dogs and cats are welcome to the event, and animals will also be available for adoption. Dogs must be well behaved, leashed, and cleaned up after at all times.
Friends for Life Barktoberfest 2048 E Baseline Road Mesa AZ 480-899-5253
http://www.azfriends.org/
This free, annual October event sponsored by Friends for Life Animal Sanctuary for our four-legged companions is a full day of games, contests, raffles, vendors, costume and talent contests, a doggy wash, and a lot more. Dogs must be well mannered, leashed, and cleaned up after at all times.
Walk to Save the Animals 620 N Mill Avenue Tempe AZ 602-273-6852
http://www.aawl.org
This annual event, sponsored by the Arizona Animal Welfare League, is usually held in October at Tempe Town Lake. Hundreds of pooches and their owners gather for this benefit walk that raises tens of thousands of dollars every year for Arizona's oldest and largest "No Kill" shelter. There will also be raffles, and a variety of vendors for pet related merchandise, services, and care. Dogs must be well behaved, leashed, and cleaned up after at all times.

Day Kennels
PetsHotel by PetsMart Day Kennel 7920 W. Bell Road Glendale AZ 623-979-0016

http://www.petsmart.com/PETsHOTEL/
This PetSmart store offers day care, day camp and overnight care. Their hours are 7 am - 9 pm M-F, Sunday hours are 7am - 7pm. You may drop off and pick up your dog at anytime that the store is open. Dogs are required to have proof of current rabies, DPT and bordatella vaccines.
PetsHotel by PetsMart Day Kennel 10030 N. 90th St. Scottsdale AZ   480-391-1647
http://www.petsmart.com/PETsHOTEL/
This PetSmart store offers day camp only. You may drop off your pet during their business hours - 7 am - 7 pm M-S, and Dunday 9 am - 5 pm. Dogs are required to have proof of up to date rabies, DPP and Bordatella vaccinations.
PetsHotel by PetsMart Day Kennel 1315 WE Elliot Rd. Tempe AZ   480-785-0587
http://www.petsmart.com/PETsHOTEL/
This PetSmart offers day care, day camp and overnight care. You may drop off your dog and pick up your dog between the hours of 7 am - 7 pm M-S and Sunday between 7 am - 7 pm. Up to date rabies, DPP and Bordatella vacines are required.

Picacho

Campgrounds and RV Parks
Picacho Peak State Park Picacho Peak Road Picacho AZ   520-466-3183
This park has a variety of trails varying in length and difficulty. The trails are open from 8 am to sunset. Dogs are allowed at no additional fee. Dogs may not be left unattended, they must be on no more than a 6 foot leash, and be cleaned up after. Dogs are not allowed on the advanced trails. The camping and tent areas also allow dogs. There is a dog walk area at the campground. There are no water hookups at the campground.

Parks
Picacho Peak State Park P. O. Box 275 Picacho AZ   520-466-3183
This park has a rich natural and cultural history, and was once used as a landmark by early explorers. The park offers picnic areas, ramadas, restrooms, a variety of trails with varying difficulty and interests, historical markers, playground, and the Civil War Re-enactment of 3 different battles. The park is open from 8:00 a.m. to 10:00 p.m. Dogs of all sizes are allowed. Dogs must be leashed and cleaned up after, and they may not be left unattended at any time. Dogs are allowed on the trails, but not in any park buildings. They also have a campground (some sites with electric) with grills and a dumpstation.

Pinetop

Accommodations
Buck Springs Resort 6126 Buck Springs Road Pinetop AZ   928-369-3554 (800-339-1909)
http://www.bucksspringsresort.com/
Sitting on 20 acres of tall pines offering lots of hiking trails, this scenic resort features 20 one bedroom cottages and 4 three bedroom townhouses around a wonderful courtyard area with benches and a small raised pavilion. There are barbecues available, and all units have a covered front porch, cable TV, a wood burning stove, and are fully equipped with all the essentials, including the kitchen. Dogs of all sizes are allowed for an additional fee of $10 per night per pet, and they must be declared at the time of reservations. Dogs may only be left alone in the room if they will be well behaved and quiet, and they must be leashed and cleaned up after at all times.
Holiday Inn Express 431E. White Mountain Blvd Pinetop AZ   928-367-6077 (877-270-6405)
Dogs of all sizes are allowed. There is a $10 per day additional pet fee. Pets may not be left unattended in the rooms.

Prescott

Accommodations
Apple Creek Cottages 1001 White Spar Prescott AZ   928-445-7321 (888-455-8003)
http://www.applecreekcottages.com
These pet-friendly cottages are one, two or three bedrooms. Pets are allowed with a refundable $35.00 deposit.
Lynx Creek Farm Bed and Breakfast SR69 and Onyx Rd Prescott AZ   928-778-9573

There is an additional $10 per day pet fee. Pets may not be left in the room unattended.
Motel 6 - Prescott 1111 East Sheldon Street Prescott AZ   928-776-0160 (800-466-8356)
One well-behaved family pet per room. Guest must notify front desk upon arrival. Guest is liable for any damages. In consideration of all guests, pets must never be left unattended in the guest rooms.
Super 8 Motel - Prescott 1105 E. Sheldon Street Prescott AZ   928-776-1282 (800-800-8000)
http://www.innworks.com/prescott
$10/stay for up to 3 dogs in one room. FREE 8-minute long distance call each night. FREE continental breakfast. Coffee maker, night light, clock/radio, safe in each room. Seasonal outdoor pool. On-site guest laundry. Kids 12 & under stay free. On Sheldon St (BR 89), West of intersection of US 89 & AZ 69.
Days Inn Prescott 7875 E Hwy 69 Prescott Valley AZ   928-772-8600 (800-329-7466)
Dogs of all sizes are allowed. There is a $50 returnable deposit required per room.
Motel 6 - Prescott Valley 8383 East US Route 69 Prescott Valley AZ   928-772-2200 (800-466-8356)
One well-behaved family pet per room. Guest must notify front desk upon arrival. Guest is liable for any damages. In consideration of all guests, pets must never be left unattended in the guest rooms.

Campgrounds and RV Parks
Granite Basin Yavapai Campground/Prescott National Forest Iron Springs Road Prescott AZ   928-443-8000
Granite Mountain Wilderness is very popular due to its proximity to Prescott (only 20 minutes by paved road) and the unique experience it offers for hikers among huge granite boulders and varying trails, rock formations, and the spectacular view of the surrounding area. Dogs of all sizes are allowed for no additional fee, and they are allowed to go everywhere their owners can go except public buildings. Dogs may only be left for short periods on the campsite if they will be quiet and well behaved, and they must be leashed and cleaned up after. The camping and tent areas also allow dogs. There is a dog walk area at the campground.
Granite Basin Yavapai Campground/Prescott National Forest Iron Springs Road Prescott AZ   928-443-8000
Granite Mountain Wilderness is very popular due to its proximity to Prescott (only 20 minutes by paved road) and the unique experience it offers for hikers among huge granite boulders and varying trails, rock formations, and the spectacular view of the surrounding area. Dogs of all sizes are allowed for no additional fee, and they are allowed to go everywhere their owners can go except public buildings. Dogs may only be left for short periods on the campsite if they will be quiet and well behaved, and they must be leashed and cleaned up after. The camping and tent areas also allow dogs. There is a dog walk area at the campground. There are no electric or water hookups at the campgrounds.
Prescott National Forest 344 S Cortez Street Prescott AZ   928-443-8000
http://www.fs.fed.us/r3/prescott/
This forest of over a million acres provides spectacular scenery, a rich cultural history, and diverse ecosystems that support a large variety of plants, animals, and recreation. Dogs of all sizes are allowed at no additional fee. Dogs may not be left unattended, and they must be leashed and cleaned up after. Dogs are allowed on the trails. This campground is closed during the off-season. The camping and tent areas also allow dogs. There is a dog walk area at the campground.
Willow Lake RV and Camping Park 1617 Heritage Park Road Prescott AZ   928-445-6311
Dogs of all sizes are allowed. There are no additional pet fees. Dogs must be leashed and cleaned up after. The camping and tent areas also allow dogs. There is a dog walk area at the campground.

Stores
PetSmart Pet Store 277 N Walker Rd Prescott AZ   928-776-9636
Your licensed and well-behaved leashed dog is allowed in the store.
Petco Pet Store 1931 SR-69 Prescott AZ   928-708-0212
Your licensed and well-behaved leashed dog is allowed in the store.

Off-Leash Dog Parks
Willow Creek Dog Park Willow Creek Road Prescott AZ   928-777-1100
This completely fenced dog park offers a separate section for small and large dogs. Amenities include picnic tables, benches, water and shade. The dog park is located next to Willow Creek Park. The park is located just north of the junction of Willow Lake and Willow Creek Roads.

Quartzsite

Accommodations
Super 8 Quartzsite 2050 Dome Rock Rd Quartzsite AZ   928-927-8080 (800-800-8000)

Dogs of all sizes are allowed. There is a $5 per night pet fee per pet. Smoking and non-smoking rooms are available for pet rooms.

Campgrounds and RV Parks
B-10 Campground 615 Main Quartzsite AZ   928-927-4393
Dogs of all sizes are allowed. There are no additional pet fees. Dogs must be leashed and cleaned up after. There are some breed restrictions. This RV park is closed during the off-season. There is a dog walk area at the campground.

Roosevelt

Parks
Tonto National Monument HC 02 Box 4602 Roosevelt AZ   928-467-2241
http://www.nps.gov/tont/index.htm
Dogs on leash are allowed in the park and the Lower Cliff Dwelling Trail. Dogs are not allowed on the Upper Cliff Dwelling Trail.

Safford

Accommodations
Days Inn Safford 520 E Hwy 70 Safford AZ   928-428-5000 (800-329-7466)
Dogs of all sizes are allowed. There is a $10 per night pet fee per pet.
Quality Inn and Suites 420 E Hwy 70 Safford AZ   928-428-3200 (877-424-6423)
Dogs of all sizes are allowed. There is a $10 per night per room additional pet fee. Dogs may not be left alone in the rooms, and they must be leashed and cleaned up after.

Campgrounds and RV Parks
Roper Lake State Park 101 E. Roper Lake Road Safford AZ   928-428-6760
This park has 2 camping sections, and offers a model Indian village, land and water recreation, and a natural hot spring. Dogs are allowed at no additional fee. Dogs may not be left unattended, and they must be leashed and cleaned up after. Dogs are not allowed in park buildings or on the beach, but they are allowed on the trails. The camping and tent areas also allow dogs. There is a dog walk area at the campground. Dogs are allowed in the camping cabins.

Sedona

Accommodations
El Portal - Sedona's Luxury Hacienda 95 Portal Lane Sedona AZ   928-203-9405 (800-313-0017)
http://www.elPortalsedona.com
There are five pet rooms at this 1910 adobe hacienda located in the center of Sedona. Pets are allowed for a $35 non-refundable cleaning fee.
Hilton 90 Ridge Trail Drive Sedona AZ   928-284-4040
Dogs up to 50 pounds are allowed. There is a $50 one time fee and a pet policy to sign at check in. Pet rooms are located on the 1st floor.
Kings Ransom Sedona Hotel 771 Hwy 179 Sedona AZ   928-282-7151 (800-846-6164)
http://www.kingsransomsedona.com/
Set on 8 scenic acres with superb views, this luxury boutique hotel also provides a great location for world class shopping, visiting art galleries, and numerous recreational activities. Some of the amenities include a 1-acre garden courtyard with a waterfall, a vast wilderness area behind the hotel for some great hiking adventures, an eatery, and all the rooms have a private balcony or patio. Dogs of all sizes are allowed for an additional fee of $15 per night per pet. Dogs must be well mannered, leashed and cleaned up after at all times, and they must be removed or crated for housekeeping. Directly adjacent to the property, the hotel created a Doggy Park complete with plastic bags and a receptacle for disposal. They ask that dogs are not walked in the courtyard, rather at the Doggy Park or on the trails behind the hotel.
L'Auberge de Sedona 301 L'Auberge Lane Sedona AZ   928-282-1661

http://www.lauberge.com
This premier destination hotel is a two-story European-style building with two fireplaces, 19 guest rooms and two junior suites (each with king beds and a private patio or balcony), a fine dining restaurant, and many amenities. Dogs of all sizes are allowed for an additional pet fee of $75 per room. Dogs must be quiet, very well behaved, leashed at all times, and cleaned up after.

Matterhorn Motor Lodge 230 Apple Ave Sedona AZ 928-282-7176
http://www.sedona.net/hotel/matterhorn/
This inn is located in the center of uptown Sedona.

Oak Creek Terrace Resort 4548 N. Hwy. 89A Sedona AZ 928-282-3562 (800-224-2229)
http://www.oakcreekterrace.com
Relax by the creek or in one of the jacuzzi rooms. Dogs are welcome with a $35 non-refundable pet fee. Ammenities include in-room fireplaces, barbeque and picnic areas, air conditioning and cable TV.

Quail Ridge Resort 120 Canyon Circle Dr Sedona AZ 928-284-9327
http://www.quailridgeresort.com/
There is a $10 per day pet fee.

Sky Ranch Lodge Airport Rd Sedona AZ 928-282-6400 (888-708-6400)
http://www.skyranchlodge.com/
There is a $10.00 per day pet fee, dogs up to 75 pounds ok.

The Views Inn Sedona 65 E Cortez Drive Sedona AZ 928-284-2487
A convenient location, clean, comfortable, and affordable, this inn also offers a pool, spa, and great views. Dogs of all sizes are allowed. There is a $10 per night per pet additional fee. Dogs must be leashed and cleaned up after.

Campgrounds and RV Parks
Rancho Sedona RV Park 135 Bear Wallow Lane Sedona AZ 928-282-7255
http://www.ranchosedona.com
Dogs of all sizes are allowed. There is a $1 per night per pet additional fee, and there are discounts for AAA or Good Sam members. Dogs may not be left unattended outside, and they must be quiet, leashed, and cleaned up after. There is a dog walk area at the campground.

Attractions
TOP 200 PLACE Adventure Company Jeep Tours 336 Hwy 179 Sedona AZ 928-204-1973
http://www.sedonajeeptours.com/
This company offers 4-wheeling fun in their convertible jeeps with a variety of tours of Sedona's spectacular red rock country. They offer the history of the amazing geological process responsible for the incredible scenery. You will also learn about the Native American and pioneer history, and the diverse plant and animal life of the area. Your well behaved dog is allowed to journey with you as long as none of the other riders object. There is also the option of renting out the jeep for your party only. If your dog is a large breed and needs a seat, there may be the cost of a child's ticket for the pet. Dogs must be leashed at all times and cleaned up after.

Red Rock Country - Coconino National Forest various Sedona AZ 928-527-3600
This park offers a colorful collection of buttes, pinnacles, mesas, canyons and red rock vistas. Over the years, this area has served as the setting of many western novels and movies and has been the subject of uncounted paintings, photographs and other works of art. Your leashed dog is allowed on the scenic Red Rock Country hiking trails with you.

Stores
Bark N' Purr Pet Care Center 30 Finley Drive Sedona AZ 928-282-4108
This pet care center provides a variety of services and supplies for your pet. They offer pet sitting or overnight care, heated floors, indoor and outdoor runs, grooming, food, and more. They are open Monday-Friday 8:30am-6:00pm, Saturday 8:30am-1:00pm, and closed Sunday.

Sedona Pet Supply 104 Coffee Pot Sedona AZ 928-203-9898
Well behaved dogs of all sizes are allowed in this pet supply store. Dogs must be on leash and under owner's control at all times. The store is open Monday-Friday from 9 am to 5:30 pm, Saturday from 9 am to 4 pm, and closed on Sunday.

Three Dog Bakery 320 N Hwy 89A Sedona AZ 928-282-5550
http://www.threedog.com
Three Dog Bakery provides cookies and snacks for your dog as well as some boutique items. You well-behaved, leashed dog is welcome.

Parks
Slide Rock State Park 6871 N Hwy 89A Sedona AZ 928-282-3034

This day use park was put on the National Register of Historic Places in 1991. In addition to sharing a rich natural and cultural history, this park provides swimming, picnicking, birdwatching, fishing (no glass bait jars please), a nature trail and access to other trails, a volleyball court, and special events and programs. Dogs of all sizes are allowed at no additional fee. Dogs are not allowed at the creek, in the water or at the swim beaches. The dogs are allowed to go as far as the top of the stairs that lead to some of these areas. They are allowed on the trails on lead. Dogs may not be left unattended at any time, including being left in automobiles. Dogs must be on leash and under control at all times, and be cleaned up after.

Outdoor Restaurants
Cucina Rustica 7000 Hwy 179 Sedona AZ 928-284-3010
http://www.cucinarustica.com/
This award winning restaurant serves Mediterranean-Italian dishes in a charming setting of Old World architecture. They open at 5pm every day, and reservations are recommended. Your pet may join you on the patio. They are not allowed to go through the restaurant. Dogs must be leashed at all times and kept close.
Troia's Pizza Pasta Amore 1885 W Hwy 89A Sedona AZ 928-282-0123
This pizzeria opens up their outside dining after Memorial Day, and your well behaved, leashed dog may join you on the patio. They suggest, however, that you call ahead to confirm they are serving outside. They are open from Tuesday to Sunday at 5 pm.

Show Low

Accommodations
Best Western Paint Pony Lodge 581 W Deuce of Clubs Show Low AZ 928-537-5773 (800-780-7234)
Dogs of all sizes are allowed. There is a $10 per night pet fee per pet. Smoking and non-smoking rooms available.
Days Inn Show Low 480 W Deuce of Clubs Show Low AZ 928-537-4356 (800-329-7466)
Dogs of all sizes are allowed. There is a $10 one time per pet fee per visit.
Motel 6 - Show Low 1941 East Duece of Clubs Show Low AZ 928-537-7694 (800-466-8356)
One well-behaved family pet per room. Guest must notify front desk upon arrival. Guest is liable for any damages. In consideration of all guests, pets must never be left unattended in the guest rooms.

Campgrounds and RV Parks
Fool Hollow Lake Rec Area 1500 N Fool Hollow Lake Road Show Low AZ 928-537-3680
Nestled among 100 foot pine trees along a lake at 6300 feet, this rec area offers an impressive list of weekend activities May through September such as parades, car shows, festivals, concerts, rodeos, and more, in addition to a variety of land and water recreation. Dogs are allowed throughout the park for no additional fee, and on the trails, as long as they are on lead at all times, and cleaned up after. The campground offers 123 camping sites, a dump station, fish cleaning station, boat ramps, picnic tables, picnic ramadas, grills, playgrounds, private showers and restrooms. The camping and tent areas also allow dogs. There is a dog walk area at the campground.
Fool Hollow Lake Rec Area 1500 N Fool Hollow Lake Road Show Low AZ 928-537-3680
Nestled among 100 foot pine trees along a lake at 6300 feet, this rec area offers an impressive list of weekend activities May through September such as parades, car shows, festivals, concerts, rodeos, and more, in addition to a variety of land and water recreation. Dogs are allowed throughout the park for no additional fee, and on the trails, as long as they are on lead at all times, and cleaned up after. The campground offers 123 camping sites, a dump station, fish cleaning station, boat ramps, picnic tables, picnic ramadas, grills, playgrounds, private showers and restrooms. The camping and tent areas also allow dogs. There is a dog walk area at the campground.
Fool Hollow Lake Recreation Area 1500 N Fool Hollow Lake Show Low AZ 928-537-3680
This park offers 100 foot pine trees and a large mountain lake. The lake is at 6,300 feet altitude and also provides a home for Great Blue Herons. Dogs of all sizes are allowed. There are no additional pet fees. Dogs may not be left unattended, they must be on no more than a 6 foot leash, and be cleaned up after. Dogs must be quiet and well behaved. Dogs are not allowed in any of the buildings. The camping and tent areas also allow dogs. There is a dog walk area at the campground.

Sierra Vista

Accommodations

Motel 6 - Sierra Vista - Fort Huachuca 1551 East Fry Boulevard Sierra Vista AZ   520-459-5035 (800-466-8356)
One well-behaved family pet per room. Guest must notify front desk upon arrival. Guest is liable for any damages. In consideration of all guests, pets must never be left unattended in the guest rooms.
Quality Inn 1631 S Hwy 92 Sierra Vista AZ   520-458-7900 (877-424-6423)
Dogs of all sizes are allowed. There is a $10 per night per pet additional fee. Dogs must be leashed, cleaned up after, and crated when left alone in the room.
Super 8 Motel - Sierra Vista 100 Fab Avenue Sierra Vista AZ   520-459-5380 (800-800-8000)
http://www.innworks.com/sierravista
$10/stay for up to 3 dogs in one room. FREE 8-minute long distance call each night. FREE continental breakfast. Coffee maker, refrigerator, night light, clock/radio, safe in each room. Seasonal outdoor pool. On-site guest laundry. Kids 12 & under stay free. I-10, Exit 302, straight on Buffalo Soldier Trail, 30 miles, through light to Fry Blvd.; Left 1 blk.

Springerville

Campgrounds and RV Parks
Apache-Sitgreaves National Forest 309 S Mountain Avenue Springerville AZ   928-333-4301
http://www.fs.fed.us/r3/asnf/
Two forests were combined creating over 2 million acres of spectacular scenery, hundreds of miles of trails, a variety of recreational pursuits, and more areas of water than any other Southwestern National Forest. Dogs of all sizes are allowed at no additional fee. Dogs may not be left unattended, and they must be leashed and cleaned up after. Dogs are allowed on the trails. The camping and tent areas also allow dogs. There is a dog walk area at the campground. There are no electric or water hookups at the campground.

St Johns

Campgrounds and RV Parks
Lyman Lake State Park On Hwy 180/191 11 miles E of St Johns St Johns AZ   928-337-4441
This park shares the ancient historic Pueblo Trail, and offers many sites of interest and villages of the Hopi people. Dogs of all sizes are allowed, and there are no additional pet fees for tent or RV sites. There is a $5 one time additional pet fee for the cabins. Dogs must be leashed and cleaned up after. The camping and tent areas also allow dogs. There is a dog walk area at the campground. Dogs are allowed in the camping cabins.

Superior

Attractions
Boyce Thompson Arboretum 37615 U.S. Highway 60 Superior AZ   520-689-2723
This is the oldest arboretum and botanical garden in the American Southwest. This 320 acre collection of deseart plants was founded in the 1920s. It is set at the foot of the Picketpost Mountain. The arboretum has two miles of walking path and is a place for children and adults to learn about our desert ecosystems. Highlights include the Heritage Rose Garden, the three acre Cactus Garden, Ayer Lake (no swimming), Magma Ridge with scenic vistas, the interpretive Herb Garden, the Eucalyptus Forest, and the two acre Demonstration Garden. The Arboretum is constantly voted "Best Day Trip" in polls from Phoenix and Tucson residents. This park is located about an hour from Phoenix and 90 minutes from north Tucson. It is at Highway 60 Milepost 223, about one hour east of Phoenix on the Superstition Freeway. From Tucson, take Highway 79 to Florence Junction and then go 12 miles east on Highway 60. Hours are daily from 8am to 4pm, except Christmas Day. Prices are $7.50 for adults, $3 for children 5 to 12 and free for children under 5 and for dogs. Pets are allowed but need to be leashed and cleaned up after. They are not allowed inside buildings.

Parks
TOP 200 PLACE Boyce Thompson Arboretum State Park 223 Hwy 60 Superior AZ   520-689-2811
This 323 acre park is Arizona's oldest and largest botanical garden. They feature the plants of the desert, a streamside forest, panoramic views, various natural habitats and wildlife, a desert lake, specialty gardens, and more. They also offer an interpretive center, a demonstration garden, visitor center, guided tours, picnic grounds

with tables, gift shop, and restrooms. Well behaved dogs of all sizes are allowed for no additional fee. They must be kept on a short lead, under owner's control at all times, and cleaned up after. Dogs are not allowed anywhere in the water or in the gift shop. They are allowed throughout the rest of the park, and may even join their owners on the guided tours. The park is open daily from 8:00 a.m. to 5:00 p.m (October 1 - April 30). Summer hours are from 6:00 a.m. to 3:00 p.m. (May 1 - September 30).

Tombstone

Accommodations

Best Western Lookout Lodge Hwy 80 W Tombstone AZ   520-457-2223 (800-780-7234)
Dogs of all sizes are allowed. There is a $20 per night pet fee per pet. Smoking and non-smoking rooms available.
Trail Rider's Inn 13 N. 7th Street Tombstone AZ   520-457-3573 (800-574-0417)
http://www.trailridersinn.com
You and your pup can walk to the historic Tombstone district from this inn. They offer large, clean, quiet rooms and cable TV. There is a $5 per day pet fee.

Campgrounds and RV Parks

Picacho Peak RV Resort 17065 E Peak Lane Picacho AZ   520-466-7841
http://www.picachopeakrv.com
Dogs of all sizes are allowed. There are no additional pet fees. Dogs may not be left unattended outside, and they must have up to date shots, and be leashed and cleaned up after. This is an adults only park. There are some breed restrictions. There is a dog walk area at the campground.
Tombstone RV Park MM 315 Hwy 80 Tombstone AZ   800-348-3829
http://www.tombstone-rv.com
Dogs of all sizes are allowed. There are no additional pet fees. Dogs may be walked in the park, but they must be taken to the dog walk areas to do their business, and cleaned up after. There is a dog walk area at the campground.

Attractions

TOP 200 PLACE 1880 Historic Tombstone 70 miles from Tucson Tombstone AZ   800-457-3423 (800-457-3423)
http://www.tombstone1880.com/
This historic Western town is one of the most famous and glamorized mining towns in America. Prospector Ed Schieffelin was told he would only find his tombstone in the San Pedro Valley. He named his first silver claim Tombstone, and it later became the name of the town. The town is situated on a mesa at an elevation of 4,540 feet. While the area became notorious for saloons, gambling houses and the O.K. Corral shootout, in the 1880s Tombstone had become the most cultivated city in the West. Surviving the Great Depression and relocation of the County Seat to Bisbee, in the 1930s Tombstone became known as "The Town Too Tough To Die." You an your leashed dog are welcome to take a step back in time and walk along the wooden sidewalks and dirt streets. Here is a side note about the town: dogs are not allowed inside the O.K. Corral shoot-out area. This historic town is a must visit when you go to Arizona!
Old Tombstone Stagecoach Tours Allen Street (between 4th and 5th Streets) Tombstone AZ   520-457-3018
You and your pooch are welcome to hop on the stagecoach and tour the old town of Tombstone. They offer horse drawn tours daily. Prices run about $10 for a 10-15 minute tour.
WF Trading Company 418 Allen St Tombstone AZ   520-457-3664
Located in the heart of historic Tombstone, this retail store allows your well-behaved leashed dog inside the store. They sell gift items, jewelry, clothing and more.

Outdoor Restaurants

O.K. Cafe 220 E. Allen Street Tombstone AZ   520-457-3980
Come here for breakfast and lunch. Dogs are allowed at the outdoor tables.

Tonalea

Parks

Navajo National Monument HC 71 Box 3 Tonalea AZ   928-672-2700
http://www.nps.gov/nava/index.htm
Dogs must be on leash and must be cleaned up after in campsites, picnic, and parking areas. Dogs are not allowed on the trails.

Tucson

Accommodations
Motel 6 - Tucson North 4630 West Ina Road Marana AZ   520-744-9300 (800-466-8356)
One well-behaved family pet per room. Guest must notify front desk upon arrival. Guest is liable for any damages. In consideration of all guests, pets must never be left unattended in the guest rooms.
Clarion Hotel Randolph Park 102 N Alvernon Way Tucson AZ   520-795-0330 (877-424-6423)
Dogs of all sizes are allowed. There is a $25 per pet per stay additional pet fee. The Do Not Disturb sign needs to be on the door if the pet is alone in the room, and they must be leashed and cleaned up after.
Comfort Suites 6935 S Tucson Blvd Tucson AZ   520-295-4400 (877-424-6423)
Dogs of all sizes are allowed. There can be up to 3 small to medium dogs or up to 2 large dogs per room. There is a $25 per pet per stay additional pet fee. Dogs must be quiet, well behaved, leashed, and cleaned up after. They request you let the front desk know when there is a pet alone in the room, and that the Do Not Disturb sign is put on the door.
Comfort Suites at Tucson Mall 515 W Automall Drive Tucson AZ   520-888-6676 (877-424-6423)
Dogs of all sizes are allowed. There is a $10 per night per pet additional fee. Dogs must be leashed and cleaned up after, and the Do Not Disturb sign put on the door if they are alone in the room.
Country Inns & Suites by Carlson 7411 N Oracle Rd Tucson AZ   520-575-9255
Dogs of all sizes are allowed. There is a $20 one time additional pet fee.
Doubletree 445 S Alvernon Way Tucson AZ   520-881-4200
Dogs up to 50 pounds are allowed. There is a $25 one time pet fee per room.
Hawthorn Suites Ltd 7007 E Tanque Verde Rd Tucson AZ   520-298-2300
There is a $25 pet fee per visit.
Hilton 10000 N Oracle Road Tucson AZ   520-544-5000
Dogs up to 50 pounds are allowed. There is a $50 one time fee per pet and a pet policy to sign at check in.
Holiday Inn Express 2548 E. Medina Rd. Tucson AZ   520-889-6600 (877-270-6405)
Dogs up to 50 pounds are allowed. There is a $100 refundable pet deposit if you are paying with cash. The hotel has a fitness center on site.
La Quinta Inn & Suites Tucson Airport 7001 South Tucson Blvd. Tucson AZ   520-573-3333 (800-531-5900)
Dogs of all sizes are allowed. There are no additional pet fees. Dogs must be leashed and cleaned up after.
La Quinta Inn Tucson Downtown 750 West Starr Pass Blvd Tucson AZ   520-624-4455 (800-531-5900)
Dogs of all sizes are allowed. There are no additional pet fees; however, there is a pet waiver to sign at check in. Dogs may not be left unattended, and they must be leashed and cleaned up after.
La Quinta Inn Tucson East 6404 E. Broadway Tucson AZ   520-747-1414 (800-531-5900)
Dogs of all sizes are allowed. There are no additional pet fees. Dogs must be leashed and cleaned up after.
Lodge on the Desert 306 North Alvernon Way Tucson AZ   520-325-3366
http://www.lodgeonthedesert.com/
This lodge offers hacienda-style rooms and many have tile covered patios and fireplaces. Amenities include garden pathways, a pool and a restaurant with an outdoor patio where your pooch can join you. Room rates range from $79 to $269 depending on the season or type of room. Rates are subject to change. Pets are welcome for an additional $15 per day pet fee and a $50 refundable pet deposit. Well-behaved dogs of all sizes are welcome. All 35 rooms and suites are non-smoking and dogs are allowed in any of the rooms.
Loews Ventana Canyon Resort 7000 North Resort Drive Tucson AZ   520-299-2020
All well-behaved dogs of any size are welcome. This upscale hotel offers their "Loews Loves Pets" program which includes special pet treats, local dog walking routes, and a list of nearby pet-friendly places to visit. There are no pet fees.
Motel 6 - Tucson - 22nd Street 1222 South Freeway Tucson AZ   520-624-2516 (800-466-8356)
One well-behaved family pet per room. Guest must notify front desk upon arrival. Guest is liable for any damages. In consideration of all guests, pets must never be left unattended in the guest rooms.
Motel 6 - Tucson - Congress Street 960 S Freeway Tucson AZ   520-628-1339 (800-466-8356)
One well-behaved family pet per room. Guest must notify front desk upon arrival. Guest is liable for any damages. In consideration of all guests, pets must never be left unattended in the guest rooms.
Motel 6 - Tucson Airport 1031 East Benson Highway Tucson AZ   520-628-1264 (800-466-8356)
One well-behaved family pet per room. Guest must notify front desk upon arrival. Guest is liable for any damages. In consideration of all guests, pets must never be left unattended in the guest rooms.
Quality Inn 1025 E Benson H Tucson AZ   520-623-7792 (877-424-6423)
Dogs of all sizes are allowed. There is a $25 per night per pet additional fee. Dogs may not be left unattended,

and they must be leashed and cleaned up after.

Red Roof Inn - Tucson North 4940 West Ina Road Tucson AZ 520-744-8199 (800-RED-ROOF)
One well-behaved family pet per room. Guest must notify front desk upon arrival. Guest is liable for any damages. In consideration of all guests, pets must never be left unattended in the guest rooms.

Red Roof Inn - Tucson South 3700 East Irvington Road Tucson AZ 520-571-1400 (800-RED-ROOF)
One well-behaved family pet per room. Guest must notify front desk upon arrival. Guest is liable for any damages. In consideration of all guests, pets must never be left unattended in the guest rooms.

Residence Inn by Marriott 6477 E. Speedway Blvd Tucson AZ 520-721-0991
Dogs of all sizes are welcome. There is a $75 one time fee, and a pet policy to sign at check in.

Sheraton Tucson Hotel & Suites 5151 East Grant Rd. Tucson AZ 520-323-6262 (888-625-5144)
Dogs of all sizes are allowed. There are no additional pet fees. Dogs are not allowed to be left alone in the room.

Studio 6 - Tucson - Irvington Rd 4950 S Outlet Center Dr Tucson AZ 520-746-0030 (800-466-8356)
One well-behaved family pet per room. Guest must notify front desk upon arrival. Guest is liable for any damages. In consideration of all guests, pets must never be left unattended in the guest rooms.

Super 8 Tucson/Dwtn/University Area 1248 N Stone St Tucson AZ 520-622-6446 (800-800-8000)
Dogs of all sizes are allowed. There is a $8 per night pet fee per pet. Smoking and non-smoking rooms are available for pet rooms.

TownePlace Suites Tucson 405 W Rudasill Road Tucson AZ 520-292-9697
Dogs of all sizes are allowed. There is a $75 one time fee per visit.

TOP 200 PLACE **Westward Look Resort** 245 East Ina Road Tucson AZ 520-297-1151 (800-722-2500)
http://www.westwardlook.com
This resort comes highly recommended from one of our readers. They said it was the most pet-friendly resort around and they can't say enough good things about it. This former 1912 guest ranch, now a desert resort hideaway, is nestled in the foothills of Tucson's picturesque Santa Catalina Mountains. It offers guests a Southwestern experience on 80 desert acres. They have walking trails at the resort, tennis, swimming pools and much more. Special room rates can be as low as $69 during certain times and seasons. There is a $50 one time additional pet fee.

Windmill Suites 4250 N Campbell Avenue Tucson AZ 623-583-0133
Dogs of all sizes are allowed. There are no additional pet fees.

Campgrounds and RV Parks

Catalina State Park 11570 N Oracle Road Tucson AZ 520-628-5798
This scenic desert recreational park has a variety of attractions plus an archaeological site to explore and there are 8 trails of varying length and difficulty. Dogs are allowed at no additional fee. Dogs must be leashed and cleaned up after. Dogs are not allowed at the Pusch Ridge Wilderness area, but they are allowed on trails. The camping and tent areas also allow dogs. There is a dog walk area at the campground.

Coronado National Forest 5700 N Sabino Canyon Road Tucson AZ 520-388-8300
http://www.fs.fed.us/r3/coronado/
This forest, with elevations ranging from 3000 feet to 10,720 feet, covers more than 1.7 million acres over twelve widely scattered mountain ranges. The rugged mountains rise from the desert floor, and are known as the "sky islands". There is recreation during all seasons. Dogs of all sizes are allowed at no additional fee. Dogs may not be left unattended, and they must be leashed and cleaned up after. Dogs are allowed on the trails, but they are not allowed in the Push Ridge Wilderness Area. The camping and tent areas also allow dogs. There is a dog walk area at the campground. There are no electric or water hookups at the campground.

Crazy Horse RV Park 6660 S Craycroft Tucson AZ 520-574-0157
http://www.crazyhorserv.com
Dogs of all sizes are allowed. There is $1 per night per pet additional fee for daily rates; $5 by the week, and $15 by the month. Dogs must be walked in designated areas only, and they must be leashed and cleaned up after. Dogs may be left in the RV only if air conditioned. Tucson pet ordinance prohibits dogs from being left in an auto or tied up at any time. There is a dog walk area at the campground.

Prince of Tucson RV Park 3501 N Freeway Tucson AZ 520-887-3501
http://www.princeoftucsonrvpark.com
Dogs of all sizes are allowed. There are no additional pet fees for the first two dogs, thereafter the fee is $2 per night per pet. Dogs may not be left unattended outside, and they must be leashed and cleaned up after. Tucson pet ordinance prohibits dogs from being left in an auto or tied up at any time. There are some breed restrictions. There is a dog walk area at the campground.

Attractions

Pima Air and Space Museum 6000 East Valencia Road Tucson AZ 520-574-0462
Dogs are allowed at the outdoor exhibits at this air museum. This museum has over 250 aircraft on display on 80 acres. Please make sure your pooch does not lift a leg on the aircraft. Have him or her take care of business before entering the museum.

TOP 200 PLACE **Trail Dust Town** 6541 E Tanque Verde Road Tucson AZ 520-296-4551

http://www.traildusttown.com/
Originally constructed as a movie set, this town has been a Tucson landmark for over 40 years, and is considered a premier "in-town" western town. It features wooden boardwalks and red brick streets, the Fiesta del Presidio carousel, a town square with a centerpiece gazebo, and a lot more. There is a variety of activities and recreation such as the Wild Wild West street shows or panning for gold. Dogs are allowed throughout the town, but they are not allowed inside the shops or museum. Dogs must be kept leashed, under owners' control at all times, and cleaned up after.

Stores

PetSmart Pet Store 10625 N Oracle Oro Valley AZ   520-797-0008
Your licensed and well-behaved leashed dog is allowed in the store.
PetSmart Pet Store 7727 E Broadway Blvd Tucson AZ   520-290-0776
Your licensed and well-behaved leashed dog is allowed in the store.
PetSmart Pet Store 4740 E Grant Ave Tucson AZ   520-322-5080
Your licensed and well-behaved leashed dog is allowed in the store.
PetSmart Pet Store 3931 W Costco Dr Tucson AZ   520-742-6363
Your licensed and well-behaved leashed dog is allowed in the store.
PetSmart Pet Store 1175 W Irvington Rd Tucson AZ   520-573-6652
Your licensed and well-behaved leashed dog is allowed in the store.
PetSmart Pet Store 4374 N Oracle Rd Tucson AZ   520-407-0146
Your licensed and well-behaved leashed dog is allowed in the store.
Petco Pet Store 4625 North Oracle Rd Tucson AZ   520-887-0111
Your licensed and well-behaved leashed dog is allowed in the store.
Petco Pet Store 7810 East Wrightstown Rd Tucson AZ   520-886-6183
Your licensed and well-behaved leashed dog is allowed in the store.
Petco Pet Store 5405 Broadway Blvd Tucson AZ   520-571-1772
Your licensed and well-behaved leashed dog is allowed in the store.

Parks

Rillito River Trail La Cholla Blvd Tucson AZ   520-877-6000
This popular paved trail stretches for miles, offering plenty of opportunity for your pooch to stretch his or her legs. Just be careful to go early in the morning or early evening if it is a hot day, as the paved path and the adjacent desert sand can become too hot for paws. A popular section of the trail is located between La Cholla Blvd. and Campbell Avenue, along the Rillito River. There is parking and restrooms available near La Cholla Boulevard.
Saguaro National Park 3693 South Old Spanish Trail Tucson AZ   520-733-5100
http://www.nps.gov/sagu/index.htm
Dogs must be on leash and must be cleaned up after on roadways and picnic areas. They are not allowed on any trails or buildings.

Off-Leash Dog Parks

Anamax Off-Leash Dog Park 17501 S. Camino de las Quintas Sahuarita AZ   520-625-2731
This dog park opened in November, 2006. Located in Anamax Park the fenced dog park has seperate areas for large and small dogs. The dog park is one acre in size and is equipped with benches, water and dog clean up bags. To get to the dog park from I-19 take the Sahuarita Rd exit west and turn south onto N La Canada Dr. Turn left onto W. Camino Cuzco and take it to Camino De Las Quintas. Turn right and the park will be on your left.
Christopher Columbus Dog Park 4600 N. Silverbell Tucson AZ   520-791-4873x0
This dog park is fenced and is about 1/3 acre in size. It has lights and is open to about 2 or 3 hours after dark. There is a separate fenced area for small dogs. The park is located just south of the intersection of Silverbell and W El Camino Del Cerro and just west of I-10 at El Camino Del Cerro.
Gene C. Reid Park Off-Leash Area 900 S. Randolph Way Tucson AZ   520-791-3204
This park offers a designated off-leash area. It is located across from the Reid Park Zoo entrance on a converted Little League field. The one acre dog park is lighted and fenced. Amenities include water, picnic tables, trees, and a separate area for small and large dogs. Dog park hours are from 7am to 9pm. Dogs must be on leash when outside the off-leash area.
Jacobs Dog Park 3300 N. Fairview Ave. Tucson AZ   520-791-4873x0
This dog park opened in Jacobs Park in 2005. The dog park is fenced and located on the west side of the park. It is open during daylight hours.
McDonald District Park Off-Leash Area 4100 N. Harrison Road Tucson AZ   520-877-6000
This park offers a designated off-leash area. Dogs must be on leash when outside the off-leash area.
Northwest Center Off-Leash Dog Park 2075 N. 6th Street Tucson AZ   520-791-4873x0
This half an acre fenced off-leash dog park was opened in 2004. It is located across 6th Street from the Northwest Center. The park features double gates and tables. The park is open during daylight hours.

Palo Verde Park Off-Leash Area 300 S. Mann Avenue Tucson AZ 520-791-4873
This park offers a designated off-leash area. Amenities of this fenced and double-gated dog park include doggie drinking fountains, picnic tables and pooper scooper dispensers. Dogs must be on leash when outside the off-leash area. The park is located at 300 S. Mann Avenue, south of Broadway, west of Kolb, and directly between Langley and Mann Avenues.
Udall Dog Park 7290 E. Tanque Verde Tucson AZ 520-791-5930
This one acre, fenced dog park has lights and is open from 6 am to 10:30 pm. It has water for dogs. The dog park opened in 2004 in Udall Regional Park. The park is located south of E. Tanque Verde Road between N Sabino Canyon Rd and N. Pantano Rd.

Outdoor Restaurants
Baggin's Gourmet Sandwiches 2741 E Speedway Blvd Tucson AZ 520-327-4342
This restaurant serves gourmet sandwiches. Dogs are allowed at the outdoor tables.
Dakota Cafe and Catering Company 6541 E Tanque Verde Rd Tucson AZ 520-298-7188
This restaurant serves American and other varieties of food. Dogs are allowed at the outdoor tables in garden area.
Eegee's 4510 E Speedway Tucson AZ 520-881-3280
This restaurant serves American food. Dogs are allowed at the outdoor tables.
El Charro Cafe 311 North Court Avenue Tucson AZ 520-622-1922
Well-behaved dogs are allowed at the outdoor tables. Choose from a selection of fajitas, tamales, chalupas, enchiladas, salads and more.
Famous Sam's Restaurant and Bar 8058 North Oracle Rd Tucson AZ 520-531-9464
Dogs are allowed at the outdoor tables, but need to enter through the patio gate. Have a server open the gate for you.
Ghini's 1803 E Prince Rd Tucson AZ 520-326-9095
This cafe serves French American food. Dogs are allowed at the outdoor tables. Water bowls and dog biscuits are provided for your pet.
Li'l Abner's Steakhouse 8500 North Silverbell Rd Tucson AZ 520-744-2800
Dogs are allowed at the outdoor tables.
Mama's Famous Pizza and Heros 7965 North Oracle Rd Tucson AZ 520-297-3993
Enjoy pizza or sandwiches at this restaurant. Dogs are allowed at the outdoor tables.
Ric's Cafe 5605 East River Rd Tucson AZ 520-577-7272
Dogs are allowed at the outdoor tables.
Saga Restaurant and Sushi Bar 2955 E Speedway Blvd Tucson AZ 520-320-0535
This restaurant serves Japanese food. Dogs are allowed at the outdoor tables.
Schlotzsky's Deli 5121 East Grant Rd Tucson AZ 520-325-5185
Dogs are allowed at the outdoor tables. Choose from a variety of hot and cold sandwiches, salads and more.
Schlotzsky's Deli 3270 East Valencia Tucson AZ 520-741-2333
Dogs are allowed at the outdoor tables. Choose from a variety of hot and cold sandwiches, salads and more.
The Cup Cafe (in Hotel Congress) 311 E Congress St Tucson AZ 520-798-1618
http://www.hotcong.com
This restaurant serves American and other types of food. Dogs are allowed at the outdoor tables.

Day Kennels
PetsHotel by PetsMart Day Kennel 4374 N. Oracle Rd. Tucson AZ 520-407-0197
http://www.petsmart.com/PETsHOTEL/
This PetSmart pet store offers day care only. You can drop off your dog between the hours of 7 am - 9pm M-S and Sunday 7 am - 7 pm. Dogs are required to have proof of up to date rabies, DPP and bordatella vacinations.

Tumacacori

Attractions
Tumacacori National Historical Park 1891 E Frontage Rd Tumacacori AZ 520-398-2341
http://www.nps.gov/tuma/index.htm
Dogs must be on leash and must be cleaned up after in the park. Dogs are not allowed in any buildings. Reservations are needed to tour the park.

Wenden

Campgrounds and RV Parks
Alamo Lake State Park Alamo Road Wenden AZ 928-669-2088
This recreational park has one of Arizona'a best fishing holes, and there is more than enough to interest nature lovers also with a wide variety of flora and fauna. Dogs are allowed at no additional fee. Dogs may not be left unattended, and they must be leashed and cleaned up after. Dogs are allowed on the trails. The camping and tent areas also allow dogs. There is a dog walk area at the campground.

Wickenburg

Accommodations
Best Western Rancho Grande 293 E Wickenburg Way Wickenburg AZ 928-684-5445 (800-780-7234)
Dogs of all sizes are allowed. There is a $8 per night pet fee per pet. Smoking and non-smoking rooms available.

Attractions
Robson's Mining World P. O. Box 3465 (On Hwy 71) Wickenburg AZ 928-685-2609
This real mining town offers museums of a grocery, barber shop, an assay office, newspaper, Post Office, and a total of more than 30 antique buildings on its' Main Street. There are miles of hiking trails to explore, or browse and wander through acres of Antique equipment, go gold panning (with instruction), enjoy cowboy style cookouts, great bird watching, or explore ancient Indian artifacts and petroglyphs. They are open from October 1st to May 1st. Dogs of all sizes are allowed throughout the town and grounds, but they are not allowed in most of the buildings or the restaurant. Dogs may not be left unattended in the town or automobiles, and they must be leashed and cleaned up after. There is also an area for RV camping.

Willcox

Accommodations
Best Western Plaza Inn 1100 W Rex Allen Dr Willcox AZ 520-384-3556 (800-780-7234)
Dogs of all sizes are allowed. There is a $15 one time per pet fee per visit. Smoking and Non-Smoking rooms are used for pets.
Days Inn Willcox 724 N Bisbee Ave Willcox AZ 520-384-4222 (800-329-7466)
Dogs of all sizes are allowed. There is a $5 per night pet fee per pet.
Motel 6 - Willcox 921 North Bisbee Avenue Willcox AZ 520-384-2201 (800-466-8356)
One well-behaved family pet per room. Guest must notify front desk upon arrival. Guest is liable for any damages. In consideration of all guests, pets must never be left unattended in the guest rooms.

Parks
Chiricahua National Monument 13063 E Bonita Canyon Rd Willcox AZ 520-824-3560
http://www.nps.gov/chir/index.htm
Dogs on leash are allowed in campsites and on paved roads. Dogs are not allowed on hiking trails in the park.

Window Rock

Accommodations
Quality Inn Navajo Nation Capitol 48 W Hwy 264 Window Rock AZ 928-871-4108 (877-424-6423)
Dogs of all sizes are allowed. There is a $50 refundable deposit if paying with cash. Dogs must be quiet, well behaved, leashed, and cleaned up after. The Do Not Disturb sign needs to be put on the door if there is a pet alone in the room.

Winslow

Accommodations

Days Inn Winslow 2035 W Old Hwy Rt 66 Winslow AZ   928-289-1010 (800-329-7466)
Dogs of all sizes are allowed. There is a $10 one time per pet fee per visit.
Econo Lodge I40 & Exit 253 North Park Dr Winslow AZ   928-289-4687
There is a $5 per day additional pet fee.
Holiday Inn Express 816 Transcon Lane Winslow AZ   928-289-2960 (877-270-6405)
Dogs up to 60 pounds are allowed. There is a $10 per day additional pet fee. The hotel has a few smoking and non-smoking pet rooms.
La Posada 303 E 2nd Street Winslow AZ   928-289-4366
Dogs of all sizes are allowed. There is a $10 one time fee per room and a pet policy to sign at check in.
Motel 6 - Winslow 520 Desmond Street Winslow AZ   928-289-9581 (800-466-8356)
One well-behaved family pet per room. Guest must notify front desk upon arrival. Guest is liable for any damages. In consideration of all guests, pets must never be left unattended in the guest rooms.

Campgrounds and RV Parks

Homolovi Ruins State Park Honahanie Road Winslow AZ   928-289-4106
This archeological recreational park explores the rich Native American history. There is a book store as well as the exhibits, and several trails. Dogs are allowed at no additional fee. Dogs must be leashed and cleaned up after. Dogs are not allowed in any of the buildings. The camping and tent areas also allow dogs. There is a dog walk area at the campground.

Attractions

TOP 200 PLACE **Homolovi Ruins State Park** State Route 87 Winslow AZ   928-289-4106
This site is Arizona's first archaeological state park. Homolovi, a Hopi word meaning 'place of the little hills,' consists of four major pueblo sites thought to have been occupied between A.D. 1200 and 1425 by ancestors of today's Hopi Indians. Homolovi sites I and II are accessible to visitors. Your leashed dog is welcome to view the sites with you. Just stay on the trail because there are rattlesnakes in the area. The park is located five miles northeast of Winslow on State Route 87. Tale I-40 to Exit 257, then go 1.3 miles north on Highway 87.

Parks

Homolovi Ruins State Park HCR 63 Box, State Route 87N Winslow AZ   928-289-4106
This park now serves as a research center recording the late migration period of the Hopi from the 1200's to the late 1300's. Park facilities include a visitor center and museum, various trails, and pullouts that provide opportunities to observe wildlife over the 4,000 acres at an elevation of 4,900 feet. Dogs are allowed to go on all the trails, the ruins, the park grounds, and the visitor's center. Dogs must be leashed or crated at all times, and they may not be left unattended in the park or automobiles. There is camping available with hook-ups, several covered picnic tables, showers, and a dump station.

Yuma

Accommodations

Comfort Inn 1691 S Riley Avenue Yuma AZ   928-782-1200 (877-424-6423)
Dogs of all sizes are allowed. There is a $10 per night per room additional pet fee. Dogs may not be left alone in the room, and they must be leashed and cleaned up after.
Holiday Inn 1901 E 18th St Yuma AZ   800-HOL-IDAY (877-270-6405)
Dogs of all sizes are allowed. There is a $10 per night pet fee per pet. Smoking and non-smoking rooms are available for pets.
Holiday Inn Express 3181 S. 4th Ave Yuma AZ   928-344-1420 (877-270-6405)
There is a $10 per day additional pet fee.
Motel 6 - Yuma - Oldtown 1640 South Arizona Avenue Yuma AZ   928-782-6561 (800-466-8356)
One well-behaved family pet per room. Guest must notify front desk upon arrival. Guest is liable for any damages. In consideration of all guests, pets must never be left unattended in the guest rooms.
Motel 6 - Yuma East 1445 East 16th Street Yuma AZ   928-782-9521 (800-466-8356)
One well-behaved family pet per room. Guest must notify front desk upon arrival. Guest is liable for any damages. In consideration of all guests, pets must never be left unattended in the guest rooms.
Quality Inn Airport 711 E 32nd Street Yuma AZ   928-726-4721 (877-424-6423)
Dogs of all sizes are allowed. There is a $25 one time per pet per stay additional fee. Dogs may only be left

unattended if they will be quiet, and a contact number is left with the front desk. Dogs must be leashed and cleaned up after.

Shilo Inn- Conference Center & Resort Hotel 1550 S Castle Dome Road Yuma AZ   928-782-9511
Dogs of all sizes are allowed. There is a $10 per night per pet additional fee.

Super 8 Yuma 1688 S Riley Ave Yuma AZ   928-782-2000 (800-800-8000)
Dogs of all sizes are allowed. There is a $10 per night pet fee per pet. Smoking and non-smoking rooms are available for pet rooms.

Campgrounds and RV Parks

Cocopah RV & Golf Resort 6800 Strand Avenue Yuma AZ   928-343-9300
http://www.cocopahrv.com
Dogs of all sizes are allowed. There are no additional pet fees. Dogs must be walked in designated pet areas only, and they must be leashed and cleaned up after. Dogs are not allowed in the golf course area. This is an adult only resort. There is a dog walk area at the campground.

Shangri-la RV Resort 10498 N Frontage Road Yuma AZ   877-742-6474
http://www.shangrilarv.com
Dogs of all sizes are allowed. There are no additional pet fees. Dogs must be walked in the designated pet areas only, and they must be leashed and cleaned up after. There are some breed restrictions. There is a dog walk area at the campground.

Westwind RV and Golf Resort 9797 E 32nd Street Yuma AZ   928-342-2992
http://www.westwindrvgolfresort.com
Dogs of all sizes are allowed. There are no additional pet fees. Dogs are also allowed in the park models in the pet section only. Dogs must stay in the designated pet areas only to be walked, and are not allowed at the office or other non-pet areas. Dogs may not be left unattended, and they must be leashed and cleaned up after. There are some breed restrictions. There is a dog walk area at the campground.

Stores

PetSmart Pet Store 1460 S Yuma Palms Pkwy Yuma AZ   928-329-7291
Your licensed and well-behaved leashed dog is allowed in the store.

Parks

Century House Museum and Gardens 240 S Madison Yuma AZ   928-782-1841
http://yumalibrary.org/ahs/index.htm
Purchased in 1890 by a pioneer merchant, this home is now a museum of the history of the era, and the beautiful Italian-style gardens and aviaries that were started back then are still maintained today. They are open from Tuesday through Saturday. Dogs are allowed to walk through the gardens with their owners, and there is no additional fee for them. Dogs must be on leash at all times, and cleaned up after. Dogs are not allowed in the museum or any of the park buildings.

Chapter 16

Colorado
Dog Travel Guide

Alamosa

Campgrounds and RV Parks
Alamosa KOA 6900 Juniper Avenue Alamosa CO   719-589-9757 (800-562-9157)
http://www.koa.com
Dogs of all sizes are allowed, however there can only be up to 3 dogs at tent and RV sites, and up to 2 dogs at the cabins. There are no additional pet fees. Dogs may not be left unattended at the cabins or outside, and they must be leashed and cleaned up after. There are some breed restrictions. The camping and tent areas also allow dogs. There is a dog walk area at the campground. Dogs are allowed in the camping cabins.

Almont

Accommodations
Harmel's Ranch Resort & Spa 6748 County Road 742 Almont CO   970-641-1740 (800-235-3402)
http://www.harmels.com
Harmels is a dude ranch that allows you to bring your leashed dog with you. They have a three night minimum in their 37 cabins. The Ranch borders on the Gunnison National Forest which allows leashed dogs on its hiking trails. There is a $10 per night pet fee. The ranch also features barbecue's, hayrides and horseback riding and has some nearby swimming holes for dogs.

Arboles

Campgrounds and RV Parks
Navajo State Park 1526 County Road 982 (Box 1697) Arboles CO   970-883-2208 (800-678-2267)
This scenic park touts a reservoir with over 15,000 acres, and offers a variety of land and water recreation in addition to the geological and historical points of interest. Dogs of all sizes are allowed at no additional fee. Dogs may not be left unattended, and they must be on no more than a 6 foot leash, and be cleaned up after. The camping and tent areas also allow dogs. There is a dog walk area at the campground. Dogs are allowed in the camping cabins.

Aspen

Accommodations
Hotel Aspen 110 W. Main Street Aspen CO   970-925-3441 (800-527-7369)
http://www.hotelaspen.com
This dog-friendly hotel is located right on Main Street in Aspen. Rooms are large and beautifully appointed and they come equipped with a wet bar, small refrigerator, coffee maker, microwave, iron, ironing board, hairdryer, humidifier, VCR, and air conditioning. Most rooms open onto terraces or balconies and some have private jacuzzis.They have a $20 per night charge for pets.
Hotel Jerome 330 E Main Street/Hwy 82 Aspen CO   970-920-1000 (800-331-7213)
This luxury hotel has been in service for more than a hundred years in the magnificent setting of the Rocky Mountains. Amenities include elegant accommodations, world class cuisine with 2 fine dining restaurants and outdoor dining in summer, 2 taverns, heated outdoor pool/Jacuzzi, underground parking, and much more. Dogs of all sizes are allowed. There is a $75 one time additional pet fee per pet. Dogs must be leashed and cleaned up after at all times.
St. Regis Resort Aspen 315 East Dean St. Aspen CO   970-920-3300
Dogs of all sizes are allowed. There is a $100 per dog one time nonrefundable fee due at check in time. Dogs are not allowed to be left alone in the room.
The Sky Hotel 709 East Durant Avenue Aspen CO   970-925-6760
Well-behaved dogs of all kinds and sizes are welcome at this pet-friendly hotel. The luxury boutique hotel offers

both rooms and suites. Hotel amenities include a heated outdoor pool, and a fitness room. There are no pet fees, just sign a pet waiver.
The St. Regis Hotel 315 East Dean Street Aspen CO   970-920-3300 (800-325-3535)
http://www.destinationaspen.com/stregis/
There is a one time $50 pet charge. The hotel can also arrange a dog sitter or dog walker if you need to leave the room and cannot take your dog.

Cross Country Ski Resorts
Aspen Cross Country Center 39551 West Highway 82 Aspen CO   970-925-2145
http://www.utemountaineer.com/AXCC.htm
This rental center allows dogs on the trail that goes around the golf course. It is 1.5 miles long and is usually groomed once a day in the morning. Dogs need to be on leash or under direct voice control. Please clean up after your pet.

Outdoor Restaurants
Ajax Tavern 685 E Durant Aspen CO   970-920-9333
Dogs are allowed at the outdoor tables.
In and Out House 233 E Main Street Aspen CO   970-925-6647
Dogs are allowed at the outdoor tables. The restaurant has outdoor tables only in the summer.
Zele Cafe 121 S Galena Street Aspen CO   970-925-5745
Dogs are allowed at the outdoor tables.

Avon

Accommodations
Comfort Inn Beaver Creek 0161 W Beaver Creek Blvd Avon CO   970-949-5511 (877-424-6423)
Dogs of all sizes are allowed. There is a $25 per room per stay additional pet fee. Dogs must be leashed and cleaned up after.

Bailey

Accommodations
Glen Isle Resort Highway 285 (near milepost marker 221) Bailey CO   303-838-5461
Dogs are welcome in the cabins (no designated smoking or non-smoking cabins). All cabins contain fully equipped kitchens, private baths, easy chairs, bedding and linens, fireplaces (wood provided) and gas heat. Resort amenities include a children's playground, games and game room and a library. The resort is within walking distance of the Pike National Forest and the Platte River. There you will find hours of dog-friendly hiking trails. There is a $5 per day pet charge. The resort is located 45 miles southwest of Denver.

Basalt

Campgrounds and RV Parks
Aspen Basalt Campground 20640 Hwy 82 Basalt CO   800-567-2773
Dogs of all sizes are allowed. There are no additional pet fees. Dogs may not be left unattended outside, and must be leashed and cleaned up after. There is a dog walk area at the campground.

Bayfield

Campgrounds and RV Parks
Blue Spruce Cabins and RV Park 1875 County Road 500 Bayfield CO   970-884-2641
Dogs of all sizes are allowed. There are no additional pet fees. Dogs may not be left out at night, or outside unattended. Dogs must be leashed and cleaned up after. There are some breed restrictions. This RV park is

closed during the off-season. The camping and tent areas also allow dogs. There is a dog walk area at the campground.

Vallecito Resort 13030 County Road 501 Bayfield CO   970-884-9458

http://www.vallecitoresort.com

Dogs of all sizes are allowed. There are no additional pet fees. Dogs must be leashed and cleaned up after. There are some breed restrictions. This RV park is closed during the off-season. The camping and tent areas also allow dogs. There is a dog walk area at the campground. Dogs are allowed in the camping cabins.

Black Hawk

Parks

Mountain City Historic Park Gregory Street Black Hawk CO   303-582-2525

Black Hawk is known for having many casinos and a large variety of seasonal attractions. Against a backdrop of being a distinct old west gold mining town with restored old buildings, an active historical society museum, and several historic mining sites, there is a city block park they consider a prime attraction. It is a stroll back in time that offers a glimpse of the intermingling of Victorian and Gothic architectural styles, and the park features other sites/statues, like the mama bear and her 3 cubs. This day use park is free of charge and is open daily. Dogs of all sizes are allowed throughout the park. Dogs must be leashed at all times, and they request that you bring supplies to clean up after your pet.

Bond

Attractions

Colorado River Runs Star Route, Box 32 Bond CO   800-826-1081

http://www.coloradoriverruns.com/

Exciting tours on the Colorado Rivers run from easy to thrilling rapids, and the scenery viewed here is unforgettable. The owners here are willing to take a dog on the river, but they must meet with the owner and their dog first, and it would have to be a private trip. The dog would also have to have its own life jacket. Tours are by reservation only and are available May through September.

Boulder

Accommodations

Boulder Outlook Motel and Suites 800 28th Street Boulder CO   303-443-3322 (800-542-0304)

This luxury hotel offers a wide variety of amenities and services, some of which include a chlorine-free heated indoor pool, a hot tub, a wall for climbing, an Adventure guide onsite to book outdoor activities, complimentary continental breakfast, restaurants, a bar, concierge level service, and a lot more. They welcome dogs and have a fully fenced in dog run complete with disposal amenities located adjacent to the designated pet rooms. They will also arrange for dog walking services or a vet if needed. Dogs of all sizes are allowed. There is a $10 per night per pet additional fee. Dogs may be left alone in the room only if they will be quiet, and they must be leashed and cleaned up after.

Days Inn Boulder 5397 South Boulder Rd Boulder CO   303-499-4422 (800-329-7466)

Dogs of all sizes are allowed. There is a $10 one time per pet fee per visit.

Foot of the Mountain Motel 200 Arapahoe Ave. Boulder CO   303-442-5688

Pets are welcome at this log cabin motel. There is an additional $5 per day pet charge. There are no designated smoking or non-smoking cabins.

Holiday Inn Express 4777 North Broadway Boulder CO   303-442-6600 (877-270-6405)

Dogs up to 90 pounds are allowed. There is a $15 per day pet fee or $30 for the stay if more than one day.

Homewood Suites 4950 Baseline Rd. Boulder CO   303-499-9922

There is a one time $50 pet charge.

New West Inn 970 28th Street Boulder CO   303-443-7800 (800-800-8000)

Dogs of all sizes are allowed. There is a $50 returnable deposit required per room. There is a $5 per night pet fee per pet. Reservations are recommended due to limited rooms for pets.

Quality Inn and Suites 2020 Arapahoe Ave Boulder CO   303-449-7550 (877-424-6423)

Dogs of all sizes are allowed. There is a $15 per night per pet additional fee, and a pet waiver to sign at check in. Dogs must be leashed, cleaned up after, and a contact number left with the front desk when they are alone in the

room.
Residence Inn by Marriott 3030 Center Green Drive Boulder CO   303-449-5545
Dogs of all sizes are allowed. There is a $50 to $75 fee per pet depending on the length of stay and a pet policy
to sign at check in.
Comfort Inn 1196 Dillon Road Louisville CO   303-604-0181 (877-424-6423)
Dogs of all sizes are allowed. There is a $10 per night per pet additional fee. Dogs may not be left alone in the
room, and they must be leashed and cleaned up after.
La Quinta Inn & Suites Denver Louisville Boulder 902 Dillon Rd. Louisville CO   303-664-0100 (800-531-
5900)
Dogs of all sizes are allowed. There are no additional pet fees. There is a pet waiver to sign at check in, and a
cell number needs to be left with the front desk if your pet is left alone in the room. Also, place the "Do Not
Disturb" sign on the door so housekeeping does not enter. There is a specified pet area where dogs are to be
taken, and they must be leashed and cleaned up after.
Quality Inn and Suites 960 W Dillon Road Louisville CO   303-327-1215 (877-424-6423)
Dogs of all sizes are allowed. There is a $15 per night per pet. Dogs must be quiet, leashed, and cleaned up
after.
Residence Inn by Marriott 845 Coal Creek Circle Louisville CO   303-665-2661
Dogs of all sizes are allowed There is a $75 one time fee, and a pet policy to sign at check in.

Attractions

TOP 200 PLACE Boulder Creek Winery 6440 Odell Place Boulder CO   303-516-9031
This is a winery that offers modern technology with old world artistry in handcrafting traditional and private
reserve wines. They also offer a variety of wine related gift items from their tasting room. Hours vary through the
seasons, and they are closed the month of January. Dogs are allowed in and around the tasting room. They are
not allowed in the winery or on the tours. Dogs must be friendly and well behaved. If your dog is under firm voice
control, they may be off lead, and please clean up after your pet.

Stores

Boulder Book Store 1107 Pearl Street Boulder CO   303-447-2074
This bookstore offers a variety of activities in addition to a large selection of reading material. Your well behaved,
house-trained, dog is welcome to join you in the store. Dogs must be leashed at all times.
Boulder Bookstore 1107 Pearl Street Boulder CO   303-447-2074
This active bookstore offers a variety of events, specials, and programs for their visitors. They are open Monday
to Friday from 10 am to 10 pm; Saturday from 9 am to 10 pm, and on Sunday from 10 am to 8 pm (closed some
holidays). Your housebroken and well behaved dog is allowed to come into the store with you. They must be
leashed at all times, and please clean up after your pet if they do their business next to the store.
PetSmart Pet Store 2982 Iris Ave Boulder CO   303-939-9033
Your licensed and well-behaved leashed dog is allowed in the store.
Petco Pet Store 2480 Arapahoe Avenue Boulder CO   303-544-1888
Your licensed and well-behaved leashed dog is allowed in the store.

Parks

Boulder Creek Path 9th street and Parallels Arapahoe Avenue Boulder CO   303-413-7200
http://www.ci.boulder.co.us
This multi-use nature and exercise trail runs about 16 miles through the city and into the adjacent mountains with
no street crossings. Some of the attractions along the way include a sculpture garden, fishing ponds, cottonwood
groves, a restored steam locomotive, city parks, a playground, and the state university. Dogs are allowed on the
trail if they are leashed and you clean up after your pet. There are trash receptacles along the way, but you will
need to bring your own clean up supplies.
Boulder Reservoir 5100 N 51st Street Boulder CO   303-441-3456
This reservoir offers a great scenic view to enjoy with your hiking. Dogs are allowed on the North Shore only, and
the trails on that side. You can access this area from 51st Street, past the main gate to the trailhead, and then
walk to the shore from there. Dogs are not allowed at any swim beach, food areas, or on boat rentals. Dogs must
be leashed and cleaned up after.
Chautauqua Park 900 Baseline Road Boulder CO   303-442-3282
http://www.chautauqua.com/
Situated on 26 gorgeous acres, this historic landmark park on the National Register, features buildings that date
back to its beginnings, beautiful gardens, and now provides a retreat experience in the heart of Bolder. Run and
preserved by the Colorado Chautauqua Association, their goal is to help build their community through social,
cultural, educational, and recreational opportunities. Dogs of all sizes are allowed throughout the park and on the
trails. They must be on leash except in off lead areas, and for your dog to be legally off lead, an off-leash tag
must be purchased. Dogs are not allowed in park buildings or on the upper section of the McClintock Trail, and

they must be cleaned up after at all times.
University of Colorado-Boulder 914 Broadway St Boulder CO   303-492-1411
http://www.colorado.edu/
Your pet may walk with you through this beautiful campus, but they must be well behaved, leashed, and cleaned up after at all times. Please bring your own clean up supplies. Dogs are not allowed in any of the buildings or in food service areas.

Off-Leash Dog Parks
East Boulder Park 5660 Sioux Drive Boulder CO   303-413-7258
This three acre dog park has separate fenced areas for small and large dogs. There is limited water access to a small lake. The city warns to be careful as water quality can vary. People need to pick up after their pets, especially near the water because of water quality issues. The dog park is located near the East Boulder Community Center.
Foothills Park Dog Park Cherry Ave at 7th St Boulder CO   303-413-7258
This 2 acre dog park is fully fenced. There are separate areas for small dogs and large dogs. The park is open during daylight hours. To get to the park from Broadway turn west onto Violet Ave, then right on 10th and left on Cherry Ave. The dog park is at the north end of Foothills Community Park.
Howard Hueston Dog Park 34th Street Boulder CO   303-413-7258
This 1.25 acre off-leash area (Voice and Sight area) is not fenced but is designated by yellow poles. Dogs must be leashed when outside the off-leash area. The park is located on 34th Street, south of Iris Avenue and east of 30th Street.
Valmont Dog Park 5275 Valmont Road Boulder CO   303-413-7258
This three acre dog park has separate fenced areas for small and large dogs. Water is available seasonally.
Louisville Community Park Dog Park 955 Bella Vista Drive Louisville CO   303-335-4735
The dog park is fully fenced and is open during daylight hours. There is a pond with reclaimed water in the dog pond. You may not want your dog to be drinking this water. You should be aware that Louisville and Denver have a complete Pit Bull ban. Boulder does not have such a ban.

Outdoor Restaurants
Half Fast Subs 1215 13th Street Boulder CO   303-449-0404
This restaurant serves Deli-type food. Dogs are allowed at the outdoor tables.
Rockies Brewing Company 2880 Wilderness Place Boulder CO   303-444-8448
http://www.boulderbeer.com/
This is Colorado's first micro-brewery with tours Monday through Friday at 2 pm. They also carry a line of logo products. There is patio seating, and your well behaved, leashed dog is welcome to join you. Please clean up after your pet.
Royal Peacock 5290 Arapahoe Avenue at 55th Street Boulder CO   303-447-1409
http://www.royalpeacocklounge.com
This restaurant serves East Indian food. Dogs are allowed at the outdoor tables.
Rudi's World Cuisine 4720 Table Mesa Drive Boulder CO   303-494-5858
http://www.rudismenu.com
Dogs are allowed at the outdoor tables. The restaurant has outdoor tables only in the summer.

Breckenridge

Accommodations
Breckenridge Wayside Inn 165 Tiger Rd. Breckenridge CO   970-453-5540 (800-927-7669)
http://www.toski.com/wayside/
Clean, comfortable motel rooms which are centrally located in Summit County, just 5 minutes to Breckenridge. Thanks to one of our readers who writes "Low-key, no-frills motel. A few miles from the heart of town but right on the main highway." Amenities include a free continental breakfast and free Hot Spiced Cider with cheese & crackers. Dogs are allowed at the motel, but not allowed in lodge area because they have three dogs of their own. There is a $20 refundable pet deposit.
Great Divide Lodge 550 Village Road Breckenridge CO   970-547-5550 (888-906-5698)
This full-service, slopeside hotel features 208 spacious, luxury guestrooms rich with amenities, 24 hour guest service, indoor and outdoor pools and hot tubs, a large sun deck, in room dining, a restaurant and lounge, expansive mountain views, and heated underground parking. Although pet friendly rooms are limited, dogs up to 45 pounds are allowed for an additional fee of $30 per night per pet, plus a $150 refundable deposit, with advance reservations. Dogs must be well behaved, leashed, and cleaned up after.

Campgrounds and RV Parks
Tiger Run RV Resort 85 Tiger Run Road Breckenridge CO   800-895-9594
http://www.tigerrunresort.com
Dogs of all sizes are allowed. There are no additional pet fees. Dogs must be leashed and cleaned up after.
There is a dog walk area at the campground.

Broomfield

Accommodations
TownePlace Suites Boulder Broomfield 480 Flatiron Blvd Broomfield CO   303-466-2200
Dogs of all sizes are allowed. There is a $75 one time pet fee per visit.

Stores
PetSmart Pet Store 16575 Washington St Broomfield CO   303-255-0644
Your licensed and well-behaved leashed dog is allowed in the store.
Petco Pet Store 12163 North Sheridan Blvd Broomfield CO   303-635-1540
Your licensed and well-behaved leashed dog is allowed in the store.

Buena Vista

Campgrounds and RV Parks
Arrowhead Point Camping Resort 33975 Hwy 24N Buena Vista CO   719-395-2323
http://www.arrowheadpointresort.com
Dogs of all sizes are allowed. There are no additional pet fees. Dogs must be leashed and cleaned up after.
There are some breed restrictions. This RV park is closed during the off-season. The camping and tent areas
also allow dogs. There is a dog walk area at the campground.
Buena Vista KOA 27700 Hwy 303 Buena Vista CO   719-395-8318 (800-562-2672)
http://www.koa.com
Dogs of all sizes are allowed, and there are no additional pet fees for tent or RV sites. There is a $5 per night per
pet additional fee for cabins. There can be up to 3 dogs at tent or RV sites, but only up to 2 dogs at the cabins.
Dogs may not be left unattended, and they must be leashed and cleaned up after. There are some breed
restrictions. This RV park is closed during the off-season. The camping and tent areas also allow dogs. There is
a dog walk area at the campground. Dogs are allowed in the camping cabins.

Burlington

Accommodations
Comfort Inn 282 S Lincoln Burlington CO   719-346-7676 (877-424-6423)
Dogs of all sizes are allowed. There is a $50 refundable deposit, plus a $10 per night per pet additional fee.
Dogs may not be left unattended, and they must be leashed and cleaned up after.

Campgrounds and RV Parks
Bonny Lake State Park 32300 Yuma County Road 2 Burlington CO   970-354-7306
Dogs of all sizes are allowed. There are no additional pet fees. Dogs must be on no more than a 6 foot leash,
and be cleaned up after. Dogs are allowed on the trails and at the beach, but not at the swim areas. The
camping and tent areas also allow dogs. There is a dog walk area at the campground. There are no water
hookups at the campground.

Canon City

Accommodations

Comfort Inn 282 S Lincoln Canon City CO   719-275-8676 (877-424-6423)
Dogs of all sizes are allowed. There are no additional fees or deposits with a credit card on file. Dogs must be well behaved, leashed, and cleaned up after. Dogs may only be left for short periods if they will be very quiet, and a contact number is left with the front desk. Dogs must be crated or removed for housekeeping.
Comfort Inn 311 Royal Gorge Blvd/H50 Canon City CO   719-276-6900 (877-424-6423)
Dogs of all sizes are allowed. There is a $10 one time fee per pet. Dogs may not be left alone in the rooms, and they must be leashed and cleaned up after.
Holiday Inn Express 110 Latigo Lane Canon City CO   719-275-2400 (877-270-6405)
Dogs of all sizes are allowed. There is a $10 per day pet fee.

Campgrounds and RV Parks
Fort Gorge RV Park 45044 Hwy 50W Canon City CO   719-275-5111
http://www.fortgorge.com
Dogs of all sizes are allowed. There are no additional pet fees. Dogs may not be left unattended, and must be leashed and cleaned up after. The camping and tent areas also allow dogs. There is a dog walk area at the campground. Dogs are allowed in the camping cabins.
Royal Gorge/Canon City KOA 559 County Road 3A Canon City CO   719-275-6116 (800-562-5689)
http://www.royalgorgekoa.net
Dogs of all sizes are allowed. There are no additional pet fees. Dogs may not be left unattended at the cabins, and they must be leashed and cleaned up after. This RV park is closed during the off-season. The camping and tent areas also allow dogs. There is a dog walk area at the campground. Dogs are allowed in the camping cabins.
Yogi Bear Jellystone Park 43595 Hwy 50 Canon City CO   719-275-2128 (800-341-4471)
http://www.royalgorgejellystone.com
Dogs of all sizes are allowed. There are no additional pet fees. Dogs may not be left unattended except for short periods. Dogs must be well behaved, quiet, leashed, and cleaned up after. There are some breed restrictions. This RV park is closed during the off-season. The camping and tent areas also allow dogs. There is a dog walk area at the campground.

Attractions
TOP 200 PLACE Buckskin Joe Frontier Town and Railway 1193 Fremont County Road 3A Canon City CO   719-275-5149
http://www.buckskinjoe.com/
This old west town takes you to back to the wild frontier through a series of activities and settings. The "little train" is open-topped and offers a big view of this dramatic gorge country. After the train ride, head back into town for a variety of activities, reenactments, food, and fun. Hours and days open vary throughout the seasons. This place is pet friendly; they even let your four-legged friends ride the train, go into all the shops, or belly up to the bar at the Silver Dollar Saloon for something cool to drink. They are not allowed in the restaurant; however, the same menu is served in the bar. They ask that you take extra care with your dog around the other animals in town and during the gunfights. Dogs must be leashed and cleaned up after at all times.
TOP 200 PLACE Royal Gorge Bridge & Park 4218 Fremont County Road 3A Canon City CO   719-275-7507
http://www.royalgorgebridge.com/
Known as the Grand Canyon of Colorado, this park offers a variety of thrill rides, several attractions such as the Mountain Man Encampment, a Visitor's Center, petting zoo, a wildlife park, the world's highest suspension bridge that offers unparalleled views of all over-but especially down, and much more. They also offer live daily entertainment, shopping, and a variety of food choices. Dogs are allowed throughout the park as long as they are kept leashed at all times, and cleaned up after. Dogs are not allowed on any of the rides.

Canyon City

Accommodations
Quality Inn & Suites 3075 E Hwy 50 Canyon City CO   719-275-8676 (877-424-6423)
Dogs of all sizes are allowed. There are no additional pet fees.

Carbondale

Accommodations
Comfort Inn and Suites 920 Cowen Drive Carbondale CO   970-963-8880 (877-424-6423)
Dogs of all sizes are allowed. There can be up to 3 small dogs, or up to 2 medium to large dogs, per room. Dogs may not be left unattended, and they must be leashed and cleaned up after.

Castle Rock

Accommodations
Comfort Suites 4755 Castleton Way Castle Rock CO   303-814-9999 (877-424-6423)
Dogs of all sizes are allowed. There is a $10 per night per room additional pet fee. Dogs must be leashed, cleaned up after, and removed or crated for housekeeping. The Do Not Disturb sign needs to be on the door if there is a pet in the room alone.
Days Inn and Suites Castle Rock 4691 Castleton Way Castle Rock CO   303-814-5825 (800-329-7466)
Dogs of all sizes are allowed. There is a $10 per night pet fee per pet.
Hampton Inn 4830 Castleton Way Castle Rock CO   303-660-9800
Dogs of all sizes are allowed. There is a $25 one time fee. Dogs are not to be left alone in the room, and they will not accept Bit Bulls.
Holiday Inn Express 884 Park Street Castle Rock CO   303-660-9733 (877-270-6405)
There is a $10 per day additional pet fee. Dogs up to 50 pounds are allowed.
Super 8 Castle Rock 1020 Park St Castle Rock CO   303-688-0800 (800-800-8000)
Dogs of all sizes are allowed. There are no additional pet fees. Dogs are not allowed to be left alone in the room. Smoking and non-smoking rooms are available for pet rooms.

Campgrounds and RV Parks
Castle Rock Campground 6527 S I 25 Castle Rock CO   303-681-3169 (800-387-9396)
http://www.castlerockcampground.com
Dogs of all sizes are allowed. There are no additional pet fees. Dogs must be well behaved, leashed, and cleaned up after. They also have lodges (deluxe cabins) where your dog is allowed at no extra fee. The camping and tent areas also allow dogs. There is a dog walk area at the campground. Dogs are allowed in the camping cabins.

Stores
PetSmart Pet Store 4565 Milestone Dr Castle Rock CO   720-733-6282
Your licensed and well-behaved leashed dog is allowed in the store.

Off-Leash Dog Parks
Glendale Open Space Dog Park 100 Third Street Castle Rock CO   303-660-7495
This area has a 5 acre off leash dog-park where you can really let them run. It is adjacent to a 1.6 mile natural multi-use trail area where dogs must be on lead because of the sensitive habitats. The Open Space area is on the east side of the highway down a short gravel drive, and the dog park area is just west of the main trailhead; southwest of the parking lot. Benches and port-a-potties are on site.

Cedaredge

Accommodations
Howard Johnson Express Inn 530 So. Grand Mesa Drive Cedaredge CO   970-856-7824 (800-446-4656)
Dogs of all sizes are welcome. There is a $10 per day pet fee per pet.

Centennial

Accommodations
Candlewood Suites 6780 South Galena St Centennial CO   303-792-5393 (877-270-6405)
Dogs up to 80 pounds are allowed. There is a $75 one time pet fee for 1-6 nights and $150 for over 7 nights.

Smoking and non-smoking rooms are available for pets.
Embassy Suites Hotel Denver Tech Center 10250 E. Costilla Avenue Centennial CO   303-792-0433
Dogs of all sizes are allowed. There is a $75 one time pet fee per visit. Dogs are not allowed to be left alone in the room.

Central City

Campgrounds and RV Parks
Gambler's Edge RV Park 605 Lake Gultch Road Central City CO   303-582-9345
http://www.gamblersedgervpark.com
Dogs of all sizes are allowed. There are no additional pet fees. Dogs must be leashed and cleaned up after. There are some breed restrictions. There is a dog walk area at the campground.

Clark

Accommodations
Steamboat Lake Marina Camper Cabins P. O. Box 867/Hwy 62 Clark CO   970-879-7019
Located in the scenic Steamboat Lake State Park at 8,100 feet on a beautiful 1,100 acre lake, this marina is now offering rental cabins for year around campers. Nestled in the pines and of log construction, the cabins each have a small refrigerator/freezer, coffee maker, some with table and chairs, and all have electric heat and fire pits. There is a convenience store at the marina, coin operated showers, flush toilets, and running water close to sites. Boat rentals are also available, and your dog is allowed to join you. Dogs of all sizes are allowed in the cabins. There is a $5 per night per pet additional fee. Dogs must be leashed and cleaned up after, and under owner's control at all times. A park pass is also required in addition to cabin fees.

Campgrounds and RV Parks
Steamboat Lake State Park 61105 Hwy 129 Clark CO   970-879-3922 (800-678-2267)
This park is one of Colorado's most popular parks with year round recreational pursuits. Although the camp areas are closed in winter, there are 18 sites for RVs at the marina. Dogs of all sizes are allowed at no additional fee. Dogs may not be left unattended, and they must have current rabies and shot records. Dogs must be on no more than a 6 foot leash, and be cleaned up after. Dogs are not allowed in public swim areas or in buildings. Dogs are allowed on the trails. The camping and tent areas also allow dogs. There is a dog walk area at the campground. There are no water hookups at the campground.
Steamboat Lake State Park 61105 Rural County Road 129 Clark CO   970-879-3922
This park sits in a lush forest setting at 8,100 feet, and offers wonderful scenery of green valleys and alpine wildflowers. A park for all seasons, there is an abundance of activities and recreation to enjoy, such as hiking, fishing, swimming, boating, and skiing. Dogs of all sizes are allowed for no additional fee. Dogs must be on no more than a 6 foot leash and cleaned up after at all times. Dogs are allowed throughout the park and on the trails; they are not allowed on the swim beach. The campground offers 198 sites, and some of the amenities include a visitor's center, an amphitheater, a marina with store, campfires, barbecue grills, tables, coin operated laundry, hot showers (even in winter), and a dump station. The State Park daily vehicle pass is not included in your reservation and must be purchased separately at the park. The camping and tent areas also allow dogs. There is a dog walk area at the campground. There are no water hookups at the campgrounds.

Attractions
TOP 200 PLACE **Steamboat Lake Marina** P. O. Box 867/County Road 62 Clark CO   970-879-7019
http://www.steamboatlakemarina.com/
Located In the scenic Steamboat Lake State Park at 8,100 feet, this marina services a 1,100 surface acre, beautiful man made lake. They offer boat rentals (seasonal), fuel, a convenience store, and freshly made foods in the summer. If requested at the time of reservation, some of the pontoon boats have gas grills on board for no extra charge. Dogs are allowed on the rentals, and they are usually most comfortable on the pontoon boats. There is no additional fee for your pet unless there is excessive cleaning needed, then, there is a $25 cleaning fee. Dogs must be under owner's control and cleaned up after at all times.

Parks
Steamboat Lake State Park 61105 Rural County Road 129 Clark CO   970-879-3922

This park sits in a lush forest setting at 8,100 feet, and offers wonderful scenery of green valleys and alpine wildflowers. A park for all seasons, there is an abundance of activities and recreation to enjoy, such as hiking, fishing, swimming, boating, and skiing. Dogs of all sizes are allowed for no additional fee. Dogs must be on no more than a 6 foot leash and cleaned up after at all times. Dogs are allowed throughout the park and on the trails; they are not allowed on the swim beach.

Clifton

Campgrounds and RV Parks
Colorado River State Park 700 32 Road Clifton CO 970-434-3388
This is an unusual park in that there are five separate areas along the Colorado River for this park, each with their own special recreational features. From Island Acres on the east, down to the river at Fruita, there is a variety of scenery, a wildlife area, and varied activities such as hiking, biking, picnicking, fishing, swimming, and more, to greet visitors. The 3 middle sections of the park are for day use only, and at each end there is camping. Dogs of all sizes are allowed for no additional fee. Dogs must be on no more than a 6 foot leash and cleaned up after at all times. Dogs are allowed throughout the park and on the trails; they are not allowed on the swim beach. The campgrounds are in the Island Acres (I-70 at exit 47) and Fruita (I-70 at exit 19) areas, and they offer flush toilets, laundry facilities, coin-operated hot showers, barbecues, campfires, a dump station, firewood for sale, and vending machines. Camping fees may be reduced in winter, and an Aspen Leaf day use pass is required in addition to applicable camping fees. The camping and tent areas also allow dogs. There is a dog walk area at the campground.
RV Ranch at Grand Junction 3238 E I 70 Business Loop Clifton CO 970-434-6644
http://www.rvranches.com
One dog of any size is allowed. There are no additional pet fees. Dogs must be leashed and cleaned up after. There are some breed restrictions. The camping and tent areas also allow dogs. There is a dog walk area at the campground.

Parks
Colorado River State Park 700 32 Road Clifton CO 970 434 3388
This is an unusual park in that there are five separate areas along the Colorado River for this park, each with their own special recreational features. From Island Acres on the east, down to the river at Fruita, there is a variety of scenery, a wildlife area, and varied activities such as hiking, biking, picnicking, fishing, swimming, and more, to greet visitors. The 3 middle sections of the park are for day use only, and at each end there is camping. Dogs of all sizes are allowed for no additional fee. Dogs must be on no more than a 6 foot leash and cleaned up after at all times. Dogs are allowed throughout the park and on the trails; they are not allowed on the swim beach.

Colorado Springs

Accommodations
Candlewood Suites 6450 North Academy Blvd Colorado Springs CO 719-533-0011 (877-270-6405)
Dogs of all sizes are allowed. There is a $35 one time pet fee for 1-6 nights and $75 for over 7 nights. Smoking and non-smoking rooms are available for pets.
Clarion Hotel 314 W Bijou Street Colorado Springs CO 719-471-8680 (877-424-6423)
Dogs of all sizes are allowed. There is a $10 per night per pet additional fee. Dogs may only be left alone in the room if they will be quiet, well behaved, and crated. Dogs must be leashed and cleaned up after.
Comfort Inn North 6450 Corporate Center Drive Colorado Springs CO 719-262-9000 (877-424-6423)
Dogs of all sizes are allowed. There can be up to 3 very small dogs or up to 2 average sized dogs per room. There is a $10 per night per pet additional fee, and a pet policy to sign at check in. Dogs must be quiet, well behaved, leashed, and cleaned up after.
Days Inn Colorado Springs 8350 Razorback Rd Colorado Springs CO 719-266-1314 (800-329-7466)
Dogs of all sizes are allowed. There is a $10 per night pet fee per pet.
Days Inn Colorado Springs 2850 S Circle Dr Colorado Springs CO 719-527-0800 (800-329-7466)
Dogs of all sizes are allowed. There is a $25 one time per pet fee per visit.
Econo Lodge Inn and Suites World Arena 1623 South Nevada Colorado Springs CO 719-632-6651
http://www.choicehotels.com/hotel/co725
This hotel has a large wooded park on site. They also have a staff veterinarian. There is no size restrictions for dogs. There is a playground for children on site. Pets and their owners may select either smoking or non

smoking rooms. There is a $20 refundable pet deposit. Pets must be crated if left in rooms and are not allowed to stay if they engage in persistent or periodic barking. Pets must be leashed while on the hotel property outside of the guest room.

La Quinta Inn & Suites Colorado Springs South AP 2750 Geyser Dr. Colorado Springs CO   719-527-4788 (800-531-5900)
Dogs up to 80 pounds are allowed. There are no additional pet fees. Leave a cell number with the front desk if your dog is alone in the room, and make arrangements with housekeeping if staying more than one day. Dogs may not be left unattended, and they must be leashed and cleaned up after.

La Quinta Inn Colorado Springs Garden of the Gods 4385 Sinton Rd. Colorado Springs CO   719-528-5060 (800-531-5900)
Dogs of all sizes are allowed. There are no additional pet fees. Dogs may not be left unattended, and they must be leashed and cleaned up after.

Motel 6 - Colorado Springs 3228 N Chestnut Street Colorado Springs CO   719-520-5400 (800-466-8356)
One well-behaved family pet per room. Guest must notify front desk upon arrival. Guest is liable for any damages. In consideration of all guests, pets must never be left unattended in the guest rooms.

Radisson Inn & Suites Colorado Springs Airport 1645 N. Newport Road Colorado Springs CO   719-597-7000
Up to 2 dogs per room are allowed. Each dog must not be larger than 50 pounds. There is a $100 refundable pet deposit and a $25 non-refundable one time pet fee per visit.

Radisson Inn Colorado Springs North 8110 North Academy Blvd Colorado Springs CO   719-598-5770
Dogs of any size are allowed. Pets are welcome but need to stay in first floor rooms. There is a $50 refundable pet deposit.

Red Roof Inn - Colorado Springs 8280 Highway 83 Colorado Springs CO   719-598-6700 (800-RED-ROOF)
One well-behaved family pet per room. Guest must notify front desk upon arrival. Guest is liable for any damages. In consideration of all guests, pets must never be left unattended in the guest rooms.

Residence Inn by Marriott 3880 N Academy Blvd Colorado Springs CO   719-574-0370
Dogs of all sizes are allowed. There is a $75 one time fee and a pet policy to sign at check in.

Residence Inn by Marriott 2765 Geyser Drive Colorado Springs CO   719-576-0101
Dogs of all sizes are allowed. There is a $75 one time fee and a pet policy to sign at check in.

Sheraton Colorado Springs Hotel 2886 South Circle Dr. Colorado Springs CO   719-576-5900 (888-625-5144)
Dogs up to 60 pounds are allowed. There are no additional pet fees. Dogs are not allowed to be left alone in the room.

Staybridge Suites 7130 Commerce Center Dr Colorado Springs CO   719-590-7829 (877-270-6405)
Dogs of all sizes are allowed. There is a $150 one time pet fee per visit. Smoking and non-smoking rooms are available for pets.

Super 8 Colorado Spring/Hwy 24 605 Peterson Rd Colorado Springs CO   719-597-4100 (800-800-8000)
Dogs of all sizes are allowed. There is a $10 per night pet fee per pet. Smoking and non-smoking rooms are available for pet rooms.

TownePlace Suites Colorado Springs 4760 Centennial Blvd Colorado Springs CO   719-594-4447
Dogs of all sizes are allowed. There is a $20 per night pet fee per pet or there is a $75 one time pet fee per visit.

Campgrounds and RV Parks

Fountain Creek RV Park 3023 W Colorado Avenue Colorado Springs CO   719-633-2192
http://www.fountaincreekrvpark.com
Dogs of all sizes are allowed. There are no additional pet fees. Dogs may not be left unattended, and must be leashed and cleaned up after. The camping and tent areas also allow dogs. There is a dog walk area at the campground.

Garden of the Gods Campground 3704 W Colorado Avenue Colorado Springs CO   719-475-9450
http://www.coloradocampground.com
Dogs of all sizes are allowed. There are no additional pet fees. Dogs must be quiet, leashed, and cleaned up after. The camping and tent areas also allow dogs. There is a dog walk area at the campground.

Attractions

TOP 200 PLACE **Pikes Peak Toll Road** P.O. Box 1575-MC060 Colorado Springs CO   719-385-PEAK (800-318-9505)
The Pikes Peak Toll Road allows you to drive your car up to the top of Pikes Peak at an altitude of over 14,000 feet. You may bring your dog with you. Dogs are not allowed on the Cog Railway. Dogs need to be on leash when outside of your car. There are a number of trails at various altitudes where leashed dogs may accompany you. Please keep in mind that the air is very thin at 14,000 feet. Before venturing up to this altitude, you should check with any appropriate doctors and veterinarians. At the summit, do not let your dog off-leash as it is very unsafe to exercise your dog at this altitude. It will take you up to around three hours to make the round trip up the mountain. To get to the toll road from Interstate 25 take Highway 24 West to the toll road.

TOP 200 PLACE **Manitou Cliff Dwellings Museum** Cliff Dwelling Road Manitou Springs CO   719-685-5242

http://www.cliffdwellingsmuseum.com/
These authentic Anasazi cliff dwellings have been preserved under a protective red sandstone overhang, and are considered a rare historical treasure. In addition to the ruins, there are reproductions of a stone mesa-top building, an Anasazi baking oven, a nature walk with well-labeled native flowers/herbs/trees, and a 3 story Pueblo-style building that houses the museum and gift shop. From June through August a snack bar and picnic patio are available. Well behaved, leased dogs are allowed throughout the preserve, and please clean up after your pet.

Stores
PetSmart Pet Store 571 N Academy Colorado Springs CO   719-570-1313
Your licensed and well-behaved leashed dog is allowed in the store.
PetSmart Pet Store 7680 N Academy Blvd Colorado Springs CO   719-531-7870
Your licensed and well-behaved leashed dog is allowed in the store.
PetSmart Pet Store 2160 Southgate Rd Colorado Springs CO   719-447-0622
Your licensed and well-behaved leashed dog is allowed in the store.
PetSmart Pet Store 2965 New Center Point Colorado Springs CO   719-637-3308
Your licensed and well-behaved leashed dog is allowed in the store.
Petco Pet Store 1820A West Uintah St Colorado Springs CO   719-578-1123
Your licensed and well-behaved leashed dog is allowed in the store.
Petco Pet Store 5720 North Academy Blvd Colorado Springs CO   719-536-0160
Your licensed and well-behaved leashed dog is allowed in the store.
Petco Pet Store 1650 East Cheyenne Mountain Blvd Colorado Springs CO   719-540-8090
Your licensed and well-behaved leashed dog is allowed in the store.
Petco Pet Store 3050 North Powers Blvd Colorado Springs CO   719-637-8777
Your licensed and well-behaved leashed dog is allowed in the store.

Parks
Garden of the Gods Park 1805 N 30th Street Colorado Springs CO   719-634-6666
http://www.gardenofgods.com
Dogs on leash are allowed in the park. You must cleanup after pets at all times. There is a section between Gateway Road and 30th Street that is fenced in for off-leash dogs. They are also allowed to sit at the outside tables of the cafe in the park.
Seven Falls 2850 S Cheyenne Rd Colorado Springs CO   719-632-0765
http://www.sevenfalls.com
Dogs on leash are allowed in the park. The park is open all year round. The park features a waterfall with hiking trails and picnic areas. There is a fee for people but dogs are free. You must cleanup after your pets. The park is located about 15 minutes from downtown Colorado Springs.

Off-Leash Dog Parks
Cheyenne Meadows Dog Park Charmwood Dr. and Canoe Creek Dr. Colorado Springs CO   719-385-2489
There is a fenced dog park in the southern portion of Cheyenne Meadows Park.
Garden of the Gods Park Off-Leash Area Gateway Road Colorado Springs CO   719-385-2489
This park has a designated off-leash area which is not fenced. The area is located east of Rock Ledge Ranch and south of Gateway Road. Dogs must be leashed when outside the off-leash area.
Palmer Park Dog Park 3650 Maizeland Road Colorado Springs CO   719-385-2489
This park has a fenced off-leash area. It is located at the old baseball field, .3 miles from the Maizeland entrance. There is also an off-leash area (Dog Run Area) in the park which is not fenced. Dogs must be leashed when outside the off-leash area.
Rampart Park Dog Park 8270 Lexington Drive Colorado Springs CO   719-385-2489
This park has a fenced off-leash area. It is located just east of the baseball diamond. Dogs must be leashed when outside the off-leash area. The area is located near Rampart High School, next to the running track.
Red Rock Canyon Off-Leash Dog Loops 31st Street at Highway 24 Colorado Springs CO   719-385-2489
At Red Rock Canyon Open Space Reserve there are two dog loops on which dogs are allowed to be off-leash if they are under voice control. These trails total about 5/8 mile in length and are located just south of the main entrance to the park. Dogs on leash are allowed on the rest of the trails in the park. To get to the reserve take Highway 24 to High Street and head south into the reserve.
Red Rock Canyon Open Space 31st Street at Highway 24 Colorado Springs CO   719-385-2489
http://www.redrockcanyonopenspace.org
The Red Rock Canyon Open Space is a beautiful series of canyons and hills in the east slope of the Rockies. In 2003 the City of Colorado Springs purchased nearly 800 acres for the purpose of providing trails, hiking, cycling,

equestrian activities and trails for people with dogs. Dogs on leash are allowed throughout the picturesque trails. There are over 10 miles of trails in the open space. However, there are two dog loops on which dogs are allowed to be off-leash if they are under voice control. These trails total about 5/8 mile in length and are located just south of the main entrance to the park.

Outdoor Restaurants
La Petite Maison Restaurant 1015 W Colorado Ave Colorado Springs CO 719-632-4887
This restaurant serves French/American cuisine. Dogs are allowed at the outdoor tables.
Poor Richard's 324 North Tejon Colorado Springs CO 719-632-7721
This restaurant serves American food. Dogs are allowed at the outdoor tables.
Whole Foods Market 7635 N Academy Blvd Colorado Springs CO 719-531-9999
This restaurant serves deli-type food. Dogs are allowed at the outdoor tables.
Stagecoach Inn 702 Manitou Ave Manitou Springs CO 719-685-9400
This restaurant serves American food. Dogs are allowed at the outdoor tables with reservations.

Day Kennels
PetsHotel by PetsMart Day Kennel 7680 N. Academy Blvd. Colorado Springs CO 719-531-0711
http://www.petsmart.com/PETsHOTEL/
This PetSmart pet store offers day care, day camp and overnight care. You may drop off your dog during the hours of 7 am - 8:45 pm M-S, Sunday 7 am - 7 pm. Dogs must have proof of current up to date rabies, DPP and bordatella vaccinations.

Cortez

Accommodations
Anasazi Motor Inn 640 S. Broadway Cortez CO 970-565-3773 (800-972-6232)
There is a $50 refundable pet deposit.
Days Inn Cortez 430 N State Hwy 145 Cortez CO 970-565-8577 (800-329-7466)
Dogs of all sizes are allowed. There is a $10 per night pet fee per pet. Pet must be kept in kennel when left alone.
Holiday Inn Express 2121 East Main Cortez CO 970-565-6000 (877-270-6405)
Dogs of all sizes are allowed. There are no additional pet fees. Dogs are not allowed to be left alone in the room. Reservations are recommended due to limited rooms for pets. Smoking and non-smoking rooms are available for pets.
Far View Lodge Mesa Verde National Park Mancos CO 970-529-4421
Far View Lodge sits on a high shoulder of the Mesa Verde, offering panoramic vistas into three states. There is a $50 refundable pet deposit. Pets are allowed in some of the standard rooms.
Morefield Lodge and Campground 34879 Hwy 160 Mancos CO 800-449-2288
Dogs of all sizes are allowed. There is a $25 per night per pet additional fee. Dogs may not be left unattended, and they must be leashed and cleaned up after. There is an RV and campground on site where dogs are allowed at no extra fee. Dogs may not be on the trails or in the camp buildings.

Campgrounds and RV Parks
Cortez Mesa Verde KOA 27432 E Hwy 160 Cortez CO 970-565-9301 (800-562-3901)
http://www.cortezkoa.com
Dogs of all sizes are allowed. There are no additional pet fees. Dogs may not be left unattended at the cabins or outside, and they must be leashed and cleaned up after. There are some breed restrictions. This RV park is closed during the off-season. The camping and tent areas also allow dogs. There is a dog walk area at the campground. Dogs are allowed in the camping cabins.
Echo Basin Ranch 43747 Co. Rd M Mancos CO 970-533-7000 (800-426-1890)
http://www.echobasin.com/rvpark.html
Dogs of all sizes are allowed. There are no additional pet fees. Dogs must be leashed or crated at all times, and be cleaned up after. This RV park is closed during the off-season. The camping and tent areas also allow dogs. There is a dog walk area at the campground.
Mesa Verde RV Resort 35303 Hwy 160 Mancos CO 970-533-7421
Dogs of all sizes are allowed. There are no additional pet fees. Dogs must be leashed and cleaned up after. There is a pet sitter on site available for $5 per pet per day. The camping and tent areas also allow dogs. There is a dog walk area at the campground. There are special amenities given to dogs at this campground.
Mesa Verde RV Resort 35303 Hwy 160 Mancos CO 970-533-7421 (800-776-7421)
http://www.mesaverdervresort.com/

Dogs of all sizes are allowed. There are no additional pet fees. Dogs must be leashed and cleaned up after. Dogs are not allowed in buildings or the pool area. The camping and tent areas also allow dogs. There is a dog walk area at the campground.

Morefield Campground 34879 Hwy 160 Mancos CO   800-449-2288
http://www.visitmesaverde.com
Dogs of all sizes are allowed, and there are no additional pet fees for tent or RV sites. There is a $25 per night per pet additional fee for the lodge. Dogs may not be left unattended at the lodge at any time. Dogs must be leashed and cleaned up after. Dogs may not be left outside unattended, and they are not allowed in the buildings or on the trails. This RV park is closed during the off-season. The camping and tent areas also allow dogs. There is a dog walk area at the campground.

Parks
Hovenweep National Monument McElmo Route Cortez CO   970-562-4282
http://www.nps.gov/hove/index.htm
Dogs must be on leash and must be cleaned up after in the park area. The park features hiking, camping, and sightseeing. The monument protects six Puebloan-era villages spread over a twenty-mile expanse of mesa tops and canyons along the Utah-Colorado border.

Cotopaxi

Campgrounds and RV Parks
Cotopaxi Arkansas River KOA 21435 Hwy 50 Cotopaxi CO   719-275-9308 (800-562-2686)
http://www.koa.com
Dogs of all sizes are allowed, and there are no additional pet fees for tent or RV sites. There is a $5 per night per pet additional fee for the cabins or motel. Dogs must be quiet, well behaved, be on no more than a 6 foot leash, and cleaned up after. Dogs may not be left unattended at any time. There are some breed restrictions. This RV park is closed during the off-season. The camping and tent areas also allow dogs. There is a dog walk area at the campground. Dogs are allowed in the camping cabins.

Craig

Accommodations
Holiday Inn Hotel and Suites 300 Colorado Hwy 13 Craig CO   970-824-4000 (877-270-6405)
Dogs of all sizes are allowed. There is a $50 returnable deposit required per room. Smoking and non-smoking rooms are available for pets.

Super 8 Craig 200 Hwy 13 South Craig CO   970-824-3471 (800-800-8000)
Dogs of all sizes are allowed. There is a $4 per night pet fee per pet. Smoking and non-smoking rooms are available for pet rooms.

Campgrounds and RV Parks
Craig KOA 2800 E Hwy 40 Craig CO   970-824-5105 (800-562-5095)
http://www.koa.com
Dogs of all sizes are allowed. There are no additional pet fees. Dogs must be leashed and cleaned up after. The camping and tent areas also allow dogs. There is a dog walk area at the campground. Dogs are allowed in the camping cabins.

Crawford

Campgrounds and RV Parks
Crawford State Park 40468 Hwy 92 N Crawford CO   970-921-5721 (800-678-2267)
Water recreation, fishing, and hiking are the main attractions at this scenic park. Dogs of all sizes are allowed at no additional fee. Dogs may not be left unattended, and they must be on no more than a 6 foot leash, and cleaned up after. Dogs are not allowed in buildings, or on the swim or ski beaches. The camping and tent areas also allow dogs. There is a dog walk area at the campground.

Crested Butte

Accommodations
The Ruby of Crested Butte 624 Gothic Avenue Crested Butte CO 970-349-1338
Dogs of all sizes are allowed. There is a pet policy to sign at check in and there are no additional fees.

Cripple Creek

Campgrounds and RV Parks
Cripple Creek/Colorado Springs W KOA 2576 County Road 81 Cripple Creek CO 719-689-3376 (800-562-9152)
http://www.cripplecreekkoa.com
Dogs of all sizes are allowed. There are no additional pet fees. Dogs may not be left unattended at the cabins or outside. Dogs must be quiet, be on no more than a 6 foot leash, and cleaned up after. This RV park is closed during the off-season. The camping and tent areas also allow dogs. There is a dog walk area at the campground. Dogs are allowed in the camping cabins.

Del Norte

Campgrounds and RV Parks
Rio Grande National Forest 13308 W Hwy 160 Del Norte CO 719-852-5941 (800-678-2267)
http://www.fs.fed.us/r2/riogrande/
With 4 ranger districts and over a million acres, this forest provides a variety of camping areas and trails. The diverse ecosystems support a large variety of plant, fish, mammal, and bird species. Dogs are allowed at no additional fee. Dogs may not be left unattended, and they must be leashed and cleaned up after in the camp areas. Dogs are allowed on the trails. The camping and tent areas also allow dogs. There is a dog walk area at the campground.

Delta

Accommodations
Comfort Inn 180 Gunnison River Drive Delta CO 970-874-1000 (877-424-6423)
Dogs of all sizes are allowed. There is a $10 per night per pet additional fee. Dogs must be leashed and cleaned up after. Dogs may be left alone in the room only if they will be quiet, well behaved, a contact number is left with the front desk, and the Do Not Disturb sign is put on the door.

Campgrounds and RV Parks
Grand Mesa, Uncompahgre and Gunnison National Forests 2250 Hwy 50 Delta CO 970-874-6600
http://www.fs.fed.us/r2/gmug/
With more than 3 million acres of public land, there is a variety of recreational pursuits. Dogs of all sizes are allowed. There are no additional pet fees. Dogs must be leashed and cleaned up after. Dogs are allowed on the trails. This campground is closed during the off-season. The camping and tent areas also allow dogs. There is a dog walk area at the campground. There are no electric or water hookups at the campground.

Denver

Accommodations
La Quinta Inn Denver Aurora 1011 S. Abilene St. Aurora CO 303-337-0206 (800-531-5900)
Dogs of all sizes are allowed. There are no additional pet fees. Dogs must be crated when left alone in the room,

and they must be leashed and cleaned up after.
Motel 6 - Denver East - Aurora 14031 East Iliff Avenue Aurora CO   303-873-0286 (800-466-8356)
One well-behaved family pet per room. Guest must notify front desk upon arrival. Guest is liable for any damages. In consideration of all guests, pets must never be left unattended in the guest rooms.
Sleep Inn Denver International Airport 15900 E 40th Avenue Aurora CO   303-373-1616 (877-424-6423)
Dogs of all sizes are allowed. There is a $10 per night per pet additional fee, and a pet policy to sign at check in. Dogs may only be left alone in the room if they will be quiet, well behaved, and the Do Not Disturb sign is put on the door. Dogs must be leashed and cleaned up after.
Cameron Motel 4500 E Evans Denver CO   303-757-2100
Dogs of all sizes are allowed. There is a $5 per night per pet additional fee. Dogs must be well behaved, leashed, and cleaned up after.
Comfort Inn 401 E 58th Avenue Denver CO   303-297-1717 (877-424-6423)
Dogs of all sizes are allowed. There is a $10 per night per pet additional fee. Dogs may not be left in the room alone at any time, and they must be leashed and cleaned up after.
Days Inn Central Denver 620 Federal Blvd Denver CO   303-571-1715 (800-329-7466)
Dogs of all sizes are allowed. There is a $50 returnable deposit required per room. There is a $25 one time pet fee per visit.
Denver East Drury Inn 4380 Peoria Street Denver CO   303-373-1983 (800-378-7946)
Dogs of all sizes are permitted. Pets are not allowed in the breakfast area of the hotel. Pets are not to be left unattended, and each guest must assume liability for damage of property or other guest complaints. There is a limit of one pet per room.
Doubletree 3203 Quebec Street Denver CO   303-321-3333
Dogs of all sizes are allowed. There is a $20 one time fee per pet. No pit bulls are allowed per Denver law.
Embassy Suites Hotel Denver - Aurora 4444 N. Havana Denver CO   303-375-0400
Dogs of all sizes are allowed. There are no additional pet fees. Dogs are not allowed to be left alone in the room.
Embassy Suites Hotel Denver - Southeast (Hampden Ave.) 7525 East Hampden Ave. Denver CO   303-696-6644
Dogs of all sizes are allowed. There is a $50 one time pet fee per visit. Dogs are not allowed to be left alone in the room.
Executive Tower Hotel 1405 Curtis Street Denver CO   303-571-0300
There is a $50 refundable pet deposit.
Four Points by Sheraton Denver Cherry Creek 600 South Colorado Blvd. Denver CO   303-757-3341 (888-625-5144)
Dogs of all sizes are allowed. There is a $50 per day per dog fee. Dogs are not allowed to be left alone in the room.
Four Points by Sheraton Denver South East 6363 East Hampden Ave. Denver CO   303-758-7000 (888-625-5144)
Dogs of all sizes are allowed. There are no additional pet fees. Dogs are not allowed to be left alone in the room.
Guest House Inn 3737 Quebec St. Denver CO   303-388-6161 (800-2-RAMADA)
There is a $100 refundable pet deposit.
Hampton Inn 5001 S Ulster Street Denver CO   303-894-9900
Well behaved dogs of all sizes are allowed. There are no additional pet fees, and a pet policy to sign at check in.
Holiday Inn 4849 Bannock Street Denver CO   303-292-9500 (877-270-6405)
Dogs up to 65 pounds are allowed. There is a $200 returnable deposit required per room. Smoking and non-smoking rooms are available for pets.
Holiday Inn 15500 East 40th Ave Denver CO   303-371-9494 (877-270-6405)
Dogs of all sizes are allowed. There is a $25 one time per pet fee per visit. Smoking and non-smoking rooms are available for pets.
Hotel Monaco Denver 1717 Champa Street at 17th Denver CO   303-296-1717
http://www.monaco-denver.com/
Well-behaved dogs of all sizes are welcome at this pet-friendly hotel. The luxury boutique hotel offers both rooms and suites. Hotel amenities include complimentary evening wine service, a 24 hour on-site fitness room, and a gift shop. There are no pet fees, just sign a pet liability form.
Hotel Teatro 1100 Fourteenth Street Denver CO   303-228-1100
http://www.hotelteatro.com/
Dogs are allowed at this luxury boutique hotel. There is no extra pet charge.
Inn at Cherry Creek 233 Clayton Street Denver CO   303-377-8577
http://www.innatcherrycreek.com/
Located in the heart of the Cherry Creek North shopping and restaurant district, this unique hotel features 35 cozy quest rooms and 2 corporate residences with an outdoor roof-top terrace that is perfect for open air parties. There are many in-room amenities, and a full service restaurant/bar that puts focus on a fresh seasonally influenced menu. Dogs of all sizes are allowed for an additional pet fee of $10 per night per room. Dogs may only be left alone in the room if they will be quiet and well behaved. Dogs must be leashed and cleaned up after at all times.
JW Marriott Denver at Cherry Creek 150 Clayton Lane Denver CO   303-316-2700 (800-228-9290)

Dogs of all sizes are welcome with treats and special attention. There is a pet registration form to fill out, and they provide bedding, personalized bowls, and a pet walking service. There are no additional fees. Dogs must be quiet, well behaved, leashed, cleaned up after, and a contact number left with the front desk if they are in the room alone.

La Quinta Inn Denver Central 3500 Park Ave. West Denver CO   303-458-1222 (800-531-5900)
Dogs of all sizes are allowed. There are no additional pet fees. Dogs must be crated with the "Do Not Disturb" sign on the door when left alone in the room, and crated or removed for housekeeping. Dogs must be leashed and cleaned up after.

La Quinta Inn Denver Cherry Creek 1975 S. Colorado Blvd. Denver CO   303-758-8886 (800-531-5900)
Dogs of all sizes are allowed. There are no additional pet fees. Dogs may not be left unattended, and they must be leashed and cleaned up after.

Loews Denver Hotel 4150 East Mississippi Ave. Denver CO   303-782-9300
All well-behaved dogs of any size are welcome. This upscale hotel offers their "Loews Loves Pets" program which includes special pet treats, local dog walking routes, and a list of nearby pet-friendly places to visit. There are no pet fees.

Marriott TownePlace Suites - Downtown 685 Speer Blvd Denver CO   303-722-2322 (800-257-3000)
http://www.towneplacesuites.com/dencb
Marriott TownePlace Suites is an all suite hotel designed for the extended stay traveler. All studio, one, and two-bedroom suites offer full kitchens and weekly housekeeping. Pets are welcome for a non-refundable fee of $20 a day up to $200.00. On-site amenities include a guest laundry, business center, fitness room and free parking.

Motel 6 - Denver 3050 West 49th Avenue Denver CO   303-455-8888 (800-466-8356)
One well-behaved family pet per room. Guest must notify front desk upon arrival. Guest is liable for any damages. In consideration of all guests, pets must never be left unattended in the guest rooms.

Motel 6 - Denver - Airport 12020 East 39th Avenue Denver CO   303-371-1980 (800-466-8356)
One well-behaved family pet per room. Guest must notify front desk upon arrival. Guest is liable for any damages. In consideration of all guests, pets must never be left unattended in the guest rooms.

Oxford Hotel 1600 17th St Denver CO   303-628-5400 (800-228-5838)
http://www.theoxfordhotel.com
This hotel is located in Denver's trendy LoDo District. Please mention that you are bringing a pet when making reservations.

Quality Inn 3975 Peoria Way Denver CO   303-371-5640 (877-424-6423)
Dogs of all sizes are allowed. There is a $10 one time additional fee per pet for small dogs, and a $20 one time additional fee per pet for large dogs. Dogs must be leashed, cleaned up after, and the Do Not Disturb sign put on the door if they are in the room alone.

Red Lion 4040 Quebec Street Denver CO   303-321-6666
Dogs of all sizes are allowed. There is a $25 one time fee per pet.

Red Roof Inn - Denver Airport 6890 Tower Road Denver CO   303-371-5300 (800-RED-ROOF)
One well-behaved family pet per room. Guest must notify front desk upon arrival. Guest is liable for any damages. In consideration of all guests, pets must never be left unattended in the guest rooms.

Residence Inn by Marriott 2777 Zuni Street Denver CO   303-458-5318
Dogs of all sizes are allowed. There is a $75 one time fee and a pet policy to sign at check in.

Staybridge Suites 4200 East Virginia Avenue Denver CO   303-321-5757 (877-270-6405)
Dogs of all sizes are allowed. There is a $75 one time additional pet fee.

Super 8 Denver/I-25 and 58th Ave 5888 N Broadway Denver CO   303-296-3100 (800-800-8000)
Dogs up to 60 pounds are allowed. There is a $25 one time per pet fee per visit. Smoking and non-smoking rooms are available for pet rooms.

The Timbers 4411 Peoria Street Denver CO   303-373-1444
Dogs of all sizes are allowed. There is a $25 per stay per room fee and a pet policy to sign at check in.

The Westin Tabor Center 1672 Lawrence St. Denver CO   303-572-9100 (888-625-5144)
Dogs up to 50 pounds are allowed. There are no additional pet fees. Dogs are not allowed to be left alone in the room.

TownePlace Suites Denver Downtown 685 Speer Blvd Denver CO   303-722-2322
Dogs of all sizes are allowed. There is a $20 per night pet fee per pet.

TownePlace Suites Denver Southeast 3699 S Monaco Parkway Denver CO   303-759-9393
Dogs of all sizes are allowed. There is a $25 per night pet fee per pet.

Denver Tech Center Drury Inn & Suites 9445 East Dry Creek Road Englewood CO   303-694-3400 (800-378-7946)
Dogs of all sizes are permitted. Pets are not allowed in the breakfast area of the hotel. Pets are not to be left unattended, and each guest must assume liability for damage of property or other guest complaints. There is a limit of one pet per room.

Hampton Inn 9231 E Arapahoe Road Englewood CO   303-792-9999
Dogs of all sizes are allowed. There is a $10 per night per pet fee and a pet policy to sign at check in.

Holiday Inn Express Hotel and Suites 7380 South Clinton St Englewood CO   303-662-0777 (877-270-6405)
Dogs of all sizes are allowed. There are no additional pet fees. Smoking and non-smoking rooms are available for pets.

Quality Suites Tech Center South 7374 S Clinton Street Englewood CO   303-858-0700
Dogs of all sizes are allowed. There is a $10 per night per pet additional fee. Dogs must be quiet, leashed, cleaned up after, and the Do Not Disturb sign put on the door if they are in the room alone.
Residence Inn by Marriott 8322 S Valley Highway Englewood CO   720-895-0200
Dogs of all sizes are allowed. There is a $75 one time fee and a pet policy to sign at check in.
Residence Inn by Marriott 6565 S Yosemite Englewood CO   303-740-7177
Dogs of all sizes are allowed. There is a $75 one time fee per pet and a pet policy to sign at check in.
Sheraton Denver Technical Center Hotel 7007 South Clinton St. Englewood CO   303-799-6200 (888-625-5144)
Dogs up to 50 pounds are allowed. There are no additional pet fees. Dogs are not allowed to be left alone in the room.
TownePlace Suites Denver Tech Center 7877 S Chester Street Englewood CO   720-875-1113
Dogs of all sizes are allowed. There is a $25 per night ($200 max) pet fee per pet.
Candlewood Suites 895 Tabor Street Golden CO   303-232-7171 (877-270-6405)
Dogs up to 80 pounds are allowed. There is a $75 pet fee for stays up to 14 days. There is a $150 pet fee for longer stays.
Clarion Collection The Golden Hotel 800 11th Street Golden CO   303-279-0100 (877-424-6423)
Dogs of all sizes are allowed. There is a $100 refundable deposit per room plus $15 per night per pet additional fee. Dogs must be leashed, cleaned up after, and the Do Not Disturb sign put on the door if they are in the room alone. Dogs must be removed or crated for housekeeping.
Comfort Suites 11909 W 6th Avenue Golden CO   303-231-9929 (877-424-6423)
Dogs of all sizes are allowed. There is a $10 per night per room additional pet fee, and a pet policy to sign at check in. Dogs may not be left alone in the rooms at any time, and they must be leashed and cleaned up after. Dogs are not allowed in the common areas.
Denver Marriott West 1717 Denver West, Marriott Blvd Golden CO   303-279-9100 (800-228-9290)
Dogs of all sizes are allowed. There is a $50 one time additional pet fee per room. Dogs must be leashed, cleaned up after, and the Do Not Disturb sign put on the door if they are in the room alone.
La Quinta Inn Denver Golden 3301 Youngfield Service Rd. Golden CO   303-279-5565 (800-531-5900)
Dogs of all sizes are allowed. There are no additional pet fees. Dogs may only be left unattended in the room if they will be quiet and well behaved.
Quality Suites at Evergreen Parkway 29300 Hwy 40 Golden CO   303-526-2000
Dogs of all sizes are allowed. There is a $50 refundable deposit plus a $10 per night per pet additional fee. Dogs must be leashed, cleaned up after, and crated when left alone in the room.
La Quinta Inn & Suites Denver Englewood/Tech Ctr 9009 E. Arapahoe Road Greenwood Village CO   303-799-4555 (800-531-5900)
Dogs of all sizes are allowed. There are no additional pet fees. Dogs must be leashed, cleaned up after, removed for housekeeping, and the front desk notified if there is a pet in the room alone.
Motel 6 - Denver South - South Tech Center 9201 East Arapahoe Road Greenwood Village CO   303-790-8220 (800-466-8356)
One well-behaved family pet per room. Guest must notify front desk upon arrival. Guest is liable for any damages. In consideration of all guests, pets must never be left unattended in the guest rooms.
Sleep Inn Denver Tech Center 9257 E Costilla Avenue Greenwood Village CO   303-662-9950 (877-424-6423)
Dogs of all sizes are allowed. There is a $25 one time additional fee per pet. Dogs must be leashed, cleaned up after, crated when left alone in the room, and removed for housekeeping.
Residence Inn by Marriott 93 W Centennial Blvd Highlands Ranch CO   303-683-5500
Dogs of all sizes are allowed. There is a $75 one time fee and a pet policy to sign at check in.
La Quinta Inn & Suites Denver Southwest Lakewood 7190 West Hampden Ave. Lakewood CO   303-969-9700 (800-531-5900)
Dogs of most sizes are allowed; no extra large dogs. There are no additional pet fees. Dogs may only be left unattended in the room if they will be very quiet and well behaved, and leave the "Do Not Disturb" sign on the door. Dogs must be leashed.
Motel 6 - Denver - Lakewood 480 Wadsworth Boulevard Lakewood CO   303-232-4924 (800-466-8356)
One well-behaved family pet per room. Guest must notify front desk upon arrival. Guest is liable for any damages. In consideration of all guests, pets must never be left unattended in the guest rooms.
Residence Inn by Marriott 7050 W Hampden Avenue Lakewood CO   303-985-7676
Dogs of all sizes are allowed. Up to 2 dogs and one cat can be in the studios, and up to 3 dogs in the 2 bedroom suites. There is a $75 one time fee and a pet policy to sign at check in.
Sheraton Denver West Hotel 360 Union Blvd. Lakewood CO   303-987-2000 (888-625-5144)
Dogs up to 80 pounds are allowed. There is a $150 one time pet fee per visit. Dogs are restricted to rooms on the 4th floor only. Dogs are not allowed to be left alone in the room.
Super 8 Lakewood/Denver Area 7240 W Jefferson Ave Lakewood CO   303-989-4600 (800-800-8000)
Dogs of all sizes are allowed. There is a $10 per night pet fee per pet. Smoking and non-smoking rooms are available for pet rooms.
TownePlace Suites Denver Southwest/Littleton 10902 W Toller Drive Littleton CO   303-972-0555

Dogs of all sizes are allowed. There is a $10 one time pet fee per visit.
Staybridge Suites 7820 Park Meadows Dr Lone Tree CO   303-649-1010 (877-270-6405)
Dogs of all sizes are allowed. There is a $20 (maximum $100 fee) per night pet fee per pet. Smoking and non-smoking rooms are available for pets.
Motel 6 - Denver - Thorton 6 West 83rd Place Thornton CO   303-429-1550 (800-466-8356)
One well-behaved family pet per room. Guest must notify front desk upon arrival. Guest is liable for any damages. In consideration of all guests, pets must never be left unattended in the guest rooms.
Sleep Inn 12101 N Grant Street Thornton CO   303-280-9818 (877-424-6423)
Dogs of all sizes are allowed. There is a $5 per night per room additional fee for up to 2 dogs, and $10 per night additional fee for 3 dogs. Dogs must be leashed, cleaned up after, and the Do Not Disturb sign put on the door if they are in the room alone.
Doubletree 8773 Yates Drive Westminster CO   303-427-4000
Well behaved pets are allowed. There can be 3 small dogs or 2 large dogs per room, and no extra large dogs are allowed. Dogs are not allowed to be left in the room, except for short periods for meals in the hotel. There are no additional pet fees and they request to keep your dogs out of the public and food areas.
La Quinta Inn & Suites Westminster Promenade 10179 Church Ranch Way Westminster CO   303-438-5800 (800-531-5900)
Dogs of all sizes are allowed. There are no additional pet fees. Dogs must be leashed and cleaned up after.
La Quinta Inn Denver Northglenn 345 West 120th Ave. Westminster CO   303-252-9800 (800-531-5900)
Dogs of all sizes are allowed. There are no additional pet fees. Dogs must be crated when left alone in the room. Dogs must be leashed and cleaned up after.
La Quinta Inn Denver Westminster Mall 8701 Turnpike Dr. Westminster CO   303-425-9099 (800-531-5900)
One large dog or 2 small to medium dogs are allowed. There are no additional pet fees. Dogs must be leashed.
The Westin Westminster 10600 Westminster Blvd. Westminster CO   303-410-5000 (888-625-5144)
Dogs of all sizes are allowed. There are no additional pet fees. Dogs are not allowed to be left alone in the room.
Motel 6 - Denver (West) 9920 West 49th Avenue Wheat Ridge CO   303-424-0658 (800-466-8356)
One well-behaved family pet per room. Guest must notify front desk upon arrival. Guest is liable for any damages. In consideration of all guests, pets must never be left unattended in the guest rooms.
Motel 6 - Denver West - Wheat Ridge S 10300 South I-70 Frontage Road Wheat Ridge CO   303-467-3172 (800-466-8356)
One well-behaved family pet per room. Guest must notify front desk upon arrival. Guest is liable for any damages. In consideration of all guests, pets must never be left unattended in the guest rooms.

Campgrounds and RV Parks

Denver Meadows RV Park 2075 Potomac Street Aurora CO   303-364-9483 (800-364-9487)
http://www.denvermeadows.com/
Dogs of all sizes are allowed. There are no additional pet fees. Dogs may not be left unattended outside, and they must be leashed and cleaned up after. This is an RV only park. There are some breed restrictions. There is a dog walk area at the campground.
Dakota Ridge RV Park 17800 W Colfax Golden CO   800-398-1625
http://www.dakotaridgerv.com
Dogs of all sizes are allowed. There is a $1 per night per pet additional fee. Dogs must be quiet, leashed, and cleaned up after. Dogs may not be put in outside pens, or be left unattended outside. There are some breed restrictions. There is a dog walk area at the campground.
Genesee Park/Chief Hosa Campground 27661 Genesee Drive Golden CO   303-526-1324
http://www.chiefhosa.com/
This is Denver's largest mountain park with 2,341 acres of trees, wildlife, recreation, and popular hiking trails. There is even a Braille Trail with interpretive signs in Braille. Some of the amenities include picnic areas, charcoal grills, a volleyball court, softball field, and a scenic overlook along I 70 where you can view the resident buffalo herd. They are open daily from 5 am to 11 pm. Dogs of all sizes are allowed. Dogs must be leashed and cleaned up after at all times. They are allowed throughout the park and on the trails; they are not allowed in park buildings. The Chief Hosa Campground was dubbed 'America's First Motor-Camping Area when it opened in 1913, and sits at 7,700 feet altitude. There are 61 sites, and amenities include gaming courts, showers, restrooms, and a dump station. This campground will not be open to concert camping. There is a $1 per night per pet additional fee for camping. This RV park is closed during the off-season. The camping and tent areas also allow dogs. There is a dog walk area at the campground.
Chatfield State Park 11500 N Roxborough Park Road Littleton CO   303-791-7275
This beautiful, multi-functional park offers resource education, diverse ecosystems, an expansive trail system It is a great retreat for camping, picnicking, hiking/biking, birding, boating and fishing. This park is also one of the most popular hot-air balloon launch areas on the Front Range. Dogs of all sizes are allowed for no additional fee. Dogs must be on no more than a 6 foot leash, and cleaned up after at all times. The exception is when dogs are used in hunting, field trials, or while being trained on lands open to such use. Dogs may be anywhere throughout the park, except they are not allowed on any swim beach, water-ski beach, or in park buildings. There are 4 camping areas with 197 sites that are within walking distance to the lake. Amenities include picnic sites with

tables and grills (also picnic sites throughout the park), flush toilets, showers, laundry, firewood, centrally located water, and a dump station. Camping permits are required in addition to the day-use park pass. The camping and tent areas also allow dogs. There is a dog walk area at the campground.

Prospect RV Park 11600 W 44th Avenue Wheat Ridge CO   303-424-4414
http://www.prospectrv.com
Dogs of all sizes are allowed. There are no additional pet fees. Dogs must be leashed and cleaned up after. There are some breed restrictions. There is a dog walk area at the campground.

Transportation Systems
RTD Regional Denver CO   303-299-6000
http://www.rtd-denver.com
Small dogs in hard-sided carriers are allowed on the buses and light rail.

Attractions
Cherry Creek Marina Boat Rentals Cherry Creek State Park Aurora CO   303-779-6144
Located just minutes from downtown Denver, this marina allows dogs on their fishing boat rentals. You and your pup can rent a boat and explore the reservoir located in the dog-friendly Cherry Creek State Park. Boat rental rates start at about $25 for 1 hour.

Larimer Square Larimer Street Denver CO
http://www.larimersquare.com/
Popular with both the locals and tourists, this area offers specialty stores, galleries, and restaurants. Some of the restaurants allow dogs at the outdoor tables, including the Del Mar Crab House and The Market Restaurant. If you want to do some shopping with your pooch, some stores allow your well-behaved dog inside including the Larimer Mission Gift Shop, Cry Baby Ranch and Z Gallerie. Look for details about the restaurants and stores in our Denver City Guide. The square is located on Larimer Street, between 14th and 15th Streets, and Market and Lawrence Streets.

Rocky Mountain Audio Guides, LLC P.O. Box 22963 Denver CO   303-898-7073
http://www.rmaguides.com/
Whether you are a local or a visitor, these self-guided audio walking tours using your cell phone are a great entertaining and healthy way to learn more about this mile high city. Tours take you along routes that include the Union Station, Market Street, D&F Tower, Larimer and Sakura Square, Coors Field, and more. The tour cost of $8 is applied directly to your credit card for a 2 mile walk, and you must make arrangements for the tour from the cell phone that you plan to use. Dogs are allowed to walk the tour with you, but they must be leashed and cleaned up after at all times. Please bring your own clean up supplies.

State Capitol Grounds 200 E Colfax Denver CO   303-866-2604
http://www.milehighcity.com/capitol/
Free guided tours are offered of this illustrious building composed of Colorado white granite with large pillars that is reminiscent of the White House, a gold leaf dome that adorns the top, stained glass windows, and many more special features. The beautifully manicured gardens and lawns that surround the Capitol building feature several memorial statues and dedications. The Colorado State Capitol is open to the public Monday through Friday from 7 a.m. to 5:30 p.m. Your pet is welcome to explore the grounds with you, but they are not usually allowed inside unless they are very small and carried only. Dogs must be friendly, leashed, and cleaned up after quickly. Disposal bags are not supplied, so please bring your own bags.

TOP 200 PLACE Tennyson Gallery and Sherlock Hound Pet Deli 4329 Stuart St Denver CO   303-433-3274
http://www.tennysongallery.com
This dog-friendly art gallery and attached pet deli makes for an interesting combination. The Tennyson Gallery is very dog-friendly. There are many events held here including Saturday morning dog socials with coffee for the people and snacks for the dogs. Sandwiches are available to be ordered from the deli across the street. On some days there are speakers at the gallery.

TOP 200 PLACE Buffalo Bills Gravesite and Museum 987 1/2 Look-Out Mountain Road Golden CO   303-526-0744
http://www.buffalobill.org/
On the top of Lookout Mountain, among the wildlife, breezes, and Ponderosa Pines, per his request, is the gravesite of Buffalo Bill Cody. Today visitors can enjoy the panoramic view from 2 observation decks adjacent to his burial site, tour the comprehensive museum and gift store, join in on one of the planned yearly events, walk along the nature trails, or just rest and enjoy the concessions that offer a variety of foods and drink. Dogs of all sizes are allowed. They must be leashed at all times, and please bring supplies to clean up after them quickly. Dogs are not allowed in the park buildings, but they are allowed on the grounds and the trails.

Lookout Mountain Park Lookout Mountain Road Golden CO   303-964-2589
Dogs on leash are allowed at this Denver mountain park. The park is over 65 acres and offers scenic views including an overlook of Denver and the plains. William "Buffalo Bill" Cody was buried in this park back in 1917. Dogs are not allowed inside the Buffalo Bill Museum. However, you and your pooch can visit the outdoor

gravesite of this popular cowboy and frontiersman. You can also take your dog on one of the many hiking trails at the park. To get to the park, take Interstate 70 west to exit 256 (marked as Buffalo Bill Grave). Follow the signs to the park (Buffalo Bills Grave). It will be a winding uphill road.

Dinosaur Ridge 16831 West Alameda Parkway Morrison CO   303-697-3466
http://www.dinoridge.org/
Leashed dogs are allowed, including on the self-guided walking tour. Dinosaur Ridge is a geographically famous National Natural Landmark, located just 15 minutes west of downtown Denver. The site features historically famous Jurassic dinosaur bones. The bones were discovered in 1877 and over 300 Cretaceous dinosaur footprints have also been found. The self-guided tour is one mile long and features 16 interpretive signs that describe fossil remains and other important features. There is no charge for the self guided walk. Booklets are available for purchase in the Visitor Center. The booklets offer more details of the walking tour. To get there from Interstate 70, take exit 259 (Morrison/Golden exit) and head south (towards Red Rocks Park) on Highway 93/26. As you near Red Rocks Park, there will be a turn off to the left for Highway 26. Follow the signs for Dinosaur Ridge.

Adventure Golf and Racefire 9650 N Sheridan Blvd Westminster CO   303-650-7587
http://www.adventuregolfandraceway.com/
This place is a great get-a-way for relaxing, or taking on any number of fun challenges. They feature 54 holes of adventure golf, a raceway, dragway, 18 and 9 hole championship regulation golf courses, and a practice facility/range. Amenities include covered picnic areas, concessions and catering, restrooms, and a clubhouse. Dogs of all sizes are allowed to be on site with their owners. They can go around the miniature golf and picnic areas, but they are not allowed at the raceways or in buildings. Dogs must be well behaved and friendly. They must be leashed at all times, and cleaned up after quickly. Please bring your own supplies.

Shopping Centers

Denver Pavilions 15th Street and Tremont Denver CO   303-260-6000
http://www.denverpavilions.com/
This open air shopping center allows leashed dogs at the outdoor areas. Located downtown, this is Denver's premier retail and entertainment complex. The center features 50 stores and restaurants in four three-story buildings linked by walkways. Dogs are also welcome to dine at the 16th Street Deli's outdoor tables, located in the shopping center. To get there from Interstate 25, exit Colfax Avenue. Cross Speer Blvd. and take the first left onto Welton Street. Cross 15th Street to the Denver Pavilions. The entrance to the underground parking garage is on the right. There is a minimal fee for parking.

TOP 200 PLACE **Aspen Grove Shopping Center** 7301 S Santa Fe Drive Littleton CO   303-794-0640
http://www.shopaspengrove.com/
This open air shopping center offers the finest of national specialty shops and restaurants in a convenient, safe, pleasing environment, and with great views of Colorado too. Your well-behaved pet is welcome here, and there are more than 2 dozen stores that display the yellow "Pet Friendly" triangle sign. There are poop-n-scoop stations throughout the mall so that you may clean up after your pet quickly. Dogs must be kept leashed at all times.

Stores

PetSmart Pet Store 5283 Wadsworth Bypass Arvada CO   303-456-1114
Your licensed and well-behaved leashed dog is allowed in the store.
PetSmart Pet Store 5520 S Parker Rd Aurora CO   303-690-4697
Your licensed and well-behaved leashed dog is allowed in the store.
PetSmart Pet Store 40 S Abilene St Aurora CO   720-859-8122
Your licensed and well-behaved leashed dog is allowed in the store.
PetSmart Pet Store 7350 S Gartrell Rd Aurora CO   303-400-4778
Your licensed and well-behaved leashed dog is allowed in the store.
Petco Pet Store 13750 East Mississippi Avenue Aurora CO   303-695-1223
Your licensed and well-behaved leashed dog is allowed in the store.
Petco Pet Store 16960 Quincy Avenue Aurora CO   303-699-5061
Your licensed and well-behaved leashed dog is allowed in the store.
Petco Pet Store 24101 East Orchard Rd Ste C Aurora CO   303-627-5710
Your licensed and well-behaved leashed dog is allowed in the store.
Cry Baby Ranch 1422 Larimer Street Denver CO   303-623-3979
http://www.crybabyranch.com/
This store offers Western gear for men, women, children and babies. They also offer unique Western-themed items including kitchen supplies, bedding, bath supplies, signs, and even lunchboxes. Well-behaved, leashed dogs are allowed inside.
Larimer Mission Gift Shop 1421 Larimer Street Denver CO   720-904-2789
This gift shop allows well-behaved, leashed dogs inside.
PetSmart Pet Store 160 Wadsworth Blvd Denver CO   303-232-0858

Your licensed and well-behaved leashed dog is allowed in the store.
PetSmart Pet Store 2780 S Colorado Blvd Stes 308 and 310 Denver CO   303-756-4199
Your licensed and well-behaved leashed dog is allowed in the store.
PetSmart Pet Store 7505 E 35th Ave Bldg 3 Denver CO   303-393-9156
Your licensed and well-behaved leashed dog is allowed in the store.
Petco Pet Store 8100 West Crestline Denver CO   303-973-7057
Your licensed and well-behaved leashed dog is allowed in the store.
Three Dog Bakery 231 Clayton Street Denver CO   303-350-4499
http://www.threedog.com
Three Dog Bakery provides cookies and snacks for your dog as well as some boutique items. You well-behaved, leashed dog is welcome.
Z Gallerie 1465 Larimer Street Denver CO   303-615-9646
http://www.zgallerie.com/
This home furnishings store allows leashed, well-behaved dogs inside.
Petco Pet Store 9425 East County Line Rd Englewood CO   303-708-0616
Your licensed and well-behaved leashed dog is allowed in the store.
Petco Pet Store 551 West Hampden Avenue Englewood CO   303-761-0363
Your licensed and well-behaved leashed dog is allowed in the store.
PetSmart Pet Store 360 S Colorado Blvd Glendale CO   303-394-4406
Your licensed and well-behaved leashed dog is allowed in the store.
Petco Pet Store 17132 W Colfax Avenue Golden CO   303-384-0013
Your licensed and well-behaved leashed dog is allowed in the store.
Three Dog Bakery 8000 E Belleview Avenue, Suite B-70 Greenwood Village CO   303-773-3647
http://www.threedog.com
Three Dog Bakery provides cookies and snacks for your dog as well as some boutique items. You well-behaved, leashed dog is welcome.
Petco Pet Store 475 South Wadsworth Lakewood CO   303-985-0050
Your licensed and well-behaved leashed dog is allowed in the store.
PetSmart Pet Store 8695 S Park Meadow Ctr Dr Littleton CO   303-799-3575
Your licensed and well-behaved leashed dog is allowed in the store.
PetSmart Pet Store 7900 West Quincy Littleton CO   303-971-0016
Your licensed and well-behaved leashed dog is allowed in the store.
PetSmart Pet Store 8222 S University Littleton CO   303-220-0215
Your licensed and well-behaved leashed dog is allowed in the store.
PetSmart Pet Store 8440 S Kipling Pkwy Littleton CO   720-922-8335
Your licensed and well-behaved leashed dog is allowed in the store.
PetSmart Pet Store 8500 W Crestline Ave Littleton CO   303-948-6364
Your licensed and well-behaved leashed dog is allowed in the store.
Petco Pet Store 7460 South University Blvd Littleton CO   720-488-5222
Your licensed and well-behaved leashed dog is allowed in the store.
PetSmart Pet Store 10600 Melody Dr Northglenn CO   720-929-9459
Your licensed and well-behaved leashed dog is allowed in the store.
Petco Pet Store 450 E 120th Avenue, Unit A2 Northglenn CO   303-255-4528
Your licensed and well-behaved leashed dog is allowed in the store.
PetSmart Pet Store 9359 Sheridan Blvd Westminster CO   303-426-4999
Your licensed and well-behaved leashed dog is allowed in the store.
Petco Pet Store 6735 West 88th Avenue Westminster CO   303-432-9230
Your licensed and well-behaved leashed dog is allowed in the store.
PetSmart Pet Store 3540 Youngfield St Wheat Ridge CO   303-424-0123
Your licensed and well-behaved leashed dog is allowed in the store.

Parks

Cherry Creek State Park 4201 South Parker Road Aurora CO   303-699-3860
http://parks.state.co.us/cherry_creek
Dogs on a 6 foot or less leash are allowed, except on wetland trails, and swim beaches. But there are plenty of dog-friendly hiking trails in this park. There is also an off-leash area in this park, located near Parker and Orchard Roads. For details of which hiking trails allow dogs, please visit one of the Entrance Stations at the park.
Bible Park Yale Avenue Denver CO   303-964-2580
This is a 70 acre park and about half of it is developed with sports fields, picnic areas and restrooms. The park has many walking trails and it is bordered by the High Line Canal Trail and the Cherry Creek Trail. The park is located at Yale Avenue and Pontiac Street. Dogs must be leashed.
City Park 17th Avenue Denver CO   303-964-2580
This park is Denver's largest city park. It covers over 300 acres and offers tennis courts, fountains, flower gardens, sports fields, a lake and more. The park is located just east of downtown on 17th Avenue and York

Street. Pets must be on a leash.

Washington Park Franklin Drive and Exposition Blvd Denver CO   303-698-4962

This park, known as Denver's premium park with over 155 acres, two lakes, formal flower gardens (one being a replica of the President Washington's garden at Mt Vernon), a historic bathhouse and gazebo, attracts all ages. A great trail system, including a 2.5 scenic loop, big open lawns, beautiful scenery, gaming courts, and planned venues also make this a great mini-get-a-way. Dogs of all sizes are allowed as long as they are on a leash. Dog are allowed throughout the park and on the trails, but they must be cleaned up after; please carry supplies.

Genesee Park/Chief Hosa Campground 27661 Genesee Drive Golden CO   303-526-1324

http://www.chiefhosa.com/

This is Denver's largest mountain park with 2,341 acres of trees, wildlife, recreation, and popular hiking trails. There is even a Braille Trail with interpretive signs in Braille. Some of the amenities include picnic areas, charcoal grills, a volleyball court, softball field, and a scenic overlook along I 70 where you can view the resident buffalo herd. They are open daily from 5 am to 11 pm. Dogs of all sizes are allowed. Dogs must be leashed and cleaned up after at all times. They are allowed throughout the park and on the trails; they are not allowed in park buildings.

The Colorado Trail 710 10th Street, #210 Golden CO   303-384-3729

http://www.coloradotrail.org/

This is Colorado's premier long distance trail at almost 500 miles stretching from Denver to Durango. Spectacular scenery greets the traveler all the way to where the trail tops out at 13,334 feet. There are 6 wilderness areas, 8 mountain ranges, abundant wildlife, lakes, creeks, and many diverse ecosystems. Dogs are allowed in all areas along the trail with the exception of the first 7 miles from the Denver side. Both points of access into this area (Waterton Canyon and Roxborough State) prohibit dogs. You may begin the trail with your dog at the S Platte River Bridge Trailhead. The Guidebook also mentions another route from the Indian Creek Campground onto the Indian Creek Equestrian Trail. Dogs must be on leash through the wilderness areas, under owners control at all times, and cleaned up after on the trail and any camp areas.

Daniels Park 1315 Welch Street Lakewood CO   303-987-7800

This 1000+ acre park is home to a Bison preserve and natural area where they can be viewed in their high-plains habitat. Some of the amenities include a picnic shelter with 8 tables, 2 barbecue grills, horseshoe pits, tennis courts, gaming courts/fields, and restrooms. Dogs must be kept leashed at all times and cleaned up after.

Chatfield State Park 11500 N Roxborough Park Road Littleton CO   303-791-7275

This beautiful multi-functional park offers resource education, diverse ecosystems, an expansive trail system. It is a great retreat for camping, picnicking, hiking/biking, birding, boating and fishing. This park is also one of the most popular hot-air balloon launch areas on the Front Range. Dogs of all sizes are allowed for no additional fee. Dogs must be on no more than a 6 foot leash, and cleaned up after at all times. The exception is when dogs are used in hunting, field trials, or while being trained on lands open to such use. Dogs may be anywhere throughout the park, except they are not allowed on any swim beach, water-ski beach, or in park buildings.

Off-Leash Dog Parks

Arvada Dog Park 17975 West 64th Parkway Arvada CO   303-421-3487

This five acre fenced dog park has separate areas for small and large dogs. It is open during daylight hours. Dogs must be leashed when not in the off-leash area. The park is located about 1/2 mile east of Highway 93. There are still 15 acres to develop as funds allow.

Grandview Park Dog Park 17500 E. Salida Street Aurora CO   303-739-7160

This park has a designated off-leash dog park. The 5 acre dog park is fenced. It is located at the west end of Quincy Reservoir, about a third of a mile east of Buckley on Quincy. Dogs must be leashed when outside of the off-leash area.

Happy Tails Dog Park 1111 Judicial Center Drive Brighton CO   303-655-2049

This dog park is fully fenced and is open during daylight hours daily. Dogs must be cleaned up after. From I-76 exit at E. 152nd Avenue and head west. Turn left onto Judicial Center Dr to the park.

Broomfield County Commons Dog Park 13th and Sheridan Blvd Broomfield CO   303-464-5509

Broomfield's first dog park is located at this temporary location. It is in the North Pod of the Broomfield County Commons. There are two separate fully fenced areas for large and small dogs. Dogs must be licensed and people must clean up after their dogs.

Beaver Ranch Bark Park 11369 Foxton Rd Conifer CO   303-829-1917

There is a 2 acre fenced dog park located in Conifer's Beach Ranch Community Park. The dog park is located at the top of the Tipi Loop Trail in the park.

Barnum Park Off-Leash Area Hooker and West 5th Denver CO   720-913-0696

This park has a designated off-leash area which is located in the northeast area of the park. It borders the 6th Avenue Freeway. Enter from the parking lot on 5th. This off-leash area is part of a pilot program for the city and county of Denver. It is in place to test the feasibility of off-leash areas in Denver parks. Volunteers observe the conditions at the parks on a regular basis and the success and future of the program will be determined at the end of the pilot program.

Berkeley Park Dog Park Sheridan and West 46th Denver CO   720-913-0696

This park has a designated fenced dog park which is located west of the lake. Enter from lake side. This dog park is part of a pilot program for the city and county of Denver. It is in place to test the feasibility of off-leash areas in Denver parks. Volunteers observe the conditions at the parks on a regular basis and the success and future of the program will be determined at the end of the pilot program.

Denver's Off Leash Dog Park 666 South Jason Street Denver CO   303-698-0076
This park is Denver's first off leash dog park. It is open from sunrise to sunset, seven days a week. The park is located directly behind the Denver Animal Control building.

Fuller Park Dog Park Franklin and East 29th Denver CO   720-913-0696
This park has a designated fenced dog park which is located at the northwest part of the park. It is west of the basketball courts. Enter from 29th Avenue. This dog park is part of a pilot program for the city and county of Denver. It is in place to test the feasibility of off-leash areas in Denver parks. Volunteers observe the conditions at the parks on a regular basis and the success and future of the program will be determined at the end of the pilot program.

Green Valley Ranch East Off-Leash Area Jebel and East 45th Denver CO   720-913-0696
This park has a designated off-leash area which is located at the southwest area of the park. This off-leash area is part of a pilot program for the city and county of Denver. It is in place to test the feasibility of off-leash areas in Denver parks. Volunteers observe the conditions at the parks on a regular basis and the success and future of the program will be determined at the end of the pilot program.

Kennedy Soccer Complex Off-Leash Area Hampden and South Dayton Denver CO   720-913-0696
This park has a designated off-leash area which is located at the southwest point of the park. Do not park inside the complex gate as it will be locked. This off-leash area is part of a pilot program for the city and county of Denver. It is in place to test the feasibility of off-leash areas in Denver parks. Volunteers observe the conditions at the parks on a regular basis and the success and future of the program will be determined at the end of the pilot program.

Centennial Park Off-Leash Area 4630 S. Decatur Englewood CO   303-762-2300
There is an off-leash area in Centennial Park. The off-leash area is not fenced and dogs must be under good voice control.

Duncan Park Off-Leash Area 4800 S. Pennsylvania Englewood CO   303-762-2300
There is an off-leash area in Duncan Park. The off-leash area is not fenced and dogs must be under good voice control.

Englewood Canine Corral 4848 S. Windermere Englewood CO   303-762-2300
The one and 1/2 acre Englewood Canine Corral is a completely fenced off-leash dog park. It has a number of benches and shade. The dog park is located on the west side of Belleview Park. To get to the dog park from Belleview Avenue head north on Windermere. The park will be on your right.

Jason Park Off-Leash Area 4200 S. Jason Englewood CO   303-762-2300
There is an off-leash area in Jason Park. The off-leash area is not fenced and dogs must be under good voice control.

Northwest Greenbelt Off-Leash Area Tejon at W Baltic Pl Englewood CO   303-762-2300
The off-leash area is not fenced and dogs must be under good voice control. To get to the off-leash area from I-25 take the Colorado Blvd exit south to Evens. Turn west on Evans Avenue to Tejon and turn south on Tejon a few blocks to the off-leash area.

Outdoor Restaurants

Baja Fresh 14301 E Cedar Avenue, Suite A Aurora CO   303-367-9700
This restaurant serves Mexican food. Dogs are allowed at the outdoor tables. The restaurant has outdoor tables only in the summer.

Armida's 840 Lincoln Denver CO   303-837-8921
http://www.armidas.com
This Mexican restaurant offers a variety of food like burritos, fajitas, flautas, and tacos. They also offer sandwiches and salads. Dogs are allowed at the outdoor tables.

Baja Fresh 555 Broaway, Suites 3,4,&5 Denver CO   720-904-0973
This restaurant serves Mexican food. Dogs are allowed at the outdoor tables. The restaurant has outdoor tables only in the summer.

Baja Fresh 99918th Street, #107 Denver CO   303-296-1800
This restaurant serves Mexican food. Dogs are allowed at the outdoor tables. The restaurant has outdoor tables only in the summer.

Corner Bakery Cafe 500 16th Street Denver CO   303-572-0170
http://www.cornerbakery.com/
Dogs are allowed at the outdoor tables.

Croc's Cafe 1630 Market Street Denver CO   303-436-1144
This Mexican restaurant allows dogs at their outdoor tables.

Del Mar Crab House 1453 Larimer Square Denver CO   303-825-4747
http://www.delmardenver.com/
Dogs need to be tied to the fence, but on the same side of the fence as your outdoor table, and your pooch can sit right next to you. This restaurant, located in Larimer Square, specializes in crab, seafood, and steaks.

Dixons Downtown Grill 1610 16th Street Denver CO 303-573-6100
This restaurant serves Southwest American style food. Dogs are allowed at the outdoor tables. A bowl of water and a dog biscuit are provided for your pet.
Gelato D'Italia 250 Detroit Denver CO 303-316-9154
Dogs are allowed at the outdoor tables. This is a popular spot for dogs and their owners. Gelato D' Italia serves a variety of gelato.
Paris Coffee Roasting 1553 Platte Street Denver CO 303-455-2451
Dogs are allowed at the outdoor tables.
Rubios Baja Grille 703 S Colorado Blvd Denver CO 303-765-0636
Dogs are allowed at the outdoor tables. The restaurant has outdoor tables only in the summer.
St Mark's Coffeehouse 2019 E 17th Ave Denver CO 303-322-8384
This restaurant serves Deli/Pastry type food. Dogs are allowed at the outdoor tables.
Strings 1700 Humboldt St Denver CO 303-831-7310
This restaurant serves Seafood and American food. Pets are allowed on the outside of the fence.
The Market 1445 Larimer Street Denver CO 303-534-5140
This restaurant, located in Larimer Square, allows dogs at their outdoor tables.
The Rock Bottom Restaurant and Brewery 1001 16th St Denver CO 303-534-7616
This restaurant and bar serves American/Asian. Dogs are allowed at the outdoor tables. A bowl of water is provided for your pet.
Wall Street Deli 1801 California Street Denver CO 303-296-6277
http://www.wallstreetdeli.com
This chain restaurant serves gourmet sandwiches, salads and soups. Dogs are allowed at the outdoor tables.
Baja Fresh 6570 S Yosemite Street Greenwood Village CO 303-741-5151
This restaurant serves Mexican food. Dogs are allowed at the outdoor tables. The restaurant has outdoor tables only in the summer.
Yia Yia's Eurocafe 8310 East Belleview Avenue Greenwood Village CO 303-741-1110
This Mediterranean restaurant features bistro specialties, pasta, pizza and more. Dogs are allowed at the outdoor tables.
Rubios Baja Grille 3620 Highlands Ranch Parkway Highlands Ranch CO 303-471-6222
Dogs are allowed at the outdoor tables. The restaurant has outdoor tables only in the summer.
Baja Fresh 5350 S Santa Fe Drive, Suite F Littleton CO 303-730-1466
This restaurant serves Mexican food. Dogs are allowed at the outdoor tables. The restaurant has outdoor tables only in the summer.
Baja Fresh 11961 Bradburn Blvd, Suite 600 Westminster CO 303-410-6677
This restaurant serves Mexican food. Dogs are allowed at the outdoor tables. The restaurant has outdoor tables only in the summer.

Events

MaxFund Lucky Mutt Strut S Downing Street and E Louisianna Avenue Denver CO 720-482-1578
http://www.maxfund.org/
This annual June event held in Washington Park benefits the MaxFund shelter, a no-kill shelter for injured, neglected, and abused animals with no known owners. Participants receive event souvenirs, and there is a variety of entertainment, raffle prizes, and canine demos. Dogs must be leashed and under owner's control and care at all times.
Wag and Train Canine Carnival 370 Kalamath Street Denver CO 720-312-5499
http://www.wagandtrain.com/
To celebrate the American Kennel Club Responsible Dog Ownership Day and to help dog rescues, local businesses joined together for a fun community outreach day. This fundraising event offers numerous family and dog activities, kids' events-crafts-and clinics, educational classes and seminars, discounted micro-chipping for dogs, an all day dog washing station, pet first aid courses, and more. Dogs must be well behaved, leashed, and cleaned up after at all times.

Dillon

Accommodations
Super 8 Dillon/Breckenridge Area 808 Little Beaver Trail Dillon CO 970-468-8888 (800-800-8000)
Dogs up to 60 pounds are allowed. There is a $15 one time per pet fee per visit. Smoking and non-smoking rooms are available for pet rooms.

Dinosaur

Colorado   - Please always call ahead to make sure that an establishment is still dog-friendly

Campgrounds and RV Parks
Dinosaur National Monument 4545 E Hwy 40 Dinosaur CO   970)374-3000
http://www.nps.gov/dino/
This park is the largest quarry of the Jurassic Period dinosaur bones ever found, and gives this 200,000+ acre, visually striking park its name. The Quarry visitor's Center is now closed, but the monument is open with much to see; there are exhibits, fossil displays, ranger led programs (in summer), many trails to explore, 2 self-guided auto tours offering spectacular scenery, and plenty of land and water recreation. The Canyon Area Visitor Center in Dinosaur, Colorado, is open daily from 8:00 a.m. to 4:00 p.m. through Labor Day; then to October 31 they are closed on the weekends, and closed from November 1st to April 30th. The park is open year round for auto touring, weather permitting; roads are not maintained and are closed when there is snow. Dogs of all sizes are allowed for no additional fee. Dogs may not be left unattended, and they must be leashed and cleaned up after at all times. Dogs are not allowed on the trails at this park or in any of the park buildings. They may get out of the vehicle when stopping along side the road on the auto tour, but may not walk along trails to get to overlooks. The Green River Campground, just 5 miles east of the Quarry, is on a first-come, first-served basis. Some of the amenities include picnic tables, fireplaces and wood for sale, drinking water, modern restrooms, and fishing. There are also campfire circle ranger talks through the summer. There are no electric or water hookups at the campgrounds.

Parks
Dinosaur National Monument 4545 E Highway 40 Dinosaur CO   970-374-3000
http://www.nps.gov/dino/index.htm
Dogs on leash are allowed in campgrounds while attended. Dogs are not allowed on hiking trails, backcountry or the visitor center.
Dinosaur National Monument 4545 E Hwy 40 Dinosaur CO   970)374-3000
http://www.nps.gov/dino/
This park is the largest quarry of the Jurassic Period dinosaur bones ever found, and gives this 200,000+ acre, visually striking park its name. The Quarry visitor's Center is now closed, but the monument is open with much to see; there are exhibits, fossil displays, ranger led programs (in summer), many trails to explore, 2 self-guided auto tours offering spectacular scenery, and plenty of land and water recreation. The Canyon Area Visitor Center in Dinosaur, Colorado, is open daily from 8:00 a.m. to 4:00 p.m. through Labor Day; then to October 31 they are closed on the weekends, and closed from November 1st to April 30th. The park is open year round for auto touring, weather permitting; roads are not maintained and are closed when there is snow. Dogs of all sizes are allowed for no additional fee. Dogs may not be left unattended, and they must be leashed and cleaned up after at all times. Dogs are not allowed on the trails at this park or in any of the park buildings. They may get out of the vehicle when stopping along side the road on the auto tour, but may not walk along trails to get to overlooks.

Divide

Campgrounds and RV Parks
Mueller State Park 21045 Hwy 67S Divide CO   719-687-2366 (800-678-2267)
This park has over 5,000 acres of some of the most beautiful land in the state. The park offers a variety of year round recreation. Dogs are allowed at no additional fee. Dogs may not be left unattended, and they must be on no more than a 6 foot leash, and be cleaned up after. Dogs are not allowed off the pavement, and they may not go on the trails. The camping and tent areas also allow dogs. There is a dog walk area at the campground. There are no water hookups at the campground.
Mueller State Park 21045 Hwy 67S Divide CO   719-687-2366 (800-678-2267)
Extending over 5,000 acres across some of the most beautiful land in the state, this park is a popular wildlife area and a joy for photographers and sightseers. For the hiker/mountain biker/horseback rider, there are more than 55 miles of scenic, year round, multi-use trails. Dogs of all sizes are allowed for no additional fee. Dogs are not allowed in the backcountry or on the nature trails; they may be walked on paved roads only. Dogs must be on no more than a 6 foot leash, and be cleaned up after. The campground is in a forested setting at 9,500 feet and offer panoramic views, 132 sites, and some tent walk-in sites. Some of the amenities include a Camper Services Building, modern restrooms, coin operated showers and laundry, campfires, barbecue grills, and a dump station. Some services are not available in winter. The camping and tent areas also allow dogs. There is a dog walk area at the campground. There are no water hookups at the campgrounds.

Dolores

Campgrounds and RV Parks

Dolores River RV Park 18680 Hwy 145 Dolores CO 970-882-7761
http://www.doloresriverrv.com
Dogs of all sizes are allowed, and there are no additional pet fees for tent or RV sites. There may be a small one time fee for pets in cabins. This RV park is closed during the off-season. The camping and tent areas also allow dogs. There is a dog walk area at the campground. Dogs are allowed in the camping cabins.

Durango

Accommodations

Days Inn Durango 1700 County Rd 203 Durango CO 970-259-1430 (800-329-7466)
Dogs of all sizes are allowed. There are no additional pet fees.
Doubletree 501 Camino Del Rio Durango CO 970-259-6580
Dogs up to 50 pounds are allowed. There is a $15 per night per room pet fee.
Holiday Inn 800 Camino Del Rio Durango CO 970-247-5393 (877-270-6405)
There is a $10 per day additional pet fee.
Rochester Hotel 726 E. Second Ave. Durango CO 970-385-1920 (800-664-1920)
http://www.rochesterhotel.com/
This beautifully renovated hotel offers fifteen spacious rooms with high ceilings, king or queen beds, and private baths, and is decorated in an Old West motif. This hotel, located in downtown Durango, was designated as "The Flagship Hotel of Colorado" by Conde' Nast Traveler. They are very pet-friendly and offer two pet rooms, with a $20 per day pet charge.

Campgrounds and RV Parks

Alpen Rose RV Park 27847 Hwy 550N Durango CO 970-247-5540
http://www.alpenroservpark.com
Dogs of all sizes are allowed. There are no additional pet fees. Dogs may not be left unattended outside, and must be quiet, leashed, and cleaned up after. There are a couple of dog sitters on site that will take care of your dog with walks, food and water, and play time for $10 per day per dog. This RV park is closed during the off-season. There is a dog walk area at the campground. There are special amenities given to dogs at this campground.
Durango East KOA 30090 Hwy 160 Durango CO 970-247-0783 (800-562-0793)
http://www.koa.com
Dogs of all sizes are allowed. There are no additional pet fees. Dogs may not be left unattended, and they must be quiet, well behaved, leashed and cleaned up after. There are some breed restrictions. This RV park is closed during the off-season. The camping and tent areas also allow dogs. There is a dog walk area at the campground. Dogs are allowed in the camping cabins.
Durango North KOA 13391 County Road 250 Durango CO 970-247-4499 (800-562-0793)
http://www.koa.com
Dogs of all sizes are allowed. There are no additional pet fees. Dogs may not be left unattended, and they must be leashed and cleaned up after. This RV park is closed during the off-season. The camping and tent areas also allow dogs. There is a dog walk area at the campground. Dogs are allowed in the camping cabins.
San Juan National Forest 15 Burnett Court Durango CO 970-247-4874
http://www.fs.fed.us/r2/sanjuan/
With over 2 and a half million acres, and home to the Anasazi Heritage Center, there are historical and geological interests as well as a variety of recreational pursuits. Dogs are allowed at no additional fee. Dogs may not be left unattended, and they must be leashed and cleaned up after. Dogs are allowed on the trails, and they may be off lead in the forest if they are under voice control. This campground is closed during the off-season. The camping and tent areas also allow dogs. There is a dog walk area at the campground. There are no water hookups at the campground.
United Campground of Durango 1322 Animas View Road Durango CO 970-247-3853
http://www.unitedcampground.com
Dogs of all sizes are allowed. There are no additional pet fees. Dogs may not be in the buildings, or at the pool, nor left unattended. Dogs must be leashed at all times, and must be cleaned up after. This RV park is closed during the off-season. The camping and tent areas also allow dogs. There is a dog walk area at the campground.

Attractions

Rent A Wreck of Durango 21760 Highway 160 West Durango CO 970-259-5858

http://www.rentawreckofdurango.com/
Go for a mountain adventure in your own rental Jeep 4x4. There are some great off-road trails which pass by several old ghost towns in Silverton, about an hour and a half drive north of Durango. Rent A Wreck of Durango allows dogs in their Jeep rentals. Don't let the name fool you, they actually do rent new 4x4 Jeep Wranglers. According to Rent A Wreck, they are the only year round off-road 4x4 rental in the area. The charge for a one day Jeep rental is approximately $110 which is pretty much the going rate for a 4x4 in Durango. There is a $20 extra pet fee if the Jeep has lots of doggie hair upon return. Reservations are not required, but it's probably a good idea to reserve a Jeep about a week in advance just in case.

Stores

Half-Price Tees 758 Main Street Durango CO 970-259-5601
Well-behaved, leashed dogs are allowed in the store.
Mountain Treasures Gifts 108 East 5th Street Durango CO 970-375-9270
Well-behaved, leashed dogs are allowed in the store.
Southwest Book Trader 175 E. 5th Street Durango CO 970-247-8479
Well-behaved, leashed dogs are allowed in the store.
The Shirt Off My Back 680 Main Street Durango CO 970-247-9644
Well-behaved, leashed dogs are allowed in the store.
Toh-Atin Gallery 145 West 9th Street Durango CO 970-247-8277
Art gallery specializing in Native American and Southwestern arts and crafts. Well-behaved, leashed dogs are allowed in the store.

Parks

Animas River Trail 32nd Avenue (at East 2nd Ave) Durango CO
The Animas River Trail is a 5 mile paved trail that runs along the river and through Durango. It is a popular trail with walkers, runners, in-line skaters and of course, dogs. If your pooch wants to cool off along the way, he or she can take a dip in the refreshing river. The north end of the trail is located at 32nd Avenue and East 2nd Avenue. Dogs must be leashed on the trail.

Off-Leash Dog Parks

Durango Dog Park Highway 160 Durango CO 970-385-2950
This dog park is located off Highway 160 West, at the base of Smelter Mountain. The designated parking area is located at the first driveway located west of the off-leash area entrance on Highway 160.

Outdoor Restaurants

Cyprus Cafe 725 East Second Avenue Durango CO 970-385-6884
http://www.cypruscafe.com
This restaurant, located in downtown Durango, welcomes dogs to their popular outdoor patio. This award-winning Mediterranean restaurant serves lunch and dinner. Try the grilled salmon sandwich, lamb, chicken salad, or gyro for lunch. If you come for the dinner, they serve a variety of entrees including rock shrimp linguini, roasted butternut squash risotto, and portabello mushroom. In addition to the delicious food, you and your pooch can enjoy the live jazz on the patio.
Durango Natural Foods Deli 575 East 8th Avenue Durango CO 970-247-8129
This deli offers organic and natural sandwiches, soups, salads and more. Dogs are allowed at the outdoor tables.

Eagle

Accommodations

Holiday Inn Express I-70 Exit 147 & Pond Rd Eagle CO 970-328-8088 (877-270-6405)
There is a $20 one time pet fee per visit.

Off-Leash Dog Parks

Eagle Dog Park Sylvan Lake Rd at Lime Park Dr Eagle CO 970-328-6354
http://www.townofeagle.org
The Eagle town off-leash area is located at the south end of Brush Creek Park. It is an unfenced area and is marked by signage. Dogs must be under clear voice control to be off-leash in the area. To get to the dog park from I-70 take the Eby Creek Rd exit south. Turn right onto Highway 6 past downtown Eagle and turn left on

Sylvan Lake Rd. Follow Sylvan Lake Rd a few miles to the park.

Eldorado Springs

Parks
Eldorado Canyon State Park 9 Kneale Road, Box B Eldorado Springs CO   303-494-3943
Famous for its geological history with rocks calculated to be over 1.5 billion years old this park has plenty to do. Some of the features/activities include technical rock climbing, picnicking by running streams, hiking trails for all abilities, fishing, biking, sightseeing, wildlife viewing, and a visitor's center. Dogs of all sizes are allowed throughout the park and on the trails. Dogs must be leashed at all times and be cleaned up after.

Estes Park

Accommodations
Holiday Inn 101 South St. Vrain Avenue Estes Park CO   970-586-2332 (877-270-6405)
Dogs of any size are allowed. There is a $10 per day additional pet fee.

Campgrounds and RV Parks
Elk Meadow Lodge and RV Resort 1665 Hwy 66 Estes Park CO   970-586-5342
http://www.elkmeadowrv.com
Dogs of all sizes are allowed. There are no additional pet fees. Dogs may not be left unattended, and they must be quiet, leashed, and cleaned up after. There are some breed restrictions. This RV park is closed during the off-season. The camping and tent areas also allow dogs. There is a dog walk area at the campground.
Estes Park KOA 2051 Big Thompson Avenue Estes Park CO   970-586-2888 (800-562-1887)
http://www.estespark-koa.com
Dogs of all sizes are allowed. There are no additional pet fees. Dogs may not be left unattended, and they must be leashed and cleaned up after. There may only be up to 2 dogs in the cabins. There are some breed restrictions. This RV park is closed during the off-season. The camping and tent areas also allow dogs. There is a dog walk area at the campground. Dogs are allowed in the camping cabins.
Manor RV Park 815 Riverside Drive Estes Park CO   970-586-3251
http://www.manorrvparkandmotel.com
Dogs of all sizes are allowed. There are no additional pet fees. Dogs must be quiet, leashed, and cleaned up after. This RV park is closed during the off-season. There is a dog walk area at the campground.
Mary's Lake Campground 2120 Mary's Lake Road Estes Park CO   970-586-4411
http://www.maryalakecampground.com
Dogs of all sizes are allowed. There are no additional pet fees. Dogs must be leashed and cleaned up after. This RV park is closed during the off-season. The camping and tent areas also allow dogs. There is a dog walk area at the campground.
Yogi Bear Jellystone Park 5495 Hwy 36 Estes Park CO   970-586-4230 (800-722-2928)
http://www.jellystoneofestes.com
Dogs of all sizes are allowed. There are no additional pet fees. Dogs must be well behaved, quiet, leashed, and cleaned up after. This RV park is closed during the off-season. The camping and tent areas also allow dogs. There is a dog walk area at the campground.

Parks
Rocky Mountain National Park 1000 Highway 36 Estes Park CO   970-586-1206
http://www.nps.gov/romo/
Dogs cannot really do much in this park, but as you drive through the park, you will find some spectacular scenery and possibly some sightings of wildlife. Pets are not allowed on trails, or in the backcountry. Pets are allowed in your car, along the road, in parking lots, at picnic areas and campgrounds. Dogs must be on a 6 foot or less leash. You can still take your dog for a hike, not in the national park, but in the adjacent Arapaho-Roosevelt National Forest.
Arapaho-Roosevelt National Forest 240 West Prospect Rd Fort Collins CO   970-498-1100
There are numerous trails in this national forest that allow dogs. Some of the trails are located off Highway 34 or Highway 36, near Estes Park. The following are examples of three trails. The North Fork Trail is over 4 miles long and is rated easy. To get there from Loveland take Highway 34 west to Drake, turn right onto County Road #43 and travel approximately 6 miles. Turn right onto Dunraven Glade Road (there will be a Forest Service access sign) and travel to the end of the road. The Lions Gulch Trail/Homestead Meadows Trail is almost 3

miles long and is rated moderate. The trailhead is located on Highway 36, seven miles east of Estes Park, or twelve miles west of Lyons. The Round Mountain Trail is about 4.5 miles long and is rated moderate to difficult. Take Highway 34 west of Loveland for approximately 12 miles. The trailhead is on the south side of the highway, across from the Viestenz-Smith Mountain Park.

Off-Leash Dog Parks
Estes Valley Dog Park off Highway 36 Estes Park CO   970-586-8191
http://www.estesvalleyrecreation.com/
The dog park is located off Highway 36. It is next to Fishcreek Road. This fenced off-leash area has lake access.

Outdoor Restaurants
Grumpy Gringo 1560 BigThompson Avenue Estes Park CO   970-586-7705
Dogs are allowed at the outdoor tables. The restaurant has outdoor tables only in the summer.
Mary's Lake Lodge 2625 Mary's Lake Road Estes Park CO   970-586-4777
Dogs are allowed at the outdoor tables.
Molly B's 200 Moraine Avenue Estes Park CO   970-586-2766
http://www.estesparkmollyb.com
Dogs are allowed at the outdoor tables. The restaurant has outdoor tables only in the summer.
Notchtop Bakery & Cafe 459 E Wonderview Avenue Estes Park CO   970-586-0272
Dogs are allowed at the outdoor tables.

Evans

Accommodations
Motel 6 - Greeley - Evans 3015 8th Avenue Evans CO   970-351-6481 (800-466-8356)
One well-behaved family pet per room. Guest must notify front desk upon arrival. Guest is liable for any damages. In consideration of all guests, pets must never be left unattended in the guest rooms.
Sleep Inn 3025 8th Avenue Evans CO   970-356-2180 (877-424-6423)
Dogs of all sizes are allowed. There is a $15 one time additional pet fee per room. Dogs must be leashed, cleaned up after, and crated when left alone in the room.

Fort Collins

Accommodations
Comfort Suites 1415 Oakridge Drive Fort Collins CO   970-206-4597 (877-424-6423)
Dogs of all sizes are allowed. There is a $15 per night per pet additional fee. Dogs must be leashed, cleaned up after, and crated when left alone in the room. Dogs are not allowed at the pool area, and they may not be given baths in the room.
Days Inn Fort Collins 3625 E Mulberry St Fort Collins CO   970-221-5490 (800-329-7466)
Dogs of all sizes are allowed. There is a $5 per night pet fee per pet.
Fort Collins Marriott 350 E Horsetooth Road Fort Collins CO   970-226-5200 (800-228-9290)
Well behaved dogs of all sizes are allowed. There is a $10 per room per stay additional pet fee. Dogs must be quiet, housebroken, leashed, cleaned up after, and a contact number left with the front desk if they are in the room alone.
Hampton Inn 1620 Oakridge Drive Fort Collins CO   970-229-5927
Well behaved dogs up to 50 pounds are allowed. There is a $25 per pet per stay fee and a pet policy to sign at check in. Dogs may not be left in the room unattended.
Hilton 425 W Prospect Road Fort Collins CO   970-428-2626
One dog up to 100 pounds or 2 pets that total 100 pounds is allowed. There is a $25 per night per pet fee.
Holiday Inn-University Park 425 W. Prospect Rd. Fort Collins CO   970-482-2626 (877-270-6405)
There are no additional pet fees.
Motel 6 - Fort Collins 3900 East Mulberry Fort Collins CO   970-482-6466 (800-466-8356)
One well-behaved family pet per room. Guest must notify front desk upon arrival. Guest is liable for any damages. In consideration of all guests, pets must never be left unattended in the guest rooms.
Quality Inn and Suites 4001 S Mason Street Fort Collins CO   970-282-9047 (877-424-6423)
Dogs of all sizes are allowed. There is a $25 one time additional pet fee per room. Dogs may not be left alone in the room, and they must be leashed and cleaned up after.

Residence Inn by Marriott 1127 Oakridge Drive Fort Collins CO   970-223-5700
Dogs of all sizes are allowed. There is a $75 one time fee and a pet policy to sign at check in.
Sleep Inn 3808 Mulberry Street Fort Collins CO   970-484-5515 (877-424-6423)
Dogs of all sizes are allowed. There is a $10 per night per pet additional fee. Dogs may not be left alone in the rooms for longer than one hour; the Do Not Disturb sign needs to be put on the door, and a contact number left with the front desk. Dogs must be leashed and cleaned up after.
Sundance Trail Guest Ranch 17931 Red Feather Lakes Rd Fort Collins CO   970-224-1222 (800-357-4930)
http://www.sundancetrail.com
This is a summer family Dude Ranch. During Fall, Winter and Spring this is a Country Lodge with horse back riding. There are no additional pet fees and the entire ranch is non-smoking.

Campgrounds and RV Parks

Arapaho Roosevelt National Forest 2150 Center Avenue, Building E Fort Collins CO   970-498-2770
http://www.fs.fed.us/r2/arnf
This park covers 22 million acres of forest and grassland in 5 states. There are about 50 campgrounds, but only 2 are open all year, and only 3 have electric hook-ups. Dogs of all sizes are allowed. There are no additional pet fees. Dogs are not allowed in any buildings, and on some of the trails as marked. Dogs must be leashed and cleaned up after. The Arapaho Roosevelt National Forest surrounds the Rocky Mountain National Park, and the National Park doesn't allow dogs in most areas. The camping and tent areas also allow dogs. There is a dog walk area at the campground. There are no water hookups at the campground.
Heron Lake RV Park 1910 N Taft Hill Fort Collins CO   877-254-4063
http://www.heronlakerv.com
Dogs of all sizes are allowed. There is a $1 per day per dog, or $5 per week per dog, additional pet fee. Dogs must be leashed and cleaned up after. There are some breed restrictions. This RV park is closed during the off-season. The camping and tent areas also allow dogs. There is a dog walk area at the campground.

Attractions

TOP 200 PLACE **Grave of Annie the Railroad Dog** 201 Peterson St Fort Collins CO
Annie, the Railroad Dog, was adopted by the Colorado and Southern Railway people in 1934. She was sick and was nursed back to health at the railway depot. For years she remained at the depot, greeting trains and visitors. Annie died in 1948 and was buried a few yards from the depot. There is a statue of Annie in front of the library at 201 Peterson St. The gravesite is at the nearby intersection of Mason Street and LaPorte Avenue. The site is designated a national landmark. Both you and your dog can view the statue and gravesite of Fort Collin's most famous dog.

Stores

PetSmart Pet Store 4432 S College Ave Fort Collins CO   970-223-9020
Your licensed and well-behaved leashed dog is allowed in the store.
Petco Pet Store 2211 South College Avenue Ste 200 Fort Collins CO   970-484-4477
Your licensed and well-behaved leashed dog is allowed in the store.

Off-Leash Dog Parks

Fossil Creek Dog Park 5821 South Lemay Avenue Fort Collins CO   970-221-6618
http://fcgov.com/parks/
This one acre dog park has a separate fenced area for small and shy dogs. Amenities include a double-gated entry and a drinking fountain. The park is located at the entrance to Fossil Creek Community Park.
Soft Gold Dog Park 520 Hickory Street Fort Collins CO   970-221-6618
The one acre fenced park is located in Soft Gold Neighborhood Park. From North College Avenue turn west on Hickory Street to the park.
Spring Canyon Dog Park Horsetooth Road Fort Collins CO   970-221-6618
http://fcgov.com/parks/
This 2 to 3 acre dog park has a separate fenced area for small and shy dogs. Amenities include water fountains, bags and trash cans. The dog park is located at the west end of Horsetooth Road. It is in the undeveloped Spring Canyon Community Park along Spring Creek.
Poudre Pooch Park Eastman Park Dr at 7th Street Windsor CO   970-674-3500
This one acre fenced dog park is located in the southwest corner of Poudre Natural Park. From I-25 take County Highway 68 east to 7th Street (County Highway 17). Head south on 7th Street to Eastman Park Dr. The park is to the west.

Outdoor Restaurants

Beau Jo's Pizza Restaurant 100 N College Ave Fort Collins CO   970-498-8898

This restaurant serves Italian/American food. Dogs are allowed at the outdoor tables on the other side of fence.

Fort Lupton

Accommodations
Motel 6 - Fort Lupton 65 South Grand Avenue Fort Lupton CO   303-857-1800 (800-466-8356)
One well-behaved family pet per room. Guest must notify front desk upon arrival. Guest is liable for any damages. In consideration of all guests, pets must never be left unattended in the guest rooms.

Fountain

Campgrounds and RV Parks
Colorado Springs South KOA 8100 Bandley Drive Fountain CO 719-382-7575 (800-562-8609)
http://www.coloradospringskoa.com
Dogs of all sizes are allowed, and there are no additional pet fees for tent or RV sites. There is a $3 per night per pet additional fee for cabins. Dogs may not be left unattended in the cabins or outside, and they must be leashed and cleaned up after. There are some breed restrictions. The camping and tent areas also allow dogs. There is a dog walk area at the campground. Dogs are allowed in the camping cabins.

Franktown

Parks
Castlewood Canyon State Park 2989 S Hwy 83 Franktown CO   303-688-5242
Located in the famous Black Forest, this day-use park offers unique sightseeing and recreational opportunities. Explore ancient ruins, a century old dam, or a variety of hiking trails that wind into the deepest regions of the canyon. There are plenty of chances for nature study, bird watching, photography, technical rock climbing, and picnicking. Amenities include rest rooms, a scenic overlook, an amphitheater, a concrete surface trail, and a Visitor's Center. Dogs are welcome throughout the park and on the trails. Dogs must be leashed and cleaned up after at all times.

Frisco

Accommodations
Holiday Inn 1129 N. Summit Blvd Frisco CO   970-668-5000 (877-270-6405)
There is a $20 one time pet fee.
Hotel Frisco 308 Main Street Frisco CO   970-668-5009 (800-262-1002)
Dogs are welcome at this classic Rocky Mountain lodge which is located on Frisco's historic Main Street. The hotel offers two dog-friendly rooms with access to the back porch and to the doggie run. Enjoy hiking and swimming with your dog right from the hotel's front door! Dog amenities include dog beds and treats. Dog sitting and walking services are also available. There is a $10 per day pet fee.
Woods Inn Second Ave and Granite St Frisco CO   970-668-2255
http://www.woodsinn.biz
The Woods Inn is located in the heart of Colorado ski country. They offer a range of accommodations, from full condo-style suites to single bunks. Breckenridge is just minutes away and Vail is not far. There is a $15 one time per stay pet charge.

Cross Country Ski Resorts
Frisco Nordic Center Highway 9 Frisco CO   970-668-0866
While dogs are not allowed on the cross-country ski trails, they are allowed on the snowshoe trails. Rent snowshoes from the center and then take your dog on one of the easy or difficult trails. The trails can take an hour or more to complete. Dogs must be leashed on the trails and are not allowed in or near the rental building. To get there from Denver, take Interstate 70 west to the Frisco/Breckenridge exit number 203. Go south on

Highway 9/Summit Blvd. for 2 miles past Frisco's main street. Go .5 miles and turn left into the Peninsula Recreation Area parking and the Nordic Log Lodge.

Fruita

Accommodations

Comfort Inn 400 Jurassic Avenue Fruita CO   970-858-1333 (877-424-6423)
Dogs up to 100 pounds are allowed. There is a pet policy to sign at check in, and there are no additional pet fees with a credit card on file. Dogs may not be left alone in the rooms, and they must be leashed and cleaned up after.
La Quinta Inn & Suites Fruita 570 Raptor Road Fruita CO   970-858-8850 (800-531-5900)
Dogs of all sizes are allowed. There are no additional pet fees. Dogs must be crated when left alone in the room, and they may not be left unattended at all between the hours or 8 pm and 9 am. Dogs must be kept leashed.

Campgrounds and RV Parks

Mountain RV Resort 607 Hwy 340 Fruita CO   970-858-3155
Dogs of all sizes are allowed, but there can only be up to 3 small dogs or 2 large dogs per site. There are no additional pet fees. Dogs must be leashed and cleaned up after. There are some breed restrictions. There is a dog walk area at the campground.

Parks

Colorado National Monument Colorado National Monument Fruita CO   970-858-3617
http://www.nps.gov/colm/index.htm
Dogs on leash are allowed in campgrounds and paved areas only. Dogs are not allowed on any hiking trails or backcountry.

Glenwood Springs

Accommodations

Hotel Colorado 526 Pine Street Glenwood Springs CO   970-945-6511 (800-544-3998)
This elegant hotel offers a superior setting and a great location near a wide variety of recreational opportunities. Dogs of all sizes are allowed. There is a $15 per night per pet additional fee. Dogs must be declared at check in, and they prefer that dogs are not left alone in the room because the hotel is also registered as a "haunted hotel". If it is necessary for a short time, a Do Not Disturb sign can be put on the door. If there is a chance they may become uncomfortable and/or bark, they request you leave a contact number at the front desk, and they must be crated unless they will be relaxed and quiet. Dogs must be well behaved, leashed, and cleaned up after.
Quality Inn and Suites on the River 2650 Gilstrap Court Glenwood Springs CO   970-945-5995 (877-424-6423)
Dogs of all sizes are allowed. There is a $10 per room per stay additional pet fee. Dogs must be leashed, cleaned up after, and the Do Not Disturb sign put on the door and a contact number left with the front desk if they are in the room alone.
Red Mountain Inn 51637 Hwy 6/24 Glenwood Springs CO   970-945-6353 (800-748-2565)
Dogs of all sizes are allowed. There is a $10 per night per pet additional fee. Dogs may only be left alone in the room if they will be well behaved and quiet, and the Do Not Disturb sign is put on the door. Dogs must be leashed and cleaned up after.

Campgrounds and RV Parks

Glenwood Canyon Resort 1308 County Road 129 Glenwood Springs CO   970-945-6737 (800-970-6737)
http://www.glenwoodcanyonresort.com/
Located on the banks of the Colorado River, this park offers some of the prettiest scenery in the state, and some great land and water recreational opportunities. Amenities include picnic tables, fire pits, restrooms, showers, laundry facilities, and a recreation room. Dogs of all sizes are allowed. There is a $5 per night per pet additional fee. Dogs must be leashed and cleaned up after. Dogs are allowed throughout the park and on the trails, but they are not allowed in park buildings. The camping and tent areas also allow dogs. There is a dog walk area at the campground.
Rock Gardens RV Resort and Campground 1308 County Road 129 Glenwood Springs CO   800-958-6737
http://www.glenwoodcanyonresort.com

Dogs of all sizes are allowed. There are no additional pet fees. Dogs must be leashed and cleaned up after. This RV park is closed during the off-season. The camping and tent areas also allow dogs. There is a dog walk area at the campground.
White River Naional Forest 900 Grand Avenue Glenwood Springs CO   970-945-2521
http://www.fs.fed.us/r2/whiteriver/
With over 2 million acres and 8 wilderness areas, this forest provides a variety of camping areas and trails. The diverse ecosystems support a large variety of plants, fish, mammals, bird species, and recreation. Dogs are allowed at no additional fee. Dogs may not be left unattended, and they must be leashed and cleaned up after in the camp areas. Dogs are not allowed in some of the wilderness areas. This campground is closed during the off-season. The camping and tent areas also allow dogs. There is a dog walk area at the campground.

Stores
Petco Pet Store 105 East Meadows Rd Glenwood Springs CO   970-945-1527
Your licensed and well-behaved leashed dog is allowed in the store.

Goodrich

Campgrounds and RV Parks
Jackson Lake State Park 26363 County Road 3 Goodrich CO   970-645-2551 (800-678-2267)
This park has been referred to as an "oasis in the plains", and there are a variety of recreational pursuits offered all year. Quiet and well behaved dogs of all sizes are allowed at no additional fee. Dogs may not be left unattended, and they must be on no more than a 6 foot leash, and be cleaned up after. Dogs are not allowed on the swim or ski beaches, or in buildings. Dogs are allowed on the trails. There is an off-leash area and a pond where dogs can swim at the North end of the park. The camping and tent areas also allow dogs. There is a dog walk area at the campground.

Grand Junction

Accommodations
Hampton Inn 205 Main Street Grand Junction CO   970-243-3222
Dogs of all sizes are allowed. There is a $25 per night per pet fee and a pet policy to sign at check in.
Holiday Inn 755 Horizon Drive Grand Junction CO   970-243-6790 (877-270-6405)
Dogs must stay in first floor rooms. They may not be left unattended at any time. Pets must also be on leash on the premises. There is no additional pet fee.
La Quinta Inn & Suites Grand Junction 2761 Crossroads Blvd. Grand Junction CO   970-241-2929 (800-531-5900)
Dogs of all sizes are allowed. There are no additional pet fees. Dogs may not be left unattended, and they must be leashed and cleaned up after. Dogs must be crated or removed for housekeeping.
Motel 6 - Grand Junction 776 Horizon Drive Grand Junction CO   970-243-2628 (800-466-8356)
One well-behaved family pet per room. Guest must notify front desk upon arrival. Guest is liable for any damages. In consideration of all guests, pets must never be left unattended in the guest rooms.
Quality Inn 733 Horizon Drive Grand Junction CO   970-245-7200 (877-424-6423)
Dogs of all sizes are allowed. There are no additional pet fees. Dogs may not be left alone in the rooms, and they must be leashed and cleaned up after.
Super 8 Grand Junction 728 Horizon Dr Grand Junction CO   970-248-8080 (800-800-8000)
Dogs of all sizes are allowed. There is a $10 per night pet fee per pet. Smoking and non-smoking rooms are available for pet rooms.

Stores
PetSmart Pet Store 2428 F Rd Grand Junction CO   970-255-9305
Your licensed and well-behaved leashed dog is allowed in the store.
Petco Pet Store 2464 US Highway 6 Grand Junction CO   970-241-8340
Your licensed and well-behaved leashed dog is allowed in the store.

Off-Leash Dog Parks
Canyon View Dog Park Interstate 70 at 24 Road Grand Junction CO   970-254-3846
The dog park is 3.2 acres and enclosed by a 6 foot fence. The dog park is open from 5 am to midnight daily. It is

located in the northern most end of Canyon View park which is just south of Interstate 70. To get to the park from I-70, take 24 Road south and turn left into the Canyon View Park. Then turn left again on the park road to the dog park.

Grand Lake

Accommodations

Mountain Lakes Lodge 10480 Hwy 34 Grand Lake CO   970-627-8448
Dogs of all sizes are allowed. There is a $10 per night per pet fee and a pet policy to sign at check in. They also provide a care package for your dog.

Greeley

Accommodations

Holiday Inn Express 2563 W 29th Street Greeley CO   970-330-7495 (877-270-6405)
There is a $25 one time pet fee.

Stores

PetSmart Pet Store 2833 35th Ave Greeley CO   970-330-3790
Your licensed and well-behaved leashed dog is allowed in the store.
Petco Pet Store 4751 West 29th St Greeley CO   970-330-5941
Your licensed and well-behaved leashed dog is allowed in the store.

Gunnison

Accommodations

Gunnison Lodging Company 412 E. Tomichi Ave Gunnison CO   970-641-0700 (866-641-0700)
http://www.gunnisonlodging.com
Your dog is welcome at the Gunnison Inn and the Cottages within easy walking distance to many amenities and parks.

Campgrounds and RV Parks

Gunnison KOA 105 County Road 50 Gunnison CO   970-641-1358 (800-562-1248)
http://www.koa.com
Dogs of all sizes are allowed, but there can only be 1 large or 2 small dogs per site. There are no additional pet fees. Dogs may not be left unattended, and they must be leashed at all times, and cleaned up after. This RV park is closed during the off-season. The camping and tent areas also allow dogs. There is a dog walk area at the campground. Dogs are allowed in the camping cabins.
Gunnison Lakeside Resort 28357 Hwy 50 Gunnison CO   970-641-0477 (877-641-0488)
This park, located within walking distance of Colorado's largest lake (Blue Mesa) offers 67 RV sites (some that accommodate big rigs), large shady, grassy sites, restrooms, showers, a gift shop, convenience store, and a wide variety of land and water recreational activities. Dogs of all sizes are allowed for no additional fee. Dogs may not be left on site alone at any time, even inside an RV. They are allowed on the trails. Dogs must be leashed and cleaned up after at all times. This rv park is closed during the offseason. The camping and tent areas also allow dogs. There is a dog walk area at the campground.
Gunnison Lakeside Resort 28357 Hwy 50 Gunnison CO   970-641-0477 (877-641-0488)
http://www.gunnisonlakeside.com/
Dogs of all sizes are allowed. There are no additional pet fees. Dogs may not be left unattended outside, and they must be well behaved, leashed at all times, and cleaned up after. This RV park is closed during the off-season. The camping and tent areas also allow dogs. There is a dog walk area at the campground.
Lake Fork Resort and RV Park 940 Cove Road Gunnison CO   970-641-3564
This resort offers 12 RV sites, fire pits, a store, playground, horseshoe pits, and a wide range of land and water recreational opportunities. Dogs of all sizes are allowed for no additional fee for tent or RV sites. There is a $5 per night per pet additional fee for the cabins. Not all the cabins are pet friendly. Dogs must be leashed and cleaned up after at all times. The camping and tent areas also allow dogs. There is a dog walk area at the

campground. Dogs are allowed in the camping cabins.

Mesa RV Resort 36128 Hwy 50 Gunnison CO   970-641-3186 (800-482-8384)
http://www.mesarvresort.com/
This mountain resort is located along Blue Mesa Lake, Colorado's largest body of water. In addition to a wide variety of land and water recreational opportunities, they also offer their knowledge of the best hunting/fishing/hiking areas, WiFi, a convenience store, luxury sites, a recreational hall, 24 hour laundry facilities, modern restroom, showers, LP gas, a dump station, and even a pet walking service. Dogs of all sizes are allowed for no additional fee. Dogs must be walked in the pet areas when in the resort, and they must be leashed and cleaned up after. This rv park is closed during the offseason. The camping and tent areas also allow dogs. There is a dog walk area at the campground.

Mesa RV Resort 36128 W Hwy 50 Gunnison CO   970-641-3186
http://www.mesarvresort.com
Dogs of all sizes are allowed. There are no additional pet fees. Dogs must be quiet, leashed, and cleaned up after. This RV park is closed during the off-season. The camping and tent areas also allow dogs. There is a dog walk area at the campground.

Attractions

Elk Creek Marina 24830 Hwy 50 Gunnison CO   970-641-0707
http://www.bluemesares.com/
This full service marina offers a variety of boat rentals, slip rentals, guided fishing expeditions, a boater's store, gift shop, a gas dock, and a boat repair facility. The marina usually opens about the 1st of May through September. Hours and times vary toward the end of the season. Dogs of all sizes are allowed to join you on one of the rental boats. There is $5 additional pet fee. Dogs must be friendly, under control, and cleaned up after.

Lake Fork Marina Lake Fork Gunnison CO   970-641-3048
http://www.bluemesares.com/
This full service marina offers a variety of boat rentals, slip rentals, guided fishing expeditions, a boater's store, gift shop, and a gas dock. The marina usually opens about the 15th of May through September. Hours and times vary toward the end of the season. Dogs of all sizes are allowed to join you on one of the rental boats. There is $5 additional pet fee. Dogs must be friendly, under control, and cleaned up after.

TOP 200 PLACE **Monarch Crest Tram** Hwy 50 between Salida and Gunnison Gunnison CO   719-539-4091
This tram's four passenger gondolas climb from the 11,312 foot Monarch Pass to the Continental Divide at an altitude of over 12,000 feet, and offer some of the most spectacular views anywhere in the world. They are open daily from 8:30 am to 5:30 pm, with few exceptions. Your dog is allowed to join you on the ride for no additional fee. Dogs must be leashed, and please bring your own poop-n-scoop supplies.

Parks

Black Canyon of the Gunnison National Park 102 Elk Creek Gunnison CO   970-641-2337
http://www.nps.gov/blca/index.htm
This unique canyon in the Rockies is narrow and deep. Dogs may view the Canyon with you from the Rim Rock Trail. Dogs on leash are allowed on roads, campgrounds, overlooks, the Rim Rock trail, Cedar Point Nature trail, and North Rim Chasm View Nature trail. They are not allowed on other hiking trails, inner canyon routes, or in the wilderness area within the park. Dogs on leash are permitted throughout the Curecanti National Recreation Area nearby.

Curecanti National Recreation Area 102 Elk Creek Gunnison CO   970-641-2337
http://www.nps.gov/cure/index.htm
Dogs on leash are allowed in all of the park areas. The park features auto touring, boating, camping, fishing, hiking, swimming, and more.

Idaho Springs

Attractions

TOP 200 PLACE **Argo Gold Mill and Museum** 2350 Riverside Drive Idaho Springs CO   303-567-2421
http://www.historicargotours.com/
An experienced guide takes you through the history of the tunnel that took 17 years to go the 4.5 miles to town, the mine and mill showing live demonstrations of crushing/milling/rock drilling, and at the end of the tour--free gold panning instructions with a pan of free gold ore to try your luck. You might also want to buy a sack of guaranteed gold or gemstone ore, as there are a variety of gems to be found. Dogs are allowed to tour the mine, mill, and grounds. Water bowls are provided for thirsty four-legged guests. Dogs must be friendly, well trained, and be able to climb stairs. Dogs must be leashed and cleaned up after at all times.

Parks

Echo Lake Park Hwy 103 Idaho Springs CO   303-697-4545
Echo Lake Park is a 617-acre park west of Denver along the Mount Evans Scenic Byway, the highest paved road in North America. Being nestled in a glacially formed hanging valley at over 10,000 feet, it also offers spectacular views. Park amenities include a stone shelter, picnic tables, and barbecue grills. Dogs of all sizes are allowed. They must be kept leashed at all times and cleaned up after.

La Junta

Accommodations

Holiday Inn Express 27994 US Hwy 50 Frontage Road La Junta CO   719-384-2900 (877-270-6405)
Dogs of any size are allowed. There is a $10 per day pet fee.

Campgrounds and RV Parks

La Junta KOA 26680 Hwy 50 La Junta CO   719-384-9580 (800-562-9501)
http://www.koa.com
Dogs of all sizes are allowed. There are no additional pet fees. Dogs must be quiet, be on no more than a 6 foot leash, and cleaned up after. There are some breed restrictions. The camping and tent areas also allow dogs. There is a dog walk area at the campground. Dogs are allowed in the camping cabins.

Attractions

Bent's Old Fort National Historic Site 35110 Highway 194 East La Junta CO   719-383-5010
http://www.nps.gov/beol/index.htm
Dogs on leash are allowed in the site area. Dogs are not allowed inside the rooms of the fort or other buildings.

LaPorte

Campgrounds and RV Parks

Fort Collins KOA 6670 N Hwy 287 LaPorte CO   970-493-9758 (800-562-2648)
http://www.koa.com
Dogs of all sizes are allowed. There are no additional pet fees. Dogs must be leashed and cleaned up after. Dogs are not allowed at the playground, the camp kitchen, or the bathrooms. This RV park is closed during the off-season. The camping and tent areas also allow dogs. There is a dog walk area at the campground. Dogs are allowed in the camping cabins.

LaVeta

Accommodations

Bearadise Cabins & RV Park 404 S Oak Street LaVeta CO   719-742-6221
Dogs of all sizes are allowed. There are no additional pet fees.

Lake George

Campgrounds and RV Parks

Eleven Mile State Park 4229 County Road 92 Lake George CO   719-748-3401 (800-678-2267)
Great fishing, hiking, waterfront camping, and various water and land recreation make this a popular park. Dogs of all sizes are allowed at no additional fee. Dogs may not be left unattended, and they must be on no more than a 6 foot leash, and be cleaned up after. Dogs are not allowed in the water anywhere. Dogs are allowed on the trails. The camping and tent areas also allow dogs. There is a dog walk area at the campground. There are no water hookups at the campground.

Lamar

Accommodations
Super 8 Lamar 1202 N Main Lamar CO   719-336-3427 (800-800-8000)
Dogs of all sizes are allowed. There are no additional pet fees. Smoking and non-smoking rooms are available for pet rooms.

Leadville

Cross Country Ski Resorts
TOP 200 PLACE **Piney Creek Nordic Center** 259 County Road 19 Leadville CO   719-486-1750
http://www.tennesseepass.com/skiing.htm
This rental center is located off Highway 24 between Leadville and Vail. Dogs are allowed on any of the 25km of groomed and maintained trails. Pets are not allowed inside the nordic center and need to be leashed when on the property. Once on the trails, dogs can be off-leash under direct voice control. Please clean up after your pet.

Limon

Campgrounds and RV Parks
Limon KOA 575 Colorado Avenue Limon CO   719-775-2151 (800-562-2129)
http://www.koa.com
Dogs of all sizes are allowed. There are no additional pet fees. Dogs must be leashed and cleaned up after. There are some breed restrictions. This RV park is closed during the off-season. The camping and tent areas also allow dogs. There is a dog walk area at the campground. Dogs are allowed in the camping cabins.

Longmont

Accommodations
Residence Inn by Marriott 1450 Dry Creek Drive Longmont CO   303-702-9933
Dogs of all sizes are allowed. There is a $50 one time fee for up to 6 nights, and a $100 one time fee after 6 days.
Super 8 Longmont/Del Camino Area 10805 Turner Blvd Longmont CO   303-772-0888 (800-800-8000)
Dogs of all sizes are allowed. There are no additional pet fees. Dogs are not allowed to be left alone in the room. Smoking and non-smoking rooms are available for pet rooms.
Super 8 Longmont/Twin Peaks Area 2446 N Main St Longmont CO   303-772-8106 (800-800-8000)
Dogs of all sizes are allowed. There is a $5-7 per night pet fee per pet depending on size. Smoking and non-smoking rooms are available for pet rooms.

Campgrounds and RV Parks
St. Vrain State Park 3525 Hwy 119 Longmont CO   303-678-9402
Dogs of all sizes are allowed. There are no additional pet fees. Dogs must be leashed and cleaned up after. The camping and tent areas also allow dogs. There is a dog walk area at the campground.

Stores
PetSmart Pet Store 1125 S Hover Rd Longmont CO   303-702-9526
Your licensed and well-behaved leashed dog is allowed in the store.
Petco Pet Store 205 Ken Pratt Blvd #280 Longmont CO   720-652-4642
Your licensed and well-behaved leashed dog is allowed in the store.

Beaches

Union Reservoir Dog Beach County Line Rd at E 9th Ave Longmont CO   303-651-8447
This is an unfenced off-leash area where dogs may swim in the Union Reservoir. Dogs may only be off-leash in the designated area and must be leashed when in the rest of the rec area. Dogs are not allowed on beaches outside of the dog beach. To get to Union Reservoir Rec Area from I-25 take Ute Hwy west to E County Line Rd and turn left (south). Turn left onto Highway 26 into the park in just over one mile.

Off-Leash Dog Parks
Longmont Dog Park #1 21st and Francis Longmont CO   303-651-8447
The fenced dog park is located at 21st and Francis Street. The city requests that dog park visitors park west of the dog park in Garden Acres Park or east of the dog park at Carr Park. From I-25 take the Ute Hwy (66) west to Francis Street and turn south to the dog park.
Longmont Dog Park #2 Airport Road at St Vrain Rd Longmont CO   303-651-8447
The fenced dog park is located at Airport Rd at the intersection with St Vrain Rd. This is just north of the Longmont Airport.

Loveland

Accommodations
Best Western Coach House 5542 E Hwy 34 Loveland CO   970-667-7810 (800-780-7234)
This hotel underwent renovation in 2006 and some of the features include an outdoor heated pool, meeting/banquet facilities, free continental breakfast, and many in room amenities. Dogs of all sizes are allowed for an additional fee of $30 per pet per stay. Dogs must be quiet, well behaved, and leashed and cleaned up after at all times.

Campgrounds and RV Parks
Johnson's Corner RV Retreat 3618 SE Frontage Road Loveland CO   970-669-8400
http://www.johnsonscornercampgrnd.com
Dogs of all sizes are allowed. There is a $1 per night per pet additional fee. Dogs must be leashed and cleaned up after. There is a dog walk area at the campground.

Stores
PetSmart Pet Store 1715 Rocky Mountain Ave Loveland CO   970-278-9178
Your licensed and well-behaved leashed dog is allowed in the store.

Marble

Cross Country Ski Resorts
TOP 200 PLACE **Ute Meadows Nordic Center** 2880 County Road 3 Marble CO   970-963-5513
http://www.utemeadows.com
This nordic center welcomes dogs on their cross country and snowshoe trails. The cross country trails are groomed. There is a $3 daily "tail-fee" for dogs and a maximum of 2 dogs per skier. Dogs can be off-leash on the trails but need to be under direct voice control. You can rent cross-country skis or snowshoes from the nordic center. If you are looking for a place to stay, the Ute Meadows Bed and Breakfast Inn allows pets. They are located next to the nordic center. This center is located 2 hours east of Grand Junction and 4 hours west of Denver. From Interstate 70, take Highway 82 south towards Aspen. Go 12 miles then at Carbondale take Highway 133 south towards Redstone. Go 5 miles past Redstone and turn left on County Road 3. Go 3 more miles and turn right just after you cross the Crystal River bridge.

Mesa Verde

Parks
Mesa Verde National Park PO Box 8 Mesa Verde CO   970-529-4465
http://www.nps.gov/meve/index.htm
Dogs on leash are allowed in the campgrounds and parking lots only. Dogs are not allowed on hiking trails or

archaeological sites. Pets cannot be left alone or in vehicles.

Monte Vista

Accommodations
Comfort Inn 1519 Grande Avenue Monte Vista CO   719-852-0612 (877-424-6423)
Dogs of all sizes are allowed. There are no additional pet fees. Dogs may not be left alone in the rooms, and they must be leashed and cleaned up after.

Montrose

Accommodations
Black Canyon Motel 1605 E. Main Street Montrose CO   970-249-3495 (800-348-3495)
http://www.innfinders.com/blackcyn/
There is a $5 per day additional pet fee.
Holiday Inn Express Hotel & Suites 1391 South Townsend Ave Montrose CO   970-240-1800 (877-270-6405)
Pets must stay in the first floor rooms. There is no additional pet fee.
Quality Inn and Suites 2751 Commercial Way Montrose CO   970-249-1011 (877-424-6423)
Dogs of all sizes are allowed. There is a $5 one time additional fee per pet for dogs under 20 pounds, and a $10 one time fee per pet for dogs over 20 pounds. Dogs must be quiet, well behaved, leashed, cleaned up after, and the Do Not Disturb sign put on the door if they are in the room alone.
San Juan Inn 1480 Highway 550 South Montrose CO   970-249-6644
There is a $12 per day pet charge.

Mosca

Parks
TOP 200 PLACE Great Sand Dunes National Park and Preserve 11999 Highway 150 Mosca CO   719-378-6300
http://www.nps.gov/grsa/index.htm
The dunes of Great Sand Dunes National Park rise over 750 feet high. Dogs are allowed throughout the park and must be on leash. You must clean up after your dog and dogs may not be left unattended in the park. Leashed dogs are also welcome in the campgrounds. The park features auto touring, camping fishing, hiking, and more.

New Castle

Campgrounds and RV Parks
Elk Creek Campgrounds 0581 County Road 241 New Castle CO   970-984-2240 (800-562-3240)
http://www.elkcreekcamping.com
Dogs of all sizes are allowed, and there are no additional pet fees for tent or RV sites. There is a $5 per night per pet additional fee for cabins. Dogs may not be left unattended, and they must be leashed and cleaned up after. There is a small fenced in area for off lead. This RV park is closed during the off-season. The camping and tent areas also allow dogs. There is a dog walk area at the campground.

Oak Creek

Campgrounds and RV Parks
Stagecoach State Park 25500 R County Road 14 Oak Creek CO   970-736-2436
Located south of Steamboat Springs in the fertile Yampa Valley, this park boasts a 780 acre reservoir with a full

service marina, and offers a wide variety of land and water recreation and activities. There are a couple of great trails to walk your dog, and they are allowed at no additional fee. Dogs must be on no more than a 6 foot leash and cleaned up after. Dogs are allowed on the trails, but they are not allowed on the swim beach. There are 92 campsites located in 4 separate campgrounds. Some of the amenities include picnic areas, restrooms, a dump station, campfires, and barbecue grills. The State Park daily vehicle pass is not included in your reservation and must be purchased separately at the park. The camping and tent areas also allow dogs. There is a dog walk area at the campground. There are no water hookups at the campgrounds.

Parks

Stagecoach State Park 25500 R County Road 14 Oak Creek CO   970-736-2436
Located south of Steamboat Springs in the fertile Yampa Valley, this park boasts a 780 acre reservoir with a full service marina, and offers a wide variety of land and water recreation and activities. There are a couple of great trails to walk your dog, and they are allowed at no additional fee. Dogs must be on no more than a 6 foot leash and cleaned up after. Dogs are allowed on the trails, but they are not allowed on the swim beach.

Ouray

Accommodations

Comfort Inn 191 5th Avenue Ouray CO   970-325-7203 (877-424-6423)
Dogs of all sizes are allowed. There is a $10 per night per pet additional fee. Dogs may only be left alone in the rooms if they will be quiet, well behaved, the Do Not Disturb sign is put on the door, and a contact number is left with the front desk. Dogs must be leashed and cleaned up after.
Ouraylodging.com 50 Third Avenue Ouray CO   970-325-7222 (800-84-OURAY)
http://www.ouraylodging.com
This 38 room hotel and condominiums are located on the river two blocks from Main Street. There is no additional pet fee.
Rivers Edge Motel 110 7th Avenue Ouray CO   970-325-4621
There is a $5 per day pet charge.

Campgrounds and RV Parks

Ouray KOA 225 County Road 23 Ouray CO   970-325-4736 (800-562-8026)
http://www.koa.com
Dogs of all sizes are allowed. There are no additional pet fees. Dogs may not be left unattended at the cabins or outside, and they are not allowed in the buildings. Dogs must be quiet, well behaved, be on no more than a 6 foot leash, and cleaned up after. There are some breed restrictions. This RV park is closed during the off-season. The camping and tent areas also allow dogs. There is a dog walk area at the campground. Dogs are allowed in the camping cabins.

Attractions

Colorado West Jeep Tours 701 Main Street/Hwy 550 Ouray CO   800-648-JEEP (5337)
Travel the majestic terrain of the San Juan Mountains with some of the most rugged terrain and back country roads above 10,000 feet in the country. When you come in they can suggest an appropriate trail for you, and provide you with a free mapping service, or there are many tour books/maps available. Dogs are allowed. They can be on a guided tour only if there are no other passengers, and they are allowed to join you on a rental jeep. There is no additional fee unless there is a lot of clean up, but they ask that you vacuum out the vehicle before returning it, so there is usually no fee. Dogs must be well behaved, under owner's control, leashed, and cleaned up after-please bring your own supplies.
San Juan Scenic Jeep Tours 210 7th Avenue Ouray CO   970-325-0089
http://www.ouraycolorado.com/scenicjeep
Being the oldest jeep tour company in what is considered the "Jeep Capitol of the World", they consider themselves old pros of the 4X4 open air tours, and they can also custom tailor tours. Some points of beauty that you will pass include waterfalls, lakes, aspen groves, fields of wildflowers, and breathtaking mountaintop views. Reservations are required, and the dog must be declared at that time. Dogs are allowed on the tours, if there are no objections (usually none) and/or if you have a private tour, for no additional fee. Dogs must be well behaved, leashed, and please brings supplies to clean up after your pet. Tours begin from the Historic Western Hotel lobby; dogs are not allowed in the hotel.

Outdoor Restaurants
Billy Goat Gruff's Beer Garden Corner of 4th and Main Ouray CO   970-325-4370

Dogs are allowed at the outdoor tables.

Pagosa Springs

Accommodations

Fireside Inn 1600 E Hwy 160 Pagosa Springs CO 970-264-9204 (888-264-9204)
They offer modern one and two bedroom cabins (built in 1996) with fireplaces, hot tubs, kitchens and more. The cabins are located on seven acres on the San Juan River. Dogs and horses are welcome. There is a $7.50 per day additional pet fee.
High Country Lodge 3821 E Hwy 160 Pagosa Springs CO 970-264-4181 (800-862-3707)
Dogs are allowed in the cabins. There is a $15 one time pet charge. All cabins are non-smoking.

Campgrounds and RV Parks

Elk Meadows River Resort 5360 E Hwy 160 Pagosa Springs CO 970-264-5482 (866-264-5482)
http://www.elkmeadowsresort.com
Dogs of all sizes are allowed. There are no additional pet fees. Dogs may not be left unattended outside unless they will be quiet and well behaved, and they must be leashed and cleaned up after. This is an RV and rental cabins park. This RV park is closed during the off-season. There is a dog walk area at the campground. Dogs are allowed in the camping cabins.

Palisade

Attractions

TOP 200 PLACE Colorado Cellars Winery 3553 E Road Palisade CO 970-464-7921
http://www.coloradocellars.com/
This winery is Colorado's oldest and largest winery, and they offer a wide variety of wines, ports, and more. They are open Monday to Friday from 9 am to 5 pm; Saturday from 10 am to 5 pm, and closed on Sunday. Dogs are allowed in and around the tasting room, but they are not allowed in the vineyards. They must be leashed, and please clean up after your pet.

Parker

Stores

PetSmart Pet Store 11183A S Parker Rd Parker CO 720-851-7790
Your licensed and well-behaved leashed dog is allowed in the store.

Pueblo

Accommodations

Hampton Inn 4703 North Freeway Pueblo CO 719-544-4700
Dogs up to 50 pounds are allowed. There is a $15 per room per stay fee.
Holiday Inn 4001 N. Elizabeth Pueblo CO 719-543-8050 (877-270-6405)
Dogs of all sizes are allowed. There is a $25 refundable pet deposit.
Motel 6 - Pueblo - Highway 50 960 Highway 50 West Pueblo CO 719-543-8900 (800-466-8356)
One well-behaved family pet per room. Guest must notify front desk upon arrival. Guest is liable for any damages. In consideration of all guests, pets must never be left unattended in the guest rooms.
Motel 6 - Pueblo I-25 4103 North Elizabeth Street Pueblo CO 719-543-6221 (800-466-8356)
One well-behaved family pet per room. Guest must notify front desk upon arrival. Guest is liable for any damages. In consideration of all guests, pets must never be left unattended in the guest rooms.
Sleep Inn 3626 North Freeway Pueblo CO 719-583-4000 (877-424-6423)
Dogs of all sizes are allowed. There is a $10 per night per pet additional fee. Dogs may not be left alone in the rooms, and they must be leashed and cleaned up after.

Campgrounds and RV Parks
Lake Pueblo 640 Reservoir Road Pueblo CO   719-561-9320 (800-678-2267)
There are over 9,000 acres at this scenic park, 2 full service marinas, a swim beach/waterpark, miles of hiking trails, and a variety of land and water recreation. Dogs of all sizes are allowed at no additional fee. Dogs may not be left unattended, and they must be on no more than a 6 foot leash, and be cleaned up after. Dogs are not allowed on the swim beach. The camping and tent areas also allow dogs. There is a dog walk area at the campground. There are no water hookups at the campground.
Pike and San Isabel National Forests 2840 Kachina Drive Pueblo CO   719-545-8737
http://www.fs.fed.us/r2/psicc/
This forest, with it's nearly 3 million acres, unique ecosystem, flora and fauna, is one of the most diverse forest in the U.S. Campgrounds are seasonal, however the park is open year round. Dogs of all sizes are allowed. There are no additional pet fees. Dogs are allowed on the trails. Dogs must be leashed and cleaned up after. This campground is closed during the off-season. The camping and tent areas also allow dogs. There is a dog walk area at the campground. There are no water hookups at the campground.
Pueblo KOA 4131 I 25N Pueblo CO   719-542-2273 (800-562-7453)
http://www.koa.com
Dogs of all sizes are allowed. There are no additional pet fees. Dogs may not be left unattended, and they must be leashed and cleaned up after. The camping and tent areas also allow dogs. There is a dog walk area at the campground. Dogs are allowed in the camping cabins.

Stores
PetSmart Pet Store 4230 N Fwy Pueblo CO   719-595-9000
Your licensed and well-behaved leashed dog is allowed in the store.
Petco Pet Store 5843 N. Elizabeth St Pueblo CO   719-543-6160
Your licensed and well-behaved leashed dog is allowed in the store.

Outdoor Restaurants
Gaetano's 910 W Hwy 50W Pueblo CO   719-546-0949
This restaurant serves fine Italian dining. Dogs are allowed at the outdoor tables.

Red Feather Lakes

Accommodations
Sundance Trail Guest Ranch 17931 Red Feather Lakes Road Red Feather Lakes CO   970-224-1222
Dogs of all sizes are allowed. There are no additional pet fees.

Attractions
Dude Ranch 17931 Red Feather Lakes Rd Red Feather Lakes CO   800-357-4930
http://www.sundancetrail.com
Dogs are allowed at the ranch. They must get along with other animals (dogs, horses, goats, sheep) and kids. This is a completely off leash ranch. It is a very dog friendly ranch.

Cross Country Ski Resorts
Beaver Meadows Resort Ranch 100 Marmot Drive #1 Red Feather Lakes CO   970-881-2450
http://www.beavermeadows.com
While this resort does not allow dogs on their cross-country trails, dogs are allowed on the snowshoe trails. Snowshoes can be rented at the resort. Once on the trails, dogs can be off-leash under direct voice control. This resort is located about 1.5 hours from Fort Collins.

Redstone

Accommodations
River's Edge 15184 Highway 133 Redstone CO   970-963-8368
Dogs of all sizes are allowed, however there can only be a maximum of 2 large or 3 small dogs to a room. There

are no additional pet fees.

Outdoor Restaurants
Crystal Club Cafe 467 Redstone Blvd Redstone CO   970-963-9515
Dogs are allowed at the outdoor tables. The restaurant has outdoor tables only in the summer.

Ridgeway

Campgrounds and RV Parks
Ridgeway State Park 28555 Hwy 550 Ridgeway CO   970-626-5822 (800-678-2267)
This park offers a sandy swim beach, a full service marina, and is known as a very accessible recreation area for people with disabilities. Dogs of all sizes are allowed at no additional fee for tent or RV sites. There is a $10 daily additional pet fee for the yurts. Dogs may not be left unattended outside, and they must be on no more than a 6 foot leash, and be cleaned up after. Dogs are not allowed in public swim areas, but they are allowed on the trails. The camping and tent areas also allow dogs. There is a dog walk area at the campground. Dogs are allowed in the camping cabins.

Rifle

Accommodations
Buckskin Inn 101 Ray Avenue Rifle CO   970-625-1741 (877-282-5754)
http://www.buckskininn.com/
Amenities include Satellite TV, multiple HBO, microwaves, refrigerators, and free local calls. There is no charge for a pet, but please let staff know when reserving a room. Pets cannot be left unattended in the rooms.

Campgrounds and RV Parks
Rifle Falls State Park 575 Hwy 325 Rifle CO   970-625-1607 (800-678-2267)
Visitors will enjoy the unusual scenery and tropical feel of this park as a result of the waterfalls and the mist they create for vegetation. Dogs of all sizes are allowed at no additional fee. Dogs may not be left unattended, and they must be on no more than a 6 foot leash, and be cleaned up after. Dogs are not allowed on the swim beach or at Harvey Gap, but they are allowed on the trails. The camping and tent areas also allow dogs. There is a dog walk area at the campground.

Salida

Accommodations
Super 8 Salida 525 W Rainbow Salida CO   719-539-6689 (800-800-8000)
Dogs of all sizes are allowed. There are no additional pet fees. Smoking and non-smoking rooms are available for pet rooms.
Woodland Motel 903 W 1st Street Salida CO   719-539-4980
One large dog or up to 3 small dogs are allowed per room. There are no additional pet fees.

Attractions
Monarch Crest Tram Hwy 50 between Salida and Gunnison Salida CO   719-539-4091
This tram's four passenger gondolas climb from the 11,312 foot Monarch Pass to the Continental Divide at an altitude of over 12,000 feet, and offer some of the most spectacular views anywhere in the world. They are open daily from 8:30 am to 5:30 pm, with few exceptions. Your dog is allowed to join you on the ride for no additional fee. Dogs must be leashed, and please bring your own poop-n-scoop supplies.

Silverthorne

Accommodations

Days Inn Summit County 580 Silverthorne Lane Silverthorne CO 970-468-8661 (800-329-7466)
Dogs of all sizes are allowed. There is a $10 per night pet fee per pet.

Silverton

Accommodations

Canyon View Motel 661 Greene Street Silverton CO 970-387-5400
Every room really does have a canyon view here. Dogs of all sizes are welcomed with complimentary biscuits, and there are no additional pet fees. Dogs may not be left alone in the room, and they must be leashed and cleaned up after.

The Wyman Hotel & Inn 1371 Greene Street Silverton CO 970-387-5372 (800-609-7845)
This hotel and inn, the recipient of several accolades for food and service and listed on the National Register of Historic Places, offer the ambiance of a bed and breakfast, and personal service for any special occasion. They feature a full gourmet breakfast each morning, and a 3-course candlelight diner each evening. Dogs of all sizes are allowed. There is a $25 one time additional pet fee per pet, and a pet policy to sign at check in. Dogs may not be left alone in the room, and they must be leashed and cleaned up after.

Campgrounds and RV Parks

Silver Summit RV Park 640 Mineral Street Silverton CO 970-387-0240
http://www.silversummitrvpark.com
Dogs of all sizes are allowed. There are no additional pet fees. Dogs may not be left unattended, and they must be quiet, leashed, and cleaned up after. This RV park is closed during the off-season. There is a dog walk area at the campground.

Attractions

TOP 200 PLACE **Triangle Jeep Rentals** 864 Greene Street Silverton CO 877-522-2354
The staff here will share their vast knowledge of this area with you by providing you with a map of the area, going over the routes with you, and offering instructions when needed. There are over 500 miles of jeep roads offering a variety of vistas, waterfalls, wildlife, ghost towns, and snow-laden peaks. Your dog is allowed to join you on the jeep rental for no additional charge. However, they are quite strict regarding dog hair. If the jeep only needs the regular clean up from the trip, there is no charge; however, if they have to clean a lot of dog hair, they charge $25 per hour-firm. There are no size or weight restrictions. Dogs must be under owner's control at all times.

Snowmass Village

Attractions

TOP 200 PLACE **Blazing Adventures** P. O. Box 5068 Snowmass Village CO 800-282-7238
http://www.BlazingAdventures.com/
This outdoor adventure company offers a wide range of exciting summer and winter guided tours; some of which include jeep tours, rafting, hiking or biking tours, sunset dinners, and fishing excursions. They couple these tours with a unique selection of environmental, educational, and historical lectures. They offer years of experience and will custom tailor your adventure according to your needs. They will allow dogs on most of the tours; however, it would have to be a "private trip". There is no additional fee for the dog, and they must be leashed at all times.

Somerset

Campgrounds and RV Parks

Paonai State Park On Hwy 133 Somerset CO 970-921-5721 (800-678-2267)
This small primitive park offers wildflowers in abundance and a small lake for recreation. There is no drinking water available here, so bring your own. Dogs of all sizes are allowed at no additional fee. Dogs may not be left unattended, and they must be leased and cleaned up after. Dogs are not allowed in public swim areas. Dogs are allowed on the trails. The camping and tent areas also allow dogs. There is a dog walk area at the campground.

There are no electric or water hookups at the campground.

South Denver

Day Kennels
PetsHotel by PetsMart Day Kennel 8695 S. Park Meadows Center South Denver CO   303-799-1624
http://www.petsmart.com/PETsHOTEL/
This PetSmart pet store offers day care, day camp and overnight care. You may drop off and pick up your dog during the hours of 7 am - 9 pm M-S, Sundays 7 am - 7 pm. Dogs are required to have proof of current rabies, DPP and bordatella vaccinations.

South Fork

Accommodations
Foothills Lodge and Cabins 0035 Silver Thread Lane South Fork CO   719-873-5969 (800-510-3897)
http://www.foothillslodgeandcabins.com
The lodge and cabins are available for people traveling with friendly pets. Pets are permitted with a signed pet policy, credit card deposit and a pet fee of $5 per day.

Steamboat Springs

Accommodations
Alpiner Lodge 424 Lincoln Ave. Steamboat Springs CO   970-879-1430 (800-538-7519)
http://www.toski.com/sli/2s.html
There is an $15 one time fee.
Comfort Inn 1055 Walton Creek Road Steamboat Springs CO   970-879-6669 (877-424-6423)
Dogs of all sizes are allowed. There is a $20 per night per pet additional fee. Dogs may not be left alone at any time, and they must be leashed and cleaned up after.
Hampton Inn 725 S Lincoln Avenue Steamboat Springs CO   970-871-8900
Dogs of all sizes are allowed. There is a $10 per night per pet fee.
Holiday Inn 3190 S. Lincoln Ave Steamboat Springs CO   970-879-2250 (877-270-6405)
http://www.basshotels.com/holiday-inn
Well-behaved dogs of all sizes are welcome. Dogs cannot be left alone in the room. There is a $10 per day pet charge. Pets are allowed in non-smoking and smoking rooms.
La Quinta Inn Steamboat Springs 3155 Ingles Lane Steamboat Springs CO   970-871-1219 (800-531-5900)
Dogs of all sizes are allowed. There is a $10 per night per stay additional fee. Dogs may not be left unattended unless they will be quiet, well behaved, and a contact number left with the front desk. Dogs must be leashed and cleaned up after.
Rabbit Ears Motel 201 Lincoln Avenue /Hwy 40 Steamboat Springs CO   970-879-1150
This motel is located across from the famous Steamboat Health and Recreation Association and their natural hot spring pools as well as several other worthy local attractions. Some of the amenities offered are a free full continental breakfast, discounted Hot Springs Pool passes, and a large gathering room. Dogs of all sizes are allowed. There is a $12 one time additional pet fee per room. Dogs may not be left alone in the room, and they must be leashed and cleaned up after.
Sheraton Steamboat Resort & Conference Center 2200 Village Inn Court Steamboat Springs CO   970-879-2220 (888-625-5144)
Dogs up to 80 pounds are allowed. There is a $25 one time nonrefundable pet fee per visit. Dogs are not allowed to be left alone in the room.

Attractions
Amaze'n Steamboat 1255 S Lincoln Avenue Steamboat Springs CO   970-870-8682
Although dogs are not allowed in the maze here, they are allowed on the grounds and in the mini golf area. Dogs must be friendly and well behaved, and they must be leashed and cleaned up after at all times.

TOP 200 PLACE Silver Bullet Gondola Rides Gondola Square Steamboat Springs CO   970-879-0740
Dogs are allowed to join their owners on this incredibly scenic ride of lush mountain sides with blankets of

wildflowers, and long distance vistas. The gondola is open daily (weather permitting), and is located at the base of Mt Werner. At the top of the mountain there are several trails to explore. Tickets are available at the Main Ticket Office or Ride Sports from 9:00am to 5:00pm; lift hours vary by season and day. Dogs are allowed to ride the gondola in the summer only and free of charge. They must be leashed at all times, and please clean up after your pet.

Parks
Fish Creek Falls Fish Creek Falls Road Steamboat Springs CO 970-879-1870
http://www.fs.fed.us/r2/mbr/
Although located in the Routt National Forest, it is only a short distance to this worthy sight. You will find a short, semi-steep trail leading to the bottom of a stunning 283 foot waterfall, or take the short walk to a scenic overlook, ramped for those with disabilities. There are picnic areas and a variety of other trails along the way-some of them more challenging. Dogs are allowed for no additional fee at this day-use park, and they are allowed on the trails. If your dog responds firmly to voice control they do not have to be on leash.

Outdoor Restaurants
Geeks Garage 730 Lincoln Ave Steamboat Springs CO 970-879-2976
Dogs are allowed at this internet/coffee shop. They serve coffee and pastries.

Sterling

Campgrounds and RV Parks
Jellystone Park 22018 Hwy 6 Sterling CO 970-522-2233 (866-964-4232)
http://www.buffalohillscampground.com
Dogs of all sizes are allowed. There are no additional pet fees. Dogs must be well behaved, quiet, leashed, and cleaned up after. For those on the road in the off season, they have electric only hook-ups. This RV park is closed during the off-season. The camping and tent areas also allow dogs. There is a dog walk area at the campground.

Strasburg

Campgrounds and RV Parks
Denver East/Strasburg KOA 1312 Monroe Strasburg CO 303-622-9274 (800-562-6538)
http://www.koa.com
Dogs of all sizes are allowed, and there are no additional pet fees for tent or RV sites. There is a $4 per night per pet additional fee for the cabins. Dogs are greeted at check in with a dog biscuit. Dogs may not be left unattended at the cabins or outside, and they must be leashed and cleaned up after. The camping and tent areas also allow dogs. There is a dog walk area at the campground. Dogs are allowed in the camping cabins. There are special amenities given to dogs at this campground.

Superior

Stores
PetSmart Pet Store 402 Center Dr Superior CO 303-543-6060
Your licensed and well-behaved leashed dog is allowed in the store.

TOWAOC

Campgrounds and RV Parks
Ute Mountain Casino RV Resort 3 WEEMINUCHE DRIVE TOWAOC CO 970-565-6544 (800-889-5072)
http://www.utemountaincasino.com/
This RV park is along side the state's first Tribal gaming facility; the largest casino in the 4 corners area. Some of

the amenities of the camp area include a convenience store, restrooms, showers, laundry facilities, sauna, indoor pool, wading pool, cable, a game room, and playground. Dogs of all sizes are allowed for no additional fee. Dogs must be leashed and cleaned up after at all times. This RV park is closed during the offseason. The camping and tent areas also allow dogs. There is a dog walk area at the campground.

Tabernash

Cross Country Ski Resorts
Devils Thumb Resort 3530 County Road 83 Tabernash CO   800-933-4339
http://www.devilsthumbranch.com
This resort was voted number one in scenery and number seven overall out of all Nordic resorts in North America by a 2003 Fischer Nordic Poll. The resort is located at the base of the Continental Divide. While dogs are not allowed in the lodge or cabins, they are allowed on a special cross-country ski trail. It is called Dog Loop and it is about an 8k to 10k groomed trail. Dogs should be leashed at the resort and on the trail. This resort is located about 2 hours northeast of Denver.

Telluride

Accommodations
Hotel Columbia Telluride 300 W. San Juan Ave. Telluride CO   970-728-0660 (800-201-9505)
http://www.columbiatelluride.com/
This full service resort hotel welcomes your best friend. They are located just two blocks from the downtown shops and restaurants. There is a $15 per day pet charge. All rooms are non-smoking.
TOP 200 PLACE Mountain Lodge Telluride 457 Mountain Village Blvd. Telluride CO   866-368-6867
http://www.mountainlodgetelluride.com
This rustic pet-friendly lodge is located in Telluride's Mountain Village Resort community with views of the San Juan Mountains. There are 125 dog-friendly rooms in the lodge. There is a $25 per day pet fee up to a maximum of $100 per stay. The lodge offers pet beds, bowls and treats to their dog visitors and have pet pick-up stations around the property.
Wyndham Peaks Resort 136 Country Club Drive Telluride CO   970-728-6800 (800-789-2220)
http://www.thepeaksresort.com/
There is a $50 per day pet charge.

Campgrounds and RV Parks
Town Park Campground 500 E Colorado Avenue Telluride CO   970-728-2173
This campground is located at the Town Park in Telluride, (refer to our listing under Telluride Town Park) a 36 acre landscaped public park and festival grounds bustling with year around activities. Dogs of all sizes are allowed throughout the park and on the trails in the summer. They are not allowed at the event center during festivals or other planned events. Dogs must be leashed at all times, and cleaned up after. Camping is on a cash/money order, first come first served basis, and during the season they fill up fast on the weekends. Dogs are allowed for no additional fee. There are 28 vehicle campsites and 5 primitive sites, coin-operated showers, and toilet facilities. This rv park is closed during the off-season. The camping and tent areas also allow dogs. There is a dog walk area at the campground. There are no electric or water hookups at the campgrounds.

Attractions
Dave's Mountain Tours P.O. Box 2736 Telluride CO   970-728-9749
http://www.telluridetours.com/summer.htm
Knowledgeable guides help visitors to experience the magic of the Colorado Rockies in their 8-passenger, open top 4X4 vehicles. Following trails to over 12,000 feet you will enjoy clear mountain streams, waterfalls, abundant wildlife, open meadows filled with flowers, ghost towns, mountain passes, dramatic 360 degree views, and more. Dogs are allowed on some of the tours; they ask that you declare the dog at the time of reservations. There are no additional fees for dogs. They must be leashed, and please bring your own poop-n-scoop supplies.

Parks
Telluride Town Park 500 E Colorado Avenue Telluride CO   970-728-2173
Town Park in Telluride is a 36 acre landscaped public park and festival grounds tucked away in a dramatic box

canyon surrounded by 12 and 13 thousand foot mountain peaks. Some of the features here include a community built play ground (Imagination Station), a kids fishing pond, gaming courts, multi-purpose ball fields, a pool, camping (refer to our listing for Town Park Campground), a concert area, picnic areas with barbecues, and a core area for special activities/events. In winter they feature a sledding hill, an ice rink pavilion, and groomed cross country ski trails. Dogs of all sizes are allowed throughout the park and on the trails in the summer. They are not allowed at the event center during festivals or other planned events. Dogs must be leashed at all times, and cleaned up after.

Events

Telluride Fur Ball 113 Lost Creek Ln # A Telluride CO   970-626-CARE (2273)
This is one of the SCHS' (Second Chance Humane Society) largest fundraisers of the year and a very popular event where pets and their owners enjoy indoor fine dining at a fancy hotel. The event is usually held in July at the Telluride Conference Center at Mountain Village, and some of the activities include a large silent auction, a guest speaker, and live music. Dogs must be current on shots, well mannered at all times and leashed and cleaned up after.

Trinidad

Accommodations

Quality Inn 3125 Toupal Drive Trinidad CO   719-846-4491 (877-424-6423)
Dogs of all sizes are allowed. There is a $15 per night per pet additional fee. Dogs must be leashed, cleaned up after, and the Do Not Disturb sign put on the door and a contact number left with the front desk if they are in the room alone.
Super 8 Trinidad 1924 Freedom Rd Trinidad CO   719-846-8280 (800-800-8000)
Dogs of all sizes are allowed. There is a $11.09 one time per pet fee per visit. Smoking and non-smoking rooms are available for pet rooms.

Vail

Accommodations

Antlers at Vail 680 W. Lionshead Place Vail CO   970-476-2471 (800-843-8245)
http://www.antlersvail.com/
This hotel and condo complex is definitely dog-friendly. They have had large doggie guests like a 250 pound mastiff. They have several pet rooms and there is a $15 per day pet charge. There are no designated smoking or non-smoking units.
Lifthouse Condominiums 555 E Lionshead Circle Vail CO   970-476-2340 (800-654-0635)
http://www.lifthousevail.com/index.cfm
Looking out upon Vail's ski runs, the Lifthouse has a great location for many other activities, and offer several in-house amenities. Dogs of all sizes are allowed for an additional fee of $25 per night per pet. Dogs must be crated or removed for housekeeping, and they must be leashed and cleaned up after at all times.

Cross Country Ski Resorts

Vail Nordic Center 1778 Vail Valley Drive Vail CO   970-479-2264
While dogs are not allowed on the cross-country ski trails they are allowed on the snowshoe trails. Dogs must be leashed on the trails. You can rent snowshoes from the Vail Nordic Center which is located at the Vail Golf Course.

Outdoor Restaurants

Bully Ranch Restaurant at Sonnenalp Resort of Vail 20 Vail Road Vail CO   970-476-5656
This restaurant serves up a casual, western-style atmosphere with a tasty Southwestern/American menu, and now they also offer a doggie gourmet menu. All well behaved, leashed dogs are welcome to join you on the lower terrace for a great dining experience. They ask that you come in through the street side entrance, and please clean up after your pet. Hours are from 11 am to 11 pm daily, unless there is a private function.

Walden

Campgrounds and RV Parks

North Park/Gould/Walden KOA 53337 Hwy 14 Walden CO   970-723-4310 (800-562-3596)
http://www.koa.com
Dogs of all sizes are allowed. There are no additional pet fees. Dogs may not be left unattended, and they must be leashed and cleaned up after. This RV park is closed during the off-season. The camping and tent areas also allow dogs. There is a dog walk area at the campground. Dogs are allowed in the camping cabins.

Wellington

Campgrounds and RV Parks

Fort Collins North/Wellington KOA 4821 E County Road 70/Owl Canyon Road Wellington CO   970-568-7486 (800-562-8142)
http://www.koa.com
Dogs of all sizes are allowed. There are no additional pet fees. Dogs must be leashed and cleaned up after. The camping and tent areas also allow dogs. There is a dog walk area at the campground. Dogs are allowed in the camping cabins.

Wentmore

Accommodations

Jack's Cabin 30 County Road 388 Wentmore CO   719-784-3160
Dogs of all sizes are allowed. There are no additional pet fees and they request you kennel your pet when out. Also do not let your pets out alone at night.

Westcliffe

Campgrounds and RV Parks

Grape Creek RV Park 56491 Hwy 69 Westcliffe CO   719-783-2588
Dogs of all sizes are allowed. There are no additional pet fees. Dogs must be leashed and cleaned up after. There is only one dog friendly cabin. This RV park is closed during the off-season. The camping and tent areas also allow dogs. There is a dog walk area at the campground. Dogs are allowed in the camping cabins.

Westminister

Accommodations

Residence Inn by Marriott 5010 W 88th Place Westminister CO   303-427-9500
Dogs of all sizes are allowed. There is a $75 one time fee and a pet policy to sign at check in.

Winter Park

Accommodations

Beaver Village Lodge 79303 Hwy 40 Winter Park CO   970-726-5741
Dogs of all sizes are allowed. There are no additional pet fees.

Chapter 17

Idaho
Dog Travel Guide

Ahsahka

Campgrounds and RV Parks
Dent Acres Rec Area P. O. Box 48/ Well Bench Road Ahsahka ID   208-476-1261 (877-444-6777)
This 677 acre park located on the Dworshak Reservoir offers a variety of land and water recreation. Dogs of all sizes are allowed at no additional fee. Dogs may not be left unattended outside, and they must be leashed and cleaned up after. Dogs are not allowed on the swim beach or in buildings. Dogs are allowed on the trails. This campground is closed during the off-season. The camping and tent areas also allow dogs. There is a dog walk area at the campground.

Almo

Campgrounds and RV Parks
City of Rocks National Reserve 3035 S Elba Almo Road Almo ID   208-824-5519 (866-634-3246)
This scenic park holds geologic and historic significance in that it is home to some of the oldest rocks in America (some over 60 stories high), so rock climbing is popular here. Dogs of all sizes are allowed at no additional fee. Dogs may not be left unattended, and they must be on no more than a 6 foot leash, and be cleaned up after. Dogs must not be allowed to dig, especially at the staging/climbing areas. Dogs are allowed on the trails. The camping and tent areas also allow dogs. There is a dog walk area at the campground. There are no electric or water hookups at the campground.

Parks
City of Rocks National Reserve PO Box 169 Almo ID   208-824-5519
http://www.nps.gov/ciro/index.htm
Dogs must be on leash and must be cleaned up after on all trails and park grounds. The park features auto touring, picnicking, camping, and hiking.

American Falls

Campgrounds and RV Parks
Massacre Rocks State Park 3592 Park Lane American Falls ID   208-548-2672 (866-634-3246)
This 1000 acre park is rich in geological and cultural history, and is home to a variety plant and animal life. It is situated on the Snake River and offers a visitor center, about 10 miles of hiking trails, a self-guided nature trail, boat launch area, seasonal weekend campfire programs, and they are host to special events held throughout the year. Dogs of all sizes are allowed for no additional fee. Dogs may not be left unattended outside and may only be left inside the camp unit if they will be quiet and comfortable. Dogs must be leashed and cleaned up after at all times. The campground offers 40 camp sites, 4 cabins, restrooms, and hot showers. Dogs are allowed in one of the cabins-also, for no additional charge. The camping and tent areas also allow dogs. There is a dog walk area at the campground. Dogs are allowed in the camping cabins. There are no water hookups at the campgrounds.

Parks
Massacre Rocks State Park 3592 Park Lane American Falls ID   208-548-2672 (866-634-3246)
This 1000 acre park is rich in geological and cultural history, and is home to a variety plant and animal life. It is situated on the Snake River and offers a visitor center, about 10 miles of hiking trails, a self-guided nature trail, boat launch area, seasonal weekend campfire programs, and they are host to special events held throughout the year. Dogs of all sizes are allowed for no additional fee. Dogs may not be left unattended outside and may only be left inside the camp unit if they will be quiet and comfortable. Dogs must be leashed and cleaned up after at all times.

Arco

Campgrounds and RV Parks

Craters of the Moon National Monument Hwy 20/26/93 18 miles SW of Arco Arco ID   208-527-3257
http://www.nps.gov/crmo
The landscape is so surreal here that an Oregon-bound pioneer in the early 1800's described this area as the 'the Devil's Vomit'. Roughly the size of Rhode Island, these young lava flows are visible from space, and the Visitor's Center is replete with information and exhibits. The park offers interpretive programs/signage, and a 7 mile scenic loop drive. Dogs are allowed in the park for no addition fee, but they must remain on the paved roads or in the camp areas. They are not allowed on the trails or back country. Dogs must be leashed and cleaned up after. Among the lava formations beyond the visitor center, is a 52 site campground available on a 1st come 1st serve basis. Some of the amenities include water (except during off season), restrooms, grills and picnic tables. The camping and tent areas also allow dogs. There is a dog walk area at the campground. There are no electric or water hookups at the campgrounds.

Parks

Craters of the Moon National Monument Hwy 20/26/93 18 miles SW of Arco Arco ID   208-527-3257
http://www.nps.gov/crmo
The landscape is so surreal here that an Oregon-bound pioneer in the early 1800's described this area as the 'the Devil's Vomit'. Roughly the size of Rhode Island, these young lava flows are visible from space, and the Visitor's Center is replete with information and exhibits. The park offers interpretive programs/signage, and a 7 mile scenic loop drive. Dogs are allowed in the park for no addition fee, but they must remain on the paved roads or in the camp areas. They are not allowed on the trails or back country. Dogs must be leashed and cleaned up after.

Ashton

Accommodations

Suoer 8 Ashton 1370 Highway 20N Ashton ID   208-652-3699 (800-800-8000)
Dogs of all sizes are allowed. There is a $10 per night pet fee per pet. Smoking and non-smoking rooms are available for pet rooms.

Athol

Campgrounds and RV Parks

Farragut State Park 13550 E Hwy 54 Athol ID   208-683-2425
With over 4,000 acres and home to the largest lake in the state, this biologically diverse park offers a variety of nature study, and land and water recreation. This park also has exhibits about their part as a Navel Training Center in WWII. Dogs of all sizes are allowed at no additional fee. Dogs may not be left unattended, and they must be quiet, well behaved, leashed and cleaned up after. Dogs are not allowed on the beach or in buildings. Dogs are allowed on the trails. The camping and tent areas also allow dogs. There is a dog walk area at the campground. Dogs are allowed in the camping cabins.
Silverwood RV Park and Campground 27843 N Hwy 95 Athol ID   208-683-3400, Ext 139
This RV park and campground has 126 sites in a beautifully wooded park setting, and sits adjacent to the Silverwood Theme Park/Boulder Beach Water Park - the Northwest's largest theme park. Some of the amenities here include a convenience store, volleyball courts, horseshoe pits, laundry facilities, showers/restrooms, picnic areas, and discounted admission tickets to the theme/water park. Dogs may be left inside your RV unit if they will be quiet, comfortable, and they are checked on regularly. There is no additional pet fee, and dogs must be leashed and cleaned up after at all times. This RV park is closed during the off-season. The camping and tent areas also allow dogs. There is a dog walk area at the campground.

Blackfoot

Accommodations

Best Western Blackfoot Inn 750 Jensen Grove Dr Blackfoot ID   208-785-4144 (800-780-7234)
Dogs of all sizes are allowed. There are no additional pet fees. Smoking and Non-Smoking rooms are used for pets.

Super 8 Blackfoot 1279 Parkway Dr Blackfoot ID   208-785-9333 (800-800-8000)
Dogs of all sizes are allowed. There is a $10 one time pet fee per visit. Smoking and non-smoking rooms are available for pet rooms.

Boise

Accommodations
Doubletree 475 W Parkcenter Blvd Boise ID   208-345-2002
Dogs of all sizes are allowed. There is a $10 per night per pet fee.
Doubletree 2900 Chinden Blvd Boise ID   208-343-1871
One dog up to 50 pounds is allowed. There is a $25 one time fee and a pet policy to sign at check in.
Econo Lodge 4060 W. Fairview Ave. Boise ID   208-344-4030 (800-553-2666)
Dogs up to 70 pounds allowed. There is a $10 per day pet fee.
Holiday Inn - Airport 3300 Vista Ave Boise ID   208-344-8365 (877-270-6405)
There is a $25 one time pet fee.
Motel 6 - Boise - Airport 2323 Airport Way Boise ID   208-344-3506 (800-466-8356)
One well-behaved family pet per room. Guest must notify front desk upon arrival. Guest is liable for any damages. In consideration of all guests, pets must never be left unattended in the guest rooms.
Red Lion 1800 Fairview Avenue Boise ID   208-344-7691
Dogs of all sizes are allowed. There is a pet policy to sign at check in and there are no additional fees.
Residence Inn by Marriott 1401 Lusk (Capitol & University) Boise ID   208-344-1200
Pets of all sizes are allowed. There is a $75 one time fee and a pet policy to sign at check in.
Rodeway Inn 1115 N Curtis Road Boise ID   208-376-2700
Dogs of all sizes are allowed. There is a $10 per night per pet fee and a pet policy to sign at check in.
Super 8 Boise 2773 Elder St Boise ID   208-344-8871 (800-800-8000)
Dogs of all sizes are allowed. There is a $25 returnable deposit required per room. Reservations are recommended due to limited rooms for pets. Smoking and non-smoking rooms are available for pet rooms.

Campgrounds and RV Parks
On the River RV Park 6000 Glenwood Boise ID   208-375-7432
http://www.camplan.com/ontheriver
Dogs up to 35 pounds are allowed. There are no additional pet fees but there may be a deposit required. Dogs must be leashed and cleaned up after. The camping and tent areas also allow dogs. There is a dog walk area at the campground.

Attractions
Ste Chapelle Winery 19348 Lowell Rd Caldwell ID   877-783-2427
http://www.stechapelle.com
Dogs on leash are allowed at the outdoor tables of this winery. It is located near Boise and is open 7 days a week. The property is great for picnicking and there is some light fare (cheese, bread,etc) available for purchase.

Stores
PetSmart Pet Store 8501 West Franklin Rd Boise ID   208-323-0385
Your licensed and well-behaved leashed dog is allowed in the store.
Petco Pet Store 179 N Milwaukee St Boise ID   208-375-7971
Your licensed and well-behaved leashed dog is allowed in the store.
Petco Pet Store 3548 South Findley Avenue Boise ID   208-344-1651
Your licensed and well-behaved leashed dog is allowed in the store.

Parks
Julia Davis Park 700 S Capital Blvd Boise ID   208-384-4228
This park of 86 acres has become known as the "cultural, historical, and artistic gateway to the heart of the city". The park offers museums, a discovery center, zoo, an outdoor sculpture garden, a band shell, playground, gaming courts, lagoon and river walking areas, and an amazing Rose Garden-given it's accreditation in 1992. Dogs of all sizes are allowed on the grounds and trails of the park. They are not allowed in the zoo or buildings. Dogs must be well mannered, and leashed and cleaned up after at all times; please bring your own supplies.
Ridge to Rivers Trail System Various Locations Boise ID   208-514-3756
The Ridge to Rivers Trail System of Boise consists of over 85 miles of trails around the Boise foothills. Many of these trails allow dogs off-leash provided that the dog is under voice control and remains within 30 feet of its

owner. Please check signs for off-leash areas. You must clean up after your dog and the number one complaint heard from users of the trails is the failure of pet owners to clean up after their dogs.

The Boise Foothills Various Locations Boise ID 208-384-4240
The city of Boise is surrounded by foothills consist of many trails and park areas. There are many areas of these parks that allow dogs. Some areas allow dogs off-leash and others allow dogs on-leash only. In off-leash areas dogs must be under voice control and within 30 feet of their owners. Please clean up after your dog as there are many complaints about people who don't clean up after their pets. One section of the foothills is the Ridge to Rivers section which has over 85 miles of trails. Ridge to Rivers is a collaborative effort between Boise and the county and federal authorities.

Off-Leash Dog Parks
Military Reserve Off-Leash Park Mountain Cove Road and Reserve St Boise ID 208-384-4240
http://www.cityofboise.org/parks
Dogs are allowed off-leash in this park. There is some shade and picnic tables.

Outdoor Restaurants
Baja Fresh 992 N Milwaukee Boise ID 208-327-0099
This restaurant serves Mexican food. Dogs are allowed at the outdoor tables. The restaurant has outdoor tables only in the summer.
Baja Fresh 980 Broadway Avenue Boise ID 208-331-1100
This restaurant serves Mexican food. Dogs are allowed at the outdoor tables. The restaurant has outdoor tables only in the summer.
Quiznos 2237 University Drive Boise ID 208-389-1177
Dogs are allowed at the outdoor tables. The restaurant has outdoor tables only in the summer.

Bonner's Ferry

Campgrounds and RV Parks
Copper Creek Campground Forest Road 2517 Bonner's Ferry ID 208-267-5561
Located 1 mile south of Eastport, this primitive 16 unit campsite offers 3 handicap sites, potable water, and pit toilets. Nearby is the Copper Falls self-guided nature trail that takes visitors to a spectacular outlook over the falls; the best viewing is in the spring. Dogs of all sizes are allowed. There are no additional pet fees. Dogs must be leashed and cleaned up after. The camping and tent areas also allow dogs. There is a dog walk area at the campground. There are no electric or water hookups at the campgrounds.

Attractions
TOP 200 PLACE **Copper Falls Self-Guided Nature Trail** Forest Road 2517 Bonner's Ferry ID 208-267-5561
Located in the Bonner's Ferry Ranger District, this great family hike of just under a mile takes you to a spectacular overlook of the Copper Falls then takes you on an easy loop back along the creek. There is an information and registration box at the trailhead that offers pamphlets. Dogs are allowed on this trail. They must be under owner's control, and leashed and cleaned up after at all times. The Copper Creek Campground nearby also allows pets.

Caldwell

Accommodations
Best Western Caldwell Inn and Suites 908 Specht Ave Caldwell ID 208-454-7225 (800-780-7234)
Dogs of all sizes are allowed. There are no additional pet fees. Smoking and Non-Smoking rooms are used for pets.
La Quinta Inn Caldwell 901 Specht Ave Caldwell ID 208-454-2222 (800-531-5900)
Dogs of all sizes are allowed. There are no additional pet fees. Dogs must be quiet, well behaved, leashed, and they request dogs be taken to the dog run out back.

Campgrounds and RV Parks
Ambassador RV Resort 615 S Mead Parkway Caldwell ID 888-877-8307

http://www.ambassadorrvresort.com
Dogs of all sizes are allowed. There are no additional pet fees. Dogs must be quiet, leashed, and cleaned up after. Dogs may not be left unattended outside. There are some breed restrictions. There is a dog walk area at the campground.

Cambridge

Parks
Weiser River Trail 3494 Rush Creek Road Cambridge ID   208-414-0452
http://weiserrivertrail.org/
This is Idaho's longest rail trail at 84 miles and it travels through rolling hills, roadless canyons, into the Payette National Forest. The trail offers a wide variety of wildlife and ever changing scenery along this multi-use trail. Dogs are allowed on this trail and they may be off lead in non-populated areas if they are under good voice control. Please clean up after your pet on the trail or in populated areas.

Challis

Attractions
Custer Motorway West end of Main Street/Hwy 93 Challis ID 208-756-5100
This driving tour of the historic Yankee Fork Mining District is a 40 mile interpretive trail with several interesting stops along the way. Many remnants of mining equipment and buildings remain. This trail is a narrow dirt road suitable for pick-ups or other high clearance vehicles. Your dog is welcome to join you on the tour, and they may get out with you at the different stops. Dogs must be under owner's control at all times.

Chubbuck

Stores
Petco Pet Store 4335 Yellowstone Avenue Chubbuck ID   208-238-0380
Your licensed and well-behaved leashed dog is allowed in the store.

Coeur D'Alene

Accommodations
Best Inn & Suites 280 W. Appleway Coeur D'Alene ID   208-765-5500
There are no pet fees. This was formerly the Comfort Inn
Best Western Coeur D'Alene Inn 414 W Appleway Coeur D'Alene ID   208-765-3200 (800-780-7234)
Dogs of all sizes are allowed. There is a $20 per night pet fee per pet. Smoking and Non-Smoking rooms are used for pets.
Days Inn Coeur D'Alene 2200 Northwest Blvd Coeur D'Alene ID   208-667-8668 (800-329-7466)
Dogs of all sizes are allowed. There is a $10 per night pet fee per pet.
La Quinta Inn & Suites Coeur D Alene East 2209 E Sherman Ave Coeur D'Alene ID   208-667-6777 (800-531-5900)
Dogs of all sizes are allowed. There are no additional pet fees. Please leash and clean up after your pet.
La Quinta Inn Coeur D Alene Appleway 280 W Appleway Coeur D'Alene ID   208-765-5500 (800-531-5900)
Dogs of all sizes are allowed. There are no additional pet fees. Please leash and clean up after your pet.
Shilo Inn 702 W. Appleway Coeur D'Alene ID   208-664-2300 (800-222-2244)
There is a $25 per stay pet charge for up to two pets.

Campgrounds and RV Parks
Coeur D'Alene KOA 10588 E Wolf Lodge Bay Road Coeur D'Alene ID   208-664-4471 (800-562-2609)
http://www.koa.com
Dogs of all sizes are allowed. There are no additional pet fees. Dogs must be quiet, leashed, and cleaned up

after. This RV park is closed during the off-season. The camping and tent areas also allow dogs. There is a dog walk area at the campground. Dogs are allowed in the camping cabins.

Blackwell Island RV Resort 800 S Marina Way Coeur d'Alene ID 208-665-1300
http://www.idahorvpark.com
Dogs of all sizes are allowed. There are no additional pet fees. Dogs must be leashed and cleaned up after. This RV park is closed during the off-season. There is a dog walk area at the campground.

Idaho Panhandle National Forest 3815 Schreiber Street Coeur d'Alene ID 208-765-7223
http://www.fs.fed.us/ipnf/
This forest of 2.5 million acres has more than 3,300 miles of hiking trails, and the various ecosystems support a large variety of plants, fish, mammals, bird species, and recreation. Dogs of all sizes are allowed at no additional fee. Dogs may not be left unattended, and they must be leashed and cleaned up after. Dogs are allowed on the trails. The camping and tent areas also allow dogs. There is a dog walk area at the campground. Dogs are allowed in the camping cabins.

Stores
Petco Pet Store 420 Wilbur Avenue Coeur D'Alene ID 208-772-7588
Your licensed and well-behaved leashed dog is allowed in the store.

Coolin

Campgrounds and RV Parks
Priest Lake State Park 3140 Indian Creek Park Road Coolin ID 208-443-6710
Steeped in history, this scenic park offers a variety of habitats, trails, and land and water recreation. Dogs of all sizes are allowed at no additional fee. Dogs may not be left unattended, and they must be quiet, be on no more than a 6 foot leash, and cleaned up after. Dogs are not allowed in the public swim area, but they are allowed at their own designated swim area and on the trails. The camping and tent areas also allow dogs. There is a dog walk area at the campground. Dogs are allowed in the camping cabins. There are no water hookups at the campground.

Cottonwood

Accommodations
TOP 200 PLACE Dog Bark Park Inn 2421 Hwy 95 Cottonwood ID 208-962-3647
http://dogbarkparkinn.com/index.htm
Definitely a unique traveling experience! The inn is built into the shape of a 30 foot tall Beagle and its 12 foot tall "puppy". They offer a 2nd floor private deck with sleeping accommodations for four, a cozy reading nook in the dog's nose, and an extended continental breakfast. The owners' obvious love of dogs shows in the folk-art style wooden canine carvings (over 60 different breeds) that are offered in their gift store. Carvings from real or still life (like pictures), and tours of the studio where they are made are also available. They are open seasonally and at times close when business may take them away, so call ahead. Dogs of all sizes are welcome for an additional $10 per night per pet. Dogs may not be left alone in the room at any time, or on the beds, and they must be well behaved, leashed and cleaned up after.

Donnelly

Cross Country Ski Resorts
TOP 200 PLACE Tamarack Resort Nordic Center 2099 West Mountain Road Donnelly ID 208-325-1002
This nordic center offers 22km of daily groomed trails and 15km of snowshoe trails. Dogs are welcome on all of the trails. They can be off-leash if under direct voice control. There is a $3 per day dog trail pass. This nordic center is located about 2.5 hours from Boise.

Driggs

Accommodations

Pine Motel Guest House 105 S MainH33 Driggs ID 208-354-2774 (800-354-2778)
This guest house is surrounded by an acre of tree covered lawn, and a big country breakfast is an option they also offer. One large dog or 2 small dogs are allowed per room. There is a $10 per night per pet additional fee. Dogs may only be left alone in the room if they will be quiet and well behaved. Dogs must be leashed and cleaned up after.

Eagle

Attractions

The Winery at Eagle Knoll 3705 North Hwy 16 Eagle ID 208-286-9463
http://www.thewineryateagleknoll.com
Dogs on leash are allowed at the outdoor tables. Open 7 days a week with hours of 11am-6pm.

Elk City

Attractions

Elk City Wagon Road/Nez Perce National Forest HC01, Box 416 Elk City ID 208-842-2245
Starting at Harpster, this historic wagon road follows the southern Nez Perce Trail, and most of the road is still rutted and narrow and more suitable for vehicles with a higher clearance. In July you can join a group tour of the road, or from June through September you can do the self-guided tour following the interpretive signage along the way. There are pullouts where you can pitch a tent; there are no campgrounds, but there are picnic and toilet facilities near the Newsome Creek Cabin. Dogs are allowed along the trail; they must be under owner's control at all times, and leashed and cleaned up after.

Glenn's Ferry

Campgrounds and RV Parks

Three Island Crossing 1083 S Three Island Park Drive Glenn's Ferry ID 208-366-2394 (866-634-3246)
This 613 acre park sits at an elevation of almost 2,500 feet on the Snake River, and it was one of the most famous river crossing areas on the historic pioneer trail. Some of the features/amenities here include an interpretive center, educational programs, historic artifacts, a self-guided tour, picnic areas, hiking trails, and a variety of other recreational pursuits. Dogs of all sizes are allowed for no additional fee. Dogs are allowed around the park and on the trails. Dogs must be well behaved, leashed and cleaned up after. The campground offers about 100 sites, with showers, flush toilets, a group shelter, and a dump station. Reservations are available from April 1st to October 31st, and is on a first come, first served basis in the off season. The camping and tent areas also allow dogs. There is a dog walk area at the campground.

Parks

Three Island Crossing 1083 S Three Island Park Drive Glenn's Ferry ID 208-366-2394 (866-634-3246)
This 613 acre park sits at an elevation of almost 2,500 feet on the Snake River, and it was one of the most famous river crossing areas on the historic pioneer trail. Some of the features/amenities here include an interpretive center, educational programs, historic artifacts, a self-guided tour, picnic areas, hiking trails, and a variety of other recreational pursuits. Dogs of all sizes are allowed for no additional fee. Dogs are allowed around the park and on the trails. Dogs must be well behaved, leashed and cleaned up after.

Grangeville

Campgrounds and RV Parks

Christmas Ranch RV Park 16967 Hwy 95S Grangeville ID 208-983-2383
http://www.christmasranchofidaho.com
Dogs of all sizes are allowed. There are no additional pet fees. When out walking with your pet, they must be on

a leash. Dogs may be off leash on site if they are under voice command and will not chase. Dogs must be cleaned up after at all times. There is a dog walk area at the campground.

Nez Perce National Forest 1005 Hwy 13 Grangeville ID 208-983-1950
http://www.fs.fed.us/r1/nezperce/
This diverse forest of 2.2 million acres provides spectacular scenery, a rich cultural history, and diverse ecosystems that support a large variety of plants animals, and recreation. Dogs of all sizes are allowed at no additional fee. Dogs may not be left unattended, and they must be leashed and cleaned up after in camp areas. Dogs are allowed on the trails except in winter when they are not allowed on the ski trails. The camping and tent areas also allow dogs. There is a dog walk area at the campground. There are no electric or water hookups at the campground.

Hagerman

Campgrounds and RV Parks

Hagerman RV Village 18049 Hwy 30 Hagerman ID 208-837-4906
Dogs of all sizes are allowed. There are no additional pet fees. Dogs must be quiet, well behaved, leashed, and cleaned up after. They are allowed in the cabins, but they may not be left unattended there, and they are not allowed on the furniture. The camping and tent areas also allow dogs. There is a dog walk area at the campground.

High Adventure River Tours RV Park 1211 E 2350 S Hagerman ID 208-837-9005 (800-286-4123)
Scenic tours, river rafting, Dutch oven cooking, and even fresh produce in season are offered here. Well behaved dogs of all sizes are allowed at no additional fee. Dogs must be well behaved, leashed, and cleaned up after. Dogs are not allowed in the buildings, but they are allowed on the trails. The camping and tent areas also allow dogs. There is a dog walk area at the campground. There are no electric or water hookups at the campground.

Parks

Hagerman Fossil Beds National Monument 221 North State Street Hagerman ID 208-837-4793
http://www.nps.gov/hafo/index.htm
Dogs must be on leash and must be cleaned up after in park. Dogs are not allowed in any buildings. The park features auto touring, hiking, fishing, boating, and more. The park contains the largest concentration of Hagerman Horse fossils in North America.

Minidoka Internment National Monument PO Box 570 Hagerman ID 208-837-4793
http://www.nps.gov/miin/index.htm
Dogs must be on leash and must be cleaned up after at the park. There are no facilities at the site but you are able to see the structures and monument of the Japanese American internment camp during WWII.

Hailey

Accommodations

Woods River Inn 601 Main Street/Hwy 75 Hailey ID 208-578-0600 (877-542-0600)
http://www.woodriverinn.com/
Located in the Sun Valley area of Idaho, this motel offers oversized, well-appointed guest rooms, and conveniences for both the vacation or business traveler. Some of the amenities include Jacuzzi, fireplace, and full kitchen suites, an indoor heated pool and hot tub, and a complimentary expanded Continental breakfast. Dogs of all sizes are welcome. There is a $25 one time additional pet fee per room, and a damage waiver to sign at check in. Dogs must be quiet, well behaved, leashed, and cleaned up after. Dogs may not be left alone in the room at any time.

Heyburn

Accommodations

Super 8 Heyburn/Burley Area 336 South 600 West Heyburn ID 208-678-7000 (800-800-8000)
Dogs of all sizes are allowed. There is a $5 per night pet fee per pet. Reservations are recommended due to limited rooms for pets. Smoking and non-smoking rooms are available for pet rooms.

Horseshoe Bend

Attractions

TOP 200 PLACE **Cascade Raft Company** 7050 Hwy 55 Horseshoe Bend ID 208-793-2221
http://www.cascaderaft.com/
This rafting company offers a variety of trips so that you can enjoy river rafting at its best; whether whitewater thrills or a cool float. They will allow a dog on board, but you must provide your own doggy lifejacket. Their season usually lasts from the end of April to the first couple of weeks in September. There is no additional fee for your pet. Dogs must be very well mannered, under owner's control at all times, leashed, and cleaned up after.

Idaho City

Campgrounds and RV Parks

Boise National Forest 3833 Hwy 21 Idaho City ID 208-373-4100 (877-444-6777)
http://www.fs.fed.us/r4/boise/
This forest has 6 ranger districts, over 2 million acres, and diverse ecosystems that support a large variety of plants, fish, mammals, bird species, and year round recreation. Dogs of all sizes are allowed at no additional fee. Dogs may not be left unattended, and they must be leashed and cleaned up after. Dogs are not allowed on the furniture in the cabins, or in any other park buildings. Dogs are allowed on the trails. This campground is closed during the off-season. The camping and tent areas also allow dogs. There is a dog walk area at the campground. Dogs are allowed in the camping cabins. There are no electric or water hookups at the campground.

Idaho Falls

Accommodations

Best Western Driftwood Inn 575 River Pkwy Idaho Falls ID 208-523-2242 (800-780-7234)
Dogs of all sizes are allowed. There is a $10 one time pet fee per visit. Smoking and Non-Smoking rooms are used for pets.
Comfort Inn 195 S Colorado Avenue Idaho Falls ID 208-528-2804 (877-424-6423)
Dogs of all sizes are allowed. There is a $10 per night per pet additional fee. Dogs may not be left alone in the rooms at any time, and they must be leashed and cleaned up after.
Comfort Inn 195 S Colorado Avenue Idaho Falls ID 208-528-2804 (877-424-6423)
Dogs of all sizes are allowed. There is a $10 per night per pet fee and a pet policy to sign at check in.
Motel 6 - Idaho Falls 1448 W Broadway Idaho Falls ID 208-522-0112 (800-466-8356)
One well-behaved family pet per room. Guest must notify front desk upon arrival. Guest is liable for any damages. In consideration of all guests, pets must never be left unattended in the guest rooms.
Shilo Conference Hotel 780 Lindsay Blvd Idaho Falls ID 208-523-0088 (800-222-2244)
There are no additional pet fees.

Campgrounds and RV Parks

Caribou-Targhee National Forest 3659 East Ririe Highway Idaho Falls ID 208-524-7500
These 2 forests were joined in the year 2000, creating 6 ranger districts, over 3 million acres, and diverse ecosystems that support a large variety of plants, animals and year round recreation. Dogs of all sizes are allowed at no additional fee. Dogs may not be left unattended, and they must be leashed and cleaned up after. Dogs are not allowed on the West Mink Trail, but they are allowed on the other trails. This campground is closed during the off-season. The camping and tent areas also allow dogs. There is a dog walk area at the campground. There are no electric or water hookups at the campground.
Targhee-Caribou National Forest 1405 Hollipark Drive Idaho Falls ID 208-524-7500
These 2 forests were joined in the year 2000, creating 7 ranger districts, over 3 million acres, and diverse ecosystems that support a large variety of plants, fish, mammals, bird species, and year round recreation. Dogs of all sizes are allowed at no additional fee. Dogs may not be left unattended, and they must be leashed and cleaned up after. Dogs are not allowed on the West Mink Trail, but they are allowed on the other trails. This campground is closed during the off-season. The camping and tent areas also allow dogs. There is a dog walk area at the campground. There are no electric or water hookups at the campground.

Stores
PetSmart Pet Store 2410 S 25th E Idaho Falls ID 208-542-9636
Your licensed and well-behaved leashed dog is allowed in the store.
Petco Pet Store 2375 E 17th St Idaho Falls ID 208-525-6166
Your licensed and well-behaved leashed dog is allowed in the store.

Island Park

Campgrounds and RV Parks
Henry's Lake State Park 3917 E 5100 N Island Park ID 208-558-7532
This high mountain lake park offers beautiful scenery and a variety of land and water recreational pursuits. Dogs of all sizes are allowed at no additional fee. Dogs may not be left unattended, and they must be on no more than a 6 foot leash, and be cleaned up after. Dogs are not allowed in buildings, but they are allowed on the trails. This campground is closed during the off-season. The camping and tent areas also allow dogs. There is a dog walk area at the campground.

Jerome

Accommodations
Best Western Sawtooth Inn and Suites 2653 South Lincoln Jerome ID 208-324-9200 (800-780-7234)
Dogs of all sizes are allowed. Smoking and Non-Smoking rooms are used for pets. There is a $50 returnable deposit required per room.

Campgrounds and RV Parks
Twin Falls/Jerome KOA 5431 Hwy 93 Jerome ID 208-324-4169 (800-562-4169)
http://www.koa.com
Dogs of all sizes are allowed. There are no additional pet fees, but they request that if you rented a cabin with a dog that you sweep the cabin out before you leave. Dogs may not be left unattended, must be leashed, and cleaned up after. There are some breed restrictions. This RV park is closed during the off-season. The camping and tent areas also allow dogs. There is a dog walk area at the campground. Dogs are allowed in the camping cabins.

Kellogg

Accommodations
Morning Star Lodge 602 Bunker Avenue Kellogg ID 208-783-1111 (866-344-2675)
This premier condominium lodge sits in the heart of the Silver Mountain Resort's new Gondola Village just steps from shopping, dinning, and a variety of recreational activities. Some of the amenities include fully furnished kitchenettes, a large community room with a big-screen TV, and rooftop hot tubs. Dogs are allowed for an additional $30 one time fee per pet. Dogs may only be left alone in the room if they will be quiet, well behaved, checked on regularly, and a contact number is left with the front desk. Dogs must be leashed and cleaned up after at all times. Dogs are also allowed on the 3.1 mile long gondola to the top of the mountain during the summer season.
Silverhorn Motor Lodge 699 W Cameron Avenue Kellogg ID 208-783-1151
http://www.silverhornmotorinn.com/
This motor lodge is just 6 blocks from Gondola Village, and a 3.1 mile long gondola (the longest single stage people carrier in the world) to the top of the mountain and spectacular views. In the summer, your pet may join you on this journey. The lodge offers an in-house restaurant, the largest hot tub in town, and spacious rooms with private baths. Dogs of all sizes are allowed for no additional fee. Dogs may not be left alone in the room unless you are somewhere in the lodge where they can reach you, and then only if they will be quiet and well mannered. Dogs must be leashed and cleaned up after at all times.
Super 8 Kellogg 601 Bunker Ave Kellogg ID 208-783-1234 (800-800-8000)
Dogs of all sizes are allowed. There are no additional pet fees. Dogs are not allowed to be left alone in the room. Smoking and non-smoking rooms are available for pet rooms.

Attractions

TOP 200 PLACE **Silver Mountain Gondola** 610 Bunker Avenue Kellogg ID 208-783-1111
http://www.silvermt.com/
This gondola is 3.1 miles long; the longest single stage people carrier in the world. Dogs are allowed on the gondola in the summer only, but they are allowed in the gondola village at the base of the mountain year round. There is no additional fee for your pet on the gondola ride, and there are a variety of hiking trails available. They are also allowed at the Morning Star Lodge here; please check our listing. Dogs must be under owner's control at all times, and be leashed and cleaned up after.

Ketchum

Accommodations

Best Western Tyrolean Lodge 260 Cottonwood Ketchum ID 208-726-5336 (800-780-7234)
Dogs of all sizes are allowed. There is a $10 per night pet fee per pet. Smoking and Non-Smoking rooms are used for pets.

Campgrounds and RV Parks

Sawtooth National Rec Area 5 N Fort Canyon Road Ketchum ID 208-837-9005
http://www.fs.fed.us/r4/sawtooth/
Located in the Sawtooth National Forest, this recreational area provides a wide variety of year round land and water activities. Dogs of all sizes are allowed at no additional fee. Dogs may not be left unattended, and they must be leashed and cleaned up after. Dogs are allowed on the trails. The camping and tent areas also allow dogs. There is a dog walk area at the campground. There are no electric or water hookups at the campground.
Smiley Creek Lodge HC 64, Box 9102/ 37 miles N of Ketchum on Hwy 75 Ketchum ID 208-774-3547 (877-774-3547)
http://www.ruralnetwork.net/~smileyck/
Dogs of all sizes are allowed. There are no additional pet fees. Dogs may not be left unattended outside, and they must be leashed and cleaned up after. The camping and tent areas also allow dogs. There is a dog walk area at the campground.
Wood River Campground/Sawtooth National Forest 12 Miles N of Ketchum on Hwy 75 Ketchum ID 208-726-7672
Dogs of all sizes are allowed. There are no additional pet fees. Dogs must be leashed and cleaned up after. This RV park is closed during the off-season. The camping and tent areas also allow dogs.

Cross Country Ski Resorts

Galena Lodge HC 64 PO Box 8326 Ketchum ID 208-726-4010
http://www.galenalodge.com
This lodge is the base camp for the North Valley Trail System. There are several cross country ski trails and snowshoe trails that allow dogs. Dogs can be off-leash on the trails but need to be under direct voice control. There is a $2 per day dog trail fee. Dogs are not allowed in the lodge. They are located about 3.5 hours from Boise.

Stores

Elephant's Perch 280 East Avenue N Ketchum ID 208-726-3497
http://www.elephantsperch.com/
This store specializes in high quality backcountry equipment and clothing. Your well mannered dog is welcome to come into the store with you. Dogs must be well trained, and under owner's control at all times.

Outdoor Restaurants

H & G's Reserve 571 4th Street E Ketchum ID 208-726-0140
Dogs are allowed at the outdoor tables. The restaurant has outdoor tables only in the summer.
Rico's Pizza 200 N Main Ketchum ID 208-726-RICO (7426)
Dogs are allowed at the outdoor tables.

Kune

Attractions

Indian Creek (Stowe) Winery 1000 North McDermott Rd Kune ID 208-922-4791
http://www.idahowine.org
Dogs on leash are allowed at the outdoor tables and lawn area. Only open Saturday (10-5) and Sunday (12-5).

Lewiston

Accommodations

Comfort Inn 2128 8th Avenue Lewiston ID 208-798-8090 (877-424-6423)
Dogs of all sizes are allowed. There is a $10 per night per room additional pet fee, and a pet policy to sign at check in. Dogs must be leashed, cleaned up after, and they prefer pets are not left alone in the room. If you must leave the pet alone in the room for a short time, a contact number must be left with the front desk.
Guest House Inn and Suites 1325 Main Street Lewiston ID 208-746-1393
This inn is located only 1 block from the Snake River and the Clearwater Rivers, and some of the amenities they offer include a complimentary continental breakfast, a cocktail lounge, seasonal outdoor pool, and a hot tub. Dogs of all sizes are welcome for an additional fee of $10 per night per pet. Dogs may not be left alone in the room at any time, and they must be leashed and cleaned up after.
Red Lion 621 21st Street Lewiston ID 208-799-1000
Dogs of all sizes are allowed. There is a $10 per night per pet fee and a pet policy to sign at check in. All pet rooms are located on the first floor.
Super 8 Lewiston 3120 North South Hwy Lewiston ID 208-743-8808 (800-800-8000)
Dogs of all sizes are allowed. There is a $5 per night pet fee per pet. Reservations are recommended due to limited rooms for pets. Smoking and non-smoking rooms are available for pet rooms.

Campgrounds and RV Parks

Hells Gate State Park 4832 Hells Gate State Park Lewiston ID 208-799-5015 (866-634-3246)
This park offers shady campsites on the Snake River along the deepest river gorge in North America, an interpretive plaza, a discovery center, tours, and various recreation. Dogs of all sizes are allowed at no additional fee. Dogs may not be left unattended, and they must be leashed at all times, and cleaned up after. Dogs are not allowed on the beach or in buildings, but they are allowed on the trails. The camping and tent areas also allow dogs. There is a dog walk area at the campground. Dogs are allowed in the camping cabins.

Attractions

Kirkwood Historic Ranch Kirkwood Road Lewiston ID 208-628-3916
http://www.fs.fed.us/hellscanyon/
This historic ranch is located in Hell's Canyon down a 4-wheel drive road, and they can also be accessed by trail or boat. If hiking, they suggest you stop at the office at the end of town and get updates and maps. The home on site of the first early ranchers is still being used by volunteers, and the bunkhouse is a museum with historic and prehistoric artifacts on display. The park features interpretive signage/exhibits, picnic tables, primitive tent camping, restrooms, and various hiking trails. Dogs of all sizes are allowed for no additional fee. Dogs may not be left unattended, and they must be leashed and cleaned up after.

Stores

Petco Pet Store 2362 Nez Perce Drive Lewiston ID 208-798-7791
Your licensed and well-behaved leashed dog is allowed in the store.

Lucile

Campgrounds and RV Parks

Riverfront Gardens RV Park MM 210.5 Hwy 95 Lucile ID 208-628-3777
This is an RV only park. Dogs of all sizes are allowed at no additional fee. Dogs must be leashed and cleaned up after. There is a dog walk area at the campground.

McCall

Accommodations

Brundage Inn 1005 W Lake Street/Hwy 55 McCall ID   208-634-2344 (800-643-2009)
This inn is an enchanting family style lodge only a few blocks from Payette Lake, and is also a perfect launching spot for bikers, hikers, and skiers. Some of the amenities include TV/VCRs with cable, kitchens, family suites, some rooms with fireplaces, outside barbecue grills and tables, and all rooms include a microwave and refrigerator. Two small dogs (10 pounds or under each) or one dog of average size is welcome for a $20 per night per pet additional fee. Dogs must be well mannered, leashed, and cleaned up after at all times. Dogs are not allowed on the furniture or beds.

The Western Mountain Lodge 415 Third St McCall ID   208-634-6300
Dogs of all sizes are allowed. There are no additional pet fees. Smoking and Non-Smoking rooms are used for pets. Dogs are not allowed to be left alone in the room.

Campgrounds and RV Parks

Payette National Forest 102 W Lake Street McCall ID   208-634-0700
http://www.fs.fed.us/r4/payette/
From the deepest river gorge in North America to elevations of almost 9,500 feet, this diverse forest of 2.3 million acres supports a large variety of plants, fish, mammals, bird species, and recreation. Dogs of all sizes are allowed at no additional fee. Dogs may not be left unattended, and they must be leashed and cleaned up after in camp areas. Dogs are not allowed in any buildings, but however they are allowed on the trails. This campground is closed during the off-season. The camping and tent areas also allow dogs. There is a dog walk area at the campground. There are no electric or water hookups at the campground.

Ponderosa State Park Miles Standish Road McCall ID   208-634-2164 (866-634-3246)
The diverse topography of his peninsula park offers a variety of naturescapes, and the park provides educational programs, guided tours, and various year round recreation. Dogs of all sizes are allowed at no additional fee. Dogs may not be left unattended, and they must be on no more than a 6 foot leash and be cleaned up after. Dogs are not allowed on ski trails in winter, on the beach, or in park buildings; they are allowed on the trails. This campground is closed during the off-season. The camping and tent areas also allow dogs.

Ponderosa State Park Miles Standish Road McCall ID   208-634-2164 (866-634-3246)
This scenic 1500+ acre park sits at an elevation of just over 5000 feet, and it covers most of a 1000-acre peninsula on Payette Lake. The park offers a wide variety of year round land and water recreation, wildlife viewing, guided walks, picnicking, and seasonal evening campfire programs. There are both dirt and hard path multi-use trails, and a nature store and visitor center. Dogs of all sizes are allowed for no additional fee. Dogs must be well behaved, leashed, and cleaned up after at all times. Dogs are allowed throughout the park and on the trails. They are not allowed on the beaches or in the park at all in the winter. Campsites can be reserved from Thursday prior to Memorial Day through Labor Day, and are on a first come first served basis during off-season, weather permitting. Amenities include restrooms, showers, picnic tables, and a dump station. This RV park is closed during the offseason. The camping and tent areas also allow dogs. There is a dog walk area at the campground.

Parks

Ponderosa State Park Miles Standish Road McCall ID   208-634-2164 (866-634-3246)
This scenic 1500+ acre park sits at an elevation of just over 5000 feet, and it covers most of a 1000-acre peninsula on Payette Lake. The park offers a wide variety of year round land and water recreation, wildlife viewing, guided walks, picnicking, and seasonal evening campfire programs. There are both dirt and hard path multi-use trails, and a nature store and visitor center. Dogs of all sizes are allowed for no additional fee. Dogs must be well behaved, leashed, and cleaned up after at all times. Dogs are allowed throughout the park and on the trails. They are not allowed on the beaches or in the park at all in the winter.

Meridian

Accommodations

Motel 6 - Meridian 1047 South Progress Avenue Meridian ID   208-888-1212 (800-466-8356)
One well-behaved family pet per room. Guest must notify front desk upon arrival. Guest is liable for any damages. In consideration of all guests, pets must never be left unattended in the guest rooms.

Campgrounds and RV Parks

Boise Meridian RV Resort 184 Pennwood Meridian ID   877-894-1357

Dogs of all sizes are allowed. There are no additional pet fees. Dogs may not be left unattended, or tied to the trees or other campsite furnishings. Dogs must be leashed and cleaned up after. There are some breed restrictions. There is a dog walk area at the campground.

The Playground RV Park 1680 Overland Road Meridian ID   208-887-1022
http://www.playgroundrv.com
Dogs of all sizes are allowed. There are no additional pet fees. Dogs must be leashed and cleaned up after. There is a dog walk area at the campground.

Stores

PetSmart Pet Store 1220 Eagle Rd N Meridian ID   208-884-0611
Your licensed and well-behaved leashed dog is allowed in the store.

Outdoor Restaurants

Baja Fresh 1440 N Eagle Road Meridian ID   208-855-2468
This restaurant serves Mexican food. Dogs are allowed at the outdoor tables. The restaurant has outdoor tables only in the summer.

Montpelier

Accommodations

Best Western Clover Creek Inn 243 N 4th St Montpelier ID   208-847-1782 (800-780-7234)
Dogs of all sizes are allowed. There is a $5 one time pet fee per visit. Smoking and Non-Smoking rooms are used for pets.

Campgrounds and RV Parks

Montpelier Creek KOA 28501 Hwy 89N Montpelier ID   208-847-0863 (800-562-7576)
http://www.koa.com
Dogs of all sizes are allowed. There are no additional pet fees. Dogs must be leashed and cleaned up after. This RV park is closed during the off-season. The camping and tent areas also allow dogs. There is a dog walk area at the campground. Dogs are allowed in the camping cabins.

Moravia

Campgrounds and RV Parks

Ro VelDo Cabins and Campgrounds 20925 Hwy J5T Moravia ID   641-437-4084
http://www.roveldo.com/
Dogs of all sizes are allowed. There are no additional pet fees for tent or RV sites. There is a $50 one time additional pet fee for the cabins, which are open all year. Dogs must be quiet, well behaved, leashed, and cleaned up after. This RV park is closed during the off-season. The camping and tent areas also allow dogs. There is a dog walk area at the campground.

Moscow

Accommodations

Hillcrest Motel 706 North Main Street Moscow ID   208-882-7579 (800-368-6564)
There is a $5 per day pet charge.
La Quinta Inn Moscow-Pullman 185 Warbonnet Drive Moscow ID   208-882-5365 (800-531-5900)
Dogs of all sizes are allowed. There are no additional pet fees. Dogs may not be left unattended at any time, and they must be leashed and cleaned up after.
Palouse Inn 101 Baker Street Moscow ID   208-882-5511
Dogs of all sizes are allowed. They have 4 pet friendly rooms; 2 of which are non-smoking. There is a $7 per night per room additional pet fee.
Super 8 Moscow 175 Peterson Dr Moscow ID   208-883-1503 (800-800-8000)
Dogs up to 80 pounds are allowed. There is a $10 per night pet fee per pet. Smoking and non-smoking rooms

are available for pet rooms.

Mountain Home

Accommodations
Best Western Foothills Motor Inn 1080 Hwy 20 Mountain Home ID 208-587-8477 (800-780-7234)
Dogs of all sizes are allowed. There is a $5 per night pet fee per pet. Smoking and Non-Smoking rooms are used for pets.
Sleep Inn 1180 Hwy 20 Mountain Home ID 208-587-9743 (877-424-6423)
Dogs of all sizes are allowed. There is a $10 per night per room additional pet fee. Dogs may not be left alone in the rooms, and they must be leashed and cleaned up after.

Campgrounds and RV Parks
Bruneau Dunes State Park 27608 Sand Dunes Road Mountain Home ID 208-366-7919 (866-634-3246)
Home to the Bruneau Dunes Observatory, and the tallest single-structured sand dune in North America at 470 feet, this high desert park offers a wide variety of nature/sky study, and land and water recreation. Dogs of all sizes are allowed at no additional fee. Dogs may not be left unattended, and they must be on no more than a 6 foot leash, and be cleaned up after in the camp areas. Dogs may be off lead out of the camp area only if they are well trained and will respond to voice command. Dogs are allowed on the trails. This campground is closed during the off-season. The camping and tent areas also allow dogs. There is a dog walk area at the campground.
Bruneau Dunes State Park 27608 Sand Dunes Road Mountain Home ID 208-366-7919 (866-634-3246)
This park is home to the tallest single-structured sand dune in North America at a height of 470 feet, and this high mountain desert park offers lakes, prairies, and marshlands to explore. There is a wide variety of land and water recreation and activities, a nature store, a 5 mile hiking trail that will present visitors with stunning views, interpretive programs, and star/space viewing at Idaho's only public observatory. Dogs of all sizes are allowed for no additional fee. Dogs must be under owner's control, and be leashed and cleaned up after at all times. Dogs are allowed on all the trails. Camping is available year round on a first-come, first-served basis (weather conditions permitting). The campground offers one of the longest camping seasons of the state parks. Amenities include restrooms, showers, a group shelter, a dump station, and lots of shade trees. The camping and tent areas also allow dogs. There is a dog walk area at the campground.
Mountain Home KOA 220 E 10th N Mountain Home ID 208-587-5111 (800-562-8695)
http://www.koa.com
Dogs of all sizes are allowed. There are no additional pet fees. Dogs must be leashed and cleaned up after. This RV park is closed during the off-season. The camping and tent areas also allow dogs. There is a dog walk area at the campground. Dogs are allowed in the camping cabins.
Mountain Home RV Park 2295 American Legion Blvd Mountain Home ID 208-890-4100
Dogs of all sizes are allowed. There are no additional pet fees. Dogs must be quiet, well behaved, and cleaned up after. Dogs may be off lead if they are under voice control. There is a dog walk area at the campground.

Parks
Bruneau Dunes State Park 27608 Sand Dunes Road Mountain Home ID 208-366-7919 (866-634-3246)
This park is home to the tallest single-structured sand dune in North America at a height of 470 feet, and this high mountain desert park offers lakes, prairies, and marshlands to explore. There is a wide variety of land and water recreation and activities, a nature store, a 5 mile hiking trail that will present visitors with stunning views, interpretive programs, and star/space viewing at Idaho's only public observatory. Dogs of all sizes are allowed for no additional fee. Dogs must be under owners control, and be leashed and cleaned up after at all times. Dogs are allowed on all the trails.

Nampa

Accommodations
Hampton Inn 5750 Franklin Road Nampa ID 208-442-0036
Dogs up to 50 pounds are allowed. There is a $20 one time fee per room and a pet policy to sign at check in. Dogs are not allowed to be left alone in the room.

Orofino

Accommodations

Helgeson Place Hotel Suites 125 Johnson Avenue Orofino ID 208-476-5729 (800-404-5729)
http://www.helgesonhotel.com/
This hotel is situated right on the Lewis and Clark trail, and they offer a great location for activities and recreation and serve a continental breakfast. Dogs of all sizes are allowed for an additional $15 per night per pet. Dogs must be quiet, well behaved, leashed, and cleaned up after.

Campgrounds and RV Parks

Clearwater National Forest 83544 Hwy 12 Orofino ID 208-476-4541
http://www.fs.fed.us/r1/clearwater/
This forest has 4 ranger districts, 1.8 million acres, and has diverse ecosystems that support a large variety of plants, fish, mammals, bird species as well as year round recreation. Dogs of all sizes are allowed at no additional fee. Dogs may not be left unattended, and they must be leashed, and cleaned up after in camp areas, and especially on the beaches. Dogs are not allowed in swim areas or in buildings. Dogs are allowed on the trails. This campground is closed during the off-season. The camping and tent areas also allow dogs. There is a dog walk area at the campground. Dogs are allowed in the camping cabins. There are no electric or water hookups at the campground.
Dworshak State Park P. O. Box 2028/Freeman Creek Road Orofino ID 208-476-5994 (866-634-3246)
This 850, acre park located on shores of Dworshak Reservoir, offers a variety of activities and land and water recreation. Dogs of all sizes are allowed at no additional fee. Dogs may not be left unattended, and they must be leashed at all times, and cleaned up after. Dogs are not allowed in the buildings or on the beaches. Dogs are allowed on the trails. The camping and tent areas also allow dogs. There is a dog walk area at the campground. Dogs are allowed in the camping cabins.

Paris

Campgrounds and RV Parks

Bear Lake State Park P. O. Box 297 Paris ID 208-847-1757 (866-634-3246)
This 966 acre park sits at an elevation of 5,900 feet, and with Bear Lake at 20 miles long and 8 miles wide, there is a wide variety of year round land and water recreation. There are various programs and activities hosted by the park, and they also offer group shelters, boat ramps, and picnicking. Dogs of all sizes are allowed for no additional fee. Dogs are not allowed in the North Beach day use area, but they are allowed down by the beach that is adjacent to the campground. Dogs must be friendly, leashed, and cleaned up after. The campground is located on the east side of the lake and offer 47 individual sites, plus three (3) group campsites. This RV park is closed during the off-season. The camping and tent areas also allow dogs. There is a dog walk area at the campground. There are no water hookups at the campgrounds.

Parks

Bear Lake State Park P. O. Box 297 Paris ID 208-847-1757 (866-634-3246)
This 966 acre park sits at an elevation of 5,900 feet, and with Bear Lake at 20 miles long and 8 miles wide, there is a wide variety of year round land and water recreation. There are various programs and activities hosted by the park, and they also offer group shelters, boat ramps, and picnicking. Dogs of all sizes are allowed for no additional fee. Dogs are not allowed in the North Beach day use area, but they are allowed down by the beach that is adjacent to the campground. Dogs must be friendly, leashed, and cleaned up after.

Pinehurst

Campgrounds and RV Parks

Kellogg/Silver Valley KOA 801 N Division Street Pinehurst ID 208-682-3612 (800-562-0799)
http://www.kelloggsilvervalleykoa.com
Dogs of all sizes are allowed. There are no additional pet fees. There is a $50 refundable deposit (or have credit card on file) for the cabin rentals. Dogs must be well behaved, may not be left unattended, must be leashed at all times, and cleaned up after. There is a fenced in dog run on site. This RV park is closed during the off-season. The camping and tent areas also allow dogs. There is a dog walk area at the campground. Dogs are allowed in the camping cabins.

Plummer

Campgrounds and RV Parks
Heyburn State Park 1291 Chatcolet Road Plummer ID   208-686-1308 (866-634-3246)
This park of about 5,500 acres with 2,300 acres of lake is rich in natural and cultural history. The park offers an interpretive center along with a wide variety of land and water activities and recreation. Dogs of all sizes are allowed at no additional fee. Dogs may not be left unattended except for short periods, and then only if they will be quiet and well behaved. Dogs must be on no more than a 6 foot leash, and be cleaned up after. Dogs are allowed on the trails. This campground is closed during the off-season. The camping and tent areas also allow dogs. There is a dog walk area at the campground. Dogs are allowed in the camping cabins.

Pocatello

Accommodations
Cavanaughs Pocatello Hotel 1555 Pocatello Creek Road Pocatello ID   208-233-2200 (800-325-4000)
There are no additional pet fees.
Holiday Inn 1399 Bench Rd Pocatello ID   208-237-1400 (877-270-6405)
Pets are allowed in the rooms with exterior entrances only. There is a $10.90 one time additional pet fee.
Motel 6 - Pocatello - Chubbuck 291 West Burnside Avenue Pocatello ID   208-237-7880 (800-466-8356)
One well-behaved family pet per room. Guest must notify front desk upon arrival. Guest is liable for any damages. In consideration of all guests, pets must never be left unattended in the guest rooms.
Red Lion 1555 Pocatello Creek Road Pocatello ID   208-233-2200
Dogs of all sizes are allowed. There are no additional pet fees.
Super 8 Pocatello 1330 Bench Rd Pocatello ID   208-234-0888 (800-800-8000)
Dogs of all sizes are allowed. There is a $2 per night pet fee per pet in smoking rooms. There is a $10 per night pet fee per pet in non-smoking rooms.

Campgrounds and RV Parks
Pocatello KOA 9815 W Pocatello Creek Road Pocatello ID   208-233-6851 (800-562-9175)
http://www.koa.com
Dogs of all sizes are allowed. There are no additional pet fees. Dogs may not be left unattended, must be leashed, and cleaned up after. The camping and tent areas also allow dogs. There is a dog walk area at the campground.

Pollock

Campgrounds and RV Parks
Canyon Pines Resort 10 Barn Road Pollock ID   208-628-4006
http://www.canyonpinesrv.com
Dogs of all sizes are allowed. There are no additional pet fees. Dogs may not be left unattended, and must be leashed and cleaned up after. The camping and tent areas also allow dogs. There is a dog walk area at the campground.

Ponderay

Accommodations
Motel 6 - Sandpoint 477255 Highway 95 North Ponderay ID   208-263-5383 (800-466-8356)
One well-behaved family pet per room. Guest must notify front desk upon arrival. Guest is liable for any damages. In consideration of all guests, pets must never be left unattended in the guest rooms.

Post Falls

Accommodations

Comfort Inn 3105 E Seltice Way Post Falls ID   208-773-8900 (877-424-6423)
Dogs of all sizes are allowed. There is a $20 per night per stay additional pet fee. Dogs may be left alone in the room if there is a contact number left at the front desk. Dogs must be leashed and cleaned up after.
Holiday Inn Express 3105 E. Seltice Way Post Falls ID   208-773-8900 (877-270-6405)
Well-behaved dogs of all sizes are welcome. There is a $20 one time pet fee.
Howard Johnson Express Inn West 3647 5th Ave. Post Falls ID   208-773-4541 (800-446-4656)
Dogs of all sizes are welcome. There is a $5 per day pet fee.
Sleep Inn 100 Pleasant View Road Post Falls ID   208-777-9394 (877-424-6423)
Dogs of all sizes are allowed. There is a $20 one time fee per room and a pet policy to sign at check in.

Campgrounds and RV Parks

Suntree RV Park 350 N Idahline Road Post Falls ID 208-773-9982
Dogs of all sizes are allowed. There is a $1 per night per pet additional fee. Dogs may not be left unattended, and they must be quiet, well behaved, leashed, and cleaned up after. There is a dog walk area at the campground.

Priest Lake Area

Accommodations

Elkin's Resort on Priest Lake 404 Elkins Road Nordman ID   208-443-2432
http://www.elkinsresort.com/
There is a $15 per day pet charge and there are no designated smoking or non-smoking cabins.
Hill's Resort 4777 W. Lakeshore Rd. Priest Lake ID   208-443-2551
http://www.hillsresort.com/
There is a $150 per week pet charge. Dogs are also allowed on the beaches.
Edgewater Resort 56 Bridge Street Sandpoint ID   208-263-3194 (800-635-2534)
There is a $5 one time pet charge.
Super 8 Sandpoint 476841 Hwy 95 North Sandpoint ID   208-263-2210 (800-800-8000)
Dogs of all sizes are allowed. There is a $5 per night pet fee per pet. Smoking and non-smoking rooms are available for pet rooms.

Attractions

Pend d'Oreille Winery 220 Cedar St Sandpoint ID   877-452-9011
http://www.powine.com
Dogs on leash are allowed at the outdoor tables of this winery. Open 7 days a week with various hours. The winery is located in Sandpoint. There is a lake close by that you can walk to.

Rexburg

Accommodations

Comfort Inn 885 W Main Street Rexburg ID   208-359-1311 (877-424-6423)
Dogs of all sizes are allowed. There are no additional pet fees. Dogs may not be left alone in the rooms at any time, and they must be leashed and cleaned up after.
Days Inn Rexburg 271 South 2nd West Rexburg ID 208-356-9222 (800-329-7466)
Dogs of all sizes are allowed. There are no additional pet fees. Pet must be kept in kennel when left alone. Reservations are recommended due to limited rooms for pets.

Riggins

Accommodations

Salmon River Motel 1203 S Hwy 95 Riggins ID 208-628-3231

http://www.salmonrivermotel.com/
This motel is situated in a deep canyon at the confluence of the Salmon River and the Little Salmon Rivers, and fishing is a favorite pastime. Amenities include clean, spacious rooms, cable TV, and a convenient location for hunters, hikers, and sightseers. Dogs up to 50 pounds are allowed for no additional fee with a credit card on file. Dogs are not allowed on the beds or furnishings, and they must be leashed and cleaned up after at all times.

Attractions
TOP 200 PLACE **Heavens Gate Observation Site/Hells Canyon** Forest Road 517 Riggins ID 208-628-3916
Located in Hell's Canyon by way of Heaven's Gate, this is one of 3 routes to the edge of the canyon. This short path winds to the Heaven's Gate Lookout and an incredible four state vista with several impressive points of interest. The Forest Road 517 is a steep gravel road that climbs from 2,500 feet to 7,200 feet and is not viable for large trailers or trucks. Dogs are permitted at the look-out point and at stops along the way. Dogs must be leashed and cleaned up after.

Salmon

Accommodations
Syringa Lodge 13 Gott Lane Salmon ID 208-756-4424 (877-580-6482)
http://syringalodge.com/
Made of large spruce logs, this beautiful lodge is located on a bluff on 19 acres of an old homestead which offers great views of the river and mountains. Some of the features/amenities include a home-cooked breakfast served in the dining room or on the sun porch, six porches, a great room with an ornate fireplace, and private baths. One dog is allowed per room for an additional $10 one time fee. Dogs must be quiet, well mannered, and leashed and cleaned up after at all times.

Campgrounds and RV Parks
Heald's Haven RV Park and Campground 22 Heald Haven Drive Salmon ID 208-756-3929
This campground offers clean, grassy sites with shade trees, and easy pull-through sites. Some of the amenities include drinking water, fire rings, restrooms, showers, handicap access, and a dump station. They are open for self-contained visitors only in the winter. Dogs of all sizes are welcome for no additional fee. Dogs must be well behaved, leashed, and cleaned up after. This RV park is closed during the off-season. The camping and tent areas also allow dogs. There is a dog walk area at the campground.
Salmon River RV Park 111 Whitetail Drive Salmon ID 208-894-4549
http://www.salmonriverrvp.com/
Dogs of all sizes are allowed. There are no additional pet fees. Dogs may not be left unattended outside, and they must be quiet, well behaved, leashed, and cleaned up after. This is an RV only park. There is a dog walk area at the campground.
Salmon-Chalis National Forest 50 Hwy 93 S Salmon ID 208-756-5100
http://www.fs.fed.us/r4/sc/
This forest has 7 ranger districts, is home to the largest wilderness area in the US with over 4.3 million acres, and has diverse ecosystems and year round recreation. Dogs of all sizes are allowed at no additional fee. Dogs may not be left unattended outside, and they must be leashed and cleaned up after. Dogs are not allowed in buildings, but they are allowed on the trails. This campground is closed during the off-season. The camping and tent areas also allow dogs. There is a dog walk area at the campground. There are no electric or water hookups at the campground.
Salmon-Chalis National Forest 1669 Hwy 93 Salmon ID 208-879-4100
http://www.fs.fed.us/r4/sc/
This forest has 7 ranger districts, is home to the largest wilderness area in the US with over 4.3 million acres, and has diverse ecosystems that support a large variety of plants, animals, and year round recreation. Dogs of all sizes are allowed at no additional fee. Dogs may not be left unattended outside, and they must be leashed and cleaned up after. Dogs are not allowed in buildings, but they are allowed on the trails. This campground is closed during the off-season. The camping and tent areas also allow dogs. There is a dog walk area at the campground. There are no electric or water hookups at the campground.

Attractions
Sacajawea Interpretive Cultural and Education Center 60 Hwy 28 Salmon ID 208-756-1188
http://sacajaweacenter.org/
This 71 acre park is located by the rivers and mountains of the Sacajawea's homeland, and is dedicated to

commemorating her, her people-the Agaidika, and the Lewis and Clark expedition. The park provides a unique outdoor experience of the past for visitors to learn about the regions history. Some of the park features include an outdoor amphitheater, a designated dog walk area provided by the local humane society, event sheds for demonstrations/vendors, a large ranch yard for festivals/events, and interpretive programs. Dogs of all sizes are welcome for no additional fee. Dogs are allowed on the grounds and trail, but not in park buildings.

Spalding

Parks
Nez Perce National Historical Park 39063 US Highway 95 Spalding ID 208-843-2261
http://www.nps.gov/nepe/index.htm
Dogs on leash are allowed in this historical park. They are not allowed in any buildings. Located in Idaho, Montana, Oregon, and Washington. The park features camping, auto touring, fishing, hiking, swimming, and more.

Spencer

Attractions
Spencer Opal Mine Main Street Spencer ID 208-374-5476
http://www.spenceropalmine.com
The opal mines here have two digging areas. The main mine, where dogs on leash are allowed, and the mini mine where they are not. This is a seasonal mine, and not all days are available for digging. They also have "free" digs every year, so call ahead for times and dates as they change.

St Anthony

Accommodations
Best Western Henry's Fork Inn 115 South Bridge St St Anthony ID   208-624-3711 (800-780-7234)
Dogs of all sizes are allowed. There is a $20 returnable deposit required per room. Smoking and Non-Smoking rooms are used for pets.

St Charles

Campgrounds and RV Parks
Bear Lake North RV Park 220 N Main St Charles ID   208-945-2941
http://www.bearlakenorth.com
Dogs of all sizes and numbers are allowed at RV sites, however only 1 dog up to 20 pounds is allowed at the cabins. There is a $1.50 per night per pet additional fee. Dogs may not be left unattended at the cabins, and they are not allowed on the beds or in the loft. The camping and tent areas also allow dogs. There is a dog walk area at the campground. Dogs are allowed in the camping cabins.

Stanley

Accommodations
Mountain Village Resort P. O. Box 150/ @ Hwy 75/21 Stanley ID   208-774-3661 (800-843-5475)
http://www.mountainvillage.com/
This 61 room lodge offers a warm, inviting decor, a natural hot springs for guests, and satellite television. Dogs of all sizes are allowed for an additional fee of $8 per night per pet. Dogs must be well behaved, leashed, cleaned up after, and the Do Not Disturb sign put on the door if they are in the room alone.

Campgrounds and RV Parks

Carmela Winery Golf Course and RV Park 1294 W Madison Stanley ID 208-366-2773
Dogs of all sizes are allowed at no additional fee. Dogs may only be left inside your RV for short periods, and only if they will be quiet and well behaved. Dogs must be leashed and cleaned up after. The park has an adjoining 65 acres nearby where your dog may run off lead if they are trained and will obey voice command. The camping and tent areas also allow dogs. There is a dog walk area at the campground.

Twin Falls

Accommodations

Best Western Apollo Motor Inn 296 Addison Ave West Twin Falls ID 208-733-2010 (800-780-7234)
Dogs of all sizes are allowed. There is a $8 per night pet fee per pet. Smoking and non-smoking rooms are available for pets.
Comfort Inn 1893 Canyon Springs Road Twin Falls ID 208-734-7494 (877-424-6423)
Dogs of all sizes are allowed. There is a $10 per night per pet additional fee. Dogs may not be left alone in the rooms at any time, and they must be leashed and cleaned up after.
Motel 6 - Twin Falls 1472 Blue Lake Boulevard North Twin Falls ID 208-734-3993 (800-466-8356)
One well-behaved family pet per room. Guest must notify front desk upon arrival. Guest is liable for any damages. In consideration of all guests, pets must never be left unattended in the guest rooms.
Red Lion 1357 Blue Lakes Blvd N Twin Falls ID 208-734-5000
Dogs up to 80 pounds are allowed. There is a $50 refundable deposit per room and a pet policy to sign at check in.

Campgrounds and RV Parks

Anderson Camp S Tipperary Eden ID 888-480-9400
http://www.andersoncamp.com
Dogs of all sizes are allowed. There are no additional pet fees. Dogs may not be left unattended, and must be quiet, leashed, and cleaned up after. The camping and tent areas also allow dogs. There is a dog walk area at the campground. Dogs are allowed in the camping cabins.
Sawthooth National Forest 2647 Kimberly Road E. Twin Falls ID 208-737-3200 (800-260-5970)
http://www.fs.fed.us/r4/sawtooth/
In addition to archaeological and historical sites and interests, this forest of more than a million acres has diverse ecosystems support a large variety of plants, animals, and recreation. Dogs of all sizes are allowed at no additional fee. Dogs may not be left unattended, and they must be leashed and cleaned up after. Dogs are allowed on the trails. This campground is closed during the off-season. The camping and tent areas also allow dogs. There is a dog walk area at the campground. There are no electric or water hookups at the campground.

Stores

PetSmart Pet Store 1505 Blue Lake Blvd Twin Falls ID 208-732-6121
Your licensed and well-behaved leashed dog is allowed in the store.

Parks

Centennial Waterfront Park 4185 North 2874 East at Blue Lakes Blvd Twin Falls ID 208-734-9491
This seasonal, day use park offers a variety of water and land recreation, picnic shelters, hiking trails, interpretive exhibits, and great scenic views. Dogs of all sizes are allowed for no additional fee. Dogs must be under owner's control, and leashed and cleaned up after at all times.
TOP 200 PLACE Shoshone Falls Park Road 3300 East Twin Falls ID 208-736-2265
The falls at this park drop 212 feet and are higher than Niagara Falls. They are considered one of the most spectacular natural beauties on the Snake River. There is a variety of land and water recreation, and some of the amenities include large shaded grass areas, picnicking, playgrounds, hiking trails, restrooms, a concession stand, boat ramp, and a scenic overlook. Dogs of all sizes are allowed for no additional fee. Dogs must be under owner's control, and leashed and cleaned up after at all times.
Twin Falls Park 3500 East Twin Falls ID 208-773-3974
This day-use park features 10 wooded acres and lawns providing excellent picnicking and sightseeing opportunities. Some of the features include a boat ramp and dock, interpretive exhibits, various land and water recreation, and picnic shelters. Dogs of all sizes are allowed for no additional fee. Dogs must be under owner's control, and leashed and cleaned up after at all times.

Outdoor Restaurants
Dunken's Microbrewery 102 Main Avenue N Twin Falls ID   208-733-8114
This microbrewery provides outside seating and service weather permitting. Your dog is welcome to join you at the outdoor seating. Dogs must be under owner's control, and leashed and cleaned up after at all times.

Wallace

Accommodations
Best Western Wallace Inn 100 Front St Wallace ID   208-752-1252 (800-780-7234)
Dogs of all sizes are allowed. There is a $15 per night pet fee for one pet and $5 for additional pet. Smoking and non-smoking rooms are available for pets.

White Bird

Accommodations
Hells Canyon Jet Boat Trips and Lodging 1 mile S of White Bird on Old Hwy 95 White Bird ID   800-469-8757
Dogs of all sizes are allowed. There are no additional pet fees. There is one pet-friendly room available, and dogs may not be left unattended in the room at any time. Dogs must be leashed and cleaned up after.

Campgrounds and RV Parks
Hells Canyon Jet Boat Trips and Lodging 1 mile S of White Bird on Old Hwy 95 White Bird ID   800-469-8757
Dogs of all sizes are allowed. There are no additional pet fees. Dogs must be leashed and cleaned up after. Dogs may be left on site on leash, but please inform the office as to how long you will be gone and if you will be on the 6 hour jet boat tour. There is a motel on site that has one pet friendly room, also at no additional fee for a pet, however, only 1 dog is allowed in the motel room at a time. The camping and tent areas also allow dogs. There is a dog walk area at the campground.

Winchester

Campgrounds and RV Parks
Winchester Lake State Park Forest Road Winchester ID   208-924-7563 (866-634-3246)
This 418 acre park, with 103 lake acres, is popular for nature study, fishing, and hiking, and offers a variety of land and water activities and recreation. Dogs of all sizes are allowed at no additional fee. Dogs may not be left unattended, and they must be well behaved, leashed and cleaned up after. Dogs are not allowed in the buildings, but they are allowed on the trails. The park has one pet-friendly yurt available. The camping and tent areas also allow dogs. There is a dog walk area at the campground.

Worley

Accommodations
Coeur d' Alene Casino Resort Hotel 27068 S Hwy 95 Worley ID   800-523-2464
http://www.cdacasino.com/
This luxury gaming resort offers over 200 finely appointed rooms, over 100,000 square feet of gaming space, several eateries, a heated swimming pool and Jacuzzi, top-name entertainment, and they have a world class golf course adjacent to the hotel. Dogs of all sizes are allowed for an additional $15 per night per pet. Dogs must be well mannered, leashed, and cleaned up after.

Chapter 18

Nevada
Dog Travel Guide

Austin

Campgrounds and RV Parks
Berlin-Ichthyosaur State Park HC 61 Box 61200 Austin NV 775-964-2440
http://parks.nv.gov/bi.htm#SITES
Once a mining area, this park sits at about 7,000 feet and came into being to protect and display North America's richest concentration and largest known Ichthyosaur fossils. It also oversees the old mining town of Berlin and the Diana Mine. There is an extensive sign/trail system that tells the history and features of this Registered Natural Landmark, a nature trail, and viewing windows at the Fossils Shelter. Dogs of all sizes are allowed for no additional fee. Dogs must be well mannered, be on no more than a 6 foot leash, and be cleaned up after. They are allowed throughout the park and on the trails; they are not allowed in park buildings. The camping and tent areas also allow dogs. There is a dog walk area at the campground. There are no electric or water hookups at the campgrounds.
Berlin-Ichthyosaur State Park HC 61 Box 61200/Hwy 844 Austin NV 775-964-2440
http://parks.nv.gov/bi.htm#TRAILS
Nestled at 7,000 feet on the Shoshone mountain range, this park preserves a true Nevada ghost town. It also features archeological sites, extensive self guided hiking trails, a nature trail to the Fossil Shelter, tours and various recreational pursuits. It is first come, first serve camping. Dogs of all sizes are allowed at no additional fee. Dogs may not be left unattended outside, and only inside if they will be quiet and comfortable. Dogs must be leashed and cleaned up after. Dogs are allowed on the trails. The camping and tent areas also allow dogs. There is a dog walk area at the campground. There are no electric hookups at the campgrounds.

Parks
Berlin-Ichthyosaur State Park HC 61 Box 61200 Austin NV 775-964-2440
http://parks.nv.gov/bi.htm#SITES
Once a mining area, this park sits at about 7,000 feet and came into being to protect and display North America's richest concentration and largest known Ichthyosaur fossils. It also oversees the old mining town of Berlin and the Diana Mine. There is an extensive sign/trail system that tells the history and features of this Registered Natural Landmark, a nature trail, and viewing windows at the Fossils Shelter. Dogs of all sizes are allowed for no additional fee. Dogs must be well mannered, be on no more than a 6 foot leash, and be cleaned up after. They are allowed throughout the park and on the trails; they are not allowed in park buildings.

Battle Mountain

Accommodations
Comfort Inn 521 E Front Street Battle Mountain NV 775-635-5880 (877-424-6423)
Dogs of all sizes are allowed. There is a $10 one time additional pet fee per room. Dogs must be leashed, cleaned up after, and the Do Not Disturb sign put on the door if they are in the room alone.

Beatty

Accommodations
Motel 6 - Beatty - Death Valley 550 US Route 95 North Beatty NV 775-553-9090 (800-466-8356)
One well-behaved family pet per room. Guest must notify front desk upon arrival. Guest is liable for any damages. In consideration of all guests, pets must never be left unattended in the guest rooms.

Campgrounds and RV Parks
Baileys Hot Springs RV Park 6 miles N of Beatty on Hwy 95 Beatty NV 775-553-2395
Visitors come from all over to enjoy the hot springs here. Dogs of all sizes are allowed at no additional fee. Dogs must be leashed and cleaned up after. There are some breed restrictions. The camping and tent areas also allow dogs. There is a dog walk area at the campground.

Attractions

TOP 200 PLACE **Rhyolite Ghost Town** off Highway 374 Beatty NV 760-786-3200
http://www.nps.gov/deva/rhyolite.htm
In 1904 two prospectors found quartz all over a hill which was "full of free gold". Soon the rush was on and camps were set up in the area including the townsite called Rhyolite. The name was derived from the silica-rich volcanic rock in the area. The most prominent mine in the area was the Montgomery Shoshone mine which prompted everyone to move to Rhyolite. This boomtown once had a 3 story building, a stock exchange, board of trade, red light district, hotels, stores, a school for 250 children, an ice plant, two electric plants, foundries, machine shops and a miner's union hospital. Today you can see several remnants of Rhyolite. The 3 story building still has some walls standing and so does an old jail. A privately owned train depot was restored and so was the Bottle House. The Bottle House was made out of whiskey bottles by a miner. This house was restored in 1925 by Paramount Pictures. Rhyolite is located 35 miles from the Furnace Creek Visitor Center in Death Valley National Park. Drive towards Beatty, Nevada. Before you reach Beatty, take a paved road north (left) from Highway 374. It will take you right into the ghost town. Pets are allowed but must be leashed. Please clean up after your pet. Remember to watch out for rattlesnakes.

Blue Diamond

Parks

Spring Mountain Ranch State Park P. O. Box 124 Blue Diamond NV 702-875-4141
http://parks.nv.gov/smr.htm
This luxury retreat offers a long and colorful history with such owners as Howard Hughes and Vera Krupp. In addition the park offers great scenery, a visitor's center, picnicking, historic sites, living history programs, guided tours, opportunities for nature study, and various trails. Dogs of all sizes are allowed at no additional fee. Dogs may not be left unattended, and they must be leashed and cleaned up after.

Boulder City

Accommodations

Best Western Lighthouse Inn and Resort 110 Ville Dr Boulder City NV 702-293-6444 (800-780-7234)
Dogs of all sizes are allowed. There is a $10 per night pet fee per pet. Reservations are recommended due to limited rooms for pets. Smoking and non-smoking rooms are available for pets.
Boulder Inn and Suites 704 Nevada Highway Boulder City NV 702-294-8888
Dogs of all sizes are allowed. There is a $10 per night pet fee per pet. Smoking and non-smoking rooms are available for pet rooms.

Campgrounds and RV Parks

Lake Mead RV Village 268 Lakeshore Road Boulder City NV 702-293-2540
http://www.lakemeadrvvillage.com/
Offering beautiful views, this RV park, conveniently located to a variety of attractions, also offers a convenience store, laundry facility, 2 boat launches, and a variety of land and water recreation. Dogs of all sizes are allowed at no additional fee. Dogs may not be left unattended at any time, and they must be quiet, well behaved, leashed at all times, and cleaned up after. This is an RV only park. There is a dog walk area at the campground.

Caliente

Campgrounds and RV Parks

Beaver Dam State Park P. O. Box 985 Caliente NV 775-726-3564
http://parks.nv.gov/bd.htm
This remote, primitive 2,393-acre park features deep canyons, pine forests, a flowing stream, numerous beaver dams, hiking, and interpretive trails. Due to flood damage and dangerous conditions, it is strongly advised to check conditions before going to the dam site and the exposed mud flats behind the dam. Dogs of all sizes are allowed at no additional fee. Dogs must be leashed and cleaned up after. Dogs are allowed on the trails. The camping and tent areas also allow dogs. There is a dog walk area at the campground. There are no electric

hookups at the campgrounds.

Parks
Kershaw-Ryan State Park P. O. Box 985/300 Kershaw Canyon Drive Caliente NV 775-726-3564
http://parks.nv.gov/kr.htm
This high mountain desert day park offers a spring-fed pond, scenic rugged landscapes, a picnic area, restrooms, trails, and various outdoor recreation. Dogs of all sizes are allowed at no additional fee. Dogs may not be left unattended, and they must be leashed and cleaned up after. Dogs are allowed on the trails. Hours may vary between the seasons, however winter hours are daily from 8 am to 4:30 pm, and summer hours are daily from 7 am to 8 pm.

Carlin

Accommodations
Comfort Inn Central 1018 Fir Street Carlin NV 775-754 -6110 (877-424-6423)
Dogs of all sizes are allowed. There is a $100 refundable cash deposit unless there is a credit card on file. Dogs must be leashed, cleaned up after, and the Do Not Disturb sign put on the door if they are in the room alone.

Carson City

Accommodations
Best Value Motel 2731 S Carson St Carson City NV 775-882-2007
There is a $30 refundable pet deposit.
Best Western Trailside Inn 1300 N Carson St Carson City NV 775-883-7300 (800-780-7234)
Dogs of all sizes are allowed. There is a $10 per night pet fee per pet. Smoking and non-smoking rooms are available for pets.
Days Inn Carson City 3103 N Carson St Carson City NV 775-883-3343 (800-329-7466)
Dogs of all sizes are allowed. There is a $10 per night pet fee per pet.
Holiday Inn Express Hotel & Suites 4055 North Carson Street Carson City NV 775-283-4055 (877-270-6405)
Dogs of all sizes are allowed. The non-smoking pet rooms are on the 3rd floor.
Motel 6 - Carson City 2749 South Carson Street Carson City NV 775-885-7710 (800-466-8356)
One well-behaved family pet per room. Guest must notify front desk upon arrival. Guest is liable for any damages. In consideration of all guests, pets must never be left unattended in the guest rooms.

Campgrounds and RV Parks
Washoe Lake State Park 4855 East Lake Blvd Carson City NV 775-687-4319
http://parks.nv.gov/wl.htm
This scenic park features a wetlands area with a viewing tower, an interpretive display, nature study and bird watching, hiking, horseback riding, water sports, boat launches, 2 comfort stations with showers, and access to trails and trailheads. Dogs of all sizes are allowed. There are no additional pet fees. Dogs may not be left unattended outside, and they must be leashed and cleaned up after. Dogs may be off lead when other people are not around and they are under voice control. Dogs are allowed on the beach and trails. The camping and tent areas also allow dogs. There is a dog walk area at the campground. There are no electric or water hookups at the campgrounds.

Stores
PetSmart Pet Store 250 Fairview Dr Carson City NV 775-841-9200
Your licensed and well-behaved leashed dog is allowed in the store.
Petco Pet Store 911 Topsy Lane #108 Carson City NV 775-267-2826
Your licensed and well-behaved leashed dog is allowed in the store.

Parks
Toiyabe National Forest Hwy 395 Carson City NV
There are several dog-friendly hiking trails on the national forest land in Carson City. These are desert-like trails, so only go with your dog when the weather is cooler. If it's hot, the sand may burn your pup's paws. Visit the

Carson Ranger Station for maps and trail information about the Toiyable National Forest. The station is located on Hwy 395, near S. Stewart Street. Dogs should be leashed.

Washoe Lake State Park 4855 East Lake Blvd. Carson City NV 775-687-4319
This park is frequently used for bird watching, hiking, horseback riding, picnicking, windsurfing, water skiing, jet skiing, fishing and during certain times of the year, hunting. There are many trails at this park for hikers, mountain bikers, and equestrians. Pets must be leashed at all times, except at the Wetlands during hunting season. The park is located off U.S. 395, 10 miles north of Carson City and 15 miles south of Reno.

Outdoor Restaurants
Comma Coffee 312 S. Carson Street Carson City NV
http://www.commacoffee.com/
This cafe serves breakfast and lunch, as well as fruit smoothies, juices, cappuccinos, lattes, mochas and more. Dogs are welcome at the outdoor patio tables.
Mom and Pop's Diner 224 S. Carson St. Carson City NV 775-884-4411
This restaurant serves breakfast, lunch and dinner. Dogs are allowed at the outdoor tables.
Quiznos 3228 N. Carson Street Carson City NV 775-882-7849
This restaurant serves a variety of sandwiches. Dogs are allowed at the outdoor tables.

Vets and Kennels
Carson Tahoe Veterinary Hospital 3389 S. Carson Street Carson City NV 775-883-8238
Weekdays 7:30 am - 6 pm. Emergencies will be seen 24 hours with an additional $60 emergency fee.

Dayton

Campgrounds and RV Parks
Dayton State Park P. O. Box 1478 Dayton NV 775-687-5678
http://parks.nv.gov/dsp.htm
The Carson River flows through this park giving visitors fishing opportunities and water activities. The park also offers hiking trails, an interpretive trail, a historic site and various recreation. Dogs of all sizes are allowed at no additional fee. Please keep dogs on a leash in populated areas and clean up after them. Dogs may not be left unattended outside, and they are not allowed in the pavilion area or on the lawns. The camping and tent areas also allow dogs. There is a dog walk area at the campground. There are no electric or water hookups at the campgrounds.

Elko

Accommodations
Best Western Gold Country Motor Inn 2050 Idaho St Elko NV 775-738-8421 (800-780-7234)
Dogs of all sizes are allowed. There is a $15 one time per pet fee per visit. Dogs are not allowed to be left alone in the room. Smoking and non-smoking rooms are available for pets.
High Desert Inn 3015 Idaho Street Elko NV 775-738-8425
There is a $15 one time pet charge.
Motel 6 - Elko 3021 Idaho Street Elko NV 775-738-4337 (800-466-8356)
One well-behaved family pet per room. Guest must notify front desk upon arrival. Guest is liable for any damages. In consideration of all guests, pets must never be left unattended in the guest rooms.
Shilo Inn 2401 Mountain City Highway Elko NV 775-738-5522 (800-222-2244)
http://www.shiloinn.com/Nevada/elko.html
There is a $10 per day pet charge.
Super 8 Elko 1755 Idaho St Elko NV 775-738-8488 (800-800-8000)
Dogs of all sizes are allowed. There is a $10 per night pet fee per pet. Smoking and non-smoking rooms are available for pet rooms.

Campgrounds and RV Parks
Double Dice RV Park 3730 Idaho Street Elko NV 775-738-5642 (888-738-3423)
This RV park offers 140 sites with amenities that include 30 or 50 amp electric, instant phone, 43 channel TV, 75 pull through sites for rigs up to 65 feet, a game room, laundry room, free email/web center, and showers. Tent sites are also available. Well-behaved leashed dogs are welcome. Please clean up after your pets. There is a $1

per night per pet additional fee. Dogs must be leashed, and taken to the dog run to relieve themselves. They are not allowed on the grass. Dogs may not be left outside, and they may be left inside only if they will be quiet and comfortable. The camping and tent areas also allow dogs. There is a dog walk area at the campground.
Wild Horse State Recreation Area HC 31, Box 26/Hwy 225 Elko NV 775-758-6493
http://parks.nv.gov/wh.htm
Located on the northeast shore of Wild Horse Reservoir, this park is popular for camping, picnicking, hunting, fishing, boating, and hiking. The park also offers a boat launch, showers and a dump station. Dogs of all sizes are allowed. There are no additional pet fees. Dogs must be well behaved, on no more than a 6 foot leash, and cleaned up after. The camping and tent areas also allow dogs. There is a dog walk area at the campground. There are no electric or water hookups at the campgrounds.

Ely

Accommodations
Best Western Main Motel 1101 Aultman Ely NV 775-289-4529 (800-780-7234)
Dogs of all sizes are allowed. There is a $20 one time pet fee per visit. Smoking and non-smoking rooms are available for pets.
Best Western Park Vue 930 Aultman Ely NV 775-289-4497 (800-780-7234)
Dogs of all sizes are allowed. There is a $20 one time per pet fee per visit. Smoking and non-smoking rooms are available for pets.
Jailhouse Motel 211 5th Street Ely NV 775-289-3033
Dogs of all sizes are allowed. There is a $10 per stay per room additional pet fee.
Motel 6 - Ely 770 Avenue O Ely NV 775-289-6671 (800-466-8356)
One well-behaved family pet per room. Guest must notify front desk upon arrival. Guest is liable for any damages. In consideration of all guests, pets must never be left unattended in the guest rooms.

Campgrounds and RV Parks
Cave Lake State Park P. O. Box 151761 Ely NV 775-728-4467
http://parks.nv.gov/cl.htm
This park, along a 32 acre reservoir at 7,300 feet, offers outstanding views, opportunities for nature study and photography, a boat launch, interpretive presentations, winter programs, hiking trails, and more. Dogs of all sizes are allowed at no additional fee. Dogs must be leashed and cleaned up after. Dogs are not allowed in buildings. They are allowed on the trails. The camping and tent areas also allow dogs. There is a dog walk area at the campground. There are no electric or water hookups at the campgrounds.
Ely Koa Hwy 93 Ely NV 775-289-3413 (800-562-3413)
http://www.koa.com/where/nv/28106/
Well landscaped grounds and location make this a popular park, with amenities that include 85 foot pull-through sites with 50 amp service, cable TV, LP gas, and wi-fi. Dogs of all sizes are allowed for no additional fee, and there is a pet waiver to sign. There is a $25 refundable pet deposit for the cabins. Dogs must be under owner's control and visual observation at all times. Dogs must be quiet, well behaved, and be on no more than a 6 foot leash at all times, or otherwise contained. Dogs may not be left unattended outside the owner's camping equipment, and must be brought inside at night. Dogs are not allowed on the grass except by the dog walk. There are some breed restrictions. The camping and tent areas also allow dogs. There is a dog walk area at the campground. Dogs are allowed in the camping cabins.
Ward Charcoal Ovens State Historic Park P. O. Box 151761 Ely NV 775-728-4460
http://parks.nv.gov/ww.htm
Although mostly known for its historic six beehive-shaped charcoal ovens, this park also offers outstanding geologic sites, trails consisting of several miles of different views and ecotypes, and various other recreation. Dogs of all sizes are allowed at no additional fee. Dogs may not be left unattended outside, and left inside only if they will be quiet and comfortable. Dogs must be on no more than a 6 foot leash and be cleaned up after. Dogs are allowed on the trails. The camping and tent areas also allow dogs. There is a dog walk area at the campground. There are no electric or water hookups at the campgrounds.

Fallon

Accommodations
Comfort Inn 1830 W Williams Avenue Fallon NV 775-423-5554 (877-424-6423)
Dogs of all sizes are allowed. There is a $10 per night per pet additional fee. Dogs must be quiet, leashed,

cleaned up after, and crated when left alone in the room.

Motel 6 - Fallon 1705 South Taylor Street Fallon NV   775-423-2277 (800-466-8356)
One well-behaved family pet per room. Guest must notify front desk upon arrival. Guest is liable for any damages. In consideration of all guests, pets must never be left unattended in the guest rooms.

Super 8 Fallon 855 W Williams Ave Fallon NV   775-423-6031 (800-800-8000)
Dogs of all sizes are allowed. There is a $5 per night pet fee per pet. Smoking and non-smoking rooms are available for pet rooms.

Parks

Walker Lake, c/o Fallon Region Headquarters 16799 Lahontan Dam Fallon NV   775-867-3001
http://parks.nv.gov/walk.htm
This rec area is on one of the last remnants of an ancient inland sea that covered the area about 10,000 years ago. There is a boat launch, shade ramadas, tables and grills along a sandy beach. Recreation includes fishing, boating, swimming and picnicking. Dogs of all sizes are allowed at no additional fee. Dogs may not be left unattended, and they must be leashed and cleaned up after.

Fernley

Accommodations

Best Western Fernley Inn 1405 E Newlands Dr Fernley NV   775-575-6776 (800-780-7234)
Dogs of all sizes are allowed. There is a $7 per night pet fee per pet. Reservations are recommended due to limited rooms for pets. Smoking and non-smoking rooms are available for pets.

Gerlach

Accommodations

Soldier Meadows Guest Ranch and Lodge Soldier Meadows Rd Gerlach NV   530-233-4881
http://www.soldiermeadows.com/
Dating back to 1865 when it was known as Camp McGarry, this historic cattle ranch lies in the Black Rock Desert about three hours north of Reno. Soldier Meadows is a family owned working cattle ranch with over 500,000 acres of public and private land to enjoy. It is one of the largest and remotest guest ranches in the nation. There are no phones, faxes, or computers here. Horseback riders can work with the cowboys, take trail rides to track wild mustangs and other wildlife, or ride out to the natural hot springs for a soak. Or you may chose to go mule deer hunting, fishing, hiking, mountain biking or 4-wheeling. The lodge offers 10 guest rooms, and one suite with a private bathroom and kitchenette. The main lodge has a common living room with a large fireplace. Pets are not allowed in the kitchen area. There is a $20 one time pet charge.

Las Vegas

Accommodations

TOP 200 PLACE Loews Lake Las Vegas Resort 101 Montelago Boulevard Henderson NV   702-567-6000
This upscale resort on the shores of Lake Mead offers all the luxuries. All well-behaved dogs of any size are welcome. This upscale hotel resort offers their "Loews Loves Pets" program which includes special pet treats, local dog walking routes, and a list of nearby pet-friendly places to visit. The hotel is about 30 minutes from the Las Vegas Strip. There is a $25 one time additional pet fee. To get to the hotel take I-215 east until it ends into Lake Mead Blvd and proceed 7 miles on Lake Mead Blvd. The hotel will be on the left and you can follow the signs.

Best Western Main Street Inn 1000 North Main St Las Vegas NV   702-382-3455 (800-780-7234)
Dogs of all sizes are allowed. There is a $15 per night pet fee per pet. Smoking and non-smoking rooms are available for pets.

Best Western Nellis Motor Inn 5330 E Craig Rd Las Vegas NV   702-643-6111 (800-780-7234)
Dogs of all sizes are allowed. There is a $10 per night pet fee per pet. Dogs are not allowed to be left alone in the room. Smoking and non-smoking rooms are available for pets.

Best Western Parkview Inn 921 Las Vegas Blvd North Las Vegas NV   702-385-1213 (800-780-7234)
Dogs of all sizes are allowed. There is a $8 per night pet fee per pet. Smoking and non-smoking rooms are

available for pets. Dogs are not allowed to be left alone in the room.

Candlewood Suites 4034 South Paradise Road Las Vegas NV 702-836-3660 (877-270-6405)
Dogs up to 80 pounds are allowed. Only one pet per room is permitted. There is a $75 one time pet fee for stays up to 14 days. For longer stays there is a $150 one time pet fee.

Homestead Las Vegas 3045 S Maryland Parkway Las Vegas NV 702-369-1414
One dog of any size is allowed. There is a $25 per night pet fee up to 3 nights for a maximum total of $75 per room.

La Quinta Inn & Suites Las Vegas Summerlin Tech 7101 Cascade Valley Ct. Las Vegas NV 702-360-1200 (800-531-5900)
Dogs of all sizes are allowed. There are no additional pet fees. Dogs may not be left unattended, and they must be leashed and cleaned up after. Dogs are not allowed in the lounge, pool area, or the courtyard.

La Quinta Inn & Suites Las Vegas West Lakes 9570 West Sahara Las Vegas NV 702-243-0356 (800-531-5900)
Dogs of all sizes are allowed. There are no additional pet fees. Dogs may not be left unattended, and they must be leashed and cleaned up after.

La Quinta Inn Las Vegas Nellis 4288 N Nellis Blvd. Las Vegas NV 702-632-0229 (800-531-5900)
Dogs of all sizes are allowed. There are no additional pet fees. Dogs must be crated if left alone in the room, and they must be leashed and cleaned up after.

Motel 6 - Las Vegas - Boulder Highway 4125 Boulder Highway Las Vegas NV 702-457-8051 (800-466-8356)
One well-behaved family pet per room. Guest must notify front desk upon arrival. Guest is liable for any damages. In consideration of all guests, pets must never be left unattended in the guest rooms.

Motel 6 - Las Vegas - I-15 5085 South Industrial Road Las Vegas NV 702-739-6747 (800-466-8356)
One well-behaved family pet per room. Guest must notify front desk upon arrival. Guest is liable for any damages. In consideration of all guests, pets must never be left unattended in the guest rooms.

Motel 6 - Las Vegas - Tropicana 195 E Tropicana Avenue Las Vegas NV 702-798-0728 (800-466-8356)
One well-behaved family pet per room. Guest must notify front desk upon arrival. Guest is liable for any damages. In consideration of all guests, pets must never be left unattended in the guest rooms.

Residence Inn by Marriott 3225 Paradise Road Las Vegas NV 702-796-9300
Dogs up to 60 pounds are allowed. There is a $75 one time fee and a pet policy to sign at check in.

Residence Inn by Marriott 370 Hughes Center Drive Las Vegas NV 702-650-0040
Dogs of all sizes are allowed. There is a $75 one time fee and a pet policy to sign at check in.

Rodeway Inn & Suites 167 E. Tropicana Ave Las Vegas NV 702-795-3311
There is a $100 refundable pet deposit.

Mount Charleston Lodge and Cabins HCR 38 Box 325 Mount Charleston NV 800-955-1314
http://www.mtcharlestonlodge.com/
The lodge sits at over 7,700 feet above sea level and about 35 miles from the Las Vegas Strip. There are several dog-friendly trails nearby for hikers. Dogs are welcome for an additional $10 per day pet charge.

Comfort Inn North 910 E Cheyenne Road North Las Vegas NV 702-399-1500 (877-424-6423)
Dogs of all sizes are allowed. There is a $10 per night per pet additional fee. Dogs must be leashed, cleaned up after, and crated when left alone in the room.

Campgrounds and RV Parks

Las Vegas KOA at Circus Circus 500 Circus Circus Drive Las Vegas NV 702-733-9707 (800-562-7270)
http://www.koa.com/where/nv/28138/
Located on the Las Vegas Strip, this RV mostly park offers 80 foot pull-through sites with 50 amp service, LP Gas, wi-fi, snack bar, swimming pool, hot tub, sauna, and guided tours. Dogs of all sizes are allowed for no additional fee. Dogs must be under owner's control and visual observation at all times. Dogs must be quiet, well behaved, and be on no more than a 6 foot leash at all times, or otherwise contained. Dogs may not be left unattended outside the owner's camping equipment, and must be brought inside at night. There are some breed restrictions. There is a dog walk area at the campground.

Oasis Las Vegas RV Resort 2711 W Windmill Lane Las Vegas NV 800-566-4707
http://www.oasislasvegasrvresort.com
This premier RV park offers beautifully landscaped sites, beachfront family pool and waterfalls, adult pool and spa, 18-hole putting course, fitness center, store, restaurant, and a variety of recreational pursuits. Dogs of all sizes are allowed at no additional fee. Dogs may not be left unattended at any time, and they must be leashed and cleaned up after at all times. There is a $50 fine if the dogs are not picked up after. Dogs are not allowed in the non-pet section of the park. There is a fenced in dog run area where they may be off lead, but still must be cleaned up after. This is an RV only park. There are some breed restrictions. There is a dog walk area at the campground. There are special amenities given to dogs at this campground.

Attractions

Historic Spring Mountain Ranch State Route 159 Las Vegas NV 702-875-4141 http://www.state.nv.us/stparks/smr.htm

Previous owners of this historic ranch include Chester Lauck of the comedy team "Lum & Abner," German actress Vera Krupp, and millionaire Howard Hughes. Guided tours through the Ranch House and other historic ranch buildings are available on weekends and holidays. The visitor center is open Monday through Friday and on holidays. Dogs on leash are allowed on the grounds, but not inside the buildings. Other amenities at this park include a tree-shaded picnic area and scenic hiking trails.

Las Vegas Strip Walking Tour 3300-3900 Las Vegas Blvd. Las Vegas NV

Since dogs are not allowed inside the buildings or attractions on the Vegas strip, we have put together an outdoor self-guided walking tour that you can take with your pooch. It is kid-friendly too! While you can take the tour any time of day, probably the best time is late afternoon or early evening because of the special effects and light shows at some of the points of interest. All places mentioned can be viewed from the sidewalk. Start the walk at the Treasure Island Hotel at 3300 South Las Vegas Blvd. In the front of this hotel you can view two battle ships duke it out. Every 90 minutes, each evening at Buccaneer Bay, musket and cannon fire are exchanged in a pyrotechnic battle between the pirate ship Hispaniola and the British frigate H.M.S. Britannia. This is a popular attraction and it can become very crowded on the sidewalk. Next stop is the Volcano in front of the Mirage Hotel at 3400 South Las Vegas Blvd. From dusk to midnight, every 15 minutes, flames shoot into the sky, spewing smoke and fire 100 feet above the water, transforming a tranquil waterfall into streams of molten lava. For a little musical entertainment, walk over to the Musical Fountains at the Bellagio Hotel at 3600 South Las Vegas Blvd. Here you will find spectacular fountains that fill a 1/4 mile long lake in front of the hotel. Every evening there is a water show that is timed to music. The show takes place every 15 minutes. For some interesting architecture, walk over to the Eiffel Tower at the Paris Hotel at 3655 South Las Vegas Blvd. While your pooch cannot go into the Paris Hotel or the tower, you can view this half size Paris replica from the street. You can also visit the Statue of Liberty right in Las Vegas. Walk over to the New York, New York Hotel at 3790 South Las Vegas Blvd. Again, your pooch cannot go inside this hotel, but you can view the replica from the street. The last stop is the Luxor Hotel at 3900 South Las Vegas Blvd. From the sidewalk you will see the large pyramid with hotel rooms inside and a large sphinx in the front of the hotel. Please note that some of the attractions might be closed during certain times of the year or during bad weather, especially when it is windy.

Old Las Vegas Mormon Fort 500 E Washington Ave Las Vegas NV 702-486-3511

http://www.state.nv.us/stparks/olvmf.htm

This park includes a remnant of the original adobe fort which housed the first permanent non-native Mormon missionary settlers in the Las Vegas Valley. They successfully diverted water from the Las Vegas Creek in 1855 for farming. There are future plans to re-create many more historic features at this park. The park is open all year and allows leashed dogs on the outside grounds.

Shopping Centers

TOP 200 PLACE District at Green Valley Ranch 2240 Village Walk Drive Henderson NV 702-564-8595

http://www.thedistrictatgvr.com/

Thanks for a reader for recommending this dog-friendly shopping district in Henderson. She says "This place is all about dogs. Each store has water and dog biscuits out front." Many stores allow dogs inside but please remember to ask first.

Stores

PetSmart Pet Store 531 N Stephanie St Henderson NV 702-898-0055

Your licensed and well-behaved leashed dog is allowed in the store.

Petco Pet Store 631 Marks St Henderson NV 702-458-1435

Your licensed and well-behaved leashed dog is allowed in the store.

Harley-Davidson Store 2605 S. Eastern Avenue Las Vegas NV 702-431-8500

http://www.lvhd.com/

Well-behaved, leashed dogs are allowed inside this store, which is the world's largest Harley dealership. Whether you own a Harley or just wish you could own one, stop by the store and take a look around. This is a popular place for locals and tourists. The store is located about 15 minutes north of downtown Las Vegas.

PetSmart Pet Store 2140 N Rainbow Las Vegas NV 702-631-8422

Your licensed and well-behaved leashed dog is allowed in the store.

PetSmart Pet Store 171 N Nellis Blvd Las Vegas NV 702-438-5771

Your licensed and well-behaved leashed dog is allowed in the store.

PetSmart Pet Store 1261 S Decatur Blvd Las Vegas NV 702-870-8200

Your licensed and well-behaved leashed dog is allowed in the store.

PetSmart Pet Store 9775 W Charleston Las Vegas NV 702-940-5200

Your licensed and well-behaved leashed dog is allowed in the store.

PetSmart Pet Store 9869 S Eastern Ave Las Vegas NV 702-951-0045

Your licensed and well-behaved leashed dog is allowed in the store.

PetSmart Pet Store 5160 S Fort Apache Rd Las Vegas NV 702-253-1431

Your licensed and well-behaved leashed dog is allowed in the store.

PetSmart Pet Store 6650 N Durango Dr Las Vegas NV 702-839-0479
Your licensed and well-behaved leashed dog is allowed in the store.
Petco Pet Store 2340 E Serene Avenue Las Vegas NV 702-914-0500
Your licensed and well-behaved leashed dog is allowed in the store.
Petco Pet Store 1631 W Craig Rd, Ste 5-8 Las Vegas NV 702-399-5850
Your licensed and well-behaved leashed dog is allowed in the store.
Petco Pet Store 3577 South Rainbow Blvd Las Vegas NV 702-253-7800
Your licensed and well-behaved leashed dog is allowed in the store.
Petco Pet Store 2091 North Rainbow Blvd Las Vegas NV 702-648-7106
Your licensed and well-behaved leashed dog is allowed in the store.
Petco Pet Store 7731 West Tropical Parkway Las Vegas NV 702-395-1177
Your licensed and well-behaved leashed dog is allowed in the store.
Scraps Dog Bakery 9310 Sun City Blvd Las Vegas NV 702-360-1927
This dog bakery makes tasty treats for your dog. The bakery is located in North Las Vegas on the west side of
the city. Your well-behaved leashed dog is welcome.
Three Dog Bakery 2110 N Rampart Blvd Las Vegas NV 702-737-3364
http://www.threedog.com
Three Dog Bakery provides cookies and snacks for your dog as well as some boutique items. You well-behaved,
leashed dog is welcome.
PetSmart Pet Store 1321 W Craig Rd North Las Vegas NV 702-938-5880
Your licensed and well-behaved leashed dog is allowed in the store.

Parks

Lake Mead National Recreation Area Lakeshore Rd/166 Boulder City NV 702-293-8907
http://www.nps.gov/lame/
This recreation area covers 1.5 million acres. The west side of the park is about 25 miles from downtown Las
Vegas. We didn't see any designated trails, but leashed dogs are allowed on many of the trails and at the lake.
To get there from Las Vegas, take Hwy 146 east to Lakeshore Rd./166. Lakeshore Rd. is the scenic drive along
Lake Mead.
Desert Breeze County Park 8425 W. Spring Mtn. Road Las Vegas NV
This county park has picnic tables, sports fields, a bike/walking path and a dog park. It is located approximately 5
miles east of downtown Las Vegas and the Strip. From Flamingo Road/589 in downtown, head west and pass
Hwy 15. Turn right on Durango Drive. Then turn right onto Spring Mountain Road and the park will be on the
corner. Dogs must be leashed, except for in the dog park.
Floyd Lamb State Park 9200 Tule Springs Road Las Vegas NV 702-486-5413
http://parks.nv.gov/fl.htm
This park offers tree-shaded groves alongside four small fishing lakes, allowing for nature study, and some of the
amenities include picnic areas with tables and grills, restrooms, group areas, a walking/bicycle path that winds
through the park, and historic sites. Dogs of all sizes are allowed at no additional fee. Dogs may not be left
unattended, and they must be leashed at all times, and cleaned up after. Times vary through the seasons, but
the winter hours are from 7 am to 5 pm, and in June and July they are open from 7 am to 8 pm.
Lorenzi Park 3333 W. Washington Ave. Las Vegas NV 702-229-6297
This park is about a mile west of downtown Las Vegas. Leashed dogs are allowed. Lorenzi Park features tennis
courts, playgrounds, picnic tables and a five acre lake.

TOP 200 PLACE **Red Rock Canyon National Area** Charleston Blvd/159 Las Vegas NV 702-363-1921
http://www.nv.blm.gov/redrockcanyon
Located just 20-25 minutes west of downtown Las Vegas is the beautiful Red Rock Canyon National
Conservation Area. This preserve has over 60,000 acres and includes unique geological formations. There is a
popular 13 mile one-way scenic loop road that winds around the park, providing sightseeing, vistas and
overlooks. Many of the hiking trails begin off this road. Leashed dogs are allowed on most of the trails. Some of
the trails they are not allowed on are more like rock climbing expeditions than hiking trails. There are a variety of
hiking trails ranging from easy to difficult. The visitor center is open daily and should have trail maps. On the
trails, be aware of extreme heat or cold. Also watch out for flash floods, especially near creeks and streams.
According to the BLM (Bureau of Land Management), violent downpours can cause flash flooding in areas
untouched by rain. Do not cross low places when water is running through a stream. The park entrance fee is $5
per vehicle and $5 per dog. To get there from downtown Las Vegas, take Charleston Blvd./159 and head west.
Spring Mountain National Recreation Area Echo Road Mount Charleston NV 702-515-5400
This 316,000 acre park, part of the Toiyabe National Forest, is located about 35 miles northwest of Las Vegas.
Mt. Charleston is located in this dog-friendly park and has many hiking trails. Temperatures here can average 25
to 30 degrees cooler than in Las Vegas. The Mary Jane Falls trail, located on Mt. Charleston, is one of the more
popular trails. The trail passes a seasonal waterfall and several small caves. The trail is about 2.4 miles and
starts at about 7840 foot elevation. To reach the trailhead, take State Route 157, travel 2 miles west of the
ranger station to Echo Road. After traveling .35 mile, take the left fork off Echo Road and continue up until the
road ends. Dogs must be on leash.

Off-Leash Dog Parks

Acacia Park Dog Park S Gibson Road and Las Palmas Entrada Henderson NV 702-267-4000
This fenced dog park is open daily from 6 am to midnight. The park is just south of I-215 at Gibson Rd.
Dos Escuelas Park Dog Park 1 Golden View Street Henderson NV 702-267-4000
This fenced dog park is open daily from 6 am to midnight. To get to the park, which is just south of I-215, take the S. Green Valley Pkwy exit and head south. Turn left onto Paseo Verde Pkwy and make a left onto Desert Shadow Trail. Turn left onto Rainbow View Street and left again onto Golden View Street. The park will be on the left.
Desert Breeze Dog Run 8425 W. Spring Mtn. Road Las Vegas NV
This dog park is fully enclosed with benches, trees, trash cans and water. There are three dog runs available, one for small dogs, one for middle sized dogs and one for larger dogs over 30 pounds. The park is located approximately 5 miles west of downtown Las Vegas and the Strip. From Flamingo Road/589 in downtown, head west and pass Hwy 15. Turn right on Durango Drive. Then turn right onto Spring Mountain Road. The dog park is located off Spring Mountain Rd., between the Community Center and Desert Breeze County Park.
Desert Inn Dog Park 3570 Vista del Monte Las Vegas NV 702-455-8200
This fenced dog park is open daily from 6 am to 11 pm. The park is located off of Boulder Highway east of the 515 freeway. From Boulder Highway take Indios Avenue east to Twain Ave. Turn right on Twain and go two blocks. Turn left on VIsta Del Monte Drive to the park.
TOP 200 PLACE **Dog Fancier's Park** 5800 E. Flamingo Rd. Las Vegas NV 702-455-8200
Dog Fancier's Park is a 12 acre park that allows canine enthusiasts to train their dogs off leash. Owner's must still have control over their dogs and may be cited if their dogs (while off leash) interfere with other animals training at the park. This dog park has benches, poop bags and water taps.
Molasky Park Dog Run 1065 E. Twain Ave Las Vegas NV 702-455-8200
This fenced dog park is open daily from 6 am to 11 pm. To get to the dog park from the Strip take Flamingo Rd east past Paradise. Turn left (north) on Cambridge St and east on Twain Ave. The dog park is located between Cambridge St and Maryland Parkway on Twain.
Shadow Rock Dog Run 2650 Los Feliz on Sunrise Mountain Las Vegas NV 702-455-8200
This is a 1.5 acre dog park with benches, poop bags and water taps.
Silverado Ranch Park Dog Park 9855 S. Gillespie Las Vegas NV 702-455-8200
This fenced dog park is open daily from 6 am to 11 pm. The park is south of the Strip off of Las Vegas Blvd. From the Strip head south on Las Vegas Blvd and turn left onto Silverado Ranch Blvd. Turn right onto Gillespie and the park will be on the right.
Sunset Park Dog Run 2601 E. Sunset Rd Las Vegas NV 702-455-8200
Located in Sunset Park, this dog park offers about 1.5 acres of land for your pooch to play. The dog park has benches, poop bags and water taps.

Outdoor Restaurants

Baja Fresh Mexican Grill 675 Mall Ring Circle Henderson NV 702-450-6551
http://www.bajafresh.com
This Mexican restaurant is open for lunch and dinner. They use fresh ingredients and making their salsa and beans daily. Some of the items on their menu include Enchiladas, Burritos, Tacos Salads, Quesadillas, Nachos, Chicken, Steak and more. Well-behaved leashed dogs are allowed at the outdoor tables.
The Brooklyn Bagel 1500 N. Green Valley Parkway Henderson NV 702-260-9511
Dogs are allowed at the outdoor tables.
Wild Oats Natural Marketplace 517 North Stephanie St. Henderson NV 702-458-9427
http://www.wildoats.com
This full service natural food market offers both natural and organic food. You can get food from the deli and bring it to an outdoor table where your well-behaved leashed dog is welcome.
Baja Fresh Mexican Grill 7930 W. Tropical Pkwy. Las Vegas NV 702-307-2345
http://www.bajafresh.com
This Mexican restaurant is open for lunch and dinner. They use fresh ingredients and making their salsa and beans daily. Some of the items on their menu include Enchiladas, Burritos, Tacos Salads, Quesadillas, Nachos, Chicken, Steak and more. Well-behaved leashed dogs are allowed at the outdoor tables.
Baja Fresh Mexican Grill 4760 W. Sahara Blvd. Las Vegas NV 702-878-7772
http://www.bajafresh.com
This Mexican restaurant is open for lunch and dinner. They use fresh ingredients and making their salsa and beans daily. Some of the items on their menu include Enchiladas, Burritos, Tacos Salads, Quesadillas, Nachos, Chicken, Steak and more. Well-behaved leashed dogs are allowed at the outdoor tables.
Baja Fresh Mexican Grill 4190 S. Rainbow Blvd. Las Vegas NV 702-876-4193
http://www.bajafresh.com
This Mexican restaurant is open for lunch and dinner. They use fresh ingredients and making their salsa and beans daily. Some of the items on their menu include Enchiladas, Burritos, Tacos Salads, Quesadillas, Nachos,

Chicken, Steak and more. Well-behaved leashed dogs are allowed at the outdoor tables.
Baja Fresh Mexican Grill 4343 N. Rancho Rd. Las Vegas NV 702-396-2553
http://www.bajafresh.com
This Mexican restaurant is open for lunch and dinner. They use fresh ingredients and making their salsa and beans daily. Some of the items on their menu include Enchiladas, Burritos, Tacos Salads, Quesadillas, Nachos, Chicken, Steak and more. Well-behaved leashed dogs are allowed at the outdoor tables.
Baja Fresh Mexican Grill 3385 Russell Rd Las Vegas NV 702-212-6800
http://www.bajafresh.com
This Mexican restaurant is open for lunch and dinner. They use fresh ingredients and making their salsa and beans daily. Some of the items on their menu include Enchiladas, Burritos, Tacos Salads, Quesadillas, Nachos, Chicken, Steak and more. Well-behaved leashed dogs are allowed at the outdoor tables.
Baja Fresh Mexican Grill 1380 E Flamingo Rd Las Vegas NV 702-699-8920
Dogs are allowed at the outdoor tables.
Baja Fresh Mexican Grill 7501 W Lake Mead Blvd # 100 Las Vegas NV 702-838-4100
Dogs are allowed at the outdoor tables.
Coffee Bean and Tea Leaf 2600 Nature Park Drive Las Vegas NV 702-933-4176
This cafe serves coffee,tea, and pastries. Dogs are allowed at the outdoor tables.
Einstein Brothers Bagels 9031 W. Sahara Ave Las Vegas NV 702-254-0919
Dogs are allowed at the outdoor tables.
In-N-Out Burger 2900 W. Sahara Ave. Las Vegas NV 800-786-1000
This fast food restaurant serves great hamburgers and fries.
Jitters Gourmet Coffee 2457 E Tropicana Las Vegas NV 702-898-0056
This coffee shop serves pastries. Dogs are allowed at the outdoor tables. Water is provided for your pet.
Mountain Ham Deli 1121 S. Decatur, Suite 100 Las Vegas NV 702-385-4267
Dogs are allowed at the outdoor tables.
Mountain Springs Saloon Highway 160 Las Vegas NV 702-875-4266
Dogs are welcome at the outdoor dining area. This bar has a limited food menu and serves a variety of beer. The bar has live music Friday and Saturday nights. They are located near the Mountain Springs Summit, about 15-20 minutes west of downtown Las Vegas.
ReJAVAnate 3300 E Flamingo Rd Las Vegas NV 702-253-7721
This cafe serves coffee and pastries. Dogs are allowed at the outdoor tables.
Starbucks 395 Hughes Center Drive Las Vegas NV 702-369-5537
http://www.starbucks.com
This coffee shop allows well-behaved leashed dogs at their outdoor tables.
Whole Foods Market 8855 West Charleston Blvd. Las Vegas NV 702-254-8655
http://www.wholefoods.com/
This natural food supermarket offers natural and organic foods. Order some food from their deli without your dog and bring it to an outdoor table where your well-behaved leashed dog is welcome. Dogs are not allowed in the store including the deli at any time.
Wild Oats Natural Marketplace 7250 W. Lake Mead Blvd Las Vegas NV 702-942-1500
http://www.wildoats.com
This full service natural food market offers both natural and organic food. You can get food from the deli and bring it to an outdoor table where your well-behaved leashed dog is welcome.

Events

Strut Your Mutt 5800 E Flamingo/Hwy 592 Las Vegas NV 702-455-8264
http://www.strutyourmuttlv.com/
This annual event (usually in November) is sponsored by the Clark County Parks and Recreation Department. It is an all day affair held at the Dog Fanciers Park. There are a long list of doggy contests, dozens of vendors for pet related merchandise, services, and care, demonstrations, doggy theater, agility courses, games, grooming, adoption, and more. Dogs must be friendly, well behaved, leashed, and cleaned up after at all times.

Vets and Kennels

A VIP Pet Resort 2675 W. Arby Avenue Las Vegas NV 702-361-8900
This kennel offers day boarding and long-term boarding. They have indoor/outdoor kennel runs and a grass exercise yard. The indoor facilities are climate controlled. The day boarding runs about $14 per day for a large dog (possibly less for a small dog). They are open Monday through Saturday from 8am-5pm and Sunday from 10am-2pm. There are no specific drop off or pick up times. However, you might want to call ahead and make a reservation just in case. The kennel is located about 5 minutes from the Strip, and the airport and their slogan is "Where Your Pets Are Treated Like Family".
Animal Emergency Service 1914 E Sahara Ave Las Vegas NV 702-457-8050
Monday - Friday 6 pm to 8 am, Saturday noon - Monday 8 am.
Pet Oasis Pet Care PO Box 271568 Las Vegas NV 702-645-1299

http://www.petoasispetcare.com
These pet sitters will come to your hotel room and stay with your pet while you take in a show or visit a casino when you can't take your pup. They are licensed, bonded, and insured.
The Animal Inn Kennels 3460 W Oquendo Road Las Vegas NV   702-736-0036
http://www.animalinnlv.com
This full-service boarding kennel is located right off of I-15. Daycare, overnight and long term boarders are welcomed. The office hours are Mon - Fri 8 am - 6 pm, Sat - Sun 8 am - 5 pm. Please call 702-736-0036 to make a reservation.

Laughlin

Accommodations
Pioneer Hotel and Gambling Hall 2200 S. Casino Drive Laughlin NV   702-298-2442 (800-634-3469)
This hotel allows dogs of all sizes. However, there are only ten pet rooms and these are all smoking rooms. There is a $100 refundable pet deposit required. We normally do not include smoking room only pet rooms but since the selection of pet friendly lodging in Laughlin is so limited we have listed this one.

Campgrounds and RV Parks
Silver View RV Resort 1501 Gold Rush Road Bullhead City AZ   928-763-5500
http://www.silverviewrvresort.com
With spectacular views from the bluffs overlooking the Colorado River, this 5 star resort offers a mini mart and deli, clubhouse, swimming pool/Jacuzzi, and laundry. Two dogs under 40 pounds or one dog over 40 pounds is allowed at no additional fee. Dogs may not be left unattended outside, and they must be leashed and cleaned up after. Dogs are not allowed on the grass areas. There is a dog run on site where pets may be off lead. There are some breed restrictions. The camping and tent areas also allow dogs. There is a dog walk area at the campground.
Big Bend of the Colorado P. O. Box 32850 Laughlin NV   702-298-1859
http://parks.nv.gov/bb.htm
Located on the shores of the Colorado River, this desert park offers a variety of land and water recreation. Dogs of all sizes are allowed at no additional fee. Dogs must be on no more than a 6 foot leash and be cleaned up after. The camping and tent areas also allow dogs. There is a dog walk area at the campground. There are no electric or water hookups at the campgrounds.
Don Laughlin's Riverside RV Resort 1650 S Casino Drive Laughlin NV   702-298-2535 (800-227-3849)
This RV only park, located across the street from the Riverside Resort Hotel, offers 740 full hookup RV sites. Amenities include laundry facilities, showers, and 24 hour security. Well-behaved leashed dogs are allowed. Please clean up after your pets. There is no pet fee. Dogs may not be left unattended outside, and left inside only if they will be quiet and comfortable. There is a dog walk area at the campground.

Lovelock

Campgrounds and RV Parks
Rye Patch State Recreation Area 2505 Rye Patch Reservoir Road Lovelock NV   775-538-7321
http://parks.nv.gov/rp.htm
Rich in natural and cultural history, this park along a 22-mile long reservoir, offers archaeological sites, and a variety of land and water recreation. Dogs of all sizes are allowed at no additional fee. Dogs may not be left unattended outside, and they must be on no more than a 6 foot leash, and cleaned up after. The camping and tent areas also allow dogs. There is a dog walk area at the campground. There are no electric or water hookups at the campgrounds.

Mesquite

Accommodations
Virgin River Hotel and Casino 100 Pionner Blvd Mesquite NV   800-346-7721
Up to three dogs of all sizes are allowed at this hotel. There is a refundable pet deposit of $25 per room. Dogs must be leashed and cleaned up after, and they may not be left unattended in the rooms unless crated.

Virgin River Hotel and Casino 100 Pioneer Blvd Mesquite NV 702-346-7777
Dogs of all sizes are allowed. There is a $25 per room additional pet fee.

Minden

Campgrounds and RV Parks
Silver City RV Resort 3165 Hwy 395N Minden NV 775-267-3359 (800-997-6393)
http://www.silvercityrvresort.com
This RV campground offers a covered pool and spa, fish pond, fitness club, store, laundry facilities, gaming, and various other recreational pursuits. Dogs of all sizes are allowed for an additional $1 per night per pet. Dogs may not be left unattended outside, and they must be leashed and cleaned up after. This is an RV only park. There are some breed restrictions. There is a dog walk area at the campground.

Outdoor Restaurants
Barone and Reed Food Company 1599 Esmeralda Avenue Minden NV 775-783-1988
This restaurant specializes in seafood, steak, and American food. Your dog is welcome to join you at one of the outside tables. They must be well behaved and leashed at all times.

Overton

Accommodations
Best Western The North Shore Inn at Lake Mead 520 N Moapa Valley Blvd Overton NV 702-397-6000 (800-780-7234)
Dogs of all sizes are allowed. There is a $10 per night pet fee per pet. Smoking and non-smoking rooms are available for pets.

Campgrounds and RV Parks
Valley of Fire State Park P. O. Box 515/ Valley of Fire Road Overton NV 702-397-2088
http://parks.nv.gov/vf.htm
Unusual red sandstone formations mark this park with a fascinating array of shapes, and they offer interpretive exhibits, numerous trails, historic sites, various recreation, and a visitor's center. Dogs of all sizes are allowed at no additional fee. Dogs may not be left unattended outside, and they must be leashed and cleaned up after. Dogs are allowed on the trails. The camping and tent areas also allow dogs. There is a dog walk area at the campground. There are no electric or water hookups at the campgrounds.

Parks
Valley of Fire State Park off Interstate 15, exit 75 Overton NV 702-397-2088
http://www.state.nv.us/stparks/vf.htm
This park derives its name from red sandstone formations, formed from great shifting sand dunes during the age of dinosaurs, 150 million years ago. Ancient trees are represented throughout the park by areas of petrified wood. There is also a 3,000 year-old Indian petroglyph. Popular activities include camping, hiking, picnicking and photography. Sites of special interest are the Altatl Rock, the Arch Rock, the Beehives, Elephant Rock, Seven Sisters, and more. There are many intriguing hikes available. Please inquire at the visitor center for suggestions on day hikes of varying length and terrain. The visitor's center is open daily, 8:30am to 4:30pm. The park is open all year. Pets are welcome, but they must be kept on a leash of not more than six feet in length. They are not allowed in the visitor center. The park is located six miles from Lake Mead and 55 miles northeast of Las Vegas via Interstate 15 and on exit 75.

Pahrump

Campgrounds and RV Parks
Lakeside Casino RV Park 5870 S Homestead Road Pahrump NV 775-751-7770 (888-558-5253)
http://www.terribleherbst.com
This lushly landscaped RV resort offers historic old west charm among its many amenities which include

watercraft rentals, laundry facilities, swimming lagoon, swimming pool and jacuzzi. Dogs of all sizes are allowed. There are no additional pet fees. Dogs may not be left unattended outside, and left inside if they will be quiet and comfortable. They must be leashed and cleaned up after. Dogs are not allowed in the lake, on the beach, or in the pool area. This is an RV only park. There are some breed restrictions. There is a dog walk area at the campground.

Panaca

Campgrounds and RV Parks
Cathedral Gorge State Park P. O. Box 176 Panaca NV   775-728-4460
http://www.parks.nv.gov/cg.htm
This park sits at 4,800 feet in a long, narrow valley and offers several trails to explore the cathedral spires and cave-like formations, including a 4 mile loop trail for accessing more remote areas. At Miller Point Overlook, there are excellent views of the canyon, and the visitor center offers interpretive displays and related information. Popular activities include nature study, photography, ranger programs, camping, hiking and picnicking. Dogs of all sizes are allowed for no additional fee. Dogs must be well mannered, be on no more than a 6 foot leash, and be cleaned up after. They are allowed throughout the park and on the trails; they are not allowed in park buildings. The camping and tent areas also allow dogs. There is a dog walk area at the campground. There are no electric or water hookups at the campgrounds.
Cathedral Gorge State Park 333 Cathedral Gorge Road Panaca NV   775-728-4460
http://parks.nv.gov/cg.htm
This park features dramatic scenic canyons, a rich history, interpretive displays, opportunities for nature study and photography, several trails and a variety of recreation. Dogs of all sizes are allowed for no additional fee. Dogs may not be left unattended for long periods, and only for a short time if they will be comfortable, quiet, and well behaved. Dogs are allowed on the trails. The camping and tent areas also allow dogs. There is a dog walk area at the campground. There are no electric or water hookups at the campgrounds.

Parks
Cathedral Gorge State Park P. O. Box 176 Panaca NV   775-728-4460
http://www.parks.nv.gov/cg.htm
A geological delight, this park sits at 4,800 feet in a long, narrow valley and offers several trails to explore the cathedral spires and cave-like formations, including a 4 mile loop trail for accessing more remote areas. At Miller Point Overlook, there are excellent views of the canyon, and the visitor center offers interpretive displays and related information. Popular activities include nature study, photography, ranger programs, camping, hiking and picnicking. Dogs of all sizes are allowed for no additional fee. Dogs must be well mannered, be on no more than a 6 foot leash, and be cleaned up after. They are allowed throughout the park and on the trails; they are not allowed in park buildings.

Pioche

Campgrounds and RV Parks
Echo Canyon State Park HC 74, Box 295 Pioche NV   775-962-5103
http://parks.nv.gov/ec.htm
This 1080-acre park, with a 65 acre reservoir, supports a good variety of plant and animal life. It offers a rich archeological and agricultural history to explore in addition to various recreational pursuits. Dogs of all sizes are allowed at no additional fee. Dogs must be leashed in the camp area, and cleaned up after. Dogs are allowed on the trails. The camping and tent areas also allow dogs. There is a dog walk area at the campground. There are no electric or water hookups at the campgrounds.
Spring Valley State Park HC74, Box 201 Pioche NV   775-962-5102
http://parks.nv.gov/sv.htm
This high desert park, along a 65 acre reservoir, offers a rich cultural history in addition to a variety of amenities and recreational pursuits. Dogs of all sizes are allowed for no additional fee. Dogs may not be left unattended, except for short periods, and then only if they will be quiet and well behaved. Dogs must be on no more than a 6 foot leash and cleaned up after. When there are not a lot of people around, dogs may be off lead if they are under voice control and will not chase. The camping and tent areas also allow dogs. There is a dog walk area at the campground. There are no electric or water hookups at the campgrounds.

Reno

Accommodations

TOP 200 PLACE **Atlantis Casino Resort Spa** 3800 S Virigina Street Reno NV 775-825-4700 (800-723-6500)
Dogs of all sizes are allowed in the Motor Lodge section of this casino hotel. There is a $25 one time fee per pet. Dogs must be kept on leash and cleaned up after. Please place the Do Not Disturb sign on the door if there is a pet alone in the room.

Days Inn Reno 701 E 7th Reno NV 775-786-4070 (800-329-7466)
Dogs of all sizes are allowed. There is a $10 per night pet fee per pet.

Holiday Inn Downtown 1000 E. 6th St. Reno NV 775-786-5151 (877-270-6405)
http://www.basshotels.com/holiday-inn
This hotel is located only 4 blocks from Reno's famous gaming strip and within walking distance to the Reno Livestock & Events Center. Amenities include a heated pool and gift shop. Well-behaved dogs of all sizes are welcome. There is a $15 per day pet charge. Pets are allowed in non-smoking and smoking rooms.

La Quinta Inn Reno 4001 Market Reno NV 775-348-6100 (800-531-5900)
Dogs of all sizes are allowed. There are no additional pet fees. Dogs must be leashed, cleaned up after, and crated or removed for housekeeping.

Motel 6 - Reno - Livestock Events Center 866 North Wells Avenue Reno NV 775-786-9852 (800-466-8356)
One well-behaved family pet per room. Guest must notify front desk upon arrival. Guest is liable for any damages. In consideration of all guests, pets must never be left unattended in the guest rooms.

Motel 6 - Reno - Virginia Plumb 1901 South Virginia Street Reno NV 775-827-0255 (800-466-8356)
One well-behaved family pet per room. Guest must notify front desk upon arrival. Guest is liable for any damages. In consideration of all guests, pets must never be left unattended in the guest rooms.

Motel 6 - Reno West 1400 Stardust Street Reno NV 775-747-7390 (800-466-8356)
One well-behaved family pet per room. Guest must notify front desk upon arrival. Guest is liable for any damages. In consideration of all guests, pets must never be left unattended in the guest rooms.

Quality Inn South 1885 S Virginia Street Reno NV 775-329-1001 (877-424-6423)
Dogs of all sizes are allowed. There is a $10 per night per pet additional fee. Dogs are not allowed in common areas, and they may not be left alone in the room. Dogs must be leashed and cleaned up after.

Residence Inn by Marriott 9845 Gateway Drive Reno NV 775-853-8800
Dogs up to 75 pounds are allowed, and up to 2 pets may be in the studios; up to 4 in the 1 and 2 bedroom suites. There is a $100 one time fee and a pet policy to sign at check in.

Rodeway Inn 2050 Market Street Reno NV 775-786-2500 (800-578-7878)
http://www.rodewayinn.com
This hotel (previously Travelodge) is about a mile from the Reno gambling strip. Amenities include a complimentary continental breakfast, heated outdoor pool, kitchenettes in some rooms, and wheelchair accessible rooms. There is a $10 per day pet charge.

Super 8 Reno/Meadowwood Courtyard 5851 S Virginia St Reno NV 775-829-4600 (800-800-8000)
Dogs of all sizes are allowed. There is a $10 per night pet fee per pet. Smoking and non-smoking rooms are available for pet rooms.

Truckee River Lodge 501 W. 1st Street Reno NV 775-786-8888 (800-635-8950)
http://www.truckee-river-lodge.com/
There is a $10 per day pet fee. All rooms in the hotel are non-smoking. There is a park across the street.

Vagabond Inn 3131 S. Virginia St. Reno NV 775-825-7134 (800-522-1555)
http://www.vagabondinn.com
This motel is located less than a couple miles from the downtown casinos and the Convention Center. Amenities include a swimming pool, 24 hour cable television, air conditioning, and more. There is a $10 per day pet fee.

Motel 6 - Reno Airport - Sparks 2405 Victorian Avenue Sparks NV 775-358-1080 (800-466-8356)
One well-behaved family pet per room. Guest must notify front desk upon arrival. Guest is liable for any damages. In consideration of all guests, pets must never be left unattended in the guest rooms.

Campgrounds and RV Parks

Bonanza Terrace RV Park 4800 Stoltz Road Reno NV 775-329-9624
http://www.bonanzaterracervpark.com/
This RV park is located two miles north of downtown Reno off Highway 395. The Bonanza Casino is across the street from the RV park. RV sites include a gravel parking pad, up to 50 amp electric, water, sewer and phone line. RVs up to 40 feet are welcome. Well-behaved, leashed, and quiet pets accompanied by their owner are welcome. There is a $1 per night pet fee. Please clean up after your pet. Dogs may not be left unattended outside. There are some breed restrictions. There is a dog walk area at the campground.

Reno KOA 2500 E 2nd Street Reno NV   775-789-2147 (800-562-5698)
http://www.koa.com/where/nv/28136/
Located at the Reno Hilton, there is an abundance of activities and recreation available, and amenities include 24 hour security, 65 foot pull through sites with 50 amp service, LP gas, snack bar, seasonal swimming pool, hot tub/sauna, mini golf, and guided tours. Dogs of all sizes are allowed for no additional fee. Dogs must be under owner's control and visual observation at all times. Dogs must be quiet, well behaved, and be on no more than a 6 foot leash at all times, or otherwise contained, and cleaned up after. Management will ask guests to leave if they do not clean up after their dogs. Dogs may not be left unattended outside the owner's camping equipment, and must be brought inside at night. There are some breed restrictions. The camping and tent areas also allow dogs. There is a dog walk area at the campground.
Reno RV Park 735 Mill Street Reno NV   775-323-3381 (800-445-3381)
This RV park is located about 4 blocks from the casinos. They offer restrooms, showers, 24 hour security, electric gates, propane available, recreation area, picnic area and more. Well-behaved leashed dogs are welcome. Please clean up after your dogs. There is no pet fee. Dogs may not be left unattended. The camping and tent areas also allow dogs. There is a dog walk area at the campground.
Rivers Edge RV Park 1405 S Rock Blvd Sparks NV   775-358-8533
(800-621-4792)
Dogs of all sizes are allowed. There are no additional pet fees. Dogs may not be left unattended outside, and they must be leashed and cleaned up after. Dogs are allowed on the trails. This is an RV only park. There is a dog walk area at the campground.

Stores

Harley Davidson of Reno 2295 Market Street Reno NV   775-329-2913
http://www.harley-davidsonreno.com/
Well-behaved leashed dogs are allowed in this store. In addition to the motorcycles, they also sell collectibles, riding gear and accessories.
PetSmart Pet Store 6675 S Virginia St Reno NV   775-852-8490
Your licensed and well-behaved leashed dog is allowed in the store.
Petco Pet Store 5565 South Virginia St Reno NV   775-829-9200
Your licensed and well-behaved leashed dog is allowed in the store.
Petco Pet Store 2970 Northtowne Lane Reno NV   775-673-9200
Your licensed and well-behaved leashed dog is allowed in the store.
Scraps Dog Bakery 3890 Mayberry Drive Reno NV   775-787-3647 (888-332-DOGS)
http://www.go-reno.com/scraps/
Your dog is welcome inside this bakery which sells cookies and goodies for your pup. They also have a general store which sells other doggie items.

Parks

Donnelly Park Mayberry Drive Reno NV
This is a small, but nice park to walk around with your dog. It is across the street from Scraps Dog Bakery and Walden's Coffee. Dogs must be leashed.
Rancho San Rafael Park 1595 N. Sierra Street Reno NV   775-828-6642
http://www.washoecountyparks.com/
Dogs are allowed in the undeveloped areas of this park. Dogs must be leashed with one exception. Dogs may be off-leash only at certain times at the multi-use pasture area. If there are special events or activities on the multi-use area then dogs are not allowed at all on the field. This includes when the hay is being cut and harvested. Portions of the field may be muddy when the pasture is being irrigated. Leashed dogs are allowed on a hiking and walking path which crosses over McCarren Blvd. It is a dirt trail which narrows to a single track trail once you cross over McCarren Blvd. Just be careful when crossing over McCarren because the speed limit on the road is about 45-50mph. To get there from Hwy 80, exit Keystone Ave. Head north on Keystone. Turn right onto Coleman Drive. Take Coleman until it almost ends and turn right into the park. Park near the Coleman intersection and the trailhead will be nearby.
TOP 200 PLACE Pyramid Lake Hwy 445 Sutcliffe NV   775-574-1000
Pyramid Lake is located in an Indian reservation, but visitors to the lake are welcomed guests of the Pyramid Lake Tribe of the Paiute Indians. Your leashed dog is also welcome. The lake is a beautiful contrast to the desert sandstone mountains which surround it. It is about 15 miles long by 11 miles wide, and among interesting rock formations. Pyramid Lake is Nevada's largest natural lake. It is popular for fishing and photography. The north end of the lake is off-limits to visitors because it is a sacred area to the Paiutes. There is a beach area near the ranger's station in Sutcliffe. Be careful when wading into the water, as there are some ledges which drop off into deeper water. Also, do not wade in the water at the south end of the lake because the dirt acts like quick sand. The lake is about 35-40 minutes north of Reno, off Hwy 445.

Off-Leash Dog Parks

Rancho San Rafael Regional Park 1595 North Sierra Street Reno NV 775-785-4512
Home to the annual Great Reno Balloon races, this huge park covers almost 600 acres of manicured turf, natural desert and wetlands, and has the largest off-leash space in the area. There is a pond and creek for dogs to play in with a walking path that surrounds it. Some of the amenities include benches, picnic areas, restrooms, and clean-up stations. Dogs must be on lead when not in the off leash areas, and there is signage indicating the areas in the park where pets are not allowed. Dogs must be cleaned up after at all times.

Sparks Marina Park 300 Howard Drive Reno NV 775-353-2376
This park has a 77 acre lake offering a wide variety of land and water activities and recreational pursuits. They also have the only fenced, off-lead dog park in the Reno area where dogs can play in the water. The off lead area is almost an acre in size on the south side of the marina and features lots of grass, 150 feet of shoreline, clean-up stations, a fire hydrant, and a doggie drinking fountain. The marina is surrounded by a walking trail almost 2 miles long that is lighted for nighttime walks with your pet. Dogs must be on leash when not in the fenced, off-lead area, and they must be cleaned up after at all times. Dogs are not allowed on any of the beaches.

Virginia Lake Dog Park Lakeside Drive Reno NV 775-334-2099
http://www.ci.reno.nv.us
This one acre dog park includes mitt dispensers. The park is located at Mountain View and Lakeside Drive, at the north field.

Whitaker Dog Park 550 University Terrace Reno NV 775-334-2099
http://www.ci.reno.nv.us
This fenced dog park is about .75 acres. Amenities include mitt dispensers.

Outdoor Restaurants

Archie's Grill 2195 N. Virginia St. Reno NV 775-322-9595
This restaurant serves breakfast, lunch and dinner. Your dog is allowed at the outdoor tables.

Baja Fresh Mexican Grill 5140 Kietzke Ln. Reno NV 775-826-8900
http://www.bajafresh.com
This Mexican restaurant is open for lunch and dinner. They use fresh ingredients and making their salsa and beans daily. Some of the items on their menu include Enchiladas, Burritos, Tacos Salads, Quesadillas, Nachos, Chicken, Steak and more. Well-behaved leashed dogs are allowed at the outdoor tables.

Java Jungle 246 W. 1st Street Reno NV 775-329-4484
Java Jungle was voted "Best Espresso and Cappuccino of Reno" in the Reno Gazette-Journal reader surveys. The wide variety of their customers include lawyers and judges on their way to the Washoe County Courthouse as well as joggers and dog walkers. It is located in downtown Reno, near the Truckee River. Dogs are welcome at the outdoor tables.

My Favorite Muffin & Bagel Cafe 340 California Ave. Reno NV 775-333-1025
This cafe was voted Reno's Best Bagels. As the name of the cafe implies, they serve bagels and muffins. Your dog is allowed at the outdoor tables.

Peg's Glorified Ham & Eggs 420 S. Sierra St. Reno NV 775-329-2600
This restaurant is located in downtown and has a few outdoor tables. Your dog is allowed at the outdoor tables.

Quiznos 4965 S. Virginia Street Reno NV 775-828-5252
They serve a variety of sandwiches. Dogs are allowed at the outdoor tables.

Walden's Coffee Co. 3940 Mayberry Drive Reno NV 775-787-3307
Your dog is welcome at the outdoor tables at coffee house. They have a variety of pastries and snacks available. The Scraps Dog Bakery is in the same shopping center (see Attractions.)

Wild Oats Natural Marketplace 5695 S. Virginia St. Reno NV 775-829-8666
http://www.wildoats.com
This full service natural food market offers both natural and organic food. You can get food from the deli and bring it to an outdoor table where your well-behaved leashed dog is welcome. Outdoor seating is seasonal.

Vets and Kennels

Animal Emergency Center 6427 S Virginia St Reno NV 775-851-3600
Monday - Friday 6 pm to 8 am, Saturday noon - Monday 8 am.

Silver Springs

Campgrounds and RV Parks

Fort Churchill State Historic Park 1000 Hwy 95A Silver Springs NV 775-577-2345
http://parks.nv.gov/fc.htm

Rich in American history, this park offers a visitor's center with exhibits and artifacts, hiking, historic and environmental education, and access to the Carson River for canoeing. Dogs of all sizes are allowed at no additional fee. Dogs may not be left unattended for long periods, and only then if they will be quiet and well behaved. Dogs must be on no more than a 6 foot leash, or crated, and cleaned up after. Dogs are allowed on the trails unless otherwise marked. The camping and tent areas also allow dogs. There is a dog walk area at the campground. There are no electric or water hookups at the campgrounds.
Silver Springs Beach 1971 Fir Street Silver Springs NV 775-577-2226
http://parks.nv.gov/lah.htm#CAMP
This park, located in the high desert of the Lahontan State Rec Area along a 17 mile reservoir, offers a variety of amenities and recreational opportunities. Dogs of all sizes are allowed at no additional fee. Dogs must be on no more than a 6 foot leash and cleaned up after. Dogs are allowed to go to the beach and on the trails. The camping and tent areas also allow dogs. There is a dog walk area at the campground. There are no electric or water hookups at the campgrounds.

Spring Creek

Campgrounds and RV Parks
South Fork State Recreation Area 353 Lower South Fork Unit 8 Spring Creek NV 775-744-4346
http://parks.nv.gov/sf.htm
Surrounded by 2,200 acres of wildlife-filled meadow lands and rolling hills, this park, with a 1,650 acre reservoir, is popular for hunting, boating, hiking, winter sports, and wildlife viewing. Friendly dogs of all sizes are allowed for no additional fee. Dogs must be on no more than a 6 foot leash and be cleaned up after. The camping and tent areas also allow dogs. There is a dog walk area at the campground. There are no electric or water hookups at the campgrounds.

Tonopah

Accommodations
Best Western Hi-Desert Inn 320 Main St Tonopah NV 775-482-3511 (800-780-7234)
Dogs of all sizes are allowed. There are no additional pet fees. Pet must be kept in kennel when left alone. Smoking and non-smoking rooms are available for pets.

Verdi

Campgrounds and RV Parks
Gold Ranch Casino and RV Resort 320 Gold Ranch Road Verdi NV 877-792-6789
http://www.goldranchrvcasino.com
A few miles from Reno, nestled among the trees of the Sierra Nevada mountain range, this modern, luxury resort offers a 24 hour convenience store, an Arco gas station, clean showers, laundry facilities, clubhouse, heated pool/spa, and wide pull through sites. Dogs of all sizes are allowed. There are no additional pet fees. Dogs may not be left unattended outside, and they must be leashed and cleaned up after. This is an RV only park. There is a dog walk area at the campground.

Virginia City

Campgrounds and RV Parks
Virginia City RV Park 355 N 'F' Street Virginia City NV 775-847-0999 (800-889-1240)
Located just two blocks from downtown Virginia City, this park offers 50 RV sites, and amenities include phone equipped spaces, showers, swimming pool, tennis courts park access, onsite market and deli, video rentals, laundry facility, slot machines and tent camping. Well-behaved leashed dogs are allowed. Please clean up after your pets, and do not leave them unattended. Reservations are accepted for busy periods. The park is open all year. The camping and tent areas also allow dogs. There is a dog walk area at the campground.

Attractions

Virginia & Truckee Railroad Co. 565 S. K Street Virginia City NV   775-847-0380
http://www.vtrailroad.com
You and your dog can ride back in time on this steam train. The train takes you on a leisurely 35 minute round trip to the historic station in the city of Gold Hill. Passengers can get off the train at Gold Hill, visit the historic old town and then board the next train. The conductor gives a narration of the many historic sites you will view from the train. Your dog is welcome to join you on either the open air railcar or the enclosed railcar. Trains operate everyday from May through October. The round trip fare is about $5 for adults and about $3 for children. Prices are subject to change. Tickets can be purchased at the railcar on C Street or next to the train depot near Washington and F Streets. The train ride is located in Virginia City, about 30-40 minutes south of Reno.

TOP 200 PLACE **Virginia City** Hwy 341 Virginia City NV   775-847-0311
http://www.virginiacity-nv.com/
This small town was built in the late 1800s and was a booming mining town. The restored Old Western town now has a variety of shops with wooden walkways. Dogs are allowed to window shop with you. Dogs are also welcome to ride the Virginia & Truckee Steam Train with you. Virginia City is located about 30-40 minutes south of Reno.

Stores

Bogie's Beer Collectibles 182 South C Virginia City NV   775-847-9300
Bogie's Beer Collectibles is a small retail store in historic Virginia City. They sell beer collectibles, brew bags and other fun collectible items. The owner is a dog lover and allows your dog inside the store. They even have a sign outside that says "Kids, Dogs & Cats Welcome in Bogie's. Please Tie Horses & Mules Outside."

Outdoor Restaurants

Firehouse BBQ 171 South C Street Virginia City NV   775-847-4774
You and your pup will be tempted to stop here for lunch or dinner after you smell the delicious BBQ. This restaurant is located in historic Virginia City. Dogs are allowed at the outdoor tables. Outdoor tables are only available in the summer.

Wells

Accommodations

Motel 6 - Wells Old Highway 40 & US 93 Wells NV   775-752-2116 (800-466-8356)
One well-behaved family pet per room. Guest must notify front desk upon arrival. Guest is liable for any damages. In consideration of all guests, pets must never be left unattended in the guest rooms.
Super 8 Wells 930 6th Street Wells NV   775-752-3384 (800-800-8000)
Dogs of all sizes are allowed. There is a $5 per night pet fee per pet. Smoking and non-smoking rooms are available for pet rooms.

Wendover

Accommodations

Super 8 Wendover 1325 Wendover Blvd Wendover NV   775-664-2888 (800-800-8000)
Dogs up to 100 pounds are allowed. There is a $7.50 per night pet fee per pet. Dogs are not allowed to be left alone in the room. Smoking and non-smoking rooms are available for pet rooms.

Campgrounds and RV Parks

Wendover KOA 651 N Camper Drive West Wendover NV   775-664-3221 (800-562-8552)
http://www.koa.com/where/nv/28130/
Located just 10 miles from the world-famous Bonneville Salt Flats and next to 2 casinos, this oasis park offers large pull through sites, seasonal heated outdoor pool, mini golf, a grocery and souvenir shop, laundry and much more. Dogs of all sizes are allowed for no additional fee. Dogs must be under owner's control and visual observation at all times. Dogs must be quiet, well behaved, and be on no more than a 6 foot leash at all times, or otherwise contained, and cleaned up after. Dogs may not be left unattended outside the owner's camping equipment or alone in the cabins, and they must be brought inside at night. There are some breed restrictions. The camping and tent areas also allow dogs. There is a dog walk area at the campground. Dogs are allowed in

the camping cabins.

Winnemucca

Accommodations

Best Western Gold Country Inn 921 W Winnemucca Blvd Winnemucca NV 775-623-6999 (800-780-7234)
Dogs of all sizes are allowed. There is a $10 per night pet fee per pet under 47 pounds. There is a $15 per night pet fee per pet over 47 pounds to 100 pounds. There is a $20 per night pet fee per pet over 100 pounds. Smoking and non-smoking rooms are available for pets.
Days Inn Winnemucca 511 W Winnemucca Blvd Winnemucca NV 775-623-3661 (800-329-7466)
Dogs of all sizes are allowed. There is a $10 one time per pet over 25 pounds fee per visit.
Holiday Inn Express 1987 W. Winnemucca Blvd Winnemucca NV 775-625-3100 (877-270-6405)
There is a $50 pet deposit and $10 of the deposit is non-refundable.
Motel 6 - Winnemucca 1600 West Winnemucca Boulevard Winnemucca NV 775-623-1180 (800-466-8356)
One well-behaved family pet per room. Guest must notify front desk upon arrival. Guest is liable for any damages. In consideration of all guests, pets must never be left unattended in the guest rooms.
Red Lion 741 W Winnemucca Winnemucca NV 775-623-2565
Dogs of all sizes are allowed. There is no fee with a credit card on file and there is a pet policy to sign at check in. Dogs are not allowed to be left alone in the room.
Santa Fe Motel 1620 W. Winnemucca Blvd Winnemucca NV 775-623-1119
There are no additional pet fees.

Campgrounds and RV Parks

Model T RV Park 1130 W Winnemucca Blvd Winnemucca NV 775-623-2588 (800-645-5658)
http://www.modelt.com/rvpark.htm
This RV only park is located in town within walking distance of many services. Amenities include laundry facilities, a seasonal pool, restrooms and showers. Well-behaved leashed pets are allowed. There is no pet fee, just please clean up after your pet. The RV park is part of the Model T Casino and Winnemucca Quality Inn. There is a dog walk area at the campground.

Chapter 19

New Mexico
Dog Travel Guide

Alamogordo

Accommodations

Best Western Desert Aire Hotel 1021 S White Sands Blvd Alamogordo NM   505-437-2110 (800-780-7234)
Dogs of all sizes are allowed. There is a $10 per night pet fee per pet. Smoking and non-smoking rooms are available for pets.
Holiday Inn Express 1401 S. White Sands Blvd Alamogordo NM   505-437-7100 (877-270-6405)
There is a $50 refundable pet deposit. There is also a $10 per day additional pet fee.
Motel 6 - Alamogordo 251 Panorama Boulevard Alamogordo NM   505-434-5970 (800-466-8356)
One well-behaved family pet per room. Guest must notify front desk upon arrival. Guest is liable for any damages. In consideration of all guests, pets must never be left unattended in the guest rooms.

Campgrounds and RV Parks

Alamogordo Roadrunner Campground 412 24th Street Alamogordo NM   877-437-3003
http://www.roadrunnercampground.com
Dogs of all sizes are allowed. There are no additional pet fees. Dogs may not be left unattended outside, and they must be leashed and cleaned up after. The camping and tent areas also allow dogs. There is a dog walk area at the campground.
Lincoln National Forest 1101 New York Avenue Alamogordo NM   505-434-7200
http://www.fs.fed.us/r3/lincoln/
Home of Smokey Bear, this forest of over a million acres has diverse ecosystems that support a large variety of plants, fish, mammals, bird species, and recreation. Dogs of all sizes are allowed at no additional fee. Dogs may not be left unattended, and they must be leashed and cleaned up after in camp areas. Dogs may be off lead in the forest if they are well trained and under voice control. Dogs are allowed on the trails. The camping and tent areas also allow dogs. There is a dog walk area at the campground. There are no electric or water hookups at the campground.
Oliver Lee Memorial State Park 409 Dog Canyon Road Alamogordo NM   505-437-8284 (888-NMPARKS 667-2757))
This oasis in the desert features historical exhibits and guided tours of a fully restored 19th century ranch house. Dogs of all sizes are allowed at no additional fee. Dogs may not be left unattended outside, and they must be, quiet, well behaved, leashed and cleaned up after. Dogs are allowed on the trails. The camping and tent areas also allow dogs. There is a dog walk area at the campground.

Albuquerque

Accommodations

Best Western American Motor Inn 12999 Central Ave NE Albuquerque NM   505-298-7426 (800-780-7234)
There is a $10 per night pet fee per pet around 50 pounds. There is a $5 per night pet fee per pet under 50 pounds. Smoking and non-smoking rooms are available for pets.
Best Western InnSuites Hotel and Suites 2400 Yale Blvd SE Albuquerque NM   505-242-7022 (800-780-7234)
Dogs of all sizes are allowed. There is a $10 one time per pet fee per visit. Smoking and non-smoking rooms are available for pets.
Brittania and WE Mauger Estate 701 Roma Ave NW Albuquerque NM   505-242-8755 (800-719-9189)
http://www.bbonline.com/nm/mauger/
This bed and breakfast has one pet room. This room has a doggie door which leads to an enclosed lawn area for your dog. There is a $30 one time additional pet fee.
Candlewood Suites 3025 Menaul Blvd Albuquerque NM   505-888-3424 (877-270-6405)
Dogs of all sizes are allowed. There is a $75 one time pet fee for 1-13 nights and $150 for over 13 nights. Pet must be kept in kennel when left alone. Smoking and non-smoking rooms are available for pets.
Casita Chamisa 850 Chamisal Road NW Albuquerque NM   505-897-4644
This unique bed and breakfast features an inviting Southwestern decor. Other amenities include an indoor heated swimming pool, a country style continental breakfast, and flower gardens and orchards to stroll through. There are also paths that lead to and along the river. Dogs of all sizes are allowed for no additional fee. Dogs may not be left alone in the room, and they must be leashed and cleaned up after at all times.

Comfort Inn Airport 2300 Yale Blvd SE Albuquerque NM 505-243-2244 (877-424-6423)
Dogs of all sizes are allowed. There is a $10 per night per pet additional fee. Dogs must be quiet, well behaved, leashed, cleaned up after, and the Do Not Disturb sign put on the door if they are in the room alone.
Comfort Inn and Suites North 5811 Signal Avenue NE Albuquerque NM 505-822-1090 (877-424-6423)
Dogs of all sizes are allowed. There is a $15 per night per room additional fee. Dogs may only be left alone in the room for a short time, and they must be crated and a contact number left with the front desk. Dogs must be leashed and cleaned up after.
Days Inn Albuquerque East 13317 Central Ave NE Albuquerque NM 505-294-3297 (800-329-7466)
Dogs of all sizes are allowed. There is a $5 per night pet fee per pet. Reservations are recommended due to limited rooms for pets.
Days Inn Albuquerque Northeast 10321 Hotel Ave NE Albuquerque NM 505-275-3297 (800-329-7466)
Dogs of all sizes are allowed. There is a $5 per night pet fee per pet.
Days Inn Albuquerque West 6031 Liff Rd NW Albuquerque NM 505-836-3297 (800-329-7466)
Dogs of all sizes are allowed. There is a $5 per night pet fee per pet under 40 pounds and $10 per pet over 40 pounds.
Econo Lodge 13211 Central Ave NE Albuquerque NM 505-292-7600
There is a $10 per day pet fee.
Hampton Inn 5101 Ellison NE Albuquerque NM 505-344-1555
Dogs of all sizes are allowed. There are no additional pet fees.
Holiday Inn Express 6100 Iliff Rd Albuquerque NM 505-836-8600 (877-270-6405)
There is a $25 one time additional pet fee. A well-behaved and quiet large dog is okay.
Holiday Inn Express 10330 Hotel Ave NE Albuquerque NM 505-275-8900 (877-270-6405)
There is a $5 per day additional pet fee.
Howard Johnson Express Inn 7630 Pan American Freeway NE Albuquerque NM 505-828-1600 (800-446-4656)
Dogs of all sizes are welcome. There is a $5 per day pet fee.
Howard Johnson Hotel 15 Hotel Circle NE Albuquerque NM 505-296-4852 (800-446-4656)
Dogs of all sizes are welcome. There is a $20 one time pet fee.
La Quinta Inn & Suites Albuquerque-Midtown 2011 Menaul Blvd NE Albuquerque NM 505-761-5600 (800-531-5900)
Dogs of all sizes are allowed. There are no additional pet fees. Dogs may only be left alone in the room if they will be quiet and well behaved, and if behavior is questionable, they must be crated. Dogs must be leashed, cleaned up after, and they are not allowed in the back patio area.
La Quinta Inn Albuquerque Airport 2116 Yale Blvd. S.E. Albuquerque NM 505-243-5500 (800-531-5900)
Dogs of all sizes are allowed. There are no additional pet fees. Dogs must be leashed and cleaned up after.
La Quinta Inn Albuquerque I-40 East 2424 San Mateo Blvd. N.E. Albuquerque NM 505-884-3591 (800-531-5900)
Dogs of all sizes are allowed. There are no additional pet fees. Dogs must be quiet, well behaved, leashed, and cleaned up after.
La Quinta Inn Albuquerque North 5241 San Antonio Dr. N.E. Albuquerque NM 505-821-9000 (800-531-5900)
Dogs of all sizes are allowed. There are no additional pet fees. Dogs must be quiet, well behaved, leashed and cleaned up after. A contact number must be left with the front desk is there is a pet alone in the room, and arrangements need to be made with housekeeping if staying more than one day.
La Quinta Inn Albuquerque Northwest 7439 Pan American Freeway N.E. Albuquerque NM 505-345-7500 (800-531-5900)
Dogs of all sizes are allowed. There are no additional pet fees. There is a pet waiver to sign at check in. Dogs must be crated if left alone in the room, and they must be leashed and cleaned up after.
Motel 6 - Albuquerque - Carlisle 3400 Prospect Avenue Northeast Albuquerque NM 505-883-8813 (800-466-8356)
One well-behaved family pet per room. Guest must notify front desk upon arrival. Guest is liable for any damages. In consideration of all guests, pets must never be left unattended in the guest rooms.
Motel 6 - Albuquerque - Midtown 1701 University Boulevard Northeast Albuquerque NM 505-843-9228 (800-466-8356)
One well-behaved family pet per room. Guest must notify front desk upon arrival. Guest is liable for any damages. In consideration of all guests, pets must never be left unattended in the guest rooms.
Motel 6 - Albuquerque East 13141 Central Avenue Northeast Albuquerque NM 505-294-4600 (800-466-8356)
One well-behaved family pet per room. Guest must notify front desk upon arrival. Guest is liable for any damages. In consideration of all guests, pets must never be left unattended in the guest rooms.
Motel 6 - Albuquerque South - Airport 1000 Avenida Cesar Chavez Southeast Albuquerque NM 505-243-8017 (800-466-8356)
One well-behaved family pet per room. Guest must notify front desk upon arrival. Guest is liable for any damages. In consideration of all guests, pets must never be left unattended in the guest rooms.
Motel 6 - Albuquerque West - Coors Road 5701 Iliff Road Northwest Albuquerque NM 505-831-8888 (800-

466-8356)
One well-behaved family pet per room. Guest must notify front desk upon arrival. Guest is liable for any damages. In consideration of all guests, pets must never be left unattended in the guest rooms.
Plaza Inn 900 Medical Arts Ave NE Albuquerque NM 505-243-5693 (800-237-1307)
There is a $25 one time pet fee.
Quality Inn and Suites 411 McKnight Avenue NW Albuquerque NM 505-242-5228 (877-424-6423)
Dogs of all sizes are allowed. There is a $10 one time additional fee per pet. Dogs must be leashed, cleaned up after, and the Do Not Disturb sign put on the door.
Quality Suites 5251 San Antonio Blvd NE Albuquerque NM 505-797-0850
Dogs of all sizes are allowed. There are no additional pet fees. Dogs may not be left alone in the room, and they must be leashed and cleaned up after.
Radisson Hotel Conference Center Albuquerque 2500 Carlisle Blvd Northeast Albuquerque NM 505-888-3311
Dogs of all sizes are allowed. There is a $25 one time pet fee.
Red Roof Inn - Albuquerque - Coors Road 6015 Iliff Road Northwest Albuquerque NM 505-831-3400 (800-RED-ROOF)
One well-behaved family pet per room. Guest must notify front desk upon arrival. Guest is liable for any damages. In consideration of all guests, pets must never be left unattended in the guest rooms.
Red Roof Inn - Albuquerque Midtown 1635 Candelaria Boulevard Northeast Albuquerque NM 505-344-5311 (800-RED-ROOF)
One well-behaved family pet per room. Guest must notify front desk upon arrival. Guest is liable for any damages. In consideration of all guests, pets must never be left unattended in the guest rooms.
Residence Inn by Marriott 3300 Prospect Avenue NE Albuquerque NM 505-881-2661
Dogs of all sizes are allowed. There is a $75 one time fee and a pet policy to sign at check in.
Sheraton Albuquerque 2600 Louisiana Blvd. NE Albuquerque NM 505-881-0000 (888-625-5144)
Dogs up to 50 pounds are allowed. There are no additional pet fees. Dogs are not allowed to be left alone in the room.
Studio 6 - ALBUQUERQUE NORTH 4441 Osuna Road NE Albuquerque NM 505-344-7744 (800-466-8356)
One well-behaved family pet per room. Guest must notify front desk upon arrival. Guest is liable for any damages. In consideration of all guests, pets must never be left unattended in the guest rooms.
Super 8 Albuquerque/East 450 Paisano St NE Albuquerque NM 505-271-4807 (800-800-8000)
Dogs of all sizes are allowed. There is a $5 per night pet fee per pet. Smoking and non-smoking rooms are available for pet rooms.
Super 8 Albuquerque/Midtown 2500 University Blvd NE Albuquerque NM 505-888-4884 (800-800-8000)
Dogs of all sizes are allowed. There is a $5 per night pet fee per pet. Smoking and non-smoking rooms are available for pet rooms.
Super 8 Albuquerque/West 6030 Iliff NW Albuquerque NM 505-836-5560 (800-800-8000)
Dogs of all sizes are allowed. There is a $5 per night pet fee per pet. Smoking and non-smoking rooms are available for pet rooms.
TownePlace Suites Albuquerque Airport 2400 Centre Avenue SE Albuquerque NM 505-232-5800
Dogs of all sizes are allowed. There is a $75 one time pet fee per visit.
Travelodge 13139 Central Ave NE Albuquerque NM 505-292-4878
There is a $5.00 per day pet fee.
Days Inn Albuquerque Bernalillo 107 N Camino Del Pueblo Ave Bernalillo NM 505-771-7000 (800-329-7466)
Dogs of all sizes are allowed. There is a $30 returnable deposit required per room.
Super 8 Bernalillo 265 Hwy 44 E Bernalillo NM 505-867-0766 (800-800-8000)
Dogs of all sizes are allowed. There is a $10 returnable deposit required per room. Smoking and non-smoking rooms are available for pet rooms.
Days Inn Albuquerque/Rio Rancho 4200 Crestview Dr Rio Rancho NM 505-892-8800 (800-329-7466)
Dogs of all sizes are allowed. There is a $10 one time per pet fee per visit.

Campgrounds and RV Parks

Albuquerque Central KOA 12400 Skyline Road NE Albuquerque NM 505-296-2729 (800-562-7781)
http://www.koa.com
Dogs of all sizes are allowed. There are no additional pet fees. Dogs may not be left unattended outside, and they must be well behaved, leashed, and cleaned up after. There are some breed restrictions. The camping and tent areas also allow dogs. There is a dog walk area at the campground. Dogs are allowed in the camping cabins.
Enchanted Trails 14305 Central Albuquerque NM 505-831-6317
http://www.enchantedtrails.com
Dogs of all sizes are allowed. There are no additional pet fees. Dogs may not be left unattended outside, and they must be leashed and cleaned up after. There is a dog walk area at the campground.
High Desert RV Park 13000 W Frontage Road SW Albuquerque NM 866-839-9035

http://www.highdesertrvpark.com
Dogs of all sizes are allowed. There are no additional pet fees. Dogs may not be penned or left unattended outside, and they must be leashed and cleaned up after. There is a dog walk area at the campground.
Albuquerque N/Bernalillo KOA 555 S Hill Road Bernalillo NM 505-867-5227 (800-562-3616)
http://www.koa.com
Dogs of all sizes are allowed. There are no additional pet fees. Dogs may not be left unattended, and they must be quiet, leashed, and cleaned up after. Dogs may not be on the grass, in the store, the bathrooms, or the cafe. There is a fenced area for off lead. The camping and tent areas also allow dogs. There is a dog walk area at the campground. Dogs are allowed in the camping cabins.
Coronado State Park 106 Monument Road Bernalillo NM 505-980-8256
Named after the conquistador they believed passed through here looking for the 7 golden cities of Cibola, this 210 acre park is also home to the pueblo ruins of Kuana. The reconstructed kiva, visitor center, and interpretive trail tells the story of the ancient agriculturists who once thrived along these banks of the Rio Grande River. Dogs of all sizes are allowed for no additional fee. Dogs must be leashed and cleaned up after. The camp area offers great views of the Sandia mountains and the Rio Grande Valley, sheltered picnic areas, and restrooms. The camping and tent areas also allow dogs. There is a dog walk area at the campground.

Attractions

Albuquerque Museum's Historic Old Town Walking Tours 2000 Mountain Road NW Albuquerque NM 505-243-7255
http://www.cabq.gov/museum
This museum offers guided walking tours of historic Old Town Tuesday through Sunday at 11 am, from mid-March through mid-December. There are also self-guided tour brochures available at the museum's admission booth. Dogs are not allowed to go inside the museum, but they are allowed on the guided tours after the 15 minute orientation at the museum.
TOP 200 PLACE New Mexico Ghost Tours 303 Romero Street NW Albuquerque NM 505-249-7827
http://www.nmghosttours.com/
The Ghost walk of Old Town Albuquerque is an outdoor walking tour that takes visitors to reputed haunted sites and the sites that is under investigation by the Southwest Ghost Hunter's Association. The tours last about an hour and a half are available year round, and knowledgeable guides, historical accuracy, and their stellar reputation has made a name for this tour. Your well-behaved dog is welcome to join you on this outdoor tour, and there is no additional fee. Dogs must be under owner's control at all times, be leashed, and please carry supplies to clean up after your pet.
Petroglyph National Monument 6001 Unser Boulevard NW Albuquerque NM 505-899-0205
http://www.nps.gov/petr/
More than 20,000 prehistoric and historic Native American and Hispanic petroglyphs (images carved in rock) stretch 17-miles along Albuquerque's West Mesa. Your leashed dog is welcome to accompany you on a dirt trail that is about 1.5 miles long and passes about 800 petroglyphs. There is no shade or water along this trail which can get very hot during the summer months. The trail starts at Unser Blvd and St. Joseph. Dogs are not allowed on the Boca Negra trail or other developed areas of the park.
Anasazi Fields 26 Camino de los Pueblitos Placitas NM 505-867-3062
http://www.anasazifieldswinery.com
Dogs on leash are allowed at the outdoor tables. Open Wednesday thru Sunday.
TOP 200 PLACE Sandia Man Cave Cibola National Forest Placitas NM 505-281-3304
Explore a cave with your dog. From the Highway 165 exit, go towards Placitas. The paved road ends and becomes an unimproved mountain road as you enter Cibola National Forest. The road is fairly rough and muddy and becomes frozen as you reach the 7-8000 foot elevation. The parking area is unmarked but it is the only one around. After paying a $3 parking fee walk north out of the parking lot and take a 10 minute hike up a wide and fairly easy, flat trail. Take a flashlight with you because not much of cave will be visible in daylight. Dogs on leash may go with you to the caves.

Stores

Book Works 4022 Rio Grande NW Albuquerque NM 505-344-8139
http://www.brwrks.com
Dogs on leash are allowed in this bookstore. Open Monday-Saturday 8am-9pm and Sunday 8am-7:30pm.
PetSmart Pet Store 10248 Coors Bypass NW Albuquerque NM 505-792-1772
Your licensed and well-behaved leashed dog is allowed in the store.
PetSmart Pet Store 350 Eubank Blvd NE Albuquerque NM 505-298-4122
Your licensed and well-behaved leashed dog is allowed in the store.
PetSmart Pet Store 1424 Mercantile Ave NE Albuquerque NM 505-341-2431
Your licensed and well-behaved leashed dog is allowed in the store.
Petco Pet Store 6300 San Mateo Blvd Albuquerque NM 505-797-1910
Your licensed and well-behaved leashed dog is allowed in the store.

Petco Pet Store 10700 Lomas NE Albuquerque NM 505-296-0978
Your licensed and well-behaved leashed dog is allowed in the store.
Three Dog Bakery 9821 Montgomery NE Ste.C Albuquerque NM 505-294-2300
http://www.threedog.com
Three Dog Bakery provides cookies and snacks for your dog as well as some boutique items. You well-behaved, leashed dog is welcome.

Parks

Petroglyph National Monument 6001 Unser Blvd NW Albuquerque NM 505-899-0205
http://www.nps.gov/petr/
This historical park is open daily from 8 am to 5 pm, and is home to an impressive display of petroglyphs. Dogs of all sizes are allowed at no additional fee. Dogs may not be left unattended, and they must be leashed and cleaned up after. Dogs are not allowed in buildings or in the Boca Negra Canyon. Dogs are allowed on the trails unless otherwise marked.
Rio Grande Nature Center State Park 2901 Candelaria Road NW Albuquerque NM 505-344-7240
This park offers a trail system allowing for wildlife viewing and nature study, hands-on activities at their Nature Center, and a glass walled library complete with the sounds of the outside wildlife. Dogs of all sizes are allowed at no additional fee. Dogs may not be left unattended, and they must be leashed and cleaned up after. Dogs are not allowed in the buildings or on the Nature Trail. Dogs are allowed on the bike trail. The gates open daily at 8 am; the nature center at 10 am, and they close at 5 pm.
Coronado State Park 106 Monument Road Bernalillo NM 505-980-8256
Named after the conquistador they believed passed through here looking for the 7 golden cities of Cibola, this 210 acre park is also home to the pueblo ruins of Kuana. The reconstructed kiva, visitor center, and interpretive trail tells the story of the ancient agriculturists who once thrived along these banks of the Rio Grande River. Dogs of all sizes are allowed for no additional fee. Dogs must be leashed and cleaned up after.

Off-Leash Dog Parks

Coronado Dog Park 301 McKnight Ave. NW Albuquerque NM 505-768-1975
http://www.cabq.gov/pets/dogpark.html
This fenced dog park is open from 6 am to 10 pm daily. It is located in Coronado Park. Please bring your own water for your dog as there is none at the park. From I-40 take Exit 159A (4th/2nd Street), head east on the frontage road and turn right onto 3rd Street to the park.
Los Altos Dog Park 821 Eubank Blvd. NE Albuquerque NM 505-768-1975
http://www.cabq.gov/pets/dogpark.html
This fenced off-leash dog park is open from 6 am to 10 pm daily. The dog park is located in Los Altos Park. Please bring your own water for your dog as none is available at the park. From I-40 take Eubank Blvd (Exit 165). Head north on Eubank 1/4 mile and the park is on the left.
Montessa Park Off-Leash Area 3615 Los Picaros Rd SE Albuquerque NM 505-768-1975
http://www.cabq.gov/pets/dogpark.html
This unfenced off-leash area is located in Montessa Park. There is minimal shade here and you need to bring water for your dog as none is provided. From I-25 take the Rio Bravo Exit and go west. Turn left on Broadway, left on Bobby Foster and left on Los Picasos to the off-leash area.
Rio Grande Park Dog Park Iron Avenue Albuquerque NM 505-873-6620
http://www.cabq.gov/gis/park.htm
Rio Grande Park offers a designated off-leash area for dogs. The dog park is located on Iron Avenue, between Alcalde Place and 14th Street.
Roosevelt Park Dog Park Hazeldine Avenue Albuquerque NM 505-873-6620
http://www.cabq.gov/gis/park.htm
Roosevelt Park offers a designated off-leash area for dogs. The park is located off Hazeldine Avenue, between Cedar and Maple Streets.
Santa Fe Village Dog Park 5700 Bogart St. NW Albuquerque NM 505-768-1975
http://www.cabq.gov/pets/dogpark.html
This fenced dog park is open from 6 am to 10 pm daily. Please bring water for your dog as none is available at the dog park. To get to the dog park from I-40 take the Unser exit (Exit 154) and go north on Unser. Turn left on Bogart to the park.
Tom Bolack Urban Forest Dog Park Haines Avenue Albuquerque NM 505-873-6620
http://www.cabq.gov/gis/park.htm
Tom Bolack Park offers a designated off-leash area for dogs. The park is located near Haines Avenue and San Pedro Drive.
USS Bullhead Dog Park 1606 San Pedro SE Albuquerque NM 505-768-1975
http://www.cabq.gov/pets/dogpark.html
This Fenced off-leash dog park is located in USS Bullhead Park. Take I-25 to Gibson Blvd, head east on Gibson to San Pedro Blvd, and turn right to the park. There is no drinking water available at the park for dogs so please

bring your own.
Rainbow Dog Park Southern Blvd at Atlantic Rio Rancho NM
This fenced dog park is located in Rainbow Park. It has water for dogs and people and has limited shade. It can get extremely hot here in the summer. There is a separate small dog area. Rainbow Park is located on the far west side of Rio Rancho north of the Petroglyph National Monument west of Albuquerque.

Outdoor Restaurants
Barelas Coffee House 1502 Fourth St SW Albuquerque NM   505-843-7577
This restaurant serves Mexican food. Dogs are allowed at the outdoor tables.
El Norteno 6416 Zuni Rd SE Albuquerque NM 505-256-1431
This restaurant serves Mexican food. Dogs are allowed at the outdoor tables.
El Patio Restaurant 142 Harvard Drive SE Albuquerque NM 505-268-4245
This restaurant serves Mexican food. Dogs are allowed at the outdoor tables.
Flying Star Cafe 3416 Central AVe SE Albuquerque NM 505-255-6633
http://www.flyingstarcafe.com
This restaurant serves a variety of cuisine. Dogs are allowed at the outdoor tables.
Kelly's Brewery 3222 Central Ave SE Albuquerque NM 505-262-2739
This restaurant and bar serves American food. Dogs are allowed at the outdoor tables. Water and dog food are provided for your pet.
Sonic Drive-In 531 Bridge Blvd SW Albuquerque NM 505-243-7880
This restaurant serves American fast food. Dogs are allowed at the outdoor tables.
Sonic Drive-In 220 Alameda Blvd NW Albuquerque NM 505-897-7538
This restaurant serves American fast food. Dogs are allowed at the outdoor tables.
Whole Foods Market 5815 Wyoming Blvd NE Albuquerque NM 505-856-0474
This restaurant serves deli-type food. Dogs are allowed at the outdoor tables.

Events
Doggie Dash and Dawdle 1801 4th St NW # A Albuquerque NM 505-255-5523, ext. 105
http://www.ahanm.org/
This pledge walk is sponsored by the Animal Humane Association of New Mexico to benefit the homeless animals in the city. It begins in the main area of Balloon Fiesta Park and is an annual Fall event for the whole family. There are various walk and runs with a variety of prizes, and hundreds of dogs and thousands of people take part. People who come without a dog can rent one for the event. There are doggy demonstrations, pet product vendors, entertainment, breed and animal rescue groups, and more. Dogs must be well behaved, be on no more than a 6 foot leash, and be cleaned up after. Extendable leashes are not allowed, and dogs need to be current on all vaccinations.

Day Kennels
PetsHotel by PetsMart Day Kennel 1429 Mercantile Drive Albuquerque NM 505-341-2440
http://www.petsmart.com/PETsHOTEL/
This PetSmart pet store offers day care, day camp and overnight care. You can drop off and pick up you dogs during the hours of 7 am - 9 pm M-S, Sunday 7 am - 7 pm. Dogs must have proof of current rabies, DPP and bordatella vaccinations.

Angel Fire

Accommodations
Angel Fire Resort 10 Miller Lane Angel Fire NM 505-377-6401 (800-633-7463)
This resort offers spacious rooms, an indoor pool, and a variety of other amenities. Dogs are welcome to stay in the hotel section of the resort, but not in the condominiums. There is a $25 one time additional fee per pet. Dogs must be well behaved, leashed and cleaned up after at all times. With a summit of 10,677 feet (base-8,600 feet), this is an active full service ski area during their winter season, but there are a variety of recreational activities to do in the summer as well with plenty of great hiking trails. Dogs are allowed to hike the trails, with the exception of the ski trails during the winter season.

Aztec

Campgrounds and RV Parks

Ruins Road RV Park 312 Ruins Road Aztec NM 505-334-3160
http://www.ruinsroadrvpark.com/
Dogs of all sizes are allowed. There are no additional pet fees. Dogs may not be left unattended outside, and they must be leashed and cleaned up after. The camping and tent areas also allow dogs. There is a dog walk area at the campground.

Attractions

TOP 200 PLACE **Aztec Museum and Pioneer Village** 125 N Main Avenue Aztec NM 505-334-9829
Three replicated buildings and 10 original buildings depict life as it was in the 1880's, and include a log cabin, a general store, post office, sheriff's office, church, bank, school, and a doctor's office. The museum displays authentic pioneer/native American artifacts. Dogs are welcome, but they must be cat and critter friendly as there are other pets in residence. They can walk through the village and surrounding area, but they are not allowed in the museum. Dogs must be well behaved, and leashed and cleaned up after at all times.

Parks

Aztec Ruins National Monument 84 County Road 2900 Aztec NM 505-334-6174
http://www.nps.gov/azru/index.htm
Dogs on leash are allowed in picnic areas and parking lot areas. Dogs are not allowed on trails.

Belen

Attractions

The Harvey House Museum 104 North First Street Belen NM 505-861-0581
The Harvey House in Belen is one of 84 houses created by Fred Harvey. These houses/restaurants were located next to the railroad and they had a renown reputation for serving fine food in an elegant manner. Eastern U.S. women were recruited to work in these eating establishments throughout the Southwest U.S. The superb food preparation and excellent dining service sustained The Harvey House through the Great Depression of the 1930s. Your well-behaved leashed dog is welcome inside this museum. The museum is adjacent to a miniature railroad museum where your dog is also welcome. The museum is located in the city of Belen, which is about an hour south of Albuquerque. It is a nice stop on the way to the dog-friendly Very Large Array (VLA) Radio Telescopes in Socorro. Admission is free, but donations are welcome.

Caballo

Campgrounds and RV Parks

Caballo Lake State Park Box 32; On Hwy 187 Caballo NM 505-743-3942 (888-NMPARKS (677-2757))
Main attractions here are the migration of Bald and Golden Eagles and 2 cactus gardens, in addition to a variety of land and water recreation. Dogs of all sizes are allowed at no additional fee. Dogs must be leashed and cleaned up after, and they are allowed on the trails. The camping and tent areas also allow dogs. There is a dog walk area at the campground.
Percha Dam State Park Box 32; on Hwy 187 Caballo NM 505-743-3942 (888-NMPARKS (677-2757))
This 80 acre park along the Rio Grande offers fishing and hiking, nature study, and a variety of land and water recreation. Dogs of all sizes are allowed at no additional fee. Dogs may not be left unattended, and they must be leashed and cleaned up after. Dogs are allowed on the trails. The camping and tent areas also allow dogs. There is a dog walk area at the campground.

Capulin

Parks

Capulin Volcano National Monument Po Box 40 Capulin NM 505-278-2201
http://www.nps.gov/cavo/index.htm
Dogs on leash are allowed only on paved areas of the park and roads. Dogs are not allowed on unpaved park trails.

New Mexico - Please always call ahead to make sure that an establishment is still dog-friendly

Carlsbad

Accommodations
Days Inn Carlsbad 3910 National Parks Hwy Carlsbad NM 505-887-7800 (800-329-7466)
Dogs of all sizes are allowed. There is a $10 per night pet fee per pet.
Holiday Inn 601 S. Canal Carlsbad NM 505-885-8500 (877-270-6405)
There is a $25 one time pet fee.
Motel 6 - Carlsbad 3824 National Parks Highway Carlsbad NM 505-885-0011 (800-466-8356)
One well-behaved family pet per room. Guest must notify front desk upon arrival. Guest is liable for any damages. In consideration of all guests, pets must never be left unattended in the guest rooms.
Super 8 Carlsbad 3817 National Parks Hwy Carlsbad NM 505-887-8888 (800-800-8000)
Dogs of all sizes are allowed. There is a $10 per night pet fee per pet. Smoking and non-smoking rooms are available for pet rooms.

Campgrounds and RV Parks
Brantley Lake State Park Capitan Reef Road Carlsbad NM 505-457-2384 (888-NMPARKS (677-2757))
With 3000 land acres and 4000 lake acres, this park offers a variety of recreational pursuits and planned activities throughout the year. Dogs of all sizes are allowed at no additional fee. Dogs must be leashed and cleaned up after in the camp areas. Dogs may be off lead in the primitive areas if they are under voice control. The camping and tent areas also allow dogs. There is a dog walk area at the campground.
Windmill RV Park 3624 National Parks Hwy (Hwy 62/180N) Carlsbad NM 505-887-1387 (888-349-7275)
http://www.windmillrvpark.com/
Dogs of all sizes are allowed. There are no additional pet fees. Dogs may not be left unattended outside, and they must be leashed and cleaned up after. This is an RV only park. There is a dog walk area at the campground.

Parks
Carlsbad Canyon National Park 727 Carlsbad Canyon Hwy 62/180 Carlsbad NM 505-785-2232
http://www.nps.gov/cave/
This national park was established to preserve the Carlsbad Caverns, and over 100 other caves housed within a fossil reef. It is also home to America's deepest and 4th longest limestone cave. Dogs are not allowed at the park, except in the parking lot and at the kennel that is on site, and they must be on leash and cleaned up after.

Carrizozo

Campgrounds and RV Parks
Valley of Fires Recreation Area P. O. Box 871 Carrizozo NM 505-648-2241
This park sits along side what is considered the youngest lava flow in the continental US (125 square miles), and although it may appear desolate from a distance, an amazing amount of plant, animal, and bird life typical of the Chihuahuan desert flourish here. An interpretive trail starts at the group shelter and leads visitors through the lava flow on a paved walkway. Dogs are allowed in the park and on the trails, but they caution to stay on paved trails. There is no additional pet fee. Dogs must be under owner's control at all times, and be leashed and cleaned up after. There are 19 campsites at the recreation area with picnic shelters, tables, grills, and potable water at each site. There is a full facility bathroom and showers in the camp area, and vault toilets throughout the park. The camping and tent areas also allow dogs. There is a dog walk area at the campground. There are no electric or water hookups at the campgrounds.

Parks
TOP 200 PLACE Valley of Fires Recreation Area U.S. 380 Carrizozo NM 505-648-2241
Valley of Fires is adjacent to the spectacular Malpais Lava Flow. It was created about 1500 years ago when Little Black Peak erupted. The lava flowed into the Tularosa Basin, filling the valley with molten rock. The lava flow is now rock that is 4-6 miles wide by 44 miles long and 160 feet deep. This lava flow is the youngest formation of this type in the continental U.S. Dogs on leash are allowed on the self-guided paved 3/4 mile each way Malpais Nature Trail. From the trail you can view the lava rock, and native plants and animals. Valley of Fires is located on U.S. Highway 380, four miles west of Carrizozo, NM. There is a minimal fee for parking.
Valley of Fires Recreation Area P. O. Box 871 Carrizozo NM 505-648-2241

This park sits along side what is considered the youngest lava flow in the continental US (125 square miles), and although it may appear desolate from a distance, an amazing amount of plant, animal, and bird life typical of the Chihuahuan desert flourish here. An interpretive trail starts at the group shelter and leads visitors through the lava flow on a paved walkway. Dogs are allowed in the park and on the trails, but they caution to stay on paved trails. There is no additional pet fee. Dogs must be under owners control at all times, and be leashed and cleaned up after.

Cedar Crest

Campgrounds and RV Parks
Turquoise Trail Campground 22 Calvary Road Cedar Crest NM 505-281-2005
Dogs of all sizes are allowed. There are no additional pet fees. Dogs must be leashed and cleaned up after. There is also an archeological museum on site. The camping and tent areas also allow dogs. There is a dog walk area at the campground.
Turquoise Trail Campground and RV Park 22 Calvary Road Cedar Crest NM 505-281-2005
This camp area features cool mountain camping with wooded sites, an archeological museum, a playground, laundry, restrooms, and hiking access to the National Forest. The camping and tent areas also allow dogs. There is a dog walk area at the campground.

Cerrillos

Accommodations
High Feather Ranch 29 High Feather Ranch Road Cerrillos NM 505-424-1333 (800-757-4410)
This award-winning, 65 acre B&B offers plenty of privacy, and luxury guest rooms amid the rustic backdrop of incredible views of thousands of acres of high mountain desert. Just off the Turquoise Trail National Scenic Byway, there are also miles of hiking and wildflower trails on the ranch, and they also host Astronomy Adventure Star parties. Some of the amenities include a bountiful gourmet breakfast, private patios, in-room fireplaces, whirlpool baths, and more. Dogs of all sizes are welcome. There is a $20 per night per pet additional fee. Dogs may only be left alone in the room for short periods if they are crated, and they must be well behaved, quiet, leashed, and cleaned up after. Dogs are not allowed on the beds or the food areas.

Attractions
TOP 200 PLACE Old Coal Mine Museum 2846 Hwy 14 Cerrillos NM 505-438-3780
Open daily, weather permitting; this museum features antique cars and trucks, an antique steam locomotive, old mining/carpentry/medical equipment, movie projectors, a mineshaft, an old working blacksmith shop, and live theater. Dogs of all sizes are allowed throughout the park. Dogs must be friendly, well behaved, and leashed and cleaned up after at all times.

Chama

Campgrounds and RV Parks
Little Creek Resort 2631 S Hwy 84/64 Chama NM 505-756-2382
http://www.littlecreekresort.com
Dogs of all sizes are allowed. There are no additional pet fees. Dogs may not be left unattended outside, and they must be leashed and cleaned up after. The camping and tent areas also allow dogs. There is a dog walk area at the campground. Dogs are allowed in the camping cabins.
Rio Chama RV Park 182 N Hwy 17 Chama NM 505-756-2303
Dogs of all sizes are allowed. There are no additional pet fees. Dogs must be leashed and cleaned up after. This RV park is closed during the off-season. There is a dog walk area at the campground.

Chimayo

Shopping Centers

TOP 200 PLACE **High Road Market Place** HC 64 Box 12/Santuario Drive Chimayo NM 505-351-1078
This marketplace highlights high quality crafts and fine art created by over 100 local artists, and once a year many open their homes and studios to share their creations and the bounty of traditional fall foods. There are maps available for other sites along the High Road between Taos and Santa Fe at the Visitor's Center in Taos, the Marketplace, and at sites along the self-guided tour. Dogs are allowed to walk the grounds of the marketplace, and some of the stores will also let them come inside. Dogs must be very well behaved, and leashed and cleaned up after at all times.

Chinle

Campgrounds and RV Parks

Canyon de Chelly National Monument Box 588, On Hwy 7 3 miles from Chinle Chinle NM 928-674-5500
http://www.nps.gov/cach
A long and rich cultural and spiritual history echoes with more than 1,500 years of habitation reflected in the numerous pictographs, petroglyphs, and from the ruins of those who once made their homes here. It is still sustaining a living community of the Navajo people, and you must have a guide to enter canyon areas. However, there are 2 paved auto routes totaling 43 miles that stop at numerous spectacular viewpoints above the canyon, and your pet is welcome to get out at these viewpoints. Dogs are not allowed on tours or on the trails. Dogs of all sizes are welcome for no additional fee, and they may not be left unattended at any time. Dogs must be leashed and cleaned up after at all times. The campground facilities include restrooms, picnic tables, water, and a dump station. Water is not available in the winter months. The camping and tent areas also allow dogs. There is a dog walk area at the campground. There are no electric or water hookups at the campgrounds.

Parks

Canyon de Chelly National Monument Box 588, On Hwy 7 3 miles from Chinle Chinle NM 928-674-5500
http://www.nps.gov/cach
A long and rich cultural and spiritual history echoes with more than 1,500 years of habitation reflected in the numerous pictographs, petroglyphs, and from the ruins of those who once made their homes here. It is still sustaining a living community of the Navajo people, and you must have a guide to enter canyon areas. However, there are 2 paved auto routes totaling 43 miles that stop at numerous spectacular viewpoints above the canyon, and your pet is welcome to get out at these viewpoints. Dogs are not allowed on tours or on the trails. Dogs of all sizes are welcome for no additional fee, and they may not be left unattended at any time. Dogs must be leashed and cleaned up after at all times.

Church Rock

Campgrounds and RV Parks

Red Rock State Park P. O. Box 10 Church Rock NM 505-722-3839
Born from pre-historic times, the spectacular red cliffs that border the park on three sides add to the ancient feeling of the area, and the museum at the park offers a glimpse of the past through interpretations of the unique cultures of the Native Americans of the region. The park's elevation is 6600 to 7000 feet, covers 640 acres, and is known as the 'Gateway to Zuni' (one of the 7 cities of Cibola sought by the Spanish). They also hold several festivals and events throughout the year. Dogs of all sizes are allowed for no additional fee. Dogs are allowed on the trails, and they must be leashed and cleaned up after at all times. The park is home to a large campground with picnic areas, restrooms, and showers. The camping and tent areas also allow dogs. There is a dog walk area at the campground.

Parks

Red Rock State Park P. O. Box 10 Church Rock NM 505-722-3839
Born from pre-historic times, the spectacular red cliffs that border the park on three sides add to the ancient feeling of the area, and the museum at the park offers a glimpse of the past through interpretations of the unique cultures of the Native Americans of the region. The park's elevation is 6600 to 7000 feet, covers 640 acres, and is known as the 'Gateway to Zuni' (one of the 7 cities of Cibola sought by the Spanish). They also hold several festivals and events throughout the year. Dogs of all sizes are allowed for no additional fee. Dogs are allowed on the trails, and they must be leashed and cleaned up after at all times.

Clayton

Accommodations

Best Western Kokopelli Lodge 702 S 1st Clayton NM   505-374-2589 (800-780-7234)
Dogs of all sizes are allowed. There is a $5 per night pet fee per pet. Smoking and non-smoking rooms are available for pets.
Super 8 Clayton 1425 Hwy 87 Clayton NM   505-374-8127 (800-800-8000)
Dogs of all sizes are allowed. There is a $7 per night pet fee per pet. Smoking and non-smoking rooms are available for pet rooms.

Campgrounds and RV Parks

Clayton Lake State Park 141 Clayton Lake Road Clayton NM   505-374-8808 (888-677-2757)
This parks' main attraction is more than 500 dinosaur footprints that have been preserved and identified. There is also a variety of land and water recreation at this high mountain desert park. Dogs of all sizes are allowed at no additional fee. Dogs may not be left unattended, and they must be quiet, well behaved, be on no more than a 10 foot leash, and be cleaned up after. Dogs are allowed on the trails. The camping and tent areas also allow dogs. There is a dog walk area at the campground.
Clayton Lake State Park 141 Clayton Road Clayton NM   505-374-8808 (800-NMPARKS (667-2757))
Rolling grasslands, volcanic rocks, and sandstone bluffs all characterize this 471 acre park with a 170 surface acre lake, but the real pull here is the internationally significant dinosaur trackway that contains more than 500 footprints dating back more than 100 million years. Many have been preserved and identified, and a boardwalk trail with extensive signage tells of the ancient visitors here. The park is also home to a variety of plant/bird/animal life, and land and water recreation. Dogs of all sizes are allowed for no additional fee. Dogs must be leashed and cleaned up after at all times. The camp area offers 33 sites, a playground area, restrooms, showers, water, and picnic tables. The camping and tent areas also allow dogs. There is a dog walk area at the campground.

Parks

TOP 200 PLACE **Clayton Lake State Park** 141 Clayton Road Clayton NM   505-374-8808 (800-NMPARKS (667-2757))
Rolling grasslands, volcanic rocks, and sandstone bluffs all characterize this 471 acre park with a 170 surface acre lake, but the real pull here is the internationally significant dinosaur trackway that contains more than 500 footprints dating back more than 100 million years. Many have been preserved and identified, and a boardwalk trail with extensive signage tells of the ancient visitors here. The park is also home to a variety of plant/bird/animal life, and land and water recreation. Dogs of all sizes are allowed for no additional fee. Dogs must be leashed and cleaned up after at all times.

Cloudcroft

Accommodations

The Lodge Resort #1 Corona Place Cloudcroft NM   505-682-2566 (800-395-6343)
http://www.thelodgeresort.com/
Weathered by a cultured and intriguing past, this elegant mountain lodge is surrounded by over 200,000 acres of national forest, and offer plush accommodations, gourmet dining, and luxurious grounds. Amenities/features include a heated pool, sauna, outdoor hot tub, lawn games, a traditional Scottish 9-hole golf course, and a variety of scenic hiking trails. There is one unit set aside in the bed and breakfast section that is separate from the main lodge where dogs are allowed. There is a $25 (plus tax) one time additional pet fee. Dogs are allowed on the trails and around the grounds; they must be leashed and cleaned up after at all times.

Clovis

Accommodations

Howard Johnson Express Inn 2920 Mabry Drive Clovis NM   505-769-1953 (800-446-4656)
Dogs up to 50 pounds are allowed. There is a $10 per day pet fee.

La Quinta Inn & Suites Clovis 4521 N. Prince St. Clovis NM 505-763-8777 (800-531-5900)
Dogs of all sizes are allowed. There are no additional pet fees. Dogs must be leashed and cleaned up after.
Dogs may not be left unattended unless they will be quiet and well behaved, and it is for a short period.

Columbus

Campgrounds and RV Parks
Pancho Villa State Park 400 W Hwy 9 Columbus NM 505-532-2711 (888-NMPARKS (667-2757))
This historical park features an extensive exhibit depicting an armed invasion by Pancho Villa and interpretive
trails that wind through extensive botanical gardens. Dogs of all sizes are allowed at no additional fee. Dogs may
not be left unattended, and they must be on no more than a 10 foot leash, and be cleaned up after. Dogs are not
allowed in the buildings, but they are allowed on the trails. The camping and tent areas also allow dogs. There is
a dog walk area at the campground.
Pancho Villa State Park 400 W Hwy 9 Columbus NM 505-531-2711
This 60 acre park with an elevation of just over 4,000 feet, shares the history of Pancho Villa, and of the armed
invasion he lead against the nation. Extensive historical exhibits/buildings are on the grounds and in the
museum/visitor center-the US Customs House-built in 1902, about the invasion and his pursuit by General
Pershing. There are also a variety of other recreational pursuits, and great hiking opportunities. Dogs of all sizes
are allowed for no additional pet fee. Dogs are allowed on all the trails and throughout the park; they are not
allowed in the museum or park buildings. Dogs must be leashed and cleaned up after at all times. The camp
area offer 62 sites, with picnic shelters, restrooms, showers, a playground, and a dump station. The camping and
tent areas also allow dogs. There is a dog walk area at the campground.

Parks
Pancho Villa State Park 400 W Hwy 9 Columbus NM 505-531-2711
This 60 acre park with an elevation of just over 4,000 feet, shares the history of Pancho Villa, and of the armed
invasion he lead against the nation. Extensive historical exhibits/buildings are on the grounds and in the
museum/visitor center-the US Customs House-built in 1902, about the invasion and his pursuit by General
Pershing. There are also a variety of other recreational pursuits, and great hiking opportunities. Dogs of all sizes
are allowed for no additional pet fee. Dogs are allowed on all the trails and throughout the park; they are not
allowed in the museum or park buildings. Dogs must be leashed and cleaned up after at all times.

Conchas Dam

Campgrounds and RV Parks
Conchas Lake State Park Box 967; On Hwy 104 Conchas Dam NM 505-868-2270 (888-NMPARKS (667-2757))
This park offers ancient sites, one of the largest lakes in New Mexico, and a variety of land and water recreation.
Dogs of all sizes are allowed at no additional fee. Dogs may not be left unattended, they must be quiet, be on no
more than a 10 foot leash and be cleaned up after. The camping and tent areas also allow dogs. There is a dog
walk area at the campground.

Deming

Accommodations
Holiday Inn Exit 85 I-10 Deming NM 505-546-2661 (877-270-6405)
There are no additional pet fees.
La Quinta Inn & Suites Deming 4300 E Pine St Deming NM 505-546-0600 (800-531-5900)
Dogs of all sizes are allowed. There are no additional pet fees. Dogs must be leashed and cleaned up after.
Motel 6 - Deming I-10 & Motel Drive Deming NM 505-546-2623 (800-466-8356)
One well-behaved family pet per room. Guest must notify front desk upon arrival. Guest is liable for any
damages. In consideration of all guests, pets must never be left unattended in the guest rooms.

Campgrounds and RV Parks
Little Vineyard 2901 E Pine Deming NM 505-546-3560

http://www.littlevineyardrvpark.com
Dogs of all sizes are allowed. There are no additional pet fees. Dogs must be leashed and cleaned up after. There is a dog walk area at the campground.
Roadrunner RV Park 2849 E Pine Street Deming NM 505-546-6960
http://www.zianet.com/roadrunnerrv
Dogs of all sizes are allowed. There are no additional pet fees. Dogs must be quiet, leashed, and cleaned up after. There is a dog walk area at the campground.
Rockhound State Park P. O. Box 1064 Deming NM 505-546-6182 (888-NMPARKS (667-2757))
This park is a favorite for rockhounds, and it also has trails varying in difficulty and elevations that offer breathtaking scenery. Dogs of all sizes are allowed at no additional fee. Dogs may not be left unattended, and they must be on no more than a 10 foot leash, and be cleaned up after. Dogs are allowed on the trails. The camping and tent areas also allow dogs. There is a dog walk area at the campground.

Dulce

Accommodations
Best Western Jicarilla Inn and Casino 233 Jicarilla Blvd/US Hwy 64 Dulce NM 505-759-3663 (800-780-7234)
Dogs of all sizes are allowed. There is a $20 returnable deposit required per room. Smoking and non-smoking rooms are available for pets.

Eagle Nest

Campgrounds and RV Parks
Cimmarron Canyon State Park 2959 Hwy 64 Eagle Nest NM 505-377-6271 (888-NMPARKS (677-2757))
This high mountain park of over 33,000 acres is also part of the Colin Neblett Wildlife Area, and offers a variety of nature study and recreation. Dogs of all sizes are allowed at no additional fee. Dogs may not be left unattended, and they must be on no more than a 10 foot leash and be cleaned up after. Dogs are allowed on the trails. The camping and tent areas also allow dogs. There is a dog walk area at the campground.

Parks
Eagle Nest Lake State Park P. O. Box 185 Eagle Nest NM 505-377-1594
This day-use park of 2,485 acres is situated at an altitude of 8,300 feet and is home to a 2,400 acre lake that is surrounded by 2 of the state's tallest peaks. There is an abundance of wildlife, great fishing, and a variety of land and water recreational opportunities. Some of the amenities include boat ramps, restrooms, and picnic areas. Dogs of all sizes are allowed throughout the park and on the trails. Dogs must be under owners control at all times, and they must be leashed and cleaned up after.

Elephant Butte

Campgrounds and RV Parks
Elephant Butte Lake Box 13; Hwy 195/171 Elephant Butte NM 505-744-5421 (888-NMPARKS (667-2757))
Scenic Elephant Butte Lake can be described as educational, recreational and pre-historic. Dogs of all sizes are allowed at no additional fee. Dogs may not be left unattended, and they must be leashed and cleaned up after. Dogs are allowed on the trails. The camping and tent areas also allow dogs. There is a dog walk area at the campground.

Farmington

Accommodations
Comfort Inn 555 Scott Avenue Farmington NM 505-325-2626 (877-424-6423)
Dogs of all sizes are allowed. There is a $10 per night per pet additional fee. Dogs may not be left alone in the

room, and they must be leashed and cleaned up after.

Days Inn Farmington 1901 E Broadway Farmington NM 505-325-3700 (800-329-7466)
Dogs of all sizes are allowed. There is a $50 returnable deposit required per room. There is a $15 per night pet fee per pet.

Holiday Inn 600 E. Broadway Farmington NM 505-327-9811 (877-270-6405)
There is a $25 one time pet fee.

Holiday Inn Express 2110 Bloomfield Blvd Farmington NM 505-325-2545 (877-270-6405)
There is a $20 one time pet fee.

La Quinta Inn Farmington 675 Scott Ave. Farmington NM 505-327-4706 (800-531-5900)
Dogs of all sizes are allowed. There are no additional pet fees. Dogs must be leashed and cleaned up after.

Motel 6 - Farmington 1600 Bloomfield Boulevard Farmington NM 505-326-4501 (800-466-8356)
One well-behaved family pet per room. Guest must notify front desk upon arrival. Guest is liable for any damages. In consideration of all guests, pets must never be left unattended in the guest rooms.

Campgrounds and RV Parks

Downs RV Park 5701 Hwy 64 Farmington NM 505-325-7094
Dogs of all sizes are allowed. There are no additional pet fees. Dogs may not be left unattended outside, and they must be leashed and cleaned up after. The camping and tent areas also allow dogs. There is a dog walk area at the campground.

Attractions

Four Corners Monument Navajo Reservation Farmington NM 928-871-6647
This monument marks the only place where 4 states meet, and it is the traditional homeland to a number of tribes, including Navajo, Apache, Ute, and Hopi nations. They feature some of their traditional foods, and display their crafts here in a typical Navajo Mall; many can be seen doing their craft on site. Picnic tables and restrooms are available, but water is not. Dogs are allowed on site and around the shops, but they must be well behaved, leashed, and cleaned up after at all times.

Stores

Petco Pet Store 3530 East Main St, Ste A Farmington NM 505-326-6376
Your licensed and well-behaved leashed dog is allowed in the store.

Faywood

Campgrounds and RV Parks

City of Rocks State Park Box 50; On Hwy 61 Faywood NM 505-536-2800 (888-NMPARKS (677-2757))
This park is home to some of the most unusual rock formations in the world, and since it is so dark the park has also implemented a Stars-N-Parks program with a Star Observatory. Cactus gardens and scenic hiking trails are also an attraction. Dogs of all sizes are allowed at no additional fee. Dogs may not be left unattended, and they must be leashed and cleaned up after. Dogs are allowed on the trails. The camping and tent areas also allow dogs. There is a dog walk area at the campground.

City of Rocks State Park P. O. Box 50 Faywood NM 505-536-2800
It took the earth millions of years to develop the rock formations that give this park it's name, and there are only 6 other places in the world where they exist. Evidence of ancient cultures now intermingles with the state's first park observatory. Along with a variety of plant/animal/bird life, and recreational opportunities, amenities include a visitor center, picnic sites, Star Parties, interpretive exhibits, and hiking trails. Dogs of all sizes are allowed for no additional fee. Dogs are allowed on all the trails, but not in park buildings. Dogs must be leashed and cleaned up after. The campground offers 52 developed sites and 10 electrical sites. Amenities include restrooms, showers, and picnic tables. The camping and tent areas also allow dogs. There is a dog walk area at the campground.

Parks

City of Rocks State Park P. O. Box 50 Faywood NM 505-536-2800
It took the earth millions of years to develop the rock formations that give this park it's name, and there are only 6 other places in the world where they exist. Evidence of ancient cultures now intermingles with the state's first park observatory. Along with a variety of plant/animal/bird life, and recreational opportunities, amenities include a visitor center, picnic sites, Star Parties, interpretive exhibits, and hiking trails. Dogs of all sizes are allowed for no additional fee. Dogs are allowed on all the trails, but not in park buildings. Dogs must be leashed and cleaned up after.

Fort Sumner

Campgrounds and RV Parks

Sumner Lake State Park HC 64, Box 125 Fort Sumner NM 505-355-2541 (888-NMPARKS (667-2757))
This historical park is popular for water activities and nature study. Dogs of all sizes are allowed at no additional fee. Dogs may not be left unattended, and they must be leashed and cleaned up after. The camping and tent areas also allow dogs. There is a dog walk area at the campground.

Attractions

Fort Sumner State Monument 3647 Billy the Kid Road Fort Sumner NM 505-355-2573
This monument was once a military site that held captive thousands of Native Americans who were forced to leave their homeland, and documents the journey they made and of their eventual return. Living history demonstrations in summer, a visitor center, and an interpretive trail allow visitors to experience the history of this site. The park is also host to a variety of events throughout the year. Dogs are welcome around the grounds and on the trial, but not in park buildings. Dogs must be under owner's control, and leashed and cleaned up after at all times.

Gallup

Accommodations

Best Western Inn and Suites at Gallup 3009 W Highway 66 Gallup NM 505-722-2221 (800-780-7234)
Dogs of all sizes are allowed. There is a $10 per night pet fee per pet. Smoking and non-smoking rooms are available for pets.
Days Inn Gallup East 1603 W Hwy 66 Gallup NM 505-863-3891 (800-329-7466)
Dogs up to 100 pounds are allowed. There is a $10 one time per pet fee per visit.
Days Inn Gallup West 3201 W Hwy 66 Gallup NM 505-863-6889 (800-329-7466)
Dogs of all sizes are allowed. There is a $10 one time per pet fee per visit. Reservations are recommended due to limited rooms for pets.
Motel 6 - Gallup 3306 West US 66 Gallup NM 505-863-4492 (800-466-8356)
One well-behaved family pet per room. Guest must notify front desk upon arrival. Guest is liable for any damages. In consideration of all guests, pets must never be left unattended in the guest rooms.
Red Roof Inn - Gallup 3304 West Highway 66 Gallup NM 505-722-7765 (800-RED-ROOF)
One well-behaved family pet per room. Guest must notify front desk upon arrival. Guest is liable for any damages. In consideration of all guests, pets must never be left unattended in the guest rooms.
Super 8 Gallup 1715 W Hwy 66 Gallup NM 505-722-5300 (800-800-8000)
Dogs of all sizes are allowed. There is a $5 per night pet fee per pet. Smoking and non-smoking rooms are available for pet rooms.

Campgrounds and RV Parks

USA RV Park 2925 W Hwy 66 Gallup NM 505-863-5021
http://www.usarvpark.com
Dogs of all sizes are allowed. There is a pet policy to sign at check in and there are no additional pet fees. County ordinance requires that, by law, dogs be walked to the dog walk area to defecate and/or urinate. Dogs may not be left unattended outside, and they must be quiet, well behaved, be on no more than a 6 foot leash, and be cleaned up after. Dogs must be walked on asphalt only-no other surfaces, and dogs are not allowed to approach other campers or their pets. Dogs are not allowed by the office, cook areas, telephones, playground, restrooms, picnic tables, or the laundries. Adults only may walk the dogs, and dog cages or pens are not allowed. There are some breed restrictions. There is a dog walk area at the campground.

Attractions

Gallup Cultural Center 201 E Hwy 66 Gallup NM 505-863-4131
Located at the Old Train Station, this cultural museum is an indoor museum, but if your dog is well behaved and house trained, they are welcome to join you inside. Dogs must be under owner's control at all times, leashed, and cleaned up after in the outside areas. They are open Monday through Friday from 8:30 to about 3 or 4:00 pm.

Grants

Accommodations
Comfort Inn 1551 E Santa Fe Avenue Grants NM   505-287-8700 (877-424-6423)
Dogs of all sizes are allowed. There is a $10 per night per pet additional fee. Dogs must be quiet, leashed, cleaned up after, and the Do Not Disturb sign put on the door if they are in the room alone.
Days Inn Grant 1504 E Santa Fe Ave Grants NM   505-287-8883 (800-329-7466)
Dogs of all sizes are allowed. There is a $10 per night pet fee per pet.
Holiday Inn Express 1496 E Santa Fe Ave Grants NM   505-285-4676 (877-270-6405)
There are no additional pet fees.
Motel 6 - Grants 1505 East Santa Fe Avenue Grants NM   505-285-4607 (800-466-8356)
One well-behaved family pet per room. Guest must notify front desk upon arrival. Guest is liable for any damages. In consideration of all guests, pets must never be left unattended in the guest rooms.
Super 8 Grants 1604 E Santa Fe Ave Grants NM   505-287-8811 (800-800-8000)
Dogs of all sizes are allowed. There is a $50 returnable deposit required per room. There is a $10 one time per pet fee per visit. Reservations are recommended due to limited rooms for pets. Smoking and non-smoking rooms are available for pet rooms.

Campgrounds and RV Parks
Coal Mine Canyon Campground 1800 Lobo CanyonRoad Grants NM   505-287-8833
Located in the Mt. Taylor District of the Cibola National Forest, this small 17 site campground also has its own short nature trail. Some of the amenities include picnic areas, restrooms, and a large deep communal sink. Dogs of all sizes are allowed for no additional fee. Dogs are allowed on the trails, but because of cactus and desert life, they caution you to keep your dog on the trails. Dogs must be leashed and cleaned up after. This RV park is closed during the off-season. The camping and tent areas also allow dogs. There is a dog walk area at the campground. There are no electric or water hookups at the campgrounds.

Parks
El Malpais National Monument 123 E Roosevelt Avenue Grants NM   505-783-4774
http://www.nps.gov/elma/index.htm
Dogs on leash are allowed on the trails. They prefer you not take pets on lava trails unless they are wearing dog boots as it will hurt their feet. Dogs are not allowed in caves or backcountry for safety reasons. The park features auto touring, hiking, and camping with a permit.

Guadalupita

Campgrounds and RV Parks
Coyote Creek State Park Box 477, MM 17 Hwy 434 Guadalupita NM   505-387-2328 (888-NMPARKS (667-2757))
This scenic park is surround by forests of spruce, pine, and fields of wildflowers, and the creek is considered to be the best stocked in the state. Dogs of all sizes are allowed at no additional fee. Dogs may not be left unattended, and they must be quiet, be on no more than a 10 foot leash, and be cleaned up after. Dogs are allowed on the trails. The camping and tent areas also allow dogs. There is a dog walk area at the campground.
Morphy Lake State Park Box 477; Morphy Lake Road Guadalupita NM   505-387-2328 (888-NMPARKS (677-2757))
This secluded, pack-in/out park with a well stocked lake, is reached by foot or a high clearance vehicle. There is no drinking water available, and it is suggested to check road conditions before going. Dogs of all sizes are allowed at no additional fee. Dogs may not be left unattended, and they must be on no more than a 10 foot leash at all times, and be cleaned up after. Dogs are allowed on the trails. This campground is closed during the off-season. The camping and tent areas also allow dogs. There is a dog walk area at the campground. There are no electric or water hookups at the campground.

Hobbs

Accommodations

Days Inn Hobbs 211 N Marland Hobbs NM 505-397-6541 (800-329-7466)
Dogs of all sizes are allowed. There is a $10 per night pet fee per pet. Reservations are recommended due to limited rooms for pets.

Howard Johnson Inn 501 N Marland Blvd. Hobbs NM 505-397-3251 (800-446-4656)
Dogs up to 50 pounds are allowed. There is a $20 refundable pet deposit.

Holloman AFB

Attractions

White Sands National Monuments PO Box 1086 Holloman AFB NM 505-679-2599
http://www.nps.gov/whsa/index.htm
Dogs must be on leash and must be cleaned up after on site. The site features auto touring and hiking in the White Sands.

Jemez Springs

Accommodations

Laughing Lizard Inn and Cafe 17526 Hwy 4 Jemez Springs NM 505-829-3108
This Inn is uniquely decorated in Southwestern decor, and offers spectacular views of the surrounding mesas. Some of the amenities include hand-painted sleeping rooms with comfortable beds, a sitting area, private baths, and a cafe with outdoor dining so that your canine companion may join you. Dogs of all sizes are allowed for no additional fee. Dogs may not be left alone in the room at any time, and they must be leashed and cleaned up after at all times.

Campgrounds and RV Parks

Fenton Lake State Park 455 Fenton Lake Road Jemez Springs NM 505-829-3630 (888-NMPARKS (667-2757))
This park, surrounded by pine forest with a 35 acre lake, sits at an elevation of 7900 feet, and offers a variety of recreation for all seasons. Dogs of all sizes are allowed at no additional fee. Dogs may not be left unattended, and they must be leashed and cleaned up after. Dogs are allowed on the trails. The camping and tent areas also allow dogs. There is a dog walk area at the campground. There are no water hookups at the campground.

La Mesa

Attractions

Stahmann Pecan Farms 22505 Hwy 28 La Mesa NM 505-526-8974
http://www.stahmanns.com/
As you are driving to the farm along Highway 28, you are greeted by miles of pecan trees. The farm offers a variety of flavored pecans, baked items, and a large gift bag selection. Although only dogs that can be carried are allowed inside the store, all dogs are allowed around the grounds and at the porch seating area. Dogs are not allowed by the food sampling table. Dogs must be under owner's control at all times, and be leashed and cleaned up after.

Las Cruces

Accommodations

Best Western Mesilla Valley Inn 901 Avenida de Mesilla Las Cruces NM 505-524-8603 (800-780-7234)
Dogs of all sizes are allowed. There are no additional pet fees. Smoking and non-smoking rooms are available for pets.

Hampton Inn 755 Avenida de Mesilla Las Cruces NM 505-536-8311
Well behaved dogs of all sizes are allowed. There are no additional pet fees.

Holiday Inn 201 University Ave Las Cruces NM   505-526-4411 (877-270-6405)
There is a $25 one time pet fee.
La Quinta Inn Las Cruces 790 Avenida de Mesilla Las Cruces NM   505-524-0331 (800-531-5900)
Dogs of all sizes are allowed. There are no additional pet fees. Dogs must be leashed and cleaned up after.
Dogs may not be left unattended at any time.
La Quinta Inn Las Cruces Organ Mountain 1500 Hickory Drive Las Cruces NM   505-523-0100 (800-531-5900)
Dogs of all sizes are allowed. There are no additional pet fees. Dogs must have current shot records, not be left alone in the room, and be leashed at all times.
Motel 6 - Las Cruces 235 La Posada Lane Las Cruces NM   505-525-1010 (800-466-8356)
One well-behaved family pet per room. Guest must notify front desk upon arrival. Guest is liable for any damages. In consideration of all guests, pets must never be left unattended in the guest rooms.
Motel 6 - Las Cruces - Telshor 2120 Summit Court Las Cruces NM   505-525-2055 (800-466-8356)
One well-behaved family pet per room. Guest must notify front desk upon arrival. Guest is liable for any damages. In consideration of all guests, pets must never be left unattended in the guest rooms.
Teakwood Inn and Suites 2600 S Valley Drive Las Cruces NM   505-526-4441
This inn features 130 spacious rooms, complimentary breakfasts, and an indoor pool. Dogs of all sizes are allowed for an additional $10 per night per pet. Dogs must be quiet, leashed, and cleaned up after at all times.
The Coachlight Inn and RV Park 301 S Motel Blvd Las Cruces NM   505-526-3301
Dogs of all sizes are allowed. There is an additional $5 per night per pet fee for small dogs, and a $10 per night per pet fee for medium to large dogs. Dogs may not be left unattended outside, and they must be leashed and cleaned up after. There is an RV only park also on site that allows dogs for no additional fee.
TownePlace Suites Las Cruces 2143 Telshor Court Las Cruces NM   505-532-6500
Dogs of all sizes are allowed. There is a $75 one time pet fee per visit.

Campgrounds and RV Parks

Hacienda RV and Rally Resort 740 Stern Drive Las Cruces NM   888-686-9090
http://www.haciendarv.com
Dogs of all sizes are allowed. There are no additional pet fees. Dogs must be leashed and cleaned up after. There is a fenced in area where dogs may be off lead. There is a dog walk area at the campground.
The Coachlight Inn and RV Park 301 S Motel Blvd Las Cruces NM   505-526-3301
http://www.zianet.com/coachlight
Dogs of all sizes are allowed. There are no additional pet fees for the RV sites. There is an additional $5 per night per pet fee for small dogs at the inn, and an additional $10 per night per pet fee for medium to large dogs. There are only 2 dogs allowed per room, and no more than 3 for the RV area. This is an RV only park. There is a dog walk area at the campground.

Attractions

LaVina Winery 4201 South Highway 28 La Union NM   505-882-7632
http://www.lavinawinery.com
Dogs on leash are allowed at the outdoor tables and property. The hours are 12pm-5pm Monday-Sunday. Bring a picnic to enjoy the day at the oldest New Mexico winery.
Blue Teal Tasting Room 1720 Avenida de Mesilla Las Cruces NM   866-336-7360
http://www.blueteal.com
Dogs on leash are allowed at the outdoor tables and on the property. Open 7 days a week. It is located in the Mesilla Valley with a view of the Organ Mountains.

Stores

PetSmart Pet Store 2200 E Lohman Ave Las Cruces NM   505-523-1154
Your licensed and well-behaved leashed dog is allowed in the store.
Petco Pet Store 3050 East Lohman Avenue Las Cruces NM   505-532-5200
Your licensed and well-behaved leashed dog is allowed in the store.

Las Vegas

Accommodations

Plaza Hotel 230 Plaza Las Vegas NM   505-425-3591 (800-328-1882)
http://plazahotel-nm.com/amenities.htm
Although built in 1882, this hotel has been beautifully restored and offers all the 21st century amenities one would expect. It is listed on the National Register of Historic Places, and its elegance and amenities make it a

premiere place for both business and vacation travelers. Amenities include a complimentary hot breakfast each morning, room service, a saloon with entertainment, a guest computer, meeting facilities, and more. Dogs of all sizes are allowed. There is a $10 per night per pet additional fee. Dogs must be crated when left alone in the room and they must be leashed and cleaned up after at all times.

Campgrounds and RV Parks
Storrie Lake State Park HC 33, Box 109 #2 Las Vegas NM 505-425-7278 (888-NMPARKS (667-2757))
This park with 1,100 acres of lake surface, offers a wide variety of water recreation, an interesting history, and plenty of trails. Dogs of all sizes are allowed at no additional fee. Dogs may not be left unattended, and they must be on no more than a 10 foot leash, and be cleaned up after. Dogs are allowed on the trails. This campground is closed during the off-season. The camping and tent areas also allow dogs. There is a dog walk area at the campground.

Lincoln

Attractions
TOP 200 PLACE **Lincoln Historic Town** Highway 380 Lincoln NM
The town of Lincoln was built in the 1800's and today it is a National Historic Landmark. The Lincoln County war took place here, which was a fight between cowboys/ranchers and banker/politicians. Billy the Kid was one of the cowboys who fled during this battle. He was later found and brought back to Lincoln. While waiting for his trial, he escaped from the Lincoln County Courthouse. Today there are over 40 historic buildings throughout the town. You and your pup can go on a self-guided walking tour of Lincoln. Just pick up a map from the Visitor Center located on Hwy 380. There is a minimal fee for the map.

Logan

Campgrounds and RV Parks
Ute Lake State Park 1800 540 Loop Logan NM 505-487-2284 (888-NMPARKS (667-2757))
Nature study, round-the-clock fishing, scenic trails, and a variety of land and water recreation make this a popular park. Dogs of all sizes are allowed at no additional fee. Dogs may not be left unattended, and they must be leashed and cleaned up after. Dogs are allowed on the trails unless otherwise marked. The camping and tent areas also allow dogs. There is a dog walk area at the campground.

Lordsburg

Accommodations
Best Western Western Skies Inn 1303 South Main Lordsburg NM 505-542-8807 (800-780-7234)
Dogs of all sizes are allowed. There is a fee of $7 for every 10 pounds the pet weighs. Smoking and non-smoking rooms are available for pets.
Holiday Inn Express 1408 South Main Lordsburg NM 505-542-3666 (877-270-6405)
Dogs of all sizes are allowed. There is a $10 per day additional pet fee. Smoking and non-smoking rooms are available for pets.

Los Alamos

Parks
Bandelier National Monument 15 Entrance Road Los Alamos NM 505-672-3861
http://www.nps.gov/band/index.htm
Dogs on leash are allowed in camping and picnic areas. Dogs are not allowed on trails.

Los Lunas

Accommodations
Days Inn Los Lunas 1919 Main St SW Los Lunas NM   505-865-5995 (800-329-7466)
Dogs of all sizes are allowed. There is a $10 one time per pet fee per visit.

Los Ojos

Campgrounds and RV Parks
Heron Lake State Park Box 159; MM 6 Hwy 95 Los Ojos NM   505-588-7470 (888-NMPARKS (667-2757))
Ideal for both winter and summer sports at 7200 feet, this scenic park also has a trail that leads to a suspension bridge that crosses the river. Dogs of all sizes are allowed at no additional fee. Dogs may not be left unattended, and they must be leashed and cleaned up after. Dogs are allowed on the trails. The camping and tent areas also allow dogs. There is a dog walk area at the campground.

Madrid

Attractions
TOP 200 PLACE Old Coal Mine Museum 2846 Highway 14 Madrid NM   505-473-0743
The Old Coal Mine Museum is located on 3 acres of what was once the epicenter of the Madrid mining operation. Here you will find a fully restored railroad engine, impressive collection of mining equipment, tools of trade, household goods and a blacksmith's shop, as well as industrial sized machinery. Dogs are welcome at this mostly outdoor museum. There is a minimal entrance fee. The museum is located in the city of Madrid, about an hour south of Santa Fe. If you are driving between Santa Fe and Albuquerque, take Highway 14 and visit this attraction in Madrid.

Maxwell

Campgrounds and RV Parks
Maxwell National Wildlife Refuge P. O. Box 276/Lake Road 13 Maxwell NM   505-375-2331
The park was established as a feeding and resting area for over 200 species of migratory birds. There has been more than 400 acres of agricultural fields planted with food for them. There is also roughly 2200 acres of short-grass prairie, 900 acres of lakes, and 200 acres of woodlands or other lands. Interpretive/environmental programs are available upon request, and there is a variety of land and water recreational opportunities plus primitive camping on the west side of Lake 13. Dogs of all sizes are allowed for no additional fee. Dogs are allowed on the trails unless otherwise marked, and they must be leashed and cleaned up after. The primitive campsite is seasonal and has a 3 day stay limit. Restrooms are located at the entrance road leading into Lake 13. This RV park is closed during the off-season. The camping and tent areas also allow dogs. There is a dog walk area at the campground. There are no electric or water hookups at the campgrounds.

Parks
Maxwell National Wildlife Refuge P. O. Box 276/Lake Road 13 Maxwell NM   505-375-2331
The park was established as a feeding and resting area for over 200 species of migratory birds. There has been more than 400 acres of agricultural fields planted with food for them. There is also roughly 2200 acres of short-grass prairie, 900 acres of lakes, and 200 acres of woodlands or other lands. Interpretive/environmental programs are available upon request, and there is a variety of land and water recreational opportunities plus primitive camping on the west side of Lake 13. Dogs of all sizes are allowed for no additional fee. Dogs are allowed on the trails unless otherwise marked, and they must be leashed and cleaned up after.

Moriarty

Accommodations

Comfort Inn 119 Route 66 E Moriarty NM 505-832-6666 (877-424-6423)
Dogs of all sizes are allowed. There are no additional pet fees. Dogs must be quiet, well behaved, leashed, cleaned up after, and the Do Not Disturb sign put on the door if they are in the room alone.
Days Inn Moriarty 1809 W Route 66 Moriarty NM 505-832-4451 (800-329-7466)
Dogs of all sizes are allowed. There is a $5 per night pet fee per pet.
Super 8 Moriarty 1611 Old Route 66 Moriarty NM 505-832-6730 (800-800-8000)
Dogs of all sizes are allowed. There is a $20 returnable deposit required per room. Reservations are recommended due to limited rooms for pets. Smoking and non-smoking rooms are available for pet rooms.

Mountainair

Campgrounds and RV Parks
Manzano Mountains State Park HC66, Box 202 Mountainair NM 505-847-2820 (888-NMPARKS (667-2757))
This park of 160 acres at 7600 foot altitude has a wide variety of trees and is an important bird fly zone. The park will also provide a field check list for the birds. Dogs of all sizes are allowed at no additional fee. Dogs may not be left unattended, and they must quiet, well behaved, be on no more than a 10 foot leash, and be cleaned up after. Dogs are allowed on the trails. This campground is closed during the off-season. The camping and tent areas also allow dogs. There is a dog walk area at the campground. There are no water hookups at the campground.

Attractions
Salinas Pueblo Missions National Monument PO Box 517 Mountainair NM 505-847-2585
http://www.nps.gov/sapu/index.htm
Dogs must be on leash and must be cleaned up after in the monument area. Dogs must not be allowed off paths.

Nageezi

Campgrounds and RV Parks
Chaco Culture National Historical Park P. O. Box 220 Nageezi NM 505-786-7014 (888-NMPARKS (667-2757))
http://www.nps.gov/chcu/
This park has a rich cultural history; it is part of the Chaco Night Sky Program, and a variety of trails here will lead you by petroglyphs and historic writings. There are no services here, so you must bring your own food and water. Dogs of all sizes are allowed at no additional fee. Dogs may not be left unattended, and they must be quiet, well behaved, leashed, and cleaned up after. Dogs are allowed on the trails unless otherwise marked. The camping and tent areas also allow dogs. There is a dog walk area at the campground. There are no electric or water hookups at the campground.
Chaco Culture National Historical Park County Road 7950 Nageezi NM 505-786-7014
http://www.nps.gov/chcu/
At one time this area was a thriving and sophisticated administrative center for ancient urban peoples, and now these sites are sacred homeland to the Pueblo, Hopi, and Navajo Nations. Most of the park and cultural sites are self guided, and there are hiking trails that will take visitors to a variety of sites, petroglyphs/historic inscriptions, and vistas. Trails are day use only, and a free hiking permit is required. There are few amenities here, so go prepared. Dogs are allowed for no additional fee. Dogs are allowed on the trails and around the park/camp areas; they are not allowed inside sites, ruins, or park buildings. Dogs must be leashed and cleaned up after. Gallo Campground offers 48 sites on a first come, first served basis in a rugged, ancient feeling environment; RVs over 30 feet cannot be provided for. There is a picnic table and fire grate with a grill at each site, and there is non-potable water, restrooms, a dump station, and drinking water at the visitor center. This RV park is closed during the off-season. The camping and tent areas also allow dogs. There is a dog walk area at the campground. There are no electric or water hookups at the campgrounds.

Parks
Chaco Culture National Historical Park County Road 7950 Nageezi NM 505-786-7014
http://www.nps.gov/chcu/
At one time this area was a thriving and sophisticated administrative center for ancient urban peoples, and now these sites are sacred homeland to the Pueblo, Hopi, and Navajo Nations. Most of the park and cultural sites are self guided, and there are hiking trails that will take visitors to a variety of sites, petroglyphs/historic inscriptions,

and vistas. Trails are day use only, and a free hiking permit is required. There are few amenities here, so go prepared. Dogs are allowed for no additional fee. Dogs are allowed on the trails and around the park/camp areas; they are not allowed inside sites, ruins, or park buildings. Dogs must be leashed and cleaned up after.

Navajo Dam

Campgrounds and RV Parks
Navajo Lake State Park 1448 Hwy 511 #1 Navajo Dam NM 505-632-2278 (888-NMPARKS (667-2757))
With over 21,000 land acres and an almost 16,000 acre lake, this park offers interpretive exhibits, 2 full service marinas, and a wide variety of land and water recreation. Dogs of all sizes are allowed at no additional fee. Dogs may not be left unattended, and they must be on no more than a 10 foot leash, and be cleaned up after. Dogs are allowed on the trails. The camping and tent areas also allow dogs. There is a dog walk area at the campground.
Navajo Lake State Park 1448 Hwy 511 (#1) Navajo Dam NM 505-632-2278
Sitting at an altitude of 6,100 feet, this 21,000 acre park is home to the state's 2nd largest lake at almost 16,000 acres. They offer a variety of land and water recreation and services, interpretive exhibits/signage, a full service marina, a wheelchair accessible fishing area, several hiking trails, 7 day use areas, camping, and a visitor center. Dogs are allowed throughout the park and on the trails. There is no additional pet fee. Dogs may not be left unattended at any time, and they must be leashed and cleaned up after at all times. The camp areas offer 246 developed sites; some of the amenities include picnic areas, restrooms, showers, a playground, and a dump station. Many of the camp sites are along the lake. The camping and tent areas also allow dogs. There is a dog walk area at the campground.

Parks
Navajo Lake State Park 1448 Hwy 511 (#1) Navajo Dam NM 505-632-2278
Sitting at an altitude of 6,100 feet, this 21,000 acre park is home to the state's 2nd largest lake at almost 16,000 acres. They offer a variety of land and water recreation and services, interpretive exhibits/signage, a full service marina, a wheelchair accessible fishing area, several hiking trails, 7 day use areas, camping, and a visitor center. Dogs are allowed throughout the park and on the trails. There is no additional pet fee. Dogs may not be left unattended at any time, and they must be leashed and cleaned up after at all times.

Pecos

Parks
Pecos National Historic Park P. O. Box 418 Pecos NM 505-757-6414
http://www.nps.gov/peco
This day-use park safeguards and preserves more than 12,000 years of cultural and geographical history of the ancient Pueblo of Pecos, the mission ruins and trails of the area, the Forked Lighting Ranch, and the site of the Civil War Battle of Glorieta Pass. Some of the amenities here include a 1-1/4 mile hiking trail, picnic areas, restrooms, and a museum. Dogs are allowed at the park for no additional fee. Dogs are allowed on the trails and around the park, but not in park buildings. Dogs must be leashed, and please clean up after your pet.

Portales

Campgrounds and RV Parks
Oasis State Park 1891 Oasis Road Portales NM 505-356-5331 (888-NMPARKS (667-2757))
This park of 193 acres, set among the cottonwood trees and shifting sand dunes, offers a small fishing lake and more than 80 species of birds. Dogs of all sizes are allowed at no additional fee. Dogs may not be left unattended outside or for long periods inside, and they must be on no more than a 10 foot leash, and be cleaned up after. Dogs are not allowed in the water, but they are allowed on the trails. The camping and tent areas also allow dogs. There is a dog walk area at the campground.

Prewitt

Campgrounds and RV Parks

Bluewater Lake State Park Box 3419/ at end of Hwy 412 Prewitt NM   505-876-2391 (877-664-7787)
This year round recreational park offers great fishing, a wide variety of birds, a visitor's center, and plenty of hiking trails. Dogs are allowed at no additional fee. Dogs must be leashed and cleaned up after. Dogs are allowed on the trails. The camping and tent areas also allow dogs. There is a dog walk area at the campground. There are no water hookups at the campground.

Radium Springs

Campgrounds and RV Parks

Leasburg Dam State Park P.O. Box 6 Radium Springs NM   505-524-4068 (888-NMPARKS (667-2757)
This park along the Rio Grande offers a variety of land and water recreation. Dogs of all sizes are allowed at no additional fee. Dogs may not be left unattended, and they must be leashed and cleaned up after. Dogs are allowed on the trails. The camping and tent areas also allow dogs. There is a dog walk area at the campground. There are no water hookups at the campground.

Ramah

Campgrounds and RV Parks

Ancient Way Outpost Campground 4018 Hwy 53 Ramah NM   505-783-4612
http://elmorro-nm.com/
This RV park also offers free wi-fi, furnished log cabins, an historic café that serves snacks or hearty, American, New Mexican and Vegetarian specialties, and a great location for exploring the many legendary sites close by, including the legendary seven cities of gold (Cibola) that Spanish explorers once sought. Dogs of all sizes are allowed for no additional fee for tent or RV sites. There is a $10 one time additional pet fee for the cabins. There is a mesa behind the park with many trails to walk your pooch. Although not allowed inside the café, there is a bench out front on the porch where you can sit, or get food to go. Dogs must be well behaved, and leashed and cleaned up after in camp and on the trails. The camping and tent areas also allow dogs. There is a dog walk area at the campground. Dogs are allowed in the camping cabins.

El Morrow National Monument HC 61 Box 43/Monument Drive Ramah NM   505-783-4226
http://www.nps.gov/elmo
Located at an elevation of over 7,000 feet, this monument boasts a massive mesa-point that rises 200 feet above the valley floor with a 1/2 mile loop trail leading to an historic pool, and more than 2000 inscriptions and petroglyphs. If you continue to the top of the mesa for a 2 mile round trip hike, you will be met with breathtaking views and the ancestral Puebloan ruins. Dogs are allowed on the trails, but they must stay on the trails, and be leashed and under owner's control at all times. Dogs must be cleaned up after in the campground area, the park, and on the trails. Pets are not permitted in the visitor center, but they ask that you stop there first before going in to get directions/instructions. There is a picnic area at the visitor center where pets are allowed. The campground has 9 primitive sites on a first come, first served basis. Amenities include picnic tables, fire pits, water, and pit toilets. Water is shut off in the winter when camping is available for no cost. The camping and tent areas also allow dogs. There is a dog walk area at the campground. There are no electric or water hookups at the campgrounds.

Parks

TOP 200 PLACE **El Morrow National Monument** HC 61 Box 43/Monument Drive Ramah NM   505-783-4226
http://www.nps.gov/elmo
Located at an elevation of over 7,000 feet, this monument boasts a massive mesa-point that rises 200 feet above the valley floor with a 1/2 mile loop trail leading to an historic pool, and more than 2000 inscriptions and petroglyphs. If you continue to the top of the mesa for a 2 mile round trip hike, you will be met with breathtaking views and the ancestral Puebloan ruins. Dogs are allowed on the trails, but they must stay on the trails, and be leashed and under owners control at all times. Dogs must be cleaned up after in the campground area, the park, and on the trails. Pets are not permitted in the visitor center, but they ask that you stop there first before going in to get directions/instructions. There is a picnic area at the visitor center where pets are allowed.

Raton

Accommodations

Motel 6 - Raton 1600 Cedar Street Raton NM 505-445-2777 (800-466-8356)
One well-behaved family pet per room. Guest must notify front desk upon arrival. Guest is liable for any damages. In consideration of all guests, pets must never be left unattended in the guest rooms.

Campgrounds and RV Parks

Sugarite Canyon State Park HCR 63, Box 386 Raton NM 505-445-5607 (888-NMPARKS (667-2757))
With 3,600 land acres at an altitude of 7,800 feet and a lake with 120 acres, this scenic park provides a variety of year round recreation. Dogs of all sizes are allowed at no additional fee. Dogs may not be left unattended outside or left in the unit for long periods, and they must be leashed and cleaned up after. Dogs are not allowed in public swim areas or in buildings. Dogs are allowed on the trails. The camping and tent areas also allow dogs. There is a dog walk area at the campground.

Sugarlite Canyon State Park HCR 63, Box 386 Raton NM 505-445-5607 (800-NMPARKS (667-2757))
This park is 3,600 acres of wildflower filled meadows (butterfly paradise), heavily wooded mountains, and interesting geological features such as the giant volcanic Caprock. There is also a 120 acre surface lake, the Coal Camp Interpretive Trail, various scenic trails to hike, a visitor center, and a variety of land and water recreation. Dogs of all sizes are allowed for no additional fee. Dogs are allowed on all the trails-except ski trails in winter and they must be leashed and cleaned up after. The campground offers 2 camp areas with 40 developed sites plus 12 with electric, restrooms, showers, tables, grills, and water. The camping and tent areas also allow dogs. There is a dog walk area at the campground.

Parks

Sugarlite Canyon State Park HCR 63, Box 386 Raton NM 505-445-5607 (800-NMPARKS (667-2757))
This park is 3,600 acres of wildflower filled meadows (butterfly paradise), heavily wooded mountains, and interesting geological features such as the giant volcanic Caprock. There is also a 120 acre surface lake, the Coal Camp Interpretive Trail, various scenic trails to hike, a visitor center, and a variety of land and water recreation. Dogs of all sizes are allowed for no additional fee. Dogs are allowed on all the trails-except ski trails in winter and they must be leashed and cleaned up after.

Red River

Accommodations

Best Western Rivers Edge 301 W River St Red River NM 505-754-1766 (800-780-7234)
Dogs of all sizes are allowed. There is a $25 one time pet fee per visit. Smoking and non-smoking rooms are available for pets.

Black Bear Inn 517 Main Street/Hwy 38 Red River NM 505-754-2262
This family owned motel sits in a scenic little valley at over 8,500 feet altitude, and is very close to a variety of recreational pursuits, restaurants, and shops. Dogs of all sizes are allowed for no additional pet fee with a credit card on file. There is only one or two dogs allowed per room depending on the size of the dog and the room. Dogs must be leashed, cleaned up after, and crated when left alone in the room.

Terrace Towers Lodge 712 West Main Street Red River NM 800-695-6343
http://www.terracetowers-lodge.com
The rooms at this lodge overlook the town of Red River and the Red River Ski Area. The lodge offers 16 two bedroom suites with a living/dining/kitchen area. Amenities include cable TV, hot tub, picnic and playground areas, guest laundry and Internet. There is a small pet fee and a limit of 2 pets per unit. There is no size or weight limit for dogs. Pets need to be leashed while on the property.

Campgrounds and RV Parks

River Ranch 1501 W Main (Hwy 38) Red River NM 505-754-2293
http://www.riverranch.com/
Dogs of all sizes are allowed. There are no additional pet fees. Dogs may not be left unattended outside, and they must be quiet, well behaved, leashed and cleaned up after. This RV park is closed during the off-season. The camping and tent areas also allow dogs. There is a dog walk area at the campground.

Cross Country Ski Resorts
TOP 200 PLACE Enchanted Forest Cross Country Ski Area P. O. Box 219 Red River NM   505-754-2374

http://www.enchantedforestxc.com/
This is the state's largest full service cross country ski area with about 20 miles of groomed areas for various skiing, and about 10 miles for snowshoeing, but they have provided an area especially for our canine companions. There are about 3 miles of a smooth, groomed trail for easier skiing/snowshoers, and varies from 6 to 12 feet that guests with or without pets may use. They expect guests to use the doggie waste bags they have provided along the way. Dogs must be leashed in the parking areas, and under strict voice command if off lead on the trails.
Enchanted Forest Cross Country Ski Area 417 West Main Street Red River NM   505-754-2374
http://www.enchantedforestxc.com
This nordic center has about 5km of special cross-country and snowshoeing trails just for dogs. The trails are groomed. Dogs need to be leashed in the parking lot area but can be off-leash under direct voice control on the trails. Doggie waste bags are provided and need to be used on the trails. This ski area is less than 1 hour from Taos.

Rodeo

Campgrounds and RV Parks
Rustys RV Ranch 22 Estrella Parkway Rodeo NM   505-557-2526
http://wwwl.caballoresort.com/home.htm
Dogs of all sizes are allowed. There are no additional pet fees. Dogs may not be left unattended outside, and they must be leashed in camp, and cleaned up after. Dogs may be off lead on the trails if they are under voice command and will not chase wildlife. The camping and tent areas also allow dogs. There is a dog walk area at the campground.

Roseburg

Attractions
Shakespeare Ghost Town Ghost Town Road Roseburg NM   505-542-9034
http://www.shakespeareghostown.com/
This historical old western town, listed as a National Historic Site, offer authentic reenactments and living history activities/programs/stories (times and months vary). They are open for tours 2 times a month and by appointment. Dogs are welcome around the grounds and the trails. Dogs must be under owner's control, and leashed and cleaned up after at all times.

Roswell

Accommodations
Best Western El Rancho Palacio 2205 E Main St Roswell NM   505-622-2721 (800-780-7234)
Dogs of all sizes are allowed. There are no additional pet fees. Smoking and non-smoking rooms are available for pets.
Comfort Inn 3595 N Main Street Roswell NM   505-623-4567 (877-424-6423)
Dogs of all sizes are allowed. There are no additional pet fees. Dogs may not be left alone in the room, and they must be leashed and cleaned up after.
Cozy Cowboy Cottage Rentals 804 W 4th Street Roswell NM   505-624-3258
The number and size of pets depends on the size and type of unit rented. There is a $250 refundable deposit per stay per unit and a pet policy to sign at check in.
Days Inn Roswell 1310 N Main St Roswell NM   505-623-4021 (800-329-7466)
Dogs of all sizes are allowed. There are no additional pet fees.
Frontier Motel 3010 N Main St Roswell NM   505-622-1400 (800-678-1401)
There are no additional pet fees.
La Quinta Inn & Suites Roswell 200 East 19th Street Roswell NM   505-622-8000 (800-531-5900)
Dogs of all sizes are allowed. There are no additional pet fees. There is a pet waiver to sign at check in. Dogs

may not be left unattended, and they must be leashed at all times and cleaned up after. Dogs must be crated or removed for housekeeping.

Motel 6 - Roswell 3307 North Main Street Roswell NM   505-625-6666 (800-466-8356)
One well-behaved family pet per room. Guest must notify front desk upon arrival. Guest is liable for any damages. In consideration of all guests, pets must never be left unattended in the guest rooms.

Campgrounds and RV Parks

Bottomless Lakes State Park HC 12, Box 1200; On Hwy 409 Roswell NM   505-624-6058 (888-NMPARKS (667-2757))
This park has 1400 acres and 7 small lakes and offers a variety of recreational pursuits. Dogs of all sizes are allowed at no additional fee. Dogs may not be left unattended, and they must be leashed and cleaned up after. The camping and tent areas also allow dogs. There is a dog walk area at the campground.

Bottomless Lakes State Park HC 12, Box 1200 (Hwy 409) Roswell NM   505-624-6058 (800-NMPARKS (667-2757))
Although thought to be 'bottomless', the deepest of the several small lakes here is Lea Lake at 90 feet, and it is the only lake that swimming is allowed in. The lakes are set among high red bluffs offering a good variety of land and water recreational opportunities. Amenities include paddle boat rentals in summer, a visitor center, a large day-use and picnic area with a playground, and a host of hiking trails. Dogs of all sizes are allowed for no additional fee. Dogs may not be left unattended at any time, including at the campground. Dogs must be quiet, on no more than a 10 foot leash, and be cleaned up after. Spacious campsites are located at both the Lea Lake Rec area and along the lower lakes. Developed camping with vault toilets and fresh water are offered at the lower lakes, and full hook-ups with hot showers and modern restrooms at Lea Lake. A dump station is also available. The camping and tent areas also allow dogs. There is a dog walk area at the campground.

Red Barn RV Park 2806 E 2nd Street Roswell NM   505-623-4897 (877-800-4897)
Dogs of all sizes are allowed. There are no additional pet fees. Dogs must be leashed and cleaned up after. There is a dog walk area at the campground.

Town and Country RV Park 331 W Brasher Road Roswell NM   505-624-1833
http://www.townandcountryrvpark.com
Dogs of all sizes are allowed. There are no additional pet fees. Dogs may not be tied up or left unattended outside, and they must be leashed and cleaned up after. The camping and tent areas also allow dogs. There is a dog walk area at the campground.

Attractions

TOP 200 PLACE **International UFO Museum & Research Center** 114 N. Main Street Roswell NM   505-625-9495
http://www.iufomrc.com/
Ever wondered if there is extraterrestrial life out there? Curious about the famous 'Roswell Incident'? The Tourism Association of New Mexico has awarded this museum the 1996 "Top Tourist Destination of New Mexico." You and your dog are absolutely welcome inside this very popular and large UFO Museum and Research Center. They have many dog visitors every day. At the museum you can view exhibits about The Roswell Incident, Crop Circles, Ragsdale Crash Site, Ancient Cultures, Worldwide Sighting Map and a Childrens Area. You can also sit and view videos (with your pup, of course) in their small theatre room. After viewing the exhibits, your pup is welcome in the gift shop too. Admission is free, but donations are always welcome.

Parks

Bottomless Lakes State Park HC 12, Box 1200 (Hwy 409) Roswell NM   505-624-6058 (800-NMPARKS (667-2757))
Although thought to be 'bottomless', the deepest of the several small lakes here is Lea Lake at 90 feet, and it is the only lake that swimming is allowed in. The lakes are set among high red bluffs offering a good variety of land and water recreational opportunities. Amenities include paddle boat rentals in summer, a visitor center, a large day-use and picnic area with a playground, and a host of hiking trails. Dogs of all sizes are allowed for no additional fee. Dogs may not be left unattended at any time, including at the campground. Dogs must be quiet, on no more than a 10 foot leash, and be cleaned up after.

Ruidoso

Accommodations

Apache Village Cabins 311 Mechem Drive Ruidoso NM   505-257-2435
Well behaved dogs of all sizes are allowed. There is a $15 per stay per room additional fee. There must also be

a credit card on file.

Hawthorne Suites Conference and Golf Resort 107 Sierra Blanca Drive Ruidoso NM 505-258-5500 (888-323-5216)

http://www.ruidosohawthorn.com/

This resort offers world class accommodations and services, and some of the amenities include the city's largest pool and Jacuzzi (enclosed in a 2-story atrium), private balconies, fireplaces, a 24 hour convenience store, a full service bar, and a complimentary full hot American breakfast. Dogs of all sizes are welcome for no additional fee or deposit; there is a pet policy to sign at check in. Dogs may not be left alone in the room at any time, and they must be leashed and cleaned up after at all times.

Motel 6 - Ruidoso 412 US 70 West Ruidoso NM 505-630-1166 (800-466-8356)

One well-behaved family pet per room. Guest must notify front desk upon arrival. Guest is liable for any damages. In consideration of all guests, pets must never be left unattended in the guest rooms.

Swiss Chalet Inn 1451 Meecham Drive Ruidoso NM 505-258-3333 (800-47-SWISS (477-9477))

http://www.sciruidoso.com/

This inn sits atop the Alto Crest nestled among towering Ponderosa Pines, and in addition to luxury and stunning views, amenities also include a complimentary continental breakfast, an indoor pool, hot tub, and easy access to several recreational activities. Dogs of all sizes are allowed for a $25 one time additional fee per pet. Dogs must be well mannered, and leashed and cleaned up after at all times.

Whispering Pines Cabins 422 Main Road Ruidoso NM 505-257-4311

Well behaved dogs of all sizes are allowed. There is a $10 one time fee per pet additional fee. Dogs are not allowed to be left alone in the room.

Best Western Pine Springs Inn 1420 Hwy 70 Ruidoso Downs NM 505-378-8100 (800-780-7234)

Dogs of all sizes are allowed. There are no additional pet fees. Smoking and non-smoking rooms are available for pets.

Sandia Park

Parks

Sandia Park Hwy 536 Sandia Park NM 505-281-3304

This day use park offers picnic areas, restrooms, and a variety of trails. Dogs are allowed on the trails and around the park. Dogs must be leashed and cleaned up after at all times.

Sandia Peak Ski Area/Summer Use Tramway Blvd Sandia Park NM 505-242-9052

http://www.sandiapeak.com/

The park's parking lot is over 10,000 feet with trails reaching an elevation of over 12,000 feet. The park is open year round, but their ski season is usually mid-December through mid-March with the exception of a couple of 2 week closures for maintenance. They have a full service base community, an extensive biking/hiking system, sand pit volleyball, picnic areas, eateries, and more. Dogs are allowed on the mountain all year, but they are not allowed on the ski trails during the ski season or on the tram or chair lift at any time. Pets may join you at the outdoor dining tables, picnic areas, and on many of the trails. Dogs must be well behaved, leashed and cleaned up after at all times.

Santa Fe

Accommodations

Hacienda Dona Andrea de Santa Fe 78 Vista del Oro Cerrillos NM 505-424-8995

http://www.hdasantafe.com

This is a large hotel on 64 acres in the mountains overlooking Santa Fe. Well behaved dogs are welcome. The hotel has a resident terrier named Daisy. There are hiking trails in the area for you to hike with your dog.

Comfort Inn 604-B S Riverside Drive Espanola NM 505-753-2419 (877-424-6423)

Dogs of all sizes are allowed. There are no additional pet fees. Dogs must be healthy and tick and flea free. Dogs may not be left alone in the room, and they must be quiet, well behaved, leashed, and cleaned up after.

Days Inn Espanola 807 S Riverside Dr Espanola NM 505-747-1242 (800-329-7466)

Dogs of all sizes are allowed. There is a $5 per night pet fee per pet.

Super 8 Espanola 811 S Riversidw Espanola NM 505-753-5374 (800-800-8000)

Dogs of all sizes are allowed. There are no additional pet fees. Smoking and non-smoking rooms are available for pet rooms.

Alexander's Inn 529 East Palace Avenue Santa Fe NM 505-986-1431 (888-321-5123)

This intimate inn offers their visitors privacy and a host of amenities, some of which include a welcome basket full of goodies, a lavish continental breakfast, an afternoon wine and cheese reception, luxurious authentic

Southwestern decor, kiva-style fireplaces, full kitchens and patios, and a guest membership at a full-service health club. Dogs of all sizes are allowed for an additional pet fee of $20 per pet per stay, and there is a pet policy to sign at check in. They even keep a supply of doggie biscuits to treat their canine visitors. Dogs must be crated if left alone in the room, be well behaved, and leashed and cleaned up after at all times.

Best Western Inn of Santa Fe 3650 Cerrillos Rd Santa Fe NM 505-438-3822 (800-780-7234)
Dogs of all sizes are allowed. There are no additional pet fees. Dogs are not allowed to be left alone in the room. Smoking and non-smoking rooms are available for pets.

Comfort Inn 4312 Cerrillos Road Santa Fe NM 505-474-7330 (877-424-6423)
Dogs of all sizes are allowed. There are no additional pet fees. Dogs may not be left alone in the room at any time, and they must be leashed and cleaned up after.

El Paradero Bed and Breakfast Inn 220 W. Manhattan Ave Santa Fe NM 505-988-1177
http://www.elparadero.com
This B&B is located just a few minute walk from the Plaza and the Railyard district. Dogs of all sizes are allowed. There is a $15 nightly pet fee for dogs.

Eldorado Hotel 309 W San Francisco Santa Fe NM 505-988-4455
http://www.eldoradohotel.com/
There is a $50 one time pet fee.

Hacienda Nicholas 320 Marcy C Santa Fe NM 505-992-8385 (888-284-3170)
Behind extra thick adobe walls, this intimate, authentic hacienda offers all the amenities of a luxury hotel. It also features a beautiful, lush garden courtyard with an outdoor kiva fireplace and an afternoon wine and cheese reception. Organic and vegetarian food is available. Dogs of all sizes are allowed for an additional pet fee of $20 per pet per stay, and a pet policy to sign at check in. They even keep a supply of doggie biscuits for their canine visitors. Dogs must be crated if left alone in the room, and they must be well behaved, and leashed and cleaned up after at all times.

Hampton Inn 3625 Cerrillos Road Santa Fe NM 505-474-3900
Dogs of all sizes are allowed. There is a pet policy to sign at check in and there are no additional pet fees. Dogs are not allowed to be left alone in the room.

Hilton 100 Sandoval Street Santa Fe NM 505-988-2811
Well behaved dogs of all sizes are allowed. There is a $50 one time fee and they request you kennel your dog for housekeeping.

Hotel Santa Fe 1501 Paseo De Peralta Santa Fe NM 505-982-1200
Dogs of all sizes are allowed. There is a $20 per night per pet additional fee.

Inn of the Anasazi 113 Washington Ave Santa Fe NM 505-988-3030 (800-688-8100)
http://www.slh.com/pages/a/aziusaba.html
There is a $20 one time pet fee.

Inn of the Five Graces 150 E. DeVargas Street Santa Fe NM 505-992-0957
This unique hotel features an intricate blending of the Orient and the Old West creating a warm and interesting luxurious background, for which they are the recipient of several accolades and awards. They offer a continental breakfast, and a number of amenities and services. The Gate House restaurant on site features a Tapas menu, and offer courtyard seating amid mature trees; dogs are allowed there also. Dogs of all sizes are allowed. There is a $50 per night per room additional pet fee. Dogs may not be left alone in the room, and they must be well behaved, leashed, and cleaned up after.

Inn on the Alameda 303 E Alameda Santa Fe NM 505-984-2121 (888-984-2121)
Peaceful, garden adobe courtyards and their 71 suites will immerse visitors in luxurious authentic Southwestern decor. They offer a continental breakfast, an afternoon wine and cheese reception, outdoor whirlpools, fireplaces/patios/balconies, and a great location for exploring the area. Dogs of all sizes are allowed for an additional fee of $20 per night per pet. Dogs may not be left alone in the rooms, and they must be leashed and cleaned up after at all times.

La Quinta Inn Santa Fe 4298 Cerrillos Rd. Santa Fe NM 505-471-1142 (800-531-5900)
Dogs of all sizes are allowed. There are no additional pet fees. Dogs may not be left unattended, and they must be leashed and cleaned up after.

Motel 6 - Santa Fe 3007 Cerrillos Road Santa Fe NM 505-473-1380 (800-466-8356)
One well-behaved family pet per room. Guest must notify front desk upon arrival. Guest is liable for any damages. In consideration of all guests, pets must never be left unattended in the guest rooms.

Park Inn and Suites 2907 Cerrillos Road Santa Fe NM 505-471-3000 (800-670-7275)
This inn features a cozy southwestern décor, and offers guest rooms, studio suites, and an Executive Suite. Their prime location places them near a variety of attractions, historic sites, shops, and areas for hiking. Some of the amenities include a complimentary waffle bar and continental breakfast daily, a seasonal outdoor pool, year around hot tub, free daily newspaper, and you can earn your 'goldpoints' here. Dogs of all sizes are allowed. There is a $10 per night per pet additional fee. Dogs must be quiet, leashed, cleaned up after, and a contact number left with the front desk if they are in the room alone.

Pecos Trail Inn 2239 Old Pecos Trail Santa Fe NM 505-982-1943
Dogs of all sizes are allowed. There are no additional pet fees.

Quality Inn 3011 Cerrillos Road Santa Fe NM 505-471-1211 (877-424-6423)
Dogs of all sizes are allowed. There can be up to 2 large or 3 small to medium dogs per room. There is a $10

per night per room additional pet fee. Dogs may not be left alone in the room at any time, and they must be leashed and cleaned up after.

Red Roof Inn - Santa Fe - Cerrillos Road 3695 Cerrillos Road Santa Fe NM 505-471-4140 (800-RED-ROOF)
One well-behaved family pet per room. Guest must notify front desk upon arrival. Guest is liable for any damages. In consideration of all guests, pets must never be left unattended in the guest rooms.

Residence Inn by Marriott 1698 Galisteo Street Santa Fe NM 505-988-7300
Dogs of all sizes are allowed. There is a $75 one time fee and a pet policy to sign at check in.

Santa Fe Sage Inn 725 Cerrillos Santa Fe NM 505-982-5952 (866-433-0335)
This Inn offers comfortable Southwestern themed rooms, an extended continental breakfast, a swimming pool, many other amenities, and a great central location to several shopping opportunities and various attractions. Dogs of all sizes are allowed. There is a $25 per pet per stay additional fee. Dogs must be leashed and cleaned up after at all times.

Sunrise Springs Inn and Retreat 242 Los Pinos Road Santa Fe NM 505-471-3600
Dogs of all sizes are allowed. There is a $25 per night per pet fee and a pet policy to sign at check in. Dogs must be crated when left in the room.

TOP 200 PLACE **Ten Thousand Waves Japanese Spa and Resort** 3451 Hyde Park Road Santa Fe NM 505-992-5003
http://www.tenthousandwaves.com
Ten Thousand Waves is a Japanese style spa in the mountains above Santa Fe with outdoor and indoor hot tubs, facials, spa services, and many types of massage. There are 13 guest houses, most with fireplaces and either enclosed courtyards or decks. Some have full kitchens and/or separate bedrooms. The resort is about ten minutes from downtown. Pets are $20 per night for one or more.

Campgrounds and RV Parks

Hyde Memorial State Park 740 Hyde Park Road Santa Fe NM 505-983-7175 (888-NMPARKS (677-2757))
Located in the Sangre de Cristo Mountains at 8500 feet, this park offers beautiful scenery, quiet settings, and year round recreation. Dogs of all sizes are allowed at no additional fee. Dogs may not be left unattended, and they must be leashed and cleaned up after. Dogs are allowed on the trails. This campground is closed during the off-season. The camping and tent areas also allow dogs. There is a dog walk area at the campground.

Rancheros de Santa Fe 736 Old Las Vegas H Santa Fe NM 800-426-9259
http://www.rancheros.com
Dogs of all sizes are allowed. There are no additional pet fees. Dogs may not be left unattended, and they must be quiet, leashed, and cleaned up after. There is a fenced in Doggy Corral for off lead. The camping and tent areas also allow dogs. There is a dog walk area at the campground. Dogs are allowed in the camping cabins.

Santa Fe National Forest 1474 Rodeo Road Santa Fe NM 505-438-7840
http://www.fs.fed.us/r3/sfe/
This forest of 1.6 million acres at an altitude of over 13,000 feet. It offers diverse ecosystems that support a large variety of plants, fish, mammals, bird species, and recreation. Dogs of all sizes are allowed at no additional fee. Dogs may not be left unattended, and they must be leashed and cleaned up after. Dogs are allowed on the trails. The camping and tent areas also allow dogs. There is a dog walk area at the campground. There are no electric or water hookups at the campground.

Santa Fe Skies RV Park 14 Browncastle Ranch Santa Fe NM 505-473-5946
http://www.santafeskiesrvpark.com
Dogs of all sizes are allowed. There are no additional pet fees. Dogs must be cleaned up after. Dogs may be off leash if they are friendly and under owner's control. Dogs must be quiet and well behaved. There is a dog walk area at the campground.

Trailer Ranch RV Resort 3471 Cerrillos Santa Fe NM 505-471-9970
http://www.trailerranch.com
Dogs of all sizes are allowed. There are no additional pet fees. Dogs must be quiet, well behaved, leashed, and cleaned up after. This is a 55 plus resort so at least one of the campers must be 55 or older. There are some breed restrictions. There is a dog walk area at the campground.

Attractions

Santa Fe Vineyards Route 1 Box 216A Espanola NM 505-753-8100
http://www.santafevineyards.com
Dogs on leash are allowed at the outdoor tables. Open 7 days a week. It is located 20 miles from Santa Fe.

El Camino Real de Tierra Adentro National Historic Trail 1100 Old Santa Fe Trail Santa Fe NM 505-988-6888
http://www.nps.gov/elca/index.htm
Dogs on leash are allowed at the roadside sites and trails. Dogs are not allowed in buildings. The trail spans New Mexico and Texas. This trail is mainly auto touring with site stops and museums.

TOP 200 PLACE **Galloping Galleries** 22B Stacy Rd Santa Fe NM 505-988-7016

http://www.gallopinggalleries.com/
This company provides CD road trips of New Mexico's landscape, history, diverse cultures, and cultural events, and then they combine them with the local myths and legends of the area. The CD's are also interlaced with music from local musicians, and includes information such as where the last chance for gas or food is, and more. This is a fun and casual way to discover New Mexico from your own car.

Historic Walking Tour of Santa Fe San Francisco Street Santa Fe NM 505-986-8388
This historic walking tour weaves a story of 1000 years of occupation by the Pueblos before the city was founded by the Spaniards more than 400 years ago. They welcome your well behaved dog to join you on all the walking portions of the tour. The only 2 places they are not allowed to go into is the St. Francis Cathedral or the Loretto Chapel so you will need to have someone remain outside with the dog. There is no additional fee, and dogs must be leashed and cleaned up after at all times. Daily tours depart from The Plaza area.

Old Spanish National Historic Trail 1100 Old Santa Fe Trail Santa Fe NM 505-988-6888
http://www.nps.gov/olsp/index.htm
Dogs on leash are allowed in the site areas. The trail features auto touring and site stops explaining the trail use to transport goods and horses between New Mexico and Los Angeles. The trail was first taken by Mexican trader Antonio Armijo in 1829.

Santa Fe National Historic Trail 1100 Old Santa Fe Trail Santa Fe NM 505-988-6888
http://www.nps.gov/safe/index.htm
Dogs on leash are allowed. Some sites are city and state owned and additional rules may apply. The trail features auto touring, hiking, and more depending on the site. The trail spans Missouri, Kansas, Oklahoma, New Mexico, and Colorado. It was used as a commercial highway connecting Missouri and Santa Fe from 1821 to 1846.

State Capitol Grounds 491 Old Santa Fe Trail Santa Fe NM 505-986-4589
http://www.legis.state.nm.us
The New Mexico capitol building is the only round capitol building in the U.S., and it was made to resemble a Zia Pueblo sun sign, which is also the state symbol. Surrounding the building are 6 ½ acres of lush gardens with more than 100 varieties of flowering plants, nut and fruit trees, sequoias, and shrubs. Dogs are welcome to explore the area with you. Dogs must be leashed and cleaned up after at all times.

Trail of Tears National Historic Park 1100 Old Santa Fe Trail Santa Fe NM 505-988-6888
http://www.nps.gov/trte/index.htm
Dogs must be on leash and must be cleaned up after. Dogs are not allowed in building sites. The trail goes through many other state parks and other locations. You must follow general rules and pet policies of any state parks and locations that trail goes through. The trail is located in Alabama, Arkansas, Georgia, Illinois, Kentucky, Missouri, North Carolina, Oklahoma, and Tennessee with mainly auto touring and site stops that allow picnicking and some hiking.

Shopping Centers

Santa Fe Premium Outlets 8380 Cerrillos Rd Ste 412 Santa Fe NM 505-474-4000
http://www.santafeoutlets.com/
This courtyard style open-air mall is located on the south end of town and offer over 25 stores and services. Well behaved, leashed dogs are welcome throughout the mall. Some stores may allow pets to enter, but it is not unusual for your four-legged companion to sniff out one of the treat bins, and there are doggy ties ups in case they are needed. Dogs must be under the owner's control at all times.

Stores

PetSmart Pet Store 3561 Zafarano Dr Santa Fe NM 505-471-5255
Your licensed and well-behaved leashed dog is allowed in the store.
Petco Pet Store 2006 Cerrillos Rd Santa Fe NM 505-424-1667
Your licensed and well-behaved leashed dog is allowed in the store.

Parks

Ski Santa Fe Hwy 475 (Artist Road/Hyde Park Road) Santa Fe NM 505-982-4429
http://www.skisantafe.com/
This park is nestled high in the beautiful Sangre de Cristo Mountains, reaches to a 12,075 foot summit, and their season here is usually from Thanksgiving to Easter. In the off season months, dogs are allowed on the mountain and the numerous trails. There are restrooms available, but no other services are available in the off season. Dogs must be under owner's control at all times, leashed, and cleaned up after on the trails. Dogs are not allowed in the ski park during the ski season.

State Capitol Grounds 491 Old Santa Fe Trail Santa Fe NM 505-986-4589
http://www.legis.state.nm.us
The New Mexico capitol building is the only round capitol building in the U.S., and it was made to resemble a Zia Pueblo sun sign, which is also the state symbol. Surrounding the building are 6 ½ acres of lush gardens with more than 100 varieties of flowering plants, nut and fruit trees, sequoias, and shrubs. Dogs are welcome to

explore the area with you. Dogs must be leashed and cleaned up after at all times.

Off-Leash Dog Parks
Frank Ortiz Park Off-Leash Area Camino Las Crucitas Santa Fe NM 505-955-2100
http://www.santafenm.gov/parks/index.asp
This off-leash area is located in Frank Ortiz park which used to be the old landfill. To get there from town, head west on Paseo De Paralta towards St. Francis. When you come to St. Francis, do not turn left or right, but instead go across to Camino Las Crucitas Street. Follow this road which takes you through the Casa Solana residential neighborhood. The park has a large field on the left where the off-leash area is located.

Outdoor Restaurants
Cloud Cliff Bakery and Restaurant 1805 Second Street Santa Fe NM 505-983-6254
This restaurant serves American cuisine. Dogs are allowed at the outdoor tables.
Il Piatto 95 W Marcy Santa Fe NM 505-984-1091
This restaurant serves Italian food. Dogs are allowed at the outdoor tables.
Whole Foods Market 753 Cerrillos Road Santa Fe NM 505-992-1700
This cafe serves deli-type food. Dogs are allowed at the outdoor tables.

Santa Rosa

Accommodations
Best Western Adobe Inn 1501 E Will Rogers Dr Santa Rosa NM 505-472-3446 (800-780-7234)
Dogs of all sizes are allowed. There are no additional pet fees. Smoking and non-smoking rooms are available for pets.
Best Western Santa Rosa Inn 3022 Historic Route 66 Santa Rosa NM 505-472-5877 (800-780-7234)
Dogs of all sizes are allowed. There is a $3.35 per night pet fee per pet. Smoking and non-smoking rooms are available for pets.
Comfort Inn 3343 Historic Route 66 Santa Rosa NM 505-472-5570 (877-424-6423)
Dogs of all sizes are allowed. There is a $10 per night per pet additional fee. Dogs must be leashed and cleaned up after, and they may only be left alone in the room if they will be quiet, well behaved, and the Do Not Disturb sign is put on the door.
Days Inn Santa Rosa 1830 Will Rogers Dr Santa Rosa NM 505-472-5985 (800-329-7466)
Dogs of all sizes are allowed. There is a $5 per night pet fee per pet.
La Quinta Inn Santa Rosa 1701 Will Rogers Dr. Santa Rosa NM 505-472-4800 (800-531-5900)
Dogs of all sizes are allowed. There are no additional pet fees as long as pets are reported at the time of registration. Dogs may not be left unattended, and they must be leashed and cleaned up after.
Motel 6 - Santa Rosa 3400 Will Rogers Drive Santa Rosa NM 505-472-3045 (800-466-8356)
One well-behaved family pet per room. Guest must notify front desk upon arrival. Guest is liable for any damages. In consideration of all guests, pets must never be left unattended in the guest rooms.

Campgrounds and RV Parks
Santa Rosa Campground 2136 Historic Hwy 66 Santa Rosa NM 505-472-3126
http://www.santarosacampground.com
Dogs of all sizes are allowed. There are no additional pet fees. Dogs may be walked anywhere in the park, but they must be taken to the dog walk to relieve themselves. Dogs must be leashed and cleaned up after. The camping and tent areas also allow dogs. There is a dog walk area at the campground. Dogs are allowed in the camping cabins.
Santa Rosa Lake State Park P.O. Box 384 Santa Rosa NM 505-472-3110 (888-NMPARKS (667-2757))
With 500 land acres and 3,800 lake acres, this park offers a variety of land and water recreation and nature study. Dogs of all sizes are allowed at no additional fee. Dogs may not be left unattended, and they must be on no more than a 10 foot leash, and be cleaned up after. Dogs are allowed on the trails. The camping and tent areas also allow dogs. There is a dog walk area at the campground.

Silver City

Accommodations
Comfort Inn 1060 E Hwy 180 Silver City NM 505-534-1883 (877-424-6423)

Dogs of all sizes are allowed. There is a $10 per night per pet additional fee. Dogs must be leashed and cleaned up after, and they may be left alone in the room only if they will be quiet, well behaved, and the Do Not Disturb sign is put on the door.

Econo Lodge 1120 Hwy 180 Silver City NM   505-534-1111 (877-424-6423)
http://www.econolodgesilvercity.com/
This lodge offers 59 deluxe rooms and 3 suites and features well kept grounds, an atrium with comfortable benches and a fountain in the middle, a hot tub, and a great indoor heated pool area. Some of the other amenities include a conference room, many in-room perks, and a free continental breakfast. Dogs of all sizes are allowed for an additional pet fee of $7 (plus tax) per night per room, and there is a pet policy to sign at check in. Dogs may not be left alone in the room, they must be leashed and cleaned up after at all times, and crated or removed for housekeeping.

Holiday Inn Express 1103 Superior St Silver City NM   505-538-2525 (877-270-6405)
Dogs of all sizes are allowed. There are no additional pet fees. Smoking and non-smoking rooms are available for pets.

Campgrounds and RV Parks

Gila National Forest 3005 Camino Del Bosque Silver City NM   505-388-8201
http://www2.srs.fs.fed.us/r3/gila/
This forest has 6 ranger districts, covers 3.3 million acres, and has diverse ecosystems that support a large variety of plants, fish, mammals, bird species, and recreation. Dogs of all sizes are allowed at no additional fee. Dogs may not be left unattended, and they must be leashed and cleaned up after. Dogs are not allowed at the cliff dwellings or on the trail to the dwellings, however, they are allowed on the other trails unless marked. The camping and tent areas also allow dogs. There is a dog walk area at the campground. There are no electric or water hookups at the campground.

Parks

Gila Cliff Dwellings National Monument HC 68 Box 100 Silver City NM   505-536-9461
http://www.nps.gov/gicl/index.htm
Dogs must be on leash and must be cleaned up after in park. Dogs are not allowed on trails leading to the caves but you may take them on other trails. They offer a free on-site kennel if you want to hike to caves. The park features camping, fishing, hiking, and more.

Socorro

Accommodations

Motel 6 - Socorro 807 South US 85 Socorro NM   505-835-4300 (800-466-8356)
One well-behaved family pet per room. Guest must notify front desk upon arrival. Guest is liable for any damages. In consideration of all guests, pets must never be left unattended in the guest rooms.

Attractions

TOP 200 PLACE **Very Large Array (VLA) Radio Telescope** U.S. Hwy 60 Socorro NM   505-835-7000
The VLA is one of the world's premier astronomical radio observatories. It consists of 27 antennas arranged in a huge Y pattern up to 22 miles across. Dogs are not allowed in the visitor's center, but you can take your pup on the self-guided walking tour. This is where part of the movie Contact, starring Jodie Foster, was filmed. The VLA is located 50 miles west of Socorro on U.S. Highway 60. From U.S. 60, turn South on NM 52, then West on the VLA access road, which is well marked. Signs will point you to the Visitor Center. The tour is free, but donations are welcome.

Steins

Attractions

TOP 200 PLACE **Steins Railroad Ghost Town** Interstate 10, Exit 3 Steins NM   505-542-9791
When traveling along I-10 in New Mexico, near the Arizona border, be sure to stop at this ghost town. Steins Railroad Ghost Town was once a thriving railroad station town named after Captain Stein, a U.S. Army officer, who was the first Anglo witness to sign a treaty with the Apaches. At the town's peak, between 1905 to 1945, Steins supported 1300 residents. Take a step back in time and walk through the preserved Old West frontier town with your pup. You can purchase some souvenirs and cold drinks at the Steins Mercantile or purchase a

guided tour for $2.50 per person. The self-guided tour is free. This is a nice place to stop when traveling along I-10. Just be sure to keep your dog leashed because there are several cats on the premises.

Sumner

Campgrounds and RV Parks
Valley View RV Park 401 E Sumner Avenue Sumner NM 505-355-2380
Dogs of all sizes are allowed. There are no additional pet fees. Dogs may not be left unattended outside, and they must be leashed and cleaned up after. This park only closes for the first 2 weeks in January each year. There is a dog walk area at the campground.

Taos

Accommodations
Adobe and Pines Inn 4107 Hwy 68 Taos NM 505-751-0947 (800-723-8267)
http://adobepines.com
This luxurious, romantic hideaway is a 170+ year old adobe hacienda that has been preserved with original architecture and transformed into lush grounds with an inviting Southwestern decor. Amenities include full gourmet breakfasts, a brook with an old stone bridge, acres of country gardens, private patios, an outdoor fire ring, spa services, and more. Dogs of all sizes are welcome. There is a $20 one time additional fee per pet. Dogs may also be walked in the large yard next door, and if your dog is under good voice control, they may be off lead in that area. On the property, dogs must be leashed and cleaned up after at all times. Dogs must be crated when left alone in the room.
Alpine Village Suites PO Box 917 Taos NM 505-776-8540 (800-576-2666)
http://www.alpine-suites.com
Located in Taos Ski Valley, this hotel offers a completely non-smoking environment. All 24 Suites and Studios have mini-kitchens, and most have private balconies with views. Many of our suites have fireplaces, and all suites have TV/VCR's, full baths and telephones. They are located steps from the lifts, restaurants, nightlife, and shopping. The Alpine Village complex houses two full service ski shops, a restaurant and bar. They welcome kids of all ages and the family pet. There is a $10 per day pet charge.
American Artist Gallery House 132 Frontier Lane Taos NM 505-758-4446 (800-532-2041)
This B&B offers southwest hospitality in a secluded, romantic setting, and they feature luxury accommodations, gourmet breakfasts, and a stunning view of Taos Mountain. Some of the amenities include Jacuzzi suites, kiva fireplaces, private bath, an outdoor hot tub, and a guest computer. Dogs of all sizes are allowed. There is a $25 additional fee per pet for the first 1 or 2 days, and then an additional $10 per pet per day thereafter. Dogs may not be left alone in the room at any time, and they must be well mannered, leashed, and cleaned up after at all times. Dogs are not allowed on the beds or furnishings, or in the common or breakfast areas. Shots must be current. Dogs are allowed on the trails surrounding the B&B.
Casa Europa 840 Upper Ranchitos Road (HC68, Box 3F) Taos NM 505-758-9798 (888-758-9798)
http://casaeuropanm.com/
This spacious 18th century, pueblo-style estate features a warm inviting Southwestern decor with enclosed garden courtyards and water fountains. Amenities include a full gourmet breakfast, afternoon snacks, an outdoor Jacuzzi and sauna, rooms with fireplaces/private baths/whirlpool tubs, and they are close to many hiking opportunities. Dogs of all sizes are allowed in the apartment suite. There is a $25 per night per pet additional fee. They ask that if you leave your pet in the room, that they are either crated or put in the Jacuzzi room. Dogs must be leashed and cleaned up after.
El Monte Sagrado Living Resort and Spa 317 Kit Carson Road Taos NM 505-758-3502 (800-828-TAOS (8267))
This retreat, with several accolades to their name, specializes in luxury accommodations with an emphasis on environmental and ecological harmony. On site are a Biolarium, lush gardens, a spa, and a decor that reflects an array of global influences inspired by Native American culture. World class cuisine is featured on site, and although dogs are not allowed in dining areas, they have an in-suite dining menu available. Dogs of all sizes are allowed. There is a $150 one time fee per stay for one dog, and an additional $75 one time fee per stay for a 2nd dog. Dogs must be quiet, well behaved, leashed, and cleaned up after at all times.
La Dona Luz Inn 114 Kit Carson Road Taos NM 505-758-4874 (800-758-9187)
http://www.ladonaluz.com/
Thanks to one of our readers for recommending this dog-friendly bed and breakfast. A large dog is welcome to stay here if they are well-behaved and if the dog owner agrees to pay for room damages caused by their dog. There is a $10 per night pet fee. This historic B&B offers 5 rooms (up a narrow spiral stairway), all with private

baths. Room rates are approximately $75 to $150 per night. This B&B has been recommended by both The New York Times and USA Today Weekend.

Quality Inn 1043 Paseo Del Pueblo Spur Taos NM 505-758-2200 (877-424-6423)
Dogs of all sizes are allowed. There is a $7 per night per pet additional fee. Dogs may only be left alone in the room for a short time if there is a contact number left with the front desk, and they must be leashed and cleaned up after.

San Geronimo Lodge 1101 Witt Road Taos NM 505-751-3776 (800-894-4119)
http://www.sangeronimolodge.com/
This lodge offers a great location to several activities/recreational pursuits, great dining, and old historic charm with all the comforts and conveniences of modern day accommodations. Amenities include a seasonal pool, home-cooked meals (special diets-no problem), an outside hot tub, and complete concierge service. Dogs of all sizes are welcome; however pet rooms are limited so be sure to phone ahead. There is a $10 refundable deposit per pet. There is a large field, and a trail from the lodge that leads to the river for some great walking areas for your canine companion. Dogs must be well behaved and social with other animals, as there are other friendly animals in residence too. Dogs must be leashed and cleaned up after.

Campgrounds and RV Parks

Carson National Forest 208 Cruz Alta Taos NM 505-758-6200
http://www.fs.fed.us/r3/carson/
This forest has 6 ranger districts, covers 1.5 million acres, is home to the states highest mountain at 13,161 feet, and it's diverse ecosystems support a large variety of plants, animals, and recreation. Dogs of all sizes are allowed at no additional fee. Dogs may not be left unattended, and they must be leashed and cleaned up after. Dogs are allowed on trails. The camping and tent areas also allow dogs. There is a dog walk area at the campground. There are no electric or water hookups at the campground.

Enchanted Moon RV Park and Campground HC 71 Box 59 Taos NM 505-758-3338
http://www.emooncampground.com/
Dogs of all sizes are allowed. There are no additional pet fees. Dogs must be leashed and cleaned up after. This RV park is closed during the off-season. The camping and tent areas also allow dogs. There is a dog walk area at the campground.

Orilla Verde Rec Area Intersection of SHwy 570 and SHwy 68 Taos NM 505-758-8851
The park is located along the Rio Grande within the steep walls of the Rio Grande Gorge, and because of the evidence of ancient cultures and the diversity of the area, it is popular among vacationers, nature enthusiasts, and anthropologist. The Taos Valley Overlook is about 900 feet above the park and offers stunning views of the gorge and Sangre de Cristo Mountains. Great fishing, whitewater rafting, picnicking, and hiking are just a few of the recreational opportunities. Dogs of all sizes are allowed for no additional fee. Dogs are allowed on the trails, and they must be well behaved, leashed, and cleaned up after. There are five campgrounds, each with tables, fire grills, restrooms, shelters, and drinking water. Primitive camping is only allowed at designated sites. The camping and tent areas also allow dogs. There is a dog walk area at the campground.

Wild Rivers Recreation Area 1120 Cerro Road Taos NM 505-770-1600
Located at the confluence of the Rio Grand and Red Rivers, this recreation area also includes an 800 foot deep volcanic canyon (the Gorge) that features diverse ecosystems, and many trails from easy to difficult to explore. There is a wide variety of plants (even 500 year old trees), animals, and bird life, and land and water recreation, including the Wild Rivers Backcountry Byway, a 13 mile, paved road that allows visitors access to several scenic views and recreational spots. Some of the amenities include a picnic area, grills, drinking water, restrooms, and a visitor center. Dogs of all sizes are allowed for no additional fee. Dogs are allowed on the trails and throughout the park; they are not allowed in buildings. Dogs must be under owner's control at all times, and they must be leashed and cleaned up after. Dogs are not permitted on Big Arsenic Trail or in any freshwater springs. Camping is available at 5 developed campgrounds, each with tables, grills, drinking water, and bathrooms. Four other trails will take visitors to primitive river campsites The camping and tent areas also allow dogs. There is a dog walk area at the campground.

Vacation Home Rentals

Artist's Casita between Taos and Ski Valley Taos NM 505-776-2373
http://www.ann-cole.com/rental.html
This charming one-bedroom casita on the Valdez Rim Road is available for rental. Dogs are welcomed at no additional fee. The rental is about twenty minutes from skiing and from downtown Taos.

Attractions

Black Mesa Winery 1502 State Hwy 68 Velarde NM 800-852-6372
http://www.blackmesawinery.com
Dogs on leash are allowed at the outdoor tables. Open 7 days a week. There is beautiful scenery in the area.

Parks

Orilla Verde Rec Area Intersection of SHwy 570 and SHwy 68 Taos NM 505-758-8851
The park is located along the Rio Grande within the steep walls of the Rio Grande Gorge, and because of the evidence of ancient cultures and the diversity of the area, it is popular among vacationers, nature enthusiasts, and anthropologist. The Taos Valley Overlook is about 900 feet above the park and offers stunning views of the gorge and Sangre de Cristo Mountains. Great fishing, whitewater rafting, picnicking, and hiking are just a few of the recreational opportunities. Dogs of all sizes are allowed for no additional fee. Dogs are allowed on the trails, and they must be well behaved, leashed, and cleaned up after.
Wild Rivers Recreation Area 1120 Cerro Road Taos NM 505-770-1600
Located at the confluence of the Rio Grand and Red Rivers, this recreation area also includes an 800 foot deep volcanic canyon (the Gorge) that features diverse ecosystems, and many trails from easy to difficult to explore. There is a wide variety of plants (even 500 year old trees), animals, and bird life, and land and water recreation, including the Wild Rivers Backcountry Byway, a 13 mile, paved road that allows visitors access to several scenic views and recreational spots. Some of the amenities include a picnic area, grills, drinking water, restrooms, and a visitor center. Dogs of all sizes are allowed for no additional fee. Dogs are allowed on the trails and throughout the park; they are not allowed in buildings. Dogs must be under owners control at all times, and they must be leashed and cleaned up after. Dogs are not permitted on Big Arsenic Trail or in any freshwater springs.

Tierra Amarilla

Campgrounds and RV Parks

El Vado Lake State Park Box 367; El Vado State Park Road Tierra Amarilla NM 505-588-7247 (888-NMPARKS (667-2757))
With over 1700 land acres and a lake with 3200 acres, this park has a variety of nature study and land and water recreation. Dogs of all sizes are allowed at no additional fee. Dogs may not be left unattended, and they must be on no more than a 10 foot leash, and be cleaned up after. Dogs are allowed on the trails. The camping and tent areas also allow dogs. There is a dog walk area at the campground. There are no water hookups at the campground.

Tijeras

Campgrounds and RV Parks

Cibola National Forest 11776 Hwy 337 Tijeras NM 505-346-3900
http://www.fs.fed.us/r3/cibola/
This forest has 6 ranger districts, almost 2 million acres with 5 wilderness areas, and diverse ecosystems that support a large variety of plants, animals, and recreation. Dogs of all sizes are allowed at no additional fee. Dogs may not be left unattended, and they must be leashed and cleaned up after. Dogs are not allowed in buildings, but they are allowed on the trails. The camping and tent areas also allow dogs. There is a dog walk area at the campground. There are no electric or water hookups at the campground.

Truth or Consequences

Accommodations

Best Western Hot Springs Inn 2270 N Date St Truth or Consequences NM 505-894-6665 (800-780-7234)
Dogs of all sizes are allowed. There are no additional pet fees. Smoking and non-smoking rooms are available for pets.
Comfort Inn and Suites 2205 N Dale Street Truth or Consequences NM 505-894-1660 (877-424-6423)
Dogs of all sizes are allowed. There are no additional pet fees. Dogs must be leashed, cleaned up after, and they may be left in the room for a short time only with the Do Not Disturb sign put on the door.
Holiday Inn 2255 N Date St Truth or Consequences NM 505-894-1660 (877-270-6405)
Dogs of all sizes are allowed. There are no additional pet fees. Smoking and non-smoking rooms are available for pets.
Marshall Hot Springs 311 Marr Street Truth or Consequences NM 505-894-9286
http://www.marshallhotsprings.com/
Hot springs feed spring-fed pools at this dog-friendly hotel. Dogs of all sizes are allowed. There is a fee of $5 per

dog per stay. All dogs receive dog biscuits and sheets for dogs that sleep on the bed.
Super 8 Truth or Consequences 2151 N Date St Truth or Consequences NM   505-894-7888 (800-800-8000)
Dogs of all sizes are allowed. There are no additional pet fees. Smoking and non-smoking rooms are available for pet rooms.

Campgrounds and RV Parks
Cielo Vista RV Resort 501 S Broadway Truth or Consequences NM   505-894-3738
Dogs of all sizes are allowed. There are no additional pet fees. Dogs may not be left unattended, and they must be quiet, well behaved, be on no more than a 6 foot leash, and cleaned up after. There is a dog walk area at the campground.

Tucumcari

Accommodations
Best Western Discovery Inn 200 East Estrella Ave Tucumcari NM   505-461-4884 (800-780-7234)
Dogs of all sizes are allowed. There is a $5 per night pet fee per pet. Smoking and non-smoking rooms are available for pets.
Best Western Pow Wow Inn 801 W Tucumcari Blvd Tucumcari NM   505-461-0500 (800-780-7234)
Dogs of all sizes are allowed. There are no additional pet fees. Smoking and non-smoking rooms are available for pets.
Comfort Inn 2800 E Tucumcari Blvd Tucumcari NM   505-461-4094 (877-424-6423)
Dogs of all sizes are allowed. There is a $6 per night per pet additional fee. Dogs must be leashed, cleaned up after, and the Do Not Disturb sign put on the door and a contact number left with the front desk if they are in the room alone.
Days Inn Tucumcari 2623 S First St Tucumcari NM   505-461-3158 (800-329-7466)
Dogs of all sizes are allowed. There is a $5 per night pet fee per pet.
Holiday Inn 3716 E. Tucumcari Blvd Tucumcari NM   505-461-3780 (877-270-6405)
There is a $6 one time pet fee.
Howard Johnson Express Inn 3604 E. Rt. 66 Blvd. Tucumcari NM   505-461-2747 (800-446-4656)
Dogs of all sizes are welcome. There is a $6 per day pet fee.
Motel 6 - Tucumcari 2900 East Tucumcari Boulevard Tucumcari NM   505-461-4791 (800-466-8356)
One well-behaved family pet per room. Guest must notify front desk upon arrival. Guest is liable for any damages. In consideration of all guests, pets must never be left unattended in the guest rooms.

Campgrounds and RV Parks
Mountain Road RV Park 1700 Mountain Road Tucumcari NM   505-461-9628
http://www.mountainroadrvpark.com
Dogs of all sizes are allowed. There are no additional pet fees. Dogs may be walked anywhere in the park, but they must be taken to one of the dog walks to relieve themselves. Dogs may not be left unattended outside, and they must be leashed and cleaned up after. The camping and tent areas also allow dogs. There is a dog walk area at the campground.

Tularosa

Attractions
Tularosa Vineyards 23 Coyote Canyon Rd Tularosa NM   505-585-2260
http://www.tularosavineyards.com
Dogs on leash are allowed at the outdoor tables and property. Tables are located under pecan trees for shade. The hours are 12pm-5pm Monday-Sunday. It is located two miles from the town of Tularosa.

Villanueva

Campgrounds and RV Parks
Villanueva State Park P. O. Box 40 Villanueva NM   505-421-2957 (888-NMPARKS (667-2757))
A scenic, riverside canyon park, there are a variety of land and water recreational pursuits and places to explore.

Dogs of all sizes are allowed at no additional fee. Dogs may not be left unattended, and they must be on no more than a 10 foot leash, and be cleaned up after. Dogs are not allowed in buildings, but they are allowed on the trails. This campground is closed during the off-season. The camping and tent areas also allow dogs. Dogs are allowed in the camping cabins.

Watrous

Attractions
Fort Union National Monument Po Box 127 Watrous NM 505-425-8025
http://www.nps.gov/foun/index.htm
Dogs must be on leash and must be cleaned up after in park areas. Dogs are not allowed off trails and into backcountry.

White's City

Accommodations
Best Western Cavern Inn 17 Carlsbad Caverns Hwy White's City NM 505-785-2291 (800-780-7234)
Dogs of all sizes are allowed. There is a $10 per night pet fee per pet. Smoking and non-smoking rooms are available for pets.
Whites City Resort 17 Carlsbad Cavern H White's City NM 505-785-2291 (800-CAVERNS(228-3767))
Dogs of all sizes are allowed. There is a $10 per night per pet additional fee for the Walnut Inn. Dogs must be quiet, well behaved, leashed, and cleaned up after. There is also a campground on site that allows dogs at no additional fee.

Campgrounds and RV Parks
White City Resort 17 Carlsbad Caverns Highway White's City NM 800-228-3767
http://www.whitecity.com/
Dogs of all sizes are allowed. There are no additional pet fees for the tent or RV sites. There is a $10 per night per pet additional fee for the Walnut Inn. Dogs must be quiet, well behaved, leashed, and cleaned up after. The camping and tent areas also allow dogs. There is a dog walk area at the campground.

Zuni

Stores
Pueblo of Zuni Arts & Crafts 1222 State Highway 53 Zuni NM 505-782-5531
http://www.ashiwi.org/Enterprise.aspx
This enterprise features authentic and intricate jewelry, pottery, paintings, textiles, and more, and is one of the most important outlets for the arts here, supporting many of the artisans of the area. Your well behaved and trained dog may go into the shop with you. Dogs must be friendly and under owner's control at all times.

Chapter 20

Oregon
Dog Travel Guide

Albany

Accommodations

Best Western Albany Inn 315 Airport Rd SE Albany OR 541-928-6322 (800-780-7234)
Dogs of all sizes are allowed. There is a $10 per night pet fee per pet. Smoking and non-smoking rooms are available for pets.
Days Inn Albany 1100 Price Road SE Albany OR 541-928-5050 (800-329-7466)
Dogs of all sizes are allowed. There is a $10 per night pet fee per pet.
Holiday Inn Express Hotel and Suites 105 Opal court Albany OR 541-928-8820 (877-270-6405)
Dogs of all sizes are allowed. There is a $30 one time pet fee per visit. Smoking and non-smoking rooms are available for pets.
La Quinta Inn & Suites Albany 251 Airport Rd SE Albany OR 541-928-0921 (800-531-5900)
Dogs of all sizes are allowed. There are no additional pet fees. There is a pet waiver to sign at check in. Dogs must be leashed and cleaned up after.
Motel 6 - Albany 2735 East Pacific Boulevard Albany OR 541-926-4233 (800-466-8356)
One well-behaved family pet per room. Guest must notify front desk upon arrival. Guest is liable for any damages. In consideration of all guests, pets must never be left unattended in the guest rooms.

Campgrounds and RV Parks

Albany/Corvallis KOA 33775 Oakville Road S Albany OR 541-967-8521 (800-562-8526)
http://www.koa.com
Dogs of all sizes are allowed. There are no additional pet fees. Dogs must be quiet, well behaved, be on no more than a 6 foot leash, and be cleaned up after. There are some breed restrictions. The camping and tent areas also allow dogs. There is a dog walk area at the campground.

Arch Cape

Accommodations

Inn Arch Cape 79340 Hwy 101 Arch Cape OR 503-738-7373
Dogs of all sizes are allowed. There is a $15 per night per pet fee and a pet policy to sign at check in.

Ashland

Accommodations

Best Western Bard's Inn 132 N Main St Ashland OR 541-482-0049 (800-780-7234)
Dogs of all sizes are allowed. There is a $15 per night pet fee per pet. Only non-smoking rooms used for pets.
Best Western Windsor Inn 2520 Ashland St Ashland OR 541-488-2330 (800-780-7234)
Dogs of all sizes are allowed. There is a $15 one time per pet fee per visit. Smoking and non-smoking rooms are available for pets.
La Quinta Inn & Suites Ashland 434 Valley View Rd Ashland OR 541-482-6932 (800-531-5900)
Dogs of all sizes are allowed. There are no additional pet fees. There is a pet waiver to sign at check in. Dogs may not be left unattended, and they must be leashed at all times, and cleaned up after.
Super 8 Ashland 2350 Ashland St Ashland OR 541-482-8887 (800-800-8000)
Dogs of all sizes are allowed. There is a $10 per night pet fee per pet. Smoking and non-smoking rooms are available for pet rooms.
Windmill Inn and Suites 2525 Ashland Street Ashland OR 541-482-8310
Dogs of all sizes are allowed. There is a pet policy to sign at check in and there are no additional pet fees.

Off-Leash Dog Parks

The Dog Park Nevada and Helman Streets Ashland OR 541-488-6002
http://www.ashland.or.us
This 2 acre fenced dog park has picnic tables and drinking water. It is located behind the Ashland Greenhouse

Oregon - Please always call ahead to make sure that an establishment is still dog-friendly

and Nursery, off Nevada, across from Helman Street.

Astoria

Accommodations
Best Western Astoria Inn 555 Hamburg Ave Astoria OR 503-325-2205 (800-780-7234)
Dogs of all sizes are allowed. There is a $10 per night pet fee per pet. Smoking and non-smoking rooms are available for pets.
Crest Motel 5366 Leif Erikson Drive Astoria OR 503-325-3141
Dogs of all sizes are allowed. There are no additional pet fees.
Holiday Inn Express Hotel and Suites 204 West Marine Dr Astoria OR 888-898-6222 (877-270-6405)
Dogs of all sizes are allowed. There is a $15 per night pet fee per pet. Only non-smoking rooms are used for pets.

Attractions
Fort Astoria 15th and Exchange Streets Astoria OR 503-325-6311
This small park has a partial replica of the fort and is located where John Jacob Astor's fur traders originally constructed their fort. There is a mural recreating the vista from the Fort in 1813, and serves as a backdrop to the recreated stockade building. Dogs may join their owners here, but they must be leashed and cleaned up after.

Parks
Lewis and Clark National Historical Park 92343 Fort Clatsop Rd Astoria OR 503-861-2471
http://www.nps.gov/lewi/index.htm
Dogs must be on leash and must be cleaned up after in the park grounds. They are not allowed in visitor center or in the rooms in the fort. The park features hiking, nature walks and more.

Baker City

Accommodations
Best Western Sunridge Inn 1 Sunridge Lane Baker City OR 541-523-6444 (800-780-7234)
Dogs of all sizes are allowed. There is a $15 per night pet fee per pet. Smoking and non-smoking rooms are available for pets.

Campgrounds and RV Parks
Oregon Trails West RV Park 42534 N Cedar Road Baker City OR 888-523-3236
Dogs of all sizes are allowed. There are no additional pet fees. Dogs must be quiet, leashed and cleaned up after. Dogs may not be left unattended. The camping and tent areas also allow dogs. There is a dog walk area at the campground.
Wallowa-Whitman National Forest 1550 Dewey Avenue Baker City OR 541-523-6391
http://www.fs.fed.us/r6/w-w/
These forests were combined creating 2.3 million acres of spectacular scenery, hundreds of miles of trails, and diverse ecosystems that support a large variety of plants, animals, and recreation. Dogs of all sizes are allowed at no additional fee. Dogs may not be left unattended, and they must be leashed and cleaned up after in camp areas. Dogs are allowed on the trails. This campground is closed during the off-season. The camping and tent areas also allow dogs. There is a dog walk area at the campground.

Bandon

Accommodations
Best Western Inn at Face Rock 3225 Beach Loop Rd Bandon OR 541-347-9441 (800-780-7234)
Dogs of all sizes are allowed. There is a $15 one time pet fee per visit and $5 for each additional pet. Smoking and non-smoking rooms are available for pets.
Driftwood Motel 460 Hwy 101 Bandon OR 541-347-9022

There is a $10 per day pet fee.
Sunset Motel 1755 Beach Loop Rd Bandon OR   541-347-2453 (800-842-2407)
http://www.sunsetmotel.com/
There is a $10 per day pet charge. All rooms are non-smoking.

Campgrounds and RV Parks
Bandon by the Sea RV Park 49612 Hwy 101 Bandon OR   541-347-5155
http://www.bandonbythesearvpark.com
Dogs of all sizes are allowed. There are no additional pet fees. Dogs must be well behaved, leashed, and cleaned up after. Dogs may be left in your RV only if they will be comfortable and quiet, and they are not allowed at the club house. There is a dog walk area at the campground.
Bullards Beach State Park 52470 Hwy 101 Bandon OR   541-347-2209 (800-452-5687)
This is a large, family-oriented park nestled among the pines along the Coquille River, and offers an historic lighthouse with tours (seasonal) as well as various recreational pursuits. When visiting the park you can bring your binoculars for viewing the wildlife refuge just across the river. Dogs of all sizes are allowed at no additional fee. Dogs may not be left unattended except for short periods, and only if they will be quiet and well behaved. Dogs must be on no more than a 6 foot leash, and cleaned up after. Dogs are allowed on the trails. The camping and tent areas also allow dogs. There is a dog walk area at the campground.

Beaches
Bullards Beach State Park Highway 101 Bandon OR   541-347-2209
Enjoy a walk along the beach at this park. Picnic tables, restrooms, hiking and campgrounds are available at the park. There is a minimal day use fees. Leashed dogs are allowed on the beach. Dogs are also allowed on hiking trails and campgrounds. They must be on a six foot or less leash at all times and people are required to clean up after their pets. On beaches located outside of Oregon State Park boundaries, dogs might be allowed off-leash and under direct voice control, please look for signs or postings. This park is located off U.S. Highway 101, 2 miles north of Bandon.
Seven Devils State Recreation Site Highway 101 Bandon OR   800-551-6949
Enjoy several miles of beach at this park. Picnic tables are available at this park. There are no day use fees. Dogs are allowed on the beach. They must be on a six foot or less leash at all times and people are required to clean up after their pets. On beaches located outside of Oregon State Park boundaries, dogs might be allowed off-leash and under direct voice control, please look for signs or postings. This park is located off U.S. Highway 101, 10 miles north of Bandon.

Parks
Bullards Beach State Park Hwy 101, 2 miles North of Bandon Bandon OR   541-347-2209
This scenic park sits at the mouth of the Coquille River on Oregon's south coast, and features a historic lighthouse that is located at the end of the beach access road. During the summer months they offer evening history, nature and entertainment programs in the park's amphitheater. Park amenities also include a variety of trails, 4.5 miles of beach, historic sites and displays, a boat launch, ADA restrooms, interpretive signage, and various land and water recreation. The park is open daily from 7 a.m. to sunset. Dogs of all sizes are allowed for no additional fee. Dogs may not be left unattended at any time, and they must be on no more than a 6 foot leash, and cleaned up after. Dogs are allowed on all the trails and throughout the park. There is camping at this park with full RV hook-ups, and dogs are allowed at tent or RV sites, but not at the yurts.

Bend

Accommodations
Best Western Inn and Suites of Bend 721 NE 3rd St Bend OR   541-382-1515 (800-780-7234)
Dogs of all sizes are allowed. There is a $10 per night pet fee per pet. Only non-smoking rooms used for pets.
Entrada Lodge 19221 Century Dr Bend OR   541-382-4080
There is a $5 per day pet fee. Pets may not be left alone in the room.
Hampton Inn 15 NE Butler Market Road Bend OR   541-388-4114
Dogs of all sizes are allowed. There is a $10 per night per pet fee. There are only 2 non-smoking pet rooms available.
Holiday Inn Express Hotel 20615 Grandview Drive Bend OR   541-317-8500 (877-270-6405)
There is a $10 per day pet fee. Pets may not be left alone in the room.
La Quinta Inn Bend 61200 S Highway 97 Bend OR   541-388-2227 (800-531-5900)
Dogs of all sizes are allowed. There are no additional pet fees. There is a pet waiver to sign at check in. Dogs must be leashed and cleaned up after. They prefer that dogs are not left unattended in the room, but if you must

be out for a short time, they must be crated.

Motel 6 - Bend 201 Northeast 3rd Street Bend OR   541-382-8282 (800-466-8356)
One well-behaved family pet per room. Guest must notify front desk upon arrival. Guest is liable for any damages. In consideration of all guests, pets must never be left unattended in the guest rooms.

Quality Inn 20600 Grandview Drive Bend OR   541-318-0848 (877-424-6423)
One dog of any size is allowed. There is a $10 per night additional pet fee. Your pet may not be left alone in the room, and must be leashed and cleaned up after.

Red Lion 1415 NE Third Street Bend OR   541-382-7011
Dogs of all sizes are allowed. There is a pet policy to sign at check in and there are no additional fees.

Red Lion 849 NE Third Street Bend OR   541-382-8384
Dogs of all sizes are allowed. There is a pet policy to sign at check in and there are no additional fees.

Sleep Inn 600 N E Bellvue Bend OR   541-330-0050 (877-424-6423)
One dog of any size is allowed. There is a $10 one time additional pet fee. Dogs may not be left alone in the room, and they must be leashed and cleaned up after.

Super 8 Bend 1275 S Hwy 97 Bend OR   541-388-6888 (800-800-8000)
Dogs of all sizes are allowed. There is a $25 returnable deposit required per room. There is a $10 one time per pet fee per visit. Smoking and non-smoking rooms are available for pet rooms.

The Riverhouse Resort 3075 N Hwy 97 Bend OR   541-389-3111
You need to sign a pet policy.

Westward Ho Motel 904 SE Third Street Bend OR   541-382-2111
Dogs only are allowed and of all sizes. There are no additional pet fees.

Comfort Suites Airport 2243 SW Yew Avenue Redmond OR   541-504-8900 (877-424-6423)
Dogs of all sizes are allowed. There can be up to 2 medium to large dogs or up to 3 small dogs per room. There is a $25 one time additional fee per pet. Dogs must be leashed, cleaned up after, and crated when left alone in the room.

Motel 6 - Redmond 2247 South US Route 97 Redmond OR   541-923-2100 (800-466-8356)
One well-behaved family pet per room. Guest must notify front desk upon arrival. Guest is liable for any damages. In consideration of all guests, pets must never be left unattended in the guest rooms.

Super 8 Redmond 3629 SW 21st Place Redmond OR   541-548-8881 (800-800-8000)
Dogs of all sizes are allowed. There is a $10 one time per pet fee per visit. Smoking and non-smoking rooms are available for pet rooms.

Sunset Realty 56805 Ventura Lane Sunriver OR   541-593-5018 (800-541-1756)
http://www.sunriverlodging.com/
This realty company offers dozens of pet friendly, fully-furnished vacation homes and condos in the Sunriver resort area of Oregon. They feature many different amenities such as private hot tubs, pool/foos tables, barbecues, fireplaces with supplies, phones in all units, cable TV, and completely equipped kitchens. Dogs are allowed for an additional fee of $10 per night per pet, or $15 per night if there is more than one pet. Dogs must be well mannered, leashed, and cleaned up after.

Campgrounds and RV Parks

Deschutes National Forest 1001 SW Emkay Drive Bend OR   541-383-5300
http://www.fs.fed.us/r6/centraloregon/
Rich in natural and cultural history, this forest is home to the Newberry National Volcanic Monument, 8 wilderness areas and hundreds of miles of trails. The park also offers many diverse scenic and recreational opportunities. Dogs of all sizes are allowed at no additional fee. Dogs must be leashed and cleaned up after. This campground is closed during the off-season. The camping and tent areas also allow dogs. There is a dog walk area at the campground.

Sisters/Bend KOA 67667 Hwy 20W Bend OR   541-549-3021 (800-562-0363)
http://www.koa.com
Dogs of all sizes are allowed. There are no additional pet fees. Dogs must be leashed and cleaned up after. This RV park is closed during the off-season. The camping and tent areas also allow dogs. There is a dog walk area at the campground.

Vacation Home Rentals

Sunray Vacation Rentals Call to Arrange Sunriver OR   541-593-3225 (800-531-1130)
http://www.sunrayinc.com
These vacation properties allow pets for a $25 fee per pet. Some homes have limits on the size and quantity of pets so be sure and check when making reservations.

Attractions

Peterson Rock Gardens 7930 SW 77th Street Redmond OR   541-382-5574
When Danish immigrant Peterson came to America at 17 he started collecting all kinds of colorful local rocks from the area of his home. It resulted in an amazing 4 acre park featuring miniature bridges, towers, terraces,

and replicas of historic buildings created out of rock and petrified wood. There is a museum featuring a variety of rock specimens, and picnic sites are available on the grounds. Well behaved dogs of all sizes are allowed. Dogs must be leashed at all times and properly cleaned up after. They are allowed throughout the park and on the trails, but not in the buildings. The museum is open daily from 9 am to 5 pm, and the park is open from 9 am to sunset.

Sunriver Nature Center 57245 River Road Sunriver OR 541-593-4394
http://www.sunrivernaturecenter.org/
This private, not-for-profit scientific and educational center features interpretive exhibits, a large scale public observatory, botanical garden, educational programs, an Astronomy store, and a nature center and trail. There are day and evening programs and times vary throughout the year. Dogs of all sizes are allowed to explore the grounds and trails with their owners, but they are not allowed in the buildings. Dogs must be leashed and cleaned up after.

Cross Country Ski Resorts

TOP 200 PLACE **Mount Bachelor Ski Resort** 13000 SW Century Drive Bend OR 800-829-2442
http://mtbachelor.com/
As one of North Americas' largest ski resorts, skiers, snowboarders, and Nordic skiers will find great conditions with plenty of snow, a large terrain, short lift lines, great value, 4 different terrain parks, and an Olympic size superpipe. Mt. Bachelor is nearly 3700 acres of varied terrain atop the high desert of the Central Cascades in the Deschutes National Forest. They also offer tubing, snowshoeing, dog sledding, and they host the North American Pond Skimming Championships each year. They are open from mid-November to Memorial Day for the ski season, and from July 1st through Labor Day for summer sight-seeing. Dogs of all sizes are allowed throughout the year. In the summer, your pet can even ride the chair lift, and is allowed throughout the park. In the winter, there are some ski trails and trails that dogs can be on. Dogs must be leashed at all times, and cleaned up after. Dogs must be friendly and well behaved.

Stores

PetSmart Pet Store 63455 N Hwy 97 Bend OR 541-330-0178
Your licensed and well-behaved leashed dog is allowed in the store.
Petco Pet Store 3197 #5 N Highway 97 Bend OR 541-382-0510
Your licensed and well-behaved leashed dog is allowed in the store.

Off-Leash Dog Parks

Big Sky Dog Park 21690 NE Neff Road Bend OR 541-389-7275
The Big Sky Off-Leash Dog Park opened in 2005. It is 3 acres and completely fenced. There are picnic tables and water for your dog. You can walk your dog on leash outside of the dog park in the 90 acre Big Sky Park with walking trails, ponds and landscaping. The park is on the east side of town on Neff Rd east of Hamby Rd.

Bridal Veil

Parks

Bridal Veil Falls State Park M.P. 28 on the Columbia River Scenic H Bridal Veil OR 800-551-6949
Located in a large timber stand, this park offers nice grassy areas, picnic tables, and restrooms, all within easy walking distance from the parking area. One trail is an upper walking/interpretive trail that takes visitors around the precipice of the cliffs of the Gorge. Sign boards along the way point out distinctive native wild plants that grow abundantly in the area. The lower trail takes visitors downhill to the base of the 120 foot Bridal Veil Falls and is about a mile round trip. They say it is dangerous to walk along the bridge over the Historic Highway to view the falls, and to PLEASE view the falls from the trail. The falls can be fully appreciated from the deck of a viewing platform. Dogs of all sizes are allowed. Dogs must be leashed at all times and cleaned up after. They are allowed throughout the park and on the trails.

Brookings

Accommodations

Whaleshead Beach Resort 19921 Whaleshead Road Brookings OR 541-469-7446 (800-943-4325)
http://www.whalesheadresort.com/

This enchanting resort features individually decorated cottages with ocean, creek, or forest settings, and there is access to the beautiful Whaleshead Beach via a 700 foot tunnel or a short drive by car (dogs are allowed on the beach under voice control or a 6 foot leash). Some of the amenities include ocean view dining and lounge, TV/VCRs, coffee makers, barbecues, and hot tubs. Dogs of all sizes are allowed for an additional fee of $10 per night per pet. Two cabins will allow 2 pets; the others will only accept 1 pet per room. Dogs must be leashed and cleaned up after, and may only be left alone in the room if they will be quiet and well behaved. There is also an RV area on site and dogs are welcome there for no additional fees or number of dog restrictions.

Campgrounds and RV Parks

At Rivers Edge RV Park 98203 S Bank Chetco River Road Brookings OR   541-469-3356 (888-295-1441)
http://www.atriversedge.com/
Dogs of all sizes are allowed. There are no additional pet fees. Dogs may not be left unattended unless they will be quiet and well behaved. Dogs must be leashed and cleaned up after. Dogs may be off lead on your site only if they are under voice command and will not chase. The camping and tent areas also allow dogs. There is a dog walk area at the campground.
Harris Beach State Park 1655 Hwy 101N Brookings OR   541-469-2021 (800-452-5687)
This park sits along the coastline making marine mammal watching a favorite here. The park also offers interpretive events, nature programs, trails, and a variety of land and water recreation. Dogs of all sizes are allowed at no additional fee. Dogs may not be left unattended; they must be on no more than a 6 foot leash or crated, and cleaned up after. Dogs are allowed on the trails. Dogs are not allowed in buildings. The camping and tent areas also allow dogs. There is a dog walk area at the campground.
Whaleshead Beach Resort 19921 Whaleshead Road Brookings OR   541-469-7446 (800-943-4325)
http://www.whalesheadresort.com/
Located in a unique ocean side resort in a forested setting, this scenic RV park features terraced spacious sites, private decks, a market and gift store, clean restrooms and showers, a laundry, and a restaurant/lounge is also on the property. Dogs of all sizes are allowed for no additional fee, and they must be declared at the time of registration. Dogs must be well behaved, and leashed and cleaned up after at all times. Dogs are also welcome at the resort in the cabins for an additional per night fee, and they are allowed on the beach under voice control or on a 6 foot leash. There is a dog walk area at the campground.

Beaches

Harris Beach State Park Highway 101 Brookings OR   541-469-2021
The park offers sandy beaches for beachcombing, whale watching, and sunset viewing. Picnic tables, restrooms (including an ADA restroom) and shaded campsites are available at this park. There is a minimal day use fee. Leashed dogs are allowed on the beach. Dogs are also allowed at the campgrounds. They must be on a six foot or less leash at all times and people are required to clean up after their pets. On beaches located outside of Oregon State Park boundaries, dogs might be allowed off-leash and under direct voice control, please look for signs or postings. This park is located off U.S. Highway 101, just north of Brookings.
McVay Rock State Recreation Site Highway 101 Brookings OR   800-551-6949
This beach is a popular spot for clamming, whale watching and walking. Picnic tables and restrooms are available at this park. There are no day use fees. Dogs are allowed on the beach. They must be on a six foot or less leash at all times and people are required to clean up after their pets. On beaches located outside of Oregon State Park boundries, dogs might be allowed off-leash and under direct voice control, please look for signs or postings. This park is located off U.S. Highway 101, just south of Brookings.
Samuel H. Boardman State Scenic Corridor Highway 101 Brookings OR   800-551-6949
Steep coastline at this 12 mile long corridor is interrupted by small sandy beaches. Picnic tables, restrooms (including an ADA restroom), and a hiking trail are available at this park. There are no day use fees. Leashed dogs are allowed on the beach. Dogs are also allowed on the hiking trail. They must be on a six foot or less leash at all times and people are required to clean up after their pets. On beaches located outside of Oregon State Park boundaries, dogs might be allowed off-leash and under direct voice control, please look for signs or postings. This park is located off U.S. Highway 101, 4 miles north of Brookings.

Parks

Azalea Park Chetcho River Road Brookings OR   541-469-2021
A labor of love by volunteers brought this beautiful park and it's long rich history to life again. They filled the garden with year-round plants with more than 400 rhododendrons, bulbs, annuals, shrubs, and ornamental trees. Now it is a place for rest and relaxation, picnics, weddings, birthday parties, reunions, civic affairs, and concerts (including the American Music Festival Free Summer Concert Series). Well behaved dogs are allowed. They must be on a lead, under the owners' control at all times, and cleaned up after. They do not provide clean up bags.

Burns

Accommodations
Days Inn Burns 577 W Monroe Burns OR   541-573-2047 (800-329-7466)
Dogs of all sizes are allowed. There is a $5 per night pet fee per pet. Reservations are recommended due to limited rooms for pets. Only non-smoking rooms are used for pets.
Silver Spur Motel 789 N Broadway Avenue Burns OR   541-573-2077
This motel features a breakfast buffet, HBO/cable TV and refrigerators/microwaves in all rooms. Dogs of all sizes are allowed for an additional fee of $5 per night per pet for 2 dogs, and an additional $5 more per night if there are more than 2. Dogs must be well behaved, leashed, cleaned up after, and crated when left alone in the room.

Canby

Off-Leash Dog Parks
Molalla River State Park Off-Leash Area Canby Ferry Road Canby OR   800-551-6949
This state park offers a designated off-leash exercise area. Dogs must be leashed in all other areas of the park. The park is located about 2 miles north of Canby.

Cannon Beach

Accommodations
Hallmark Inns 1400 S Hemlock Cannon Beach OR   503-436-1566
Dogs of all sizes are allowed. There is a $12 per night per pet additional fee.
Surfsand Resort 148 W. Gower Cannon Beach OR   503-436-2274 (1-800-547-6100)
http://www.surfsand.com/
This resort offers views of Haystack Rock and the Pacific Ocean from oceanfront and ocean-view rooms. The Surfsand is a nice vacation spot for families and couples. The hotel caters to four-legged family members and they host an annual "For Fun" Dog Show. The resort is entirely non-smoking and it is located near a dog-friendly restaurant called The Local Scoop. There is a $12 per day pet fee.
The Haystack Resort 3361 S. Hemlock Cannon Beach OR   503-436-1577 (1-800-499-2220)
http://www.haystackresort.com/
Every room and suite at the Haystack Resort offers complete ocean views. Your pet is always welcome. They are located near a dog-friendly restaurant called "The Local Scoop. There is a $10 per day additional pet fee.
The Inn at Cannon Beach 3215 S. Hemlock Cannon Beach OR   503-436-9085 (800-321-6304)
There is a $10 per day pet fee. A maximum of two pets per room is allowed.

Campgrounds and RV Parks
Cannon Beach RV Resort 340 Elk Creek Road Cannon Beach OR   800-847-2231
http://www.cbrvresort.com
Dogs of all sizes are allowed. There are no additional pet fees. Dogs may not be left unattended, and they must be well behaved, leashed, and cleaned up after. There is a dog walk area at the campground.
Sea Ranch RV Park and Stables 415 1st Street Cannon Beach OR   503-436-2815
http://www.searanchrv.com
Dogs of all sizes are allowed. There is a $2 per night per pet additional fee. Dogs may not be left unattended, and they must be leashed and cleaned up after. Dogs must be friendly to other animals because there are a variety of animals on site, including a free range bunny population. The camping and tent areas also allow dogs. There is a dog walk area at the campground.

Beaches
Arcadia Beach State Recreation Site Highway 101 Cannon Beach OR   800-551-6949
This sandy ocean beach is just a few feet from where you can park your car. Picnic tables and restrooms are available at this park. There are no day use fees. Dogs are allowed on the beach. They must be on a six foot or less leash at all times and people are required to clean up after their pets. On beaches located outside of Oregon

State Park boundaries, dogs might be allowed off-leash and under direct voice control, please look for signs or postings. This park is located off U.S. Highway 101, 3 miles south of Cannon Beach.

TOP 200 PLACE **Ecola State Park** Highway 101 Cannon Beach OR 503-436-2844
According to the Oregon State Parks Division, this park is one of the most photographed locations in Oregon. To reach the beach, you will need to walk down a trail. Restrooms, hiking and primitive campgrounds are available at this park. There is a $3 day use fee. Leashed dogs are allowed on the beach. Dogs are also allowed on hiking trails and campgrounds. They must be on a six foot or less leash at all times and people are required to clean up after their pets. On beaches located outside of Oregon State Park boundaries, dogs might be allowed off-leash and under direct voice control, please look for signs or postings. This park is located off U.S. Highway 101, 2 miles north of Cannon Beach.

Hug Point State Recreation Site Highway 101 Cannon Beach OR 800-551-6949
According to the Oregon State Parks Division, people used to travel via stagecoach along this beach before the highway was built. Today you can walk along the original trail which was carved into the point by stagecoaches. The trail is located north of the parking area. Visitors can also explore two caves around the point, but be aware of high tide. Some people have become stranded at high tide when exploring the point! This beach is easily accessible from the parking area. Picnic tables and restrooms are available at this park. There are no day use fees. Dogs are allowed on the beach. They must be on a six foot or less leash at all times and people are required to clean up after their pets. On beaches located outside of Oregon State Park boundaries, dogs might be allowed off-leash and under direct voice control, please look for signs or postings. This park is located off U.S. Highway 101, 5 miles south of Cannon Beach.

Tolovana Beach State Recreation Site Highway 101 Cannon Beach OR 800-551-6949
Indian Beach is popular with surfers. There is a short walk down to the beach. Picnic tables are available at this park. There are no day fees. Dogs are allowed on the beach. They must be on a six foot or less leash at all times and people are required to clean up after their pets. On beaches located outside of Oregon State Park boundaries, dogs might be allowed off-leash and under direct voice control, please look for signs or postings. This park is located off U.S. Highway 101, 1 mile south of Cannon Beach.

Carlton

Attractions
Anne Amie Vineyards 6580 NE Mineral Springs Road Carlton OR 503-864-2991
http://www.anneamie.com/home.htm
With the goal to make the finest Pinot Noir in the world, this beautiful winery also offers a wide variety of activities throughout the year. Your pet may join you on the patio and around the picnic areas. Dogs are not allowed in the tasting room or in the vineyards. Dogs must be well behaved, leashed, and cleaned up after at all times. They also ask that you do not bring your pet on holiday weekends because of the large crowds. The tasting room is open from 9 am to 5 pm daily.

Carson

Attractions
Wind River Experimental Forest/Arboretum 1262 Hemlock Road Carson OR 509-427-3200
This arboretum, located in the Gifford Pinchot National Forest, was designed as a research facility for the adaptability of foreign tree species in relation to the northwestern United States. As a result of various testing of terrestrial and aquatic ecosystems, they feature a wide variety of plant and animal species. In addition to containing a section of the Pacific Crest Trail, there is also a 1.5 mile interpretive trail. Dogs are allowed throughout the park; please keep to paths. Dogs must be leashed and cleaned up after.

Cascade Locks

Accommodations
Best Western Columbia River Inn 735 Wanapa St Cascade Locks OR 541-374-8777 (800-780-7234)
Dogs of all sizes are allowed. There is a $10 per night pet fee per pet. Smoking and non-smoking rooms are available for pets.

Campgrounds and RV Parks

Cascade Locks/Portland East KOA 841 NW Forest Lane Cascade Locks OR   541-374-8668 (800-562-8698)
http://www.koa.com
Dogs of all sizes are allowed. There are no additional pet fees. Dogs may not be left unattended at any time, must be leashed, and cleaned up after. There are some breed restrictions. This RV park is closed during the off-season. The camping and tent areas also allow dogs. There is a dog walk area at the campground. Dogs are allowed in the camping cabins.

Port of Cascade Locks and Marine Park 355 WaNaPa Street Cascade Locks OR   541-374-8619
http://www.portofcascadelocks.org/
The Marine Park here is a 23-acre scenic paradise, perfect for picnics, camping, weddings and outdoor events for groups up to 1000 people. This park is also home to the Sternwheeler Columbia Gorge and the Cascade Locks Historical Museum. They offer a visitors' center, gift shop, 37-slip marina, public boat launch, a playground, RV accommodations, a recently remodeled Gorge Pavilion, and a foot bridge that accesses the adjacent three-acre Thunder Island. Although dogs are not allowed on any of the boats here, they are allowed in the camp area and around the park. Dogs must be leashed and cleaned up after at all times. The camping and tent areas also allow dogs. There is a dog walk area at the campground.

Port of Cascade Locks and Marine Park 355 WaNaPa Street Cascade Locks OR   541-374-8619
http://www.portofcascadelocks.org/
The Marine Park here is a 23-acre scenic paradise, perfect for picnics, camping, weddings and outdoor events for groups up to 1000 people. This park is also home to the Sternwheeler Columbia Gorge and the Cascade Locks Historical Museum. They offer a visitors' center, gift shop, 37-slip marina, public boat launch, a playground, RV accommodations, a recently remodeled Gorge Pavilion, and a foot bridge that accesses the adjacent three-acre Thunder Island. Although dogs are not allowed on any of the boats here, they are allowed in the camp area and around the park. Dogs must be leashed and cleaned up after at all times. The camping and tent areas also allow dogs. There is a dog walk area at the campground.

Cave Junction

Accommodations

Junction Inn 406 Redwood Hwy Cave Junction OR   541-592-3106
There is a $5 per day additional pet fee. They normally put dogs in smoking rooms, but will make exceptions.

Parks

Oregon Caves National Monument 19000 Caves Highway Cave Junction OR   541-592-2100
http://www.nps.gov/orca/index.htm
Dogs must be on leash and must be cleaned up after on all trails. They are not allowed in any caves.

Central Point

Campgrounds and RV Parks

Medford/Gold Hill KOA 12297 Blackwell Road Central Point OR   541-855-7710 (800-562-7608)
http://www.koa.com/where/or/37109/
Dogs of all sizes are allowed. There are no additional pet fees. Dogs must be quiet, well behaved, leashed, and cleaned up after. Dogs may not be left unattended, and may be left outside alone only if they are in an enclosed pen. There are some breed restrictions. The camping and tent areas also allow dogs. There is a dog walk area at the campground. Dogs are allowed in the camping cabins.

Charleston

Campgrounds and RV Parks

Charleston Marina RV Park 63402 King Fisher Road Charleston OR   541-888-2548
Dogs of all sizes are allowed. There are no additional pet fees. Dogs may not be left unattended, and they must be leashed and cleaned up after. This RV park is closed during the off-season. The camping and tent areas also allow dogs. There is a dog walk area at the campground.

Coos Bay

Accommodations

Motel 6 - Coos Bay 1445 Bayshore Drive Coos Bay OR   541-267-7171 (800-466-8356)
One well-behaved family pet per room. Guest must notify front desk upon arrival. Guest is liable for any damages. In consideration of all guests, pets must never be left unattended in the guest rooms.
Red Lion 1313 N Bayshore Drive Coos Bay OR   541-267-4141
Dogs of all sizes are allowed. There is no fee if a credit card is on file; if cash, it is a $40 refundable deposit.

Campgrounds and RV Parks

Lucky Loggers RV Park 250 E Johnson Coos Bay OR   541-267-6003
Dogs of all sizes are allowed. There are no additional pet fees. Dogs must be leashed and cleaned up after. There is a dog walk area at the campground.
Sunset Bay State Park 89814 Cape Arago Coos Bay OR   541-888-4902 (800-452-5687)
This picturesque park, along the Oregon coast, features sandy beaches sheltered by towering sea cliffs, interpretive and nature programs, a network of hiking trails, and a variety of land and water recreation. Dogs of all sizes are allowed at no additional fee, and they must have current tags, rabies, and shot records. Dogs may not be left unattended; they must be on no more than a 6 foot leash, and cleaned up after. Dogs are allowed on the trails except where marked. Dogs are not allowed in Shore Acres. The camping and tent areas also allow dogs. There is a dog walk area at the campground.

Attractions

Cape Arago Lighthouse Chief's Island Coos Bay OR
Someday the lighthouse may be open to the public with an interpretive center so that visitors can enjoy up close the rich history of the Oregon Coast. But for now, the lighthouse may be viewed from about 1 mile away. From US 101 Coos Bay, turn west onto West Commercial Ave and proceed 0.2 miles, Turn left (south) onto North 5th Stand, continue a 05 miles. Turn right onto W Central Ave and go 0 5 miles. Bear right onto Ocean Blvd and continue 2.6 miles. Turn left onto Newmark Ave and go 0.6 miles. Turn left onto Empire Blvd (which becomes Cape Arago Hwy) and continue south/west another eight miles (passing through the town of Charleston en route). Shortly after you pass the entrance to the camping area and before you reach Shore Acres, there will be a pullout area on your right from which you can get a distant view of the lighthouse. If you take Cape Arago Highway to Cape Arago State Park you have gone too far.
New Carissa Shipwreck North Spit Beach Coos Bay OR   800-547-7842
http://www.oregon.gov/DSL/LW/ncar.shtml
The 600-foot bulk freighter went aground roughly one mile north of the jetty, on Feb. 4, 1999, and several winter storms prevented the ship from being towed back to sea successfully causing the hull to eventually split into two parts. The bow was towed out to sea and sunk, and the stern is still mired in the sand on the North Spit. To get there, watch for the Oregon Dunes National Recreation Area, Horsefall Beach sign, approximately one-half mile north of the green McCullough bridge outside North Bend, OR. on US Highway 101. Turn west (left if northbound, right if southbound on US 101) and follow the Transpacific Parkway. You'll cross railroad tracks near the Weyerhaeuser facility. Bear right and cross the second set of railroad tracks, then bear left past the Horsfall Beach turnoff. The boat ramp is approximately three and one-half miles farther, and about 100 yards farther is the entrance to the North Spit road to the New Carissa on the right. The BLM requires visitors to keep pets on leash at all times. Also visitors with pets must stay in the wet sand portion of the beach, that is exposed at low tide, to avoid disturbing the nesting shorebirds.

Beaches

Sunset Bay State Park 89814 Cape Arrago H Coos Bay OR   541-888-4902
This scenic park's beautiful sandy beaches are protected by the towering sea cliffs surrounding them, and the day-use and picnic facilities are only a short walk from the beach allowing for easy access for beachcombing, fishing, swimming, and boating. There is a network of hiking trails that connect Sunset Bay with nearby Shore Acres and Cape Arago State Parks. These trails give the hiker opportunities to experience the pristine coastal forests, seasonal wildflowers, and the spectacular ocean vistas of the area. There is a fully enclosed observation building that has interpretive panels describing the history of the Simpson estate along the way. From points along the trail you can see views of Gregory Point and the Cape Arago lighthouse. The park is open year round from 8 a.m. until sunset. Dogs on lead at all times are allowed, and pets must be cleaned up after. Dogs may not be left unattended at any time. There is a campground here that offer a variety of activities and recreation.

Parks

Cape Arago State Park End of Cape Arago H Coos Bay OR 800-551-6949
Cape Arago sits on a scenic headland jetting out into the ocean, making it a premium place for watching ships, marine mammals, birds, terrestrial wildlife, and the off-shore colonies of seals and sea lions at Shell Island. The trail is closed March 1- June 30 to protect seal pups. There is a network of hiking trails that connect Cape Arago with nearby Sunset Bay and Shore Acres State Parks. These trails give the hiker opportunities to experience the coastal forests, seasonal wildflowers, and the spectacular ocean vistas of the area. There is a fully enclosed observation building that has interpretive panels describing the history of the Simpson estate along the way. From points along the trail you can see views of Gregory Point and the Cape Arago lighthouse. The park is open year round from 8 a.m. until sunset. Dogs on lead at all times are allowed, and pets must be cleaned up after. Dogs may not be left unattended at any time. There is a campground here that offers a variety of activities and recreation.

Shore Acres State Park Coos Bay Road Coos Bay OR 541-888-3732
Perched on rugged sandstone cliffs high above the ocean, Shore Acres is a combination of beautiful natural and constructed features. There is a garden here that has flowers from all over the world. Although pets are not allowed in the garden, they are allowed throughout the day use areas and trails, and may be left in your auto (weather permitting) while you tour the gardens. There is a network of hiking trails that connect Sunset Bay with nearby Shore Acres and Cape Arago State Parks. These trails give the hiker opportunities to experience the pristine coastal forests, seasonal wildflowers, and the spectacular ocean views. There is a fully enclosed observation building that has interpretive panels describing the history of the Simpson estate along the way. From points along the trail you can see views of Gregory Point and the Cape Arago lighthouse. The park is open year round from 8 a.m. until sunset.

Corvallis

Accommodations
Holiday Inn Express 781 NE Second Street Corvallis OR 541-752-0800 (877-270-6405)
Dogs of all sizes are allowed. There is a $15 per night pet fee per pet. Only non-smoking rooms are used for pets.

Motel 6 - Corvallis 935 Northwest Garfield Avenue Corvallis OR 541-758-9125 (800-466-8356)
One well-behaved family pet per room. Guest must notify front desk upon arrival. Guest is liable for any damages. In consideration of all guests, pets must never be left unattended in the guest rooms.

Super 8 Corvallis 407 NW 2nd Street Corvallis OR 541-758-8088 (800-800-8000)
Dogs of all sizes are allowed. There is a $25 returnable deposit required per room. Smoking and non-smoking rooms are available for pet rooms.

Campgrounds and RV Parks
Siuslaw National Forest 4077 SW Research Way Corvallis OR 541-750-7000
http://www.fs.fed.us/r6/siuslaw/
This very diverse and productive forest of over 630,000 acres has unique and varying ecosystems to explore and offers a wide variety of land and water recreation. Dogs of all sizes are allowed at no additional fee. Dogs may not be left unattended, and they must be leashed and cleaned up after. Dogs are not allowed in public swim areas or buildings. Dogs are allowed on the trails. The camping and tent areas also allow dogs. There is a dog walk area at the campground. There are no water hookups at the campground.

Stores
Petco Pet Store 2365 NW Kings Blvd Corvallis OR 541-766-8997
Your licensed and well-behaved leashed dog is allowed in the store.

Off-Leash Dog Parks
Bald Hill Park Dog Park Oak Creek Drive Corvallis OR 541-766-6918
http://www.ci.corvallis.or.us
There is a designated off-leash area located west of this park. People must clean up after their pets.

Chip Ross Park Dog Park Lester Avenue Corvallis OR 541-766-6918
http://www.ci.corvallis.or.us
This park has a designated off-leash area. People must clean up after their pets. The park is located at the end of Lester Avenue.

Crystal Lake Sports Field Dog Park Crystal Lake Drive Corvallis OR 541-766-6918
http://www.ci.corvallis.or.us
From March to November only, dogs can play off-leash at the non-improved turf areas. People must clean up after their pets. This sports field area is located off Crystal Lake Drive, adjacent to Williamette Park.

Walnut Park Dog Park Walnut Boulevard Corvallis OR   541-766-6918
http://www.ci.corvallis.or.us
This park has a designated off-leash area which is located in the southwest corner of the park. People must clean up after their pets.
Williamette Park Dog Park SE Goodnight Avenue Corvallis OR   541-766-6918
http://www.ci.corvallis.or.us
This park has a designated off-leash area. People must clean up after their pets. The park is located southeast of Corvallis, off Highway 99W on southeast Goodnight Avenue.
Woodland Meadow Park Dog Park Circle and Witham Hill Drive Corvallis OR   541-766-6918
http://www.ci.corvallis.or.us
This park has a designated off-leash area which is located in the upper portion of the park. People must clean up after their pets.

Cottage Grove

Accommodations
Comfort Inn 845 Gateway Blvd Cottage Grove OR   541-942-9747 (877-424-6423)
Dogs of all sizes are allowed. There is a $10 per night per pet additional fee. Dogs must be quiet, well behaved, leashed, and cleaned up after. Dogs may only be left for a short time in the room, and the Do Not Disturb sign put on the door with a contact number left at the front desk if they are in the room alone.
Holiday Inn Express 1601 Gateway Blvd Cottage Grove OR   541-942-1000 (877-270-6405)
There is a $10 per day pet fee for each pet.

Crater Lake

Campgrounds and RV Parks
Crater Lake National Park P.O. Box 7/S Entrance Road Crater Lake OR   541-594-2211
http://www.nps.gov/crla/
This beautiful and historical lake park is a very diverse area. It is almost 90% wilderness and supports a large variety of plants, fish, mammals, bird species, and recreation. Dogs of all sizes are allowed at no additional fee. Dogs may not be left unattended, and they must be leashed and cleaned up after. Dogs are not allowed in buildings or in the Rim Village area in the winter. Dogs are allowed on the trails. This campground is closed during the off-season. The camping and tent areas also allow dogs. There is a dog walk area at the campground.

Parks
Crater Lake National Park PO Box 7 Crater Lake OR   541-594-3100
http://www.nps.gov/crla/index.htm
Dogs must be on leash and must be cleaned up after in park. Dogs must remain in the developed portions of the park and are not allowed on the dirt trails or in the backcountry. They are allowed on the roads and the sidewalks. There is a road and sidewalk surrounding Crater Lake so you and your dog may view the lake and walk quite a ways around it. Dogs are not allowed in any buildings. Dogs are allowed in the campgrounds on leash in the park.

Creswell

Accommodations
Best Western Creswell Inn 345 E Oregon Ave Creswell OR   541-895-3341 (800-780-7234)
Dogs of all sizes are allowed. There is a $10 one time per pet fee per visit. Smoking and non-smoking rooms are available for pets.

Culver

Campgrounds and RV Parks

Madras/Culver KOA 2435 SW Jericho Lane Culver OR   541-546-3046 (800-562-1992)
http://www.koa.com
Dogs of all sizes are allowed, and there are no additional pet fees for up to 2 dogs. If there are more than 2 dogs, the fee is $2 per night per pet. Dogs must be leashed and cleaned up after. There are some breed restrictions. This RV park is closed during the off-season. The camping and tent areas also allow dogs. There is a dog walk area at the campground.

The Cove Palisades State Park 7300 SW Jordan Road Culver OR   541-546-3412 (800-452-5687)
This high desert park features a myriad of water and land recreational opportunities, 10 miles of hiking trails, a designated off-leash area for your dog, historic sites, and special events and programs throughout the year. Dogs of all sizes are allowed at no additional fee. Dogs may not be left unattended, and they must be on no more than a 6 foot leash and cleaned up after. Dogs are not allowed in any of the swim areas, in buildings, or where posted as such. Dogs are allowed on the trails. The camping and tent areas also allow dogs. There is a dog walk area at the campground. There are special amenities given to dogs at this campground.

Parks

Cove Palisades State Park 7300 SW Jordan Road Culver OR   541-546-3412
This popular year round recreational park features a myriad of land and water recreational opportunities, a store, restaurant, marina and rental services, a variety of planned activities and celebrations, and nearly 10 miles of hiking trails that give access to areas rich in wildlife and splendid scenery. This park also has a designated off-leash area for your pet at the Deschutes campground. A leash no longer than 6 feet is required elsewhere in the park. Dogs of all sizes are allowed, but they must be cleaned up after and under owners' control at all times. For those wanting to camp, there is a full service campground at this park.

Depoe Bay

Accommodations

Trollers Lodge 355 SW Hwy 101 Depoe Bay OR   541-765-2287
Dogs of all sizes are allowed. There is an $8 per night per pet additional fee.

Attractions

TOP 200 PLACE **Dockside Charters Whale Watching** PO Box 1308/ Coast Guard Place Depoe Bay OR 541-765-2445
http://www.docksidedepoebay.com/
Experienced professionals, wanting their visitors to have the best time they can, thought ocean charters should be a more personal experience, and have implemented several ideas to make the trips fun and enjoyable. Although dogs are not allowed on the fishing charters, they are allowed on the whale watching tours. This is the closest port along the path of the migrating Gray Whales and the summer feeding grounds for numerous other whales. Dogs up to about 70 pounds are allowed for no additional fee. Dogs must be friendly and well behaved. They must be on a leash at all times. The cruises are approximately an hour and a half, and run seasonally. Schedules and times vary.

Beaches

Fogarty Creek State Recreation Area Highway 101 Depoe Bay OR   800-551-6949
This beach and park offer some of the best birdwatching and tidepooling. Picnic tables and hiking are available at this park. There is a $3 day use fees. Leashed dogs are allowed on the beach. Dogs are also allowed on hiking trails. They must be on a six foot or less leash at all times and people are required to clean up after their pets. On beaches located outside of Oregon State Park boundaries, dogs might be allowed off-leash and under direct voice control, please look for signs or postings. This park is located off U.S. Highway 101, 2 miles north of Depoe Bay.

Detroit

Campgrounds and RV Parks

Detroit Lake State Recreation Area 44000 N Santiam Hwy SE Detroit OR   503-854-3346 (800-452-5687)
This scenic park sits along a beautiful 400-foot-deep lake located in the Cascade Mountains. It features nature

programs, interpretive tours and exhibits, various special events, and a variety of land and water recreation. Dogs of all sizes are allowed at no additional fee. Dogs may not be left unattended, and they must be on no more than a 6 foot leash, and cleaned up after. Dogs are allowed on the trails. This campground is closed during the off-season. The camping and tent areas also allow dogs. There is a dog walk area at the campground.

Diamond Lake

Accommodations
Diamond Lake Resort 350 Resort Drive Diamond Lake OR   541-793-3333
http://www.diamondlake.net
This resort is located on the eastern shore of Diamond Lake. Recreation in the summer includes hiking in the nearby dog-friendly national forest, fishing and water sports. Winter recreation activities include dog-friendly cross-country skiing. Pets are allowed in the cabins and motel rooms, including non-smoking rooms. Well-behaved dogs of all sizes are welcome. There is a $5 per day pet fee. Pets cannot be left alone in the rooms or cabins.

Campgrounds and RV Parks
Diamond Lake RV Park 3500 Diamond Lake Loop Diamond Lake OR   541-793-3318
http://www.diamondlakervpark.com
Dogs of all sizes are allowed, but only 2 large or 3 small dogs are allowed per site. There are no additional pet fees. Dogs must be leashed and cleaned up after. This RV park is closed during the off-season. There is a dog walk area at the campground.

Cross Country Ski Resorts
TOP 200 PLACE **Diamond Lake Resort** 350 Resort Drive Diamond Lake OR   541-793-3333
http://www.diamondlake.net
This resort has 8 miles of groomed cross-country ski trails and 50 miles of ungroomed trails. They rent skis and snowmobiles. The cross-country ski and snowmobiles trails are separate. Dogs are allowed on almost all of the cross-country ski trails. Pets need to be leashed at the resort and on the trails. If you are looking for a place to stay, the resort allows pets in both their cabins and motel rooms.

Dundee

Attractions
Erath Winery 9409 NE Worden Hill Road Dundee OR   503-538-3318
http://www.erath.com/
This vineyard harvests 115 acres of grapes in the Dundee Hills of Oregon's Willamette Valley, and they are well known for their high quaility wines and Chef Series, which is the pairing of 4 to 5 course meals with complementary wines. They are open from 11 am to 5 pm daily. Dogs of all sizes are allowed to explore the grounds with their owners, but they are not allowed in any of the buildings. Dogs must be leashed and cleaned up after.
Sokol Blosser Winery 5000 Sokol Blosser Lane Dundee OR   503-864-2282
http://www.sokolblosser.com/
This scenic winery produces wines made in the Willamette Valley's Dundee Hills. They received their USDA organic certification in 2005, and both the vineyards and winery are run using sustainable and environmentally friendly practices. The winery is open from 11 am to 5 pm daily. Well behaved dogs of all sizes are allowed. There are cats on site so they need to be cat friendly. Dogs may explore the grounds with their owners, but they are not allowed in the buildings. Dogs must be leashed and cleaned up after.

Enterprise

Accommodations
Ponderosa Motel 102 E Greenwood Enterprise OR   541-426-3186
Dogs up to 100 pounds are allowed. There is a $10 per night per pet additional fee. Dogs are not allowed to be

left alone in the room.

Estacada

Off-Leash Dog Parks
Milo McIver State Park Off-Leash Area Springwater Road Estacada OR   503-630-7150
This state park offers a designated off-leash exercise area. Dogs must be leashed in all other areas of the park. The park is located on Springwater Road, 4 miles west of Estacada.

Eugene

Accommodations
Best Western New Oregon Motel 1655 Franklin Blvd Eugene OR   541-683-3669 (800-780-7234)
Dogs of all sizes are allowed. There is a $30 returnable deposit required per room. Smoking and non-smoking rooms are available for pets.
Days Inn Eugene 1859 Franklin Blvd Eugene OR   541-342-6383 (800-329-7466)
Dogs of all sizes are allowed. There are no additional pet fees. Reservations are recommended due to limited rooms for pets.
Hilton 66 E 6th Avenue Eugene OR   541-342-2000
Dogs up to 100 pounds are allowed. There is a $25 per stay fee.
La Quinta Inn & Suites Eugene 155 Day Island Rd Eugene OR   541-344-8335 (800-531-5900)
Dogs of all sizes are allowed. There are no additional pet fees, but there must be a credit card on file. Dogs may not be left unattended, and they must be leashed and cleaned up after.
Motel 6 - Eugene South - Springfield 3690 Glenwood Drive Eugene OR   541-687-2395 (800-466-8356)
One well-behaved family pet per room. Guest must notify front desk upon arrival. Guest is liable for any damages. In consideration of all guests, pets must never be left unattended in the guest rooms.
Red Lion 205 Coburg Road Eugene OR   541-342-5201
Dogs of all sizes are allowed. There is a pet policy to sign at check in and there is a $10 per night pet fee per pet.
Residence Inn by Marriott 25 Club Road Eugene OR   541-342-7171
Dogs of all sizes are allowed. There is a $75 one time fee and a pet policy to sign at check in.
Valley River Inn 1000 Valley River Way Eugene OR   541-687-0123
Dogs of all sizes are allowed. There are no additional pet fees. Dogs are not allowed to be left alone in the room, and pet rooms are located on the 1st floor.
Valley River Inn 1000 Valley River Way Eugene OR   541-687-0123
Dogs of all sizes are allowed and pet rooms are located on the 1st floor. There are no additional pet fees and dogs are not allowed to be left alone in the room.

Campgrounds and RV Parks
Premier RV Resorts 33022 Van Duyn Road Eugene OR   541-686-3152 (888-701-8451)
http://www.premierrvresorts.com
Dogs of all sizes are allowed. There are no additional pet fees. Dogs must be leashed and cleaned up after. There is a small fenced in area for off lead. There is a dog walk area at the campground.
Shamrock RV Village 4531 Franklin Blvd Eugene OR   541-747-7473
Dogs of all sizes are allowed. There are no additional pet fees. Dogs must be leashed and cleaned up after. There are some breed restrictions. There is a dog walk area at the campground.

Attractions
King Estate Winery 80854 Territorial Road Eugene OR   541-942-9874
http://www.kingestate.com
This winery's Visitor Center offers complimentary wine tasting and winery tours and features fresh baked breads and artisan cheeses daily. They have a food and wine pairing menu Wednesday through Sunday that features local, organic items that fully complement the King Estate wines. The winery is open 7 days a week from 11:00 to 6:00 p.m.; Sunday through Thursday from 11:00 to 7:00 p.m., Friday and Saturday. Well behaved dogs of all sizes are allowed. Dogs must be leashed, cleaned up after, and under owners' control at all times. Dogs are not allowed in the buildings or in the fields.

Stores

PetSmart Pet Store 2847 Chad Dr Eugene OR   541-683-3353
Your licensed and well-behaved leashed dog is allowed in the store.
Petco Pet Store 1169 Valley River Drive Eugene OR   541-485-7900
Your licensed and well-behaved leashed dog is allowed in the store.

Off-Leash Dog Parks
Alton Baker Park Off-Leash Area Leo Harris Parkway Eugene OR   541-682-4800
This park offers a designated off-leash area. The dog park is located off Martin Luther King Jr. Boulevard on Leo Harris Parkway, behind Autzen Stadium. Park in lot 8.
Amazon Park Off-Leash Area Amazon Parkway Eugene OR   541-682-4800
This park offers a designated off-leash area. The park is located off Amazon Parkway, at 29th Avenue.
Candlelight Park Off-Leash Area Royal Avenue Eugene OR   541-682-4800
This park offers a designated off-leash area. The park is located off Royal Avenue, at Candlelight.
Morse Ranch Park Off-Leash Area 595 Crest Drive Eugene OR   541-682-4800
This park offers a designated off-leash area.

Florence

Accommodations
Ocean Breeze Motel 85165 Hwy 101S Florence OR   541-997-2642
Dogs of all sizes are accepted on an individual basis, but no cats. There is an $8 per night per pet fee plus a $50 refundable deposit, and a credit card must be on file. Dogs are not allowed to be left alone in the room, and they ask you cover the furniture.

Campgrounds and RV Parks
Jessie M Honeyman Memorial State Park 84505 Hwy 101S Florence OR   541-997-3641 (800-452-5687)
This park has the second largest overnight camping area in the state and features two miles of sand dunes, two natural freshwater lakes, an ATV area, interpretive and nature programs, and a variety of land and water recreation. Dogs of all sizes are allowed at no additional fee. Dogs may not be left unattended, and they must be on no more than a 6 foot leash, and cleaned up after. Dogs are allowed on the trails, but they are not allowed in buildings or yurts. The camping and tent areas also allow dogs. There is a dog walk area at the campground.
Mercer Lake Resort 88875 Bay Berry Lane Florence OR   800-355-3633
http://www.mloregon.com/
Dogs of all sizes are allowed. There is a $5 per night per pet additional fee. Dogs may not be left unattended, and they must be leashed and cleaned up after. This is an RV only park. There is a dog walk area at the campground.

Vacation Home Rentals
Whales Watch Vacation Rentals 88572 2nd Ave Florence OR   541-999-1493 (800-760-1866)
http://www.whaleswatch.com
Whales Watch Vacation Rentals homes are located on Heceta Beach. Enjoy your time at the coast with all the comforts of home. Some of the vacation homes allow dogs - when you reserve a house you need to request a dog-friendly home. There may be additional pet fees. Cats are not permitted at any of the houses.

Beaches
Carl G. Washburne Memorial State Park Highway 101 Florence OR   541-547-3416
This park offers five miles of sandy beach. Picnic tables, restrooms, hiking and campgrounds are available at this park. There is a day use fee. Leashed dogs are allowed on the beach. Dogs are also allowed on hiking trails and campgrounds. They must be on a six foot or less leash at all times and people are required to clean up after their pets. On beaches located outside of Oregon State Park boundaries, dogs might be allowed off-leash and under direct voice control, please look for signs or postings. This park is located off U.S. Highway 101, 14 miles north of Florence.
Heceta Head Lighthouse State Scenic Viewpoint Highway 101 Florence OR   800-551-6949
Go for a walk above the beach or explore the natural caves and tidepools along the beach. This is a great spot for whale watching. According to the Oregon State Parks Division, the lighthouse located on the west side of 1,000-foot-high Heceta Head (205 feet above ocean) is one of the most photographed on the Oregon coast. Picnic tables, restrooms and hiking are available at this park. There is a $3 day use fee. Leashed dogs are allowed on the beach. Dogs are also allowed on hiking trails. They must be on a six foot or less leash at all times and people are required to clean up after their pets. On beaches located outside of Oregon State Park

boundaries, dogs might be allowed off-leash and under direct voice control, please look for signs or postings. This park is located off U.S. Highway 101, 13 miles north of Florence.

Garibaldi

Accommodations
Comfort Inn 502 Garibaldi Avenue Garibaldi OR 503-322-3338 (877-424-6423)
Dogs of all sizes are allowed. There is a $10 one time additional fee per pet. Dogs may not be left alone in the room, and they must be leashed and cleaned up after.

Gaston

Attractions
Elk Cove Vineyards 27751 NW Olson Road Gaston OR 503-985-7760
http://elkcove.com/contact_us.html
This vineyard is a family owned and operated winery, and one of Oregon's oldest and most respected wine producers. The vineyards now cover over 120 acres on three separate sites in the Northern Willamette Valley. The tasting room is open from 10 am to 5 pm daily except major holidays. Well behaved dogs of all sizes are allowed. Dogs must be leashed at all times and cleaned up after. They are allowed to walk around the grounds with their owners; they are not allowed in the buildings or the fields.

Gearhart

Accommodations
Gearhart Ocean Inn 67 N Cottage Avenue Gearhart OR 503-738-7373
Dogs of all sizes are allowed. There is a $15 per night per pet fee and a pet policy to sign at check in.

Gold Beach

Accommodations
Econo Lodge 29171 Eltensburg Ave Gold Beach OR 541-247-6606
There is a $5 one time pet fee.
Jot's Resort 94360 Wedderburn Loop Gold Beach OR 541-247-6676 (800-FOR-JOTS)
http://www.jotsresort.com/
There is a $10 per day pet fee. Pets are allowed in the deluxe rooms overlooking the river.

Campgrounds and RV Parks
Four Seasons RV Resort 96526 N Bank Road Gold Beach OR 800-248-4503
http://www.fourseasonsrv.com
Dogs of all sizes are allowed. There are no additional pet fees. Dogs must be leashed and cleaned up after. There is a dog walk area at the campground.
Indian Creek Resort 94680 Jerry's Flat Road Gold Beach OR 541-247-7704
http://www.indiancreekresort.net
Dogs of all sizes are allowed, and there are no additional pet fees for tent or RV sites. There is a $20 one time additional pet fee for cabins. Dogs may not be left unattended outside, and they must be leashed and cleaned up after. Dogs must be quiet and well behaved. The camping and tent areas also allow dogs. There is a dog walk area at the campground. Dogs are allowed in the camping cabins.
Turtle Rock RV Resort 28788 Hunter Creek Loop Gold Beach OR 541-247-9203
http://www.turtlerockresorts.com
Dogs of all sizes are allowed. There are no additional pet fees for one pet, either at the tent and RV sites or the cabins. For more than one dog there is a $4 per night per pet additional fee for the tent and RV sites, and a $15 per night per pet additional pet fee for the cabins. Dogs must be leashed and cleaned up after. The camping and

tent areas also allow dogs. There is a dog walk area at the campground. Dogs are allowed in the camping cabins.

Beaches

Pistol River State Scenic Viewpoint Highway 101 Gold Beach OR 800-551-6949
This beach is popular for ocean windsurfing. There has even been windsurfing national championships held at this beach. Picnic tables and restrooms are available here. There are no day use fees. Dogs are allowed on the beach. They must be on a six foot or less leash at all times and people are required to clean up after their pets. On beaches located outside of Oregon State Park boundaries, dogs might be allowed off-leash and under direct voice control, please look for signs or postings. This park is located off U.S. Highway 101, 11 miles south of Gold Beach.

Gold Hill

Campgrounds and RV Parks

Valley of the Rouge State Park I 5 AT Exit 45B Gold Hill OR 541-582-1118 (800-452-5687)
This scenic park sits along the river made famous by novelist and avid fisherman Zane Grey. It offers a self-guided interpretive walking trail, nature programs, and a variety of land and water recreation. Dogs of all sizes are allowed at no additional fee. Dogs may not be left unattended, be on no more than a 6 foot, and cleaned up after in camp areas. Dogs are allowed on the trails, and they may be off lead there if they will not chase and they are under voice command. The camping and tent areas also allow dogs. There is a dog walk area at the campground.

Government Camp

Cross Country Ski Resorts

Timberline Ski Resort Timberline Road Government Camp OR 503-622-7979
http://timberlinelodge.com/
Timberline is popular for the skiing and snowboarding, but there are many other year round activities and recreational pursuits such as hiking the trails, taking snowshoeing trips, or lodge tours, and exploring. Dogs of all sizes are allowed on the resort grounds. Dogs are not allowed in any of the buildings, and they must be leashed at all times, and cleaned up after. Although dogs are not allowed on the groomed ski trails, they are allowed on some of the snowshoeing and hiking trails. There will be informational signs at the trailheads. Dogs are not allowed to stay in the lodging at Timberline.

Grants Pass

Accommodations

Best Western Grants Pass Inn 111 NE Agness Ave Grants Pass OR 541-476-1117 (800-780-7234)
Dogs of all sizes are allowed. There is a $10 one time per pet fee per visit. Smoking and non-smoking rooms are available for pets.
Comfort Inn 1889 NE 6th Street Grants Pass OR 541-479-8301 (877-424-6423)
Dogs of all sizes are allowed. There is a $10 per night per pet additional fee. Dogs must be quiet, leashed, cleaned up after, and the Do Not Disturb sign put on the door and a contact number left with the front desk if they are in the room alone.
Holiday Inn Express 105 NE Agness Ave Grants Pass OR 541-471-6144 (877-270-6405)
There is a $5 per day per pet additional pet fee. Pets are allowed in the 1st and 2nd floor rooms.
La Quinta Inn & Suites Grants Pass 243 NE Morgan Lane Grants Pass OR 541-472-1808 (800-531-5900)
Dogs of all sizes are allowed. There are no additional pet fees. Dogs must be leashed and cleaned up after. Dogs may only left for short periods, and only then if they will be quiet and well behaved. If they disturb other quests when you are away, they add a $25 fee.
Motel 6 - Grants Pass 1800 NE 7th Street Grants Pass OR 541-474-1331 (800-466-8356)
One well-behaved family pet per room. Guest must notify front desk upon arrival. Guest is liable for any damages. In consideration of all guests, pets must never be left unattended in the guest rooms.
Redwood Motel 815 NE 6th Street Grants Pass OR 541-476-0878

http://www.redwoodmotel.com
Dogs of all sizes are allowed for a $10 additional pet fee. There are limited pet rooms so you need to tell the hotel about your pet when making reservations.
Super 8 Grants Pass 1949 NE 7th St Grants Pass OR 541-474-0888 (800-800-8000)
Dogs of all sizes are allowed. There is a $25 returnable deposit required per room. Smoking and non-smoking rooms are available for pet rooms.

Campgrounds and RV Parks
Jack's Landing RV Resort 247 NE Morgan Lane Grants Pass OR 541-472-1144
http://www.jackslandingrv.com
Dogs of all sizes are allowed. There are no additional pet fees. Dogs may not placed in outdoor pens or be left unattended. They may be left in the RV if comfortable and quiet. Dogs must be leashed and cleaned up after. There is a dog walk area at the campground.
Siskiyou National Forest 2164 NE Spalding Avenue Grants Pass OR 541-471-6500 (877-444-6777)
http://www.fs.fed.us/r6/rogue-siskiyou/
Rogue River and Siskiyou National Forests were combined creating 1.8 million acres of spectacular scenery, hundreds of miles of trails, and diverse ecosystems that support a large variety of plants, animals, and recreation. Dogs of all sizes are allowed at no additional fee. Dogs may not be left unattended, and they must be leashed and cleaned up after in camp areas. Dogs are allowed off lead in the forest if they will not chase and if they are under strict voice control. This campground is closed during the off-season. The camping and tent areas also allow dogs. There is a dog walk area at the campground.

Vacation Home Rentals
Grants Pass Vacation Rental . com Call to Arrange Grants Pass OR 541-660-5673
http://www.GrantsPassVacationRental.com
Grants Pass Vacation Rental is centrally located in Grants Pass. This 3 bedroom, 2 bath home offers a fenced yard for your dog or kids, wireless Internet and a Nautilus work out system.

Gresham

Accommodations
Quality Inn and Suites 2323 NE 181st Avenue Gresham OR 503-492-4000 (877-424-6423)
Dogs of all sizes are allowed. There is a $10 per night per pet additional fee. Dogs must be quiet, leashed, cleaned up after, and the Do Not Disturb sign put on the door if they are in the room alone.
Super 8 Gresham/Portland Area 121 NE 181st Ave Gresham OR 503-661-5100 (800-800-8000)
Dogs of all sizes are allowed. There is a $10 per night pet fee per pet. Smoking and non-smoking rooms are available for pet rooms.

Stores
PetSmart Pet Store 430 NW Eastman Pkwy Gresham OR 503-669-8405
Your licensed and well-behaved leashed dog is allowed in the store.
Petco Pet Store 2000 NE Burnside St Gresham OR 503-674-8558
Your licensed and well-behaved leashed dog is allowed in the store.

Haines

Attractions
Eastern Oregon Museum 610 3rd Street Haines OR 541-856-3380
This museum was founded in 1959 to preserve the memory and spirit of the men and women who prospected, homesteaded, and eventually settled in Northeastern Oregon, and to share this rich pioneer history with present and future generations. The museum has over 10,000 nostalgic artifacts, and several outer historic buildings including a one room school house. The school is still furnished and complete in 1800's style. The Museum is open to the public Thursday through Monday from May 15 through September 15. Hours of operation are from 9:30 am to 4:30 pm; the off season is from 10:00 am to 4:00 pm., Monday through Thursday. Dogs of all sizes are allowed to explore this historic site with their owners, but they are not allowed inside buildings. Dogs must be well behaved, friendly, leashed at all times, and cleaned up after.

Halsey

Accommodations
Best Western Pioneer Lodge 33180 Hwy 228 Halsey OR   541-369-2804 (800-780-7234)
Dogs of all sizes are allowed. There is a $5 per night pet fee per pet. Smoking and non-smoking rooms are available for pets.

Hammond

Campgrounds and RV Parks
Astoria/Seaside KOA 1100 Northwest Ridge Road Hammond OR   503-861-2606 (800-562-8506)
http://www.astoriakoa.com
Dogs of all sizes are allowed. There is a $2 per night per pet additional fee. Dogs may not be left unattended, must be leashed, and cleaned up after. There are some breed restrictions. The camping and tent areas also allow dogs. There is a dog walk area at the campground. Dogs are allowed in the camping cabins.
Fort Stevens State Park 100 Peter Ierdale Hammond OR   503-861-1671 (800-452-5687)
Born out of the need for military defense this historic park offers programs and exhibits on its history, a nature/visitor center, several trails, various habitats, and a variety of land and water recreation. Dogs of all sizes are allowed at no additional fee. Dogs may not be left unattended, and they must be on no more than a 6 foot leash, and cleaned up after. Dogs are allowed off lead on South Beach, and they are allowed on the trails. The camping and tent areas also allow dogs. There is a dog walk area at the campground.

Harbor

Accommodations
Best Western Beachfront Inn 16008 Boat Basin Rd Harbor OR   541-469-7779 (800-780-7234)
Dogs of all sizes are allowed. There is a $10 per night pet fee per pet. Smoking and non-smoking rooms are available for pets. Reservations are recommended due to limited rooms for pets.

Hines

Accommodations
Comfort Inn 504 N Hwy 20 Hines OR   541-573-3370 (877-424-6423)
Dogs of all sizes are allowed. There can be 1 large or 2 small dogs per room. There is a $10 per night per pet additional fee, and a pet policy to sign at check in. There is also a $50 refundable deposit if paying by cash. Dogs may not be left alone in the room at any time, and they must be leashed and cleaned up after. Dogs are not allowed in the pool or lobby areas. There are only 4 dog friendly rooms available; 2 non-smoking.
Comfort Inn 504 N Hwy 20 Hines OR   541-573-3370 (877-424-6423)
Dogs of all sizes are allowed, but there can only 1 large dog or 2 small dogs per room. There are only 2 non-smoking rooms available. There is a $10 per night per room fee and a pet policy to sign at check in.

Hood River

Accommodations
Best Western Hood River Inn 1108 E Marina Way Hood River OR   541-386-2200 (800-780-7234)
Dogs of all sizes are allowed. There is a $12 per night pet fee per pet. Dogs are not allowed to be left alone in the room. Smoking and non-smoking rooms are available for pets. Pets are not allowed in Suites.
Columbia Gorge Hotel 4000 Westcliff Dr Hood River OR   541-386-5566 (800-345-1921)
http://www.columbiagorgehotel.com/
Dogs of all sizes are allowed. There is a $25 pet charge.

Pheasant Valley's Bed & Breakfast and Winery 3890 Acree Drive Hood River OR   541-387-3040 (877-386-BEDS (2337))
This Bed and Breakfast offers a two bedroom cottage that is complete with a kitchen, living and dining area, bath, private covered deck, and a campfire. They feature a full sized breakfast, and a great view of Mt Hood. They offer summer/winter rates for monthly, weekly, or nightly. Dogs of all sizes are allowed for no additional fee. Dogs may not be left unattended at any time, and they must be leashed and properly cleaned up after. If your pet is used to being on the furniture or bed, they request the furnishings be covered with a clean mat or blanket. Set in this picturesque setting is also an award-winning winery, and a certified organic pear and apple orchard Dogs are not allowed in the main B&B.

Attractions
TOP 200 PLACE **Pheasant Valley Vineyard** 3890 Acree Drive Hood River OR   866-357-WINE (9463)
http://www.pheasantvalleywinery.com/
This winery gets rave reviews for their award-winning wines and picturesque setting. There is a certified organic pear and apple orchard also on site, and a very nice Bed and Breakfast Inn. Wine gift packs, accessories, and souvenirs are available in their gift shop. They are open daily April through October from 11 am to 6 pm, and from November through March from 11 am to 5 pm. Well behaved, friendly dogs of all sizes are allowed. Dogs must be leashed, cleaned up after, and under owners' control at all times. They are not allowed in the buildings, but they can be out on the covered patio or lawns, and walked around with their owners. They are not allowed at the Bed and Breakfast Inn; however, they have a 2 bedroom, full sized cottage where up to 2 dogs (no size restriction) are allowed for no additional fee.

Hornbrook

Campgrounds and RV Parks
Blue Heron RV Park 6930 Copco Road Hornbrook OR   530-475-3270
http://www.klamathranchresort.com
Dogs of all sizes are allowed. There is a $1 per night per pet additional fee. Dogs must be leashed and cleaned up after. There is a dog walk area at the campground.

John Day

Campgrounds and RV Parks
Malheur National Forest 431 Patterson Bridge Road John Day OR   541-575-3000
http://www.fs.fed.us/r6/malheur/
This 1.7 million acre forest offers spectacular scenery, hundreds of miles of trails, and diverse ecosystems that support a large variety of plants, animals, and recreation. Dogs of all sizes are allowed at no additional fee. Dogs may not be left unattended, and they must be leashed and cleaned up after. This campground is closed during the off-season. The camping and tent areas also allow dogs. There is a dog walk area at the campground. There are no electric or water hookups at the campground.

Joseph

Accommodations
Mountain View Motel and RV Park 83450 Joseph H Joseph OR   541-432-2982
Dogs of all sizes are allowed. There are no additional pet fees. There are some breed restrictions.

Campgrounds and RV Parks
Park at the River 59879 Wallowa Lake H Joseph OR   541-432-8800
http://www.eaglecapchalets.com
Dogs of all sizes are allowed. There are no additional pet fees. Dogs may not be left unattended, and must be well behaved, leashed, and cleaned up after. Dogs are not allowed at any of the rentals. There is a dog walk area at the campground.

Kimberly

Parks
John Day Fossil Beds National Monument 32651 Highway 19 Kimberly OR   541-987-2333
http://www.nps.gov/joda/index.htm
Dogs must be on leash and must be cleaned up after. Dogs are only allowed in the developed areas and a few designated trails.

Klamath Falls

Accommodations
Best Western Klamath Inn 4061 South Sixth St Klamath Falls OR   541-882-1200 (800-780-7234)
Dogs of all sizes are allowed. There is a $10 one time per pet fee per visit. Smoking and non-smoking rooms are available for pets.
Cimarron Motor Inn 3060 S Sixth St Klamath Falls OR   541-882-4601
There is a $5 one time fee for pets.
CrystalWood Lodge 38625 Westside Road Klamath Falls OR   541-381-2322
Located in the Southern Oregon Cascades, this lodge welcomes all well-behaved dogs. There is no pet fee.
Motel 6 - Klamath Falls 5136 South 6th Street Klamath Falls OR   541-884-2110 (800-466-8356)
One well-behaved family pet per room. Guest must notify front desk upon arrival. Guest is liable for any damages. In consideration of all guests, pets must never be left unattended in the guest rooms.
Quality Inn 100 Main Street Klamath Falls OR   541-882-4666 (877-424-6423)
Dogs of all sizes are allowed. There is a $10 per night per pet additional fee. Dogs may not be left alone in the room, and they must be quiet, leashed and cleaned up after.
Shilo Suites Hotel 2500 Almond St Klamath Falls OR   541-885-7980
There is a $10 per day pet fee.
Super 8 Klamath Falls 3805 Hwy 97N Klamath Falls OR   541-884-8880 (800-800-8000)
Dogs of all sizes are allowed. There is a $25 returnable deposit required per room. Smoking and non-smoking rooms are available for pet rooms.

Campgrounds and RV Parks
Fremont- WINEMA National Forest 2819 Dahlia Street Klamath Falls OR   541-883-6714
http://www.fs.fed.us/r6/frewin/
The Fremont-Winema National Forests were combined creating 2.3 million acres of spectacular scenery, hundreds of miles of trails, and diverse ecosystems that support a large variety of plants, animals, and recreation. Dogs of all sizes are allowed at no additional fee. Dogs may not be left unattended, and they must be leashed and cleaned up after in camp areas. Dogs may be off lead in the forest if they will not chase and they are under voice control. Dogs are not allowed in buildings. This campground is closed during the off-season. The camping and tent areas also allow dogs. There is a dog walk area at the campground. There are no electric or water hookups at the campground.
Klamath Falls KOA 3435 Shasta Way Klamath Falls OR   541-884-4644 (800-562-9036)
http://www.koa.com
Dogs of all sizes are allowed. There are no additional pet fees. Dogs may not be left unattended, and they must be leashed and cleaned up after. There is a large fenced in area where dogs may run off lead. The camping and tent areas also allow dogs. There is a dog walk area at the campground.

LaPine

Campgrounds and RV Parks
LaPine State Park 15800 State Recreation Road LaPine OR   541-536-2071 (800-452-5687)
This park, home to the oldest tree in Oregon aged about 500 years, offers access to 2 rivers, 10 miles of trails, a museum, and a variety of land and water recreation. Dogs of all sizes are allowed at no additional fee. Dogs may not be left unattended, and they must be on no more than a 6 foot leash, and cleaned up after. Dogs are allowed on trails unless otherwise marked. The camping and tent areas also allow dogs. There is a dog walk area at the campground.

Lakeview

Campgrounds and RV Parks
FREEMONT-Winema National Forest 1301 S G Street Lakeview OR   541-947-2151
http://www.fs.fed.us/r6/frewin/
The Fremont-Winema National Forests were combined creating 2.3 million acres of spectacular scenery, hundreds of miles of trails, and diverse ecosystems that support a large variety of plants, animals, and recreation. Dogs of all sizes are allowed at no additional fee. Dogs may not be left unattended, and they must be leashed and cleaned up after. This campground is closed during the off-season. The camping and tent areas also allow dogs. There is a dog walk area at the campground. There are no electric or water hookups at the campground.

Parks
Hart Mountain National Antelope Refuge P.O. Box 111, 18 South G Street (Fish and Wildlife Complex) Lakeview OR   541-947-3315
This 278,000-acre refuge has one of the west's most expansive wildlife habitats free of domestic livestock. Originally this park was set aside in the 1930s for the conservation of pronghorn antelope, and now acts for protection and restoration of native ecosystems for the public's enjoyment and education. There is also a wide variety of land and water recreation available. Potable water, compressed air, and restrooms are available at the refuge headquarters. Dogs of all sizes are allowed. Dogs may not be left unattended, and all pets must be leashed. Dogs used for hunting during the waterfowl or upland bird hunts, are permitted to be unleashed as long as they remain under strict voice control. Dogs are allowed on the trails (trails not maintained). There is primitive camping here, but none of them have any RV hook-ups, drinking water, firewood, or fire rings.

Langlois

Campgrounds and RV Parks
Bandon/Port Orford KOA 46612 Hwy 101 Langlois OR   541-348-2358 (800-562-3298)
http://www.koa.com
Dogs of all sizes are allowed. There are no additional pet fees. Dogs must be leashed and cleaned up after. There are some breed restrictions. The camping and tent areas also allow dogs. There is a dog walk area at the campground.

Lebanon

Campgrounds and RV Parks
Premier RV Resort 31958 Bellinger Scale Road Lebanon OR   541-259-0070
Dogs of all sizes are allowed. There are no additional pet fees. Dogs may not be left unattended, and must be leashed and cleaned up after. There is a fenced dog run area for off lead. There is a dog walk area at the campground.

Lincoln City

Accommodations
Chinook Winds Casino Resort Hotel 1501 NW 40th Place Lincoln City OR   541-996-5825 (877-4BEACH1 (423-2241))
This hotel offers ocean front property located right next to the casino. They offer an indoor heated swimming pool, sauna, spa, a full service restaurant and lounge with live entertainment on weekends, and a complimentary shuttle to the casino. Dogs of all sizes are allowed for an additional fee of $15 per night per pet. Dogs may not be left unattended, and they must be leashed and cleaned up after. Dogs are allowed in the front lobby and around most of the grounds. There are also special dog walk areas. Dogs are not allowed in the casino, the pool, or in food service areas.

Ester Lee Motel 3803 SW Hwy 101 Lincoln City OR 541-996-3606
Dogs of all sizes are allowed in the cottages but not the motel. There is a $7 per night per pet fee and a pet policy to sign at check in.
Motel 6 - Lincoln City 3517 N Highway 101 Lincoln City OR 541-996-9900 (800-466-8356)
One well-behaved family pet per room. Guest must notify front desk upon arrival. Guest is liable for any damages. In consideration of all guests, pets must never be left unattended in the guest rooms.

Beaches
D River State Recreation Site Highway 101 Lincoln City OR 800-551-6949
This beach, located right off the highway, is a popular and typically windy beach. According to the Oregon State Parks Division, this park is home to a pair of the world's largest kite festivals every spring and fall which gives Lincoln City the name Kite Capital of the World. Restrooms are available at the park. Dogs are allowed on the beach. They must be on a six foot or less leash at all times and people are required to clean up after their pets. On beaches located outside of Oregon State Park boundaries, dogs might be allowed off-leash and under direct voice control, please look for signs or postings. This park is located off U.S. Highway 101 in Lincoln City.
Roads End State Recreation Site Highway 101 Lincoln City OR 800-551-6949
There is a short trail here that leads down to the beach. Picnic tables are available at this park. There are no day use fees. Dogs are allowed on the beach. They must be on a six foot or less leash at all times and people are required to clean up after their pets. On beaches located outside of Oregon State Park boundaries, dogs might be allowed off-leash and under direct voice control, please look for signs or postings. This park is located off U.S. Highway 101, 1 mile north of Lincoln City.

Madras

Accommodations
Best Western Rama Inn 12 SW 4th St Madras OR 541-475-6141 (800-780-7234)
Dogs of all sizes are allowed. There is a $10 per night pet fee per pet. Smoking and non-smoking rooms are available for pets.
Sweet Virginia's Bed and Breakfast 407 6th Street Metolius OR 541-546-3031
The house was built in 1915 at a time when Metolius, Oregon was a booming railroad town. The city is smaller now. Three guest rooms are available. Well-behaved dogs are welcome and the owners have two dogs on the property. They have two large fenced yards. Dog beds and other supplies are available.

Manzanita

Beaches
Nehalem Bay State Park Highway 101 Manzanita OR 503-368-5154
The beach can be reached by a short walk over the dunes. This park is a popular place for fishing and crabbing. Picnic tables, restrooms (including an ADA restroom), hiking and camping are available at this park. There is a $3 day use fee. Leashed dogs are allowed on the beach. Dogs are also allowed on hiking trails and campgrounds. They must be on a six foot or less leash at all times and people are required to clean up after their pets. On beaches located outside of Oregon State Park boundaries, dogs might be allowed off-leash and under direct voice control, please look for signs or postings. This park is located off U.S. Highway 101, 3 miles south of Manzanita Junction.
Oswald West State Park Highway 101 Manzanita OR 800-551-6949
The beach is located just a quarter of a mile from the parking areas. It is a popular beach that is frequented by windsurfers and boogie boarders. Picnic tables, restrooms, hiking, and campgrounds are available at this park. There are no day use fees. Leashed dogs are allowed on the beach. Dogs are also allowed on hiking trails and campgrounds. They must be on a six foot or less leash at all times and people are required to clean up after their pets. On beaches located outside of Oregon State Park boundaries, dogs might be allowed off-leash and under direct voice control, please look for signs or postings. This park is located off U.S. Highway 101, 10 miles south of Cannon Beach.

McKenzie Bridge

Campgrounds and RV Parks

Willamette National Forest 57600 McKenzie H McKenzie Bridge OR   541-822-3381
http://www.fs.fed.us/r6/willamette/
This forest has over a million and a half acres of high mountains, cascading streams, narrow canyons, and diverse ecosystems that support a large variety of plants, animals, and recreation. Dogs of all sizes are allowed at no additional fee. Dogs may not be left unattended, and they must be leashed and cleaned up after in camp. Dogs may be off lead on the trails only if they will not chase, and if they are under strict voice command. The camping and tent areas also allow dogs. There is a dog walk area at the campground. There are no electric or water hookups at the campground.

McMinnville

Accommodations

Red Lion 2535 NE Cumulus Avenue McMinnville OR   503-472-1500
Dogs of all sizes are allowed. There is a $10 per night per pet fee and a pet policy to sign at check in.

Stores

Petco Pet Store 2370 NE Highway 99W McMinnville OR   503-474-4252
Your licensed and well-behaved leashed dog is allowed in the store.

Medford

Accommodations

Motel 6 - Medford North 2400 Biddle Road Medford OR   541-779-0550 (800-466-8356)
One well-behaved pet is welcome. There are no additional pet fees. Pets may not be left unattended in the room.
Motel 6 - Medford South 950 Alba Drive Medford OR   541-773-4290 (800-466-8356)
One well-behaved family pet per room. Guest must notify front desk upon arrival. Guest is liable for any damages. In consideration of all guests, pets must never be left unattended in the guest rooms.
Red Lion 200 N Riverside Avenue Medford OR   541-779-5811
Dogs of all sizes are allowed. There are no additional pet fees.
Reston Hotel 2300 Crater Lake Hwy Medford OR   541-779-3141
http://www.restonhotel.com/
There is a $20 one time pet fee.
Windmill Inn 1950 Biddle Road Medford OR   541-779-0050
Dogs of all sizes are allowed. There are no additional pet fees.

Campgrounds and RV Parks

Rogue River National Forest 333 W 8th Street Medford OR   541-858-2200 (877-444-6777)
http://www.fs.fed.us/r6/rogue-siskiyou/
Rogue River and Siskiyou National Forests were combined creating 1.8 million acres of spectacular scenery, hundreds of miles of trails, and diverse ecosystems that support a large variety of plants, animals, and recreation. Dogs of all sizes are allowed at no additional fee. Dogs may not be left unattended, and they must be leashed and cleaned up after in camp areas. Dogs are allowed off lead in the forest if they will not chase and if they are under strict voice control. This campground is closed during the off-season. The camping and tent areas also allow dogs. There is a dog walk area at the campground. There are no water hookups at the campground.

Stores

PetSmart Pet Store 3279 Crater Lake Hwy Medford OR   541-772-5564
Your licensed and well-behaved leashed dog is allowed in the store.

Off-Leash Dog Parks

Bear Creek Park Dog Park Highland Drive Medford OR   541-774-2400
http://www.ci.medford.or.us
This park offers a 2 acre fenced off-leash area. Amenities include water and a picnic table. Dogs must be on leash when not in the dog park. People must clean up after their pets. The park is located at the corner of

Highland Drive and Barnett Road, near I-5, exit 27.

Monmouth

Attractions
Airlie Winery 15305 Dunn Forest Road Monmouth OR   503-838-6013
http://www.airliewinery.com/
Located along the coastal edge of Oregon's Willamette Valley, this 32 acre winery has a nice pond and picnic area. It hosts several events and fun activities throughout the year. The tasting room hours are Saturday and Sunday, 12p.m. to 5 p.m. and other times by appointment. They welcome your well behaved dog, and if they are under voice control they may be off lead around the grounds. They are not allowed in the buildings.

Mosier

Campgrounds and RV Parks
Memaloose State Park Box 472 Mosier OR   541-478-3008 (800-452-5687)
This oasis like park offers interpretive exhibits and events, nature programs, various day and night programs and a variety of land and water recreation. Dogs of all sizes are allowed at no additional fee. Dogs may not be left unattended unless they will be quiet and well behaved, and they must be on no more than a 6 foot leash, and cleaned up after. Dogs are allowed on the trails unless otherwise marked, and they may be off lead on trails if they are under strict voice command. This campground is closed during the off-season. The camping and tent areas also allow dogs. There is a dog walk area at the campground.

Mount Hood

Accommodations
Cooper Spur Mountain Resort 10755 Cooper Spur Rd Mount Hood OR   541-352-6692
http://www.cooperspur.com
There are designated pet rooms. There is a $20 one time per stay additional pet fee.

Myrtle Creek

Campgrounds and RV Parks
On the River Golf & RV Resort 111 Whitson Lane Myrtle Creek OR   541-679-3505
http://www.ontherivergolf-rv.com/
Dogs of all sizes are allowed. There are no additional pet fees. Dogs may not be left unattended outside, and they must be leashed and cleaned up after. There are some breed restrictions. The camping and tent areas also allow dogs. There is a dog walk area at the campground.

Neskowin

Beaches
Neskowin Beach State Recreation Site Highway 101 Neskowin OR   800-551-6949
Not really any facilities (picnic tables, etc.) here, but a good place to enjoy the beach. Dogs are allowed on the beach. They must be on a six foot or less leash at all times and people are required to clean up after their pets. On beaches located outside of Oregon State Park boundaries, dogs might be allowed off-leash and under direct voice control, please look for signs or postings. This park is located off U.S. Highway 101 in Neskowin.

Netarts

Campgrounds and RV Parks

Netarts Bay RV Park and Marina 2260 Bilyeu Avenue Netarts OR 503-842-7774
http://www.netartsbay.com
Dogs of all sizes are allowed. There are no additional pet fees. Dogs must be leashed and cleaned up after. There are some breed restrictions. There is a dog walk area at the campground.

Netarts Bay

Accommodations

Terimore Lodging by the Sea 5105 Crab Avenue Netarts Bay OR 503-842-4623 (800-635-1821)
http://www.oregoncoast.com/terimore/
Located off the beaten path, and in one of the most beautiful areas along the coast, this inn offers ocean views, TV with HBO/ESPN, and some of the units have kitchens and fireplaces. Dogs of all sizes are allowed for an additional fee of $7 per night for one dog and $10 per night for two dogs. Dogs may only be left for a short time if they will be quiet, well behaved, and a contact number is left with the front desk. Dogs must be leashed and cleaned up after at all times.

Newberg

Attractions

Rex Hill Vineyards 30835 N Hwy 99W Newberg OR 800-739-4455
http://www.rexhill.com/visit.htm
This scenic winery in Oregon's Willamette Valley is a beautiful blending of the old and new, and is known for the gardens that flow up along the drive leading to the winery. They end in a breathtaking tiered amphitheater of color and are perfect for a simple afternoon picnic or elegant evening wedding. Tasting room hours are from 11 to 5 PM daily (winter), and from 11-5 PM Monday-Thursday & 10-5 PM Friday-Sunday (summer). Well behaved dogs of all sizes are allowed to explore the grounds with their owners, but they are not allowed in the buildings. Dogs must be leashed and cleaned up after.

Newport

Accommodations

Hallmark Resort 744 SW Elizabeth St Newport OR 541-265-2600
http://www.ohwy.com/or/h/hallresn.htm
There is a $5 per day pet fee, Dogs are allowed on the first floor only.
La Quinta Inn & Suites Newport 45 SE 32nd Street Newport OR 541-867-7727 (800-531-5900)
Dogs of all sizes are allowed. There are no additional pet fees. Dogs may not be left unattended, and they must be well behaved, leashed and cleaned up after.
Shilo Oceanfront Resort 536 SW Elizabeth St Newport OR 541-265-7701
There is a $10 per day pet fee.

Campgrounds and RV Parks

Beverly Beach State Park 198 NE 123rd Street Newport OR 541-265-9278 (800-452-5687)
This forest-sheltered campground sits along the Oregon coast providing a long sandy seashore to explore. It provides nature programs, trails, interpretive programs, and a variety of recreational pursuits. Dogs of all sizes are allowed at no additional fee. Dogs may not be left unattended, and they must be on no more than a 6 foot leash, and cleaned up after. Dogs are allowed on trails unless otherwise marked. The camping and tent areas also allow dogs. There is a dog walk area at the campground.

Stores

Bella's Pet Boutique 1688 N Coast H Newport OR 877-412-3552
This store is located in the Sea Town Shopping Center in the Northern most courtyard. You'll find a wide variety

of dog clothes and raingear available, wholesome treats (and a few decadent ones!), toys, fragrances, jewelry, bedding, and more. All well behaved, leashed dogs are welcome to come in and explore the store with their owners.

Beaches

Agate Beach State Recreation Site Highway 101 Newport OR 800-551-6949
This beach is popular with surfers. Walk through a tunnel to get to the beach. According to the Oregon State Parks Division, many years ago Newport farmers led cattle westward through the tunnel to the ocean salt. Picnic tables and restrooms are available at this park. There is no day use fees. Dogs are allowed on the beach. They must be on a six foot or less leash at all times and people are required to clean up after their pets. On beaches located outside of Oregon State Park boundaries, dogs might be allowed off-leash and under direct voice control, please look for signs or postings. This park is located off U.S. Highway 101, 1 mile north of Newport.
Beverly Beach State Park Highway 101 Newport OR 541-265-9278
To get to the beach, there is a walkway underneath the highway that leads to the ocean. Picnic tables, restrooms (including an ADA restroom), a walking trail and campgrounds are available at this park. There is a day use fee. Leashed dogs are allowed on the beach. Dogs are also allowed on the walking trail and campgrounds. They must be on a six foot or less leash at all times and people are required to clean up after their pets. On beaches located outside of Oregon State Park boundaries, dogs might be allowed off-leash and under direct voice control, please look for signs or postings. This park is located off U.S. Highway 101, 7 miles north of Newport.
Devils Punch Bowl State Natural Area Highway 101 Newport OR 800-551-6949
This is a popular beach for surfing. Picnic tables, restrooms and hiking are available at this park. There are no day use fees. Leashed dogs are allowed on the beach. Dogs are also allowed on hiking trails. They must be on a six foot or less leash at all times and people are required to clean up after their pets. On beaches located outside of Oregon State Park boundaries, dogs might be allowed off-leash and under direct voice control, please look for signs or postings. This park is located off U.S. Highway 101, 8 miles north of Newport.
South Beach State Park Highway 101 Newport OR 541-867-4715
This beach offers many recreational opportunities like beachcombing, fishing, windsurfing and crabbing. Picnic tables, restrooms (including an ADA restroom), hiking (including an ADA hiking trail), and campgrounds are available at this park. There is a day use fee. Leashed dogs are allowed on the beach. Dogs are also allowed on hiking trails and campgrounds. They must be on a six foot or less leash at all times and people are required to clean up after their pets. On beaches located outside of Oregon State Park boundaries, dogs might be allowed off-leash and under direct voice control, please look for signs or postings. This park is located off U.S. Highway 101, 2 miles south of Newport.

Parks

Yaquina Head Outstanding Natural Area 750 Lighthouse Drive Newport OR 541-574-3100
Home to the tallest lighthouse in Oregon, this day-use park also offers an interpretive center, and the headlands provide visitors with one of the most accessible wildlife and ocean viewing locations on the Pacific Coast. The lighthouse is undergoing restoration, and may not be available to the public for a time to come; the grounds are open all year from sunrise to sunset. Dogs of all sizes are allowed. They must be on no more than a 6 foot leash, cleaned up after, and friendly. Dogs are allowed on the trails and down to the beach, but they are not allowed in the bird nesting areas or where otherwise posted.

Outdoor Restaurants

Rogue Ale Public House 748 SW Bay Blvd Newport OR 541-265-3188
This restaurant and bar serves American. Dogs are allowed at the outdoor tables. They offer a doggie menu for your pet.

North Bend

Campgrounds and RV Parks

Oregon Dunes KOA 68632 Hwy 101 North Bend OR 541-756-4851 (800-562-4236)
http://www.koa.com
Dogs of all sizes are allowed. There are no additional pet fees. Dogs must be leashed and cleaned up after, and walked by an adult. Dogs are not allowed to be left unattended outside, but they may be left in your auto or RV if they will be comfortable and quiet. The camping and tent areas also allow dogs. There is a dog walk area at the campground.

Oakridge

Accommodations
Best Western Oakridge Inn 47433 Hwy 58 Oakridge OR   541-782-2212 (800-780-7234)
Dogs of all sizes are allowed. There is a $10 one time per pet fee per visit. Smoking and non-smoking rooms are available for pets.

Ontario

Accommodations
Holiday Inn 1249 Topadera Ave Ontario OR   541-889-8621 (877-270-6405)
Dogs of all sizes are allowed. There is a $10 per night pet fee per pet. Reservations are recommended due to limited rooms for pets. Smoking and non-smoking rooms are available for pets.
Motel 6 - Ontario 275 NE 12th Street Ontario OR   541-889-6617 (800-466-8356)
One well-behaved family pet per room. Guest must notify front desk upon arrival. Guest is liable for any damages. In consideration of all guests, pets must never be left unattended in the guest rooms.

Otis

Campgrounds and RV Parks
Lincoln City KOA 5298 NE Park Lane Otis OR   541-994-2961 (800-562-2791)
http://www.koa.com
Dogs of all sizes are allowed. There is a pet policy to sign at check in and there are no additional pet fees. Dogs must be leashed and cleaned up after. There are some breed restrictions. The camping and tent areas also allow dogs. There is a dog walk area at the campground.

Pacific City

Campgrounds and RV Parks
Cape Kiwanda RV Resort 33305 Cape Kiwanda Drive Pacific City OR   503-965-6230
http://www.capekiwandarvpark.com
Dogs of all sizes are allowed. There are no additional pet fees. Dogs must be leashed and cleaned up after. There is a dog walk area at the campground.

Beaches
Bob Straub State Park Highway 101 Pacific City OR   800-551-6949
This is a nice stretch of beach to walk along. Picnic tables and restrooms (including an ADA restroom) are available at this park. There are no day use fees. Dogs are allowed on the beach. They must be on a six foot or less leash at all times and people are required to clean up after their pets. On beaches located outside of Oregon State Park boundaries, dogs might be allowed off-leash and under direct voice control, please look for signs or postings. This park is located off U.S. Highway 101 in Pacific City.
Cape Kiwanda State Natural Area Highway 101 Pacific City OR   800-551-6949
This beach and park is a good spot for marine mammal watching, hang gliding and kite flying. Picnic tables are available at this park. There are no day use fees. Dogs are allowed on the beach. They must be on a six foot or less leash at all times and people are required to clean up after their pets. On beaches located outside of Oregon State Park boundaries, dogs might be allowed off-leash and under direct voice control, please look for signs or postings. This park is located off U.S. Highway 101, 1 mile north of Pacific City.

Pendleton

Accommodations

Holiday Inn Express 600 SE Nye Ave Pendleton OR 541-966-6520 (877-270-6405)
There is a $10 one time pet fee per pet.
Motel 6 - Pendleton 325 Southeast Nye Avenue Pendleton OR 541-276-3160 (800-466-8356)
One well-behaved family pet per room. Guest must notify front desk upon arrival. Guest is liable for any damages. In consideration of all guests, pets must never be left unattended in the guest rooms.
Red Lion 304 SE Nye Avenue Pendleton OR 541-276-6111
Dogs of all sizes are allowed. There is a $20 refundable deposit if paying with cash and no fee with a credit card on file. There is a pet policy to sign at check in.

Campgrounds and RV Parks

Umatilla National Forest 2517 SW Hailey Avenue Pendleton OR 541-278-3716
http://www.fs.fed.us/r6/uma/
This forest of nearly 1.4 million acres provides spectacular scenery, a rich cultural history, and diverse ecosystems that support a large variety of plants, animals, and recreation. Dogs of all sizes are allowed at no additional fee. Dogs may not be left unattended; they must be quiet, well behaved, be on no more than a 6 foot leash, and cleaned up after in camp areas. Dogs are allowed on the trails. This campground is closed during the off-season. The camping and tent areas also allow dogs. There is a dog walk area at the campground. Dogs are allowed in the camping cabins. There are no electric or water hookups at the campground.

Port Orford

Campgrounds and RV Parks

Port Orford RV Village 2855 Port Orford Loop Port Orford OR 541-332-1041 (800-332-1041)
http://www.portorfordrv.com/
In addition to being close to many points of interest, this RV park features a rec room with a full kitchen, showers, heated bathrooms, a car wash area, fish cleaning station, cable TV, and laundry facilities. Dogs of all sizes are welcome for no additional fee. Dogs must be friendly as there are other animals in residence. Dogs may be left inside an RV unit only if they will be quiet and well behaved; they are not allowed to be left unattended outside at any time. Dogs must be leashed and cleaned up after. The camping and tent areas also allow dogs. There is a dog walk area at the campground.

Attractions

Prehistoric Gardens 36848 Hwy 101S Port Orford OR 541-332-4463
You and your dog can be transported back through time to the age when monster dinosaurs roamed more than 70 million years ago. The pathways are lined with 24 life sized dinosaurs, some towering over 40 feet from your head. There is a gift and souvenir Shop located just outside the Gardens area, featuring items in keeping with the prehistoric theme. Dogs of all sizes are allowed for no additional fee. Dogs must be leashed and cleaned up after at all times. Dogs are not allowed in the buildings. They are allowed throughout the park on the trails and at the picnic areas. The park is open from 9 am to dusk 7 days a week from March 1st to October 31st. During the off season, they are only open on the weekends.

Beaches

Cape Blanco State Park Highway 101 Port Orford OR 541-332-6774
Take a stroll on the beach or hike on over eight miles of trails which offer spectacular ocean vistas. Picnic tables, restrooms, hiking and campgrounds are available at this park. There is a minimal day use fee. Leashed dogs are allowed on the beach. Dogs are also allowed on hiking trails and campgrounds. They must be on a six foot or less leash at all times and people are required to clean up after their pets. On beaches located outside of Oregon State Park boundaries, dogs might be allowed off-leash and under direct voice control, please look for signs or postings. This park is located off U.S. Highway 101, 9 miles north of Port Orford.
Humbug Mountain State Park Highway 101 Port Orford OR 541-332-6774
This beach is frequented by windsurfers and scuba divers. A popular activity at this park is hiking to the top of Humbug Mountain (elevation 1,756 feet) . Picnic tables, restrooms, hiking and campgrounds are available at this park. There is a minimal day use fee. Leashed dogs are allowed on the beach. Dogs are also allowed on hiking trails and campgrounds. They must be on a six foot or less leash at all times and people are required to clean up after their pets. On beaches located outside of Oregon State Park boundaries, dogs might be allowed off-leash and under direct voice control, please look for signs or postings. This park is located off U.S. Highway 101, 6 miles south of Port Orford.

Portland

Accommodations

Hawthorn Inn & Suites 2323 NE 181st Ave Gresham OR   503-492-4000 (800-527-1133)
There is a $10 per stay pet fee.
Red Lion 3500 NE Cornell Road Hillsboro OR   503-648-3500
Dogs of all sizes are allowed. There is a $10 per night per room fee up to a maximum charge of $50 and a pet policy to sign at check in.
Residence Inn by Marriott 18855 NW Tanasbourne Drive Hillsboro OR   503-531-3200
Dogs of all sizes are allowed. There is a $10 per night fee and a pet policy to sign at check in.
TownePlace Suites Portland Hillsboro 6550 NE Brighton St Hillsboro OR   503-268-6000
Dogs of all sizes are allowed. There is a $10 per night pet fee per pet.
Crowne Plaza 14811 Kruse Oaks Dr Lake Oswego OR   503-624-8400 (877-270-6405)
There is a $20 per day pet fee per pet. Dogs are allowed on the second floor which has some smoking and non-smoking rooms.
Residence Inn by Marriott 15200 SW Bangy Road Lake Oswego OR   503-684-2603
Dogs of all sizes are allowed. There is a $75 one time fee and a pet policy to sign at check in.
5th Avenue Suites 506 S.W. Washington Portland OR   503-222-0001
http://www.5thavenuesuites.com/
Well-behaved dogs of all sizes are welcome at this pet-friendly hotel. The luxury boutique hotel offers both rooms and suites. Hotel amenities include complimentary evening wine service, and a 24 hour on-site fitness room. There are no pet fees, just sign a pet liability form.
Days Inn Portland North 9930 N Whitaker Road Portland OR   503-289-1800 (800-329-7466)
Dogs of all sizes are allowed. There is a $15 one time per pet fee per visit.
Four Points by Sheraton Portland Downtown 50 Southwest Morrison Portland OR   503-221-0711 (888-625-5144)
Dogs of all sizes are allowed. There are no additional pet fees. Dogs are not allowed to be left alone in the room.
Hilton 921 SW Sixth Avenue Portland OR   503-226-1611
Dogs up to 50 pounds are allowed. There is a $25 one time fee and a pet policy to sign at check in.
Hotel Lucia 400 SW Broadway Portland OR   503-228-7221
There is a $35 non-refundable one time pet fee.
Hotel Vintage Plaza 422 SW Broadway Portland OR   503-228-1212
http://www.vintageplaza.com/
Well-behaved dogs of all sizes are welcome at this pet-friendly hotel. The luxury boutique hotel offers both rooms and suites. Hotel amenities include complimentary evening wine service, complimentary high-speed Internet access in all guest rooms, 24 hour room service and an on-site fitness room. There are no pet fees, just sign a pet liability form.
La Quinta Inn & Suites Portland Airport 11207 NE Holman St. Portland OR   503-382-3820 (800-531-5900)
Dogs of all sizes are allowed. There are no additional pet fees, but a credit card must be on file. Dogs must be quiet, leashed, cleaned up after, and crated if left alone in the room. Dogs are not allowed in the pool or breakfast areas.
La Quinta Inn & Suites Portland Northwest 4319 NW Yeon Portland OR   503-497-9044 (800-531-5900)
Dogs of all sizes are allowed. There are no additional pet fees. Dogs must be leashed, cleaned up after, and the Do Not Disturb sign on the door if there is a pet alone in the room.
La Quinta Inn Portland Convention Center 431 NE Multnomah Portland OR   503-233-7933 (800-531-5900)
Dogs of all sizes are allowed. There are no additional pet fees. Dogs must be leashed and cleaned up after. Dogs must be crated if left alone in the room.
Mallory Hotel 729 SW 15th Portland OR   503-223-6311 (800-228-8657)
http://www.malloryhotel.com/
There is a $10 one time fee for pets.
Motel 6 - Portland Central 3104-06 Se Powell Boulevard Portland OR   503-238-0600 (800-466-8356)
One well-behaved family pet per room. Guest must notify front desk upon arrival. Guest is liable for any damages. In consideration of all guests, pets must never be left unattended in the guest rooms.
Motel 6 - Portland Mall - 205 9225 Southeast Stark Street Portland OR   503-255-0808 (800-466-8356)
One well-behaved family pet per room. Guest must notify front desk upon arrival. Guest is liable for any damages. In consideration of all guests, pets must never be left unattended in the guest rooms.
Motel 6 - Portland North 1125 North Schmeer Road Portland OR   503-247-3700 (800-466-8356)
One well-behaved family pet per room. Guest must notify front desk upon arrival. Guest is liable for any damages. In consideration of all guests, pets must never be left unattended in the guest rooms.
Quality Inn Portland Airport 8247 NE Sandy Blvd Portland OR   503-256-4111 (877-424-6423)
Dogs of all sizes are allowed. There is a $15 per night per pet additional fee. Dogs must be leashed, cleaned up

after, crated or removed for housekeeping, and the Do Not Disturb sign put on the door if they are in the room alone.

Red Lion 5019 NE 102nd Street Portland OR   503-252-6397
Dogs of all sizes are allowed. There is a $15 per stay per room fee for 2 pets any size. There is an additional $15 per stay if more than 2. There is a pet policy to sign at check in.

Residence Inn by Marriott 1710 NE Multnomah Street Portland OR   503-288-1400
Dogs of all sizes are allowed. There is a $50 one time fee and a pet policy to sign at check in.

Residence Inn by Marriott 2115 SW River Parkway Portland OR   503-552-9500
Well behaved dogs of all sizes are allowed. There is a $10 per night per pet fee and a pet policy to sign at check in.

Sleep Inn East 2261 NE 181 Avenue Portland OR   503-618-8400 (877-424-6423)
Dogs of all sizes are allowed. There is a $10 per night per pet additional fee. Dogs must be quiet, well behaved, leashed, cleaned up after, and the Do Not Disturb sign put on the door if they are in the room alone.

Staybridge Suites 11936 NE Glenn Widing Drive Portland OR   503-262-8888 (877-270-6405)
There is a $25 non-refundable pet fee plus an additional pet fee of $10 per day.

Super 8 Portland/Airport 11011 NE Holman Portland OR   503-257-8988 (800-800-8000)
Dogs of all sizes are allowed. There is a $25 returnable deposit required per room. Smoking and non-smoking rooms are available for pet rooms.

The Benson Hotel 309 SW Broadway Portland OR   503-228-2000
Dogs up to 75 pounds are allowed. There is a $75 one time additional pet fee per room.

The Heathman Hotel 1001 SW Broadway at Salmon Portland OR   503-241-4100
Dogs of all sizes are allowed. There is a pet policy to sign at check in and there are no additional pet fees.

The Mark Spencer Hotel 409 SW 11th Avenue Portland OR   503-224-3293
Dogs of all sizes are allowed. There is a $10 per night per pet additional fee.

The Westin Portland 750 Southwest Alder St. Portland OR   503-294-9000 (888-625-5144)
Dogs of all sizes are allowed. There is a $50 one time pet fee per visit. Dogs are not allowed to be left alone in the room.

Best Western Northwind Inn and Suites 16105 SW Pacific Hwy Tigard OR   503-431-2100 (800-780-7234)
Dogs of all sizes are allowed. There is a $10 per night pet fee per pet under 40 pounds. There is a $15 per night pet fee per pet over 40 pounds. Smoking and non-smoking rooms are available for pets.

Embassy Suites Hotel Portland - Washington Square 9000 S.W. Washington Square Road Tigard OR 503-644-4000
Dogs of all sizes are allowed. There is a $25 one time pet fee per visit and an additional $10 per night per pet fee. Dogs are not allowed to be left alone in the room.

Motel 6 - Portland S- Lake Oswego -Tigard 17950 Southwest McEwan Road Tigard OR   503-620-2066 (800-466-8356)
One well-behaved family pet per room. Guest must notify front desk upon arrival. Guest is liable for any damages. In consideration of all guests, pets must never be left unattended in the guest rooms.

Red Roof Inn - Portland Tigard - Lake Oswego 17959 Southwest McEwan Road Tigard OR   503-684-0760 (800-RED-ROOF)
One well-behaved dog up to about 80 pounds is allowed. There are no additional pet fees.

Comfort Inn and Suites 7640 SW Warm Springs Street Tualatin OR   503-612-9952 (877-424-6423)
Dogs of all sizes are allowed. There is a $10 per night per pet additional fee. Dogs must be quiet, leashed, cleaned up after, and crated if they are in the room alone.

Comfort Inn 8855 SW Citizen Drive Wilsonville OR   503-682-9000 (877-424-6423)
Dogs of all sizes are allowed. There is a $10 per night per room additional pet fee for one dog. There is a $15 per night per room additional pet fee for two dogs. Dogs must be leashed, cleaned up after, and the Do Not Disturb sign put on the door and the front desk informed if they are in the room alone.

Holiday Inn Select 25425 SW 95th Ave Wilsonville OR   503-682-2211 (877-270-6405)
There is a $15 one time pet fee.

La Quinta Inn Wilsonville 8815 SW Sun Place Wilsonville OR   503-682-3184 (800-531-5900)
Dogs of all sizes are allowed. There are no additional pet fees. Dogs must be leashed, cleaned up after, and crated for housekeeping.

Super 8 Wilsonville/Portland Area 25438 SW Parkway Ave Wilsonville OR   503-682-2088 (800-800-8000)
Dogs of all sizes are allowed. There is a $25 returnable deposit required per room. Smoking and non-smoking rooms are available for pet rooms.

Campgrounds and RV Parks

Portland Fairview RV Park 21401 NE Sandy Blvd Fairview OR   503-661-1047
http://www.portlandfairviewrv.com
Dogs of all sizes are allowed. There are no additional pet fees. Dogs must be quiet, friendly, well behaved, leashed, and cleaned up after. Dogs may not be left unattended outside. There are some breed restrictions. There is a dog walk area at the campground.

Rolling Hills RV Park 20145 NE Sandy Blvd Fairview OR   503-666-7282

Dogs of all sizes are allowed. There are no additional pet fees. Dogs may not be left unattended or chained outside alone. Dogs must be leashed and cleaned up after. There are some breed restrictions. There is a dog walk area at the campground.

Jantzen Beach RV Park 1503 N Hayden Island Drive Portland OR   503-289-7626
http://www.jantzenbeachrv.com/
One dog of any size is allowed. There are no additional pet fees. Dogs may not be left unattended outside, and they must be leashed and cleaned up after. This is an RV only park. There are some breed restrictions. There is a dog walk area at the campground.

RV Park of Portland 6645 SW Nyberg Road Tualatin OR   503-692-0225 (800-856-2066)
http://www.rvparkofportland.com/
Dogs of all sizes are allowed, but only 1 dog may be over 40 pounds, and St. Bernards are not allowed. There are no additional pet fees. Dogs may not be left unattended outside, and they must be leashed and cleaned up after. There are some breed restrictions. There is a dog walk area at the campground.

Transportation Systems

Tri-Met 4012 SE Center Portland OR   503-238-RIDE (7433)
http://www.trimet.org
A small dog in a carrier is allowed on the rail and bus lines at no additional fee.

Attractions

Oak Knoll Winery 29700 SW Burkhalter Rd. Hillsboro OR   530-648-8198
http://www.oakknollwinery.com/
As one of Oregon's pioneering wineries, it has played a vital role in helping to shape Oregon's national and international wine reputation. They invite you to browse, enjoy, and learn about Oak Knoll and the wines they make here in Oregon's Willamette Valley. Dogs of all sizes are allowed to join their owners in exploring the vineyard, but they are not allowed in the buildings or in the fields. Dogs must be well behaved, leashed, and cleaned up after at all times. Office hours are from 8:30 a.m. to 5:00 p.m. PST Monday through Friday. Tasting room hours are from May to September, 11 a.m. to 6 p.m. Monday through Friday, and from 11 a.m. to 5 p.m. Saturday and Sunday. From October to April they are open daily from 11am to 5 p.m.

Crystal Springs Rhododendron Garden SE 28th Avenue and Woodstock Portland OR   503-771-8386
http://www.rhodies.org/
Originally this garden began as a test, and now visitors can enjoy more than 2000 species of hybrid rhododendrons, azaleas, magnolias and related plants growing in garden like settings. In addition to offering extraordinary vistas of flowers and plants, the garden is surrounded almost completely by water in a grove of towering trees that feature three spectacular waterfalls and a high fountain. The garden is open daily from dawn to dusk March to October. The garden is also the site of many flower shows and plant sales, and now there are wheelchair accessible routes. Dogs of all sizes are allowed. Dogs must be well behaved, leashed at all times, and please bring bags to clean up after your pet and dispose of waste properly.

TOP 200 PLACE Hoyt Arboretum 4000 SW Fairview Blvd Portland OR   503-865-8733
http://www.hoytarboretum.org/
Hoyt Arboretum covers 185 ridge top acres, is home to a collection of trees representing more than 1,100 species gathered from around the world, and features 12 miles of trails winding through what they call "a living museum". The Visitor Center is at the heart of the Arboretum and they offer maps, trail guides, and park information. There are tours, classes, and special events throughout the year also. Free guided tours, part of Portland Parks and Recreation's Green Walk series, are offered the first Saturday of each month from April through October. The grounds are open 6:00 a.m. to 10:00 p.m. daily. The Visitor Center is open from 9 a.m. to 4 p.m. Monday through Friday; 9 a.m. to 3 p.m. on Saturday; and closed Sundays and major holidays. They say that all dogs are welcome in the Arboretum "as long as they are accompanied by a sensible human", and if your pet(s) is thirsty after the drive, they have a water dish out front to greet them. Dogs must be friendly, well behaved, leashed, and cleaned up after. Dogs are allowed throughout the park on all the trails.

TOP 200 PLACE Oaks Park Amusement Park 7100 SE Oaks Parkway Portland OR   503-233-5777
http://www.oakspark.com/
Surrounded by stately Oak trees, and one of the oldest continuously operating amusement parks in America, this amusement park really has something for everyone. They've got thrill rides, kid's rides, bumper cars, carnival games, a roller skating rink, all the usual carnival treats, and many events and celebrations throughout the year. The park is closed on Monday and the hours and times vary month by month. Your pet is allowed to join you at the park for no additional fee. They are not allowed in buildings. Dogs must be friendly, well behaved, leashed at all times, and cleaned up after. Owners assume full responsibility for their pet.

Peninsula Rose Garden 700 N Portland Blvd Portland OR   503-823-7529
Bought by the city in the early 1900's this neighborhood park is typical of that era, complete with an historic octagonal bandstand overlooking one of the areas most beautiful formal rose gardens with almost 9000 plantings on a two-acre site. Other amenities at this park include a fountain, paved paths, picnic sites, restrooms, disabled access, a playground, public garden, soccer/softball fields, basketball court, an outdoor stage, tennis

court, and outdoor wading pool. Dogs of all sizes are allowed for no additional fee. Dogs may not be left unattended at any time, and they must be leashed and cleaned up after at all times. Dogs must display tags showing proof of current license and rabies vaccination. Dogs must be well behaved and show no aggressive behavior.

Portland Saturday Market 108 West Burnside Portland OR 503-222-6072
http://www.saturdaymarket.org/
This is the largest outdoor arts and crafts market in continuous operation in the United States. It is also one of Portland's top tourist attractions. You will find over 350 artisans, live music and lots of food vendors. There are also many pet-related booths that sell anything from dog cookies, bandanas, and dog beds to waterproof fleece-lined dog coats. Well-behaved leashed dogs are allowed. This market is open Saturdays from 10am to 5pm and on Sundays from 11am to 4:30pm. The market is located between Front Avenue and SW 1st Avenue under the Burnside Bridge.

TOP 200 PLACE **Portland Walking Tours** SW Broadway and Yamhill Portland OR 503-774-4522
Take an award-winning guided outdoor walking tour of Portland. Their most popular tour is called The Best of Portland. This 2 to 2.5 hour morning tour features an overview of Portland including history, architecture, artwork, and more. The tour goes through downtown Portland, the Cultural District, Historic Yamhill and along the riverfront. Tours are held rain or shine on Friday, Saturday and Sunday at 10:30am and 3pm, from April through November. The cost is $15 per person and free for dogs and young children. At the beginning of the tour, the guide will ask if everyone is okay with dogs. If there is anyone in your tour that is uncomfortable around dogs, you might have to keep your pooch away from that person by staying on the other side of the group. The overwhelming majority of people on these tours are okay with dogs. All tours leave from the Pioneer Courthouse Square. Please note that they strongly recommend reservations, even a week or two in advance.

The Grotto NE 85th and Sandy Blvd. Portland OR 503-254-7371
http://www.thegrotto.org/
This is a 62 acre Catholic Shrine and botanical garden. While dogs are not allowed on the upper level, they are allowed outdoors on the first level, both in the plaza and in the botanical garden. The Grotto holds special events throughout the year, including a Blessing of the Animals each July. Well-behaved leashed dogs are allowed. The main public entrance to the Grotto is located on Sandy Blvd (Hwy 30) at Northeast 85th Avenue. It is near the junction of the I-205 and I-84 freeways just minutes from downtown Portland.

Stores

PetSmart Pet Store 12375 SW Walker Rd Beaverton OR 503-644-7901
Your licensed and well-behaved leashed dog is allowed in the store.
Petco Pet Store 4037 SE 117th Avenue, Ste C Beaverton OR 503-644-6558
Your licensed and well-behaved leashed dog is allowed in the store.
Petco Pet Store 18200 NW Evergreen Parkway Beaverton OR 503-614-8070
Your licensed and well-behaved leashed dog is allowed in the store.
PetSmart Pet Store 889 NE 25th Ave Hillsboro OR 503-615-5900
Your licensed and well-behaved leashed dog is allowed in the store.
Petco Pet Store 2151 SE Tualatin Valley Highway, Building B Hillsboro OR 503-640-4449
Your licensed and well-behaved leashed dog is allowed in the store.
Healthy Pet 16140 SW Boones Ferry Road Lake Oswego OR 503-636-3186
Healthy foods and all natural products are the focus at this store, and they carry a line of fun gifts and supplies for your pet. They are open from 10 am to 7 pm Monday through Friday; 10 am to 6 pm on Saturday, and from 11:30 am to 5 pm on Sunday. Your well behaved, leashed, pet is welcome to explore the store with you.
Petco Pet Store 333 S State St, Ste A Lake Oswego OR 503-635-5324
Your licensed and well-behaved leashed dog is allowed in the store.
Jari's Dog Boutique 3000 SE Courtney Road Portland OR 503-233-1967
Look for the big purple building to find this pet gift and grooming store. Dogs of all sizes are allowed to come in and explore as long as they are on lead. They are open daily from 11 am to 6 pm.
Lexidog Boutique and Social Club 416 NW 10th Avenue Portland OR 503-243-6200
http://www.lexidog.com/
This shop offers a variety of toys, treats, and various pet supplies; bring your pet in to explore. They also provide a pet sitting service. They must be leashed and well behaved.
PetSmart Pet Store 9450 SE 82nd Ave Portland OR 503-777-0176
Your licensed and well-behaved leashed dog is allowed in the store.
Petco Pet Store 14410 SE Division St Portland OR 503-761-0553
Your licensed and well-behaved leashed dog is allowed in the store.
Petco Pet Store 1132 North Hayden Meadows Portland OR 503-735-1778
Your licensed and well-behaved leashed dog is allowed in the store.
Petco Pet Store 10730 SE 82nd Avenue Portland OR 503-654-4479
Your licensed and well-behaved leashed dog is allowed in the store.
Petco Pet Store 6655 NE Glisan St Portland OR 503-233-8541
Your licensed and well-behaved leashed dog is allowed in the store.

PetSmart Pet Store 7500 SW Dartmouth St Tigard OR   503-684-3234
Your licensed and well-behaved leashed dog is allowed in the store.
Petco Pet Store 11705 SW Pacific Highway Tigard OR   503-684-0648
Your licensed and well-behaved leashed dog is allowed in the store.
Petco Pet Store 8775 Tualatin Sherwood Rd Tualatin OR   503-885-9224
Your licensed and well-behaved leashed dog is allowed in the store.
PetSmart Pet Store 8311 SW Jack Burns Blvd Wilsonville OR   503-570-6145
Your licensed and well-behaved leashed dog is allowed in the store.

Parks

Forest Park NW 29th Ave & Upshur St to Newberry Rd Portland OR   503-823-7529
This city park is the largest city park in the US at almost 5,000 acres. A forested park, it has a massive tree canopy with substantial undergrowth, allowing the park to serve as a natural air purifier, water collector, and erosion controller. Some of the amenities include a natural area, guided tours, hiking/biking/equestrian trails, a vista point, and more than 112 bird and 62 mammal species. Dogs of all sizes are allowed throughout the park. Dogs must be friendly, well behaved, leashed and cleaned up after at all times, and displaying tags showing proof of current license and rabies vaccination. Dogs must be under owner's control at all times.
Portland Rose Gardens various locations Portland OR   503-823-7529
There are three main rose gardens in Portland. The International Rose Test Garden in Washington Park is one of the world's most famous rose gardens. It is a popular tourist site with great views and more than 8,000 roses. Ladd's Addition Rose Garden, located at SE 16th and Harrison, displays over 3,000 roses. The Peninsula Park Rose Garden, located at N. Ainsworth between Kerby and Albina, offers more than 8,800 fragrant roses. Dogs may accompany you to all of the rose gardens, but pets must be leashed and you are required to clean up after your dog.
Powell Butte Nature Park SE 162nd Avenue and Powell Blvd Portland OR   503-823-7529
This 592 acre park is an extinct volcano and is Portland's second largest park. There are over 9 miles of hiking trails which are popular with mountain bicyclists, horseback riders, and hikers. Dogs must be leashed and people must clean up after their dogs.
Tom McCall Waterfront Park Naito Parkway Portland OR   503-823-7529
This waterfront park follows the Willamette River, between SW Clay and NW Glisan. The park offers walking and bicycling trails. Dogs are allowed but must be leashed and people need to clean up after their pets.
Washington Park SW Park Place Portland OR   503-823-7529
This 129 acre park offers hiking trails and a popular rose garden. Dogs must be leashed and people must clean up after their dogs.

Off-Leash Dog Parks

Hazeldale Park Dog Park Off 196th, N of Farmington Beaverton OR
http://www.thprd.org
This fenced dog park has a separate section for small dogs and large dogs. Thanks to one of our readers for recommending this dog park.
North Clackamas Park 5440 SE Kellog Ck Drive Milwaukie OR   503-794-8002
The North Clackamas Dog Park is fully fenced and open during daylight hours. There is water for your dog at the dog park. Dogs must be on-leash whenever they are outside of the fenced dog area.
Brentwood Park Dog Park 60th Street and Duke Portland OR   503-823-PLAY
This fenced off-leash dog park is next to the Joseph Lan School. There is some shade. The dog park hours are 5 am to 12 midnight daily. The dog park has been "adopted" and supported by the Friends of Brentwood Off-Leash Association.
Chimney Dog Park 9360 N. Columbia Blvd Portland OR   503-823-7529
This entire 16-acre park is designated as an off-leash area. The park has meadows and trails but is not fenced and no water is available. The park is open year-round and is located next to the City Archives Building.
East Delta Park Off-Leash Area N. Union Court Portland OR   503-823-7529
This 5 acre off-leash fenced field has trees and benches, but no water. It is open during the dry season only, from May through October. Dogs are allowed off-leash, but not on the sports fields. The park is located off exit 307 on I-5 across from the East Delta Sports Complex.
Gabriel Park and Off-Leash Area SW 45 Ave and Vermont Portland OR   503-823-7529
This popular regional park offers trails, a natural area and picnic tables. Dogs are not allowed on the playgrounds, sports fields, tennis courts, or in the wetlands and creeks. They are allowed in the rest of the park but must be leashed, except for the designated off-leash area. There is a 1.5 acre fenced dog park that has trees, picnic tables and water. The dog park is only open during the dry season, from May through October.
Normandale Off-Leash Dog Park NE 57th Ave at Halsey St Portland OR   503-823-7529
This fenced dog park is located in Narmandale Park. It is open from 5 am to 12 midnight daily.
Portland's Unfenced Off-Leash Dog Areas Various Portland OR   503-823-PLAY
Portland has a number of parks with unfenced off-leash dog areas. These parks are available for unleashed

dogs from 5 am to 12 midnight daily. The parks are Alberta Park (NE 22 and Killingsworth), Cathedral Park (N. Edison and Pittsburg), Fernhill Park (NE 37 and Ainsworth), Lents Park (SE 92 and Holgate), Mt Tabor Park (SE Lincoln - east of SE 64), Portland International Raceway (N. Denver and Victory Blvd), Williamette Park (SW Macadam and Nebraska) and Wilshire Park (NE 33 and Skidmore). Portland has additional off-leash areas that have limited hours and other restrictions. Many of the limited off-leash hours at the additional parks are during the early morning and the evening hours. For a list of these parks you should check the Portland City Web Site at http://www.portlandonline.com/parks/index.cfm?c=39523. Most of the Portland Parks allow leashed dogs at all times.

Rooster Rock State Park Off-Leash Area I-84 Portland OR 503-695-2261
This state park offers a designated off-leash exercise area. Dogs must be leashed in all other areas of the park. The park is located on I-84, 22 miles east of Portland (exit 25).

West Delta Park Off-Leash Area N. Expo Road & Broadacre Portland OR 503-823-7529
This 3 acre field has a portion which is fenced. No water is available. It is open year-round but the ground gets soggy after heavy rains. Dogs are allowed off-leash. The park is located off exit 306B on I-5 next to the entrance to Portland International Raceway (PIR).

Ash Street Dog Park 12770 SW Ash Avenue Tigard OR 503-639-4171
This small, 100x100 foot fenced dog park is located off of Burnham Street on Ash Avenue. There is limited parking. The dog park is open during daylight hours. From the 217 Freeway exit on 99W and head west. Turn left on SW Hall Blvd (south) and right on Burnham Street after crossing the train tracks. From I-5 North, take 217 and follow the above directions.

Potso Dog Park Wall Street at Hunziker Street Tigard OR 503-639-4171
Potso Dog Park is named for the "first dog" of Coe Manufacturing which allowed the city to use a 4 acre site for the dog park. The fenced dog park has a separate, smaller area for small dogs. This dog park is open only on weekends in the fall and winter and daily during the summer.

Summerlake Park Dog Park 11450 SW Winterlake Drive Tigard OR 503-639-4171
The Summerlake Park Dog Park is 2/3 of an acre in size and fenced. It is open daily year round during daylight hours. From SW Scholls Ferry Rd take SW 130th Street to the park.

Mary S. Young Dog Park Hwy 43 West Linn OR 503-557-4700
This unfenced area in the Mary S. Young State Park is a designated off-leash area. It is about 9 miles from Portland on Highway 43 heading towards Lake Oswego/West Linn. The park has tables, benches, restrooms and water.

Memorial Park Off-Leash Dog Park 8100 SW Wilsonville Road Wilsonville OR 503-682-3727
The Memorial Park Dog Park is fully fenced and has a path around the perimeter for jogging. The dog park is open during daylight hours daily. From I-5 take the Wilsonville Rd exit. Go east on Wilsonville Road. Turn right onto Memorial Drive. The park is on the left.

Outdoor Restaurants

Iron Mutt Coffee Company 530 SW 205th Avenue Beaverton OR 503-869-3205
http://www.ironmuttcoffee.com
The mission of this company was to combine their love of coffee and companion pets. Pet related features offered by Iron Mutt include complimentary water and biscuits for your pet, a custom enclosed outdoor dog run, special pet treats and spoils for purchase, a great patio comfortable for both pets and people, and they host fundraisers to help animals. There is also a brag wall showcasing customer's pets, hand-painted animal motif murals, and custom portraits of animals along the walls. Your pet is welcome to join you on their patio. The patio is usually open weather permitting. Dogs are not allowed inside the building and need to come on leash, but they can be off lead in the gated area. Summer hours are Monday-Wednesday from 6:30am to 7pm; Thursday-Friday from 6:30am to 9pm; Saturday from 8am to 9pm, and Sunday from 8am to 7pm.

Monteaux's Public House 16165 SW Regatta Lane Beaverton OR 503-439-9942
http://www.monteauxs.com/
This restaurant offers a variety of food like salads, soups, burgers, sandwiches, pastas, chicken and meat entrees and omelets. Well-behaved leashed dogs are allowed at the outdoor tables. Thanks to one of our readers for recommending this restaurant. The restaurant is located on Walker Road, two blocks west of 158th Street.

Baja Fresh Mexican Grill 1121 W. Burnside St. Portland OR 503-595-2252
http://www.bajafresh.com/
This Mexican restaurant chain offers a variety of items on their menu including burritos, tacos, salads, quesadillas, fajitas, and enchiladas. Well-behaved leashed dogs are allowed at the outdoor tables.

Baja Fresh Mexican Grill 1505 NE 40th Ave Portland OR 503-331-1000
http://www.bajafresh.com/
This Mexican restaurant chain offers a variety of items on their menu including burritos, tacos, salads, quesadillas, fajitas, and enchiladas. Well-behaved leashed dogs are allowed at the outdoor tables.

Berlin Inn German Restaurant and Bakery 3131 SE 12th and Powell Portland OR 503-236-6761
http://www.berlininn.com/poochmenu2.htm
This dog-friendly restaurant welcomes dogs at their outdoor tables with a bowl of cool water. They even have a

special doggie menu with cookie treats and Warm Patio Pooch Platters like the Mutt Mix (two grilled turkey hotdogs sliced and tossed with assorted biscuits). They have basic Patio Puppy Rules like do not tie your dog to the chairs or tables, all dogs need to be kept under control and do not let your dog disturb other guests. The restaurant's people food includes authentic German dishes including chicken, beef and vegetarian entrees. The in-house bakery offers sponge cake tortes and strudels. This restaurant also offers a wide variety of wines. They are open Wednesday through Sunday.

City Thai 6341 S.W. Capitol Highway Portland OR 503-293-7335
This Middle Eastern fast food restaurant has patio dining. Well-behaved leashed dogs are allowed at the outdoor tables.

Crackerjacks 2788 NW Thurman @ 28th Avenue Portland OR 503-222-9069
Chosen by Portland residents as the best place to grab a beer and pizza, this restaurant has an outdoor patio, and your well behaved dog may sit out there with you. Dogs must be leashed and properly cleaned up after.

Equinox Restaurant 830 N Shaver Street Portland OR 503-460-3333
This restaurant features various cuisine of the world, coupled with a wine list and specialty cocktails to reflect the menu. Your pet is welcome to join you at one of the tables just outside the courtyard of the restaurant. They service these tables, and provide them for guests with pets. Dogs must be well behaved, leashed at all times, and cleaned up after in the vicinity of the building. They open Wednesday through Sunday at 5 p.m., and closed Monday and Tuesday.

Jake's Famous Crawfish 401 SW 12th Ave. Portland OR 503-226-1419
http://www.mccormickandschmicks.com
This seafood restaurant is part of the McCormick & Schmick's chain. Well-behaved leashed dogs are allowed at the outdoor tables.

La Costita Restaurant II 7405 SE Barbur Blvd, Suite 110 Portland OR 503-293-1899
http://www.lacostita.com/
This Mexican restaurant offers a nice patio so that your pet can join you. Dogs must be very well behaved and friendly. They must be leashed at all times and properly cleaned up after.

TOP 200 PLACE **Lucky Labrador Brewing Co.** 915 SE Hawthorne Blvd. Portland OR 503-236-3555
http://www.luckylab.com
This dog-friendly brew pub has a labrador retriever as their mascot and on their beer labels. At the outside seating area, your pooch can relax at your feet while you unwind with some beer or food. The pub offers a nice variety of food including veggie and meat sandwiches, bentos (chicken or veggies over rice), soup and more. Of course, if you love beer, you will also have to try their ales like the Black Lab Stout, the Dog Day India Pale Ale or the Top Dog Extra Special Pale Ale. And if you visit during the month of October, don't miss their Dogtoberfest usually held on a Saturday. They celebrate the pub's anniversary on this day. The highlight of the day is the dog wash, which helps to raise money for dog-related causes or dog organizations. For treats, humans can try a special Dogtoberfest ale and doggies can get dog cookies and biscuits. The pub might even have a band for musical entertainment as well. Please keep pets leashed.

Lucky Labrador Public House 7675 SW Capitol Highway Portland OR 503-244-2537
http://www.luckylab.com/lab_mult.html
This restaurant is a spin-off from the original Lucky Labrador Brewing Co. Dogs are welcome at the outdoor tables. The restaurant serves pizza, salads, and drought ale direct from their brewery in southeast Portland. They are located on Capitol Highway, near 31st Street. Please keep pets leashed.

MacTarnahan's Taproom 2730 NW 31st Avenue Portland OR 503-228-5269
http://www.portlandbrew.com/
A pioneer in craft brewing, they utilize old-world brewing vessels to a state-of-the-art bottling system, to create award winning brews. They offer them with a full menu of classic Brew House Cuisine including kettle-brewed soups, apple wood grilled plates and rotisserie dishes. Your pet is welcome to join you on the patio, which is accessed from the outside. Pets must be well behaved, under owner's control, leashed, and cleaned up after.

Old Lompoc 1616 NW 23rd Ave Portland OR 503-225-1855
This restaurant and bar serves American. Dogs are allowed at the outdoor tables.

Old Market Pub & Brewery 6959 SW Multnomah Blvd Portland OR 503-244-0450
This brewery offers handcrafted brews, burgers, pizza, sandwiches, pastas, and other main-course dishes, as well as a range of appetizers and snacks. It is a very pleasant spacious pub inside, and they also provide picnic tables on the patio out front next to the entrance. They are open daily from 11:30 am to Midnight. Your well behaved dog may join you on the patio. Dogs must be leashed and cleaned up after.

Rubios Baja Grille 1307 NE 102nd Avenue, Suite K Portland OR 503-258-8340
Dogs are allowed at the outdoor tables.

The Blue Moon Tavern and Grill 432 NW 21st Ave Portland OR 503-223-3184
This restaurant and bar serves American. Dogs are allowed at the outdoor tables.

Tin Shed Garden Cafe 1438 NE Alberta St Portland OR 503-288-6966
This restaurant serves American food. Dogs are allowed at the outdoor tables.

Vita Cafe 3024 NE Alberta Portland OR 503-335-8233
This natural food restaurant specializes in vegan dishes, but they also offer meat too. Organic foods and ingredients are used whenever possible. Well-behaved leashed dogs are allowed at the outdoor tables.

Widmer Brothers Gasthaus 955 N Russell Street Portland OR 503-281-3333
They only serve their own beers at this pub, which has been quoted as "fabulous", and the large menu has an emphasis on burgers and German food. They are open Monday to Thursday from 11 am to 11 pm; Friday to Saturday from 11 am to 1 am, and Sunday from Noon to 9 pm. They have an outdoor patio where your well behaved pet may join you. Dogs must be leashed, under owner's control, and cleaned up after.
Wild Oats Natural Marketplace 3535 15th Ave. Portland OR 503-288-3414
http://www.wildoats.com
This natural food market has a deli with outdoor seats. Well-behaved leashed dogs are allowed at the outdoor tables. They are located on 15th Avenue at Fremont.
Wild Oats Natural Marketplace 6344 SW Capitol Highway Portland OR 503-244-3110
http://www.wildoats.com
This natural food market has a deli with a couple of outdoor seats. Well-behaved leashed dogs are allowed at the outdoor tables. The deli is located in the Hillsdale Shopping Center.
Wild Oats Natural Marketplace 2825 East Burnside Street Portland OR 503-232-6601
http://www.wildoats.com
This natural food market has a deli with outdoor seats. Well-behaved leashed dogs are allowed at the outdoor tables.

Events
Dogtoberfest 915 SE Hawthorne Blvd Portland OR 503-228-7281
http://dovelewis.org/
This yearly October event is sponsored by Dove Lewis Emergency and ICU Hospital to raise money for the Dove Lewis Blood Bank. While your pup is getting a first rate washing and towel dry (minimum donation of $5), you can enjoy a Dogtoberfest brew at the Lucky Labrador Brew Pub where this event is held.

Princeton

Parks
Malheur National Wildlife Refuge 3691 Sodhouse Lane Princeton OR 541-493-2612
This park consists of more than 185,000 acres of prime wildlife habitat, and is famous for its diversity and spectacular concentrations of wildlife. This park also protects 120,000 acres of a vast complex of wetlands. Birdwatchers and wildlife enthusiasts can enjoy the more than 320 species of birds, 58 species of mammals, 10 species of native fish, and a number of reptiles on the refuge. Dogs of all sizes are allowed. Dogs must be leashed at all times and properly cleaned up after. Dogs must remain in the car on the Central Patrol Road (a scenic drive road). They are allowed throughout the park and on the trails. The refuge and museum are open daily from dawn to dusk. The office and visitor center are open Monday through Thursday, 7:00 a.m. to 4:30 p.m., and Friday from 7:00 a.m. to 3:30 p.m. With the help of volunteers, the visitor center is open most weekends during spring and summer. They are closed on the weekends in winter.

Prineville

Accommodations
Best Western Prineville Inn 1475 NE Third St Prineville OR 541-447-8080 (800-780-7234)
Dogs of all sizes are allowed. There are no additional pet fees. Smoking and non-smoking are available for pets.

Campgrounds and RV Parks
Ochoco National Forest 3160 SE 3rd Street Prineville OR 541-416-6500 (877-444-6777)
The Ochoco and Deschutes Forests were combined creating 2.5 million acres of spectacular scenery, hundreds of miles of trails, diverse ecosystems and recreation. Dogs of all sizes are allowed at no additional fee. Dogs may not be left unattended, and they must be leashed and cleaned up after in camp areas. Dogs may be off lead in the forest on the trails if they will not chase wildlife and if they are under strict voice control. Dogs are not allowed in buildings. This campground is closed during the off-season. The camping and tent areas also allow dogs. There is a dog walk area at the campground. There are no electric or water hookups at the campground.
Prineville Reservoir State Park 19020 SE Parkland Drive Prineville OR 541-447-4363 (800-452-5687)
This park and reservoir offer a wide variety of land and water recreation, nature programs, trails, and interpretive events and tours. Dogs of all sizes are allowed at no additional fee. Dogs may not be left unattended, and they must be on no more than a 6 foot leash, and cleaned up after. Dogs are not allowed in cabins or in the cabin area. Dogs are allowed on the trails. The camping and tent areas also allow dogs. There is a dog walk area at

the campground.

Stores
Casteel Dog Boutique 735 N Main Street Prineville OR   541-447-3862
This pet gift and grooming store offers pet grooming supplies, foods, and various petwear. The store is open Monday to Friday from 8:30 to 4:30., and closed Saturday and Sunday. Dogs must be well behaved and on a leash.

Reedsport

Accommodations
Best Western Salbasgeon Inn and Suites of Reedsport 1400 Hwy Ave US 101 Reedsport OR   541-271-4831 (800-780-7234)
Dogs of all sizes are allowed. There is a $10 per night pet fee per pet under 40 pounds. There is a $15 per night pet fee per pet over 40 pounds. Reservations are recommended due to limited rooms for pets. Smoking and non-smoking are available for pets.
Economy Inn 1593 Highway Ave 101 Reedsport OR   541-271-3671
There is a $5 per day pet fee.
Loon Lake Lodge and RV Resort 9011 Loon Lake Road Reedsport OR   541-599-2244
Well behaved and friendly dogs of all sizes are allowed. There are no additional pet fees.

Rockaway Beach

Accommodations
Ocean Locomotion 19130 Alder Rockaway OR   503-355-2093
Dogs only are allowed and of all sizes. You can have up to 3 dogs if they are under 50 pounds and up to 2 dogs if they are over 50 pounds. There is a $5 per night per pet fee and a pet policy to sign at check in.

Beaches
Manhattan Beach State Recreation Site Highway 101 Rockaway Beach OR   800-551-6949
The beach is a short walk from the parking area. Picnic tables are available at this park. There are no day use fees. Dogs are allowed on the beach. They must be on a six foot or less leash at all times and people are required to clean up after their pets. On beaches located outside of Oregon State Park boundaries, dogs might be allowed off-leash and under direct voice control, please look for signs or postings. This park is located off U.S. Highway 101, 2 miles north of Rockaway Beach.

Roseburg

Accommodations
Best Western Douglas Inn 511 SE Stephens Roseburg OR   541-673-6625 (800-780-7234)
Dogs of all sizes are allowed. There are no additional pet fees. Smoking and non-smoking are available for pets.
Best Western Garden Villa Inn 760 NW Garden Valley Blvd Roseburg OR   541-672-1601 (800-780-7234)
Dogs of all sizes are allowed. There is a $15 per night pet fee per pet. Smoking and non-smoking are available for pets.
Holiday Inn Express 375 Harvard Blvd Roseburg OR   541-673-7517 (877-270-6405)
There is a $5 one time pet fee. Pets are allowed in the first floor rooms only.
Motel 6 - Roseburg 3100 Northwest Aviation Roseburg OR   541-464-8000 (800-466-8356)
One well-behaved family pet per room. Guest must notify front desk upon arrival. Guest is liable for any damages. In consideration of all guests, pets must never be left unattended in the guest rooms.
Quality Inn Central 427 NW Garden Valley Blvd Roseburg OR   541-673-5561 (877-424-6423)
Dogs of all sizes are allowed. There is a $100 refundable deposit plus a $7 per night per room additional pet fee. Dogs may only be left alone in the room if they will be quiet and well behaved. Dogs must be leashed, cleaned up after, and the Do Not Disturb sign put on the door if they are in the room alone.
Sleep Inn and Suites 2855 NW Edenbower Blvd Roseburg OR   541-464-8338 (877-424-6423)
Dogs of all sizes are allowed. There is a $10 one time additional fee per pet. Dogs may not be left alone in the

room unless they will be quiet and well behaved. Dogs must be leashed, cleaned up after, and the Do Not Disturb sign put on the door if they are in the room alone.

Super 8 Roseburg 3200 NW Aviation Dr Roseburg OR 541-672-8880 (800-800-8000)
Dogs of all sizes are allowed. There is a $25 returnable deposit required per room. Smoking and non-smoking rooms are available for pet rooms.

Windmill Inn 1450 NW Mulholland Drive Roseburg OR 541-673-0901
Dogs of all sizes are allowed. There is a pet policy to sign at check in and there are no additional pet fees.

Campgrounds and RV Parks
Rising River RV Park 5579 Grange Road Roseburg OR 541-679-7256
Dogs of all sizes are allowed. There are no additional pet fees. Dogs may not be left unattended outside, and they must be leashed and cleaned up after. There are some breed restrictions. There is a dog walk area at the campground.

Umpqua National Forest 2900 Stewart Parkway Roseburg OR 541-750-7000 (877-444-6777)
http://www.fs.fed.us/r6/umpqua/
This forest of almost a million acres is home to one of the largest developed recreational facilities within the Forest Service. It offers a diverse topography that provides for a wide variety of habitats, naturescapes and recreational activities. Dogs of all sizes are allowed at no additional fee. Dogs may not be left unattended; they must be quiet, well behaved, be on no more than a 6 foot leash, and cleaned up after in camp areas. Dogs are allowed on the trails, but they say to use caution on the horse and ATV trails. The camping and tent areas also allow dogs. There is a dog walk area at the campground. There are no electric or water hookups at the campground.

Attractions
Hillcrest Vineyards 240 Vineyard Lane Roseburg OR 541-673-3709
http://www.hillcrestvineyard.com
This vineyard is one of Oregon's oldest continuously open wineries in Oregon. They are known for aging their red and white wines longer than most American wineries, then releasing them at the peak of maturity and complexity. There is no charge for tour or tasting. They are open daily, year round, from 11 a.m. to 5 p.m. Well behaved dogs of all sizes are allowed to walk the grounds with their owners, but they are not allowed in the tasting room or in the fields. Dogs must be leashed at all times and cleaned up after.

Spangle Vineyards 491 Winery Lane Roseburg OR 541-679-9654
Your pet is welcome to join you in exploring the grounds, or you can just sit and enjoy the scenery from the deck. Dogs must be leashed and cleaned up after. Dogs are not allowed in the tasting room or in the pond.

Rouge River

Attractions
Rouge River Palmerton Arboretum W Evans Creek Road Rouge River OR 541-582-4401
This 5 acre Arboretum features almost 90 species of trees and shrubs from all over the world, and 40 species of mature trees including Japanese pines, Mediterranean cedars, redwoods, and other trees native to the Pacific Northwest. There is a variety of other labeled plants, shrubs and trees, in addition to several kinds of azaleas and rhododendrons. There is also a duck pond, playground, and picnic area. Dogs of all sizes are allowed throughout the park except in buildings. Dogs must be well behaved, friendly, leashed at all times, and properly cleaned up after. The park is open daily from dawn to dusk.

Salem

Accommodations
Best Western Black Bear Inn 1600 Motor Court NE Salem OR 503-581-1559 (800-780-7234)
Dogs of all sizes are allowed. There is a $10 one time per pet fee per visit. Smoking and non-smoking are available for pets.

Best Western Pacific Highway Inn 4646 Portland Rd NE Salem OR 503-390-3200 (800-780-7234)
Dogs of all sizes are allowed. There is a $20 per night pet fee per pet. Reservations are recommended due to limited rooms for pets. Smoking and non-smoking are available for pets.

Holiday Inn Express 890 Hawthorne Ave SE Salem OR 503-391-7000 (877-270-6405)
There is a $15 per day pet fee.

Motel 6 - Salem 1401 Hawthorne Avennue Northeast Salem OR 503-371-8024 (800-466-8356)

One well-behaved family pet per room. Guest must notify front desk upon arrival. Guest is liable for any damages. In consideration of all guests, pets must never be left unattended in the guest rooms.
Phoenix Inn - Salem South 4370 Commercial St SE Salem OR   503-588-9220 (800-445-4498)
There is a $10 per day pet charge.
Red Lion 3301 Market Street Salem OR   503-370-7888
Dogs of all sizes are allowed. There is a $10 per night per pet additional fee.
Residence Inn by Marriott 640 Hawthorne Avenue SE Salem OR   503-585-6500
Dogs of all sizes are allowed. There is a $75 one time fee and a pet policy to sign at check in.
Super 8 Salem 1288 Hawthorne NE Salem OR   503-370-8888 (800-800-8000)
Dogs of all sizes are allowed. There is a $25 returnable deposit required per room. There is a $10 one time per pet fee per visit. Reservations are recommended due to limited rooms for pets. Smoking and non-smoking rooms are available for pet rooms.

Campgrounds and RV Parks
Premier RV Resorts 4700 Hwy 22 Salem OR   503-364-7714 (503-364-7714)
http://www.premierresorts.com
Dogs of all sizes are allowed. There are no additional pet fees. Dogs must be quiet, well behaved, leashed, and cleaned up after. Dogs may not be left unattended outside. There is a dog walk area at the campground.
Salem Campground 3700 Hager's Grove Road Salem OR   503-581-6736 (800-826-9605)
http://www.salemrv.com
Dogs of all sizes are allowed. There are no additional pet fees. Dogs must be leashed and cleaned up after. There are some breed restrictions. There is a dog walk area at the campground.

Attractions
Ankeny Vineyard Winery 2565 Riverside Road S Salem OR   503-378-1498
http://www.ankenyvineyard.com/
This winery is located in the heart of Oregon's Willamette Valley overlooking the Ankeny National Wildlife Refuge, and climate provides a perfect growing condition for the grapes here. They are open from Noon to 5 pm Wednesday to Sunday. Dogs are welcome to come explore with their owners. Dogs must be friendly and well behaved, and if they get along with their friendly pooch, they can go run free and wear themselves out.
TOP 200 PLACE **The Oregon Garden** 879 W Main Street Silverton OR   877-674-2733
http://www.oregongarden.org
Popular and educational, this 80 acre botanical garden displays thousands of plants in more than 20 specialty gardens. There is an amphitheater for their annual summer concert series, picnic areas and a café, a seasonal tram that allows you to get on and off anywhere in the gardens, and they are also host to many other planned events and activities throughout the year. Some of the spectacular scenery includes an educational forest with a 400 year old Oak tree, a children's garden, a refreshing water garden, a rose garden with a fountain and a view, a sensory garden, the Lewis and Clark garden, and many more, but unusual for public gardens-there is a Pet-Friendly Garden where "Max" the yellow lab (statue) welcomes all the canine guests. Dogs of all sizes are allowed throughout the park for no additional fee, and they can ride the tram too. Dogs must be on no more than an 8 foot leash, be well behaved, and cleaned up after at all times.

Stores
PetSmart Pet Store 2925 Lancaster Dr NE Salem OR   503-362-5325
Your licensed and well-behaved leashed dog is allowed in the store.
Petco Pet Store 628 Lancaster Drive NE Salem OR   503-391-1828
Your licensed and well-behaved leashed dog is allowed in the store.

Off-Leash Dog Parks
Minto-Brown Island Park 2200 Minto Island Road Salem OR   503-588-6336
http://www.cityofsalem.net
This park offers a designated area for dogs to play off-leash. The area is not fenced. Dogs must be leashed when outside the off-leash area.
Orchard Heights Park 1165 Orchard Heights Road NW Salem OR   503-588-6336
http://www.cityofsalem.net
This park has a small designated area where dogs can play off-leash. Dogs must be leashed when outside the off-leash area.

Sandy

Accommodations

Best Western Sandy Inn 37465 Hwy 26 Sandy OR 503-668-7100 (800-780-7234)
Dogs of all sizes are allowed. There is a $10 per night pet fee per pet. Smoking and non-smoking are available for pets.

Campgrounds and RV Parks

Mount Hood National Forest 16400 Champion Way Sandy OR 503-668-1700
http://www.fs.fed.us/r6/mthood/
This beautiful forest of more than a million acres offers hundreds of miles of trails, interpretive programs, and diverse ecosystems that support a large variety of plants, animals, and recreation. Dogs of all sizes are allowed at no additional fee. Dogs may not be left unattended, and they must be leashed and cleaned up after. Dogs are allowed on the trails. This campground is closed during the off-season. The camping and tent areas also allow dogs. There is a dog walk area at the campground. There are no electric or water hookups at the campground.

Seaside

Accommodations

Motel 6 - Seaside 2369 South Roosevelt Drive Seaside OR 503-738-6269 (800-466-8356)
One well-behaved family pet per room. Guest must notify front desk upon arrival. Guest is liable for any damages. In consideration of all guests, pets must never be left unattended in the guest rooms.
Seaside Convention Center Inn 441 Second Ave Seaside OR 503-738-9581 (800-699-5070)
http://www.seasideccinn.com/
There is a $10.00 per day pet charge.
The Best Western Ocean View Resort 414 North Prom Seaside OR 800-234-8439 (800-780-7234)
http://www.oceanviewresort.com
Dogs of all sizes are allowed. There is a $20 per night additional pet fee. The pet rooms are on the first and second floors.

Beaches

Del Rey Beach State Recreation Site Highway 101 Seaside OR 800-551-6949
There is a short trail to the beach. There is no day use fee. Dogs are allowed on the beach. They must be on a six foot or less leash at all times and people are required to clean up after their pets. On beaches located outside of Oregon State Park boundaries, dogs might be allowed off-leash and under direct voice control, please look for signs or postings. This park is located off U.S. Highway 101, 2 miles north of Gearhart.

Parks

Jewel Meadows Wildlife Area 79878 Hwy 202 Seaside OR 503-755-2264
The reserve is for all the wildlife and birds here and it provides a winter habitat and supplemental feeding area for the Roosevelt elk, which are most visible from November through April. The largest viewing area is at the headquarters, and they offer parking for eighty vehicles and an RV lane, a central interpretive kiosk, a large lawn area, picnic tables, brochures, and flush toilets (the only toilets in the park). There are four elk viewing areas in the reserve along Hwy 202. Dogs are may journey this reserve with their owners, and they are allowed to go on the short trails to the viewing areas. Dogs must be on leash at all times, be well behaved, and quiet so as not to disturb the wildlife.

Sisters

Accommodations

Best Western Ponderosa Lodge 500 Hwy 20 West Sisters OR 541-549-1234 (800-780-7234)
Dogs of all sizes are allowed. There is a $15 one time pet fee per visit. Smoking and non-smoking are available for pets. Reservations are recommended due to limited rooms for pets. This hotel loves dogs and will give you a welcome basket for your dog.

Springfield

Accommodations
Motel 6 - Eugene North - Springfield 3752 International Court Springfield OR   541-741-1105 (800-466-8356)
One well-behaved family pet per room. Guest must notify front desk upon arrival. Guest is liable for any
damages. In consideration of all guests, pets must never be left unattended in the guest rooms.

St Helens

Accommodations
Best Western Oak Meadows Inn 585 S Columbia River Hwy St Helens OR   503-397-3000 (800-780-7234)
Dogs of all sizes are allowed. There is a $10 one time per pet fee per visit. Smoking and non-smoking are
available for pets.

St Paul

Campgrounds and RV Parks
Champoeg State Heritage Area Champoeg Road St Paul OR   503-678-1251, ext 221 (800-452-5687)
Located on the banks of the Willamette River, this scenic park has a rich historic past, and offers historic tours,
living history demonstrations, nature and history programs, and a wide variety of land and water activities. Dogs
of all sizes are allowed at no additional fee. Dogs may not be left unattended, and they must be on no more than
a 6 foot leash, and cleaned up after. Dogs are not allowed in buildings. There is a large off-leash area located at
the west end of the park for your pet to run. The camping and tent areas also allow dogs. There is a dog walk
area at the campground. There are special amenities given to dogs at this campground.

Sutherlin

Campgrounds and RV Parks
Hi-Way Haven RV Park 609 Fort McKay Road Sutherlin OR   541-459-4557 (800-552-5699)
http://www.hiwayhaven.com/
This nicely kept RV only park offers amenities such as a picnic area, barbecue facilities, a recreation room, a
convenience store, planned activities, and more, but they also offer another rare treat. The park is built on the
site of a drive in theater and is licensed to show classic films, which they usually do on Saturday night for no
additional charge. Dogs of all sizes are allowed for no additional fee, and they offer 2 large dog walk/exercise
areas. Dogs may not be left alone outside at any time, and may be left in your unit only if they will be quiet and
well behaved. Your dog's food and water may not be left outside, and dogs are not allowed on the lawn just in
front of the movie screen, but they can be in your vehicle if you pull up to watch the movie. There is a dog walk
area at the campground.

The Dalles

Accommodations
Best Western River City Inn 112 W Second St The Dalles OR   541-296-9107 (800-780-7234)
Dogs of all sizes are allowed. There is a $10 per night pet fee per pet. Smoking and non-smoking are available
for pets.
Comfort Inn Columbia Gorge 351 Lone Pine Drive The Dalles OR   541-298-2800 (877-424-6423)
Dogs of all sizes are allowed. There is a $10 per night per pet additional fee. Dogs may be left alone in the room
for just a short time, and only if they will be quiet and well behaved. Dogs must be leashed and cleaned up after.
Motel 6 - The Dalles 2500 West 6th Street The Dalles OR   541-296-1191 (800-466-8356)
One well-behaved family pet per room. Guest must notify front desk upon arrival. Guest is liable for any

damages. In consideration of all guests, pets must never be left unattended in the guest rooms.

Outdoor Restaurants
Holstein's 3rd and Taylor The Dalles OR 541-298-2326
This restaurant serves American food. Dogs are allowed at the outdoor tables.

Tillamook

Campgrounds and RV Parks
Cape Lookout State Park 13000 Whiskey Creek Road W Tillamook OR 503-842-4981 (800-452-5687)
This lush coastal forest park offers spectacular views, marine watching, hiking trails, interpretive tours, historic programs, and a variety of recreational pursuits. Dogs of all sizes are allowed at no additional fee. Dogs may not be left unattended, and they must be on no more than a 6 foot leash, and cleaned up after. Dogs are allowed on trails unless otherwise marked. The camping and tent areas also allow dogs. There is a dog walk area at the campground.

Beaches
Cape Lookout State Park Highway 101 Tillamook OR 503-842-4981
This is a popular beach during the summer. The beach is a short distance from the parking area. It is located about an hour and half west of Portland. Picnic tables, restrooms (including an ADA restroom), hiking trails and campgrounds are available at this park. There is a $3 day use fee. Leashed dogs are allowed on the beach. Dogs are also allowed on hiking trails and campgrounds. They must be on a six foot or less leash at all times and people are required to clean up after their pets. On beaches located outside of Oregon State Park boundaries, dogs might be allowed off-leash and under direct voice control, please look for signs or postings. This park is located off U.S. Highway 101, 12 miles southwest of Tillamook.
Cape Meares State Scenic Viewpoint Highway 101 Tillamook OR 800-551-6949
The beach is located south of the scenic viewpoint. The viewpoint is situated on a headland, about 200 feet above the ocean. According to the Oregon State Parks Division, bird watchers can view the largest colony of nesting common murres (this site is one of the most populous colonies of nesting sea birds on the continent). Bald eagles and a peregrine falcon have also been known to nest near here. In winter and spring, this park is an excellent location for viewing whale migrations. Picnic tables, restrooms and hiking are available at this park. There are no day use fees. Leashed dogs are allowed on the beach. Dogs are also allowed on hiking trails. They must be on a six foot or less leash at all times and people are required to clean up after their pets. On beaches located outside of Oregon State Park boundaries, dogs might be allowed off-leash and under direct voice control, please look for signs or postings. This park is located off U.S. Highway 101, 10 miles west of Tillamook.

Troutdale

Accommodations
Comfort Inn and Suites 477 NW Phoenix Drive Troutdale OR 503-669-6500 (877-424-6423)
Dogs of all sizes are allowed. There is a $10 per night per pet additional fee. Dogs may be left alone in the room for just a short time, and only if a contact number is left with the front desk. Dogs must be quiet, well behaved, leashed, and cleaned up after.
Holiday Inn Express 1000 NW Graham Road Troutdale OR 503-492-2900 (877-270-6405)
Dogs of all sizes are allowed. There is a $10 per first night pet fee per pet and $5 for each additional night. Smoking and non-smoking rooms are available for pets.
Motel 6 - Portland East - Troutdale 1610 Nw Frontage Road Troutdale OR 503-665-2254 (800-466-8356)
One well-behaved family pet per room. Guest must notify front desk upon arrival. Guest is liable for any damages. In consideration of all guests, pets must never be left unattended in the guest rooms.

Waldport

Campgrounds and RV Parks
Waldport/Newport KOA 1330 NW Pacific Coast H Waldport OR 541-563-2250 (800-562-3443)
http://www.koa.com

Dogs of all sizes are allowed. There are no additional pet fees. Dogs must be on no more than a 6 foot leash (retractable leashes are not allowed), and cleaned up after. There are some breed restrictions. The camping and tent areas also allow dogs. There is a dog walk area at the campground. There are special amenities given to dogs at this campground.

Beaches

Beachside State Recreation Site Highway 101 Waldport OR   541-563-3220
Enjoy miles of broad sandy beach at this park or stay at one of the campground sites that are located just seconds from the beach. Picnic tables, restrooms (including an ADA restroom), and hiking are also available at this park. There is a day use fees. Leashed dogs are allowed on the beach. Dogs are also allowed on hiking trails and campgrounds. They must be on a six foot or less leash at all times and people are required to clean up after their pets. On beaches located outside of Oregon State Park boundaries, dogs might be allowed off-leash and under direct voice control, please look for signs or postings. This park is located off U.S. Highway 101, 4 miles south of Waldport.

Governor Patterson Memorial State Recreation Site Highway 101 Waldport OR   800-551-6949
This park offers miles of flat, sandy beach. It is also an excellent location for whale watching. Picnic tables and restrooms are available at this park. There are no day use fees. Dogs are allowed on the beach. They must be on a six foot or less leash at all times and people are required to clean up after their pets. On beaches located outside of Oregon State Park boundaries, dogs might be allowed off-leash and under direct voice control, please look for signs or postings. This park is located off U.S. Highway 101, 1 mile south of Waldport.

Warrenton

Accommodations

Shilo Inn 1609 E Harbor Drive Warrenton OR   503-861-2181 (800-222-2244)
There is a $10 per day pet fee.

Beaches

Fort Stevens State Park Highway 101 Warrenton OR   503-861-1671
http://www.oregonstate.org/park_179.php
There are miles of ocean beach. Picnic tables, restrooms (including an ADA restroom), hiking and campgrounds are available at this park. There is a $3 day use fee. Leashed dogs are allowed on the beach. Dogs are also allowed on hiking trails and campgrounds. They must be on a six foot or less leash at all times and people are required to clean up after their pets. On beaches located outside of Oregon State Park boundaries, dogs might be allowed off-leash and under direct voice control, please look for signs or postings. This park is located off U.S. Highway 101, 10 miles west of Astoria.

Welches

Campgrounds and RV Parks

Mt Hood Village 65000 E Hwy 26 Welches OR   800-255-3069
http://www.mhcrv.com
One dog of any size is allowed, and there are no additional pet fees for tent or RV sites. There is a $10 one time additional pet fee for the cabin. Dogs must be quiet, well behaved, leashed, and cleaned up after. There are some breed restrictions. The camping and tent areas also allow dogs. There is a dog walk area at the campground. Dogs are allowed in the camping cabins.

Parks

Mt Hood National Forest 65000 E Hwy 26 (Visitors' Center) Welches OR   888-622-4822
http://www.mthood.info/usdafs/index.html
With more than a million acres, and 189,200 acres of designated wilderness, this forests' diverse ecosystems support a large variety of plants, fish, mammals, bird species, and recreation. Dogs of all sizes are allowed for no additional fee. Dogs are allowed throughout the forest, except at the Timberline Lodge, park buildings, or public swim areas. Dogs are allowed on some of the cross country ski trails. Dogs may not be left unattended at any time, and they must be leashed and cleaned up after. There are also several campground areas and a beautiful scenic drive to the top of Mt Hood.

Wilderville

Campgrounds and RV Parks
Grants Pass/Redwood Hwy KOA 13370 Redwood H Wilderville OR   541-476-6508 (800-562-7566)
http://www.koa.com/where/or/37106/
Dogs of all sizes are allowed. There are no additional pet fees. Dogs may not be tied to the picnic tables, and they must be leashed and cleaned up after. Dogs must be taken to the specified dog walk area to do their business. There are some breed restrictions. The camping and tent areas also allow dogs. There is a dog walk area at the campground.

Winchester Bay

Campgrounds and RV Parks
The Marina RV Resort End of Marina Way Winchester Bay OR   541-271-0287
http://www.marinarvresort.com
Dogs of all sizes are allowed. There are no additional pet fees. Dogs may not be left unattended, and they must be well behaved, leashed and cleaned up after. There is a dog walk area at the campground.

Winston

Attractions
Wildlife Safari Kennels 1790 Safari Road Winston OR   541-679-6761
http://www.wildlifesafari.org/
Wildlife Safari is fun destination for all ages where you can view animals in their natural habitat and roaming freely as they do in the wild. Watch animals from Africa, Asia and South America, as well as many native to North America, up close and personal from the safety of your car. This is also a world renowned medical and research facility, and a nationally recognized educational facility for veterinary and biological sciences. You can visit their Village after your drive where you can relax in beautiful gardens, eat in the White Rhino Restaurant, or explore the unique Casbah Gift Shop. Since dogs are not allowed in the animal park or the village, they provide free kennel service. There is an attendant on duty at all times until closing. Locks are available for $5 if you do not have a padlock. The runs are all outdoors and covered. They also request you bring your pets food. The park is open March 25 to October 15 from 9 am to 5 pm; from October 16 to March 24 they are open from 9 am to 4 pm.

Woodburn

Accommodations
Best Western Woodburn 2887 Newberg Hwy Woodburn OR   503-982-6515 (800-780-7234)
Dogs of all sizes are allowed. There is a $10 one time per pet fee per visit. Smoking and non-smoking are available for pets.
La Quinta Inn & Suites Woodburn 120 Arney Rd NE Woodburn OR   503-982-1727 (800-531-5900)
Dogs of all sizes are allowed. There are no additional pet fees. Dogs must be leashed and cleaned up after. Dogs may only be left alone in the room if they will be quiet and well behaved, and they must be crated.
Super 8 Woodburn 821 Evergreen Rd Woodburn OR   503-981-8881 (800-800-8000)
Dogs of all sizes are allowed. There is a $50 returnable deposit required per room. There is a $10 one time per pet fee per visit. Smoking and non-smoking rooms are available for pet rooms.

Yachats

Accommodations

Adobe Resort 1555 US 101 Yachats OR   541-547-3141
http://www.adoberesort.com/
There is a $10 per day pet charge.
See Vue Hotel 95590 Hwy 101 Yachats OR   541-547-3227
Dogs of all sizes are allowed. There is an $8 per night per pet additional fee.
Shamrock Lodgettes US 101 Yachats OR   541-547-3312 (800-845-5028)
Pets are allowed in cabins only. There is an additional $5 per day charge. All units are non-smoking and have fireplaces.
The Fireside Inn Hwy 101 Yachats OR   800-336-3573 (800-336-3573)
http://www.overleaflodge.com/fireside/
There is a $9 per day per pet charge. Dogs cannot be left unattended in the room. All rooms are non-smoking.

Beaches

Neptune State Scenic Viewpoint Highway 101 Yachats OR   800-551-6949
During low tide at this beach you can walk south and visit a natural cave and tidepools. Or sit and relax at one of the picnic tables that overlooks the beach below. Restrooms (including an ADA restroom) are available at this park. There are no day use fees. Dogs are allowed on the beach. They must be on a six foot or less leash at all times and people are required to clean up after their pets. On beaches located outside of Oregon State Park boundaries, dogs might be allowed off-leash and under direct voice control, please look for signs or postings. This park is located off U.S. Highway 101,
Yachats State Recreation Area Highway 101 Yachats OR   800-551-6949
This beach is a popular spot for whale watching, salmon fishing, and exploring tidepools. Picnic tables and restrooms are available at this park. There are no day use fees. Dogs are allowed on the beach. They must be on a six foot or less leash at all times and people are required to clean up after their pets. On beaches located outside of Oregon State Park boundaries, dogs might be allowed off-leash and under direct voice control, please look for signs or postings. This park is located off U.S. Highway 101 in Yachats.

Chapter 21

Utah
Dog Travel Guide

American Fork

Accommodations
Quality Inn and Suites 712 S Utah Valley Drive American Fork UT   801-763-8383 (877-424-6423)
Dogs of all sizes are allowed. There are no additional pet fees. Dogs must be well behaved, leashed, cleaned up after, crated or removed for housekeeping, and the Do Not Disturb sign put on the door if they are in the room alone.

Stores
PetSmart Pet Store 472 N 990 West American Fork UT   801-756-0192
Your licensed and well-behaved leashed dog is allowed in the store.

Parks
Timpanogos Cave National Monument RR 3 Box 200 American Fork UT   801-756-5238
http://www.nps.gov/tica/index.htm
Pets on leash are allowed on the Canyon Nature trail. Dogs are not allowed on the cave trail. There is an on-site kennel with water provided for free if you decide to go on the cave trail.

Beaver

Accommodations
Best Western Butch Cassidy Inn 161 South Main Beaver UT   435-438-2438 (800-780-7234)
Dogs of all sizes are allowed. There is a $5 per night pet fee per pet. Smoking and non-smoking are available for pets.
Best Western Paradise Inn 1451 North 300 West Beaver UT   435-438-2455 (800-780-7234)
Dogs of all sizes are allowed. There are no additional pet fees. Smoking and non-smoking are available for pets.
Motel 6 - Beaver 1345 North 450 West Beaver UT   435-438-1666 (800-466-8356)
One well-behaved family pet per room. Guest must notify front desk upon arrival. Guest is liable for any damages. In consideration of all guests, pets must never be left unattended in the guest rooms.

Campgrounds and RV Parks
Beaver KOA 1428 Manderfield Road Beaver UT   435-438-2924 (800-562-2912)
http://www.koa.com
Dogs of all sizes are allowed. There are no additional pet fees. Dogs must be leashed and cleaned up after. This RV park is closed during the off-season. The camping and tent areas also allow dogs. There is a dog walk area at the campground. Dogs are allowed in the camping cabins.

Blanding

Accommodations
Best Western Gateway Inn 88 East Center Blanding UT   435-678-2278 (800-780-7234)
Dogs of all sizes are allowed. There is a $50 returnable deposit required per room. Smoking and non-smoking are available for pets.
Four Corners Inn 131 E Center St Blanding UT   435-678-3257
http://www.moabutah.com/fourcornersinn/
There are no additional pet fees. Dogs are not allowed on the beds.

Campgrounds and RV Parks
Goosenecks State Park 660 West 400 North/End of Hwy 316 Blanding UT   435-678-2238 (800-322-3770)
This park shares 300 million years of geologic history with its visitors from an observation shelter located at 1000

feet over the San Juan River. From here you can see the path of the river's erosion. Dogs are allowed at no additional fee. Dogs may be off lead if there is voice control. The camping and tent areas also allow dogs. There is a dog walk area at the campground. There are no electric or water hookups at the campground.

Bluff

Campgrounds and RV Parks
Cadillac Ranch 640 E Main Bluff UT 800-538-6195
Dogs of all sizes are allowed. There are no additional pet fees. Dogs must be leashed and cleaned up after. The camping and tent areas also allow dogs. There is a dog walk area at the campground.

Brigham City

Accommodations
Howard Johnson Inn 1167 S Main St. Brigham City UT 435-723-8511 (800-446-4656)
Dogs of all sizes are welcome. There are no additional pet fees.

Attractions
Transcontinental Railroad National Back Country Byway P. O. Box 897 Brigham City UT 801-471-2209
This was the place where the Transcontinental Railroad joined the east and the west on May 10, 1869, and in its heyday, there were 28 sidings, stations, and towns built along the Promontory Branch. In 1904 this branch of the railway was replaced for a shorter route, towns became abandoned, and this area became a Back Country Byway. Now there are over 30 sites that are interpreted along this grade that begins south of Promontory near the Golden Spike National Historic Site and travels west to Lucin. There are no facilities or services along this almost 90 mile grade, so plenty of gas (if by auto) and water is needed. Dogs are allowed on this trail. They request that animals (or people) do no digging. There is free primitive camping on BLM land, and when in a camp area where there are other visitors, dogs must be leashed and cleaned up after.

Bryce Canyon

Accommodations
Best Western Ruby's Inn Utah Hwy 63 Bryce UT 435-834-5341 (800-780-7234)
Dogs of all sizes are allowed at the hotel and the attached campground. There are no additional pet fees. Smoking and non-smoking are available for pets. This hotel is the closest and most convenient pet-friendly hotel to Bryce and Red Canyon.
Bryce Junction Inn 3090 E Highway 12 & Jct 89 Panguitch UT 435-676-8886
This hotel is open from March 15 to Nov 15 and closed during the winter.. Dogs of all sizes are allowed. There are no additional pet fees.
Bryce Way Motel 429 N Main St Panguitch UT 435-676-2400
Pets are allowed for a $5 per night additional pet fee.The hotel is in Panguitch which is about 20 miles from Bryce.
Marianna Inn Motel 699 N Main St Panguitch UT 435-676-8844
Dogs of all sizes are allowed for a $5 per night additional pet fee. The hotel is in Panguitch which is about 20 miles from Bryce.

Campgrounds and RV Parks

Ruby's Inn Campground and RV Park 1280 S Hwy 63 Bryce Canyon UT 435-834-5301 (866-866-6616)
http://www.brycecanyoncampgrounds.com/
This scenic camp area is a great place to stay when visiting the Bryce Canyon National Park, offer over 200 shaded campsites, and large pull-through sites to accommodate modern RV's. Some of the amenities include showers, clean restrooms, a large Laundromat, heated pool, a post office, dump station, 2 stores, and various recreational activities. The campground is located near Ruby's Inn, and they ask that you check in there at the front desk for camp sites. Dogs of all sizes are allowed for no additional fee. Dogs must be quiet, well behaved, leashed and cleaned up after at all times. They are not allowed to be left unattended outside the RV, and they

may not be left inside tents alone. Dogs are not allowed in Bryce Canyon, on the rim or on trails. Dogs are allowed throughout the campgrounds, and on the connecting ATV trails. This rv park is closed during the off-season. The camping and tent areas also allow dogs. There is a dog walk area at the campground.

Cannonville/Bryce Valley KOA Hwy 12 at Red Rocks Road Cannonville UT   435-679-8988 (888-562-4710)
http://www.brycecanyonkoa.com
Dogs of all sizes are allowed. There are no additional pet fees. Dogs must be well behaved, leashed, and cleaned up after. This RV park is closed during the off-season. The camping and tent areas also allow dogs. There is a dog walk area at the campground. Dogs are allowed in the camping cabins.

Kodachrome Basin State Park P. O. Box 238/Kodachrome Drive Cannonville UT   435-679-8562 (800-322-3770)
Multi-colored and red tinged rock formations against incredible blue skies give rise to this park's name. It boasts the world's only collection of 'sand pipes'; oddly shaped sandstone pillers that rise from 6 to 170 feet from the ground. There are several short trails in the park that lead to very scenic views, a visitor's center, a camping supply store, and guided tours. Dogs are allowed at no additional fee. They must be on no more than a 6 foot leash, they are not allowed in park buildings, but they can be around the park and on the trails. Dogs may not be left unattended, and they must be cleaned up after. Located in a natural amphitheater among desert vegetation, this well maintained campground offers a pavilion area with picnic tables, fire pit, barbecue grills, fresh spring water, modern restrooms, showers, dump station, and firewood. They are open year round, but water is shut off in winter. Campers do not have to pay an additional day use fee for the park. The camping and tent areas also allow dogs. There is a dog walk area at the campground. There are no electric or water hookups at the campgrounds.

Panguitch KOA 555 Main Street Panguitch UT   435-676-2225 (800-562-1625)
http://www.koa.com
Dogs of all sizes are allowed. There are no additional pet fees. Dogs must be leashed and cleaned up after. This RV park is closed during the off-season. The camping and tent areas also allow dogs. There is a dog walk area at the campground.

Paradise RV Park 2153 N Hwy 89 Panguitch UT   435-676-8348
Dogs of all sizes are allowed at the tent and RV sites. Only small, lightly furred dogs are allowed at the cabins. There are no additional pet fees. Dogs may not be left unattended, and they must be leashed and cleaned up after. This RV park is closed during the off-season. The camping and tent areas also allow dogs. There is a dog walk area at the campground. Dogs are allowed in the camping cabins.

Red Canyon Campground 3279 Scenic Highway 12 Panguitch UT   435-676-2690
This campground sits at 7,400 feet altitude in a Ponderosa Pine setting, and is surround by striking Pink Limestone formations. Sites are available on a first-come, first-served basis, and there are a variety of extensive trail systems for multi-use, many scenic overlooks, and a visitor's center. Some of the amenities include drinking water, a modern restroom and showers, gaming courts, fire rings and grills, paved sidewalks, free cable TV, and a dump station. Dogs of all sizes are allowed for no additional fee. Dogs must be well behaved, leashed, and cleaned up after at all times. Dogs are allowed throughout the park and on the trails by the park. They are not allowed in park buildings, or on the trails leading into the Bryce Canyon National Park. This rv park is closed during the off-season. The camping and tent areas also allow dogs. There is a dog walk area at the campground. There are no electric or water hookups at the campgrounds.

Red Canyon Park P. O. Box 80/Hwy 12 Panguitch UT   435-676-9300
The beautiful Red Canyon Park can serve as a dog-friendly substitute to see the rock formations that make Bryce Canyon famous. Dogs are not allowed on any trails at Bryce Canyon but are allowed on leash throughout Red Canyon Park. The park sits at a 7,400 foot altitude in a Ponderosa Pine setting surrounded by striking red and pink Limestone formations that rival those of the National Park. There are a variety of extensive trail systems for multi-use, many scenic overlooks (one allows visitors to see 3 different states), and a visitor's center. Dogs of all sizes are allowed for no additional fee. Dogs must be well behaved, leashed, and cleaned up after at all times. Dogs are allowed throughout the park and on the trails by the park. They are not allowed in park buildings, or on the trails leading into the nearby Bryce Canyon National Park. Camp sites are available on a first-come, first-served basis. Some of the amenities include drinking water, modern restroom and showers, gaming courts, fire rings and grills, paved sidewalks, free cable TV, and a dump station. This RV park is closed during the off-season. The camping and tent areas also allow dogs. There is a dog walk area at the campground.

Red Canyon RV Park 3279 Hwy 12 Panguitch UT   435-676-2690
http://www.redcanyon.net/rc_rvpark
Dogs of all sizes are allowed. There are no additional pet fees. Dogs must be leashed and cleaned up after. This RV park is closed during the off-season. The camping and tent areas also allow dogs. There is a dog walk area at the campground.

Parks

Bryce Canyon National Park PO Box 640201/ On Hwy 63 Bryce UT   435-834-5322
http://www.nps.gov/brca/
This park is famous for it's unique geology, creating vast and unusual limestone formations throughout the region. Dogs are not allowed on any of the trails, the shuttle, the viewpoints, or the visitor's center. The park is

open 24 hours a day year round. There are 2 campgrounds; Loop A, the north campground, is open all year, and the Sunset campground is only open for the season. There are no hookups at either campground. Dogs can walk along the road in the campground. There are no additional fees for the dogs. Dogs may not be left unattended, they must be leashed at all times, and cleaned up after.
Kodachrome Basin State Park P. O. Box 238/Kodachrome Drive Cannonville UT   435-679-8562 (800-322-3770)
Multi-colored and red tinged rock formations against incredible blue skies give rise to this park's name. It boasts the world's only collection of 'sand pipes'; oddly shaped sandstone pillers that rise from 6 to 170 feet from the ground. There are several short trails in the park that lead to very scenic views, a visitor's center, a camping supply store, and guided tours. Dogs are allowed at no additional fee. They must be on no more than a 6 foot leash, they are not allowed in park buildings, but they can be around the park and on the trails. Dogs may not be left unattended, and they must be cleaned up after.

TOP 200 PLACE Red Canyon Park P. O. Box 80/Hwy 12 Panguitch UT   435-676-9300
The beautiful Red Canyon Park can serve as a dog-friendly substitute to see the rock formations that make Bryce Canyon famous. Dogs are not allowed on any trails at Bryce Canyon but are allowed on leash throughout Red Canyon Park. The park sits at a 7,400 foot altitude in a Ponderosa Pine setting surrounded by striking red and pink Limestone formations that rival those of the National Park. There are a variety of extensive trail systems for multi-use, many scenic overlooks (one allows visitors to see 3 different states), and a visitor's center. Dogs of all sizes are allowed for no additional fee. Dogs must be well behaved, leashed, and cleaned up after at all times. Dogs are allowed throughout the park and on the trails by the park. They are not allowed in park buildings, or on the trails leading into the nearby Bryce Canyon National Park.

Canonville

Campgrounds and RV Parks
Kodachrome Basin State Park P.O. Box 180069/ Cottonwood Road Canonville UT   435-679-8562 (800-322-3770)
This park offers a unique desert beauty as a result of geological activity that created the many trails and massive, colorful sandstone chimneys. Dogs are allowed at no additional fee. Dogs may not be left unattended, and they must be on no more than a 6 foot leash, and be cleaned up after. Dogs are allowed on the trails. The camping and tent areas also allow dogs. There is a dog walk area at the campground. There are no electric or water hookups at the campground.

Cedar City

Accommodations
Days Inn Cedar City 1204 South Main Cedar City UT   435-867-8877 (800-329-7466)
Dogs of all sizes are allowed. There is a $10 per night pet fee per pet.
Holiday Inn Express Hotel and Suites 1555 S Old Highway 91 Cedar City UT   435-865-7799 (877-270-6405)
Dogs of all sizes are allowed. There is a $10 one time per pet fee per visit. Only non-smoking rooms are used for pets.
Motel 6 - Cedar City 1620 West 200 North Cedar City UT   435-586-9200 (800-466-8356)
One well-behaved family pet per room. Guest must notify front desk upon arrival. Guest is liable for any damages. In consideration of all guests, pets must never be left unattended in the guest rooms.
Super 8 Cedar City 145 N 1550 West Cedar City UT   735-586-8880 (800-800-8000)
Dogs of all sizes are allowed. There is a $9 per night pet fee per pet. Smoking and non-smoking rooms are available for pet rooms.

Campgrounds and RV Parks
Cedar City KOA 1121 N Main Cedar City UT   435-586-9872 (800-562-9873)
http://www.cedarcitycampgrounds.com
There can be up to 3 dogs of any size for the tent or RV sites, and there are no additional pet fees. There is a $5 per night per pet additional fee for the cabins, and only up to 2 dogs are allowed. Dogs may not be left unattended, and they must be leashed and cleaned up after. There are some breed restrictions. The camping and tent areas also allow dogs. There is a dog walk area at the campground. Dogs are allowed in the camping cabins.
Dixie National Forest 1789 N Wedgewood Lane Cedar City UT   435-865-3700
http://www.fs.fed.us/dxnf

This is the largest National Forest in Utah and dogs of all sizes are allowed. There are no additional pet fees. Dogs may not be left unattended, and they must be leashed and cleaned up after. Dogs are allowed on all the trails, but they are not allowed on the beaches or in the water. This campground is closed during the off-season. The camping and tent areas also allow dogs. There is a dog walk area at the campground.

Parks

Cedar Breaks National Monument 2390 West Highway 56 Ste #11 Cedar City UT 435-586-9451
http://www.nps.gov/cebr/index.htm
Dogs must be on leash and must be cleaned up after on paved areas and in campgrounds. Dogs are not allowed on hiking trails or the backcountry.

Clearfield

Accommodations

Traveller's Inn 572 N Main St Clearfield UT 801-825-8000
Dogs of all sizes are allowed. There is a $10 per night pet fee per pet. Smoking and non-smoking rooms are available for pet rooms.

Coalville

Accommodations

Best Western Holiday Hills 210 South 200 West Coalville UT 435-336-4444 (800-780-7234)
Dogs of all sizes are allowed. There is a $15 per night pet fee per pet. Smoking and non-smoking are available for pets.

Cortez

Campgrounds and RV Parks

Hovenweep Campground/Hovenweep National Monument On Hwy 10 (McElmo Route) Cortez UT 970-562-4282 (800-322-3770)
http://www.nps.gov/hove/
This park is the safeguard for six prehistoric, Puebloan-era villages, and offers a variety of historical, geological, and scenic sites. Dogs are allowed at no additional fee. Dogs may not be left unattended outside, and they must be leashed and cleaned up after. Dogs are allowed on the trails, and they must stay on the trails. The camping and tent areas also allow dogs. There is a dog walk area at the campground. There are no electric or water hookups at the campground.

Dinosaur National Monument

Accommodations

Frontier Motel 75 S 200 E Roosevelt UT 435-722-2201
There are no additional pet fees.
Motel 6 - Vernal 1092 West Highway 40 Vernal UT 435-789-0666 (800-466-8356)
One well-behaved family pet per room. Guest must notify front desk upon arrival. Guest is liable for any damages. In consideration of all guests, pets must never be left unattended in the guest rooms.
Sage Motel 54 W Main St Vernal UT 435-789-1442
There is a $5 one time pet fee.

Campgrounds and RV Parks

Ashley National Forest 355 N Vernal Avenue Vernal UT 435-789-1181 (877-444-6777)
http://www.fs.fed.us/r4/ashley/
Dogs of all sizes are allowed. There are no additional pet fees. Dogs may not be left unattended, and they must

be leashed and cleaned up after. This campground is closed during the off-season. The camping and tent areas also allow dogs. There is a dog walk area at the campground.

Red Fleet State Park 8750 North Highway 191 Vernal UT 435-789-4432 (877-UTPARKS (877-2757))
Red Fleet is almost 2,000 acres with a reservoir of 750 water acres, and sits in what is known as 'the heart of Dinosaurland' at an elevation of 5,500 feet. Tracks believed to be more than 200 million years old can be reached by hiking a rather strenuous 1.25 mile trail of several up and down sections. There is a variety of land and water recreation, hiking trails, wildlife viewing, and camping and/or picnicking. Day use permits cover personal watercraft launches, and annual passes are available at the visitor's center. Park hours are shortened for the winter. Dogs are allowed throughout the park, on the trails, and on the beach. Dogs must be on a maximum 6 foot leash, and they are not allowed in park buildings. Dogs must be well behaved, and cleaned up after at all times. The campground overlooks a sandstone and desert landscape, and they offer modern restrooms, picnic sites, and drinking water. Campers do not have to pay an additional day use fee for the park. The camping and tent areas also allow dogs. There is a dog walk area at the campground. There are no electric or water hookups at the campgrounds.

Vernal/Dinosaurland KOA 930 N Vernal Avenue Vernal UT 435-789-2148
http://www.koa.com/where/ut/44152/
Dogs of all sizes are allowed. There are no additional pet fees. Dogs may not be left unattended at any time, and they must be quiet, leashed, and cleaned up after. Only 2 dogs at a time are allowed in the cabins, and up to 3 dogs at the tent or RV sites. There are some breed restrictions. This RV park is closed during the off-season. The camping and tent areas also allow dogs. There is a dog walk area at the campground. Dogs are allowed in the camping cabins.

Parks
Red Fleet State Park 8750 North Highway 191 Vernal UT 435-789-4432 (877-UTPARKS (877-2757))
Red Fleet is almost 2,000 acres with a reservoir of 750 water acres, and sits in what is known as 'the heart of Dinosaurland' at an elevation of 5,500 feet. Tracks believed to be more than 200 million years old can be reached by hiking a rather strenuous 1.25 mile trail of several up and down sections. There is a variety of land and water recreation, hiking trails, wildlife viewing, and camping and/or picnicking. Day use permits cover personal watercraft launches, and annual passes are available at the visitor's center. Park hours are shortened for the winter. Dogs are allowed throughout the park, on the trails, and on the beach. Dogs must be on a maximum 6 foot leash, and they are not allowed in park buildings. Dogs must be well behaved, and cleaned up after at all times.

Draper

Stores
Petco Pet Store 195 East 12300 South Draper UT 801-495-4201
Your licensed and well-behaved leashed dog is allowed in the store.

Escalante

Campgrounds and RV Parks
Escalante State Park 710 N Reservoir Road Escalante UT 435-826-4466 (800-322-3770)
This park, along the Wide Hollow Reservoir, has a couple of popular trails; The Petrified Forest Trail which winds through lava flows and petrified wood, and for more of a challenge there is the Sleeping Rainbows trail. Dogs are allowed at no additional fee. Dogs may not be left unattended, and they must be leashed and cleaned up after. Dogs are allowed on the trails. The camping and tent areas also allow dogs. There is a dog walk area at the campground. There are no electric or water hookups at the campground.

Eureka

Attractions
Tintic Mining Museum 241 W Main Street Eureka UT 435-433-6842
http://www.utah.com/museums/
This museum is located at the historic Eureka City Hall and features a history room, mining artifacts, a mineral

display, library, and self guided tours. This town was the center of a strong mining industry for gold, lead, silver, copper, and other minerals. The phone number listed is the home number of the curator, and they are open by appointment from 10 am to 4 pm most days. Well behaved, social dogs are allowed to explore the museum and the mining sites with their owners; just let them know when you call that you have a pet. Dogs must be leashed and cleaned up after at all times.

Farmington

Campgrounds and RV Parks
Lagoon RV Park and Campground 375 N Lagoon Drive Farmington UT 801-451-8000 (800-748-5246)
http://www.lagoonpark.com/camping.php
This RV park and campground offers such amenities as a general store, laundry, restrooms with showers, a sandwich shop, a gourmet ice cream parlor, and a bicycle/walking trail around a large lagoon. Reservations are recommended, and they usually start taking them about mid-February. This park also sits along side the Lagoon Amusement Park and Pioneer Village, a world class amusement park of over 100 acres with dozens of rides and attractions, and dogs are allowed in some of the areas there. Dogs of all sizes are allowed for no additional fee for camping or the park. Dogs may not be left unattended at the campsite, and they must be leashed and cleaned up after at all times. This rv park is closed during the off-season. The camping and tent areas also allow dogs. There is a dog walk area at the campground.

Attractions
TOP 200 PLACE **Lagoon Amusement Park and Pioneer Village** 375 N Lagoon Drive Farmington UT 801-451-8000
http://www.lagoonpark.com/
This amusement park offers dozens of rides and attractions, shops, games, a state-of-the-art waterpark, 2 high-tech go-kart tracks, an X-Venture Zone (extreme rides), a lagoon, and lots of delicious eating. They also offer an active live entertainment program, and the Pioneer Village, an 1800's frontier community with all the artifacts to transport you back in time. They are open daily from about May 5th to August 22, and then open mostly weekends until closed for the season. Dates and times are subject to change and closing times may vary. They have an extended opening for FRIGHTMARES, from September 29th to October 28th, opening on Friday's at 6 pm and on the weekend at 11 am. This yearly event offers several spooky fun activities for all ages. Dogs of all sizes are allowed to explore this fun place. They are not allowed in the waterpark, on the rides or in buildings, but they are allowed on the midway, around the grounds, and through the village. Dogs must be leashed and cleaned up after at all times. There is also a full service RV and campground on site where dogs are allowed for no additional fee.

Filimore

Accommodations
Best Western Paradise Inn and Resort 905 N Main Filimore UT 435-743-6895 (800-780-7234)
Dogs of all sizes are allowed. There are no additional pet fees. Smoking and non-smoking are available for pets.

Fillmore

Campgrounds and RV Parks
Fillmore KOA 900 S 410 W Fillmore UT 435-743-4420 (800-562-1516)
http://www.koa.com
Dogs of all sizes are allowed, and there can be up to 3 dogs at the tent and RV sites. Two small dogs only are allowed at the cabins, and they must stay off the beds. There are no additional pet fees. Dogs are not allowed at the playground or the pool, and they must be leashed and cleaned up after. There are some breed restrictions. This RV park is closed during the off-season. The camping and tent areas also allow dogs. There is a dog walk area at the campground. Dogs are allowed in the camping cabins.

Garden City

Campgrounds and RV Parks

Bear Lake State Park Box 184/ Off Hwy 30 Garden City UT   435-946-3343 (800-322-3770)
This beautiful lake park is located high in the Rocky Mountains and is open year round. Dogs are allowed at no additional fee. Dogs may not be left unattended, and they must be leashed and cleaned up after. Dogs may be off lead when out of the camp areas if there is voice control. Dogs are allowed on the trails unless otherwise marked. This campground is closed during the off-season. The camping and tent areas also allow dogs. There is a dog walk area at the campground.

Bear Lake/Garden City KOA 485 N Bear Lake Blvd Garden City UT   435-946-3454 (800-562-3442)
http://www.koa.com
Dogs of all sizes are allowed. There are no additional pet fees. Dogs may not be left unattended, and they must be leashed and cleaned up after. There is an off leash dog run area. The tent and RV sites are seasonal, and the cabins stay open all year. There are some breed restrictions. The camping and tent areas also allow dogs. There is a dog walk area at the campground. Dogs are allowed in the camping cabins.

Glendale

Campgrounds and RV Parks

Glendale KOA 11 Koa Street Glendale UT   435-648-2490 (800-562-8635)
http://www.koa.com
Dogs of all sizes are allowed. There are no additional pet fees. Dogs must be leashed and cleaned up after. There is a fenced in dog run for off lead. This RV park is closed during the off-season. The camping and tent areas also allow dogs. There is a dog walk area at the campground.

Green River

Accommodations

Holiday Inn Express 965 East Main Street Green River UT   435-564-4439 (877-270-6405)
Dogs up to 60 pounds are allowed. There is a $5 per day additional pet fee. The hotel has a few pet rooms.
Motel 6 - Green River 946 East Main Street Green River UT   435-564-3436 (800-466-8356)
One well-behaved family pet per room. Guest must notify front desk upon arrival. Guest is liable for any damages. In consideration of all guests, pets must never be left unattended in the guest rooms.
Super 8 Green River 1248 E Main Green River UT   435-564-8888 (800-800-8000)
Dogs of all sizes are allowed. There is a $5 per night pet fee per pet. Reservations are recommended due to limited rooms for pets. Smoking and non-smoking rooms are available for pet rooms.

Campgrounds and RV Parks

Goblin Valley State Park P.O. Box 637 Green River UT   435-564-3633 (800 322-3770)
A vast unearthly landscape greets visitors with thousands of intricately eroded sandstone creations, that someone obviously thought looked like goblins. The movie Galaxy Quest was filmed here because of this unusual scenery. There are plenty of places to hike to and through, a visitor observation shelter, visitor's center, and picnicking. They are open daily year round. Dogs are allowed at no additional fee. They must be on no more than a 6 foot leash, and they are not allowed in park buildings. Dogs may not be left unattended, and they must be cleaned up after. Camping is allowed in designated areas only, and they offer modern restrooms, showers, covered tables, drinking water, and a dump station. The camping and tent areas also allow dogs. There is a dog walk area at the campground. There are no electric or water hookups at the campgrounds.

Green River State Park 125 Fairway Avenue Green River UT   435-564-3633 (800-322-3770)
This park has it's own recreational activities and a golf course, but is is also a central point to access other recreational areas and trails. Dogs are allowed at no additional fee. Dogs may not be left unattended, and they must be leashed and cleaned up after. Dogs are allowed on the trails. This campground is closed during the off-season. The camping and tent areas also allow dogs. There is a dog walk area at the campground. There are no electric or water hookups at the campground.

United Campground of Green River 910 E Main Street Green River UT   435-564-8195
Dogs of all sizes are allowed. There are no additional pet fees. Dogs must be leashed and cleaned up after. The camping and tent areas also allow dogs. There is a dog walk area at the campground.

Parks

Goblin Valley State Park P.O. Box 637 Green River UT 435-564-3633 (800 322-3770)
A vast unearthly landscape greets visitors with thousands of intricately eroded sandstone creations, that someone obviously thought looked like goblins. The movie Galaxy Quest was filmed here because of this unusual scenery. There are plenty of places to hike to and through, a visitor observation shelter, visitor's center, and picnicking. They are open daily year round. Dogs are allowed at no additional fee. They must be on no more than a 6 foot leash, and they are not allowed in park buildings. Dogs may not be left unattended, and they must be cleaned up after.

Hanksville

Campgrounds and RV Parks

Goblin Valley State Park P.O. Box 637/Hanksville Road Hanksville UT 435-564-3633 (800-322-3770)
Goblin Valley is so named as a result of the unusual rock formations and the scenery of the park. Dogs are allowed at no additional fee. Dogs may not be left unattended, and they must be leashed and cleaned up after. Dogs are allowed on the trails. The camping and tent areas also allow dogs. There is a dog walk area at the campground. There are no electric or water hookups at the campground.

Harrisville

Stores

Petco Pet Store 390 East 525 North Harrisville UT 801-528-5043
Your licensed and well-behaved leashed dog is allowed in the store.

Huntington

Campgrounds and RV Parks

Huntington State Park P.O. Box 1343/ On Hwy 10 Huntington UT 435-687-2491 (800-322-3770)
The beautiful reservoir here is surrounded by sandstone cliffs, and a variety of recreation is available. Dogs are allowed at no additional fee. Dogs may not be left unattended, and they must be leashed and cleaned up after. Dogs are allowed on the trails. The camping and tent areas also allow dogs. There is a dog walk area at the campground. There are no electric or water hookups at the campground.

Huntsville

Campgrounds and RV Parks

Snowbasin: A Sun Valley Resort 3925 E. Snowbasin Road Huntsville UT 801-620-1000 (888-437-5488)
http://www.snowbasin.com/index_s.asp
Located in the spectacular Wasatch-Cache National Forest, Snowbasin's 2,959 vertical feet truly offer terrain to suit everyone's needs. There are 17 designated trails of varying degrees of difficulty, and a variety of recreational pursuits. Amenities include two eateries, a summer concert series and other planned activities, some picnic tables along the trails, a new Disc Golf course, and they offer a trail map to show you the ideal rest, viewing, and picnic areas. Dog of all sizes are allowed for no additional fee. They are not allowed up on the mountain or on the ski runs in the winter, or in park buildings. They are allowed at the plaza, on several of the all season trails, and at the Nordic area. There are some unpopulated areas where dogs may be off lead if they are under firm voice control. Dogs must be leashed and cleaned up after on the trails and at the resort. There is a dog walk area at the campground.

Parks

Snowbasin: A Sun Valley Resort 3925 E. Snowbasin Road Huntsville UT 801-620-1000 (888-437-5488)
http://www.snowbasin.com/index_s.asp
Located in the spectacular Wasatch-Cache National Forest, Snowbasin's 2,959 vertical feet truly offer terrain to

suit everyone's needs. There are 17 designated trails of varying degrees of difficulty, and a variety of recreational pursuits. Amenities include two eateries, a summer concert series and other planned activities, some picnic tables along the trails, a new Disc Golf course, and they offer a trail map to show you the ideal rest, viewing, and picnic areas. Dog of all sizes are allowed for no additional fee. They are not allowed up on the mountain or on the ski runs in the winter, or in park buildings. They are allowed at the plaza, on several of the all season trails, and at the Nordic area. There are some unpopulated areas where dogs may be off lead if they are under firm voice control. Dogs must be leashed and cleaned up after on the trails and at the resort.

Ivins

Campgrounds and RV Parks
Snow Canyon State Park 1002 Snow Canyon Drive Ivins UT   435-628-2255
This park ranges from 3,100 to almost 5,000 feet altitude, and covers about 7,100 acres. Rarely snowed in, they are open year round, and some of the features offered are 16 miles of hiking trails, technical rock climbing, wildlife viewing, camping, and plenty of photo ops of this visually striking area. Dogs of all sizes are allowed at no additional fee. They must be on no more than a 6 foot leash, and they are not allowed in park buildings. Dogs may not be left unattended outside an RV or tent, or inside a tent, and they must be cleaned up after quickly. Dogs are allowed around the campground, and on the Whiptail Trail and the West Canyon Rim Trail only. The campground offers 33 sites, modern restrooms, showers, drinking water, picnicking, and a dump station. Campers do not have to pay an additional day use fee for the park. The camping and tent areas also allow dogs. There is a dog walk area at the campground.

Parks
Snow Canyon State Park 1002 Snow Canyon Drive Ivins UT   435-628-2255
This park ranges from 3,100 to almost 5,000 feet altitude, and covers about 7,100 acres. Rarely snowed in, they are open year round, and some of the features offered are 16 miles of hiking trails, technical rock climbing, wildlife viewing, camping, and plenty of photo opportunities at this visually striking area. Dogs of all sizes are allowed at no additional fee. They must be on no more than a 6 foot leash, and they are not allowed in park buildings. Dogs may not be left unattended outside an RV or tent, or inside a tent, and they must be cleaned up after quickly. Dogs are allowed around the campground, and on the Whiptail Trail and the West Canyon Rim Trail only.

Kanab

Accommodations
Best Western Red Hills 125 W Center Kanab UT   435-644-2675 (800-780-7234)
Dogs of all sizes are allowed. There is a $10 per night pet fee per pet. Smoking and non-smoking are available for pets.
Holiday Inn Express 815 E. Hwy 89 Kanab UT   435-644-8888 (877-270-6405)
There are no addtional pet fees.
Parry Lodge 89 East Center Street Kanab UT   435-644-2601 (800-748-4104)
http://www.infowest.com/parry/
There are 3 non-smoking pet rooms. There is a $5 per day pet fee.
Shilo Inn 296 West 100 North Kanab UT   435-644-2562 (800-222-2244)
http://www.shiloinns.com/Utah/kanab.html
There is a $10 one time pet fee.
Super 8 Kanab 70 South 200 West Kanab UT   435-644-5500 (800-800-8000)
Dogs of all sizes are allowed. There is a $10 per night pet fee per pet. Smoking and non-smoking rooms are available for pet rooms.

Campgrounds and RV Parks
Coral Pink Sand Dunes State Park P.O. Box 95/Coral Springs Road Kanab UT   435-648-2800 (800-322-3770)
This park offer a unique geologic feature since it is the only major sand dune field on the Colorado Plateau. There is plenty of hiking and ATV trails. Dogs are allowed at no additional fee. Dogs may not be left unattended, and they must be leashed and cleaned up after. Dogs are allowed on the trails with the exception of the ATV trails. The camping and tent areas also allow dogs. There is a dog walk area at the campground. There are no electric or water hookups at the campground.

Coral Pink Sand Dunes State Park 2500 Sand Dunes Road Kanab UT   435-648-2800
A phenomenon known as the Venturi Affect helped to created these 10,000 to 15,000 year old dunes, and the beautiful contrasting colors of this park really showcase its unique geological features. The park, at an elevation of almost 6,000 feet, is open daily year round, and they offer hiking and interpretive trails, off-roading, picnicking, and a visitor's center. There is also an interesting and diverse population of insects and other desert wildlife. Dogs are allowed for no additional fee, and they are allowed throughout the park and on all the trails. Dogs may not be left unattended, and they must be on no more than a 6 foot leash and cleaned up after at all times. Camping is allowed only in designated campsites. Some of the amenities include modern restrooms, showers, tables, drinking water, and a dump station. Campers do not have to pay an additional day use fee for the park. The camping and tent areas also allow dogs. There is a dog walk area at the campground. There are no electric or water hookups at the campgrounds.
Kanab RV Corral 483 S 100 E Kanab UT   435-644-5330
http://www.kanabrvcorral.com
Dogs of all sizes are allowed. There are no additional pet fees. Dogs may not be left unattended, and they must be leashed and cleaned up after. There is a dog walk area at the campground.

Attractions

TOP 200 PLACE **Frontier Movie Town** 297 W Center Street Kanab UT   800-551-1714
http://www.frontiermovietown.com/
Some 300 movies and TV shows were filmed here, giving it the name of "Utah's Little Hollywood", where several movie sets were left behind with lots of memorabilia. They offer a gift shop, museum, an Old West Costume rental shop, an all you can eat cowboy-style dinner buffet with tin plates and cups (or have coffee and a light snack from their cook shack), and a photo shop. Friendly dogs of all sizes are allowed. They can walk through the gift shop to get to the Frontier Movie Town. Your pet is welcome to join you at the picnic tables, on the grass under the trees, and around the park. They keep a bucket of doggy treats and water available for four-legged travelers. Dogs must be leashed and cleaned up after at all times, and they are not allowed in the cook shack.

Stores

Denny's Wigwan 78 E Center Kanab UT   435-644-2452
http://www.dennyswigwam.com/index.html
Located in a land rich in history and legends, and the backdrop for over 100 western movies, this American trading post and western wear store began as a family affair. They offer one of the largest inventories of Native American jewelry in the Southwest, clothing, memorabilia, many one-of-a-kind items, replica firearms, and gifts unique to the land. Well behaved, leashed, dogs are welcome to explore the store with their owners. Dogs must do their business outside and be cleaned up after quickly.
Willow Creek Books & Coffee 263 S 100 E Kanab UT   435-644-8884
http://www.willowcanyon.com/
This coffee/book shoppe is also connected to an outdoor gear and apparel store, but they have a bench, chairs, and a table out front where you are allowed to sit with your pet and enjoy some refreshments. Dogs must be well behaved, leashed, and cleaned up after quickly. Summer hours are 7:30 am to 8 pm, and in winter from 7:30 am to about 6 pm.

Parks

Coral Pink Sand Dunes State Park 2500 Sand Dunes Road Kanab UT   435-648-2800
A phenomenon known as the Venturi Affect helped to created these 10,000 to 15,000 year old dunes, and the beautiful contrasting colors of this park really showcase its unique geological features. The park, at an elevation of almost 6,000 feet, is open daily year round, and they offer hiking and interpretive trails, off-roading, picnicking, and a visitor's center. There is also an interesting and diverse population of insects and other desert wildlife. Dogs are allowed for no additional fee, and they are allowed throughout the park and on all the trails. Dogs may not be left unattended, and they must be on no more than a 6 foot leash and cleaned up after at all times.

Lake Powell

Campgrounds and RV Parks
Bullfrog Resort and Marina Campground On Hwy 276 Lake Powell UT   435-684-7000 (800-322-3770)
Every Summer this park has interpretive programs about the ancestral Puebloans who lived here, and about the geology and wildlife of the area, but there are also activities year round. There is a car ferry that travels across the lake and dogs are allowed on the 30 minute ride. For ferry crossing times call (435)684-3000. Dogs are also allowed in the rentals, on the trails (unless otherwise marked), and on rented boats. Dogs must be leashed and

cleaned up after. Dogs are not allowed at the ruins. The camping and tent areas also allow dogs. There is a dog walk area at the campground.

Village Center at Halls Crossing Marina End of Hwy 276 Lake Powell UT   435-684-7000 (800-322-3770)
Every Summer this park has interpretive programs about the ancestral Puebloans who lived here, and about the geology and wildlife of the area, but there are activities year round. There is a car ferry that travels across the lake and dogs are allowed on the 30 minute ride. For ferry crossing times call (435)684-3000. Dogs are also allowed in the rentals, on the trails (unless otherwise marked), and on the rented houseboats. Dogs must be leashed and cleaned up after. Dogs are not allowed at the ruins. The camping and tent areas also allow dogs. There is a dog walk area at the campground.

Parks

Natural Bridges National Monument HC 60 Box 1 Lake Powell UT   435-692-1234
http://www.nps.gov/nabr.index.htm
Dogs must be on leash and must be cleaned up after in campgrounds and paved areas. Dogs are not allowed on hiking trails or in the backcountry.

Logan

Stores

PetSmart Pet Store 1050 N Main St Logan UT   435-755-0244
Your licensed and well-behaved leashed dog is allowed in the store.

Manila

Campgrounds and RV Parks

Flaming Gorge National Recreation Area, Ashley Nat'l Forest P.O. Box 279/ Hwy 191 Manila UT   435-784-3445
The Flaming Gorge area is a diverse land of scenic beauty, and is administered by the Ashley National Forest. Against a backdrop of brilliant red cliffs runs the 91 mile reservoir offering over 300 miles of shoreline, boat ramps, full service marinas and lodges, and a wide variety of land and water recreation. The 'Gorge', although an aquatic paradise, it is most famous for its fishing. There is a host of land recreational pursuits as well with plenty of trails to walk with your pet. The trails wind through meadows, tree-covered slopes, mountain peaks above timberline, and the five-mile Canyon Rim Trail is accessible from three areas. Day use permits and annual passes are available at the visitor's center. Dogs of all sizes are allowed for no additional fee. Dogs must be on a leash in campgrounds, picnic areas, and trailheads at all times. Dogs are not allowed in park buildings, they must be under owner's control, and cleaned up after. Your dog is welcome to camp with you at the campgrounds; amenities include picnic tables, drinking water, fire rings, grills, water, and toilets. Campers do not have to pay an additional day use fee for the park. This RV park is closed during the off-season. The camping and tent areas also allow dogs. There is a dog walk area at the campground.

Flaming Gorge/Manila KOA Hwy 43 & 3rd W Manila UT   435-784-3184 (800-562-3254)
http://www.koa.com
Dogs of all sizes are allowed. There is a $10 cash only refundable pet deposit. Dogs must be leashed and cleaned up after. This RV park is closed during the off-season. The camping and tent areas also allow dogs. There is a dog walk area at the campground. Dogs are allowed in the camping cabins.

Parks

Flaming Gorge National Recreation Area, Ashley Nat'l Forest P.O. Box 279/ Hwy 191 Manila UT   435-784-3445
The Flaming Gorge area is a diverse land of scenic beauty, and is administered by the Ashley National Forest. Against a backdrop of brilliant red cliffs runs the 91 mile reservoir offering over 300 miles of shoreline, boat ramps, full service marinas and lodges, and a wide variety of land and water recreation. The 'Gorge', although an aquatic paradise, it is most famous for its fishing. There is a host of land recreational pursuits as well with plenty of trails to walk with your pet. The trails wind through meadows, tree-covered slopes, mountain peaks above timberline, and the five-mile Canyon Rim Trail is accessible from three areas. Day use permits and annual passes are available at the visitor's center. Dogs of all sizes are allowed for no additional fee. Dogs must be on a leash in campgrounds, picnic areas, and trailheads at all times. Dogs are not allowed in park buildings, they must be under owner's control, and cleaned up after.

Midvale

Accommodations
Motel 6 - Salt Lake City South - Midvale 7263 South Catalpa Road Midvale UT   801-561-0058 (800-466-8356)
One well-behaved family pet per room. Guest must notify front desk upon arrival. Guest is liable for any damages. In consideration of all guests, pets must never be left unattended in the guest rooms.

Stores
Petco Pet Store 1090 East Fort Union Blvd Midvale UT   801-352-1510
Your licensed and well-behaved leashed dog is allowed in the store.

Midway

Campgrounds and RV Parks
Wasatch Mountain State Park 1281 Warm Springs Road Midway UT   435-654-1791 (800-322-3770)
This recreational park is open year round, has a 36 hole golf course, and is Utah's most developed state park. Dogs are allowed at no additional fee. Dogs must be leashed and cleaned up after. Dogs are allowed on the trails, but they are not allowed on the golf course. This campground is closed during the off-season. The camping and tent areas also allow dogs. There is a dog walk area at the campground. There are no electric or water hookups at the campground.
Wasatch Mountain State Park Box 10/1281 Warm Springs Drive Midway UT   435-654-1791
This nearly 22,000 acre preserve sits at 6,000 feet, is one of Utah's newest golf destination with two 18 hole championship courses, and offers many year round recreational pursuits; with activities varying by the season. They hosted the 2002 Olympic Winter Games at Soldier Hollow, and the venue remains open to the public featuring a variety of activities and events. There are also a couple of historic sites to explore, and campfire and junior ranger programs. The Wasatch Park Café is located in the Mountain Clubhouse, and there is a snack bar and full-service catering too. Dogs are allowed at no additional fee. They must be on a maximum 6 foot leash, and they are not allowed in park buildings or on the golf courses. They are allowed on the trails. Dogs must be well behaved, and cleaned up after at all times. The park has 139 camping/picnicking areas, modern restrooms, hot showers, and your pet is welcome. There is even a pond where small children can go fishing. Campers do not have to pay an additional day use fee for the park. The phone number directly to the campgrounds is 435-654-3961. The camping and tent areas also allow dogs. There is a dog walk area at the campground.

Parks
Wasatch Mountain State Park Box 10/1281 Warm Springs Drive Midway UT   435-654-1791
This nearly 22,000 acre preserve sits at 6,000 feet, is one of Utah's newest golf destination with two 18 hole championship courses, and offers many year round recreational pursuits; with activities varying by the season. They hosted the 2002 Olympic Winter Games at Soldier Hollow, and the venue remains open to the public featuring a variety of activities and events. There are also a couple of historic sites to explore, and campfire and junior ranger programs. The Wasatch Park Café is located in the Mountain Clubhouse, and there is a snack bar and full-service catering too. Dogs are allowed at no additional fee. They must be on a maximum 6 foot leash, and they are not allowed in park buildings or on the golf courses. They are allowed on the trails. Dogs must be well behaved, and cleaned up after at all times.

Moab

Accommodations
Apache Hotel 166 S 400 East Moab UT   435-259-5727 (800-228-6882)
http://www.moab-utah.com/apachemotel/
There is a 1 dog limit per room. There are no additional pet fees.
Bowen Motel 169 N Main St Moab UT   435-259-7132
There is a $5 per day pet fee.
Comfort Suites 800 S Main S treet Moab UT   435-259-5252 (877-424-6423)

Dogs of all sizes are allowed. There is a $10 per night per pet additional fee. Dogs must be quiet, well behaved, leashed, cleaned up after, and the Do Not Disturb sign put on the door and a contact number left with the front desk if they are in the room alone.

La Quinta Inn Moab 815 S. Main St. Moab UT   435-259-8700 (800-531-5900)
Dogs of all sizes are allowed. There are no additional pet fees. There is a pet waiver to sign at check in. Dogs must be leashed, cleaned up after, and crated if left alone in the room. Dogs are not allowed in the food areas, and they must be walked at the designated pet walk area.

Moab Valley Inn 711 S Main St Moab UT   435-259-4419 (800-831-6622)
http://www.moabvalleyinn.com/
There is a $10 per day per room additional pet fee.

Motel 6 - Moab 1089 North Main Street Moab UT   435-259-6686 (800-466-8356)
One well-behaved family pet per room. Guest must notify front desk upon arrival. Guest is liable for any damages. In consideration of all guests, pets must never be left unattended in the guest rooms.

River Canyon Lodge 71 W 200 N Moab UT   435-259-8838
Dogs of all sizes are allowed. There is a $10 one time fee per pet for pets under 10 pounds. There is a $15 one time fee per pet for pets 15 to 20 pounds, and a $20 one time fee per pet for pets over 21 pounds. There is a pet policy to sign at check in.

Sleep Inn 1051 S Main Street Moab UT   435-259-4655 (877-424-6423)
Dogs of all sizes are allowed. There is a $50 refundable pet deposit per room. Dogs may only be left alone in the room if they will be quiet and well behaved. Dogs must be leashed and cleaned up after.

The Gonzo Inn 100 W 200 S Moab UT   435-259-2515
Dogs of all sizes are allowed. There is a $25 per night per room fee and a pet policy to sign at check in.

Campgrounds and RV Parks

Arch View Resort 10 miles N of Moab on Hwy 191 Moab UT   435-259-7854
http://www.archviewresort.com
Dogs of all sizes are allowed. There are no additional pet fees. Dogs must be quiet, well behaved, leashed, and cleaned up after. This RV park is closed during the off-season. The camping and tent areas also allow dogs. There is a dog walk area at the campground. Dogs are allowed in the camping cabins.

Canyonlands Campground 555 S Main Street Moab UT   800-522-6848
http://www.canyonlandsrv.com
Dogs of all sizes are allowed. There are no additional pet fees. Dogs may not be left unattended, and they must be quiet, leashed, and cleaned up after. The camping and tent areas also allow dogs. There is a dog walk area at the campground.

Dead Horse Point State Park P.O. Box 609/At End of Hwy 313 Moab UT   435-259-2614 (800-322-3770)
This park, Utah's Grand Canyon, is known for having the most spectacular views in all of the Utah parks. Dead Horse Point towers over 2000 feet over the Colorado River. Dogs must be leashed in the campground and cleaned up after. Dogs are allowed on the trails. The camping and tent areas also allow dogs. There is a dog walk area at the campground. There are no water hookups at the campground.

Dead Horse Point State Park P. O. Box 609/ Hwy 131 Moab UT   435-259-2614
Dead Horse Point, towering 2,000 feet above the Colorado River, offers breathtaking views of the canyon country and the pinnacles and buttes of Canyon Lands National Park. The park, at an elevation of almost 6,000 feet, is open year round, and they offer hiking and interpretive trails, picnicking, and a visitor's center. Dogs are allowed at no additional fee. They must be on no more than a 6 foot leash, and they are not allowed in park buildings. Dogs may not be left unattended, and they must be cleaned up after. Dogs are allowed throughout the park and on the trails. The campground offers a modern restroom, drinking water, tables, and a dump station. There is limited water here as it must be trucked in, so they ask that you fill your water tanks before arriving. Campers do not have to pay an additional day use fee for the park. The camping and tent areas also allow dogs. There is a dog walk area at the campground. There are no water hookups at the campgrounds.

Moab KOA 3225 S Hwy 191 Moab UT   435-259-6682 (800-562-0372)
http://www.koa.com
Dogs of all sizes and numbers are allowed, and there is a $5 one time fee for tent or RV sites. Dogs may not be left unattended outside, or inside an RV unless there is air conditioning. There is a $5 one time fee for the cabins also, only 2 dogs are allowed, and they must be crated if left. Dogs must be quiet, leashed, and cleaned up after. There are some breed restrictions. This RV park is closed during the off-season. The camping and tent areas also allow dogs. There is a dog walk area at the campground. Dogs are allowed in the camping cabins.

Squaw Flat Campground/Canyonlands National Park End of Hwy 211 Moab UT   435-259-4711 (Needles) (800-322-3770)
http://www.nps.gov/cany/
This park provides a colorful landscape of sedimentary sandstone created by the erosion of the Colorado River and it's tributaries. Dogs are allowed on the main roads and in the campground. Dogs are not allowed on the trails, in the back country, or on the 4-wheel drive trails. Dogs must be leashed and cleaned up after. The closest services and gas are about 50 miles away in Monticello. The camping and tent areas also allow dogs. There is a dog walk area at the campground. There are no electric or water hookups at the campground.

Attractions

TOP 200 PLACE **Red River Canoe Company** 1371 Main Street/N Hwy 191 Moab UT 800-753-8216
http://www.redrivercanoe.com/
There are several types of tours through this visually striking area on the waterways of the Colorado Plateau, guided and unguided. They open daily at 8:30 am from March through October. Dogs are not allowed on guided tours, but they are allowed on self-guided canoe rentals. There are many places on the river to pull over along the way for you and your pooch to hike, picnic, or just explore. Dogs must be under owners control at all times, and be sure to pack enough water and food for your pet as well.

Parks

Arches National Park PO Box 907 Moab UT 435-719-2299
http://www.nps.gov/arch/index.htm
Pets on leash with cleanup are allowed in the campsites and paved areas of the parks. Dogs are not allowed on any trails or backcountry. They are allowed unattended if well-behaved in the Devil's Garden campground.
Canyonlands National Park 2282 SW Resource Blvd Moab UT 435-719-2313
http://www.nps.gov/cany/index.htm
Pets on leash are allowed in developed areas, such as campgrounds, paved roads, and the Potash/Shafer Canyon road between Moab and the Island in the Sky. They are not allowed on hiking trails or in the backcountry.
Dead Horse Point State Park P. O. Box 609/ Hwy 131 Moab UT 435-259-2614
Dead Horse Point, towering 2,000 feet above the Colorado River, offers breathtaking views of the canyon country and the pinnacles and buttes of Canyon Lands National Park. The park, at an elevation of almost 6,000 feet, is open year round, and they offer hiking and interpretive trails, picnicking, and a visitor's center. Dogs are allowed at no additional fee. They must be on no more than a 6 foot leash, and they are not allowed in park buildings. Dogs may not be left unattended, and they must be cleaned up after. Dogs are allowed throughout the park and on the trails.

Monument Valley

Accommodations

Goulding's Lodge 1000 Main Street Monument Valley UT 435-727-3231
http://www.gouldings.com/
Well-behaved leashed dogs of all sizes are welcome. There is a $50 refundable pet deposit. The rooms offer views of Monument Valley. The lodge is located north of the Arizona and Utah border, adjacent to the Navajo Tribal Park in Monument Valley. Thanks to one of our readers for recommending this lodging.

Campgrounds and RV Parks

Gouldings RV Park 1000 Main Street Monument Valley UT 435-727-3235
Both tent sites and full hookup RV sites are offered at this campground. Rates are from $16 to $26 per site per night. The rates are for two people. There is a $3 per night extra fee per additional person. Well-behaved leashed pets are welcome. Campground amenities includes a view of Monument Valley, heated indoor pool, laundromat, hot showers, grocery store, playground and cable TV. The campground is located north of the Arizona and Utah border, adjacent to the Navajo Tribal Park in Monument Valley. They are open year round with limited service from November 1 to March 14. There is a dog walk area at the campground.

Attractions

TOP 200 PLACE **Goulding's Tours** 1000 Main Street Monument Valley UT 435-727-3231
This tour company has Navajo Indian guides which take you on a full day or half day tour of the area. The tours include Anasazi ruins, petroglyphs, movie locations, 1,000 foot monoliths, rug weaving and Indian hogans. Tour prices for half a day are $40 per person and full day are $70 per person. Children under 8 years old receive a discount off the adult price. Well-behaved leashed dogs are allowed on the tours. There is no charge for a small dog but if you have a larger dog that takes up more space, they may charge extra. You can make a reservation by calling or by signing up at the pet-friendly Goulding's Lodge or campgrounds.

Parks

TOP 200 PLACE **Monument Valley Navajo Tribal Park** P. O. Box 360289 Monument Valley UT 435-727-

5870
Rich in natural and cultural history, this great valley is home to sandstone masterpieces towering to 1,000 feet and surrounded by miles of mesas and buttes, shrubs, trees, and windblown sand. There is a scenic drive through this park; the hours for Summer-(May-Sept) 6:00am - 8:30pm, and Winter-(Oct - Apr) 8:00am - 4:30pm. In summer, the visitor center features the Haskenneini Restaurant, which specializes in both native Navajo and American cuisines, and film/snack/souvenir shop. There are year-round restroom facilities. Dogs of all sizes are allowed for no additional fee. Dogs must be leashed at all times, cleaned up after, and under owner's control. Dogs are allowed throughout the park; they are not allowed in buildings.

Morgan

Campgrounds and RV Parks
East Canyon State Park 5535 South Highway 66 Morgan UT   801-829-6866 (877-UTPARKS (887-2757))
Rich in pioneer history, this oasis sits in a mountainous desert at 5,700 feet, and offers a variety of trails, land and water recreation/activities, food service, wildlife viewing, and historic sites. The Donner/Reed party, the Mormons, the Overland Stage, and the Pony Express all utilized the East Canyon. Now there is boating and year round fun, fishing, camping, and it provides a great get away for travelers. A day-use permit covers your own watercraft launches, and annual passes are available at the visitor's center. Dogs are not allowed on the boat rentals. Dogs of all sizes are allowed at no additional fee, and may be walked anywhere in the park, but they are not allowed on the private property/trails that boundary the park. They must be on a maximum 6 foot leash, and they are not allowed in park buildings. Dogs must be well behaved, and cleaned up after at all times. The camp area offers modern restrooms, hot showers, picnic sites, and your pet is welcome. The camping and tent areas also allow dogs. There is a dog walk area at the campground.

Parks
East Canyon State Park 5535 South Highway 66 Morgan UT   801-829-6866 (877-UTPARKS (887-2757))
Rich in pioneer history, this oasis sits in a mountainous desert at 5,700 feet, and offers a variety of trails, land and water recreation/activities, food service, wildlife viewing, and historic sites. The Donner/Reed party, the Mormons, the Overland Stage, and the Pony Express all utilized the East Canyon. Now there is boating and year round fun, fishing, camping, and it provides a great get away for travelers. A day-use permit covers your own watercraft launches, and annual passes are available at the visitor's center. Dogs are not allowed on the boat rentals. Dogs of all sizes are allowed at no additional fee, and may be walked anywhere in the park, but they are not allowed on the private property/trails that boundary the park. They must be on a maximum 6 foot leash, and they are not allowed in park buildings. Dogs must be well behaved, and cleaned up after at all times.

Nephi

Accommodations
Best Western Paradise Inn of Nephi 1025 S Main Nephi UT   435-623-0624 (800-780-7234)
Dogs of all sizes are allowed. There is a $7.50 per night pet fee per pet. Only non-smoking rooms used for pets. Reservations are required due to limited rooms for pets.
Motel 6 - Nephi 2195 South Main Street Nephi UT   435-623-0666 (800-466-8356)
One well-behaved family pet per room. Guest must notify front desk upon arrival. Guest is liable for any damages. In consideration of all guests, pets must never be left unattended in the guest rooms.

Ogden

Accommodations
Comfort Inn 877 N 400 W Layton UT   801-544-5577 (877-424-6423)
Dogs of all sizes are allowed. There is a $25 refundable deposit per pet. Dogs must be leashed, cleaned up after, crated or removed for housekeeping, and the Pet In Room sign put on the door if they are in the room alone.
Hampton Inn 1702 N Woodland Park Drive Layton UT   801-775-8800
Dogs of all sizes are allowed. There are no additional pet fees. There is a pet policy to sign at check in and they only have a few non-smoking rooms available. Dogs are not allowed to be left alone in the room.

Holiday Inn Express 1695 Woodland Park Dr Layton UT   801-773-3773 (877-270-6405)
Dogs of all sizes are allowed. There are no additional pet fees for smoking rooms and a one time fee of $50 for smoking rooms.
La Quinta Inn Salt Lake City Layton 1965 North 1200 W. Layton UT   801-776-6700 (800-531-5900)
Dogs of all sizes are allowed. There are no additional pet fees. Dogs must be quiet, well behaved, leashed, and cleaned up after.
TownePlace Suites Salt Lake City/Layton 1743 Woodland Park Drive Layton UT   801-779-2422
Dogs of all sizes are allowed. There is a $75 one time pet fee per visit.
Best Western Country Inn 1335 W 12th St Ogden UT   801-394-9474 (800-780-7234)
Dogs of all sizes are allowed. There are no additional pet fees. Reservations are required due to limited rooms for pets. Smoking and non-smoking are available for pets.
Comfort Suites 2250 S 1200 W Ogden UT   801-621-2545 (877-424-6423)
Dogs of all sizes are allowed. There are no additional pet deposits required with a credit card on file; there is a $50 refundable pet deposit if paying by cash. Dogs must be quiet, leashed, cleaned up after, and a contact number left with the front desk if there is a pet alone in the room.
Holiday Inn Express Hotel & Suites 2245 S. 1200 West Ogden UT   801-392-5000 (877-270-6405)
There are no additional pet fees.
Motel 6 - Ogden 1455 Washington Boulevard Ogden UT   801-627-4560 (800-466-8356)
One well-behaved family pet per room. Guest must notify front desk upon arrival. Guest is liable for any damages. In consideration of all guests, pets must never be left unattended in the guest rooms.
Red Roof Inn - OGDEN - RIVERDALE 1500 West Riverdale Road Ogden UT   801-627-2880 (800-RED-ROOF)
One well-behaved family pet per room. Guest must notify front desk upon arrival. Guest is liable for any damages. In consideration of all guests, pets must never be left unattended in the guest rooms.
Super 8 Ogden 1508 W 2100 South Ogden UT   801-731-7100 (800-800-8000)
Dogs of all sizes are allowed. There is a $25 returnable deposit required per room. Smoking and non-smoking rooms are available for pet rooms.

Campgrounds and RV Parks
Cherry Hill RV Resort 1325 S Main Kaysville UT   801-451-5379
http://www.cherryhill.com
Dogs of all sizes are allowed. There are no additional pet fees. Dogs must be well behaved, leashed, and cleaned up after. Dogs may only be left alone if they will be quiet and comfortable. The camping and tent areas also allow dogs. There is a dog walk area at the campground.

Attractions
Utah Botanical Center 725 South Sego Lily Drive Kaysville UT   801-593-8969
http://utahbotanicalcenter.org/
This amazing education center's goal is to provide a more sustainable future by preserving and understanding our precious natural resources. In addition to innovative research, they provide educational, recreational, interactive experiences, and a real connection to the outdoors. Some attractions are still in development. There is a pavilion that serves as a community gathering place, the Utah house (a model home), an education greenhouse and nursery, many natural areas, ponds, and trails. In development is a children's discovery garden, arboretum, a wetlands education center, auditorium, a visitor's courtyard with shops, exhibits, an observation tower, and much more. Well behaved dogs are allowed for no additional fee. Dogs must be leashed and cleaned up after at all times. Dogs are allowed on the trails and throughout the park; they are not allowed in buildings or sectioned off areas.

Stores
PetSmart Pet Store 859 Hill Field Layton UT   801-543-0217
Your licensed and well-behaved leashed dog is allowed in the store.
Petco Pet Store 4153 Riverdale Rd Ogden UT   801-394-5400
Your licensed and well-behaved leashed dog is allowed in the store.
PetSmart Pet Store 1145 W Riverdale Rd Riverdale UT   801-392-0119
Your licensed and well-behaved leashed dog is allowed in the store.

Orem

Accommodations
La Quinta Inn & Suites Orem University Parkway 521 W. University Parkway Orem UT   801-226-0440 (800-

531-5900)
Dogs of all sizes are allowed. There are no additional pet fees. Dogs must be quiet, leashed, and cleaned up after.
La Quinta Inn Orem/Provo North 1100 West 780 North Orem UT   801-235-9555 (800-531-5900)
Dogs of all sizes are allowed. There are no additional pet fees. Dogs may not be left unattended, and they must be quiet, well behaved, leashed and cleaned up after.

Stores
PetSmart Pet Store 20 W University Pkwy Orem UT   801-224-0026
Your licensed and well-behaved leashed dog is allowed in the store.
Petco Pet Store 85 South State St Orem UT   801-434-8819
Your licensed and well-behaved leashed dog is allowed in the store.

Park City

Accommodations
Best Western Landmark Inn 6560 N Landmark Dr Park City UT   435-649-7300 (800-780-7234)
Dogs of all sizes are allowed. There is a $10 per night pet fee per pet. There is a $50 returnable deposit required per room. Only non-smoking rooms used for pets.
Holiday Inn Express Hotel & Suites 1501 West Ute Blvd Park City UT   435-658-1600 (877-270-6405)
Dogs of all sizes are allowed. There is a $10 per day additional pet fee and a $50 refundable pet deposit.
Radisson Inn Park City 2121 Park Avenue Park City UT   435-649-5000
Dogs of all sizes are allowed. There is a $15 per day additional pet fee.
The Gables Hotel 1335 Lowell Avenue, PO Box 905 Park City UT   435-655-3315 (800-443-1045)
http://www.thegablespc.com
Pets receive a Pet Gift basket upon arrival. Amenities include an outdoor jacuzzi, sauna and laundry facilities. Rates start at $85.00 per night. There is a $20 per night additional pet fee. There is a $100 refundable pet deposit upon arrival.

Campgrounds and RV Parks
Park City RV Resort 2200 Rasmussen Road Park City UT   435-649-2535
http://www.parkcityrvresort.com
This resort offers a convenient location with dramatic mountain views, concrete pads or acres of grassy sites, and a creek with a bridge. Some of the amenities include showers, fire pits, a club house, game room, a climbing wall, summer concerts, and a variety of other land and water recreation. Dogs of all sizes are allowed at no additional fee. There is a pet policy to sign at check-in. Dogs are allowed in most of the park and on the trails; they are not allowed in any building, in the horseshoe pit area, or the grass areas on the upper level. Your dog must go with you if you leave the campground. Dogs must be on a leash at all times, and cleaned up after immediately. There is also a fenced in dog run on site. There are some breed restrictions. The camping and tent areas also allow dogs. There is a dog walk area at the campground.

Stores
Petco Pet Store 6030 Market St, Ste 130 Park City UT   435-575-0250
Your licensed and well-behaved leashed dog is allowed in the store.

Outdoor Restaurants
Wild Oats Natural Marketplace 1748 W Redstone Center Drive Park City UT   435-575-0200
http://www.wildoats.com
This natural and organic grocery store has a deli with a variety of dishes, entrees, salads, sandwiches and more. Well-behaved leashed dogs are allowed at the outdoor tables.

Parowan

Accommodations
Days Inn Parowan 625 W 200 South Parowan UT   435-477-3326 (800-329-7466)
Dogs of all sizes are allowed. There is a $10 per night pet fee per pet. Reservations are recommended due to

limited rooms for pets.

Payson

Accommodations
Comfort Inn 830 N Main Street Payson UT   801-465-4861 (877-424-6423)
Dogs of all sizes are allowed. There are no additional pet fees. Dogs may be left in the room alone only if they will be quiet. Dogs must be leashed, cleaned up after, and a contact number left with the front desk when they are in the room alone.

Peoa

Campgrounds and RV Parks
Rockfort State Park 9040 North Highway 302 Peoa UT   435-336-2241 (877-UTPARKS (887-2757))
This state park offers a wide variety of land and water recreation year round, miles of hiking trails, and opportunities for nature study. The park is located at an elevation of 6,000 feet, covers 770 acres with the reservoir at over a thousand water acres, and is home to many wildlife species. The Rockport Sports and Recreation offers boat rentals, and a general store and grill. Dogs ride free and are allowed to join you on one of the watercraft rentals. The pontoon boats appear to be their favorite because of the nice flat bottom. Day use hours are from 6 am until they close the gates at 11 pm, daily. A day-use permit covers your own watercraft launches, and annual passes are available at the visitor's center. Dogs are allowed at no additional fee. They must be on a maximum 6 foot leash, and they are not allowed in park buildings. Dogs must be well behaved, and cleaned up after at all times. Camping is allowed in any one of 5 developed and primitive campgrounds and your pet is welcome. Services for the campground close for the winter, but if no services are needed, they will allow for RV camping. Campers do not have to pay an additional day use fee for the park. The camping and tent areas also allow dogs. There is a dog walk area at the campground.
Rockfort State Park 9040 N Hwy 302 Peoa UT   435-336-2241
This state park offers a wide variety of land and water recreation year round, miles of hiking trails, and opportunities for nature study. The park is located at an elevation of 6,000 feet, covers 770 acres with the reservoir at over a thousand water acres, and is home to many wildlife species. Day use hours are from 6 am until they close the gates at 11 pm, daily. A day-use permit covers watercraft launches, and annual passes are available at the visitor's center. Dogs are allowed at no additional fee. They must be on a maximum 6 foot leash, and they are not allowed in park buildings. Dogs must be well behaved, and cleaned up after at all times. Camping is allowed in any one of 5 developed and primitive campgrounds, and your pet is welcome. Services for the campground close for the winter, but if no services are needed, they will allow for RV camping. The camping and tent areas also allow dogs. There is a dog walk area at the campground.

Parks
Rockfort State Park 9040 North Highway 302 Peoa UT   435-336-2241 (877-UTPARKS (887-2757))
This state park offers a wide variety of land and water recreation year round, miles of hiking trails, and opportunities for nature study. The park is located at an elevation of 6,000 feet, covers 770 acres with the reservoir at over a thousand water acres, and is home to many wildlife species. The Rockport Sports and Recreation offers boat rentals, and a general store and grill. Dogs ride free and are allowed to join you on one of the watercraft rentals. The pontoon boats appear to be their favorite because of the nice flat bottom. Day use hours are from 6 am until they close the gates at 11 pm, daily. A day-use permit covers your own watercraft launches, and annual passes are available at the visitor's center. Dogs are allowed at no additional fee. They must be on a maximum 6 foot leash, and they are not allowed in park buildings. Dogs must be well behaved, and cleaned up after at all times.

Perry

Campgrounds and RV Parks
Brigham City/Perry South KOA 1040 W 3600 S Perry UT   435-723-5503 (800-562-0903)
http://www.koa.com
Dogs of all sizes are allowed. There are no additional pet fees. Dogs must be leashed and cleaned up after.

There are some breed restrictions. This RV park is closed during the off-season. The camping and tent areas also allow dogs. There is a dog walk area at the campground.

Price

Accommodations
National 9 641 W. Price River Drive Price UT   435-637-7000
There is a $5 per day pet fee.

Campgrounds and RV Parks
Manti-La Sal National Forest 599 W. Price River Dr. Price UT   435-636-3500
http://www.fs.fed.us/r4/mantilasal/
This forest of more than 1.4 million acres, with elevations from 5,000 feet to over 12,000 feet, provides a variety of landscapes and year round recreational opportunities. Dogs are allowed at no additional fee. Dogs may not be left unattended, and they must be leashed and cleaned up after when in camp areas. Dogs may be off lead in the forest if there is voice control. Dogs are allowed on the trails. This campground is closed during the off-season. The camping and tent areas also allow dogs. There are no electric or water hookups at the campground.

Promontory

Attractions
TOP 200 PLACE **Golden Spike National Historical Site** 6200 N 22300 W Promontory UT   435-471-2209
http://www.nps.gov/gosp/home.html
This historic site commemorates the driving of the last spike on May 10, 1869 of the first transcontinental railroad, and illustrates the social, economic, and political impacts this accomplishment has meant to the growth and westward development of America. The Visitor's Center is open daily from 9 am to 5 pm. The activities range from regularly scheduled ranger programs, engine house tours, living history programs, reenactments, films to view, picnicking, a 1 ½ mile walking trail, and locomotive demonstrations are offered seasonally. Dogs are welcome throughout the park, with the exception of the Visitor's Center. Dogs must be leashed and cleaned up after at all times.

Provo

Accommodations
Days Inn Provo 1675 N 200 West Provo UT   801-375-8600 (800-329-7466)
Dogs of all sizes are allowed. There is a $5 per night pet fee per pet.
Hampton Inn 1511 S 40 East Provo UT   801-377-6396
Dogs of all sizes are allowed. There is a $20 one time cleaning fee and a pet policy to sign at check in.
Sleep Inn 1505 South 40 East Provo UT   801-377-6597 (877-424-6423)
Dogs of all sizes are allowed. There is a $10 per night per pet additional fee. Dogs may only be left alone in the room for very shorts periods, and they must be leashed and cleaned up after. Please put the Do Not Disturb sign on the door and leave a contact number with the front desk if there is a pet in the room alone.

Campgrounds and RV Parks
Lakeside RV Campground 4000 W Center Street Provo UT   801-373-5267
http://www.lakesidervcampground.com
Dogs of all sizes are allowed. There are no additional pet fees. Dogs may not be left unattended at any time, and they must be quiet, leashed, and cleaned up after. Dogs are not allowed in the store, at the pool, or at the playground. The camping and tent areas also allow dogs. There is a dog walk area at the campground.
Provo KOA 320N 2050 W Provo UT   801-375-2994 (800-562-1894)
http://www.koa.com
Dogs of all sizes are allowed. There are no additional pet fees. Dogs may not be left unattended at the cabins, and they must be leashed and cleaned up after. The camping and tent areas also allow dogs. There is a dog walk area at the campground. Dogs are allowed in the camping cabins.

Uinta National Forest 88 W 100 N Provo UT   801-377-5780 (877-444-6777)
http://www.fs.fed.us/r4/uinta
Dogs of all sizes are allowed. There are no additional pet fees. Dogs may not be left unattended, and they must be quiet, well behaved, leashed, and cleaned up after. This campground is closed during the off-season. The camping and tent areas also allow dogs. There is a dog walk area at the campground. There are no water hookups at the campground.

Utah Lake State Park 4400 West Center Street Provo UT   801-375-0733
This park sits at an altitude of 4,500 feet, is Utah's largest freshwater lake at 96,600 acres, offers several species of fish, and a good variety of land and water recreation. Some of the amenities include a full service marina, food service, and a visitor's center. Dogs are allowed at no additional fee. They must be on no more than a 6 foot leash, and they are not allowed in park buildings. They are allowed on the trails and the beach. Dogs may not be left unattended, and they must be cleaned up after quickly. There are 71 sites for camping, and some of the amenities are modern restrooms, showers, drinking water, fishing area for the disabled, and a dump station. Campers do not have to pay an additional day use fee for the park. This RV park is closed during the off-season. The camping and tent areas also allow dogs. There is a dog walk area at the campground.

Parks

Utah Lake State Park 4400 West Center Street Provo UT   801-375-0733
This park sits at an altitude of 4,500 feet, is Utah's largest freshwater lake at 96,600 acres, offers several species of fish, and a good variety of land and water recreation. Some of the amenities include a full service marina, food service, and a visitor's center. Dogs are allowed at no additional fee. They must be on no more than a 6 foot leash, and they are not allowed in park buildings. They are allowed on the trails and the beach. Dogs may not be left unattended, and they must be cleaned up after quickly.

Richfield

Accommodations

Days Inn Richfield 333 N Main St Richfield UT   435-896-6476 (800-329-7466)
Dogs of all sizes are allowed. There is a $10 per night pet fee per pet.

Campgrounds and RV Parks

Fishlake National Forest 115 East 900 North Richfield UT   435-896-9233 (877-444-6777)
http://www.fs.fed.us/r4/fishlake
Dogs of all sizes are allowed. There are no additional pet fees. Dogs may not be left unattended, and they must be leashed and cleaned up after. Dogs are allowed on the trails. This campground is closed during the off-season. The camping and tent areas also allow dogs. There is a dog walk area at the campground.

Richfield KOA 600 W 600 S Richfield UT   435-896-6674 (888-562-4703)
http://www.koa.com
Dogs up to about 75 pounds are allowed. There are no additional pet fees. Dogs may not be left unattended, and they must be quiet, leashed, and cleaned up after. There are some breed restrictions. This RV park is closed during the off-season. The camping and tent areas also allow dogs. There is a dog walk area at the campground.

Salina

Accommodations

Super 8 Salina/Scenic Hills Area 1500 South 80 East Salina UT   435-529-7483 (800-800-8000)
Dogs of all sizes are allowed. There is a $10 per night pet fee per pet. Smoking and non-smoking rooms are available for pet rooms.

Salt Lake City

Accommodations

Holiday Inn Express 12033 South Factory Outlet Drive Draper UT   801-571-2511 (877-270-6405)
Dogs of all sizes are allowed. There are no additional pet fees.

Best Western Timpanogos Inn 195 South 850 East Lehi UT   801-768-1400 (800-780-7234)

Dogs of all sizes are allowed. There is a $10 per night pet fee per pet. Smoking and non-smoking are available for pets.

Motel 6 - Salt Lake City South - Lehi 210 South 1200 East Lehi UT   801-768-2668 (800-466-8356)
One well-behaved family pet per room. Guest must notify front desk upon arrival. Guest is liable for any damages. In consideration of all guests, pets must never be left unattended in the guest rooms.

Studio 6 - Salt Lake City - Fort Union 975 East 6600 South Murray UT   801-685-2102 (800-466-8356)
One well-behaved family pet per room. Guest must notify front desk upon arrival. Guest is liable for any damages. In consideration of all guests, pets must never be left unattended in the guest rooms.

Best Western Garden Inn 154 West 600 South Salt Lake City UT   801-521-2930 (800-780-7234)
Dogs of all sizes are allowed. There is a $20 one time pet fee per visit for one pet and $10 additional fee for another pet. Smoking and non-smoking are available for pets.

Candlewood Suites 2170 W. North Temple Salt Lake City UT   801-359-7500 (877-270-6405)
Dogs of all sizes are allowed. There is a $25 one time pet fee for up to 6 days and additional fees for more days.

Candlewood Suites 6990 South Park Centre Drive Salt Lake City UT   801-567-0111 (877-270-6405)
Dogs up to 80 pounds are allowed. There is a $25 one time pet fee per pet for up to 6 days. There is a $75 one time additional pet fee for stays from 7 - 29 days.

Comfort Inn 200 N Admiral Bird Road Salt Lake City UT 801-537-7444 (877-424-6423)
Dogs of all sizes are allowed. There is a $20 one time additional fee per pet.

Comfort Inn Airport/International Center 200 N Admiral Byrd Blvd Salt Lake City UT   801-746-5200 (877-424-6423)
Dogs of all sizes are allowed. There is a $20 per night per pet additional fee. Dogs must be leashed, cleaned up after, and the Do Not Disturb sign put on the door if they are in the room alone.

Days Inn Salt Lake City Airport 1900 West North Temple St Salt Lake City UT   801-539-8538 (800-329-7466)
Dogs of all sizes are allowed. There are no additional pet fees. Reservations are recommended due to limited rooms for pets.

Days Inn Salt Lake City Central 315 West 3300 South Salt Lake City UT   801-486-8780 (800-329-7466)
Dogs of all sizes are allowed. There are no additional pet fees.

Hilton 5151 Wiley Post Way Salt Lake City UT 801-539-1515
Dogs of all sizes are allowed. There is a $50 deposit, $25 of which is refundable, and there is a pet policy to sign at check in.

Hotel Monaco Salt Lake City 15 West 200 South Salt Lake City UT   801-595-0000
http://www.monaco-saltlakecity.com/
Well-behaved dogs of all sizes are welcome at this pet-friendly hotel. The luxury boutique hotel offers both rooms and suites. Hotel amenities include complimentary evening wine service, 24 hour room service and a 24 hour on-site fitness room. There are no pet fees, just sign a pet liability form.

La Quinta Inn & Suites Salt Lake City Airport 4905 W. Wiley Post Way Salt Lake City UT   801-366-4444 (800-531-5900)
Dogs of all sizes are allowed. There are no additional pet fees. Dogs must be leashed, cleaned up after, and crated when left alone in the room.

Motel 6 - Salt Lake City Downtown 176 W 600th S Street Salt Lake City UT   801-531-1252 (800-466-8356)
One well-behaved family pet per room. Guest must notify front desk upon arrival. Guest is liable for any damages. In consideration of all guests, pets must never be left unattended in the guest rooms.

Motel 6 - Salt Lake City West - Airport 1990 West North Temple Street Salt Lake City UT   801-364-1053 (800-466-8356)
One well-behaved family pet per room. Guest must notify front desk upon arrival. Guest is liable for any damages. In consideration of all guests, pets must never be left unattended in the guest rooms.

Red Lion 161 W 600 S Salt Lake City UT   801-521-7373
Well behaved dogs of all sizes are allowed. There is a $50 refundable deposit.

Residence Inn by Marriott 285 W Broadway (300S) Salt Lake City UT   801-355-3300
Dogs of all sizes are allowed. There is a $75 one time fee and a pet policy to sign at check in.

Residence Inn by Marriott 6425 S 3000 East Salt Lake City UT   801-453-0430
Well behaved dogs of all sizes are allowed. There is a $75 one time fee and a pet policy to sign at check in.

Residnece Inn by Marriott 4883 W Douglas Corrigan Way Salt Lake City UT   801-532-4101
Dogs of all sizes are allowed. There is a $75 one time fee and a pet policy to sign at check in. They also request you make arrangements for housekeeping.

Salt Lake City Centre Travelodge 524 S West Temple Salt Lake City UT   801-531-7100
There is a $10 per day pet fee.

Sheraton City Centre Hotel, Salt Lake City 150 West 500 South Salt Lake City UT   801-401-2000 (888-625-5144)
Dogs up to 80 pounds are allowed. There are no additional pet fees. Dogs are not allowed to be left alone in the room.

Comfort Inn 8955 S 255 West Sandy UT   801-255-4919 (877-424-6423)
Dogs of all sizes are allowed. There is a $10 per night per pet additional fee. Dogs must be leashed, cleaned up after, and the Do Not Disturb sign put on the door if they are in the room alone.

Comfort Suites 10680 Automall Drive Sandy UT 801-495-1317 (877-424-6423)
Dogs of all sizes are allowed. There is a $10 per night per room additional fee. Dogs may not be left alone in the room, and they must be leashed and cleaned up after.
Residence Inn by Marriott 270 W 10000S Sandy UT 801-561-5005
Dogs of all sizes are allowed. There is a $75 one time fee and a pet policy to sign at check in.
Sleep Inn 10676 S 300 W South Jordan UT 801-572-2020 (877-424-6423)
Dogs of all sizes are allowed. There is a $5 per night per pet additional fee. Dogs may only be left alone in the room if they will be quiet. Dogs must be leashed, cleaned up after, and a contact number left with the front desk if they are in the room alone.
Super 8 South Jordan/Sandy/SLC Area 10722 South 300 West South Jordan UT 801-553-8888 (800-800-8000)
Dogs of all sizes are allowed. There is a $10 per night pet fee per pet. Dogs are not allowed to be left alone in the room. Smoking and non-smoking rooms are available for pet rooms.
Baymont Inn & Suites Salt Lake City/West Valley 2229 W. City Center Court West Valley City UT 801-886-1300 (800-531-5900)
Dogs of all sizes are allowed. There are no additional pet fees. Dogs must be quiet, well behaved, leashed and cleaned up after, and the Do Not Disturb sign put on the door if there is a pet in the room alone.
Hampton Inn 2393 S 800 West Woods Cross UT 801-296-1211
Dogs of all sizes are allowed. There are no additional pet fees.
Motel 6 - Salt Lake City North-Woods Cross 2433 South 800 West Woods Cross UT 801-298-0289 (800-466-8356)
One well-behaved family pet per room. Guest must notify front desk upon arrival. Guest is liable for any damages. In consideration of all guests, pets must never be left unattended in the guest rooms.

Campgrounds and RV Parks

Sunset Campground Farmington Canyon Farmington City UT 877-444-6777
This campground is located at an elevation of 6,400 feet in the Wasatch-Cache National Forest, east of Farmington City and north of Salt Lake City. There are 16 camp sites with tables, fire circles and grills. Campground amenities include toilets and drinking water but no trash cans or RV hookups. The maximum vehicle length allowed is 28 feet. Sites are paved with pull-thru capabilities. Some of the sites are shaded and wheelchair accessible. Dogs must be leashed at the campgrounds and on the 1/2 mile Sunset Trail. Please clean up after your pets. All camp sites are first come, first serve and no reservations are accepted. The campground is open from June through October. To get there from Salt Lake City, head north on Interstate 15 and take the Farmington Exit. At the stop sign, turn right. Go to 100 East Street and turn left (heading north). Take this road 5.3 miles up the canyon (Farmington Canyon) to the campground.
Salt Lake City KOA 1400 W North Temple Salt Lake City UT 801-355-1214 (800-562-9510)
http://www.koa.com/where/ut/44143/
Dogs of all sizes are allowed. There are no additional pet fees. Dogs may not be left unattended, and they must be quiet, well behaved, leashed, and cleaned up after. The camping and tent areas also allow dogs. There is a dog walk area at the campground.
Wasatch -Cache National Forest 3285 East 3800 S Salt Lake City UT 801-466-6411 (800-322-3770)
http://www.fs.fed.us/r4/wcnf/
There are ample recreational opportunities in this forest of over a million acres comprised of high desert and alpine landscapes with 6 ranger districts. Dogs are allowed at no additional fee. Dogs may not be left unattended, and they must be leashed and cleaned up after. Dogs are allowed on the trails, but they are not allowed in any watershed areas. The camping and tent areas also allow dogs. There is a dog walk area at the campground. There are no water hookups at the campground.
Quail Run RV Park 9230 S State Street Sandy UT 801-255-9300
http://www.quailrunrvpark.com
Dogs of all sizes are allowed. There are no additional pet fees. Dogs must be quiet, well behaved, leashed, and cleaned up after. Dogs may not be left unattended, or chained to the lamp posts or trees.

Attractions

California National Historic Trail 324 South State Street Ste 200 Salt Lake City UT 801-741-1012
http://www.nps.gov/cali/index.htm
Dogs must be on leash and must be cleaned up after to stop at trail sites and points of interest on this trail. Dogs are not allowed in buildings. Mainly an auto touring event. This trail represents the 250,000 plus gold-seekers and farmers who traveled to the gold fields and rich farmlands of California during the 1840s and 1850s. Considered to be the greatest mass migration in American history.

TOP 200 PLACE **Carriage for Hire** across from Crossroads Mall Salt Lake City UT 801-363-8687
Take a carriage ride through downtown Salt Lake City. Most of the carriages will allow a well-behaved dog. The horse and carriages cost about $40 for a half hour ride. They give rides on weekdays from about 10am to 4pm and then again from 6pm to 11pm. During the weekends they are usually open for carriage rides all day.

KUTV2 Main Street News Studio 299 South Main Street Salt Lake City UT   801-973-3000
http://www.kutv.com
This TV station offers a unique sidewalk vantage for watching the filming of live news broadcasts. You and your pooch can watch from the sidewalk. There are several live broadcast opportunities daily. Just be aware that it might get a little crowded and you and your pooch might need to stand back so your dog can have more room.
Olympic Cauldron Park 451 South 1400 East Salt Lake City UT   801-972-7800
This city park is home to the 72 foot tall 2002 Olympic Winter Games Cauldron that burned during the Games. Large outdoor panels tell the story of the 17 days of the Olympic Games. Dogs on leash are allowed at the park. Please clean up after your pet.
Oregon National Historic Trail 324 South State Street Ste 200 Salt Lake City UT   801-741-1012
http://www.nps.gov/oreg/index.htm
Dogs must be on leash and must be cleaned up after at all site stops. Dogs are not allowed in buildings. The trail starts in Independence, Missouri and follows through to Oregon City, OR and is mainly auto touring.
Pony Express National Historic Trail 324 South State Street Ste 200 Salt Lake City UT   801-741-1012
http://www.nps.gov/poex/index.htm
Dogs on leash are allowed in the site areas. Dogs are not allowed in any buildings. Trail consists of auto touring and site stops from Missouri to California.
Pony Express Trail National Back Country Byway BLM, 2370 South 2300 W Salt Lake City UT   801-977-4300
There are several ways to enjoy this part of the historic Pony Express trail in Utah that runs for about 133 miles, including by auto, hiking, biking, or horseback. This was also the route used for the Overland Stage Company, and incorporates a piece of the Lincoln Highway-the nation's first coast to coast auto road. A good place to stop on your travels is the visitor information site located 1.8 miles west of Faust Junction. There are a number of interpretation sites along the way and the tour begins at Lehi on Highway 73, south of Salt Lake and proceeds west to Ibapah. Local guides/brochures are usually available at each trail site. The byway should be a passable gravel road most of the time, except when unstable due to rain or snow. There are no facilities on this back road, so bring plenty of gas (if auto), water, and food. Dogs are allowed on this trail. They request that animals (or people) do no digging. If your dog is under voice control, they may be off lead except when in populated areas, and please clean up after your pet.

TOP 200 PLACE **Wheeler Historic Farm** 6351 S 900 E Salt Lake City UT   801-264-2241
http://www.wheelerfarm.com
This historical, working farm (a restoration of the turn of the century dairy farm of Henry J. Wheeler) represents the rural lifestyle in Salt Lake County from 1890-1920 and showcases the best farming methods of the Progressive Era. It is comprised of 75 acres and is on both the state and National Register of Historic Places. They offer a variety of planned seasonal activities, farmhouse tours, historic demonstrations, exhibits, and environmental educational programs. The grounds are open from dawn to dusk everyday, and office hours are from 9 am to 5 pm, Monday through Saturday. Friendly dogs on leash are welcome, and please clean up after your pet.

Shopping Centers

The Gateway Shopping District 400 W 100 S Salt Lake City UT   801-456-0000
http://www.shopthegateway.com/home.html
This is Salt Lake City's only open air mall, and it delivers the ultimate in shopping, entertainment, and dining with more than 105 restaurants and stores. The mall is a beautifully restored 1908 Union Pacific Train Depot featuring early French Renaissance architecture and original artwork. The Olympic Legacy Plaza features a classic clock tower overlooking the "dancing waters" of the Olympic Snowflake Fountain, and you will find a variety of shops for all budgets. Regular hours for the Gateway are Monday through Saturday from 10 am to 9 pm, and on Sunday from noon to 6 pm. There may be extended hours during the summer and holidays. Dogs of all sizes are welcome to explore the mall with their owners, and maybe even some of the stores. Dogs must be well behaved, and leashed and cleaned up after at all times.
Gardner Village Shopping Center 1100 W 7800 S West Jordan UT   801-566-8903
http://www.gardnervillage.com/
Gardner Village, listed on the National Historic Register, reflects the outlines of a once bustling early Utah mill industry. The cabins, houses, and buildings adjacent to and including the Old Gardner Mill, have all been restored. You can experience some of Utah's colorful history through the vintage pioneer architecture, antique fixtures, the red brick paths, and the more than 20 shops or eateries. The village is open from January 1 to March 31, Monday to Saturday from 10 am to 6 pm, and from April 1 to December 30, Monday to Saturday from 10 am to 8 pm. The village is closed on Sunday. Well behaved dogs are welcome to explore this historic open mall with their owners. They are not allowed in the stores, unless invited in. Dogs must be leashed and cleaned up after at all times.

Stores

PetSmart Pet Store 5576 S Redwood Rd Murray UT   801-965-9362

Your licensed and well-behaved leashed dog is allowed in the store.
PetSmart Pet Store 3191 E 3300 S Salt Lake City UT 801-487-9290
Your licensed and well-behaved leashed dog is allowed in the store.
PetSmart Pet Store 389 West 1830 S Salt Lake City UT 801-466-0313
Your licensed and well-behaved leashed dog is allowed in the store.
Petco Pet Store 1165 E Wilmington Salt Lake City UT 801-474-2610
Your licensed and well-behaved leashed dog is allowed in the store.
PetSmart Pet Store 10329 S State St Sandy UT 801-495-3700
Your licensed and well-behaved leashed dog is allowed in the store.
Petco Pet Store 181 North 545 West West Bountiful UT 801-397-5287
Your licensed and well-behaved leashed dog is allowed in the store.
PetSmart Pet Store 7378 Plaza Center Dr West Jordan UT 801-260-0368
Your licensed and well-behaved leashed dog is allowed in the store.
Petco Pet Store 6842 S Redwood Rd West Jordan UT 801-561-0055
Your licensed and well-behaved leashed dog is allowed in the store.
PetSmart Pet Store 3061-A S 5600 W West Valley City UT 801-840-2728
Your licensed and well-behaved leashed dog is allowed in the store.

Parks

Big Water Trail Mill Creek Canyon Road Salt Lake City UT 801-466-6411
This Wasatch-Cache National Forest trail is located in Mill Creek Canyon. It is a 3 mile trail, rated easy, and takes about 2 hours one way. The trail starts at an elevation of 7600 feet and climbs 1240 feet up to an elevation of 8840 feet. The trail leads up to Dog Lake, which is a popular destination. Please note that while dogs are allowed on the trail, they are not allowed in Big Cottonwood Canyon which is just past Dog Lake. These rules are strictly enforced by many Salt Lake City agencies including the Sheriff's Office. On the trail, dogs must be leashed on EVEN numbered calendar days. On ODD numbered days, dogs are permitted off-leash on the trail. Dogs still need to be leashed at all times in developed sites which include parking lots, trailheads, picnic sites, campgrounds and cabins. This is also a popular trail for mountain biking but no biking is permitted on ODD numbered days. Please remember to pick up after your dog. The trail is located southeast of downtown Salt Lake City. Take I-80 east heading out of Salt Lake City. Take Highway 215 south and exit at Mill Creek Canyon Road (3800 South Wasatch Blvd). Head east towards the mountains. Drive about 9.1 miles up the canyon to the parking lot. Please note that the upper parking lots can fill up quickly on the weekends.

TOP 200 PLACE **Ensign Peak Trail** Ensign Vista Drive Salt Lake City UT 801-972-7800
Located just a short drive from downtown, this .5 mile trail offers panoramic views of the valley and the lake. It also offers some historical value. This peak was used by Indians, pioneers and explorers. Brigham Young, along with eight other pioneers, climbed to this summit on July 26, 1847, two days after the Mormon pioneers arrived in the Salt Lake Valley. They used this peak to view their surroundings. The trail leads up to a stone monument located at the peak. The elevation gain is about 400 feet. Dogs must be on a leash. To get there, drive north on East Capitol Blvd. and go past the State Capitol Building. Continue for about 8 blocks and then turn left on Ensign Vista Drive.

Liberty Park 589 East 1300 South Salt Lake City UT 801-972-7800
This large popular city park offers walking paths, several nice playgrounds, picnic areas, tennis courts and a children's amusement park with a carousel, miniature car and plane rides and more. The park also has a variety of events during the summer. Dogs are allowed at the park, including at many of the events. There will be signs posted where dogs are not allowed, like a few children's water areas. Pets must be leashed and please clean up after them.

Memory Grove Park 300 N. Canyon Road/130 East Salt Lake City UT 801-972-7800
This park features a replica of the Liberty Bell as well as memorials to Utah's veterans. A bridge connects Memory Grove to City Creek Park which features a stone-lined stream. Dogs on leash are allowed at the park. Please clean up after your pet.

Millcreek Canyon East End of 3800 S. Salt Lake City UT 801-236-3400
http://www.fs.fed.us/r4/wcnf/faq/
In the Millcreek Canyon area of the Wasatch-Cache National Forest dogs are allowed off-leash on odd numbered days. They must be leashed on even numbered days. There are many trails to take which are mostly quite strenuous. The Salt Lake Overlook Trail, for example, climbs 1,250 feet in 1.75 miles. Once there you will get a nice view of the city to the west. To get to Millcreek Canyon exit I-215 at 3300 or 3900 South. Go to 3800 S. and head east to the canyon.

Salt Lake State Marina 13312 W Hwy 202 Salt Lake City UT 801-250-1898
This well-developed marina with water, electricity, and a pumpout station, is located on the South shore of the Great Salt Lake in the Great Salt Lake State Park. Some of the amenities include modern restrooms, drinking water, wildlife viewing, beautiful scenery, picnicking, and a variety of year round land and water recreation. Dogs of all sizes are allowed to explore the area with their owners. They are allowed all along the waterfront, picnic areas, and the beach. Dogs must be friendly, and leashed and cleaned up after at all times.

Sugarhouse Park 1300 East 2100 South Salt Lake City UT 801-467-1721

Sugar House Park, a favorite recreation place, is one of the city's largest and most beautiful parks. Some of the attractions include a trail that outlines the park's outer edge, paved trails, a creek that runs through the park to a duck pond on the west end, pavilions for barbecues, playgrounds, sport fields/courts, hills (perfect for sledding in winter),and acres of grass. There are also several events held here each year such as the 4th of July fireworks, and the Strut Your Mutt fundraiser (for homeless pets) usually held in May. The park is open daily from 8 am to 10 pm. Dogs of all sizes are welcome throughout the park, but they must be leashed and cleaned up after at all times.

Sunset Trail 100 East Street Salt Lake City UT
This Wasatch-Cache National Forest trail has been rated as a hike that is suitable for families with children. It is . 5 miles one way, rated easy, and takes about 20 minutes one way. The trail starts at an elevation of 6400 feet and goes down to the falls at an elevation of 6120 feet. The waterfalls are the main attraction on this trail. The trail also provides views of Farmington Canyon. No bicycles, motorized vehicles or skiing is allowed on this trail. Dogs are allowed but must be leashed. Please remember to clean up after your pets. To get there from Salt Lake City, go north on I-15 and take the Farmington exit. At the stop sign turn right/east and go to 100 East Street and turn left/north. Follow the road into Farmington Canyon and go 5.3 miles up the canyon to Sunset Campground.

This is the Place State Park 2601 Sunnyside Avenue Salt Lake City UT 801-582-1847
http://www.thisistheplace.org/
This is the Place" Heritage Park marks the end of the 1,300 mile journey of the first Mormon settlers into the Salt Lake Valley in 1847, and is home to the Old Deseret Village (seasonal), a living history museum/town depicting life of that era. The monument, erected in 1947 and sitting just south of the village, is over 60 feet tall, 86 feet long, and acknowledges the early Spanish explorers and missionaries, the trappers, the Donner-Reed party, and the Mormon pioneers. The park is open year round from dawn to dusk for day use. There is picnicking, a visitor's center and museum (hours vary), a Mormon handicraft store, modern rest rooms, drinking water, and hiking trails nearby. Dogs of all sizes are allowed at the monument and around the park; they are not allowed in the Old Deseret Village. Dogs must be leashed and cleaned up after at all times.

Off-Leash Dog Parks

Herman Frank's Park 700 E 1300 S Salt Lake City UT
This park has a designated off-leash area. Dogs must be leashed when outside the leash free area.
Jordan Park 1060 South 900 West Salt Lake City UT 801-972-7800
This park has a designated off-leash area. Dogs must be leashed when outside the leash free area.
Lindsey Gardens 9th Avenue and M Street Salt Lake City UT 801-972-7800
This park has a designated off-leash area. Dogs must be leashed when outside the leash free area.
Memory Grove Park 485 N. Canyon Road Salt Lake City UT 801-972-7800
This park has a designated off-leash area which is located in the Freedom Trail area. Dogs must be leashed when outside the leashed area. The park is located east of the Utah State Capitol.
Parley's Gulch 2700 East Salt Lake City Salt Lake City UT 801-269-7499
The Parley's Gulch area behind Tanner Park is now an official off-leash area. However, Tanner Park is not and dogs must be leashed there. This is mostly an unfenced area. The off-leash dog area is around the intersection of the I-80 and I-215 freeways. There is a fence between the off-leash areas and the freeways.
Sandy City Dog Park 9980 South 300 East Sandy UT 801-568-2900
This fenced, one acre dog park has benches, trees for shade and a walking trail. From I-15 exit at S 106th. Head east to State Street and head north (left) on State Street to E Sego Lily Dr. Turn right on Sego Lily Dr. Turn right on South 300 East to the park.
Millrace Off-Leash Dog Park 5400 South at 1100 West Taylorsville UT 801-963-5400
The fenced, Millrace Park Dog Park is open during the summer from 7 am to 10 pm and during the winter from 7 am to 7 pm. The park will be closed during bad weather and possibly after bad weather. Beginning in July, 2006 the dog park requires an annual permit to use the park. It costs $10 for Taylorsville residents and $25 for non-residence. To get a tag call 801-269-7499 or visit http://www.slcoanimalservices.org.

Outdoor Restaurants

Atlantic Cafe & Market 325 S Main St. Salt Lake City UT 801-524-9900
This cafe allows well-behaved leashed dogs at their outdoor tables.
Cafe Pierpont 122 West Pierpont Avenue Salt Lake City UT 801-364-1222
http://www.gastronomyinc.com/pierpont
This family friendly restaurant offers a variety of Mexican dishes. They have chicken, beef, and seafood entrees. Well-behaved leashed dogs are allowed at the outdoor patio tables. The patio is open May through September.
Rubios Baja Grille 358 S 700 E, Suite F Salt Lake City UT 801-363-0563
Dogs are allowed at the outdoor tables. The restaurant has outdoor tables only in the summer.
Rubios Baja Grille 1160 E 2100 S Salt Lake City UT 801-466-1220
Dogs are allowed at the outdoor tables. The restaurant has outdoor tables only in the summer.
Wild Oats Natural Marketplace 645 E 400 South Salt Lake City UT 801-355-7401

http://www.wildoats.com
This natural and organic grocery store has a deli with a variety of dishes, entrees, salads, sandwiches and more. Well-behaved leashed dogs are allowed at the outdoor tables. They have some picnic tables on the lawn.

Events
Strut Your Mutt 2100 South 1300 East Salt Lake City UT   801-364-0370
http://www.utahpets.com
This is an annual event which is sponsored by No More Homeless Pets in Utah. It is usually held in May at the Sugarhouse Park. Thousands of pets and their owners take part for fun and prizes. In addition to a nice mile and a half walk with your pet there will be contests, giveaways, vendors, an agility course, and more. Dogs must be well mannered, have current ID Tags on, be leashed and cleaned up after at all times. Dogs may not be in heat or younger than 4 months old.

Scipio

Accommodations
Super 8 Scipio 230 West 400 North Scipio UT   435-758-9188 (800-800-8000)
Dogs of all sizes are allowed except puppies. There is a $10 per night pet fee per pet. Reservations are recommended due to limited rooms for pets. Smoking and non-smoking rooms are available for pet rooms.

Sevier

Campgrounds and RV Parks
Fremont Indian State Park 3820 W Clear Creek Canyon Road Sevier UT   435-527-4631
Historical, recreational, scenic, and geologically popular can all describe this park. You can pick up a trail guide at the visitor's center that will guide you to rock art panels, geological wonders, dramatic viewpoints, bubble caves, and a favorite trail takes you to an amazing canyon overlook area. There is an ATV trail system that runs through the park, but the hiking trails are for non-motorized use only. There is also a visitor's center and a museum of the Indian village uncovered here. Dogs are allowed at no additional fee. They must be on a maximum 6 foot leash at all times, and they are not allowed in park buildings. Dogs are allowed on all the trails and at the overlook areas. Dogs must be well behaved, and cleaned up after at all times. The Castle Rock Campground is the only place you can camp in the park, and it offers a scenic setting complete with a creek, flush toilets, and your pet is welcome. Campers do not have to pay an additional day use fee for the park. The camping and tent areas also allow dogs. There is a dog walk area at the campground. There are no electric or water hookups at the campgrounds.

Parks
Fremont Indian State Park 3820 W Clear Creek Canyon Road Sevier UT   435-527-4631
Historical, recreational, scenic, and geologically popular can all describe this park. You can pick up a trail guide at the visitor's center that will guide you to rock art panels, geological wonders, dramatic viewpoints, bubble caves, and a favorite trail takes you to an amazing canyon overlook area. There is an ATV trail system that runs through the park, but the hiking trails are for non-motorized use only. There is also a visitor's center and a museum of the Indian village uncovered here. Dogs are allowed at no additional fee. They must be on a maximum 6 foot leash at all times, and they are not allowed in park buildings. Dogs are allowed on all the trails and at the overlook areas. Dogs must be well behaved, and cleaned up after at all times.

Springville

Accommodations
Best Western Cotton Tree Inn of Springville 1455 N 1750 West Springville UT   801-489-3641 (800-780-7234)
Dogs of all sizes are allowed. There is a $10 one time per pet fee per visit. Smoking and non-smoking are available for pets.

St George

Accommodations
Motel 6 - St. George 205 N 1000 E Street St George UT   435-628-7979 (800-466-8356)
One well-behaved family pet per room. Guest must notify front desk upon arrival. Guest is liable for any damages. In consideration of all guests, pets must never be left unattended in the guest rooms.

Campgrounds and RV Parks
Snow Canyon State Park 1002 Snow Canyon Drive (Hwy 18) St George UT   435-628-2255 (800-322-3770)
Sand dunes, quiet beauty, and many trails bring visitors to this park. Dogs are allowed at no additional fee. Dogs may not be left unattended, and they must be leashed and cleaned up after. Dogs are allowed on the Whiptail Trail and the West Canyon Trail only. The camping and tent areas also allow dogs. There is a dog walk area at the campground.
Templeview RV Resort 975 S Main St George UT   800-381-0321
http://www.templeviewrv.com
Dogs of all sizes are allowed. There are no additional pet fees unless the stay is monthly; then there is a $5 additional pet fee. Dogs must be leashed and cleaned up after. The camping and tent areas also allow dogs. There is a dog walk area at the campground.

Stansbury Park

Attractions
Benson Grist Mill 325 Hwy 138 Stansbury Park UT   435-882-7678
http://www.bensonmill.org/
Over 150 years old, this restored mill is now widely recognized as one of the more intact pioneer era industrial buildings in Utah. This significant landmark was added to the National Register of Historic Sites in 1972, and there are also other interesting buildings at the mill. A replica of the Miller's home showcases a unique rock fireplace, and provides a museum and tourist information center. Benson Mill is open Monday through Saturday from 10 am to 4 pm; closed Sunday. Well behaved dogs are allowed for no additional fee. They are allowed throughout the grounds, but they are not allowed in the buildings. Dogs must be leashed and cleaned up after at all times.

Sterling

Campgrounds and RV Parks
Palisade State Park 2200 Palisade Road Sterling UT   435-835-7275 (800-322-3770)
The Palisade Reservoir of 70 acres provides many water sports. There is a golf course, driving range, several trails, and Six-Mile Canyon for the off-roaders. Dogs are allowed at no additional fee. Dogs may not be left unattended, and they must be leashed and cleaned up after. Dogs are allowed on the trails. The camping and tent areas also allow dogs. There is a dog walk area at the campground.

Syracuse

Campgrounds and RV Parks
Antelope Island State Park 4528 West 1700 South Syracuse UT   801-773-2941 (800-322-3770)
This park is Utah's largest island with over 28,000 acres, and is reached via a 2 lane causeway. This park has a unique history, with biological, geological, and plenty of recreational opportunities to pursue. Dogs are allowed at no additional fee. Dogs may not be left unattended, and they must be leashed and cleaned up after. Dogs are allowed on all but 2 of the trails and the beach. The camping and tent areas also allow dogs. There is a dog walk area at the campground. There are no electric or water hookups at the campground.

Parks

Antelope Island State Park 4528 West 1700 South Syracuse UT   801-773-2941
This park is easily accessed over a 7-mile paved causeway, or by boat and an abundance of flora and fauna, a bison herd, and numerous migrating birds are some of the things that await you. The visitor center offers information on the island's unique biology, geology and history, and some of the amenities include white sandy beaches, a sailboat marina, nearly 40 miles of hiking and multi-use trails, wildlife viewing, picnicking, and, because of the distance from the city and its lights, stargazing. Hours vary throughout the year. Dogs of all sizes are allowed at no additional fee. Dogs are not allowed on the beach, park buildings, or on Prairie Creek Trail; other trails are okay. Dogs must be on no more than a 6 foot leash and cleaned up after at all times.

Torrey

Accommodations
Comfort Inn at Capitoal Reef 2424 Hwy 24 Torrey UT   435-425-3866 (877-424-6423)
Dogs of all sizes are allowed. There is a $20 one time additional fee per pet, and a pet policy to sign at check in. Dogs may not be left alone in the room unless it is for a short time, they will be quiet, and you are in the building. Dogs must be leashed and cleaned up after.
Days Inn Torrey 675 E Hwy 24 Torrey UT   435-425-3111 (800-329-7466)
Dogs of all sizes are allowed. There is a $10 per night pet fee per pet. Only non-smoking rooms are used for pets.
Super 8 Torrey/Capitol Reef Area 600 East Hwy 24 Torrey UT   435-425-3688 (800-800-8000)
Dogs of all sizes are allowed. There are no additional pet fees. Reservations are recommended due to limited rooms for pets. Only non-smoking rooms are used for pets.

Parks
Capitol Reef National Park HC 70 Box 15 Torrey UT   435-425-3791
http://www.nps.gov/care/index.htm
Dogs on leash are allowed in campsites and on paved road areas. Dogs are not allowed on hiking trails or in the backcountry.

Virgin

Campgrounds and RV Parks
Zion River Resort 730 E Hwy 9 Virgin UT   800-838-8594
http://www.zionriverresort.com
Dogs of all sizes are allowed. There are no additional pet fees. Dogs must be leashed and cleaned up after. There is a fenced in area where dogs may run off lead. There is a dog walk area at the campground.

Washington

Stores
Petco Pet Store 765 West Telegraph St Washington UT   435-986-9704
Your licensed and well-behaved leashed dog is allowed in the store.

Wendover

Accommodations
Motel 6 - Wendover 561 East Wendover Boulevard Wendover UT   435-665-2267 (800-466-8356)
One well-behaved family pet per room. Guest must notify front desk upon arrival. Guest is liable for any damages. In consideration of all guests, pets must never be left unattended in the guest rooms.

Willard

Campgrounds and RV Parks

Willard Bay State Park 900 West 650 North #A/ On Hwy 315 Willard UT   435-734-9494 (800-322-3770)
Willard Bay has 2 marinas open to the public, and is a freshwater reservoir providing fresh water for farming as well as recreation. Dogs are allowed at no additional fee. Dogs may not be left unattended, and they must be leashed and cleaned up after. Dogs are allowed on the trails. The camping and tent areas also allow dogs. There is a dog walk area at the campground.

Zion National Park

Accommodations

Motel 6 - Hurricane 650 West State Street Hurricane UT   435-635-4010 (800-466-8356)
One well-behaved family pet per room. Guest must notify front desk upon arrival. Guest is liable for any damages. In consideration of all guests, pets must never be left unattended in the guest rooms.
Driftwood Lodge 1515 Zion Park Blvd Springdale UT   435-772-3262 (888-801-8811)
http://www.driftwoodlodge.net/index.html
There is a $10 one time pet fee.
El Rio Lodge 995 Zion Park Blvd Springdale UT   435-772-3205 (888-772-3205)
http://www.elriolodge.com/
This small 10 room motel is located in the Zion canyon with 360 degree views of the fascinating landscape of deep canyons, soaring cliffs, and geological surprises. (The Pa-rus Trail is the only trail that dogs are allowed on in the park.) They offer affordable prices, and clean, comfortable rooms with a great location to eateries and other attractions. Dogs of all sizes are allowed for an additional pet fee of $15 per night per room. Dogs may not be left alone in the room at any time, and they must be leashed and cleaned up after.

Campgrounds and RV Parks

Brentwood RV Resort 15N 3700W Hurricane UT   800-447-2239
http://www.zionsgaterv.com
One dog of any size is allowed. There are no additional pet fees. Dogs must be leashed and cleaned up after. There is a dog walk area at the campground.
Quail Creek State Park Hwy 318 M.P. #2 Hurricane UT   435-879-2378 (800-322-3770)
This park provides a variety of year round recreation, and the man-made reservoir here is known for the warmth of its water in the summer. Dogs are allowed at no additional fee. Dogs must be on no more than a 6 foot leash and be cleaned up after. Dogs are not allowed on the beach between the grass areas. The camping and tent areas also allow dogs. There is a dog walk area at the campground. There are no hookups at the campground.
Red Cliffs Recreation Area 4.5 miles from Leeds on I-15 Leeds UT   435-688-3246
This recreational site has 10 campsites among the bright colored canyon walls of the area. Dogs are allowed at no addtional fee, and they must be leashed and cleaned up after. Information and maps can be gotten from the BLM office at 345 E. Riverside Drive, St. George, Utah. The camping and tent areas also allow dogs. There is a dog walk area at the campground. There are no electric or water hookups at the campground.
Zion Canyon Campground & Resort 479 Zion Park Blvd Springdale UT   435-772-3237
http://www.zioncamp.com
Dogs of all sizes are allowed. There are no additional pet fees. Dogs may not be left inside a tent or outside on any site unattended, and they may be left in an RV only if there is air conditioning. Dogs must be quiet, well behaved, leashed, and cleaned up after. There are some breed restrictions. The camping and tent areas also allow dogs. There is a dog walk area at the campground.

Parks

Zion National Park State Route 9 Springdale UT   435-772-3256
http://www.nps.gov/zion/
Dogs are allowed on one walking trail at this national park. Dogs on a 6 foot or less leash are allowed on the Pa'rus Trail which is a 1.5 mile long trail that runs from the South Campground to Canyon Junction. You and your pooch can also enjoy a 10-12 mile scenic drive on the Zion-Mount Carmel Highway which goes through the park. If you are there from November through March, you can also take your car on the Zion Canyon Scenic Drive. If you arrive during the summer months, the Zion Canyon Scenic Drive is closed and only allows park shuttle buses. Other pet rules include no pets on shuttle buses, in the backcountry, or in public buildings. Pets are allowed in the campgrounds and along roadways.

Chapter 22

Washington
Dog Travel Guide

Aberdeen

Accommodations
America's Best Value 521 W Wishkah Aberdeen WA   360-532-5210
Dogs of all sizes are allowed. There is a $10 per night pet fee.

Anacortes

Accommodations
Anacortes Inn 3006 Commercial Ave Anacortes WA   360-293-3153
http://www.ohwy.com/wa/a/anactinn.htm
There is a $10 per night pet fee.
Fidalgo Country Inn 7645 St Route 20 Anacortes WA   360-293-3494
There is a $20 per day pet charge. There are 2 pet rooms.

Campgrounds and RV Parks
Fidalgo Bay Resort 4701 Fidalgo Bay Road Anacortes WA   360-293-5353
http://www.fidalgobay.com
Dogs of all sizes are allowed. There are no additional pet fees. Dogs may not be left unattended, and they must be quiet, well behaved, leashed at all times, and cleaned up after. Dogs may not be kenneled outside. This is an RV only park. There is a dog walk area at the campground.
Pioneer Trails RV Resort 7337 Miller Road Anacortes WA   360-293-5355
http://www.pioneertrails.com
Dogs of all sizes are allowed. There is a $2 per night per pet additional fee. Dogs must be leashed and cleaned up after. Dogs are not allowed in the covered wagons. There are some breed restrictions. There is a dog walk area at the campground.

Anatone

Campgrounds and RV Parks
Fields Spring State Park 992 Park Road Anatone WA   509-256-3332
This state park has a variety of year round land and water recreational activities. Dogs of all sizes are allowed at no additional fee. Dogs may not be left unattended, and they must be leashed and cleaned up after. Dogs are allowed on the trails, but they are not allowed at any public swim areas. The camping and tent areas also allow dogs. There is a dog walk area at the campground. There are no electric or water hookups at the campground.

Ashford

Campgrounds and RV Parks
Mount Rainier National Park Tahoma Woods Star Route (H706) Ashford WA   360-569-2211
http://www.nps.gov/mora/
This park is home to Mount Rainier, an active volcano encrusted by ice, and at 14,411 feet it towers 8,000 feet above the surrounding Cascades peaks and creates it own weather. There is a variety of land and water recreation. Dogs are allowed at no additional fee. Dogs must be leashed and cleaned up after. Dogs are not allowed in any of the buildings, or on any of the trails except for the Pacific Coast Trail. Dogs must otherwise stay on the roads and parking lots of the camp areas. This campground is closed during the off-season. The camping and tent areas also allow dogs. There is a dog walk area at the campground. There are no electric or water hookups at the campground.

Parks
Mount Rainer National Park Tahoma Woods State Route Ashford WA 360-569-2211
http://www.nps.gov/mora/index.htm
Dogs must be on leash where they are allowed. Dogs are only allowed on roads, parking lots, and campgrounds. They are not allowed on trails, snow, in buildings, or any wilderness areas. There is a small portion of Pacific Crest Trail near the park's eastern boundary that allows pets on leash.

Auburn

Campgrounds and RV Parks
Flaming Geyser State Park 23700 SE Flaming Geyser Road Auburn WA 253-931-3930
This 475 acre day-use park, located only 8 miles from Seattle's waterfront, offers lots of activities, and land and water recreation. There are large open lawns, over 200 picnic sites with tables, multi-use trails, and a self-guided ADA accessible Salmon Interpretive Trail, but it's main features are its' two geysers and other bubbling springs. Dogs of all sizes are allowed. Dogs must be on no more than an 8 foot leash and be cleaned up after at all times. The park has provided clean-up stations throughout the park. Pets are not permitted on designated swimming beaches. There is a dog walk area at the campground.

Parks
Flaming Geyser State Park 23700 SE Flaming Geyser Road Auburn WA 253-931-3930
This 475 acre day-use park, located only 8 miles from Seattle's waterfront, offers lots of activities, and land and water recreation. There are large open lawns, over 200 picnic sites with tables, multi-use trails, and a self-guided ADA accessible Salmon Interpretive Trail, but it's main features are its' two geysers and other bubbling springs. Dogs of all sizes are allowed. Dogs must be on no more than an 8 foot leash and be cleaned up after at all times. The park has provided clean-up stations throughout the park. Pets are not permitted on designated swimming beaches.

Bagley

Campgrounds and RV Parks
Jellystone Park 11354 County Hwy X Bagley WA 608-996-2201 (800-999-6557)
http://www.jellystonebagley.com
Dogs of all sizes are allowed. There are no additional pet fees. Dogs must be leashed and cleaned up after. This RV park is closed during the off-season. The camping and tent areas also allow dogs. There is a dog walk area at the campground.
Wyalusing State Park 13081 State Park lane Bagley WA 608-996-2261 (888-WIPARKS (947-2757))
This park holds historical significance as one of Wisconsin's oldest parks. It has over 24 miles of trails, including a canoe trail, water and land recreation, an interpretive center, and more. Dogs are allowed at no additional fee. Dogs may not be left unattended, and they must be leashed and cleaned up after. Dogs are not allowed in the picnic areas, in buildings, on cross-country ski trails once there is snow, or on the Sugar Maple Nature trail. Dogs are allowed on the hiking trails, and they may be off lead when out of the camp area if there is voice control. The camping and tent areas also allow dogs. There is a dog walk area at the campground. There are no water hookups at the campground.

Bainbridge Island

Campgrounds and RV Parks
Fay Bainbridge State Park 15446 Sunrise Drive NE Bainbridge Island WA 206-842-3931 (888-226-7688)
This 17 acre marine camping park, with 1,420 feet of saltwater shoreline, offers excellent scenery and a host of water and land recreation. Dogs of all sizes are allowed at no additional fee. Dogs may not be left unattended, and they must be leashed and cleaned up after. Dogs are not allowed in park buildings, however they are allowed on the trails. The camping and tent areas also allow dogs. There is a dog walk area at the campground.

Attractions

Bainbridge Island Vineyards 8989 Day Road East Bainbridge Island WA   206-842-9463
http://www.bainbridgevineyards.com/
Along with a list of dry, sweet, and fruit wines, this vineyard produces the only Pinot Noir grown in the Puget
Sound Appellation. Dogs of all sizes are allowed on the grounds, but it is important they are social and friendly
with the other dogs and animals that make their home here. Dogs must be leashed and cleaned up after.

Beaches
Fay Bainbridge State Park Sunset Drive NE Bainbridge Island WA   360-902-8844
This park is located on the northeast side of Bainbridge Island on Puget Sound. On a clear day, you can see Mt.
Rainer and Mt. Baker from the beach. Picnic tables, restrooms and campgrounds are available at this park.
Leashed dogs are allowed on the beach. Pets are not permitted on designated swimming beaches. However,
there is usually a non-designated swimming beach area as well. Dogs are also allowed at the campgrounds.
They must be on a eight foot or less leash at all times and people are required to clean up after their pets. To get
there from From Poulsbo, take Hwy. 305 toward Bainbridge Island. Cross the Agate Pass Bridge. After three
miles, come to stoplight and big brown sign with directions to park. Turn left at traffic light onto Day Rd. NE.
Travel approximately two miles to a T-intersection. Turn left onto Sunrise Drive NE, and continue to park
entrance, about two miles away.

Off-Leash Dog Parks
Eagledale Park Off-Leash Dog Park 5055 Rose Avenue NE Bainbridge Island WA   206-842-2306
This one acre dog park is located in Eagledale Park which is at Rose Avenue a few blocks south of Eagle
Harbor Dr NE.

Outdoor Restaurants
Bainbridge Thai Cuisine 330 Madison Avenue S Bainbridge Island WA   206-780-2403
http://www.royalthai-cuisine.com/
Claims of being the best Thai food available, they also provide outside dining for their customers. Your pet is
welcome to join you on the patio. Dogs must be well behaved, leashed, and please clean up after your pet.
Emmy's VegeHouse 100 Winslow Way W Bainbridge Island WA   206-855-2996
This restaurant is takeout only and serves up Vietnamese vegetarian takeout. There are tables outside where
you can sit with your pet and enjoy your meal. They are open from 11 am to 7:30 pm Monday to Friday, only to 7
pm on Saturday, and closed Sunday. Dogs must be well behaved, leashed, and cleaned up after.
Pegasus Coffee House 131 Parfitt Way Bainbridge Island WA   206-842-6725
http://www.pegasuscoffeehouse.com/
This coffee house welcomes your pet on their patio area. Dogs must be well behaved, leashed, and cleaned up
after.
Subway 278 E Winslow Way Bainbridge Island WA   206-780-5354
This sub shop is located in an open air mall, and your pet is welcome to join you at the outside tables. Dogs of all
sizes are welcome. Dogs must be leased, and please clean up after your pet.

Bay Center

Campgrounds and RV Parks
Bay Center/Willapa Bay KOA 457 Bay Center Road Bay Center WA   360-875-6344 (800-562-7810)
http://www.koa.com/where/wa/47121.html
Dogs of all sizes are allowed. There are no additional pet fees. Dogs may not be left unattended outside, must
be quiet, leashed, and cleaned up after. Dogs are met at the door with doggy treats. Dogs are not allowed on the
playground, at the cabins, or in the buildings. There are some breed restrictions. This RV park is closed during
the off-season. The camping and tent areas also allow dogs. There is a dog walk area at the campground. There
are special amenities given to dogs at this campground.

Bellevue

Accommodations
Candlewood Suites 15805 SE 37th Street Bellevue WA   425-373-1212 (877-270-6405)
Dogs of all sizes are allowed. There is a $75 one time additional pet fee.
Residence Inn by Marriott 14455 NE 29th Place Bellevue WA   425-882-1222

Dogs of all sizes are allowed. There is a $75 one time fee and a pet policy to sign at check in.
Sheraton Bellevue Seattle East Hotel 100 112th Avenue SE Bellevue WA   425-455-3330 (888-625-5144)
Dogs of all sizes are allowed. There are no additional pet fees. Dogs are not allowed to be left alone in the room.

Stores
Petco Pet Store 15600 NE 8th St, Ste 01 Bellevue WA   425-641-9333
Your licensed and well-behaved leashed dog is allowed in the store.
Petco Pet Store 4080 Factoria Blvd SE Bellevue WA   425-641-5203
Your licensed and well-behaved leashed dog is allowed in the store.

Bellingham

Accommodations
Aloha Motel 315 N Samish Way Bellingham WA   360-733-4900
One dog of any size is allowed. There is an additional $5 per night pet fee.
Days Inn Bellingham 125 E Kellogg Rd Bellingham WA   360-671-6200 (800-329-7466)
Dogs of all sizes are allowed. There is a $7 per night pet fee per pet.
Holiday Inn Express 4160 Guide Meridian Bellingham WA   360-671-4800 (877-270-6405)
There is a $10 one time pet fee.
Motel 6 - Bellingham 3701 Byron Street Bellingham WA   360-671-4494 (800-466-8356)
One well-behaved family pet per room. Guest must notify front desk upon arrival. Guest is liable for any
damages. In consideration of all guests, pets must never be left unattended in the guest rooms.
Quality Inn Baron Suites 100 E Kellogg Road Bellingham WA   360-647-8000 (877-424-6423)
Dogs of all sizes are allowed. There is a $25 one time additional pet fee per room for a 1 to 15 days stay. Dogs
may not be left alone in the room, and they must be leashed and cleaned up after.
Island Vacation Rentals 1695 Seacrest Drive Lummi Island WA   360-758-7064
Well behaved adult dogs over a year old, and of all sizes, are allowed. There is a pet policy to sign at check in
and there are no additional fees.

Campgrounds and RV Parks
Bellingham RV Park 3939 Bennett Drive Bellingham WA   360-752-1224
http://www.bellinghamrvpark.com
Dogs of all sizes are allowed. There are no additional pet fees. Dogs must be leashed and cleaned up after.
There are some breed restrictions. The camping and tent areas also allow dogs. There is a dog walk area at the
campground.
Larrabee State Park 245 Chuckanut Drive Bellingham WA   360-676-2093
This year round recreational park features 8,100 feet of saltwater shoreline, 2 freshwater lakes, and many miles
of trails to explore. The I-5 route is suggested for larger RVs. Dogs of all sizes are allowed at no additional fee.
Dogs may not be left unattended, and they must be leashed and cleaned up after. Dogs are allowed on the trails,
but not in any buildings. The camping and tent areas also allow dogs. There is a dog walk area at the
campground.
Lynden/Bellingham KOA 8717 Line Road Lynden WA   360-354-4772 (800-562-4779)
http://www.koa.com
Dogs of all sizes are allowed. There are no additional pet fees. Dogs must be well behaved, leashed, and
cleaned up after. The camping and tent areas also allow dogs. There is a dog walk area at the campground.

Attractions
Sehome Hill Arboretum 25th Street and McDonald Parkway Bellingham WA   360-676-6985
http://www.ac.wwu.edu/~sha/index.html
This 180 natural forest park remains one of the last refuges for the diverse population of birds, animal, and plant
life indigenous to the area. Sitting atop a hill in the heart of the city, there is one man-made structure on site-an
80 foot observation tower providing outstanding views, and to which all the trails lead. There are almost 6 miles
of gravel hiking/interpretive trails, and a large tunnel cut into a rock that hikers can walk through. Dogs of all
sizes are allowed. Dogs must be leashed and cleaned up after at all times. Dogs and visitors must stay on
established paths.
Victoria San Juan Cruises 355 Harris Avenue, Ste 104 Bellingham WA   800-443-4552
http://www.whales.com/
This commuter ferry offers daily service in the summer months between Bellingham, Washington and Friday
Harbor on San Juan Island. Dogs are allowed on the commuter ferry only, and not on the sightseeing or dinner
cruises. Dogs are allowed to be on leash during the crossing if they are comfortable with the boat and will be well

behaved; otherwise they need to be crated. There is no additional fee for your pet.

Stores

PetSmart Pet Store 4379 Guide Meridian St Bellingham WA 360-738-9653
Your licensed and well-behaved leashed dog is allowed in the store.
Petco Pet Store 189 East Bakerview Rd Bellingham WA 360-715-3785
Your licensed and well-behaved leashed dog is allowed in the store.

Parks

Maritime Heritage Park West Holly Street Bellingham WA 360-676-6985
This park of over 11 acres offers a lush green setting, open play areas, picnic facilities, a playground, fishing area, a fish hatchery, and an amphitheater. They are open year round, and to get there drive west on Holly Street from downtown Bellingham and the park will be on your right. Dogs of all sizes are allowed throughout the park, but they are not allowed in any of the buildings. Dogs must be leashed and cleaned up after at all times.

Birch Bay

Accommodations

Madrona West Home Vacations Call to Arrange Birch Bay WA 360-738-32233
Well behaved adult dogs over a year old, and of all sizes are allowed. There is a pet policy to sign at check in and there are no additional pet fees.

Blaine

Campgrounds and RV Parks

Birch Bay State Park 5105 Helwig Blaine WA 360-371-2800 (888-226-7688)
Year around recreation is offered at this park. There are 194 acres with over 8,200 feet of saltwater shoreline, a rich archeological history, miles of trails, and a variety of land and water activities. Dogs of all sizes are allowed at no additional fee. Dogs may not be left unattended at any time, they must be on no more than a 6 foot leash, and be cleaned up after. Dogs are allowed on the trails, but they are not allowed on the beach. The camping and tent areas also allow dogs. There is a dog walk area at the campground.

Attractions

M.V. Plover Ferry Marine Drive / Blaine Moorage Dock at Gate II Blaine WA 360-332-5742
http://www.mvplover.org/
The M.V. Plover Ferry is the located at the Blaine Marina, and is the oldest passenger foot-ferry in Washington State. The ferry runs every Friday, Saturday, and Sunday, Memorial Day through Labor Day, shuttling up to 17 passengers and their gear across the Drayton Harbor. There is no charge for pet or person for this ferry service; however donations are greatly appreciated. Dogs of all sizes are allowed, and they must be leashed and cleaned up after at all times.

Beaches

Birch Bay State Park Grandview Blaine WA 360-902-8844
This beach, located near the Canadian border, offers panoramic coastal views. Picnic tables, restrooms (including an ADA restroom), and campgrounds (including ADA campsites) are available at this park. Leashed dogs are allowed on the beach. Pets are not permitted on designated swimming beaches. However, there is usually a non-designated swimming beach area as well. Dogs are also allowed in the campgrounds. They must be on a eight foot or less leash at all times and people are required to clean up after their pets. This park is located 20 miles north of Bellingham and ten miles south of Blaine. From the south take exit #266 off of I-5. Go left on Grandview for seven miles, then right on Jackson for one mile, then turn left onto Helweg. From the north take exit #266 off of I-5, and turn right onto Grandview.

Parks

Peace Arch State Park P. O. Box 87 Blaine WA 360-332-8221
This gorgeous, 20 acre day-use park features lush lawns, expansive gardens (they plant more than 20,000

flowers annually), outstanding views of the ocean and the surrounding area, and an impressive Peace Arch that stands astride the boundary of the United States and Canada. The arch commemorates treaties and agreements that arose from the War of 1812. Some of the amenities include picnic areas, interpretive programs/signs, recreational programs, horticultural displays, and peace concerts. Dogs of all sizes are allowed throughout the park, but not in buildings or planted areas. Dogs must be leashed and cleaned up after at all times-please bring supplies.

Bothell

Campgrounds and RV Parks
Lake Pleasant RV Park 24025 Bothell Everett Hwy SE Bothell WA   425-487-1785
Dogs of all sizes are allowed. There are no additional pet fees. Dogs must be leashed and cleaned up after. There are some breed restrictions. There is a dog walk area at the campground.

Bremerton

Accommodations
Super 8 Bremerton 5068 Kitsap Way Bremerton WA   360-377-8881 (800-800-8000)
Dogs of all sizes are allowed. There is a $15 returnable deposit required per room. There is a $10 one time pet fee per visit. Smoking and non-smoking rooms are available for pet rooms.

Campgrounds and RV Parks
Illahee State Park 3540 Bahia Vista Bremerton WA   360-478-6460 (888-CAMP OUT (226-7688))
This park is a marine camping park with almost 1800 feet of saltwater frontage. There is only 1 site that has hook-ups. Dogs of all sizes are allowed. There are no additional pet fees. Dogs may not be left unattended, and they must be leashed and cleaned up after. Dogs are allowed on the trails, but not in any buildings. The camping and tent areas also allow dogs. There is a dog walk area at the campground. There are no electric or water hookups at the campground.

Stores
Petco Pet Store 4209 Wheaton Way Bremerton WA   360-377-9112
Your licensed and well-behaved leashed dog is allowed in the store.

Off-Leash Dog Parks
Bremerton Bark Park 1199 Union Avenue Bremerton WA   360-473-5305
http://www.visitkitsap.com/kitsap.asp
This fenced off-leash dog park is located at Pendergast Park. It opened in November, 2005. To get to the park from Hwy 16 or Hwy 3, head towards Bremerton, take the Loxie Eagans Blvd exit off of Hwy 3 and go west onto Werner Road. Turn left on Union Street and the park will be on the right. This location is considered a temporary location for the park so check to see if it has moved.

Burbank

Parks
McNary National Wildlife Refuge 311 Lake Road Burbank WA   509-547-4942
http://nwr.mcnary.wa.us/
This refuge of over 15,000 acres provides a wide variety of habitats for a priceless diversity of fish, wildlife, birds, and plants. It extends along the east bank of the Columbia River from the junction of the Snake River to the mouth of the Walla Walla River then downstream into Oregon. Dogs of all sizes are welcome. Dogs must be under owner's control and leashed at all times, and please bring supplies to clean up after your pet. The exception to dogs being off lead is when they are assisting waterfowl hunters in retrieving downed birds during hunting season. Dogs, nor people, are allowed at Sanctuary Pond or off the roads or trails at any time.

Burley

Off-Leash Dog Parks
Bandix Dog Park Bandix Road SE at Burley-Olalla Rd Burley WA
http://www.visitkitsap.com/kitsap.asp
This very large 30 acre off-leash park opened in July, 2004. It is not fenced and dogs that use it should follow voice commands well. The dog park is located on Bandix Road SE south of Burley-Olalla Rd and North of Nelson (Stevens) Road near State Highway 16. From State Highway 16 take Burley-Olalla Rd east to Bandix Road SE and turn right. The park will be on the right. The dog park is sponsored and maintained by Kitsap Dog Parks, Inc.

Burlington

Campgrounds and RV Parks
Burlington/Anacortes KOA 6397 N Green Road Burlington WA   360-724-5511 (800-562-9145)
http://www.koa.com
Dogs of all sizes are allowed. There are no additional pet fees. Dogs must be well behaved, quiet, be on no more than a 6 foot leash, and be cleaned up after. Dogs may not be left unattended at any time and can not be on the beds in the cabins. The camping and tent areas also allow dogs. There is a dog walk area at the campground. Dogs are allowed in the camping cabins.

Stores
PetSmart Pet Store 1969 Marketplace Dr Burlington WA   360-757-1616
Your licensed and well-behaved leashed dog is allowed in the store.

Castle Rock

Campgrounds and RV Parks
Seaquest State Park Spirit Lake H Castle Rock WA   206-274-8633 (888-226-7688)
There are 475 acres at this year round recreational park with 8 miles of hiking trails, over a mile of lake shoreline, and a variety of activities. Dogs of all sizes are allowed at no additional fee. Dogs may not be left unattended at any time, they must be on no more than a 6 foot leash, and be cleaned up after. Dogs are allowed on the trails. The camping and tent areas also allow dogs. There is a dog walk area at the campground.

Centralia

Accommodations
Motel 6 - Centralia 1310 Belmont Avenue Centralia WA   360-330-2057 (800-466-8356)
One well-behaved family pet per room. Guest must notify front desk upon arrival. Guest is liable for any damages. In consideration of all guests, pets must never be left unattended in the guest rooms.

Chehalis

Campgrounds and RV Parks
Scotts RV Park 118 h 12 Chehalis WA   360-262-9220
Dogs of all sizes are allowed. There are no additional pet fees. Dogs may not be left unattended, must be leashed, and cleaned up after. The camping and tent areas also allow dogs. There is a dog walk area at the campground. Dogs are allowed in the camping cabins.

Attractions

TOP 200 PLACE **Chehalis-Centralia Railroad** 1101 Sylvenus Street Chehalis WA   360-748-9593
http://www.steamtrainride.com/index.html
Operating over a nine mile section of tract through scenic hills, farmland, and many wooden trestles, this restored steam powered train will provide a pleasant, relaxing journey back in time. This company currently runs only one of a few steam powered standard gauge tourist railroads in the state. Your pet is welcome to join you for no additional fee when they are not very busy and/or when the train cars are not full. Dogs must be well behaved, leashed, and please bring supplies to clean up after your pet.

Chelan

Transportation Systems

Lake Chelan Boat Company 1418 W Woodin Ave Chelan WA   509-682-4584
http://www.ladyofthelake.com/
Daily service passenger boats provide round-trip service between Chelan and Stehekin, with a few scheduled stops in between, from about mid-March through October 31st, and then reduced service during the winter. Dogs up to 100 pounds are allowed. Dogs must remain in a crate in the luggage area on the outside deck with the owner present at all times while underway. There is an additional fee of $13.00 round-trip in the owner's cage or $24.00 round-tip in a boat company cage.

Attractions

TOP 200 PLACE **Chelan Airways** 1328 West Woodin Ave/Hwy Alt 97 Chelan WA   509-682-5555
http://www.chelanairways.com/
This company has been providing air transportation and sightseeing tours for over 60 years to the Lake Chelan area, an area that offers spectacular contrasts in geography and topography. Cradled in the deepest gorge in North America, the lake begins deep inside the North Cascades and reaches 55 miles into the desert of N. Central Washington. Dogs are allowed on the small planes if they will be comfortable and well behaved. There is no additional fee if they do not take a paying seat. Dogs must be leashed and please carry supplies to clean up after your pet.
The Tour Boat Lake Chelan Marina Chelan WA   509-682-8287
http://www.thetourboat.com
Dogs on leash are allowed on the boat tours. Tours of Lake Chelan with scenic stops, picnicking, etc can be purchased with small groups or individual pricing.

Cheney

Campgrounds and RV Parks

Klinks Williams Lake Resort 18617 Williams Lake Road Cheney WA   509-235-2391
http://www.klinksresort.com
Dogs of all sizes are allowed. There are no additional pet fees. Dogs must be friendly, well behaved, leashed, and cleaned up after. Dogs are not allowed at the beach. There are some breed restrictions. This RV park is closed during the off-season. The camping and tent areas also allow dogs. There is a dog walk area at the campground.

Parks

Cheney Turnbull National Wildlife Refuge 26010 S Smith Road Cheney WA   509-235-4723
Home to one of the most unique ecosystems in the world, this refuge provides a variety of habitats to a large animal and bird population. Some of the features here include a 5-mile auto tour, interpretive signage, environmental education sites, plenty of multi-use trails, and about 2,300 acres for public use. Dogs of all sizes are allowed for no additional fee. They must be kept on the trails and in public use areas. Dogs must be leashed and cleaned up after at all times.

Chewelah

Attractions
49 Degrees North Mountain Resort 3311 Flowery Trail Road Chewelah WA   509-935-6049
http://www.ski49n.com/
Although dogs are not allowed at this resort in the winter, this is a beautiful place to visit in the summer months. With almost 2 million acres and breathtaking views, you can find a variety of recreational pursuits. Dogs must be leashed and cleaned up after at all times. Dogs are not allowed in the buildings or food service areas.

Clarkston

Accommodations
Motel 6 - Clarkston 222 Bridge Street Clarkston WA   509-758-1631 (800-466-8356)
One well-behaved family pet per room. Guest must notify front desk upon arrival. Guest is liable for any damages. In consideration of all guests, pets must never be left unattended in the guest rooms.

Campgrounds and RV Parks
Granite Lake RV Resort 306 Granite Lake Drive Clarkston WA 509-751-1635
http://www.granitelakervresort.com
Dogs of all sizes are allowed. There is no fee for one dog. If you have a 2nd dog there is an additional fee of $1 per day. Dogs may not be left unattended, and if needed, there is a dog sitter on site. Dogs may walk along the river, and they must be leashed and cleaned up after. There are some breed restrictions. There is a dog walk area at the campground.

Attractions
TOP 200 PLACE Snake Dancer Excursions 1550 Port Drive, Suite B (Below Roosters Landing) Clarkston WA   509-758-8927
http://www.snakedancerexcursions.com/
These jet boat tours of the Hells Canyon have been offering a variety of scenic tours since 1970. Some of the features/amenities include whitewater rapids, historic sites, exposed lava flows, petroglyphs, incredible scenery, abundant wildlife, and a tasty home-made buffet style lunch. Dogs are allowed on some of the tours (if ok with other passengers) for no additional fee, or you can schedule a customized tour. You must provide your pooch with their own doggy life jacket. Dogs must be attended to at all times, well behaved, leashed, and cleaned up after.

Colville

Campgrounds and RV Parks
Colville National Forest 765 Main (Forest Supervisor's Office) Colville WA   509-684-7000
http://www.fs.fed.us/r6/colville/
Dogs of all sizes are allowed. There are no additional pet fees. Dogs may not be left unattended, and they must be leashed and cleaned up after. There are some beaches that dogs are allowed on, but they are not allowed at any of the public swim areas. Dogs are allowed on the trails unless otherwise marked. This campground is closed during the off-season. The camping and tent areas also allow dogs. There is a dog walk area at the campground. There are no electric or water hookups at the campground.

Concrete

Campgrounds and RV Parks
Concrete/Grandy Creek KOA 7370 Russell Road Concrete WA   360-826-3554 (888-562-4236)
http://www.koa.com
Dogs of all sizes are allowed. There are no additional pet fees. Dogs may not be left unattended at any time, must be leashed, and cleaned up after. There are some breed restrictions. This RV park is closed during the off-season. The camping and tent areas also allow dogs. There is a dog walk area at the campground. Dogs are allowed in the camping cabins.

Copalis Beach

Accommodations
Iron Springs Ocean Beach Resort P. O. Box 207 Copalis Beach WA   360-276-4230
http://www.ironspringsresort.com
Iron Springs is a 100 acre resort on the Washington Coast located halfway between Copalis and Pacific Beach.
They offer individual cottages with fireplaces and great ocean views. The cottages are nestled among the rugged
spruce trees on a low lying bluff overlooking the Pacific Ocean. They are located near miles of sandy beaches.
There is a $15.00 per day charge for pets. There are no designated smoking or non-smoking cabins. They are
located 130 miles from Seattle and 160 miles from Portland.

Beaches
Griffith-Priday State Park State Route 109 Copalis Beach WA   360-902-8844
This beach extends from the beach through low dunes to a river and then north to the river's mouth. Picnic tables
and restrooms are available at this park. Dogs are allowed on the beach. They must be on a eight foot or less
leash at all times and people are required to clean up after their pets. This park is located 21 miles northwest of
Hoquiam. From Hoquiam, go north on SR 109 for 21 miles. At Copalis Beach, at the sign for Benner Rd., turn
left (west).

Cougar

Campgrounds and RV Parks
Lone Fir Motel and RV Resort 16806 Lewis River Road Cougar WA   360-238-5210
http://www.lonefirresort.com
Dogs of all sizes and numbers are allowed, and there are no additional pet fees for the tent and RV sites. There
is a $10 per night per pet additional fee for the motel and only 2 dogs are allowed per room. Dogs must be quiet,
well behaved, leashed, and cleaned up after. The camping and tent areas also allow dogs. There is a dog walk
area at the campground. Dogs are allowed in the camping cabins.

Coulee City

Campgrounds and RV Parks
Sun Lakes Park Resort 34228 Park Lake Road NE Coulee City WA   509-632-5291
http://www.sunlakesparkresort.com
Dogs of all sizes are allowed. There is a $7 per night per pet additional fee for the cabins, tent or RV sites. Dogs
may not be left unattended, are not allowed at the swim beach, and must be leashed and cleaned up after. There
is an area where the dogs are also allowed to go swim. This RV park is closed during the off-season. The
camping and tent areas also allow dogs. There is a dog walk area at the campground. Dogs are allowed in the
camping cabins.
Sun Lakes State Park Hwy 17, 2 miles W of Coulee City Coulee City WA   509-632-5583 (888-226-7688)
This park is home to one of the great geological wonders of North America; a stark cliff is the only remnant of a
once grand waterfall 10 times the size of Niagara Falls. There is also more than 4,000 acres with over 73,000
feet of shoreline to explore. Dogs of all sizes are allowed at no additional fee. Dogs may not be left unattended at
any time, they must be on no more than a 6 foot leash, and be cleaned up after. Dogs are allowed on the trails,
but not at any public swim areas or buildings. This campground is closed during the off-season. The camping
and tent areas also allow dogs. There is a dog walk area at the campground. There are no water hookups at the
campground.
Sun Lakes-Dry Falls State Park 34875 Park Lake Road NE Coulee City WA   509-632-5538 (888-CAMPOUT
(226-7688))
This park is full of beautiful natural formations, but its real attraction is the gigantic dried-up waterfall now
standing as a dry cliff 400 feet high and 3.5 miles long; once 10 times larger than Niagara Falls. The park has a
visitor's center by the falls, and some of the park amenities include 15 miles of hiking trails, interpretive activities,
2 boat ramps, 9 lakes, a park store, a 9 hole golf course, and a miniature golf course. Dogs of all sizes are
allowed for no additional fee. Dogs must be under physical control at all times, leashed, and cleaned up after.
Dogs are not allowed in park buildings or on designated swimming beaches. The campground offers about 200

campsites, fire pits, restrooms, showers, a dump station, and laundry facilities. The camping and tent areas also allow dogs. There is a dog walk area at the campground. There are no electric or water hookups at the campgrounds.

Parks
Sun Lakes-Dry Falls State Park 34875 Park Lake Road NE Coulee City WA   509-632-5538 (888-CAMPOUT (226-7688))
This park is full of beautiful natural formations, but its real attraction is the gigantic dried-up waterfall now standing as a dry cliff 400 feet high and 3.5 miles long; once 10 times larger than Niagara Falls. The park has a visitor's center by the falls, and some of the park amenities include 15 miles of hiking trails, interpretive activities, 2 boat ramps, 9 lakes, a park store, a 9 hole golf course, and a miniature golf course. Dogs of all sizes are allowed for no additional fee. Dogs must be under physical control at all times, leashed, and cleaned up after. Dogs are not allowed in park buildings or on designated swimming beaches.

Coulee Dam

Campgrounds and RV Parks
Lake Roosevelt National Recreation area Spring Canyon Road Coulee Dam WA   509-633-9441
http://www.nps.gov/laro
This year round recreational area has 28 campgrounds around the lake, miles of trails, and a variety of fun activities. Dogs of all sizes are allowed at no additional fee. Dogs may not be left unattended, and they must be leashed and cleaned up after. Dogs are allowed on the trails, but not in any day use or public swim areas. The camping and tent areas also allow dogs. There is a dog walk area at the campground. There are no electric or water hookups at the campground.

Parks
Lake Roosevelt National Recreation Area 1008 Crest Drive Coulee Dam WA   509-738-6266
http://www.nps.gov/laro/index.htm
Dogs must be on leash and must be cleaned up after. The park features boating, auto touring, camping, fishing, hiking, and more.

Coupeville

Campgrounds and RV Parks
Fort Ebey State Park 400 Hill Valley Drive Coupeville WA   360-678-4636 (888-226-7688)
Popular, historical, educational, recreational, and pre-historic, all describe this scenic park that offer interpretive programs and several miles of trails. Dogs of all sizes are allowed at no additional fee. Dogs may not be left unattended, and they must be leashed and cleaned up after. Dogs are allowed on the trails. The camping and tent areas also allow dogs. There is a dog walk area at the campground.

Parks
Ebey's Landing National Historic Reserve 162 Cemetery Road Coupeville WA   360-678-6084
http://www.nps.gov/ebla/index.htm
Dogs on a 6 ft leash are allowed at this reserve. There are two off leash areas that you will need a map from the visitor's center to find. The park features camping, auto touring, boating, fishing, hiking, and more.

Off-Leash Dog Parks
Patmore Pit Off-Leash Area Patmore Rd At Keystone Hill Rd Coupeville WA   360-321-4049
http://www.fetchparks.org
This large forty acre meadow is partially fenced. There is also a fenced agility area with toys, water and cleanup bags. To get to the park from SR 20 take Patmore Road west to Keystone Hill Rd. Turn left (south) on Keystone Hill to the park. It will be on the right side.

Covington

Stores
Petco Pet Store 27111 167th Place SE, Ste 113 Covington WA   253-638-1064
Your licensed and well-behaved leashed dog is allowed in the store.

Des Moines

Beaches
Saltwater State Park Marine View Drive Des Moines WA   360-902-8844
This state beach is located on Puget Sound, halfway between the cities of Tacoma and Seattle (near the Sea-Tac International Airport). Picnic tables, restrooms and campgrounds are available at this park. Leashed dogs are allowed on the beach. Pets are not permitted on designated swimming beaches. However, there is usually a non-designated swimming beach area as well. Dogs are also allowed at the campgrounds. They must be on a eight foot or less leash at all times and people are required to clean up after their pets. To get there from the north, take exit #149 off of I-5. Go west, then turn south on Hwy. 99 (sign missing). Follow the signs into the park. Turn right on 240th at the Midway Drive-in. Turn left on Marine View Dr. and turn right into the park.

Electric City

Campgrounds and RV Parks
Coulee Playland Resort 401 Coulee Blvd E (Hwy 155) Electric City WA   509-633-2671
http://www.couleeplayland.com
Dogs of all sizes are allowed. There are no additional pet fees. Dogs may not be left unattended outside, and they must be leashed and cleaned up after. This RV park is closed during the off-season. The camping and tent areas also allow dogs. There is a dog walk area at the campground.
Steamboat Rock State Park Banks Lake Electric City WA   509-633-1304 (888-CAMPOUT (226-7688))
This park with more than 3,500 acres along Banks Lake is an oasis in desert surroundings, and a variety of activities and recreation are offered. Dogs of all sizes are allowed at no additional fee. Dogs may not be left unattended, and they must be leashed and cleaned up after. Dogs are not allowed in public swim areas or in buildings. Dogs are allowed on the trails. The camping and tent areas also allow dogs. There is a dog walk area at the campground.

Ellensburg

Accommodations
Comfort Inn 1722 Canyon Road Ellensburg WA   509-925-7037 (877-424-6423)
Dogs up to 60 pounds are allowed. There is a $10 per night per pet additional fee. Dogs may not be left alone in the room, and they must be leashed and cleaned up after.
Super 8 Ellensburg 1500 Canyon Rd Ellensburg WA   509-962-6888 (800-800-8000)
Dogs of all sizes are allowed. There is a $10 one time per pet fee per visit. Smoking and non-smoking rooms are available for pet rooms.

Campgrounds and RV Parks
Ellensburg KOA 32 Thorp Hwy S Ellensburg WA   509-925-9319 (800-562-7616)
http://www.koa.com
Dogs of all sizes are allowed. There are no additional pet fees. Dogs may not be left unattended, must be leashed, and cleaned up after. Dogs are allowed at the river, but the river is very swift. The camping and tent areas also allow dogs. There is a dog walk area at the campground.

Ephrata

Campgrounds and RV Parks

Oasis RV Park and Golf 2541 Basin Street SW Ephrata WA 509-754-5102
Dogs of all sizes are allowed. There are no additional pet fees. Dogs may not be left unattended, must be well behaved, leashed, and cleaned up after. This RV park is closed during the off-season. There is a dog walk area at the campground.

Everett

Accommodations

Days Inn Seattle/ Everett 1602 SE Everett Mall Way Everett WA 425-355-1570 (800-329-7466)
Dogs of all sizes are allowed. There is a $10 one time per pet fee per visit.
Motel 6 - Everett North 10006 Evergreen Way Everett WA 425-347-2060 (800-466-8356)
One well-behaved family pet per room. Guest must notify front desk upon arrival. Guest is liable for any damages. In consideration of all guests, pets must never be left unattended in the guest rooms.
Motel 6 - Everett South 224 128th Street Southwest Everett WA 425-353-8120 (800-466-8356)
One well-behaved family pet per room. Guest must notify front desk upon arrival. Guest is liable for any damages. In consideration of all guests, pets must never be left unattended in the guest rooms.

Campgrounds and RV Parks

Lakeside Park 12321 Hwy 99S Everett WA 425-347-2970
Dogs of all sizes are allowed. There are no additional pet fees. Dogs may not be left unattended at any time, must be leashed, and cleaned up after. The camping and tent areas also allow dogs. There is a dog walk area at the campground.
Maple Grove RV Resort 12417 Hwy 99 Everett WA 425-423-9608
http://www.maplegroverv.com
Dogs of all sizes are allowed. There are no additional pet fees. Dogs may not be tied up outside alone, and they must be leashed and cleaned up after. There is a dog walk area at the campground.

Stores

PetSmart Pet Store 1130 SE Everett Mall Way Everett WA 425-267-3401
Your licensed and well-behaved leashed dog is allowed in the store.
Petco Pet Store 1203 SE Everett Mall Way, Ste F Everett WA 425-290-6533
Your licensed and well-behaved leashed dog is allowed in the store.

Beaches

Howarth Park Dog Beach 1127 Olympic Blvd. Everett WA 425-257-8300
Most of the park and beach areas require that dogs are on-leash and there are fines for violations. There is an off-leash beach area north of the pedestrian bridge that crosses the railroad tracks. Your dog should be under excellent voice control at this beach if it is off-leash due to the nearby train tracks. In addition, the train may spook a dog. There are also some trails for leashed dogs. The park is open from 6 am to 10 pm.
Howarth Park Dog Park 1127 Olympic Blvd. Everett WA 425-257-8300
Most of the park and beach areas require that dogs are on-leash and there are fines for violations. There Is an off-leash beach area north of the pedestrian bridge that crosses the railroad tracks. Your dog should be under excellent voice control at this beach if it is off-leash due to the nearby train tracks. In addition, the train may spook a dog. There are also some trails for leashed dogs. The park is open from 6 am to 10 pm.

Off-Leash Dog Parks

Loganberry Lane Off-Leash Area 18th Ave. W. Everett WA 425-257-8300
This is a small unfenced off-leash area which is about 1/2 acre in size. It is wooded with trails. The hours at the park are 6 am to 10 pm.
Lowell Park Off-Leash Area 46th St at S 3rd Ave. Everett WA 425-257-8300
This is a small but fenced off-leash area. The hours at the park are 6 am to 10 pm. The off-leash dog park is located north of the tennis courts in Lowell Park. From I-5 you can exit at 41st Street, head east and then turn south on 3rd Ave to the park.

Everson

Attractions

Mt Baker Vineyards 4298 Mt Baker H Everson WA   360-592-2300
This scenic vineyard offers views of Mt Baker and a picnic area. Dogs are allowed, but there are other dogs on site, so pets must be friendly and social with people and animals. Dogs must be leashed and cleaned up after at all times. They are not allowed in buildings.

Federal Way

Accommodations

Super 8 Federal WAy 1688 S 348th St Federal Way WA   253-838-8808 (800-800-8000)
Dogs of all sizes are allowed. There is a $10 per night pet fee per pet. Smoking and non-smoking rooms are available for pet rooms.

Campgrounds and RV Parks

Dash Point State Park 5700 SW Dash Point Road Federal Way WA   253-661-4955 (888-CAMP OUT (226-7688))
This park has 11 miles of trails and 3,301 feet of saltwater shoreline on Puget Sound. Dogs of all sizes are allowed. There are no additional pet fees. Dogs may not be left unattended, they must be on no more than an 8 foot leash, and be cleaned up after. Dogs are allowed on the trails and beach but not in buildings. This campground is closed during the off-season. The camping and tent areas also allow dogs. There is a dog walk area at the campground.
Dash Point State Park 5700 SW Dash Point Road Federal Way WA   253-661-4955 (888-CAMPOUT (226-7688))
This 398-acre park, with 3,301 feet of saltwater shoreline on the Puget Sound, offers an amphitheater, interpretive programs, nature study, and a variety of land and water recreation. Dogs of all sizes are allowed at no additional fee. Dogs may not be left unattended, and they must be on no more than an 8 foot leash, and be cleaned up after. Dogs are not allowed in buildings, but they are allowed on the trails unless otherwise marked. The camping and tent areas also allow dogs. There is a dog walk area at the campground.

Stores

PetSmart Pet Store 31705 Pacific Hwy S Federal Way WA   253-529-4693
Your licensed and well-behaved leashed dog is allowed in the store.
Petco Pet Store 31419 Pacific Highway South Federal Way WA   253-839-7423
Your licensed and well-behaved leashed dog is allowed in the store.

Beaches

Dash Point State Park Dash Point Rd. Federal Way WA   360-902-8844
This beach offers great views of Puget Sound. Picnic tables, restrooms, 11 miles of hiking trails and campgrounds are available at this park. Leashed dogs are allowed on the beach. Pets are not permitted on designated swimming beaches. However, there is usually a non-designated swimming beach area as well. Dogs are also allowed on hiking trails and campgrounds. They must be on a eight foot or less leash at all times and people are required to clean up after their pets. This park is located on the west side of Federal Way in the vicinity of Seattle. From Highway 5, exit at the 320th St. exit (exit #143). Take 320th St. west approximately four miles. When 320th St. ends at a T-intersection, make a right onto 47th St. When 47th St. ends at a T-intersection, turn left onto Hwy. 509/ Dash Point Rd. Drive about two miles to the park. (West side of street is the campground side, and east side is the day-use area.)

Off-Leash Dog Parks

French Lake Dog Park 31531 1st Ave S Federal Way WA   253-835-6901
The French Lake Dog Park is a large, 10 acre off-leash area. It has a pond and picnic benches. To get to the park take I-5 to the S. 320th Street exit. Head west on 320th Street to 1st Way and head north to the park.

Ferndale

Accommodations
Super 8 Ferndale/Bellingham Area 5788 Barrett Ave Ferndale WA   360-384-8881 (800-800-8000)
Dogs of all sizes are allowed. There is a $10 one time per pet fee per visit. Smoking and non-smoking rooms are available for pet rooms.

Campgrounds and RV Parks
The Cedars RV Resort 6335 Portal Way Ferndale WA   360-384-2622
http://www.holidaytrailsresorts.com
Dogs of all sizes are allowed. There is a $2 per night per pet additional fee. Dogs must be leashed and cleaned up after, and they are not allowed at the playground or in the buildings. The camping and tent areas also allow dogs. There is a dog walk area at the campground.

Fife

Accommodations
Emerald Queen Hotel and Casino 5700 Pacific Hwy East Fife WA   253-922-3555 (888-820-3555)
Dogs of all sizes are allowed. There is a $25 pet fee per day. You will need to make reservations early due to limited pet rooms.
Motel 6 - Tacoma - Fife 5201 20th Street East Fife WA   253-922-1270 (800-466-8356)
One well-behaved family pet per room. Guest must notify front desk upon arrival. Guest is liable for any damages. In consideration of all guests, pets must never be left unattended in the guest rooms.
Quality Inn 5601 Pacific Hwy E Fife WA   253-926-2301 (877-424-6423)
Dogs of all sizes are allowed. There can be up to 2 large dogs or 3 small dogs per room. There is a $10 per night per pet additional fee. Dogs may not be left alone in the room, and they must be leashed and cleaned up after.

Forks

Accommodations
Kalaloch Ocean Lodge 157151 Hwy. 101 Forks WA   360-962-2271
http://www.kalaloch.com
Perched on a bluff, overlooking the Pacific Ocean, sits the Kalaloch Lodge located in Olympic National Park. The Olympic National Forest is also located nearby. Dogs are not allowed in the lodge, but they are welcome in the cabins. This resort offers over 40 cabins and half of them have ocean views. There are no designated smoking or non-smoking cabins. Thanks to one of our readers who writes "This is a great place where you can rent cabins situated on a bluff overlooking the Pacific Ocean. Great for watching storms pound the beaches and walking wide sand beaches at low tide. Near rain forest with wooded hikes and lakes throughout. Not all units allow dogs, but you can still get a good view." There is a $12.50 per day pet fee.

Freeland

Beaches
Double Bluff Beach 6400 Double Bluff Road Freeland WA   360-321-4049
http://www.fetchparks.org
South of Freeland and on Whidbey Island, this unfenced off-leash area also includes a dog beach. This is one of the largest off-leash beaches in the U.S. The off-leash beach is about 2 miles long. On clear days you can see Mt Rainier, the Seattle skyline and many ships. The beach nearest the parking lot is an on-leash area and the off-leash beach starts about 500 feet from the lot. There will be steep fines for dogs that are unleashed in an inappropriate area. From WA-525 watch for a sign for Double Bluff Road and it south. The road ends at the beach.

Off-Leash Dog Parks
Marguerite Brons Dog Park WA 525 at Bayview Rd Freeland WA   360-321-4049
http://www.fetchparks.org
This large thirteen acre off-leash park is fully fenced. Most of the park is wooded with trails through the trees.

Some of the park is an open meadow. To get to the park from Freeland take WA-525 south and turn right on Bayview Rd. The park is on the left in about 1/2 mile.

Gig Harbor

Accommodations
Best Western Wesley Inn of Gig Harbor 6575 Kimball Gig Harbor WA   253-858-9690 (800-780-7234)
Dogs of all sizes are allowed. There is a $10 per night pet fee and pets are only allowed up to 5 nights. Pets are allowed on the first floor only.

Campgrounds and RV Parks
Gig Harbor RV Resort 9515 Burnham Drive NW Gig Harbor WA   253-858-8138
Dogs of all sizes are allowed. There are no additional pet fees. Dogs may not be left outside alone, must be leashed at all times, and cleaned up after. The camping and tent areas also allow dogs. There is a dog walk area at the campground.

Stores
Petco Pet Store 5190 Borgen Blvd, Ste 201 Gig Harbor WA   253-858-1606
Your licensed and well-behaved leashed dog is allowed in the store.

Gold Bar

Campgrounds and RV Parks
Wallace Falls State Park 14503 Wallace Lake Road Gold Bar WA   360-793-0420
Because of the outstanding scenery in this 678 acre park and the overlooks at Wallace Falls (265 feet), it is a favorite of hikers. There are numerous other waterfalls, a rock climbing wall, hiking trails, an interpretive trail, picnic tables, 3 back country lakes, and a river that offer a wide variety of recreational pursuits. Dogs of all sizes are allowed for no additional fee. Dogs must be under physical control at all times, leashed, and cleaned up after. Pets are not permitted in park buildings or at designated swimming beaches. Tent camping is available at 7 beautiful, private walk-in sites on a first come first serve basis. Sites have picnic tables, campfire rings, drinking water, and a restroom. The camping and tent areas also allow dogs. There is a dog walk area at the campground. There are no electric or water hookups at the campgrounds.

Parks
Wallace Falls State Park 14503 Wallace Lake Road Gold Bar WA   360-793-0420
Because of the outstanding scenery in this 678 acre park and the overlooks at Wallace Falls (265 feet), it is a favorite of hikers. There are numerous other waterfalls, a rock climbing wall, hiking trails, an interpretive trail, picnic tables, 3 back country lakes, and a river that offer a wide variety of recreational pursuits. Dogs of all sizes are allowed for no additional fee. Dogs must be under physical control at all times, leashed, and cleaned up after. Pets are not permitted in park buildings or at designated swimming beaches.

Grayland

Beaches
Grayland Beach State Park Highway 105 Grayland WA   360-902-8844
This 412 acre park offers beautiful ocean frontage and full hookup campsites (including ADA campsites). Leashed dogs are allowed on the beach. Dogs are also allowed at the campgrounds. They must be on a eight foot or less leash at all times and people are required to clean up after their pets. This park is located five miles south of Westport. From Aberdeen, drive 22 miles on Highway 105 south to Grayland. Traveling through the town, watch for park signs.

Greenbank

Events

Wag n' Walk Festival 760 E Wonn Road Greenbank WA   360-321-WAIF (9243)
http://www.waifanimals.org/
This annual September festival, usually held at Greenbank Farm for everything ?Dog", is sponsored by the
Whidbey Animals Improvement Foundation (WAIF) and directly benefits the shelter's animals. It is a full day of
activities with demonstrations, vendors, contests, games, adoption hopefuls, and more. Dogs must be leashed
and cleaned up after at all times, and they may not be in heat or younger than 4 months old.

Hood River

Accommodations

Inn of the White Salmon 172 W Jewett White Salmon WA   509-493-2335 (800-972-5226)
http://www.gorge.net/lodging/iws/
There is a $10 per day pet fee. All rooms are non-smoking.

Hoodsport

Attractions

Hoodsport Winery 23522 N Hwy 101 Hoodsport WA   360-877-9894
http://www.hoodsport.com/
This small award wining winery is located on the rural Olympic Peninsula, and offers a great view of the Hood
Canal and the Olympic Mountains. Well behaved, happy dogs are welcome here. Dogs must be leashed and
cleaned up after at all times.

Hyak

Cross Country Ski Resorts

Gold Creek SnoPark Interstate 90 Hyak WA   360-902-8844
This Washington State Park offers both ski and snowshoe rentals. The trails at this SnoPark are not groomed
and no motorized vehicles are allowed on the trails. Dogs must be leashed at all times. To use these trails you
will need a Washington SnoPark permit or an Oregon or Idaho snow park permit. Many sporting goods stores
sell the SnoPark permits. You also call the State Park office at 360-902-8500 or purchase permits online at
https://wws2.wa.gov/parks/ecomm/sno/dsnostp0.asp .

Ilwaco

Campgrounds and RV Parks

Ilwaco/Long Beach KOA 1509 Hwy 101 Ilwaco WA   360-642-3292 (800-562-3258)
http://www.koa.com
Dogs of all sizes are allowed. There are no additional pet fees. Dogs must be leashed and cleaned up after.
There is an off leash fenced in area for dogs also. There are some breed restrictions. This RV park is closed
during the off-season. The camping and tent areas also allow dogs. There is a dog walk area at the campground.

Beaches

Cape Disappointment State Park Highway 101 Ilwaco WA   360-902-8844
This park offers 27 miles of ocean beach and 7 miles of hiking trails. Enjoy excellent views of the ocean,
Columbia River and two lighthouses. Picnic tables, restrooms (including an ADA restroom), hiking and
campgrounds (includes ADA campsites) are available at this park. Leashed dogs are allowed on the beach.
Dogs are also allowed on hiking trails and campgrounds. They must be on a eight foot or less leash at all times
and people are required to clean up after their pets. This park is located two miles southwest of Ilwaco. From

Seattle, Take I-5 south to Olympia, SR 8 west to Montesano. From there, take U.S. Hwy. 101 south to Long Beach Peninsula.

Kelso

Accommodations
Motel 6 - Kelso - Mt St Helens 106 Minor Road Kelso WA   360-425-3229 (800-466-8356)
One well-behaved family pet per room. Guest must notify front desk upon arrival. Guest is liable for any damages. In consideration of all guests, pets must never be left unattended in the guest rooms.
Red Lion 510 Kelso Drive Kelso WA   360-636-4400
Dogs of all sizes are allowed. There is a $25 one time fee per stay and a pet policy to sign at check in.
Super 8 Kelso/Longview Area 250 Kelso Dr Kelso WA   360-423-8880 (800-800-8000)
Dogs of all sizes are allowed. There is a $10 one time per pet fee per visit. Smoking and non-smoking rooms are available for pet rooms.

Kennewick

Accommodations
Best Western Kennewick 4001 W 27th Avenue Kennewick WA   509-586-1332 (800-780-7234)
Dogs of all sizes are allowed. There is a $10 per night pet fee per pet.
La Quinta Inn & Suites Kennewick 4220 W 27th Place Kennewick WA   509-736-3326 (800-531-5900)
Dogs of all sizes are allowed. There are no additional pet fees. Dogs may not be left unattended at any time, and they must be leashed and cleaned up after.
Red Lion 1101 N Columbia Center Blvd Kennewick WA   509-738-0611
Dogs of all sizes are allowed. There is a pet policy to sign at check in and no additional fees.
Super 8 Kennewick/Tri-Cities Area 626 N Columbia Center Blvd Kennewick WA   509-736-6888 (800-800-8000)
Dogs of all sizes are allowed. There is a $10 per night pet fee per pet. Smoking and non-smoking rooms are available for pet rooms.
Royal Hotel 1515 George Washington Way Richland WA   509-946-4121
There is a $25 one time pet fee.

Attractions
Badger Mountain Vineyards 1106 S Jurupa Street Kennewick WA   800-643-WINE (9463)
http://www.badgermtnvineyard.com/
A favorable location, climate, volcanic soil, and organic technique, coupled with a commitment to produce 100% organic wines, have brought this winery national and international recognition for their consistent high quality. The tasting room is open daily from 10 am to 5 pm. Dogs are allowed to explore the grounds with their owner, but they are not allowed in any of the buildings. Dogs must be leashed and cleaned up after.

Stores
PetSmart Pet Store 6807 W Canal Dr Kennewick WA   509-735-3101
Your licensed and well-behaved leashed dog is allowed in the store.

Kent

Accommodations
Howard Johnson Inn 1233 North Central Kent WA   253-852-7224 (800-446-4656)
Well-behaved dogs up to 80 pounds are allowed. There is a $15 one time additional pet fee.
TownePlace Suites Seattle Southcenter 18123 72nd Avenue South Kent WA   253-796-6000
Dogs of all sizes are allowed. There is a $10 per night pet fee per pet or $150 per stay.

Campgrounds and RV Parks
Seattle/Tacoma KOA 5801 S 212th Street Kent WA   253-872-8652 (800-562-1892)

http://www.seattlekoa.com
Dogs of all sizes are allowed. There are no additional pet fees. Dogs must have current shot records, be leashed, and cleaned up after. Dogs may be left in your RV if they will be quiet and comfortable. There are some breed restrictions. The camping and tent areas also allow dogs. There is a dog walk area at the campground.

La Conner

Outdoor Restaurants
Whiskers 128 South 1st Street La Conner WA 360-466-1008
This restaurant serves American and seafood. Dogs are allowed at the outdoor tables.

LaPush

Campgrounds and RV Parks
Lonesome Creek RV Park 490 Ocean Drive LaPush WA 360-374-4338
Dogs of all sizes are allowed. There are no additional pet fees. Dogs must be leashed and cleaned up after. The camping and tent areas also allow dogs. There is a dog walk area at the campground.

Leavenworth

Accommodations
Quality Inn and Suites 185 Hwy 2 Leavenworth WA 509-548-7992 (877-424-6423)
Dogs of all sizes are allowed. There is a $15 per night per pet additional fee. Dogs must be well behaved, leashed, cleaned up after, and crated when left alone in the room.

Campgrounds and RV Parks
Lake Wenatchee State Park 21588A Hwy 207 Leavenworth WA 509-662-0420 (888-CAMPOUT (226-7688))
This 489 acre park along a glacier fed lake offers an amphitheater, interpretive programs, nature study, a variety of trails, and various land and water activities and recreation. Dogs of all sizes are allowed at no additional fee. Dogs may not be left unattended, and they must be leashed and cleaned up after. Dogs are not allowed in buildings, but they are allowed on the trails. The camping and tent areas also allow dogs. There is a dog walk area at the campground.
Leavenworth/Wenatchee KOA 11401 Riverbend Drive Leavenworth WA 509-548-7709 (800-562-5709)
http://www.pinevillagekoa.com
Dogs of all sizes are allowed. There are no additional pet fees. Dogs must be leashed and cleaned up after. Dogs may be left unattended if they are quiet and well behaved. There are some breed restrictions. This RV park is closed during the off-season. The camping and tent areas also allow dogs. There is a dog walk area at the campground.

Long Beach

Accommodations
Super 8 Long Beach 500 Ocean Beach Blvd Long Beach WA 360-642-8988 (800-800-8000)
Dogs of all sizes are allowed. There is a $5.39 per night pet fee per pet. Smoking and non-smoking rooms are available for pet rooms.

Campgrounds and RV Parks
Andersen's RV Park on the Ocean 1400 138th Street (Hwy 103) Long Beach WA 800-645-6795
http://www.andersensrv.com/
Dogs of all sizes are allowed. There are no additional pet fees. Dogs may not be left unattended unless they will be very quiet and well behaved. Dogs must be leashed and cleaned up after. Dogs may be off lead along the beach only if they will respond to voice command. This is an RV only park. There is a dog walk area at the

campground.

Longview

Stores
Petco Pet Store 200 Triangle Center, Ste 230 Longview WA   360-636-1444
Your licensed and well-behaved leashed dog is allowed in the store.

Lopez Island

Campgrounds and RV Parks
Spencer Spit State Park 521A Baker View Road Lopez Island WA   360-468-2251 (888-CAMPOUT (226-7688))
There is a 45 minute ferry ride from Anacordes to this park, and dogs must remain on the car deck during the crossing. This is a marine and camping park along the Strait of Juan de Fuca, and beachcoming and nature study are favorites here. Pets must be on a leash and under physical control at all times. Dogs are not permitted on designated swimming beaches. Dogs are allowed on the trails. The camping and tent areas also allow dogs. There is a dog walk area at the campground. There are no electric or water hookups at the campground.

Beaches
Spencer Spit State Park Bakerview Road Lopez Island WA   360-902-8844
Located in the San Juan Islands, this lagoon beach offers great crabbing, clamming and beachcombing. Picnic tables, restrooms, campgrounds and 2 miles of hiking trails are available at this park. Leashed dogs are allowed on the beach. Pets are not permitted on designated swimming beaches. However, there is usually a non-designated swimming beach area as well. Dogs are also allowed on hiking trails and campgrounds. They must be on a eight foot or less leash at all times and people are required to clean up after their pets. This park is located on Lopez Island in the San Juan Islands. It is a 45-minute Washington State Ferry ride from Anacortes. Dogs are allowed on the ferry. Once on Lopez Island, follow Ferry Rd. Go left at Center Rd., then left at Cross Rd. Turn right at Port Stanley and left at Bakerview Rd. Follow Bakerview Rd. straight into park. For ferry rates and schedules, call 206-464-6400.

Lynnwood

Accommodations
Embassy Suites Seattle - North/Lynnwood 20610 44th Ave. West Lynnwood WA   425-775-2500
Dogs of all sizes are allowed. There is a $50 one time pet fee per visit. Only 5 rooms available for pets.
La Quinta Inn Lynnwood 4300 Alderwood Mall Blvd Lynnwood WA   425-775-7447 (800-531-5900)
Dogs of all sizes are allowed, and 2 dogs per room are preferred, but 3 dogs are ok if they are small dogs. There are no additional pet fees. Dogs may not be left unattended, and they must be leashed and cleaned up after. Dogs are not allowed in any of the food areas.
Residence Inn by Marriott 18200 Alderwood Mall Parkway Lynnwood WA   425-771-1100
Two dogs are allowed per room, however they will not accept extra large dogs, and they must be well behaved. There is a $15 per night per room fee to a maximum total of $75 per stay and a pet policy to sign at check in.

Campgrounds and RV Parks
Twin Cedars RV Park 17826 Hwy 99N Lynnwood WA   425-742-5540
Dogs of all sizes are allowed. There are no additional pet fees. Dogs may not be left unattended, must be leashed, and cleaned up after. Dogs may be off leash at the dog run if they are well behaved. There is a dog walk area at the campground.

Stores
PetSmart Pet Store 18820 Hwy 99 Lynnwood WA   425-672-4422
Your licensed and well-behaved leashed dog is allowed in the store.
Petco Pet Store 2617 196th St SW, Ste 141 Lynnwood WA   425-673-7060

Washington - Please always call ahead to make sure that an establishment is still dog-friendly

Your licensed and well-behaved leashed dog is allowed in the store.

Mead

Campgrounds and RV Parks
Mount Spokane State Park 26107 Mount Spokane Park Drive Mead WA 509-238-4258 (888-CAMPOUT (226-7688))
This almost 14,000 acre park offers over one hundred miles of hiking trails, interpretive activities and a variety of year round recreation. Dogs of all sizes are allowed at no additional fee. Dogs may not be left unattended, they must be on no more than an 8 foot leash, and be cleaned up after. Dogs are not allowed in building, however, they are allowed on the trails. This campground is closed during the off-season. The camping and tent areas also allow dogs. There is a dog walk area at the campground. There are no electric or water hookups at the campground.
Mount Spokane State Park 26107 N Mount Spokane Park Drive Mead WA 509-238-4258
This camping park of almost 14,000 acres, reaches an elevation of over 5,880 feet, and at times you can see great views of Washington, Idaho, and Montana. They offer interpretive activities, a variety of recreational pursuits, and over 100 miles of multi-use trails for spring/summer/fall that becomes cross-country ski trails in winter. Dogs are allowed on hiking trails except in winter. Dogs must be under physical control at all times, leashed, and cleaned up after. The campground is on a first come first served basis, and has 12 standard campsites with water and a flush restroom. This RV park is closed during the off-season. The camping and tent areas also allow dogs. There is a dog walk area at the campground. There are no electric or water hookups at the campgrounds.

Parks
Mount Spokane State Park 26107 N Mount Spokane Park Drive Mead WA 509-238-4258
This camping park of almost 14,000 acres, reaches an elevation of over 5,880 feet, and at times you can see great views of Washington, Idaho, and Montana. They offer interpretive activities, a variety of recreational pursuits, and over 100 miles of multi-use trails for spring/summer/fall that becomes cross-country ski trails in winter. Dogs are allowed on hiking trails except in winter. Dogs must be under physical control at all times, leashed, and cleaned up after.

Mercer Island

Parks
Luther Burbank Park 2040 84th Avenue SE Mercer Island WA 206-205-7532
This 77 acre park offers great views of Lake Washington and is popular for boating and fishing. There are almost 3 miles of walking paths. Dogs on leash are allowed. There is also a special off-leash area for dogs located at the north end of the park. To get there from I-5, take I-90 East to Mercer Island and take the Island Crest Way exit (#7). At the top of the ramp, turn right on SE 26th Street. At the stop sign turn left on 84th Avenue SE and drive straight to the park after another stop sign at SE 24th Street.

Metaline Falls

Campgrounds and RV Parks
Crawford State Park Boundary Road Metaline Falls WA 509-446-4065
This state park is a 49 acre, forested day-use park featuring a tourable cave-the 3rd largest limestone cavern in the state. There is a restroom, one kitchen shelter (without electricity), and 2 sheltered and 11 unsheltered picnic tables available on a first come first served basis. This park closes in September and reopens in April. Dogs of all sizes are welcome at the park, but they may not go into the cave. Dogs must be leashed and cleaned up after at all times. There is a dog walk area at the campground.

Parks
Crawford State Park Boundary Road Metaline Falls WA 509-446-4065
This state park is a 49 acre, forested day-use park featuring a tourable cave-the 3rd largest limestone cavern in the state. There is a restroom, one kitchen shelter (without electricity), and 2 sheltered and 11 unsheltered picnic

tables available on a 1st come 1st served basis. This park closes in September and reopens in April. Dogs of all sizes are welcome at the park, but they may not go into the cave. Dogs must be leashed and cleaned up after at all times.

Moclips

Accommodations
Hi-Tide Resort 4849 Railroad Avenue Moclips WA   800-662-5477
Dogs of all sizes are allowed. There is a $12 per night per pet additional fee.
Ocean Crest Resort 4651 SR 109 Moclips WA   360-276-4465
http://www.ohwy.com/wa/o/ocecrere.htm
There is a $15 per day pet fee. Pets are allowed in some of the units. All rooms are non-smoking.

Monroe

Accommodations
Best Western Baron Inn 19233 Highway 2 Monroe WA   360-794-3111 (800-780-7234)
Dogs of all sizes are allowed. There is a $15 per day pet fee. Additional fees for more than two pets. The hotel is all non-smoking.

Montesano

Campgrounds and RV Parks
Lake Sylvia State Park 1812 Lake Sylvia Road Montesano WA   360-249-3621 (888-CAMPOUT (226-7688))
This 233-acre camping park with 15,000 feet of freshwater shoreline is rich with logging lore and history. It offers 5 miles of hiking trails, and a variety of land and water recreation. Dogs of all sizes are allowed at no additional fee. Dogs may not be left unattended, and they must be quiet, well behaved, be on no more than an 8 foot leash, and be cleaned up after. Dogs are not allowed in public swim areas, buildings, or in the Environmental Learning Center area. This campground is closed during the off-season. The camping and tent areas also allow dogs. There is a dog walk area at the campground. There are no electric or water hookups at the campground.

Moses Lake

Accommodations
Best Western Lakeside Inn 3000 Marina Dr Moses Lake WA   509-765-9211 (800-780-7234)
Dogs of all sizes are allowed. There are no additional pet fees. Dogs are not allowed to be left alone in the room.
Holiday Inn Express 1745 E Kittleson Moses Lake WA   509-766-2000 (877-270-6405)
Dogs of all sizes are allowed. There are no additional pet fees. Smoking and non-smoking rooms are available for pets.
Motel 6 - Moses Lake 2822 West Driggs Drive Moses Lake WA   509-766-0250 (800-466-8356)
One well-behaved family pet per room. Guest must notify front desk upon arrival. Guest is liable for any damages. In consideration of all guests, pets must never be left unattended in the guest rooms.

Mount Baker - Glacier

Vacation Home Rentals
TOP 200 PLACE Mt. Baker Lodging 7463 Mt. Baker Highway Glacier WA   360-599-2453 (1-800-709-7669)
http://www.mtbakerlodging.com/
Private vacation rental homes located at the gateway to Mt. Baker. There are a wide variety of rental homes to

choose, from honeymoon getaways and family cabins, to accommodations for group retreats and family reunions. All properties are privately owned, unique and completely self-contained.

Mount Vernon

Accommodations
Best Western College Way Inn 300 W College Way Mount Vernon WA   360-424-4287 (800-780-7234)
Dogs of all sizes are allowed. There is a $15 pet fee.
Comfort Inn 1910 Freeway Drive Mount Vernon WA   360-428-7020 (877-424-6423)
Dogs of all sizes are allowed. There is a $10 per night per pet additional fee. Dogs must be leashed, cleaned up after, and the Do Not Disturb sign put on the door if they are in the room alone.
Days Inn Mt Vernon 2009 Riverside Dr Mount Vernon WA   360-424-4141 (800-329-7466)
Dogs of all sizes are allowed. There is a $10 per night pet fee per pet.

Stores
Petco Pet Store 201 East College Way, Ste B Mount Vernon WA   360-424-5999
Your licensed and well-behaved leashed dog is allowed in the store.

Mountlake Terrace

Accommodations
Studio 6 - SEATTLE - MOUNTLAKE TERRACE 6017 244th Street SW Mountlake Terrace WA   425-771-3139 (800-466-8356)
One well-behaved family pet per room. Guest must notify front desk upon arrival. Guest is liable for any damages. In consideration of all guests, pets must never be left unattended in the guest rooms.

Campgrounds and RV Parks
Mt. Baker-Snoqualmie National Forest 21905 64th Avenue W Mountlake Terrace WA   425-775-9702 (800-627-0062)
http://www.fs.fed.us/r6/mbs/
Snoqualmie National Forest extends more than 140 miles along the west side of the Cascade Mountains and offers a wide variety of recreational activities year round. Dogs of all sizes are allowed at no additional fee. Dogs may not be left unattended, and they must be leashed and cleaned up after. Dogs are allowed on the trails, but not in public swim areas. This campground is closed during the off-season. The camping and tent areas also allow dogs. There is a dog walk area at the campground. There are no electric or water hookups at the campground.

Mukilteo

Accommodations
TownePlace Suites Seattle North/Mukiteo 8521 Mukilteo Speedway Mukilteo WA   425-551-5900
Dogs up to 75 pounds are allowed. There is a $10 per night pet fee per pet.

Nine Mile Falls

Campgrounds and RV Parks
Riverside State Park Charles Road Nine Mile Falls WA   509-465-5064 (888-CAMPOUT (226-7688))
This 10,000-acre park along the Spokane Rivers offers interpretive centers, 55 miles of scenic hiking trails, opportunities for nature study, and a variety of land and water recreation. Dogs of all sizes are allowed at no additional fee. Dogs may not be left unattended, and they must be leashed at all times, and cleaned up after. Dogs are not allowed in the natural heritage area or in the Spokane River. Dogs are allowed on the trails. The camping and tent areas also allow dogs. There is a dog walk area at the campground.

Nordland

Campgrounds and RV Parks
Fort Flager State Park 10541 Flagler Road Nordland WA   360-385-1259 (888-CAMPOUT (226-7688))
This historic, 784-acre marine park, sits atop a high bluff overlooking the Puget Sound, and offers a museum, interpretive programs, several miles of trails, and land and water activities. Dogs are allowed at no additional fee. Dogs may not be left unattended, and they must be leashed and cleaned up after. Dogs are not allowed in any of the buildings, but they are allowed on the trails. The camping and tent areas also allow dogs. There is a dog walk area at the campground.

North Cascades National Park

Parks
North Cascades National Park State Route 20 Newhalem WA   360-856-5700
http://www.nps.gov/noca
Dogs are allowed on one of the hiking trails, the Pacific Crest Trail. This scenic hiking trail runs through the park and is rated moderate to difficult. The trail is located off Highway 20, about one mile east of Rainy Pass. At the Bridge Creek Trailhead, park on the north side of the highway and then hike north (uphill) or south (downhill). A Northwest Forest Pass is required to park at the trailhead. The cost is about $5 and can be purchased at the Visitor's Center in Newhalem. For a larger variety of trails, including a less strenuous hike, dogs are also allowed on trails at the adjacent Ross Lake National Recreation Area and the Lake Chelan National Recreation Area. Both recreation areas are managed by the national park.

Oak Harbor

Campgrounds and RV Parks
Deception Pass State Park 41227 State Route 20 Oak Harbor WA   360-675-2417 (888-CAMPOUT (226-7688))
Rich in natural and cultural history, this 4,134 acre marine and camping park is home to a large variety of plant/animal/bird life, and offers ample land and water recreational opportunities. Some of the amenities/features include salt and freshwater shorelines, 3 lakes, 2 amphitheaters, 6 fire circles, interpretive activities/signage, a museum, hiking trails plus a 1.2 mile ADA hiking trail, and breath-taking viewing areas. Dogs of all sizes are allowed for no additional fee. Dogs must be under physical control, leashed, and cleaned up after at all times. Dogs are not allowed on designated swimming beaches. Camping is available year round, although some sites may be closed for winter. Amenities include picnic tables (some sheltered), over 200 camp sites, restrooms, showers, and dump stations. The camping and tent areas also allow dogs. There is a dog walk area at the campground.
North Whidbey RV Park 565 W Coronet Bay Road Oak Harbor WA   360-675-9597
http://www.northwhidbeyrvpark.com
Dogs of all sizes are allowed. There are no additional pet fees. Dogs may not be left unattended, or tied up outside alone. Dogs must be leashed and cleaned up after. There is a dog walk area at the campground.

Beaches
Fort Ebey State Park Hill Valley Drive Oak Harbor WA   360-902-8844
This 600+ acre park is popular for hiking and camping, but also offers a saltwater beach. Picnic tables and restrooms (including an ADA restroom) are available at this park. Leashed dogs are allowed on the saltwater beach. Dogs are also allowed on hiking trails and campgrounds. They must be on a eight foot or less leash at all times and people are required to clean up after their pets. To get to the park from Seattle, take exit #189 off of I-5, just south of Everett. Follow signs for the Mukilteo/ Clinton ferry. Take the ferry to Clinton on Whidbey Island. Dogs are allowed on the ferry. Once on Whidbey Island, follow Hwy. 525 north, which becomes Hwy. 20. Two miles north of Coupeville, turn left on Libbey Rd. and follow it 1.5 miles to Hill Valley Dr. Turn left and enter park.
Joseph Whidbey State Park Swantown Rd Oak Harbor WA   360-902-8844
This 112 acre park offers one of the best beaches on Whidbey Island. Picnic tables, restrooms, and several miles of hiking trails (including a half mile ADA hiking trail) are available at this park. Leashed dogs are allowed on the beach. Pets are not permitted on designated swimming beaches. However, there is usually a non-

designated swimming beach area as well. Dogs are also allowed on hiking trails. They must be on a eight foot or less leash at all times and people are required to clean up after their pets. To get there from the south, drive north on Hwy. 20. Just before Oak Harbor, turn left on Swantown Rd. and follow it about three miles.

Parks

Deception Pass State Park 41227 State Route 20 Oak Harbor WA   360-675-2417 (888-CAMPOUT (226-7688))
Rich in natural and cultural history, this 4,134 acre marine and camping park is home to a large variety of plant/animal/bird life, and offers ample land and water recreational opportunities. Some of the amenities/features include salt and freshwater shorelines, 3 lakes, 2 amphitheaters, 6 fire circles, interpretive activities/signage, a museum, hiking trails plus a 1.2 mile ADA hiking trail, and breath-taking viewing areas. Dogs of all sizes are allowed for no additional fee. Dogs must be under physical control, leashed, and cleaned up after at all times. Dogs are not allowed on designated swimming beaches.

Off-Leash Dog Parks

Clover Valley Dog Park Oak Harbor at Ault Field Rd Oak Harbor WA   360-321-4049
http://www.fetchparks.org
This two acre fenced dog park is located north of the city of Oak Harbor on Whidbey Island. The dog park is located next to the Clover Valley Baseball Park. From SR 20 head west about one mile on Ault Field Road to the park.
Oak Harbor Dog Park Technical Park at Goldie Rd Oak Harbor WA   360-321-4049
http://www.fetchparks.org
This one acre fenced dog park is located north of the city of Oak Harbor on Whidbey Island. From SR 20 head west on Ault Field Rd. Turn left on Goldie Rd and turn left on Technical Drive. Follow Technical Drive to the park.

Ocean Park

Accommodations

Charles Nelson Guest House 26205 Sandridge Road Ocean Park WA   360-665-3016 (888-862-9756)
http://www.charlesnelsonbandb.com
This B&B is within walking distance of the Pacific Ocean and features a view of Willapa Bay. There is a large field nearby for dog walking. There is a $25 one time pet fee.
Coastal Cottages of Ocean Park 1511 264th Place Ocean Park WA   360-665-4658 (800-200-0424)
The cottages are located in a quiet setting and have full kitchens and fireplaces. There is a $5 per day pet charge. There are no designated smoking or non-smoking rooms.

Campgrounds and RV Parks

Ocean Park Resort 25904 R Street Ocean Park WA   360-665-4585
http://www.opresort.com
Dogs of all sizes and numbers are allowed, and there are no additional pet fees. There is a $7 per night per pet additional fee for the motel, and only 2 dogs are allowed per room. Dogs must be leashed and cleaned up after. There are some breed restrictions. The camping and tent areas also allow dogs. There is a dog walk area at the campground.

Attractions

Willapa Bay Oyster House Interpretive Center 3311 275th Street Ocean Park WA   360-665-4547
This interpretive center offers the chronology of the 150 year oyster industry in this region. The walls of the center are covered with quotes, old photographs, and a 20 foot mural of the bay. There are many artifacts and tools of the oyster trade on display, including a 14 foot double-ended dinghy built in the late 1920's. This is also one of the few places to go down to the shores of the bay that is not on private property. Your dog is allowed at the center and on the grounds. Dogs must be under owner's control at all times, leashed, and cleaned up after. They are open from Memorial Day weekend through the last weekend in September.

Beaches

Pacific Pines State Park Highway 101 Ocean Park WA   360-902-8844
Fishing, crabbing, clamming and beachcombing are popular activities at this beach. Picnic tables and a restroom are available at this park. Dogs are allowed on the beach. They must be on a eight foot or less leash at all times and people are required to clean up after their pets. This park is located approximately one mile north of Ocean

Park. From north or south, take Hwy. 101 until you reach Ocean Park. Continue on Vernon St. until you reach 271st St.

Ocean Shores

Accommodations
The Polynesian Condominium Resort 615 Ocean Shores Blvd Ocean Shores WA   360-289-3361
There is a $15 per day fee for pets. Pets are allowed on the ground floor only.

Beaches
Damon Point State Park Point Brown Avenue Ocean Shores WA   360-902-8844
Located on the southeastern tip of the Ocean Shores Peninsula, this one mile long beach offers views of the Olympic Mountains, Mount Rainer, and Grays Harbor. Picnic tables are available at this park. Dogs are allowed on the beach. They must be on a eight foot or less leash at all times and people are required to clean up after their pets. To get there from From Hoquiam, take SR 109 and SR 115 to Point Brown Ave. in the town of Ocean Shores. Proceed south on Point Brown Ave. through town, approximately 4.5 miles. Just past the marina, turn left into park entrance.
Ocean City State Park State Route 115 Ocean Shores WA   360-902-8844
Beachcombing, clamming, surfing, bird watching, kite flying and winter storm watching are all popular activities at this beach. Picnic tables, restrooms, and campgrounds (including ADA campgrounds) are available at this park. Leashed dogs are allowed on the beach. Dogs are also allowed at the campgrounds. They must be on a eight foot or less leash at all times and people are required to clean up after their pets. This park is located on the coast one-and-a-half miles north of Ocean Shores on Hwy. 115. From Hoquiam, drive 16 miles west on SR 109, then turn south on SR 115 and drive 1.2 miles to the park.

Okanogan

Campgrounds and RV Parks
Okanogan National Forest 1240 South Second Avenue Okanogan WA   509-826-3275
http://www.fs.fed.us/r6/oka/
This forest of a million and a half acres has a variety of water and land recreation year round. Dogs are allowed at no additional fee. Dogs may not be left unattended, and they must be leashed and cleaned up after. Dogs are not allowed in the back country, and on many of the trails. Dogs must remain on paved areas or on marked trails. This campground is closed during the off-season. The camping and tent areas also allow dogs. There is a dog walk area at the campground. There are no electric or water hookups at the campground.

Olympia

Accommodations
Super 8 Lacey/Olympia Area 112 College St SE Lacey WA   360-459-8888 (800-800-8000)
Dogs of all sizes are allowed. There is a $10 per night pet fee per pet. Smoking and non-smoking rooms are available for pet rooms.
West Coast Inn 2300 Evergreen Park Drive Olympia WA   360-943-4000
There is a $45.00 one time pet fee.
Best Western Tumwater Inn 5188 Capitol Blvd Tumwater WA   360-956-1235 (800-780-7234)
Dogs of all sizes are allowed. There is a $10 per night pet fee per pet.
Comfort Inn 1620 74th Avenue SW Tumwater WA   360-352-0691 (877-424-6423)
Dogs up to 100 pounds are allowed. There is a $10 per night per room additional pet fee, and a pet policy to sign at check in. Dogs must be leashed, cleaned up after, and the Do Not Disturb sign put on the door if they are in the room alone. Dogs must be quiet, well behaved, and crated or removed for housekeeping.
Motel 6 - Tumwater - Olympia 400 West Lee Street Tumwater WA   360-754-7320 (800-466-8356)
One well-behaved family pet per room. Guest must notify front desk upon arrival. Guest is liable for any damages. In consideration of all guests, pets must never be left unattended in the guest rooms.

Campgrounds and RV Parks

Olympic National Forest 1835 Black Lk Blvd SW Olympia WA 360-956-23300
http://www.fs.fed.us/r6/olympic/
This park is a unique geographic province in that it contains 5 different major landscapes, and is home to an astounding diversity of plants, animals, and recreational pursuits. The campground at Round Creek is the only camp area that stays open year round. Dogs of all sizes are allowed at no additional fee. Dogs may not be left unattended, and they must be leashed and cleaned up after. Dogs are allowed on the trails. The camping and tent areas also allow dogs. There is a dog walk area at the campground. Dogs are allowed in the camping cabins. There are no electric or water hookups at the campground.

Stores
PetSmart Pet Store 719 Sleater-Kinney Rd SE Lacey WA 360-493-0228
Your licensed and well-behaved leashed dog is allowed in the store.
Petco Pet Store 1530 Black Lake Blvd Olympia WA 360-956-0698
Your licensed and well-behaved leashed dog is allowed in the store.

Olympic National Park

Attractions
Olympic National Park 600 East Park Avenue Port Angeles WA 360-565-3130
http://www.nps.gov/olym/
Pets are not permitted on park trails, meadows, beaches or in any undeveloped area of the park. There is one exception. Dogs are allowed on leash, during daytime hours only, on Kalaloch Beach along the Pacific Ocean and from Rialto Beach north to Ellen Creek. For those folks and dogs who want to hike on a trail, try the adjacent dog-friendly Olympic National Forest.

Parks
Olympic National Forest 1835 Black Lake Blvd. SW Olympia WA 360-956-2402
http://www.fs.fed.us/r6/olympic/
Leashed dogs are allowed on the national forest trails. Of particular interest is the Mt. Mueller Trail which offers great views of the Strait of Juan de Fuca and the mountains. Maps for this 13 mile loop trail and other trails can be picked up for free at a Forest Ranger Station including the one located at 551 Forks Avenue South, Forks, Washington.

Othello

Accommodations
Best Western Lincoln Inn 1020 East Cedar St. Othello WA 509-488-5671 (800-780-7234)
Dogs of all sizes are allowed. There is a $10.95 per night pet fee.

Parks
Columbia National Wildlife Refuge 735 E Main Street 24 Othello WA 509-488-2668
http://www.fws.gov/columbiarefuge/
This refuge of about 30,000 acres is located within the Columbia Basin of central Washington, and provides a variety of diverse environments that supply critical habitats for numerous species. To tour the refuge drive NW from Othello on McManamon Road, then turn North on Morgan Lake Road (the major north/south public road that takes you through the center of the refuge). There are maps available at the Main Street office, and at almost every parking area inside the refuge. Dogs are welcome, but they must be under owner's control and leashed at all times. Please bring supplies to clean up after your pet.

Otis Orchards

Campgrounds and RV Parks
Spokane KOA N 3025 Barker Road Otis Orchards WA 509-924-4722 (800-562-3309)
http://www.koa.com

Dogs of all sizes are allowed. There are no additional pet fees. Dogs may not be left unattended, can be on no more than a 6 foot leash, and must be cleaned up after. There are some breed restrictions. The camping and tent areas also allow dogs. There is a dog walk area at the campground. Dogs are allowed in the camping cabins.

Pacific Beach

Accommodations
Pacific Beach Inn 12 First Street S Pacific Beach WA   360-276-4433
http://www.pbinn.com/main_page.htm
Offering 12 intimate rooms, most with a full ocean view, this great get-a-way sits on the edge of one of the most majestic beaches in the world. Dogs of all sizes are allowed for an additional fee of $10 per night per pet. Dogs may not be left alone in the room at any time, and they must be leashed and cleaned up after.
Sand Dollar Inn & Cottages 56 Central Avenue Pacific Beach WA   360-276-4525
http://www.sanddollarinn.net
This inn and cottages has one and two bedroom pet friendly units. Some of the units have kitchens. Some have fenced yards or a dog kennel. There is a $10 per night pet fee.
Sandpiper Ocean Beach Resort 4159 State Route 109 Pacific Beach WA   360-276-4580
Thanks to one of our readers who writes "A great place on the Washington Coast with miles of sand beach to run." There is a $13 per day pet fee. All rooms are non-smoking.
Pacific Beach Inn 12 First Street South Pacific Beach WA   360-276-4433
Dogs of all sizes are allowed. There is a $10 per night per pet additional fee.

Campgrounds and RV Parks
Pacific Beach State Park On Hwy 109 Pacific Beach WA   360-276-4297 (888-CAMPOUT (226-7688))
This 10 acre camping park, with 2,300 feet of ocean shoreline, offers a variety of land and water recreation. Dogs of all sizes are allowed at no additional fee. Dogs may not be left unattended, and they must be quiet, well behaved, be on no more than an 8 foot leash, and be cleaned up after. Dogs are not allowed in public swim areas or buildings. Dogs are allowed on the trails. This campground is closed during the off-season. The camping and tent areas also allow dogs. There is a dog walk area at the campground.

Beaches
Pacific Beach State Park State Route 109 Pacific Beach WA   360-902-8844
The beach is the focal point at this 10 acre state park. This sandy ocean beach is great for beachcombing, wildlife watching, windy walks and kite flying. Picnic tables, restrooms (including an ADA restroom), and campgrounds (some are ADA accessible) are available at this park. Leashed dogs are allowed on the beach. Dogs are also allowed in the campgrounds. They must be on a eight foot or less leash at all times and people are required to clean up after their pets. This park is located 15 miles north of Ocean Shores, off SR 109. From Hoquiam, follow SR 109, 30 miles northwest to the town of Pacific Beach. The park is located in town.

Pasco

Accommodations
Best Western Pasco Inn Northeast Corner St Andrews Loop Pasco WA   509-543-7722 (800-780-7234)
Dogs of all sizes are allowed. There is a $10 per night per pet fee. Dogs are not allowed to be left alone in the room.
Red Lion 2525 N 20th Avenue Pasco WA   509-547-0701
Dogs of all sizes are allowed. There are no additional pet fees, and dogs are not allowed to be left alone in the room.
Sleep Inn 9930 Bedford Street Pasco WA   509-545-9554 (877-424-6423)
Dogs of all sizes are allowed. There is a $10 (plus tax) per night additional fee for 1 dog, and a $15 per night (plus tax) additional fee for two dogs. Three dogs may be allowed if all the dogs are under 20 pounds. Dogs must be leashed, cleaned up after, crated when left alone in the room, and the Do Not Disturb sign put on the door and a contact number left with the front desk is they are in the room alone.

Campgrounds and RV Parks
Sandy Heights RV Park 8801 St Thomas Drive Pasco WA   877-894-1357

Dogs of all sizes are allowed. There are no additional pet fees. Dogs must be leashed and cleaned up after. There are some breed restrictions. There is a dog walk area at the campground.

Paterson

Attractions
Columbia Crest Winery Columbia Crest Drive Paterson WA 509-875-2061
http://www.columbia-crest.com/
Open 7 days a week (except holidays), this winery offers complimentary wine tasting and self guided tours of the winery. Well behaved dogs are welcome at the winery, but they are not allowed in buildings or fields. Dogs must be leashed and cleaned up after.

Pendleton

Campgrounds and RV Parks
Mountain View RV Park 1375 SE 3rd Street Pendleton WA 866-302-3311
http://www.nwfamilyrvresorts.com
Dogs of all sizes are allowed. There are no additional pet fees. Dogs must be leashed and cleaned up after. There are some breed restrictions. The camping and tent areas also allow dogs. There is a dog walk area at the campground.

Port Angeles

Accommodations
Red Lion 221 N Lincoln Port Angeles WA 360-452-9215
Dogs of all sizes are allowed. There is a pet policy to sign at check in and there are no additional fees.
Super 8 Port Angeles 2104 E 1st Street Port Angeles WA 360-452-8401 (800-800-8000)
Dogs of all sizes are allowed. There is a $10 one time per pet fee per visit. Smoking and non-smoking rooms are available for pet rooms.

Campgrounds and RV Parks
Log Cabin Resort 3183E Beach Road Port Angeles WA 360-928-3325
http://www.logcabinresort.net/home.htm
This resort style park offers spectacular scenery, a variety of accommodations as well as recreational pursuits. Dogs of all sizes are allowed at no additional fee for RV sites, however there is a $10(plus tax)per night per pet additional fee for the rustic cabins. Dogs may not be left unattended, and they must be leashed and cleaned up after. Dogs are not allowed on the trails in the Olympic National Forest area. There is a dog walk area at the campground. Dogs are allowed in the camping cabins.
Olympia National Park 600 East Park Avenue Port Angeles WA 360-452-4501
http://www.nps.gov/olym/
From rainforest to glacier capped mountains, this forest's diverse and impressive eco-system is home to 8 plants and 15 animals that are not found anywhere else on earth. It also provides an abundant variety of year round recreational pursuits. Dogs of all sizes are allowed at no additional fee. Dogs may not be left unattended, and they must be leashed and cleaned up after. Dogs are allowed in the camp areas and the parking lot at Hurricane Ridge; dogs are not allowed on the trails. The camping and tent areas also allow dogs. There is a dog walk area at the campground. There are no electric or water hookups at the campground.
Port Angeles/Swquim KOA 80 O'Brien Road Port Angeles WA 360-457-5916 (800-562-7558)
http://www.portangeleskoa.com
Dogs of all sizes are allowed. There are no additional pet fees. Dogs may not be left unattended, must be on no more than a 6 foot leash, and cleaned up after. There are some breed restrictions. This RV park is closed during the off-season. The camping and tent areas also allow dogs. There is a dog walk area at the campground.

Beaches
Kalaloch Beach Olympic National Park Port Angeles WA 360-962-2283
http://www.nps.gov/olym/

Dogs are allowed on leash, during daytime hours only, on Kalaloch Beach along the Pacific Ocean and from Rialto Beach north to Ellen Creek. These beaches are in Olympic National Park, but please note that pets are not permitted on this national park's trails, meadows, beaches (except Kalaloch and Rialto beaches) or in any undeveloped area of the park. For those folks and dogs who want to hike on a trail, try the adjacent dog-friendly Olympic National Forest. Kalaloch Beach is located off Highway 101 in Olympic National Park.

Port Orchard

Accommodations
Days Inn Port Orchard 220 Bravo Terrace Port Orchard WA   360-895-7818 (800-329-7466)
Dogs of all sizes are allowed. There is a $10 per night pet fee per pet.
Holiday Inn Express 1121 Bay Street Port Orchard WA   360-895-2666 (877-270-6405)
Dogs of all sizes are allowed. There is a $15 one time additional pet fee.

Parks
Howe Farm Historic Park and Off-Leash Dog Area Long Lake Rd at Sedgwick Rd Port Orchard WA   360-337-5350
http://www.visitkitsap.com/kitsap.asp
Howe Farm County Park is a Historic Farm with Walking Trails. Dogs are allowed on leash at outside areas of the park. In addition, there is a 5.5 acre off-leash area. This area is not fenced and dogs should be under voice control and well-behaved. To get to Howe Farm take Hwy 16 to Sedgwick. Head east on Sedgwick for three miles to Long Lake Road. Turn left on Long Lake Rd to the park.

Off-Leash Dog Parks
Howe Farm Historic Park and Off-Leash Dog Area Long Lake Rd at Sedgwick Rd Port Orchard WA   360-337-5350
http://www.visitkitsap.com/kitsap.asp
Howe Farm County Park is a Historic Farm with Walking Trails. Dogs are allowed on leash at outside areas of the park. In addition, there is a 5.5 acre off-leash area. This area is not fenced and dogs should be under voice control and well-behaved. To get to Howe Farm take Hwy 16 to Sedgwick. Head east on Sedgwick for three miles to Long Lake Road. Turn left on Long Lake Rd to the park.

Port Townsend

Campgrounds and RV Parks
Point Hudson Resort Marina and RV Park 103 Hudson Port Townsend WA   360-385-2828
http://www.portofpt.com
Dogs of all sizes are allowed. There are no additional pet fees. Dogs must be leashed and cleaned up after. Dogs are allowed to go to the beach, and if you bring them in the office they usually have doggy treats on hand. There is a dog walk area at the campground. There are special amenities given to dogs at this campground.

Attractions
Puget Sound Express/Point Hudson Marina 227 Jackson Street Port Townsend WA   360-385-5288
http://www.pugetsoundexpress.com/
P.S. Express offers a variety of fun and interesting guided tours for whale watching and general sightseeing around the Olympic Peninsula and San Juan Islands. Dogs are allowed to go on some of the tours, but only if they already have their doggy sea-legs. Dogs must be boat and marine-life comfortable as sometimes the whales are close. There is a $10 additional fee for the dog. Dogs must be well behaved, leashed, and please bring supplies to clean up after your pet.
TOP 200 PLACE Sidewalk Tours Old City Hall Port Townsend WA   360-385-1967
You can enjoy these expertly guided living history walking tours of this culturally rich area with your pooch. Dogs usually take the tour of the waterfront where they get a few pit stops at the water along the way. Tours begin at the Old City Hall on Water and Madison Streets and are by appointment. Dogs must be friendly, leashed, and please bring supplies to clean up after your pet when in town.

Prosser

Campgrounds and RV Parks
Wine Country RV Park 330 Merlot Drive Prosser WA   800-726-4969
http://www.winecountryrvpark.com
Dogs of all sizes are allowed. There are no additional pet fees. Dogs must be quiet, well behaved, leashed, and cleaned up after. No stakes are allowed put in the ground to tie your pet to. Dogs are allowed to run in the field across the street unleashed as long as there is control by the owner. The camping and tent areas also allow dogs. There is a dog walk area at the campground.

Pullman

Accommodations
Holiday Inn Express 1190 SE Bishop Blvd Pullman WA   509-334-4437 (877-270-6405)
There are no additional pet fees. Pets are allowed in the first floor rooms.
Quality Inn Paradise Creek SE 1400 Bishop Blvd Pullman WA 509-332-0500 (877-424-6423)
Dogs of all sizes are allowed. There are no additional pet fees for one of the 4 pet friendly rooms, and a $35 one time additional pet fee per room for non-pet friendly rooms. There is a pet policy to sign at check in. Dogs must be quiet, well behaved, leashed, cleaned up after, and a contact number left with the front desk if they are in the room alone.

Puyallup

Accommodations
Best Western Park Plaza 620 South Hill Park Dr Puyallup WA   253-848-1500 (800-780-7234)
Dogs of all sizes are allowed. There is a $25 per room pet fee.
Holiday Inn Express & Suites 812 South Hill Park Drive Puyallup WA   253-848-4900 (877-270-6405)
Dogs of all sizes are allowed. There is a $25 one time pet fee.

Stores
PetSmart Pet Store 120 31st Ave Puyallup WA   253-845-8988
Your licensed and well-behaved leashed dog is allowed in the store.
Petco Pet Store 3717 South Meridian St Puyallup WA   253-446-1501
Your licensed and well-behaved leashed dog is allowed in the store.

Renton

Stores
Petco Pet Store 10583 SE Carr Rd Renton WA   425-271-8347
Your licensed and well-behaved leashed dog is allowed in the store.

Richland

Accommodations
Days Inn Richland 615 Jadwin Ave Richland WA   509-943-4611 (800-329-7466)
Dogs of all sizes are allowed. There is a $10 per night pet fee per pet.
Holiday Inn Express Hotel and Suites 1970 Center Parkway Richland WA   509-737-8000 (877-270-6405)
Dogs of all sizes are allowed. There is a $10 per night pet fee per pet. Only non-smoking rooms are used for pets.

Motel 6 - Richland - Kennewick 1751 Fowler Street Richland WA   509-783-1250 (800-466-8356)
One well-behaved family pet per room. Guest must notify front desk upon arrival. Guest is liable for any damages. In consideration of all guests, pets must never be left unattended in the guest rooms.

Campgrounds and RV Parks
Horn Rapids RV Resort 2640 Kings Gate Way Richland WA   509-375-9913
http://www.hornrapidsrvresort.com
Dogs of all sizes are allowed. There are no additional pet fees. Dogs must be leashed and cleaned up after. There is a dog run and a dog bathing area on site. There is a dog walk area at the campground.

Ritzville

Accommodations
La Quinta Inn Ritzville 1513 Smitty's Blvd. Ritzville WA   509-659-1007 (800-531-5900)
Dogs of all sizes are allowed. There are no additional pet fees. Dogs must be quiet, well behaved, leashed and cleaned up after. Dogs must be walked at the designated pet walk area, and they are not allowed in the lobby during breakfast hours.

Rochester

Campgrounds and RV Parks
Outback RV Park 19100 Huntington Rochester WA   360-273-0585
http://www.outbackrvpark.com
Dogs of all sizes are allowed. There are no additional pet fees. Dogs may not be left unattended at any time, or tied up outside alone. Dogs must be leashed and cleaned up after. There is a dog walk area at the campground.

Ruston

Attractions
TOP 200 PLACE **Fort Nisqually** 5400 N Pearl Street Ruston WA   253-591-5339
http://www.fortnisqually.org/
Located in Point Defiance Park, this living history museum recreates life in the early 1800's in the first European settlement on Puget Sound. Workers from all over came to this area for the fur trade and brought with them quite a diverse trade and agricultural market. The fort also plays host to other events during the year, and their hours vary with the seasons. Dogs are welcome at the park, and at this mostly outdoor museum. Dogs are not allowed to go inside any of the buildings, and they must be leashed and cleaned up after at all times.

Parks
Point Defiance Park 5400 N Pearl Street Ruston WA   253-305-1016
Spectacular views, saltwater beaches, and a natural forest are only a few of the features at this 702 acre park. Other features include a zoo and aquarium, gardens, hiking trails, a living history museum of the 1st fort here (Fort Nisqually), special events and educational programs, a marina, a family picnic and playground area, and more. Dogs are allowed at this park for no additional fee. They must be leashed and cleaned up after at all times. Dogs are allowed throughout the park with the exception of the zoo area.

San Juan Island

Accommodations
Blair House Bed and Breakfast 345 Blair Street Friday Harbor WA   360-378-5907 (800-899-3030)
http://www.friday-harbor.net/blair/
Blair House is located in Friday Harbor, Washington on San Juan Island, just five short blocks from the ferry

landing. The two acre grounds are wooded and landscaped. The Blair House Cottage is 800 square feet of private living where you, your children and your pets are welcome. You will need to take a car ferry to the island.
The Inn at Friday Harbor   Friday Harbor WA   360-378-4000 (800-752-5752)
http://www.theinns.com/
There is a $50.00 one time pet fee. You need to take a car ferry to the island.

Campgrounds and RV Parks

Lakedale Resort 4313 Roche Harbor Road Friday Harbor WA   360-378-2350
http://www.lakedale.com
Dogs of all sizes are allowed. There is a $2 per night per pet additional fee for tent or RV sites. There is a $20 per night per pet additional fee for the lodge, however, depending on size and number, the fee for the lodge is flexible. Dogs may not be left unattended, and they must be quiet, well behaved, leashed, and cleaned up after. A ferry from Anacortes off I 5, or other ferries in the area will transport your pet on the car deck only. The camping and tent areas also allow dogs. There is a dog walk area at the campground. Dogs are allowed in the camping cabins.
San Juan Island National Historical Park 4668 Cattle Point Road-Visitor Center Friday Harbor WA   360-378-2240
http://www.nps.gov/sajh/
This scenic park commemorates the peaceful resolution of the 19th century boundary dispute between the US and Great Britain. It has become a popular educational, historical, and recreational destination offering many features and activities-even whale watching. Dogs are allowed throughout the park and on the trails. Dogs must be well behaved, leashed, and cleaned up after. There is a dog walk area at the campground.

Attractions

TOP 200 PLACE San Juan Island National Historic Park 125 Spring Street Friday Harbor WA   360-378-2902
http://www.nps.gov/sajh/
Leashed dogs are welcome on the hiking trails. Some of the trails are self-guided tours of the area and buildings. Dogs on leash are also allowed at South Beach, which is located at the American Camp. Dogs are not allowed inside the Visitor's Center.

Beaches

South Beach 125 Spring Street Friday Harbor WA   360-378-2902
http://www.nps.gov/sajh/
Dogs on leash are allowed at South Beach, which is located at the American Camp in the San Juan Island National Historic Park.

Parks

San Juan Island National Historical Park 4668 Cattle Point Road-Visitor Center Friday Harbor WA   360-378-2240
http://www.nps.gov/sajh/
This scenic park commemorates the peaceful resolution of the 19th century boundary dispute between the US and Great Britain. It has become a popular educational, historical, and recreational destination offering many features and activities-even whale watching. Dogs are allowed throughout the park and on the trails. Dogs must be well behaved, leashed, and cleaned up after.

Outdoor Restaurants

Friday's Crabhouse 65 Front Street Friday Harbor WA   360-378-8801
This eatery is located just off the ferry landing, and there is a patio outside where you and your pooch can take a break. You can access the patio from outside, and they provide service to your table. Dogs must be well behaved, leashed, and cleaned up after.
SJ Coffee Roasting Company 18 Cannery Landing Friday Harbor WA   360-378-44431
Located next to the ferry landing, this coffee shop also offers additional treats. Outside tables are offered for guests, and your pet may join you there. Dogs must be well behaved, leashed, and cleaned up after.
Vic's Driftwood Drive In 25 2nd Street Friday Harbor WA   360-378-VICS (8427)
Good inexpensive food for breakfast, lunch, and dinner, and they offer outdoor patio service. Dogs are allowed at the outside tables. They must be well behaved, leashed, and please clean up after your pet.

Seattle

Accommodations

Alexis Hotel 1007 First Avenue Seattle WA   206-624-4844
http://www.alexishotel.com/
Well-behaved dogs up to 200 pounds are welcome at this pet-friendly hotel. The luxury boutique hotel offers both rooms and suites. Hotel amenities include complimentary evening wine service, 24 hour room service and an on-site fitness room. This hotel is located near the historic Pioneer Square and Pike's Place Market. There are no pet fees, just sign a pet liability form.
Best Western Executive Inn 200 Taylor Ave N Seattle WA   206-448-9444 (800-780-7234)
Only 1 pet up to 50 pounds is allowed. There is a $35 one time pet fee. The entire hotel is non-smoking.
Crowne Plaza Downtown 1113 Sixth Avenue Seattle WA   206-464-1980 (877-270-6405)
http://www.basshotels.com/holiday-inn
Well-behaved dogs of all sizes are welcome. There is a $50 one time per stay pet fee and you will need to sign a pet waiver. Pets are allowed in non-smoking and smoking rooms. A dog-friendly park is located nearby.
Doubletree 18740 International Blvd Seattle WA   206-246-8600
Dogs of all sizes are allowed. There are no additional pet fees and pet rooms are located on the 1st floor.
Holiday Inn Express Hotel & Suites 19621 International Blvd Seattle WA   206-824-3200 (877-270-6405)
Dogs of all sizes are allowed. There is a $50 one time additional pet fee. There is a $75 refundable pet deposit.
Hotel Monaco Seattle 1101 4th Avenue Seattle WA   206-621-1770
http://www.monaco-seattle.com/
Well-behaved dogs of all sizes are welcome at this pet-friendly hotel. The luxury boutique hotel offers both rooms and suites. Hotel amenities include complimentary evening wine service, complimentary high speed Internet access in all guest rooms, 24 hour room service and a 24 hour on-site fitness room. There are no pet fees, just sign a pet liability form.
Hotel Vintage Park 1100 Fifth Avenue Seattle WA   206-624-8000
http://www.hotelvintagepark.com/
Well-behaved dogs of all sizes are welcome at this pet-friendly hotel. The luxury boutique hotel offers both rooms and suites. Hotel amenities include complimentary evening wine service, complimentary high speed Internet access, and 24 hour room service. There are no pet fees, just sign a pet liability form.
La Quinta Inn & Suites Seattle Downtown 2224 8th Avenue Seattle WA   206-624-6820 (800-531-5900)
Dogs of all sizes are allowed. There are no additional pet fees. Dogs may not be left unattended, and they must be leashed and cleaned up after.
La Quinta Inn Seattle Sea-Tac 2824 S. 188th St. Seattle WA   206-241-5211 (800-531-5900)
Dogs of all sizes are allowed. There are no additional pet fees. Dogs must be leashed, cleaned up after, and attended to or removed for housekeeping.
Motel 6 - Seattle Sea - Tac Airport South 18900 47th Avenue South Seattle WA   206-241-1648 (800-466-8356)
One well-behaved dog up to about 75 pounds is allowed. There are no additional pet fees.
Motel 6 - Seattle Airport 16500 Pacific Highway South Seattle WA   206-246-4101 (800-466-8356)
One well-behaved family pet per room. Guest must notify front desk upon arrival. Guest is liable for any damages. In consideration of all guests, pets must never be left unattended in the guest rooms.
Motel 6 - Seattle South 20651 Military Road Seattle WA   206-824-9902 (800-466-8356)
One well-behaved family pet per room. Guest must notify front desk upon arrival. Guest is liable for any damages. In consideration of all guests, pets must never be left unattended in the guest rooms.
Pensione Nichols Bed and Breakfast 1923 1st Avenue Seattle WA   206-441-7125 (800-440-7125)
http://www.seattle-bed-breakfast.com
Thanks to one of our readers who writes: "A charming and very dog-friendly place to stay in downtown Seattle." Large dogs are allowed to stay here if they are well-behaved. This B&B also requires that you do not leave your dog in the room alone. The Pensione Nichols is the only bed-and-breakfast located in the retail and entertainment core of downtown Seattle. Housed in a remodeled, turn-of-the-century building in the historic Smith Block, Pensione Nichols overlooks the Pike Place Market. This B&B has 10 guest rooms and suites (the suites have private bathrooms). Rates are approximately $75 (guest rooms) to $175 (suites).During the summer, there is a 2 night minimum.
Quality Inn and Suites 225 Aurora Avenue North Seattle WA   206-728-7666 (877-424-6423)
Dogs off all sizes are allowed. There is a $25 one time additional fee per pet. Dogs may not be left alone in the room, and they must be leashed and cleaned up after.
Red Lion 18220 International Blvd Seattle WA   206-246-5535
Dogs of all sizes are allowed. There is a $10 per night per room additional pet fee.
Red Lion 11244 Pacific Highway S Seattle WA   206-762-0300
Dogs of all sizes are allowed. There is a $35 deposit, $15 of which is refundable per pet, and a pet policy to sign at check in.
Red Roof Inn - SEATTLE - AIRPORT 16838 International Boulevard Seattle WA   206-248-0901 (800-RED-ROOF)

One well-behaved family pet per room. Guest must notify front desk upon arrival. Guest is liable for any damages. In consideration of all guests, pets must never be left unattended in the guest rooms.

Residence Inn by Marriott 800 Fairview Avenue North Seattle WA 206-624-6000
Well behaved dogs of all sizes are allowed. There is a $10 per night per pet fee and a pet policy to sign at check in.

Residence Inn by Marriott 16201 W Valley Highway Seattle WA 425-226-5500
Dogs of all sizes are allowed. There is a $75 one time fee and a pet policy to sign at check in.

Seattle Pacific Hotel 325 Aurora Avenue N Seattle WA 206-441-0400 (888-451-0400)
http://www.seattlepacifichotel.com/
Located just minutes from some of Seattle's most impressive sites; this hotel offers 59 nicely-appointed rooms with many in-room amenities, a free continental breakfast, and a seasonal outdoor pool and Jacuzzi. Dogs of all sizes are allowed. There is a $15 per night per pet additional fee for dogs under 15 pounds, and a $25 per night per pet additional fee for dogs over 15 pounds. Dogs must be leashed, cleaned up after, and crated or removed for housekeeping.

Sheraton Seattle Hotel 1400 6th Ave. Seattle WA 206-621-9000 (888-625-5144)
Dogs up to 80 pounds are allowed. There are no additional pet fees. Dogs are not allowed to be left alone in the room.

Super 8 Seattle/Sea-Tac Intl Arpt 3100 S 192nd Seattle WA 206-433-8188 (800-800-8000)
Dogs of all sizes are allowed. There is a $25 returnable deposit required per room. Smoking and non-smoking rooms are available for pet rooms.

University Inn 4140 Roosevelt Way NE Seattle WA 206-632-5055
Dogs only are allowed and up to 80 pounds. There is a $20 per night per room fee and a pet policy to sign at check in. Dogs are not to be left unattended.

Vagabond Inn by the Space Needle 325 Aurora Ave N Seattle WA 206-441-0400
This motel is located just several blocks from the Space Needle, the waterfront and Washington St. Convention Center. The motel has a heated swimming pool and jacuzzi, 24 hour cable television and more. There is a $10 per day pet charge

W Seattle 1112 4th Avenue Seattle WA 206-264-6000
Dogs of all sizes are allowed. There is a $20 per night pet fee per pet. Dogs are not allowed to be left alone in the room.

Campgrounds and RV Parks

Blake Island State Park P.O. Box 42650 Seattle WA 360-731-8330
A highlight of this 475 acre marine-camping park, reachable only by tour or private boat, is its 5 mile sandy shoreline offering outstanding views of the Olympic Mountains, volcanoes, and the Seattle skyline. In addition to offering a rich history, features/amenities include interpretive trails and activities, miles of hiking trails, a host of land and water recreation, and an impressive variety of plant, animal, and marine life. The park is also home to Tillicum Village where you can enjoy a Northwest Indian dining and cultural experience. Dogs of all sizes are allowed for no additional fee around the park and the village (except for the longhouse). Dogs must be leashed at all times, and cleaned up after. They are not allowed on designated swimming beaches. Camping is on a first come first served basis. There are barbecue grills located in the day use area. They offer a dump station, restrooms (one ADA), and a shower area. There are specific camp sites on the west end of the island for canoers and kayakers, as well as some additional primitive sites. The camping and tent areas also allow dogs. There is a dog walk area at the campground. There are no electric or water hookups at the campgrounds.

Blue Sky RV Park 9002 302nd Avenue SE Seattle WA 425-222-7910
http://www.blueskypreston.com
Dogs of all sizes are allowed. There are no additional pet fees. Dogs may not be left tied up outside alone, and must be leashed and cleaned up after. There is a dog walk area at the campground.

Transportation Systems

King County Metro Regional Seattle WA 206-553-3000
http://transit.metrokc.gov
Both small and large dogs are allowed on the street cars and buses. Small dogs that fit in their owner's lap ride for free. Large dogs are charged the same fare as their owner and should not occupy a seat. One large dog per bus is allowed. Large dogs should ride on the floor of the bus, preferably under the seat. It is up to the driver as to whether or not your dog will be allowed if you have a very large dog, if there is another animal already onboard or if the bus or street car is excessively crowded. Dogs must be leashed.

Washington State Ferries Pier 52 Seattle WA 206-464-6400
http://www.wsdot.wa.gov/ferries/
The Washington State Ferries is the nation's largest ferry system and the state's number one tourist attraction. This ferry service offers many ferry routes, including Seattle to Bainbridge Island, Seattle to Bremerton, Edmonds to Kingston, Anacortes to Friday Harbor (San Juan Islands), and Anacortes to Sidney in British Columbia, Canada. Please see our Washington State Ferry listing in our Victoria, British Columbia, Canada City Guide for

customs requirements for both people and dogs. While leashed dogs are allowed on the ferry routes mentioned above, the following pet regulations apply. On the newer ferries that have outside stairwells, dogs are allowed on the car deck and on the outdoor decks above the car deck. If the ferry has indoor stairwells, dogs are only allowed on the deck where they boarded the ferry. For example, if your dog comes onto the ferry in your car, he or she has to remain on the car deck. If you walk onto the ferry with your dog, your pooch is allowed on the outside deck where you boarded but cannot go onto other decks. In cases where your pet has to remain on the car deck, you can venture to the above decks without your pet to get food at the snack bars. However, the ferry system recommends in general that you stay with your pooch in the car. For any of the ferries, dogs are not allowed inside the ferry terminals. Ferry prices for people and autos are determined by the route and peak times, but in general tickets for people can start under $10 round trip, and more for autos. Dogs ride free!

Attractions

Carl English Jr Botanical Garden 3015 NW 54th Street Ballard WA   206-783-7059
This beautiful garden is located at the Lake Washington Ship Canal and Ballard Locks. After the construction of the locks, this barren land was transformed by our first horticulturist, Carl English Jr. into a spectacular botanical garden. He combined elegant English landscaping style with more than 570 species and 1,500 varieties of flowers/plants from around the world. Dogs are allowed throughout the park, but neither dogs nor people are allowed off the designated paths. They especially want dogs to stay away from the flower beds. Dogs must be leashed and cleaned up after at all times.

Kenmore Air Seaplanes 6321 Northeast 175th Kenmore WA   800-543-9595
http://www.kenmoreair.com/seaplanes.html
Well-behaved, leashed dogs are allowed on these seaplanes. Small dogs can sit on your lap. For larger dogs, you will need to purchase an extra seat. To board the seaplanes, you will need to walk up a step ladder. Since seaplanes are usually noisier inside than large commercial airplanes, the staff or pilot usually hands out earplugs to help keep the noise down. Seaplanes fly lower than commercial airliners and therefore you are able to see a lot more sights than if you where flying at over at 30,000 feet. They offer many scheduled flight routes to or from Seattle including the San Juan Islands, Oak Harbor, Victoria and Vancouver. Or you and your pooch can try the 20 minute sightseeing tour of Seattle. Charter packages are also available. For trips to or from Canada, customs regulations apply. You can hop aboard their seaplanes at the Kenmore Air Harbor at 6321 N 175th Street in Kenmore, or at the Lake Union Terminal at 950 Westlake Avenue in Seattle.

Blake Island Adventure Cruise/Tillicum Village 2992 SW Avalon Way Seattle WA   206-933-8600
http://www.tillicumvillage.com/
Located in the Blake Island State Park, this adventure company also offers ferry service from Pier 55 to the island. They offer tours around the island, entertainment, educational programs, Native American artist and performers, and Whole Chinook salmon cooked Northwest Coast Indian style around an open alder-wood fire. The dinners are served buffet style in a huge cedar longhouse. Dogs are allowed in the village and the park, but they are not allowed in the longhouse. Dogs are allowed to ferry over on the back deck of the boat, but they are not allowed on the island tours. Dogs must be leashed and cleaned up after at all times.

Emerald Country Carriages Piers 55-56 Seattle WA   425-868-0621
Emerald Country Carriages allows well-behaved dogs on their elegant horse and carriage rides. They offer both open and closed carriages which seat up to six. The standard tour includes the waterfront and Pioneer Square. You can catch one of their white and burgundy carriages on the waterfront, between Piers 55 and 56. The cost is about $35 for a standard 30 minute tour and an extra $10 if you make a reservation in advance.

TOP 200 PLACE **Fun Forest Amusement Park** 305 Harrison Street Seattle WA   206-728-1586
http://www.funforest.com
This amusement park sits at the base of the Seattle Space needle and was originally the midway for the 1962 World's Fair. In addition to the midway and a host of thrill rides, there is an entertainment pavilion and the Seattle Center House, a vast food court. Days and hours of operation vary with the seasons. There is no admission fee, and dogs are welcome throughout the park, with the exception of the Center House food court. Dogs must be well behaved, and leashed and cleaned up after at all times.

Kubota Garden 9817 55th Avenue S Seattle WA   206-684-4584
http://www.kubota.org/
The breathtaking beauty of these gardens gives way to a deep appreciation for the garden artists (the Kabota family) who worked to make this lush environment. Among the streams, waterfalls, ponds, rock outcroppings, and luxuriant plant life, are the paths that take you to the next amazing setting. There are a couple of picnic tables, and a large lawn area, but there is no drinking water. Dogs are allowed here, but they must be leashed and cleaned up after at all times, and please bring your own clean up supplies for your pet.

Lake Washington Ship Canal and Ballard Locks 3015 NW 54th St. Seattle WA   206-783-7059
Visitors come here to watch boats, migrating salmon, or to stroll through the spectacular botanical gardens that cover 7 acres and contains more than 500 species of plant life. A rare treat here are the underground windows that offer a close up view of migrating salmon and steelhead. There are free guided tours, a theater program, interpretive exhibits, museum/visitor center, cultural/historic sites, and plenty of hiking areas. Dogs are allowed throughout the park, but neither dogs nor people are allowed off the designated paths. They especially want dogs to stay away from the flower beds. Dogs must be leashed and cleaned up after at all times.

Pioneer Square First Street and Yesler Way Seattle WA
Pioneer Square is Seattle's oldest neighborhood. It is preserved as a National Historic District. Please note that dogs are not allowed on the Underground Tour at Pioneer Square. In this district, you can stroll through the area and see the historic buildings, or better yet, take an elegant horse and carriage ride from Emerald Country Carriages.

Seattle Center Mercer Street and Broad St. Seattle WA   206-684-7200
http://www.seattlecenter.com/
The Seattle Center is a 74 acre urban park which was home to the 1962 World Fair. While your pooch cannot go into the buildings, he or she is allowed to walk around the center with you and spot out several points of interest. The famed Seattle Space Needle resides at the center and is always a good photo opportunity. You and your pooch can also visit the Sculpture Garden and watch jugglers, musicians, face painters, and more. Pets must be on leash. If you have a doggie that happens to be under 20 pounds, you can even carry him or her on the Seattle Monorail.

Washington Park Arboretum 4300 Arboretum Drive E Seattle WA   206-543-8800
http://depts.washington.edu/wpa/
Featuring over 70 years of stewardship and 230 acres of beautifully groomed gardens, the arboretum also offers facility rentals, educational programs, and constantly changing colors throughout the year. They are open dawn to dusk 7 days a week (visitor center from 10 am to 4 pm) and admission is free. Dogs of all sizes are welcome. It is important to keep your pet on the paths, and they must be leashed and cleaned up after at all times.

Woodland Park Rose Garden 700 N 50th Street Seattle WA   206-684-4863
Featuring over 70 years of stewardship and 230 acres of beautifully groomed gardens, the arboretum also offers facility rentals, educational programs, and constantly changing colors throughout the year. This garden is also a certified American Rose Test Garden, one of only 24 in the country. They are open dawn to dusk 7 days a week (visitor center from 10 am to 4 pm) and admission is free. Dogs of all sizes are welcome. It is important to keep your pet on the paths, and they must be leashed and cleaned up after at all times.

Stores

PetSmart Pet Store 13000 Aurora Ave N Seattle WA   206-361-1634
Your licensed and well-behaved leashed dog is allowed in the store.
Petco Pet Store 809 NE 45th St Seattle WA   206-548-1400
Your licensed and well-behaved leashed dog is allowed in the store.
Petco Pet Store 8728 Holman Rd NW Seattle WA   206-784-0524
Your licensed and well-behaved leashed dog is allowed in the store.
Petco Pet Store 4732 California Avenue SW Seattle WA   206-932-9003
Your licensed and well-behaved leashed dog is allowed in the store.
Petco Pet Store 1241 North 205th Seattle WA   206-546-1234
Your licensed and well-behaved leashed dog is allowed in the store.
Three Dog Bakery 1408 1st Avenue Seattle WA   206-364-9999
You can purchase all kinds of fresh home-made treats for your pooch at this dog cookie bakery.
Three Dog Bakery 1408 1st Avenue Seattle WA   206-364-9999
http://www.threedog.com
Three Dog Bakery provides cookies and snacks for your dog as well as some boutique items. You well-behaved, leashed dog is welcome.

Beaches

TOP 200 PLACE **Sand Point Magnuson Park Dog Off-Leash Beach and Area** 7400 Sand Point Way NE Seattle WA   206-684-4075
This leash free dog park covers about 9 acres and is the biggest fully fenced off-leash park in Seattle. It also offers an access point to the lake where your pooch is welcome to take a dip in the fresh lake water. To find the dog park, take Sand Point Way Northeast and enter the park at Northeast 74th Street. Go straight and park near the playground and sports fields. The main gate to the off-leash area is located at the southeast corner of the main parking lot. Dogs must be leashed until you enter the off-leash area.

Parks

Blake Island State Park P.O. Box 42650 Seattle WA   360-731-8330
A highlight of this 475 acre marine-camping park, reachable only by tour or private boat, is its 5 mile sandy shoreline offering outstanding views of the Olympic Mountains, volcanoes, and the Seattle skyline. In addition to offering a rich history, features/amenities include interpretive trails and activities, miles of hiking trails, a host of land and water recreation, and an impressive variety of plant, animal, and marine life. The park is also home to Tillicum Village where you can enjoy a Northwest Indian dining and cultural experience. Dogs of all sizes are allowed for no additional fee around the park and the village (except for the longhouse). Dogs must be leashed at all times, and cleaned up after. They are not allowed on designated swimming beaches.

Discovery Park 3801 W. Government Way Seattle WA 206-386-4236
Discovery Park is located northwest of downtown Seattle. It has over 500 acres and is the city's largest park. It offers views of both the Olympic and Cascade mountain ranges. Dogs on leash are allowed on about 7 miles of trails except for beaches, ponds, wetlands and the Wolf Tree Nature Trail.
Sand Point Magnuson Park 7400 Sand Point Way NE Seattle WA 206-684-4075
The park is northeast of Seattle and is located across the lake from the city of Kirkland. This park has about 350 acres and is Seattle's second largest park. You will find over four miles of walking trails along Lake Washington, through grassy fields, trees and brush. Dogs are not allowed in the water at Lake Washington, except at the off-leash area.

Off-Leash Dog Parks
Golden Gardens Dog Park 8498 Seaview Place NW Ballard WA 206-684-4075
This 2.2 acre fenced dog park is in the upper part of Golden Gardens Park. The park is open from 6 am to 11:30 pm. To get to the park from I-5 take the 85 St exit and head west. When 85 Street ends turn right and go under the railroad tracks to the park.
Luther Burbank Dog Park 2040 84th Avenue SE Mercer Island WA 206-236-3545
The unfenced, off-leash dog area is on the north side of the park on the shore of Lake Washington. There are places for your dog to take a dip in Lake Washington in the off-leash areas. Dogs are allowed on leash in the rest of the park. To get there from I-5, take I-90 East to Mercer Island and take the Island Crest Way exit (#7). At the top of the ramp, turn right on SE 26th Street. At the stop sign turn left on 84th Avenue SE and drive straight to the park after another stop sign at SE 24th Street.
Genesee Park Dog Park 46th Avenue S & S Genesee Street Seattle WA 206-684-4075
This fully fenced dog park in Genesee Park has double gates, a drinking fountain for dogs and a kiosk for community notices.
I-5 Colonnade Dog Park E. Howe Street at Lakeview Blvd Seattle WA 206-684-4075
There is a narrow but fenced off-leash dog park located underneath the I-5 Freeway. Since the dog park is under the freeway it stays dry during most rain. The dog park shares the 7 acre park sight with a mountain bike course. The park is open from 4 am to 11:30 pm. The park is located just beneath the I-5 Freeway at E. Howe Street between Lakeview Blvd and Franklin Ave E.
I-90 "Blue Dog Pond" Off-Leash Area S Massachusetts Seattle WA 206-684-4075
This dog park is located at the northwest corner of the intersection of Martin Luther King Jr. Way S and S Massachusetts. The park has a large sculpture of a blue dog.
Jose Rizal Park Off-Leash Area 1008 12th Avenue S Seattle WA 206-684-4075
This park offers a designated off-leash area. The park is located at 1008 12th Avenue S on North Beacon Hill. Parking is available on 12th South.
Northacres Park Off-Leash Area North 130th Street Seattle WA 206-684-4075
This park is located west of I-5 at North 130th Street. The park is south of North 130th Street and the off-leash area is in the northeast corner of the park. Parking is available on the west side of the park on 1st NE and on the south side of the park on N 125th.
Plymouth Pillars Dog Park Boren Avenue at Pike Street Seattle WA 206-684-4075
The off-leash dog park opened in January of 2006. The dog park is 10,000 square feet and is a narrow and curved design. The surface is rock. The park is located above the I-5 freeway. To get to the park from the freeway take exits 166 or 165. The park is located on Boren Avenue between Pike Street and Pine Street.
Regrade Park Off-Leash Area 2251 3rd Avenue Seattle WA 206-684-4075
This small off-leash area in Regrade Park is located in downtown at 2251 3rd Avenue at Bell Street.
Sand Point Magnuson Park Dog Off-Leash Area 7400 Sand Point Way NE Seattle WA 206-684-4946
This leash free dog park covers about 9 acres and is the biggest fully fenced off-leash park in Seattle. It also offers an access point to the lake where your pooch is welcome to take a dip in the fresh lake water. To find the dog park, take Sand Point Way Northeast and enter the park at Northeast 74th Street. Go straight and park near the playground and sports fields. The main gate to the off-leash area is located at the southeast corner of the main parking lot. Dogs must be leashed until you enter the off-leash area.
Westcrest Park 8806 8th Avenue SW Seattle WA 206-684-4075
This dog park in Westcrest Park is over 4 acres in size. It is located in West Seattle.
Woodland Park Off-Leash Area W Green Lake Way N Seattle WA 206-684-4075
This park has a designated off-leash area.

Outdoor Restaurants
Crave 1621 12th Avenue Seattle WA 206-388-0526
Dogs on leash are allowed at the tables on the patio. They open the patio for the summer months. Order inside and take your food to your table outside.
Lombardi's Cucina 2200 N.W. Market Street Seattle WA 206-783-0055
This restaurant offers traditional Italian cuisine. Well-behaved dogs are allowed at the outdoor tables. If they are busy, they will try to find a spot away from the crowd for your pooch.

Madison Park Cafe 1807 42nd Street Seattle WA   206-324-2626
Dogs on leash are allowed at this eatery's full service cobblestone courtyard. They open the courtyard for the summer months.
Maggie Bluff's Marina Grill 2601 W. Marina Place Seattle WA   206-283-8322
This restaurant, open for breakfast and lunch, serves hamburgers, salads, pastas, and more. Dogs are allowed at the outdoor tables. Heaters are usually available.
Pink Door 1919 Post Aly Seattle WA   206-443-3241
Dogs on leash are allowed at the tables on both the patio and the deck. Full table service is offered outside during the summer.
Portage Bay Cafe 4130 Roosevelt Way NE Seattle WA   206-547-8230
Open for breakfast and lunch, this cafe allows dogs are their outdoor tables. A children's menu is available.
Torero's Mexican Restaurant 401 Broadway E Seattle WA   206-860-1363
Dogs on leash are allowed at the tables on the patio. Full table service is offered.

Events
Paws Walk 7400 Sand Point Way NE Seattle WA   425-787-2500
This benefit for the animals is a rain or shine annual event, usually held in September with hundreds of participants and dogs. The event is held at Seattle's dog-friendly Sandpoint Magnuson Park. There are vendors, dog micro-chipping, adoptions, a kids zone, agility course and more. Dogs must have ID Tags on, be leashed and cleaned up after at all times, and they may not be in heat or younger than 4 months old.

Seattle Area

Accommodations
Motel 6 - Seattle East - Issaquah 1885 15th Place NW Issaquah WA   425-392-8405 (800-466-8356)
One well-behaved family pet per room. Guest must notify front desk upon arrival. Guest is liable for any damages. In consideration of all guests, pets must never be left unattended in the guest rooms.
La Quinta Inn Seattle Bellevue Kirkland 10530 NE Northup Way Kirkland WA   425-828-6585 (800-531-5900)
Dogs of all sizes are allowed. There are no additional pet fees. Dogs must be leashed, cleaned up after, and the Do Not Disturb sign put on the door if there is a dog alone in the room.
Motel 6 - Seattle North - Kirkland 12010 120th Place Northeast Kirkland WA   425-821-5618 (800-466-8356)
One well-behaved family pet per room. Guest must notify front desk upon arrival. Guest is liable for any damages. In consideration of all guests, pets must never be left unattended in the guest rooms.
Holiday Inn Express 19801 7th Avenue NE Poulsbo WA   360-697-4400 (877-270-6405)
There is a $10 per day pet fee.
Residence Inn by Marriott 7575 164th Avenue NE Redmond WA   425-497-9226
Dogs of all sizes are allowed. There is a $75 one time fee and a pet policy to sign at check in.

Campgrounds and RV Parks
Issaquah Highlands 10610 Renton Issaquah Road Issaquah WA   425-392-2351
Dogs of all sizes are allowed. There are no additional pet fees. Dogs must be leashed and cleaned up after. The camping and tent areas also allow dogs. There is a dog walk area at the campground.
Eagle Tree RV Park 16280 Hwy 305 Poulsbo WA   360-598-5988
http://www.eagletreerv.com
Dogs of all sizes are allowed. There are no additional pet fees. Dogs may not be tied up outside alone, must be leashed, and cleaned up after. There are some breed restrictions. There is a dog walk area at the campground.

Stores
PetSmart Pet Store 1505 11th Ave NW Issaquah WA   425-557-6651
Your licensed and well-behaved leashed dog is allowed in the store.
Petco Pet Store 975 NW Gilman Blvd Issaquah WA   425-392-9664
Your licensed and well-behaved leashed dog is allowed in the store.
Petco Pet Store 12040 NE 85th St Kirkland WA   425-889-8319
Your licensed and well-behaved leashed dog is allowed in the store.
Petco Pet Store 7215 170th Avenue NE Redmond WA   425-861-3907
Your licensed and well-behaved leashed dog is allowed in the store.
PetSmart Pet Store 17845 Garden Way NE Unit 11 Woodinville WA   425-424-2098
Your licensed and well-behaved leashed dog is allowed in the store.

Beaches
Off-Leash Area and Beach 498 Admiral Way Edmonds WA 425-771-0230
http://www.olae.org
The Off-leash area and beach in Edmonds gives dogs a place to run free, swim and meet other dogs. The area is maintained and supported by O.L.A.E. and overseen by the City of Edmonds Parks and Rec Dept. From I-5 follow signs to the Edmonds Ferry until Dayton Street. Turn west on Dayton Street and then south on Admiral Way. The off-leash area is south of Marina Beach.

Parks
Marymoor Park and Off-Leash Area 6046 West Lake Sammamish Pkwy NE Redmond WA 206-296-8687
This park offers 640 acres of land for recreational activities. Some special areas in the park include a velodrome (for bicyclist training and racing), a climbing rock, a model airplane flying field, and the historic Willowmoor Farm. Dogs on leash are allowed at the park. There is also a 40 acre off-leash dog exercise area where dogs can run free while under voice control. To get there from I-5 or I-405, take State Route 520 east to the West Lake Sammamish Pkwy exit. At the bottom of the ramp, go right (south) on W. Lake Sammamish Parkway NE. The park entrance is the next left at the traffic light.

Off-Leash Dog Parks
Golden Gardens Park Dog Park 8498 Seaview Place NW Ballard WA 206-684-4075
This fenced dog park is located in the upper park.
Raab Dog Park 18349 Caldart Ave Poulsbo WA 360-779-9898
The fenced, off-leash area is located in Raab Park. Raab Park overlooks downtown Poulsbo and also has a nature trail and a running or walking track. From Washington 305 Turn east on NE Hostmark St and then south on Caldart Ave to the park.
Marymoor Park Off-Leash Area 6046 West Lake Redmond WA 206-205-3661
This park has a designated off-leash area for dogs. The off-leash area is forty acres in size but most of the 640 acre park is not designated off-leash so check the signs. There are a number of trails with bridges through the off-leash area and a stream for dogs to play in. To get to the park from I-5 or I-405, take State Route 520 east to the West Lake Sammamish Parkway exit. At the bottom of the ramp, go right/southbound on W. Lake Sammamish Parkway NE. The park entrance is the next left at the traffic light.
Grandview Park Dog Park Seatac WA 425-881-0148
http://www.soda.org
This is a very large 37 acre fenced dog park. There are picnic benches and, on nice days, you can see Mt Rainier. The park is mostly grassy fields. To get to the Grandview Dog Park take I-5 to Kent-Des Moines Rd (Route 516) and head east on 516. Turn north on Military Rd and east on S 228th Street to the park.

Outdoor Restaurants
Baja Fresh 2192 148th Avenue NE Redmond WA 425-298-0866
Dogs on leash are allowed at the outdoor tables. Order inside and bring your food to your table outside.
Taste the Moment 8110 164th Avenue NE Redmond WA 425-556-98 38
Dogs on leash are allowed at the tables on the deck. Full table service is offered, and they are open from 11 am to 9 pm Wednesday through Sunday, and closed Monday and Tuesday.
Victors Celtic Coffee Company 7993 Gilman Street Redmond WA 425-881-6451
Dogs on leash are allowed on the benches or at the tables on the outside deck. Order inside and take your food out to your table.

Sedro-Wooley

Campgrounds and RV Parks
North Cascades National Park 810 State Route 20 Sedro-Wooley WA 360-856-5700
http://www.nps.gov/noca/
Know as the North American Alps, the North Cascades National Park is home to an astounding diversity of plants and animals, and provides a variety of recreational pursuits. Dogs of all sizes are allowed at no additional fee. Dogs may not be left unattended, and they must be leashed and cleaned up after. Dogs are allowed at the Ross Lake National Recreation area, and on close-in trails. Dogs are not allowed in the back country. This campground is closed during the off-season. The camping and tent areas also allow dogs. There is a dog walk area at the campground. There are no electric or water hookups at the campground.

Sedro-Woolley

Parks
Lake Chelan National Recreation Area 810 State Route 20 Sedro-Woolley WA   360-856-5700
http://www.nps.gov/lach/index.htm
Dogs must be on leash and must be cleaned up after in this National Recreation Area. They are not allowed on the Picture Lake Boardwalk, Table Mountain Trail or the National Park Proper. They are allowed on the rest of the trails and the Stehekin Shuttle bus tours. Features camping, boating, fishing, and hiking. Accessed only by ferry or floatplane.
Ross Lake National Recreation Area 810 State Route 20 Sedro-Woolley WA   360-856-5700
http://www.nps.gov/rola/index.htm
Dogs on leash are allowed in the park area and lake. The park features boating, camping, fishing, hiking, and more. It sits in the North Cascade Mountains.

Sequim

Accommodations
Quality Inn and Suites 142 River Road Sequim WA   360-683-2800
Dogs of all sizes are allowed. There is a $10 per night per pet additional fee. Dogs must be quiet, well behaved, leashed, cleaned up after, and the Do Not Disturb sign put on the door if they are in the room alone.
Sunset Marine Resort 40 Buzzard Ridge Road Sequim WA   360-681-4166
Dogs of most sizes are allowed; no extra large dogs. There is a $15 per night per pet fee and a pet policy to sign at check in.

Campgrounds and RV Parks
Rainbows End RV Park 261831 Hwy 101 Sequim WA   360-683-3863
http://www.rainbowsendrvpark.com
Dogs of all sizes are allowed. There are no additional pet fees. Dogs may not be left unattended, must be leashed, and cleaned up after. There is, however, a large fenced in doggy play yard where they can run off leash. The camping and tent areas also allow dogs. There is a dog walk area at the campground.

Shelton

Accommodations
Super 8 Shelton 2943 Northview Circle Shelton WA   360-426-1654 (800-800-8000)
Dogs of all sizes are allowed. There is a $15 per night pet fee per pet under 20 pounds or $25 per pet over 20 pounds. Smoking and non-smoking rooms are available for pet rooms.

Silverdale

Accommodations
Red Lion 3073 NW Bucklin Hill Road Silverdale WA   360-698-1000
Dogs of all sizes are allowed. There is a $20 per night per room fee and a pet policy to sign at check in.

Stores
PetSmart Pet Store 9588 Ridgetop Blvd NW Silverdale WA   360-692-1514
Your licensed and well-behaved leashed dog is allowed in the store.

Skamania

Campgrounds and RV Parks
Beacon Rock State Park 34841 h 14 Skamania WA   360-427-8265
Beacon Rock, the core of an ancient volcano, provides technical rock climbing, and the more than 20 miles of trails offers some outstanding panoramic views at this park. Dogs of all sizes are allowed at no additional fee. Dogs may not be left unattended, and they must be leashed and cleaned up after. Dogs are not allowed in any park buildings, but they are allowed on the trails. This campground is closed during the off-season. The camping and tent areas also allow dogs. There is a dog walk area at the campground. There are no electric or water hookups at the campground.
Beacon Rock State Park 34841 State Route 14 Skamania WA   509-427-8265
Beacon Rock is actually the core of an ancient volcano, and the mile-long trail to its summit gives the viewer a stunning panoramic view of the Columbia River Gorge. With over 4,600 acres, more than 20 miles of multi-use trails, and 9,500 feet of freshwater shoreline, there is an abundance of plant and wildlife, and land and water recreation. Dogs of all sizes are allowed for no additional fee. Dogs must be under physical control at all times, leashed, and cleaned up after. Dogs are not allowed on designated swimming beaches. The park's main campground is seasonal, but there are 2 campsites near the moorage area available year round on a first come first served basis. The camp, being an older camp, is more suited to tent camping rather than RV, and there are only a limited number of sites that will accommodate rigs over 20 feet. There is a restroom and showers. This RV park is closed during the off-season. The camping and tent areas also allow dogs. There is a dog walk area at the campground. There are no electric or water hookups at the campgrounds.

Parks
Beacon Rock State Park 34841 State Route 14 Skamania WA   509-427-8265
Beacon Rock is actually the core of an ancient volcano, and the mile-long trail to its summit gives the viewer a stunning panoramic view of the Columbia River Gorge. With over 4,600 acres, more than 20 miles of multi-use trails, and 9,500 feet of freshwater shoreline, there is an abundance of plant and wildlife, and land and water recreation. Dogs of all sizes are allowed for no additional fee. Dogs must be under physical control at all times, leashed, and cleaned up after. Dogs are not allowed on designated swimming beaches.

Snoqualmie

Attractions
TOP 200 PLACE **Northwest Railway Museum** 38625 SE King Street Snoqualmie WA   425-888-3030
http://www.trainmuseum.org/
This is the largest and most comprehensive railway museum in the state, and they offer interpretive programs/displays on the history, operation, and importance of the railway. Although dogs are not allowed in the buildings or on the train, they are allowed around the grounds. Dogs must be leashed and cleaned up after.

Spokane

Accommodations
Best Western Tradewinds North N 3033 Division Spokane WA   509-326-5500 (800-780-7234)
Dogs of all sizes are allowed. There are no additional pet fees. All rooms are non-smoking.
Cavanaughs River Inn N 700 Division St Spokane WA   509-326-5577
There are no additional pet fees.
Comfort Inn North 7111 N Division Street/Hwy 395 Spokane WA   509-467-7111 (877-424-6423)
Dogs of all sizes are allowed. There is a $7 per night per pet additional fee. Dogs may only be left alone in the room if they will be quite, it is for just a short time, and a contact number is left with the front desk. Dogs must be leashed and cleaned up after.
Doubletree 322 N Spokane Falls Court Spokane WA   509-455-6900
Dogs of all sizes are allowed. There is a $25 per room per stay additional pet fee.
Holiday Inn 1616 South Windsor Dr Spokane WA   509-838-1170 (877-270-6405)
Dogs up to 50 pounds are allowed. There is a $50 refundable pet deposit. The entire hotel is non-smoking.
Holiday Inn Express 9220 E Mission Spokane WA   509-927-7100 (877-270-6405)
Dogs of all sizes are allowed. There are no additional pet fees. Smoking and non-smoking rooms are available for pets.

Howard Johnson Inn South 211 Division St. Spokane WA   509-838-6630 (800-446-4656)
Dogs of all sizes are welcome. There is a $10 per day pet fee.
La Quinta Inn & Suites Spokane 3808 N Sullivan Rd Spokane WA   509-893-0955 (800-531-5900)
Dogs of all sizes are allowed. There are no additional pet fees. Dogs must be leashed, cleaned up after, and
crated when left alone in the room.
Motel 6 - Spokane East 1919 North Hutchinson Road Spokane WA   509-926-5399 (800-466-8356)
One well-behaved family pet per room. Guest must notify front desk upon arrival. Guest is liable for any
damages. In consideration of all guests, pets must never be left unattended in the guest rooms.
Motel 6 - Spokane West-Airport 1508 South Rustle Street Spokane WA   509-459-6120 (800-466-8356)
One well-behaved family pet per room. Guest must notify front desk upon arrival. Guest is liable for any
damages. In consideration of all guests, pets must never be left unattended in the guest rooms.
Red Lion 303 W North River Drive Spokane WA   509-326-8000
Dogs of all sizes are allowed. There is a $10 per stay fee, and there must be a credit card on file. There is a pet
policy to sign at check in.
Red Lion 700 N Division Spokane WA   509-326-5577
Dogs of all sizes are allowed. There is a pet policy to sign at check in and there are no additional fees.
Red Lion 515 W Sprague Avenue Spokane WA   509-838-2711
Dogs of all sizes are allowed. There is a $100 refundable deposit per room and a pet policy to sign at check in.
Rodeway Inn 901 W 1st Sreet Spokane WA   509-399-2056
Dogs of all sizes are allowed. There are no additional pet fees. Dogs are not allowed to be left alone in the room.
Super 8 Spokane/Airport/West W 11102 Westbow Blvd Spokane WA   509-838-8800 (800-800-8000)
Dogs of all sizes are allowed. There is a $15 one time per pet fee per visit. Smoking and non-smoking rooms are
available for pet rooms.
The Davenport Hotel 10 S Post Street Spokane WA   509-455-8888 (800-899-1482)
http://www.thedavenporthotel.com/#
This hotel offers a long, rich history and feature 1, 2, and 3 bedroom luxury guest rooms and suites with many in-
room amenities, world class dining including a Champagne Sunday Brunch, indoor pool and Jacuzzi, and they
even offer an historic walking tour. They are also home to the popular Peacock Room Lounge that showcases a
giant stained-glass peacock ceiling, and provides great nightlife entertainment. Dogs of all sizes are allowed for
no additional fee. Dogs may only be left alone in the room if they will be quiet and well behaved, and they must
be leashed and cleaned up after at all times.

Campgrounds and RV Parks

Alderwood RV Resort 14007 N Newport H Spokane WA   509-467-5320
http://alderwoodrv.com
Dogs of all sizes are allowed. There are no additional pet fees. Dogs may not be left outside alone, and outside
pens for pets are not allowed. Dogs must be leashed and cleaned up after. The camping and tent areas also
allow dogs. There is a dog walk area at the campground.

Stores

PetSmart Pet Store 9950 N Newport Hwy Spokane WA   509-466-4566
Your licensed and well-behaved leashed dog is allowed in the store.
Petco Pet Store 6302 North Division Spokane WA   509-487-3242
Your licensed and well-behaved leashed dog is allowed in the store.
Petco Pet Store 2805 East 29th Avenue Spokane WA   509-532-0185
Your licensed and well-behaved leashed dog is allowed in the store.

Parks

Riverfront Park 507 N Howard Spokane WA   509-625-6600
http://www.spokaneriverfrontpark.com/
Once the site of the 1974 World's Fair, this 110 acre, lush, urban park in downtown Spokane offers an array of
recreational pursuits, special events, food, and entertainment on a backdrop of the scenic Spokane Falls. They
are also home to a 1909 Looff Carrousel and a seasonal outdoor skating rink. Dogs are allowed throughout the
park with the exception of special events and some holidays. Dogs must be well behaved, leashed, and please
bring supplies to clean up after your pet.

Off-Leash Dog Parks

SCRAPS Dog Park 26715 E Spokane Bridge Rd Spokane WA   509-477-2532
http://www.spokanecounty.org/animal
This 3 1/2 acre fenced dog park is located in the new Gateway Park. It is the first off-leash dog park in Spokane
County. Gateway Park is just north of I-90 at the Idaho state line. The Park was built on the abandoned rest area.

Spokane Valley

Accommodations
Comfort Inn Valley 905 N Sullivan Road Spokane Valley WA   509-924-3838 (877-424-6423)
Dogs of all sizes are allowed. There are no additional pet fees with a credit card on file, and a $50 refundable deposit if paying by cash. There is a pet policy to sign at check in. Dogs may not be left alone in the room, and they must be leashed and cleaned up after.
Doubletree 1100 N Sullivan Road Spokane Valley WA   509-924-9000
Dogs of all sizes are allowed. There is a $50 refundable deposit per pet and a pet policy to sign at check in. Dogs are not allowed to be left alone except for short periods while having meals at the hotel.
Super 8 Spokane Valley 2020 North Argonne Rd Spokane Valley WA   509-928-4888 (800-800-8000)
Dogs of all sizes are allowed. There is a $15 one time per pet fee per visit. Smoking and non-smoking rooms are available for pet rooms.

Campgrounds and RV Parks
Trailer Inns RV Park 6021 E 4th Spokane Valley WA   509-535-1811
http://www.trailerinnsrv.com
Dogs of all sizes are allowed. There are no additional pet fees for up to 2 dogs, and there is no deposit unless you stay by the month. If there are more than 2 dogs, the fee is $3 per night per pet. Dogs may not be left unattended, must be leashed, and cleaned up after. There is a dog walk area at the campground.

Stanwood

Campgrounds and RV Parks
Wenberg State Park 15430 E Lake Goodwin Road Stanwood WA   360-652-7417 (888-CAMPOUT (226-7688))
This 46 acre camping park, with 1,140 feet of freshwater shoreline, offers great fishing and a variety of land and water recreation. Dogs of all sizes are allowed at no additional fee. Dogs may not be left unattended, and they must be leashed at all times, and cleaned up after. Dogs are not allowed in public swim areas or in buildings. The camping and tent areas also allow dogs. There is a dog walk area at the campground.

Tacoma

Accommodations
Days Inn Tacoma Mall 6802 Tacoma Mall Blvd Tacoma WA   253-475-5900 (800-329-7466)
Dogs of all sizes are allowed. There is a $30 one time per pet fee per visit. Only non-smoking rooms are used for pets.
La Quinta Inn & Suites Seattle Tacoma 1425 E. 27th St. Tacoma WA   253-383-0146 (800-531-5900)
Dogs of all sizes are allowed. There are no additional pet fees. Dogs must be quiet, well behaved, leashed and cleaned up after.
Motel 6 - Tacoma South 1811 South 76th Street Tacoma WA   253-473-7100 (800-466-8356)
One well-behaved family pet per room. Guest must notify front desk upon arrival. Guest is liable for any damages. In consideration of all guests, pets must never be left unattended in the guest rooms.
Sheraton Tacoma Hotel 1320 Broadway Plaza Tacoma WA   253-572-3200 (888-625-5144)
Dogs of all sizes are allowed. There are no additional pet fees. Dogs are not allowed to be left alone in the room.

Stores
PetSmart Pet Store 10210 59th Ave SW Lakewood WA   253-584-7920
Your licensed and well-behaved leashed dog is allowed in the store.
Petco Pet Store 5700 100th St SW Lakewood WA   253-984-6903
Your licensed and well-behaved leashed dog is allowed in the store.
PetSmart Pet Store 3326 S 23rd St Tacoma WA   253-396-0507
Your licensed and well-behaved leashed dog is allowed in the store.
Petco Pet Store 3801 S Steele St Tacoma WA   253-475-8555

Your licensed and well-behaved leashed dog is allowed in the store.
Urban Dogs 1717 Dock Street Tacoma WA   253-573-1717
http://www.urban-dogs.com/
Neat playtoys, good nutritious food, designer clothes/collars/leads, and comfy beds are just some of the treats to find at this store. They are open from 11 am to 6 pm daily. Your pet is welcome to shop with you, and if they are well behaved and respond to voice command, they may be off lead in the store.

Off-Leash Dog Parks
Rogers Park Off-Leash Dog Park E L St At E Wright Ave Tacoma WA   253-305-1060
This fenced dog park is located in Rogers Park. From I-5 you can take the Portland Avenue Exit. Head east of E Wiley Ave (parallels the I-5 South) and turn south on E Valley View Terrace to the park on your left.

Toppenish

Campgrounds and RV Parks
Yakama Nation RV Resort 280 Buster Road Toppenish WA   509-865-2000
http://www.yakamanation.com
Dogs of all sizes are allowed. There are no additional pet fees. Dogs must be leashed and cleaned up after. In addition to tent and RV sites, they have teepee sites, and dogs are allowed there also. There are some breed restrictions. The camping and tent areas also allow dogs. There is a dog walk area at the campground.

Tukwila

Stores
PetSmart Pet Store 17585 Southcenter Pkwy Tukwila WA   206-575-2373
Your licensed and well-behaved leashed dog is allowed in the store.

Union Gap

Accommodations
Super 8 Union Gap/Yakima Area 2605 Rucklin Rd Union Gap WA   509-248-8880 (800-800-8000)
Dogs of all sizes are allowed. There is a $25 returnable deposit required per room. Smoking and non-smoking rooms are available for pet rooms.

Attractions
TOP 200 PLACE **Central Washington Agricultural Museum** 4508 Main Street Union Gap WA   509-457-8735
Located on 15 acres in a city park, this museum has collected an extensive history of Central Washington's agriculture, which is still recognized as one of the most productive agricultural areas in the nation. They constructed an outer ring of semi-open buildings to display numerous exhibits, and farm equipment. There is also an operating windmill and a railroad exhibit. Dogs are allowed to walk the grounds, but they are not allowed in enclosed buildings. Dogs must be leashed, and please have supplies to clean up after your pet. Hours vary with the season.

Stores
PetSmart Pet Store 1403 E Washington Ave Union Gap WA   509-469-9933
Your licensed and well-behaved leashed dog is allowed in the store.

Vancouver

Accommodations

Comfort Inn 13207 NE 20th Avenue Vancouver WA   360-574-6000 (877-424-6423)
Dogs of all sizes are allowed. There is a $10 per night per pet additional fee. Dogs may not be left alone in the room, and they must be leashed and cleaned up after.
Quality Inn and Suites 7001 NE Hwy 99 Vancouver WA   360-696-0516 (877-424-6423)
Dogs of all sizes are allowed. There is a $10 per night per pet additional fee. Dogs must be leashed, cleaned up after, and crated if they are in the room alone. Dogs may only be left unattended for short periods.
Red Lion 100 Columbia Street Vancouver WA   360-694-8341
Dogs of all sizes are allowed. There is an additional $25 per pet per stay fee.
Red Lion 1500 NE 134th Street Vancouver WA   360-566-1100
Dogs of all sizes are allowed. There is a $25 per stay per room fee and a pet policy to sign at check in.
Residence Inn by Marriott 8005 NE Parkway Drive Vancouver WA   360-253-4800
Dogs of all sizes are allowed. There is a $75 one time fee and a pet policy to sign at check in.
Staybridge Suites 7301 NE 41st St Vancouver WA   360-891-8282 (877-270-6405)
There is a $50 refundable pet deposit and an additional pet fee of $10 per day.

Campgrounds and RV Parks

Gifford Pinchot National Forest 10600 N.E. 51st Circle Vancouver WA   360-891-5000
http://www.fs.fed.us/gpnf/
There are 67 campgrounds in this forest, and it is also home to the Mount St. Helens National Volcanic Monument. Dogs are not allowed out of the car at the monument. Dogs of all sizes are allowed, and there are no additional pet fees. Dogs may not be left unattended, and they must be quiet, leashed, and cleaned up after. Dogs must be walked in designated areas. This campground is closed during the off-season. The camping and tent areas also allow dogs. There is a dog walk area at the campground. There are no electric or water hookups at the campground.
Vancouver RV Park 7603 NE 13th Avenue Vancouver WA   360-695-1158
http://www.vancouverrvparks.com
Dogs of all sizes are allowed. There are no additional pet fees. Dogs may not be left unattended or tied up alone outside. Dogs must be quiet, well behaved, leashed, and cleaned up after. There are some breed restrictions. The camping and tent areas also allow dogs. There is a dog walk area at the campground.

Attractions

Fort Vancouver National Historic Site 612 E Reserve St Vancouver WA   800-832-3599
http://www.nps.gov/fova/index.htm
Dogs must be on leash and must be cleaned up after in this National historic site. They are not allowed in the buildings or the fort.
Fort Vancouver National Historical Reserve 1501 E Evergreen Blvd Vancouver WA   360-696-7655
This reserve is a premier historical archaeological site in the Pacific Northwest with a long natural and cultural history. They keep this history alive by offering living history demonstrations, and a variety of educational programs and exhibits. They are open from 9 am to 5 pm daily. Dogs of all sizes are allowed to explore the grounds with their owners, but they are not allowed in any buildings or at the fort site. There is also a large grassy area for your pet to explore. Dogs must be leashed and cleaned up after.
McLoughlin House National Historic Site 612 E Reserve St Vancouver WA   800-832-3599
http://www.nps.gov/mcho/index.htm
Dogs must be on leash and must be cleaned up after. Dogs are not allowed in the house. Part of the Fort Vancouver National Historic Site in Oregon and Washington.

Stores

PetSmart Pet Store 7603 NE Vancouver Plaza Dr Vancouver WA   360-256-7082
Your licensed and well-behaved leashed dog is allowed in the store.
PetSmart Pet Store 130 SE 192nd Ave Vancouver WA   360-256-8667
Your licensed and well-behaved leashed dog is allowed in the store.
Petco Pet Store 305 SE Chkalov, Ste B Vancouver WA   360-944-2055
Your licensed and well-behaved leashed dog is allowed in the store.
Petco Pet Store 8820 NE 5th Avenue Vancouver WA   360-574-8884
Your licensed and well-behaved leashed dog is allowed in the store.
Petco Pet Store 11505 NE Fourth Plain Rd Vancouver WA   360-253-5540
Your licensed and well-behaved leashed dog is allowed in the store.

Off-Leash Dog Parks

Ross Off-Leash Rec Area NE Ross St at NE 18th St Vancouver WA   360-619-1111
This nearly 9 acre fenced dog park was a joint project between BPA (which donated land), DOGPAW and the city of Vancouver. It is Vancouver's first off-leash dog park. To get to the park, exit I-5 at Highway 99 and head

north. Turn right onto NE Ross St to NE 18th St and the park.

Vantage

Campgrounds and RV Parks

Iron Horse State Park P. O. Box 1203 Vantage WA   509-856-2700
This linear park of over 1,600 acres celebrates its railroading history, spans several geological zones, protects several ecosystems and their inhabitants, and provides a variety of recreational pursuits. It is also home to Snoqualmie Pass Tunnel (seasonal) that is almost 2 miles long-bring your flashlight, and the Iron Horse Trail that is over 100 miles long following along the route of the railroad. Dogs are allowed for no additional fee. Pets must be on a leash, under physical control at all times, and cleaned up after (even on trails). Dogs are not allowed on any designated swimming beaches. Camping is allowed on a first come first served basis, and there are four primitive campgrounds along the trail, each with 3 to 4 sites, a picnic table and a vault toilet. There is also camping available by the trail near the U. S. Forest Service at Tinkham, Denny Creek, Lake Kachess, and Crystal Springs. The camping and tent areas also allow dogs. There is a dog walk area at the campground. There are no electric or water hookups at the campgrounds.

Parks

Iron Horse State Park P. O. Box 1203 Vantage WA   509-856-2700
This linear park of over 1,600 acres celebrates its railroading history, spans several geological zones, protects several ecosystems and their inhabitants, and provides a variety of recreational pursuits. It is also home to Snoqualmie Pass Tunnel (seasonal) that is almost 2 miles long-bring your flashlight, and the Iron Horse Trail that is over 100 miles long following along the route of the railroad. Dogs are allowed for no additional fee. Pets must be on a leash, under physical control at all times, and cleaned up after (even on trails). Dogs are not allowed on any designated swimming beaches.

Veradale

Stores

PetSmart Pet Store 15615 E Broadway Ave Veradale WA   509-927-9223
Your licensed and well-behaved leashed dog is allowed in the store.
Petco Pet Store North 10 - Sullivan Rd Veradale WA   509-927-2670
Your licensed and well-behaved leashed dog is allowed in the store.

Walla Walla

Accommodations

Holiday Inn Express 1433 W Pine Street Walla Walla WA   509-525-6200 (877-270-6405)
Dogs of all sizes are allowed. There is a $10 per day additional pet fee.
La Quinta Inn Walla Walla 520 North 2nd Avenue Walla Walla WA   509-525-2522 (800-531-5900)
Dogs of all sizes are allowed. There are no additional pet fees. Dogs must be leashed and cleaned up after. The Do Not Disturb sign must be put on the door and the front desk informed if there is a dog alone in the room.
Super 8 Walla Walla 2315 Eastgate St N Walla Walla WA   509-525-8800 (800-800-8000)
Dogs of all sizes are allowed. There is a $25 returnable deposit required per room. There is a $10 one time per pet fee per visit. Smoking and non-smoking rooms are available for pet rooms.

Campgrounds and RV Parks

Fairway RV Resort 50 W George Street (entrance Burns St) Walla Walla WA   509-525-8282
http://www.fairwayrvresort.com
Dogs of all sizes are allowed. There are no additional pet fees for 2 dogs. If there are more than 2 dogs, then the fee is $1 per night per pet additional. Dogs may not be left unattended or staked outside alone, they must be leashed, and cleaned up after. The camping and tent areas also allow dogs. There is a dog walk area at the campground.

Attractions

Whitman Mission National Historic Site 328 Whitman Mission Road Walla Walla WA   509-522-6357
http://www.nps.gov/whmi/index.htm
Dogs must be on leash and must be cleaned up after on park grounds. They are not allowed in buildings. Open 8am-4:30pm year round. The park features nature walks, and bird watching. This site commemorates the courage of Marcus and Narcissa Whitman, the role the Whitmans played in establishing the Oregon Trail, and the challenges encountered when two different cultures met.

Wenatchee

Accommodations

Holiday Inn Express 1921 N. Wenatchee Ave Wenatchee WA   509-663-6355 (877-270-6405)
Dogs up to 50 pounds are allowed. There are no additional pet fees. Pets are allowed on the 3rd floor only and can not be left alone in the room.
La Quinta Inn & Suites Wenatchee 1905 N Wenatchee Ave Wenatchee WA   509-664-6565 (800-531-5900)
Dogs of all sizes are allowed. There are no additional pet fees. Dogs may not be left unattended, and they must be leashed and cleaned up after.
Red Lion 1225 N Wenatchee Avenue Wenatchee WA   509-663-0711
Dogs of all sizes are allowed. There is a pet policy to sign at check in and there are no additional fees.

Campgrounds and RV Parks

Wenatchee National Forest 215 Melody Lane (forest HQ) Wenatchee WA   509-664-9200
http://www.fs.fed.us/r6/wenatchee/
This forest is divided into 6 ranger districts and covers 2.2 million acres with a variety of trails totaling about 2,500 miles. Dogs of all sizes are allowed at no additional fee. Dogs may not be left unattended, and they must be leashed and cleaned up after in camp areas. Dogs are allowed on the trails, but they are not allowed in public swim areas or any buildings. The camping and tent areas also allow dogs. There is a dog walk area at the campground. There are no electric or water hookups at the campground.

Stores

Petco Pet Store 516 Valley Mall Parkway East Wenatchee WA   509-886-5518
Your licensed and well-behaved leashed dog is allowed in the store.

Westport

Campgrounds and RV Parks

Totem RV Park 2421 N Nyhus Westport WA   360-268-0025 (888-TOTEMRV (868-3678))
http://www.totemrv.com
Dogs of all sizes are allowed. There are no additional pet fees. Dogs may not be left unattended, and they must be quiet, well behaved, leashed, and cleaned up after. If you would like to view this area from their tower, the site is westportcam.com. The camping and tent areas also allow dogs. There is a dog walk area at the campground.

Beaches

Twin Harbors State Park Highway 105 Westport WA   360-902-8844
This beach is popular for beachcombing, bird watching, and fishing. Picnic tables, restrooms (including an ADA restroom), and campgrounds (includes ADA campgrounds) are available at this park. Leashed dogs are allowed on the beach. Dogs are also allowed at the campgrounds. They must be on a eight foot or less leash at all times and people are required to clean up after their pets. This park is located three miles south of Westport on Highway 105. From Aberdeen,
Westport Light State Park Ocean Avenue Westport WA   360-902-8844
Enjoy the panoramic view at this park or take the easy access trail to the beach. Swimming in the ocean here is not advised because of variable currents or rip tides. Picnic tables, restrooms (including an ADA restroom), and a 1.3 mile paved trail (also an ADA trail) are available at this park. Leashed dogs are allowed on the beach. Dogs are also allowed on the paved trail. They must be on a eight foot or less leash at all times and people are required to clean up after their pets. This park is located on the Pacific Ocean at Westport, 22 miles southwest of Aberdeen. To get there from Westport, drive west on Ocean Ave. about one mile to park entrance.

White Pass

Cross Country Ski Resorts

TOP 200 PLACE **White Pass Ski Area** 48935 Hwy 12 White Pass WA 509-672-3101
http://www.skiwhitepass.com/
This snow/ski resort offers a wide variety of terrain for all ability levels, ski/snowboard instruction, and they are family oriented and offer fun events throughout the year. Dogs are allowed at this resort and can be on the trails. During their winter season, dogs are only allowed on the cross country ski trails after 3:30 on Thursday, Friday, and Saturday, and all day on Monday through Wednesday. During the summer (off-season months) there is unlimited use. Dogs may be unleashed when on the cross country trails if they will respond to voice control. Dogs must be leashed and cleaned up after at all times when in the resort area.

White Salmon

Campgrounds and RV Parks

Bridge RV Park & Campground 65271 Hwy 14 White Salmon WA 509-493-1111
http://www.bridgerv.com/
Dogs of all sizes are allowed. There is a $1 per night per pet additional fee. Dogs may not be left unattended, and they must be quiet, well behaved, leashed, and cleaned up after. The camping and tent areas also allow dogs. There is a dog walk area at the campground.

Winthrop

Accommodations

Best Western Cascade Inn 960 Hwy 20 Winthrop WA   509-996-3100 (800-780-7234)
Dogs of all sizes are allowed. There is a $10 per night pet fee per pet. Reservations preferred for pets ahead of time. Non-smoking rooms king and queen beds only used.
The Winthrop Inn 960 Hwy 20 Winthrop WA   509-996-2217
One well behaved dog up to 70 pounds is allowed. There is a $7 per night additional pet fee. They request you bring your dog's sleeping mat and that you keep them leashed while on the grounds. There is a beach on the river close by where the dogs can run unleashed.

Campgrounds and RV Parks

Winthrop/N Cascades National Park KOA 1114 Hwy 20 Winthrop WA 509-996-2258 (800-562-2158)
http://www.methownet.com/koa
Dogs of all sizes are allowed. There are no additional pet fees. Dogs must be leashed and cleaned up after. Dogs may be left unattended if they are quiet and well behaved, and you can also tie your pet by the office. This RV park is closed during the off-season. The camping and tent areas also allow dogs. There is a dog walk area at the campground. Dogs are allowed in the camping cabins.

Woodland

Accommodations

Cedars Inn 1500 Atlantic Avenue Woodland WA   360-225-6548 (800-444-9667)
Frequently referred to as Woodland's Best, this Inn has parking that will accommodate RVs and 18-wheelers, and they offer 60 spacious, nicely-appointed rooms with many in-room amenities, and a deluxe complimentary breakfast. Dogs of all sizes are allowed for an additional one time fee of $10 per pet. There may be a discount available for guests there for the dog shows. Dogs may not be left alone in the room at any time, and they must be leashed and cleaned up after.

Campgrounds and RV Parks

Columbia Riverfront RV Park 1881Pike Road Woodland WA   360-225-8051
http://www.columbiariverfrontrvpark.com
Dogs of all sizes are allowed. There are no additional pet fees for up to 2 pets. If there are more than 3 dogs, then the fee is an additional $1 per night per pet. Dogs must be leashed and cleaned up after, and they are allowed at the beach. There are some breed restrictions. There is a dog walk area at the campground.

Yakima

Accommodations
Best Western Ahtanum Inn 2408 Rudkin Rd Yakima WA   509-248-9700 (800-780-7234)
Dogs up to 60 pounds are allowed. There is a $10 per night pet fee per pet. Smoking and non-smoking rooms available.
Clarion Hotel and Conference Center 1507 N First Street Yakima WA   509-248-7850 (877-424-6423)
Dogs of all sizes are allowed. There is a $10 per night per pet additional fee, and a pet policy to sign at check in. Dogs must be leashed, cleaned up after, and the Do Not Disturb sign put on the door if they are in the room alone.
Motel 6 - Yakima 1104 North 1st Street Yakima WA   509-454-0080 (800-466-8356)
One well-behaved family pet per room. Guest must notify front desk upon arrival. Guest is liable for any damages. In consideration of all guests, pets must never be left unattended in the guest rooms.
Red Lion 607 E Yakima Avenue Yakima WA   509-248-5900
Dogs of all sizes are allowed. There is a $5 per night per pet fee and a pet policy to sign at check in.
Red Lion 9 N 9th Street Yakima WA   509-452-6511
Dogs of all sizes are allowed. There is a $5 per night per pet fee and a pet policy to sign at check in.

Campgrounds and RV Parks
Trailer Inns RV Park 1610 N 1st Street Yakima WA   509-452-9561
http://www.trailerinns.com
Dogs of all sizes are allowed. There are no additional pet fees. Dogs may not be left unattended, or tied up outside alone. Dogs must be leashed and cleaned up after. The camping and tent areas also allow dogs. There is a dog walk area at the campground.
Yakima KOA 1500 Keys Road Yakima WA   509-248-5882 (800-562-5773)
http://www.koa@html.com
Dogs of all sizes are allowed. There are no additional pet fees. Dogs must be well behaved, leashed, and cleaned up after. There are some breed restrictions. The camping and tent areas also allow dogs. There is a dog walk area at the campground. Dogs are allowed in the camping cabins.

Attractions
TOP 200 PLACE **McAllister Museum of Aviation** 2008 S 16th Avenue Yakima WA   509-457-4933
http://mcallistermuseum.org/
Operating for 73 years, this flight school was one of the longest running flight schools in the Northwest. Now a museum, they host various events throughout the year, and on Saturdays you will usually find local pilots hanging out there who love to share their aviation history. Dogs are allowed to explore the museum with you. Dogs must be well behaved, leashed, and please have supplies to clean up after your pet.

Stores
Petco Pet Store 201 East Yakima Avenue Yakima WA   509-576-9771
Your licensed and well-behaved leashed dog is allowed in the store.

Zillah

Accommodations
Comfort Inn 911 Vintage Valley Parkway Zillah WA   509-829-3399 (877-424-6423)
Dogs of all sizes are allowed. There is a $10 per night per pet additional fee. Dogs may only be left alone in the room if they will be quiet and well behaved. Dogs must be leashed, cleaned up after, and the Do Not Disturb sign put on the door if they are in the room alone.

Chapter 23

Yellowstone - Grand Teton
Dog Travel Guide

Yellowstone - Grand Teton (Wyoming)

Accommodations

Colter Bay Cabins Jackson Lake Grand Teton National Park WY   800-628-9988
http://www.gtlc.com/
There are over 200 log cabins and a number of tent cabins. Pets are allowed and there are no additional pet fees.

Jackson Lake Lodge Jackson Lake Grand Teton National Park WY   800-628-9988
http://www.gtlc.com/
Dogs are allowed in the classic rooms. There is a $10 per night additional pet fee.

Flat Creek Inn 1935 N H 89/26 Jackson WY   307-733-5276
Dogs of all sizes are allowed. There are no additional pet fees.

Motel 6 - Jackson 600 South Highway 89 Jackson WY   307-733-1620 (800-466-8356)
One well-behaved family pet per room. Guest must notify front desk upon arrival. Guest is liable for any damages. In consideration of all guests, pets must never be left unattended in the guest rooms.

Quality 49er Inn and Suites 330 W Pearl St Jackson WY   307-733-7550
There are no additional pet fees.

Quality Inn and Suites 49'er 330 W Pearl Street Jackson WY   307-733-7550 (877-424-6423)
Dogs of all sizes are allowed. There are no additional pet fees. Dogs may not be left alone in the room at any time, and they must be leashed and cleaned up after.

Painted Buffalo Inn 400 West Broadway Jackson Hole WY   307-733-4340
http://www.paintedbuffalo.com/
There is a $10 one time pet fee.

Snow King Resort 400 E Snow King Ave Jackson Hole WY   307-733-5200 (800-522-5464)
There is a $100 pet deposit. $50 of this is refundable.

Chico Hot Springs Resort #1 Chico Road Pray WY   406-333-4933 (800-HOT-WADA)
http://www.chicohotsprings.com/
"We're pet-friendly, so bring your four-legged friends along." This resort has a lodge and cabins which sit on 150 acres. There are miles of hiking trails for you and your pup. They are located 30 miles from the north Yellowstone National Park entrance. There is a $10 per day pet fee.

Green Creek Inn 2908 Yellowstone Hwy Wapiti WY   307-587-5004
There is a $5 per day pet fee.

Canyon Western Cabins   Yellowstone National Park WY   307-344-7311
http://travelyellowstone.com
Dogs are allowed in the Cabins only. There are no additional pet fees. The Cabins are open seasonally from about May to September each year.

Flagg Ranch Village Hwy 89 Yellowstone South Entrance Yellowstone National Park WY   307-543-2861 (800-443-2311)
http://www.flaggranch.com/
Dogs are allowed in cabins. This is a seasonal hotel and is not open year round. There is a $5 per day additional pet fee.

Lake Lodge Cabins Lake Lodge Yellowstone National Park WY   307-344-7311
http://travelyellowstone.com
Dogs are allowed in the Cabins only. There are no additional pet fees. The Cabins are open seasonally from about May to September each year.

Lake Yellowstone Cabins Lake Yellowstone Yellowstone National Park WY   307-344-7311
http://travelyellowstone.com
Dogs are allowed in the Cabins only. There are no additional pet fees. The Cabins are open seasonally from about May to September each year.

Mammoth Hot Springs Cabins Mammoth Hot Springs Yellowstone National Park WY   307-344-7311
http://travelyellowstone.com
Dogs are allowed in the Cabins only. There are no additional pet fees. The Cabins are open seasonally from about May to September each year.

Old Faithful Lodge Cabins Old Faithful Yellowstone National Park WY   307-344-7311
http://travelyellowstone.com
Dogs are allowed in the Cabins only. There are no additional pet fees. The Cabins are open seasonally from about May to September each year. These cabins are within easy walking distance of Old Faithful.

Pioneer Cabins   Yellowstone National Park WY   307-344-7311
http://travelyellowstone.com
Dogs are allowed in the Cabins only. There are no additional pet fees. The Cabins are open seasonally from

about May to September each year.

Campgrounds and RV Parks

Campgrounds in Grand Teton Various Grand Teton National Park WY 800-628-9988
Dogs on leash are allowed in campgrounds thoughout Grand Teton National Park. Pets may not be left
unattended and must be cleaned up after.

Colter Bay Campground Colter Bay Grand Teton National Park WY 800-628-9988
This RV Park is located in Grand Teton National Park. It is the only RV Park in the park with electric hookups
and the only one that will handle campers over 30 feet in length. Dogs on leash are allowed in the RV park.

Lizard Creek Campground North End of Park Grand Teton National Park WY 800-672-6012
This RV Park and campground is located at the north end of Grand Teton National Park. This RV park has no
electric hookups but does have water and dumping. RVs less than 30 feet in length are allowed. The
campground is open seasonally from about June to September. Dogs on leash are allowed in the campground.
No reservations are accepted, it is first come first serve.

Signal Mountain 16 Miles north of Jenny Lake Grand Teton National Park WY 800-672-6012
This RV Park and campground is located at the north end of Grand Teton National Park. This RV park has no
electric hookups but does have water and dumping. RVs less than 30 feet in length are allowed. The
campground is open seasonally from about May to October. Dogs on leash are allowed in the campground. No
reservations are accepted, it is first come first serve.

Bridger-Teton National Forest 340 Cash Street Jackson WY 307-739-5500
http://www.fs.fed.us/btnf
This park covers 3.4 million acres, and it is first come first serve for camping. Dogs of all sizes are allowed.
There are no additional pet fees. Although it is not advised, dogs may be off lead in the forest if you have voice
control. Dogs must be cleaned up after at all times, and they must be on leash in the camp areas. The camping
and tent areas also allow dogs. There is a dog walk area at the campground. There are no electric or water
hookups at the campground.

Jackson South/Hoback Junction KOA 9705 S H 89 Jackson WY 307-733-7078 (800-562-1878)
http://www.koa.com
Dogs of all sizes are allowed. There are no additional pet fees. Dogs may not be left unattended, and must be
quiet, leashed, and cleaned up after. There are some breed restrictions. This RV park is closed during the off-
season. The camping and tent areas also allow dogs. There is a dog walk area at the campground. Dogs are
allowed in the camping cabins.

Virginian RV Resort 750 W Broadway Jackson WY 307-733-7189
http://www.virginianlodge.com
Dogs of all sizes are allowed. There are no additional pet fees. Dogs must be leashed and cleaned up after. This
RV park is closed during the off-season. There is a dog walk area at the campground.

Teton Village/Jackson West KOA 2780 Moose Wilson Road Teton Village WY 307-733-5354 (800-652-
9043)
http://www.koa.com
Dogs of all sizes are allowed. There are no additional pet fees. Dogs may not be left unattended, and they must
be leashed and cleaned up after. There are some breed restrictions. This RV park is closed during the off-
season. The camping and tent areas also allow dogs. There is a dog walk area at the campground. Dogs are
allowed in the camping cabins.

Yellowstone Park/West Entrance KOA 3305 Targhee Pass H W Yellowstone WY 406-646-7606 (800-562-
7591)
http://www.yellowstonekoa.com
Dogs of all sizes are allowed. There are no additional pet fees. Dogs may not be left unattended in the cabins,
and they must be leashed and cleaned up after. There are some breed restrictions. This RV park is closed
during the off-season. The camping and tent areas also allow dogs. There is a dog walk area at the campground.
Dogs are allowed in the camping cabins.

Campsites in Yellowstone National Park Throughout Yellowstone National Park WY 307-344-7311
All Yellowstone campgrounds allow pets. Pets must be leashed at all times. Pets may not be left unattended,
may not bark continuously, and must be cleaned up after. Pets are not allowed on park trails and must not be
more than 100 feet from a roadway or parking area outside of the campground.

Fishing Bridge RV Park Lake Yellowstone Yellowstone National Park WY 307-344-7311
http://travelyellowstone.com
This RV Park is located in the middle of Yellowstone National Park on the north side of Lake Yellowstone. It is
open seasonally from May through October. Dogs are required to be on leash at all times.

Attractions

Amaze'n Jackson Hole 85 Snow King Ave Jackson WY 307-734-0455
Your dog may accompany you as you try to find your way through this outdoor maze in time to receive a prize.

Cross Country Ski Resorts

Jackson Hole Nordic Center 3395 West Village Drive Teton Village WY 307-739-2629
http://www.jacksonhole.com
This nordic center is located at the Jackson Hole Mountain Resort. The groomed trails are at the base of the Teton Village. Dogs are allowed on 7 out of 17 kilometers of groomed trails. Pets can be off-leash but need to be under direct voice control.

Parks

Shoshone National Forest 808 Meadow Lane Cody WY 307-527-6241
There are numerous dog-friendly trails in the forest, many of which are located between the town of Cody and Yellowstone National Park. One of the trails is the Eagle Creek Trail, which is about 16 miles long, at an elevation of 6700 to 9900 feet with a hiking difficulty of moderate. This trail is located off Highways 14 and 16, between Cody and Yellowstone.

Bridger-Teton National Forest various Jackson WY 307-739-5500
This national forest offers over 1200 miles of trails for you and your pooch to enjoy. You can take a short hike or take a week-long backpacking trip. There are many trails near Jackson and Buffalo. Here are two trails located near Jackson. The first is Cache Creek Trail which is about 6 miles long and follows the creek. It is a popular trail and offers good views of the town and surrounding area. You might spot wildlife like moose, deer, elk and more during the summertime. This hike has a gentle grade which makes it a good trail for the entire family. To get there from the town square, travel east on Broadway to Redmond Street. Follow Redmond to Cache Creek Drive then follow Cache Creek Drive to parking lot. Another trail is the Black Canyon Overlook/Pass Ridge Trail. This trail is rated moderate and is about 2 miles long. The trail follows the ridge and travels through meadows and forest, with views of Jackson Hole and the surrounding mountains. To get there from Jackson, follow Highway 22 West to the summit of Teton Pass. Park at the top of Teton Pass on the left. The trailhead is well marked on the south side of the road at the parking area.

Grand Teton National Park Moose WY 307-739-3300
http://www.nps.gov/grte/
Grand Teton National Park offers spectacular views of the jagged Teton Range, meadows, pine trees and beautiful blue lakes. This national park limits pets mostly to where cars can go. Pets are allowed in your car, on roads and within 50 feet of any road, campgrounds, picnic areas and parking lots. Pets are not allowed on any hiking trails, in the backcountry, on swimming beaches, or in any visitor centers. However, dogs are allowed on paths in the campgrounds, and can ride in a boat on Jackson Lake only. Dogs must be on a 6 foot leash or less, caged, crated, or in your car at all times. Pets cannot be left unattended or tied to an object. An activity you can do with your pet is to take a scenic drive. There are three scenic drives in the park. Many turnouts along the road offer exhibits on park geology, wildlife and plants. The Teton Park Road follows along the base of the Teton Range from Moose to Jackson Lake Junction. The Jenny Lake Scenic Drive skirts along Jenny Lake and offers great views of the Grand Teton peaks. This drive is one-way and starts just south of String Lake. You can reach this scenic drive by driving south at the North Jenny Lake Junction. Another scenic drive is the Signal Mountain Summit Road which climbs 800 feet to offer panoramic views of the Teton Range, Jackson Hole valley and Jackson Lake. For accommodations within the park, dogs are welcome in some of the Colter Bay Cabins and in some rooms at the Jackson Lake Lodge. For hiking trails that are dog-friendly, try the nearby Bridger-Teton National Forest.

Yellowstone National Park various Yellowstone National Park WY 307-344-7381
http://www.nps.gov/yell
Yellowstone National Park was established in 1872 and is America's first national park. Most of the park is at a high altitude of 7,500 feet or greater. The park is home to a wide variety of wildlife including grizzly bears, wolves, bison, elk, deer, coyotes and more. Yellowstone is also host to many natural scenic attractions including the popular Old Faithful geyser. There are numerous other geysers, hot springs, mudpots, and fumaroles which are all evidence of ongoing volcanic activity. Included in this park is Yellowstone Lake, which is the largest high-altitude lake in North America. While the lake looks stunning with its brilliantly blue water, it does have many hot hydrothermal spots, so people are advised not to swim in most of the lake areas and pets are prohibited from swimming. Traveling to Yellowstone Park with a pet can be pretty restrictive, but you will still be able to view most of the popular sights that tourists without pets usually come to see. While pets are not allowed on the trails, in the backcountry, in thermal areas, or on the boardwalks, you will still be able to view Old Faithful from about 200 feet back. Even at that distance, Old Faithful can look pretty spectacular. And if you drive the Grand Loop Road, you will be able to view some points of interest and perhaps see some wildlife including black bears, grizzly bears, bison and elk. Dogs are allowed in parking areas, campgrounds and within 100 feet of roads. Pets must be on a 6 foot or less leash or crated or caged at all times. Pets are not allowed to be left unattended and tied to an object. However, they can remain in your car while you view attractions near roads and parking areas. The park officials do require that you provide sufficient ventilation in the car for your pet's comfort and survival. For accommodations within the park, dogs are welcome in some of the park's cabins. There are some dog-friendly cabins within easy walking distance of Old Faithful. If you are looking for some dog-friendly hiking trails, there are numerous dog-friendly trails in the nearby Shoshone National Forest, located between the town of

Cody and Yellowstone National Park.

Outdoor Restaurants

Betty Rock Coffee House & Cafe 325 Pearl Avenue Jackson WY   307-733-0747
Dogs are allowed at the outdoor tables. The restaurant has outdoor tables only in the summer.
Cafe Two 45 245 W Pearl Street Jackson WY   307-734-0245
Dogs are allowed at the outdoor tables. The restaurant has outdoor tables only in the summer.
Firehole Grill 611 Highway 20 West Yellowstone WY   406-646-4948
Dogs are allowed at the outdoor tables. This restaurant is open for breakfast, lunch and dinner.
Petes Rocky Mountain Pizza and Pasta Canyon Street and Madison Ave. West Yellowstone WY   406-646-7820
Enjoy pizza, pasta, chicken, salads and more. Dogs are allowed at the outdoor tables.
Pearl Street Bagels Fish Creek Center Wilson WY   307-739-1261
Dogs are allowed at the outdoor tables.

Yellowstone - Grand Teton (Montana)

Accommodations

Pioneer Motel 515 Madison Avenue West Yellowstone MT   406-646-9705
Well behaved dogs up to 60 pounds are allowed. There are no additional pet fees. Dogs are not allowed on the beds, must be leashed on the property, and are not allowed to be left alone in the room.

Campgrounds and RV Parks

Lionshead RV Resort 1545 Targhee Pass H W Yellowstone MT   406-646-7662
http://www.lionsheadrv.com
Dogs of all sizes are allowed. There are no additional pet fees. Dogs must be leased and cleaned up after. This RV park is closed during the off-season. The camping and tent areas also allow dogs. There is a dog walk area at the campground.
Madison Arm Resort 5475 Madison Arm Road West Yellowstone MT   406-646-9328
http://www.madisonarmresort.com/
Dogs of all sizes are allowed. There are no additional pet fees. Dogs may not be left unattended, and they must be leashed at all times, and cleaned up after. This RV park is closed during the off-season. The camping and tent areas also allow dogs. There is a dog walk area at the campground.
Yellowstone Grizzly RV Park 210 S Electric Street West Yellowstone MT   406-646-4466
http://www.grizzlyrv.com
Dogs of all sizes are allowed. There are no additional pet fees. Dogs must be quiet, well behaved, leashed, and cleaned up after. Dogs may not be left unattended. There is a forest nearby where they can run if they are under voice command. This RV park is closed during the off-season. The camping and tent areas also allow dogs. There is a dog walk area at the campground. Dogs are allowed in the camping cabins.

Chapter 24

Dog-Friendly Highway Guides

Highway 1 Accommodation Listings

California Listings

Dogs per Room

Westport

Howard Creek Ranch Inn B&B	707-964-6725	40501 N. Highway 1 Westport CA	1+

Fort Bragg

Beachcomber Motel	707-964-2402	1111 N. Main Street Fort Bragg CA	1+
Cleone Gardens Inn	707-964-2788	24600 N. Hwy 1 Fort Bragg CA	1+
Delamere Seaside Cottages	707-964-3175	16821 Ocean Drive Fort Bragg CA	1+
Harbor View Seasonal Rental	760-438-2563	Call to arrange. Fort Bragg CA	1+
Quality Inn and Suites Tradewinds	707-964-4761	400 S Main Street - Exit H 1/Main Street Fort Bragg CA	1+
The Rendezvous Inn and Restaurant	707-964-8142	647 North Main Street Fort Bragg CA	3+

Mendocino

Abigails Bed & Breakfast	707-937-4892	P.O. Box 150, 499 Howard St. Mendocino CA	1+
Coastal Getaways	707-937-9200	10501 Ford Street POB1355 Mendocino CA	1+
Inn at Schoolhouse Creek	707-937-5525	7051 N. Highway 1 Mendocino CA	1+
Little River Inn	707-937-5942	7901 Highway One Mendocino CA	1+
MacCallum House	707-937-0289	45020 Albion Street Mendocino CA	1+
Mendocino Coast Reservations	707-937-5033	Call to Arrange Mendocino CA	1+
Mendocino Seaside Cottages	707-485-0239	10940 Lansing St Mendocino CA	1+
Pacific Mist Inn and Cabins	707-937-1543	6051 Highway One Mendocino CA	1+
Stanford Inn by the Sea and Spa	707-937-5615	44850 Comptche Ukiah Rd and Highway One Mendocino CA	1+
Sweetwater Spa & Inn	707-937-4076	44840 Main Street Mendocino CA	1+

Gualala

Ocean View Properties	707-884-3538	P.O. Box 1285 Gualala CA	1+
Sea Ranch Vacation Homes	707-884-4235	P.O. Box 246 Gualala CA	1+
Serenisea Vacation Homes	707-884-3836	36100 Highway 1 S. Gualala CA	1+
Surf Motel	707-884-3571	39170 S. Highway 1 Gualala CA	1+

Inverness

Rosemary Cottage	415-663-9338	75 Balboa Ave Inverness CA	1+

Point Reyes Station

Point Reyes Station Inn Bed and Breakfast	415-663-9372	11591 Highway One, Box 824 Point Reyes Station CA	1+
Tree House Bed and Breakfast Inn	415-663-8720	73 Drake Summit, P.O. Box 1075 Point Reyes Station CA	1+

San Francisco

Campton Place Hotel	415-781-5555	340 Stockton Street San Francisco CA	1+
Crowne Plaza - Union Square	415-398-8900	480 Sutter Street San Francisco CA	1+
Days Inn - Lombard St	415-922-2010	2358 Lombard Street San Francisco CA	1+
Four Seasons Hotel San Francisco	415-633-3000	757 Market St. San Francisco CA	1+
Harbor Court Hotel	415-882-1300	165 Steuart Street San Francisco CA	2
Holiday Inn Select	415-433-6600	750 Kearny Street San Francisco CA	2
Hotel Cosmo	415-673-6040	761 Post Street San Francisco CA	1+
Hotel Diva	800-553-1900	440 Geary Street - Exit 9th Street/Civic Center San Francisco CA	1
Hotel Metropolis	800-553-9100	25 Mason Street - Exit 9th Street/Civic Center San Francisco CA	1
Hotel Palomar	415-348-1111	12 Fourth Street San Francisco CA	1+
Hotel Triton	415-394-0500	342 Grant Avenue San Francisco CA	1+
Hotel Union Square	800-553-1900	114 Powell Street - Exit 9th Street/Civic Center San Francisco CA	1
Kensington Park Hotel	800-553-9100	450 Post Street - Exit I 80 San Francisco CA	1
Marina Motel - on Lombard Street	415-921-9406	2576 Lombard St. San Francisco CA	1+
Monticello Inn	415-392-8800	127 Ellis Street San Francisco CA	1+
Palace Hotel	415-512-1111	2 New Montgomery Street San Francisco CA	1+
Prescott Hotel	415-563-0303	545 Post Street San Francisco CA	1+
San Francisco Marriott Fisherman's Wharf	415-775-7555	1250 Columbus Avenue San Francisco CA	2
Serrano Hotel	415-885-2500	405 Taylor Street San Francisco CA	3+
Sheraton Fisherman's Wharf Hotel	415-362-5500	2500 Mason St. San Francisco CA	1+
The Laurel Inn	415-567-8467	444 Presidio Ave. San Francisco CA	1+
The Palace Hotel	415-512-1111	2 New Montgomery St. San Francisco CA	1+
The W San Francisco	415-777-5300	181 3rd St. San Francisco CA	1+

Half Moon Bay

Comfort Inn	650-712-1999	2930 N Cabrillo H Half Moon Bay CA	3+
Holiday Inn Express	650-726-3400	230 S Cabrillo Hwy Half Moon Bay CA	1+

Santa Cruz

Edgewater Beach Motel	831-423-0440	525 Second Street Santa Cruz CA	1+
Guesthouse International	831-425-3722	330 Ocean Street Santa Cruz CA	1+
Redtail Ranch by the Sea	831-429-1322	Call to Arrange. Santa Cruz CA	1+

Watsonville

Best Western Rose Garden Inn	831-724-3367	740 Freedom Blvd Watsonville CA	2

Highway Guides - Please always call ahead to make sure that an establishment is still dog-friendly

Motel 6 - Watsonville - Monterey Area	831-728-4144	125 Silver Leaf Drive Watsonville CA	1+
Red Roof Inn - Watsonville	831-740-4520	1620 West Beach Street Watsonville CA	1+
Monterey			
Best Western The Beach Resort	831-394-3321	2600 Sand Dunes Dr Monterey CA	2
El Adobe Inn	831-372-5409	936 Munras Ave. Monterey CA	1+
Hyatt Regency Monterey	831-372-1234	1 Old Golf Course Road - Exit Monterey Peninsula Monterey CA	2
Monterey Fireside Lodge	831-373-4172	1131 10th Street Monterey CA	1+
Motel 6 - Monterey	831-646-8585	2124 North Fremont Street Monterey CA	1+
Carmel			
Best Western Carmel Mission Inn	831-624-1841	3665 Rio Rd Carmel CA	2
Carmel Country Inn	831-625-3263	P.O. Box 3756 Carmel CA	1+
Casa De Carmel	831-624-2429	Monte Verde & Ocean Ave Carmel CA	1+
Coachman's Inn	831-624-6421	San Carlos St. & 7th Carmel CA	1+
Cypress Inn	831-624-3871	Lincoln & 7th Carmel CA	1+
Happy Landing Inn	831-624-7917	Monte Verde at 6th Carmel CA	2
Hofsas House Hotel	831-624-2745	San Carlos Street Carmel CA	1+
Lincoln Green Inn	831-624-7738	PO Box 2747 Carmel CA	1+
Sunset House	831-624-4884	Camino Real and Ocean Ave Carmel CA	1+
The Forest Lodge Cottages	831-624-7055	Ocean Ave. and Torres St. (P.O. Box 1316) Carmel CA	1+
The Tradewinds at Carmel	831-624-2776	Mission Street at 3rd Avenue Carmel CA	1+
Vagabond's House Inn B&B	831-624-7738	P.O. Box 2747 Carmel CA	1+
Wayside Inn	831-624-5336	Mission St & 7th Ave. Carmel CA	1+
Big Sur			
Big Sur Vacation Retreat	831-624-5339 Ext 13	off Highway One Big Sur CA	1+
San Simeon			
Best Western Cavalier Oceanfront Resort	805-927-4688	9415 Hearst Dr San Simeon CA	2
Motel 6 - San Simeon - Hearst Castle Area	805-927-8691	9070 Castillo Drive San Simeon CA	1+
Silver Surf Motel	805-927-4661	9390 Castillo Drive San Simeon CA	1+
Cambria			
Cambria Shores Inn	805-927-8644	6276 Moonstone Beach Drive Cambria CA	2
The Big Red House	805-927-1390	370- B Chelsea Lane Cambria CA	1+
Morro Bay			
Bayfront Inn	805-772-5607	1150 Embarcadero Morro Bay CA	1+
Days Inn	805-772-2711	1095 Main Street Morro Bay CA	1+
Motel 6 - Morro Bay	805-772-5641	298 Atascadero Road Morro Bay CA	1+
Pleasant Inn Motel	805-772-8521	235 Harbor Street Morro Bay CA	1+
San Luis Obispo			
Holiday Inn Express	805-544-8600	1800 Monterey Street San Luis Obispo CA	1+
Motel 6 - San Luis Obispo North	805-549-9595	1433 Calle Joaquin San Luis Obispo CA	1+
Motel 6 - San Luis Obispo South	805-541-6992	1625 Calle Joaquin San Luis Obispo CA	1+
Sands Suites & Motel	805-544-0500	1930 Monterey Street San Luis Obispo CA	1+
Vagabond Inn	805-544-4710	210 Madonna Rd. San Luis Obispo CA	1+
Pismo Beach			
Motel 6 - Pismo Beach	805-773-2665	860 4th Street Pismo Beach CA	1+
Oxford Suites	805-773-3773	651 Five Cities Drive Pismo Beach CA	1+
Sea Gypsy Motel	805-773-1801	1020 Cypress Street Pismo Beach CA	1+
Lompoc			
Days Inn - Vandenberg Village	805-733-5000	3955 Apollo Way Lompoc CA	1+
Motel 6 - Lompoc	805-735-7631	1521 North H Street Lompoc CA	1+
Quality Inn and Suites	805-735-8555	1621 N H Street - Exit H 246 Lompoc CA	1+
Goleta			
Motel 6 - Santa Barbara - Goleta	805-964-3596	5897 Calle Real Goleta CA	1+
Santa Barbara			
Best Western Beachside Inn	805-965-6556	336 W Cabrillo Blvd Santa Barbara CA	2
Casa Del Mar Hotel	805-965-4418	18 Bath Street Santa Barbara CA	1+
Fess Parkers Doubletree Resort	805-564-4333	633 E Cabrillo Blvd - Exit Milpas Street Santa Barbara CA	3+
Four Seasons Resort	805-969-2261	1260 Channel Dr. Santa Barbara CA	1+
Montecito Del Mar	805-962-2006	316 W Montecito St Santa Barbara CA	1+
Motel 6 - Santa Barbara - Beach	805-564-1392	443 Corona Del Mar Santa Barbara CA	1+
Motel 6 - Santa Barbara - State Street	805-687-5400	3505 State Street Santa Barbara CA	1+
San Ysidro Ranch	805-969-5046	900 San Ysidro Lane Santa Barbara CA	1+
Secret Garden Inn & Cottages	805-687-2300	1908 Bath Street Santa Barbara CA	1+
Ventura			
Crowne Plaza Hotel - Ventura Beach	805-648-2100	450 E Harbor Blvd Ventura CA	1+
La Quinta Inn Ventura	805-658-6200	5818 Valentine Rd. - Exit Victoria Ventura CA	3+

Motel 6 - Ventura Beach	805-643-5100	2145 East Harbor Boulevard Ventura CA	1+
Motel 6 - Ventura South	805-650-0080	3075 Johnson Drive Ventura CA	1+
Vagabond Inn	805-648-5371	756 E. Thompson Blvd. Ventura CA	1+
Oxnard			
Casa Sirena Hotel and Resort	805-985-6311	3605 Peninsula Rd Oxnard CA	1+
Residence Inn by Marriott	805-278-2200	2101 W Vineyard Avenue - Exit Vinyard Avenue Oxnard CA	3+
Vagabond Inn	805-983-0251	1245 N. Oxnard Blvd. Oxnard CA	1+
Santa Monica			
LeMerigot Hotel-A JWMarriott Beach Hotel and Spa	310-395-9700	1740 Ocean Avenue Santa Monica CA	3+
Loews Santa Monica Beach Hotel	310-458-6700	1700 Ocean Avenue Santa Monica CA	1+
Sheraton Delfina Santa Monica Hotel	310-399-9344	530 West Pico Blvd. Santa Monica CA	2
The Fairmont Miramar Hotel Santa Monica	310-576-7777	101 Wilshire Blvd - Exit Ocean Avenue Santa Monica CA	1+

Interstate 5 Accommodation Listings

Washington Listings (Interstate 5)

Dogs per Room

Ferndale			
Super 8 Ferndale/Bellingham Area	360-384-8881	5788 Barrett Ave - Exit 262 Ferndale WA	2
Bellingham			
Days Inn Bellingham	360-671-6200	125 E Kellogg Rd - Exit 256 Bellingham WA	2
Holiday Inn Express	360-671-4800	4160 Guide Meridian Bellingham WA	1+
Motel 6 - Bellingham	360-671-4494	3701 Byron Street Bellingham WA	1+
Quality Inn Baron Suites	360-647-8000	100 E Kellogg Road - Exit H 539N Bellingham WA	2
Mount Vernon			
Best Western College Way Inn	360-424-4287	300 W College Way - Exit 227 College Way Mount Vernon WA	2
Comfort Inn	360-428-7020	1910 Freeway Drive - Exit 227/College Way Mount Vernon WA	3+
Days Inn Mt Vernon	360-424-4141	2009 Riverside Dr - Exit 227 Mount Vernon WA	2
Everett			
Days Inn Seattle/ Everett	425-355-1570	1602 SE Everett Mall Way - Exit 189 Everett WA	2
Motel 6 - Everett North	425-347-2060	10006 Evergreen Way Everett WA	1+
Motel 6 - Everett South	425-353-8120	224 128th Street Southwest Everett WA	1+
Lynnwood			
Embassy Suites Seattle - North/Lynnwood	425-775-2500	20610 44th Ave. West Lynnwood WA	1
La Quinta Inn Lynnwood	425-775-7447	4300 Alderwood Mall Blvd - Exit 181 Lynnwood WA	1+
Residence Inn by Marriott	425-771-1100	18200 Alderwood Mall Parkway - Exit 183 Lynnwood WA	1+
Seattle			
Best Western Executive Inn	206-448-9444	200 Taylor Ave N - Exit Danny Way Seattle WA	1
Doubletree	206-246-8600	18740 International Blvd - Exit 152 Seattle WA	3+
Holiday Inn Express Hotel & Suites	206-824-3200	19621 International Blvd Seattle WA	1+
La Quinta Inn & Suites Seattle Downtown	206-624-6820	2224 8th Avenue - Exit Mercer Seattle WA	3+
La Quinta Inn Seattle Sea-Tac	206-241-5211	2824 S. 188th St. - Exit 152 Seattle WA	3+
Quality Inn and Suites	206-728-7666	225 Aurora Avenue North - Exit 167/Mercer Street Seattle WA	2
Red Lion	206-762-0300	11244 Pacific Highway S - Exit 158 Seattle WA	2
Residence Inn by Marriott	206-624-6000	800 Fairview Avenue North - Exit 167/Seattle Center/Mercer Street Seattle WA	3+
Super 8 Seattle/Sea-Tac Intl Arpt	206-433-8188	3100 S 192nd - Exit 152 Seattle WA	2
Federal Way			
Super 8 Federal WAy	253-838-8808	1688 S 348th St - exit 142b Federal Way WA	2
Fife			
Emerald Queen Hotel and Casino	253-922-3555	5700 Pacific Hwy East Fife WA	1
Quality Inn	253-926-2301	5601 Pacific H E - Exit 137 to 54th Avenue Fife WA	1+
Tacoma			
Days Inn Tacoma Mall	253-475-5900	6802 Tacoma Mall Blvd - Exit 129 Tacoma WA	2
La Quinta Inn & Suites Seattle Tacoma	253-383-0146	1425 E. 27th St. - Exit Portland Avenue Tacoma WA	2
Puyallup			
Best Western Park Plaza	253-848-1500	620 South Hill Park Dr - Take Hwy 512 Towards Puyallup Exit 9 Puyallup WA	2
Holiday Inn Express & Suites	253-848-4900	812 South Hill Park Drive Puyallup WA	1+
Olympia			
Super 8 Lacey/Olympia Area	360-459-8888	112 College St SE - Exit Exti 109 Lacey WA	2
West Coast Inn	360-943-4000	2300 Evergreen Park Drive Olympia WA	1+

Highway Guides - Please always call ahead to make sure that an establishment is still dog-friendly

Best Western Tumwater Inn	360-956-1235	5188 Capitol Blvd - Exit 102 Tumwater WA	3+
Comfort Inn	360-352-0691	1620 74th Avenue SW - Exit 101 (Not H 101) Tumwater WA	3+
Motel 6 - Tumwater - Olympia	360-754-7320	400 West Lee Street Tumwater WA	1+
Centralia			
Motel 6 - Centralia	360-330-2057	1310 Belmont Avenue Centralia WA	1+
Kelso			
Motel 6 - Kelso - Mt St Helens	360-425-3229	106 Minor Road Kelso WA	1+
Red Lion	360-636-4400	510 Kelso Drive - Exit 39 Kelso WA	3+
Super 8 Kelso/Longview Area	360-423-8880	250 Kelso Dr - Exit 39 Kelso WA	2
Vancouver			
Comfort Inn	360-574-6000	13207 NE 20th Avenue - Exit 7 Vancouver WA	3+
Quality Inn and Suites	360-696-0516	7001 NE H 99 - Exit 4/78th Street Vancouver WA	3+
Red Lion	360-694-8341	100 Columbia Street - Exit 1B City Center Vancouver WA	3+
Red Lion	360-566-1100	1500 NE 134th Street - Exit 7 Vancouver WA	3+
Residence Inn by Marriott	360-253-4800	8005 NE Parkway Drive Vancouver WA	3+
Staybridge Suites	360-891-8282	7301 NE 41st St Vancouver WA	1+

Oregon Listings (Interstate 5)   Dogs per Room

Portland			
Crowne Plaza	503-624-8400	14811 Kruse Oaks Dr Lake Oswego OR	1+
Residence Inn by Marriott	503-684-2603	15200 SW Bangy Road - Exit 292E Lake Oswego OR	3+
Days Inn Portland North	503-289-1800	9930 N Whitaker Road - Exit 306b Portland OR	2
Hilton	503-226-1611	921 SW Sixth Avenue - Exit 300 Portland OR	2
La Quinta Inn Portland Convention Center	503-233-7933	431 NE Multnomah - Exit 302A/Broadway Portland OR	3+
Best Western Northwind Inn and Suites	503-431-2100	16105 SW Pacific Hwy - Exit 294 Tigard OR	2
Comfort Inn and Suites	503-612-9952	7640 SW Warm Springs Street - Exit 289 Tualatin OR	2
Comfort Inn	503-682-9000	8855 SW Citizen Drive - Exit 283 Wilsonville OR	2
Holiday Inn Select	503-682-2211	25425 SW 95th Ave Wilsonville OR	1+
La Quinta Inn Wilsonville	503-682-3184	8815 SW Sun Place - Exit 286 Wilsonville OR	3+
Super 8 Wilsonville/Portland Area	503-682-2088	25438 SW Parkway Ave - Exit 286 Wilsonville OR	2
Woodburn			
Best Western Woodburn	503-982-6515	2887 Newberg Hwy - Exit 271 Woodburn OR	2
La Quinta Inn & Suites Woodburn	503-982-1727	120 Arney Rd NE - Exit 271 Woodburn OR	3+
Super 8 Woodburn	503-981-8881	821 Evergreen Rd - Exit 271 Woodburn OR	2
Salem			
Best Western Black Bear Inn	503-581-1559	1600 Motor Court NE - Exit 256 Salem OR	2
Best Western Pacific Highway Inn	503-390-3200	4646 Portland Rd NE - Exit 258 Salem OR	2
Holiday Inn Express	503-391-7000	890 Hawthorne Ave SE Salem OR	1+
Motel 6 - Salem	503-371-8024	1401 Hawthorne Avennue Northeast Salem OR	1+
Phoenix Inn - Salem South	503-588-9220	4370 Commercial St SE Salem OR	1+
Red Lion	503-370-7888	3301 Market Street Salem OR	1+
Residence Inn by Marriott	503-585-6500	640 Hawthorne Avenue SE Salem OR	2
Super 8 Salem	503-370-8888	1288 Hawthorne NE - Exit 256 Salem OR	2
Corvallis			
Holiday Inn Express	541-752-0800	781 NE Second Street - Exit 228 Corvallis OR	2
Super 8 Corvallis	541-758-8088	407 NW 2nd Street - Exit 228 Corvallis OR	2
Albany			
Best Western Albany Inn	541-928-6322	315 Airport Rd SE - Exit 234 Albany OR	2
Days Inn Albany	541-928-5050	1100 Price Road SE - Exit 233 Albany OR	2
Holiday Inn Express Hotel and Suites	541-928-8820	105 Opal court - Exit 234 Albany OR	2
La Quinta Inn & Suites Albany	541-928-0921	251 Airport Rd SE - Exit 234 Albany OR	3+
Motel 6 - Albany	541-926-4233	2735 East Pacific Boulevard Albany OR	1+
Eugene			
Best Western New Oregon Motel	541-683-3669	1655 Franklin Blvd - Exit 192 Eugene OR	2
Days Inn Eugene	541-342-6383	1859 Franklin Blvd - Exit 192 Eugene OR	2
Hilton	541-342-2000	66 E 6th Avenue - Exit 194B Eugene OR	2
La Quinta Inn & Suites Eugene	541-344-8335	155 Day Island Rd - Exit 194 Eugene OR	3+
Motel 6 - Eugene South - Springfield	541-687-2395	3690 Glenwood Drive Eugene OR	1+
Red Lion	541-342-5201	205 Coburg Road - Exit 195 Beltline W Eugene OR	3+
Residence Inn by Marriott	541-342-7171	25 Club Road Eugene OR	3+
Valley River Inn	541-687-0123	1000 Valley River Way - Exit 195B W Eugene OR	3+
Creswell			
Best Western Creswell Inn	541-895-3341	345 E Oregon Ave - Exit 182 Creswell OR	2
Cottage Grove			
Comfort Inn	541-942-9747	845 Gateway Blvd - Exit 174 Cottage Grove OR	3+
Holiday Inn Express	541-942-1000	1601 Gateway Blvd Cottage Grove OR	1+

Roseburg

Best Western Douglas Inn	541-673-6625	511 SE Stephens - Exit 124 Roseburg OR	2
Best Western Garden Villa Inn	541-672-1601	760 NW Garden Valley Blvd - Exit 125 Roseburg OR	2
Holiday Inn Express	541-673-7517	375 Harvard Blvd Roseburg OR	1+
Motel 6 - Roseburg	541-464-8000	3100 Northwest Aviation Roseburg OR	1+
Quality Inn Central	541-673-5561	427 NW Garden Valley Blvd - Exit 125 Roseburg OR	2
Sleep Inn and Suites	541-464-8338	2855 NW Edenbower Blvd - Exit 127 Roseburg OR	2
Super 8 Roseburg	541-672-8880	3200 NW Aviation Dr - Exit 127 Roseburg OR	2

Grants Pass

Best Western Grants Pass Inn	541-476-1117	111 NE Agness Ave - Exit 55 Grants Pass OR	2
Comfort Inn	541-479-8301	1889 NE 6th Street - Exit 58 W Grants Pass OR	3+
Grants Pass Vacation Rental . com	541-660-5673	Call to Arrange Grants Pass OR	1+
Holiday Inn Express	541-471-6144	105 NE Agness Ave Grants Pass OR	1+
La Quinta Inn & Suites Grants Pass	541-472-1808	243 NE Morgan Lane Grants Pass OR	3+
Motel 6 - Grants Pass	541-474-1331	1800 NE 7th Street Grants Pass OR	1+
Redwood Motel	541-476-0878	815 NE 6th Street Grants Pass OR	1+
Super 8 Grants Pass	541-474-0888	1949 NE 7th St - Exit 58 Grants Pass OR	2

Medford

Motel 6 - Medford North	541-779-0550	2400 Biddle Road Medford OR	1+
Motel 6 - Medford South	541-773-4290	950 Alba Drive Medford OR	1+
Red Lion	541-779-5811	200 N Riverside Avenue - Exit 27 Medford OR	3+
Reston Hotel	541-779-3141	2300 Crater Lake Hwy Medford OR	1+

Ashland

Best Western Bard's Inn	541-482-0049	132 N Main St - Exit 19 Ashland OR	2
Best Western Windsor Inn	541-488-2330	2520 Ashland St - Exit 14 Ashland OR	2
La Quinta Inn & Suites Ashland	541-482-6932	434 Valley View Rd - Exit 19 Ashland OR	3+
Super 8 Ashland	541-482-8887	2350 Ashland St - Exit 14 Ashland OR	2

California Listings   (Interstate 5)   Dogs per Room

Yreka

Best Western Miner's Inn	530-842-4355	122 E Miner St - Central Yreka Exit Yreka CA	3+
Comfort Inn	530-842-1612	1804 E Fort Jones Road - Exit 773 Yreka CA	1
Days Inn	530-842-1612	1804 B Fort Jones Rd Yreka CA	1+
Motel 6 - Yreka	530-842-4111	1785 South Main Street Yreka CA	1+

Mount Shasta

Railroad Park Resort	530-235-4440	100 Railroad Park Road Dunsmuir CA	1+
Dream Inn Bed and Breakfast	530-926-1536	326 Chestnut Street Mount Shasta CA	1+
Econo Lodge	530-926-3145	908 S. Mt. Shasta Blvd. Mount Shasta CA	1+
Mount Shasta Ranch Bed and Breakfast	530-926-3870	1008 W. A. Barr Rd. Mount Shasta CA	1+
Mountain Air Lodge	530-926-3411	1121 S Mount Shasta Blvd Mount Shasta CA	1+
Swiss Holiday Lodge	530-926-3446	2400 S. Mt. Shasta Blvd. Mount Shasta CA	1+
Comfort Inn Central	530-938-1982	1844 Shastina Drive - Exit S Weed Weed CA	1+
Holiday Inn Express	530-938-1308	1830 Black Butte Drive Weed CA	1+
Lake Shastina Golf Resort	530-938-3201	5925 Country Club Drive Weed CA	1+
Motel 6 - Weed - Mount Shasta	530-938-4101	466 North Weed Boulevard Weed CA	1+

Redding

Best Western Hospitality House Motel	530-241-6464	532 N Market St - Exit Market St Redding CA	3+
Fawndale Lodge and RV Resort	800-338-0941	15215 Fawndale Road Redding CA	1+
Holiday Inn Express	530-241-5500	1080 Twin View Blvd Redding CA	1+
La Quinta Inn Redding	530-221-8200	2180 Hilltop Drive - Exit 677/Cypress Avenue Redding CA	3+
Motel 6 - Redding Central	530-221-1800	1640 Hilltop Drive Redding CA	1+
Motel 6 - Redding North	530-246-4470	1250 Twin View Boulevard Redding CA	1+
Motel 6 - Redding South	530-221-0562	2385 Bechelli Lane Redding CA	1+
Ponderosa Inn	530-241-6300	2220 Pine St - Exit Cypress St Redding CA	2
Quality Inn	530-221-6530	2059 Hilltop Drive - Exit Cypress Avenue Redding CA	2
River Inn	530-241-9500	1835 Park Marina Drive Redding CA	1+
Shasta Lodge	530-243-6133	1245 Pine Street Redding CA	1+

Anderson

AmeriHost Inn	530-365-6100	2040 Factory Outlets Dr Anderson CA	1+

Red Bluff

Comfort Inn	530-529-7060	90 Sale Lane - Exit H 99/H 36 Red Bluff CA	3+
Motel 6 - Red Bluff	530-527-9200	20 Williams Avenue Red Bluff CA	1+
Travelodge	530-527-6020	38 Antelope Blvd Red Bluff CA	1+

Corning

Best Western Inn-Corning	530-824-2468	2165 Solano St - Corning Exit Corning CA	2
Comfort Inn	530-824-5200	910 H 99W - Exit Corning Road Corning CA	2
Holiday Inn Express Hotel & Suites	530-824-6400	3350 Sunrise Way Corning CA	1+

Willows

Best Western Golden Pheasant Inn	530-934-4603	249 N Humboldt Ave Willows CA	3+
Days Inn	530-934-4444	475 N Humboldt Ave Willows CA	1+
Motel 6 - Willows	530-934-7026	452 Humboldt Avenue Willows CA	1+
Williams			
Comfort Inn	530-473-2381	400 C Street - Exit Williams Williams CA	3+
Holiday Inn Express Hotel and Suites	530-473-5120	374 Ruggieri Way - Exit E Street Williams CA	2
Motel 6 - Williams	530-473-5337	455 4th Street Williams CA	1+
Woodland			
Holiday Inn Express	530-662-7750	2070 Freeway Drive Woodland CA	1+
Motel 6 - Woodland - Sacramento Area	530-666-6777	1564 East Main Street Woodland CA	1+
Sacramento - Days Inn	530-666-3800	1524 East Main Street Woodland CA	1+
Sacramento			
Clarion Hotel Mansion Inn	916-444-8000	700 16th Street - Exit J Street Sacramento CA	1
Holiday Inn	916-338-5800	5321 Date Ave - Exit Madison Ave Sacramento CA	2
Holiday Inn Express	916-444-4436	728 16 Street Sacramento CA	1+
La Quinta Inn Sacramento Downtown	916-448-8100	200 Jibboom St. - Exit Richards Blvd Sacramento CA	3+
Stockton			
Holiday Inn	209-474-3301	111 East March Lane - Exit March Lane Stockton CA	2
La Quinta Inn Stockton	209-952-7800	2710 W. March Ln. - Exit W March Lane Stockton CA	3+
Residence Inn by Marriott	209-472-9800	March Lane and Brookside - Exit March Lane and turn W Stockton CA	3+
Travelodge	209-466-7777	1707 Fremont St Stockton CA	1+
Lathrop			
Days Inn	209-982-1959	14750 South Harlan Rd Lathrop CA	1+
Westley			
Days Inn	209-894-5500	7144 McCracken Rd Westley CA	1+
Econo Lodge	209-894-3900	7100 McCracken Rd Westley CA	1+
Super 8 Westley/Modesto Area	209-894-3888	7115 McCracken Road - I 580 Exit to Westley Westley CA	2
Gustine			
Motel 6 - Santa Nella - Los Banos	209-826-6644	12733 South Highway 33 Gustine CA	1+
Santa Nella			
Holiday Inn Express	209-826-8282	28976 W. Plaza Drive Santa Nella CA	1+
Los Banos			
Best Western Executive Inn	209-827-0954	301 West Pacheco Blvd - Exit Hwy 152 Los Banos CA	2
Days Inn	209-826-9690	2169 East Pacheco Blvd Los Banos CA	1+
Sunstar Inn	209-826-3805	839 W. Pacheco Blvd Los Banos CA	1+
Firebaugh			
Best Western Apricot Inn	559-659-1444	46290 W Panoche Rd - Exit Panoche Rd Firebaugh CA	2
Coalinga			
Best Western Big Country Inn	559-935-0866	25020 West Dorris Ave - Exit SRI 98 Coalinga CA	2
Motel 6 - Coalinga East	559-935-1536	25008 West Dorris Avenue Coalinga CA	1+
Pleasant Valley Inn	559-935-2063	25278 W Doris St Coalinga CA	1+
Kettleman City			
Best Western Kettleman City Inn and Suites	559-386-0804	33410 Powers Dr - Kettleman City Exit Kettleman City CA	2
Super 8 Kettleman City	559-386-9530	33415 Powers Drive - Hwy 41 Exit to Bernard Dr Kettleman City CA	2
Lost Hills			
Days Inn	661-797-2371	14684 Aloma St Lost Hills CA	1+
Motel 6 - Lost Hills	661-797-2346	14685 Warren Street Lost Hills CA	1+
Buttonwillow			
Motel 6 - Bakersfield - Buttonwillow	661-764-5153	20638 Tracy Avenue Buttonwillow CA	1+
Gorman			
Econo Lodge	661-248-6411	49713 Gorman Post Rd Gorman CA	1+
Santa Clarita			
Residence Inn by Marriott	661-290-2800	25320 The Old Road - Exit Lyons Avenue L Santa Clarita CA	3+
Hollywood - West LA			
Hilton Burbank	818-843-6000	2500 Hollywood Way - Exit Hollywood Way Burbank CA	3+
Anaheim Resort Area			
Anaheim Marriott	714-750-8000	700 W Convention Way - Exit Katella Avenue Anaheim CA	3+
Hilton	714-750-4321	777 Convention Way - Exit Katella Avenue Anaheim CA	2
Staybridge Suites	714-748-7700	1855 South Manchester Avenue Anaheim CA	1+
Fullerton Marriott at California State University	714-738-7800	2701 E Nutwood Avenue - Exit H 57 Fullerton CA	3+
Anaheim Marriott Suites	714-750-1000	12015 Harbor Blvd - Exit Chapman Avenue Garden Grove CA	3+
Residence Inn by Marriott	714-591-4000	11931 Harbor Blvd - Exit Chapman Ave Garden Grove CA	3+
Orange County South			

Doubletree	949-661-1100	34402 Pacific Coast Highway - Exit H 1 Dana Point CA	3+
Candlewood Suites	949-788-0500	16150 Sand Canyon Ave Irvine CA	1+
Residence Inn by Marriott	949-380-3000	10 Morgan - Exit Alton Parkway-Right Irvine CA	3+
Holiday Inn	949-361-3000	111 S. Ave. De Estrella San Clemente CA	1+
San Diego County North			
Inns of America	760-931-1185	751 Raintree Carlsbad CA	1+
Quality Inn and Suites	760-931-1185	751 Raintree Drive - Exit Poinsetta Lane Carlsbad CA	2
Residence Inn by Marriott	760-431-9999	2000 Faraday Avenue - Exit Palomar Airport Road Carlsbad CA	3+
Hilton	858-792-5200	15575 Jimmy Durante Blvd - Exit Via de LaValle Del Mar CA	2
Best Western Encinitas Inn and Suites at Moonlight Beach	760-942-7455	85 Encinitas Blvd - Exit Encinitas Blvd Encinitas CA	1+
Holiday Inn Express	760-944-3800	607 Leucadia Blvd Encinitas CA	1+
La Quinta Inn San Diego - Oceanside	760-450-0730	937 N. Coast Highway - Exit Coast H Oceanside CA	3+
San Diego			
Coronado Island Marriott Resort	619-435-3000	2000 Second Street - Exit R on Glorietta Blvd after Coronado Bridge Coronado CA	3+
Andrea Villa Inn	858-459-3311	2402 Torrey Pines Rd La Jolla CA	1+
Residence Inn by Marriott	858-587-1770	8901 Gilman Drive - Exit Gilman Drive La Jolla CA	1+
San Diego Marriott La Jolla	858-587-1414	4240 La Jolla Village Drive - Exit La Jolla Drive La Jolla CA	3+
Hotel Solamar	619-531-8740	453 6th Avenue - Exit Front Street San Diego CA	2
Red Lion	619-297-1101	2270 Hotel Circle N - Exit Taylor Street San Diego CA	2
Residence Inn by Marriott	619-881-3600	1865 Hotel Circle S - Exit Hotel Circle/Taylor Street San Diego CA	3+
Staybridge Suites	858-453-5343	6639 Mira Mesa Blvd San Diego CA	1+
Staybridge Suites	619-795-4000	1110 A Street San Diego CA	1+

Interstate 10 Accommodation Listings

California Listings (Interstate 10)   Dogs per Room

Pomona - Ontario			
Country Inns & Suites by Carlson	909-937-6000	231 North Vineyard Avenue Ontario CA	1+
La Quinta Inn & Suites Ontario Airport	909-476-1112	3555 Inland Empire Blvd - Exit Haven Ontario CA	3+
Residence Inn by Marriott	909-937-6788	2025 Convention Center Way - Exit Vineyard Ave Ontario CA	3+
San Bernardino			
TownePlace Suites Ontario Airport	714-256-2070	9645 Milliken Avenue - Milliken Ave Exit Rancho Cucamonga CA	2
Best Western Sandman Motel	909-793-2001	1120 W Colton Ave - Exit Tennessee Ave Redlands CA	2
Best Western Empire Inn	909-877-0690	475 W Valley Blvd - Exit Riverside Rialto CA	3+
Hilton	909-889-0133	285 E Hospitality Lane - Exit Waterman N San Bernardino CA	2
Banning			
Travelodge	909-849-1000	1700 W. Ramsey Street Banning CA	1+
Palm Springs			
Comfort Suites	760324-5939	69151 E Palm Canyon Drive/H 111 - Exit Date Palm Drive S Cathedral City CA	3+
Best Western Date Tree Hotel	760-347-3421	81-909 Indio Bvd - Monroe St exit to Indio Blvd Indio CA	2
Holiday Inn Express	760-342-6344	84-096 Indio Springs Pkwy Indio CA	1+
Palm Shadow Inn	760-347-3476	80-761 Highway 111 Indio CA	1+
Comfort Suites	760-360-3337	39-585 Washington Street - Exit Washington Street Palm Desert CA	2
Residence Inn by Marriott	760-776-0050	38305 Cook Street - Exit Cook Street Palm Desert CA	3+
Hilton	760-320-6868	400 E Tahquitz Canyon Way - Exit 111/Palm Springs Palm Springs CA	2
Palm Springs Hotels Caliente Tropics Resort	800-658-5975	411 E. Palm Canyon Drive Palm Springs CA	1+
Super 8 Lodge - Palm Springs	760-322-3757	1900 N. Palm Canyon Drive Palm Springs CA	1+
Blythe			
Best Western Sahara Motel	760-922-7105	825 W Hobson Way - Exit Lovekin Blvd Blythe CA	3+
Comfort Suites Colorado River	760-922-9209	545 N Hobson Way - Exit 7th Street Blythe CA	1+
Holiday Inn Express	760-921-2300	600 W Donlon St - Exit Lovekin Blvd Blythe CA	2
Motel 6 - Blythe	760-922-6666	500 West Donlon Street Blythe CA	1+

Arizona Listings (Interstate 10)   Dogs per Room

Ehrenberg			
Best Western Flying J Motel	928-923-9711	I-10 Exit 1, S Frontage Rd - Exit 1 Ehrenberg AZ	2
Quartzsite			
Super 8 Quartzsite	928-927-8080	2050 Dome Rock Rd - Exit 17 Quartzsite AZ	2
Buckeye			
Days Inn Buckeye	623-386-5400	25205 West Yuma Rd - Exit 114 Buckeye AZ	2

Highway Guides - Please always call ahead to make sure that an establishment is still dog-friendly

Phoenix

Clarion Hotel Phoenix Tech Center	480-893-3900	5121 E La Puenta Avenue - Exit Elliot Road Phoenix AZ	2
Days Inn Phoenix Airport	602-244-8244	3333 E Van Buren - Exit Hwy 202 to Exit 32nd Phoenix AZ	2
Holiday Inn - West	602-484-9009	1500 N 51st Ave Phoenix AZ	1+
Holiday Inn Express Hotel & Suites	480-785-8500	15221 S. 50th St Phoenix AZ	1+
Super 8 Phoenix/West I-10	602-415-0888	1242 N 53rd Ave - 51st Ave Exit Phoenix AZ	2

Phoenix Area

Comfort Inn	480-705-8882	255 N Kyrene Road - Exit Chandler Blvd Chandler AZ	3+
Best Western Inn Phoenix-Glendale	623-939-9431	7116 N 59th Ave - Exit 59th Ave N Glendale AZ	3+
Best Western Phoenix Goodyear Inn	623-932-3210	55 N Litchfield Rd - Exit 128 Goodyear AZ	2
Hampton Inn	623-536-1313	2000 N Litchfield Road - Exit 128/Litchfield Road Goodyear AZ	3+
Holiday Inn Express	623-535-1313	1313 N. Litchfield Rd Goodyear AZ	1+
Super 8 Goodyear/Phoenix Area	623-932-9622	1710 N Dysart Rd - Exit 129 Goodyear AZ	2
Holiday Inn Express Hotel & Suites	623-853-1313	16771 N. 84th Avenue Peoria AZ	1+
Candlewood Suites	480-777-0440	1335 W Baseline Road Tempe AZ	1+
Country Inns & Suites by Carlson	480-345-8585	1660 W Elliot Rd Tempe AZ	1+
Residence Inn by Marriott	480-756-2122	5075 S. Priest Drive - Exit Baseline Road Tempe AZ	2
TownePlace Suites Tempe	480-345-7889	5223 S Priest Drive - Baseline Rd Exit Tempe AZ	2

Casa Grande

Days Inn Casa Grande	520-426-9240	5300 N Sunland Gin Rd - Exit 200 Casa Grande AZ	2
Holiday Inn	520-426-3500	777 N Pinal Ave Casa Grande AZ	1+
Super 8 Casa Grande	520-836-8800	2066 E Florence Blvd - Exit 194 Casa Grande AZ	2

Eloy

Red Roof Inn - Eloy	520-466-2522	4015 West Outer Drive Eloy AZ	1+

Tucson

Clarion Hotel Randolph Park	520-795-0330	102 N Alvernon Way - Exit Speedway Blvd Tucson AZ	3+
Comfort Suites	520-295-4400	6935 S Tucson Blvd - Exit Kino Parkway Tucson AZ	1+
Comfort Suites at Tucson Mall	520-888-6676	515 W Automall Drive - Exit 254 Tucson AZ	3+
Doubletree	520-881-4200	445 S Alvernon Way - Exit 258 Tucson AZ	2
Hilton	520-544-5000	10000 N Oracle Road - Exit Tangerine Tucson AZ	2
Holiday Inn Express	520-889-6600	2548 E. Medina Rd. Tucson AZ	1+
La Quinta Inn & Suites Tucson Airport	520-573-3333	7001 South Tucson Blvd. - Exit Valencia Road/Airport Tucson AZ	3+
La Quinta Inn Tucson Downtown	520-624-4455	750 West Starr Pass Blvd - Exit 259 Tucson AZ	3+
La Quinta Inn Tucson East	520-747-1414	6404 E. Broadway - Exit Broadway Tucson AZ	3+
Quality Inn	520-623-7792	1025 E Benson H - Exit 262/Benson H S Tucson AZ	2
Residence Inn by Marriott	520-721-0991	6477 E. Speedway Blvd - Exit Speedway Tucson AZ	2
Super 8 Tucson/Dwtn/University Area	520-622-6446	1248 N Stone St - Exit 257 Tucson AZ	2
TownePlace Suites Tucson	520-292-9697	405 W Rudasill Road - E to Orange Grove Exit Tucson AZ	2

Benson

Motel 6 - Benson	520-586-0066	637 South Whetstone Commerce Drive Benson AZ	1+
Super 8 Benson	520-586-1530	855 N Ocotillo Rd - Exit 304 Benson AZ	2

Willcox

Best Western Plaza Inn	520-384-3556	1100 W Rex Allen Dr - Exit 340 Willcox AZ	2
Days Inn Willcox	520-384-4222	724 N Bisbee Ave - Exit 340 Willcox AZ	2
Motel 6 - Willcox	520-384-2201	921 North Bisbee Avenue Willcox AZ	1+

New Mexico Listings   (Interstate 10)

Dogs per Room

Lordsburg

Best Western Western Skies Inn	505-542-8807	1303 South Main - Exit 22 Lordsburg NM	2
Holiday Inn Express	505-542-3666	1408 South Main - Exit 22 Lordsburg NM	2

Deming

Holiday Inn	505-546-2661	Exit 85 I-10 Deming NM	1+
La Quinta Inn & Suites Deming	505-546-0600	4300 E Pine St - Exit 85 Deming NM	3+
Motel 6 - Deming	505-546-2623	I-10 & Motel Drive Deming NM	1+

Las Cruces

Best Western Mesilla Valley Inn	505-524-8603	901 Avenida de Mesilla - Exit 140 Las Cruces NM	3+
Hampton Inn	505-536-8311	755 Avenida de Mesilla - Exit 140 Las Cruces NM	2
Holiday Inn	505-526-4411	201 University Ave Las Cruces NM	1+
La Quinta Inn Las Cruces	505-524-0331	790 Avenida de Mesilla - Exit 140 Las Cruces NM	3+
La Quinta Inn Las Cruces Organ Mountain	505-523-0100	1500 Hickory Drive - Exit 140 Las Cruces NM	3+
The Coachlight Inn and RV Park	505-526-3301	301 S Motel Blvd - Exit 139 Las Cruces NM	2

Interstate 15 Accommodation Listings

Montana Listings (Interstate 15)   Dogs per Room

Shelby
Comfort Inn	406-434-2212	455 McKinley - Exit 363/Jct H 2 & H 15 Shelby MT	3+

Conrad
Super 8 Conrad	406-278-7676	215 N Main St - Exit 339 Conrad MT	2

Great Falls
Comfort Inn	406-454-2727	1120 9th St S - Exit 10th Avenue S Great Falls MT	1+
Days Inn Great Falls	406-727-6565	101 14th Ave NW - Exit 280 Great Falls MT	2
Hampton Inn	406-453-2675	2301 14th Street SW - Exit 10th Avenue, then exit 0 Great Falls MT	3+
Holiday Inn	406-727-7200	400 10th Ave S. Great Falls MT	1+
La Quinta Inn & Suites Great Falls	406-761-2600	600 River Drive South - Exit 280 Great Falls MT	3+
Super 8 Great Falls	406-727-7600	1214 13th Street South - Exit 278 Great Falls MT	3+

Helena
Comfort Inn	406-443-1000	750 Fee Street - Exit Capital W Helena MT	2
Days Inn Helena	406-442-3280	2001 Prospect Ave - Capitol Area Exit Helena MT	2
Hampton Inn	406-443-5800	3000 Highway 12E - Exit 192A Helena MT	3+
Holiday Inn	406-443-2200	22 N. Last Chance Gulch Helena MT	1+
Red Lion	406-443-2100	2301 Colonial Drive - Exit Capitol Helena MT	3+
Super 8 Helena	406-443-2450	2200 11th Ave - Exit 192 or 192b Helena MT	2

Butte
Comfort Inn	406-494-8850	2777 Harrison Avenue - Exit 127/Harrison Avenue Butte MT	3+
Super 8 Butte	460-494-6000	2929 Harrison Ave - Exit 127 or 127a Butte MT	2

Dillon
Best Western Paradise Inn	406-683-4214	650 N Montana St - Exit 63 Dillon MT	3+
Comfort Inn	406-683-6831	450 N Interchange - Exit 63 Dillon MT	2
Super 8 Dillon	406-683-4288	550 N Montana St - Exit 63 to Hwy 41 Dillon MT	2

Idaho Listings (Interstate 15)   Dogs per Room

Idaho Falls
Best Western Driftwood Inn	208-523-2242	575 River Pkwy - Exit 118 Idaho Falls ID	2
Comfort Inn	208-528-2804	195 S Colorado Avenue - Exit 118 W Idaho Falls ID	3+

Blackfoot
Best Western Blackfoot Inn	208-785-4144	750 Jensen Grove Dr - Exit 93 Blackfoot ID	3+
Super 8 Blackfoot	208-785-9333	1279 Parkway Dr - Exit 93 Blackfoot ID	2

Pocatello
Holiday Inn	208-237-1400	1399 Bench Rd Pocatello ID	1+
Super 8 Pocatello	208-234-0888	1330 Bench Rd - Exit 71 Pocatello ID	2

Utah Listings (Interstate 15)   Dogs per Room

Brigham City
Howard Johnson Inn	435-723-8511	1167 S Main St. Brigham City UT	1+

Ogden
Comfort Inn	801-544-5577	877 N 400 W - Exit 331 Layton UT	2
Hampton Inn	801-775-8800	1702 N Woodland Park Drive - Exit 335 E Layton UT	3+
Holiday Inn Express	801-773-3773	1695 Woodland Park Dr - Exit 335 Layton UT	2
La Quinta Inn Salt Lake City Layton	801-776-6700	1965 North 1200 W. - Exit 332 Layton UT	3+
TownePlace Suites Salt Lake City/Layton	801-779-2422	1743 Woodland Park Drive - Exit 335 Layton UT	2
Best Western Country Inn	801-394-9474	1335 W 12th St - Exit 347 Ogden UT	2
Comfort Suites	801-621-2545	2250 S 1200 W - Exit 343/21st Street Ogden UT	3+
Holiday Inn Express Hotel & Suites	801-392-5000	2245 S. 1200 West Ogden UT	1+
Motel 6 - Ogden	801-627-4560	1455 Washington Boulevard Ogden UT	1+
Red Roof Inn - OGDEN - RIVERDALE	801-627-2880	1500 West Riverdale Road Ogden UT	1+
Super 8 Ogden	801-731-7100	1508 W 2100 South - Exit 346 Ogden UT	1+

Clearfield
Traveller's Inn	801-825-8000	572 N Main St - Exit 338 Clearfield UT	2

Salt Lake City
Holiday Inn Express	801-571-2511	12033 South Factory Outlet Drive Draper UT	1+
Best Western Timpanogos Inn	801-768-1400	195 South 850 East - Exit 282 Lehi UT	2
Best Western Garden Inn	801-521-2930	154 West 600 South - Exit 600 S Salt Lake City UT	2
Candlewood Suites	801-359-7500	2170 W. North Temple Salt Lake City UT	1+
Candlewood Suites	801-567-0111	6990 South Park Centre Drive Salt Lake City UT	1+
Days Inn Salt Lake City Central	801-486-8780	315 West 3300 South - Exit 306 Salt Lake City UT	2

Highway Guides - Please always call ahead to make sure that an establishment is still dog-friendly

Red Lion	801-521-7373	161 W 600 S - Exit 600th Salt Lake City UT	3+
Comfort Inn	801-255-4919	8955 S 255 West - Exit 295/90th S Sandy UT	3+
Comfort Suites	801-495-1317	10680 Automall Drive - Exit 293 E/10600th S Sandy UT	1+
Residence Inn by Marriott	801-561-5005	270 W 10000S - Exit 106th S Sandy UT	3+
Sleep Inn	801-572-2020	10676 S 300 W - Exit 293/10600S South Jordan UT	3+
Super 8 South Jordan/Sandy/SLC Area	801-553-8888	10722 South 300 West - Exit 297 South Jordan UT	2
Hampton Inn	801-296-1211	2393 S 800 West - Exit 318 Woods Cross UT	3+
Orem			
La Quinta Inn & Suites Orem University Parkway	801-226-0440	521 W. University Parkway - Exit 269 Orem UT	3+
La Quinta Inn Orem/Provo North	801-235-9555	1100 West 780 North - Exit 272 Orem UT	3+
Provo			
Days Inn Provo	801-375-8600	1675 N 200 West - Exit 272 Provo UT	2
Hampton Inn	801-377-6396	1511 S 40 East - Exit 266 Provo UT	3+
Sleep Inn	801-377-6597	1505 South 40 East - Exit 266/University Avenue Provo UT	3+
Springville			
Best Western Cotton Tree Inn of Springville	801-489-3641	1455 N 1750 West - Exit 265 Springville UT	2
Scipio			
Super 8 Scipio	435-758-9188	230 West 400 North - Exit 188 Scipio UT	2
Nephi			
Best Western Paradise Inn of Nephi	435-623-0624	1025 S Main - Exit 222 Nephi UT	2
Motel 6 - Nephi	435-623-0666	2195 South Main Street Nephi UT	1+
Beaver			
Best Western Butch Cassidy Inn	435-438-2438	161 South Main - Exit 109S or 112N Beaver UT	2
Best Western Paradise Inn	435-438-2455	1451 North 300 West - Exit 112 Beaver UT	2
Motel 6 - Beaver	435-438-1666	1345 North 450 West Beaver UT	1+
Cedar City			
Holiday Inn Express Hotel and Suites	435-865-7799	1555 S Old Highway 91 - Exit 57 Cedar City UT	2
Super 8 Cedar City	735-586-8880	145 N 1550 West - Exit 59 Cedar City UT	2

Nevada Listings   (Interstate 15)

Dogs per Room

Mesquite			
Virgin River Hotel and Casino	800-346-7721	100 Pionner Blvd - Exit 122 Mesquite NV	3+
Overton			
Best Western The North Shore Inn at Lake Mead	702-397-6000	520 N Moapa Valley Blvd - Exit 93 Overton NV	3+
Las Vegas			
Best Western Main Street Inn	702-382-3455	1000 North Main St - Exit 43 Las Vegas NV	2
Best Western Nellis Motor Inn	702-643-6111	5330 E Craig Rd - Exit 48 Las Vegas NV	3+
Best Western Parkview Inn	702-385-1213	921 Las Vegas Blvd North - Exit Las Vegas Blvd Las Vegas NV	3+
Candlewood Suites	702-836-3660	4034 South Paradise Road Las Vegas NV	1+
La Quinta Inn Las Vegas Nellis	702-632-0229	4288 N Nellis Blvd. - Exit Craig Las Vegas NV	3+
Residence Inn by Marriott	702-796-9300	3225 Paradise Road - Exit East at Sahara Las Vegas NV	3+
Residence Inn by Marriott	702-650-0040	370 Hughes Center Drive - Exit E Flamingo Blvd Las Vegas NV	3+
Rodeway Inn & Suites	702-795-3311	167 E. Tropicana Ave Las Vegas NV	1+
Comfort Inn North	702-399-1500	910 E Cheyenne Road - Exit 46/Cheyenne W North Las Vegas NV	3+

California Listings   (Interstate 15)

Dogs per Room

Barstow			
Days Inn	760-256-1737	1590 Coolwater Lane Barstow CA	1+
Econo Lodge	760-256-2133	1230 E. Main Street Barstow CA	1+
Holiday Inn Express	760-256-1300	1861 W. Main St. Barstow CA	1+
Holiday Inn Express Hotel and Suites	760-253-9200	2700 Lenwood Road - Exit Outlet Center Dr Barstow CA	2
Motel 6 - Barstow	760-256-1752	150 Yucca Avenue Barstow CA	1+
Quality Inn	760-256-6891	1520 E Main Street - Exit E Main Street and go W Barstow CA	2
Red Roof Inn - Barstow	760-253-2121	2551 Commerce Parkway Barstow CA	1+
Super 8 Barstow	760-256-8443	170 Coolwater Lane - E Main Exit Barstow CA	2
Victorville			
Days Suites	760-948-0600	14865 Bear Valley Rd Hesperia CA	1+
Howard Johnson Express Inn	760-243-7700	16868 Stoddard Wells Rd. Victorville CA	1+
Motel 6 - Victorville	760-243-0666	16901 Stoddard Wells Road Victorville CA	1+
Red Roof Inn - Victorville	760-241-1577	13409 Mariposa Road Victorville CA	1+
Temecula			
Comfort Inn-Wine Country	951-296-3788	27338 Jefferson Avenue - Exit Winchester Road W Temecula CA	3+

Motel 6 - Temecula - Rancho California	951-676-7199	41900 Moreno Drive Temecula CA	1+
San Diego I-15 Corridor			
Castle Creek Inn Resort	760-751-8800	29850 Circle R Way Escondido CA	1+
San Diego County North			
Best Western Country Inn (San Diego)	858-748-6320	13845 Poway Rd - Exit Poway Rd Poway CA	2
San Diego			
La Quinta Inn San Diego Rancho Penasquitos	858-484-8800	10185 Paseo Montril - Exit Rancho Penasquitos/Poway Road San Diego CA	2
Residence Inn by Marriott	858-635-5724	12011 Scripps Highland Drive - Exit Scripps Poway Parkway San Diego CA	3+

Interstate 25 Accommodation Listings

Wyoming Listings (Interstate 25)   Dogs per Room

Buffalo			
Comfort Inn	307-684-9564	65 H 16E Buffalo WY	3+
Motel 6 - Buffalo	307-684-7000	100 Flat Iron Drive Buffalo WY	1+
Super 8 Buffalo	307-684-2531	655 E Hart St - Exit Hwy 16 Buffalo WY	2
Casper			
Days Inn Casper	307-234-1159	301 East E Street - Exit 188a Casper WY	2
Hampton Inn	307-235-6668	400 West F Street - Exit 188A Casper WY	2
Holiday Inn	307-235-2531	300 West F Street Casper WY	1+
Motel 6 - Casper	307-234-3903	1150 Wilkins Circle Casper WY	1+
Quality Inn and Suites	307-266-2400	821 N Poplar Street - Exit 188B/N Poplar Street Casper WY	3+
Super Casper West	307-266-3480	3838 Cy Ave - Exit 188b Casper WY	2
Evansville			
Comfort Inn	307-235-3038	480 Lathrop Road Evansville WY	2
Sleep Inn and Suites	307-235-3100	6733 Bonanza Road - Exit 182/Hat Six Road Evansville WY	2
Super 8 Casper East	307-237-8100	269 Miracle St - Exit 185 Evansville WY	2
Douglas			
Best Western Douglas Inn and Conf Cntr	307-358-9790	1450 Riverbend Dr - Exit 140 Douglas WY	2
Holiday Inn Express Hotel and Suites	307-358-4500	900 West Yellowstone Highway - exit 140 Douglas WY	2
Wheatland			
Best Western Torchlite Motor Inn	307-322-4070	1809 N 16th St - N Wheatland (Exit 80) Wheatland WY	2
Motel 6 - Wheatland	307-322-1800	95 16th Street Wheatland WY	1+
Vimbo's Motel	307-322-3842	203 16th St Wheatland WY	1+
Cheyenne			
Days Inn Cheyenne	307-778-8877	2360 W Lincolnway - Exit 9 Cheyenne WY	2
La Quinta Inn Cheyenne	307-632-7117	2410 W. Lincolnway - Exit 9 Cheyenne WY	3+

Colorado Listings (Interstate 25)   Dogs per Room

Fort Collins			
Comfort Suites	970-206-4597	1415 Oakridge Drive - Exit 265/Harmony Road Fort Collins CO	3+
Days Inn Fort Collins	970-221-5490	3625 E Mulberry St - Exit 269B Fort Collins CO	2
Fort Collins Marriott	970-226-5200	350 E Horsetooth Road - Exit 265/Harmony Road Fort Collins CO	3+
Hampton Inn	970-229-5927	1620 Oakridge Drive - Exit 265/Harmony Road Fort Collins CO	3+
Hilton	970-428-2626	425 W Prospect Road - Exit 268/Prospect Road Fort Collins CO	1+
Quality Inn and Suites	970-282-9047	4001 S Mason Street - Exit 265W/Harmony Road Fort Collins CO	3+
Residence Inn by Marriott	970-223-5700	1127 Oakridge Drive - Exit 265W Fort Collins CO	3+
Sleep Inn	970-484-5515	3808 Mulberry Street - Exit 269B Fort Collins CO	2
Greeley			
Holiday Inn Express	970-330-7495	2563 W 29th Street Greeley CO	1+
Longmont			
Residence Inn by Marriott	303-702-9933	1450 Dry Creek Drive - Exit Longmont Longmont CO	2
Super 8 Longmont/Del Camino Area	303-772-0888	10805 Turner Blvd - Exit 240 Longmont CO	2
Super 8 Longmont/Twin Peaks Area	303-772-8106	2446 N Main St - Exit 243 Longmont CO	2
Denver			
Comfort Inn	303-297-1717	401 E 58th Avenue - Exit 215/58th Avenue Denver CO	2
Days Inn Central Denver	303-571-1715	620 Federal Blvd - Exit 209b Denver CO	2
Hampton Inn	303-894-9900	5001 S Ulster Street - Exit 199/Belleview Avenue Denver CO	3+
Holiday Inn	303-292-9500	4849 Bannock Street - Exit 215 or 214b Denver CO	2
La Quinta Inn Denver Central	303-458-1222	3500 Park Ave. West - Exit 213 Denver CO	3+

La Quinta Inn Denver Cherry Creek	303-758-8886	1975 S. Colorado Blvd. - Exit 204 Denver CO	3+
Residence Inn by Marriott	303-458-5318	2777 Zuni Street - Exit Speer Blvd N Denver CO	3+
Staybridge Suites	303-321-5757	4200 East Virginia Avenue Denver CO	1+
Super 8 Denver/I-25 and 58th Ave	303-296-3100	5888 N Broadway - Exit 215 Denver CO	2
TownePlace Suites Denver Downtown	303-722-2322	685 Speer Blvd - Speer Blvd Exit Denver CO	2
TownePlace Suites Denver Southeast	303-759-9393	3699 S Monaco Parkway - Hampden Ave Exit Denver CO	2
Denver Tech Center Drury Inn & Suites	303-694-3400	9445 East Dry Creek Road Englewood CO	1+
Hampton Inn	303-792-9999	9231 E Arapahoe Road - Exit 197E Englewood CO	3+
Holiday Inn Express Hotel and Suites	303-662-0777	7380 South Clinton St - Dry Creek Exit Englewood CO	2
Quality Suites Tech Center South	303-858-0700	7374 S Clinton Street - Exit Dry Creek Road Englewood CO	3+
Residence Inn by Marriott	720-895-0200	8322 S Valley Highway - Exit County Line Road Englewood CO	3+
Residence Inn by Marriott	303-740-7177	6565 S Yosemite - Exit Arapahoe Englewood CO	3+
TownePlace Suites Denver Tech Center	720-875-1113	7877 S Chester Street - Dry Creek Exit Englewood CO	2
Candlewood Suites	303-232-7171	895 Tabor Street Golden CO	1+
Comfort Suites	303-231-9929	11909 W 6th Avenue - Exit 6th Avenue Golden CO	2
La Quinta Inn & Suites Denver Englewood/Tech Ctr	303-799-4555	9009 E. Arapahoe Road - Exit Arapahoe Greenwood Village CO	2
Sleep Inn Denver Tech Center	303-662-9950	9257 E Costilla Avenue - Exit 197/Arapahoe Road Greenwood Village CO	2
Residence Inn by Marriott	303-683-5500	93 W Centennial Blvd - Exit Broadway Highlands Ranch CO	3+
Sleep Inn	303-280-9818	12101 N Grant Street - Exit 223/120th Avenue Thornton CO	3+
La Quinta Inn Denver Northglenn	303-252-9800	345 West 120th Ave. - Exit 233 Westminster CO	3+
Castle Rock			
Comfort Suites	303-814-9999	4755 Castleton Way - Exit 184/Meadows Parkway Castle Rock CO	3+
Days Inn and Suites Castle Rock	303-814-5825	4691 Castleton Way - Exit 184 Castle Rock CO	2
Hampton Inn	303-660-9800	4830 Castleton Way - Exit 184W Castle Rock CO	3+
Holiday Inn Express	303-660-9733	884 Park Street Castle Rock CO	1+
Super 8 Castle Rock	303-688-0800	1020 Park St - Exit 182 Castle Rock CO	2
Colorado Springs			
Candlewood Suites	719-533-0011	6450 North Academy Blvd - S to Exit 150 Colorado Springs CO	2
Clarion Hotel	719-471-8680	314 W Bijou Street - Exit 142/Bijou Street Colorado Springs CO	3+
Comfort Inn North	719-262-9000	6450 Corporate Center Drive - Exit 149/Woodman Road W Colorado Springs CO	1+
Days Inn Colorado Springs	719-266-1314	8350 Razorback Rd - Academy Blvd Exit to Rt 83 Colorado Springs CO	2
Days Inn Colorado Springs	719-527-0800	2850 S Circle Dr - Exit 138 Colorado Springs CO	2
Econo Lodge Inn and Suites World Arena	719-632-6651	1623 South Nevada Colorado Springs CO	1+
La Quinta Inn Colorado Springs Garden of the Gods	719-528-5060	4385 Sinton Rd. - Exit 145 Colorado Springs CO	3+
Residence Inn by Marriott	719-574-0370	3880 N Academy Blvd - Exit 146 Colorado Springs CO	3+
Residence Inn by Marriott	719-576-0101	2765 Geyser Drive - Exit 138 Colorado Springs CO	3+
Staybridge Suites	719-590-7829	7130 Commerce Center Dr - Exit 149 Colorado Springs CO	2
TownePlace Suites Colorado Springs	719-594-4447	4760 Centennial Blvd - Exit 146 Colorado Springs CO	2
Pueblo			
Hampton Inn	719-544-4700	4703 North Freeway - Exit 102 Pueblo CO	3+
Holiday Inn	719-543-8050	4001 N. Elizabeth Pueblo CO	1+
Sleep Inn	719-583-4000	3626 North Freeway - Exit 101 Pueblo CO	2
Trinidad			
Quality Inn	719-846-4491	3125 Toupal Drive - Exit 11 Trinidad CO	3+
Super 8 Trinidad	719-846-8280	1924 Freedom Rd - Exit 15 Trinidad CO	2

New Mexico Listings (Interstate 25)

Dogs per Room

Raton			
Motel 6 - Raton	505-445-2777	1600 Cedar Street Raton NM	1+
Santa Fe			
Best Western Inn of Santa Fe	505-438-3822	3650 Cerrillos Rd - Exit 278 Santa Fe NM	3+
Comfort Inn	505-474-7330	4312 Cerrillos Road - Exit 278/Cerrillos Road Santa Fe NM	2
El Paradero Bed and Breakfast Inn	505-988-1177	220 W. Manhattan Ave Santa Fe NM	1+
Hampton Inn	505-474-3900	3625 Cerrillos Road - Exit 278N Santa Fe NM	3+
Hilton	505-988-2811	100 Sandoval Street - Exit Saint Francis Santa Fe NM	3+
La Quinta Inn Santa Fe	505-471-1142	4298 Cerrillos Rd. - Exit 278/Cerrillos Road Santa Fe NM	3+
Park Inn and Suites	505-471-3000	2907 Cerrillos Road - Exit 278 Santa Fe NM	3+
Quality Inn	505-471-1211	3011 Cerrillos Road - Exit 278/Cerrillos Road Santa Fe NM	1+
Residence Inn by Marriott	505-988-7300	1698 Galisteo Street - Exit H 285N Santa Fe NM	2
Albuquerque			

761

Best Western InnSuites Hotel and Suites	505-242-7022	2400 Yale Blvd SE - Exit 222A Albuquerque NM	2
Comfort Inn Airport	505-243-2244	2300 Yale Blvd SE - Exit 222A Albuquerque NM	3+
Comfort Inn and Suites North	505-822-1090	5811 Signal Avenue NE - Exit 233/Alameda Street Albuquerque NM	2
Hampton Inn	505-344-1555	5101 Ellison NE - Exit 231 L Albuquerque NM	3+
Howard Johnson Express Inn	505-828-1600	7630 Pan American Freeway NE Albuquerque NM	1+
La Quinta Inn Albuquerque Airport	505-243-5500	2116 Yale Blvd. S.E. Albuquerque NM	3+
La Quinta Inn Albuquerque North	505-821-9000	5241 San Antonio Dr. N.E. - Exit 231 Albuquerque NM	3+
La Quinta Inn Albuquerque Northwest	505-345-7500	7439 Pan American Freeway N.E. - Exit San Antonio Albuquerque NM	2
Quality Suites	505-797-0850	5251 San Antonio Blvd NE - Exit 231/San Antonio Drive Albuquerque NM	3+
Super 8 Albuquerque/Midtown	505-888-4884	2500 University Blvd NE - Exit 227 Albuquerque NM	2
TownePlace Suites Albuquerque Airport	505-232-5800	2400 Centre Avenue SE - Exit 222 Albuquerque NM	2
Days Inn Albuquerque Bernalillo	505-771-7000	107 N Camino Del Pueblo Ave - Exit 242 Bernalillo NM	2
Super 8 Bernalillo	505-867-0766	265 Hwy 44 E - Exit 242 Bernalillo NM	2
Days Inn Albuquerque/Rio Rancho	505-892-8800	4200 Crestview Dr - Exit 233 Rio Rancho NM	2
Los Lunas			
Days Inn Los Lunas	505-865-5995	1919 Main St SW - Los Lunas Exit Los Lunas NM	2
Socorro			
Motel 6 - Socorro	505-835-4300	807 South US 85 Socorro NM	1+
Truth or Consequences			
Best Western Hot Springs Inn	505-894-6665	2270 N Date St - Exit 79 Truth or Consequences NM	3+
Comfort Inn and Suites	505-894-1660	2205 N Dale Street Truth or Consequences NM	3+
Holiday Inn	505-894-1660	2255 N Date St - Exit 79 Truth or Consequences NM	2
Super 8 Truth or Consequences	505-894-7888	2151 N Date St - Exit 79 Truth or Consequences NM	2
Las Cruces			
Holiday Inn	505-526-4411	201 University Ave Las Cruces NM	1+
TownePlace Suites Las Cruces	505-532-6500	2143 Telshor Court - Exit 6 Las Cruces NM	2

Interstate 40 Accommodation Listings

California Listings (Interstate 40)

Dogs per Room

Barstow			
Days Inn	760-256-1737	1590 Coolwater Lane Barstow CA	1+
Econo Lodge	760-256-2133	1230 E. Main Street Barstow CA	1+
Holiday Inn Express	760-256-1300	1861 W. Main St. Barstow CA	1+
Holiday Inn Express Hotel and Suites	760-253-9200	2700 Lenwood Road Barstow CA	2
Motel 6 - Barstow	760-256-1752	150 Yucca Avenue Barstow CA	1+
Quality Inn	760-256-6891	1520 E Main Street - Exit E Main Street and go W Barstow CA	2
Red Roof Inn - Barstow	760-253-2121	2551 Commerce Parkway Barstow CA	1+
Super 8 Barstow	760-256-8443	170 Coolwater Lane - E Main Exit Barstow CA	2
Needles			
Days Inn and Suites	760-326-5836	1215 Hospitality Lane Needles CA	1+
Econo Lodge	760-326-3881	1910 N. Needles Hwy Needles CA	1+
Motel 6 - Needles	760-326-3399	1420 J Street Needles CA	1+
Travelers Inn	760-326-4900	1195 3rd Street Hill Needles CA	1+

Arizona Listings (Interstate 40)

Dogs per Room

Kingman			
Best Western Kings Inn and Suites	928-753-6101	2930 E Route 66 - Exit 53 Kingman AZ	3+
Days Inn	928-757-7337	3381 E Andy Devine - Andy Devine Ave Exit Kingman AZ	2
Days Inn Kingman/West	928-753-7500	3023 Andy Devine - Exit 53 Kingman AZ	2
Motel 6 - Kingman East	928-757-7151	3351 East Andy Devine Avenue Kingman AZ	1+
Motel 6 - Kingman West	928-753-9222	424 West Beale Street Kingman AZ	1+
Quality Inn	928-753-4747	1400 E Andy Devine Avenue - Exit 53/Andy Devine Avenue Kingman AZ	3+
Super 8 Kingman	928-757-4808	3401 E Andy Devine Ave - Andy Devine Hwy Exit Kingman AZ	2
Grand Canyon			
Days Inn Williams	928-635-4051	2488 W Rt 66 - Exit 161 Williams AZ	2
Holiday Inn	928-635-4114	950 N. Grand Canyon Blvd Williams AZ	1+
Quality Inn Mountain Ranch & Resort	928-635-2693	6701 E Mountain Ranch Road - Exit 171 Williams AZ	2
Flagstaff			
Best Western Kings House Motel	928-774-7186	1560 East Route 66 - Exit 198 Flagstaff AZ	2

762

Comfort Inn	928-774-2225	2355 S Beulah Blvd - Exit 195 Flagstaff AZ	3+
Days Inn Flagstaff East	928-527-1477	3601 E Lockett Rd - Exit 201 Flagstaff AZ	2
Days Inn Flagstaff Hwy 66	928-774-5221	1000 West Rte 66 - Exit 195B Flagstaff AZ	2
Holiday Inn	928-714-1000	2320 E Lucky Lane Flagstaff AZ	1+
Howard Johnson Inn	800-437-7137	3300 E. Rt. 66 Flagstaff AZ	1+
La Quinta Inn & Suites Flagstaff	928-556-8666	2015 South Beulah Blvd. - Exit 195 Flagstaff AZ	2
Quality Inn	928-226-7111	2500 E Lucky Lane - Exit 198 Flagstaff AZ	2
Quality Inn	928-774-8771	2000 S Milton Road - Exit 195 Flagstaff AZ	3+
Residence Inn by Marriott	928-526-5555	3440 N. Country Club Drive - Exit 201 Flagstaff AZ	1+
Sleep Inn	928-556-3000	2765 S Woodlands Village Blvd - Exit 195 Flagstaff AZ	2

Winslow

Days Inn Winslow	928-289-1010	2035 W Old Hwy Rt 66 - Exit 252 Winslow AZ	2
Econo Lodge	928-289-4687	I40 & Exit 253 North Park Dr Winslow AZ	1+
Holiday Inn Express	928-289-2960	816 Transcon Lane Winslow AZ	1+
Motel 6 - Winslow	928-289-9581	520 Desmond Street Winslow AZ	1+

New Mexico Listings   (Interstate 40)

Dogs per Room

Gallup

Best Western Inn and Suites at Gallup	505-722-2221	3009 W Highway 66 - Exit 16 Gallup NM	3+
Days Inn Gallup East	505-863-3891	1603 W Hwy 66 - Exit 20 Gallup NM	2
Days Inn Gallup West	505-863-6889	3201 W Hwy 66 - Exit 16 Gallup NM	2
Motel 6 - Gallup	505-863-4492	3306 West US 66 Gallup NM	1+
Red Roof Inn - Gallup	505-722-7765	3304 West Highway 66 Gallup NM	1+
Super 8 Gallup	505-722-5300	1715 W Hwy 66 - Exit 20 Gallup NM	2

Grants

Comfort Inn	505-287-8700	1551 E Santa Fe Avenue - Exit 85 Grants NM	3+
Days Inn Grant	505-287-8883	1504 E Santa Fe Ave - Exit 85 Grants NM	2
Holiday Inn Express	505-285-4676	1496 E Santa Fe Ave Grants NM	1+
Motel 6 - Grants	505-285-4607	1505 East Santa Fe Avenue Grants NM	1+
Super 8 Grants	505-287-8811	1604 E Santa Fe Ave - Exit 85 Grants NM	2

Albuquerque

Best Western American Motor Inn	505-298-7426	12999 Central Ave NE - Exit 167S Albuquerque NM	2
Days Inn Albuquerque East	505-294-3297	13317 Central Ave NE - Exit 167 Albuquerque NM	2
Days Inn Albuquerque Northeast	505-275-3297	10321 Hotel Ave NE - Exit 165 Albuquerque NM	2
Days Inn Albuquerque West	505-836-3297	6031 Liff Rd NW - Exit 155 Albuquerque NM	2
Holiday Inn Express	505-836-8600	6100 Iliff Rd Albuquerque NM	1+
Holiday Inn Express	505-275-8900	10330 Hotel Ave NE Albuquerque NM	1+
Howard Johnson Hotel	505-296-4852	15 Hotel Circle NE Albuquerque NM	1+
La Quinta Inn & Suites Albuquerque-Midtown	505-761-5600	2011 Menaul Blvd NE - Exit Carlisle Albuquerque NM	3+
La Quinta Inn Albuquerque I-40 East	505-884-3591	2424 San Mateo Blvd. N.E. - Exit San Mateo N Albuquerque NM	3+
Quality Inn and Suites	505-242-5228	411 McKnight Avenue NW - Exit 159 D University Albuquerque NM	3+
Residence Inn by Marriott	505-881-2661	3300 Prospect Avenue NE - Exit Carlisle Blvd N Albuquerque NM	3+
Super 8 Albuquerque/East	505-271-4807	450 Paisano St NE - Exit 166 Albuquerque NM	2
Super 8 Albuquerque/Midtown	505-888-4884	2500 University Blvd NE - Exit 159a or 159d Albuquerque NM	2
Super 8 Albuquerque/West	505-836-5560	6030 Iliff NW - Exit 155 Albuquerque NM	2
Days Inn Albuquerque/Rio Rancho	505-892-8800	4200 Crestview Dr - Exit 155 Rio Rancho NM	2

Moriarty

Comfort Inn	505-832-6666	119 Route 66 E - Exit 196 Moriarty NM	3+
Days Inn Moriarty	505-832-4451	1809 W Route 66 - Exit 194 Moriarty NM	2
Super 8 Moriarty	505-832-6730	1611 Old Route 66 - Exit 194 or 197 Moriarty NM	2

Santa Rosa

Best Western Adobe Inn	505-472-3446	1501 E Will Rogers Dr - Exit 275 Santa Rosa NM	3+
Best Western Santa Rosa Inn	505-472-5877	3022 Historic Route 66 - Exit 277 Santa Rosa NM	2
Comfort Inn	505-472-5570	3343 Historic Route 66 - Exit 277/Will Rogers Blvd Santa Rosa NM	2
Days Inn Santa Rosa	505-472-5985	1830 Will Rogers Dr - Exit 275 Santa Rosa NM	2
La Quinta Inn Santa Rosa	505-472-4800	1701 Will Rogers Dr. Santa Rosa NM	3+
Motel 6 - Santa Rosa	505-472-3045	3400 Will Rogers Drive Santa Rosa NM	1+

Tucumcari

Best Western Discovery Inn	505-461-4884	200 East Estrella Ave - Exit 332 Tucumcari NM	3+
Best Western Pow Wow Inn	505-461-0500	801 W Tucumcari Blvd - Exit 329 Tucumcari NM	3+
Comfort Inn	505-461-4094	2800 E Tucumcari Blvd - Exit 335 W Tucumcari NM	2
Days Inn Tucumcari	505-461-3158	2623 S First St - Exit 332 Tucumcari NM	2
Holiday Inn	505-461-3780	3716 E. Tucumcari Blvd Tucumcari NM	1+
Howard Johnson Express Inn	505-461-2747	3604 E. Rt. 66 Blvd. Tucumcari NM	1+
Motel 6 - Tucumcari	505-461-4791	2900 East Tucumcari Boulevard Tucumcari NM	1+

Highway 49 Accommodation Listings

California Listings

Dogs per Room

Downieville
Downieville Carriage House Inn	530-289-3573	110 Commercial Street Downieville CA	1+

Nevada City
The Outside Inn	530-265-2233	575 E. Broad Street Nevada City CA	1+

Grass Valley
Swan Levine House Bed and Breakfast	916-272-1873	328 South Church Street Grass Valley CA	1+

Auburn
Motel 6 - Auburn	530-888-7829	1819 Auburn Ravine Road Auburn CA	1+
Travelodge	530-885-7025	13490 Lincoln Way Auburn CA	1+

Coloma
Golden Lotus Bed and Breakfast Inn	530-621-4562	1006 Lotus Road Coloma CA	1+

Placerville
Best Western Placerville Inn	530-622-9100	6850 Greenleaf Dr Placerville CA	2
Fleming Jones Homestead B&B	530-344-0943	3170 Newtown Road Placerville CA	1+

Drytown
Old Well Motel	209-245-6467	15947 State Highway 49 Drytown CA	1+

Jackson
Amador Motel	209-223-0970	12408 Kennedy Flat Rd Jackson CA	1+
Jackson Gold Lodge	209-223-0486	850 N. State Hwy 49 Jackson CA	1+

Angels Camp
Best Western Cedar Inn and Suites	209-736-4000	444 S Main St Angels Camp CA	2

Columbia
Columbia Gem Motel	209-532-4508	22131 Parrotts Ferry Rd Columbia CA	1+

Sonora
Best Western Sonora Oaks	800-532-1944	19551 Hess Avenue Sonora CA	2
Sonora Aladdin Motor Inn	209-533-4971	14260 Mono Way (Hwy 108) Sonora CA	1+

Jamestown
Royal Hotel Bed and Breakfast	209-984-5271	18239 Main Street Jamestown CA	1+
The National Hotel	209-984-3446	18183 Main Street Jamestown CA	1+

Highway 50 Accommodation Listings

California Listings

Dogs per Room

Rancho Cordova
AmeriSuites	916-635-4799	10744 Gold Center Dr. Rancho Cordova CA	1+
Best Western Heritage Inn	916-635-4040	11269 Point East Dr Rancho Cordova CA	3+
Inns of America	916-351-1213	12249 Folsom Blvd Rancho Cordova CA	1+
Motel 6 - Sacramento - Rancho Cordova East	916-635-8784	10694 Olson Drive Rancho Cordova CA	1+
Residence Inn by Marriott	916-851-1550	2779 Prospect Park Drive Rancho Cordova CA	2

Folsom
Lake Natoma Inn	916-351-1500	702 Gold Lake Drive Folsom CA	1+

Placerville
Best Western Placerville Inn	530-622-9100	6850 Greenleaf Dr Placerville CA	2
Fleming Jones Homestead B&B	530-344-0943	3170 Newtown Road Placerville CA	1+

South Lake Tahoe
3 Peaks Resort and Beach Club - South Lake Tahoe Hotel	800-957-5088	931 Park Avenue South Lake Tahoe CA	1+
7 Seas Inn	530-544-7031	4145 Manzanita Ave South Lake Tahoe CA	1+
Alder Inn	530-544-4485	1072 Ski Run Blvd South Lake Tahoe CA	1+
Buckingham Properties Lake Tahoe	530-542-1114	Call to Arrange South Lake Tahoe CA	1+
Colony Inn at South Lake Tahoe	530-544-6481	3794 Montreal Road South Lake Tahoe CA	1+
Fireside Lodge	530-544-5515	515 Emerald Bay Rd. South Lake Tahoe CA	1+
Hal & Pat's Lake Tahoe Mountain Home	520-405-0242	3745 Forest Ave. South Lake Tahoe CA	1+
Hollys Place	530-544-7040	1201 Rufus Allen Blvd. South Lake Tahoe CA	3+
Inn at Heavenly B&B	530-544-4244	1261 Ski Run Boulevard South Lake Tahoe CA	1+
Motel 6 - South Lake Tahoe	530-542-1400	2375 Lake Tahoe Boulevard South Lake Tahoe CA	1+
Spruce Grove Cabins & Suites	530-544-0549	P.O. Box 16390 South Lake Tahoe CA	1+
Stonehenge Vacation Properties	800-822-1460	Call to Arrange. South Lake Tahoe CA	1+

| Tahoe Keys Resort | 530-544-5397 | 599 Tahoe Keys Blvd   South Lake Tahoe CA | 1+ |
| TahoeWoods Lodging | 415-444-0777 | See Website or Call   South Lake Tahoe CA | 1+ |

Nevada Listings

Dogs per Room

Carson City

Best Value Motel	775-882-2007	2731 S Carson St Carson City NV	1+
Best Western Trailside Inn	775-883-7300	1300 N Carson St Carson City NV	3+
Days Inn Carson City	775-883-3343	3103 N Carson St Carson City NV	2
Holiday Inn Express Hotel & Suites	775-283-4055	4055 North Carson Street Carson City NV	1+
Motel 6 - Carson City	775-885-7710	2749 South Carson Street Carson City NV	1+

Fallon

Comfort Inn	775-423-5554	1830 W Williams Avenue Fallon NV	2
Motel 6 - Fallon	775-423-2277	1705 South Taylor Street Fallon NV	1+
Super 8 Fallon	775-423-6031	855 W Williams Ave Fallon NV	3+

Ely

Best Western Main Motel	775-289-4529	1101 Aultman Ely NV	3+
Best Western Park Vue	775-289-4497	930 Aultman Ely NV	3+
Motel 6 - Ely	775-289-6671	770 Avenue O Ely NV	1+

Interstate 70 Accommodation Listings

Utah Listings   (Interstate 70)

Dogs per Room

Richfield

| Days Inn Richfield | 435-896-6476 | 333 N Main St - Exit Hwy 89 Richfield UT | 2 |

Salina

| Super 8 Salina/Scenic Hills Area | 435-529-7483 | 1500 South 80 East - Exit 54 Salina UT | 2 |

Green River

Holiday Inn Express	435-564-4439	965 East Main Street Green River UT	1+
Motel 6 - Green River	435-564-3436	946 East Main Street Green River UT	1+
Super 8 Green River	435-564-8888	1248 E Main - Exit 158 or 162 Green River UT	2

Colorado Listings   (Interstate 70)

Dogs per Room

Grand Junction

Hampton Inn	970-243-3222	205 Main Street - Exit 37 Grand Junction CO	3+
Holiday Inn	970-243-6790	755 Horizon Drive Grand Junction CO	1+
La Quinta Inn & Suites Grand Junction	970-241-2929	2761 Crossroads Blvd. - Exit Horizon Drive Grand Junction CO	3+
Quality Inn	970-245-7200	733 Horizon Drive - Exit 31S Grand Junction CO	2
Super 8 Grand Junction	970-248-8080	728 Horizon Dr - Exit 31 Grand Junction CO	2

Rifle

| Buckskin Inn | 970-625-1741 | 101 Ray Avenue   Rifle CO | 3+ |

Glenwood Springs

| Quality Inn and Suites on the River | 970-945-5995 | 2650 Gilstrap Court - Exit 114 Glenwood Springs CO | 3+ |

Eagle

| Holiday Inn Express | 970-328-8088 | I-70 Exit 147 & Pond Rd Eagle CO | 1+ |

Vail

| Antlers at Vail | 970-476-2471 | 680 W. Lionshead Place   Vail CO | 1+ |

Frisco

Holiday Inn	970-668-5000	1129 N. Summit Blvd Frisco CO	1+
Hotel Frisco	970-668-5009	308 Main Street Frisco CO	1+
Woods Inn	970-668-2255	Second Ave and Granite St Frisco CO	1+

Dillon

| Super 8 Dillon/Breckenridge Area | 970-468-8888 | 808 Little Beaver Trail - Exit 205 Dillon CO | 2 |

Silverthorne

| Days Inn Summit County | 970-468-8661 | 580 Silverthorne Lane - Exit 205 Silverthorne CO | 2 |

Denver

Sleep Inn Denver International Airport	303-373-1616	15900 E 40th Avenue - Exit 283 Aurora CO	3+
Comfort Inn	303-297-1717	401 E 58th Avenue - Exit I 25 Denver CO	2
Denver East Drury Inn	303-373-1983	4380 Peoria Street Denver CO	1+
Doubletree	303-321-3333	3203 Quebec Street - Exit 278/Quebec Street Denver CO	2
Holiday Inn	303-371-9494	15500 East 40th Ave - Exit 283 Denver CO	2
JW Marriott Denver at Cherry Creek	303-316-2700	150 Clayton Lane - Exit Colorado Blvd Denver CO	3+
Quality Inn	303-371-5640	3975 Peoria Way - Exit Peoria Way Denver CO	3+

Red Lion	303-321-6666	4040 Quebec Street - Exit 278 Denver CO	3+
Staybridge Suites	303-321-5757	4200 East Virginia Avenue Denver CO	1+
Clarion Collection The Golden Hotel	303-279-0100	800 11th Street - Exit H 85 Golden CO	3+
Denver Marriott West	303-279-9100	1717 Denver West, Marriott Blvd - Exit 263 Golden CO	3+
La Quinta Inn Denver Golden	303-279-5565	3301 Youngfield Service Rd. - Exit 264 Golden CO	3+
Quality Suites at Evergreen Parkway	303-526-2000	29300 H 40 - Exit H 40 Golden CO	2
Burlington			
Comfort Inn	719-346-7676	282 S Lincoln - Exit 437 Burlington CO	3+

Interstate 80 Accommodation Listings

California Listings (Interstate 80)   Dogs per Room

San Francisco			
Holiday Inn Select	415-433-6600	750 Kearny Street - Bay Bridge Exit San Francisco CA	2
Kensington Park Hotel	800-553-9100	450 Post Street - Exit 7th Street San Francisco CA	1
Vallejo			
Motel 6 - Vallejo - Maritime North	707-552-2912	597 Sandy Beach Road Vallejo CA	1+
Motel 6 - Vallejo - Six Flags East	707-642-7781	458 Fairgrounds Drive Vallejo CA	1+
Motel 6 - Vallejo - Six Flags West	707-643-7611	1455 Marine World Parkway Vallejo CA	1+
Vacaville			
Best Western Heritage Inn	707-448-8453	1420 E Monte Vista Ave - Exit Monte Vista Ave Vacaville CA	3+
Motel 6 - Vacaville	707-447-5550	107 Lawrence Drive Vacaville CA	1+
Residence Inn by Marriott	707-469-0300	360 Orange Drive - Exit Orange Drive Vacaville CA	3+
Dixon			
Best Western Inn Dixon	707-678-1400	1345 Commercial Way - Exit Pitt School Rd Dixon CA	2
Davis			
Best Western University Lodge	530-756-7890	123 B Street - Davis-Richards Exit Davis CA	2
Econo Lodge	530-756-1040	221 D Street Davis CA	1+
Howard Johnson Hotel	530-792-0800	4100 Chiles Road Davis CA	1+
Motel 6 - Davis - Sacramento Area	530-753-3777	4835 Chiles Road Davis CA	1+
University Inn Bed and Breakfast	530-756-8648	340 A Street Davis CA	1+
University Park Inn & Suites	530-756-0910	1111 Richards Blvd. Davis CA	1+
Sacramento			
Best Western Rocklin Park Hotel	916-630-9400	5450 China Garden Rd - Exit Rocklin Rd Rocklin CA	2
Best Western Roseville Inn	916-782-4434	220 Harding Blvd - Exit Douglas Blvd West to Harding Roseville CA	3+
Oxford Suites	916-784-2222	130 N Sunrise Ave Roseville CA	1+
Residence Inn by Marriott	916-772-5500	1930 Taylor Road - Exit Atlantic/Eureka Roseville CA	3+
Doubletree	916-929-8855	2001 Point West Way - Exit Arden Way Sacramento CA	3+
Holiday Inn Express	916-444-4436	728 16 Street Sacramento CA	1+
Residence Inn by Marriott	916-649-1300	2410 W El Camino Avenue - Exit West El Camino Avenue Sacramento CA	3+
Auburn - Gold Country North			
Travelodge	530-885-7025	13490 Lincoln Way Auburn CA	1+
Lake Tahoe			
The Inn at Truckee	530-587-8888	11506 Deerfield Drive Truckee CA	1+

Nevada Listings (Interstate 80)   Dogs per Room

Reno			
Days Inn Reno	775-786-4070	701 E 7th - Wells Ave Exit Reno NV	2
Super 8 Reno/Meadowwood Courtyard	775-829-4600	5851 S Virginia St - S Virginia St Exit Reno NV	2
Truckee River Lodge	775-786-8888	501 W. 1st Street Reno NV	1+
Fernley			
Best Western Fernley Inn	775-575-6776	1405 E Newlands Dr - Exit 48 Fernley NV	3+
Winnemucca			
Best Western Gold Country Inn	775-623-6999	921 W Winnemucca Blvd - Exit 176 Winnemucca NV	3+
Days Inn Winnemucca	775-623-3661	511 W Winnemucca Blvd - Exit 176 or 178 Winnemucca NV	2
Holiday Inn Express	775-625-3100	1987 W. Winnemucca Blvd Winnemucca NV	1+
Motel 6 - Winnemucca	775-623-1180	1600 West Winnemucca Boulevard Winnemucca NV	1+
Red Lion	775-623-2565	741 W Winnemucca - Exit 178 Winnemucca NV	3+
Santa Fe Motel	775-623-1119	1620 W. Winnemucca Blvd Winnemucca NV	1+
Battle Mountain			
Comfort Inn	775-635-5880	521 E Front Street - Exit 229/Allen Road Battle Mountain NV	2
Elko			

Best Western Gold Country Motor Inn	775-738-8421	2050 Idaho St - Exit 303 Elko NV	2
High Desert Inn	775-738-8425	3015 Idaho Street Elko NV	1+
Motel 6 - Elko	775-738-4337	3021 Idaho Street Elko NV	1+
Shilo Inn	775-738-5522	2401 Mountain City Highway Elko NV	1+
Super 8 Elko	775-738-8488	1755 Idaho St - Exit 303 Elko NV	2
Wells			
Motel 6 - Wells	775-752-2116	Old Highway 40 & US 93 Wells NV	1+
Super 8 Wells	775-752-3384	930 6th Street - Exit 351 or 352a Wells NV	2
Wendover			
Super 8 Wendover	775-664-2888	1325 Wendover Blvd - Exit 410 Wendover NV	2

Utah Listings   (Interstate 80) Dogs per Room

Wendover			
Motel 6 - Wendover	435-665-2267	561 East Wendover Boulevard Wendover UT	1+
Salt Lake City			
Candlewood Suites	801-359-7500	2170 W. North Temple Salt Lake City UT	1+
Comfort Inn Airport/International Center	801-746-5200	200 N Admiral Byrd Blvd - Exit 113/5600 W Salt Lake City UT	2
Days Inn Salt Lake City Airport	801-539-8538	1900 West North Temple St - Redwood Rd Exit Salt Lake City UT	2
Hilton	801-539-1515	5151 Wiley Post Way - Exit 114 Salt Lake City UT	3+
La Quinta Inn & Suites Salt Lake City Airport	801-366-4444	4905 W. Wiley Post Way - Exit 114 Salt Lake City UT	3+
Residence Inn by Marriott	801-355-3300	285 W Broadway (300S) - Exit North Temple to 300W Salt Lake City UT	3+
Residnece Inn by Marriott	801-532-4101	4883 W Douglas Corrigan Way - Exit 114 Salt Lake City UT	2
Park City			
Best Western Landmark Inn	435-649-7300	6560 N Landmark Dr - Exit 145 Park City UT	2
Holiday Inn Express Hotel & Suites	435-658-1600	1501 West Ute Blvd Park City UT	1+
Radisson Inn Park City	435-649-5000	2121 Park Avenue Park City UT	1+
The Gables Hotel	435-655-3315	1335 Lowell Avenue, PO Box 905 Park City UT	1+
Coalville			
Best Western Holiday Hills	435-336-4444	210 South 200 West - Exit 164 Coalville UT	2

Interstate 84 Accommodation Listings

Oregon Listings   (Interstate 84) Dogs per Room

Portland			
La Quinta Inn Portland Convention Center	503-233-7933	431 NE Multnomah Portland OR	3+
Residence Inn by Marriott	503-288-1400	1710 NE Multnomah Street - Exit Lloyd Blvd Portland OR	2
Residence Inn by Marriott	503-552-9500	2115 SW River Parkway - Exit R on Naito Parkway/Front Ave Portland OR	3+
Sleep Inn East	503-618-8400	2261 NE 181 Avenue - Exit 13 Portland OR	3+
Gresham			
Quality Inn and Suites	503-492-4000	2323 NE 181st Avenue - Exit 13 Gresham OR	3+
Super 8 Gresham/Portland Area	503-661-5100	121 NE 181st Ave - Exit 13 Gresham OR	2
Troutdale			
Comfort Inn and Suites	503-669-6500	477 NW Phoenix Drive - Exit 17 Troutdale OR	2
Holiday Inn Express	503-492-2900	1000 NW Graham Road - Exit 17 Troutdale OR	2
Motel 6 - Portland East - Troutdale	503-665-2254	1610 Nw Frontage Road Troutdale OR	1+
Cascade Locks			
Best Western Columbia River Inn	541-374-8777	735 Wanapa St - Exit 44 Cascade Locks OR	2
Hood River			
Best Western Hood River Inn	541-386-2200	1108 E Marina Way - Exit 64 Hood River OR	2
Columbia Gorge Hotel	541-386-5566	4000 Westcliff Dr Hood River OR	1+
Pheasant Valley's Bed & Breakfast and Winery	541-387-3040	3890 Acree Drive - Exit 62 Hood River OR	2
The Dalles			
Best Western River City Inn	541-296-9107	112 W Second St - Exit 84 The Dalles OR	2
Comfort Inn Columbia Gorge	541-298-2800	351 Lone Pine Drive - Exit 87 The Dalles OR	2
Motel 6 - The Dalles	541-296-1191	2500 West 6th Street The Dalles OR	1+
Pendleton			
Holiday Inn Express	541-966-6520	600 SE Nye Ave Pendleton OR	1+
Motel 6 - Pendleton	541-276-3160	325 Southeast Nye Avenue Pendleton OR	1+
Red Lion	541-276-6111	304 SE Nye Avenue - Exit 210 Pendleton OR	3+

Baker City			
Best Western Sunridge Inn	541-523-6444	1 Sunridge Lane - Exit 304 Baker City OR	2
Ontario			
Holiday Inn	541-889-8621	1249 Topadera Ave - Exit 376b Ontario OR	2
Motel 6 - Ontario	541-889-6617	275 NE 12th Street Ontario OR	1+

Idaho Listings   (Interstate 84)

Dogs per Room

Caldwell			
Best Western Caldwell Inn and Suites	208-454-7225	908 Specht Ave - Exit 29 Caldwell ID	3+
La Quinta Inn Caldwell	208-454-2222	901 Specht Ave - Exit 29 Caldwell ID	3+
Nampa			
Hampton Inn	208-442-0036	5750 Franklin Road - Exit Garrity Nampa ID	3+
Boise			
Doubletree	208-345-2002	475 W Parkcenter Blvd - Exit 54 Boise ID	3+
Holiday Inn - Airport	208-344-8365	3300 Vista Ave Boise ID	1+
Residence Inn by Marriott	208-344-1200	1401 Lusk (Capitol & University) - Exit 53 Boise ID	3+
Super 8 Boise	208-344-8871	2773 Elder St - Exit 53 Boise ID	3+
Mountain Home			
Best Western Foothills Motor Inn	208-587-8477	1080 Hwy 20 - Exit 95 Mountain Home ID	3+
Sleep Inn	208-587-9743	1180 H 20 - Exit 95/H 20E Mountain Home ID	1+
Jerome			
Best Western Sawtooth Inn and Suites	208-324-9200	2653 South Lincoln - Exit 168 Jerome ID	3+
Twin Falls			
Best Western Apollo Motor Inn	208-733-2010	296 Addison Ave West - Exit 173 Twin Falls ID	2
Comfort Inn	208-734-7494	1893 Canyon Springs Road - Exit 173/H 93S Twin Falls ID	3+
Red Lion	208-734-5000	1357 Blue Lakes Blvd N - Exit 173 Twin Falls ID	2
Heyburn			
Super 8 Heyburn/Burley Area	208-678-7000	336 South 600 West - Exit 208 Heyburn ID	2

Utah Listings   (Interstate 84)

Dogs per Room

Ogden			
Comfort Inn	801-544-5577	877 N 400 W Layton UT	2
Hampton Inn	801-775-8800	1702 N Woodland Park Drive Layton UT	3+
Holiday Inn Express	801-773-3773	1695 Woodland Park Dr Layton UT	2
La Quinta Inn Salt Lake City Layton	801-776-6700	1965 North 1200 W. Layton UT	3+
TownePlace Suites Salt Lake City/Layton	801-779-2422	1743 Woodland Park Drive Layton UT	2
Best Western Country Inn	801-394-9474	1335 W 12th St Ogden UT	2
Comfort Suites	801-621-2545	2250 S 1200 W Ogden UT	3+
Holiday Inn Express Hotel & Suites	801-392-5000	2245 S. 1200 West Ogden UT	1+
Motel 6 - Ogden	801-627-4560	1455 Washington Boulevard Ogden UT	1+
Red Roof Inn	801-627-2880	1500 West Riverdale Road Ogden UT	1+
Super 8 Ogden	801-731-7100	1508 W 2100 South Ogden UT	1+

Interstate 90 Accommodation Listings

Washington Listings   (Interstate 90)

Dogs per Room

Bellevue			
Candlewood Suites	425-373-1212	15805 SE 37th Street Bellevue WA	1+
Ellensburg			
Comfort Inn	509-925-7037	1722 Canyon Road - Exit 109 Ellensburg WA	2
Super 8 Ellensburg	509-962-6888	1500 Canyon Rd - Exit 109 Ellensburg WA	2
Moses Lake			
Best Western Lakeside Inn	509-765-9211	3000 Marina Dr - Exit #176 Moses Lake WA	2
Holiday Inn Express	509-766-2000	1745 E Kittleson - Exit 179 Moses Lake WA	2
Motel 6 - Moses Lake	509-766-0250	2822 West Driggs Drive Moses Lake WA	1+
Ritzville			
La Quinta Inn Ritzville	509-659-1007	1513 Smitty's Blvd. - Exit 221 Ritzville WA	2
Spokane			
Best Western Tradewinds North	509-326-5500	N 3033 Division - Exit Hwy 2 Exit Division Spokane WA	3+
Comfort Inn North	509-467-7111	7111 N Division Street/H 395 - Exit 281 N Spokane WA	3+
Doubletree	509-455-6900	322 N Spokane Falls Court - Exit 281 Spokane WA	2

Holiday Inn	509-838-1170	1616 South Windsor Dr Spokane WA	1+
Howard Johnson Inn	509-838-6630	South 211 Division St. Spokane WA	1+
La Quinta Inn & Suites Spokane	509-893-0955	3808 N Sullivan Rd - Exit 291B Spokane WA	3+
Red Lion	509-326-8000	303 W North River Drive - Exit 281 Spokane WA	2
Red Lion	509-326-5577	700 N Division - Exit 281 Spokane WA	3+
Red Lion	509-838-2711	515 W Sprague Avenue - Exit Division N Spokane WA	3+
Super 8 Spokane/Airport/West	509-838-8800	W 11102 Westbow Blvd - Exit 272 Spokane WA	2
Spokane Valley			
Comfort Inn Valley	509-924-3838	905 N Sullivan Road - Exit 291/Sullivan Road Spokane Valley WA	3+
Doubletree	509-924-9000	1100 N Sullivan Road - Exit 291B Spokane Valley WA	3+
Super 8 Spokane Valley	509-928-4888	2020 North Argonne Rd - Exit 287 Spokane Valley WA	2

Idaho Listings   (Interstate 90)

Dogs per Room

Post Falls			
Comfort Inn	208-773-8900	3105 E Seltice Way - Exit 7 Post Falls ID	2
Holiday Inn Express	208-773-8900	3105 E. Seltice Way Post Falls ID	1+
Howard Johnson Express Inn	208-773-4541	West 3647 5th Ave. Post Falls ID	1+
Coeur D'Alene			
Best Western Coeur D'Alene Inn	208-765-3200	414 W Appleway - Exit 12 Coeur D'Alene ID	3+
Days Inn Coeur D'Alene	208-667-8668	2200 Northwest Blvd - Exit 11 Coeur D'Alene ID	2
La Quinta Inn & Suites Coeur D Alene East	208-667-6777	2209 E Sherman Ave - Exit Sherman Avenue Coeur D'Alene ID	3+
La Quinta Inn Coeur D Alene Appleway	208-765-5500	280 W Appleway - Exit 12 Coeur D'Alene ID	3+
Kellogg			
Super 8 Kellogg	208-783-1234	601 Bunker Ave - Exit 49 Kellogg ID	2
Wallace			
Best Western Wallace Inn	208-752-1252	100 Front St - Exit 61 and 62 Wallace ID	2

Highway 99 Accommodation Listings

California Listings

Dogs per Room

Red Bluff			
Comfort Inn	530-529-7060	90 Sale Lane Red Bluff CA	3+
Motel 6 - Red Bluff	530-527-9200	20 Williams Avenue Red Bluff CA	1+
Travelodge	530-527-6020	38 Antelope Blvd Red Bluff CA	1+
Chico			
Esplanade Bed & Breakfast	530-345-8084	620 The Esplanade Chico CA	1+
Holiday Inn	530-345-2491	685 Manzanita Ct Chico CA	1+
Motel 6 - Chico	530-345-5500	665 Manzanita Court Chico CA	1+
Music Express Inn Bed and Breakfast	530-891-9833	1091El Monte Avenue Chico CA	1+
Super 8 Chico	530-345-2533	655 Manzanita Ct - Cohasset Rd Exit Chico CA	2
Yuba City			
Days Inn	530-674-1711	700 N Palora Ave Yuba City CA	1+
Motel 6 - Yuba City	530-790-7066	965 Gray Avenue Yuba City CA	1+
Sacramento			
Lake Natoma Inn	916-351-1500	702 Gold Lake Drive Folsom CA	1+
Motel 6 - Sacramento - North Highlands	916-973-8637	4600 Watt Avenue North Highlands CA	1+
AmeriSuites	916-635-4799	10744 Gold Center Dr. Rancho Cordova CA	1+
Best Western Heritage Inn	916-635-4040	11269 Point East Dr Rancho Cordova CA	3+
Inns of America	916-351-1213	12249 Folsom Blvd Rancho Cordova CA	1+
Motel 6 - Sacramento - Rancho Cordova East	916-635-8784	10694 Olson Drive Rancho Cordova CA	1+
Residence Inn by Marriott	916-851-1550	2779 Prospect Park Drive Rancho Cordova CA	2
Best Western Rocklin Park Hotel	916-630-9400	5450 China Garden Rd Rocklin CA	2
Best Western Roseville Inn	916-782-4434	220 Harding Blvd Roseville CA	3+
Oxford Suites	916-784-2222	130 N Sunrise Ave Roseville CA	1+
Residence Inn by Marriott	916-772-5500	1930 Taylor Road Roseville CA	3+
Candlewood Suites	916-646-1212	555 Howe Ave Sacramento CA	1+
Canterbury Inn Hotel	916-927-0927	1900 Canterbury Rd Sacramento CA	1+
Clarion Hotel Mansion Inn	916-444-8000	700 16th Street Sacramento CA	1
Doubletree	916-929-8855	2001 Point West Way Sacramento CA	3+
Holiday Inn	916-338-5800	5321 Date Ave Sacramento CA	2
Holiday Inn Express	916-444-4436	728 16 Street Sacramento CA	1+
Inn At Parkside	916-658-1818	2116 6th Street Sacramento CA	1+

La Quinta Inn Sacramento Downtown	916-448-8100	200 Jibboom St. Sacramento CA	3+
Motel 6 - Sacamento South	916-689-6555	7407 Elsie Avenue Sacramento CA	1+
Motel 6 - Sacramento Central	916-383-8110	7850 College Town Drive Sacramento CA	1+
Motel 6 - Sacramento Downtown	916-457-0777	1415 30th Street Sacramento CA	1+
Motel 6 - Sacramento North	916-331-8100	5110 Interstate Avenue Sacramento CA	1+
Motel 6 - Sacramento Southwest	916-689-9141	7780 Stockton Boulevard Sacramento CA	1+
Motel 6 - Sacramento-Old Sacramento North	916-441-0733	227 Jibboom Street Sacramento CA	1+
Red Lion	916-922-8041	1401 Arden Way Sacramento CA	3+
Red Roof Inn - Sacramento	916-927-7117	3796 Northgate Boulevard Sacramento CA	1+
Residence Inn by Marriott	916-649-1300	2410 W El Camino Avenue Sacramento CA	3+
Residence Inn by Marriott	916-920-9111	1530 Howe Avenue Sacramento CA	3+
Sheraton Grand Sacramento Hotel	916-447-1700	1230 J St. (13th & J St) Sacramento CA	2
Motel 6 - Sacramento West	916-372-3624	1254 Halyard Drive West Sacramento CA	1+
Stockton			
Holiday Inn	209-474-3301	111 East March Lane Stockton CA	2
La Quinta Inn Stockton	209-952-7800	2710 W. March Ln. Stockton CA	3+
Motel 6 - Stockton - Charter Way West	209-946-0923	817 Navy Drive Stockton CA	1+
Motel 6 - Stockton - I-5 Southeast	209-467-3600	1625 French Camp Turnpike Road Stockton CA	1+
Motel 6 - Stockton North	209-951-8120	6717 Plymouth Road Stockton CA	1+
Residence Inn by Marriott	209-472-9800	March Lane and Brookside Stockton CA	3+
Travelodge	209-466-7777	1707 Fremont St Stockton CA	1+
Motel 6 - Tracy	209-836-4900	3810 North Tracy Boulevard Tracy CA	1+
Modesto			
Motel 6 - Modesto	209-522-7271	1920 West Orangeburg Avenue Modesto CA	1+
Red Lion	209-521-1612	1612 Sisk Road - Exit Carpenter/Briggsmore Modesto CA	3+
Vagabond Inn	209-577-8008	2025 W Orangeburg Ave Modesto CA	1+
Turlock			
Motel 6 - Turlock	209-667-4100	250 South Walnut Avenue Turlock CA	1+
Merced			
Motel 6 - Merced North	209-384-2181	1410 V Street Merced CA	1+
Travelodge	209-722-6225	1260 Yosemite Park Way Merced CA	1+
Vagabond Inn	209-722-2737	1215 R Street Merced CA	1+
Chowchilla			
Days Inn	559-665-4821	Hwy 99 & Robertson Blvd Chowchilla CA	1+
Madera			
Days Inn	559-674-8817	25327 Ave 16 Madera CA	1+
Madera Valley Inn	559-664-0100	317 North G St Madera CA	3+
Motel 6 - Madera	559-675-8697	22683 Avenue 18 1/2 Madera CA	1+
Fresno			
Comfort Inn	559-275-2374	5455 W Shaw Avenue - Exit Shaw Avenue Fresno CA	2
Econo Lodge	559-485-5019	445 N Parkway Dr Fresno CA	1+
Holiday Inn Express and Suites	559-277-5700	5046 N. Barcus Rd Fresno CA	1+
Quality Inn	559-275-2727	4278 W Ashlan Avenue - Exit Ashlan Avenue Fresno CA	3+
TownePlace Suites Fresno	559-435-4600	7127 N Fresno St - Herndon Exit Fresno CA	2
Visalia			
Holiday Inn	559-651-5000	9000 W. Airport Drive Visalia CA	1+
Tulare			
Days Inn	559-686-0985	1183 N Blackstone St Tulare CA	1+
Howard Johnson Express Inn	559-688-6671	1050 E Rankin Ave Tulare CA	1+
Motel 6 - Tulare	559-686-1611	1111 North Blackstone Drive Tulare CA	1+
Delano			
Shilo Inn	661-725-7551	2231 Girard Street Delano CA	1+
Bakersfield			
Best Western Heritage Inn (Buttonwillow)	661-764-6268	253 Trask St Bakersfield CA	2
Best Western Hill House	661-327-4064	700 Truxton Ave Bakersfield CA	2
Days Hotel and Golf	661-324-5555	4500 Buck Owens Blvd Bakersfield CA	1+
Doubletree	661-323-7111	3100 Camino Del Rio Court - Exit H 58/Rosedale H Bakersfield CA	3+
Holiday Inn Select	661-323-1900	801 Truxton Avenue Bakersfield CA	2
La Quinta Inn Bakersfield	661-325-7400	3232 Riverside Dr. - Exit Buck Owens Bakersfield CA	3+
Motel 6 - Bakersfield Convention Center	661-327-1686	1350 Easton Drive Bakersfield CA	1+
Motel 6 - Bakersfield East	661-366-7231	8223 East Brundage Lane Bakersfield CA	1+
Motel 6 - Bakersfield South	661-834-2828	2727 White Lane Bakersfield CA	1+
Quality Inn	661-325-0772	1011 Oak Street - Exit California Avenue E Bakersfield CA	2
Red Lion	661-327-0681	2400 Camino Del Rio Court - Exit H 58/Rosedale H Bakersfield CA	3+
Residence Inn by Marriott	661-321-9800	4241 Chester Lane - Exit W on California Ave Bakersfield CA	3+
Rio Bravo Resort	661-872-5000	11200 Lake Ming Rd Bakersfield CA	1+

Highway 101 Accommodation Listings

Washington Listings (Highway 101)
Dogs per Room

Olympia

Super 8 Lacey/Olympia Area	360-459-8888	112 College St SE Lacey WA	2
West Coast Inn	360-943-4000	2300 Evergreen Park Drive Olympia WA	1+
Best Western Tumwater Inn	360-956-1235	5188 Capitol Blvd Tumwater WA	3+
Comfort Inn	360-352-0691	1620 74th Avenue SW Tumwater WA	3+
Motel 6 - Tumwater - Olympia	360-754-7320	400 West Lee Street Tumwater WA	1+

Shelton

Super 8 Shelton	360-426-1654	2943 Northview Circle - 1st Shelton Exit Shelton WA	2

Sequim

Quality Inn and Suites	360-683-2800	142 River Road - Exit N on River Road Sequim WA	2

Port Angeles

Red Lion	360-452-9215	221 N Lincoln Port Angeles WA	3+
Super 8 Port Angeles	360-452-8401	2104 E 1st Street Port Angeles WA	2

Forks

Kalaloch Ocean Lodge	360-962-2271	157151 Hwy. 101 Forks WA	3+

Aberdeen

America's Best Value	360-532-5210	521 W Wishkah Aberdeen WA	2

Oregon Listings (Highway 101)
Dogs per Room

Astoria

Best Western Astoria Inn	503-325-2205	555 Hamburg Ave Astoria OR	2
Holiday Inn Express Hotel and Suites	888-898-6222	204 West Marine Dr Astoria OR	2

Seaside

Motel 6 - Seaside	503-738-6269	2369 South Roosevelt Drive Seaside OR	1+
Seaside Convention Center Inn	503-738-9581	441 Second Ave Seaside OR	1+
The Best Western Ocean View Resort	800-234-8439	414 North Prom Seaside OR	1+

Cannon Beach

Surfsand Resort	503-436-2274	148 W. Gower Cannon Beach OR	1+
The Haystack Resort	503-436-1577	3361 S. Hemlock Cannon Beach OR	1+
The Inn at Cannon Beach	503-436-9085	3215 S. Hemlock Cannon Beach OR	1+

Lincoln City

Chinook Winds Casino Resort Hotel	541-996-5825	1501 NW 40th Place - Exit Logan Road Lincoln City OR	3+
Motel 6 - Lincoln City	541-996-9900	3517 N Highway 101 Lincoln City OR	1+

Newport

Hallmark Resort	541-265-2600	744 SW Elizabeth St Newport OR	1+
La Quinta Inn & Suites Newport	541-867-7224	45 SE 32nd Street - Exit SE 32nd Street Newport OR	2
Shilo Oceanfront Resort	541-265-7701	536 SW Elizabeth St Newport OR	1+

Yachats

Adobe Resort	541-547-3141	1555 US 101 Yachats OR	1+
Shamrock Lodgettes	541-547-3312	US 101 Yachats OR	1+
The Fireside Inn	800-336-3573	Hwy 101 Yachats OR	1+

Florence

Whales Watch Vacation Rentals	541-999-1493	88572 2nd Ave Florence OR	1+

Reedsport

Best Western Salbasgeon Inn and Suites of Reedsport	541-271-4831	1400 Hwy Ave US 101 Reedsport OR	2
Economy Inn	541-271-3671	1593 Highway Ave 101 Reedsport OR	1+

Coos Bay

Motel 6 - Coos Bay	541-267-7171	1445 Bayshore Drive Coos Bay OR	1+
Red Lion	541-267-4141	1313 N Bayshore Drive Coos Bay OR	3+

Bandon

Best Western Inn at Face Rock	541-347-9441	3225 Beach Loop Rd Bandon OR	2
Driftwood Motel	541-347-9022	460 Hwy 101 Bandon OR	1+
Sunset Motel	541-347-2453	1755 Beach Loop Rd Bandon OR	1+

Harbor

Best Western Beachfront Inn	541-469-7779	16008 Boat Basin Rd Harbor OR	2

California Listings (Highway 101)   Dogs per Room

Redwood National and State Parks			
Motel Trees	707-482-3152	15495 Highway 101 South Klamath CA	1+
Arcata			
Best Western Arcata Inn	707-826-0313	4827 Valley West Blvd Arcata CA	1
Comfort Inn	707-826-2827	4701 Valley W Blvd - Exit Guintoli Lane Arcata CA	3+
Hotel Arcata	707-826-0217	708 Ninth Street Arcata CA	1+
Motel 6 - Arcata - Humboldt University	707-822-7061	4755 Valley West Boulevard Arcata CA	1+
Quality Inn	707-822-0409	3535 Janes Road - Exit Giuntoli/Janes Road W Arcata CA	2
Super 8 Arcata	707-822-8888	4887 Valley W Blvd - Giuntoli Lane Exit Arcata CA	2
Eureka			
Best Western Bayshore Inn	707-268-8005	3500 Broadway Eureka CA	2
Discovery Inn	707-441-8442	2832 Broadway Eureka CA	1+
Motel 6 - Eureka	707-445-9631	1934 Broadway Street Eureka CA	1+
The Eureka Inn	707-442-6441	518 Seventh Street Eureka CA	1+
Fortuna			
Best Western Country Inn	707-725-6822	2025 Riverwalk Dr Fortuna CA	2
Avenue Of The Giants			
Miranda Gardens Resort	707-943-3011	6766 Avenue of the Giants Miranda CA	1+
Ukiah			
Days Inn	707-462-7584	950 North State St Ukiah CA	1+
Motel 6 - Ukiah	707-468-5404	1208 South State Street Ukiah CA	1+
Sonoma			
Russian River Getaways	707-869-4560	14075 Mill Street, P.O. Box 1673 Guerneville CA	1+
Best Western Dry Creek Inn	707-433-0300	198 Dry Creek Rd - Exit Dry Creek Rd Healdsburg CA	2
Duchamp Hotel	707-431-1300	421 Foss Street Healdsburg CA	1+
Doubletree	707-584-5466	One Doubletree Drive - Exit Golf Course Circle Rohnert Park CA	1+
Best Western Garden Inn - Santa Rosa	707-546-4031	1500 Santa Rosa Avenue Santa Rosa CA	1+
Days Inn	707-568-1011	3345 Santa Rosa Ave Santa Rosa CA	1+
Holiday Inn Express	707-545-9000	870 Hopper Ave Santa Rosa CA	1+
Los Robles Lodge	707-545-6330	1985 Cleveland Ave Santa Rosa CA	1+
Santa Rosa Motor Inn	707-523-3480	1800 Santa Rosa Ave Santa Rosa CA	1+
Marin - North Bay			
Inn Marin	415-883-5952	250 Entrada Drive Novato CA	1+
Travelodge	415-892-7500	7600 Redwood Blvd Novato CA	1+
Quality Inn	707-664-1155	5100 Montero Way - Exit Pengrove Petaluma CA	1+
San Francisco			
Days Inn - Lombard St	415-922-2010	2358 Lombard Street San Francisco CA	1+
Hotel Diva	800-553-1900	440 Geary Street - Exit 9th Street/Civic Center San Francisco CA	1
Hotel Metropolis	800-553-9100	25 Mason Street - Exit 9th Street/Civic Center San Francisco CA	1
Hotel Union Square	800-553-1900	114 Powell Street - Exit 9th Street/Civic Center San Francisco CA	1
Kensington Park Hotel	800-553-9100	450 Post Street - Exit I 80 San Francisco CA	1
Marina Motel - on Lombard Street	415-921-9406	2576 Lombard St. San Francisco CA	1+
Palo Alto - Peninsula			
Doubletree	650-344-5500	835 Airport Blvd - exit Airport Blvd Burlingame CA	2
San Francisco Airport Marriott	650-692-9100	1800 Old Bayshore H - Exit Millbrae E Burlingame CA	2
Vagabond Inn	650-692-4040	1640 Bayshore Highway Burlingame CA	1+
Residence Inn by Marriott	650-940-1300	1854 El Camino West - Exit Shoreline Blvd Mountain View CA	3+
Tropicana Lodge	650-961-0220	1720 El Camino Real Mountain View CA	1+
Hotel Sofitel	650-598-9000	223 Twin Dolphin Dr Redwood City CA	1+
Staybridge Suites	650-588-0770	1350 Huntington Avenue San Bruno CA	1+
Howard Johnson Express Inn	650-589-9055	222 South Airport Blvd. South San Francisco CA	1+
La Quinta Inn San Francisco Airport	650-583-2223	20 Airport Blvd. - Exit Airport Blvd South San Francisco CA	3+
Vagabond Inn	650-589-9055	222 S. Airport Blvd South San Francisco CA	1+
San Jose			
Residence Inn by Marriott	650-559-7890	4460 El Camino Real - Exit San Antonino Road W Los Altos CA	3+
Clarion Hotel San Jose Airport	408-453-5340	1355 N 4th Street - Exit H 880S San Jose CA	1
Fairmont Hotel	408-998-1900	170 S Market Street - Exit H 87 San Jose CA	2
Santa Clara Marriott	408-988-1500	2700 Mission College Blvd - Exit Great America Parkway Santa Clara CA	3+
Comfort Inn	408-244-9000	1071 E El Camino Real - Exit Lawrence Expressway Sunnyvale CA	1
Residence Inn by Marriott	408-720-1000	750 Lakeway - Exit Lawrence Expressway S Sunnyvale CA	3+
Residence Inn by Marriott	408-720-8893	1080 Stewart Drive - Exit Lawrence Expressway Sunnyvale CA	3+
Staybridge Suites	408-745-1515	900 Hamlin Court Sunnyvale CA	3+
The Maple Tree Inn	408-720-9700	711 El Camino Real Sunnyvale CA	1+
TownePlace Suites Sunnyvale Mountain View	408-733-4200	606 S Bernardo Avenue - Mountain View Alviso Rd/CA-237 Exit Sunnyvale CA	2

Woodfin Suite Hotel	408-738-1700	635 E. El Camino Real Sunnyvale CA	1+
Morgan Hill			
Residence Inn by Marriott	408-782-8311	18620 Madrone Parkway - Exit Cochrane Road Morgan Hill CA	2
Salinas			
Motel 6 - Salinas North - Monterey Area	831-753-1711	140 Kern Street Salinas CA	1+
Motel 6 - Salinas South - Monterey Area	831-757-3077	1257 De La Torre Boulevard Salinas CA	1+
Residence Inn by Marriott	831-775-0410	17215 El Rancho Way - Exit W Laurel Drive Salinas CA	2
King City			
Motel 6 - King City	831-385-5000	3 Broadway Circle King City CA	1+
San Luis Obispo			
Oxford Suites	805-773-3773	651 Five Cities Drive Pismo Beach CA	1+
Sea Gypsy Motel	805-773-1801	1020 Cypress Street Pismo Beach CA	1+
Sands Suites & Motel	805-544-0500	1930 Monterey Street San Luis Obispo CA	1+
Vagabond Inn	805-544-4710	210 Madonna Rd. San Luis Obispo CA	1+
Santa Maria			
Best Western Big America	805-922-5200	1725 North Broadway Santa Maria CA	3+
Holiday Inn Hotel & Suites	805-928-6000	2100 North Broadway Santa Maria CA	1+
Motel 6 - Santa Maria	805-928-8111	2040 North Preisker Lane Santa Maria CA	1+
Solvang			
Motel 6 - Buellton - Solvang Area	805-688-7797	333 McMurray Road Buellton CA	1+
Quality Inn	805-688-0022	630 Avenue of the Flags - Exit Avenue of the Flags Buellton CA	3+
Rodeway Inn	805-688-0022	630 Ave of Flags Buellton CA	1+
Santa Ynez Valley Marriott	805-688-1000	555 McMurray Road - Exit 246 Buellton CA	2
Royal Copenhagen Inn	800-624-6604	1579 Mission Drive Solvang CA	1+
Wine Valley Inn	805-688-2111	1554 Copenhagen Drive - Exit H 246/Mission Solvang CA	3+
Santa Barbara			
Holiday Inn Express Hotel and Suites	805-566-9499	5606 Carpinteria Ave Carpinteria CA	2
Motel 6 - Santa Barbara-Carpinteria North	805-684-6921	4200 Via Real Carpinteria CA	1+
Motel 6 - Santa Barbara-Carpinteria South	805-684-8602	5550 Carpinteria Avenue Carpinteria CA	1+
Motel 6 - Santa Barbara - Goleta	805-964-3596	5897 Calle Real Goleta CA	1+
Best Western Beachside Inn	805-965-6556	336 W Cabrillo Blvd Santa Barbara CA	2
Casa Del Mar Hotel	805-963-4418	18 Bath Street Santa Barbara CA	1+
Fess Parkers Doubletree Resort	805-564-4333	633 E Cabrillo Blvd - Exit Milpas Street Santa Barbara CA	3+
Four Seasons Resort	805-969-2261	1260 Channel Dr. Santa Barbara CA	1+
Montecito Del Mar	805-962-2006	316 W Montecito St Santa Barbara CA	1+
Motel 6 - Santa Barbara - Beach	805-564-1392	443 Corona Del Mar Santa Barbara CA	1+
Motel 6 - Santa Barbara - State Street	805-687-5400	3505 State Street Santa Barbara CA	1+
San Ysidro Ranch	805-969-5046	900 San Ysidro Lane Santa Barbara CA	1+
Secret Garden Inn & Cottages	805-687-2300	1908 Bath Street Santa Barbara CA	1+
Ventura - Oxnard			
Motel 6 - Camarillo	805-388-3467	1641 East Daily Drive Camarillo CA	1+
Casa Sirena Hotel and Resort	805-985-6311	3605 Peninsula Rd Oxnard CA	1+
Residence Inn by Marriott	805-278-2200	2101 W Vineyard Avenue - Exit Vinyard Avenue Oxnard CA	3+
Vagabond Inn	805-983-0251	1245 N. Oxnard Blvd. Oxnard CA	1+
Crowne Plaza Hotel - Ventura Beach	805-648-2100	450 E Harbor Blvd Ventura CA	1+
La Quinta Inn Ventura	805-658-6200	5818 Valentine Rd. - Exit Victoria Ventura CA	3+
Motel 6 - Ventura Beach	805-643-5100	2145 East Harbor Boulevard Ventura CA	1+
Motel 6 - Ventura South	805-650-0080	3075 Johnson Drive Ventura CA	1+
Vagabond Inn	805-648-5371	756 E. Thompson Blvd. Ventura CA	1+
Thousand Oaks			
Thousand Oaks Inn	805-497-3701	75 W. Thousand Oaks Blvd. Thousand Oaks CA	1+
San Fernando Valley			
Hilton	818-595-1000	6360 Canoga Avenue - Exit Canoga Avenue Woodland Hills CA	2
Warner Center Marriott	818-227-6126	21850 Oxnard Street Woodland Hills CA	1+
Warner Center Marriott Woodland Hills	818-887-4800	21850 Oxnard Street - Exit Topanga Canyon Blvd Woodland Hills CA	3+

Highway 395 Accommodation Listings

Alturas			
Best Western Trailside Inn	530-233-4111	343 N Main St Alturas CA	2
Susanville			
Budget Host Frontier Inn	530-257-4141	2685 Main St Susanville CA	1+

River Inn	530-257-6051	1710 Main St Susanville CA	1+

Reno

Atlantis Casino Resort Spa	775-825-4700	3800 S Virigina Street - Exit Moana Lane Reno NV	3+
Days Inn Reno	775-786-4070	701 E 7th Reno NV	2
Holiday Inn Downtown	775-786-5151	1000 E. 6th St. Reno NV	1+
La Quinta Inn Reno	775-348-6100	4001 Market - Exit 65A Reno NV	3+
Motel 6 - Reno - Livestock Events Center	775-786-9852	866 North Wells Avenue Reno NV	1+
Motel 6 - Reno - Virginia Plumb	775-827-0255	1901 South Virginia Street Reno NV	1+
Motel 6 - Reno West	775-747-7390	1400 Stardust Street Reno NV	1+
Quality Inn South	775-329-1001	1885 S Virginia Street Reno NV	2
Residence Inn by Marriott	775-853-8800	9845 Gateway Drive - Exit 60/South Meadows Parkway Reno NV	1+
Rodeway Inn	775-786-2500	2050 Market Street Reno NV	1+
Super 8 Reno/Meadowwood Courtyard	775-829-4600	5851 S Virginia St Reno NV	2
Truckee River Lodge	775-786-8888	501 W. 1st Street Reno NV	1+
Vagabond Inn	775-825-7134	3131 S. Virginia St. Reno NV	1+

Carson City

Best Value Motel	775-882-2007	2731 S Carson St Carson City NV	1+
Best Western Trailside Inn	775-883-7300	1300 N Carson St Carson City NV	3+
Days Inn Carson City	775-883-3343	3103 N Carson St Carson City NV	2
Holiday Inn Express Hotel & Suites	775-283-4055	4055 North Carson Street Carson City NV	1+
Motel 6 - Carson City	775-885-7710	2749 South Carson Street Carson City NV	1+

Coleville

Andruss Motel	530-495-2216	106964 Highway 395 Coleville CA	1+

Lee Vining

Inn at Lee Vining	760-647-6300	45 2nd St Lee Vining CA	1+
Murphey's Hotel	760-647-6316	51493 Hwy 395 Lee Vining CA	1+

June Lake

Big Rock Resort	760-648-7717	Big Rock Road at Boulder Drive June Lake CA	1+
Double Eagle Resort and Spa	760-648-7004	5587 Highway 158 June Lake CA	1+
June Lake Villager Inn	760-648-7712	Boulder Dr & Knoll Ave June Lake CA	1+

Mammoth Lakes

Convict Lake Resort	760-934-3800	HCR - 79, Box 204 - Exit Convict Lake Mammoth Lakes CA	3+
Crystal Crag Lodge	760-934-2436	P.O. Box 88 Mammoth Lakes CA	1+
Edelweiss Lodge	760-934-2445	1872 Old Mammoth Road Mammoth Lakes CA	3+
Mammoth Creek Inn	760-934-6162	663 Old Mammoth Road Mammoth Lakes CA	1+
Motel 6 - Mammoth Lakes	760-934-6660	3372 Main Street Mammoth Lakes CA	1+
Shilo Inn	760-934-4500	2963 Main Street Mammoth Lakes CA	1+
Sierra Lodge	760-934-8881	3540 Main Street Mammoth Lakes CA	1+
Swiss Chalet	760-934-2403	3776 Viewpoint Road Mammoth Lakes CA	1+
Villa De Los Pinos #3	760-722-5369	3252 Chateau Rd Mammoth Lakes CA	1+

Bishop

Comfort Inn	760-873-4284	805 N Main Street - Exit Main Street Bishop CA	3+
Motel 6 - Bishop	760-873-8426	1005 North Main Street Bishop CA	1+
Rodeway Inn	760-873-3564	150 E Elm Street Bishop CA	1+
Vagabond Inn	760-873-6351	1030 N Main Street Bishop CA	1+

Big Pine

Big Pine Motel	760-938-2282	370 S Main St Big Pine CA	1+
Bristlecone Motel	760-938-2067	101 N. Main St. Big Pine CA	1+

Independence

Independence Courthouse Motel	760-878-2732	157 N Edwards Street Independence CA	1+
Ray's Den Motel	760-878-2122	405 N Edwards St Independence CA	1+
Wilder House Bed & Breakfast	760-878-2119	325 Dusty Lane Independence CA	1+

Lone Pine

Alabama Hills Inn	760-876-8700	1920 South Main Lone Pine CA	1+
Best Western Frontier Motel	760-876-5571	1008 S Main St Lone Pine CA	3+

Olancha

Ranch Motel	760-764-2387	2051 S Highway 395 Olancha CA	1+

Ridgecrest

Motel 6 - Ridgecrest	760-375-6866	535 South China Lake Boulevard Ridgecrest CA	1+

Index - Please always call ahead to make sure that an establishment is still dog-friendly

Book Contents and Pages

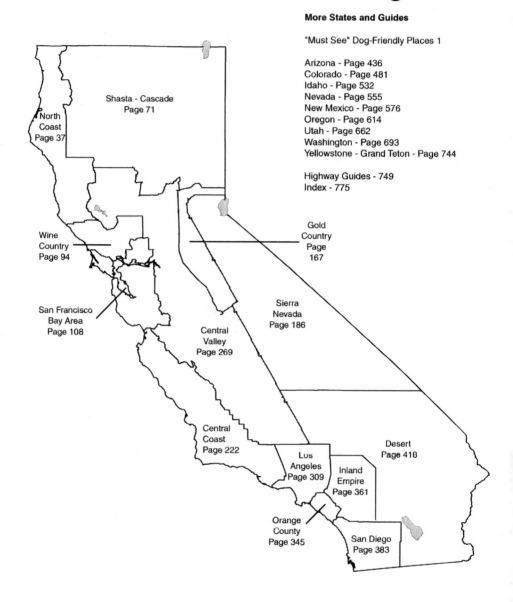